RASHI'S COMMENTARY ON PSALMS

This publication is
made possible
by a generous gift
from an anonymous donor

In honor of
David Smith

RASHI'S COMMENTARY
ON PSALMS

BY

MAYER I. GRUBER

2007 • 5768
The Jewish Publication Society
Philadelphia

Copyright © 2004 by Koninklijke Brill NV, Leiden, The Netherlands
First published in cloth in 2004 by Koninklijke Brill NV

First paperback edition 2007 by The Jewish Publication Society

Manufactured in the United States of America

ISBN 13: 978-0-8276-0872-6
ISBN 10: 0-8276-0872-1

Library of Congress Cataloging-in-Publication Data
Rashi, 1949-1105
    [Perush Rahsi le-sefer Tehilim. English & Hebrew]
    Rashi's Commentary on Psalms / by Mayer Gruber.
       p. cm. — (The Brill reference library of Judaism. ISBN 1571-5000 ; v. 18)
    Includes bibliographical references and indexes.
    ISBN 90-04-13251-1 (alk. paper)
      1. Bible, O.T. Psalms—Commentaries—Early works to 1800. I. Gruber, Mayer I.
    (Mayer Irwin) II. Title. III. Series.

BS1429.R3717 2003
223'.207—dc22

Reprinted from the original cloth edition in

THE BRILL REFERENCE LIBRARY
OF JUDAISM

In loving memory

of

ABE FRIEDMAN

(October 29, 1921 - April 29, 1994)

TABLE OF CONTENTS

TABLE OF ABBREVIATIONS

AB	The Anchor Bible
AHW	Wolfram von Soden, *Akkadisches Handwörterbuch*
Akk.	Akkadian, a Semitic language spoken in ancient Mesopotamia between the middle of the 3[d] millenium B.C.E. and the beginning of the Common Era
ANEP[2]	James B. Pritchard, ed., *The Ancient Near East in Pictures Relating to the Old Testament*, 2[d] ed. with Supplement
ANET[3]	James B. Pritchard, ed., *Ancient Near Eastern Texts Relating to the Old Testament*, 3[d] ed. with Supplement
AOS	American Oriental Series
Aram.	Aramaic, a Semitic language, in which much Jewish sacred literature was written, including parts of the biblical books of Daniel and Ezra, a sentence in Jeremiah and two words in Genesis
BDB	Francis Brown, S. R. Driver, and Charles A. Briggs, *A Hebrew and English Lexicon of the Old Testament*
Ben Yehuda, Dict.,	Eliezer Ben Yehuda, *A Complete Dictionary of Ancient and Modern Hebrew*
BGM	Robert Gordis, *The Book of God and Man*
BH[3]	Rudolph Kittel, ed., *Biblica Hebraica*, 3d ed.
BHS	W. Rudolph and H. P. Rüger, *Biblica Hebraica Stuttgartensia*, 2[d] ed.
B-L	Hans Bauer and Pontus Leander, *Historische Grammatik der hebräischen Sprachen des Alten Testamentes*
Briggs	Charles Augustus Briggs and Emilie Grace Briggs, *A Critical and Exegetical Commentary on the Book of Psalms*
BT	Babylonian Talmud
BZAW	Beihefte zur Zeitschrift für die alttestamentliche Wissenschaft
CAD	A. Leo Oppenheim, ed., *The Assyrian Dictionary of the Oriental Institute of the University of Chicago*
CB	The Cambridge Bible for Schools and Colleges

CTA	Andrée Herdner, *Corpus des tablettes en cunéiformes alphabétiques découvertes à Ras Shamra de 1929 à 1939*
Dahood	Mitchell Dahood, *Psalms*
Driver, Deut.	S. R. Driver, *A Critical and Exegetical Commentary on Deuteronomy*
Driver, Tenses³	S. R. Driver, *A Treatise on the Use of the Tenses in Hebrew*, 3d ed.
Ehrlich	Arnold Ehrlich, *Die Psalmen*
Ehrlich, Mikrâ ki-Pheschuto	Arnold Ehrlich, *Mikrâ ki-Pheschuto*
EI	*Eretz-Israel*
EJ	*Encyclopaedia Judaica*
EM	*Encyclopedia Miqra'it*
Eng.	English
Gaster, *MLC*	Theodor H. Gaster, *Myth, Legend, and Custom in the Old Testament*
Gk.	Greek
GKC	Wilhelm Gesenius, *Gesenius' Hebrew Grammar*, ed. E. Kautzsch, 2ᵈ Engl. ed., revised by A. E. Cowley
Gruber, *Aspects*	M. I. Gruber, *Aspects of Nonverbal Communication in the Ancient Near East*
Heb.	Hebrew
HG	G. Bergsträsser, *Hebräische Grammatik*
HUCA	*Hebrew Union College Annual*
IB	George A. Buttrick, ed., *The Interpreter's Bible*
IDB	George A. Buttrick, ed., *The Interpreter's Bible Dictionary*
JANES	*Journal of the Ancient Near Eastern Society*
JAOS	*Journal of the American Oriental Society*
Jastrow, *Dict.*	Marcus Jastrow, *A Dictionary of the Targumim, the Talmud Babli and Yerushalmi, and the Midrashic Literature*
JBL	*Journal of Biblical Literature*
JE	I. Singer, ed., *The Jewish Encyclopedia* (1901)
JPS	Max L. Margolis, ed., The Holy Scriptures (1917)
JQR	*Jewish Quarterly Review*
JSS	*Journal of Semitic Studies*
JT	Jerusalem Talmud
KAI	H. Dönner and W. Röllig, *Kanaanäische und aramäische Inschriften*

K-B	Ludwig Koehler and Walter Baumgartner, *Lexikon in Veteris Testamenti Libros* (1903)
*K-B*³	Ludwig Koehler and Walter Baumgartner, *Hebräisches und aramäisches Lexikon zum Alten Testament*, 3d ed.
KJV	The Authorized Version of 1611, commonly called the King James Bible
Krauss, *Lehnwörter*	Samuel Krauss, *Greichische und Lateinische Lehnwörter im Talmud, Midrasch und Targum*
KTU	Manfried Dietrich, Oswald Loretz, Joaquín Sanmartín, *The Cuneiform Alphabetic Texts*
Liddell & Scott	Henry George Liddell and Robert Scott, *A Greek-English Lexicon*
LXX	Septuagint, the oldest Jewish translation of the Bible into Greek
Maarsen	I. Maarsen, *Parschandatha*
Mahberet Menahem	Menahem ben Saruq, *Mahberet*, ed. Sáenz-Badillos
Mahberet Menahem, ed. Filipowski	*Sefer Mahberet Menahem*, ed. H. Filipowski
Mandelkern	Solomon Mandelkern, *Veteris Testamenti Concordantiae*
Mekilta	Jacob Z. Lauterbach, Mekilta de-Rabbi Ishmael
MGWJ	*Monatsschrift für Geschichte und Wissenschaft des Judentums*
NEB	The New English Bible
NIC	The New International Commentary
NJV	New Jewish Version of the Bible = *Tanakh: A New Translation of the Holy Scriptures*
NRSV	The New Revised Standard Version of the Bible
NT	New Testament
Orlinsky, *Notes*	Harry M. Orlinsky, *Notes on the New Translation of the Torah*
OTL	Old Testament Library
PAAR	*Proceedings of the American Academy for Jewish Research*
PRE	Pirke de Rabbi Eliezer
PRK	Pesikta de Rav Kahana
RB	*Revue Biblique*
REJ	*Revue des Etudes Juives*

R.H.	Rosh ha-Shanah, the Jewish New Year and the Tractate of Mishnah, Tosefta and Talmuds, which treats of that festival
Rogerson and McKay	J. W. Rogerson and J. W. McKay, *Psalms 51-100.*
RSV	The Revised Standard Version of the Bible
Speiser, *Genesis*	E. A. Speiser, *Genesis*
Teshuvot Dunash	Dunaš Ben Labrat, *Tešubot de Dunaš Ben Labrat,* ed. Sáenz-Badillos
Teshuvot Dunash, ed. Filipowski	*Sepher Teshuvot Dunash Ben Labrat,* ed. H. Filipowski
TJ	Targum Jonathan, Rabbinic Judaism's official Aramaic Targum [translation] of the Early and Later Prophets
T.O.	Targum Onkelos, Rabbinic Judaism's official Aramaic Targum [translation] of the Pentateuch
UF	*Ugarit Forschungen*
Ugar.	Ugaritic, an ancient Semitic language of inscriptions from the 2^d millenium B.C.E. found primarily at Ras Shamra on the Syrian coast
UT	Cyrus H. Gordon, *Ugaritic Textbook*
VT	*Vetus Testamentum*
Weiser	Artur Weiser, *The Psalms: A Commentary*
ZAW	*Zeitschrift für die alttestamentliche Wissenschaft*

PREFACE

I am delighted to record my sincere thanks to Professor Jacob Neusner, Research Professor of Religion and Theology and Senior Fellow, Institute of Advanced Theology at Bard College, Annandale-on-Hudson, New York, Editor of the Brill Reference Library of Judaism, for inviting me to publish this book in this series. I thank Brill Academic Publishers, and especially Senior Acquisitions Editor Joed Elich, and Religion and Social Sciences Editor Ivo Romein, for bringing this project to fruition.

I am pleased also to record my sincere thanks to my three adult sons—Rabbi David Shalom Gruber, Mr. Jehiel Benjamin Gruber, and Rabbi Hillel Boaz Gruber—for their important contribution many years ago as children to the research that lies behind this book. Over a period of several years my sons filed the index cards that served as a dictionary of the exegetical, linguistic and theological terminology employed by Rashi in his Commentary on Psalms. I utilized this dictionary to make certain that my translation and notes reflected both Rashi's consistent use of certain expressions and his homonymous usage of some of those same expressions. My eldest son David also helped me in the preparation of the cumulative bibliography at the end of this volume.

I am pleased to acknowledge my indebtedness to Prof. Robert A. Harris of the Jewish Theological Seminary of America in New York City for his critical review of my earlier *Rashi's Commentary on Psalms 1-89*.[*] Several leading questions posed in that review inspired me to write section IV of the introduction to the present work, which describes the totality of Rashi's literary output.

Special thanks are due the Austrian National Library in Vienna for granting me permission to publish both the text of Rashi's Commentary on Psalms found in Austrian National Library Cod. Hebr. 220 and my translation of that text. I record my deep appreciation to Dr. Michael Carasik for transcribing the Hebrew text from the

---

[*] Robert A. Harris, Review of *Rashi's Commentary on Psalms 1-89 (Books I-III)* by Mayer I. Gruber, in *Hebrew Studies* 40 (1999), pp. 331-334.

manuscript. I am sincerely grateful to the Jewish Publication Society of America for permission to quote freely from their *Tanakh: A New Translation of the Holy Scriptures According to the Traditional Hebrew Text* (Philadelphia, 1985). I am pleased to record my sincere thanks to Mr. Binyamin Richler, Director of the Institute for Microfilms of Hebrew Manuscripts at the Jewish National and University Library at the Givat Ram Campus of the Hebrew University of Jerusalem, and to his entire staff for their constant help and encouragement. They went out of their way to bring to my attention data concerning new manuscript discoveries useful to my work.

The map, which accompanies the notes to Rashi's Commentary on Psalm 24, was prepared by Mr. Patrice Kaminski of the Department of Bible & Ancient Near East at Ben-Gurion University of the Negev.

I am most grateful to the late Rosemary Krensky of Chicago, Illinois and, may they be distinguished for long life, Jerome and Lillian Mann of Golf, Illinois, for their generous grants to the American Associates of Ben-Gurion University of the Negev in support of this project. I am pleased to acknowledge generous grants from the I. Edward Kiev Library Foundation and the Committee on Research & Publications of the Faculty of Humanities & Social Sciences of Ben-Gurion University of the Negev in support of the writing of this book. Prof. Byron L. Sherwin, former Vice President for Academic Affairs of Spertus Institute of Judaica in Chicago, arranged for a generous grant from the Rosaline Cohn Scholars Fund in support of the transcription of the Hebrew text of Rashi's Commentary on Psalms. Special thanks are due Margo and Amiel Schotz and Judith Bodenheimer of WordByte for their formatting earlier versions of both the English and Hebrew text of this book.

A large part of the translation and notes contained in this volume was prepared during the academic year 1985-1986. I express my sincere thanks to Ben-Gurion University of the Negev for granting me sabbatical leave during that period. I thank Spertus College of Judaica for an appointment as Visiting Professor of Biblical Studies during that year, and the University of Chicago for an appointment as Visiting Scholar in the Department of Near Eastern Languages & Literatures. Special thanks to my late and beloved wife Judith Friedman Gruber (1948-1993), may her memory be for a blessing, for having proofread several versions of the translation and notes and sections I, and VI-X of the introduction and for her many stylistic improvements. Judith Appleton offered many stylistic improvements for sections II-V of the introduction, the foreword to the Hebrew section, the bibliography, and the preface.

The introduction and indices were completed during the years 1999-2003 in the midst of my other teaching, research and administrative obligations at Ben-Gurion University of the Negev. I record with both gratitude and pride the encouragement I have received from my colleagues, students and university administration here in Beersheva during these especially fruitful years. My daughters—Tamara Ditza Gruber and Shlomit Malka Gruber—have been most encouraging and supportive.

For their encouragement and advice in ways too numerous to mention I record my thanks to Prof. Moshe Held, Dr. Sarah Kamin and Prof. Harry M. Orlinsky—may their memory be for a blessing, and, may they be distinguished for long life—Prof. Abraham Gross, Prof. Avraham Grossman, Prof. Victor Avigdor Hurowitz, Prof. Daniel J. Lasker, Prof. Jordan Penkower, Prof. Nahum M. Sarna, Prof. Lawrence Schiffman, Prof. Zipora Talshir, and Prof. Elazar Touito. Special thanks are due my students at Ben-Gurion University of the Negev who have been demanding but fair critics. I alone am responsibile for any errors in this work.

As indicated in the Table of Abbreviations, references in the notes to *Mahberet Menahem and Teshuvot Dunash* without any qualification refer to the Sáenz-Badillos editions of those works. References to the important Filipowski editions of those two works are specifically designated as such. Likewise, references to the text and annotations in Isaac Maarsen's edition of the Hebrew text of Rashi's Commentary on Psalms appear simply as "Maarsen" while references to other works by Maarsen include additional details.

I am pleased to dedicate this volume to the memory of Abe Friedman, dear father of my late beloved wife Judith and devoted grandfather of my precious sons and daughters. Finally, I thank God Almighty for having enabled me to complete this *Rashi's Commentary on Psalms*. I fervently pray that I may be privileged to publish other works of scholarship for the glory of God and the edification of humankind.

MAYER I. GRUBER
Beersheva, Israel

INTRODUCTION

I. Rashi's Life: An Overview

Rashi (Heb. RŠY, רש״י) is the acronym for Rabbi Shlomo Yitzhaki, i.e., Rabbi Solomon son of Isaac.[1] He was born in the city of Troyes, the capital of the province of Champagne in Northern France. On the basis of a *responsum* of R. Solomon b. Jehiel Luria (1510-1571) it is commonly held that Rashi was born in the year of

---

[1] The acronym *RŠY* was also popularly interpreted to mean Rabban shel Yisrael "the Teacher of Israel" (V. Aptowitzer, *Introductio ad Sefer Rabiah* [Jerusalem: Mekize Nirdamim, 1938], p. 395; Samuel M. Blumenfield, *Master of Troyes: A Study of Rashi the Educator* [New York: Behrman House for the Jewish Institute of Religion, 1946], p. 3; Esra Shereshevsky, *Rashi: The Man and His World* [New York: Sepher-Hermon, 1982], p. 1), an allusion to the fact that Rashi's commentaries on the Bible and the Babylonian Talmud have been for the Jews during the past nine centuries the two most influential corpora of sacred texts after the Bible and the Talmud themselves. The apostate Raymond Martini (1220-1285) seems to have been the first to misinterpret the initials *RŠY* as Rabbi Salomo Yarhi (also spelled Jarhi). See Maurice Liber, *Rashi*, trans. Adele Szold (Philadelphia: Jewish Publication Society, 1906), p. 34. The misinterpretation was taken over by the German Christian Hebraist Sebastian Münster (1489-1552) in his list of the six hundred and thirteen commandments taken from the Sepher Mitzvot Gadol by the thirteenth century R. Moses b. Jacob of Coucy. Consequently, Rashi was so designated by various Christian and Jewish authors from the sixteenth to the nineteenth centuries. These authors include Johann Breithaupt in his Latin translation of Rashi's commentaries on the Pentateuch (Gotha: Andrea Schalius, 1710), the Prophets, Job, and Psalms (Gotha: Andrea Schalius, 1713). Hayyim Joseph David Azulai (b. Jerusalem c. 1724; d. Leghorn 1807) in his Hebrew treatise, *The Names of the Great Ones* suggested that Rashi was called Yarhi because "Rashi or his father was originally from Lunel." [Note that the provençal city of Lunel was designated in Heb. Yeriho, i.e., Jericho, because the latter name was perceived to be derived from Heb. *yārēaḥ* 'moon' while the name Lunel was perceived to be derived from the French equivalent lune]. Subsequently it was believed that Rashi was none other than R. Solomon Hacohen of Lunel mentioned in *The Itinerary of Benjamin of Tudela*, ed. Marcus Nathan Adler (London: H. Frowde, 1907), p. 4. In fact, all we know of the latter Solomon is that he was one of the prominent Jews of Lunel when Benjamin the Traveller passed through there in 1160 C.E. See Leopold Zunz, "Heisst Raschi Jarchi?" *Israelitische Annalen* (1839), pp. 328-315, reprinted in L. Zunz, *Gesammelte Schriften* (Berlin: Louis Gerschel Verlag, 1875), pp. 100-105; see also Maurice Liber, "Rashi," JE 10:324. Recently Menahem Banitt, *Rashi: Interpreter of the Biblical Letter* (Tel Aviv: Chaim Rosenberg School of Jewish Studies, Tel Aviv University, 1985), pp. 166-168 argued that the designation of Rashi as Yitzhaki rather than b. Yitzhak points to the Italian origin of the family.

the death of Rabbenu Gershom,[2] i.e., in the year of Creation 4800, i.e., 1039/40 C.E.[3] However, it has been argued as follows that in fact Rashi was born in 1030 C.E.:

Our knowledge of Rashi's birth is based on the statement that he was born in the year of Rabbenu Gershom's death. It has been widely assumed that Rabbenu Gershom died in 1040; but more accurate documents suggest that Rabbenu Gershom died in 1028.[4] Another historical source, the *Sefer Yuhasin*, states that Rashi lived seventy-five years,[5] which would place Rashi's birth at about 1030. This last statement can be easily harmonized with the former statement concerning the specific date 1028 on the ground that the author of *Sefer Yuhasin* used round numbers.[6]

Apart from the fact that his name was Isaac all we know for certain of Rashi's father is that Rashi refers in his commentary on Tractate Avodah Zarah of the Babylonian Talmud fol. 75a to his father's interpretation of a difficult passage as follows:

> [The latter is] the interpretation[7] of my father my teacher may his repose be glory,[8] and I agree with it,[9] and the former [interpretation] is the interpretation of my teacher,[10] and it is unacceptable to me....

---

[2] On Rabbenu Gershom b. Judah of Mainz (960-1028) see below.

[3] Shereshevsky, *Rashi: The Man and His World*, p. 7; Herman Hailperin, *Rashi and the Christian Scholars* (Pittsburgh: University of Pittsburgh Press, 1963), p. 25.

[4] The sources are the ms. called Siddur Rashi dated 5042 Anno Mundi, i.e., 1282 C.E., and p. 198b of Ms. Parma de Rossi 175 of Rashi's commentary on the Pentateuch dated (in that ms., p. 198a) 1305 C.E.; see Shereshevsky, p. 20; contrast Avraham Grossman, *The Early Sages of France* (2[d] ed.; Jerusalem: Magnes, 1996), pp. 122-123.

[5] The *Sefer ha-Yuhasin* was written by Abraham b. Samuel Zacuto (1452-c.1515). Completed at Tunis in 1504, the work was first published in Constantinople in 1566. See now Abraham b. Samuel Zacuto, *Sefer ha-Yuhasin*, ed. A. H. Freimann (2[d] ed.; Frankfurt am Main: Wahrman, 1924), p. 217b.

[6] Hailperin, p. 25; see also Aptowitzer, *Introductio ad Sefer Rabiah*, p. 395 cited Hailperin, p. 270, nn. 48-49; see also Shereshevsky, *Rashi: The Man and His World*, pp. 19-21.

[7] Heb. *lĕšôn;* on the many nuances of the Heb. term *lāšôn* (in the construct singular the form is *lĕšôn*) *see* below.

[8] Heb. *mĕnûḥātô kābôd;* moderns would say "may he rest in peace" or "may his memory be for a blessing."

[9] Heb. *wĕhu' nir'eh bĕ'ênay,* lit., "it seems in my eyes [to be correct]," a formulaic expression throughout the Talmud commentaries of Rashi and Tosafot.

[10] See below, for Rashi's designations of his various teachers.

Since Rashi's father Isaac has been referred to at least once as "the holy one," it is widely assumed that Rashi's father must have been martyred for his stubborn adherence to the ancestral faith.[11] Of Rashi's mother we know that she was the sister of the *paytan*, i.e., the composer of synagogal hymns, R. Simeon b. Isaac the Elder of Mainz (b. 950 C.E.), who was known also as Rabbi Simeon the Great.[12] Rashi quotes this uncle in his commentary on the Babylonian Talmud at Shabbat 85b.[13] There we read as follows:

> My teachers did not explain it thus, for they interpreted these *qĕrānôt* [to mean] 'borders'. I have many hesitations about it [their interpretation]. In the entire Talmud I am acquainted with *qĕrānôt* only [in the sense of] 'corners'. I have found support for myself [with respect to the meaning of the noun *qĕrānôt* in Rabbinic Heb.] in the work written by[14] R. Simeon the Elder my mother's brother on the basis of the oral teaching of[15] Rabbenu Gershom, the Patriarch[16] of the Exile.[17] The refutation by which my teacher R. Isaac b. Judah[18] attempted to refute it with three arguments was not correct in my eyes.

It is assumed that "Rashi received the education typical of his day."[19]

---

[11] Yehudah Leib HaKohen (Fischman) Maimon, ed., *Sefer Rashi* (Jerusalem: Mosad ha-Rav Kook, 1955), p. 8; Shereshevsky, *Rashi: The Man and His World*, p. 21.

[12] See S. M. Chones, *Toledot HaPoskim* (Warsaw, 1910), p. 207; quoted Shereshevsky, Rashi: The Man and His World, p. 21.

[13] Not p. 85a as given by Shereshevsky, *Rashi: the Man and His World*, p. 28, n. 7.

[14] Heb. *bysôdô šel*. Rashi's frequent use of the verb *yāsad* 'compose, write' (see Rashi's Commentary on Psalms at Ps. 42:1; 42:5c; 45:1; 57:1; 87:1; 88:1; 120:1) should suggest that *yĕsôdô šel R*. Mošeh Haddaršan (see Rashi's Commentary on Psalms at Ps. 45:2; 60:4; 62:13; 68:17; 80:6) means simply 'the book or the work by R. Moses the Interpreter' (not Preacher!; on the nuances of the verb *dāraš* in Rashi's Hebrew see Sarah Kamin, *Rashi's Exegetical Categorization* (Jerusalem: Magnes, 1986), pp. 136-157). The use of the expression *bysôdô šel* 'in the work written by' to refer to a lost commentary on the Talmud by Rashi's uncle R. Simeon the Elder should put to rest the notion that R. Moses Ha-Darshan wrote a book called *Yesod*. The source of that erroneous view concerning R. Moses Ha-Darshan is Abraham Epstein, *Moses ha-Darschan aus Narbonne* (Vienna: Alkalay, 1891), p. 10.

[15] Heb. *mippî*.

[16] Heb. *'ăbî*.

[17] I.e., the Jewish communities on either side of the Rhine, from which originated Ashkenazi Jewry; on the importance of Rabbenu Gershom b. Judah see below.

[18] On the importance of R. Isaac b. Judah in Rashi's life see below.

[19] Hailperin, p. 25

What precisely this should mean is uncertain as the author of the
latter writes

> Rashi either was sent to the Jewish school, or what seems to have
> been the commoner custom, his father likely engaged a young man
> as a resident tutor.[20]

On the basis of descriptions of the practice among Ashkenazi Jews
a generation or so after Rashi it is assumed that when Rashi was
five years of age he was brought to the school at dawn on the festival of Shavuot where the following would take place:

> They would then bring a slate upon which was written the first [four]
> letters of the [Hebrew] alphabet...and the final four letters of the al-
> phabet in reverse... and the sentence, "The law which Moses com-
> manded us" (Deut. 33:4), then the additional sentence, "Torah shall
> be my faith," and the first verse of the Book of Leviticus. The Rabbi
> would then read each letter and the child would read each letter af-
> ter him. Then the Rabbi would put a little honey on the slate and
> the boy would lick the honey which was on the letter with his
> tongue."[21]

Just as we do not know whether Rashi's earliest education was ob-
tained at home or at a school sponsored by the Jewish community
of Troyes so do we not know to what extent the course of study
resembled that described by R. Eleazar b. Judah of Worms (1160-
1238) or in the thirteenth century *Hukke Hatorah* as suggested by
Blumenfield.[22]

It seems to be agreed that regardless of the nature and extent of
his formal elementary education, by the time Rashi was thirty years
of age he had completed his monumental commentary on the
Pentateuch. At this point he left his native Troyes to study in the
established Jewish academies of Mainz and Worms. It is agreed
that Rashi's aim in studying at those *yeshivot* was to acquire the tools
necessary for preparing the definitive commentary on the Babylonian Talmud without which the latter would have been for all but a
select few in every generation a closed book.[23] Rashi's commentary

---

[20] Ibid., p. 26
[21] Blumenfield, p. 37 quoting *Sefer Asufot*; I have made minor corrections in
the English style; cf. Hailperin, p. 26.
[22] Blumenfield, pp. 39-41.
[23] Hailperin, p. 27; see also Solomon Zeitlin, "Rashi and the Rabbinate,"
JQR, n.s., 31(1940-41), pp. 35-36.

made possible the Babylonian Talmud's serving as the central object of study in Jewish higher education for almost nine centuries after the death of its author. At Mainz Rashi studied at the *yeshivah*, which had been presided over by Rabbenu Gershom b. Judah (960-1028), "the Light of the Exile," of whom Rashi said, "All Ashkenazic Jewry are the disciples of his disciples."[24] Rashi's teachers at Mainz were indeed Rabbenu Gershom's direct disciples, Rabbi Jacob son of Yakar, whom Rashi called *môrî hazzāqēn* 'my old teacher' and 'my teacher in Scripture'[25] and Rabbi Isaac son of Judah, whom Rashi called *môreh ṣedeq* 'virtuous teacher'.[26] Apparently, Rashi quite early surpassed the latter teacher in his expertise in *halakah* as the latter addressed some thirty-eight questions on Jewish law to Rashi.[27] After the death of R. Jacob son of Yakar Rashi continued his studies at the Worms *yeshivah* headed by R. Isaac b. Eliezer *segan Leviyyah*,[28] whom Rashi calls "our holy teacher."[29]

It has been argued that during his student days in the Rhineland Rashi returned to his native Troyes for every major Jewish holiday. This fact would explain why it is that when Rashi was queried concerning an aspect of the liturgical practice on the major holidays he could cite only the practice of Troyes, expressing ignorance of the procedure in Mainz and Worms.[30]

About the year 1070 Rashi returned from Worms to his native Troyes where he is said to have founded a *yeshivah*.[31] Troyes at that time probably had a total population of not more than ten thou-

---

[24] Joël Mueller, ed., *Réponses faites par de célèbres rabins français et lorrains du XI et XII siècle* (Vienna: Alkalay, 1881), #21.

[25] Hailperin, p. 27; Israel Ta-Shma, "Jacob Ben Yakar," *EJ* 9:1224; for the sources see Shereshevsky, *Rashi: the Man and His World*, p. 26.

[26] See Rashi's commentary to BT Yoma 16b; for additional sources see Shereshevsky, *Rashi: the Man and His World*, p. 34, n. 63.

[27] See Israel Elfenbein, *Responsa Rashi* (New York: Shulsinger, 1943), p. xxii for the list.

[28] I.e., a member of the tribe of Levi; to this day many of those who trace their ancestry to this tribe bear the family name Segal, an abbreviation of *segan Leviyyah*, because a member of the tribe of Levi functions as a *segan*, i.e., 'assistant' to the priests.

[29] For the sources see Israel Ta-Shma, "Isaac Ben Eliezer," *EJ* 9:18-19.

[30] Irving A. Agus, *The Heroic Age of Franco-German Jewry* (New York: Yeshiva University, 1969), p. 27; p.46, n. 56; cf. Mahzor Vitry, p. 358.

[31] Hailperin, p. 27; Joshua Bloch, "Rashi: The Great Expounder of the Bible and Talmud," in *Rashi, His Teaching and Personality*, ed. Simon Federbusch (New York: Cultural Division of the World Jewish Congress, 1958), p. 52; see also below, pp. 11–22.

sand persons.[32] Baron argues that Rashi may "have had with him [in Troyes] no more than some 100-200 Jewish fellow citizens."[33]

Hence, argues Baron:

> We may visualize this tiny settlement as consisting of persons living in close quarters around their synagogue and constantly marrying among themselves. What Jacob Tam tells of the equally significant community of Orléans several decades later, namely that, with the exception of the rabbi, all its Jews were related to one another by blood or by marriage, undoubtedly applied also to the community over which Rashi presided. This constant mingling, incidentally, explains to us the otherwise strange phenomenon that almost all of Rashi's disciples and friends recorded in the sources appear to have been related to him in some degree or other.[34]

Baron concludes, therefore:

> Rashi was the leader of a predominantly rural Jewish community whose influence beyond the borders of the town was based partly upon its incipient commercial relations with more distant localities, partly upon the centralized power of the counts of Champagne residing in their Troyes castle and, most of all, upon Rashi's own intellectual preëminence.[35]

Moreover, says Baron:

> The renowned academy..., over which Rashi presided, need not have resembled in its externals any of the later regular Jewish institutions of higher learning. We may simply envisage Solomon Yizhaki as the owner of a vineyard, which he cultivated with the assistance of his family,[36] spending most of his free time—vineyards may allow for a good deal of free time—teaching a few pupils, mostly members of

---

[32] Salo W. Baron, "Rashi and the Community of Troyes," in *Rashi Anniversary Volume*, ed. H. L. Ginsberg (New York: American Academy for Jewish Research, 1941), p. 59.

[33] Ibid.; Baron explains (there, n. 18) that he arrives at these figures "on the basis of some extant tax records in France as well as Germany"; Louis Rabinowitz, *The Social Life of the Jews of Northern France in the XII–XIV Centuries* (2ᵈ ed.; New York: Hermon, 1972), pp. 30-32 arrives at similar figures on the basis of a variety of sources.

[34] Baron, p. 59.

[35] Ibid., p. 58.

[36] See Liber, *Rashi*, p. 56; Agus, p. 173; Israel S. Elfenbein, "Rashi in His Responsa," in *Rashi, His Teachings and Personality*, ed. Federbusch, p. 67; contrast Haym Soloveitchik, "Can Halakhic Texts Talk History?" *AJS Review* 3 (1978), 172, n. 54.

his own family, discussing with them the fine points in Bible and Talmud and, perhaps with their assistance, compiling and revising his bulky commentaries.[37]

"It is astounding," says Baron, "with what vigor such a tiny community managed to pursue its independent intellectual career and to spread its influence over a vast area of northern France and western Germany."[38] It is even more significant and more astounding that such a small community should have exerted through the writings of Rashi and his disciples an influence on world Jewry and beyond Jewry comparable only, perhaps to that of the Bible and the Talmud before him and the Kabbalah and Modern Zionism after him.

Between 1070 and his death in 1105 Rashi completed his commentaries on the Early and Later Prophets and all of the Hagiographa except Ezra-Nehemiah and Chronicles.[39] Likewise, it was during this period that he wrote commentaries on most of the Babylonian Talmud. He is reported to have died while writing the word 'pure' in his commentary to BT Makkot 19b.[40] Apparently incomplete at the time of his death was the commentary on the biblical Book of Job.[41] Also belonging to the most mature phase of Rashi's scholarly productivity is the Commentary on the Book of Psalms here presented with English translation and supercommentary.

It has been argued that Rashi's failure to comment on Pss. 121, 128, 134 derives from his failure to live long enough to complete the commentary.[42] The assumption that the Commentary on the Book of Psalms belongs to the latest phase of Rashi's creativity is supported by (1) his treatment in the Commentary on the Book of Psalms of the phenomenon today variously called "the expanded

---

[37] Baron, p. 60; but see below, pp. 19–20.

[38] Ibid.

[39] Hailperin, p. 31; see also the sources cited there; for details see below, pp. 63–75.

[40] So it is recorded there in the parentheses, which separate the last words of Rashi's commentary from the first words of the commentary of Rabbi Judah b. Nathan; for critical analysis of this account see below, pp. 38–41.

[41] I. Maarsen, *Parshandatha: The Commentary of Rashi on the Prophets and Hagiographs* [sic], Part III. Psalms (Jerusalem, 1936), p. viii, n. 3; Moshe Sokolow, "Establishing the Text of Rashi's Commentary on the Book of Job," *PAAJR* 48 (1981), p. 35.

[42] Maarsen, p. viii; Benjamin J. Gelles, *Peshat and Derash in the Exegesis of Rashi*, Études sur le judaisme médiéval, tome IX (Leiden: E. J. Brill, 1981), pp. 138–139.

colon" or "staircase parallelism" and which Rashi himself is said to have called "Samuel verses" because he learned about the poetic structure of these verses from his grandson R. Samuel b. Meir (Rashbam);[43] and (2) his tendency in the commentary before us to

---

[43] It is well known that when Rashi first wrote his commentary on Ex. 15:6 he wrote as follows: "YOUR RIGHT HAND, YOUR RIGHT HAND. [The expression is repeated] twice for when Israel perform God's will the left [hand] becomes [strong like the] right [hand] (cf. *Mekhilta*, vol. 2, p. 41). YOUR RIGHT HAND, O LORD, IS GLORIOUS IN POWER to save Israel, and Your second right hand SHATTERS THE FOE. Now it seems to me that the same right hand [that is GLORIOUS IN POWER (v. 6a)] SHATTERS THE FOE (v. 6b), a feat which a human cannot perform, [i.e.], two acts with one hand." However, as noted by A. Berliner, *Raschi: Der Kommentar des Salomo b. Isak über den Pentateuch.* (2ᵈ ed.; Frankfurt-am-Main: J. Kaufmann, 1905), p. ix, what immediately follows in all editions of Rashi's commentary is an interpretation based upon the following comment of his grandson Samuel b. Meir at Ex. 15:6: "This verse is like 'The rivers lifted up, O LORD, the rivers lifted up their voices' (Ps. 93:3); 'How long will the wicked, O LORD, how long will the wicked exult' (Ps. 94:3); 'Surely, Your enemies, O LORD, surely Your enemies will perish' (Ps. 92:10). [In each of these verses] the first part does not complete its thought before the second part repeats [its words] and completes its thought; note that the first part names the subject." Summarizing these words present editions of Rashi's commentary on Ex. 15:6 add the following words: "The real meaning of the verse [*pĕšûṭô šel miqrā;* since Rashi here follows Rashbam's interpretation the expression must be understood according to Rashbam's usage; on Rashi's usage of the term see Kamin, *Rashi's Exegetical Categorization*, pp. 111-136] is 'As for the predicate of [the subject] YOUR RIGHT HAND, O LORD, which is glorious IN POWER, it is [that] YOUR RIGHT HAND SHATTERS THE FOE.' A number of Scripture verses [exemplify] its literary form [i.e., expanded colon or staircase parallelism]: [E.g.], 'Surely, Your enemies, O LORD, surely Your enemies perish' and [the verses that are] like them." Berliner explains that Rashi added this comment and the full list of examples cited by Rashbam (these have been eliminated in most mss. and printed editions) because he had come to accept his grandson's understanding of the stylistic device today called "staircase parallelism" or "expanded colon". That this is precisely what happened is demonstrated by the remark in ms. Bodleian 271 and in ms. Vienna 32 of the comments of the Tosaphists on the Pentateuch at Gen. 49:22: "The aforementioned interpretation is from the work [*yĕsôd;* i.e., the Pentateuch commentary] of R. Samuel [b. Meir]. When his grandfather, Rabbi Solomon [i.e., Rashi] would come to those verses, he would call them Samuel verses after his [the Rashbam's] name" (cited by Samuel Poznanski, *Kommentar zu Ezechiel und den XII kleinen Propheten von Eliezer aus Beaugency* [Warsaw: Mekize Nirdamim, 1913], p. xlv [in Hebrew]). Hence, when Rashi adopts Rashbam's approach in his exegesis of Ps. 96:7 (see our discussion there) and takes for granted this approach in his commentary at Ps. 29:1; 93:3 Rashi testifies to the psalter commentary's belonging together with the revised commentary on Ex. 15:6 to the latter phase of Rashi's creativity when he had the good fortune to be able to learn from his grandson, Samuel b. Meir (c.1080-1158). Important modern treatments of the stylistic device in question are Samuel. E. Loewenstamm, "The Expanded Colon in Ugaritic and Biblical Verse," *JSS* 14 (1969),

allude briefly to the exegesis of biblical verses on which he has commented at length in his commentary on the Babylonian Talmud.[44]

Rashi had three daughters, whose names were Miriam, Jochebed, and Rachel. The last also bore the French name Bellasez. Miriam married Rabbi Judah b. Nathan, who completed Rashi's commentary on BT Makkot.[45] Jochebed married R. Meir son of Samuel. They had four sons: R. Samuel b. Meir, Rabbenu Isaac, Rabbi Solomon, and Rabbenu Jacob, who is commonly called Rabbenu Tam on the basis of Gen. 25:27, which states, *Ya'aqob 'iš tām* "Jacob was a mild man."[46]

It has been argued that the First Crusade (1096) had no impact on Rashi's life.[47] Weinryb argued, however, that Rashi's introduction to the Book of Genesis, in which he insists that the Torah begins with Creation in order to demonstrate that God as Creator had the right to take away the land of Israel from the Canaanites and give it to Israel, may have been inspired by the First Crusade, which was an attempt to assert Christian sovereignty over the land

---

pp. 176-196; Y. Avishur, "Addenda to the Expanded Colon in Ugaritic and Biblical Verse," *UF* 4 (1972), pp. 1-10; E. L. Greenstein, "Two Variations of Grammatical Parallelism in Canaanite Poetry and Their Psycholinguistic Background," *JANES* 6 (1974), 96-105; Chaim Cohen, "Studies in Early Israelite Poetry I: An Unrecognized Case of Three-Line Staircase Parallelism in the Song of the Sea," *JANES* 7 (1975), pp. 14-17; E. L. Greenstein, "One More Step on the Staircase," *UF* 9 (1977), pp. 77-86.

[44] See, e.g., his comments on Ps. 112:8; 120:3; 127:2, 3, 4; 140:9. All of Rashi's comments on biblical verses embedded in his commentary on the Babylonian Talmud have been systematically arranged according to the order of the verses in the Hebrew Bible by Yoel Florsheim, *Rashi on the Bible in His Commentary on the Talmud* (3 vols.: Jerusalem: Rubin Mass, 1981-1991) [in Hebrew].

[45] See below, p. 39.

[46] Concerning these scholars and their contributions see Shereshevsky, *Rashi: The Man and His World*, pp. 22-25; concerning Rashbam see Ezra Zion Melamed, *Biblical Commentators* (2 vols.; Jerusalem: Magnes, 1975), 1:358-448; Sara Japhet and Robert Salters, *The Commentary of R. Samuel Ben Meir Rashbam on Qoheleth* (Jerusalem: Magnes, 1985); E. Touito, "Concerning Rashbam's Method in His Commentary on the Pentateuch," *Tarbiz* 48 (1979), pp. 248-73 (in Hebrew); id., "Rashbam's Method in His Commentary on the Legal Portions of the Pentateuch," *Mile't* 2 (1984), pp. 275-288 (in Hebrew). On Isaac see Shlomoh Zalman Havlin, "Isaac Ben Meir," *EJ* 9:23-24; on Solomon see Israel. Ta-Shma, "Solomon Ben Meir," *EJ* 15:125; on Rabbenu Tam see id., "Tam, Jacob b. Meir," *EJ* 15:779-81.

[47] Hailperin, p. 21; contrat Abraham Grossman, "Rashi's Commentary on Psalms and Jewish-Christian Polemics," in *Studies in the Bible and Education Presented to Professor Moshe Ahrend*, ed. Dov Rappel (Jerusalem: Touro College Press, 1996), pp. 59-74

of Israel.[48] It has been also arued that Rashi's comment on Num. 16:3 where Rashi has Korah say to Moses, "If you have taken royalty for yourself, then at least you should not have chosen the priesthood for your brother," alludes to the investiture struggle, waged in Europe during the years 1075-1122.[49]

Because the study of both the Pentateuch and the Babylonian Talmud were inextricably linked to the study of Rashi's commentaries in the culture of the East European Jew, Jews grew up assuming that Rashi, like all of their teachers, spoke Yiddish and that the 3,000 French glosses in Rashi's commentaries must represent an old form of Yiddish.[50] It is against this background that one can appreciate the emphasis in the modern biographies of Rashi on the following: (1) Rashi and his fellow Jews dressed just like their Christian neighbors; (2) Rashi and his fellow Jews spoke the same Northern Old French as did their Christian neighbors; special Jewish languages such as Judeo-Spanish and Yiddish emerged only in the fifteenth century; (3) Rashi and his fellow Jews did not live in a ghetto; the first ghetto was built in Venice in the sixteenth century.[51]

---

[48] Bernard D. Weinryb, "Rashi Against the Background of His Epoch," in *Rashi Anniversary Volume*, ed. H. L. Ginsberg (New York: American Academy for Jewish Research, 1941), pp. 41-42. Maarsen, p. xii sees in Rashi's remark in his comment at Ps. 90:14, "the troubles which we have endured during these OUR DAYS," a reference to the Crusades; similarly Shereshevsky, *Rashi: The Man and His World*, p. 241 with respect to Rashi's comment on Ps. 73:14, "Continually each morning new troubles are devised."

[49] Weinryb, pp. 40-41.

[50] So M. Ahrend in the introduction to his lecture, "Concerning Rashi's Approach to Lexicography," (in Hebrew) presented at the Colloque Israélo-Français sur Rachi (March 8, 1988).

[51] Hailperin, pp. 16-17; Rabinowitz, p. 237; similarly Liber, *Rashi*, pp. 19-23.

II. Rashi's School and Disciples

As we noted, Rashi is said to have set up his own school or *yeshivah* in Troyes in approximately 1070 when he was only thirty years old.[1] The first students, who boarded in Rashi's own home, were Simhah of Vitry,[2] Shemayah,[3] Judah b. Abraham,[4] Judah b. Nathan,[5] and

---

[1] See above, p. 5.

[2] Simhah's son Samuel married Rashi's granddaughter who was the daughter of R. Meir and Jochebed (see Grossman, *The Early Sages of France*, p. 171). This granddaughter was the sister of R. Samuel b. Meir (known by his acronym Rashbam; concerning him see Sarah Jafet and Robert B. Salters, *The Commentary of R. Samuel Ben Meir* Rashbam *on Qoheleth* (Jerusalem: Magnes, 1985), pp. 11-16). Samuel the son of R. Simhah of Vitry was the father of R. Isaac the Elder of Dampierre; concerning the latter and his overwhelming influence on the commentaries called *Tosafot* found in the outer margins of the standard editions of the Babylonian Talmud see E. E. Urbach, *The Tosaphists: Their History, Writings and Methods* (4th enlarged ed.; 2 vols.; Jerusalem: Bialik Institute, 1980), 1:226-260 (in Hebrew). Unquestionably, the most important contribution of R. Simhah of Vitry was his *Mahzor Vitry*, which is best described as an annotated prayerbook with appendices. As explained by Grossman, *The Early Sages of France*, pp. 395-403, such an annotated prayerbook had already been composed by R. Yosef Tov Elem (concerning this predecessor of Rashi see below, pp. 119.). However, as Grossman emphasizes, it was the disciples of Rashi—R. Shemayah, R. Simhah of Vitry, R. Jacob b. R. Samson, R. Samuel b. Perigors [Concerning R. Samuel b. Perigors see Grossman, *The Early Sages of France,,* p. 172. Perhaps R. Samuel's father was the R. Perigors of France; according to R. Abraham Ibn Daud, *The Book of Tradition*, 78-81, R. Perigors of France was one of the important teachers of Isaac b. Baruch Albalia (1035-1094), the poet, astronomer and talmudist, who served as court astrologer to King al-Mu'tawid of Seville], who developed the genre of the annotated prayerbook called *Mahzor*. Grossman, *The Early Sages of France*, pp. 402-403, argues that the main impetus to the development of this genre, which was typical of French Jewry in the generations following Rashi, was Rashi's having dared both to question established liturgical practices and to establish new ones. Typical of Rashi's concern with such matters is his *responsum* (Elfenbein, *Responsa Rashi* # 18; see also *Mahzor Vitry* #345) as to why during the High Holy Days one concludes the 11th blessing of the Eighteen Benedictions with the formula *hammelek hammišpāṭ* (see Birnbaum, *Daily Prayer Book*, pp. 93-94) where elementary Hebrew grammar (see *GKC* # 127) would seem to require the formula *melek hammišpāṭ* 'the just King'. Rashi remarks that the accepted formula in which the definite article precedes both of the two elements in the construct genitive chain is probably a mistake and that the correct and original form was probably *melek hammišpāṭ*. However, suggests Rashi, the accepted formula was probably formed on the analogy of the formula which conludes the third blessing of the Eighteen Benedictions during the Ten Days of Penitence, *hammelek haqqadoš* 'the Holy King' (see Birnbaum, there, pp. 89-90) in which however the two elements are not construct genitive but noun

followed by attributive adjective. Moreover, Rashi points out, exceptional cases of the use of the prefixed definite article before both elements of a construct chain are found already in the Bible as in Jer. 31:40 [*ha'emeq happĕgārîm*] ; 2 Kgs. 16:14 [*hammizbēaḥ hannĕḥôśet*] and Jer. 32:12 [*hassēper hammiqnāh*] (cf. *GKC* # 127h). Like modern Jewish prayerbooks, *Mahzor Vitry* provides a version of the daily, Sabbath, festival and high holy day prayers including the songs prescribed to be sung at the Sabbath dinner table. In addition to an extensive selection of liturgical poems (Heb. *piyyutim*), *Mahzor Vitry* also provides rules for the writing of the texts contained in *tefillin* and *mezuzot*, Like modern day Rabbis' Manuals and unlike modern daily prayerbooks, *Mahzor Vitry* formulae for such legal documents as the bill of divorce (Heb. *get*) and the marriage contract (*ketubbah*) and even the formula for the writ of emancipation of a female slave; see S. Hurwitz, ed., *Machsor* [*sic*] *Vitry* (2ᵈ ed.; Nürnberg: J. Bulka, 1923), p. 792. In the Middle Ages the Church forbade Jewish ownership of Christian slaves. Jews, like Christians, did, however, own slaves, who were non-Christians from Eastern Europe, hence the designation in Medieval Latin of men and women from Eastern Europe as *slavi* and *slavae* respectively. Just as in the antebellum United States of America being a slave and being of African birth or descent were synonymous so in Medieval Europe being a slave and being of Eastern European origin were synonymous; hence from the single Latin term *slavus* we have the two English derivates 'slave' referring to a man or woman held as a chattel and 'Slav' referring to a person who speaks a language belonging to that family of languages prominent among which are Russian, Ukranian, Polish, and Serbian. Consequently, in Medieval Hebrew the term 'Canaanite' (alluding to the paradigmatic slave, Canaan, in Gen. 9:25-27) designates Slavs and their language(s). Concerning French Jews' owning slaves in the time of Rashi see Hans Georg von Mutius, *Rechtsentscheide Rachis aus Troyes (1040-1105)*, Judentum und Umwelt, vols. 15/I-15/II (2 vols.; Frankfurt am Main: Peter Lang, 1986-87), vol. 1, p. 16; Simḥah Assaf, "Slaves and the Slave Trade Among Jews in the Middle Ages," in Simḥah Assaf, *Be-OhaleyYa'akov* (Jerusalem: Mossad Harav Kook, 1943), pp. 223-256. That *Mahzor Vitry* provides the formula for writing a writ of emancipation for a female slave indicates not only that Jews, like their Christian neighbors, held slaves but also that at least some Jewish slaveowners, including the intellectual and spiritual elite associated with Rashi, endeavored to abide by the humanitarian rules adumbrated in Hebrew Scripture and spelled out in *halakah*. In light of this detail, which is alluded to by the inclusion in *Mahzor Vitry* of the formula for a writ of emancipation, the interpretation by Rashi, Ibn Ezra and Nahmanides in their biblical commentaries of Deut. 23:16, "You shall not surrender a runaway slave to his owner," as applying, *inter alia*, to Gentiles whom Jews held as chattels means the following: 1) their interpretation was more than an academic exercise; 2) their interpretation suggests that the Torah taught by Rashi and his circle and the other aforementioned culture heroes of medieval Rabbinic Judaism continued to be that very Torah, which in the words of Judah M. Rosenthal, "The Slavery Controversy and Judaism," *Conservative Judaism* 31, no. 3 (1977), p. 69, "distinguishes itself by demanding a humane treatment of slaves." Rosenthal, in his posthumously published article, pp. 69-79 bends over backwards to show that not all ancient, medieval and modern rabbis taught the Torah's highest ideals. This should not be surprising. What appears to be of far greater significance is the fact that the aforementioned exegesis of Deut. 23:16 shows that living in societies where Jews did own Gentile slaves, Jewish communal leaders insisted on interpreting literally an ancient biblical law, which was light years ahead of the modern world on the eve of the American Civil War. *Mahzor Vitry* intersperses its recording R. Simhah's understanding of the correct text of the prayers and blessings with citation of sources, rules and explanations of the subtle meanings of liturgical formulae. Grossman, *The Early Sages of France*, p. 171 points out that R. Simhah made extensive use of the no longer extant *Mahzor* produced by R. Shemayah (see below, n. 3). Grossman, there, p. 172, explains, "R. Simhah took from it [the *Mahzor* of R. Shemayah] much of Rashi's teaching as well as the teaching of the Babylonian Geonim and the early sages of Ashkenaz. To these he added [the traditions] which he personally received from Rashi." Grossman, there, p. 170 quotes from a *responsum* of Rabbenu Tam that *Mahzor Vitry* is especially valuable because "it contains explanations of most of the matters [pertaining to liturgy] from *Seder Rav Amram* [the oldest complete Jewish prayerbook; it was compiled by Rav Amram, who was head of the academy of Sura from 856 to 874 C.E.; see David Hedegard, ed., *Seder R. Amram Gaon, Part I* (Lund; Lindstedt, 1951), p. xx; Tryggve Kronholm, ed., *Seder R. Amram Gaon, Part II* (Lund: CWK Gleerup, 1974), p. xxiii], *Halakot Gedolot* [written by Simeon Qayyara, this codification of *halakah*, is regarded as the single most important *halakic* work of the Gaonic period; see Esriel Hildesheimer, *Sefer Halakhot Gedolot, edited from mss. and with introduction and notes* (3 vols; Jerusalem: Mekize Nirdamim, 1971-1988), Rabbenu Solomon [i.e., Rashi] and the other Geonim [see below, n. 5] and it can be found in most places." Interestingly enough, notwithstanding the fact that the book was not published until 1893 [ed. S. Hurwitz (Berlin: Itzkowski), eight medieval mss. of this work survived and they include two of the oldest surviving Hebrew mss. from the Middle Ages. New York JTS Ms. 8334 completed in the year 1204 C.E. and Sassoon Ms. 535 from the middle of the 12th century C.E. are especially important witnesses to the original form of *Mahzor Vitry*. See I. Ta-Shma, "Concerning Some Matters Pertaining to Mahzor Vitry," *Alei Sefer* 11 (1984), pp. 81-89 (in Hebrew); David Solomon Sassoon, *Ohel David* (2 vols.: Oxford: Oxford University Press, 1932), 1:311; Grossman, *The Early Sages of France*, p. 172, n. 180.

[3] R. Shemayah may have come to Troyes from Italy (see Grossman, *The Early Sages of France*, p. 351-52), and he became Rashi's disciple c. 1080 (there, p. 352). He was probably born c. 1060, and he died somewhere in France c. 1130 (see there, p. 352). According to Rabbenu Tam, one of R. Shemayah's daughters married one of Rashi's grandsons, most likely Rabbi Samuel b. Meir (Rashbam) c. 1100. Moreover, R. Shemayah himself informs us that at that daughter's wedding Rashi delivered the charge to the bride and groom, in which Rashi chose as his text a line from one of the liturgical poems of Eliezer ha-Kalir. There is some evidence that R. Shemayah had two daughters and a son; see Grossman, there, pp. 348-349, 352. For many years R. Shemayah lived in Rashi's house and ate at his table, and he served as Rashi's personal secretary (see Grossman, there, p. 353). Shemayah referred to Rashi usually as "Rabbi," i.e., "my mentor" but not infrequently as "the saint" or "our saintly rabbi" (there, p. 353) while Rashi referred to Shemayah in his personal correspondence as "my brother". Just as in the letters of Middle Eastern kings of the Bronze and Iron Ages "my brother" as against "my servant" means "my ally" as against "my vassal," so in the context of Rashi's letters to Shemayah "my brother" means "my esteemed colleague" as against "my disciple". R. Shemayah edited Rashi's personal correspondence, and he wrote fascinating commentaries on the liturgical poems of R. Eliezer ha-Kalir (see Grossman, there, pp. 355-58; see notes there for citation of the medieval mss. containing these commentaries). He helped Rashi edit the final versions of Rashi's commentaries

on Isaiah and Ezekiel, and he was present and available for consultation when Rashi edited the final version of his Commentary on Psalms. Among Shemayah's most important contributions are his extensive glosses on the Commentary of Rashi on the Pentateuch contained in Leipzig Stadtbibliothek, Ms. Wagenseil, B.H. fol. 1, which was produced by a scribe named R. Makir b. Creshbia [on the spelling of this name see Grossman, *The Early Sages of France*, p. 360; cf. Blondheim, "Liste des manuscrits des commentaires bibliques de Raschi," *REJ* 91 (1931), p. 85] who included also some of his own and some of his father's interpretations of Rashi as well; see Grossman, *The Early Sages of France*, p. 360. The glosses in this ms. contain not only the valuable and largely untapped insights of R. Shemayah but also important material which R. Shemayah received orally from Rashi himself. See the extensive discussion in Grossman, *The Early Sages of France*, p. 359-366; id., "Marginal Notes and Addenda of R. Shemaiah and the Text of Rashi's Bible Commentary," *Tarbiz* 60 (1991), pp. 67-98 (in Hebrew); id. "MS Leipzig 1 and Rashi's Commentary on the Bible," *Tarbiz* 61 (1992), pp. 205-315 (in Hebrew); contrast E. Touito, "Does MS Leipzig 1 Really Reflect the Authentic Version of Rashi's Commentary on the Pentateuch?" *Tarbiz* 61 (1992), pp. 85-115 (in Hebrew). The views of Grossman, who assigns to the ms. a 13th century dated and Touito, who assigns a 14th century date, were held by Leopold Zunz and Franz Delitzsch respectively in the 19th century; see Blondheim, "Liste des manuscrits des commentaires bibliques de Raschi," p.85.

⁴ The latter was the very close friend and associate of R. Shemayah. In setting down in writing Rashi's version of the Passover Haggadah, which still awaits full and proper publication, R. Shemayah states, "I Shemayah and R. Judah b. R. Abraham heard these things from the mouth of the saint, may his memory be for good, and may he who is at rest be honored"; see Grossman, *The Early Sages of France*, p. 237; p. 404, n. 177; see also Raphael Rabbinovicz, *Variae Lectiones in Mischnam et in Talmud Baylonicum (Diqduqe Soferim), Pars. VI. Tract. Psachim* (Munich: E. Huber, 1874), p. 195b. In his glosses on Rashi's Pentateuch Commentary found in Leipzig Stadtbibliothek, Ms. Wagenseil, B.H. fol. 1, p. 122b, Shemayah reports that in arriving at his reconciliation of the apparent contradiction between Ex. 25:15, "the staves will not move therefrom" and Num. 4:14, "they will place the staves," Rashi was inspired by a question addressed to him by Judah b. Abraham; see Grossman, *The Early Sages of France*, pp. 171, 196, n. 230. Mahzor Vitry Ms. Munich 346, p. 92a and Ms. Paris 646 report that it was Shemayah who discovered that the statement "Your promise is trustworthy and abides forever" (cf. Birnbaum, *High Holyday Prayer Book*, pp. 35-36: "and thy word is true and permanent forever") is based upon PRK [see ed. Mandelbaum, pp. 33-34, Pisqa A; see below, pp. 34, n. 24] and that he showed this to his colleague R. Judah b. Abraham; cf. Grossman, *The Early Sages of France*, p. 398.

⁵ R. Judah b. Nathan (his acronym is Riban) wrote commentaries on most of the tractates of BT and a commentary on the Pentateuch; see J. N. Epstein, "The Commentaries of R. Jehudah ben Nathan and the Commentaries of Worms," *Tarbiz* 4 (1932), p. 13 (in Hebrew). In fact, the commentary on BT Makkot 19b-24a in the current editions of BT belongs to Riban's complete commentary on Makkot; see id., "The Commentaries of R. Jehudah ben Nathan and the Commentaries of Worms," *Tarbiz* 4(1933), p. 183 (in Hebrew). The commentary on Tractate Nazir attributed to Rashi on the standard editions of BT is also from the pen of Riban (see id., "The Commentaries of R. Jehudah ben Nathan and the Commentaries of Worms," *Tarbiz* 4 (1933), p. 153 (in Hebrew). Reuven Margolis, *Nizozey Or* (Jerusalem: Mossad Harav Kook, 1965), p. 98 assigns to Riban also the commen-

Meir b. Samuel.[6] It is reported in a Bodleian Library manuscript quoted by Grossman that it once happened that without Rashi's knowledge Rashi's maidservant purchased flour on a festival day for preparing food for the *yeshivah* students resident in Rashi's home.[7]

---

tary on BT Horayot, which the standard editions attribute to Rashi; contrast J. N. Epstein, "The Commentary on Horayot Attributed to Rashi," *Tarbiz* 3 (1932), pp. 218-225 (in Hebrew); Epstein holds that the latter commentary belongs to the Mainz Commentary on BT. The little that is known concerning the biography of Riban includes the tradition that he married Rashi's daughter Miriam. They had two children, a son and a daughter. The son of Miriam and Riban was Rabbi Yom Tov bar Judah, who is also called Rabbi Yom Tov of Falaise. He was a contemporary of Rashbam. It is Rabbenu Tam's answer to a question sent by R. Yom Tov that supplies the information that Rashi's third daughter was Rachel (Rabbenu Tam refers to her as "our [Rabbenu Tam's and R. Yom Tov's] aunt") who was married to and later was divorced by a certain R. Eliezer; see Grossman, *The Early Sages of France*, p. 125. Riban's and Miriam's daughter was Elvina, whose testimony to certain dietary practices is cited in some versions of the so-called *Teshuvot Maimuniyyot* [these are responsa of Franco-German origin, which form an appendix to the the *Haggahot Maimuniyyot* and hence an appendix to the standard editions of Maimonides, Mishneh Torah. Shlomoh Zalman Havlin, "Haggahot Maimuniyyot," *EJ* 7:1110-1112, following Urbach, *Tosaphists*, pp. 434-436, explains that this work is a collection of marginal notes to 9 out of the 14 books of Moses Maimonides (1135-1204), Mishneh Torah. This collection of glosses was composed late in the 13th century by R. Meir ha-Kohen of Rothenburg, brother-in-law of the famous Ashkenazic *halakic* authority, Mordecai b. Hillel, and disciple of R. Meir of Rothenburg. The purpose of Meir ha-Kohen's glosses and the appended responsa was to attach to Maimonides' compendium of Talmudic *halakah* the legal traditions of Ashkenazic Judaism. Current editions of this work are based upon the edition printed at Venice by Daniel Bomberg in 1524. Scholars generally prefer the readings in that edition to those found in other early editons.] to Maimonides' Mishneh Torah, Laws of Forbidden Foods #5 [see Epstein, "The Commentaries of R. Jehudah ben Nathan," p 12, n. 8]. The current editions read instead "Miriam the granddaughter of Rabbenu Shelomo (i.e., Rashi) while Urbach, *Tosafists*, vol.1 p. 38 argues that the correct reading is "Miriam the daughter of Rabbenu Shelomo" (i.e., Rashi).

[6] He married Rashi's daughter Jochebed, who bore him four sons. The eldest son was Rabbi Samuel b. Meir, commonly known by his acronym, Rashbam. The youngest son was Rabbenu Tam. Concerning Rabbi Meir b. Samuel see Grossman, *The Early Sages of France*, pp. 168-170 and the literature cited there.

[7] M. Breuer, "Toward the Investigation of the Typology of Western *Yeshivot* in the Middle Ages," in *Studies in the History of Jewish Society in the Middle Ages and in the Modern Period Presented to Professor Jacob Katz on his Seventy-Fifth Birthday*, ed. E. Etkes and Y. Salmon (Jerusalem: Magnes, 1980), pp. 49-53 (in Hebrew) argues that the *yeshivot* of France and Germany both during Rashi's student days and during Rashi's years as head of a *yeshivah* in Troyes were located in the respective homes of the heads of those *yeshivot*. Breuer contends that each student had his own bedroom located on an upper floor; that the students ate their meals with the head of the *yeshivah* and his family at the family's dining table; that the class sessions took place in the family's living room, which was called on the basis of Jer. 36:22;

When the matter was brought to Rashi's attention he permitted the use of the flour after the fact.[8] From the flowery introduction to a series of *halakic* questions addressed to Rashi by two of his disciples, Azriel son of R. Nathan[9] and Joseph son of R. Judah[10] we learn that the school over which Rashi presided was called *Yeshivat Ge'on Ya'aqov*, which is to say the *yeshivah* which is the Glory of Jacob, i.e., of the Jewish People, who are the descendants of Jacob the Patriarch and that Rashi's title was *Rosh Yeshivat Ge'on Ya'aqov*, head of the *yeshivah* which is the Glory of Jacob.[11] This means that Rashi

---

Am. 3:16 "the winter house." The latter room, Breuer, p. 51, explains, "was the largest room in the house and the only room which was provided with a heating stove. In the fall and winter most of the domestic activities were carried on here, and the family members sat there and ate their meals there." On the basis of John Thomas Smith, Patrick Arthur Faulkner, and Anthony Emery, *Studies in Medieval Domestic Architecture*, ed. M. J. Swanton (London:Royal Archaeological Institute, 1975), p. 85f. and Ludolf Veltheim-Lottum, *Kleine Weltgeschichte des Städtischen Wohnhauses*, vol. 1 (Heidelberg:L. Schneider, 1952), pp. 204f. Breuer, p. 51, n. 38 argues that the size of the so-called winter house or living room, which, in Breuer's view, doubled as the the *bet midrash* or lecture hall of the typical medieval Ashkenazic *yeshivah*, was 7 square meters. Moreover, Breuer suggests, the reason that Ashkenazic women of the era of Rashi and Tosaphot were so knowledgeable in *halakah* is that the *bet midrash* was, in fact, their living room. Breuer concludes, therefore, that a typical *yeshivah* of the era in question had no more than ten students and that in many cases the number of students was even smaller. In fact, R. Meir of Rotenberg in his famous *responsum* (cited below, n. 32), which refers to the yeshivah students' bording in his own palatial home distinguishes between 'the winter house' and 'the *bet midrash*'. Breuer cites as an additional reason for the small number of students evidence that the municipal authorities limited the number of students (see, with Breuer, p. 51, Karl Bücher, *Die Bevölkerung von Frankfort a. M. im XIV. und XV. Jahrhundert* (Tübingen : H. Laupp, 1886), p. 543 n. 3; p. 568). Breuer, p. 52 is forced to conclude that reports that some *yeshivot* such as that headed by R. Jacob Moellin (Maharil (c. 1360-1427)] had at one time more than fifty students must simply be exaggerated and unreliable. Contrast the evidence assembled by Norman Golb, *The Jews in Medieval Normandy* (Cambridge: Cambridge University Press, 1998), pp. 192-198; 563-576.

[8] Grossman, *The Early Sages of France*, p. 166; see also the discussion there, n. 156.

[9] Joël Müller, *Réponses faites de célèbres rabins français et lorrains du XI. et XII. siècle* (Vienna: Loevy & Alkalay, 1881), p. 9b, n. 1 to #15 (in Hebrew) notes that R. Azriel son of R. Nathan was "a relative of Rashi, perhaps brother of Rashi's son-in-law R. Judah b. Nathan" [on whom see above, n. 4].

[10] At this juncture all we know of R. Joseph son of Judah is that he was "a dear friend of Rashi" (so also Müller, *Réponses*, p. 4a, n. 1 to # 6); the basis for the latter assertion is Rashi's statement in the *responsum* to which we refer here, which was previously published in Müller as *responsum* #15, q.v.

[11] Elfenbein, *Responsa Rashi*, p. 93 #73; for a clear refutation of the possibility that in its biblical context in Am. 8:7 the Hebrew expression 'glory of Jacob' is a divine epithet see Shalom M. Paul, *Amos*, Hermeneia (Minneapolis: Fortress, 1999),

deliberately adopted for the name of his academy the name borne by the world famous *yeshivah*, which in Rashi's time stood in Baghdad and was headed by R. Isaac b. Moses b. Sakri.[12] and which traced its origins to the academy founded by Rav in 219 at Sura in Babylonia.[13] As late as the middle of the 11th century C.E. this academy and its sister academy, Pumbeditha, were together seen by Jews throughout the world as the spiritual umbilicus of Judaism.[14] They were, *mutatis mutandi*, the medieval Jewish counterpart of the English Oxbridge (a term frequently used at the end of the 20th century C.E. to refer collectively to Oxford and Cambridge Universities vis-à-vis the rest of English academe). Almost until the time of Rashi these academies were widely perceived as the unrivaled successors to the pre-70 C.E. Sanhedrin and the post-70 C.E. Jewish self-governing

---

pp. 259-60; for 'glory of Jacob' in Hebrew Scripture unequivocally as an epithet of the Israelite people see Nah. 2:3; Ps. 47:5.

[12] Abraham Ibn Daud in his *Sefer Ha-Qabbalah* [see Gerson D. Cohen, *A Critical Edition With a Translation and Notes of the Book of Tradition (Sefer Ha-Qabbalah) by Abraham Ibn Daud* (Philadelphia: Jewish Publication Society, 1967), pp. 82-83] written 1160/61 C.E. tells us the following concerning R. Isaac b. Moses b. Sakri: "Indeed, he was called 'al-Haber' ['the Colleague]. R. Isaac b. R. Moses, surnamed Ben-Sakri of the community of Denia [a seaport in Valencia in Eastern Spain; in the 11th century it became capital of a powerful Muslim kingdom ruled by the al-Mujahid dynasty. When Isaac b. Moses Ibn Sakri set out for Baghdad he was succeeded as rabbi of Denia by R. Isaac b. Reuben Al Bargeloni; see Haim Beinart, "Denia," *EJ* 5:1534-1535; contrast Ibn Daud, who clearly did not think well of him]. On occasion he is called 'Rabbi' and on occasion 'Haber.' However, he was not a colleague of these men, nor did he attain any office in their days. He [finally] left Denia for the East, where he was appointed gaon and occupied the see of Rabbenu Hai, of blessed memory. Incidentally, we note that [by that time] all of Iraq had been left without a remnant of native talmudic scholarship." David Solomon Sasoon, *A History of the Jews in Baghdad* (Letchworth: Solomon David Sassoon, 1949), p. 60 points out that with the death of Hai Gaon on the 6th day of Passover in the year 1038 C.E. it was perceived by Jews far and wide that "the Torah [itself] was caried to the grave and buried." In the period that followed various Jewish leaders in diverse locations called their institutions *Yeshivat Ge'on Ya'aqov* and themselves *Rosh Yeshivat Ge'on Ya'aqov* See Samuel Poznański, *Babylonische Geonim im nachgaonäischen Zeitalter nach handschriftlichen und gedruckten Quellen*, Schriften der Lehranstalt für die Wissenschaft des Judentums, Band IV, Heft 1.1 (Berlin: Mayer & Müller, 1914), pp. 84, 92, 96, 103; etc. It is assumed that R. Isaac died c. 1100 or some time thereafter; so Sassoon, p. 60.

[13] David M. Goodblatt, *Rabbinic Instruction in Sassanian Babylonia*, Studies in Judaism in Late Antiquity, vol. 9, ed. Jacob Neusner (Leiden: E. J. Brill, 1975), pp. 11-44 analyzes the Gaonic literary sources of this claim.

[11] For 1050 as the end of the Gaonic period see Poznański, *Babylonische Geonim*, p. 3.

entity founded by Johanan b. Zakkai at Yavneh while the Temple
was still in flames.[15]

The naming of his academy *Ge 'on Ya 'aqov* "Glory of Jacob" (Am.
6:8; 8:7; Nah. 2:3; Ps. 47:5) and Rashi's referring to himself by the
title "Gaon"[16] both suggests that part of the greatness of Rashi seems
to have been his accurate perception of his goals and accomplish-
ments as a legitimate successor of Hai Gaon and, as such, a teacher,
spiritual leader, decisor and commentator, whose literary legacy
would be no less formative for the future of Judaism than the legacy
of the Tannaim and the Amoraim, i.e., the authorities responsible
for Mishnah-Tosefta on the one hand and the two Talmuds on the
other hand.

The virtually canonical biography[17] of Rashi summarized above

---

[15] Concerning the Yavnean Sanhedrin see Jacob Neusner, *A Life of Yohanan ben
Zakkai ca. 1-80 C.E.* (2d ed.; Leiden: E. J. Brill, 1970), pp. 203-226 and the authorities cited there. Goodblatt, *Rabbinic Instruction*, pp. 13-16 discusses ancient and
medieval sources, which trace the origin of the academies of Sura and Pumbeditha
not to students of the students of the Yavnean Sanhedrin but to sages who arrived in Babylonia with King Jehoiachin in 597 B.C.E. (cf. 2 Kgs. 24:14-16); see
with Goodblatt Sifre Deuteronomy, ed. Finkelstein, p. 370.

[16] *Responsa Rashi*, ed. Elfenbein #115, pp. 245, 246. Isadore Twersky, *Introduction to the Code of Maimonides* , Yale Judaica Sries, vol. 22 (New Haven & London:
Yale University Press, 1980), p. 66, n. 113 and p. 82 refers to Maimonides' applying
the term Gaon to post-Talmudic sages in France and Spain, and he gives the
impression that it was Maimonides' audacity that led him to defy, as it were, the
authority of Louis Ginzberg, *Geonica* (2 vols.; New York: Jewish Theological Seminary of America, 1909), 1:148, n. 2 in applying such a title to a person of other
than Asian-African provenance and of a date later than that of Isaac Alfasi of Fez
(1013-1073). The facts 1) that Rashi's contemporaries called him Gaon and 2) that
Rashi himelf called his academy *Ge'on Ya'aqov* suggest that Maimonides simply
reflected the nomenclature which had been adopted by Jews throughout the world.
These Jews of the high Middle Ages saw their communities as the legitimate successor states, as it were, which inherited and shared the mantle of spiritual leadership with the erstwhile Babylonian academies of Sura and Pumbeditha in
Baghdad. The latter academies had for several generations been looked upon as
world Jewry's functional equivalent of Latin Christianity's Rome. It is fair to say
that their own and their contemporaries' conceptualization of the communal and
spiritual leadership of both Rashi and Maimonides as the legitimate successors of
Hai Gaon and his academy played an important role in their writings' having become together with Hebrew Scripture and the Babylonian Talmud the essential
literary canon of world Jewry for the greater part of the last millenium. For the
widespread use throughout the world in Rashi's era of the title *Yeshivat Ge'on Ya'aqov*
for Jewish institutions of learning and of the titles *Gaon* and *Rosh Yeshivat Ge'on Ya'aqov*
for the heads of such institutions see above n. 12.

[17] For the virtual canonicity of that presentation see passim in Emily Taitz,
The Jews of Medieval France, Contributions to the Study of World History, no. 45
(Westport, Ct.: Greenwood Press, 1994); and see also Hailperin, *Rashi and the Chris-*

and presented so lucidly by Baron treats Rashi as a vitner by pro-
fession and as the head of an academy of Jewish learning as an avo-
cation.[18] Unfortunately, when Baron wrote that biography the corpus
of Rashi's *Responsa*[19] had not yet been published. The bulk of the
latter corpus, which was published and annoted by Elfenbein,[20] has
now beem considerably augmented by Grossman's detailed examination of additional yet unpublished *responsa* by Rashi.[21] These
responsa shed much light on Rashi's personality,[22] and they considerably alter the picture of Rashi's school painted so vividly by Baron.
Baron's portrayal of Rashi an amateur and of Rashi's *yeshivah* as a
hobby[23] fails to reckon with the facts, which can be culled from
examination of Rashi's *responsa*.[24] Moreover, it fosters the widely
accepted notion that religious instruction, the study of sacred texts
whether from a historical or theological perspective, and humanis-
tic learning in general are all leisure activities. Careful reading of
the *responsa* reveal, however, that Rashi himself succeeded by his
professionalism in his very careful and by no means subtle design for
making his *yeshivah* an intellectual and spiritual center for all of world
Jewry and, indeed, for all persons both friendly and hostile, who
wished to understand Judaism.[25] In a scathing critique of Baron's
biography of Rashi, Robert Liberles[26] suggests that Baron's conten-

---

tian Scholars, p. 268, nn. 10-11; Grossman, *The Early Sages of France*, p. 121, n. 1; p.
130, n. 31; and see especially Breuer, "Toward the Investigation," p. 49, n. 26.

[18] See above, pp. 6–7.

[19] See now Israel Elfenbein, *Responsa Rashi* (New York: Shulsinger, 1943).

[20] See previous note.

[21] See passim in Grossman, *The Early Sages of France*, pp. 127-159; see also
Soloveitchik, "Can Halakhic Texts Talk History?" pp. 153-196.

[22] See Elfenbein, *Responsa Rashi* pp. xiii-xvi.

[23] Baron, p. 60.

[24] See above, nn. 6-9, and see the extensive discussion in Grossman, *The Early
Sages of France*, pp. 166-168.

[25] Concerning Rashi's familiarity with Christian beliefs and his systematic ar-
gumentation against specific Christian beliefs see below, pp. 130–131; 177; 178,
n. 6; and passim in index s.v. Christianity and s.v. Messiah; and see below at Pss.
105; 110; 118; see also Hailperin, especially pp.43-61; 178; 318, n. 312; Grossman,
"Rashi's Commentary on Psalms and the Jewish-Christian Polemic," pp. 59-74;
Eleazar Touito, "Rashi's Commentary on Genesis 1-6 in the Context of Judeo-
Christian Controversy," *HUCA* 61 (1990), pp. 159-183.

[26] Robert Liberles, *Salo Wittmayer Baron: Architect of Jewish History*, Modern Jewish Masters Series, vol. 5 (New York & London: New York University Press, 1995),
pp. 288-294. Liberles, there, p. 288 contends that Baron's essay on Rashi 1) "totally lacks an inner unity"; 2) "has virtually no beginning"; and 3) "there is no
conclusion". *Mirabile dictu*, Liberles, there, p. 288 claims that in Baron's essay "there

tion that Rashi became the principal spokesperson of French Jewry "by virtue of his learning, rather than by that of any recognized position"[27] was meant to foster the notion that in Baron's own era— World War II—the institutionalized communal leaders of American Jewry should yield their authority to that of the men of learning such as Baron himself, whose authority derived not from any office but only from their learned lectures and publications.[28]

Various references in Rashi's *Responsa* to Rashi's students living in his house and eating at his table[29] suggest that also Breuer's portrayal of the *bet midrash* or 'study house' as, in fact, the *yeshivah* head's living room,[30] may be plausible unless and until archaeological evidence will have demonstrated otherwise. In fact, Breuer's depiction of the Ashkenazic *yeshivah* of the high Middle Ages as typically occupying space within the home of the head of the *yeshivah*[31] is challenged by the archaeological evidence concerning the *yeshivah* of Rouen presented by Norman Golb.[32] Golb argues that the communal

---

was certainly no direct attempt at relevance to the times [in which Baron wrote in the essay]" This latter contention is contradicted by Liberles' insistence, there, p. 294 that the appearance "around the time of [the Japaneese attack on the U.S. airbase at] Pearl Harbor [December 7, 1941] of an entire series of essays by Baron on medieval rabbis "was not accidental, and in their own way these essays were not oblivious to the world events of the time." Concerning the importance of Liberles' book see Jacob Neusner, review of *Salo Wittmayer Baron: Architect of Jewish History* , by Robert Liberles, *Religion* 26 (1996), pp. 286-290.

[27] Baron, p. 60, cited above, p. 17 and in Liberles, p. 293.

[28] Liberles, pp. 293-294.

[29] See for example Elfenbein, *Responsa Rashi* #87; for additional examples see below, p. 23, n. 6.

[30] See above, p. 13, n. 7.

[31] Breuer, pp. 49-53.

[32] Golb , *The Jews in Medieval Normandy*, pp. 154-169 and the literature cited there, pp. 157-166, nn. 42-52. Golb, there, pp. 176-195 argues that "The Ancient Rules of Study" (referred to above, n. 4 by the Hebrew title *Hukke Hatorah*) preserved in a single ms., dated 1309 C.E., i.e., Oxford Bodleian Ms. Opp. 342, pp. 196-199 and published, *inter alia*, in Norman Golb, *History and Culture of the Jews of Rouen in the Middle Ages* (Tel Aviv: Dvir, 1976) pp. 181-184 (in Hebrew) reflects an original "twelve rules," which "were issued by a regional council meeting in a major northwestern European city, very likely Rouen, no later than some time in the tenth, or at the latest, the eleventh century" (Golb, *The Jews in Normandy*, p. 190). This covenant or constitution, as it were, required the maintenance of a *midrash*, i.e., a Jewish school of higher learning or *yeshivah*, in every town. Golb argues that a later, 12th century recension of the *Hukke haTorah*, reflected in that same ms., "while reiterating the principle that a *midrash* should be built near the synagogue, required the foundation of a higher academy of this kind only in the principle city of each 'kingdom'—...an academic building was to be purchased from communal funds, while every year outlying Jewish communities would send

nature of such *yeshivot* is reflected in the Latin designation of the *yeshivah* of Rouen as *scola Routhomagi,* i.e., "the [official] *yeshivah* of Rouen," which is semantically parallel to Rashi's designation of the official *yeshivah* of Rome by the Aramaic *mĕtîbtā' dĕmātā' Rômî* "the [official] *yeshivah* of the city of Rome."[33]

Combining the textual evidence cited by Breuer concerning Ashkenazic *yeshivot,* the textual and archaeological evidence cited by Golb with two matters of no small importance, namely, 1) that Rashi and many of the other European *yeshivah* heads with whom Rashi

---

'contributions' in unspecified amounts for the upkeep of the higher school in the main city." Breuer, "Toward the Investigation," p. 52 sees R. Meir of Rothenburg's school, which, according to Breuer, was housed in R. Meir's own "palatial home" (cf. Golb, *The Jews in Normandy,* p. 192, n. 39) described in his Responsum, *Sefer She'elot uTeshuvot...Maharam* (Cremona: Vinceno Conti, 1557) #108 [a complete English translation is found in Irving Agus, *Rabbi Meir of Rothenburg* (2 vols.; Philadelphia: Dropsie College, 1947), 1:264-265, text #213] as typical. Golb, pp. 192-193, on the other hand, argues for two parallel systems of education, to which we might compare, *mutatis mutandi,* the public and private colleges and universties in the modern United States of America: "eminent scholars such as Meir of Rotheburg (thirteenth century) had yeshiboth in their own names [Reading Prof. Golb's words in the light of Breuer's study quoted above, I was inclined by my training as a biblical scholar to emend this word to "homes" based on the graphic similarity between the initial h of "homes" and the initial n of "names," and I assumed that Prof. Golb's secretary or a typesetter misreading initial n for h then misread o as a. Fortunately, I asked Prof. Golb (electronic communication dated 3 August, 2000) if, in fact, my conjectural emendation had correctly restored his intent. Prof. Golb kindly replied with his explanation that, in fact, Jews were forbidden by their own rules (see for example *Hukke haTorah* cited above) to conduct the classes of a *yeshivah* in a residence] evidently not connected in any way with a public system of support. Judah b. Qalonymus had a school of this kind at Mainz before and immediately after the first Crusade. The system of public support for the acadmies and the very concept of communal ownership of the institutions of higher learning were parallel phenomena of long standing, encouraged and indeed mandated by the formulation of both the first and the second recensions of the Rules [i.e., *Hukke Hatorah* referred to above]. Thus in Provence, alongside the school of Master Meshullam at Béziers (thirteenth century), and the several schools evidently in the hands of private scholars mentioned by Benjamin of Tudela (*circa* 1165)—i.e. those at Montpellier, Lunel and Posquières—there were also higher academic institutions of an emphatically communal nature, such as those at Marseilles and Narbonne. As the monumental proportions of the academic structure discovered at Rouen demonstrate [see Golb, there, p. 160, figure 44, which indicates an area of 14 X 9.5 meters], the yeshibah of the capital of Normandy was of a communal nature: it was clearly designed to serve the needs of a relatively large number of students, who would have been drawn not only from Rouen but also from the outlying towns of Normandy.... Academies of this type doubtlessly were built in other important cities such as Paris, Reims and Troyes."

[33] Golb, *The Jews in Medieval Normandy,* p. 196; for the reference in Rashi's *responsum* see Elfebein, *Responsa Rashi,* #41.

corresponded bore the title *ga'ôn* ; and 2) that the *yeshivah,* which Rashi
founded and maintained, perhaps throughout his tenure as *ga'ôn,* in
his own home, bore the pretentious title of *yeshivat ge'on Ya'aqov,* it is
reasonable to conclude that Rashi's principle vocation was, with all
due respect to Prof. Salo Baron,[34] of blessed memory, and with all
due respect to Prof. Haym Soloveitchik,[35] may he be distinguished
for life, neither vintner nor egg salesperson but *rē's mĕtibtā',* which is
Aramaic for 'head of the *yeshivah'.* This, of course, means that the
communal funds paid on behalf of *yeshivah* students referred to in
the *Hukke haTorah* went not only to buy manuscripts but also to keep
Rashi and his wife and daughters adequately fed, clothed and jew-
elled (see M. Shabbat 6:1)[36] as befit the status of a *Ga'ôn* and his
family! So long as the historical setting of Rashi belonged to the realm
of myth it could be imagined that Rashi's encyclopedic learning,
teaching, exegesis and extensive written correspondence with other
Ge'onim were all carried on "on the side" while he made a living in
some other manner. Close reading of Rashi's *responsa* together with
the greater knowledge of the historical background of the era uncovered during the sixty years since the appearance of Baron's influential essay enables us to see Rashi as a Jewish and academic
professional, part of whose deliberate program was to create that
very professionalism, which in due course led to the building in
medieval France of monumental *yeshivot,* of which so far we only know
archaeologically the one uncovered by accident at Rouen.

---

[34] See above.

[35] See below.

[36] Concerning women's clothing in Rashi's time and place described in Rashi's
commentaries on BT see Moché Catane, *La Vie en France au XIe siècle d'après les
écrits de Rachi* (Jerusalem: Editions Gallia, 1994), pp. 99-100; concerning women's
jewelry in Rashi's time and place see there, pp. 100-102; concerning cosmetics
see there, pp. 102-103.

III. The Viticulture Question

As I pointed out above, it has long been taken for granted that Rashi engaged in viticulture.[1] However, Haym Soloveitchik's assertion, "Indeed the presumption is against anyone being a winegrower in Troyes. Its chalky soil is inhospitable to viticulture... "[2] followed by his almost flippant declaration, "Rashi may nevertheless have been a vintner; but by the same measure he may have been an egg salesman,"[3] has led subsequent scholars to reopen the questions as to 1) how precisely Rashi made a living; and 2) what role if any viticulture may have played in the life of the Jews of Troyes, whose soil Soloveitchik has declared to be "inhospitable to viticulture."[4] Soloveitchik declares, it would appear, on the basis of his independent study of medieval *responsa* that being an egg salesman and being a vintner were equally plausible careers for Rashi. Therefore, scholarly integrity demands that any discussion of Rashi's biography treat both the viticulture question and the egg question dispassionately.

In fact, a perusal of the published *responsa* of Rashi reveals that, in fact, eggs were very close, if not to Rashi's heart, at least to his palate. Rashi's famous disciple Shemayah tells us that on more than one occasion he had seen that Rashi was served grilled meat[5] or spiced meat or fried eggs with honey[6] and that Rashi would pronounce the benediction "by whose will all things came into being"[7] and consume these foods prior to beginning the meal with the benediction over bread.[8] Shemayah explains that Rashi informed him

---

[1] See above; see also Solomon Zeitlin, "Rashi and the Rabbinate," *JQR*, n.s., 31 (1940-1941), p. 55.

[2] Soloveitchik, "Can Halakhic Texts Talk History?" p. 172, n. 54, cited above, p. 6, n. 36.

[3] Soloveitchik, "Can Halakhic Texts Talk History?" p. 172.

[4] See Taitz, pp. 56, 228 and the sources cited there; cf. Grossman, *The Early Sages of France*, p. 135.

[5] For the different possible textual readings and their respective meanings see Elfenbein, p. 114 #86, nn. 4-5.

[6] Elfenbein, *Responsa Rashi*, pp. 114-15 #86; similarly, there, pp. 310-11 #270 it is reported, possibly by Shemayah (see there, p. 310, n. 1), that one of Rashi's favorite foods was nuts fried with honey and that the name of this delicacy in Old Northern French is *ab-bstr*.

[7] See Birnbaum, *Daily Prayer Book*, p. 773.

[8] Elfenbein, *Responsa Rashi*, p. 115.

[concerning the reason he did not wash his hands and recite the appropriate benediction for washing the hands and then the benediction over bread followed by the consumption of a small piece of bread before eating the aforementioned foods] :

> This [eggs fried with honey etc.] is much more enjoyable to me than bread, and I like bestowing my benedictions to laud my Creator with respect to [the food] which I love.[9]

What this *halakic* text tells us about Rashi and eggs is that fried eggs mixed with honey were among his favorite foods, which he enjoyed so much that he ate them as an appetizer before the meal itself which began with the washing of the hands and the benediction over bread. Fried eggs mixed with honey[10] were among the food items for which Rashi had no patience to wait. Notwithstanding Rashi's enjoyment of fried eggs, neither this text nor any other text so far published intimates that Rashi was engaged in either the retail or wholesale trade in eggs. On the other hand, the following responsum demonstrates that Rashi received eggs and other comestibles for his personal consumption from others:

> It happened to me, Solomon ha-Yitzhaqi. A Gentile sent me[11] cakes and eggs on the eighth day of Passover. The Gentile entered the courtyard and called to my wife, and my wife sent a messenger[12] to the synagogue. Thereupon[13] I gave instructions to keep the eggs in a corner until the evening. In the evening [after the end of Passover] I permitted their use allowing the amount of time that it would have taken [to bring them to my house had they set out for my house] after this time [when the holiday has already ended].[14] However, [in my initial instructions issued on the eighth day of Passover from the synagogue to which my wife sent a messenger] I did not accept [from

---

[9] Ibid.

[10] The text of the *responsum* refers, in fact, to eggs fried *in* honey. In light of the commentary of Nissim Gerondi at the top of BT Nedarim 52b, it appears that "fried in honey" is a literary convention in Rabbinic Hebrew for "mixed in honey and fried [in oil]."

[11] Heb. *šiggēr;* see next note.

[12] Heb. *šiggĕrāh.*

[13] Heb. *halaktî,* lit., "I went," here employed as an auxilliary verb implying "thereupon" like the verb *qām* 'stand up' frequently in Biblical Hebrew; concerning the usage in Biblical Hebrew see Orlinsky, *Notes,* pp. 34-35, 99, 100, 101 and passim.

[14] This ruling is based on the principle attributed to R. Papa in BT Beṣa 24a: If a Gentile brought a Jew a present at night just after the end of a Jewish festival, the Jew may benefit from the gift only after there has elapsed sufficient time for the Gentile to have prepared the gift after the end of the festival.

the Gentile] the bread. The Gentile wanted to abandon it [the bread] on the property of my neighbors, but I did not want it [the bread which the Gentile brought on Passover] for we determined about it[15] that it became leaven when it was still in his possession [during the Passover holiday] and that it was forbidden for me and for any Jew for benefit and for eating.[16]

Several of Rashi's *responsa* suggest that he and other Jewish residents of Troyes from time to time owned pregnant cows and ewes.[17] None of these accounts suggest that either Rashi or the other Jews mentioned in these *responsa* owned herds of cattle or flocks of sheep. The one cow or sheep was probably the family's source of dairy products. In each of the recorded instances Rashi advised divesting oneself of ownership in favor of a Gentile so as to avoid being subject to the biblical precept of redeeming the firstborn male of a cow or ewe, which cannot be accomplished in the absence of the Temple (see Deut. 12:6, 17; 14:23). In the one instance where one of Rashi's Jewish neighbors made the mistake of acquiring and slaughtering for meat from a Gentile professional shepherd the lamb born of a ewe of which the Jew was legal owner Rashi decided that the only recourse was to bury the slaughtered lamb half on Rashi's property and half on the other Jew's property so that the act of burying all that meat would be less conspicuous and the Jews would not be suspected by their neighbors of engaging in some kind of witchcraft.[18]

According to Rashi's own testimony he acquired and ate eggs. To date, however, there is no evidence whatsover that he was an egg salesman. Likewise, we have seen, on one occasion Rashi did disposses himself of the ownership of a pregnant cow. Rashi's erst-

---

[15] I.e., the bread.

[16] Elfenbein, *Responsa Rashi*, #114, p. 142; the ruling that Jews cannot use after Passover products (earlier referred to as cakes) which became leaven (through the admixture of flower and water which were not baked into unleavened bread within a period of 18 minutes) during the Passover holiday may not be consumed after Passover is based upon M. Pesaḥim 2:1-2 according to which after Passover a Jew may not benefit from leaven which was owned by a Jew during Passover but a Jew may benefit from leaven which was owned by a Gentile during Passover. Rashi's point in the *responsum* is that by virtue of the Gentile's having abandoned the leaven on Jewish property it was no longer in the category of leaven in the possession of a Gentile during Passover; it entered the category of leaven belonging to a Jew during Passover; hence Rashi forbade the Jews to benefit from it after Passover.

[17] Elfenbein, *Responsa Rashi*, pp. 202-03, responsa nos. 182-184; contrast Taitz, p. 85.

[18] Elfenbein, *Responsa Rashi*, p. 202 #182.

while ownership of this cow did not, we have seen, turn Rashi into a cowboy or rancher. Likewise, the various testimonies to Rashi's familiarity with the details of wine production in Rashi's *responsa* as well as in his commentaries to BT Shabbat 18a and Jer. 25:30 do not prove that Rashi actually cultivated vineyards either for private use or for commercial purposes.[19] As argued by Soloveitchik, all the texts bearing upon Rashi's familiarity with wine production serve only to demonstrate that, in fact, the Jews of Troyes in Rashi's era had to produce their own wine because *halakah* prohibited Jews from consuming wine produced by Gentiles.[20] The reference in a Rashi *responsum* to a wine barrel that bore Rashi's seal[21] no more makes Rashi a commercial producer or either wine or grapes than does his pregnant cow make him a cowboy. On the other hand, Rashi's *responsum* referring to a Jewish borrower who pledged a vineyard as collateral[22] is one of a number of texts,[23] which suggest that So-

---

[19] Contrast Catane, *La Vie en France aus 11e siècle d'après les écrits de Rachi*, pp. 130-31; cf. Taitz, pp. 72-77.

[20] Soloveitchik, "Can Halakhic Texts Talk History?" pp. 172-73.

[21] The source is Oxford Bodleian Ms. Opp. 276, p. 35a, cited Grossman, *The Early Sages of France*, p. 132; p. 135, n. 45.

[22] Elfenbein, *Responsa Rashi*, p. 66, responsum no. 61; cited by Taitz, p. 84.

[23] Note the "ordinance of Rashi" in Louis Finkelstein, *Jewish Self Government in the Middle Ages* (2[d] printing; New York: Feldheim, 1964), p. 147, which specifically exempts from taxation by the self-governing Jewish community of greater Troyes household items, houses, vineyards, and fields; see the discussion in Robert Chazan, *Medieval Jewry in Northern France: A Political and Social History* (Baltimore & London: Johns Hopkins University Press, 1973), p. 16. See also the account of the case that came before R. Joseph b. Samuel Tob-Elem (Bonfils) at the end of the 10th and the beginning of the 11th century concerning the attempt of the community of Troyes to ignore the community's traditional exemption of vineyards from taxation in respect of the vineyard owned by a certain Leah. Fortunately for Leah, the learned R. Joseph agreed with her. See Chazan, pp. 15-16. Irving Agus, *Urban Civilization in Pre-Crusade Europe* (2 vols.; New York: Yeshiva University Press, 1965), pp. 438-446 anticipates Soloveitchik's attempt to play down the importance of vineyards in the economic life of the Jews of Troyes in the time of Rashi, and he goes so far as to argue from silence that Leah was at that time the only owner of a substantial vineyard. In any case both the litigation in question and the reference to vineyards along with household goods and houses in the so-called "ordinance of Rashi" should put to rest Soloveitchik's contention that the soil of greater Troyes was inhospitable to viticulture. See also the numerous references to wine production in Rashi's commentary on BT where Rashi frequently contrasts the *realia* referred to in BT with the corresponding *realia* in 11th-12th century C.E. Troyes; these sources are listed and analyzed in Catane, *La Vie en France aus 11e siècle d'apres les écrits de Rachi*. pp. 130-133; see also the references in Rashi's responsa to Jews' hiring Christians to carry wine casks; see Elfenbein, *Responsa Rashi*, #160; #260; see Taitz, p. 84.

loveitchik may have gone too far in arguing that one of the reasons that Rashi could not have been a vintner is that the region in which he lived did not support viticulture.[24]

---

[24] Soloveitchik, "Can Halakhic Texts Talk History?" p. 172, n. 54.

IV. Rashi's Literary Output

A. Rashi's Liturgical Poetry

At least ten liturgical poems, all of which belong to the genre of *seliḥot*,[1] have been attributed to Rashi. As early as 1855 Zunz stated that only eight of these were actually composed by Rashi.[2] Ten years later Zunz established the accepted list of seven *seliḥot*,[3] which are now commonly regarded as from the pen of Rashi.[4] Five of these seven are alphabetical acrostics beginning with the first letter of the Hebrew alphabet, *aleph*, and ending with the final letter of the Hebrew alphabet, *taw* while two are alphabetical acrostics beginning with *taw* and ending with *aleph*. The closing lines of all seven poems contain the colophon identifying the author. In the *seliḥah 'Elohei haṣṣēbā 'ôt* "God of Hosts," the author signs his name *šlmh br yṣḥq*, i.e., Solomon son of Isaac, while in the *seliḥot 'Az Terem Nimtahu* "Then were not yet stretched out" and *Torah Ha-temimah* 'The Perfect Torah" the author signs his name Solomon son of Rabbi Isaac. At the end of the *seliḥah 'Ak Lelohim Napshi Dommi* "Howbeit be silent to God, my soul" the author signs his name "Solomon son of Isaac the Young (*hṣ'yr*), may he live". At the end of the *seliḥah 'Appeka Hasheb* "Turn away Your anger" Rashi signs his name "Solomon the Young (*hṣ'yr*), son of Rabbi Isaac while at the conclusion of *Tefilah Leqaddemeka* he signs his name "Solomon the son of Rabbi Isaac, the Young." Comparison with the other colophons indicates that the attributive adjective "the young" refers to Rashi and not to his father. The longest of the colophons appears at the end of the *seliḥah Ophan Ehad Baareṣ*

---

[1] For explanation of the genre *seliḥot*, singular *seliḥah*, and the subcategories relevant to the compositions attributed to Rashi see below.

[2] Leopold Zunz, *Die synagogale Poesie des Mittelalters* (2 vols.; Berlin: J. Springer, 1855; reprint, Hildesheim: Georg Olms, 1967), 1:181.

[3] Id., *Literaturgeschichte der synagogalen Poesie* (Berlin: Louis Gerschel, 1865), pp. 252-54; contrast Grossman, *The Early Sages of France*, pp. 248-49.

[4] Abraham Meir Haberman, *Piyute Rashi* (Jerusalem: Schocken, 1940); id., "Piyute Rashi," in *Sefer Rashi*, 2d ed., edited by Yehudah Leib ha-Kohen (Fischman) Maimon (Jerusalem: Mossad Harav Kook, 1956), pp. 592-610; Jefim Hayyim Schirmann in Ismar Elbogen, *Jewish Liturgy: A Comprehensive History*, trans. Raymond P. Scheindlin (Philadelphia: Jewish Publication Society/New York: Jewish Theological Seminary of America, 1993), p. 258.

"One Wheel[5] Upon Earth". This colophon, which is found in lines 23-41 of the 42 line poem, is spread over slightly less than than half of the lines of the poem. The colophon in question reads as follows: "Solomon son of Rabbi Isaac, the Young (*hqtn*); may he grow in [knowledge of] Torah and in good deeds." These colophons suggest that five of the seven liturgical poems, Rashi's authorship of which is a matter of scholarly consensus, must have been written early on in Rashi's literary career, probably before Rashi wrote his commentaries on the Babylonian Talmud and certainly long before the Commentary on Psalms, which has been shown to belong to the closing years of Rashi's career.[6]

Liturgical poems belong to the genre *selihot* are poems which frame the liturgical chanting of part of Ex. 34:6-7:

> The LORD, the LORD, God, Merciful, Gracious, Patient, Abounding in kindness [to persons who lack merit acruing from virtuous behavior][7] and [Abounding in] faithfulness [to reward persons whose bevhavior is virtuous],[7] Who keeps in mind] the kindness [which a person performs before God][7] [with respect to the virtuous] for [two][8] thousands of generations [of virtuous persons' descendants], Who forgives premeditated crimes,[7] and [Who forgives] acts of rebellion performed just to make God angry,[7] and [Who forgives] sin, and Who acquits [the penitent].[9]

---

[5] If in the popular imagination the heavens are populated with angels, in the imagination of Jewish liturgy inspired initially by Hebrew Scripture and subsequently by mystical circles mentioned in Rabbinic literature (see, e.g., Mishnah Hagigah 2:1 and Tosefta and Talmuds *ad loc.*) there are also *seraphim*, who are mentioned in Isa. 6 and various other creatures including "wheels" mentioned in Ezek. 3; see, *inter alia*, Gerschom Scholem, *Jewish Gnosticism, Merkabah Mysticism and Talmudic Tradition* (2d ed.; New York: Schocken, 1965); Ithamar Gruenwald, *From Apocalypticism to Gnosticism*, Beiträge zur Erforschung des Alten Testaments und des antiken Judentums, vol. 14 (Frankfurt am Main: Peter Lang, 1988); David Joel Halperin, *The Merkabah in Rabbinic Literature*, AOS, no. 62 (New Haven: American Oriental Society, 1980); id., *The Faces of the Chariot* (Tübingen: J. C.B. Mohr, 1988). Joseph Dan, "Rashi and the Merkabah," in *Rashi 1040-1990: Homage aL Ephraim E. Urbach*, ed. Gabrielle Sed-Rajna (Paris: Editions du Cerf, 1993), pp. 259-264 concludes (p. 264), ". . .at this time we have no proof that Rashi and his school were aware of the details of the mystical endeavor of the ancient Jewish mystics in Late Antiquity."

[6] See above, pp. 7–9 and the sources cited there; cf. Grossman, *The Early Sages of France*, p. 182, n. 204; p. 223, n. 299; see below, 57.

[7] See Rashi at Ex. 34:6-7.

[8] See Rashi at Ex. 34:7, s.v. "for thousands."

[9] See Rashi at Ex. 34:7, s.v. "And who will by no means clear the guilty."

This text is chanted liturgically (1) as many as five times in each of the five prayer services of the Day of Atonement; (2) during or prior to the *shaharit* service on every other fast with the exception of the Ninth of Av; (3) at special penitential services held during each weekday between the New Year and the Day of Atonement; (4) among Ashkenazic Jews at daily penitential services beginning on the Sunday (or late Saturday Night) at least four days before the New Year; (5) among Sephardic and Oriental Jews at daily penitential services beginning on the second day of the month (Elul) prior to the New Year. The basis for this practice is a *midrash* found in BT Rosh ha-Shanah 17b. The latter text explains that in the aftermath of the Israelites' worship of the golden calf God forgave Israel and announced the thirteen attributes of divine mercy. In so doing, God demonstrated to Moses how whenever in the future the people of Israel should sin and be in need of divine forgiveness a prayer leader should come forward and enwrap himself[10] in the prayer shawl and recite these thirteen attributes so as to influence God to forgive the people of Israel. The recitation of the thirteen attributes from Ex. 34:6-7 so as to exclude the final clauses of v. 7, which speak not of forgiveness but of divine retribution extending up to three and four generations is, in fact, anticipated by several passages in the Prophets and Hagiographa. For example, Joel 2:13:

> For He is Gracious and Merciful,
> Patient, Abounding in kindness,
> And He renounces punishment.

Similarly, we read in Jon. 4:2

> For I knew that You are
> God, Gracious and Merciful,
> Patient and Abounding in kindness,
> And renouncing punishment.

Likewise, we read in Neh. 9:17

> But You, being God, Forgiving,
> Gracious and Merciful,

---

[10] My feminist leanings notwithstanding, I am still waiting to be convinced that it would be correct to assume that this Talmudic text assumes that the prayer leader might be either male or female.

Patient and Abounding in kindness,
Did not abandon them.[11]

One of Rashi's *seliḥot* is commonly recited to this day on the morning before Rosh ha-Shanah in the Ashkenazi rite shared by many Orthodox and Conservative congregations throughout the world.[12] This is the *seliḥah*, whose first line is *'Elohei haṣṣĕbā 'ôt* "God of Hosts." This *seliḥah* belongs to the subcategory of *petiḥah* 'opening'. This is to say that this liturgical poem is the very first in a series of twenty-three separate poems recited during the Seliḥot Service on the morning before the Eve of Rosh ha-Shanah.[13] Interestingly, in the rite of the three Northern Italian cities of Asti, Fossano and Monclavo, known from the initial Hebrew letters of the names of these three cities as the rite of Apam,[14] Rashi's *seliḥah*, *'Elohei haṣṣĕbā 'ôt* "God of Hosts" is the *petiḥah* for the Evening (*'Arvit*) Service of the Day of Atonement. Another of Rashi's *seliḥot* is commonly recited to this day on the morning of the Fast of Gedaliah[15] in the Ashkenazi rite. This is the *petiḥah 'Az Terem Nimtahu* "Then were not yet stretched out."[16] Rashi's *seliḥah Tefillah Leqaddemĕkā* "A Prayer with which to come before You" survived in the liturgy only in Prague's famous Altneuschul.[17]

To round out our picture of Rashi's multifacted creativity we include here an annotated English rendering of Rashi's *seliḥah* "God of Hosts" recited on the morning before the New Year:

---

[11] Yochanan Muffs, *Love & Joy* (New York and Jerusalem: Jewish Theological Seminary of America, 1992), pp. 22-24 with respect to Ps. 99:6 and Ps. 103, in which he sees what he calls "recycling" of Ex. 34:6-7.

[12] See, e.g., Abraham Rosenfeld, *The Authorised Selichot for the Whole Year* (London: n.p., 1969), p. 136.

[13] Abraham. Z. Idelsohn, *Jewish Liturgy and Its Development* (New York: Henry Holt & Co., 1932), p. 253.

[14] Daniel J. Goldschmidt, *On Jewish Liturgy* (Jerusalem: Magnes, 1980), pp. 80-121 (in Hebrew) describes the written sources of the liturgy of French Jewry prior to the expulsion of the Jews from France in 1394. He notes that this rite survived in the North Italian cities of Asti, Fassano and Moncalo.

[15] The third day of the month of Tishri, i.e., the third day of the year commencing with *Rosh ha-Shanah*, the New Year. The Fast of Gedaliah commemorates the tragic political assassination of the Jewish governor of Judah, Gedaliah son of Ahikam in 586 B.C.E. This event put an end to the last shred of Judean political autonomy. For the historical background see 2 Kgs. 25:25. The fast is referred to in Zech. 8:19 as "the fast of the tenth [month]."

[16] See Rosenfeld, p. 191.

[17] Elbogen, p. 258.

RASHI'S *SELIḤAH* "GOD OF HOSTS"

1a God[18] of Hosts, worshipped by the supernal beings,[19]

1b You said, "Return rebellious children";[20]

2a "Come to Me with thanksgiving and songs" (cf. Ps. 100:3, 4),

2b "Seek My face (cf. Ps. 27:8) with crying and supplication" (Jer. 3:21).

3a Even when the prayer of persons praying[21] is silenced (cf. Lam. 3:8)

3b The doors are wide open for the repentant.[22]

4a Your promise is forever (cf. Ps. 119:89).[23]

---

[18] The structure of the alphabetical acrostic going from *'aleph* to *taw* indicates that the first word of the poem must be *'el* 'God' and not *yy*, an abbreviation for the tetragrammaton liturgically read as *'ădonāy* 'LORD'. Contrast the standard printings of the Selihot according to the Ashkenazic, Lithuanina and Polish rites found in synagogues and libraries as well as Rosenfeld, p. 136. Daniel Goldschmidt in his critical edition, *Seder Ha-Selihot According to the Lithanian Rite* (Jerusalem: Mossad Harav Kook, 1965), p. 65 (in Hebrew) brackets the opening word *yy*. Moreover, by not referring to this word in his commentary, he hints that it is a spurious addition to Rashi's poem. Haberman, *Piyyute Rashi*, p. 9 reads not *yy* but *'ădonāy* 'My Lord' as in Am. 3:13 and elsewhere. So also Yaakov Lavon, trans., *The Complete ArtScroll Selichos*, ed., with a commentary by Avie Gold, ArtScroll Mesorah Series, edited by Meir Zlotowitz and Nosson Scherman (New York: Mesorah Publications, 1996), p. 294. Were this the correct reading, the word would not destroy the alphabetic acrostic, and there would be no need to bracket it. However, the additional word is problematic for the additional reason that it results in the first hemistich's having five stresses while every other line has only four stresses (if we assume with Goldschmidt that all other apparent exceptions are to be treated as either proclitics followed by *maqqeph* or enclitics preceded by *maqqeph*).

[19] Heb. *nôrā' bā'elyônîm*, which is a paraphrase of "The LORD Most High is awesome" in Ps. 47:3; with Goldschmidt, *Seder Ha-Selihot*, p. 65 note that *'elyônîm* in the sense 'supernal beings, heavenly host' is found in Rabbinic literature in BT Ketubbot 104a and elsewhere.

[20] Paraphrase of Jer. 3:14. Rashi substitutes *sarbānîm* for the prophet's *šôbēbîm* for the sake of the rhyme *nîm* repeated at the end of each of the 48 hemistichs.

[21] Heb *hegyônîm*. Goldschmidt, *Seder Ha-Selihot*, p. 65 notes that this form seems to be based upon the phrase *hegyôn libbî* in Ps. 19:15. For Rashi to base the expression *hegyônîm* in the sense 'persons praying' upon Biblical Heb. *hegyôn libbî*, Rashi had to have understood the latter phrase to mean 'utterance' notwithstanding Rashi's interpreting it to mean 'thought' in his commentary at Ps. 1:2 (see below, p. 173 and p. 175, nn. 10, 12). The *selihah* under discussion testifies to the fact that at least at the time he composed this poem Rashi was fully aware that *hegyôn libbî* in Ps. 19:15 means 'utterance', an idea that was rediscovered by H. L. Ginsberg in the second half of the twentieth century.

[22] Literally, "the doors for the repentant are open windows"; for Hebrew *gallê* 'doors of/for' see with Goldschmidt, BT Shabbat 81a. With Goldschmidt note that the Hebrew expression *pĕtûḥîm kawwānîm* 'open windows' is based upon Aram. *kewwîn pĕtîḥān* 'windows open' in Dan. 6:11.

[23] Here ends the suppliant's quoting God's promises to the penitent contained in or alluded to in Hebrew Scripture; see next note.

4b   The paths to You kindly provided are everlasting and un-
     changing (cf. Mal. 3:6).[24]
5a   Look! We approach You like poor (Jer. 3:22) and impoverished
     knocking on the door for charity[25] (and) moaning like doves.[26]
5b   The charity is Yours (Dan. 9:7), and the iniquities are ours.
6a   We return to you in shame
6b   [knocking] on Your doors[27] (and) moaning like doves (Isa.
     38:14)
7a   Remember us, and recall us for a full life.
7b   Cleanse our stains pure and white (cf. Isa. 1:18).
8a   May the sins of our youth (Ps. 25:7) be wiped away like [pass-
     ing] clouds
8b   Renew our days like the former days (cf. Lam. 5:21)
9a   Remove uncleanness (Zech. 13:2), and put an end to malicious
     deeds (cf. Dan. 9:24)
9b   Pour pure (and) faithful water (Ezek. 36:25; Isa. 33:16; Jer.
     2:13; cf. Job. 6:15)
10a We acknowledge (Jer. 14:20) our wickedness: (we are) thorns
     and thistles (Ezek. 2:6)
10b Our stiffneckedness is as [great as] the stoutness of oak trees.
11a We planted a vineyard spoiled by weeds (cf. Jer. 2:21)
11b Its face was covered with brambles and thorns (cf. Prov.
     24:31)
12a Experienced in doing evil; glued to idols
12b Avid for bribes, greedy for graft (cf. Isa. 1:23)
13a Quickly we polluted the marriage chamber.[28]

---

[24] Here as frequently in the liturgy of the High Holy Days (New Year and Day
of Atonement) God's eternal promise referred to in Ps. 119:89 is understood to
be the promise God made to Adam in the myth recorded in PRK, ed. Mandelbaum
pp. 333-334 (Pisqa 23:1). Briefly, according to this myth, just as Adam, humankind personified, was forgiven on the New Year for his having eaten the forbidden fruit in the Garden of Eden so will God grant forgiveness to all Adam's
descendants for all their sins every year on the New Year. Concerning the allusions to this myth in the High Holy Day liturgy see Max Arzt, *Justice and Mercy*
(New York: Holt, Rinehart & Winston, 1963), pp. 55-56; see above, p. 14, n. 4.
[25] The classic posture of the seeker of alms is to knock on the door; cf. the
more ancient posture of standing outside the door with hand outstretched discussed
in Gruber, *Aspects*, pp. 45-50. On the nuance 'charity, alms' for Heb. ṣĕdāqāh Rabbinic Hebrew and the possible Biblical Hebrew roots of this nuance see below,
p. 477, n. 7 and the authorities cited there.
[26] For the comparison of the wailing of a mourner/ suppliant to the sound of
a dove see Isa. 38:14; 59:11; Nah. 2:8; for the comparison of the wailing of mourners
to the sound of doves in Akkadian literature see *CAD*, S, p. 379b, s.v. *summatu* 'dove'.
[27] Taking the poet's "on your doors" as an elliptical allusion to "knocking on
your doors" in line 5; contrast Lavon: "murmuring like doves around Your doors."
[28] The reference is to the sin of worshipping the golden calf (Ex. 32), which
took place at the foot of Mt. Sinai, which was the metaphoric marriage chamber

13b From then on we have been (Isa. 59:14; Jer. 7:24) steadily
     losing ground.
14a The sacrifices of doubly fat lambs[29] ceased
14b [Likewise] the fragrance of the incense[30]
15a Captain of fifty,[31] advisor and official (Isa. 3:3)[32]

---

in which the marriage of the Holy One Blessed be He (the bridegroom) and the Congregation of Israel (the bride) took place. Hos. 1-3, followed by Jeremiah (see, e.g., Jer. 2-3) and Ezekiel (Ezek. 16; 23) introduced into Israelite thought both 1) the comparison of the relationship between God and Israel to marriage (as in Rabbinic *midrash* on Canticles); and 2) the comparison of Israel's apostasy to adultery. For the idea that the Giving of the Torah at Mt. Sinai constituted the consummation of God's marriage to Israel cf., with Gold, p. 295, Mishnah Ta'anit 4:1: ". . .'on his [King Solomon's] wedding day' (Cant. 3:11). This refers [allegorically] to the Giving of the Torah [at Mt. Sinai]." For the comparison of Israel's worship of the golden calf to a bride's commiting adultery during the wedding dinner see Rashi at Cant. 1:12.

[29] As noted by Rashi in his commentary at 1 Sam. 15:9 the term *wĕhammišnîm* in that verse is an *hapax legomenon* in Biblical Hebrew. The rendering *wĕsamînayyā'* found in TJ and in the Peshitta may well reflect a reading *wĕhaššĕmēnîm* 'and the fatlings' in the Hebrew *Vorlage*; this has already been suggested by Qimhi in his commentary at 1 Sam. 15:9. The latter exegesis suggests that the *hapax legomenon* may be the result of errant scribal metathesis. Rashi, on the other hand, in his commentary at 1 Sam. 15:9, accepting the principle of *lectio difficilior*, explains the *hapax legomenon* as follows: "I think that the epression *mišnîm* is a form of [the word *mišneh* 'double' in the phrase] 'double money' (in Gen. 43:12). [The animal is called *mišneh* 'double'] because it is double [*kāpul*] with respect to [its] flesh and fat." Regardless of the order in which Rashi wrote the *seliḥah* and the commentary on the Book of Samuel, it is reasonable to assume with Lavon and Gold, p. 295 that if Rashi inserted the *hapax legomenon* in the *seliḥah*, Rashi at the time concurred with the assumption spelled out in his Samuel commentary that the word is not simply a plural of the word *mišneh* in the sense 'two year old lamb'. Moreover, there is no mention anywhere in Hebrew Scripture of sacrificing a two year old lamb; for the sacrifice of one year old lambs see Num. 7:17 and passim; 28:3 and passim; 29:2 and passim.

[30] So Rosenfeld, p. 136. This rendering of the Heb. phrase *qĕtoret samĕmānîm* 'incense made up of ingredients' reflects the usage of the noun *samĕmānîm* in Rabbinic Hebrew with respect to the subject of 'incense'; see dictionaries. Lavon and Gold, p. 295 render the entire line as follows: "the satisfying aroma [of the flour-offerings and wine libations]; the spice-compounded incense," and they point out that in Hebrew Scripture the phrase *rēăḥ nihôăḥ* 'satisfying aroma' (NJV: "a pleasing odor") "refers to either animal and meal-offerings or wine libations. Since the animal offerings are already mentioned in the preceding stich, this one must mean the flour offerings and the wine libations." Concerning *rēăḥ nihôăḥ* in Biblical Heb. see, e.g., Num. 29:2, 6.

[31] BT Hagigah 14a, q.v., offers a variety of interpretations of the three expressions from Isa. 3:3; see next note; and cf. Lavon and Gold, p. 296. In the present context the three terms are probably meant to conjure up the officialdom of ancient Israel at the height of its political power in the age of the Davidic monarchy; see below, n. 35.

[32] If concerning 'captain of fifty' and 'advisor' BT Hagigah 14a offers a var-

15b Assistant priest and high priest,[33] Levites and Aaronides.[34]

16a Look how we stand before You poor and impoverished.[35]

16b Anxious in spirit (Isa. 63:10), bitter like wormwood (Prov. 5:4)

17a We recall You in [our] trouble.

17b Worried and mournful because of the fear of Your decree.

18a Make spring up for the faithful a branch of kindness (Jer. 33:15).

18b Command the expiation of former iniquities (Job. 7:21; Ps. 79:8).

19a May the voice of the one who sings aloud[36]put an end to litigation.[37]

---

iety of interpretations, it is noteworthy that it interprets *nĕśû' pānîm* 'official' according to its primary, literal meaning 'a person to whom deference is shown' and suggests two Tannaitic culture heroes as quintessential persons to whom deference is shown, namely, Rabbi Haninah b. Dosa, to whom God showed deference and Rabbi Abbahu to whom Caesar showed deference. On the primary, literal meaning of Heb. *nĕśû' pānîm* and its various nuances see Gruber, "The Many Faces of Hebrew *nāśá' pānîm*," pp. 256-257.

[33] Heb. *māśûaḥ*, lit., 'annointed' appears as a technical term for the high priest of the First Temple era in Mishnah Megillah 1:9; cf. Goldschmidt, p. 66, n.

[34] The use of the term Aaronides for 'priests', who are descendants of Aaron just as Levites are descendants of Levi and Israelites descendants of Israel is a typical poetic convention of medieval Hebrew poetry; see Yonah David, *Lexicon of Epithets in Hebrew Liturgical Poetry* (Jerusalem: Rubin Mass, 2001), p. 23 (in Hebrew).

[35] The poverty referred to here in this veritable plea of poverty before the heavenly Judge consists of 1) the loss of the sacrificial system referred to in line 14; 2) Israel's loss of political power as described in Isa. 3:3; and 3) the loss of the priestly hierarchy, whose task was to expiate the sins of Israel. Consequently, in lines 19-21 the poet asks God to show special consideration for the limited number of treasures upon which Israel can still rely: a) the voice of the prayer leader; b) the humility of those who pray; c) God's promise to the patriarchs.

[36] In Isa. 6:4 *qôl haqqōrē'*, 'the voice of the one who sings aloud' refers back to Isa. 6:3 where it is said of the seraphs (perhaps only two?): "One would sing aloud [*wĕqārā'...wĕ'āmar*] to the other: 'Holy, holy, holy is the LORD of Hosts! The whole earth is full of His Glory.'" In the present context 'the voice of the one who sings aloud' is the voice of the prayer leader. Cf. Rosenfeld, p. 136, n. 6; cf. Lavon, p. 297: "the voice of the chazzan"; contrast Goldschmidt, p. 66, n.: "I.e., the voice of the Holy One Blessed be He. . . ." One of the recurrent themes in the prayers of the High Holy Days is the idea that the prayer leader or *hazzan* has the potentiality of influencing God to change His/Her mind and thus to revoke unpleasant decrees against sinners. Consequently, in several prayers both the congregation (see Birnbaum, *High HolyDay Prayerbook,* p. 380 from "Our God". to "God of Israel") and the prayer leader (see there, pp. 212, 230-31, 326, 380 from "I firmly hope" to "my Saviour") ask God to turn this potentiality into actuality. See next note.

[37] The verb and direct object, "will put an end to litigation" is taken from Prov. 18:18 where the noun *midyānîm* 'litigation' is an abstract noun derived from the common Semitic verbal root *dyn* 'plead, litigate, judge'. Since Rashi in his commentary at Prov. 18:18 does not comment on the first half of the verse,

19b Silence the prosecuting attorney,[38] and hush the defamers.

20a May our humble spirit and our broken and contrite hearts

20b be accepted as a substitute for the fat of sacrifices.

21a Fulfill for the descendants the oath [You swore] to the patriarchs.

21b Hear from Your [heavenly] abode the prayers[39] of those who sing aloud to You.[40]

22a Prepare their hearts so that they will be prepared to revere You.

22b Make Your ear hearken to their plea for mercy

23a Again extricate Your people from the mire.

23b May Your ancient love come toward us quickly.

24a May those who depend on Your compassion be acquitted in their trial.

24b Praying for Your kindness and relying on Your mercy.

Goldschmidt's statement, p. 66, n., that Rashi there and here in our *selihah* treats *midyānîm* as people, sc., litigants, is baseless. In fact, here in the *selihah*, as in Proverbs, the noun *midyānîm* denotes 'litigation'. While Prov. 18:17-19 clearly speaks of civil litigation between mortals, our *selihah* refers to God's litigation with mortals, especially during the High Holy Days. Our *selihah* hopes through the charm of Rashi's poetry and the melodious singing voice of the prayer leader to influence the Holy One Blessed be He to withdraw His case so that Israel will go unpunished. The expression "put an end to litigation" occurs also in Birnbaum, *High Holyday Prayerbook*, p. 367; in that context the verb *yašbît* serves as a jussive, i.e., a third person imperative; however, Birnbaum, p. 368 paraphrases as follows: "remove thou our foe"; note also that in *High Holyday Prayerbook*, there, the reading is *midayyĕnēnû* 'our litigant', i.e., Satan in his role as heavenly prosecuting attorney as in Job. 1-2.

[38] I.e., Satan; see previous note; note also that the expression "defamers" is a poetic synonym of "prosecuting attorney" just as 'hush' is a synonym for 'silence', and that line 19b of the poem represents an example of synonymus parallelism; perhaps 'defamers' in the plural refers to mortals and heavenly beings in the employ of Satan, the defamer *par excellence* as in Job. 1-2.

[39] Heb. *šau'at*; cf. Ps. 145:19: "He will hearken to *šau'atām* 'their prayer/shout', and He will save them."

[40] Heb. *qōrĕ'ykā*; see above, n. 36.

B. Rashi's Exegetical Compositions

1. Rashi's Commentary on the Babylonian Talmud

a. The Scope of Rashi's Commentary on the Talmud

It is now almost taken for granted that the commentaries printed in the inner margin of the standard editions of the Babylonian Talmud to the following tractates were not actually written by Rashi: Ta'anit, Nedarim, Nazir, Horayot, Bava Batra from pp. 29b to the end; and Makkot from p. 19b to the end.[1] It was long assumed that Rashi simply did not live long enough to complete his monumental commentary on the Talmud. This impression seems to be supported by the following note in the *editio princeps* of the Babylonian Talmud (Venice: Bomberg, 1521) at Bava Batra 29a:

> Up to here commented Rashi, may the memory of the righteous be for a blessing. From here on commented R. Samuel b. Meir.

Even stronger support for this view is provided by the Pesaro (1510) edition of BT at that same juncture of the commentaries of Rashi and Rashbam at Bava Batra 29a:

> Here died Rashi, may his memory be for a blessing.

Similarly, in the *editio princeps* of BT (Venice: Bomberg, 1520-1523) at Makkot 19b we read as follows:

---

[1] Grossman, *The Early Sages of France*, pp. 216-18; concerning the commentaries to Nazir, Makkot and Horayot, which are widely recognized as from the pen of Rashi's grandson Rabbi Judah b. Nathan (Riban), see above, p. 14 n. 4; concerning the commentary on Ta'anit wrongly attributed to Rashi in the standard editions of of BT see below, p. 106, n. 3; concerning the possibility that Rashi's own commentary on Ta'anit may have been discovered see Grossman, *The Early Sages of France*, p. 216, n. 275; concerning the commentary on Nedarim wrongly attributed to Rashi in the standard editions of BT see Grossman, there. For the possibility that additional commentaries (Temurah and Me'ilah) or parts thereof (Zebahim 68a-78a; Menahot, Chapters 7-8; Bekorot 57bff.) attributed to Rashi in the standard editions of BT are not, in fact, from the pen of Rashi see Grossman, there, p. 217, n. 277; concerning the debate as to whether or not Rashi is the author of the commentary attributed to him in the standard editions of BT Sanhedrin, Chapter 11 ("All Israel have a portion in the posteschatological era....") see the extensive literature cited in Grossman, there, n. 278.

Rashi, whose body was pure,[2] and whose soul departed in purity commented no further; from here on it [the commentary] is the text[3] of his disciple R. Judah b. R. Nathan.

Observing that Rashi's commentary on BT Moʿed Qaṭan is missing from the standard editions of BT but survives in a single ms. published by Kupfer,[4] Grossman suggests that 1) Rashi did, in fact,

---

[2] The literal meaning of this clause is that immediately before his death Rashi immersed himself in a *miqweh*. As suggested by Berliner, "Beiträge," p. 16 the inspiration for this idea is that Rashi died immediately after commenting on the phrase in BT Makkot 19b: "Since he bathed, he is pure."

[3] Heb. *lĕšôn;* on this ubiquitous word and its multiple meanings in Rashi's commentaries see below, pp. 140–145 and passim. It should be observed that in Medieval Rabbinic Hebrew quotations are often introduced by *wĕzeh lĕšônô*, which is the Heb. functional equivalent of Eng., 'and I quote". Likewise, in Medieval Rabbinic Hebrew the functional equivalent of closing quotation marks is the expression *ʿad kāʾn lĕšônô*. In light of these usages and in light of medieval copyists' penchant for creating eclectic versions of Rashi's commentaries by utilizing as many mss. as they could get their hands on (see below, pp. 158–161) it seems reasonable to draw the following conclusion: The copyist responsible for the current version of the commentary on the inner margins of BT Makkot has attempted to compile a complete commentary on BT Makkot. Since his manuscript sources supply Rashi's commentary only as far as p. 19a, he completes the commentary by copying out from the commentary of Rabbi Judah b. R. Nathan on BT Makkot 19bff.

[4] Efraim F. Kupfer, *R. Salomon Izḥaqi (Raši) Commentarius in Tractatum Moʿed Katan ad Fidem Codicis Hispansiensis* (Jerusalem: Mekize Nirdamim 1961); see also the discussion in Grossman, *The Early Sages of France*, p. 216, n. 276. On the other hand, Yoel Florsheim, "Rashi's Commentary on Môʿed Qaṭan," *Tarbiz* 51 (1982), pp. 421-444 (in Hebrew); id, "More Concerning Rashi's Commentary on Tractate Môʿed Qaṭan," *Sinai* 63 (2000), pp. 174-181 (in Hebrew) argues that 1) indeed, Rashi composed a complete commentary on Môʿed Qaṭan; but 2) this commentary as so far not been found; 3) the ms. published by Kupfer is a collection of quotations from Rashi's commentary compiled from various sources. However, Adiel Schremer, "Concerning the Commentaries on Môʿed Qaṭan Attributed to Rashi," in *Atara Lʾ Haim: Studies in the Talmud and Medieval Rabbinic Literature in Honor of Professor Haim Zalman Dimitrovsky*, edited by Daniel Boyarin, Shamma Friedman, Marc Hirshman, Menahem Schmelzer, Israel M. Ta-Shma (Jerusalem: Magnes, 2000), pp. 534-554, on the other hand, argues that Rashi never composed a commentary on Môʿed Qaṭan. Schremer's contention that, in fact, Rashi never composed a commentary on Moʿed Qaṭan would seem to be challenged by the fact that Rashi himself in his Pentateuch Commentary at Lev. 19:19 writes as follows: "[The sesame plants may be plucked on the intermediate days of the festivals of Passover and Tabernacles] because it is fit for use on account of the *naʿăzî* 'seeds' which they contain. [As for the *naʿăzî* 'seeds'] which we explain as a term referring to [*lĕšôn*] *kāmûš* 'worn out'; *flestrir* 'to wither' [in O.F.; cf. Rashi at Ps. 1:3]." Charles Chavel, *Rashi's Commentaries on the Torah* (Jerusalem: Mossad Harav Kook, 1982), p. 374 (in Hebrew) states, "I do not know what this is that Rashi writes here. Perhaps he changed his mind with respect to his comment there [in the commentary found in the inner margins of standard printed editions of BT Moʿed

comment on most and possibly all of BT; 2) the commentaries on Ta'anit, Nedarim, Nazir, Horayot, and the latter parts of the commentaries on Bava Batra and Makkot were lost; 3) the vivid imagination of later copyists, followed by the printers, supplied the plausible explanation, eventually treated as fact by modern scholars,[5] that Rashi died in the middle of his writing the commentaries on Bava Batra and Makkot[6] and that he simply did not live long enough to write commentaries on Ta'anit, Nedarim, Nazir, and Horayot.[7]

One may well compare the fanciful explanation that Rashi died in the middle of writing his commentaries on BT Bava Batra and Makkot with Gordis's explanation for the appearance of what Gordis calls the "Hymn to Wisdom" as Chapter 28 of the Book of Job. Gordis argues that Job. 28 cannot be either an original part of the speech assigned to Job in Job. 27 nor originally part of the original third speech of Zophar, which many scholars reconstruct from parts of Job. 26-27.[8] "Nevertheless," Gordis points out, "...the 'Hymn to Wisdom' is eminently worthy of the genius of the author of Job."[9] This leads directly to Gordis's conclusion:

> Its position in our present text is therefore best explained by the assumption that it represents an early treatment in lyrical form of the basic theme with which the author was to be concerned throughout his life, and to which he was later to devote his masterpiece [the Book

---

Qatan]: "they are fit to be made into oil." Apparently, Chavel forgot that it had long been known that the commentary found in the inner margins of standard printed editions of BT Mô'ed Qatan is not from the pen of Rashi. Similarly, Morris Abraham Rosenbaum and Maurice Silbermann in collaboration with. A. Blashki and L. Joseph, *Pentateuch with Targum Onkelos, Haftaroth and Rashi's Commentary Translated into English and Annotated* (5 vols.; London: Shapiro Valentine & Co., 1932), vol. 3, p. 180. The problem can, of course, be resolved by examining the Kupfer edition, which on p. 39 quotes BT Mô'ed Qatan 12b, "*lnzy* WHICH ARE CONTAINED THEREIN" and comments, "*kĕmûšîn* which are contained therein are fit for eating." Naturally, Kupfer, there, n. 44 compares Rashi's commentary on Lev. 19:19. Obviously, Rashi's referring in his commentary on Lev. 19:19 to the commentary on BT Mô'ed Qatan attributed to Rashi by Kupfer and Grossman touches upon the fascinating question as to the order in which Rashi wrote and reedited his various exegetical compositions; see, e.g., Yoel Florsheim, "Concerning Rashi's Biblical Exegesis," *Sinai* 59 (1996), pp. 71-72 (in Hebrew); Gelles, pp. 136-138; Liber, *Rashi*, pp. 90-91.

[5] Berliner, "Beiträge," p. 14 notes that this view was adopted but later rejected by Samuel David Luzzatto.
[6] Grossman, *The Early Sages of France*, pp. 217-18.
[7] So Gelles, p. 137.
[8] *BGM*, p. 102.
[9] Ibid.

of Job; clarification by M.I.G.]—the mystery of the universe and of man's suffering in it.[10]

Just as copyists and printers accounted for the fact that they only had part of Rashi's commentary on BT Bava Batra and Makkot by the assumption that Rashi died in the course of writing commentaries to those tractates so did Gordis account for the appearance of Job. 28 in the middle of two speeches of Job by reconstructing the biography of the common author of the Book of Job and the originally independent "Hymn to Wisdom" in Job. 28. The common assumption of both Gordis and the copyists/printers of BT is that there is a rational explanation complete with a human interest angle for anomalies in the transmission of ancient and medieval texts. Since there is no independent evidence to support either Gordis's accounting for the appearance of the "Hymn to Wisdom" in Job. 28 or the copyists'/printers' explanation for their printing the commentary of R. Samuel b. Meir to BT Bava Batra from folio 29a onward and that of R. Judah b. R. Nathan to Makkot from folio 19b onward, we are dealing not with history/biography but with the tendency of human imagination to provide a simple solution to every problem. There is an essential difference between the pseudo-biography exemplified both by Gordis and by the copyists/printers of BT on the one hand and *midrash* on the other. The difference is that the authors of *midrash* utilize simple solutions born of imagination to teach extremely profound lessons in human behavior and theology without any illusion that such solutions constitute a reconstruction of history or biography.

Three pertinent analogies support Grossman's view that, in fact, Rashi produced a commentary on the entire Babylonian Talmud and that since parts of it were lost, editors of manuscripts followed by the editors of the earliest printed editions systematically provided other medieval commentaries to the tractates or parts thereof, for which they did not have access to Rashi's commentary. The three pertinent analogies are 1) Samuel ben Meir's Commentary on the Babylonian Talmud; 2) Samuel ben Meir's Commentary on the Book of Job; and 3) Rashi's Commentary on the Book of Job.

Since the common printed editions of BT supply the commentary of R. Samuel b. Meir (Rashbam) only to the tenth chapter of

---

[10] Ibid.

Tractate Pesaḥim and to Bava Batra from p. 29a where the commentary of Rashi breaks off, it was, perhaps, commonly assumed
that Rashbam had, in fact, written his commentary on Bava Batra
deliberately to provide a commentary on the portion of Bava Batra,
which Rashi, owing to his demise[11], had not been able to complete.[12]
However, more than 120 years ago Rosin[13] made the following observations concerning Rashbam's commentaries on BT: 1) parts of
Rashbam's Commentary to Tractate 'Avodah Zarah are quoted in
Temim Deʿim ;[14] 2) Isaac b. Moses of Vienna (c. 1180-c.1250 C.E.)
refers to Rashbam's Commentary on Tractate Niddah in his *halakic*
compendium *Or Zarua;*[15] 3) various *halakic* authorities of the later
Middle Ages refer to commentaries (Heb. *pitrônê*) of Rabbenu Samuel
[i.e., Rashbam] on the following tractates of BT: 'Erubin,[16] Beṣah,
Hagigah, Menaḥot; 4) various authors of the later Middle Ages quote
a no longer extant (or not yet rediscovered?) Commentary on Mishnah Avot.[17] Urbach added to this short list of tractates of BT, on
which Rashbam is known to have written commentaries, the following: Berakot,[18] Shabbat,[19] Yoma,[20] Yebamot,[21] Nedarim,[22] Giṭṭin,[23]

---

[11] See above.

[12] David Rosin, ed., *The Torah Commentary of R. Samuel b. Meir* (Breslau: Schottlaender, 1882), p. xiii (in Hebrew) points out that in fact there are two surving
commentaries of Rashbam on BT Bava Batra 29a-54b: a shorter commentary,
which was printed in the Pesaro edition of BT, and a longer commentary, which
is found in all other printed editions of BT.

[13] Rosin, *The Torah Commentary of Rabbi Samuel b. Meir*, pp. xii-xiv.

[14] *Temim Deʿim* is the collected responsa of R. Abraham b. David of Posquières
(c. 1125-1198 C.E.). See *Temim Deʿim* (Lemberg: Herz Grossman, 1812) #105 (p.
11a); #108 (p. 11b) for the quotations from the commentary on BT 'Avodah Zarah
by Samuel b. Meir, there called Samuel of Ramerupt (there spelt Ramerug). A
printed edition of portions of Rashbam's commentary on BT 'Avodah Zarah copied
out from a medieval ms. was published by Abraham Epstein in *Ozar Tob* (=
hebräische Beilage zum *Magazin für die Wissenschaft des Judentums*) 14 (1887), pp.
1-7; cf. Urbach, *Tosaphists,* vol. 1, p. 50; for additional testimony to Rashbam's
Commentary on BT 'Avodah Zarah see Urbach, *Tosaphists,* vol. 1, p. 55.

[15] Significant additional testimony to Rashbam's Commentary on BT Niddah
including that of R. Meir of Rothenberg, Ra'aviah, Tosaphot, and R. Judah b.
R. Kalonymos is listed in Urbach, *Tosaphists,* vol. 1, p. 56

[16] More testimony to Rashbam's Commentary on 'Erubin is listed by Urbach,
Tosaphists, vol. 1, p. 52, nn. 53, 54.

[17] See Urbach, *Tosaphists,* vol. 1, p. 51, nn. 46-47.

[18] See Urbach, *Tosaphists,* vol. 1, p. 51 citing Hagahot Maimoniyot to Moses
Maimonides, Mishneh Torah, Laws of Sabbath 20:16 as well as Tosaphot to BT
Berakot.

[19] Note, with Urbach, *Tosaphists,* vol. 1, p. 52 that British Museum Heb. Ms.
409 records a commentary of Rashbam on BT Shabbat, Chapters 7 and 9; for

Makkot[24] and Hullin.[25] Sarah Japhet notes that a proper study of both the extant of Rashbam's contribution to the exegesis of BT and the characteristics of his Talmudic exegesis is yet to be written.[26]

Just as the printed editions of BT supply Rashi's commentary on BT Bava Batra up to p. 29a and Rashbam's commentary on that tractate from p. 29a to the end of the tractate (p. 54b) so, it is now established, the Rabbinic Bible published by Daniel Bomberg at Venice beginning in 1548 and 1568 follows a number of medieval mss. (Munich Heb. Ms. 5; Ms. Parma de Rossi 181; Vatican Ms. Ebr. 94) in supplying Rashi's commentary to Job. 1:1-40:25 and continuing without warning with Rashbam's commentary on Job. 40:26-42:17.[27] Given the evidence 1) that Rashi's commentary on Job did not end at Job. 40:25;[28] 2) that Rashbam penned a frequently

---

quotations of Rashbam's Commentary on BT Shabbat in Tosaphot to BT Shabbat see Urbach, *Tosaphists* , vol. 1, n. 48.

[20] Urbach, *Tosaphists*, vol. 1, n. 62 quoting Sefer ha-Yashar by Rabbenu Jacob Tam, Chapters 561, 562, 564 and Tosaphot to BT Yoma 60a, s.v. "Two".

[21] Urbach, *Tosaphists*, vol. 1, p. 53, n. 67 citing Sefer Ra'abiah, Chapter 973.

[22] Urbach, *Tosaphists*, vol. 1, p. 53.

[23] Ibid.

[24] Urbach, *Tosaphists*, vol. 1, p. 53 citing Tosaphot on BT Makkot, Chapter 3; moreover, Urbach, there, points out that when the Tosaphot on BT Makkot from p. 20a onward employ the term (*ha*) *qunteres* '(the) commentary *par execellence*' they refer not to Rashi but to Rashbam.

[25] See Urbach, *Tosaphists*, vol. 1, pp. 51, 55.

[26] Sara Japhet, *The Commentary of Rabbi Samuel ben Meir (Rashbam) On the Book of Job* (Jerusalem: Magnes, 2000), pp. 9-10 [in Hebrew].

[27] See Avraham Shoshana, *The Book of Job with the Commentaries of RaSHI, Rabbenu Jacob b. Meir Tam, and a disciple of Rashi* (Jerusalem: Ofeq Institute, 5760 [=1999]), pp. v-vi. Japhet, *The Commentary of Rabbi Samuel ben Meir (Rashbam) On the Book of Job*, pp. 19-22, showed that the commentary commonly appended to Rashi's Commentary on Job from Job. 40:26 was taken verbatim from a complete commentary on Job found in the 12th century C.E. Hebrew manuscript of Northern French origin known as Ms. New York Jewish Theological Seminary L 778, pp. 142b-155a. Moreover, she argued (there, pp. 22-36) on the basis of numerous attributions by later medieval authorities of verbatim quotations from that commentary to Rashbam that, in fact, this complete commentary on Job was authored by Rashbam. In fact, to write out (print) Rashi's commentary up to Job. 40:25 and to continue with Rashbam from Job. 40:25 is only *one of several* traditions. As noted already by Sokolow, "Establishing," p. 23, n. 25, the 1515 Saloniki edition of the Rabbinic Bible provides Rashi's commentary up to Job. 40:20 and continues with the commentary of R. Jacob Nazir. The custom reflected in the Saloniki edition is anticipated by Ms. Bodleian Opp. 34 (13th cent.). Ms. Bodleian 142 (1328 C.E.) and Ms. New York JTS : 782 (15th cent.) provide Rashi as far as Job. 40:25 and continue with the commentary of R. Jacob Nazir from Job. 40:26.

[28] The various views and the evidence for each of them are discussed with great detail and with equal clarity in Grossman, *The Early Sages of France*, p. 223-231.

quoted commentary on the entire Book of Job, whose proper identification was confirmed only by Japhet's definitive work on the subject in 2000 C.E.;[29] 3) that Rashbam composed commentaries on a
large part of BT, it is reasonable to conclude that future research
in medieval Hebrew manuscripts will totally vindicate Grossman in
his conjecture that the impression that Rashi and Rashbam had each
commented on only part of BT Bava Batra derives from the fact
that compilers of the mansucripts, which formed the basis of our
printed editions, had access to Rashi on Bava Batra only up to p.
29a. It was these editors/publishers who created the false impression that Rashbam's commentary on the latter part of BT Bava Batra
was designed as a stand-in, as it were, for the final portion of Rashi's
commentary on that tractate, the writing of which had been pre-
empted by Rashi's sudden demise.

Moreover, almost a century ago Abraham Berliner showed that
Rashi had, in fact, composed a complete commentary on BT Nedarim.[30] Since by the time of the Geonim, Tractate Nedarim rarely
formed part of the curriculum of the *yeshivot*, Rashi's commentary
on that tractate was not extensively copied and did not reach a wide
audience. Consequently, this commentary disappeared. Among those
who saw and quoted Rashi's commentary on BT Nedarim are Isaac
b. Moses of Vienna in his *halakic* compendium Or Zarua and the
latter's son Hayyim (late13th century Germany) in his responsa;[31]
Joseph Ben Lev (b. Monastir, Herzogovina 1505; d. Constaninople
1580);[32] and Menahem Azariah of Pano (1548-1620).[33]

Berliner likewise points out that the numerous quotations from
Rashi in Rashbam's commentary on BT Bava Batra prove that
Rashbham had access to a complete commentary by Rashi on that

---

[29] See Japhet, *The Commentary of Rabbi Samuel ben Meir (Rashbam) on the Book of Job* , pp. 22-36; for dissenting views see Martin Lockshin, "'Rashbam' on Job: A Reconsideration," *Jewish Studies Quarterly* 8 (2001), pp. 80-104; Michael S. Rosen, "The Hebrew Commentary on Job in Ms. Jewish Theological Seminary, New York L 778 Attributed by Some to R. Samuel ben Meir: An Analysis of Its Sources and Consideration of Its Authorhsip" (Ph.D. diss., University of London, 1994).

[30] Berliner, "Beiträge," p. 15.

[31] Ibid.

[32] See *Responsa of Joseph Ben Lev* (4 vols.; Amsterdam: Moses Frankfurt, 1626), vol. 1, p. 35b (responsum # 51); vol. 2, p. 52ᵈ (responsum # 104) [in Hebrew]. This collection of responsa was republished as *Responsa of Joseph Ben Lev* (4 vols.; Bene Berak, S.L.A., 1988).

[33] See *Responsa of Rabbenu Menahem Azariah of Pano* (Jerusalem: Salomon, 1963), p. 43 (#26); p. 127 (#66)

tractate. Moreover, Berliner notes, numerous quotations from Rashi's commentary on BT Bava Batra in *Sefer ha-Yashar* by Rashi's grandson Jacob, commonly known as Rabbenu Tam[34] and in the responsa of Rabbi Meir of Rothenberg (c. 1215- 1293) testify to these authors' familiarity with Rashi's complete commentary on BT Bava Batra.[35]

In the same vein, Berliner notes that numerous quotations in the *responsa* of Rabbi Yom Tov b. Abraham of Seville, commonly known by the acronym Ritba (1250-1330), prove that the latter had access to Rashi's complete commentary on BT Makkot.[36]

b. The Characteristics of Rashi's Commentary on
the Babylonian Talmud

In composing his monumental commentary on Hebrew Scripture, Rashi had access to a *textus receptus*;[37] the notes of the Massoretes;[38] exegetical and lexicographical traditions preserved in Targum Onkelos to the Pentateuch, Targum Jonanthan to the Prophets,[39] and the so-called 'Second Targum' to the Scroll of Esther;[40] two

---

[34] Berliner, "Beiträge," p. 15.

[35] Ibid.

[36] Ibid; similarly, Jonah Fraenkel, *Rashi's Methodology in His Exegesis of the Babylonian Talmud* (2^d ed.; Jerusalem: Magnes, 1980), pp. 307-308 cites numerous medieval authors, who quote in the name of Rashi the commentary attributed to Rashi in the printed editions of BT on Sanhedrin, Chapter XI, i.e., "All Israel have a portion in the posteschatological era... ," to prove that the latter commentary is, in fact, the work of Rashi; in addition, Fraenkel, there, pp. 322-335 argues on the basis of the characteristics of that commentary that it is, indeed, the work of Rashi.

[37] In its proper and original use the term *textus receptus*, lit., 'received text' refers to the form of the Greek text of the New Testament published by the Elzevir brothers in 1633 with the following declaration: *"Textum ergo habes, nunc ab omnibus receptum: in quo nihil immutatum aut corruptum damus,"* which means, "Therefore you have a text accepted by all, in which we have presented neither emendation nor error"; see Ira Maurice Price, *The Ancestry of Our English Bible*, 3d rev. ed. by William A. Irwin and Allen P. Wikgren (New York: Harper & Brothers, 1956), p. 204. When Daniel Boyarin, review of *A Manual of Babylonian Jewish Aramaic*, by David Marcus, in *JNES* 42 (1983), p. 297, faults Marcus for reprinting passages from "the *textus receptus*," he extends the meaning of the latter term since it is clear from 1) the numerous marginal corrections; 2) the marking of innumerable additions with square brackets; and 3) the marking of doubtful passages with parentheses that the standard edition of the Babylonian Talmud (22 vols.; Vilna: Romm, 1885) blantantly claims to present both error and emendation.

[38] See, e.g., Rashi at Ps. 10:10b; 42:9b; 80:3c; 123:4.

[39] See index s.v. Targum Onkelos; Targum Jonathan.

[40] See passim in Rashi's Commentary on the Scroll of Esther; see Michael

reasonably good dictionaries of Biblical Hebrew;[41] additional lexicographical insights provided by R. Moses the Interpeter of Narbonne;[42] the written and oral traditions transmitted by earlier French Jewish exegetes and translators;[43] and a plethora of data available in Rabbinic literature,[44] liturgical poetry[45] and traditions and insights conveyed by his teachers.[46] As pointed out by Maurice Liber, Rashi had few of these kinds of data at his disposal when he composed his even more monumental commentary on BT.[47]

The attempt to establish and preserve a *textus receptus* of Hebrew Scripture and a canonical set of variants known as *qeri* pre-dates the Christian Era.[48] For the Babylonian Talmud, on the other hand, there is to this day no *textus receptus*, and modern attempts to create critical editions of inidividual tractates have been totally sporadic.[49] Berliner pointed out that because the technique of preparing animal skins for writing was not yet widely known in France and Germany when Rashi was growing up books were extremely rare in France and Germany. Consequently, one of Rashi's esteemed teachers, R. Eliezer the Great of Mainz, testified that he had never stud-

---

Carasik, "Rashi's Commentary to the Book of Esther Translated into English with Supercommentary, Chapters 1-3" (M.A. Thesis, Spertus College of Judaica, 1986).

[41] These are, of course, *Mahberet Menahem* and *Teshuvot Dunash;* see passim in the index at the end of this work.

[42] See e.g., Rashi at Ps. 45:2c; 60:4b; 62:13a; 68:17a; 80:65.

[43] See e.g., Rashi at Ezek. 26:21; Ps. 9:1; 68:32a.

[44] See in Rashi's commentary at Gen. 3:8 and in the introduction to his commentary on Song of Songs Rashi delineation of the criteria he used in selecting from the abundance of data contained in the rabbinic corpora.

[45] See e.g., Rashi at Ps. 42:5.

[46] See e.g., Rashi at Ps. 73:12; 76:11.

[47] Liber, *Rashi,* pp. 135-142.

[48] See Robert Gordis, *The Biblical Text in the Making,* (augmented edition; New York: Ktav, 1972); concerning Rashi's reference to such a *textus receptus* of Hebrew Scripture and the Rabbinic terminology for such a *textus receptus* see Rashi at Ps. 9:1 and the discussion below, p. 203.

[49] Rare examples of these include Henry Malter, *The Treatise Ta'anith of the Babylonian Talmud Critically Edited on the Basis of Twenty-four Manuscripts, Quotations by Old Authorities and Early Editions, and Provided with Notes Containing the Critical Apparatus* (New York: American Academy for Jewish Research, 1930; Baruch Na'eh, *Gemara Shelemah: Tractate Pesahim from the Babylonian Talmud* (Jerusalem: Torah Shelemah Institute, 1960); and last, but by no means least, *The Babylonian Talmud with Variant Readings: Tractate Gittin (II)*. Edited by Rabbi Hillel Porush. Director Rabbi Joshua Hutner. Jerusalem: Yad Harav Herzog/Instiute for the Complete Israeli Talmud, 2001. The latter volume is the 15th volume in an ongoing project to reprint the text of the entire BT according to the standard printed editions together with all variant readings.

ied Tractate 'Avodah Zarah of the Babylonian Talmud.[50] It has been suggested that Rashi left his native Troyes for Mainz primarily to gain access to reliable copies of BT. Rashi himself testifies that he made use of the copy of BT which Rabbenu Gershom (c. 1000) had copied out from manuscripts brought to Europe from the Middle East.[51] Rashi, however, took pains, mostly on the basis of conjecture (like modern biblical scholars with the Hebrew Bible!) to correct the text of BT. In fact, subsequent editions of BT bear the imprint of Rashi's numerous conjectural emendations.[52]

The first dictionary of the Hebrew and Aramaic employed in Rabbinic literature was the Arukh by R. Nathan b. Jehiel of Rome, which was completed in 1105, the year of Rashi's death. As demonstrated by Berliner, both R. Nathan and Rashi learned much of their Talmudic lexicography from two common sources. These were the Mainz Commentary on the Talmud,[53] which in turn was based upon the commentary of Rabbenu Gershom, and the Worms Commentary on the Talmud. Rashi's contemporary, R. Kalonymos b. Shabbetai, who became head of the Worms yeshivah in 1070, passed on to R. Nathan data from the Worms Commentary.[54]

In addition to establishing a usable text of BT and virtually creating his own dictionary in his head or in writing [his equivalent of index cards has not survived] at the very same time that R. Nathan b. Jehiel created the Arukh, Rashi made use of the Mainz and Worms Commentaries[55] and the written commentaries of his three mentors— Rabbi Jacob son of Yakar of Mainz,[56] R. Isaac b. Judah of Mainz,[57] and R. Isaac b. Eliezer of Worms[58] as well as of the material he had

[50] Berliner, "Beiträge," p. 2.
[51] Simon Schwarzfuchs, "Reshit darko shel Rashi," in *Rashi Studies*, ed. Zvi Arie Steinfeld (Ramat-Gan: Bar-Ilan University Press, 1993), pp. 177-183; cited Grossman, *The Early Sages of Fance*, p. 220; see also the sources cited above, p. 4, n. 23.
[52] Liber, *Rashi*, p. 139.
[53] Grossman, *The Early Sages of Fance*, p. 220; Liber, *Rashi*, p. 140; Jonah Fraenkel, "Rashi's Commentary to the Babylonian Talmud," *EJ* 13:1564; Isaac Hirsch Weiss, *Dor Dor Wedorshayw* (5 vols.; New York & Berlin: Platt & Munkus, 1924), 4:323-324.
[54] Grossman, *The Early Sages of France*, p. 221 points out that parts of this commentary are found in current printings of the Talmud *in addition to* Rashi's commentary on the following tractates: Menaḥot, Hullin, Bekorot; 'Arakin, Temurah, Keritot, Me'ilah, and Tamid.
[55] Berliner, "Beiträge," p. 3.
[56] With Berliner, "Beiträge," p. 44, n. 3; see Rashi at BT Gittin 82a.
[57] Berliner, "Beiträge," p. 7; see Rashi at BT Rosh ha-Shanah 28a; 32a.

committed to memory during his student days in Mainz and Worms or which he had otherwise received orally from teachers and contemporaries.[59] Just as Rashi systematically studied BT and created and made extensive use in his commentary of a Babylonian Jewish Aramaic-Rabbinic Hebrew lexicon,[60] so did he create and utilize a dictionary of BT's exegetical terminology.[61] As in his biblical commentaries so also in his Commentary on BT Rashi made use of the term *lĕšôn* to designate, variously, "a synonym of"; "an expression referring to"; and "a cognate of."[62] As in his biblical commentaries, so also in his Commentary on BT, Rashi takes for granted the ubiquity of biliteral roots in the Semitic languages.[63]

As in his biblical commentaries, Rashi rarely identifies his sources in his BT Commentary. Nevertheless, it is known that the basis of Rashi's commentary on each tractate of BT is what he had learned from the particular mentor who had first guided him through that tractate.[64]

Rashi succeeded in writing in Rabbinic Hebrew liberally peppered with Aramaisms[65] and some 1100 glosses in French and other Eu-

---

[58] Berliner, "Beiträge," p. 7; concerning all three of these mentors see above, pp. 3–5.

[59] Cf. Berliner, "Beiträge," p. 7.

[60] Fraenkel, *Rashi's Methodology*, pp, 96-100 reconstructs some of this dictionary.

[61] See Fraenkel, *Rashi's Methodology*, pp. 163-201. Fraenkel, there, p. 200 explains that Rashi explains the first time they occur in BT—following the usual order (for what is nowadays "the usual order of the tractates within BT see Hermann L. Strack, *Introduction to the Talmud and Midrash* [Philadelphia: Jewish Publication Society of America, 1931], pp. 365-366; and note with Strack, there, p. 366, nn. 1, 5, 6 and p. 253, n. 9 that with respect to the Middle Ages the terminology "the usual order of the tractates within the Babylonian Talmud" is highly elusive")—terms, which are employed consistently throughout the corpus of BT; for specific examples see Fraenkel, there, pp. 170, 172, 178, 181. On the other hand, Fraenkel, there, pp. 163-200 demonstrates, Rashi explains in detail each instance of an expression employed in an unexpected meaning.

[62] Concerning these nuances in Rashi's' biblical commentaries see below pp. 140–145, and see passim in the index; concerning these nuances in Rashi's Commentary on the Babylonian Talmud see Fraenkel, *Rashi's Methodology*, pp. 95-100.

[63] Concerning this assumption in Rashi's biblical commentaries see below, p. 399, n. 9; concerning such etymologies in Rashi's Commentary on BT see Fraenkel, *Rashi's Methodology*, pp. 106-109.

[64] Berliner, "Beiträge," p. 7-8 points out that the basis of Rashi's commentaries on Shabbat and Hullin was what he learned from R. Issac b. Eliezer while the basis for the commentary on Bava Qama was what he learned from R. Issac b. Judah; the basis for the commentary on 'Erubin was what he learned from R. Jacob b. Yakar; cf. Liber, *Rashi*, p. 137.

ropean languages[66] a running commentary on a large part of BT. The principle task, which this commentary fullfills almost perfectly to this very day, is to lead the student, whose native language is neither Rabbinic Hebrew nor Babylonian Jewish Aramaic, through the syntax of BT, telling us where a question ends and where an answer begins; defining an obscure expression; filling in phrases and entire sentences, including allusions to Scripture, which the highly elliptical language of Mishnah and BT leave to the imagination of the educated reader. As in his biblical commentaries, Rashi frequently quotes the text being commented upon and incorporates his commentary into that text.

M. Liber in his biography of Rashi, published more than a century ago, includes eleven pages of Mishnah and BT in translation with Rashi's commentary incorporated into the Rabbinic text and separated from that text by brackets.[67] In so doing, Liber replicates in writing in Modern French (or in Adele Szold's English translation) the experience of *yeshivah* students and Jewish seminarians over the last nine centuries reading BT and using Rashi's commentary to fill in the ellipses. Hopefully, the following two excerpts from Szold's English version will graphically illustrate precisely how Rashi's Commentary on BT works:

> However, it is taught in a Baraita: "It once happened that R. Nehorai accompanied a witness to give evidence concerning him at Usha" [at the time when the Sanhedrin had its seat in that city, and the new moon was proclaimed there]. R. Nehorai was accompanied by another witness, and if this witness is not mentioned, it is out of regard for R. Nehorai [for R. Nehorai is mentioned only that we may infer from his case that so prominent authority inclined to leniency in the circumstances stated; but it is not fitting for us to appeal to the authority of his less important companion]. Rab Ashi replies: There was already another witness at Usha [who knew the one that was coming to give evidence], and R. Nehorai went to join him.... (BT Rosh ha-Shanah 22a).[68]

It has likewise been shown [that the motive of the Mishnah in declar-

---

[65] Cf. Fraenkel, *Rashi's Methodology*, p. 96.

[66] See Catane, *Recueil des Gloses*, p. 252; he derives this inexact figure from the fact that many of the glosses are repeated. In addition, it should be noted that the 2462 entries include in Catane's handbook include glosses found in the commentaries, which have wrongly been attributed to Rashi.

[67] See Liber, *Rashi*, pp. 144-155.

[68] Ibid., pp. 144-145

ing the stolen Lulab unfit for use on the second day of the festival, is
that it would be the fulfilment of a regulation through the commission of a transgression]. Rabbi Ammi says: ... (BT Sukkah 29b).[69]

What we learn from these examples is precisely how Rashi composes
for an ancient text a very sophisticated commentary, which, first and
foremost, provides the necessary information, which BT, rightly or
wrongly, assumed that the reader had at her/his fingertips. It is no
wonder, therefore, that it has been suggeseted that without Rashi's
commentary BT might have been forgotten.[70]

c. The Problem of Rashi's "Editions" of his Talmud Commentary

A question which has occupied students of Rashi no less than the
scope of his original commentary on BT is the meaning of the traditions recorded by Rashi's disciples concerning two or three editions of Rashi's commentary on BT.[71] Briefly, the issue revolves
around the following data: a) numerous references in the writings
of Rashi's disciples to a first and later [Aram. batrā'] (or is it last?)
edition;[72] b) quotations of Rashi's *halakic* opinions which are at variance with the extant text of Rashi's Commentary on BT;[73] c) the
assertion by R. Moshe Ibn Danon that Rashi had produced three
editions of his Commentary on BT.[74] One of the most widely held
solutions may be summarized as follows: 1) the first edition based
upon the dialogic lessons Rashi gave in his *yeshivah* were edited by
Rashi's [early] disciples, R. Judah b. Nathan and R. Shemayah; 2)

---

[69] Ibid., p. 147.

[70] Menahem b. Zerah (c, 1312-1385) in his *Zedah la-Derek*, quoted by Liber, *Rashi*, p. 158.

[71] See Victor Aptowitzer, "Concerning the History of Rashi's Commentary on the Talmud: Part Two," in *Sefer Rashi*, ed. Yehudah Leib ha-Kohen Fishman Maimon (Jerusalem: Mossad Harav Kook, 1941), pp. 306-314 (in Hebrew); Shamma Friedman, "Rashi's Talmudic Commentaries and the Nature of their Revisions and Recensions," in *Rashi Studies*, ed. Zvi Arie Steinfeld (Ramat-Gan: Bar-Ilan University Press, 1993), pp. 147-175 (in Hebrew); Epstein, "The Commentaries of R. Jehudah ben Nathan and the Commentaries of Worms," pp. 11-34; 153-192; Fraenkel, *Rashi's Methodology*, pp. 1-15; Lipschuetz, *Rashi*, pp. 64-78.

[72] Aptowitzter, "Concerning the History," pp. 306-314.

[73] Ibid., pp. 314-318.

[74] See the extensive discussion in Friedman, "Rashi's Talmudic Commentaries," p. 149; see below, p. 117.

the final [third] edition was the one Rashi produced in his last years when he went over and corrected the draft prepared by the aforementioned disciples; 3) not many copies were made of the final edition; hence many authorities quoted from the earlier versions.[75]

Empirical evidence for such a development is now provided by the data, which Jordan Penkower assembled concerning Rashi's commentary on Ezek. 42:1 in his edition of Rashi's Commentary on Ezekiel included in Menachem Cohen, *Mikra'ot Gedolot 'Haketer': Ezekiel.* (Ramat Gan: Bar-Ilan University Press, 2000), p. 282. In the original version of his commentary on Ezek. 42:1 Rashi contradicted himself. In responding to the tenth in the series of thirteen questions concerning Rashi's Commentaries on Jeremiah and Ezekiel raised by R. Samuel of Auxerre (*Mikra'ot Gedolot 'Haketer': Ezekiel,* p. 321) Rashi admitted that he had contradicted himself. Consequently, Rashi rewrote his commentary on that verse. In the revised version of this commentary Rashi eliminated the contradiction.

Given the widely held view that Rashi was still composing both his commentary on BT and his commentary on the Hagiographa at the time of his death,[76] it is reasonable to conclude that with respect to some of the tractates of BT we may have in our current printed editions only the first or the second of three or more editions.[77] However, given the abundant testimony by Rashi himself,[78] and by his disciples, that Rashi himself produced written commentaries to the Pentateuch, the Prophets and large parts of the

---

[75] Aptowitzer,"Concerning the History of Rashi's Commentary on the Talmud: Part Two," p. 320.

[76] For the contention that some of Rashi's commentaries on tractates of BT were written before Rashi's commentaries on some of the Prophets and Hagiographa see Berliner, "Beiträge," p. 10; see also, above, p. 7; see also Gelles, pp. 136-137. Fraenkel, *Rashi's Methodology,* p. 284 argues that among Rashi's relatively earlier works were his commentaries on Berakot, Sanhedrin, Bekorot, 'Arakin, and Keritot. He holds that among Rashi's latest works were his commentaries on Soṭah, Giṭṭin, Bava Qama, Bava Mesi'a, Bava Batra, Shevu'ot and Hullin. Moreover, he argues that the order in which Rashi composed his commentaries has nothing to do with the order in which the various tractates were studied in Rashi's yeshivah because, he emphasizes, the commentaries were not based upon lecture notes; see below, n. 80.

[77] Friedman, "Rashi's Talmudic Commentaries, p. 168.

[78] See Rashi's *responsa* nos. 9 and 10 to R. Samuel of Auxerre in Menachem Cohen, ed., *Mikra'ot Gedolot ha'Keter': Ezekiel* (Ramat-Gan: Bar Ilan University Press, 2000), p. 321. These *responsa* relate specifically to requests for clarification of issues related to a commentary which both R. Samuel and Rashi agree that Rashi himself has *written.*

Hagiographa,[79] and the Babylonian Talmud,[80] no credence is to be given to the suggestion of Banitt that what we know as Rashi's commentaries were, in fact, the notes compiled by unnamed disciples from Rashi's lectures.[81]

2. Rashi's Biblical Commentaries*

a. Their Scope

Surviving medieval manuscripts of Rashi's Pentateuch commentary outnumber surviving manuscripts of Rashi's commentary on the entirety of Hebrew Scripture at a ratio of almost 10:1.[82] Likewise,

---

[79] See in the Commentary on the Pentateuch by Rashi's grandson, Rabbi Samuel b. Meir at Num. 34:2; see also Tosaphot to BT Menaḥot 75a, s.v. "like a chi": "He [Rashi] drew in his commentary [on the Prophetic Books] a kind of *tet* while in the commentary on the Pentateuch he explained *gimmel.*" See the discussion of this text in Mayer I. Gruber, "Notes on the Diagrams in Rashi's Commentry to the Book of Kings," *Studies in Bibliography and Booklore* 19 (1994), p. 31. In his Commentary on Genesis 37:49 R. Samuel b. Meir writes, "Now also our Rabbi, Solomon, my mother's father who has enlightened the eyes of the [Jews in] Exile, who composed a commentary on [Heb. *pērēš*] Pentateuch, Prophets and Hagiographa...."

[80] References to Rashi's autograph edition of his commentaries on various tractates of BT are found, *inter alia,* in Tosaphot at 'Erubin 17b; 50a; Ketubbot 78a; Qiddushin 26b; 'Avodah Zarah 56a Hullin 137b.

[81] Banitt, *Rashi: Interpeter of the Biblical Letter,* p. 4, n. 14: "The very expression 'R.'s commentary' poses a stylistic problem with unpredictable consequences. One should eliminate the personality of the compiler in the study of the text and thereby avoid the lure of the all too easy transfer of textual problems to matters of genius, character or idiosyncracies. It is simply more convenient to write 'R. says' than, for instance, 'the text of the commentary compiled by R., as written down by his students, reads.'" See also Banitt, there, p. 10, n. 18: "We should remember that, on the whole, the commentaries are a compilation of notes taken at lessons conducted in French...." See also there, p. 139, n. 40; contrast Fraenkel, *Rashi's Methodology,* p. 284.

* I am most grateful to Dr. Jordan Penkower and Dr. Avraham Avigad for their constructive criticism of two earlier version of this chapter. I alone am responsible for whatever shortcomings remain.

[82] This figure is based on David S. Blondheim, "Liste des manuscrits des commentaires bibliques de Raschi," *REJ* 91 (1931), pp. 71-101; 155-174. Blondheim lists a total of 332 manuscripts, of which 17 are mss. of commentaries on the entire 24 books of Hebrew Scripture while 160 are commentaries on the Pentateuch alone; see Blondheim, there, pp. 72-73. The percentage of mss., which include commentaries on the Pentateuch alone, is considerably greater if we take into consideration the many private and public collections of Yemenite manuscripts, which came into existence in the last seventy years since the publication of

the published supercommentaries on Rashi's Pentateuch commentary outnumber published commentaries on Rashi's commentary on the Hagiographa (exclusive of the Five Scrolls) at a ratio of 50:4.[83] The reason is very simple: while most of the surviving manuscripts of Rashi's biblical commentaries are found in public institutions, the manuscripts themselves were produced by and for Jews, for whom the study of Rashi's commentary on the Pentateuch each Sabbath was a matter of holy obligation.[84] The codes of Jewish religious law testify to no similar obligation to study Rashi's commentaries on other books of Holy Scripture

While believing and practicing Jews may have negelcted Rashi's commentaries on the Prophets and Hagiographa (with the significant exception of the Five Scrolls),[85] Rashi's own original design

---

Blondheim's list; also, note should be taken of numerous Yemenite manuscripts containing the three biblical books of Canticles, Ruth and Ecclesiastes with Targum (i.e., Aramaic translation) and Rashi's commentary; see, e.g., Norman J. Golb, *Spertus College of Judaica Yemenite Manuscripts: An Illustrated Catalogue* (Chicago: Spertus College of Judaica Press, 1972), pp. 1-7.

[83] This figure is based upon 1) the list of 200 published supercommentaries on Rashi enumerated in Israel Shapiro, "Commentaries on Rashi on the Torah," *Bitzaron* 2 (1940), pp. 426-436 (in Hebrew); and 2) the four supercommentaries on Rashi's commentaries on the Prophets and Hagiographa enumerated below, pp. 155-156. Aron Freimann, "Manuscript Supercommentaries on Rashi's Commentary on the Pentateuch," in *Rashi Anniversary Volume,* ed. H. L. Ginsberg (New York: American Academy for Jewish Research, 1941), pp. 73-114 lists fifty-two more supercommentaries by named authors and thirty-seven anonymous ones and two commenatries on the supercommentary of Elijah Mizrahi of Constantinople (c. 1450-1526). One of these was written by Nathan b. Samson Spira Ashkenaza of Grodno (d. 1577) [Ms. Oxford Bodleian 210, fol. 1-260] while the other (see Freimann, there, p. 79 for data) was written by Amram al-Biz (1796-1856) from Safru in Morocco.

[84] *Arba'ah Turim* (Four Columns) by Jacob b. Asher (d. 1340) of Toledo and *Shulhan Aruk* (The Set Table) by Joseph Qaro (b. Toledo 1488, d. Saphed 1575)— both declared in division Orah Hayyim ('Daily Life'), Chapter 285 [for additional halakic authorities who treat Rashi's biblical commentaries as canonical see Hayyim Joseph David Azulai, *Birke Yoseph* (Vienna: Adalberte della Torre, 1859) *ad loc* (i.e., p. 67b)] that a Jew may fulfill the obligation to read twice each Sabbath the weekly portion of the Pentateuch in Hebrew and once the rendering of that portion in the official (believed to have been divinely inspired) Aramaic translation (*Targum*) by substituting Rashi's Hebrew commentary for the Aramaic translation. The aforementioned codes thus give specifically to Rashi's commentary on the Pentateuch a canonical status, which, in many Jewish cirlces, this commentary retains to this day.

[85] Two (sc. Lamentations and Esther) of the Five Scrolls are prescribed to be sung liturgically as part of divine service on the Fast of the Ninth of Av and Purim respectively. To be precise, the religious obligation to hear the public reading of

seems to have been a series of commentaries on the entire twenty-four books of Hebrew Scripture. Banitt already pointed out that Rashi's commentaries were designated "in the gallicized Hebrew of R[ashi] and his contemporaries *contèrs* [86] 'a compilation of notes'."[87] Such an understanding of the nature and purpose of Rashi's insightful, albeit almost totally episodic, treatment of Hebrew Scripture corresponds, of course, to the medieval Christian counterpart, a marginal commentary on Scripture compiled largely from the Church Fathers (just as Rashi's commentary is largely compiled from the Rabbis of the Mishnah, Babylonian Talmud and cognate works) known as *Glossa ordinaria*. Banitt notes that, in fact, medieval Christians "considered it [Rashi's Bible commentaries] the Jewish counterpart to their Glossa ordinaria," and they referred to Rashi's Bible Commentary as either *glossa hebraica* or *glossa Salomonis*.[88] When we recall Rashi's frequent challenges to Christian interpretations, especially in his commentaries on Isaiah, Psalms and Daniel,[89] we can-

---

the Sroll of Esther in the synagogue on Purim is taken for granted in Mishnah Rosh ha-Shanah 3:7. This same obligation is the principal subject of Mishnah Megillah 1-2. The public reading of the Scroll of Lamentations as part of the worship service on the eve of the Fast of the Ninth of Av commemorating the destruction of both the First and the Second Temple (see Mishnah Ta'anit 4:6) is taken for granted in *Shulhan Aruk*, Orah Hayyim 559:2-3. This practice is unknown both to the *Arba'ah Turim* (see above n. 84) and to Maimonides. The earliest source, whch prescribes the reading of the Scroll of Lamentations on the Ninth of Av is Tractate Soferim (8th cent. C.E.) 18:4: "Some [communities] read the Book of Lamentations in the evening while others postpone it to the morning after the reading of the Torah." Each of the other three—Song of Songs; Ruth; Ecclesiastes—is sung respectively in some of the Ashkenazi synagogues prior to the reading of the pentateuchal portion at the morning service respectively on the Sabbath during (or seventh day of) Passover, Shavuot (Hebrew Pentecost); and the Sabbath during (or first day of) Tabernacles (Sukkot). In view of the liturgical use of the "Five Scrolls" it is understandable that the very popular supercommentary on Rashi, *Siphte Hakamim* 'The Lips of the Wise" composed by Shabbetai Bass (1641-1718) comments on both the Pentateuch and the entire Five Scrolls.

[86] In Modern Hebrew this French term is read as *quntres*; likewise, the Gk. loanword in Rabbinic Hebrew πίναξ 'writing tablet' [see Saul Lieberman, *Hellenism in Jewish Palestine* (New York: Jewish Theological Seminary of America, 1950), pp. 203-208] is commonly read in Hebrew as *pinqas*. Both of these Jewish pronunciations of Indo-European nouns reflect the pan-Semitic tendency (Phoenician and Modern Arabic are partial exceptions in this regard) to avoid consonant clusters; on this linguistic phenomenon see Sabatino Moscati, *An Introduction to the Comparative Grammar of the Semitic Languages* (Wiesbaden: Harrassowitz, 1969), pp. 60-61.

[87] Banitt, *Rashi: Interpreter of the Biblical Letter*, pp. 43, 131.

[88] Ibid., p. 131, n. 1.

[89] See, in addition to the extensive literature cited below, p. 130, n. 14, Gross-

,

not escape the conclusion that Rashi deliberately intended that his commentary would be the definitive Jewish counterpart to the Christian *Glossa ordinaria*.[90] This, of course, means that Rashi's design called for a commentary on all twenty-four books of Hebrew Scripture. Our contention that, in fact, this was Rashi's design is supported by the following:

> R[ashi']s term for Talmud is *Mishnah* 'the second annunciation' as he defines *Mishnah* in [his commentary] in Zach [*sic*; i.e., Zech.] ix:12, 'annunciation' or 'testament'. In other words, the terminology concerning the work confirms what the diptychal aspect of it suggested, namely that the ambitious young man had in view to set up the twin pedestals of Jewish doctrine in their all-embracing interconnection against the Christian concept of a *New* Testament 'refiguring', and in our mind [i.e., the collective Jewish mind according to Rashi according to Banitt] 'disfiguring', the therefore called *Old* Testament. For the Jew, the Torah was given and written in order to lead the people of Israel along the right path on the national level and in their practical day-to-day life (R[ashi at] Gen i:1), the details of which were exposed orally and compiled in the Mishnah (Talmud).[91]

Already in his monumental, *The Names of the Great Ones*,[92] Hayyim Joseph David Azulai asserted:

> Rashi commented on all of Hebrew Scripture [Heb. *tanakh*]. However, the commentary on Chronicles [in our current Rabbinic Bibles] is not by Rashi as I wrote boldly[93] in my small book *The Gate of Joseph*, p. 104.[94] And the facts are not in accordance with [what is stated in] *Qorey ha-Dorot*, p. 8 and p. 9.[95]

---

man, "Rashi's Commentary on Psalms and the Anti-Christian Polemic," pp. 59-74 (in Hebrew); Taitz, pp. 83-84.

[90] Banitt, *Rashi: Interpreter of the Biblical Letter*, pp. 131-132.

[91] Ibid.; the same dyptichal view of Judaism, which Banitt found by reading between the lines of Rashi, is fully articulated in Jacob Neusner, *Between Time and Eternity: The Essentials of Judaism* (Encino & Belmont, Calif.: Dickenson Publishing, 1975), pp. 5-15.

[92] Concerning this book (referred to already above, p. 1, n. 1) and its author Azulai [1724-1806] (commonly known by his acronym *hhyd'* (pronounced *hahida*) see below, p.118, n. 115.

[93] Heb. *běʿaniyúti*, lit., 'in my humility'; it is unlikely that Azulai would say here that his removing the Chronicles commentary from the corpus of works attributed to Rashi was an act of youthful humility. Therefore, I construe the expression as a euphemism for youthful arrogance; contrast Rashi's use of the term *ʿônyî* 'my [youthful] humility' in his *responsum* concerning the nuances of the particle *ki*, and see our discussion, below, p. 102, n. 110.

[94] *Shaar Yoseph Hay on Tractate Horayot* (Leghorn: A. Santini & Co., 1756).

[95] Hayyim Joseph David Azulai, *The Names of the Great Ones*, ed. Issac Benjacob

Azulai goes on to explain that 1) a comment found in the commentary on Chronicles in the Rabbinic Bible[96] is attributed in Tosaphot to BT Yoma 9a to the students of Rav Saadiah;[97] 2) someone asserted that the commentary on Job commonly attributed to Rashi was not written by Rashi because a) an unidentified scholar found that in his copy of the commentary Rashi was quoted [Azulai adds that he did not find such a comment in his copy]; and b) the language of the commentary on Job does not seem to be that of Rashi;[98] and 3) notwithstanding that someone may have raised the question as to whether the commentary on the Prophets commonly thought to be Rashi's commentary was, in fact, penned by Rashi, Tosaphot refer again and again to that very commentary as having been written by Rashi.[99]

As for whether or not the commentary on Job. 1:1-40:24 was written by Rashi, Sokolow argues:

> Basically, no one ever questioned the attribution to Rashi of the commentary on Job [printed in the Rabbinic Bible and attested in numerous medieval mss].[100]

(Vilna: Rom, 1832), p. 83a. Azulai refers here to the chronicle of authors and works spanning the long period from the traditional date of the close of the Babylonian Talmud [i.e., 499 C.E., which probably corresponds more than coincidentally to the end of the Middle Ages in western historiography] to his own time by David Conforte (1617 or 1618-c.1690) and published without the author's name by David Ashkenazi at Venice in 1746. This is the edition that Azulai would have seen. The now standard edition is R. David Conforte, *Liber Kore ha-Dorot*, ed. David Cassel (Berlin: A. Asher, 1846). See Moshe Nahum Zobel, "Conforte, David," *EJ* 5:891-893.

[96] The reference is to the comment in Pseudo-Rashi at 1 Ch. 5:36. However, this comment is found in all three of the commentaries on Chronicles under consideration. A. L. Pines, "Concerning the Identity of the Author of the Commentary on Chronicles Attributed to Rashi." *Beit Mikra* 23 (1978), p. 122; p. 244 (in Hebrew [indeed, the article was published twice; once in small type and one in normal type]) points out that the specific comment is a quotation from Sifre; consequently it cannot serve as the basis for dating one or another commentary on Chronicles, in which it is cited.

[97] Max Seligsohn, "Saadia ben Nahmani," *JE* 10:586 notes that this Saadia was a liturgical poet of the 11th and 12th centuries and that perhaps he was also a Bible commentator. Note that *JE* refers to all persons bearing the name Saadia(h) by the spelling Saadia while *EJ* with equal consistency employs the form Saadiah.

[98] Azulai, *The Names of the Great Ones*, p. 83a.

[99] Sources which Azulai himself, *The Names of the Great Ones*, p. 83b cites, are Tosaphot at BT Sukkah 5b, s.v. bĕšāliš; Yoma 98a, s.v. Rab Nahman; Sanhedrin 89b, s.v. Elijah.

[100] Moshe Sokolow,"Establishing the Text of Rashi's Commentary to the Book of Job," *PAAJR* 48 (1981), p. 22.

Moreover, just as Azulai had defended the authenticity of the commentaries on the prophetic books commonly attributed to Rashi on
the basis of their being quoted in the name of Rashi by Tosaphot
to the Talmud so does Sokolow defend the authenticity of the commentary on Job by reference to numerous witnesses to that commentary in 1) other biblical commentaries by Rashi; 2) Rashi's
commentary on the Babylonian Talmud; and 3) the writings of other
medieval Hebrew exegetes.

In addition, Soklow stresses that almost fifty of the medieval mss.
in Blondheim's list of 332 mss. witness to Rashi's commentary on
the Book of Job.[101] To this impressive figure one may compare the
simple fact that of seventeen mss. of Rashi's commentary, as it were,
on all of Hebrew Scripture, only eleven of these contain a commentary on Chronicles. Moreover, these eleven mss. attest to three distinct commentaries, one of which is the commentary designated
"commentary on Chronicles attributed to Rashi" in the final volume of the Second Rabbinic Bible published by Daniel Bomberg
in Venice in 1525.[102]

Maarsen, followed by Sokolow, held that Rashi composed the
commentaries on Psalms, Proverbs and Job toward the end of his
career. He considered the absence in the more reliable mss. of commentaries by Rashi on Pss. 121; 128; 134[103] as well as Rashi's commentary on Job's reaching in most of the mss. and printed editions
only to Job. 40:24 as evidence that Rashi's simply did not live long
enough to complete these commentaries.[104]

---

[101] Sokolow, "Establishing the Text," pp. 23-25; see also Shoshana, pp. 19-
20. The evidence cited by Shoshana includes, *inter alia,* Joseph Qara's quoting in
his commentary on Job (see Moshe Ahrend, ed., *The Commentary of Rabbi Yosef Qara
on the Book of Job* [Jerusalem: Mossad Harav Kook, 1989]) Rashi's commentary
on Job. 17:6; 18:2; 22:20; 27:6; and Nahmanides' quoting, in his commentary on
Job, Rashi's commentary on Job. 1:21; 3:3; 12:21; 36:9; see also Jordan S.
Penkower, "The End of Rashi's Commentary on Job: The Manuscripts and the
Printed Editions" (forthcoming), which examines the evidence of all the surviving
mss. (47 complete mss. and several fragmentary mss.) and the printed editions.
[102] Concerning these three commentaries see below, pp. 63–69.
[103] See below, pp. 701, 713, 723 and see also the discussion, p. 443.
[104] Maarsen, p. vii; Sokolow, "Establishing the Text," p. 22, n. 22; contrast
Grossman, "Rashi's Commentary on Psalms and Jewish-Christian Polemics," p.
72 (in Hebrew). Grossman, who dates the composition of Rashi's Commentary
on Psalms after the First Crusade (1096) because of the multiplicity of anti-Christian polemics in the commentary (see Grossman, there, p. 74) argues (there, p.
72) that the absence of comments on Ps. 128 and the shortness of the comments
on Pss. 34; 119 [his judgment; not ours]; 134 derive from the fact that, "Rashi

In a later chapter we refer to Rashi's Commentary on Psalms as
a kind of Rashi in miniature.[105] Indeed, Rashi's terminology in this
commentary and the issues with which he deals over and over again
including lexicographical innovations[106] and his correction of older
and (in Rashi's opinion) errant French translations of biblical terms
and roots[107] leave no room for doubt that it was Rashi who composed the Commentary on the Book of Psalms, which is here tran-
scribed, translated and annotated. However, as we shall see, the
commentaries on Ezra-Nehemiah and on Chronicles attributed to
Rashi in some of the medieval mss. and in the current printings of
the Rabbinic Bible (*Mikra'ot Gedolot*) present two distinct but fascinating stories.

Grossman in his entry "Rashi," in the *Encyclopaedia Judaica* (1972)
suggests that there were, in fact, two opinions on the, as it were, single
question as to who composed the commentaries on Ezra-Nehemiah
and Chronicles attributed to Rashi in the standard Rabbinic Bible:

> The comments ascribed to him [Rashi, in the standard editions of the
> Rabbinic Bible on Job, from 40:25, on Ezra, Nehemiah and Chronicles
> are not his, being different in style and method of exegesis. Accord-
> ing to Poznański, Rashi did not manage to comment on these, since
> in writing his commentary he followed the order of the books in the
> Bible.[108] Lipschuetz,[109] however, contends that the exegesis on these
> books is substantially Rashi's but was recast and augmented by his
> pupils.[110]

---

saw no need to explain things that seemed to him self-understood." Grossman,
The Early Sages of France, pp. 182-183 contends, "Rashi composed a commentary
on the entire Book of Job. However, for some reason his commentary to the end
of the book was lost." For the complete story see Penkower, "The End of Rashi's
Commentary on Job" (forthcoming).

[105] See below, pp. 127–130.

[106] See below, p. 128, n. 6.

[107] See Banitt, *Rashi: Interpreter of the Biblical Letter*, pp. 6-30.

[108] Cf. Poznański, *Kommentar zu Ezechiel und den XII kleinen Propheten von Eliezer
aus Beaugency* , p. xiv, n. 1; and see below.

[109] Cf. Eliezer Meir Lipschuetz, *Rashi* (Warsaw: Tushiya, 1914); and see below.

[110] Avraham Grossman, "Rashi—Bible Exegesis," *EJ* 13:1559; contrast id., *The
Early Sages of France*, p. 182: "Apparently, Rashi composed commentaries on all
the books of the Hebrew Bible, However, the commentaries printed under his name
on Ezra, Nehemiah and Chronicles and the end of Job (from Job 40:25ff.) are not
his. These commentaries are different from his [sic] other commentaries with respect to their style and their exegetical character. Sometimes, even the names of
the authorities quoted therein prove that they are later than Rashi." See now also
Avraham Grossman, "The School of Literal Jewish Exegesis in Northern France,"

in *Hebrew Bible/Old Testament: The History of Its Interpretation, Vol. I: From the Beginnings to the Middle Ages (Until 1300)*, edited by Magne Saebø (Göttingen: Vandenhoeck & Ruprecht, 2000), p. 333. Since Rashi's grandson, Rabbi Samuel b. Meir, in his commentary at Deut. 17:18, appears to quote Rashi's commentary on Chronicles, one might be tempted to accept the view of Joseph Weisse, "Concerning Rashi's Commentary to Chronicles: Its Author, Date and Content," *Kerem Chemed* 5 (1841), p. 238 (in Hebrew) that Rashi's Commentary on Chronicles was lost. For this reason, it might appear, other commentaries were copied out in its place in eleven medieval manuscripts and ultimately also in the Rabbinic Bible, and these commentaries were ultimately attributed to Rashi. This phenomenon corresponds, of course, to the loss of Rashi's commentaries on BT Nedarim, a large part of BT Bava Batra, and the end of BT Makkot. On the evidence for Rashi's having composed a commentary on BT Nedarim and for his having completed the commentaries on Bava Batra and Makkot see above, pp. 40–45. As to the spurious reference to Rashi's Commentary on Chronicles in *The Torah Commentary of Rabbi Samuel b. Meir*, ed. Rosin, p. 216 at Deut. 17:18, s.v. *mišneh hattôrāh*, the facts are as follows: R. Samuel b. Meir comments there on the enigmatic Hebrew expression, *mišneh hattôrāh*, which NJV renders "a copy of this Teaching" and which LXX renders δευτερονόμιον, from which is derived the Vulgate's rendering *Deuteronomium*, the immediate source of Eng. Deuteronomy. The latter name for the "Fifth Book of Moses," like the designation of the fifth book of the Pentateuch in Rabbinic literature as *mišneh tôrāh* (e.g., BT Megillah 31b) assumes that the Hebrew expression designates the fifth book of the Pentateuch and that the name refers to the fact that with a few noteworthy exceptions Deuteronomy seems to repeat injunctions found in the previous three books of the Pentateuch and is a kind of "second law". This interpretation of *mišneh hattôrāh* construes *mišneh* as the ordinal number 'second'. Rabbi Samuel b. Meir, on the other hand, writes as follows (according to Rosin's text): "My grandfather exegeted it [the Hebrew exrpression *mišneh hattôrāh*] in Chronicles [*dibrê hayyāmîm*] "two Torah Scrolls." This interpretation treats Heb. *mišneh* as the cardinal number 'two, double' as in Gen. 43:12; Ex. 16:5, 22; Deut. 15:18. It is possible, of course, that Rashi might have responded in his commentary to 2 Ch. 34:14-15 concerning the exegetical question arising from Hilkiah's finding a Book of the Torah in the Temple in 622 B.C.E. (cf. 2 Kgs. 22:8). The exegetical question is, "Why was a Torah Scroll found in the Temple?" The answer is to be found in Tosefta Sanhedrin 4:5, which is quoted with minor variations in BT Sanhedrin 21b: "'He [the king] shall write for himself *mišneh hattôrāh* '(Deut. 17:18) [means] 'he shall write specifically for himself two Torah Scrolls [*tôrôt*], one which accompanies him and one which is placed in his archives [Tosefta reads 'his house'].'" Conceivably, Rashi, in the alleged commentary on Chronicles accounts for the finding of a Torah Scroll in the Temple because it was left there by a pre-Josianic king who was attempting to fulfill Deut. 17:18 as interpreted by the *baraitha* in BT Sanhedrin 21b. Since, however, Rashi offers precisely the same interpretation of *mišneh hattôrāh* in his commentary at Deut. 17:18 it is strange that his grandson, Rabbi Samuel b. Meir, in his commentary on Deut. 17:18 would quote Rashi's commentary on Chronicles rather than Rashi's commentary on Deut. 17:18. The latter commentary reads as follows: "'*et mišneh hattôrāh*. Two Torah Scrolls, one which is placed in his archives and one which accompanies him." Rosin, p. 216, n. 10 suggests that the reading in his ms. of Rabbi Samuel b. Meir's commentary *bdbry hymym* "in Chronicles" is simply a scribal error for *kdbry hkmym* "according to the interpretation of the (Rabbinic) Sages [in the *baraitha*]; it is no less likely that the reading *bdbry hymym* "in Chronicles" derives from an original *bdbrym* "in Deuteronomy".

In fact, what Lipschuetz states is as follows:

> Rashi wrote a commentary on the entire Bible except for Chronicles. It apears that the commentary [commonly attributed to Rashi] on Chronicles stems from one of the disciples of R. Saadiah. This [unnamed commentator] was a great man, who lived in the Rhineland.[111]

No less intriguing than the false attribution to Lipschuetz in the *EJ* entry *"Rashi"* of the view that the commentaries on Ezra-Nehemiah and Chronicles attributed to Rashi in the so-called Rabbinic Bible is based upon one penned by Rashi himself is the view attributed to Poznański in that same *EJ* entry. What Poznański himself wrote is as follows:

> That the commentary on Ezra and Nehemiah [commonly attributed to Rashi] is not Rashi's can be ascertained on the basis of its style, language and exegetical method. Geiger wanted to attribute it [the aforementioned commentary to Ezra-Nehemiah] to R. Joseph Qara, but his arguments are not sufficiently strong. That the commentary [on Chronicles commonly attributed to Rashi] is not by Rashi was already noted by Azulai [see] and others. Its author was, so it appears, from Germany, and he lived in Narbonne.[112]

Interestingly, Lipschuetz and Poznański refer to two distinct commentaries, which served to complete, as it were, Rashi's Bible Commentary in different manuscripts. Lipschuetz refers to the 10th century commentator attested in Rostock Heb. Ms. 32 and published by Kirchheim[113] while Poznański refers to the 12th century commentator printed in the Rabbinic Bible and attested also in several mss.[114]

----

[111] Lipschuetz, *Rashi* , p. 188. These assertions go back to Weisse, "Concerning Rashi's Commentary to Chronicles: Its Author, Date and Content," pp. 232-244 (in Hebrew); Leopold Zunz, *Zur Geschichte und Literatur* (Berlin: Veit und Comp., 1845), pp. 62, 73. Lipschuetz, *Rashi* , p. 188, n. 8 cites the attribution given in Tosaphot at BT Yoma 9a. Moreover, Lipschuetz, there, p. 188 contends that Rashi composed the commentary on Ezra-Nehemiah [attributed to him in the Rabbinic Bible] but that his disciples had revised it and added to it. Obviously, the question arises as to why they should have revised specifically the commentary to Ezra-Nehemiah so that 1) this exceedingly verbose commentary differs markedly from Rashi's terse exegetical style; and 2) it consistently contradicts Rashi's known views.

[112] Poznański, *Kommentar zu Ezechiel und den XII kleinen Propheten von Eliezer aus Beaugency* , p. xiv, n. 1.

[113] See below, n. 117.

[114] See below.

Ultimately, Rashi came to be regarded as the canonical author of a commentary on Chronicles in the so-called Rabbinic Bible by virtue of the attribution of that commentary in the common editions of the Rabbinic Bible. Jordan Penkower suggested to me (personal oral commuication, June 2, 2002) that in the course of their work, Bomberg's team of Hebrew typesetters under the supervision of Jacob Ben Hayyim Ibn Adonijah realized that the Chronicles Commentary used to complete, as it were, Rashi's Bible Commentary in the manuscript they copied out, could not possibly have been composed by Rashi. Consequently, while the running heads in the Second Rabbinic Bible (Venice: Bomberg, 1525) attribute the commentary to Rashi, the title page, which was prepared at the end of their work, refers to that same commentary as "a commentary attributed to Rashi." Unfortunately, later editions shorten that title to "commentary of Rashi."

Unwittingly, by treating the errant attribution to Rashi of the commentary to Chronicles as a matter of religious principle, the foolish thereby endow with the authority of Rashi that commentary's view that significant parts of some biblical books are the work solely of human hands and human foibles. This latter view adumbrates modern biblical criticism, which employs evidence of contradiction, anachronism, lack of historicity and multiple mortal authorship to undermine the authority of Hebrew Scripture.[115] When Rashi, on

---

[115] See Benedict Spinoza, *Tractatus Theologico-Politicus*, trans. Samuel Shirley (Leiden: E. J. Brill, 1989), pp. 49-299; Julius Wellhausen, *Prolegomena to the History of Ancient Israel*, translated by J. Sutherland Black and Allan Menzies with reprint of the article "Israel" from the *Encyclopaedia Britannica* (Edinburgh: Adam & Charles Black, 1883), pp. 1-13; Elizabeth Cady Stanton, ed., *The Woman's Bible* (2 vols.; New York: European Publishing Co., 1895-1898). Judah the Pious is quoted in the commentary written down by his son R. Moshe Zaltman and published on the basis of two medieval manuscripts; see Isaac S. Lange, ed, *The Torah Commentaries of R. Judah the Pious* (Jerusalem: By the editor, 1975); see the extensive discussion of the passages in the latter commentary, which appear to adumbrate modern biblical criticism in Gershon Brin, "Studies in R. Judah the Pious' Exegesis to the Pentateuch," *Te'udah* 3 (1983), pp. 224-225 (in Hebrew); see also Israel Ta-Shma, "Bible Criticism in Early Medieval Franco-Germany," in *The Bible in Light of Its Interpreters: Studies in Memory of Sarah Kamin*, ed. Sara Japhet (Jerusalem: Magnes, 1994), pp. 453-459 (in Hebrew); David Halivni, *Peshat and Derash* (New York & Oxford: Oxford University Press, 1991), pp. 141-142; Harav Moshe Feinstein, *Igrot Moshe*: Yoreh De'ah, Part III (Bnei Braq, n.p., 1981), Chapters 114 and 115. Harav Feinstein argues that the suggestion that anything found in the Pentateuch was written by anyone other than Moses is heresy. Consequently, in his view, Rabbi Judah the Pious, being an Orthodox rabbi, could not have said the things attrib-

---

uted to him in the commentary published by Lange. Halivni, on the other hand, holds that so long as the post-Mosaic additions to the Torah identified by Rabbi Judah the Pious and by R. Joseph b. Eliezer Bonfils were provided by prophets who served as God's stenographers, the belief that there were such additions does not constitute heresy. In fact, R. Judah the Pious, R. Joseph b. Eliezer Bonfils and the authors of the three medieval commentaries on Chronicles, which were wrongly attributed to Rashi, share the common belief that 1) Moses would not contradict himself; 2) Moses would not compose anachronistic statements. In fact, these beliefs were shared by modern biblical critics, such as Julius Wellhausen, who saw in the Pentateuch's alleged anachronisms and contradictions proof that the Pentateuch, which enjoins circumcision, Sabbath and laws of purity, which Christianity had rejected, was not the God-given Torah, which Jesus had promised not to abolish but to fulfill (Matt. 5:17). While modern biblical critics have *utilized* the Pentateuch's alleged anachronisms, alleged contradictions, and alleged lack of historicity to undermine its claim upon Christianity, the medieval rabbis, whom Ta-Shma treats as biblical critics, sought to *eliminate* Moses' contradictions and anachronims by demonstrating that all passages, which seem to post-date Moses or contradict him, were, in fact, added by divine authority at a later date by later prophets. R. Joseph b. Eliezer Bonfils, *Sophnath Paneah* , ed. David Herzog (2 vols.; Heidelberg: Carl Winters, 1911-1930) is a supercommentary on the Pentateuch Commentary by Abraham Ibn Ezra. Typical of Bonfils' *alternative* to Pentateuchal criticism is the following comment on Gen. 12:6, "And the Canaanite was then in the land": "It is not possible that Moses would say 'then' for reason suggests that the word 'then' was written when the Canaanite was not in the land [of Israel]. Now we know that the Canaanite did not depart from there until after the death of Moses when Joshua conquered it [the land of Israel]. Therefore, it seems that Moses did not write this word ['then'] here. Rather, Joshua or another of the prophets wrote it. Similarly, we find in the Book of Proverbs (Prov. 25:1), 'These also are the proverbs of Solomon, which the men of Hezekiah king of Judah copied out.' Since Solomon composed the Book [of Proverbs], why should there be mentioned there Hezekiah who was born several generations later [according to the accepted chronology, Hezekiah's reign began two centuries after the death of Solomon!]? What happened was that this [Prov. 25-29] was an oral tradition going back to Solomon. Therefore, they [the men of Hezekiah] wrote it, and it was regarded as though Solomon had written it." In the same way, there was a revelation that in the time of Abraham the Canaanite was in the land [of Israel], and one of the prophets wrote it here [in Gen. 12:6]. Since we are required to believe in the words of revelation [*qabbalah;* it is likely that here as in Rabbinic literature the term *qabbalah* designates post-Mosaic biblical lore; see Norman M. Bronznick, "Qabbalah as a Metonym for the Prophets and Hagiographa," *HUCA* 38 (1967), pp. 285-295; in the 13th century C.E. the term *qabbalah* was co-opted by a school of Jewish mystics in Provence and Spain to designate and lend legitimacy to their new trend; on this development see José Faur, "A Crisis of Categories: Kabbalah and the Rise of Apostasy in Spain," in *The Jews of Spain and the Expulsion of 1492,* ed. Moshe Lazar and Stephen Haliczer, Henry J. Leir Library of Sephardica (Lancaster, Cal.: Labyrinthos, 1997), pp. 42-45] and in the words of prophecy, what difference does it make to me whether Moses wrote it or another prophet wrote it since the words of all of them true, and they are in the category of prophecy… ? When the Torah warned, 'Do not add to it…' (Deut. 13:1), it warned only about the number of commandments and principles but not about words. Consequently, if a prophet added a word or several words to clarify

the other hand, attributes to "the holy sprit," the authorship of Ezek.
1:2-3, which employs a system of chronology different from that
consistently employed by the Prophet Ezekiel himself, Rashi employs
multiple authorship not to undermine the authority of Scripture but
rather to demonstrate that apparent inconsistencies can be traced
to the presence of a divine voice along side of the human voice of
the prophet/psalmist. In the same way, Rashi in his Commentary
on Psalms at Ps. 37:25 and in his Talmud Commentary at BT Hullin
60a concerning Ps. 104:31 distinguishes between a divine voice, which
intrudes itself into the words of the psalmist, and the human voice
of the psalmist himself.[116]

b. Pseudo-Rashi on Chronicles

Nineteenth century and early twentieth century *Wissenschaft des Juden-*
tums bequeathed an extensive and fascinating scholarly literature

---

a matter as he heard from revelation, this is not an addition [interdited by Deut.
13:1]." Unlike R. Judah the Pious and R. Joseph b. Eliezer Bonfils, who hold that
Scripture contains divinely revealed additions to the books penned initially by Moses
and other traditional authors, the three commentaries on Chronicles, which have
wrongly been attributed to Rashi, refer to purely *human* authorship of Chronicles.
These commentators attempt to solve the apparent self-contradiction of divinely
inspired Scripture by intimating that while the history of Israel told in Genesis to
Kings was written by Moses and the Prophets under divine inspiration, Chronicles'
contradictory account is the work of Ezra working on his own purely human authority from a bad set of index cards. Far from constituting biblical criticism in
the modern sense, the authors of the three medieval commentaries on Chronicles
engage in defusing the weapons, which might be utilized by biblical criticism. Not
surprisingly, the post-modern minimalists who contend that pre-exilic Israel as
portrayed in Samuel and Kings is a post-exilic fantasy, regard Chronicles not as
a reworking of, *inter alia*, Samuel-Kings (this view is taken for granted in Zipora
Talshir, "From the Desk of the Author of Chronicles," *Cathedra* 102 [December
2001], pp. 188-190; see also Isaac Kalimi, *The Book of Chronicles: Historical Writing
and Literary Devices*, Biblical Encyclopaedia Library, vol. 18 [Jerusalem: Mossad
Bialik, 2000] [in Hebrew]; Sara Japhet, *The Ideology of the Book of Chronicles And Its
Place in Biblical Thought* [Jerusalem: Mossad Bialik, 1977] [in Hebrew]; concerning
the deference shown to King David in Chronicles see Japhet, pp. 993-401) but
rather an alternative account written at about the same time as the Pentateuch
and the so-called Former Prophets in the Persian Era. See, e.g., James Linville,
"Rethinking the 'Exilic' Book of Kings," *JSOT* 75 (1997), pp. 21-42; Robert P.
Carroll, "Razed Temple and Shattered Vessels," *JSOT* 75 (1997), pp. 93-106; A.
Graeme Auld, "What Was the Main Source of the Book of Chronicles?" in *The
Chronicler as Author: Studies in Text and Texture*, ed. M. Patrick Graham and Steven
L. McKenzie, JSOT Supplement Series, no. 263 (Sheffield: Sheffield Academic
Press, 1999), pp. 91-99.
    [116] See the extensive discussion below, p. 129, n. 9.

concerning the intriguing and provocative commentary on Chronicles
attributed to Rashi in the standard Rabbinic Bible.[117] At the end of
the twentieth century century Israel Ta-Shma further advanced our
understanding of this provocative commentary with two additional
studies.[118]

These studies present the following picture: The commentary on
Chronicles found in Munich Heb. ms. 5 [1233 C.E.] is attested also
in two 14th century mss., namely, Madrid National Library Hebrew
Ms. 5470 and Milan Ambrosiano Heb. Ms. C119.[119] The author of
that commentary lived and worked during the period 1140-1210.
His teachers included R. Samuel b. Qalonymos, who was a student
of R. Joseph Qara (1060-1130)) and the mentor of R. Judah the Pious,
the author of *Sefer Hasidim*.[120] In one place the author of this commentary refers to his student, Rabbi Jacob bar Shabbetai. The latter, it appears, was born in Greece c. 1135, and he was educated in
Germany in the second half of the 12th century. He then settled in
Provence where he composed a long supercommentary on Rashi's
Commentary on the Pentateuch.[121] The author of the Chronicles
commentary found in Munich Heb. Ms. 5 made extensive use of
the commentary later attributed to Rashi in the standard Rabbinic
Bible. Almost a century ago, Jacob Nahum Epstein assigned the latter
commentary to Rabbi Samuel the Pious, the mentor of the author
of the Chronicles commentary found in Munich Heb. Ms. 5.[122] This

---

[117] Zunz, *Zur Geschichte und Literatur*, p. 62; Weisse, "Concerning Rashi's Commentary to Chronicles: Its Author, Date and Content," pp. 232-244 (in Hebrew);
Abraham Berliner, "Analeketen zu dem Raschi-Commentare," *MGWJ* 12 (1863),
pp. 393-398; Victor Aptowitzer, "Deux problemes d'histoire littéraire," *REJ* 55
(1908), pp. 84-95; Raphael Kirchheim, *Ein Commentar zur Chronik aus dem 10ten
Jahrhundert* (Frankfurt-am-Main: H. L. Brünner, 1874); Jacob N. Epstein, "L'auteur
du commentaire des chroniques," *REJ* 58 (1909), pp. 189-199; Asher Weiser, "The
Commentary on Chronicles Attributed to Rashi," *Beit Mikra* 22 (1967), p. 362-
364 (in Hebrew).
[118] In addition to Ta-Shma, "Bible Criticism in Early Medieval Franco-Germany," pp. 453-459, see id., "The Commentary on Chronicles in Ms. Munich
5," in *From the Collections of the Institute for Microfilmed Hebrew Manuscripts*, ed. Avraham
David (Jerusalem: Jewish National & University Library, 1996), pp. 135-141; see
also Raphael Weiss, "The Book of Chronicles Among our Medieval Commentaries," in Raphael Weiss, *Mishshut baMiqra* (Jerusalem: Rubenstein, 1976), pp. 96-
98 (in Hebrew); Isaac Kalimi, "History of Inerpretaton: The Book of Chronicles
in Jewish Interpretation," *RB* 105 (1998), pp. 34-35.
[119] Ta-Shma, "The Commentary on Chronicles," p. 135.
[120] Ibid., pp. 136-137.
[121] Ibid.
[122] Epstein, "L'auteur du commentaire des chroniques," pp. 189-199; see also

Rabbi Samuel the Pious of Speyer wrote the first part of *Sefer Hasidim*. He also wrote commentaries on the Pentateuch, Mekilta, Sifra, some tractates of BT and a commentary on the biblical Book of Samuel. He refers to his commentary on Samuel in his commentary on 1 Ch. 12:18.[123] Rabbi Samuel the Pious of Speyer made extensive use of the 10th century commentary on Chronicles published by Kirchheim on the basis of Rostock Heb. Ms. 32.[124]

Two significant exegetical principles characterize all three of these commentaries on Chronicles—the 10th century commentary published by Kirchheim; the 12th century commentary by R. Samuel the Pious found in the standard Rabbinic Bible where it is attributed to Rashi; and the 13th century commentary by R. Samuel's student, Solomon b. Samuel of Würzburg, found in Munich Heb. Ms. 5. The first of these exegetical principles is that Chronicles and Ezra-Nehemiah were composed by Ezra the Scribe, who made use of genealogical lists found among the Jewish exiles in Babylonia. Insofar as these lists did not always agree with each other, either with respect to the spelling of individual names or with respect to

Ta-Shma, "The Commentary on Chronicles," p. 137. Jordan S. Penkower informed me (personal electronic communication, 29 April 2002) that the commentary attributed to Rashi in the current editions of the Rabbinic Bible also completes Rashi's Bible commentaries in several mss.; these include Cambridge, St. John's College Heb. ms. 3; Leiden Scaliger 1; New York, Jewish Theological Seminary Ms. L 778; Paris, Bibliothèque Nationale Heb. ms. 164; for additional information see the forthcoming study by Jordan S. Penkower.

[123] Epstein, "L'auteur du commentaire des chroniques," pp. 195-196.

[124] Ibid., p. 199; Kirchheim, *Ein Commentar zur Chronik aus dem 10ten Jahrhundert* pp. ii, iv, notes that Turin Heb. Ms. 124 attributed this commentary to R. Abraham Ibn Ezra. Since the Turin ms. seems to have been destroyed in the 1904 C.E. fire, it is impossible to determine whether or not that ms. contained the 10th century commentary we find in Ms. Rostock 32. Avraham Avigad of the Institute for Microfilms of Hebrew Manuscripts at the Jewish National and University Library in Jerusalem pointed out to me (personal, oral communication 29 March 2003) that Munich Hebrew ms. #5 provides the unique commentary authored by Solomon b. Samuel of Würzburg (1233 C.E.), the scribe who penned that ms., only as far as 1 Ch. 29:11. From there on Solomon b. Samuel copied out the 10th century commentary published by Kirchheim from Ms. Rostock 32. Authorities to which the 10th century commentary refers include Judah b. Quraysh [spelled Qurays in the ms. in question] (1 Ch. 2:6, 15; 3:3, 24; 6:33; 24:6) [concerning him see Dan Becker, *The Risāla of Judah ben Quraysh: A Critical Edition*, Texts and Studies in the Hebrew Language and Related Subjects, vol. 7 (Tel-Aviv: Tel-Aviv University, 1984), pp. 9-17]; Jiream of Magdiel (1 Ch. 6:33; 8:7); "the Easterners" (1 Ch. 9:3); "the people of Kairouan" [in Tunisia] (1 Ch. 6:33; 8:7). At 1 Ch. 23:3 the 10th century commentary states, "and in the Book of Jubilees which Rav Saadiah Gaon of Fayyum brought from the library of the *yeshivah....*"

the length of the respective family trees, Ezra simply placed some
of these lists one after the other while he broke up others and distributed parts of them in various places in Chronicles and Ezra-
Nehemiah.[125] The three medieval exegetes find support for the first
exegetical principle in the tradition recorded in the Jerusalem Talmud (JT Ta'anit 4:2, wrongly referred to in all three commentaries
as "the end of JT Megillah"!), according to which Ezra found three
versions of the Torah and attempted to create a standard edition of
the Torah by reconciling these three divergent witnesses.[126] On this
basis, the authors of the three successive medieval commentaries on
the Book of Chronicles account for Ezra's finding and recording
doublets such as the list which appears in 1 Ch. 9:2ff and with slight
variations again in Neh. 11:3ff.[127]

The second exegetical principle invoked by the three medieval
commentaries on Chronicles, including the one attributed to Rashi
in the standard Rabbinic Bible, is that the author of Chronicles

---

[125] See, for example, Pseudo-Rashi at 1 Ch. 7:13: "What he [Ezra] found he
wrote, and what he did not find he did not write. From [the genealogical list of]
the Naphtalites he found no more [than what is recorded in 1 Ch. 1:13]. This is
the reason that this entire genealogical list [1 Ch. 1-10] contains so many gaps.
He [Ezra] skipped from one document to the other and combined them. What
he could not write in this book [Chronicles] he wrote in the Book of Ezra [i.e.,
Ezra-Nehemiah]. Know [that this is so] for it is stated further on (1 Ch. 9:1), 'All
Israel was registered by genealogies, and these are in the Book of the Kings of
Israel, and Judah was taken nto exile to Babylon....' [This verse provides the]
answer [pitārôn]: if you want to know the genealogy of the ten [northern] tribes,
go to Halah and Habor, the River Gozan and the towns of Media (see 2 Kgs.
17:6) for their [the northern kingdom's] Book of Chronicles went into exile with
them. As for Judah, on the other hand ['ăbāl], I [Ezra to whom Samuel the Pious
our commentator assigns the authorship of both Ezra-Nehemiah and Chronicles
and in whose name he speaks here] found their book in Babylon, and what I found
I wrote." See also Pseudo-Rashi [i.e., Samuel the Pious] at 1 Ch. 9:1: "ALL IS-
RAEL WAS REGISTERED BY GENEALOGIES, which is to say that even
though I [Ezra] mentioned part of their genealogy, and I did not mention all of
them, IN FACT THEY ARE RECORDED IN THE BOOK OF THE KINGS
OF ISRAEL. That book is not extant among us. The same applies to [kěmô] the
Book of Jashar (Josh. 10:13; 1 Sam. 1:18) and the Book of the Wars of the LORD
(Num. 21:14). With reference to the assumption that Ezra has broken up genealogical lists and placed parts of some of them in the Book of Ezra [i.e., Ezra-
Nehemiah] and the remainder in Chronicles see, with Ta-Shma, "The Commentary
on Chronicles," p. 138; Kirchheim, *Ein Commentar zur Chronik aus dem 10ten Jahrhundert*
at 1 Ch. 9:3 (p. 29).
[126] See Pseudo-Rashi (i.e., Samuel the Pious) at 1 Ch. 8:29.
[127] See also Pseudo-Rashi (i.e., Samuel the Pious) at 1 Ch. 3:10; 17:15; 19:11;
21:4.

wanted to glorify the Davidic dynasty. This is the reason that he omitted from his retelling of the biography of David embarassing incidents such as King David's affair with Bathsheba, the wife of Uriah the Hittite. With respect to this exegetical principle let the author of the commentary wrongly attributed to Rashi in the standard Rabbinic Bible—and assigned to R. Samuel the Pious (12th century) by Epstein (and hereinafter called Pseudo-Rashi)—speak for himself:

1 Ch. 3:6
THEN IBHAR, ELISHAMA, ELIPHELET, NOGAH, NEPHEG, JAPHIA, ELISHAMA, ELIADA, AND ELIPHELET—NINE. [2] Samuel (5:14) counts Eliphelet only once and enumerates altogether seven [sons in the parallel text], and here he [Ezra] enumerates nine. Now this is the reason: his [David's] son Eliphelet died, and later there was born to him another son whom he also named Eliphelet, whom he [Ezra] counts as a[nother] name. Also here he [Ezra] counts Elishama twice. In the same manner we can say that he [Elishama] died, and another son was born to him [David], and also one [other] of these [nine sons] died, and there remained seven. Now as for the fact that he [Ezra] provides only seven names but he enumerates nine [sons] is for the glory of David who had many sons. Indeed, all of the Book [of Chronicles] was written for the glory of David and his progeny.

1 Ch. 9:1:
AND THAT TIME WHEN DAVID SAW THAT THE LORD ANSWERED HIM.... This perciope is not written in [the Book of] Samuel, and it is written here for the glory of David who made an altar....

1 Ch. 15:29:
MICHAEL DAUGHTER OF SAUL....Since the Book of Chronicles was [written] for the glory of David, it is not written here what Michal said to David, as it is written in [the Book of] Samuel], "Did not the king of Israel do himself honor today exposing himself today in the sight of the slavegirls of his officials as one of the riffraf might expose himself" (2 Sam. 6:20) for it was a deprecation of David that a woman said this to him.

1 Ch. 19:11
AND THE REST OF THE TROOPS HE [Joab] PUT UNDER THE COMMAND OF HIS BROTHER ABSHAI.... [This refers] to Abishai for [in] the entire [Book of] Chronicles it [this name] is written Abshai, and we also pronounce it Abshai with two exceptions according to the Massorah.[128] Therefore, throughout this book [he is

---

[128] Neither the Second Rabbinic Bible (1525) nor BHS nor *Jerusalem Crown*:

called] Abshai for all this book was written for the glory of David,
and it would not be honor for him to call his sister's son Abishai,
which means, "I am as important as David for [Abishai literally
means] "My father [like David's] is Jesse." Throughout the Book of
Samuel [he is called] Abishai with the exception of one Abshai.[129]
1 Ch. 21:4
AFTER THIS FIGHTING WITH THE PHILISTINES BROKE
OUT AT GEZER. What has been omitted here in this chapter is
written in [the Book of] Samuel (2 Sam. 21:15): "Again war broke
out between the Philistines and Israel, and David and the men with
him went down and fought the Philistines...." This also was not written here [in Chronicles] because of the glory of David for indeed it is
written there (in 2 Sam. 21:15), "and David grew weary"; and it is
written (also there), "and Ishbi-benob, who was a descendant of the
Raphah...and he wore new armor, and he tried to kill David." Were
it not for the fact that Abishai son of Zeruiah helped him, he would
have fallen into the hand of Ishbi-benob. It is because of this disgrace
that he [Ezra] did not write it [the account contained in 2 Sam.
21:15-17] here (in 1 Ch. 21:4).

The Commentary on Chronicles attributed to Rashi in the Rabbinic
Bible is clearly not from the pen of Rashi because 1) the author posits
a totally human origin of a sacred book, which Rashi, following the
sages of the Babylonian Talmud, would have ascribed to divine inspiration; 2) the author employs exegetical terminology, which is

---

The Bible of the Hebrew University of Jerusalem, ed. Yosef Opher (Jerusalem: Ben-Zvi,
2000) attest to the vocalization of the proper name *'bšy* Abishai anywhere in
Chronicles. The reason is very simple. All three of these printed editions are based
on mss., which reflect the traditions of Tiberias (in the land of Israel) and Spain.
Pseudo-Rashi, on the other hand, probably refers to Ashkenazi textual traditions.
In fact, Jordan S. Penkower (personal electronic communication, 16 April 2002)
confirmed this impression with the following data: 1) Benjamin Kennicott, *Vetus
Testamentum Hebraicum cum Variis Lectionibus* (2 vols.; Oxford: Clarendon Press, 1776-
1780), vol. 2, p. 646 (referring to 1 Ch. 2:16); p. 662 (referring to 1 Ch. 11:20); p.
671 (referring to 1 Ch. 18:12); p. 672 (referring to 1 Ch. 19:11); p. 672 (referring
to 1 Ch. 19:15), cites various Ashkenazi mss., which have the form Abishai in most
of the five verses in Chronicles; 2) British Library Ms. Or. 2091 reads Abishai in
the first three of the five instances in Chronicles; 3) Ms. Paris 6 reads Abishai in
two cases; in one case the consonantal text is *'byšy* while the vocalization is Abishai;
in two cases (1 Ch. 2:16; 18:12) the first *yod* is erased so that the consonantal text
is Abishai while the vocalization is Abishai. For additional details see the forthcoming study by Jordan S. Penkower.
[129] Mandelkern, pp. 1350-1351 indicates that in current printed editions of
the Bible the form *'bšy* appears in 1 Ch. 2:16; 11:20; 18:12; 19:11, 15 as well as in
2 Sam. 10:10 while the form *'byšy* occurs in 1 Sam. 26:6, 8, 9; 2 Sam. 10:14;
16:9, 11; 18:2, 5, 12; 19:22; 21:17.

distinct from that of Rashi;[130] 3) at 2 Ch. 3:15 and 22:11 the commentator cites Rashi's Commentary on Kings (i.e., 1 Kgs. 7:15 and 2 Kgs. 2:11, respectively) employing the formula, "Rabbenu Solomon, may the memory of the righteous be for a blessing, explained...";[131] 4) at 2 Ch. 35:18 he cites an interpretation known to be that of Rashi at 2 Kgs. 23:22, and he states, "This interpretation disturbs me very much, and I do not accept it";[132] and 5) he cites none of Rashi's teachers[133] while he cites as his teachers persons who lived two generations after Rashi[134] such as R. Isaac b. Samuel of Narbonne (1 Ch. 9:39; 18:3, 5; 2 Ch. 24:14)[135] and R. Eliezer b. Meshullam of Narbonne (2 Ch. 4:31; 16:35; 2 Ch. 3:4; 13:2; 27:2; 35:18; 36:12).[136]

c. Pseudo-Rashi on Ezra-Nehemiah

Unlike the commentary on Chronicles attributed to Rashi in the Rabbinic Bible, the Commentary on Ezra-Nehemiah, which the

---

[130] See Weisse, "Concerning Rashi's Commentary to Chronicles," p. 235; Epstein, "L'auteur du commentaire des chroniques," p. 198. Typical of the differences in terminology between Rashi and the Commentary on Chronicles attributed to Rashi in the Rabbinic Bible are the latter's more frequent use of the term *pittārôn* (e.g. 1 Ch. 12:21; 13:6, 8, 10; 16:19) rather than *pērûš* to mean 'explanation' and Pseudo-Rashi's frequent use of *dûgmā'* (1 Ch. 12:22, 23; 13:5; 15:22, 27; 16:6, 7, 8,10, 21), *dûgmat* (1 Ch. 16:3) and *dûgmatô* (1 Ch. 12:24; 16:26) where Rashi would have written *kĕmô*.

[131] Weisse, "Concerning Rashi's Commentary to Chronicles," pp. 236-237.

[132] Ibid., p. 237.

[133] Ibid., p. 236; Epstein, "L'auteur du commentaire des chroniques," pp. 189-192; Zunz, *Zur Geschichte und Literatur*, p. 73.

[134] Weisse, "Concerning Rashi's Commentary to Chronicles," pp. 236-238; Epstein, "L'auteur du commentaire des chroniques," pp. 189-190; in addition it has been noted by Weisse, "Concerning Rashi's Commentary to Chronicles," pp. 234, 240; Epstein, "L'auteur du commentaire des chroniques," p. 192 that the commentary on Chronicles attributed to Rashi in the Rabbinic Bible cannot have been written by Rashi because the vernacular glosses in that commentary are mostly Germanic rather than Old Northern French; so also Kalimi, "History of Interpretation," pp. 34-35; on the other hand, Aptowitzer, "Deux problemes d'histoire littéraire," pp. 85, discounted this last argument. He argued on the basis of variations between earlier and later printed editions of the commentary that the language of the glosses might well reflect the provenance of the copyists rather than that of the commentator himself.

[135] See Max Seligsohn, "Isaac ben Samuel of Narbonne," *JE* 6:630.

[136] Concerning Eliezer's father, Meshullam (b. c. 1120), who was a contemporary of Rashi's grandson, Rabbenu Jacob Tam see Israel Ta-Shma, "Meshullam b. Nathan of Melun," *EJ* 11:1403-1404; Max Seligsohn, "Meshullam b. Nathan of Melun," *JE* 8:503-504.

Rabbinic Bible attributes to Rashi, employs exegetical terminology, which is virtually identical to that of Rashi. Moreover, in consonance with Rashi's declaration in his commentary at Gen. 3:8 and in the introduction to his Commentary on Song of Songs, it seeks to utilize compositions found in Rabbinic literature in order to elucidate the literal meaning of Hebrew Scripture. However, the Commentary on Ezra-Nehemiah, which is attributed to Rashi in the Rabbinic Bible, cannot have been written by Rashi for two reasons. First, Rashi's Bible commentaries are unique in medieval Rabbinic literature because of their terse, telegraphic style, which is reminiscent of Tannaitic Midrash (Sifra on Leviticus; Sifre on Numbers; Sifre on Deuteronomy). This style renders Rashi's Bible commentaries virtually incomprehensible to those without the benefit of either a) extensive training in ancient Rabbinic literature; b) university-level courses in rapid reading of Rashi's commentaries; or c) an annotated translation into a modern language. The commentary on Ezra-Nehemiah attributed to Rashi in the Rabbinic Bible, on the other hand, is exceedingly verbose. Consequently, while the authentic commentaries of Rashi occupy one third of the space of the commentaries of Abraham Ibn Ezra on any given book, the commentary on Ezra-Nehemiah attributed to Rashi is three times as long as the commentary of Ibn Ezra on that same book. In addition, Yoel Florsheim demonstrated that the commentary on Ezra-Nehemiah attributed to Rashi constantly offers interpretations, which blatantly contradict the ones offered by Rashi in his commentaries on the Babylonian Talmud with respect to the very same passages in Ezra-Nehemiah.[137] While on some occasions Rashi may change his mind, in general Rashi will repeat the same comment again and again each time he discusses a particular word or passage.[138]

Pseudo-Rashi at Ez. 2:2 contends that the root *g'l* is a biform of

---

[137] Florsheim, 3:264-285.

[138] Typical are a) Rashi's discussions of the ambiguity of the Hebrew particle *ki* in his commentary at Gen. 18:15; Num. 20:29; Deut. 7:17; and his famous *responsum* concerning the multiple meanings of the particle *ki*; see below, pp. 94–105 for an annotated translation of the *responsum*; b) Rashi's comparing the ambiguity of Hebrew Scripture written by a single divine author to the multiplicity of rock fragments generated by a single hammer in his commentary to BT Shabbat 88b; Sanhedrin 34a; in his commentary on the Bible at Gen. 33:20 and Ex. 6:1 and in his famous *responsum* concerning the ambiguity of the Hebrew particle *ki*; and c) Rashi's comment on the name Jeduthun in his introduction to his Commentary on Psalms and again at Ps. 39:1; 62:1; and 77:1.

the root *g'l* 'reject'[139] while Rashi in his commentaries on both BT and Hebrew Scripture consistently treated these as distinct roots, interpreting *g'l* 'sullied, disqualified'.[140] Rashi in his commentary on BT at Bava Qama 50a explains that the word *'ušiyyā'* in Ez. 4:12 denotes 'foundations'. Pseudo-Rashi at Ez. 4:12, on the other hand, interprets this term to mean 'walls'.[141] Rashi in his commentary on BT at Berakot 16a and Rosh ha-Shanah 4a interprets the word *nidbāk* in Ez. 6:4 to mean a course of stones serving as the foundation of a building while Pseudo-Rashi at Ez. 6:4 interprets this term to mean a wooden wall.[142] Rashi in his commentary on BT at Yoma 31b and in his commentary on Num. 2:17 treats *'al-yādô*, which appears twice in Neh. 3:2 as consisting of the preposition *'al-yād* meaning 'near' combined with the 3d person singular pronominal suffix while Pseudo-Rashi at Neh. 3:2 interprets that very same prepositional phrase as consisting of the preposition *'al* with the word *yādô* functioning as object of the preposition.[143] It is a matter of detail but one of a significant number of matters of detail, which add up to the conclusion that the commentary on Ezra-Nehemiah attributed to Rashi in the Rabbinic Bible could only have been written by a verbose writer who often disagreed with some of Rashi's well-known interpretations. None of the instances where Pseudo-Rashi on Ezra-Nehemiah contradicts Rashi on BT can be accounted for by the necessity of Rashi commenting on BT to accommodate himself to BT's eisegesis of a biblical text. On the contrary, in each of the instances cited here it is Rashi in his commentary on BT who explains more plausibly the meaning of the biblical expression in its biblical context.

In his commentary on BT at Bava Meṣi'a 75a Rashi writes as follows concerning the meaning of the expression *wĕ'arîk*:

> Proper [*ṭôb*]. Its [Aramaic] cognate [Heb. *dōmeh lô*] is found in the Book of Ezra (Ez. 4:14): "the nakedness of the king it is not *'arîk* for us to

---

[139] On the latter root see Robert M. Galatzer-Levy and Mayer I. Gruber, "What an Affect Means: A Quasi-Experiment About Disgust," *The Annual of Psychoanalysis* 20 (1992), pp. 80-83; cf. Jacob Milgrom, *Leviticus 23-27*, Anchor Bible, vol. 3B (New York: Doubleday, 2000), pp. 2301-2302.

[140] Florsheim, 3:268-269, q.v., cites, *inter alia*, Rashi's commentaries at BT Qiddushin 70a concerning Ez. 2:2 and at Lev. 26:11; 2 Sam. 1:21; and Job. 21:10 concerning the root *g'l*.

[141] Florsheim, 3:272.

[142] See ibid., p. 275.

[143] See ibid., pp. 280-281.

see," and its meaning is, "It is not nice [yāpeh] for us to to see the king's disgrace."

Likewise in his commentary on BT Sukkah 44b Rashi writes as follows concerning the phrase "'arîk or not 'arîk":

> Proper [ṭôb] to do so or not. [The word 'arîk is] an expression denoting 'something appropriate' [hāgûn], and in Ezra (Ez. 4:14) there is an example of it: "It is not proper for us to see the king's nakedness."

Reflecting Rashi's interpretation, Pseudo-Rashi at Ez. 4:14 writes as follows:

> THE NAKEDNESS OF THE KING. The king's disgrace. IT IS NOT MEET ['arîk]. It is not appropriate [hāgûn] for us to see. 'arîk [means] 'appropriate'. It is the same word that is attested [in the phrase] "'arîk or not 'arîk" in Tractate Sukkah (44b).

The latter comment is clearly based upon Rashi's commentary on BT Sukkah 44b. As noted by Florsheim, the style, however, is clearly not that of Rashi.[144] Pseudo-Rashi here fully spells out all the ideas, which Rashi expresses telegraphically and which translations into modern languages flesh out by the use of bracketed expressions.

In his commentary on BT at Makkot 23b Rashi explains that when Neh. 10:39 states, "An Aaronite priest must be with the Levites when the Levites collect the tithe... ," it is because of what we say in [BT] Yevamot [86b]: Ezra the Scribe punished the Levites because they did not ascend with him [from Babylonia], and he commanded them to bring the tithes to the Temple storeroom so that the priests and the Levites would share equally in the first tithe [assigned by Num. 18:20-24 to the Levites] as it is written in Ezra (i.e., Neh. 10:39), "An Aaronite priest shall be with the Levites when the Levites collect the tithe." Pseudo-Rashi, on the other hand, offers a totally different explanation as to why the Levites had to collect the tithes and bring them to the Temple (the domain of the priests): "The Levites would tithe a tithe of the tithe [cf. Num. 18:18:25-32], and they would bring it to the priests who would not leave [rd. 'ōzĕbîm rather than 'ōzĕrîm 'helping'] the Temple."[145]

One of the most famous examples of homonyms in Biblical Hebrew is the rare verb 'zb 'help', which looks like the common verb

---

[144] See ibid., p. 275.
[145] See ibid., p. 284 for a very different treatment of the problem.

'*zb* 'abandon'. Rashi in his commentary at Ex. 23:5 writes as follows:

> You should read the clause "AND YOU SHALL REFRAIN FROM HELPING ['*ăzôb*] HIM?" as a question.[146] This [verb] *ăzîbāh* is a verb referring to [*lĕšôn*] help. It is attested also in[147] the expression "bond and redeemed" (1 Kgs. 10:14).[148] It is attested also in[149] "They rendered help to Jerusalem up to the broad wall [of the city], [which means that] they filled it up with earth to help [*la'ăzōb*], i.e.,[150] 'to aid' the strengthening of the wall.

Pseudo-Rashi at Neh. 3:8 demonstrates both 1) his familiarity with Rashi's interpretation (in his commentary at Ex. 23:5) of the material reality referred to in Neh. 3:8; and 2) his thorough unfamiliarty with the philological problem presented by the apparent use in a context referring to providing help of a verb, which normally means 'abandon'. This is what Pseudo-Rashi writes in his commentary at Neh. 3:8:

> AND THEY...[*wayya'azĕbû*]. They filled it with earth UP TO THE BROAD WALL in order to strenghthen it.

One would have to conclude that while Rashi, followed by most modern dictionaries of Biblical Hebrew, recognizes '*zb* I 'abandon' and '*zb* II 'help', Pseudo-Rashi on Ezra-Nehemiah refers to an otherwise unrecognized '*zb* III 'fill with earth'.

Finally, it should be noted that Pseuo-Rashi at Ez. 4:10 wrongly interprets as a place name the Aramaic expression *kĕ'enet*, a cognate of the more common *kĕ'an* and *kĕ'ēt*, all of which mean literally,

---

[146] Many questions in Biblical Hebrew, Rabbinic Hebrew, and Babylonian Jewish Aramaic are not introduced by any of the various interrogative particles such as *hă*, '*im*, *kî*, *lāmmāh; maddû'ă*. Read apart from their context, many questions might, therefore, be construed as declarative clauses. As commentator *par excellence*, Rashi here makes the exegetical judgment and supplies the marginal comment *bittĕmîhāh* meaning 'in the form of a question'.

[147] Rashi expresses "It is attested also in" by means of the Hebrew expression *wĕkēn*.

[148] Apparently, a merism referring to all Israel, both him/her who was temporarily enslaved in payment of a debt ('*āṣûr*) and he/she who had been helped ('*āzûb*) by a relative who had redeemed them (see Lev. 25:47-55).

[149] See above, n. 147.

[150] Exegetical *waw*; see the discussion below, p. 139-140, and see index, s.v. "explicative (or exegetical) *waw*."

'now'[151] and which indicate the transition from the salutation section of a letter to the body of the letter.[152] The absurdity of Pseudo-Rashi's interpretation of $kĕ'enet$ as a place name is exceeded only by this commentator's interpretion of $šĕlam~ûkĕ'ēt$, properly, "Greetings And now... ," in Ez. 4:17 as *two* place names[153] It is hard to imagine that Rashi, who authored the still definitive commentary on the Babylonian Talmud, and whose lexical and grammatical insights continue to awe and inspire the most creative biblical philologists almost 900 years after his death,[154] would write such foolishness. Indeed, to insist that Rashi is the author of the commentary on Ezra-Nehemiah wrongly ascribed to him in the Rabbinic Bible simply insults the master commentator, without whom the Babylonian Talmud would have become a closed book. The common assertion that the commentary on Ezra-Nehemiah was written or completed by Rashi's students[155] is no less an insult to Rashi's famous disciples— R. Samuel b. Meir, Rabbenu Tam and R. Joseph Qara—whose exegetical and lexicographical contributions of the very first order, are established beyond a shadow of doubt.[156] Interestingly, at Ez.

---

[151] See *BDB*, p. 1107a; and concerning the form $kĕ'an$ see Rashi at Dan. 3:15; Pseudo-Rashi at Ez. 4:13 and passim.

[152] See Joseph A. Fitzmyer, "Some Notes on Aramaic Epistolography," *JBL* 93 (1974), p. 216: "The initial greeting is often followed by $k'n$, $wk'n$, $k't$, $wk't$, $k'nt$, 'and now', a word that either introduces the body of the message or is repeated in the course of it as a sort of message divider; it marks logical breaks in the letter and has often been compared to English 'stop' in telegrams." The corresponding expression in ancient Hebrew epistolography is $wĕ'attāh$ 'and now' found in 2 Kgs. 5:6; 10:2, "the marker of tranistion between address and body"; so Dennis Pardee, *Handbook of Ancient Hebrew Letters*, Society of Biblical Literature: Sources for Biblical Study (Chico: Scholars Press, 1982), p. 169.

[153] Fitzmyer, "Some Notes on Aramaic Epistolography," pp. 214-216 explains that $šĕlam$ there means 'Greetings!'

[154] See, e.g., Chaim (Harold) Cohen, "Jewish medieval commentary on the Book of Genesis and modern biblical philology, Part I: Gen 1-18," *JQR*, n.s., 81 (1990), pp. 1-11.

[155] So, for example, Moshe Greenberg, "Tanakh—Commentary: French Commentators," *EM* 9:695 (in Hebrew).

[156] Concerning R. Joseph Qara see, *inter alia*, Ahrend, *The Commentary of Rabbi Yosef Qara on the Book of Job*, pp. 1-79 (in Hebrew); Poznański, *Kommentar zu Ezechiel und den XII kleinen Propheten von Eliezer aus Beaugency*, pp. xxiii-xxxix; Simon Eppenstein, "Studien über Joseph ben Simeon Kara als Exeget," *Jahrbuch der Jüdisch-Literarischen Gesellschaft* 4 (1906), pp. 238-268; Abraham Geiger, *Parschandatha: Die nordfranzösische Exegetschule* (Leipzig: Leopold Schnauss, 1855), pp. 21-33; Grossman, *The Early Sages of France*, pp. 254-346; and see the extensive literature cited there, p. 254, n. 1 and p. 611; concerning the brilliantly innovative biblical exegesis of Rabbenu Jacob Tam see Shoshana, *The Book of Job*, pp. 74-102; Poznański, *Kom-*

7:12 Pseudo-Rashi offers an entirely different interpretation of *kĕ'enet*. There he contends that the phrase *gĕmîr ûkĕ'enet* means 'wherewithal', and he neither compares nor contrasts *kĕ'enet* in the latter context to *kĕ'enet* in Ez. 4:10. It appears, therefore, that the commentary on Ezra-Nehemiah attributed to Rashi in the Rabbinic Bible is not the work of a scholar with a design—such as Rashi demonstrates in his Commentary on Song of Songs or as R. Samuel the Pious indicates in his Commentary on Chronicles—but of a beginning student or group of beginning students, who gathered together data from here and there including Rashi's Commentary on the Babylonian Talmud and his/their own sophomoric guesses. Modern exegetes and students who seek to utilize the contributions of the great Hebrew commentators of the Middle Ages need to be informed both 1) that the commentary on Ezra-Nehemiah attributed to Rashi in the Rabbinic Bible is not from the pen of Rashi; and 2) on what basis this assertion is made.

3. Rashi's Commentaries on Liturgical Poetry

Anticipating by more than nine centuries Robert Gordis' advocacy of what Gordis called "the vertical aspect" of comparative Semitic lexicography,[157] Rashi utilized post-biblical Hebrew texts, including medieval Hebrew liturgical poetry[158] to shed light on words whose meanings might be obscure in Hebrew Scripture but clear as day in later texts. Urbach pointed out that most of the early sages of the Rhineland and Northern France, who are so well known as commentators on the Bible and the Talmud, renders of decisions in *halakah*, and community leaders were also poets, who composed li-

---

mentar zu Ezechiel, pp. li-lv; Geiger, pp. 35-37; concerning the brilliant biblical philology of Rashbam see Japhet, *The Commentary of Rabbi Samuel Ben Meir (Rashbam) On the Book of Job*, pp. 209-276; Poznański, *Kommentar zu Ezechiel*, pp. xxxix-l; David Rosin, *R. Samuel b. Mëir (Rashbam) als Schrifterklärer*, Jahresbericht des Jüdisch-Theologischen Seminars Fraenkel'scher Stiftung (Breslau: F. W. Jungfer, 1880), pp. 128-155; Martin I. Lockshin, *Rabbi Samuel ben Meir's Commentary on Genesis: An Annotated Translation* (Lewiston: Edwin Mellen Press, 1989); id., *Rashbam's Commentary on Exodus: An Annotated Translation*, Brown Judaic Studies, no. 310 (Atlanta: Scholars Press, 1997); *Rashbam's Commentary on Leviticus and Numbers: An Annotated Translation*, Brown Judaic Studies, no. 330 (Providence, Brown University, 2001).

[157] Gordis, *Job*, pp. xvii-xviii.

[158] See, e.g., his commentary at Ps. 42:5e (see below, p. 336 and our discussion p. 342, n. 34; see also Rashi at Ex. 26:15; Cant. 4:10.

turgical poetry.[159] Urbach noted also that the compositions of earlier composers of liturgical poetry (*payyetanim*) served as models for
these Franco-German liturgical poets. It should not be surprising,
therefore, Urbach argued, that these German and French scholars
were just as dedicated to the exegesis of liturgical poetry as they were
to the exegesis of the Bible and the Talmud.[160] Apparently, "the first
of the German sages to write commentaries to *piyyutim* was Meshullam
b. Moses of Mainz."[161] As these German and French scholars were
fully aware that liturgical poetry was based upon *midrash*,[162] it should
be no less surprising that among the first French commentators on
liturgical poetry was Rabbi Moses the Interpreter of Narbonne.[163]
The first northern French commentator on liturgical poetry was
Rabbi Menahem bar Helbo, whose fragmentary biblical commentaries also antedate Rashi.[164]

Rashi held that the inclusion of medieval liturgical poetry (*piyyutim*)
in the liturgy was a legally sanctioned practice known to Jewish communities all over the world and not to be questioned. While Abraham
Ibn Ezra (1089-1164 C.E.) in his commentary on Koh. 5:1 argued
that people should not include in their prayers liturgical poems that
they did not understand, Rashi, on the other hand, held that people
are obligated to learn and to teach the meaning of the liturgical

---

[159] Ephraim Ellimelech Urbach, ed., *Sefer Arugat Habosem, autore R. Abraham b.
R. Azriel (saec XIII) Tomus IV: Prolegomen et Indices* (Jerusalem: Mekize Nirdamim,
1963), p. 3; in n. 1 there Urbach calls attention to the list of medieval commentators on liturgical poetry in Leopold Zunz, *Die Ritus des synagogalen Gottesdienstes* (2d
ed.; Berlin: L. Lamm,1919), pp. 194-201; concerning Rashi's liturgical poetry see
above, pp. 29–37.
[160] Urbach, *Arugat Habosem*, pt. iv, p. 3.
[161] Avraham Grossman, "Exegesis of the Piyyut in Eleventh Century France,"
in *Rashi et la culture juive en France du Nord au moyen âge*, ed. Gilbert Dahan, Gérad
Nahon, Elic Nicolas (Paris and Louvain: E. Peeters, 1997), p. 273, n. 21; id., *The
Early Sages of Germany* (2d ed.; Jerusalem: Magnes, 1988), pp. 389-390 (in Hebrew).
[162] Urbach, *Arugat Habosem*, pt. iv, p. 3, n. 2 cites *Sefer ha-Pardes* # 175.
[163] Urbach, *Arugat Habosem*, pt. iv, p. 3, n. 3 cites the fragments of R. Moses
the Interpreter's commentaries on liturgical poetry discussed in Epstein, *Moses ha-
Darshan aus Narbonne* , pp. 234-236.
[164] For fragments of R. Menaham bar Helbo's commentaries on liturgical poetry
see Urbach, *Arugat Habosem*, pt. iv, p. 3, n. 5; Grossman, *The Early Sages of France*,
pp. 521-522; id., "Exegesis of the Piyyut in Eleventh Century France," p. 262;
for fragments of his biblical commentaries see Samuel N. Poznański, "Fragments
from the Biblical Exegesis of Menachem bar Helbo," in *Nahum Sokolow Jubilee Volume* (Warsaw: Shuldberg, 1904), pp. 389-439 (in Hebrew); an appendix to the latter
article, pp. 437-439 includes fragments of R. Menaham bar Helbo's commentaries
on liturgical poetry.

poems.[165] It is fully understandable, therefore, that Rashi would have exegeted for himself and others medieval liturgical poetry:

> The [surviving] fragments of Rashi's commentaries [on liturgical poetry] relate to the *piyyutim* of Eleazar Qallir, Solomon ha-Bavli, Meshullam b. Kalonymos and Elijah the Elder of Le Mans."[166]

Moreover, Grossman explains:

> ...his [i.e., Rashi's] manner of expounding the *piyyut* was much akin to his manner of expounding the Bible.[167]

In addition, as in his commentary on BT, Rashi, like many 19th and 20th century C.E. biblical scholars, assumed that when the received text made no sense it should be restored by means of conjectural emendation.[168]

In other words, Rashi gave prime consideration to lexicography, grammar and syntax. He opposed reading into the *piyyutim* meanings which were not there.[169] This idea is a logical consequence of Rashi's belief that people are obligated both to include the *piyyutim* in the liturgy and to understand them. Otherwise, it should not make any difference if, as in many modern synagogues of all Jewish denominations, one either ignores what is being recited or one makes up eisegeses, often passed off as exegeses, more or less as one goes along.

Rashi conveyed to his pupils the importance of uncovering and deciphering the allusions to *midrash* in medieval liturgical poetry. Consequently, Shemayah testifies that Rashi greatly rejoiced when "Shemayah discovered the rabbinic legend serving as the basis of one of Qallir's verses."[170]

It should not be surprising, therefore, that Rashi also penned commentaries on medieval Hebrew liturgical poetry.[171] Grossman,

---

[165] See Urbach, *Arugat Habosem*, pt. iv, pp. 6-7 and the literature cited there.

[166] Grossman, "Exegesis of the Piyyut in Eleventh Century France," p. 263.

[167] Ibid., p. 264.

[168] Cf. Grossman, *The Early Sages of France*, p. 527.

[169] Grossman, "Exegesis of the Piyyut in Eleventh Century France," p. 264; id., *The Early Sages of France*, p. 250

[170] Ibid., p. 264; the source supplied in n. 5 there is Ms. Parma de Rossi 665, fol. 85a.

[171] Moritz Steinschneider, *Jewish Literature of the Eighth to the Eighteenth Century* (London: Longman, Brown, Green, Longmans & Roberts, 1857), pp. 166-168.

however, invokes the argument from silence that insofar as no fragments of Rashi's commentaries on *piyyutim* have so far been identified, one may conclude

> with a fair measure of confidence that Rashi did not commit his in-
> terpretations [of *piyyutim*] to writing, but he passed them on by word
> of mouth to his pupils.[172]

Grossman points to three forms in which literally scores of Rashi's
commentaries on *piyyutim* are cited in the writings of his chief disciple, Shemayah: "Rashi said"; "I heard"; and anonymously.[173]

I present here my annotated translations of two of the six examples
of Rashi's commentaries on liturgical poetry that have survived in
the writings transmitted by his disciples and which are quoted by
Grossman.[174] The first example is Rashi's commentary on l. 22 of
Tohelet Yisrael "The hope of Israel" by Solomon the Babylonian the
Younger.[175] The line of poetry reads as follows:

> Our guilt has accumulated to an eighth [*tomen*] and a twentieth [*'uklā'*].
> You, O LORD will not put an end [*tiklā'*][176] to Your mercy.[177]

---

[172] Grossman, "Exegesis of the Piyyut in Eleventh Century France," p. 263.

[173] Grossman, *The Early Sages of France*, pp. 249-250; see also there, pp. 522-
528. Especially important manuscript sources cited by Grossman are the 13th
century C. E. "R. Simeonis Commentarius in Machazor," which is Ms. Parma
de Rossi 655 and the 13th century Ashkenazi commentary on the *Mahzor*, [i.e.,
the prayerbook complete with the liturgical poetry; the Jewish prayerbook without the addition of the liturgical poetry is called *Siddur*] written out by Eliyyah
bar Binyamin and found on pp. 423-425 of Oxford Bodleian Ms. Opp. 171.

[174] The first of the two examples is quoted in Grossman, *The Early Sages of France*,
p. 525; the second is quoted there, p. 524; additional examples are quoted in
Grossman, there, pp. 525-528.

[175] Solomon ben Judah was a 10th century C.E. Hebrew liturgical poet, who
appears to have lived in Northern Italy a generation before Rabbenu Gershom.
He was the teacher of Meshullam b. Kalonymos. Ezra Fleischer, "Solomon ben
Judah ha-Bavli," *EJ* 15:124 suggests that Rashi calls him *ha-Bavli* "the Babylonian"
because his family was of oriental origin. The author of 25 *selihot*, Solomon ben
Judah is best known for his *yoṣer* [liturgical poem for the Shaharit or Morning
Service] for the first day of Passover, whose first line is *Or Yesha Mesharim*; see *The
Festival Prayers According to the Ritual of the German and Polish Jews* with a new trans-
lation by the Rev. David A. De Sola, vol. 1: Passover Service (London: P. Vallentine,
1881), pp. 97-100; see also notes, there, pp. 423-424; and see above, n. 166.

[176] This pseudo-Aramaic form of the Heb. verb *kly* reflects the poet's familiarity with the Aramaic noun *kl'h* 'destruction' as the equivalent of Heb. *klyyh* (see
Jastrow, *Dict.*, p. 638b); it is deliberately employed to rhyme with the noun *'uklā'*
in the previous clause; moreover the expression 'put an end to Your mercy' is
probably inspired by the clause "Your mercies never come to an end" in the

Rashi's comment including the lemma reads as follows:

TO AN EIGHTH [*tomen*] AND A TWENTIETH [*'ŭklā'*]. [These two obscure terms] are small measures [of quantity] as we say in [BT] Soṭah [8b].[178] [The line, therefore means] OUR GUILT HAS ACCUMU-LATED TO [such an extant] that it reaches [*šettimṣā'*][179] all the measures which are counted with respect to transgressions from the largest measure to the smallest measure... All the measures which they [the Tannaim in the *baraitha* quoted in BT Soṭah 8b] mentioned with re-spect to transgressions can be counted in our hands, and with respect to all of them YOU WILL NOT PUT AN END TO YOUR MERCY. [This comment is] from the mouth of *Rabbi*[180] [i.e., my mentor,

---

penultimate benediction of the so-called Eighteen Benedictions; see Birnbaum, *Daily Prayer Book*, p. 92.

[177] My translation of line 22 of the *seliḥah*; the Hebrew text of this *seliḥah* is found in Daniel Goldschmidt, *Seder Ha-Selihot According to the Lithuanian Rite* (Jerusa-lem: Mossad Harav Kook, 1965), pp. 203-205 (in Hebrew); the quoted line is found there on p. 205.

[178] Elaborating on the principle set forth in M. Soṭah 1:7 "In accord with the measure which a person metes out they [Heaven, i.e., God] mete out to him," T. Soṭah 3:1, quoted in BT Soṭah 8b interprets the obscure expression in Isa. 27:8 *bĕsa'ssāh* to mean "if a person metes out in a significant measure" [Heb. *bisě'āh*; such an inexact interpretation of Heb. *sě'āh* is reflected in LXX's μέτρον 'mea-sure'; notwithstanding the fact that the precise metric equivalents of most weights and measures referred to in the literatures of the ancient Near East and Rabbinic literature vary from time to time and place to place, 1 *sě'āh* consistently equals 6 *qab;* if we follow Daniel Sperber, "Weights and Measures in the Talmud," *EJ* 16:390 in equating one Jerusalemite *qab with* 699.4 cc., then 1 *sě'āh* equals 4.1964 liters], and it answers in the affirmative the question is to whether heavenly-sent retribu-tion is forthcoming also for meting out inappropriate behavior in smaller amounts such as *tomen* 'an eighth of a *qab*' [assuming that a Jerusalemite *qab* is 699.4 cc., a *tomen* is 87.425 cc.;] and *'uklā'* 'a twentieth of a *qab*' [assuming again that a Jerusalemite *qab* is 699.4 cc., an *'uklā'* is 34.97 cc.]. Rashi in the commentary here quoted assumes that Rabbi Solomon the Babylonian in line 22 of his *seliḥah* al-ludes to BT Soṭah 8b.

[179] Note that Heb. *mṣ'*, which often means 'find' in both Biblical and Rabbinic Hebrew, is here attested in the primary sense 'reach', which is the common meaning of the Aramaic cognate *mṭ'* and the Ugaritic cognate *mġy*.

[180] The ms. employs the abbreviation *m.r.*, which Grossman, *The Early Sages of France*, p. 525 interprets as standing for *mippî rabbî* "from the mouth of my men-tor"; this expression is quite distinct from "I wrote" (Rashi referring to himself in Elfenbein, *Responsa Rashi* #10) and from "he wrote" (Elfenbein, *Responsa Rashi* #237) as well as from "My strength is sapped and my voice is too weak to relate all the troubles I have experienced one after another. Consequently, my hand is too weak to write to my relative R. Azriel and to my dear friend and colleague R. Joseph a responsum to their words in my own handwriting. I am dictating to one of my colleagues, and he is writing... " (Elfenbein, *Responsa Rashi*, p. 96, #73). All of these three formulae attest to the fact that under normal circumstances Rashi him-self recorded his writings. Precisely when the distinct formula *mippî rabbî* is com-

Rashi].[181] There are some who interpret [the obscure words] *tomen* and *'ûklā'* [as follows]: [*tomen* in the phrase] is a form of the word [Heb. *lĕšōn*][182] *tam*, i.e.,[183] *kĕlayyāh* 'coming to an end' [while] *'ûklā'* is a cognate of [Heb. *kĕmô*][184] [the verb in the clause] *nitʾakkēl habbāśār* "the flesh has wasted away."[185] [Proof of the cogency of the latter interpretations of the two obscure words *tomen* and *'ûklā'* in the *seliḥah* can be found in] "until all that generation... was gone [*tom*]" (Num. 32:13) and *nitʾakkĕlû* [meaning] "they [the coins] disappeared" (BT Bekorot 49a). However, R[abbi 'my mentor', i.e., Rashi] does not concur.[186]

The second example of Rashi's oral commentary on liturgical poetry, which is cited in a medieval ms. and which Grossman published in his *Early Sages of France* pertains to a passage in a liturgical poem for the Festival of Shavuot (also called Weeks or Hebrew Pentecost) from the pen of Elijah b. Menahem the Elder. Assuming that most readers of these lines are not experts in or even students of the arcane discipline of Medieval Jewish liturgical poetry, I preface the passage from the medieval commentary, in which Rashi's oral commentary is quoted, with a few words about the poet, the poetic genre, the poem and the poem's allusions to Mishnah and BT, with-

---

pared with the numerous references to Rashi himself writing and drawing (see Rashbam at Num. 34: 2 and Tosaphot at BT Menahot 75a, s.v. "like a *chi*," and see Rashi himself in the ninth of his *responsa* to R. Samuel of Auxerre [see above, p. 51–52]) one senses corroboration of Grossman's contention that the writer refers specifically to an oral rather than a written commentary of Rashi on the liturgical poem under disucssion. On the other hand, the numerous references to Rashi himself writing and drawing and his extensive apology in *Responsa Rashi #73* provide ample testimony that Rashi was in the habit of himself committing his works to writing in Hebrew. Such testimony should put to rest the speculation of Banitt, *Rashi: Interpreter of the Biblical Letter*, p. 4, n. 14 that in fact Rashi's Bible commentaries were not written but "compiled by R[ashi], as written down by his students" and p. 10, n. 18: 'We should remember that, on the whole, the commentaries are a compilation of notes taken at lessons conducted in French."

[181] Grossman, *The Early Sages of France*, p. 525.

[182] Note the exegetical vocabulary shared by Shemayah and by Rashi's commentaries on the Bible; on the various nuances of the exegetical and grammatical term *lāšôn* in Rashi's biblical commentaries see below, pp. 140–145 and passim.

[183] My rendering of exegetical *waw*; on this phenomenon in Rashi's language see below, p. 139–140 and the literature cited there.

[184] Concerning the usage of Heb. *kĕmô* in this sense in Rashi's biblical commentaries see below, p. 140.

[185] M. Sanhedrin 7:6.

[186] The Hebrew text here translated and annotated is found in Grossman, *The Early Sages of France*, p. 525; Grossman's source is Ms. Oxford Bodleian, Opp. 171 (a 13th century commentary on Hebrew liturgical poetry), p. 100a; see Grossman, there, p. 525, n. 78.

out which neither the poem nor the commentary makes sense.

Elijah b. Menahem the Elder was a Jewish liturgical poet who lived in France, probably at Le Mans in the 10th century C.E. A pupil of Rabbenu Gershom,[187] he is said to have married the daughter of Sherira (906-1006 C.E.), who served as Gaon of Pumbeditha from 968 to 1006 C.E.[188] His two famous works are 1) "Seder ha-Ma'arakhah," which is a compilation of biblical passages arranged for recitation on each day of the week; and 2) "Azharot," which is a poem concerning the 613 commandments,[189] containing 176 four-line strophes. This poem is quoted in Tosaphot at BT Sukkah 49a; Yoma 8a; Bava Batra 145b; Makkot 3b; Niddah 30a.[190] The genre Azharot, to which R. Elijah's composition belongs, was first mentioned by R. Natronai b. Hilai, the Gaon of Sura (853-858 C.E.).[191] The genre in question is a category of liturgical poems for the Festival of Shavuot, in which the poet enumerates the 613 commandments. The term 'azharôt seems to reflect a) the opening word of the early piyyut of unknown authorship, the first line of which reads "A warning ['azharah] You gave Your people at the outset";[192] and b) the combined numerical value of the Hebrew letters of the word 'azharot 'warnings', which is 613. The authors of the earliest exem-

---

[187] On the importance of Rabbenu Gershom (968-1028 C.E.) for Rashi see above, p. 5.

[188] Max Seligsohn, "Elijah ben Menahem Ha-Zaken," JE 5:131-132; with the latter see Solomon Luria, Responsa (Jerusalem: Yahdayw, 1983) #29 (in Hebrew); see also Mordecai Sluçki, ed., 'Azharot leHag ha-Shavuot leRabbenu Elijah ha-Zaken (Warsaw: Halter, 1900), title page; note that the aforementioned responsum of Solomon Luria (b. Posen 1510; d. Lublin 1573) asserts that Rabbenu Gershom "received it [Torah] from Rav Hai Gaon"; by this assertion not only does Solomon Luria, who claims descent from Rashi, imitate the "chain of tradition" found in M. Avot 1 but also he asserts that Rabbenu Gershom and hence all of Ashkenazic Jewry stand in a line of apostolic succession that leads from the Babylonian academies of the Amoraic period through Hai Gaon. Clearly, Solomon Luria learned well the lesson that Rashi himself taught not so subtly by calling himself ga'ôn and his academy Yeshivat Ge'on Ya'aqov; see above, pp. 16–18.

[189] The idea that Judaism consists of 613 commandments—248 "do's" corresponding to the number of bones in the body according to the anatomists of the Roman Era, and 365 "don't's" corresponding to the number of days in a solar year—goes back to Rav Simlai (second half of the 2d cent. C.E.) in BT Makkot 23b. Moses Maimonides (1135-1204) in his Book of the Commandments, followed by numerous authorities of the 13th century C.E., attempts to determine precisely what are the 613 commandments.

[190] Abraham Meir Haberman, "Azharot, Azharah," EJ 3:1007-1008.

[191] Ibid.

[192] Ibid.

plars of the genre are unknown. These compositions were attributed
to the heads of the Baghdad academies; hence they were called either *'azharot derabbanan* "warnings by our rabbis" or *'azharot demetivtā'*
qaddisā' derabbanan de-Pumbedita "azharot stemming from the holy
yeshivah of the rabbis of Pumbedita,"[193] i.e., the Baghdad academy
headed in the time of Rabbenu Gershom (960-1028 C.E.) by Sherira
Gaon (968-998 C.E.) and his son Hai Gaon (998-1038), who was
regarded as the spiritual head of all Jewry.[194] This academy was
regarded as having been founded at Pumbedita c. 259 C.E. by the
Amora Rabbi Judah b. Ezekiel (220-299 C.E.), who was the disciple
of Samuel of Nehardea (c. 165-257 C.E.). It is no wonder that our
French Jewish poet would be supplied if not with a genealogy trac-
ing his descent to the heads of the Babylonian academies, then at
least with a marriage alliance with one of the *ge'ônim*, i.e., heads of
the Baghdad academies. More than 60 poems belonging to the genre
'azharot are presently known. Moreover, poems belonging to this genre
are attested not only for Shavuot but also for the Sabbath before
Sukkot (Tabernacles) , the Sabbath before Passover, the New Year,
Hanukkah, Purim, and New Moon.[195]

The relevant section of the Azharot of R. Elijah b. Menahem the
Elder reads as follows:

> As for one who raises a hand against father or mother[196]
> Or prophecies in the name of a false god[197]
> so as to offend Me [*lĕnaqqĕšî*],
> Kidnapper[198] and false prophet[199]
> And an elder who rebels against a ruling based on My [i.e., the offi-
> cial legal] interpretation of [an equivocal] Scripture,[200] a man who
> has sexual intercourse with someone else's wife or with the daughter
> of a priest,[201] and the people who are convicted of testifying falsely to
> these [the eight aforementioned offenses] are by virtue of My [the
> speaker is, as it were, God] creating an analogy [Heb. *bĕhaqqîšî*],[202] I

---

[193] Ibid.

[194] See above, pp. 17, n. 12.

[195] Haberman, "Azharot, Azharah," *EJ* 3:1007-1008.

[196] See Ex. 21:15.

[197] See Deut. 13:2-6.

[198] See Ex. 21:16.

[199] See Deut. 18:20-22.

[200] See the *baraitha* quoted in BT Sanhedrin 87a, which is discussed in detail
in n. 204 below.

[201] See Lev. 20:10 and the discussion in BT Sanhedrin 50b.

[Heb. *napšî*, lit., 'my neck']²⁰³ choose(s) strangulation [as their penalty].²⁰⁴

Here is the portion of R. Shemayah's commentary on the latter poem, which Grossman quotes as an illustration of R. Shemayah's quoting what appears to be an oral commenary of Rashi on R. Elijah's *'Azharot:*

IN THE NAME OF A FALSE GOD SO AS TO OFFEND ME [*lĕnaqqĕšî*]. [This infinitive with accusative pronominal suffix] is a cognate of [Heb. *lĕšôn*]²⁰⁵ *mōqēš* 'trap' in consonance with Targ[um] Onke-

---

²⁰² Mordecai Sluçki in his commentary *Hiddur Zaken* , points out that the analogy to which the poem refers is found in BT Sanhedrin 90a: "I do not know whether the persons convicted of false testimony are treated as analogous [with respect to the specific form of capital punishment] to him [the paramour] or to her [the priest's daughter]. When he [Scripture in Deut. 19:19] says 'to have done to his brother' it teaches [by implication] 'to his brother but not to his sister'."

²⁰³ Frequently in Biblical Hebrew the expression *napšî* in its extended meaning 'my person' is employed as periphrasis for the personal pronoun 'I'; see Orlinsky, *Notes*, p. 105. However, Menahem Ibn Saruq, at least according to the witness of Filipowski's edition of *Mahberet Menahem* (the reference is not fond in the Sáenz-Badillos edition) already noted that the primary meaning of Heb. *nepeš* is 'neck'; see *Mahberet Menahem*, ed. Filipowski, p. 49 s.v. *bt* IV; and see the discussion in Gruber, "Hebrew *da'abon nepeš*, " p. 365. Clearly, R. Elijah ben Judah's recognition that the primary meaning of *nepeš* is 'neck' accounts for his clever play on words "I/My neck choose(s) strangulation."

²⁰⁴ *'Azharot leHag ha-Shavuot leRabbenu Elijah ha-Zaken*, ed. Sluçki, pp. 38-39. Note that the source of this list is M. Sanhedrin 11:1: "The following are strangled: One who strikes one's father or one's mother; one who kidnaps and Israelite person; an elder who rebels against the ruling of a *bet din* [i.e., the governmental authority of a self-governing Jewish community operating under the law of the Mishnah; while Obadiah of Bertinoro (d. 1510 C.E.) holds that the rebellious elder in question is one who fails to comply with the decision of the Sanhedrin sitting in the chamber of hewn stone in the Temple at Jerusalem, a *baraitha* quoted in BT Sanhedrin 87a defines the rebellious elder as one who disagrees with a legal tradition of the Talmudic sages, which is based upon an equivocal biblical text; this understanding of the Mishnah is reflected in our poet's expression *ûmamrê bĕmidrāšî*, which may reasonably be rendered "one who rebels against (a legal decision based upon or associated with) an eisegetical interpretation of a biblical text, which I authorized (by the power, which I invested in Sages by virtue of their eisegetical interpretation of Deut. 17:9-11)]; a false prophet (see above, n. 199); and a person who prophesies in the name of idolatrous worship (see above, n. 197), and a man who has sexual intercourse with someone else's wife, and those convicted of false testimony with respect to a priest's daughter [who was married; so BT Sanhedrin 50b; see Lev. 20:10] and the man who allegedly had sex with her."

²⁰⁵ Concerning the nuances of the exegetical term *lĕšôn* in Rashi's biblical commentaries see below, pp. 140-145 and passim in our annotations to Rashi's Commentary on Psalms.

los, which translates [into Aramaic] "lest you become ensnared" [Heb.
pen tinnāqēš] (Deut. 12:30) *dilm[ā']* *tittāqal* 'lest you be entrapped' [em-
ploying a] verb referring to [Heb. *lĕšôn*] a trap. However, the quotation of [*lĕšôn*] our mentor [Heb. *rabbēnû* referring here to Rashi]
interpreted it [the infinitive with accusative pronominal suffix *lĕnaqqĕšî*]
as a cognate of [*lĕšôn*] [the verb in the clause] *dā' lĕdā' nāqšān* "they
knock one another" (Dan. 5:6) for he [Rashi][206] says, "We do not find
a *nun* in any form of [the root from which is derived the verb] *yûqāš*
[hypothetical singular of the verb *yûqāšîm* "they are trapped" (Koh.
9:12) even as a preformative [*yĕsôd nōpēl*],[207] but we do find *nun* in a
verbal root referring to [*lĕšôn*] tearing up and knocking [*qišqûš*], for
we say (in Dan. 5:6), "they knock one another...."[208]

In both instances we see that both Rashi and his disciple Shemayah
share with many modern biblical exegetes including the writer of
these lines the heartfelt conviction that understanding the precise
nuance and origin of each and every word is the *sine qua non* for
understanding any text.[209] Indeed, my annotated translations of the
two fragments of Rashi's commentaries on medieval liturgical poetry seem fully to confirm the contention of Urbach and Grossman
that Rashi exegeted liturgical poetry from the same linguistic perspective from which he approached biblical texts.

---

[206] Grossman, *The Early Sages of France*, p. 524.

[207] See the discussion of this term at Ps. 119:5; see also p. 402, n. 37.

[208] The source of this commentary, quoted in Grossman, *The Early Sages of France*, p. 524, is Ms. Oxford Bodleian, Opp. 171, p. 49a

[209] With respect to Rashi's emphasis on philology as the key to truth see Banitt, *Rashi: Interpreter of the Biblical Letter*, pp. 131-166.

C. Rashi's Responsa

Rashi's literary output includes approximately 350 *responsa*,[1] mostly to the rather typical questions in *halakah*, addressed to rabbis in every generation, such as 1) whether or not one may slaughter cattle and sheep with a knife part of whose blade is defective although not in the part of the blade with which one slaughters the animal;[2] 2) what should be done with the head and the legs of a lamb that were cooked in the same pot in the case where the head had been salted to remove the blood and the legs had not been salted to remove the blood;[3] and 3) whether a Jewish man may appoint a Gentile to deliver a bill of divorce to his wife.[4]

In addition to the the thirty-six responsa, widely assigned to Rashi, whose attribution to Rashi Elfenbein shows to be spurious,[5] Grossman shows that the attribution to Rashi in Elfenbein's collection of the following groups of *reponsa* is also spurious: a) 52-54, 67-68, 102, 107, 122-126, 150-156, which were composed by Rashi's teachers, R. Isaac b. Judah and R. Isaac the Levite;[6] b) 75-79 (which were written by R. Solomon b. Samson of Worms);[7] c) 50, 51, 55, 61, which stem from German rabbis of the generation before Rashi;[8] and d)

---

[1] See Elfenbein, *Responsa Rashi;* cf. Grossman, *The Early Sages of France*, pp. 239-243.

[2] Elfenbein, *Responsa Rashi*, #133; the answer is that the knife may not be used lest the slaughterer inadvertantly slaughter with the defective part of the blade; cf. Shulhan Aruk, Yoreh Deah 6:1.

[3] Elfenbein, *Responsa Rashi*, #138; the answer, of course is that the entire contents of that pot is not kosher; my eldest son, Rabbi David Shalom Gruber (e-mail communication 7 May 2001), suggests to me that Shulhan Aruk does not devote a specific paragraph to this question because the answer is quite obvious: the head was rendered non-kosher by being cooked together with the legs from which the blood had not been purged; cf. Shulhan Aruk, Yoreh Deah 69:11 and commentaries thereon.

[4] Elfenbein, *Responsa Rashi*,# 203; the answer is that he may not since the delivery of a bill of divorce is a religious rite, which requires that only Jews officiate; cf. Mishnah Giṭṭin 2:5; see also Shulhan Aruk, Even ha-Ezer 141:31.

[5] See Elfenbein, *Responsa Rashi* , pp. 349-73.

[6] Elfenbein, *Responsa Rashi*, #203; the answer is that he may not since the delivery of a bill of divorce is a religious rite, which requires that only Jews officiate; cf. Mishnah Giṭṭin 2:5; see also Shulhan Aruk, Even ha-Ezer 141:31.

[7] Grossman, *The Early Sages of France*, p. 240, n. 352.

[8] Ibid., p. 241; see also id., *The Early Sages of Ashkenaz:* (2^d ed.; Jerusalem: Magnes, 1988), p. 341 (in Hebrew).

39-41, which stem not from Rashi but from an Italian rabbi, R. Solomon *the* Isaaki, who was an older contemporary of Rashi.[9]

On the other hand, Grossman points out,[10] missing from Elfenbein's useful collection are 1) a number of previously published *responsa* of Rashi;[11] and 2) a number of *reponsa*, which Avraham Grossman and Simcha Emanuel have promised to publish from medieval manuscripts.[12]

Grossman holds that Rashi himself did not prepare an edition of his *responsa* because Rashi's writing numerous *responsa* was an activity of Rashi's last years when Shemayah, who had helped Rashi immensely in the editing of his commentaries, had left Troyes.[13] Nevertheless, Grossman points out, many medieval *halakic* authorities refer to Rashi's *responsa* as a complete corpus to whch they had access. Early collections of Rashi's *responsa* prepared by his disciples include a corpus of a few score of Rashi *responsa* included in the Mahzor of Shemayah.[14]

A late copy of what must have been an early collection of *responsa* by Rashi is contained within New York JTS Ms. Rab. 1087 (Elkan Adler Collection Ms. 2717), a 15th century manuscript of Near Eastern origin. While this 65 page ms. is primarily a collection of the *responsa* of R. Solomon b. Abraham Adret (c. 1235-1310), ten pages (i.e., 42b-52b) contain 30 of Rashi's respona.[15]

Especially interesting are the *responsa* of Rashi, which deal with biblical exegesis. These *responsa* fall into three groups: a) #21 in Elfenbein's edition, which deals with Isa. 45:1; b) the responsa addressed to R. Samuel of Auxerre concerning various passages in Jeremiah and Ezekiel;[16] c) the responsa concerning various *cruces* in the Book of Psalms, which were recently edited and published by Jordan Penkower;[17] and d) the long *responsum* addressed to R. Nathan b. Makhir concerning the variety of meanings of the ubiquitous particle *kî* in Biblical Hebrew. The latter *responum*, which is trans-

---

[9] Grossman, *The Early Sages of France*, pp. 241-243 and the extensive literature cited there.
[10] Grossman, *The Early Sages of France*, p. 243.
[11] Ibid.
[12] Grossman, *The Early Sages of France*, p. 239, n. 348.
[13] Ibid., p. 239, n. 349.
[14] Ibid., pp. 239-240; on this work by Shemayah see above, p. 13, n. 2.
[15] Elfenbein, p. xlvii; cf. Grossman, *The Early Sages of France*, p. 240.
[16] See below, pp. 89–92.
[17] See below, pp. 92–94.

lated and annotated below,[18] is a programmatic essay, in which Rashi demonstrates that the primary means for determining the meaning of any word in any text is its usage in context. Moreover, this essay by Rashi demonstrates the soundness of the conclusions of Kamin and Banitt concerning the meaning of Rashi's exegetical terminology and methodology as expounded by Rashi in his commentaries at Gen. 3:8 33:20; Ex. 6:9; and in Rashi's introduction to his commentary on Song of Songs.[19]

Rashi's responsum concerning Isa. 45:1 reads as follows:

> As for the one who asked [concerning] "Thus said the LORD to His Messiah, concerning [Heb. *lĕ*] Cyrus" (Isa. 45:1),[20] who is the Messiah to whom the King [i.e., God] complained[21] concerning Cyrus? My friend[22] did not explain what was difficult [for him]. If it had

---

[18] See below, pp. 94–105; to the category of *responsa* concerning matters of exegesis and grammar belong also Elfenbein, *Responsa Rashi*, #18, which is discussed above, p. 11, n. 1; q.v.

[19] See Kamin, *Rashi's Exegetical Categorization*, pp. 182-183; Banitt, *Rashi: Interpreter of the Biblical Letter*, p. 48.

[20] Elfenbein, p. 16, n. 1

[21] Ibid., n. 2 explains that the enquiry to Rashi refers here to the exegesis of Isa. 45:1 attributed to Rab Nahman son of Rab Hisda in BT Megillah 12a. There we read as follows: Rab Nahman the son of Rab Hisda expounded: "What is the meaning of what is written in Scripture, 'Thus said the LORD to His Messiah, to [Heb. *lĕ*] Cyrus whose right hand I have grasped' (Isa. 45:1)? Now was Cyrus the Messiah? On the contrary, the Holy One Blessed be He said to the Messiah, 'I am complaining to you about Cyrus.' I said, 'He shall build My Temple, and he shall gather in My exiles' (cf. Isa. 44:28; 45:13; Ezra 1:2), but he said, 'Anyone of you of all His people...let him go up' (Ezra 1:3) [This is to say that Cyrus, instead of carrying out the twofold mission referred to in Isa. 44:28; 45:13 and by Cyrus himself in Ezra 1:2, abdicated responsibility and called for volunteers among the Jewish exiles to carry out the twofold mission; so Rashi in his comment on Rab Nahman's exegesis in Rashi's commentary on BT Megillah 12a, s.v. "Anyone of you."]. Rashi points out in his commentary on BT Megillah 12a, s.v. "I am complaining to you" that Rab Nahman's exegesis is supported by the Massoretic accents. Rashi points out that the disjunctive accent *zarqa*, which appears on the word 'to His Messiah' in Isa. 45:1, is normally followed by the disjunctive accent *seghol* on the following word. In Isa. 45:1 this is not the case for the following word 'to Cyrus' is joined not by *seghol* to the previous word 'to His Messiah' but separated from 'to Cyrus' by its being pointed with the conjunctive accent *ma'arik* [this is the term commonly used today among Jews of Near Eastern origin for the conjunctive accent called *munaḥ* in texts and textbooks of Ashkenazi origin]. Rashi contends that the purpose of the unexpected conjunctive accent is to separate the words "concerning [[Heb. *lĕ*] Cyrus, whose right hand I have grasped" from "Thus said the LORD to His Messiah."

[22] Heb. *ḥābîbî*; Dr. Jordan Penkower (oral communication, January 8, 2001) explained to me that it was Rashi's frequent use of this epithet in referring to the

been interpreted for him with respect to Messiah who is going to be revealed in the future, speedily in our days, if he [the enquirer] would say that perhaps in the time of Isaiah [to whom Rashi apparently attributes all the anonymous speeches in the Book of Isaiah except for Isa. 8:19-20, which Rashi attributes to Beeri, the father of Hosea][23] he [the Messiah] was not [yet] born, [I would respond that] Cyrus also was not [yet] in the world, and he [Isaiah] prophesied concerning him.

Rashi noted in his Commentary on Psalms at Ps. 2:1; 84:10; and 105:15[24] that the philological meaning of Biblical Heb. *māšîaḥ* has nothing to do with the postbiblical belief in a Messiah and that therefore no one should be taken in by the Christian argument that biblical references to *māšîaḥ* support the Christian belief that the Christian Christ is foretold in Hebrew Scripture. How then can Rashi dare to suggest that at Isa. 45:1 Hebrew Scripture refers specifically to the long-awaited Messiah of Judaism? There seem to be three reasons for this apparent discrepancy between a) Rashi's rather consistent attempt in his biblical commentaries to defuse possible references to Messiah; and b) Rashi's countenancing of a referece to the Messiah in Isa. 45:1. First, Rashi's consistent argument against Christian interpretations of the word *māšîaḥ* Hebrew Scripture is based upon 'literal meaning', i.e., scientific philology. Second, the enquirer himself alludes to the interpretation attributed to Rab Nahman son of Rab Hisda in BT Megillah 12a, which itself interprets "his Messiah" in Isa. 45:1 as a reference to the eschatological king, whom Jews awaited at least since the Roman period. Third, the only reasonable alternative to Rab Nahman's interpretation, which, after all, belongs to the Rabbinic canon, which sets apart Judaism from Christianity, is the interpretation of 'his Messiah' as referring to Cyrus: this obvious alternative itself undermines the Christian attempt to see in every biblical reference to *māšîaḥ* a prophecy concerning Jesus. Fourth, while Rashi's Bible commentaries were certainly meant from the beginning a) to encourage Jews, who were

---

addressee of his *responsa* concerning Jeremiah and Ezekiel that led him to understand that the addressee had to be an individual, R. Samuel of Auxerre as indicated in Vatican Ms. Ebr. 94, p. 174v, rather than a group, "the sages of Auxerre," as indicated in other mss. and in Elfenbein, p. 1.

[23] See the discussion below, p. 130, n. 9.

[24] See the discussion in our notes on Rashi's commentary on each of those verses, and see also our subject index, s.v. Christianity, Messiah.

being bombarded with Christian propaganda, to remain faithful to their ancestral faith; and b) to answer or challenge Christianity,[25] the *responsum* #21 was a private communication to another rabbi, who was thoroughly immersed in the Judaism of BT and its exegesis of Hebrew Scripture.

Interestingly, in his commentary at Isa. 45:1 Rashi characteristically provides two alternative interpretations—the first of which seeks to defuse the weapon which Christianity might employ in its war to win Jewish souls—and the second of which is a paraphrase of Rab Nahman the son of Rab Hisda's exegesis. The entire comment reads as follows:

> TO HIS *māšîăḥ*. Every substantive referring to high status is called 'annointment'.[26] It is the same usage as is reflected in[27] "I grant them to you as a perquisite [Heb *lĕmôšĕḥāh*].
>
> Now our rabbis said: "The Holy One Blessed be He said to King Messiah, 'I am complaining to you about Cyrus'" as it is found in [BT] Tractate Megillah [12a].

Here as in Rashi's commentary at Ps. 2:2 "King Messiah" is Rashi's technical term for the eschatological Messiah of Davidic descent, distinct from Biblical Heb. *māšîăḥ*, which, according to Rashi, rarely, if ever, refers to the eschatological Messiah.

Typical of Rashi's *responsa* addressed to R. Samuel of Auxerre are the following:

> #1. [He replied]: Money shall be purchased (Jer. 32:43).[28] [In this clause the verb *wĕniqnāh*] is[29] future tense.[30] [The clause means], "A FIELD shall again be purchased IN THIS LAND." [The verbal form] *niqnāh*

---

[25] See our discussion below, at Ps. 2, n. 6 and especially the study by Touito cited there.

[26] Cf. Rashi's almost verbatim comment at Ps. 105:15, and see our discussion there.

[27] Heb. *kĕmô*.

[28] Heb. *wĕniqnāh hakkesep*; Rashi, like many medieval Hebrew writers, quotes biblical and rabbinic texts from memory (personal oral communication from Prof. David Weiss Halivni); hence he introduces his answer to a question about the grammatical form of the verb clause, "the field will be purchased" with a misquotation of the clause, reading 'the money' instead of 'the field'. Note that NJV renders "fields," correctly construing *haśśādeh*, lit., 'the field', as a collective noun.

[29] Writing Rabbinic Hebrew, Rashi expresses the copula by *hû'*; see below, pp. 137–139.

[30] Heb. *lĕšôn 'ātîd* ; see also Rashi at Gen. 29:3; see Kronberg, p. 40; Englander, "Grammatical Elements and Terminology in Rashi," pp. 389-390.

'it was purchased' is the same grammatical form as[31] are *nibnāh* 'it was built'; *na'ăśāh* 'it was done'; *niglāh* 'it was revealed'. When it [this verbal form][32] has no [prefixed] *waw*, it is[33] past tense.[34] Examples of this latter grammatical form[35] [include the following]: "It was built [*nibnāh*] of whole stone brought [from the quarry]" (1 Kgs. 6:7);[36] "...a vision [*ḥāzôn*][37] was revealed [*niglāh*] to Daniel" (Dan. 10:1). Now the *waw* turns it [the perfect form of the verb][38] into future tense.[39] Examples of this latter grammatical form[40] [include the following]: "The Glory of the LORD shall be revealed [*wĕniglāh*] (Isa. 40:5), [wherein the verb *wĕniglāh* means] "and it shall be revealed". Likewise *wĕniqnāh* [in Jer. 32:43 means] "and it shall be purchased".

#2 [He replied] *qārĕ'û ṣôm* "THEY PROCLAIMED A FAST" (Jer. 36:9 [corresponds in meaning to Mishnaic Hebrew] *gāzĕrû ta'ănît* 'they ordained a fast' [cf. M. Ta 'anit 1: 5]. Since they [the people of Judah

---

[31] Rashi's technical term for expressing, "it is the same grammatical form as is reflected in" is the Heb. preposition *kĕmô*; on this usage in Rashi's biblical commentaries see below, p. 140.

[32] The third person perfect *niphal* of roots whose third root letter is now understood to be *yod;* see; cf. Englander, "Rashi's View of the Weak, 'ayin-'ayin and pe-nun Roots," pp. 405-416; id., "Grammatical Elements and Terminology in Rashi," p. 389.

[33] Heb. *hû'* ; see above, n. 29.

[34] Heb. *lĕšôn 'ābar;* see below, p. 142; Kronberg, p. 40.

[35] Heb. *kĕmô* ; cf. n. 31.

[36] Elliptical rendering of Heb. *massā'* based upon Rashi's commentary at 1 Kgs. 6:7.

[37] Elfenbein and Penkower both note that the biblical text contains the word *dābār* 'word', the familiar term for divine revelation found throughout the prophetic literature of the Hebrew Bible (see, e.g., Jer. 1:2, 4, 11, 13; 2:1 and passim) rather than *ḥāzôn* 'vision' (see, e.g., Isa. 1:1; Nah. 1:1); for the equation of *ḥāzôn* 'vision' and *dābār* 'word' cf. Ezek. 7:26, "They shall seek vision from a prophet" with Jer. 18:18, "...and a word from a prophet." On the tendency of medieval Hebrew exegetes to misquote texts from memory see above n. 28.

[38] Heb. *hōpĕkô.* According to Leslie McFall, *The Enigma of the Hebrew Verbal System: Solutions from Ewald to the Present Day* (Sheffield: Almond Press, 1982), p. 10, Elias Levita (1468-1549) in his Biblical Hebrew Grammar published in 1518 and the Biblical Hebrew Grammar produced by Abraham de Balmes (c. 1450-1523) "were the first to introduce the term *waw hippuk* to denote the *waw* conversive." In fact, it appears that they were anticipated by (and possibly influenced by) Rashi in his first *responsum* to R. Samuel of Auxerre.

[39] Instructors of Bible in Israeli universities who find it necessary to explain again and again this most ubiqitous feature of Biblical Hebrew prose which their students should have learned in primary school should 1) take comfort in the fact that Rashi's esteemed colleague, Rabbi Samuel of Auxerre, shared their students' seeming ignorance or faulty memory; and 2) take comfort that Israel's Bible exegete *par excellence*, like them, had to field questions of the most elementary sort; and 3) emulate Rashi's patient and respectful treatment of his esteemed colleague's questions.

[40] Heb. *kĕmô;* see above, n 31.

described in Jer. 36:9] were afraid because of Nebuchadnezzar the virtuous [were] fasting before the Holy One Blessed be He while the wicked [were fasting] before idols [ʿăbôdāh zārāh].[11]

#3. [He replied]: "THEY MADE FOR THEM[42] CAKES IN HER LIKENESS lĕhaʿăṣîbāh" (Jer. 44:19) refers to the fact that[43] they were in the habit of making an image out of dough in the form of a star.[44]

---

[11] Lit., 'strange worship'; the antithetic parallelism proves that for Rashi the Rabbinic term is the functional equivalent of Biblical Hebrew 'ĕlôhîm aḥērîm 'other gods'; cf. Kadushin, Rabbinic Mind[3], pp. 206-207.

[42] Elfenbein notes that the biblical text reads "We made for her" rather than "they made for them"; cf. nn. 28 and 37.

[43] Heb. še.

[44] Similarly, John Arthur Thompson, The Book of Jeremiah, New International Commentary on the Old Testament (Grand Rapids: William B. Eerdmans Publishing Co., 1980), p. 680: "...they were making special crescent cakes (kawwan), which were stamped with the image of the goddess." Thompson, there, n. 11 invites the reader to compare Am. 5;26. In fact Am. 5:26 contains no reference to cakes but only to a celestial deity Kiyyun, which is probably to be identified with Saturn, one of whose Akkadian epithets is Kaymānu 'the Steady' (see CAD, K, p. 38a). Samuel D. Luzzatto, Erlläuterungen über einen Theil der Prophet und Hagiographen (Lemberg; A. Isaak Menkes, 1876), p. 114 (in Hebrew), writes as follows concerning kawwānîm 'cakes' in Jer. 44:19: "People say that they are cakes in the form of the moon, who is the queen of heaven, and that was the custom among some of the nations" (my translation from Luzzatto's Hebrew). Rashi, it appears, is in very good company. However, Heb. kawwānîm, attested only in Jer. 7: 18; 44:19, is probably best derived from Akk. kamānu 'a sweetened cake' (see CAD, K, pp. 110-111). In fact, Moshe Held, "Studies in Biblical Lexicography in the Light of Akkadian," EI 16 (1982), pp. 76-77 (in Hebrew) cites two Akkadian texts, one of which commands the preparation of kamānu -cakes in honor of Ishtar and the other of which records the declaration, "I have prepared in honor of you (the goddess Ishtar) an offering of pure milk (and) pure kamānu -cakes baked in ashes." Moreover, Held shows there that the kamānu is, in fact matzah 'unleavened bread' baked in ashes or on wood charcoal and dipped in honey or jam. In addition, Held, there, p. 77 argues that mlkt hšmym "queen of heaven" in the consonantal text of Jer. 44:19 corresponds to the Sumerian name of Ishtar, (N)INNANA, which was literally rendered into Akkadian as šarrat šamê "queen of heaven" or bēlet šamê "Lady Heaven." There is no indication that Akk. kamānu was associated with any particular deity or that its shape represented any deity. What seems to have led Rashi and others to assume that the kawwānîm baked by the Jewish devotees of Ishtar in post-586 B.C.E. Egypt were "stamped with the image of the goddess" is the problematic expression lĕhaʿăṣ bāh , which NJV renders "in her likeness" adding in a note, "Meaning of Heb. uncertain"; concerning Rashi's treatment of this expression see below. William McKane, Jeremiah, vol. 2, ICC (Edinburgh: T & T Clarke, 1996), p. 1077 notes that Aquila's rendering of Heb. lh'ṣbh by means of Gk. εἰς κάκωσιν 'to cause pain/grief' [corresponding to Heb. lĕhakʿîsēnî 'just to make Me angry" in Jer. 11:17; 44:8; Ezek. 16:26; and elsewhere] derives the expression lh'ṣbh from the verb 'ṣb 'aggrieve' (Ps. 56:6; 78:40). Aquila's interpretation of lh'ṣbh as an infinitive is supported by MT's vocalization without mappiq in the final h. Consequently, vocalized MT, Aquila and comparative Semitic lexicography all concur in the relegation to the philological dustbin of "cakes made in the image of Ishtar"; contrast Yair

This practice corresponds to[45] "idols by their skill" (Hos. 13:2) [i.e.], statues according to their form.[46] [When they say], "and it should be[47] in her likeness" (Jer. 44:19), i.e.,[48] to capture her likeness [lĕḥaṣ-līmāh], [the Biblical Hebrew expression lĕhaʿăṣîbāh 'in her likeness'] is an expression referring to likeness, image (cf. Gen. 1:26). "myyndlyy in Old French.[49]

#4 [He replied]: "IN THE ELEVENTH YEAR ON THE TENTH DAY OF THE FIRST MONTH" (Ezek. 26:1). Since he [the prophet] did not explain which month, you must assume that it was the first day of the year and that the month was Tishri.[50]

Jordan Penkower has rendered a most valuable service to students of Rashi by publishing for the first time Rashi's *responsa* concerning difficult passages in the Book of Psalms found in St. Petersburg Ms.

Hoffman, *Jeremiah*, Mikra LeYisrael (2 vols.; Tel Aviv: Am Oved/Jerusalem: Magnes, 2001), 1:252-253 (in Hebrew).

[45] Heb. kĕmô.

[46] With reference to Heb. ʿăṣabbîm 'statues' see Mayer I. Gruber, "Azabbim 'idols'," in *Dictionary of Deities and Demons in the Bible*, ed. Karel van der Toorn, Bob Becking, and Pieter W. van der Horst (2d ed.; Leiden: E. J. Brill, 1999), pp. 127-128.

[47] Heb. wyh'

[48] Heb. kĕlômar.

[49] Elfenbein, *Responsa*, p. 1, n. 3 notes that Blondheim missed this gloss. The reason is that Blondheim discussed the French glosses in Rashi's commentaries according to the order of their appearance in Rashi's commentaries on the Bible and the Talmud, and he did not devote a treatise to the French glosses contained in Rashi's *responsa*. Dr. Kirsten Fudeman of the Dept. of French at Ithaca College in Ithaca, New York explains to me (electronic communication, 29 October 2001) that in the written transmission of Rashi's Old French glosses, even in the best manuscripts, *nun* often represents an original *gimmel* while *daleth* often represents an original *resh;* hence she suggests that the gloss "myyndlyy is probably a corruption of an original "imagerie," in the sense 'to make a representation/image'. Interestingly, *Le Glossaire de Bâle*, ed. Menahem Banitt (3 vols.; Jerusalem: Israel Academy of Sciences and Humanities, 1972), vol. 2, p. 145 #4052 glosses Heb. lh'ṣbh with O.F. adolozèr corresponding to Modern French à inquiéter, i.e., Eng. 'to perturb' echoing Aquila's interpretation while *Le Glossaire de Leipzig*, ed. Menahem Banitt (3 vols.; Jerusalem: Israel Academy of Sciences and Humanities, 1998), vol. 2, p. 623, entries 7950-7951 suggests that Heb. lh'ṣbh corresponds in meaning to O.F,. à aformer or O.F. à anvoter 'to create an image'; the latter interpretations correspond to that of Rashi at Jer. 44:19.

[50] If indeed the prophet meant "the first month," he would have intended the month we call Nisan, i.e., the month in which Passover falls, which is "the first month" in Ezek. 45:21. It follows, therefore, that the month we call Tishri, the month in which the New Year and Day of Atonement fall, would be for Ezekiel as for Lev. 23 and Num. 29 "the seventh month". Rashi, the patient instructor, has here assumed the posture of absent-minded professor.

Evr. I C 6, p. 94a.[51] Here is our translation of the three questions concerning Psalms:

1) With respect to the one who requested that I explain to him what I explained with respect to MYRRH AND ALOES AND CASSIA (Ps. 45:9b) MORE THAN IVORY PALACES (Ps. 45:9c), may the palaces, which are FROM ME be better; they MADE YOU REJOICE more than those who pay the reward of your worthy recompense. [An alternative explanation of] *myny* [treated above as meaning 'from me'] is simply 'FROM them' ['them' is implied but not stated in the verse, according to this second explanation]; it corresponds in meaning to[52] *mēhem* 'from them'.[53] [All of] which is to say: THEY [will have] MADE YOU REJOICE in those palaces, which they will give you in Paradise, pleasure palaces.[54]

2) Letters in some psalms in alphabetical order [i.e., the alphabetical acrostics in Pss. 9-10; 24; 34; 37; 111; 112; 119; 145]—I do not know its rationale.[55]

3) THEY DEALT CORRUPTLY; THEY BEHAVED ABOMINABLY (Ps. 53:2) [The subject of these verbs is] the Edomites who do everything to destroy Your Temple.[56]

---

[51] See Menachem Cohen, ed., *Mikra' ot Gedolot 'Haketer': Ezekiel* (Ramat-Gan: Bar-Ilan University Press, 2001), p. 321.

[52] Heb. *kĕmô*; see above, n. 27.

[53] See, e.g., Gen. 11:6; 19:9 and many more times in Biblical Hebrew. The latter interpretation of *myny* (standard Hebrew text reads instead *minnî*, which Mandelkern, p. 693 treats as an *hapax legomenon*) assumes that the form in question is the same biform of the preposition *min* that is attested twice in Judg. 5:14; twice in Isa. 46:3 and twenty-seven more times, mostly in Job; see Mandelkern, there.

[54] Cf. Rashi's commentary on Ps. 45:9, below, p. 351.

[55] This suggests that when Rashi himself writes *seliḥot,* which are alphabetical acrostics and when he includes his own name in the concluding lines of those poems, he is simply following a literary convention, and he does not seek to convey some additional information by means of the form. However, by stating that with respect to biblical psalms, "I do not know the reason," he leaves open the possibility that some or all of the biblical writers who composed alphabetical acrostics may actually have sought to convey some additional levels of meaning, of which Rashi, at least, was unaware.

[56] In his commentary at Ps. 14:1 and again at Ps. 53:1 Rashi suggests that these near duplicate psalms, both of which speak of a benighted person who thinks that there is no God, refer respectively to Nebuchadnezzar, who destroyed the First Temple, and Titus, who destroyed the Second Temple. Perhaps, Rashi refers to these two Temples by employing the plural *bytyk* here in the *responsum.* It is likewise possible that 'the Edomites' is emloyed here to refer to the Romans under the leadership of Titus. It is also possible that here in the *responsum* the plural *bytyk* 'Your houses' may refer to Jewish homes and synagogues and schools which were destroyed by the Christian Crusaders and that 'the Edomites' refers to those Christians.

NOT EVEN ONE (Ps. 53:4) among all his troops who will protest.[57]

Perhaps the most fascinating of Rashi's *responsa* touching upon biblical exegesis is Rashi's answer to R. Nathan b. Makhir concerning four possible meanings of the particle *kî* in Biblical Hebrew.[58] There we read as follows:

> As for this that R. Simeon b. Lakish said, "[The Hebrew particle] *kî* is employed in four meanings [*lĕšônôt*]: "if," "perhaps," "but," "for."[59] Now the question was raised as to why he [R. Simeon b. Lakish] inverted the order [of these meanings} and did not mention it [the subject of the four meanings of the Hebrew particle *kî*] according to the order in which they appear in Targum Onkelos to the Torah: "for," "perhaps," "but," "if."
>
> According to the formulation of his question I [Rashi] understood that thus he had heard from his teachers: [that R. Simeon b. Lakish meant that] the person who translated the Torah in Targum Onkelos [translated the particle *kî*] in four [distinct] meanings. Moreover, they [his teachers] explained to him [the enquirer] the four [meanings] which the translators [of Targum Onkelos] employed: *kî yiqqārē'* "if it happened" [where Targum Onkelos renders] *kî* "if" [Aram. *'î*] (Deut.

---

[57] An almost verbatim repetition of Rashi's commentary at Ps. 53:4d, q.v.; cf. also Rashi at Ps. 14:3a. It is difficult to say whether or not the phraseology chosen here is a deliberate conflation of those two comments of Rashi.

[58] Elfenbein, *Responsa* #251, pp. 293-297; see also Benjamin Menashe Levin, "Rashi's *Responsum* Concerning '*kî* is employed in four meanings'," in *Sefer Rashi*, ed. Yehudah Leib ha-Kohen Fishman Maimon (Jerusalem: Mossad Harav Kook, 1941), pp. 489-495 and the literature cited there, pp. 491-492. The ambiguity of the ubiquitous particle *kî* continues to fascinate biblical scholars and lexicographers to this day; see Anneli Aejmelaeus, "Function and Interpretation of *kî* in Biblical Hebrew," *JBL* 105 (1986), pp. 193-209 ; James Muilenberg, "The Linguistic and Rhetorical Usages of the Particle *kî* in the Old Testament," *HUCA* 32 (1961), pp. 135-160; Anton Schoors, "The Particle *kî* ," *Oudtestamentische Studien* 21 (1981), pp. 240-276; Barry Bandstra, "The Syntax of the Particle 'KY' in Biblical Hebrew and Ugaritic" (Ph.D. diss., Yale University, 1982); Bernard M. Levinson and Molly M. Zahn, "Revelation Regained: The Hermeneutics of *ky* and *im* in the Temple Scroll," *DSD* 9 (2002), pp. 295-346 and the extensive literature cited there; M. Weinberg, "Die Partikel *kî* nach der Auslegung dest Talmuds," *Jahrbuch der Jüdisch-Literarischen Gesellschaft* (*Sitz: Frankfurt a.M.*) 14 (1921), pp. 191-207; see also the extensive contributions to the subject by the Medieval Hebrew grammarians from Spain and Provence and the sages of Mainz cited in Levin, "Rashi's *Responsum* Concerning *kî*," pp. 489-491.

[59] With Elfenbein, *Responsa*, p. 293, n. 1, note that the quotation from R. Simeon b. Lakish is found in BT Rosh ha-Shanah 3a; Ta'anit 9a; Gittin 90a; see below; for medieval sources see Elfenbein, there.

22:6);[60] *kî to'mar* "perhaps you will say" [where Targum Onkelos renders] *dilmā'* "perhaps" (Deut. 7:17);[61] "rather you must open" [where Targum Onkelos renders] *'ellā'* "rather" (Deut. 15:8);[62] "for Aaron had breathed his last" [where Targum Onkelos renders] "for" [Aram. *dĕhā'*] (Num. 20:29).[63]

Now what bothers him [the enquirer] is that the order of the respective appearances of the respective meanings [of the Hebrew particle *kî* in the Torah is not thus [as in the list quoted above]. Already twenty years have passed during which I do not exegete them [the respective biblical usages of the Hebrew particle *kî*] in consonance with the Targum [i.e., the official Aramaic translation of the Torah] by Onkelos. The reason [for my deviation from Targum Onkelos] is that I was challenged with respect to the issue at hand by the question as to why he [R. Simeon b. Lakish] did not enumerate [as follows] "that" [Aram. *'arê*]; "when" [Aram. *kĕdê*] "indeed" [Aram. *bĕram*]; "perhaps" [Aram. *dilmā'*]. [In fact] most of them [the occurrences in the Pentateuch of the Hebrew particle *kî* we find translated into Aramaic in Targum Onkelos "that" [Aram. *'arê*]:[64]

[Typical of this treatment of Heb. *kî* by Targum Onkelos are the following]: "when they have" [Heb. *kî yihyeh lāhem*] (Ex. 18:15) [which Targum Onkelos renders] "when they have [Aram. *kĕdĕ hăwê lĕhôn*]; "indeed you laughed" [Heb. *kî ṣāḥaqtĕ*] (Gen. 18:16) [which Targum Onkelos renders] "indeed you laughed" [*bĕram ḥayyĕk*]; "for your tool" [Heb. *kî ḥarbĕkā* (Ex. 20:21) [which Targum Onkelos renders] *dĕlā'*[65] *tĕrîm ḥarbāk* "that you should not lift up your sword."

Now as for whoever renders into Aramaic "for he had breathed his last" (Num. 20:29) by means of *dĕhā'* 'that',[66] I am totally amazed

---

[60] Contrast Alexander Sperber, ed., *The Bible in Aramaic Based on Old Manuscripts and Printed Texts: Vol. I: The Pentateuch According to Targum Onkelos* (Leiden: E. J. Brill, 1959), which reads *'ărê*.

[61] Here again Sperber reads *'ărê* ; Bernard Grossfeld, *The Targum Onkelos to Deuteronomy*, Translated with Apparatus and Notes, The Aramaic Bible, vol. 9, ed. Martin McNamara (Wilmington, Delaware: Michale Glazier, 1988), p. 36 renders "if," reflecting Aramaic *'ărê* as in Sperber's edition based upon British Library Ms. Or. 2363, and he, like Sperber, *The Bible in Aramaic, vol. 1*, p. 304 cites *dylm'* as a variant reading (see Sperber and Grossfeld for details of the specific mss.). Neither Sperber nor Grossfeld refers either to Rashi's *responsum* discussed here or to BT Rosh ha-Shanah 3a.

[62] Here again Sperber reads *'ărê*.

[63] Here again Sperber reads *'ărê*.

[64] Cf. nn. 60-63, above; with reference to the twenty years see the discussion in Gelles, pp. 139-142; Gelles concludes that the *responsum* discussed here was written circa 1090; similarly, Isaac Maarsen, "Raschi's Kommentar zu Sprüche und Job," *MGWJ* 83 (1939), pp.443-444.

[65] Sperber, vol. 1, p. 123, q.v., reads *lā'*, but he calls attention to mss., which support the reading *dĕlā'*.

[66] With Sperber, vol. 1, note that this reading is attested in Ms. Sasoon 282

about them for one should not render it into Aramaic as *dĕhā' mît* "that
he died" unless one translates [earlier in that same verse] "the entire
congregation saw," for thus we say (BT Rosh ha-Shanah 3a), "Do not
read *wyr'w* 'they saw'[67] but rather *wyyr'w* 'they were afraid'[68] in accord with the view of R. S[imeon] ben Lakish." The reason [that rendering *kî* by means of *dĕhā'* 'that' requires that one also read later in
that verse *wyr'w* 'they saw']⁶⁹ is that if you read "they saw," the expression *dĕhā'* 'that' is not used with⁷⁰ "for he had breathed his last"
because it [i.e., "for he had breathed his last"] supplies a rationale
only for what is stated earlier [i.e.], why "they saw": [namely], "because Aaron died the pillar of cloud came upon his feet."⁷¹ On the
contrary [Heb. *'ellā'*], it [the particle *kî* in Num. 20:29] is employed
to mean 'that' [Heb. *'ăšēr*]. This is the usage reflected in⁷² "that [*kî*]
the tree was good for food" (Gen. 3:6); "she saw him that [*kî*] he was
beautiful" (Ex. 2:2); "that [*kî*] the people had fled" (Ex. 14:5); "that
[*kî*] Jacob had fled" (Gen. 31:22). Likewise here (in Num. 20:29), "They
saw that Aaron died, and they mourned him."⁷³ Now even when they
render into Aramaic "and they saw" I am still thoroughly amazed about
them. Why did they [the scribes responsible for certain recensions of
Targum Onkelos]⁷⁴ decide to make the Aramaic version of it [Num.

---

and in the *Biblia Hebraica* published at Ixar in 1490 while British Library Ms. Or.
2363, which is the basis for Sperber's edition of Targum Onkelos, supports Rashi's
judgment that the reading should be *'ărê*.

⁶⁷ Hence Targum Onkelos renders *waḥăzô*, which Bernard Grossfeld, *The Targum
Onkelos to Leviticus and the Targum Onkelos to Numbers*, Translated with Apparatus and
Notes, The Aramaic Bible, vol. 8, ed. Martin McNamara (Wilmington, Delaware:
Michale Glazier, 1988), p. 124 renders "realized."

⁶⁸ *Mirabile dictu*, neither *BH³* nor *BHS* nor the standard critical commentaries
reflect any awareness of this reading.

⁶⁹ So the standard Hebrew text.

⁷⁰ Heb. *'ēnô nōpēl 'al*; concerning this expression see below, p. 138, n. 9; p. 265,
n. 10; p. 296, n. 9; p. 320, n. 2; p. 339, n. 4; and see below, p. 75, n. 97.

⁷¹ This is to say that it no longer covered Aaaron's body; cf. Rashi's Pentateuch
Commentary at Num. 21:1 and Rashi's source, which is BT Rosh ha-Shanah 3a.
There it is explained that when Aaaron died the pillar of cloud (this is the term
employed in Ex. 13:22; 14:19; 33:9-10; Deut. 31:15) or as it is called in Rashi's
Commentary at Num. 21:1 and in BT Rosh ha-Shanah "clouds of Glory."

⁷² This entire clause is expressed in Rashi's Hebrew by the preposition *kĕmô*;
concerning this usage of Heb. *kĕmô* in Rashi's Commentary on Psalms see below,
pp. 140–141.

⁷³ Rashi here paraphrases Num. 20:30 which states, "all Israel mourned
Aaron...." Concerning the transitive use of the verbal root *bky* 'weep, cry' to mean
'mourn' see Gruber, *Aspects*, pp. 402-418.

⁷⁴ Cf. Elfenbein, *Responsa Rashi*, p. 293, n. 12; cf. also Alexander Sperber, *The
Bible in Aramaic Based on Old Mansucripts and Printed Texts, Vol. IVB: The Targum and
the Hebrew Bible* (Leiden: E. J. Brill, 1973), p. 414: "We have now the Targum
Onkelos in its various recensions (according to Volume I). Any reading taken from
any Onkelos-text is just as representative of Onkelos as another one from any other

20:29] different from many instances of *kî* in the Torah which like them provide a reason for something stated previously? For example, "He blessed the seventh day and He hallowed it because [*kî*] He rested thereon" (Gen. 2:3); "for He had not sent rain" (Gen. 2:5); "for from man she was taken" (Gen. 2:23); "for during his lifetime the earth was divided" (Gen. 10:25). With respect to each of these [cases of Biblical Heb. *kî* the [Aramaic] expression [Heb. *lāšôn*] *děhā'* is appropriate;[75] and so in many other cases.

Now, with respect to "On the contrary, you must open your hand" (Deut. 15:8), [the question arises as to] why did he [Onkelos] see fit to deviate from so many other cases of *kî* in the Torah in which [the respective clauses introduced by *kî* serve to contradict what is stated previously so as to say [Heb. *lē'mōr*] "it is not so but rather."[76] Examples of this latter usage include the following:[77]

"On the contrary, you laughed" (Gen. 18:15b), [in which Heb. *kî ṣāḥaqtě* means] "it is not so [as you Sarah stated in Gen. 18:15a, 'I did not laugh']; on the contrary [Heb. *'ellā'*] you laughed"; "You shall not worship their gods...on the contrary, you shall utterly destroy them..." (Ex. 23:24); "You shall not make a covenant...;[78] on the contrary, you shall tear down their altars... (Ex. 34:12-13).

Moreover [Heb. *wě*] all instances of *kî* joined tô *'im* as in[79] "on the contrary, you will bless me" (Gen. 32:27); "on the contrary, when he comes..." (Gen. 42:15); "on the contrary, according to my word" (1 Kgs. 17:1) are synonyms of "on the contrary" [Heb. *'ellā'*]. It is the same usage as is attested in[80] "On the contrary, you shall open..." (Deut. 15:8). [This usage of *kî*, which, as we have seen, is frequently attested in the Pentateuch] is attested also in the Hagiographa: "not only against the king; on the contrary against all the officials" (Esth. 1:16). Now what made them [the translators responsible for Targum Onkelos] see fit to treat differently [with respect to their Aramaic ren-

---

text. There does not exist such a thing as an 'authoritative' Onkelos-text; each one of the texts I used for the edition is to be considered as representing Onkelos just as the other text, no matter, whether we think of manuscripts or printed editions." In these words Sperber seems to concur with Rashi's judgment expressed in the *responsum* under consideration that the authorship of the so-called Targum Onkelos may be referred to either in the singular (referring to a a consensus among recensions of Targum Onkelos) or in the plural (referring to a variety of recensions, not all of which agree, for example, with Targum Onkelos as cited in BT Rosh ha-Shanah 3a).

[75] Heb. *nōpēl 'ălêhem*; see above, n. 70.

[76] Heb. *lō' kēn kî kēn*.

[77] The equivalent of this long clause in Rashi's Hebrew is a single word, *kěgôn*.

[78] Rashi's paraphrase of the Bible's "Beware lest you make a covenant...."

[79] Heb. *kěgôn*.

[80] Rashi expresses this entire clause by means of the single word *kěmô*; on this usage of the preposition *kěmô* in Rashi's Hebrew see above, n. 72.

dering of the Hebrew particle *kî*] *kî yiqqārē'* "if it happened" (Deut. 22:6) [in which they render the Hebrew particle *kî*] by means of the Aramaic word[81] *'î* unlike most instances of *kî* in the Torah which are [respectively, examples of] a word referring to possibility[82] [which is to say] "perhaps it happens; perhaps it does not happen" correspond-ing to every instance of *'im* in the Bible? [Examples of this usage of the Hebrew particle *kî* include the following]: "if it gores" (Ex. 21:28); "if it injures" (Ex. 21:35); "if one of you offers" (Lev. 1:2); "if you hear concerning one of your cities" (Deut. 13:13); "if you encounter" (Ex. 23:4); "if a man have" (Deut. 21:18); [and likewise] "if it happened" (Deut. 22:6).

Now I answer [Heb. *wĕ'ōmēr 'ănî*]: On the basis of this common understanding, they [the copyists responsible for common editions of Targum Onkelos] habitually translated them as follows: "*kî* you shall open" (Deut. 15:8) 'on the contrary' (*ellā'*); "*kî* you will say" (Deut. 7: 17), 'perhaps' (*dilmā'*); "*kî* it happened" (Deut. 22:6), 'if' (*'î*). When their teachers explained to them these four meanings of *kî* [includ-ing] "*kî* he had breathed his last" (Num. 20:29) [which they rendered by means of Aram.] *dĕhā'* 'that', with which we are dealing [here], they did not explain it for the purpose of thus translating them into Ara-maic. On the contrary, they interpreted them as though it were im-possible for them [the several biblical instances of the particle *kî*] to be employed except in these meanings, and they mentioned one ex-ample for each meaning. They [the copyists] took hold of them [the four distinct and conventional Aramaic renderings of Heb. *kî*], and they gave them their fixed places in the Targum. However, I say that all of them should be rendered *'arê*. Moreover, just as *kî* varies in mean-ing in Hebrew so does *'arê* vary in Aramaic in that it has those four [meanings]. Now Rabbi Simeon b. Lakish did not set out to teach about the literal meaning of the various usages of them [i.e., the par-ticle *kî*] and to declare to you: "there is *kî* which is employed to pro-vide a reason; and there is *kî* which is employed to contradict and to reconcile; and there is *kî* which constitutes 'a word referring to possi-bility' just like [the various nuances of] *'im* , to which I referred above. Moreover, there is *kî* , which is an interrogative particle; and the last usage of it [the particle *kî* which needs to be mentioned] is the mean-ing of "lest." For example, "*kî* you say to yourself" (Deut. 7:17). If you interpret it like every other *kî* in the Torah, the verse which follows will constitute a *non sequitur*. "You need have no fear of them" (Deut. 7:18) does not fit with[83] either the meaning *dĕhā'* 'that' or the mean-ing *'im* 'if'.

---

[81] The equivalent of this prepositional phrase in Rashi's Hebrew is *bilĕšôn*.

[82] These five words are expressed in Rashi's Hebrew by the two words *lĕšôn tālûy*.

[83] Heb. *'ên nōpēl 'ālāyw*; cf. nn. 70, 75 above.

[With respect to] *"kî* you say...many...you need have no fear of them" (Deut. 7:17-18), it follows logically[84] that if you do *not* say, you need to fear. The identical syntactical usage is reflected in[85] *"kî* you see your adversary's donkey" (Ex. 23:5). You have no choice [but to agree that in all of these cases the particle *kî*] serves as a synonym of [Heb. *lĕšôn*] *pen* 'lest'. The same meaning is reflected in[86] "you should not see another person's bull...."[87] Likewise here (in Ex. 23:5) ["*kî* you see your adversary's donkey..." means] "you should not see your adversary's donkey...and refrain...." Now if you interpret it[88] [i.e., the particle *kî* in Ex. 23:5] in any other way, the following verse will constitute a *non sequitur.*

The "word" of our Creator "is like... a hammer which shatters rock" (Jer. 23:29; it has a variety of meanings; but Scripture never loses its literal meaning.[89]

---

[84] The equivalent of these three words in the original language of Rashi's *responsum* is the Babylonian Jewish Aramaic particle *hā'*.

[85] Heb. *wĕkēn.*

[86] Heb. *kĕmô.*

[87] Ironically, just as Rashi here argues that in many cases the particle *kî* is to be treated as a negative particle equivalent to *lō'* at the beginning of Deut. 22:1 so does NJV treat the negative particle *lō'* at the beginning of Deut. 22:1 as though it were here synonymous with one of the more common nuances of *kî*, namely, 'if'.

[88] Heb. *tidrĕšennû* ; concerning Rashi's use of the the verb *dāraš* to mean simply 'interpret' without any negative connotation see below, p. 179, n. 2.

[89] Similarly Rashi also in his Pentateuch Commentary at Gen. 33:20 and at Ex. 6:9; similarly also Rashi in the introduction to his Commentary on Canticles. With Kamin, *Rashi's Exegetical Characterizaton*, pp. 180-182 note that the comparison of homonymous usages of words in Hebrew Scripture composed by a single divine author to the multiplicity of variegated pieces of stone produced by a single hammer striking a single rock derives from "a Tanna of the School of Rabbi Ishmael" quoted in BT Sanhedrin 34a. The basic point of the long *responsum* here translated and the aforementioned comments of Rashi as well as the Tannaitic source is the very simple truth, all too often lost upon some of the greatest Semitic lexicographers and biblical exegetes: the recognition of homonyms and their nuances is the main task of biblical exegesis. Almost every attempt to bring home this point in articles in journals of biblical exegesis and in papers read at conferences of societies of biblical exegesis is greeted by at least one learned scholar, having left her/his brains at home, asking the equivalent of, "Can we be certain that the ancient author knew the difference between a pen for confining animals and a writing implement or between an alphabetic symbol and a missive?" Consequently, the master pedagogue here procedes methodically and painstakingly to demonstrate the untenable consequences of avoiding this simple truth with respect to the variety of nuances of the ubiquitous particle *kî*. Rashi, here following the Tanna of the School of Rabbi Ishmael, indicates that there is no point whatsoever of talking about rational literal exegesis, as opposed to eisegesis and gibberish, without recognizing homonymity. Cf. Mayer I. Gruber, Review of *Away from the Father's House: The Social Location of the na'ar and na'arah in Ancient Israel* by Carolyn S. Leeb, in *JQR* , n.s. 93 (2003), pp. 20-23. The apparent paradox pre-

In addition[90] [the particle *kî* in] "for [*kî*] you will serve their gods"
(Ex. 23:33b)[91] serves in the meaning of *pen* 'lest' [as is demonstrated
by the immediate context]: "They should not dwell in your land lest
[*pen*] they cause you to sin against Me" (Ex. 23: 33a). [This is to say
that the literal meaning of the following clause (Ex. 23:33b) is "lest
you serve...." So we have learned from his words[92] that whoever needs
to interpret [*lidrōš*][93] *kî* by means of one of the four [Aramaic] synonyms [*lĕšōnōt*] must interpret it according to the synonym which is
appropriate to it [the specific case].[94] Now we have relied on his words
to interpret [*lidrōš*] the passage referring to [Heb. *bĕ*] the pillar of cloud
that came upon the feet of Aaron[95] when we said that [the particle *kî*
in the clause] "for he had breathed his last" serves to supply a rationale.[96] Now we have learned that two of the four [Aramaic] synonyms
of [Heb.] *kî* are equally appropriate[97] [with respect to Num. 20:29].
Whoever sets out to interpret in the one manner may [plausibly] interpret, and whoever sets out to interpret in the other manner may
[plausibly] interpret. On the basis of this observation we understand
the rational basis for the controversy between the School of Shammai
and Rabbi Akiba in Tractate Giṭṭin (Mishnah Giṭṭin 9:10): "The School
of Shammai opine that a man may not divorce his wife unless he find
her guilty of adultery....Rabbi Akiva opines [that a man may divorce
his wife] even if he found another woman more beautiful than her,
for it is stated in Scripture, 'if she fails to please him' (Deut. 24:1),
which means [Heb. *še-*] she is not beautiful, 'or if he found in her guilt
of adultery.'" [The rational basis of Rabbi Akiva's exegesis is] the fact

---

sented by 'literal meaning' that requires recognition of 'homonymity' is aptly expressed by the comparison with the variegated pieces of stone produced by a single
hammer. The point of this comparison is to bring home the simple truth that the
literal meaning of a word or phrase in context is often far removed from the primary dictionary definition of the the word or phrase. In fact, it often appears that
midrash in the sense of creative writing by the Tannaim and Amoraim, is inspired
by the sheer absurdity alluded to by the primary meaning of an idiom; the classic
illustration of this is the *midrash* on Gen. 12:5 quoted by Rashi in his commentary
there; cf. Kamin, *Rashi's Exegetical Characterizaton*, p. 184. Concerning the dire consequences of nineteenth century biblical lexicography's reticence to recognize
homonyms see Mayer I. Gruber, "Nuances of the Hebew Root '*ny*," in *Menachem
Cohen Festschrift*, ed. Shmuel Vargon (Ramat-Gan: Bar-Ilan University Press, 2004
[in Hebrew].

[90] Heb. *wĕ'ap*.

[91] NJV; contrast KJV: "for if".

[92] R. Simeon b. Lakish in BT Rosh ha-Shanah 3a; see above, n. 59.

[93] Concerning Rashi's use of the verbal root *drš* to mean 'interpret' see above
n. 88; and see also below, p. 179, n. 2.

[94] Heb. *lāšōn hannōpēl 'ālāyw*; see above, nn. 70, 75.

[95] I.e., Num. 20:29; see above.

[96] See above.

[97] Heb. *nōpĕlim 'al*.

that there is [in Biblical Hebrew the use of the particle] *'im* [plausbily translated by the School of Shammai in its primary meaning 'if'] as a substitute for *'ô* 'or'.[98] Examples [of this usage of the particle *'im* as a synonym of [Heb. *bimĕqôm*] *ô* 'or'] include "or graceful wing and feathers" (Job 39:13)[99] and likewise all [instances of the particle *'im*] which are juxtaposed to to the interrogative [prefixed particle *h*] : "open or [*'im*] fortified" (Num. 13:19b); "good or [*'im*] bad" (Num. 13:19a); Does a wild ass bray... or [*'im*] does a bull bellow" (Job. 6:5).[100]

Moreover, we have learnt that [the particle] *kî* can refer to possibility like the vast majoriy of instances of[101] *'im* in the Pentateuch. Rabbi Ammi relied on this fact when he said, "No oath imposed by judges[102] incurs liability for an oath of utterance of the lips, for it is stated in Scripture, 'or [*kî*] she [Heb. *nepeš* 'a person'] swears' (Lev. 5:4), [i.e.] of her own volition, which is to say [Heb. *kĕlômar*] 'if [*'im*] she swears' for it is not written [there in Lev. 5:4] 'if [*'im*] she should be adjured' or 'if [*kî*] they administer the oath to him' (BT Shebu'ot 49b) Now since it is treated by him [R. Ammi] as a crux, it is certain that it [Lev. 5:4] is an instance of a reference to the future.[103] The

---

[98] Rashi here paraphrases in Hebrew the Aramaic of the anonymous Talmud, which reads as follows: "With respect to what do they [the School of Shammai and Rabbi Akiba] disagree? [The answer to this rhetorical question is as follows]: With respect to the ruling of Resh Lakish. Indeed, Resh Lakish stated that [the particle] *kî* is employed in four meanings: 'if', 'perhaps', 'but', 'for'. The School of Shammai hold [Aram. *sābĕrî* 'opine', a translation of Mishnah's *'ōmĕrîm*, lit., 'they say', which supports our rendering 'opine'; cf. passim in Gruber, "The Mishnah as Oral Torah"], "*kî* he found in her guilt of adultery" (Deut. 24:1) [means] "'for' [Aram. *dĕhā'*] he found in her guilt of adultery" while Rabbi Akiba holds, "*kî* he found in her guilt of adultery" (Deut. 24:1) [means] "Or [Aram. *'i nammî*] he found in her guilt of adultery." In other words, according to the anonymous Babylonian Talmud, the School of Shammai interpret *kî* in Deut. 24:1 according to one of the four meanings delineated by R. Simeon b. Lakish while Rabbi Akiba, anticipating Rashi, holds that the nuances of *kî* in Biblical Hebrew are not limited to the four cited by R. Simeon b. Lakish and include also the meaning 'or'.

[99] Cf. Tur-Sinai, *The Book of Job*, p. 544: "or graceful pinions and feathers"; Rashi here anticipates Tur-Sinai's treatment of Job. 39:13b as the second part of a double rhetorical question.

[100] For other references to double rhetorical questions in Rashi's exegetical writings see Rashi at Jer. 14:22; 23:20; Job. 27:10; and see below, p. 556 n. 26.

[101] "Like the vast majority of instances of" corresponds in Rashi's Hebrew to *kĕkôl*, lit., 'like all instances of'. When one reads Rashi's assertion concerning the ubiquity of Biblical Heb. *'im* in the sense 'if' in the present context where this assertion is juxtaposed with the assertion that Biblical Heb. *'im* can also mean 'or', one cannot escape the conclusion that for Rashi as for Mishnah 'Erubin 7:11 (see BT 'Erubin 81a) Heb. *kol*, literally 'all' actually means 'many' just as the 'no' of the proverbial Middle Eastern bureaucrat or of the father or mother without advanced parenting skills means only 'maybe'.

[102] See Mishnah, Shebu'ot 6:1.

[103] Heb. *lĕšôn 'ātîd*. In other contexts this identical Hebrew exrpession may

same phenomenon [of the particle *kî* introducing a clause which refers to the future] is reflected in[104] "When you enter the land" (Lev.
23:10); "when it is too far" (Deut. 12:21); "when you build" (Deut.
22:8). [In the latter verse the particle *kî* must mean 'when' and refer
to the future] because it is not possible that you will not build.[105] [Like-
wise with respect to], "And when you ask, 'What shall we eat [during
the seventh year]?'" (Lev. 25:20), you will ask that in the future.[106]
Now most [instances of the particle]*kî* in the Pentateuch serve as a
synonym of [Heb. *mĕqôm*] *ka'ăšēr* 'when'. Here (Lev. 5:4) also *kî tiššābaʿ*
[means "when she swears"], and they who adjure you are the court.[107]
Therefore it is necessary to say, and in accord with the view of R.
Simeon b. Lakish, that there is [in addition to *kî* in the meaning 'when']
kî whose meaning is an expression referring to possibility [i.e., "if"].
Moreover, "she swears" here is an instance where *kî* is [an expression referring to] possibility for[108] she [the hypothetical person referred
to in Lev. 5:4] said [the oath] on her own volition. Likewise, *kî yiqqārē'*
"chance upon" (Deut. 22:6) excludes the case of one which was in-
vited. [Deuteronomy 22:6] means "if [*'im*] you chance upon"; [i.e],
"if it happened [*yiqreh*] to you." [It is][109] an expression referring to
chance [*miqreh*].

   With respect to all these instances I did not critically examine what
I heard from the mouths of my mentors, for in my humility I ran swiftly
to serve them.[110] However, we have endeavored to explain properly

---

denote 'future tense' as it does in Modern Hebrew; see, e.g., Rashi at Gen. 29:3
where, as in Modern Hebrew, *lĕšôn ʿātîd* 'future tense' is contrasted with both *lĕšôn*
ʿābar 'past tense' and *lĕšôn hôwweh* 'present tense'. In the present instance, however, the issue is not grammar, and the construct noun *lĕšôn* means 'expressing
referring to' (see below, pp. 144–145) rather than 'tense'.

   [104] The entire clause is expressed in Rashi's Hebrew by means of the preposition *kĕmô* ; cf. above, nn. 72, 80.

   [105] I.e., in this instance *kî* cannot refer to a possibility because there is no possibility that the people of Israel would enter the Land of Israel and not build houses
therein.

   [106] When you [the people of Israel] will have been settled in the land and come
to the end of the first sabbatical cycle.

   [107] See above.

   [108] Construing Rashi's *û* as, perhaps, an exegetical *waw*.

   [109] What Rashi states here can be said both of the particle *kî* and of the verbal root *qr'*, which here in Deut. 22:6 and in a number of other cases serves as a
synonym of the verb *qārāh* 'happen'; see the discussion in the commentary of R.
Samuel b. Meir at Ex. 1:10.

   [110] Here Rashi argues that having showed his mentors the greatest possible
honor during their respective lifetimes, he is entitled to contradict them when they
have misunderstood both Scripture and ancient Rabbinic exegesis. Heb. *ʿonyî* 'my
humility' or 'my poverty' refers here to Rashi's younger days when he first began
to engage in biblical exegesis, at least twenty years before the writing of the present
responsum; see above. In his younger days his intellectual poverty [*ʿonî*]relative to
the intellectual wealth of the mature Rashi may have justified his deference to his

the words[111] of the sages of Israel for I know them intimately. Their language is fluent and melifluous, and they spoke clearly. Now as for those who make a pretense of engaging in exegesis employing imprecise language,[112] because of the impatience[113] resulting from our intellectual poverty insofar as we have not stood in their [the Rabbinic sages'] council (cf. Jer. 23:18) [to learn how] to explain things correctly.[114]

Now if my dear friend should say, "There are additional usages of the particle[115] *kî*, for most of them [the attestations of the particle *kî* in Biblical Hebrew] serve as synonyms of[116] *'ăšēr* 'that'. Examples of this usage include the following:[117] "that the tree was good" (Gen. 3:6) "that he was beautiful" (Ex. 2:2); "that the people was in flight" (Ex. 14:5); "that Jacob had fled" (Gen. 31:22); "that he had not prevailed against him" (Gen. 32:26); "that they were naked" (Gen. 3:7). In additon, there are instances [of the particle *kî*] serving as a synônym ôf *ka'ăšēr* 'when'. Examples of this usage include the following:[118] "when Pharaoh's horse" (Ex. 15:19); "It so happened when we arrived" (Gen. 43:21); "it so happened when we came back" (Gen. 44:24); "it may happen when the Egyptians see you" (Gen. 12:12). All of these [examples of the particle *kî* in the meaning *'ăšēr* 'that'] belong to the se-

---

teachers, whom he had surpassed by the time he wrote the present *responsum*.

[111] Our rendering of Heb. *lĕyaššēb dābār 'al 'ôpnāyw* is derived from Banitt, *Rashi: Interpreter of the Biblical Letter*, p. 48; q.v.

[112] With Elfenbein note that the expression 'imprecise language' is based upon *lĕšôn 'illĕgîm* in Isa. 32:4; note also that the expression *ṣaḥ* 'fluent' is also derived from that verse. It is likely, therefore, that the expression *miharti* 'I ran' in the previous line was also inspired by *nimhārîm* 'thoughtless' in that same verse. The point which Rashi seeks to bring home is that slavish repetition of the wrong ideas of one's mentors is not humility; it is foolishness.

[113] Heb. *qôṣer rûaḥ* , the expression found in Ex. 6:9 where it is commonly translated 'broken spirit'. There it refers to the inability of the Hebrew slaves in Egypt to respond to Moses' account of the theophany described in Ex. 6:2-8. For Rashi, as for biblical exegetes in modern times as well, it is frustrating that poverty of thought no less than the broken spirit of political and economic oppression makes persons impatient both to hear anything new and to pay attention to the exciting (to the scholar but not always to her/his audience/peers) rediscovery of the antique.

[114] Heb. *lĕhôšîb dābār 'al mĕkônô*, a synonym of *lĕyaššēb dābār 'al 'ôpnāyw* ; see Banitt, *Rashi: Interpreter of the Biblical Letter*, p. 48; and see above, n. 111.

[115] Heb. *lĕšôn*.

[116] Synonym of, frequently expressed by the term *lĕšôn* (see below, p. 143), is here expressed by Heb. *bimqôm* 'in place of'.

[117] These seven words in English correspond to Heb. *kĕgôn*.

[118] These seven words in English correspond to Heb. *kĕmô* ; comparsion with the previous note leads, inevitably to the conclusion, that, in additon to its variety of other meanings (see below, p. 140), the preposition *kĕmô* in Rashi's Hebrew can also be a substitute for *kĕgôn*.

mantic field of *'im* 'if' for there is [the particle] *'im*, which serves as a synonym of[119] *'ǎšēr* 'that'.

Examples of this usage include the following:[120] "She is one; therefore I say,[121] 'He destroys the blameless and the guilty' *'im* 'that' a scourge suddenly brings death" (Job. 9:22-23). [In the latter passage the clause] "*'im* a scourge suddenly brings death" [corresponds in meaning to] "*'ǎšēr* 'that' a scourge suddenly brings death"; she [i.e. 'the scourge...' referred to in Job. 9:23a] is the one [referred to in Job. 9:22a]: "who destroys the blameless and the guilty." [Since, in Rashi's view Job. 9:22a-23a constitutes a nominal sentence whose subject is 'she' in v. 22a and whose predicate is 'one' in that same half of a verse while the clause introduced by *'im* constitutes an adjectival clause modifying the predicate nominative 'one'] it is impossible to interpret[122] [it, the particle *'im*] as 'a word referring to possibility'.[123] [Other instances of *'im* meaning 'that' include the following]: "that his days are determined" (Job. 14:5); "that I look forward to Sheol being my home" (Job. 17:13). Now *'im* , which serves as a synonym for *ka'ǎšēr* 'when' [is exemplified by] "*wĕ'im* you bring a meal offering of first fruits." Whether you like it or not, [the particle *'im* there] is not [a word referring to] possibility, for, in fact, the meal offering of the sheaf of new grain [Heb. *hā'ōmēr*][124] is an obligation.[125] Its meaning [i.e., the meaning of Lev. 2:14] is "when you bring..." The same usage is reflected in "*wĕ'im* there will be a jubilee" (Num. 36: 4) [which means] "and when [*wĕka'ǎšēr*] there will be a jubilee. [In all of these cases the particle] *'im* is not [an expression referring to] possibility. And thus we learned in a Tannaitic source: "R. Simeon [b. Johai] opines that every single instance of [the particle] *'im* [in Hebrew Scripture] is [an expression referring to choice [Heb. *rĕšût*] except for three instances: "when you bring" (Lev. 2:14); "when you lend

---

[119] The Hebrew clause is *mĕsammēš bilšôn*, which corresponds semantically to the clause *mĕsammĕšîm bimqôm* , referred to in n. 116 above. The interchangeability of the two clauses demonstrates the interchangeability of the two expressions *bimqôm* and *bilšôn*.

[120] See above, n. 118.

[121] Heb. *'āmartî* so MT; here in the *responsum* Elfenbein reads without comment *'āmartem,* which can be construed as a precative perfect meaning, "you should say."

[122] Heb. *lidrôš;* concerning Rashi's use of the verbal root *d-r-š* in the sense 'interpret' without any negative connotations see the discussion, below, p. 179, n. 2; see also above, nn. 88, 93.

[123] Heb. *lĕšôn tālûy.*

[124] See Rashi's commentary at Lev. 2:14, which connects the offering mentioned there with the obligatory "sheaf of waving" offered on the second day of the Feast of Unleavened Bread according to the Pharisaic-Rabbinic understanding of Lev. 23:15.

[125] I.e., the opposite of 'possibility'; see Rashi at Lev. 2:14.

money" (Ex. 22:24); "when an altar of stone" (Ex. 20:22).[126] [The latter biblical text means] "when you will build for me an altar" because ultimately it will be built in accord with what is stated in the Bible, "You shall build it of unhewn stones" (Deut. 27:6). The same usage [of '*im* meaning 'when' rather than 'if'] is reflected in "'*im* someone uproots him from his place" (Job. 8:18), [which means] "when someone uproots him from his place". This is not a matter of possibility because, after all, he [Bildad] speaks about the fate of those who forget God (see Job. 8:13).

---

[126] Rashi's source is Mekilta at Ex. 22:24

D. Rashi as Storyteller*

In his Hebrew article on stories which Rashi retells in his commentary on the Talmud, Luis Landa delineates eighteen distinct narratives found either in the Talmud commentaries commonly accepted as being from the pen of Rashi or in Talmud commentaries concerning which there is a reasonable consensus that Rashi wrote these as well.[1] Landa takes into consideration the generally accepted view that the commentaries assigned to Rashi in the standard editions of BT on Taʿanit and Nedarim are not, in fact, from the pen of Rashi.[2] However, Landa relies on J. P. Guttel, who argues that, in fact, the so-called Pseudo-Rashi on Taʿanit is based upon a commentary written by Rashi himself.[3] Landa also includes in his list of eighteen stories also the narrative of "Rab Safra and the Buyer" in the commentary on the inner margin of BT Makkot 24a, notwithstanding the note in the Vilna edition of BT that from p. 21a through the

---

*Long after I had completed this chapter, Prof. Jacob Neusner shared with me prior to their publication his series of groundbreaking studies on Rabbinic narrative found in *Rabbinic Narrative: A Documentary Perspective,* Brill Reference Library of Judaism (4 vols.; Leiden: Brill, 2003). *Inter alia,* Neusner shows that in Rabbinic literature the Hebrew term *maʿăśeh* usually denotes 'legal precedent' and only rarely denotes 'narrative'. Not surprisingly, I found that the stories [*maʿăśîm;* plural of *maʿăśeh*] which experts in the field of Medieval Hebrew Literature discovered in Rashi's Commentary on the Babylonian Talmud, are mostly short accounts of legal precedents and only rarely compositions worthy of the name narrative. This fact should not be surprising since, after all, Rashi's language is Rabbinic Hebrew rather than Yiddish in which the Hebrew loanword *mayse* commonly denotes 'story'. Yiddish, of course, did not yet exist when Rashi composed his commentary on BT; see below.

[1] Luis Landa, "Rashi's Stories in the Rashi Commentary Printed in the Babylonian Talmud," *Eshel Beer Sheva* 3 (1986), pp. 101-17 (in Hebrew).

[2] Ibid., p. 101, n. 2; see also Grossman, *The Early Sages of France,* p. 216.

[3] Landa, p. 101, n. 2; see J. P. Guttel, "Remarques sur le Pseudo-Rasi' de Taʿanit," *REJ* 125 (1966), pp. 93-100; Eli Yassif, *The Hebrew Folktale: History, Genre, Meaning* (Jerusalem: Mossad Bialik/Ben-Gurion University of the Negev Press, 1994), p. 288 (in Hebrew) takes it for granted that the story found in the commentary printed in the inner margins of BT at Taʿanit 8a was written by Rashi; contrast David Halivni, "The First Three Pages of the Commentary on Taʿanit Attributed to Rashi," *Sinai* 43 (1958), pp. 211-222 (in Hebrew); id.,"Concerning the Identity of the Commentary on Taʿanit Assigned to Rashi," *Sinai* 44 (1959), pp. 23-25 (in Hebrew); see also Grossman, *The Early Sages of France,* p. 216, n. 275 and the extensive literature cited there.

end of BT Makkot, i.e., p. 24b, the commentary was written by R. Judah b. Nathan rather than Rashi.[4]

Landa points out that for six of the eighteen stories, i.e., 33.333%, of the stories, Rashi's Talmud commentary is the primary source in Hebrew.[5] These six stories are seen to represent a significant contribution of Rashi to the corpus of medieval Hebrew *belles lettres*.[6] Consequently, Rashi is now recognized in university curricula in Medieval Hebrew Literature as a prose writer worthy of note.[7] Landa admits that two of the six stories are found in the commentary assigned to Rashi in the standard printings of Babylonian Talmud, Tractate Nedarim.[8] The latter commentary, it is now generally agreed, belongs to the "Mainz Commentary".[9] Therefore, our English translation of four stories Rashi contributed to the corpus of Medieval Hebrew prose narrative is included here to round out the picture of the versatile Rashi, better known as community leader, *yeshivah* head, *decisor,* and liturgical poet, as well as commentator on Bible, Talmud, and liturgical poetry. Here follow our annotated translations of the four stories, which fulfill two important criteria: 1) the only Hebrew source of the story is Rashi's Commentary on the Babylonian Talmud; and 2) these stories are found in those sections of the commentary on the inner margins of the standard editions of the Babylonian Talmud, which are universally regarded as having been written by Rabbi Solomon Yitzhaki.

I. In BT Qiddushin 80b there is a discussion as to whether or not grief sufficiently supresses what moderns would call the libido (Heb.

---

[4] See Grossman, *The Early Sages of France*, p. 216, n. 275 and the literature cited there.

[5] Landa, p. 106.

[6] One cannot help but wonder if one of the reasons that Rashi came to be perceived as a writer of fiction on the basis of some four anecdotes, all but one of which is about two to three lines in length, is the fact that three out of the four stories are comments on a Talmudic text which refers to *maʿăśeh.*. This term clearly means 'legal precedent' in each of its three Talmudic contexts. However, in the East European *yeshivah* world, the place of origin of Bialik and his latter-day spiritual heirs who have sought to treat ancient and medieval sacred Jewish texts as *belles lettres*, the term in question was read as Yiddish *mayse* meaning 'story, legend'.

[7] See, for example, Yassif, *The Hebrew Folkltale*, pp. 288-90; id., "Sefer ha-Ma'asim," *Tarbiz* 53 (1984), pp. 427-428 (in Hebrew); cf. Urbach, *Tosafot*, p. 137.

[8] Landa, p. 106.

[9] See Grossman, *The Early Sages of France*, p. 216, n. 275 and the literature cited there.

yēṣer) so that a mixed group of men and women may carry a dead infant to the cemetary without engaging in illicit sex on the way. By association[10] BT points out

> *ma'ăśeh* 'legal precedent/story': Ten [men] carried her [i.e., an unnamed woman] in a bier.[11]

Rashi comments as follows:

> TEN MEN TOOK HER [a certain woman] OUT IN A BIER relying on the assumption [of the bystanders] that she was dead. They had sex[12] with her, and she was [in fact] a married woman.[13]

II. In BT Sanhedrin 19a we read as follows:

> Rammi bar Abba reported that Rabbi Jose [b. Halafta][14] legislated[15] in Sepphoris that a woman should not go around in the market place

---

[10] It has long been taken for granted that one of the major organizing principles of Rabbinic literature beginning with its first document, the Mishnah, is what is now commonly called "free association"; see, for example, Hermann L. Strack, *Introduction to the Talmud and Midrash*, (Philadelphia: Jewish Publication Society, 1931), pp. 24-25; similarly, more recently, Adin Steinsaltz, *Talmud: The Steinsaltz Edition: A Reference Guide* (New York: Random House, 1989), p. 7. However, Jacob Neusner, *How Adin Steinsaltz Misrepresents the Talmud: Four False Propositions from his "Reference Guide"*, University of South Florida Studies in the History of Judaism, no. 190 (Atlanta: Scholars Press, 1998), pp. 221-253 argues most convincingly that "free association" is a thoroughly inappropriate designation for the associative principle of organization, employed in the basic documents of Rabbinic literature. Günter Stemberger, *Introduction to the Talmud and the Midrash*, trans. and ed. Markus Bockmuehl (2^d ed.; Edinburgh: T. & T. Clark, 1996), pp. 122-124, stresses the predominantly thematic arrangement of Mishnah, frequently interrupted by associations of substance, form, or the tradent's identity.

[11] Heb. *miṭṭāh;* the regular term in Rabbinic Heb. for 'bier'; see dictionaries.

[12] Heb. *qilqĕlû.* The verb *qilqēl* in this sense is ellipsis for *qilqēl ma'ăśayw* 'he perverted his behavior', i.e., 'he acted perversely', which is the semantic equivalent of Biblical Heb. *hišḥit darkô* in Gen. 6:12 (and cf. Qimḥi at Isa. 1:4); see Jastrow, *Dict.*, p. 1382.

[13] This means that the act was not simply fornication, which may be less than virtuous behavior, but adultery, which is a capital offense; see, e.g., Lev. 20:10; Deut. 22:22.

[14] The law in question is one of three established by Rabbi Jose at Sepphoris according to the testimony of Rammi bar Abba in BT Sanhedrin 19a. Rabbi Jose, the reputed author of Seder Olam (see below, p. 278, n. 6), was born at Sepphoris. In addition, he is said to have established a school there. It was at Sepphoris also that his father is reported to have legislated; see T. Ta'anit 1:13.

[15] Heb. *hitqîn* ; on this usage see Gruber, "The Mishnah as Oral Torah," pp. 117-119; see also Martin S. Jaffee, "The Taqqanah in Tannaitic Literature: Jurisprudence and the Construction of Rabbinic Memory," *JJS* 41 (1990), pp. 204-225.

with her child following her because of a *ma'áśeh* 'legal precedent'.

Rashi comments as follows:

WITH HER CHILD FOLLOWING HER. Her little son should not walk behind her but in front of her. BECAUSE OF A LEGAL PRE-CEDENT: Licentious men kidnapped him [her child] from behind her back, and they put him in a house.[16] When she [the mother] returned home and did not see him she began to cry out and to weep. One of them [the licentious kidnappers] came and said, "Come, and I will show him to you." She entered his house after him, and they had sex[17] with her.

III. The Story of Beruria[18]

It is reported in BT Avodah Zarah 18b that R. Meir (fl. c. 135-175 C.E.) suddenly fled from Palestine to Babylonia. It is further reported that it is a matter of controversy as to why he did so:

---

[16] So *editio princeps* of BT (Venice: Bomberg, 1520-23). The Vilna (Vilna: Romm, 1880-1886) edition reads "his house," which makes no sense in context. So much for the attempt within the academic field of Hebrew literature to create a subdiscipline devoted to the stories attributed to Rashi in the Vilna edition of the Babylonian Talmud!

[17] Heb. *'innû 'ôtāh;* the very same expression that occurs in this meaning in Deut. 22:24 with respect to consensual sex initiated by a man; on the use of the verbal root *'ny* in the meaning 'have sex' in Biblical Heb., Rabbinic Heb. and in Rashi's Commentary on Genesis see Mayer I. Gruber, "A Reexamination of the Charges Against Shechem son of Hamor," *Beit Mikra* 44 (1999), pp. 119-127 (in Hebrew); id., "Nuances of the Hebrew Root 'ny," in *Menachem Cohen Festschrift*, ed. Shmuel Vargon (Ramat-Gan: Bar-Ilan University Press, 2004); Noah Hakam, "'*nh*," *Tarbiz* 69 (2000), pp. 441-444; Amos Frisch, "*wĕ'anĕtāh*," *Tarbiz* 69 (2000), pp. 445-447.

[18] See David Goodblatt, "The Beruriah Traditions," *JJS* 26 (1975), pp. 68-86; see also Daniel Boyarin, *Carnal Israel* (Berkeley: University of California Press, 1993), pp. 181-96 and the extensive literature cited there. Boyarin, there, p. 190 reads "the text of Beruria's end [described by Rashi] as being generated specifically in the intertextual web of the Babylonian talmudic tradition." Boyarin's "theory is that Beruria's story is generated as the dark double of the story of her sister, out of the matrix of the Babylonian understanding of R. Eliezer [M. Sotah 3:4]—that there is an essential nexus between a woman studying Torah and the breakdown of the structure of monogamy" (Boyarin, there, p. 191). What Boyarin calls "the intertextual web of Talmudic tradition" is, in fact, the perception that all persons quoted on the page of the Vilna edition of the Babylonian Talmud— the Tannaim, the Amoraim and the medieval exegetes printed in a distinct typeface in the margins—were all contemporaries participating in a symposium or dinner table conversation. Unfortunately, this perception of what takes place on a page of Talmud is accepted and propogated by persons with some philological and historical training who call it "intertextuality". Far more fruitful is the en-

There are some who say that it was because of the *maʿaśeh* 'what happened with' Beruria.

Rashi comments as follows:

AND THERE ARE SOME WHO SAY[19] THAT IT WAS BECAUSE OF WHAT HAPPENED WITH BERURIA. Once she made fun of the sages' dictum (Qiddushin 80a), "Women are light headed." He [Rabbi Meir, her husband] said to her, "I swear by your life that ultimately[20] you will agree with their words." He [R. Meir] commanded one of his disciples to test her with respect to fornication. He [the disciple] pressured her for many days until she agreed. When she came to her senses she strangled herself. Rabbi Meir ran away because of [his] shame [at what he had perpetrated].

IV. The Fox and the Wolf

It is noted in BT Sanhedrin 38b that R. Johanan [b. Napha (d. 279 C.E.)] reported that R. Meir had in his repertoire three hundred fox fables, of which we [i.e., the collective memory of Rabbinic Ju-

deavor of Haim Schwarzbaum, *The Mishle Shuʿalim (Fox Fables) of Rabbi Berechiah Ha-Nakdan: A Study in Comparative Folklore and Fable Lore* (Kiron: Institute for Jewish and Arab Folklore Research, 1979), p. 411, n. 21 to see Rashi's Beruria story as but one of many examples found in world literature of what folklorists call Motif K 2052.4, the virtuous woman who falls into temptation. Neither Beruria nor the Babylonian Talmud nor R. Eliezer should be blamed for Rashi's employing a well-known folklore motif to answer the exegetical question, "What was the case with respect to Beruria that led R. Meir to run away from Palestine to Babylonian?" In the same vein, Rashi utilizes a story told in his own time in his attempt to supply another missing story associated with R. Meir in the commentary at BT Sanhedrin 38b cited below. As for Boyarin's "intertextual web," Goodblatt, "The Beruriah Tradtions," p. 26, eighteen years before Boyarin's learned treatise, observed: "All the anecdotes which portray Beruriah as possessing an advanced education are of Babylonian Amoraic origin....it was in Sassanian Babylonia that the existence of a woman learned in rabbinic tradition was a possibility, however uncommon. The remaining Beruriah pericopae, which come from various times and places including second century Palestine, do not require us to ascribe to her an advanced rabbinic education." See also Tal Ilan, *Integrating Women into the Second Temple History* (Tübingen: J.C.B. Mohr, 1999), pp. 189-94; Ilan (there, p. 189) concurs with the folklorists in seeing Rashi's Beruria story as "Rashi's personal contribution"; moreover, she argues (there, p. 194) that Rashi's "story of Beruriah in contrast with [BT] Qiddushin confirms rather than denies the veracity of the statement that women are light-headed."

[19] *Editio princeps* reads here "And there is one who says."

[20] Heb. *sôpēk*; lit., 'your end'; this expression corresponds functionally to New Zealand English 'at the end of the day' and Standard English, 'in the long run'.

daism] have only three.[21] [The three tales, continues R. Johanan, were presented in the form of a *midrash*, which quotes the following three biblical verses]: "Parents ate sour grapes, and children's teeth are in pain" (Ezek. 18:18); "Scales are honest, and weights are honest" (Lev. 19:35); "A virtuous one is rescued from trouble, and a wicked one is below him" (Prov. 11:8).[22]

Apparently, R. Johanan and the anonymous author/editor[23] of the Babylonian Talmud relied on the collective memory to preserve all three of R. Meir's fables associated with the three biblical verses cited by R. Johanan. Unfortunately, none of the tales has so far been recovered from ancient manuscripts. Consequently, Rashi in his Commentary at BT Sanhedrin 38b, supplies the following fable in which the fox, like the early Amoraim of Genesis Rabbah,[24] preaches a sermon utilizing verses from Prophets, Torah and Hagiographa:[25]

---

[21] Schwarzbaum, *Mishle Shuʿalim*, p. 556, n. 10 suggests that BT assumes that its original target audience is familiar with three of the fables. Moreover, he suggests, there, n. 11 that the formula "three hundred fox fables" derives from the biblical account of Samson's having caught three hundred foxes (Judg. 15:4); on the motif of "three hundred fox fables" in Rabbinic literature see Schwarzbaum, there, pp. xxii-xxiv.

[22] Both my highly literal translation of Prov. 11:8 and my tendentious rendering of the two clauses from Lev. 19:35 are designed to reflect the meanings the quotations are given in the story told by Rashi.

[23] Concerning the authorship/editing of the Babylonian Talmud see the extensive discussion in Jacob Neusner, *Where the Talmud Comes from: A Talmudic Phenomenology*, South Florida Studies in the History of Judaism, no. 120 (Atlanta: Scholars Press, 1995), pp. 1-10; see also Richard Kalmin, *Sages, Stories, Authors, and Editors in Rabbinic Babylonia*, Brown Judaic Studies, no. 300 (Atlanta: Scholars Press, 1994); David Kraemer, *The Mind of the Talmud* (New York: Oxford University Press, 1990).

[24] See Jacob Mann, *The Bible as Read and Preached in the Old Synagogue*, vol. 1 (Cincinnati: By the author, 1940), p. 12 concerning this aspect of Genesis Rabbah.

[25] Unfortunately, oral exegetical tradition did not preserve any of R. Meir's fox fables. Hence, as pointed out by Schwarzbaum, *Mishle Shuʿalim*, p. 552, R. Hai Gaon (939-1038) and Rashi (1040-1105) each supplies a distinct fox fable, current in his time and place, 10th-11th cent. Iraq and 11th-12th century France respectively. Following Zipporah Shukry, "The Wolf and the Fox in the Well," *Laographia* 22 (1963), pp. 491-97, Schwarzbaum stresses the fact that the mechanism of drawing water from a well, which is central both to the plot of Rashi's version and the exegesis of the verses from Leviticus and Proverbs [my point, not Schwarzbaum's], "using two counterbalanced buckets rather than lowering and raising a bucket by hand, as prevalent in the Talmudic age, testifies to the Mediaeval-European setting of our fable. In addition, reference to the 'courtyard of the Jews' and his description of the greedy wolf, also point to the mediaeval European background of the fable under consideration." Hai Gaon's substitution of a medieval Middle Eastern fable and Rashi's substitution of a medieval European

"PARENTS ATE SOUR GRAPES (Ezek. 18:18)." The fable[26] is as
follows: The fox deceitfully persuaded the wolf to enter the Jewish
quarter [of the town] on the Eve of the Sabbath and to prepare with
them what is required for [the three festive Sabbath] meal[s] and to
eat with them on the Sabbath. However, when he was about to enter
[the Jewish quarter] they [the Jews] beat him with clubs. He [the wolf]
went [with intent] to kill the fox. He [the fox] explained to him [the
wolf]: "They only beat you because of your father who once went to
help them [the Jews] to prepare a meal and he ate every good dish."
He [the wolf] asked him [the fox], "Am I being beaten up because of
my father?" He [the fox] replied, "Yes. 'The parents ate sour grapes...'
(Ezek. 18:18), but come with me and I will show you a place to eat to
satiety." He came to a well at whose edge was located a tree on which
a rope was hung, and at each end of the rope was tied one of two
pails. The fox entered the upper pail so that it became heavy and
descended below while the [previously] lower pail ascended. The wolf
asked him [the fox], "Why do you enter there?" He [the fox] replied,
"Here there is meat and cheese to eat to satiety." He [the fox] showed
him [the wolf] the reflection of the moon in the water. It was a round
image that looked like round cheese. He [the wolf] asked him [the
fox], "How can I descend?" He [the fox] said to him [the wolf], "Get
into the upper pail." He [the wolf] entered so that it became heavy
and descended while the pail in which the fox was located ascended.
He [the wolf] said to him [the fox], "How can I ascend?" He [the
fox] said to him [the wolf], "A virtuous one is rescued from trouble,
and a wicked one is under him" (Prov. 11:8). Is it not thus written [in
the Torah], " Scales are honest and weights are honest" (Lev. 19:35)?

The lesson taught here by Rashi, if not by R. Meir, is as follows:
"You, Mr. Wolf, do not ascend. You, being wicked, stay down (Prov.
11:8) in the well. Is it not written in the Torah, "Scales are honest
and weights are honest"? To put it another way, the story which

---

fable for the lost 2nd century C.E. fable may rightly be compared to the practice
discussed by Thucydides, *History of the Peloponnesian War Books I and II* with an English
Translation by Charles Foster Smith, Loeb Classical Library (rev. ed.; Cambridge,
Mass.: Harvard University Press/ London: William Heinemann Ltd., 1928), pp.
38-39 (Book I. xxii.1-2): "As to the speeches that were made by different men,
either when they were about to begin the war or when they were already engaged
therein, it has been difficult to recall with strict accuracy the words actually spoken, both for as regards that which I myself heard, and for those who from various other sources have brought me reports. Therefore the speeches are given in
the language in which, as it seemed to me, the several speakers would express, on
the subjects under consideration, the sentiments most befitting the occasion, at
the same time I have adhered as closely as possible to what was actuallly said."
[26] Heb. *mashal*.

Rashi places in the mouth of R. Meir reaffirms the assertion of the Prophet Ezekiel speaking in the name of God in Ezek. 18 to the effect that the oft-repeated proverb, "Parents ate sour grapes, and children's teeth are in pain" does not reflect reality. Reality, according to Ezekiel and according to R. Meir and according to Rashi is that, contrary to appearances, justice ultimately does prevail.[27]

Missing from Landa's list of stories told by Rashi in his Commentary on the Babylonian Talmud is Rashi's famous explanation as to why women must light the Hanukkah lamp. In BT Shabbat 23a it is recorded:

A woman certainly should kindle [the Hanukkah lamp] for R. Joshua b. Levi[28] said, "Women are obligated with respect to the [kindling of the] Hanukkah lamp because they were also involved in that miracle.

Rashi's comment on THEY WERE INVOLVED IN THAT MIRACLE reads as follows:

Greeks decreed that all virgins who got married must first have intercourse with the ruler,[29] and the miracle was performed by a woman.

---

[27] Concerning the assertion in Rabbinic literature that justice does prevail within historical time on this earth see Jacob Neusner, *How the Rabbis Liberated Women*, University of South Florida Studies in the History of Judaism, no. 191 (Atlanta: Scholars Press, 1998), pp. 80-83.

[28] One of the most prominent of the Palestinian Amoraim of the first post-Tannaitic generation; he lived in the 1st half of the 3d cent. C.E.

[29] The Hebrew term for 'official' in Rashi's typically telegraphic version of the narrative is *ṭipsar*, which is attested in Biblical Hebrew in Jer. 51:27 where NJV renders the relevant clause, "Designate a marshal against her". The Hebrew term (attested also in the plural *wĕṭapsarayik* 'and your marshals' in Nah. 3:17) is derived from Akk. *ṭupšarru*, which, in turn, is derived from Sumerian *DUB.SAR* 'scribe'. The term *ṭipsar* is one of several terms for 'official' in Hebrew Scripture, whose primary meaning is 'scribe'. This semantic development probably reflects the fact that in Western Asia in the Iron Age the preponderance of scribes in governmental bureaucracy made 'scribe' and 'official' synonymous. *Mutatis mutandi*, the preponderance of clergymen in the medieval English bureaucracy explains the Modern English term 'clerk', originally a specialized form of 'cleric', i.e., 'clergyman'. Other Biblical Hebrew terms for 'official' whose literal meaning is 'scribe' include *šōṭēr* (Ex. 5:6, 10; Deut. 16:18; etc.; related to Akk. *šaṭāru* 'to write') and *sōper* (2 Kgs. 18:18, 37; Ez. 7:6, 11; etc.). Recently, Alain Boureaux, *The Lord's First Night: The Myth of the Droit de Cuissage*, trans. from French by Lydia G. Cochrane (Chicago: University of Chicago Press, 1998) demonstrated that the concept of *jus prima noctis*, lit., 'the right of the first night', i.e., the idea that medieval lords demanded and were given by law the privilege of of deflowering their vassals' virgin brides is pure fantasy.

This laconic summary of a medieval story about antiquity is rather typical of Rashi's so-called stories cited by Landa and others and here translated and annotated. This last story is a condensation of one of the medieval Jewish versions of the Story of Judith, which, like many other stories derived from Second Temple Jewish litera- ture, begin to circulate among the Jews of France a generation be- fore Rashi.[30] A more comprehensible version, which may closely resemble the version, which Rashi summarizes, was published by Jellinek. The relevant sections of the story read as folows:

> In the period of the evil Greek kingdom[31] they decreed... , and they also decreed that as for whoever marries a woman, she should have intercourse first with the official[32] and afterwards return to her hus- band. They [the Jews] obeyed this rule for three years and eight months until the daughter of Johanan the High Priest was married. When they brought her to that ruler, she dishevelled her hair and tore her garments and stood naked before all the people. Thereupon Judah and his brothers were filled with anger at her, and they said, "Remove her for death by burning[33] because she has been so arro- gant as to be naked in front of all this people, and because of the danger to human life [involved in the Jews' taking this matter into their own hands]; let the matter not be revealed to the government." Then she [Johanan's daughter] said to him [Judah Maccabbee], "What is going on? I will shame myself before my brothers and my neighbors, but I will not shame myself in front of an unclean and un- circumcised person with whom you wish to betray me[34] and whom

---

[30] For the enigmatic and exciting story of how Jewish Second Temple litera- ture reached Rashi and his contemporaries in France in the 11th century C.E. see Steven Ballaban, "The Enigma of the Lost Second Temple Literature: Routes of Recovery," Ph.D. diss., Cincinnati: Hebrew Union College-Jewish Institute of Religion, 1994; see also Israel Ta-Shma, *Rabbi Moshe ha-Darshan and the Apocryphal Literature*, Studies in Jewish History and Literature (Jerusalem: Touro College, 2001) [in Hebrew]; Shulamith Ladermann, "Parallel Texts in a Byzantine Christian Treatise and Sections of Midrash Attributed to Rabbi Moshe Hadarshan," *Tarbiz* 70 (2001), pp. 213-226 (in Hebrew); concerning medieval Hebrew narratives con- cerning Judith see Ballaban, pp. 79ff.

[31] This is the same term for the Seleucid Empire employed in the liturgical meditation for the Festival of Hanukkah *'al hannissîm* ; see Birnbaum, *Daily Prayer Book*, p.171.

[32] Heb. *hegmôn*, a loanword from Gk. ἡγεμών 'leader'; this is the term employed also in the liturgical poem by Joseph b. Solomon cited in n. 35 below.

[33] The penalty prescribed in Lev. 21:9 for a priest's daughter who commits adultery.

[34] Heb. *m'l* , which is employed in both Hebrew Scripture and Rabbinic lit- erature to refer to sacrilege.

you wish to bring to have sex with me." As soon as Judah and his associates heard this, they decided to kill the official.[35]

The story continues with the Jews' killing the official, the Greek king's responding by laying seige to Jerusalem, and Judith's cutting off the king's head in the manner described in the Book of Judith in the Apocrypha.[36]

---

[35] My translation of the Hebrew narrative entitled "A Midrash for Hanukkah" found in Adolf Jellinek, *Bet ha-Midrash* (2[d] ed.; 6 vols.; Jerusalem: Bamberger & Wahrmann, 1938), vol. 1, p. 133; the complete narrative is found on pp. 132-136; a digest of this text is presented with a French translation in Andre Marie Dubarle, *Judith: Formes et Sens de Diverses Traditions* (2 vols.; Rome: Institut Biblique Pontifical, 1966), vol. 2, pp. 110-13; with Jellinek, p. 132, n., cf. the liturgical poem composed by Joseph b. Solomon of Carcassone, France (11th cent.) to be inserted in the first of the two benedictions before *Shema* on the first Sabbath during Hanukkah in *Ozar Ha-Tefillot* (Vilna: Rom, 1928), vol. 2, appendix, p. 28a (relevant sections of this liturgical poem are reprinted with French translation in Dubarle, *Judith*, vol. 2, pp. 162-67). and the liturgical poem composed by Menahem b. Makir to be inserted in the first of the two benedictions before *Shema* on the second Sabbath during Hanukkah in *Ozar Ha-Tefillot*, vol. 2, appendix, p. 29b. Concerning the poem by Joseph b. Solomon, "I thank you for getting angry," see Jefim Hayyim Schirmann, "Joseph ben Solomon of Carcassone," *EJ* 10:237. For a comprehensive list of medieval Hebrew recensions of the story of Judith see Dubarle, *Judith*, vol. 1, pp. 80-110; vol. 2, pp. 98-177.

[36] See, in the Apocrypha, Judith 13:8.

V. *Rashi as* Parshandatha

With reference to my work on this *Rashi's Commentary on Psalms* I was asked by a former teacher if I thought that this commentary alone would have qualified Rashi to the epithet *Parshandatha*.[1] This interesting question inspired me to present here what is known about this epithet.

According to Esth. 9:6 Parshandatha is the name of the first of the ten sons of the wicked Haman who sought to annihilate the Jewish people. It is universally agreed that this is an authentic personal name employed during the time of the Achaemenid phase of Persian history, which is portrayed in the Scroll of Esther.[2] In fact, a well-known cylinder seal impression from that period bears the inscription *ḥtm pršndt br 'rtdt* 'the seal of Parshandatha the son of Arthadatha'.[3]

The attribution of this name to one of the sons of the wicked Haman did not stifle the imagination of some unknown person in the late Middle Ages to see in this name the Hebrew word *parshan* 'commentator' followed by the Aramaic word *dātā'* 'the Torah'.[4]

---

[1] Prof. Moshe Greenberg, personal written communication, dated December 18, 1998.

[2] See Ran Zadok, "Notes on Esther," *ZAW* 98 (1986), pp. 108-09; the name has been interpreted as Old Iranian *Pršanta-dāta-* meaning 'born to a multicolored person'; see Zadok, p. 109.

[3] The seal impression was first published in Charles Jean Vogüé, *Corpus Inscriptionum Semiticarum, Pars Secunda: Inscriptiones Aramaices Continens, Tomus I: Tabulae* (Paris: E Reipublicae Typographeo, 1889), Tab. VI #100; it is indicated there that the provenance of the seal is uncertain.

[4] Old Persian *dāta* 'law' is the source of both Aramaic *dātā'* 'the law' in Ezra 7:12 and passim in Ezra and Dan. and of Heb. *dāt* in Esth. 1:19; 2:8; 3:8 and passim (see standard dictionaries of Biblical Hebrew and Biblical Aramaic). Comparison of Ezra 7:6, which employs the Hebrew expression "The Torah of Moses, which the LORD God gave," and Ezra 7:12, which employs the Aramaic expression "the law [*dātā'*] of the God of Heaven," indicates that already in the Persian Era (539-333 B.C.E.) of Jewish history Heb. *tôrāh* 'divine instruction' and Aram. *dātā'* 'law' were seen as equivalents. This equivalence made it possible for medieval writers to interpret the Persian proper name *Parshandatha* to mean 'commentator on the Torah'. Moreover, it is likely that the establishment in the Achaemenid Era of the equivalence of Heb. *tôrāh* and Aram. *dātā'* 'law' accounts for the employment of Gk. νόμος 'law' to render Heb. *tôrāh* in LXX and indirectly for the employment of Gk. νόμος 'law' in the form of the Gk. loanword *nāmûsā'* 'law' to render Heb. *tôrāh* in the Syriac translation of the Bible called Peshitta (1st-2nd centuries C.E.)

and in the combination a phrase meaning "commentator on the Torah". Rabbi Abraham b. Samuel Zacuto (1452-c.1515), best known to the world at large for his copper astrolabe and for his astronomical tables used by both Christopher Columbus and Vasco Da Gama[5] testifies to the application to Rashi of the title *Parshandatha* in his *Sefer Yuhasin*, a collection of biographical data concerning Jewish sages from the period of the Second Temple down to the author's era. Zacuto writes as follows:

> The great luminary who composed commentaries on the Talmud and the Scriptures, Rashi the Frenchman, *Parshandatha*, and his disciple R. Simchah of Vitry,[6] who composed[7] *Mahzor Vitry*[8] died in the year [5]865 [Anno Mundi; i.e., 1105 C.E.], and Rashi lived seventy-five years.[9]

Urbach suggests that Zacuto may have derived this tradition from R. Isaac Aboab II. Born in Spain in 1433, R. Isaac died in Oporto, Portugal in 1493. R. Isaac was also the teacher of Rabbi Moses Ibn Danon.[10] It is this Rabbi Moses Ibn Danon who is cited by Hayyim Joseph David Azulai in his monumental work on medieval Jewish sages, *The Names of the Great Ones*, as the source for Rashi's epithet *Parshandatha*:

> Rashi wrote three editions [of his commentary] on the [Babylonian] Talmud, and the third edition is the one we possess.[11] He [Rashi] was careful in his choice of language for he hinted at several innovative interpretations by the choice of a single letter. Those who came after him [Rashi] said:

---

[5] See Francisco Cantera y Burgos, *El judio Salmantino Abraham Zacut; notas para la historia de la astronomia en la España medieval* (Madrid: Bermejo, 1931).

[6] See above, pp. 11.

[7] Heb. '*āśāh*, lit., 'made'; cf. below, n.23.

[8] See above, pp. 12–13.

[9] Abraham b. Samuel Zacuto, *Sefer ha-Yuhasin*, ed. A. H. Freimann, p. 217; see above, p. 1. With reference to Rashi's date of birth in 1030 required by Zacuto's chronology, see the extensive literature cited there.

[10] Ephraim E. Urbach, "How Did Rashi Merit the Title Parshandata?" in *Rashi 1040-1990: Hommage à Ephraim E. Urbach*, ed. Gabrielle Sed-Rajna (Paris: Editions du Cerf, 1993), p. 391 (in Hebrew).

[11] Shamma Friedman, "Rashi's Talmudic Commentaries and the Nature of the Revisions and Recensions," pp. 147-75 explains that neither Azulai nor Ibn Danon claims that Rashi wrote three distinct editions of his commentary in the modern sense. Rather, argues Friedman, Rashi, with the help of his closest disciples, twice entered minor stylistic changes, which resulted in that concise style of writing for which Rashi is so famous; see also above, pp. 13–14.

All the French commentaries throw into the trash [Heb. 'ashpatha]^{12}
Except for Parshan Datha and Ben Poratha
The meaning of [the second line of this poetic couplet] is "Except for
Rashi, commentator on the Torah,^{13} and Rabbenu Joseph Tov Elem."
Thus wrote Harav Moses son of Danon from Portugal, the disciple
of the *ga'on*,^{14} our teacher Harav I. Aboab in his *Kelalim*.^{15}

Urbach, in his posthumously published study concerning the application of the epithet *Parshandatha* to Rashi, also quotes directly from
an unidentified ms. of Isaac Aboab II's still unpublished *Kelalim*, from
which, as we have seen, Azulai quotes in his *The Names of the Great
Ones*. The passage from Isaac Aboab's work, quoted in Urbach's
translation, reads as follows:

The exegetes who came after him [Rashi] said of his commentary:
"Cast all of the commentaries of France^{16} on the refuse-heap save

---

^{12} Note the rhyme: *sarephathah* (= of France) *ashpatha*, *Datha*, *Poratha*.

^{13} With Grossman, *The Early Sages of France*, p. 177, it seems reasonable to conclude that R. Moses Ibn Danon and the other Spanish Jewish authorities cited
refer to the positive evaluation of Rashi among Spanish Jewish exegetes, which
emerged in the 14th cent. Concerning the reluctance of Spanish Jewish exegetes
to take Rashi's Pentateuch commentary seriously prior to that time, see Abraham
Gross, "Spanish Jewry and Rashi's Commentary on the Pentateuch," in *Rashi Studies*,
ed. Zvi Arie Steinfeld (Ramat-Gan: Bar-Ilan University Press, 1993), pp. 27-55
(in Hebrew).

^{14} While in Modern Hebrew this term is used to mean 'genius, an intellectual
gifted person', in the context of Judaism in the Late Middle Ages, the term *ga'on*
refers to a major player in Jewish intellectual and spiritual life, whose accomplish-
ments make him a worthy successor of the heads of the Babylonian academies of
Sura and Pumbeditha; see above, p. 18, n. 16.

^{15} Hayyim Joseph David Azulai, *The Names of the Great Ones*, ed. Yizhaq Isaac
Benjacob (Vilna: Romm, 1852), p. 83a (in Hebrew). Urbach, "How Did Rashi,"
p. 389 cites the *editio princeps* of Azulai's work (pt. 1, Leghorn: G. Falorni, 1774, p.
70a). Azulai's comprehensive listing of more than 3300 Hebrew books and authors was redesigned and made user friendly by Benjacob, whose edition, regarded
as the definitive critical edition, is frequently reprinted. In fact, Benjacob combined two separate works by Azulai—*Va'ad La Hakamim* (lst ed., Leghorn: E.
Sahadun, 1796) and *The Names of the Great Ones* (vol. 1, Leghorn: G. Falorni, 1774;
vol. 2, Leghorn: A. I. Castello & E. Sahadun, 1784), whose treatment of both per-
sonalities and books overlapped. In Benjacob's edition the material is rearranged
in two distinct alphabetical lists of 1) great people; and 2) great books. On the
book *Kelalim* by Rabbi Moses Ibn Danon see below, n. 18.

^{16} Heb. *ṣārēpātāh*; see below, n. 30. Here, as in the long poem discussed below,
pp. 121–125, the final syllable which, at first glance, corresponds to the locative *h*
in Biblical Hebrew, serves simply to creative a feminine form of the Phonecian
place name *ṣārēpat*; in both poems the feminine form is employed for the sake of
the rhyme; cf. n. 31 below with reference to Jotbathah; cf. also biblical *'ephrātāh*
where the final syllable is not locative *h* in Ps. 132:6; Ruth 4:11; 1 Ch. 2:50; 4:4.

those of Parshandatha and of Ben Poratha."[17] What they meant was, except for the commentaries of Rashi and of Rabbenu Tov-Elem, of blessed memory....[18]

In light of the wording of the traditions presented by R. Moses Ibn Danon, Abraham b. Samuel Zacuto and Hayyim Joseph David Azulai it is clear beyond a shadow of doubt that a generation or so after Rashi he was called *Parshandatha*, i.e., exegete of the Torah *par excellence*, because of his definitive third edition of his commentary on the Babylonian Talmud. It is equally clear that R. Moses Ibn Danon and Hayyim Joseph David Azulai juxtapose Rashi and Rabbenu Joseph Tov Elem because the two of them had written commentaries on the Babylonian Talmud.

In each of the three sources cited above in which Rashi is called *Parshandatha*, i.e., commentator on the Torah *par excellence*, it is first and foremost his definitive commentary on the Babylonian Talmud that makes Rashi commentator on the Torah, which is to say the essential and quintessential compendium of divine revelation/Jewish spiritual baggage. It should not be surprising, therefore, that he is juxtaposed in two of the three quotations from the dawn of the modern era with the author of another monumental commentary on the Talmud,[19] which, for better or worse, has been lost. With

---

[17] Just as the epithet Parshandatha applied to Rashi is derived from the name of Haman's eldest son attested in Esth. 9:7, so is the epithet Ben Poratha derived from the name of Haman's fourth son Poratha attested in Esth. 9:8. According to Zadok, p. 109, the biblical name Poratha is derived from Old Iranian Paru-ra-tha meaning "having many chariots".

[18] Urbach, "How Did Rashi," p. 391. Urbach's posthumously published article does not identify the as yet unpublished ms. of R. Moses Ibn Danon's *Kelalim*, from which Urbach quotes. However, Friedman, "Rashi's Talmudic Commentaries," p. 149, n. 8 indicates that the two medieval mss. of *Kelalim*, which include the quoted passage, are Oxford Bodleian Ms. Or. 620 and Parma Ms. de Rossi 1226. R. A. May, ed., *Catalogue of the Hebrew Manuscripts in the Bodleian Library, Supplement of Addenda and Corrigenda to Vol. I A of Neubauer's Catalogue) Compiled Under the Direction of Malachi Beit-Arie* (Oxford: Clarendon Press, 1994), p. 133 #850 notes that the work was composed in Arabic in Fez and translated into Hebrew by Jedidiah b. Moses at San Marino in Italy in 1566 C.E.

[19] Urbach, "How Did Rashi," p. 392, asserts, "Rabbi Isaac Lattes testifies to Josef Tov Elem's having written a commentary on the Written Law." Grossman, *The Early Sages of France*, p. 64 questions the validity of this assertion. The words of Rabbi Isaac Lattes in their context suggest that the Josef Tov Elem referred to by Lattes is not the Josef Tov Elem of the first half of the eleventh century whom Rashi quotes (see below, p. 120). The latter Joseph Tov Elem came from Provence to lead the communities of Anjou and Limoges in the North of France; see

Urbach[20] and with Simeon Hurwitz[21] it is worth noting that Rashi himself quotes his older contemporary Rabbenu Joseph Tov Elem three times in his own commentary on BT. In his commentary on BT at Ketubbot 14a Rashi writes, "I found among the words of Rabbi Joseph Tov Elem...." In his commentary on BT at Hullin 114b Rashi writes, "I read the words of Rabbi Joseph Tov Elem, may his memory be for a blessing, which I read in a *responsum* in his handwriting...." Finally, in his commentary on BT at 'Arakin 2b Rashi writes, "I found in a [liturgical poem of the category] *Silluq*,[22] which Harav Joseph Tov Elem composed...."[23]

Finally, mention should be made of the poem attributed to Abraham Ibn Ezra (1089-1164)[24] in Bodleian Library Ms. Pococke

---

Grossman, *The Early Sages of France*, pp. 46-81. Rabbi Isaac Lattes of Provence in his history of Judaism entitled *Schaare Zion* completed in 1372 states, "Now the sage R. Joseph Tov Elem wrote many worthy books, and he commented on the Written Torah in a very worthy commentary." See Isaac de Lattes, *Schaare Zion*, ed. Solomon Buber (Jaroslau: Eisig Gräber, 1885), p. 43; Adolf Neubauer, *Medieval Jewish Chronicles*, vol. 2 (Oxford: Clarendon Press, 1895), p. 237; Shlomo Zalman Havlin, *Scha'arei Ziyyon of Rabbi Isaac Lattes Edited from Oxford MS Mich. 602 and Russian State Library MS Guenzburg 1336*, with introductions, indexes, explanations, notes and comments, p. 175. This publication is an addendum to Rabbi Menahem ha-Meiri, *History of the Oral Law* (2d ed.; Jerusalem & Cleveland: Ofeq Institute, 1995) [in Hebrew]. Careful attention to Isaac de Lattes' geographical and chronological scheme shows that the Josef Tov Elem whom he describes as the author of an important commentary on The Written Law belongs not to the French scholars who preceded Rashi (p. 172) but to the Provençal scholars who followed Rashi (p. 175). Jehiel b. Solomon Heilprin (1660-1746) states in his *Seder ha-Dorot* [first edition; Karslruhe: Loter, 1769], ed. Naphtali Masileison (Warsaw: Lewin-Epstein, 1878), p. 195 that R. Joseph Tov Elem belongs to the generation of Rashi's teachers and that he had written an halakic compendium called *Ben-Poratha*.

[20] Urbach, "How Did Rashi," p. 392.

[21] S. Hurwitz, ed., *Machsor Vitry* , p. 30.

[22] Ismar Elbogen, *Jewish Liturgy: A Comprehensive History*, trans. Raymond Scheindlin (Philadelphia: Jewish Publication Society/New York: Jewish Theological Seminary of America, 1993), p. 171 explains that a *silluq* is a long...poem bearing the heading "and so may our Kedushah ascend to You, for You are..."; it serves as a transition [from the cycle of liturgical poems inserted into the first three benedictions of the ' *Amidah;* collectively, these insertions are called *Qerovot;* see Elbogen, p. 170] the *kedushah*. The most famous *Silluq* employed in the liturgy of modern synagogues of all trends is *Unetanneh Tokef* "Let us tell how utterly holy this day is"; see Birnbaum, *High Holyday Prayer Book*, pp. 361-364.

[23] Heb. *'āśāh*, lit., 'made'; cf. above, n. 7.

[24] Urbach, "How Did Rashi," pp. 390-91, notes that numerous poems of unknown authorship were attributed by copyists to Abraham Ibn Ezra. Once the attribution to Ibn Ezra is no longer taken seriously, there is no reason to suggest that the poem actually refers to Rashbam (= R. Samuel b. Meir), who was a contemporary of Ibn Ezra. Concerning the latter suggestion, see the learned com-

74^2, whose *terminus ab quo* is 1586 C. E.[25] Here is my trascription of the entire poem from the microfilm at the Institute for Microfilms of Hebrew Manuscripts at the National and University Library at the Hebrew University of Jerusalem, followed by my own annotated translation:

עוד לו מרובע ופשוט בשבח רבנו שלמה יצחקי

כוכב דרך..	מצרפתה..	מחנה ערך..	על יטבתה
שלום באו..	והוא וצבאו..	מסיני או..	מצין אתא
מאיתיאל..	ויקותיאל..	בא כשמואל.	מרמתה
אור כל סומא..	בו כל צמא.	נופת מימי..	מתקו שתה
פירוש נורא..	שם לתורה.	על כן נקרא.	פרשן דתא
ספרו גואל.	אל כל שואל.	ובישראל הוא..	תרצתה
יקיר פותר.	בקיר חותר.	עינו סתר.	יה ראתה
הנסוכה.	לו ערכה.	גם ממלכה.	לו יאתה
מלאך קונה..	אצלו חונה.	חזק מתני..	במתניתא

Another poem of his,[26] each of whose lines is divided into four parts,[27] and entirely made of up fully voweled syllables:[28]

---

mentary on the poem included in David Rosin, *Reime und Gedichte des Abraham Ibn Esra: Aussergottesdienstliche Poesie, Heft IV = Jahresbericht des jüdisch-theologischen Seminars Fraenkael'scher Stiftung* 7 (Breslau: Schottlaender, 1891), pp. 223-226.

[25] May, *Catalogue*, p. 360 #1986 suggests, tentatively, that the ms. may have been written at Salonica in Greece.

[26] Presumably Abraham Ibn Ezra (1089-1164) to whom is attributed the first of the two poems found on p. 192a of the ms. Concerning the implausability of the attribution of the Parshan Datha poem to Ibn Ezra, see above, n. 24

[27] Nehemya Allony, *The Scansion of Medieval Hebrew Poetry: Dunash, Yehuda Halevi and Abraham Ibn Ezra* (Jerusalem: Mahbarot Lesifrut & Mossad Harav Kook, 1951), p. 93 (in Hebrew) explains that the genre *merubba‘* has the following characteristics: 1) each line is divided into four stichs; 2) two or all of the first three stichs contain an internal rhyme; 3) the fourth and final stich of each line contains the common rhyme for the entire poem. Allony, there, p. 281 points out that the Heb. term *merubba‘* was coined by Abraham Ibn Ezra in his *Sefer Zakut* 141:1 and that Ibn Ezra created the term on the basis of an Arabic cognate employed by Judah Halevi. See also Allony, there, p. 94; Jefim Hayyim Schirmann, *Hebrew Poetry in Spain and Provence, vol. 2* (2^d ed.; Jerusalem: Mossad Bialik/Tel Aviv: Dvir, 1971), p. 736 (in Hebrew). Dr. David Talshir of the Dept. of Hebrew Language at Ben-Gurion University explaind to me that the aforementioned Arabic term is *rb' 'y*; the plural form is *rb' 'y't*; the latter form is, of course, reflected in the title of the famous *Rubaaiyát of Omar Khayyam*. An English version of part of the latter "collection of quatrains by the 11th-12th century Persian poet, mathematician and astronomer, Omar ibn Ibrahim al-Khayyami" ("Rubaaiyát of Omar Khayyam" in *Encyclopedia Americana* [1991 edition], vol. 23, p. 823) was published anonymously by the English writer and translator Edward FitzGerald (1809-1883) in 1859. Eventually, the *Rubaaiyát* was recognized as FitzGerald's most important contribution

A star arose from[29] France;[30] he pitched his camp at Jotbathah.[31]
Blessed[32] be the arrival of him and his host. He has come[33] from

---

to world literature (see Thomas Assad, "FitzGerald, Edward," in *Encylopedia Americana* [1991 edition], vol. 11, p. 339).

[28] Heb. *pāšûṭ*; i.e., a poem which contains neither *shewa mobile* nor half vowels (*ḥataph*) but only long and short vowels. The opposite of *pāšûṭ* (here in the nuance 'simple') in the context of Medieval Hebrew poetics is understandably *murkab* 'complex'. See Schirmann, *Hebrew Poetry in Spain and Provence, vol. 2* , pp. 711, 714, 736.

[29] Cf. Num. 24:17: "A star arose from Jacob."

[30] Heb. *ṣārĕpātāh*, feminine form of the proper name *ṣārĕpāt*, which refers in 1 Kgs. 17:8-24 to a Phoenician town located c. 6 miles south of Sidon; the place name is mentioned also in Ob. 1:20 while the Elijah narrative is referred to again in NT Lk. 4:26 where the name is spelled Sarepta. The modern name for the town is Sarafand. The Akkadian form of the name of the town, Sariptu, derived from the verb *ṣarāpu* 'to dye', suggests that like the place names Canaan (= Hurrian *kinaḫḫu*) and Phoenicia (from Gk. φοῖνιξ), which denote 'purple,' the place name Zarephath refers to the importance of the production of wool garments with the purple dye (Heb. *tĕkēlet*) produced from the blood of the murex snail. On Biblical Heb. *ṣārĕpāt* see Arvid S. Kapelrud, "Zarephath," *IDB* 4: 935. The oldest surviving written source attesting to the use of the Heb. place name *ṣārĕpat* to refer to France is Rashi's commentary at Ob. 1:20. Rashi, in turn, assigns the use of Heb. *ṣārĕpat* to designate "the kingdom which is called France in Old Northern French" to the *pōtĕrîm*, i.e., "the schoolmasters who taught the Bible to the young, and not so young in their mother tongue" (Banitt, *Rashi: Interpreter of the Biblical Letter*, p. 8). On Rashi as the source for *ṣārĕpat* as the Hebrew name for France, see Abraham Even-Shoshan, *Ha-Millon Ha-Hadash* (3 vols.; Jerusalem: Kiryat Sepher, 1970, 2:1156; see also Ben Yehuda, *Dict.*, p. 5656; Canaani, vol. 14, p. 5108. In that same comment at Ob. 1:20, Rashi attributes to TJ the use of Heb. *sĕpārād* to designate Spain. Note that the end of every line of the poem ends in the sound *ātā*, with the possible exception of the ninth and final line. The purpose of the rhyme scheme is that every line should rhyme with the designation of the poem's hero as Parshan Datha at the end of the fifth and middle line of the poem. This scheme assumes that there is no distinction between the pronunciation of *ātāh* (lines 1a and 1b) and *ātā'* (line 5). One of the main characteristics of Medieval Hebrew poetry, which have seriously challenged translators of this poetry into English, is the ease with which the medieval Hebrew poet using the marked feminine ending *āh* and the various pronominal suffixes can write scores of lines with the same rhyme.

[31] Cf. Num. 33:33b: "They encamped at Jotbathah"; contrast NJV, which, following KJV, misconstrues the final *āh* of Jotbathah as locative *heh* and therefore creates the form Jotbath. The author of our poem correctly understands that the biblical place name is Jotbathah. According to Deut. 10:7 Jotbathah was an oasis. It has been "identified with modern Tabeh seven miles south of Eilat on the western shore of the Gulf of Aqaba"; see Moshe Weinfeld, *Deuteronomy 1-11*, AB, vol. 5 (New York: Doubleday, 1991), p. 420

[32] Heb. *šĕlôm*; our vocalization as a construct assumes that the noun 'peace, well-being, greetings' is part of a construct-genitive chain in which the genitive is *bō'ô* 'the arrival of him'. For Heb. *šālôm* 'well-being' and its Semitic cognates in the secondary sense, 'greetings' especially in epistolary literature, see passim in Sally Ahl, "Epistolary Texts from Ugarit: Structural and Lexical Correspondences in Epistles in Akkadian and Ugaritic" (Ph.D. diss., Brandeis University, 1973).

Sinai or from Zin.[34]
From Ithiel[35] and Jekuthiel[36] he came like Samuel from Ramah.[37]
Through him[38] there is light for every blind person.[39]
Through him every thirsty person drank honey from his sweet water.[40]
He provided for the Torah an awesome commentary.
Therefore, they named him Parshan Datha.
His book provides answers[41] to all who ask, and in all Israel it is the accepted solution.[42]

---

[33] The choice of the two synonymous roots *bw'//'ty* ' come' conjures up the memory of Deut. 33:2 where the parallelism also suggests that Ribeboth-kodesh there is an epithet for Mt. Sinai. It is equally well known that in Jewish exegetical tradition, Zin and Sinai are synonymous; our poet alludes to this synonymity here (see next note). Here the poet intimates that while the Torah exegete *par excellence* may, physically, have been born in France, his commentary is so close to the true and correct meaning of the Torah that it can be said that his spiritual origin is with the Torah itself at Mt. Sinai!

[34] George Ernest Wright, "Sinai, Mount," *IDB* 4:376-78; Joseph Mihelic, "Sin, Wilderness of," *IDB* 4:376 and id., "Zin, Wilderness of," *IDB* 4:958-59 typify the modern discipline of biblical geography in recording diverse theories as to the location of Mt. Sinai and the wildernesses of Sin and Zin. In Rabbinic tradition recorded in BT Shabbat 89a and quoted by Rashi in his commentary at Ps. 29 Zin and Mt. Sinai are identical. Similarly, LXX and Vulgate generally treat both Zin and Sin as identical, except in Num. 34:3-4 and Josh. 15:1, 3.

[35] The addressee of the words of Agur according to Prov. 30:1. Rashi in his commentary there construes both Agur and Ithiel as epithets of King Solomon.

[36] A proper name attested in 1 Ch. 4:18. According to BT Megillah 13a (cf. also Leviticus Rabbah 1:3; see Rosin, p. 223, n. 6) the three names—Jered, Heber and Jekuthiel—of sons of Pharaoh's daughter Bithiya—are, in fact, three epithets of Moses.

[37] Ramah was the home of Samuel the Prophet during the years he judged Israel according to 1 Sam. 7:17; when Samuel annointed King Saul (see 1 Sam. 7:17-10:1); and when he annointed King David (1 Sam. 15:34-16:13). The point is that Rashi is portrayed here as a political and spiritual leader of all Israel like Moses, Samuel, and Solomon. The simile "*like* Samuel from Ramah" rules out the conjecture of Rosin that the poet refers to R. Samuel b. Meir who lived in Ramerupt.

[38] Rashi, by virtue of his enlightening commentaries.

[39] Light is a metaphor for instruction, knowledge, education (Ps. 119:105; Prov. 6:23) juxtaposed with "blind," as a metaphor for ignorant; see Rashi at Lev. 19:14.

[40] For eating and drinking as metaphors for learning, receiving an education, see Prov. 9; for the comparison of Torah to honey, see Ps. 19:11; 119:103.

[41] Heb. *gō'ēl*; lit., 'redeems'.

[42] Heb. *tirṣātāh*, an expanded form of the place name Tirzah, one of the capitals of the Northern Kingdom, which in Cant. 6:4 is placed on a par with Jerusalem (see Gordis, *Song of Songs & Lamentations*, pp. 23, 65, 92)) as it was, in fact, during the reigns of Baasha (900-877 B.C.E) Elah (877-876 B.C.E.), and Zimri (876 B.C.E.) and during the first six years of the reign of Omri (876-869 B.C.E.), who built the new capital city of Samaria; see 1 Kgs. 15:21, 33; 16:8, 15; 23-24.

The endeared[43] solves.[44] He breaks[45] through the wall.
The LORD's secret he saw.[46]
Divine wisdom[47] was spread out[48] for him.
Also kingship[49] was for him appropriate.
An angel of the Creator abides with Him,[50]

However, in the present context *tirṣātāh* serves as a form of the Rabbinic Heb. noun *ṭērûṣ* meaning 'answer to a question' or 'solution to a dilemma'.

[43] Heb. *yāqîr.* In Jer. 31:19 this epithet is applied to Ephraim, who was adopted by Jacob and given by the latter the status of Joseph's firstborn son; see Gen. 48:19-20.

[44] Heb. *pōtēr;* in Gen. 41 this term designates an interpreter of dreams; the term is used frequently in Rashi's commentaries to mean 'exegete'; see, e.g., Rashi at Ps. 68:32; see above, n. 30, and see index, s.v. *pōtērîm.*

[45] Heb. *ḥōtēr,* which rhymes with *pōtēr* in the previous clause.

[46] According to Ezek. 8:8 Ezekiel the Prophet was transported in a vision from Babylonia to Jerusalem and shown a small breach in the wall of the Temple. The prophet was thereupon commanded to break through the wall in order to see the abominations being carried out within the Temple of the LORD. Here the master commentator's breaking through barriers of time and layers of eisegesis to expose the true meaning of sacred texts is compared to Ezekiel's exposing the abominations carried out in the Jerusalem Temple before its destruction in 586 B.C.E.

[47] This is probably an allusion to Personified Wisdom's having been a confidant (NJV's rendering of *'āmôn* Prov. 8:30) of God at the time of Creation. Personified Wisdom filtered through Ps. 119, Late Second Temple Judaism and Rabbinic Judaism is, of course, personified Torah in the form of an angel. Concerning *'āmôn* in Prov. 8:30 see Victor Avigdor Hurowitz, " Nursling, Advisor Architect? *'āmôn* and the Role of Wisdom in Proverbs 8, 22-31," *Biblica* 80 (1999), pp. 391-400.

[48] Heb. *'ărûkāh;* cf. the title Shulhan Aruk, lit. 'set table' for the halakic compendium by Joseph Qaro (1564), and cf. the setting of a table and the serving of a banquet as metaphors for the dissemination of knowledge in Prov. 9.

[49] Heb. *hannĕsūkāh;* literally, 'kingship'; this may be an allusion to Rashi's role in the establishment of Jewish self-government; see Grossman, *The Early Sages of France,* pp.147-160; Taitz, pp. 65-94; Zeitlin, "Rashi and the Rabbinate," pp. 31-46; 55-58; for the interpretation of the term *hannĕsūkāh* in light of Prov. 8:23 see Rosin, *Reime und Gedichte,* p. 224, n. 4. In Prov. 8:23 personified Wisdom claims, "I was granted dominion [Heb. *nissaktî*] from of old" (this interpretation is supported by Rashi's comment there; q.v.). Rosin suggests that the poet's ascribing 'dominion' to Rashi alludes to Rashi's embodying the primordial divine Wisdom, which already in Ps. 119 (q.v.) is identical with the Jewish Torah. Rosin, n. 4 emends to *hannĕsākāh;* I have presented the text as it appears in the single manuscript copy. I have rejected all the conjectural emendations as well as Rosin's pseudo-critical discussion of the merits of the mistakes/emendations contained in the earlier copies made from the ms. by Solomon Schechter and Baer Goldberg when microfilms of the ms. did not yet exist.

[50] Rashi is, of course, the angel; for *qōneh* 'Creator' as an allusion to Gen. 14:19, 22 and for *ḥôneh* 'abides' predicated of an angel in Ps. 34:8 see Rosin, p. 224, nn. 7-8.

[and He says to that angel, which is personified wisdom]:[51]
"Be strong[52] in Mishnah."[53]

At this juncture it is impossible to determine whether this poem's
application to Rashi of the epithet *Parshandatha* is influenced by the
circle associated with Isaac Aboab II or whether this poem is evidence of that epithet's having been applied outside the circle associated with Isaac Aboab II. In any case, the suggestion that this poem
refers not to Rashi but to R. Samuel b. Meir (Rashbam) as *Parshandatha* is based solely on the no longer accepted attribution of the poem

---

[51] Another reference to Rashi as the angel.

[52] Heb. *ḥazzēq môtnēy*, lit., 'make strong the sinews of' calls to mind *šibrôn motnayim*
in Ezek. 21:11. Held, "Studies in Comparative Semitic Lexicography," p. 405,
demonstrated that the lattter expression refers to the loosening of the musculature linking the upper part of the [human] body with the lower part." In addition, he showed that the biblical expression corresponds semantically to the
stereotypical description of a frightened person/deity in Ugaritic poetry: "below
her tendons break//above her face sweats". Our anonymous poet's choice of the
anatomical idiom 'strengthen the sinews of the strong musculature which links the
upper part of the body with the lower part' links him to the poetry of the Late
Bronze Age, in which tightened muscles were perceived to denote confidence (see
Held, there, p. 406). The anonymous poet's choice of the construct *môtnê* rather
than the ôrdinary dual *môtnayim* is dictated by the internal rhyme in line 9, in
which the first three of the four elements in line 9 thus end in the syllable *ê*. Note
that in each of the nine lines of the poem, with the exception of line 1 in which
the rhyme *atah* is shared by the second and fourth of the four elements, the first
three elements share an internal rhyme (line 2 *ow*; line 3 *el*; line 4 *ey*; line 5 *ah*;
line 6 *el*; line 7 *ter*; line 8 *chah*), while in line 1 the first and third elements end in
the syllable *rach*. On this basis and on the basis of having checked the microfilm
of the ms. in the Institute for Microfilms of Hebrew Manuscripts at the National
Library in Jerusalem, I reject both Schechter's reading *motnô* and Rosin's conjectural emendation *motneh*. Our assumption that in the anonymous poet's Hebrew
dialect *môtnê* rhymes with *qoneh* and *hôneh* is supported by the rhyme of *ṣāmē'* and
mêmê in line 4.

[53] The Aramaic form *matnîtā'* almost fits the rhyme scheme and and almost
rhymes with *paršan dātā'* at the end of the fifth and middle line of the nine line
poem. How delightful it would be to find manuscript evidence of a pronunication
matnîātā. This reference to Mishnah confirms the impression that Rashi was ac-
corded the epithet Parshandatha primarily because of his monumental commentary on the *magnum opus* of Rabbinic Judaism, the Babylonian Talmud, which
purports to be a commentary on the Mishnah. Moreover, it should be remembered that Rashi and his disciples refer to Rabbinic Hebrew, the language not
only of Mishnah and Tosefta but of most normative statements in the Babylonian
Talmud—be they Tannaitic or Amoraic—as Mishnah language (see below, pp.
143–144; p. 510, n. 29; see also Banitt, *Rashi: Interpreter of the Biblical Letter*, p. 131:
"R[ashi]'s term for Talmud is *mishneh* 'the second annunciation'"; see our discussion of this contention, above, pp. 54–55.

to Abraham Ibn Ezra.[54] The latter, it is well known, corresponded in both prose and poetry with his contemporary, Rashi's grandon Jacob, commonly known as Rabbenu Tam.[55] This poem, whatever its origin, is additional testimony to a tradition, which Rabbi Moses Ibn Danon traces to the generations immediately after Rashi. They so admired Rashi for his commentary on the Babylonian Talmud that they called him *Parshandatha*, meaning, "Commentator on the Torah *par excellence*."

---

[54] See the extensive discussion in Urbach, "How Did Rashi, pp. 390-91; see also Rosin, *Reime und Gedichte,* pp. 225-226.

[55] For the exchange of poems see, *inter alia*, Leon J. Weinberger, *Twilight of a Golden Age: Selected Poems of Abraham Ibn Ezra* (Tuscaloosa & London: University of Alabama Press, 1997), pp. 6-7; for the Hebrew texts pertaining to the same exchange of poems see, *inter alia*, Benzion Dinur, *Israel in the Diapora,* vol. 2, bk. 3 (Tel Aviv: Dvir/Jerusalem: Bialik Institute, 1968), p. 83 (in Hebrew).

VI. The Importance of Rashi's Commentary on Psalms

Martin Luther aptly called the Book of Psalms "a little Bible," i.e., "an entire summary of it [the whole Bible] in one little book."[1] Indeed, the Book of Psalms contains most of the characteristic ideas and types of poetry scattered throughout the rest of Hebrew Scripture. Most scholars agree that the Book of Psalms contains some of the earliest (Ps. 18; 29; 68) and some of the latest (Ps. 119; 126; 137),[2] both the longest (Ps. 119) and the shortest (Ps. 117) chapters in the Hebrew Bible. The psalter contains both ahistorical, universalistic wisdom teaching (Ps. 1; 37; 49) characteristic of Proverbs, Job, and Ecclesiastes[3] and rehearsal of the history of the people of Israel (Ps. 106; 107; etc.).

Just as the Book of Psalms contains, *inter alia*, a sampling of most of the varieties of writing contained in Hebrew Scripture so does Rashi's Commentary of the Book of Psalms contain a sampling of

---

[1] Martin Luther, "Preface to the Psalter" (1531), in *Works of Martin Luther* (6 vols.; Philadelphia: Muhlenberg Press, 1932), vol. 6, p. 385.

[2] Peter C. Craigie, *Psalms 1-50*, Word Biblical Commentary, vol. 19 (Waco, Texas: Word Books, 1983), p. 172 writes, "There is some degree of unanimity among scholars that Ps. 18 is ancient, to be dated in the eleventh or tenth century B.C.... The evident antiquity of the psalm, taken in conjunction with the content of the title, make it most reasonable to suppose that the original form of Ps. 18 comes from the time of David or shortly thereafter." Of Ps. 29 Craigie writes (there, p. 246), "It is one of the earliest in the Psalter, to be dated provisionally in the eleventh/tenth centuries B.C." On the dating of Ps. 68 see the classic study by William F. Albright, "A Catalogue of Early Hebrew Lyric Poems (Psalm LXVIII)," *HUCA* 23 (1950-51), pp. 1-39. With reference to the post-Exilic dating of Ps. 119 see Avi Hurvitz, *The Transition Period in Biblical Hebrew: A Study in Post-Exilic Hebrew and its Implications for the Dating of Psalms* (Jerusalem: Bialik, 1972), pp. 130-152; Jon D. Levenson, "The Sources of Torah: Psalm 119 and the Modes of Revelation in Second Temple Judaism," in *Ancient Israelite Religion*, ed. Patrick D. Miller, et al. (Philadelphia: Fortress, 1987), pp. 559-574. On the post-Exilic setting of Ps. 126:1, "When the LORD restored Zion's fortunes/exile" see Leslie C. Allen, *Psalms 101-150*, Word Biblical Commentary, vol. 21 (Waco Texas: Word Books, 1983), pp. 169-75. Even Yehezkel Kaufmann, *The Religion of Israel*, trans. and abr. Moshe Greenberg (Chicago & London: University of Chicago Press, 1960), p. 311 admits that Ps. 137 requires an exilic dating.

[3] Concerning the criteria for delineating wisdom psalms see, *inter alia*, Roland E. Murphy, "A Contribution to the Classification of Wisdom Psalms," in *Congress Volume: Bonn 1962*, VTS, vol. 9 (Leiden: E. J. Brill, 1963), pp. 156-177; Avi Hurvitz, "Wisdom Vocabulary in the Hebrew Psalter: A Contribution to the Study of Wisdom Psalms," *VT* 38 (1988), pp. 41-51.

most of the various concerns typical of Rashi's commentaries on the books of Hebrew Scripture: *midrash aggadah*,[4] *midrash halakah*,[5] lexicography,[6] grammar,[7] syntax,[8] source criticism,[9] and attention to lite-

---

[4] *Midrash aggadah* or *aggadic midrash* has been defined as "an independent literary creation [of the Talmudic rabbis] based upon one or more biblical texts, whose purpose is to raise people's consciousness with respect to the ideas and institutions of Judaism"; so Mayer I. Gruber, "The Midrash in Biblical Research," in *The Solomon Goldman Lectures: Perspectives in Jewish Learning*, vol. 2, ed. Nathaniel Stampfer (Chicago: Spertus College of Judaica Press, 1979), p. 72; similarly, Gary G. Porton, "Defining Midrash," in *The Study of Ancient Judaism*, ed. Jacob Neusner (New York: Ktav, 1981), p. 62; see also Jacob Neusner, *Midrash as Literature: The Primacy of Documentary Discourse* (Lanham, Md.: University Press of America, 1987). For a survey of Rabbinic and post-Rabbinic documents containing *midrash aggadah* see Moshe David Herr, "Midrash," *EJ* 11:1507-1514. Examples of Rashi's comments, which consist of Rabbinic *midrash aggadah* are found in Rashi's Commentary on the Book of Psalms at Ps. 1:1; 1:2a; 1:3c; 4:7a; 4:8; 6:11; 7:1; 7:15; etc. For a listing of most of the identifiable instances where Rashi's comment consists of or is clearly based upon *midrash aggadah* or *midrash halakah* (see next note) see the work by Zohory cited below, p. 157. For the term *midrash aggadah* in Rashi's Commentary on the Book of Psalms see, e.g., at Ps. 12:7c; 12:9; 42:9b; 147:17; for the expression *midrāšô* 'a *midrash* based upon it' see, e.g., Rashi at Ps. 78:47; 78:48b; for the term *midrash* see also Rashi at Ps. 26:13. For the significance of these terms in Rashi's Bible commentaries see Kamin, *Rashi's Exegetical Categorization*, pp. 139-157.

[5] *Midrash halakah* or *halakic midrash* has been defined as "an independent literary creation [of the Talmudic rabbis] based upon one or more biblical texts... [whose] purpose...is...to lend support to a view of the *halakah* on a particular subject"; so Gruber, "The Midrash in Biblical Research," p. 72. It may be natural that narrative and prophetic texts and psalms should have inspired the composition of *midrash aggadah* and that legal texts of the Pentateuch should figure prominently in *midrash halakah*. Nevertheless, it should be noted that a *midrash halakah* can be based upon a narrative or prophetic text or a psalm while a *midrash aggadah* can be based upon a legal text of the Bible. Examples of *midrash halakah* found in Rashi's Commentary on the Book of Psalms can be located at Ps. 26:6; 55:18; 81:5; 92:9; 101:1; 111:8; etc.

[6] See, e.g., Ps. 1:1; 1:2b; 1:3c; 2:9a-b; 2:12b; 4:4; 4:7; 4:9b; 5:1; 5:9; 5:13; etc. It is fair to say that the two most prominent elements in Rashi's Commentary on the Book of Psalms are explanations of words and inspirational comments drawn from Rabbinic *midrash aggadah*. Following Maarsen, I have attempted in my annotations to identify the sources of Rashi's lexicographical comments in *Mahberet Menahem, Teshuvot Dunash* ,and elsewhere. In addition, I have tried to place Rashi's lexicographical comments in dialogue with both ancient (Septuagint, Vulgate, etc.) and modern biblical lexicography and to call attention to suggestions which are especially worthy of consideration in the light of recent research. See, e.g., our discussion of Rashi's comment on *yāpîaḥ* 'HE TESTIFIES' at Ps. 12:6; our discussion of Rashi's comment on *tômîk* 'YOU CAST (MY LOT)' at Ps. 16:5; Rashi's comment on *misgĕrôtêhem* 'THEIR PRISONS' at Ps. 18:46b; Rashi's comment on *hawwôt* 'destruction' at Ps. 55:12; etc. It should be observed that for lexicographical data Rashi employs Targum Onkelos to the Pentateuch (see, e.g., at Ps. 18:46; 58:9; 72:9), Targum Jonathan to the Prophets (i.e., Joshua, Judges, Samuel and

Kings; Isaiah; Jeremiah, Ezekiel, and The Book of the Twelve Prophets) [see, e.g., at Ps. 60:4; 68:28; 89:45], *Mahberet Menahem, Teshuvot Dunash*, and a work written by Rashi's contemporary, R. Moses the Interpreter of Narbonne (see above, p. 3, n. 14). *Mahberet Menahem* is a dictionary of Biblical Heb. composed in Cordova, Spain in the 10th cent. C.E. by Menahem b. Saruq, who was the Hebrew secretary to Hasdai Ibn Shaprut. The latter served as physician, head of the customs service and diplomat in the service of Caliph Abd al Rahman III (912-961 C.E.) from 925 to 975. In this capacity Hasdai negotiated treates between the Umayyad Empire headed by the caliph and the Holy Roman Empire, the Kingdom of Leon, and the Kingdom of Navarre. Allegedly, he corresponded also with King Joseph of the Khazars. *Teshuvot Dunash* is a monograph length highly critical review of *Mahberet Menahem* written by Menahem's contemporary and rival Dunash Ibn Labrat, who succeeded in having Hasdai ibn Shaprut banish Menahem from his post of Hebrew secretary and replace him with none other than Dunash Ibn Labrat. Dunash, who introduced the Arabic metre into Hebrew poetry, authored the acrostic hymns *Děway hāsēr* "Banish Grief" (see Philip Birnbaum, *Daily Prayer Book* [New York: Hebrew Publishing Company, 1949], p. 755) and *Děrôr yiqrā'* "May He proclaim liberation". As we point out at Ps. 48, n. 18; Ps. 55, n. 18; Ps. 58, n. 29; Ps. 68, n. 92, Rashi never refers to the Psalms Targum printed in current editions of the so-called Rabbinic Bible (Miqra'ot Gedolot). For Rashi, who follows the Babylonian Talmud, Targum Onkelos and Targum Jonathan were the canonical (see our discussion at Ps. 40, n. 25; Ps. 42, n. 48) Aramaic versions of Hebrew Scripture. In addition to employing comparisons with Aramaic and with Arabic (see Rashi at Ps. 45:2; 60:14; 68:17; 74:6) and Mishnaic Heb. (see Rashi at Ps. 12:7; 32:10; 37:35; 60:5; 68:24; 72:2; 76:11; 80:13b; 80:14; 89:52), Rashi attempts to establish the meaning of obscure words in Biblical Heb. also by reference to cognates in Medieval Heb. poetry (see Rashi at Ps. 42:5; 119:5). Concerning the sources of Rashi's biblical lexicography see also Banitt, *Rashi: Interpreter of the Biblical Letter*, pp. 144-66. Nissan Netzer, "Comparison with Mishnaic Hebrew—One of Rashi's Strategies in His Biblical Commentary," in *Rashi Studies*, ed. Zvi Arie Steinfeld (Ramat Gan: Bar-Ilan University Press, 1993), pp. 107-36 (in Hebrew) demonstrates that in numerous cases Rashi offers explanations of Biblical Heb. vocabulary on the basis of Rabbinic Hebrew, which are original to Rashi.

[7] Most of Rashi's grammatical comments in his Commentary on the Book of Psalms have been listed and analyzed in Henry Englander, "A Commentary on Rashi's Grammatical Comments," *HUCA* 17 (1942-43), pp. 480-87; see also the additional studies by Englander cited below, p. 142, nn. 18-21; p. 146, n. 30.

[8] See, e.g., Rashi at Ps. 27:3; 58:6; 81:8; 90:6-7; 91:2-3, 8-9; 146:5. Frequently Rashi states or intimates that a biblical passage is *miqrā' měsûrās* 'inversion', which is to say that the word order does not correspond to the syntax; see, e.g., Rashi at Ps. 22:30, 31; 36:2; 45:6; 59:9; 93:5; 113:5-6, and see Shereshevsky, *Rashi: The Man and His World*, pp. 92-99; id., "Inversion in Rashi's Commentary," in *Gratz College Anniversary* Volume, ed. I. David Passow and S. T. Lachs (Philadelphia: Gratz College, 1971), pp. 263-68; William Chomsky, "Some Traditional Principles in Biblical Exegesis," in *Essays on the Occasion of the Seventieth Anniversary of Dropsie University 1909-1979*, ed. Abraham I. Katsh and Leon Nemoy (Philadelphia: Dropsie University, 1979), pp. 33-34.

[9] In his commentary at Ps. 45:2 Rashi notes that "the psalmist begins" the psalm at v. 2, which means that the superscription at v. 1 is from the pen of someone else. At Ps. 37:25 Rashi, following BT Yevamot 16b, notes that while Ps. 37 is attributed to King David at Ps. 37:1, v. 25 of that psalm, "I have been young and

rary devices such as virtual quotations[10] and change of speakers,[11] metaphors[12] and synonymous parallelism.[13]

Rashi's Commentary on the Book of Psalms has frequently been noted as containing significant data on Jewish-Christian intellectual relations before and during the era of the First Crusade.[14] Rashi's

---

am now old," could not have been authored by David, "for David was not so old." Therefore, Rashi, following BT, assigns the authorship of v. 25 to "the prince of the world"; similarly at BT Hullin 60a the authorship of Ps. 104:31 is attributed to "the prince of the world"; see our discussion at Ps. 37, nn. 24-25. Suffice it to say that the belief in the divine inspiration of Holy Scripture requires neither the Rabbis of the Talmud nor Rashi to accept as dogma the attributions of authorship found in BT Bava Batra 14b-15a. This fact suggests that in their search for means of reconciling historical criticism of the Bible with the belief in the divine origin of Scripture contemporary Bible scholars would do well to immerse themselves in Rabbinic and Medieval Hebrew biblical exegesis. In line with what he does at Ps. 45:2 Rashi separates the latter part of Judg. 5:31, "And the land was tranquil forty years," from the Song of Deborah. In his commentary at Ezek. 1:2-3 Rashi denies to Ezekiel but not to divine inspiration the authorship of Ezek. 1:2-3, which refers to Ezekiel in the 3d person and employs a different system of chronology than is employed in Ezek. 1:1. In his commentary at Isa. 8:19 Rashi quotes a dictum of R. Simon found in Leviticus Rabbah 6:5; 15:2; Yalqut Shim'oni pt. 2 #413 and elsewhere, according to which Isa. 8:19-20 are prophecies spoken by Beeri, the father of Hosea the Prophet. These verses were, he says, "attached to [the Book of] Isaiah because they were not extensive enough to constitute a separate Book [of the Prophet Beeri]." Obviously, this dictum suggests that single authorship of the Book of Isaiah is not a dogma for either the Talmudic rabbis or for Rashi. Concerning the Mosaic or Joshuan authorship of Deut. 34:5-12 see Rashi, following Sifre Deuteronomy and BT Bava Batra 15a, at Deut. 34:5. In his commentary at Ps. 72:20, "End of the prayers of David son of Jesse," Rashi states that this verse means that at this point, Ps. 72:19, David's compositions "have been concluded." "If so," continues Rashi, "this psalm is not written in its [chronologically] proper place." The reason is that eighteen psalms of David (Ps. 86; 101; 103; 108-110; 122; 124; 131; 133; 138-145) follow Ps. 72 in the Book of Psalms.

[10] See, inter alia, Rashi at Ps. 2:2; 20:7; 28:7; 30:9-12; 47:9; 62:12-13; 68:12-13; 87:3; 91:9; 137:5; 145:11. The classic modern contribution to the understanding of this feature of ancient Hebrew rhetoric is Robert Gordis, "Quotations as a Literary Usage in Biblical, Rabbinic, and Oriental Literature," HUCA 22 (1949), 157-219. The recognition of this feature of ancient Hebrew rhetoric is applied with particular brilliance in Naphtali H. Tur-Sinai, The Book of Job: A New Commentary (Jerusalem: Kiryath Sepher, 1967) and in H. L. Ginsberg, "Job the Patient and Job the Impatient," in Congress Volume: Rome 1968, VTS, vol. 17 (Leiden: E. J. Brill, 1969), pp. 88-111.

[11] See, inter alia, Rashi at Ps. 52:11; 75:4; 118:21, 26; 145:6; see also Rashi's calling attention to change of addressees at Ps. 45:17, 18; 48:10, 13; etc.

[12] See, e.g., Rashi at Ps. 3:8; 12:9; 18:21; 23:2, 5; 31:11b; 45:5; 98:8; see also our discussion of lāšôn 'metaphor' and dûgmāh 'metaphor' below, p. 145.

[13] See our discussion, below, pp. 150–154.

[14] See Hailperin; Shereshevsky, Rashi: The Man and His World, pp. 120-129; id., "Rashi and Christian Interpretations," JQR, n.s., 61 (1970), pp. 76-86; Judah M.

grandson, R. Samuel b. Meir (Rashbam) makes it clear that the distinction drawn time and again in Rashi's commentaries between what "our rabbis interpreted" [dārĕšû rabbôtênû] and "its literal meaning" [pĕšûṭô] paved the way for the use by subsequent schools of Jewish biblical exegesis, probably beginning with R. Samuel b. Meir, of a distinction between pĕšaṭ 'the original and true meaning of the Bible to be uncovered by the exegete' and dĕraš 'eisegesis'.[15] It is well known that in several cases in his Commentary on the Book of Psalms (Ps. 2:1; 9:1; 21:2; 40:7-8; 80:16; 88:1; 98:8; 105:1; 110; etc) Rashi attempts to defuse or neutralize Christian teaching to the effect that Hebrew Scripture prophesies the passion, the death, and the resurrection of Jesus of Nazareth.[16] Rashi states explicitly in his commentary at Ps. 2:1 and again at Ps. 21:2 that the philologically correct interpretation should serve as a refutation of the claims of the Christians.[17] It is not surprising that several medieval mss. of our commentary, which for several centuries have been in the possession of Christian libraries, have lines drawn through or erasures at such points in the commentary.[18]

It has been suggested that the interest of Rashi and of his followers who went beyond Rashi's search for the literal meaning (mašmā'ô; pĕšûṭô) in their search for the original and true meaning of Scripture in context (pĕšaṭ)[19] grew out of the attempt to refute the Christians

---

Rosenthal, "Anti-Christian Polemics in the Biblical Commentaries of Rashi," in Judah M. Rosenthal, *Studies and Texts in Jewish History, Literature and Religion* (2 vols.; Jerusalem: Rubin Mass, 1967), pp. 114-115 (in Hebrew); Erwin Isaak Jacob Rosenthal, "Anti-Christian Polemic in Medieval Bible Commentaries," *JJS* 11 (1960), 115-135; Yitzhak Baer, "Rashi and the Historical Reality of His Time," *Tarbiz* 20 (1950), 320-332 (in Hebrew); see also Daniel J. Lasker, *Jewish Philosophical Polemics Against Christianity in the Middle Ages* (New York: Ktav, 1977).

[15] See the commentary of R. Samuel b. Meir (Rashbam) at Gen. 37:2. Concerning the distinction between pĕšaṭ and dĕraš as employed by Rashbam followed by Abraham Ibn Ezra (1089-1164) and Moses Nahmanides (1135-1204) and others and pĕšûṭô and midrāšô employed by Rashi see Kamin, *Rashi's Exegetical Categorization*, pp. 263-274; on the distinction between pĕšaṭ and pĕšûṭô see also Banitt, *Rashi: Interpreter of the Biblical Letter*, p. 1, n. 6; contrast Touito, "The Exegetical Method of Rashbam," p. 64.

[16] See the works cited in n. 14, and see our discussion of the aforementioned passages in Rashi's Commentary on the Book of Psalms.

[17] See our discussion there, and see especially the study by Touito cited at Ps. 2, n. 6.

[18] See ms. Parma de Rossi 181/1; ms. Parma de Rossi 32; ms. Milano-Ambrosiano 25/1.

[19] See above, n. 15.

of the eleventh and twelfth centuries, whose biblical interpretation
was primarily allegorical.[20]

It has been demonstrated, however, that precisely at the period
of the emergence of the Northern French school of Jewish biblical
exegesis (eleventh and twelfth centuries C.E.) there emerged also
among the Christians of Western Europe an interest in recovering
the literal sense of Holy Scripture.[21] Therefore, the question arises
as to what it was that drove scholars among both the Jews and the
Christians at that juncture to suggest that pure exegesis was at least
as worthy as allegory for the Christian and midrash for the Jew. The
most cogent answer to this question would seem to be that it was
the general spirit of the times.[22] Touito has noted that the general
spirit of the times is reflected in the fact that Christian biblical exegesis of the period employs the three terms sensa, littera, and
sententia as the semantic equivalents of the Hebrew terms pitārôn,
pērûš, and nimmûq respectively.[23]

It has been noted for some time that the Jews of Northern France
of the eleventh and twelfth centuries C.E. differed from their Christian neighbors only in the matter of their religion.[24] It should not
be surprising, therefore, that Jewish Bible exegetes, like their Christian counterparts, would reflect the intellectual currents of the times.
This is to say that it is not enough to note that the attempt of R.
Samuel b. Meir to draw a clear distinction between pěšaṭ 'exegesis'
and děraš 'eisegesis' has numerous contemporary parallels among the
Christians of his day. Nor is it sufficient to note that there is some
evidence of mutual influence of Jewish and Christian biblical exegesis
at that period.[25]

None of these brilliant observations touches upon the real question as to why Rashi should have employed the distinction between
the literal meaning of a Heb. word in biblical Heb. from the mean-

---

[20] See Shereshevsky, *Rashi: The Man and His World*, pp. 119-129; Touito, "The
Exegetical Method of Rashbam," pp. 48-53.

[21] See Beryl D. Smalley, *The Study of the Bible in the Middle Ages* (3d ed.; Oxford:
Blackwell, 1984); see also Touito, "The Exegetical Method of Rashbam," pp. 53-
59.

[22] Touito, "The Exegetical Method of Rashbam," p. 62.

[23] Ibid.

[24] See Rabinowitz, *The Social Life of the Jews of Northern France in the XII-XIV
Centuries*, p. 237; Blumenfield, pp. 9-10; see also José Faur, "The Legal Thinking
of Tosafot: An Historical Approach," *Dine Yisrael* 43 (1975), pp. xliii-lxxii.

[25] See Touito, "The Exegetical Method of Rashbam," pp. 63-74.

ing that word acquired in post-biblical Heb. (e.g., *māšîaḥ* in Ps. 2:2; 105:15) in the debate as to which of the two religions, Christianity or Judaism, is the true spiritual heir of ancient Israel. Clearly, the debates between Jews and Christians on this question employed different strategies at different periods. Why then, beginning with the era of Rashi does it make so much difference to both Jews and Christians to draw a distinction between what Hebrew Scripture itself has to say (*pĕšûṭô*) and what traditional lore has to say about Scripture (*midrāšô*)? The answer seems to be that Rashi was born into a world in which one of the main issues that was debated was the issue as to whether *universalia ante rem* or *universalia post rem*.[26] The former position, which was associated in the 11th cent. C.E. with Anselm, the Archbishop of Caterbury (d. 1109), has been explained to mean "that truth or reality consists of a series of forms in the mind of God, and what we see and know are only reflections of these realities and are of secondary importance."[27] The latter position, which was advocated in the 11th cent. C.E. by Roscellinus (d. 1122), has been explained to mean that "the sole reality is difference."[28] The former position, which was called realism, means for biblical studies that the distinctions scholars draw between the meaning of terms in biblical literature and their meaning in rabbinic (or patristic) literature is of no consequence since both biblical and rabbinic literature teach the same indivisible truth. The view called nominalism, according to which the sole reality is difference, should mean for biblical studies that one should only be interested in the objective meaning of a word or phrase in its specific context. Rashi's manifold references to both the literal meaning of a verse and its treatment in rabbinic midrash and R. Samuel b. Meir's insistence that both his own special interest in "the true meanings newly discovered each day"[29] and the interest in the functional meaning of Scriptural expressions in Rabbinic lore are both legitimate branches of Torah learning[30] are congruent with the doctrine associated with Peter Abelard (1079-1142) and called Conceptualism. According to this doctrine, summarized by

---

[26] See Robert Hoyt, *Europe in the Middle Ages* (New York: Harcourt Brace, 1957), pp. 308-11.

[27] Frederick B. Artz, *The Mind of the Middle Ages* (3d ed.; New York: Knopf, 1966), p. 255.

[28] Ibid., p. 256.

[29] See Rashbam at Gen. 37:2.

[30] See Rashbam at Ex. 21:1.

the formula *universalia in re,* both the individual entity and universals truly exist and are worthy of investigation[31]

Notwithstanding the fact that Rashi's comment on Ps. 49:11b that when the foolish and ignorant die "the body *and* the soul perish" is the earliest reference to the teaching of Avicenna in a Hebrew source,[32] it would be radical for any scholar to suggest that Rashi, traditionally conceived as unexposed to philosophy, had knowledge of the major intellectual currents in his environment. Since, however, it has been assumed that "Rashi himself engaged in debates with the Christian clergy,"[33] it is hard to believe that his arrival at a view of the nature of truth congruent with Abelard's Conceptualism was purely coincidental. In biblical scholarship such a coincidence involving writers living several centuries and many miles apart, writing distantly related but mutually unintelligible languages, is generally considered an obvious case of direct influence.[34] Therefore, from the perspective of biblical scholarship the emergence of twofold interpretation of Scripture, which permeates Rashi's Bible commentaries, is certainly to be sought in the cultural milieu of Northern France of the late 11th and early 12th centuries.

It is not here suggested that Rashi had to be familiar with the way in which the issue of universals and distinctions was debated by the philosophers such as Roscellinus and Anselm nor that he had heard of Abelard's compromise solution. What is suggested here is that just as the Freudian model of the tripartite mind is common knowledge among the masses of people in contemporary New York and Jerusalem although they have never studied in an institute for psychoanalysis so must the most important intellectual debate in Western Europe in the era of Rashi have filtered down to the famed rabbi of Troyes.[35]

---

[31] Artz, p. 258.

[32] See below, Ps. 49, n. 25.

[33] Shereshevsky, *Rashi: The Man and His World,* p. 120.

[34] See the standard commentaries on Gen. 1-11; see also John B. Geyer, "Twisting Tiamat's Tail: A Mythological Interpretation of Isaiah XIII 5 and 8," *VT* 37 (1987), pp. 164-179; Wilfred G. E. Watson, "Reflexes of Akkadian Incantations in Hosea," *VT* 34 (1984), pp. 242-247.

[35] It should be noted that "...in every field of culture from Iceland to the Holy Land, Latin Christendom [at the period in question] was made up culturally of a series of provinces of northern France"; so Artz, p. 228. Moreover, Artz points up (p. 231), "the philosophy of Abelard during his lifetime had reached to the bottom of Italy." See now also Pierre Riché, "Courants de Pensé dans la France du XIe Siècle," in *Rashi Studies,* ed. Zvi Arie Steinfeld (Ramat-Gan: Bar-Ilan University Press, 1993), pp. xxxi-xxxvi.

A modern counterpart to the influence of the general intellectual climate upon Rashi and his Christian contemporaries is the impact of both Hegelian thought and German Romanticism upon nineteenth and twentieth century biblical studies.[36]

Rashi's Commentary on the Book of Psalms is especially worthy of study for two reasons: (1) The Book of Psalms continues to be a primary sourcebook for both liturgy and private devotion among both Jews and Christians of every variety. Consequently, both Christian interpretation of references to *māsîaḥ* as referring to Jesus and Rashi's response to such exegesis continue to be of more than historical interest to both Jews and Christians. (2) Because Rashi's Bible commentaries have attained an almost canonical status in the Jewish community his commentaries continue to be of particular interest to three groups of people: (a) Jews, who want to study Hebrew Scripture from the standpoint of 'traditional', i.e., canonical Jewish exegesis; (b) Modern Jewish Bible scholars, teachers, and students who wish to learn from Rashi, the master teacher, the means by which Bible scholarship can be at once scientific and inspirational; and (c) Christian Bible scholars, teachers, and students, who wish to rediscover the Jewish roots of their faith, including the various traditions of Hebrew exegesis of Hebrew Scripture.

In addition, it should be noted that Rashi's Commentary on Psalms has long been considered one of Rashi's better works. In fact, Hailperin considers it Rashi's second best biblical commentary, surpassed only by Rashi's commentary on Genesis.[37]

---

[36] On the latter influences on modern biblical scholarship see Joseph L. Blenkinsopp, *Prophecy and Canon* (Notre Dame: University of Notre Dame Press, 1977), pp. 1-23; id., *A History of Prophecy in Israel* (Philadelphia: Westminster, 1983), p. 28.

[37] Hailperin, p. 231; p. 350, n. 726; contrast the utter dismissal of Rashi's commentaries on the Prophets and Hagiographa as "rudimentary" by Haym Soloveitchik, "Rashi," in *Dictionary of the Middle Ages*, ed. Joseph R. Strayer (13 vols.; New York: Scribner's, 1988), 10:259.

a. The Method

I present here a classic document of Medieval Jewish Biblical exegesis written in a variety of late 11th-12th century C.E. Medieval Rabbinic Hebrew[1] translated into standard idiomatic 21st century C.E. English. In presenting an idiomatic translation I apply to the rendition into contemporary English the method previously employed with great success in the translation of all of Hebrew Scripture by the Jewish Publication Society[2] and lucidly expounded in Harry M. Orlinsky, *Notes on the New Translation of the Torah*.[3] Idiomatic translation is to be distinguished from word-for-word translation, which ignores idioms, differences in semantic capacity, and figures of speech as it is to be distinguished from paraphrase. Word-for-word translation is exemplified by KJV while paraphrase is exemplified for Biblical Heb. and Aramaic and for New Testament Greek by the *Good News Bible*[4] and for Akkadian[5] by A. Leo Oppenheim, *Letters*

---

[1] On the use of Rabbinic Heb. "for all written purposes" among the Jews of Medieval France see Chaim Rabin, "Massorah and 'Ad Litteras'," *Hebrew Studies* 26 (1985), p. 88. With reference to Jewish authorship of entire compositions in Old Northern French penned in Hebrew characters see Kirsten Fudeman, "Father, Mother, Other Tongue" (forthcoming) and the literature cited there.

[2] *Tanakh: A New Translation of the Holy Scriptures* (Philadelphia: Jewish Publication Society, 1985).

[3] (Philadelphia: Jewish Publication Society, 1969), pp. 10-39; see also E. A. Speiser, *Genesis*, AB, vol. 1 (Garden City, N.Y.: Doubleday, 1964), introduction, pp. lxiii-lxxi; for examples of idiomatic renderings of texts in a variety of ancient Semitic languages and extensive justification of those renderings see Mayer I. Gruber, *Aspects of Nonverbal Communication in the Ancient Near East*, Studia Pohl, no 12 (2 vols.; Rome: Biblical Institute Press, 1980), and see the review by Dale A. Patrick in *JBL* 102 (1983), p. 289.

[4] (New York: American Bible Society, 1976). Typical of the *Good News Bible*'s paraphrasing rather than translation is the following: At Ps. 23:6 where NJV faithfully renders the Hebrew, "and I shall dwell in the house of the LORD for many long years" the Good News Bible paraphrases, "and your house will be my home as long as I live." Likewise, at Ps. 27:12 where NJV faithfully renders the Hebrew, "...for false witnesses and unjust accusers have appeared against me," Good News Bible paraphrases, "who attack me with lies and threats."

[5] The dominant Semitic language of ancient Iraq from the middle of the third millenium B.C.E. until the beginning of the Christian Era and frequently an international language of trade, diplomacy and culture until it was replaced in those functions by Aramaic after the middle of the eighth century B.C.E.

from Mesopotamia.[6] Oppenheim, for example, accepts what he calls

> the necessity of rendering Akkadian verbs by English substantives
> and vice versa, of replacing pronouns by proper names and vice
> versa, of omitting and adding demonstrative pronouns and personal
> suffixes....of supplying objects to eliptically used transitive Akkadian
> verbs, and of making those changes where necessary without at-
> tempting to indicate the differences between Akkadian and English
> by typographical means. In short, to recreate the thought sequence
> which carries the message of the letter and to make each letter into
> the meaningful and intelligible document the writer had in mind.[7]

The first requirement of an idiomatic translation of any prose text
into Modern English is that for the most part the word order of
Modern English must be followed[8] The reason is that since Modern English—unlike Classical Latin, for example—does not employ
case endings to indicate whether a noun is employed as the subject,
direct object or indirect object, the syntactical function of the noun
can be ascertained only by virtue of the word order. In order that
an English translation be comprehensible, it is equally important that
the verbal predicate normally follow the subject and that the direct
object follow the verb. Literal translation, on the other hand, would
require that the word order verbal predicate-subject-object be followed for Biblical Hebrew prose; the word order subject-verbal pre-
dicate-object for Mishnaic Hebrew; the word order subject-
object-verbal predicate for Sumerian, Akkadian, Latin and literary
German. It is worthy of note that even the very literal KJV generally follows English rather than Hebrew word order. All the more
so, must an idiomatic translation follow the word order of the language into which one is translating in order to convey meaning.

The Hebrew Bible and other ancient Semitic languages are re-
plete with examples of what the grammarians call the "nominal sentence". The latter expression designates a sentence in which there

---

[6] (Chicago & London: University of Chicago Press, 1967); see there, pp. 54-
67.

[7] Ibid., p. 66.

[8] Contrast Edward L. Greenstein, "Theories of Modern Bible Translation,"
Prooftexts 3 (1983), p. 18. It should be observed, however, that the standard word
order of the aforementioned languages is abandoned in poetic texts in all of those
languages because of the requirements of meter, rhyme, alphabetic acrostics, chiastic
parallelism, and other poetic devices. In such cases, it would seem, there is no
justification for the translator's adhering to standard English prose word order.

is no verb but in which two nouns or a pronoun and a noun or a noun (or pronoun) and an adjective are juxtaposed. The first noun (or pronoun) corresponds functionally to the English subject while the second noun or pronoun or adjective corresponds to the English predicate nominative or predicate adjective. Typical of the usage in question is Ps. 24:6a, *zeh dôr*, which KJV renders "This is the generation." The italicization of the word 'is' in KJV's rendering informs the reader that 1) Biblical Heb. has no equivalent of the present tense of the verb 'to be' and 2) the functional equivalent of the ancient Semitic nominal sentence in English is a sentence consisting of a noun or pronoun subject followed by a form of the present tense of the verb to be (am, is, are) followed by a predicate noun or adjective. KJV's addition of the verb 'is' between the demonstrative pronoun subject *zeh* 'this' and the predicate noun *dôr* 'generation' corresponds functionally to Rashi's treatment of the same clause. Rashi writes *zeh...hû 'dôr*, which our translation renders into Modern English, "This one is the generation." Now a so-called literal rendering of Rashi's comment based upon the lexicon of Biblical Heb. would be "This he generation," which conveys no meaning whatsoever in English. Moreover, in the lexicon of Rabbinic Heb., which is the major lexical component of the language of Rashi's Commentary on the Book of Psalms,[9] the Biblical Heb. personal

---

[9] Rashi's Hebrew also includes various Gallicisms, i.e., usages of Hebrew words based upon nuances of their equivalents in Rashi's spoken language, Old Northern French. Typical are *nōpēl 'al* and *nōpēl bĕ*, which reflect Old French *cheoir*, lit., 'fall' in its extended meaning 'happen, apply, fit' (so Banitt, *Rashi: Interpreter of the Biblical Letter*, p. 14, n.37). These are employed by Rashi to mean 'be in harmony with' (Ps. 16:1), 'is (not) employed with' (Ps. 31:13) and 'refers to' (Ps. 119:113); see also at Ps. 15:4; 45:8; 118:12. Another important example is the use of the verb *yśb* in the *pi'el pu'al*, and *hitpa'el* conjugations to mean respectively 'make fit, reconcile' and 'be appropriate, reconciled'. This usage is found in Rashi's Commentary on Psalms at Ps. 8:8; 12:7c; 51:7; and 64:2 with respect to midrashim, which can or cannot 'be reconciled' with the Scriptural contexts to which they refer. The verb is found in Rashi's Commentary on Psalms at Ps. 16:7 and 141:6 in the sense 'explain properly' and in the expression *'ên libbî mityaśśēb* 'I am not pleased' (with an interpretation) in Rashi's Commentary on Psalms at Ps. 68:34 'and 78:63. Kamin, *Rashi's Exegetical Categorization*, pp. 57-110; 209-261 and Gelles, *Peshat and Derash in the Exegesis of Rashi*, pp. 14; 144-146 devote considerable attention to this important exegetical expression in Rashi's Bible commentaries (especially famous are Rashi's comments at Gen. 3:8; Ex. 23:2 and in his introduction to the Commentary on the Song of Songs). Banitt, *Rashi: Interpreter of the Biblical Letter*, p. 48, n. 61 explains, "Being used now for centuries, this connotation of *yaśśēb* 'explain properly' does not seem odd anymore, but R[ashi] was the first to use *yaśśēb, mĕyuśśāb* in this sense. It is a clear gallicism." Banitt, there derives it

pronouns can serve both in their primary biblical function and also as the *copula*,[10] i.e., the functional equivalent of the present tense forms of the verb 'to be' in English.

Since the dialect in which Rashi wrote his Commentary on the Book of Psalms—like authentic Mishnaic Hebrew—employs the Biblical Heb. and Mishnaic Heb. personal pronouns both as equivalent of Eng. 'he', 'we', 'they' etc. and as *copulae*, an idiomatic translation must distinguish between these usages in translation. In the annotations I call attention to the appearance of the forms in question as *copulae*. I do so because I assume that many readers are familiar with the typically biblical usage of the words in question and less familiar with the Rabbinic Heb. usage, which appears alongside of the older usage in late Biblical Heb., in ancient Rabbinic Heb., and, as I have noted, in Rashi's Heb.[11]

Prof. Orlinsky points out that "traditional [i.e., literal] translations of the Bible might well be designated 'And' Bibles; hardly a sentence goes by without an 'and' or two, sometimes more."[12] In my translation of Rashi's Hebrew I follow NJV's precedent in rendering Heb. *wě, û, wa* according to context as 'moreover' (Ps. 23:1; 102:4; 133:1; etc.), 'however' (Ps. 89:1; 105:8; etc.), 'now' (Ps. 87:6b; 91:2;107:4; etc.), 'hence' (Ps. 51:8), 'thus' (Ps. 48:3) and the like. In addition, I call attention again and again in the notes to Rashi's use of the explicative or exegetical *waw*, which is to say, the apparently conjunctive *waw* employed to mean 'i.e.'. As noted by Shereshevsky and by Lehman,[13] Rashi both calls attention to this usage in Biblical Heb. and employs it in the language of his commentaries.[14] Some of the

---

"from [French] *seoir* 'sit, set establish' but also, and this is the point, 'suit, fit, become'." Concerning other Gallicisms in Rashi's vocabulary and syntax see Leopold Zunz, "Salomon ben Isaac, genannt Raschi," *Zeitschrift für die Wissenschaft des Judenthums*, 1822, pp. 327-329; Menahem Banitt, "Rashi's Commentary to Scripture and Vernacular Translations," in *Benjamin de Vries Memorial Volume*, ed. Ezra Zion Melamed (Tel Aviv: Tel Aviv University Research Authority and Stichtung Fronika SandersFonds, 1968), pp. 252-267 (in Hebrew).

[10] See Abba Bendavid, *Biblical and Rabbinic Hebrew* (rev. ed.; 2 vols.; Tel Aviv: Dvir, 1967-71), vol. 1, pp. 704-769 (in Hebrew).

[11] Examples of personal pronouns employed as copulae in Rashi's Commentary on the Book of Psalms and which are cited in our annotations, are found in the commentary, at Ps.19:7; 24: 6; 39:7; 59:13; 135:7; etc.

[12] Orlinsky, *Notes*, p. 19.

[13] Shereshevsky, *Rashi: The Man and His World*, p. 81; Manfred R. Lehman, "Studies in the Exegetical *waw*," *Sinai* 85 (1977), pp. 200-10 (in Hebrew).

[14] On the exegetical *waw* in Biblical Heb. see, in addition to the studies cited

many examples of the exegetical *waw* employed in Rashi's Commentary on the Book of Psalms are found at Ps. 30:6; 39:6; 40:3; 41:9; 45:2, 9; 47:10; 58:3; 59:1; 110:6; 129:6; etc.

Now if Rashi does, as we have seen, consciously employ the well known *wĕ* 'and' alongside of the less well known (to persons who have systematically investigated Biblical Hebrew) *wĕ* meaning 'i.e.' and the well known *hû'* 'he' alongside of the less well known *hû'* 'is' should be no less surprising that he often employs the preposition *kĕmô*, lit., 'like' and the construct noun *lĕšôn*, lit., 'tongue of' interchangeably and that he employs both of these latter two words in a variety of nuances, which are scientifically delineated and systematically differentiated in our idiomatic translation.

The stereotypic sentence "x *kĕmô* y" repeated hundreds of times in the commentaries of Rashi and other Medieval Hebrew Biblical exegetes means literally that x (a word in the verse being explicated by the commentator) 'is like' y (a word in Biblical Heb. or some other language not found in the verse. The two words may be 'synonymous' (Ps. 9:1; 10:3, 8; 18:6; 32:7; 55:14; 69:21; 712:20; 116;19; etc.), 'words derived from the same root' (i.e., cognates) [5:9; 10:5; 18:43; 27:9; 55:9; 69:22; 72:17; 81:13; 90:10; 119:66; etc.], examples of the same class of irregular verbs (Ps. 72:20), examples of the same grammatical form (Ps. 68:15; 77:10; 124:3), or two attestations of the very same word (Ps. 6:3; 48:14; 56:2; 62:2; 80:9, 13, 14; 94:4; 102:7; 143:4; etc.)

Now it might be reasonable to suggest that by rendering the preposition *kĕmô* by the noun 'synonym' or the noun 'cognate' or the expression 'the same word (adjective, noun) as is attested in' my translation has gone beyond idiomatic translation and become a mere paraphrase. The justification for my seemingly far-fetched idiomatic renderings of the preposition *kĕmô* is that in many of its nuances the latter expression is interchangeable with corresponding nuances of the construct noun *lĕšôn*. Hence, it should not be surprising that in JTS Bible ms. 690, which is a collection, recovered from the bindings of books, of 13th century C.E. French glosses on difficult Hebrew words, the designations l standing for *lĕšôn* 'a synonym of' and

---

in n. 13, Hendrik Antonie Brongers, "Alternative Interpretationen des sogennanten Waw Copulativum," *ZAW* 90 (1978), pp. 273-277; David W. Baker, "Further Examples of the Waw Explicativum," *VT* 30 (1980), pp. 129-136; B. A. Mastin, "waw explicativum in 2 Kings viii 9," *VT* 34 (1984), pp. 353-355.

k standing for *kĕmô* are employed interchangeably. Likewise, in Rashi's Commentary on the Book of Psalms at Ps. 7:15 where Vienna Heb. ms. 220 reads *lĕšôn*, ms. JTS L778 reads *kĕmô* while at Ps. 6:8 where Vienna Heb. ms. 220 reads *lĕšôn* ms. JTS L778 attests to an original *kĕmô*, which has been crossed out and corrected with a supralineal *lĕšôn*. It turns out that in the late Rabbinic Heb. of which Rashi's Commentary on the Book of Psalms is an exemplar, *kĕmô* is not only a preposition but also a noun just as *hû '* is a personal pronoun but not only that and just as *wĕ* is a coordinate conjunction but not only that.

Nevertheless, many scholars asked me why I should assume that in Rashi's dialect of Heb. *lāšôn* meaning 'tongue' is to be distinguished from *lāšôn* meaning 'dialect' and from *lāšôn* meaning 'synonym' etc. The answer is that the use of a single noun *lāšôn* in all of these and additional senses is well established long before Rashi in Rabbinic Heb. and Aram.[15] Moreover, the various usages of the term *lāšôn* in Rabbinic Heb. and Aram. linguistic terminology closely correspond to and probably derive from the usage of Akkadian *lišānu*, which, in turn goes back to the usage of Sumerian EME.[16] It appears that Rashi and other Medieval Heb. exegetes go further in refining the usage of the term *lĕšôn*. Isaac Avinery already noted:

> The meanings of *lāšôn* have become very extended in Rashi's commentaries. In addition to the [previously] established meaning *lāšôn* is found in his commentary in the meaning 'tense' (*lĕšôn 'ābar* 'past tense'); conjugation of a verb (*lĕšôn hiph'il* 'hiphil conjugation') 'form', 'meaning', 'root'; etc. Often you will find the word *lāšôn* five times in his commentary to a single verse and in different meanings (Ex. 1:17; 3:22), and in his commentary to [Babylonian Talmud, Tractate] Qiddushin, folio 6 *lāšôn* occurs about twenty times.[17]

The use of the expressions *lĕšôn yĕwānî*, and *lĕšôn 'ărābî* to denote respectively 'Greek' (Ps. 42:5) and 'Arabic' (Ps. 60:4) is rooted in the ancient usage of the term *lāšôn* and its cognates in Hebrew, Aramaic and Akkadian and their semantic equivalent in Sumerian, EME, as in the expressions EME·URI, *lišān Akkadî*, which denote 'Akkadi-

---

[15] See *Aruch Completum*, ed. Alexander Kohut (2ᵈ ed.; Vienna & Berlin: Menorah, 1926), vol. 5, pp. 60-61; Jacob Levy, *Wörterbuch über die Talmudim und Midraschim*, ed. H. L. Fleischer, 2ᵈ ed. ed. Lazarus Goldschmidt (4 vols; Berlin & Vienna: Harz, 1924), vol. 2, pp. 527-531; Jastrow, *Dict.* , p. 720.

[16] See *CAD*, L, pp. 209-215; *AHW*, p. 556.

[17] *Hechal Rashi*, vol. 1 (rev. ed.; Jerusalem: Mosad HaRav Kook, 1979), p. 728.

an' in Sumerian and Akkadian respectively. As noted by Avineri, Rashi and other Medieval Hebrew Bible commentators use the term *lāšôn* also to designate 'tense', 'conjugation', and 'form'. Thus, for example, at Ps. 2:4 Rashi notes that three imperfect forms of the verb are all *lĕšôn hōweh*, i.e., 'present tense' (in meaning).[18] Moreover, as demonstrated by Englander, Rashi employs the expression *lĕšôn ṣiwwûy* to designate both 'the imperative form of the verb' and 'the imperfect employed as a jussive (i.e., a third-person imperative).[19] Englander also notes that in Rashi's Hebrew *lĕšôn nip'al* does not mean 'niphal conjugation' but 'passive voice'; hence, as Englander demonstrates, Rashi designates forms in the *niphal* conjugation, which are reflexive in meaning as *lĕšôn hitpa'el*, i.e., 'reflexive'.[20] It should not be surprising, therefore, that in his commentary at Ps. 58:4 Rashi should employ the expression *lĕšôn nip'ălû* , i.e., 'passive plural'[21] to refer to a group of forms, which are now known to be *qal* passives.[22]

Just as Rashi's use of the term *lāšôn* in the expression *lĕšôn 'ărābî* goes back to an ancient usage of Akk. *lišānu* so, it appears, Rashi's use of the term *lāšôn* to denote 'synonym' and to denote 'cognate' should probably be traced back to the use of Sumerian EME and Akk. *lišānu* respectively to designate what is commonly called a 'synonym list',[23] but which, in fact, is a list of words whose precise relation to each other (occupations, birds, women, kinship terms, synonyms, etc.) varies from list to list.[24] It is reasonable to assume

---

[18] Concerning other meanings of the grammatical term *lĕšôn hōweh* in Rashi's Bible commentaries see Henry Englander, "Grammatical Elements and Terminology in Rashi," *HUCA* 14 (1939), pp. 408-409.

[19] Henry Englander, "Grammatical Elements and Terminology in Rashi's Bible Commentaries, Part I," *HUCA* 11 (1936), p. 367; id., "Grammatical Elements and Terminology in Rashi," *HUCA* 14 (1939), p. 390.

[20] "Grammatical Elements and Terminology in Rashi," *HUCA* 14 (1939), p. 393.

[21] Cf. Englander, "Grammatical Elements and Terminology in Rashi's Bible Commentaries, Part 1," p. 386, n. 139.

[22] See our discussion at Ps. 58:4.

[23] See *CAD*, L, p. 213; *AHW*, p. 556.

[24] See A. Leo Oppenheim, *Ancient Mesopotamia*, rev. ed. completed by Erica Reiner (Chicago & London: University of Chicago Press, 1977), pp. 243-49; Antoine Cavigneaux, "Lexikalische Listen," *Reallexikon der Assyriologie*, vol. 6 (Berlin & New York: Walter de Gruyter, 1980-83), pp. 608-41; Joachim Krecher, "Kommentare," *Reallexikon der Assyriologie*, vol. 6, pp. 188b-191a; Miguel Civil, "Lexicography," in *Sumerological Studies in Honor of Thorkild Jacobsen on His Seventieth Birthday*, Assyriological Studies, no. 20 (Chicago & London: University of Chicago Press, 1975), pp. 123-57.

that the use of *lāšôn* in Medieval Rabbinic Heb. to designate variously 'synonym', 'biform', 'cognate', 'expression refering to' and the like has evolved from the use of Akk. *lišānu* to refer first to a list of words that are somehow related and subsequently to refer to any of the diverse relationships that adhere to words juxtaposed in such lists.[25]

At any rate, on the basis of usage, I determined that in his commentary at Ps. 11:6 and Ps. 77:5 Rashi employs the formulaic expression "x *lěšôn* y" to mean "x is a biform of y." At Ps. 11:6 Rashi states *pahîm lěšôn pěhāmîm*, which means in context, "The word *pahîm* is a biform of the common word *pěhāmîm*, which means 'coals'." Likewise, at Ps. 77:5 Rashi states *šěmûrôt lěšôn 'ašmûrôt laylāh*, which means that *šěmûrôt* is a biform without prothetic *'aleph* of the word *'ašmûrôt* which designates in both Biblical and Rabbinic Heb. the subdivisions of the night determined by the changing of the guards atop the city walls.

In Rashi's commentary at Ps. 18:3; 22:8, 25; 68:24; 72:16; 76:4; 88:8; and elsewhere the word *lěšôn* appears in the formulaic expression 'x *lěšôn* y', in which x and y are synonyms. On the basis of the recurring usage I concluded that in such contexts the word *lěšôn* designates x as a synonym of y and that the formula should be translated "x is a synonym of y." For example, at Ps. 18:3 Rashi states, *ûměṣûdātî lěšôn mibṣār*, which can only mean "'MY FORTRESS' is a synonym of 'fortification'" just as in the comment which follows there *ṣûrî lěšôn selaʿ* can only mean "'MY ROCK' is a synonym of 'rock'."

At Ps. 12:7, commenting on the expression *běʿālîl*, Rashi states, *lěšôn gilluy hûʾ billěšôn mišnāh*, which means, "[The enigmatic expression] *ʿālîl* [which is attested in the Bible only at Ps. 12:7] is [employed as] a synonym of [the common word] *gilluy* 'manifest' in Mishnaic Hebrew." Rashi refers here to Mishnah Rosh ha-Shanah 1:5, and here as at Ps. 32:10; 37:35; 60:5; 68:24; 72:2; 76:11; 80:13, 14; 89:52, Rashi employs the expression *lěšôn mišnāh*, to designate

---

[25] I hope to demonstrate this fully at a later date. For the present it should be sufficient to note that Akk. *lišānu* designates both 'lexical list' and 'commentary' (see the authorities cited in n. 23). It is agreed that in the cultural sphere of ancient Mesopotamia the latter genre developed from the former (see the authorities cited in n. 24). Nevertheless, it appears that the use of *lišānu* in late stages of ancient Mesopotamian civilization to refer to these two genres demonstrates the reasonableness of our assertion that in Rashi's language the use of the identical term *lāšôn* to refer to distinct linguistic phenomena does not mean that Rashi does not distinguish them from one another.

what is commonly called Mishnaic Hebrew to this day. It is especially interesting to note that at Ps. 68:24 the term designates an
expression found not in the Mishnah but in the Tosefta while at
Ps. 76:11 the expression *lĕšôn mišnāh* refers to an expression found
in a *baraitha* quoted in the Babylonian Talmud. This usage suggests
that indeed *lĕšôn mišnāh* in Rashi's dialect means 'Mishnaic Hebrew',
i.e., the dialect of Hebrew found in the Mishnah but not only in
the Mishnah and that the expression in question cannot possibly refer
to the Mishnah as such. Subsequent to my having made this point
in a presentation at the Society of Biblical Literature International
Meeting in Jerusalem in August 1986, Prof. Pinchas Peli, of blessed
memory, shared with me a letter addressed to him in October 1986
by the late Prof. Saul Lieberman. In that letter, Prof. Lieberman
already demonstrates that *lĕšôn mišnāh* in the Hebrew of Rashi and
the Tosafists means Mishnaic Hebrew.

Another meaning of the term *lĕšôn* in Rashi's Hebrew is 'a cognate of', a usage illustrated, *inter alia*, by Rashi's Commentary on
the Book of Psalms at Ps. 6:7; 6:8; 7:5; 10:10; 16:5; 18:48; 21:7; 39:6;
44:5; etc. For example, at Ps. 6:7 Rashi states, *'aśheh lĕšôn śĕḥî ûmā'ôs*,
which means, "[The verb] *'aśheh* 'I STAIN' is a cognate of [the noun
śĕḥî 'filth' in the expression] *śĕḥî ûmā'ôs*, filth and refuse" (Lam. 3:45).
Likewise, at Ps. 39:6 Rashi writes, *ḥeled lĕšôn ḥălûdāh*, which means,
"[The Biblical Heb. noun] *ḥeled* 'SPAN' is a cognate of [the Rabbinic Heb. noun] *ḥălûdāh* 'rust'." With respect to this usage of the
expression *lĕšôn* as with respect to every item of Rashi's vocabulary,
I determined the meaning on the basis of usage in context, and I
found that it was the most suitable rendering in numerous other
contexts as well.

In many places in Rashi's Bible commentaries the term *lĕšôn* links
neither synonyms nor cognates but instead diverse parts of speech,
which are semantically related. In such cases the term *lĕšôn* denotes
'a noun/verb/ word/expression referring to' Examples of this usage are found in Rashi's Commentary on the Book of Psalms at Ps.
1:3; 18:35, 46; 20:4; 33:7; 34:11; 35:16; 48:8; 60:4; 89:45; 91:1; etc.
At Ps. 1:3, for example, Rashi states, *lō' yibbôl lĕšôn kāmûš*, which
means, "[The verb in the clause] *lō' yibbôl* 'IT NEVER FADES' is
an expression referring to '[being] worn out'." At Ps. 18:46 Rashi
states *wayaḥrĕgû lĕšôn 'êmāh*, which means "*wayaḥrĕgû* is a verb referring to 'fear'." At Ps. 91:1 Rashi states *šadday lĕšôn ḥōzeq* "[The divine name] Shaddai is an epithet referring to strength." The

rendering adopted in each of these and many additional cases on the basis of usage recommends itself since in none of these cases are the two words joined by the expression *lĕšôn* precise synonyms; they do, however, 'refer to' some common idea.

In a number of instances content and context require that the formula "x *lĕšôn* y" be rendered "x is a metaphor for y" Examples of this usage are found in Rashi's Commentary on the Book of Psalms at Ps. 23:2; 23:5; 31:11; 45:5; 98:8; etc. At Ps. 23:2 Rashi states, "Since he [the psalmist] began [the psalm] comparing his sustenance to the pasturage of cattle when he stated, 'THE LORD IS MY SHEPHERD', the metaphor [*hallāšôn*] 'ABODES OF GRASS' is fitting." At Ps. 45:5 Rashi states, "...he [the psalmist] referred to the study of Torah by the metaphor of [*bilĕšôn*] war." Particularly interesting is Rashi's comment at Ps. 98:8 where the psalmist states, "LET THE RIVERS CLAP THEIR HANDS." Rashi writes, "The prophets spoke metaphorically [*bilĕšôn šehā'ōzen šōmaʿat*]. [The psalmist here does] not [mean], 'Would that the RIVERS had HANDS.' Rather, LET THE RIVERS CLAP THEIR HANDS is a metaphor for [*lĕšôn*] happiness and joy."[26]

It should be noted also that the term *lĕšôn dibbûr* corresponds to the modern linguistic term *verbum dicendi*, i.e., 'verb of saying' in Rashi's Commentary at Ps. 12:6; 21:3; 45:2; etc. as does *lĕšôn haggādāh* in Rashi's Commentary at Ps. 19:3 while *lĕšôn niʿanûâ ʿ* corresponds to the modern linguistic term verbum movendi, i.e., 'verb of motion' in Rashi's Commentary at Ps. 45:2.

Notwithstanding the abudant evidence that *lĕšôn* can designate 'conjugation' and 'tense' and 'form' and notwithstanding the fact that the use of *lĕšôn* to mean 'synonym of' and 'word referring to' go back to the use of Sumerian EME and Akkadian *lišānu* to designate lists of words, scholars have asked me, "Is it reasonable to assume that Rashi would have used the same expression intending such diverse meanings?" The answer is in the affirmative for at least three reasons. First, the various contexts require the diverse meanings and nuances of *kĕmô* and *lĕšôn* given in my translation, and these meanings would certainly recommend themselves on the basis of usage had Rashi employed other terms with no known cognates. Second,

---

[26] In Rashi's commentary at Ps. 12:9 'metaphor' is referred to by the Hebrew term *dûgmāh* rather than the term *lāšôn*. Concerning the term *dûgmāh* in Rashi's commentaries see Sarah Kamin, "*Dûgmāh* in Rashi's Commentary on Song of Songs," Tarbiz 52 (1983), pp. 41-58 (in Hebrew).

Rashi was more likely than his modern readers to countenance homonyms since the basic dictionary of Biblical Hebrew, to which he
constantly referred, *Mahberet Menahem* posited numerous homonymous
biliteral and even monoliteral roots where later Biblical lexicography posited considerably fewer distinct trilteral roots. Third, all languages including Biblical and Rabbinic Heb., Rashi's native Old
Northern French, and even Modern Hebrew and Modern English
employ homonyms constantly, and people less gifted than Rashi
manage to distinguish, for example, between 'foot' as a unit in the
scanning of English or Greek or Latin or Akkadian poetry, the anatomical 'foot', and the 'foot' as a measure of length or between 'letter' as one of twenty-six alphabetic symbols and 'letter' as a missive
delivered through the postal service. Rashi himself distinguishes at
Ps. 2:1 between the King Messiah [Heb. *māšîăḥ*] of Rabbinic Judaism and the basic meaning of the noun *māšîăḥ* in Biblical Heb. 'a
king', such as "David himself".[27]

With respect to such exegetical expressions as *dārĕšû rabbôtênû* 'our
rabbis interpreted' (Ps. 2:1; 22:1 29:10; 64:2; 78:63; etc.) I have made
use of the findings of Sarah Kamin.[28] With respect to the expression *happōtĕrîm* 'the French-Jewish exegetes' (Ps. 68:32) I incorporated
the findings of Baneth.[29] With respect to the grammatical terminology I made use of the findings of Englander.[30] In specific instances

---

[27] This discussion of the nuances of the term *lāšôn* in Rashi's biblical commentaries is expanded from my paper, "The Nuances of the Term *lāšôn* in Rashi's
Commentary on the Book of Psalms," presented at the Society of Biblical Literature International Meeting held at Jerusalem in August 1986. Independent con-
firmation of the methodology here employed is provided by Nissan Netzer, "The
Term 'Leshon X' for the Purpose of Providing Semantic Differentiation in Rashi's
Commentary on the Bible," in *Proceedings of the Tenth World Congress of Jewish Studies (Jerusalem, August 16-24, 1989)* [Jerusalem: World Union of Jewish Studies, 1990],
Division D, Volume 1, pp. 93-100 (in Hebrew).

[28] See Kamin, *Rashi's Exegetical Categorization*, pp. 136-157; and see our remarks
at Ps. 2:1; 22:1; 29:10 and passim. Kamin demonstrates that the distinction between *pĕšaṭ* 'the true and original contextual meaning' and *dĕraš* 'eisegesis', which
is characteristic of Biblical exegesis in Hebrew to this day, was introduced by R.
Samuel b. Meir, and that the negative connotations associated with the verbal root
drš are not found in Rashi's use of the verb, which means simply 'interpret'; see
Kamin, pp. 263-274; Banitt, *Rashi: Interpreter of the Biblical Letter*, pp. 1-2.

[29] See Menahem Baneth, "Les Poterim," *REJ* 125 (1966), 21-33; see also Banitt
(=Baneth), *Rashi: Interpreter of the Biblical Letter*, p. 8 and the literature cited there,
n. 11.

[30] In addition to the studies cited in nn. 18 and 19 above, see Henry Englander,
"Rashi's View of the Weak, *'ayin-'ayin* and *pe-nun* Roots," *HUCA* 7 (1930), pp. 399-
437; id., "Grammatical Elements and Terminology in Rashi's Biblical Com-

where I found that the conclusions of earlier researchers were inapplicable I indicate this in the notes.

b. The Lemmas

There are three means of translating the lemmas, i.e., Rashi's citing of verses from the Book of Psalms before each comment. One method is to translate each lemma according to the understanding presupposed by Rashi. Unfortunately, however, it is not possible to know in every instance how Rashi understood a verse. His comment, especially if it is of a theological nature, may be applicable to several interpretations of the literal meaning of the verse. Another method, which is followed, for example, in Sara Japhet and Robert B. Salters, *The Commentary of R. Samuel ben Meir (Rashbam) on Qoheleth*, is to present all the lemmas according to a standard English translation; those that differ appreciably from the understanding presupposed by the commentator are discussed in the notes. Since, however, more than half of Rashi's comments presuppose an understanding of the biblical text, which differs from those found in standard translations, a third method recommended itself.

As far as possible I sought to render the lemma according to the understanding presupposed by Rashi's comment. Where Rashi's understanding of the lemma could not be determined or coincided with NJV I have adopted the latter's rendering of the lemma. I gratefully acknowledge my indebtedness to the Jewish Publication Society for permission to make extensive use of this version. In specific instances where my rendering of the lemma follows the margin of the NJV I have called attention to this in the notes. In a very few instances where Rashi's interpretation of the lemma differs radically from standard translations and/or from common sense and/or truth I preface the rendering of the lemma according to Rashi's understanding with a rendering in parentheses of the lemma as commonly or properly (in the opinion of this writer) interpreted. All such instances are discussed in the notes.

The lemmas and Rashi's references back to the biblical text he is

---

mentaries, Part II—Rashi's Vowel Terminology," HUCA 12-13 (1937-38), pp. 505-21; id., "Rashi as Bible Exegete and Grammarian," *CCAR Yearbook* 50 (1940), pp. 342-59; id., "A Commentary on Rashi's Grammatical Comments," *HUCA* 17 (1942-43), pp. 427-98; note that pp. 480-87 deal with the grammatical comments in Rashi's commentary on the psalter.

analyzing are printed in capitals to set them apart from Rashi's comments and amplifications. It should be noted, however, that while in some mss. of Rashi's Commentary on the Book of Psalms each lemma is distinguished from the comment by the underlining of the lemma (e.g., Corpus Christi College Oxford ms. 165) or, as in most printed editions, the setting off of the lemma from the comment by means of a dot, most mss. including Vienna Hebrew ms. 220, provide no such typographical distinction between lemma and comment. It should also be observed that one of the most variable elements from ms. to ms. of Rashi's Commentary on the Book of Psalms is the length of the lemma, i.e., just how much of the verse is quoted before each comment.

c. The Purpose

The purpose of this translation is to enable English readers who may be interested either in what Rashi's Commentary on the Book of Psalms can tell them about Hebrew Scripture and Biblical Hebrew in general and about the psalter in particular or in what Rashi's Commentary on the Book of Psalms can tell them about Medieval Jewish biblical exegesis in general and about Rashi's exegesis in particular. It is the translator's hope that this idiomatic translation will be utilized by persons with no knowledge of Hebrew, by persons who know Biblical and or Modern Hebrew but for whom Medieval Rabbinic Hebrew would otherwise be a closed book, and also by persons who may utilize the translation to gain entry to the world of Medieval Rabbinic Hebrew. I hope that this translation will make it possible for English readers to utilize Rashi's Commentary on the Book of Psalms in order to understand and appreciate the psalms and to understand the history of biblical exegesis, grammar, and lexicography. I hope also that my translation and supercommentary will enable many readers to learn how to read and understand Rashi's dialect of Hebrew and to utilize the understanding thereby acquired to read and understand other Medieval Hebrew commentaries, annotated translations of which are not yet available.

The three purposes of the annotations are as follows: (1) to call the attention of the reader to the translator's treatment of idiomatic expressions in Rashi's commentary such as those that have been discussed briefly in this section of the introduction; (2) so far as possible to identify Rashi's sources and to analyze his treatment of these sources; (3) to distinguish between comments that represent the response of a biblical exegete to philological problems in the biblical text and those that are expressions of Rabbinic or Medieval Judaism superimposed upon the biblical text. Where Rashi seems to respond primarily to a philological difficulty this difficulty is explained, and Rashi's response is analyzed and compared to the responses of other ancient, medieval, and modern exegetes. Where Rashi's comments respond primarily to extra-biblical agenda such as Jewish-Christian polemics, folkloristic beliefs or Rabbinic dogma, the specific agenda is identified and elucidated.

VIII. Synonymous Parallelism in Rashi's Exegesis

James L. Kugel in his brilliant and highly accalimed work on biblical poetry raises the question as to why parallelism "was 'forgotten' by the Jews."[1] He explains that it was "the principle of biblical 'omnisignificance'"[2] that led the Talmudic rabbis to assert again and again, "B always means someting beyond A."[3] Moreover, Kugel writes:

> Rashi feels the necessity, just as the Rabbis had, to explain any form of repetition or other apparently superfluous usages—and to explain them not as a feature of rhetoric, but as signifying something.[4]

Benjamin J. Gelles in his very learned book about Rashi asks, "Why did Rashi fail to take note of the existence of parallelism?"[5] Gelles answers his own question in these words:

> ...the phenomenon of parallelismus membrorum shows that there are a great many instances in which the same idea is expressed twice in different words. In short, this form of expression is a case of form for form's sake. To accept such a claim would render a large section of Scripture redundant from the point of view of content....[6]

Rashi in his commentary on Ps. 9:5, responding to the juxtaposition of two synonymous nouns *mišpāṭî wĕdînî* 'MY RIGHT AND MY CLAIM', follows a midrash found in Midrash Tehillim at Ps. 9:5, and he writes as follows:

---

[1] *The Idea of Biblical Poetry* (New Haven & London: Yale University Press, 1981), p. 97.

[2] Ibid., p. 104.

[3] Ibid., p. 101; note that 'A' and 'B' are terms which Kugel employs respectively for each of two parallel clauses in the poetry of the Hebrew Bible.

[4] Ibid., p. 173. In his oral response to my paper, "Synonymous Parallelism in Rashi's Exegesis of the Psalter," presented at the XIIth Congress of the International Organization for the Study of the Old Testament in Jerusalem in August 1986, Prof. Kugel referred in the quoted passage specifically to Rashi's treatment of "staircase parallelism". It should be noted, therefore, that Kugel's description of what "Rashi feels" concerning "staircase parallelism" is at odds with the evidence summarized above, p. 8, n. 43; q.v.

[5] Gelles, p. 101.

[6] Ibid.

têbôt kĕpûlôt bammiqrā' w'ên ḥillûq bênêhen
In the Bible there are precise synonyms juxtaposed.

Gelles argues that Rashi substitutes the expression *têbôt kĕpûlôt* 'synonymous words' for the expression *dĕbārîm kĕpûlîm* 'synonymous expressions' found in the midrash because "synonymity in principle applies for him [Rashi] only to individual words."[7] In fact, the midrash states concerning Ps. 9:5, *zeh 'ĕḥad miḥămiššāh dĕbārîm kĕpûlîm bammiqrā'* "This is one of five instances of duplication in the Bible."[8] It is Rashi, on the other hand, who asserts that juxtaposition of precise synonyms is a feature of the Bible in general and of Ps. 9:5 in particular.[9]

In any case, Rashi in his commentary at Ps. 9:5, following the midrash, illustrates this last point by citing two additional examples. These are Job. 16:19, "In heaven is my witness//and he who can testify for me is on high," and Job. 40:18 in which the nouns *ăṣāmāyw* and *gĕrāmāyw*, both meaning 'his bones' are employed in synonymous parallelism. Rashi's use of the midrash to support his contention that *mišpāṭî wĕdînî* in Ps. 9:5 are "precise synonymous juxtaposed" should make it clear that Rashi here does not demonstrate his having felt the necessity "to explain any form of repetition...as signifying something." Moreover, Rashi's making this point in connection with Ps. 9:5 shows that he was fully aware of the appearance of synonyms both in direct juxtaposition and in parallel clauses.

Rashi, especially in his Commentary on the Book of Psalms, treats the 10th cent. C.E. dictionary of Biblical Hebrew, *Mahberet Menahem* as a standard reference work just as modern scholars and students treat BDB or the 17th edition of Gesenius-Buhl. Hence, it goes without saying that Rashi was aware of Menahem's having made

---

[7] Ibid., pp. 99-102.

[8] The midrash, q.v., cites Ps. 9:5; Job. 16:19; 39:5; 40:18; and Ps. 71:18.

[9] In Rashi's responsum to the query addressed him by R. Samuel of Auxerre (see Cohen, *Mikrao't Gedolot 'HaKeter': Exekiel*, p. 321, #13) as to why Ezek. 47-48 employs two distinct terms *naḥālāh* 'heritage' (Ezek. 47:14) and *'ăḥúzāh* 'property' 'to refer to the stake of the people of Israel in the land of Israel, Rashi explains: *šĕnêhem šāwîm wĕderek hammiqra'ôt likpôl lĕšônām* "They are synonymous, and it is the manner of biblical verses to duplicate their language." According to Gelles, p. 102, "Rashi [in this *responsum*] could only have had in mind individual synonymous words, and beyond this, no further kind of literary device." *Mirabile dictu*, Rashi's proof of his contention consists of Job. 16:19 (quoted below in the text of our introduction) and Ps. 35:18, in the first of which the duplication represents two synonymous clauses in chiastic parallelism!

the point in his entry "ab IV that synonymous parallelism is often the key to determining the meaning of rare words.[10] Moreover, in his commentary on Ps. 68:14, Rashi states explicitly that the a-b words *kānāp* and *'ebrāh* are synonyms,[11] and he quotes Menahem's contemporary and rival Dunash ben Labrat to the effect that *yĕraqraq hārûṣ* must denote 'gold' since the noun *hārûṣ* and the noun *kesep* 'silver' found in the previous clause constitute a fixed word-pair.[12]

At Ps. 6:7 we read *'asheh bĕkôl-laylāh miṭṭātî//bĕdimmʿātî ʿarśî 'amseh*, in which at least one thing is certain, namely, that *miṭṭātî//ʿarśî* constitute a fixed pair of synonyms.[13] Now if, in fact, the portion of Ps. 6:7, just cited, is an instance of synonymous parallelism, then the two verbs *'asheh* and *'amseh*, must be treated as synonymous. Now if the feeling Kugel attributes to Rashi were manifest here, then, of course, Rashi could not treat these verbs as synonymous. What, in fact, does Rashi say about this verse? He says that the first of the two parallel clauses means, "I dirty my bed with tears" and that the second of the two parallel clauses means, "I make it wet, and I make it liquid like water." While Rashi does not treat the verbs *'asheh* and *'amseh*, as lexical equivalents, he clearly asserts that both clauses record the words of an individual, who cries his/her eyes out so that his/her bed sheets are stained with tears. By asserting that not only the second clause but also the first clause refers to tears, Rashi has anticipated Kugel's observation that the *caesura* or *'etnahtaʿ* should be treated not so much as an equals sign but as an arrow pointing in both directions.[14]

In his commentary to BT Rosh ha-Shanah 18a Rashi states explicitly that Ps. 33:15 is in synonymous parallelism with Ps. 33:14: *wĕ 'aqqĕrā' dilĕʿēl minnēh qā 'mĕhaddar* "It goes over [what is stated in] the verse which precedes it."[15]

At Ps. 36:6 we read, "O LORD, Your faithfulness reaches to heaven; Your steadfastness to the sky." Here the pairs of a-b words are *hasdĕkā//'ĕmûnātĕkā* 'faithfulness//steadfastness' and *šāmayim//*

---

[10] See *Mahberet Menahem*, p. 17; on the importance of *Mahberet Menahem* for Rashi see Nehemias Kronberg, *Raschi als Exeget* (Breslau: Schatzky, 1882), pp. 15-22.

[11] See Rashi also at Ps. 91:4.

[12] See Rashi and our discussion there, n. 42

[13] This fixed pair is found in Biblical Heb. also at Am. 3:12; 6:4; see Qimhi at Am. 3:12.

[14] See Kugel, p. 8.

[15] See our discussion at Ps. 33, n. 9.

šĕḥāqîm 'heavens/ /sky'. Were it true that Rashi must explain each and every word as signifying something, we might expect a sharpening of the distinction between ḥesed 'faithfulness' and 'ĕmûnāh 'steadfastness; and between šamayim 'heavens' and šĕḥāqîm 'sky'. In fact, Rashi's comment points to the fact that the two terms 'heavens' and 'sky' are a-b words designating the supraterrestrial realm, and his comment will make no sense unless we understand 'faithfulness' and 'steadfastness' as synonyms. Rashi's comment reads as follows:

> Because of these wicked people You take away FAITHFULNESS from the lower regions, and You elevate YOUR STEADFASTNESS TO THE SKY to remove it from people.

At Ps. 50:11 we read, "I know every bird of the mountains, while field creepers are with me."[16] A scholar, who is obsessed with finding a-b words everywhere might insist that mountain birds//field creepers constitute a fixed pair like heaven//earth, eat//drink, silver //gold. What would such a scholar do with 'I know' and 'with me'? Significantly, Rashi, who has been alleged to be "scrupulous in reading B as a distinction over against A,"[17] writes as follows in his commentary at Ps. 50:11: 'immādî' ănî yōdēa' 'et-kullām, which means, "'WITH ME' means 'I know all of them'." This comment means that Rashi in his commentary at Ps. 50:11 has anticipated the discovery in the 1980's of what has been designated either "nominal verbal parallelism" or "noun-verb parallelism".[18]

At Ps. 80:18 we read, "May Your hand be upon Your right hand man//the one You have taken as Your own." A sharp reading would distinguish between 'Your right hand man' and 'the one You have taken as Your own'. Rashi, however, writes as follows:
MAY YOUR HAND BE UPON YOUR RIGHT HAND MAN, [i.e.], upon Esau, who is about to collect payment from him [i.e.] Israel. THE ONE YOU HAVE TAKEN AS YOUR OWN so that his "abode" will be "among the fat places of the earth" (Gen. 27:39).

---

[16] Contrast NJV's rendering, and see our discussion there.

[17] Kugel, p. 173.

[18] See Adele Berlin, *The Dynamics of Biblical Parallelism* (Bloomington: University of Indiana Press, 1985), pp. 54-56; Wilfred G. E. Watson, *Classical Hebrew Poetry: A Guide to Its Techniques*, JSOT Supplement Series, no. 26 (Sheffield: JSOT Press, 1984), pp. 157-158; Daniel Grossberg, "Noun/Verb Parallelism: Syntactic or Asyntactic?" *JBL* 99 (1980), pp. 481-488; see also Rashi at Ps. 69:21.

The two expressions quoted from Gen. 27:39 are addressed in Gen. 27:39 to Esau. By identifying both 'YOUR RIGHT HAND MAN' and 'THE ONE YOU HAVE TAKEN AS YOUR OWN' with Esau, Rashi treats the two phrases as synonymous parallelism.

In his commentary at Ps. 141:7 Rashi states explicitly that the two verbs there juxtaposed *plḥ* and *bqʿ* are synonyms. Likewise, in his commentary at Ps. 144:7 where the verbs *pĕṣēnî wĕhaṣṣîlēnî* 'Rescue me, and save me' are juxtaposed, Rashi comments, "*pĕṣēnî* is a verb referring to *haṣṣālāh* 'saving'."[19] The examples cited here are typical examples of Rashi's exegesis, which demonstrate that Rashi was far from unaware both of the parallelistic nature of biblical poetry and of the tendency of biblical writers to juxtapose precise synonyms. Moreover, since Rashi seems to have some interesting contributions to a subject of great interest to contemporary Bible scholars, it seems especially important that the record be set straight. Ironically, reading 'B' as distinct in meaning from 'A', for which Rashi, quoting Rabbinic midrash, has been criticized as primitive and naive,[20] is now increasingly advocated in the academic study of Hebrew Scripture as the proper way to read biblical poetry.[21]

---

[19] For additional cases of synonymous parallelism recognized by Rashi see Rashi at Ps. 55:20; 105:8, 20; 107:10; and see in the subject index, s.v., synonymous parallelism..

[20] Cf. Joshua Baker and Ernest W. Nicholas, eds. and trans., *The Commentary of Rabbi David Kimhi on Psalms CXX-CL* (Cambridge: Cambridge University Press, 1973), pp. xxvi-xxviii.

[21] See in addition to Kugel, pp. 1-58; Robert Alter, *The Art of Biblical Poetry* (New York.: Basic Books, 1985), pp. 3-26; see also Mayer I. Gruber, "The Meaning of Biblical Parallelism: A Biblical Perspective," *Prooftexts* 13 (1993), pp. 289-293. Examples of Rashi's reading 'A' as distinct from 'B' include Rashi's comments on the pairs 'land//world' and 'seas//rivers' at Ps. 24:1-2 and his comments on 'sons of a person'//'sons of a man' at Ps. 49:3; see also passim in the commentary below. Interestingly, contrary to the conventional wisdom that rabbinic midrash requires reading 'B' as distinct from 'A', note that rabbinic *midrash halakah* actually requires that *kesse'* in Ps. 81:4 be understood as a synonym of *ḥôdeš* 'new moon'; to render the former noun as 'full moon' (so NJV despite NJV's general tendency to read parallel clauses according to the formula 'A = B') is to suggest that the *shofar* or ram's horn is sounded in Jewish ritual both on the New Year and on the Festival of Tabernacles. Such an interpretation is unacceptable in *midrash halakah* and in Rashi's Commentary on the Book of Psalms because it is at odds with the cultural reality that the shofar is sounded in Jewish ritual on the New Year and not on the Festival of Tabernacles.

IX. Previous Studies

While there are hundreds of important and worthwhile super-commentaries on Rashi's Commentary on the Pentateuch, there are only seven important treatments of Rashi's Commentary on the Book of Psalms prior to the present annotated English translation. The oldest of these super commentaries on the Psalter Commentary is the 13th-14th century manuscript (Ms. F. 12. 135) in the library of Trinity College of Cambridge University. This supercommentary on the Prophets and Hagiographa is written in Hebrew with frequent Germanic glosses (Old Yiddish?) just as Rashi's Bible and Talmud commentaries are written in Hebrew with frequent glosses in Old Northern French. The supercommentary in question consists of ten folio pages of vellum, of which the last third of p. 9a and two thirds of p. 9b are comments on Rashi's Commentary on the Book of Psalms. This supercommentary clarifies the meaning of words and phrases in Rashi's Hebrew employing alternate Hebrew words and phrases, whole sentences in Hebrew, and Germanic words and phrases. It should be of great comfort to modern students of Rashi's Bible commentaries, who are often intimidated by Rashi's frequent references to Talmudic writings, that our 13th-14th century super-commentator found it necessary in his time to identify as such the titles of tractates and chapters of the Mishnah and Talmud.

Fortunately, this 13-14th century supercommentary has been published.[1] For no apparent reason, the published version of this *Sefer Pitronot Rashi* includes transcription of the entire text, but it includes photocopies of the ms. only up to line 683 while the psalter supercommentary begins on line 712 and ends on line 751.

The next important work on Rashi's Commentary on the Book of Psalms is contained in the annotated Latin translation of Rashi's commentaries on the Later Prophets, Psalms, and Job prepared by Johann Friedrich Breithaupt (Gotha: Andrea Schalii, 1713). This monumental work identifies most of the Biblical and the Rabbinic sources employed by Rashi, attempts to clarify Rashi's Old French glosses by reference to their Latin cognates, and places Rashi's commentary in dialogue with Patristic exegesis of the Psalter and the

---

[1] Joseph Bar-El, *Sefer Pitronot Rashi* (Tel Aviv: Papyrus, 1992).

Rabbinic Hebrew lexicography of John Buxtorf (d. 1629). Breithaupt's lasting contribution to the identification of Rashi's sources can be seen on every page of Maarsen's edition (see below). In many cases an obscure Hebrew phrase in Rashi's Commentary on the Book of Psalms can be deciphered by reference to Breithaupt's rendering, which surely embodies an old Jewish exegetical tradition.

The nineteenth century bequeathed two short supercommentaries on Rashi's Commentary on the Psalms. The first of these is the slightly more than two and one-half pages (pp. 10a-12b) of the supercommentary on Rashi's commentary on the Prophets and Hagiographa, *Nisyonot Avraham* by Avraham Luria (Vilna: Mann, 1821). The second of these is the fifteen pages (pp. 29a-36b) of the supercommentary on the Prophets and Hagiographa, *'Ateret* Zvi by Jacob b. Zvi Hirsch of Mir (Vilna and Grodno: Jewish Community of Vilna Press, 1834). Early in the twentieth century a third supercommentary on Rashi's Commentary on the Psalms was published, like the latter two in Eastern Europe. This third commentary is *Shem Ephraim*, a supercommentary on Rashi's commentaries on all books of the Bible composed by Ephraim Zalman Margalioth (Munkascz: Kahn, 1913). The abiding value of all three of these attempts to elucidate Rashi's Commentary on the Psalms is adequately demonstrated by their utilization in Maarsen's work and in our own annotations.

The appearance of the third volume of *Parshandatha: The Commentary of Rashi and the Prophets and Hagiographs* (sic), edited on the basis of several manuscripts and editions by I. Maarsen, Chief Rabbi of the Hague (Amsterdam: M. Herzberger, 1936) marks a turning point in the study of Rashi's Commentary on the Book of Psalms. For the first time we have a serious attempt to identify the authentic manuscript tradition of the commentary and to combine the publication of a reliable text of the commentary with variant readings, identification of Biblical, Rabbinic, and Medieval sources referred to or alluded to by Rashi. Moreover, Maarsen successfully brings to bear on the study of Rashi's Commentary on the Book of Psalms the results of the modern study of Rashi including Arsène Darmsteter, *Les Gloses françaises de Raschi dans la Bible* (Paris: Durlacher, 1909). Maarsen was fortunate in his choice of Oxford Bodleian ms. Opp. 34 the basis of his text, for this text presents essentially the standard text found in most of the sixty-one mss. of Rashi's Commentary on the Psalms, which I was able to examined before choosing Austrian State Library Heb. ms. 220 as the basis for the published version of my translation and supercommentary. Unfortunately, Maarsen was extremely inaccurate both in his listing of variant readings in his critical apparatus and in his copying out the text of Opp. 34. See below for my discussion of why I chose Vienna 220 rather than Opp. 34.

The seventh important contribution to our understanding of Rashi's Commentary on the Book of Psalms is Menahem Zohory, *The Sources of Rashi: Halakic and Aggadic Midrashim in his Commentaries: Psalms* (Jerusalem: Cane, 1987) [in Hebrew]. As a perusal of my annotations will reveal, there are many instances where Zohory identified a Rabbinic source for a comment of Rashi's, which Maarsen and Breithaupt had failed to locate and which without Zohory I would have had to state, "I was unable to locate the source of this comment." On the other hand, Zohory seems to have gone too far in his attempt to identify known Rabbinic sources for many of Rashi's comments for which the Rabbinic source may be still unknown, lost beyond recovery, or nonexistent. Zohory's work at its best supplies the text of Rashi's commentary based on the standard printed editions followed by midrashim, which seem to have been utilized by Rashi, followed by a sentence indicating whether Rashi employs the midrash verbatim, summarizes it, or vaguely alludes to an idea found in the midrash. In many instances Zohory briefly summarizes the idea found in Rashi and his Rabbinic sources. Unlike Maarsen's annotations and unlike the present work, Zohory's useful handbook fails to reckon with the fact that Rashi's exegesis of the Book of Psalms is more than a patchwork of Rabbinic materials. Rashi brings to bear on biblical lexicography and grammar not only halakic and aggadic midrash but also comparative Semitic dialectology, which includes reference to the vocabulary of Tannaitic and Amoraic Hebrew, Targumic Aramaic, the vocabulary of Medieval Hebrew poetry (see, for example, at Ps. 42:5), and Arabic (see Ps. 45:2; 60:4; 68:17; 74:6).

In two additional works Zohory himself has remedied his failure to reckon with Rashi's reliance on both medieval Hebrew lexicography and the vocabulary of medieval Hebrew poetry.[2]

---

[2] Menahem Zohory, *Grammarians and their Writings in Rashi's Commentaries* (Jerusalem: Carmel, 1994) [in Hebrew]. which lists the quotations from *Mahberet Menahem* and *Teshuvot Dunash* in Rashi's Bible commentaries, and id., *Quotations from Moshe ha-Darshan and the Liturgical Poems of Elazar ha-Qaliri in Rashi's Commentaries* (Jerusalem: Carmel, 1995) [in Hebrew]; see also id., *Rashi's Sournces: Midrash Halakah and Midrash Aggadah in his Commentaries: Addenda and Corrigenda* (Jerusalem: Carmel, 1994) [in Hebrew]; the addenda pertaining to Ps. 149:6 are found there, p. 22.

X. The Choice of a Hebrew Text

One of the axioms of the modern study of ancient and medieval Hebrew writings is that the standard printed editons are corrupt and need to be replaced by new editions[1] of one of of three types. These types are (a) accurate publication of the most accurate ancient or medieval ms.;[2] (b) publication of a critical edition, which presents both a transcription of the best available early ms. and an apparatus, which records all variant readings from other old mss. and from quotations of the work by medieval writers;[3] and (c) publication of an eclectic text on the basis of several early mss.[4]

In his critical edition of Rashi's Commentary on Psalms I. Maarsen notes that in the printed editions of that commentary numerous passages are marked with the Hebrew abbrevation, i.e., 'absent in other editions' or printed within parentheses or marked with the expression "I found" or "another version" or "in other commentaries."[5] Since Maarsen did not find these kinds of additions to the text of Rashi's Commentary on Psalms in any of the six 13th-14th

---

[1] With respect to the Bible commentaries of Rashi see Mordechai Leib Katzenelenbogen, *Joshua and Judges with the Commentary of Rashi* (Jerusalem: Mossad Harav Kook, 1987), pp. 1-6 (in Hebrew); see also the remarks of Avraham Daron, ed., *R. David Qimhi, The Complete Commentary on Psalms* (Jerusalem: Mossad Harav Kook, 1979), pp. 5-6 (in Hebrew).

[2] See Katzenelenbogen, *Joshua and Judges with the Commentary of Rashi.*

[3] This approach has been most successfully applied in the editing of Rabbinic works of late antiquity, of which there have survived a relatively small number of complete medieval mss. Classic examples are Saul Lieberman, *The Tosefta* (4 vols.; New York: Jewish Theological Seminary of America, 1955-1988); Bernard Mandelbaum, *Pesikta de Rav Kahana* (2[d], augmented ed.; 2 vols.; New York: Jewish Theological Seminary of America, 1987); and Louis Finkelstein, *Sifra on Leviticus* (5 vols.; New York: Jewish Theological Seminary of America, 1983-1991). It is reasonable to believe that the same method may successfully be applied in the near future to the texts of medieval Hebrew Bible commentaries for which tens and hundreds of old mss. exist. The *sine qua non* for doing this work properly will be the digital publication of the manuscripts so that they can be compared by scholars and their assistants on the computer screen. This technique has already been applied most successful to the study of cuneiform tablets of the Ugaritic epics recovered from Ras Shamra. The author is most grateful to Prof. Steven A. Wiggins for his having demonstrated to him the workings of the latter project.

[4] Chaim Dov Chavel, *The Torah Commentaries of Rabbenu Moses b. Nahman* (corrected ed.; 2 vols.; Jerusalem: Mossad Harav Kook, 1982).

[5] Maarsen, *Parshandatha: Part III: Psalms*, p. xiii

century mss., which he utilized in preparing his edition, he concluded: (1) that these additions are not from the pen of Rashi but corrections by his disciples; (2) that the person who writes, "I found" introducing an addition is not Rashi but a copyist or printer.[6]

Katzenelenbogen points out that in fact the parentheses accompanied by the expression מא״א "absent in other editions" were first introduced into Rashi's commentaries on the Prophets and Hagiographa in the Lublin edition of 1623. The aforementioned abbreviation was meant to designate all passages in the Rashi commentaries, which were found in the Rabbinic Bible published by Daniel Bomberg (Venice, 1547) but which were lacking in the medieval Rashi ms. owned by Baruch Segal of Lublin.[7]

Maarsen, following I. H. Weiss,[8] was uncertain as to whether the expression māṣā'tî 'I found' was introduced by the copyist(s) of medieval mss. or by the editors of the early printed editions. My examination of medieval mss. of Rashi's Commentary on the Book of Psalms demonstrates conclusively that the expression originates with the medieval scribes and that it was copied from the mss. into the early printed editions. Moroever, I believe that I have discovered the origin of this expression. Most medieval mss. of Rashi's Commentary on the Book of Psalms contain no commentary on Pss. 121, 128, 134. Several medieval mss. contain no commentary on Ps. 67. Most of the medieval mss. contain only the brief comment on Ps. 136 found in Austrian State Library Heb. ms. 220, the text of which is reproduced below. When Menahem, the scribe responsible for the Commentary on Psalms in the latter ms., and many other medieval scribes reach, for example, Ps. 128, on which according to the best of their knowledge, there is no commentary of Rashi, the scribes simply record the opening line of the psalm in question and they proceed to the opening line of the next psalm and then to Rashi's commentary on that psalm. Other scribes completely pass over the psalms for which they have no Rashi commentary.[9] A consequence

---

[6] Ibid., p. xv.

[7] Katzenelenbogen, pp. 1-3.

[8] The Life of R. Salomon b. Isaac," *Beth Ha-Talmud* 2 (1882), pp. 260-61 (in Hebrew); contrast Menahem Cohen, ed., *Mikra'ot Gedolot 'Haketer': Joshua-Judges & General Introduction* (Ramat Gan: Bar-Ilan University Press, 1992), p. 93, n. 73 (in Hebrew).

[9] E.g., Oxford Bodleian ms. Opp. 34 and Oxford Corpus Christi College ms. 165.

of the latter practice is that the scribe may misnumber the psalms following the omitted psalm. This is what happens in London British Library ms. 1155 at Ps. 129 and in Cambridge St. John's College ms. A3 at Ps. 122 as also in Petrograd ms. Firkovich I. 16 there. Most wisely, therefore, does the scribe responsible for Oxford Bodleian ms. Can. Or. 60 explain at Ps. 128:

> As for this psalm, I did not find [*lō' māṣā'tî*] a commentary on it. However, I have recorded it so as to find the [correct] number of psalms.

The scribe responsible for Oxford Opp. Add. fol. 24 tells us the same thing with respect to Ps.121. He also states at both Ps. 128 and at Ps. 134 *wělō' māṣā'tî lô pêrûš* "I did not find a commentary on it." The scribe responsible for Oxford Bodleian ms. Can. Or. 60 tells us the following at Ps. 67:

> *ăbāl zeh hammizmôr 'en lô pêrûš kělal ûkělal*
> This psalm, however, has no commentary at all.[10]

Interestingly enough, when the 15th century scribe who added Rashi's commentary on Psalms to London British Library ms. Harley 150, reaches Ps. 121 and again when he reaches Ps. 128 not only does he provide a commentary but also he both prefaces and concludes each of these comments with the expression *māṣā'tî* 'I found (a Rashi commentary here)'. It is reasonable to conclude, therefore, that the several scribes responsible for the aforementioned mss. attempted to assemble from diverse manuscript sources a complete Rashi commentary on the entire psalter. Most of the scribes were successful in finding comments of Rashi on all the psalms except Pss. 121, 128, 134. Two scribes, whose mss. have reached us, apologized for their lack of success and one—the scribe responsible for ms. Harley 150—was bold enough to declare that he had found what others had not found. Without the evidence of the latter ms., which was examined neither by Maarsen nor by I. H. Weiss, it is understandable that the latter scholars might have attributed the origin of the expression 'I found' to the editors of the printed editions. It is to the credit of both these scholars that they left open the question as to whether this expression goes back to the mss. or originates

---

[10] Similarly, Oxford Bodleian Opp. Add. Fol. 24 states at Ps. 67: "This psalm, however, has no commentary."

with the printed editions. It should now be clear, however, that while the expression" א"סא originates with the Lublin (printed) edition of 1623 the expression *māṣā'tî* was copied into the printed editions from the mss.

The conventional wisdom seems to have been that the standard printed editions of Rashi's Commentary on the Book of Psalms with their numerous passages marked א"סא and *māṣā'tî* present us with an eclectic text based on a variety of mss. According to this conventional wisdom, examination of the best early mss. should provide us with access to the authentic and distinct traditions going back to Rashi and his earliest disciples, and it should enable us to reconstruct the original text of the commentary. However, the presence of the expressions 'I did not find' and 'I found' within the ms. tradition combines with additional evidence to suggest that even the best mss.—those without numerous marginal and supralinear additions and corrections—represent eclectic texts.

The expression 'additions' found in the standard printed editions of the commentary at Ps. 127:4 cannot be the invention of the editors of the printed editions since it is found in the mss. including Oxford Bodleian ms. Bodl. 18 at Ps. 134 and in Vienna 220 at Ps. 139:16. Precisely because many of the old mss. were produced by scribes who sought and either found or did not find in older mss. Rashi's comments on the entire psalter we find the following: The passage designated below as RASHI'S INTRODUCTION TO THE PSALTER appears in Petrograd ms. Firkovich 1/15 in expanded form following Rashi's commentary on Ps. 1:6 but prefaced by Ps. 1:1 and followed by the scribe's observation, "I found that it was thus written outside."[11] In Vienna 220 Menahem the scribe prefaces the commentary on psalms with a declaration that the commentary on Psalms follows the commentary on Proverbs. Since, in fact, in Vienna 220 the commentary on Psalms follows the commentary on Ruth, we conclude that the declaration in question was copied from an earlier ms. in which Rashi's commentary on Psalms followed the commentary on Proverbs.

Nevertheless, Maarsen's suggestion that the additions found in the standard printed editions but absent from the six mss. he used are of questionable authenticity and that the printed editions are there-

<hr/>

[11] See our discussion in our n. 1 to RASHI'S INTRODUCTION TO THE PSALTER; see below, p. 166.

fore not a reliable representation of Rashi's Commentary on Psalms as it appears in the oldest surviving mss. has been confirmed by my examination of virtually all the extant mss. of the commentary,[12] most of them from the 13th and 14th centuries. While mss. differ from each other as to spelling of words, the length of the lemmas, the order of a series of comments on a single verse, most of these mss. represent essentially the same text as is found in the manuscript chosen by Maarsen, namely Oxford Bodlein ms. Oppenheim 34. Were my translation to appear independently of the Hebrew text, it could be argued that it should be based on the best Hebrew text previously available to the public, namely, Maarsen's edition. Since, however, Brill Academic Publishers made it possible for me to publish the translation together with the Hebrew text of the commentary, it is now possible to progress beyond Maarsen's edition. The latter edition because of its tremendous number of typographical errors does not accurately represent Oppenheim 34. For the same reason Maarsen's critical apparatus does not accurately represent the mss. quoted therein. Obviously, I could have gone back and reproduced the Hebrew text of Opp. 34, which Maarsen miscopied. However, my examination of virtually all the extant mss. convinced me to choose

---

[12] Blondheim, "Liste de manuscrits des commentaires bibliques de Raschi," lists sixty-one 13th-14th-15th century mss. containing all or part of Rashi's Commentary on the Book of Psalms as well as the 17th cent. ms. JTS L781, which is of Italian origin. The provenance of almost all of the mss. in Blondheim's list is Ashkenaz (i.e., France and Germany) while a small minority are of Spanish or Italian provenance. During my visit to England in February 1988 I was able to examine in the Dept. of Oriental Books at the Bodleian Library microfilms of the three mss. from the Firkovich collection of the Leningrad State Library cited in Blondheim's list. During that visit I was able to examine at the Bodleian the various mss. referred to above as well as the Corpus Christi ms., the several mss. in the British Library to which reference has been made and the several mss. at Cambridge University. I am especially grateful to Mr. Richard Judd, Assistant Librarian at the Department of Oriental Books at the Bodleian Library, to Mrs. Christine Butler, Assistant Archivist at the Archives of Corpus Christi College Oxford, Prof. Stefan Reif, Director of the Taylor-Schechter Genizah Research Unit at the Cambridge University Library and to the members of the library staffs of Trinity College, Westminster College, and St. John's College of Cambridge University for their help and encouragement. In addition to the mss. at Oxford, Cambridge, and the British Library, which I was able to examine at first hand, I was priveleged to make use of the microfilm collection at the Institute for Microfilms of Hebrew Manuscripts at the National Library at the Hebrew University of Jerusalem. I am most appreciative of the the unstinting help and encouragement I received from the Institute's former and present directors, Prof. Israel Ta-Shma and Mr. Binyamin Richler, respectively, and the entire staff of the Institute.

instead Vienna 220 for the following reasons: (1) Vienna 220 is typical of the textual tradition represented by a majority of the mss.,
especially the older ones; (2) Vienna 220, unlike Opp. 34, represents
a single textual tradition as it has virtually no marginal or supralinear additions or corrections. Opp. 34, on the other hand, in its present
condition,, represents with respect to the psalter commentary several textual traditions from the hand of several scribes. (3) Vienna
220's triple columns of beautiful, clear script with abundant white
space between columns makes this ms. particularly aesthetic; (4) the
psalter commentary in Vienna 220 meets the two established primary criteria for the choice of a particular ms. for an edition of a
Rashi commentary: (a) generally clear (uncorrupted) readings; and
(b) as few as possible (only one in this case) passages designated as
"additions";[13] (5) having chosen Vienna 220 for the above reasons,
I was privileged to attend the Colloque Israélo-Française sur Rachi
at Bar-Ilan University March 7-9, 1988. This conference enabled
me to consult with a number of experts on Rashi mss., who confirmed my conviction that Vienna 220 was the proper choice. In
the interim a number of scholarly publications have confirmed my
judgment concerning the exemplary nature of this manuscript.[14] I
am most grateful to Dr. Eva Irblich, Director of the Dept. of Manuscripts and Incunabula at the Austrian National Library in Vienna
for granting me permission to publish the text of this ms.

I may, of course, be challenged. Sadly, more than ten years ago
someone who sought to derail my academic career asserted that I
was incompetent for not having used "Ms. Maarsen". There is, of
course, no "Ms. Maarsen"; there is a flawed critical edition prepared
by I. S. Maarsen, to which I refer, usually with utmost respect, on
almost every page of my supercommentary. Hopefully, intelligent

---

[13] See the discussion in Cohen, *Mikra'ot Gedolot 'Haketer': Joshua-Judges*, pp. 84-
85.
[14] See, e.g., Richard Steiner, "Saadia vs. Rashi: On the Shift from Meaning—
Maximalism to Meaning-Minimalism in Medieval Biblical Lexicology." *JQR*, n.s.,
88 (1998), pp. 213-258; Cohen, *Mikra'ot Gedolot 'Haketer': Joshua and Judges*, appendix, p. 84; id., *Mikra'ot Gedolot 'Haketer': Ezekiel*, p. 8; for the acepted criteria for
preferring a particular manuscript see also Abraham J. Levy, *Rashi's Commentary on
Ezekiel 40-48* (Philadelphia: Dropsie College, 1931), pp. 1-64. Note that many
scholars refer to Vienna Hebrew Ms. 200 as Vienna 23, whch is the number not
of the ms. but of the library catalogue entry where it is described in Arthur Zacharias Schwarz, *Die Hebräische Handschriften der Nationalbibliothek in Wien* (Vienna:
Ed. Strache, 1925), pp. 28-29.

readers will be guided by the authority of reason rather than by hearsay. I should not be suprised if someone should fault my work for my not have utilized Turin National Library Hebrew mss. A. I.2, AII.2 and A. IV. 27. Intelligent readers will, I believe, understand that the latter three mss. were unavailable to me becase they were completely destroyed in the fire which raged at the Turin National Library in 1904, forty years before I was born. It is conceivable that when the work of restoration is completed on Turin ms. A. II. 16, most of which survived fire and flood, scholars will be able to suggest that it was a shame that I did not used that ms. Likewise, it is reasonable to assume that the mss. of the former Jewish Theological Seminary at Wroclaw now housed at the Jewish Historical Institute in Warsaw may suggest some improved readings. Hopefully, additional mss. of Rashi's commentaries will be located and will increase our knowledge. In fact, almost every time I visit the National and University Library on the Givat Ram Campus in Jerusalem I am approached by one or another member of the staff of the Institute for Microfilms of Hebrew Manuscripts with a suggestion that I might want to examine some additional manuscript or fragment that has come to light.

Some readers may be surprised that the Hebrew text of Rashi's Commentary on the Book of Psalms does not appear in this edition in the so-called Rashi script. In fact, the latter script, which would have been strange to Rashi himself, came to be associated with Rashi's commentaries because the first dated printed edition of Rashi's Commentary on the Pentateuch (Reggio di Calabria, 1475) employed that script. Abraham ben Garton ben Isaac, who produced that editio princeps, which was the first dated Hebrew printed book, employed that script probably because it was the handwriting he had learned in his native Spain. It is not the script of the majority of the surviving medieval mss. of this commentary, which, as we have noted, originate in Rashi's native Ashkenaz (France and Germany).[15]

---

[15] Concerning the use of the Spanish script in the *editio princeps* of Rashi's Pentateuch commentary see Malachi Beit-Arié, "The Relationship Between Early Hebrew Printing and Handwritten Books: Attachment or Detachment," *Scripta Hierosylamitana* 29 (1989), pp. 6-7; contrast Mayer I. Gruber, "Light on Rashi's Diagrams from the Asher Library of Spertus College of Judaica," in *The Solomon Goldman Lectures, Volume VI,* edited by Mayer I. Gruber (Chicago: Spertus College of Judaica Press, 1993), p. 80.

RASHI'S INTRODUCTION TO THE PSALTER
IN ENGLISH WITH NOTES[1]

And may He who dwells among Proverbs prosper me in the Book of Psalms.[2]

(HAPPY IS THE MAN).[3]

'ašrê hā'îš THE LAUDATIONS OF A MAN'.[4] This book is composed of ten poetic genres [each identifiable by a characteristic introductory expression]: leading,[5] instrumental music,[6] psalm,[7] song,[8] hallel [i.e., 'praise'],[9] prayer,[10] berakah [i.e., 'blessing'],[11] thanksgiving,[12] laudations,[13] Hallelujah.[14] These correspond numerically to the ten people who composed [the 150 compositions contained in] it: Adam,[15] Melchizedek,[16] Abraham,[17] Moses,[18] David,[19] Solomon,[20] Asaph,[21] and three sons of Korah.[22] Opinion is divided concerning Jeduthun.[23] Some say that he [Jeduthun in the titles of Ps. 39:1; 62:1; 72:1] was a person such as was written about in [1] Chronicles [16:38][24] while others explain that Jeduthun in this book is only [an acronym] referring to the judgments [haddatôt wĕhaddînîn],[25] i.e., the tribulations,[26] which overtook him [King David] and Israel.

RASHI'S INTRODUCTION, NOTES

[1] Both the mss. and the printed editions of Rashi's commentary preface Rashi's introduction to the psalter with the first two words of Ps. 1. In fact, these two words serve in the Hebrew Bible as the title of the Book of Psalms just as Bĕrē'šît 'IN THE BEGINNING' serves in the Hebrew Bible as the title of the Book of Genesis and just as Wĕ'ēlleh haddĕbārîm 'THESE ARE THE WORDS' serve in the Hebrew Bible as the title of the Book of Deuteronomy. A number of biblical books do begin with actual titles. These include Isaiah, Jeremiah, Amos, and Proverbs. Because Rashi's introduction is traditionally placed after the first two words of Ps. 1, it is not surprising that Jacob b. Zvi Hirsch of Mir in his supercommentary 'Ateret Zvi (Vilna & Grodno: Jewish Community of Vilna Press,1834) would attempt to prove that this introduction is simply a gloss on the word 'ašrê. In a number of mss. (e.g., Oxford Bodleian ms. 295; Corpus Christi ms. 165) the scribe sets Rashi's introduction to the psalter apart from Rashi's commentary on Ps. 1 by prefacing each of these with the first two words of Ps. 1:1 in bold letters. In Ms. Firkovich I/15 what we call RASHI'S INTRODUCTION TO THE PSALTER appears in expanded form following Rashi's commentary on Ps. 1:6. It should be noted, however, that the introduction in question is prefaced by HAPPY IS THE MAN WHO HAS

NOT FOLLOWED (v. 1a) and followed by the scribe's observation, "I found that it was written thus outside," which suggests that the scribe, R. Isaac son of R. Judah Nur, who copied out Ms. Firkovich I/15 in 1429 C.E. has incorporated into the body of Rashi's commentary at Ps. 1:6 the introduction, which originally appeared separately.

² This line is peculiar to Vienna 220. It is altogether inappropriate here because the commentary, which immediately precedes it in that ms. is Rashi's commentary on Ruth. Apparently, the scribe responsible for our ms. has copied this line from an earlier Rashi ms., in which the commentary on the Book of Proverbs preceded that on the Book of Psalms. In a similar vein Ms. Firkovich I/15 prefaces Rashi's commentary on Ps. 1:1 with these words "I shall begin to copy out (Heb. *laḥrôt*; the root *ḥrt* occurs only once in the Hebrew Bible, at Ex. 31:16 where "God's writing" is said to have been "incised [*ḥārût*] upon the tablets") the commentary on Writings (*Ketuvim*) with the help of God 'who is enthroned upon Cherubim (*Keruvim*)' [Ps. 99:1].'

³ The conventional rendering of the lemma.

⁴ Rendering of the lemma according to the interpretation given by Rashi, below.

⁵ Heb. *niṣṣûāḥ*; see Rashi at Ps. 4:1. Rashi refers to the expression *lamĕnaṣṣēāḥ* 'FOR THE LEADER', which occurs in the titles of fifty-four psalms (Ps. 4; 5; 6; 8; 9;11; 12;13; 14; 18; 19; 20; 21; 22; 31; 36; 40; 41; 42; 44; 45; 46; 47; 49; 51; 52; 53; 54; 55; 56; 57 ; 58; 59; 60; 61; 62; 64; 65; 66; 67; 68; 69; 70; 75; 76; 77; 80; 81; 84 ; 85; 88; l09; 139; 140).

⁶ Heb. *niggûn*. Here Rashi refers to the expression *binĕgînôt* 'WITH IN-STRUMENTAL MUSIC' found in the titles at Ps. 4:1; 6:1; 54:1; 55:1; 67:1; 76:1. The related expression *'al nĕgînat* 'WITH INSTRUMENTAL MUSIC' is found in Ps. 61:1.

⁷ Heb. *mizmôr*, which is found in the titles of fifty-seven psalms: Ps. 3; 4; 5; 6; 8; 9; 12; 13; 15; 19; 20; 21; 22; 23; 24; 29; 30; 31; 38; 39; 40; 41; 47; 48; 49; 50; 51; 62; 63; 64; 65; 66; 67; 68; 73; 75; 76; 77; 79; 80; 82; 83; 84; 85; 87; 88; 92; 99; 100; 101; 108; 109; 110; 139; 140; 141; 143. Heb. *mizmôr* is the common term for 'psalm', i.e., a chapter from the Book of Psalms, in the Jerusalem Talmud; see JT Berakot 4:3; Shabbat 16:1; Ta'anit 2:2. Similarly, in the Peshitta the Book of Psalms is designated *kĕtābā' dĕmazmûrê* ; see Nahum M. Sarna, "Psalms, Book of," *EJ* 13:1304.

⁸ Heb. *šîr*, which appears in the titles of thirty-five psalms: Ps. 30; 33; 40; 45; 46; 48; 65; 66; 67; 68; 75; 76; 83; 87; 88; 92; 96; 98; 108; 120; 121; 122; 123; 124; 125; 126; 127; 128; 129; 130; 131; 132; 133; 134; 149.

⁹ Rashi's formulation of the "ten poetic genres' takes for granted the view of R. Joshua b. Levi and R. Hisda quoting R. Johanan [b. Napha] at BT Pesaḥim 117a that *hallel* and *hallelujah* are distinct terms designating distinct genres. See Nahum M. Sarna, "Hallelujah," *EJ* 7:1199-1200. As the singular imperative *hallel* is unattested in any psalm title, the term *hallel* (as distinct from *hallelujah*) must refer to Ps. 117, whose opening words are *hallĕlû 'et-YHWH* 'Praise the LORD'.

¹⁰ The term *těpillāh* 'prayer' occurs in the titles of five psalms in the standard Hebrew text of the Book of Psalms (Ps. 17; 86; 90; 102; 142). In the Psalms Scroll from Qumran Cave #11 Ps. 145 is designated *těpillāh lěDāwîd* 'a prayer of David' rather than 'a psalm of David' as in the standard Hebrew text. The latter title, it should be noted, is the only example in a psalm title of the expression *těhillāh* 'a song of praise' (so NJV there), whose plural *těhillîm*, is the common designation of the Book of Psalms in the Babylonian Talmud (e.g., Bava Batra 14a) and in Medieval and Modern Hebrew.

¹¹ Ps. 104 begins with the words *bārěkî napšî 'et-YHWH* "Bless the LORD, O my soul" while Ps. 103 begins with the words "Of David. Bless the LORD, O my soul." Ps. 144 begins with the words "Of David. Blessed [*bārûk*] is the LORD, my rock."

¹² Heb. *hôdā'āh*; here reference is made to the five psalms (Ps. 105; 106; 107; 118; 136), which open with the imperative *hôdû* 'give thanks' (so JPS following KJV; a rendering which is consonant with Rashi's comment on *tôdāh* at Ps. 100:1); NJV renders 'praise'.

¹³ Heb. *'ašrê*, rendered here according to Rashi's interpretation at Ps. 1:1, q.v. NJV consistently renders "Happy". This expression is the first word of Ps. 1 and of Ps. 119; it appears as the first word of a psalm introduced by another title in Ps. 32:1; 41:2; 112:1; 128:1.

¹⁴ Nine psalms (Ps. 111; 112; 113; 135; 146; 147; 148; 149; 150) are introduced by the word Hallelujah. Rashi's observation that the Book of Psalms is an anthology made up of ten poetic genres is clearly based upon Midrash Tehillim at Ps. 1 #6; on the latter text see William G. Braude, trans., *The Midrash on Psalms* (2 vols.; New Haven: Yale University Press, 1959), vol. 2, p. 399, n. 27. With respect to the idea that literary genres can be recognized by their opening formulae it is interesting to compare the words of Hermann Gunkel, *The Psalms: A Form-Critical Introduction*, trans. Thomas M. Horner with introduction by James Muilenberg, Facet Books Biblical Series, no. 19 (Philadelphia: Fortress, 1967), p. 11: "That we attach importance to beginnings and endings may be explained by the fact that they are a distinguishing mark of literary works in general, but especially of those in Israel." To this day the standard commentaries and encyclopedia articles concerning the Book of Psalms pay special attention to the three phenomena noted by Rashi in his introduction here: (1) the Book of Psalms is an anthology composed of a variety of literary genres; (2) the various psalms are introduced by a variety of recurring opening formulae; (3) the Book of Psalms contains poetic compositions contributed by a variety of authors from various eras; some of these authors are mentioned by name in the psalm titles.

¹⁵ Ps. 139. The attribution of Ps. 139 to Adam probably derives from 139:16, "Your eyes saw my *golem* (NJV: "unformed limbs")," where the latter expression means a body without a soul, an apt description of Adam as described in Gen. 2:7a before "He blew into his nostrils the breath of life, and Adam became a living being" (Gen. 2:7b). See Rashi at BT Bava Batra

14b, and see the various midrashim, which attribute Ps. 139 to Adam, in Midrash Tehillim there.

[16] Ps. 110; see Ps. 110:4.

[17] In Rabbinic tradition Ethan the Ezrahite, to whom Ps. 89 is attributed at Ps. 89:1, is none other than Abraham; see Rashi there (contrast Rashi at Ps. 88:1, s.v., OF HEMAN THE EZRAHITE). According to 1Kgs. 5:11 Ethan the Ezrahite was one of the wisest people in the world, wiser than whom was Solomon.

[18] Ps. 90 is attributed to Moses at Ps. 90:1; Rashi there, q.v., following various midrashim, attributes also Pss. 91-100 to Moses. Note that Heman the Ezrahite, to whom Ps. 88 is attributed (see Ps. 88:1, and see Rashi there), appears in the list of the ten authors of the Book of Psalms in BT Bava Batra 14b. However, the version of the list of ten psalmists quoted by Rashi here from Midrash Tehillim omits Heman the Ezrahite, possibly on the basis of the view of Rav (d. 247 C.E.) that Heman 'trusted' is an epithet of Moses referring to Num. 12:7b: "He is trusted [ne'ĕmān] throughout My household" (BT Bava Batra 15a).

[19] Seventy-three psalms (Ps. 3-9; 11-32; 34-41; 51-65; 68-70; 86; 101; 103; 108-110; 122; 124; 131; 133; 138-145) are attributed to David in the Book of Psalms.

[20] Ps. 72; 127, q.v.

[21] Ps. 50; 73-83.

[22] Ps. 42; 44-49; 84-85; 87-88; see Rashi at Ps. 42:1. At this point ms. Firkovich 1/15 adds the following: "And they correspond numerically to the ten utterances with which the world was created, and they correspond numerically to the ten commandments. At the place where Moses concluded [the Pentateuch], [i.e.] with 'HAPPY ARE YOU, O ISRAEL' (Deut. 33:29), the psalmist began with ten poetic genres [the first of which is 'HAPPY']. Thus he [the psalmist] concluded [the Book of Psalms] with ten repetitions of the word Hallelujah [in the psalm entitled] 'Praise God in His sanctuary' (Ps. 150). And the Sages, may their memory be for a blessing, ordained ten biblical verses for each of the [three parts of the New Year service called respectively] Sovereignty, Remembrance, and Shofar Verses." Rashi's remark that the ten poetic genres correspond numerically to the ten authors, which is based upon an anonymous midrash in Midrash Tehillim at Ps. 1 #6, might be taken to imply that the multiplicity of literary genres or stylistic features in a biblical book suggests multiple authorship. The expanded version of Rashi's Introduction found in ms. Firkovich 1/15 demonstrates that the association of ten authors with ten genres is no less and no more than the association of both of these with the ten commandments, which is simply free association.

[23] Rashi's list of the ten psalmists is taken from Midrash Tehillim at Ps. 1 #6; cf. BT Bava Batra 14b; 15a.

[24] This controversy, recorded in Koheleth Rabbah at Eccles. 7:19 involves Rav (d. 247 C.E.) and R. Johanan b. Napha (d. 279 C.E.). The former holds that Jeduthun refers to an actual person while R. Johanan holds the other view.

²⁵ This Heb. expression, which means literally 'the laws and the ordinances', is a compound based upon the Persian and Akkadian terms for 'law', *dâta* and *dînu* respectively. The expression entered Heb. via Esth. 1:13 where the expression *dāt wādîn* denoting 'law' combines the Persian and Akkadian terms just as Eng. 'will and testament' combines Anglo-Saxon and Norman French legal terminology. In the midrash, to which Rashi refers here, the term 'the laws and the ordinances' corresponds in meaning to classical Biblical Heb. *šĕpāṭîm*, lit., 'judgments', which may denote 'punishments, tribulations' as in Ex. 12:12; Ezek. 5:10; etc. Similarly, Rabbinic Heb. *gĕzêrôt* 'laws' often means 'punishments' or 'tribulations'; see dictionaries.

²⁶ Heb. *purʿānûyôt*, lit., 'exactions of punishment'; see dictionaries of Rabbinic Heb.

RASHI'S COMMENTARY ON PSALMS
IN ENGLISH WITH NOTES

PSALM I

1   (HAPPY IS THE MAN).[1]
        THE LAUDATIONS OF THE MAN.[2] These are the com-
        mendations ['iššûrāyw], i.e.,[3] the praises of a person ['ādām]:[4]
        WHO DID NOT WALK IN THE COUNSEL OF THE
        WICKED....[5]
        For as a result of the fact that HE DID NOT WALK [IN
        THE COUNSEL OF THE WICKED], HE DID NOT
        STAND [IN THE PATH OF HABITUAL SINNERS],[6] and
        as a result of the fact that HE DID NOT STAND [IN THE
        PATH OF HABITUAL SINNERS], HE DID NOT SIT [IN
        THE SEAT OF SCORNERS].[7]

2a   RATHER, THE LORD'S TORAH IS HIS DELIGHT.[2]
        Note [that on the basis of the antithetic parallelism of vv. 1
        and 2] you learn that the SEAT OF SCORNERS leads to
        neglect of Torah.[8]

2b   (AND HE RECITES HIS TEACHING).[9]
        AND HE THINKS ABOUT[10] HIS TORAH.[2] [On the ba-
        sis of the ambiguity of the pronoun 'HIS' in the expression
        'HIS TORAH', which may refer either to 'the LORD' or to
        the subject of the verb 'HE THINKS ABOUT', which is the
        more proximate antecedent, we may infer that with respect
        to] one who is beginning [the study of the Torah] it is called
        'the LORD's Torah' but [with respect to] a person who has
        exerted himself over it, it is called his [the student's own]
        Torah.[11] yehgeh 'HE THINKS'. Every form of the verb hāgāh
        [refers to an activity seated] in the lēb 'heart'.[12] Thus Scrip-
        ture states:[13] "and my heart's thought before You" (Ps. 19:15);
        "your heart will think, 'terror'" (Isa. 33:18); "For their heart
        thinks 'destruction'" (Prov. 24:2).

3c   WHOSE FOLIAGE NEVER FADES. Even his [the Torah
        student's] foolishness [lit., 'refuse'] is worthwhile. [I.e.], the
        idle conversation of Torah students is worthy of study.[14] [The
        verb in the clause] lō 'yibbôl 'IT NEVER FADES' is an ex-
        pression referring to '[being] worn out';[15] flestrir 'to wither up'
        in Old French.[16]

5   THEREFORE....

[Verse 5] is joined [by the conjunction 'THEREFORE'] to the following verse [v. 6].[17]

6   FOR THE LORD KNOWS.... [In keeping with the previous comment, Rashi now paraphrases vv. 5-6 in reverse order]: Insofar as He KNOWS THE WAY OF THE RIGHTEOUS, which is continually before Him to recognize them [sic] while THE WAY OF THE WICKED is hateful in His eyes so that He removes it from His presence, THEREFORE there will be no resurrection for the WICKED on the Day of Judgment, nor are THE HABITUAL SINNERS (v. 1b) [to be listed] in the assembly of the RIGHTEOUS.[18]

PSALM I, NOTES

[1] Conventional rendering of the lemma.

[2] Rendering of the lemma according to the understanding presupposed by Rashi's comment here.

[3] Exegetical *waw*.

[4] Rashi's point is that the difficult form *'ašrê* with which the psalm opens is to be taken as the plural construct of a supposed singular segholate noun *'ešer* 'laudation' derived from the *pi'el* verb *'iššēr* 'laud', which appears in synonymous parallelism with the verb *hillēl* 'praise' in Prov. 31:28; Cant. 6:9 and in antithetic parallelism with the verb *bāz* 'insult' in Prov. 14:21. Cf. the supercommentary of Abraham Luria, Nisyonot Abraham (Vilna, 1821), p. 10b. Rashi's comment here presupposes his recognition of the synonymous parallelism in Prov. 31:28 and Cant. 6:9. Concerning Rashi's recognition of synonymous parallelism see the discussion at Ps. 9, n. 12. Most interpreters (LXX, Vulgate, Qimhi, NJV, et al.) treat the word *'ašrê* as an adjectival noun related etymologically and semantically to the noun *'ošer* 'happiness' (Gen. 30:13); hence the conventional rendering "Happy is the man who...." The latter interpretation is supported by various instances of the word *'ašrê* in synonymous parallelism with other expressions meaning 'happy' (Ps. 128:2; Prov. 16:20).

[5] Most interpreters (see previous note) take the word *'ašrê* as an adjectival noun, the subject of a nominal sentence, whose predicate is the noun *'îš* 'MAN'. Hence they take the clauses introduced by the relative particle *'ăšer* 'who, that' as a relative clause modifying the predicate. Rashi, on the other hand, takes the construct pl. noun *'ašrê* 'laudations of' (see previous note) as the subject of a nominal sentence, whose predicate is the noun clause 'WHO DID NOT WALK....'

[6] Rashi does not quote the bracketed portion; I have supplied it for clarity.

[7] The psalmist employs three verbs referring to postures–walk, stand, sit–idiomatically to denote 'be associated with' (cf. NJV). Rashi's comment, based upon a midrash in Midrash Tehillim here, cleverly takes the three verbs in their literal meanings to refer to successive postures. Sev-

eral mss. of Rashi's commentary (Florence Plut. 3. 8; Milan-Ambrosiano 25, 1; Oxford Bodleian 321; Oxford Bodleian 364; Firkovich I/15; Israel Museum [ms. Rothschild] 180/51/1) add here the following: "Some say that it [THE LAUDATIONS OF THE MAN] refers to Abraham, WHO DID NOT WALK IN THE COUNSEL OF THE WICKED. The latter are the generation of the division [of humankind into different nations and languages; i.e., the people who conspired to build the tower of Babel (Gen. 11:1-9): Nimrod and his associates (see Gen. 10:8-12). AND HE DID NOT STAND IN THE PATH OF HABITUAL SINNERS. The latter are Abimelech's people in consonance with what is stated in the Bible, 'Surely, there is no fear of God in this place' (Gen. 20:11), for they are suspected of adultery for they asked [Abraham upon his arrival] about his [lit., 'the'] wife and not concerning the food [Abraham would like to be served] as is normal with respect to lodgers. AND HE DID NOT SIT IN THE SEAT OF SCORNERS. The latter are the people of Sodom in consonance with what is stated in the Bible, 'At scoffers He scoffs' (Prov. 3:34). Now they [the people of Sodom] were scoffers in accord with what is stated in the Bible: 'But he seemed to his sons-in-law as one who jests' (Gen. 19:14), for they were making fun of him. However, the literal meaning of the biblical text does not seem to be thus." To this comment of Rashi cf. Midrash Tehillim at Ps. 1 #13; Yalqut Shim'oni #614; BT Avodah Zarah 18b-19a.

⁸ With Maarsen cf. BT 'Avodah Zarah 19a.

⁹ Correct rendering of lemma; see below, n. 12.

¹⁰ Heb. yehgeh rendered in accord with Rashi's exegesis; see below, n. 12.

¹¹ Rashi's comment here is based upon the midrash attributed to Rava (299-352 C.E.) in BT 'Avodah Zarah 19a.

¹² From the frequent association of the verb hāgāh and its derivatives with the noun lēb 'heart', which often denotes the seat of 'thinking' and which thus often serves as the functional equivalent of 'mind', Rashi concludes that the verb hāgāh always refers to an activity of that organ, i.e., 'thinking'. Similarly Harold Louis Ginsberg, "Lexicographical Notes," in Hebräische Wortforschung, VTS, vol. 16 (Leiden: E. J. Brill, 1967), p. 80 notes that while Ludwig Koehler and Walter Baumgartner [K-B, p. 224] "made a laudable attempt to eliminate all interpretations of this root [hgy] as denoting silent meditation…. At Ps. xlix, 4, however, he [Koehler] evidently found himself unable to overcome the difficulty of the combination of hāgūt with leb and gave the meaning as 'cogitation' ('Sinnen')." Ginsberg, however, solved this difficulty by pointing out (there, p. 80) that "'throat' as the organ of speech is nearly always expressed in biblical Hebrew by lēb."

¹³ Lit., 'as you state'.

¹⁴ Cf. BT 'Avodah Zarah 19b.

¹⁵ Heb. kāmûš. Here Rashi explains a relatively obscure biblical Heb. expression by reference first to a semantic equivalent in Rabbinic Heb. and then to a semantic equivalent in Old French, the spoken language of Rashi.

¹⁶ The equivalent of Modern French flétrir.

[17] Rashi's point is that v. 5 is joined by the conjunction 'THEREFORE' to v. 6 rather than to v. 4.

[18] Cf. the midrash attributed to R. Johanan [b. Napha] in Midrash Tehillim here.

PSALM II

1a WHY DO NATIONS ASSEMBLE?[1] Our rabbis interpreted[2] the subject of the chapter[3] as a reference to the King Messiah.[4] However, according to its basic meaning[5] and for a refutation of the Christians[6] it is correct to interpret it as a reference to David himself in consonance with what is stated in the Bible, "When the Philistines heard that Israel had annointed [*māšĕḥû*] David as king over them" (2 Sam. 5:17), "the Philistines gathered their troops..." (1 Sam. 28:4), and they fell into his [David's] hand. It is concerning them [the Philistines alluded to in 2 Sam. 5 and in 1 Sam. 28] that he [David] asked [here in Ps. 2:1], "WHY DO NATIONS ASSEMBLE so that all of them are gathered together?"

1b (AND PEOPLES PLOT).[7]
AND PEOPLES THOUGHT [*yehgû*][8] in their hearts[9] VAIN THINGS, namely:[10]

2a KINGS OF THE EARTH TAKE THEIR STAND.[11]

2b AND REGENTS INTRIGUE [*nôsĕdû*] TOGETHER....
Now what is the counsel [*'ēṣāh*]?[12]
[The counsel is as follows]:

3 "LET US REMOVE THEIR CORDS." These [CORDS] are the straps with which the yoke is attached.[13]

4 *yiṣḥaq* 'LAUGHS'; *yil'ag* 'MOCKS'; [*yĕ*]*dabbēr* 'SPEAKS'.
[Although these verbs appear to be future tense forms] they function [here] as present tense [forms].[14]

5 THEN HE SPEAKS TO THEM. Now what is the speech? He says,[15]

6 "BUT I HAVE INSTALLED MY KING."
[In other words, vv. 1-6 mean the following]: "WHY did you ASSEMBLE seeing that I have appointed for Me this one [King David] to reign [*linsok*], i.e., to be king,[16] over My holy Mt. Zion?"

7a LET ME TELL OF THE DECREE. David said, "It is an established DECREE, [which][17] I accept upon myself to TELL this and to announce":

7b THE LORD SAID TO ME through the agency of [the prophets] Nathan, Gad, and Samuel,[18]

7c 'YOU ARE MY SON'[19] [i.e.], the head of Israel, who are called sons [of God, as, for example in Ex. 4:22]: "My son, My first-born son" (Ex. 4:22), and they will be sustained [by you],[17] for all of them depend on you.

7d I, by making you king over them, HAVE FATHERED YOU THIS DAY so that [you] are called My son and are dear to Me, thereby for their sake in accord with what is stated in the Bible, "Thus David knew that the LORD had established him as king over Israel, and that his kingship was highly exalted for the sake of His people Israel" (1 Ch. 14:2). We have found also that those among the kings of Israel who are dear to Him He called 'sons' as it is stated in the Bible concerning Solomon, "He shall be a son to Me, and I will be a father to him" (cf. 1 Ch. 17:13).[20]

8 ASK IT OF ME, [i.e.], Pray to Me whenever you are about to wage war against your enemies.

9a YOU CAN SMASH THEM [těro'ēm]. [I.e.], 'you can shatter them' [těroṣěṣēm].[21] WITH AN IRON MACE. This is [a metaphor for] the sword.

9b YOU CAN SHATTER THEM [těnappěṣēm]. [I.e.], You can break them in pieces [těšabběrēm]. This is the meaning [of nippûṣ][17] throughout the Bible. [It refers to] pottery, which is broken into sherds.[22]

10 SO NOW, O KINGS, BE PRUDENT. The Israelite prophets are merciful people who admonish the nations of the world to turn away from their evil, for the Holy One Blessed be He welcomes[23] both evil people and good people.[24]

11 WITH TREMBLING. When there arrives that TREMBLING concerning which it is written, "Trembling has taken hold of the godless" (Isa. 33:14), you will rejoice, and you will be happy if you will have served the LORD.[25]

12a KISS [našqû] PURITY.[8] Arm yourselves[26] with purity of heart.[27]

12b LEST HE BE ANGRY [i.e.], LEST He be wroth.[28]

12c AND YOUR WAY BE DOOMED. This corresponds to the text in which it is stated, "But the way of the wicked is doomed" (Ps. 1:6).

12d WHEN HIS ANGER WILL BURN AGAINST YOU FOR A SHORT TIME. WHEN for a brief moment HIS ANGER

WILL BURN AGAINST YOU suddenly and at that same time

12e   THE LAUDATIONS OF THOSE WHO TAKE REFUGE IN HIM.

The praiseworthy qualities of [*"iššûrê*][29] THOSE WHO TAKE REFUGE IN HIM will be recognizable.

PSALM II, NOTES

1   Rendering of the lemma according to NJV, which reflects Rashi's exegesis; contrast LXX, whose interpretation is taken for granted in the New Testament at Acts 4:25, which RSV renders as follows: "Why did the Gentiles rage... ?"

2   Heb. *rabbôtênû dārĕšû*; Kamin, *Rashi's Exegetical Categorization*, pp. 136-39 demonstrates that in Rashi's commentaries the verb *dāraš* means simply 'interpret' (see, however, our discussion at Ps. 27, n. 2; Ps. 62, n. 2). It does not have the negative connotations, which it is given in the commentaries of Samuel b. Meir, Abraham Ibn Ezra and Nahmanides.

3   Heb. *'inyān*; similarly Michael A. Signer, "King/Messiah: Rashi's Exegesis of Psalm 2," *Prooftexts* 3 (1983), p. 274.

4   As noted by Maarsen here, Rashi here alludes to BT Berakot 7b where we read as follows: Rabbi Johanan [b. Napha] said that Rabbi Simeon b. Yohai said, "Bad child-rearing in a person's home is worse than the war of Gog and Magog. Thus it is stated in the Bible [in Ps. 3:1 with respect to the former], 'A psalm of David when he fled from his son Absalom,' and it is written [also with respect to bad child-rearing] in the Bible verse following that one [i.e., in Ps. 3:2], 'O LORD, my foes are so many! Many are those who attack me.' With reference to the war of Gog and Magog, however, it is written in the Bible [in Ps. 2:1], 'Why do nations assemble, and peoples plot vain things?' but it is not written, 'my adversaries are so many!'" Note that in Rabbinic theology the 'war of Gog and Magog' is the eschatological war, which is to precede the arrival of "King Messiah"; see "Gog," in *The Illustrated Dictionary and Concordance of the Bible*, ed. Geoffrey Wigoder (New York: Macmillan, 1986), p. 403.

5   Heb. *kĕmašmā'ô*; rendering according to Banitt, *Rashi: Interpreter of the Biblical Letter*, p. 1; see his discussion of this and related exegetical terms in n. 6 there; contrast Signer, p. 274: "according to its context in the narrative of Scripture"; in fact, not only do *mašmā'ô* and *šĕmû'ô* always refer in Rabbinic literature (see Max Kadushin, *A Conceptual Approach to the Mekilta* [New York: Jonathan David Publishers for the Jewish Theological Seminary of America, 1969], pp. 2-6) and in Rashi's commentaries to 'primary, literal meaning' but also, as demonstrated by Kamin, *Rashi's Exegetical Categorization*, pp. 111-208, *pĕšûṭô* in Rashi's Bible commentaries normally means simply 'literal meaning' and nothing more; see also Banitt, *Rashi: Interpreter of the Biblical Letter*, pp. 1-2.

6   Heb. *tĕšûbat hammînîn*; so correctly Signer, p. 274; see the extensive evidence that in Rashi's commentaries *mînîn (or mînîm)* means 'Chris-

tian' in Awerbuch, *Christlich-jüdische Begegnung im Zeitalter der Frühscholastik*, pp. 101-130. E. Touito, "Concerning the Meaning of the Term *těšûbat hammînîm* in the Writings of our French Rabbis," *Sinai* 99 (1986), pp. 144-48 (in Hebrew) demonstrates on both linguistic and historical grounds that in the writings of Rashi and his disciples *těšûbat hammînîm* often means 'a challenge to the Christians' rather than 'a reply to the Christian'. The rendering of *mînîm* here "Jewish converts to Christianity" found in Hailperin, Rashi and the Christian Scholars, p. 60 is no longer tenable. Solomon Zeitlin, "Rashi," *American Jewish Yearbook* 41 (1939-1940), p. 124 writes as follows: "I examined a manuscript in the library in Moscow in which the reading of this passage is as follows: 'Many of the disciples of Jesus apply this passage to Messiah, but in order to refute the Minim this passage should be applied to David.'" This version of Rashi demonstrates conclusively that Heb. *mînîm* here can only mean 'Christians'. Moreover, it supports the idea that the search for the literal meaning [*pěšûṭô*] by Rashi and the real, original meaning [*pěšaṭ*] by Rashi's disciples was motivated by the belief that the Bible understood on its own terms would demonstrate that Judaism rather than Christianity is the only legitimate heir to the legacy, which is commonly called "the Old Testament"; see, in addition to the important literature cited by Signer, p. 273, n. 3, Touito, "The Exegetical Method of Rashbam Against the Background of the Historical Reality of His Time," pp. 48-74; Sarah Kamin, "Rashi's Commentary on the Song of Songs and the Jewish-Christian Polemic," *SHNATON* 7-8 (1984), pp. 218-48 (in Hebrew); Shereshevsky, *Rashi: The Man and His World*, pp. 119-32. Rashi here suggests that it was not science for science's sake that led him to point out that in Biblical Heb. *māšîaḥ* is not an allusion to the eschatological "King Messiah" of late Second Temple era and later Judaism but simply a synonym of the noun *melek* 'king'; see Rashi also at Ps. 105:15. That Rashi should have found it necessary to diffuse the Christian belief that *měšîḥô* in Ps. 2:2 refers to "His Messiah" can be explained as follows: in the LXX *māšîaḥ*, lit., "Annointed One" is *christos* (similarly in the Vulgate, *christus)*. Moreover, the New Testament Book of Acts 4:25-27 declares explicitly that Ps. 2:1-2, which asks, "Why did the Gentiles rage... against the Lord and against his *christos*," refers to there having been "gathered together against... Jesus...both Herod and Pontius Pilate, with the Gentiles and the peoples of Israel" (Acts 4:25-27; RSV). While a comparison of eisegetical traditions may be serviceable in interfaith dialogue, the defense of the contention that Jewry rather than Christendom was the legitimate child of Hebrew Scripture made it necessary for Rashi and his disciples to seek out the primary meaning of the biblical word and to show that this supported the Jew's adherence to the ancestral faith rather than the adoption of the Christian faith. Note that Rashi's demonstration that *měšîḥô* in Ps. 2:2 denotes 'HIS ANNOINTED KING' rests upon 2 Sam. 5:17, which refers to David's having been 'annointed...king'.

⁷   Correct rendering of the lemma (so NJV and NRSV), which reflects Ginsberg's demonstration that the verb *hāgāh* means 'utter'; see NJV margin, and see Ps. 1, n. 12.

⁸ Rendering of the lemma according to the understanding presupposed by Rashi's comment.

⁹ Here Rashi alludes to a point he has already made at Ps. 1:2, q.v., namely, that in his view the verb *hāgāh* always refers to an activity seated in the 'heart', namely, 'to think'; see Rashi and our discussion at Ps. 1:2.

¹⁰ Heb. *'ăšēr*. By the addition of this word Rashi suggests that v. 2a is the thought introduced by the verb of thinking *yehgû* in v. 1b.

¹¹ Rashi here substitutes the *nitpa'el* for the psalmist's *hitpa'el* perfect.

¹² Rashi suggests that v. 3 is the quotation introduced by the *verbum dicendi nôsēdû* 'TOOK COUNSEL, INTRIGUED'. Moreover, he suggests that this verb is a cognate of the noun *sôd* 'counsel' (see Ps. 55:15). The latter point is made explicit in other Rashi mss.

¹³ I.e., v. 3 employs the metaphor of the removal of the yoke to refer to rebellion against God. On yoke metaphors in Hebrew Scripture see C. Umhau Wolf, "Yoke," *IDB* 4: 924b-925a.

¹⁴ In Medieval and Modern Heb. the future tense form is characterized by the use of a prefix to indicate the person while the past tense form is characterized by the use of a suffix to indicate the person. I5n Biblical Hebrew, however, the prefixed form of the verb (*yaqtul*) frequently denotes the past. Thus in Biblical Heb. the tense of a given form is determined by context and may be a matter of debate; hence Rashi's comment here. On the ambiguity of the tenses in Biblical Heb. see William Chomsky, *David Kimhi's Hebrew Grammar* (New York: Bloch Publishing Co. for the Dropsie College for Hebrew and Cognate Learning, 1952), p. 340; Abba Bendavid, *Biblical Hebrew and Mishnaic Hebrew* (2 vols.; Tel Aviv: Dvir, 1967-1971), vol. 2, pp. 527-50 (in Hebrew); Moshe Held, The YQTl-QTL (QTL-YQTL) Sequence of Identical Verbs in Biblical Hebrew and in Ugaritic," in *Studies and Essays in Honor of Abraham A. Neuman* (Leiden: E. J. Brill for Dropsie College, 1962), p. 282; "Symposium: The *yiqtol* in Biblical Hebrew," *Hebrew Studies* 29 (1988), pp. 7-42.

¹⁵ Rashi notes that v. 6 is a quotation and that normally between the verb *dibbēr* 'speak' and the quotation there intervenes a form of the verb *'āmar* 'say'; for this latter phenomenon see Lev. 15:1-2; 16:1-2; 17:1-2; 18:1-2 and *passim*.

¹⁶ Rashi's comment suggests that *nissaktî* 'I INSTALLED', a synonym of *māšahtî*, lit., 'I anointed' is simply the causative *pi'el* of the verb *nāsak* 'to reign', which here means simply *limlok* 'to be king, to rule'; note Rashi's use of the explicative *waw* (see introduction, and see *passim* in Rashi's commentary on the Book of Psalms) between *linsok* and *limlok*. Cf. Rashi's attempt to defuse the explosive verb *māšah* 'anoint' in his commentary at Ps. 105:15.

¹⁷ The bracketed expression is missing in our Rashi ms.

¹⁸ Here Rashi responds to the exegetical question, "Under what circumstances did God say such a thing to David?" With reference to Rashi's answer cf. 2 Sam. 7:4-16; Ps. 89:20.

¹⁹ Cf. 2 Sam. 7:14; Ps. 89:28.

[20]   Here Rashi quotes the two clauses in the reverse of the order from which they appear in the Bible. Here again Rashi's purpose is to defuse the explosive reference to *mĕšîḥô* 'HIS ANOINTED ONE' as 'MY SON', which was important ammunition in the Christian arsenal in the war against the Jew's adherence to the ancestral faith. The Apostle Paul declares in Acts 13:33 that Ps. 2:2 is fulfilled by the birth of Jesus. Rashi shows that at least three distinct figures in Jewish history—the people of Israel collectively, King David, and King Solomon—have all been addressed by God as "My son". Hence no Jew need be intimidated into giving up the ancestral faith because of the assertion that only one historical figure, namely Jesus of Nazareth, is known to Christians as the "son of God".

[21]   *BDB*, p. 949, s.v. r" II explains that the latter is an Aram. loanword in Hebrew; the classical Heb. etymological equivalent is *rṣṣ*; the two forms go back to proto-Semitic *rḍḍ*.

[22]   See Judg. 7:19; Jer. 48:12; cf. also Isa. 27:9.

[23]   Heb. *pōšēṭ yādô*, lit., 'stretches forth his hand'; cf. Akk. *qāta tarāṣu* 'stretch forth the hand' referring to a gesture of welcome; on the latter see Mayer I. Gruber, "Akkadian *labān appi* in the Light of Art and Literature," *JANES* 7 (1975), p. 77, n. 25; on the semantic equivalent of late Heb. *pāšaṭ yād* and Akk. *qāta tarāṣu* see Gruber, *Aspects*, p. 50; Shalom David Sperling, "Studies in Late Hebrew Lexicography in the Light of Akkadian" (Ph.D. diss., Columbia University, 1973), p. 124.

[24]   Rashi's source here is Midrash Tanḥuma, Bálak #1.

[25]   Here Rashi responds to the exegetical crux pointed out by Alfred Bertholet, "Eine crux interpretum: Ps. 2 11f," *ZAW* 28 (1908), pp. 58-59, namely, the impossibility that one individual or group can rejoice while trembling. Rashi's response to this crux is to distinguish here two groups of people, one of which will REJOICE and one of which will TREMBLE; contrast NJV, which treats the imperative *gîlû* not as the well-known verb meaning 'rejoice' but as a homonym meaning 'tremble'.

[26]   Heb. *zarĕzû*; Rashi suggests that the verb employed in v. 12a is not *nšq* I 'kiss' but the less common homonym *nšq* II, which means 'fight' and from which is derived the noun *nešeq* 'weapon' (see *K-B*³, p. 690).

[27]   Heb. *bôr lēbāb*; other editions of Rashi read here *bar lēbāb* 'the pure of heart', which serves as an epithet of King David. Rashi here, like LXX, Vulgate, and NJV, took *bar* to be an abstract noun derived from the verb *brr* 'purify'; cf. *Mahberet Menahem*, p. 89, s.v. *br* III; contrast Luther and KJV, who follow Ibn Ezra in interpreting *bar* as the Aramaic word meaning 'son' as in Prov. 31:2; so already Peshitta. Since in Rashi's time v. 12 was not interpreted in Christian Europe to mean "Kiss the son," there was no reason for him to react to Christological extensions of such an interpretation.

[28]   Rashi explains that the relatively rare verb *'ānap* is a synonym of the more common verb *qāṣap*; see now Gruber, *Aspects*, p. 547, n. 1; p. 553.

[29]   Concerning Rashi's interpretation of the word *'ašrê* 'LAUDATIONS' here see Rashi at Ps. 1:1 and our discussion there.

PSALM III

1   A PSALM OF DAVID WHEN HE FLED. Aggadists have composed many homilies on the expression [WHEN HE FLED] while our Rabbis said in the Talmud [BT Berakot 7a], "From the time when the prophet [Nathan] said to him [David], 'I am about to bring upon you trouble from within your own family' (2 Sam. 12:11) he was in turmoil 'lest a slave or a bastard who will not be merciful to me will attack me'.[1] As soon as he knew that it [the attacker] would be his own son, he rejoiced." There is an aggadic midrash to the effect that when he [David] saw his strategy succeed, his servants and the Cherethites and the Pelethites, who were [the functional equivalent of the] sanhedrin,[2] supported his being sovereign over them when he said to them, "Arise, let us flee...before Absalom" (2 Sam. 15: 14). What is written there? [What is written there is the following: "The king's servants told the king], 'Whatever my lord the king chooses your servants are here [at your disposal]'" (2 Sam. 15:15). Thus when he [David] came to Mahanaim and Shobi son of Nahash and Machir son of Ammiel and Barzillai the Gileadite came forth to meet him, they supplied him [David] with food there.

2   GREAT[3] ARE THOSE WHO ATTACK ME. [They are] people great[4] in [knowledge of] Torah, great in wealth, great in physical stature like Saul and the Raphaites,[5] Doeg and Ahitophel.

3b   "THERE IS NO DELIVERANCE FOR HIM THROUGH GOD."
Because he had intercourse with another man's wife.[6]

3a[7]   THEY SAY *lĕnapši* 'TO ME'. [I.e.], *'al napši* 'OF ME'.[8]

6   I LAY DOWN, AND I SLEPT. My heart is stopped up by vexation and fear.
I AWOKE from my vexation because I trusted in the LORD who SUSTAINS ME.

8d   YOU BREAK THE TEETH OF THE WICKED. ['THE TEETH' is a metaphor for] their might.

8c   FOR YOU SLAP ALL MY ENEMIES ON THE CHEEK. [This gesture of striking a person on the cheek is] a gesture [lit., striking] of contempt[9] as it is in "Let him give his cheek to his smiter" (Lam. 3:30); "they shall strike with a club [the ruler of Israel] on the cheek" (Mic. 4:14). There is an aggadic midrash [which treats the striking referred to in Ps. 3:8 as] verbal abuse as it is in "He gave his last instructions to his household, and he hanged himself" (2 Sam. 17:23).[10]

9   DELIVERANCE IS THE LORD'S. It is incumbent upon Him [the LORD] to vindicate His devotees and His people [Israel], and it is incumbent upon His people [Israel] to bless and to thank Him. SELAH.[11]

PSALM III, NOTES

[1] Marginal note in BT Berakot points out that some editions of BT add the explanation "A normal son shows mercy to his father."

[2] On Cherethites and Pelethites in the Bible see Jonas C. Greenfield, "Cherethites and Pelethites," *IDB* 1:557a; on Cherethites and Pelethites in midrash aggadah see Louis Ginzberg, "Cherethites," *JE* 4:11b.

[3] Heb. *rabbîm*, which can mean either 'many' (so NJV) or 'great' as understood in Rashi's comment, which follows.

[4] Heb. *gĕdôlîm*, which can only mean 'great'; see previous note.

[5] For reference to the Rephaim who threatened David see 2 Sam. 21:16, 18, 20, 22; 1 Ch. 20:6, 8. On Rephaim in Ugaritic and Biblical literature see S. David Sperling, "Rephaim," *EJ* 14:79-80; Simón B. Parker, "Rephaim," *IDB Supplementary Volume*, p. 739. On Rephaim being giants see Deut. 2:11; 3:11; Josh. 12:4.

[6] The reference is to David's having committed adultery with Bathsheba, the wife of Uriah, as described in 2 Sam. 11. With Zohory, p. 24 note that the interpretation of Ps. 3:3 as a reference to Doeg's and Ahitophel's referring to the Bathsheba affair derives from Midrash Tehillim here. Note also that the attempt to whitewash David's behavior with respect to Bathsheba as in Rashi's commentary at 2 Sam. 11 is not the consistent approach of either the Talmudic rabbis or of Rashi; hence it will be taken for granted in many of Rashi's comments on Psalms that in fact David committed adultery with Bathsheba; see passim in the commentary below.

[7] Note that in our Rashi ms. the two parts of the verse are treated in reverse order; so also at v. 8 below.

[8] Rashi, followed by NJV, holds that in the present context the prefixed preposition *lĕ* means not 'to' but 'of, concerning'; for numerous attestations of this usage of *lĕ* see *BDB*, p. 516a.

[9] See Gruber, *Aspects*, p. 291.

[10] For the rendering of this verse cf. NEB. The midrash is attributed to R. Levi in Midrash Tehillim here.

[11] This final comment, a paraphrase of v. 9b, YOUR BLESSING BE UPON YOUR PEOPLE, SELAH, takes '*al* there to mean 'it is incumbent upon'. Thus Rashi treats vv. 9a-b as contrasting parallelism.

PSALM IV

1   FOR THE LEADER; WITH INSTRUMENTAL MUSIC, A PSALM. David composed this psalm so that the Levites who lead the INSTRUMENTAL MUSIC for the song upon the [Levites'] stage would recite it. The verbal root 'leading' [*niṣṣuăḥ*] refers to those who take charge of an enterprise as in the passage where it is said, "They appointed Levites twenty years of age and older to lead the work on the Temple of the LORD" (Ez. 3:8).

2c   YOU FREED ME FROM DISTRESS in the days that passed over me,

2d   but now [I ask], HAVE MERCY ON ME AND HEAR MY PRAYER.[1]

3   SONS OF A NOBLE.[2] Sons of Abraham, Isaac, and Jacob, who are called 'noble' ['*îš*]. [The term 'noble'] is applied to Abraham [in Gen. 20:7]: "Return the noble's wife." [The term 'noble'] is applied to Isaac [in Gen. 24:65]: "Who is this noble?" [The term 'noble'] is applied to Jacob [in Gen. 25:27]: "Jacob was an unblemished noble."[3]

HOW LONG WILL MY GLORY BE MOCKED? How long will you insult me [by saying], "I saw Jesse's son" (1 Sam. 22:9); "when he [Jonathan] makes a pact with Jesse's son" (1 Sam. 22:8); "You side with Jesse's son" (1 Sam. 20:30)? Do I not have a name?[4]

YOU HAVE RECOURSE TO FRAUDS. You go in pursuit to find fraudulent accusations as did the liars who were slandering me while pretending friendship and similarly the informers who were in the time of Saul [who told Saul in 1 Sam. 23:19], "Indeed, David is hiding out...at the hill of Hachilah...." There are many similar references in the Bible.

4   SINGLES OUT [*hiplāh*]. [I.e.], 'distinguishes' [*hibdîl*].

5   TREMBLE [*rigĕzû*]. [I.e.], 'quake' [*hirĕdû*] in the presence of the Holy One Blessed be He, AND SIN NO MORE. SAY IN YOUR HEART UPON YOUR BED. Keep in mind[6] that the Holy One Blessed be He has so warned you.

6a   SACRIFICE SACRIFICES OF JUSTICE. Make your deeds

just so that thereby you will be like those who present sacrifices.[7]

6b   AND TRUST IN THE LORD so that He will bestow blessings upon you, "and do not sin" (v. 5) against Him for the sake of the money you expect to receive as a reward from Saul.

7a   MANY SAY, "WHO WILL SHOW US BENEFIT?" so that we may be affluent and so that we may achieve [our] desire as they [the Gentiles do].[8]

7b   RAISE UP OVER US. Raise up over us a flag [nēs],[9] your shining face. [The verb nĕsāh] is a synonym of [the expression hērîm nēs 'lift up a flag' as in] "lift up a flag" (Isa. 62:10); "I shall raise My flag" (Isa. 49:22).

8   I, however, am not jealous of them [the Gentiles, says King David,] because YOU PUT JOY INTO MY HEART WHEN THEIR [the Gentiles'] GRAIN AND WINE SHOW INCREASE, [for] I am certain that if He [the LORD does] so much for those who make Him angry how much more [will He do] in the time to come, which is the day of their recompense, for those who perform His will.[10]

9a   SAFE TOGETHER. If Israel be SAFE TOGETHER, LET ME LIE DOWN AND I SHALL SLEEP. [I.e.], I would lie down and I would sleep securely, and I would not be afraid of any adversary or enemy.

9b   ALONE [AND SECURE].[11] [The latter phrase] is a synonym of 'secure and quiet'. [The reason for the psalmist's being secure and quiet although he is alone] is that he need not post security guards [to spend the night] with him.

PSALM IV, NOTES

[1] On the problem of the apparent change of tenses from past to present see Dahood, *Psalms*, 1:23 and the literature cited there.

[2] Heb. *bĕnê 'îš*, which may mean 'members of the clss or group man', i.e., 'men' (so NJV), may, however, mean 'sons of an *'îš*. With reference to *'îš* 'lord, noble' note the use of *'îš* as a synonym of *ba'al* 'lord, husband' in Gen. 30:18; Judg. 14:15; 2 Kgs. 4:1; Hos. 2:9; Ruth 2:11; etc.; see also R. Moses Qimhi on *'îšîm* 'affluent people' in Prov. 8:4, and note *'îšî* 'my lord' in Mishnah Yoma 1:3.

[3] With Zohory note that Rashi's source is Midrash Tehillim here.

[4] With Zohory note that Rashi's source is Midrash Tehillim here.

[5] Heb. *zayyāpîm;* the word is probably chosen deliberately on the basis

of 1 Sam. 23:19a where *wayya'ălû zipîm* "The Ziphites went up" may be interpreted "The liars [*zayyāpîm*] went up."

⁶ Heb. *hăšîbû 'al lĕbabĕkem;* cf. Deut. 4:39.

⁷ I.e., to say, the practice of justice is a form of worship; for the same idea see Mic. 6:6-8.

⁸ With Zohory note that Rashi's source is Midrash Tehillim here.

⁹ Taking Heb. *nĕsāh* 'raise' as a denominative verb derived from the noun *nēs* 'flag'.

¹⁰ With Zohory note that Rashi's source is Midrash Tehillim here.

¹¹ Our Rashi ms. does not quote the bracketed portion of the verse; I have supplied it for clarity.

PSALM V

1   ON *NEHILOTH*. Menahem [b. Jacob Ibn Saruq] explained that all of the terms *nehiloth, alamoth* (Ps. 46:1), *gittith* (Ps. 8:1; 81:1; 84:1), and *Jeduthun* (Ps. 39:1; 62:1; 77:1) are names of musical instruments and that the melody for the psalm was made appropriate to the music characterisitc of the particular instrument named in the title of the particular psalm.[1] An aggadic midrash on the Book [of Psalms] interpreted *nehiloth* as a synonym of *naḥălāh* 'inheritance',[2] but this is not the meaning of the word. Moreover, the subject matter of the psalm does not refer to inheritance. It is possible to interpret *nehiloth* as a synonym of *gayyāsôt* 'military troops' as is suggested by the expression *nāḥîl šel děbôrîm* 'swarm of bees'.[3] [Thus our psalm could be understood as] a prayer referring to enemy troops who attack Israel. The poet has composed this psalm on behalf of all Israel.

2a   GIVE EAR TO MY SPEECH when I have the strength to ask of You what I need, but when I do not have the strength to pray to You and anguish is locked in my heart

2b   UNDERSTAND MY THOUGHT [i.e.], understand the thought of my heart; so is it interpreted in a midrash.[4] Throughout the Bible every example of [the verb] *bînāh* has the stress under the *bêt* [i.e., on the penultimate syllable].[5]

3a   HEAR MY VOICE...AT DAYBREAK. AT DAYBREAK I call to You concerning them because that is the time appointed for the punishment of the wicked just as it is said, "Each morning I will destroy all the wicked of the land" (Ps. 101:8); "Be their arm every morning" (Isa. 33:2); "Each morning it [disaster] will pass by" (Is. 28:19).

3b   AT DAYBREAK I PLEAD BEFORE YOU concerning this, AND WAIT for You to punish them.

5a   FOR YOU ARE NOT...WHO DESIRES WICKEDNESS, and it pleases You to eliminate the wicked from the world.

5b   EVIL CANNOT ABIDE WITH YOU. It will not abide near You.

6   *hōlĕlîm* 'MAD PEOPLE'.[6] [I.e.], 'people who act like imbeciles'.

7   MURDEROUS, DECEITFUL MEN. This refers to Esau and
       his progeny.
8   BUT I, THROUGH YOUR ABUNDANT LOVE, ENTER
       YOUR HOUSE to bow down to acknowledge You FOR
       YOUR ABUNDANT LOVE that You have worked wonders
       for us so as to cause us to experience vindication from them
       [Esau and his progeny].
9   MY WATCHFUL FOES. [I.e.], those who look at me with
       enmity ['ōyyĕnay] watching to see if we [Israel] will rebel against
       You so that You will abandon us. [The word] šôrĕrāy 'MY
       WATCHFUL FOES' comes from the same root as [the verb
       'ăšûrennû 'I will see him' in Num. 24:17]: "I will see him but
       not soon."
10   FOR THERE IS NO SINCERITY ON THEIR LIPS. They
       appear to be friends, but they are enemies. THEIR HEART
       IS MALICE. Their design is treachery. THEIR THROAT
       IS AN OPEN GRAVE [ready] to swallow the wealth of other
       persons like a grave, which swallows the body. THEIR
       TONGUE MAKES SMOOTH TALK [i.e.], words of flat-
       tery.
11   BY THEIR OWN DEVICES, which they devise against Is-
       rael, and
12a   then ALL WHO TAKE REFUGE IN YOU WILL RE-
       JOICE.
12c   AS YOU SHELTER THEM [i.e.], as You put a shield and
       a canopy over them.
12d   WILL EXULT IN YOU when they see that
13a   YOU BLESS THE RIGHTEOUS MAN [i.e.], Jacob and his
       progeny.
13c   LIKE A SHIELD, which encompasses three sides of a per-
       son, rāṣôn 'FAVOR' [i.e.], naḥat rûaḥ 'satisfaction'; apaiement
       in O.F.[7]
13b   ENCOMPASSING HIM [i.e.], You encircle him. The verb
       employed here is the same verb as is employed in "Saul and
       his men were surrounding David and his men... " (1 Sam.
       23:2).

PSALM V, NOTES
  [1] *Mahberet Menahem*, p. 116, s.v. *gt;* p. 282, s.v. *'lm* IV makes this general point but, as noted by Maarsen here, not with reference to *nehiloth.*
Note that the latter expression occurs only in Ps. 5:1.

² Midrash Tehillim here.

³ Mishnah Bava Qama 10:2.

⁴ I.e., Midrash Tehillim here. Note that both Rashi and NJV treat the noun *ḥāgîg*, which is found only here and at Ps. 39:4, as a cognate of the verb *hāgāh*; concerning the latter verb see our discussion at Ps. 1:2. Note that Rashi here follows his view expressed there that the verbal root in question refers to cogitation while NJV here follows the view that the root in question refers to speaking.

⁵ Other editions of Rashi read as follows: Throughout the Bible every example of *bînāh* has the stress under the *nun* [i.e., on the final syllable as in most feminine nouns] except for this case and for the other identical example *bînāh šimĕʿāh zōʾt* "Understand, listen to this" (Job. 34:16). The form here attested is not a noun but a synonym of [the verb] *hăbēn* 'understand' just as in "Surely understand [*bîn tābîn*] what is before you" (Prov. 23:1). Therefore [in the two exceptional cases] the stress is under the *bêt* [i.e., penultimate].

⁶ Ad hoc rendering to reflect Rashi's interpretation, which connects the participle with the abstract noun *hôlēlôt* 'madness' attested in Eccles. 1:17; 2:12; 7:25; 9:3; see BDB, p. 239b.

⁷ See Darmsteter, "Les Gloses Françaises de Raschi dans la Bible," *REJ* 55 (1908), p. 82; for the glossing of Heb. *rāṣôn* by O.F. *apaiement* = Modern French *apaisement*, cognate of Eng. 'appeasement', see Rashi also at Gen. 33:10; Lev. 19:3; Isa. 60:10; Ps. 89:18; 145:16; Prov. 11:27; see also the important discussion in Banitt, *Rashi: Interpreter of the Biblical Letter*, pp. 24, 29, 38, 56.

PSALM VI

1　ON THE *SHEMINITH*. There is a harp with eight strings, which is called a *sheminith*.[1] Thus we find in [The Book of] Chronicles so-and-so and his sons[2] "leading the music on the *sheminith*" (1 Ch. 15:21).

3　*'ûmlal* 'FEEBLE', i.e., 'injured and poor in strength'; [it means] *confondous* in O.F.[3] It is the same adjective as is attested in [the plural in] "the feeble Jews" (Neh. 3:4).[4]

4b　WHILE YOU, O LORD—O, HOW LONG will You look [upon my affliction] without healing me?[5]

5　O LORD, TURN from Your anger; RESCUE ME from my disease.

7b　EVE RY NIGHT I STAIN MY BED. [The verb] *'aśḥeh* 'STAIN' is a cognate of [the noun *sěḥî* in the expression] *sěḥî ûmā'ôs* "filth and refuse" (Lam. 3:45) and [the noun *sûḥāh* 'refuse' in] "its corpses were like refuse in the streets" (Isa. 5:25).[6] [STAIN MY BED means] 'dirty my bed with

7c　tears' while I MELT MY COUCH [means] 'I make it wet, and I make it liquid like water'.

8a　*'āśěšāh* 'IT BECOMES GLASSY' is a cognate of [the noun *'ǎšāšît* [which means] *lanterne* in O.F.[7] [The psalmist speaks of] an eye, whose perception of light is weak so that it seems to him [the person whose eye is here described] that he is looking through [foggy] glass, which is [placed] before his eye.[8]

8b　WORN OUT. My eye has grown old and become aged with respect to its weakening perception of light.[9]

8c　BECAUSE OF ALL MY FOES [*ṣôrěrāy*]. [I.e.], because of the troubles [*ṣārôt*] with which they show hostility to me.

11　WILL BE FRUSTRATED AND STRICKEN WITH TER-ROR....

11b　To what refers THEY WILL TURN BACK, BUT THEY WILL BE SHAMED a second time? R. Johanan (b. Napha) said, "In the time to come the Holy One Blessed be He will judge the Gentiles, and they will be sentenced to Gehenna. When they protest against Him, the Holy One Blessed be He will restore them [to the earth], and He will again call attention to their Gospels, and He will judge them, and they will be found guilty, and He will return them to Gehenna. This [double sentencing] is the double shame [alluded to by the words THEY WILL TURN BACK, BUT THEY WILL BE SHAMED]."[10] R. Samuel bar Naḥmani says, "In the time to come each nation will call to its god, but none will answer. Then they will call again, [this time] to the Holy One Blessed be He, who will say to them, 'Had you called to me in the first place, I would have answered you. Now, however, you have made idolatry primary and Me subordinate. Therefore, I shall not answer you, in accord with what is stated in the Bible (in Ps. 18:42), "They cried out, but there was no deliverer," which refers to [the unsuccessful appeal to] idolatry, while afterwards [it is stated there. "they cried] to the LORD, but He did not answer."' Therefore it is stated, THEY WILL TURN BACK, BUT THEY WILL BE SHAMED."[11]

PSALM VI, NOTES

[1] Lit., 'eighth'; see *Mahberet Menahem*, p. 383, s.v. *šmn* III; p. 616, s.v. *gt;* see also BT 'Arakin 13b; Pesikta Rabbati 21.

[2] Rashi's paraphrase of a list of six obscure proper names there in 1 Ch. 15:21.

[3] See Greenberg, *Foreign Words*, p. 180.

[4] Cf. Rashi at Isa. 24:4, and see Maarsen there.

[5] See Midrash Tehillim here.

[6] Contrast Mahberet Menahem, p. 362, s.v. *šḥ* III, which is quoted in many editions of Rashi here. Menahem treats *'aśheh* as the *hiphil* causative of the verb 'to swim'; so KJV and JPS here; similarly already Vulgate.

[7] I.e., Eng. 'lantern'; see Catane, *Recueil* #20, 65, 796, 939; for O.F. *lanterne* glossing *'ăšāšît* see Rashi's commentary also at Ps. 31:10; Berakot 25b; 53a; Shabbat 23a.

[8] Hence the comparison with a lantern, whose light is surrounded by glass.

[9] Cf. Gruber, *Aspects*, pp. 387-388.

[10] Rashi's source here is Yalqut Shim'oni, pt. 2 #714 at Ps. 31:1; cf. Midrash Tehillim here and at Ps. 31:1; see Maarsen here. Concerning the use of *gilāyôn* 'document' to mean "Gospel" see in addition to Mishnah Yadayim 2:13 cited by Maarsen here the dicta attributed to R. Meir and R. Johanan [b. Napha] in BT Shabbat 116a: R. Meir calls it [the Christian Gospel] Gk. εὐαγγέλιον *'āwen-gilāyôn* 'wrong-doing document'; R. Johanan calls it *'āwôn-gilāyôn* 'transgression document'. These dicta were removed from the Vilna edition of BT by Christian censors.

[11] Rashi's source is Midrash Tehillim here.

PSALM VII

1   *SHIGGAYON* OF DAVID. Menahem [b. Jacob Ibn Saruq] said that also this [term *SHIGGAYON*] is one of the names for a musical form, which is named for a musical instrument, and thus did he explain the expression *'al Shigionoth* (Hab. 3:1).[1] Our rabbis, however, have treated the term as a synonym of *mišgeh* '[confession of] error',[2] which one confessed and beseeched concerning error [*šiggāyôn*]. [In this case, according to the latter interpretation, the error is] that he [David] composed a hymn of victory on the occasion of the fall of Saul in accord with what is stated in the Bible, "Then David sang to the LORD..." (2 Sam. 22:1). However, the content of the psalm does not support such an interpretation because it [the context] speaks about the affairs of the Gentiles: "As for the LORD, may He punish the Gentiles" (Ps. 7:9).[3] I, however, say that he [David] composed it with reference to the machinations of Ishbibenob (2 Sam. 21:16), who attacked him [David] as a punishment for [the death of] Saul, as our rabbis have explained, [sc.], that the Holy One Blessed be He said to him [David], "Doeg the Edomite was banished on account of you (see 1 Sam. 21-22); Saul and his sons were killed on account of you. [Would you rather your dynasty end or that you be delivered into the power of the enemy?" He replied, "Master of the world, I would rather be delivered into the power of the enemy than that my dynasty should end"] as it is stated in [BT, Tractate Sanhedrin, Chapter] "Portion [in the World to Come"; i.e., Chapter Eleven].[4] Now David altered his prayer, and he prayed that he should not fall into the power of the enemy. Thus its [the word *šiggāyôn's*] meaning is *mišgeh* '[confession of] error', [which] David sang to the LORD because he erred in requesting that the Holy One Blessed be He hand him over to the enemy as punishment for Saul's having been killed on his account. Another eqaully plausible *midrash aggadah* [5] [suggests that the term SHIGGA-YON is employed in our psalm] in reference to the error [*šiggāyôn*] involving the hem of Saul's garment, which he [David] cut off (1 Sam. 24:6).[6] CUSH. [This term, which

denotes Ethiopian, is an appropriate epithet for Saul because]
just as an Ethiopian is dark[7] with respect to his skin so was
Saul dark with respect to his deeds.[8]

3b   [The participle] *pōrēq* 'RENDING IN PIECES' is a cognate
of [the imperative *pārĕqû* 'take off' in] "Take off the golden
rings" (Ex. 32:2).

4   IF I HAVE DONE what is explicated in the following clause.[9]

5a   IF I HAVE DEALT EVIL TO MY ALLY. [I.e.], if I have
dealt with him according to his just deserts.

5b   I FREELY RELEASED MY ENEMY. My thought concerning his garment[10] when I cut the hem of his garment was
whether to destroy or to remove it or to leave it alone. But
did I act with malice? On the contrary. [It was my intent] to
inform him that when I had the opportunity to kill him I did
not kill him. [The verb] *wā'ăhallĕṣāh* 'I RELEASED' is a verb
referring to removal of garments.[11]

7a   RISE...IN YOUR ANGER against my enemies such as Ishbi
and his co-conspirators and the Philistines so that I shall not
be handed over to them.

7b   ASSERT YOURSELF. I.e., glorify Yourself so as to show
angry vindication when You get angry with them.

7c   BESTIR YOURSELF ON MY BEHALF so that I may be
able to execute

7d   upon them THE JUDGMENT of vindication, which YOU
HAVE ORDAINED. Now where in the Bible HAVE YOU
ORDAINED? [You have done so in Ps. 2:9 where You have
said to me, "King David], You can smash them with an iron
mace" [and in Ex. 23:22 where You have said], "I will be
an enemy to your enemies." I found this [interpretation of
v. 7] in a midrash.[12]

8a   WHEN THE ASSEMBLY OF PEOPLES GATHERS
ABOUT YOU. If the armies of the Gentiles beg You[13] to
save them, do not hearken to their voice. Remove Yourself
from them, and return to be enthroned in Your place on
high.[14]

8b   PLEASE RETURN ON HIGH to show them that Your
power prevails.[15]

9a   AS FOR THE LORD, MAY HE JUDGE THE PEOPLES.
[I.e., Please, LORD], remove the punishment [*dîn*] from us
and give it to the Gentiles. [The verb *yādîn*] is a verb referring to punishments.[16]

9b   VINDICATE ME, O LORD, ACCORDING TO THE
      RIGHTEOUSNESS... THAT ARE MINE. [I.e.], VINDI-
      CATE Israel on the basis of the good deeds to their credit
      and not on the basis of their transgressions.

10   ESTABLISH THE RIGHTEOUS; You are HE WHO
      PROBES THE MIND AND CONSCIENCE. [Thus You
      know] who is righteous so that You may establish him. GOD
      THE RIGHTEOUS. That is Your Name.

12   šōpēṭ ṣaddîq, [which could mean 'VINDICATES THE
      RIGHTEOUS'],[17] [means] 'Judge, who is just'[18]

13   The Holy One Blessed be He WHETS HIS SWORD against
      him, and He will BEND HIS BOW.[19]

14   AND FOR HIM, [i.e.], for the wicked HE, the Holy One
      Blessed be He, READIES DEADLY WEAPONS.

15a   HE HATCHES EVIL. [The verb yĕhabbēl 'HE HATCHES']
      is a verb referring to pregnancy and birth[20] as in "It was there
      your mother conceived you [ḥibbĕlatĕkā]" (Cant. 8:5).

15b   CONCEIVES MISCHEIF, AND GIVES BIRTH TO
      FRAUD. Whatever he produces and for whatever he labors
      betrays him, for it does not remain in his possession. A prov-
      erb says, "Whatever fraud begets a curse marries."[21]

18   I SHALL PRAISE THE LORD FOR HIS JUSTICE when
      the final sentence is passed to punish the wicked for their
      wickedness.[22]

PSALM VII, NOTES

[1] *Mahberet Menahem*, p. 360, s.v. šg II: "Shiggayon of David, which he
sang to the LORD, concerning Cush, a Benjaminite" (Ps. 7:1) refers to
singing as its context demonstrates. It is possible that the expression 'al
šiggyônôt in the "Prayer of Habakkuk" (Hab. 3:1) is from the same root and
that it is synonymous with 'al hannĕgînôt 'with music'. Moreover, the close
of its [the Prayer of Habakkuk's] context demonstrates that this is so, [for
it states], "for the leader; with instrumental music [binĕgînôtāy]."

[2] Cf. Dahood, *Psalms*, l:41: "Both LXX and Vulg. simply translate it
psalmus, 'a psalm', but some modern scholars relate it to the root denoting
'to go astray, err' and define it 'dithyramb'." See Franz Delitzsch, *Biblical
Commentary on the Psalms*, trans. Francis Bolton (3 vols.; Edinburgh: T. &
T. Clark, 1971), vol. 1, pp. 138-139 and the literature cited there.

[3] Rendering reflects Rashi's interpretation; see below, v. 9.

[4] BT Sanhedrin 95a. The bracketed portion is not cited by Rashi, but
it must be supplied for the reader to understand the connection between
the portion quoted by Rashi and the interpretation of Heb. šiggāyôn, which
Rashi seeks to derive from the passage.

[5] Heb. *dābār 'aḥēr;* cf. the discussion of this Rabbinic Heb. expression in Max Kadushin, *The Rabbinic Mind* [3] (New York: Bloch, 1972), pp. 71-72.

[6] Cf. Midrash Tehillim here.

[7] Cf. Midrash Tehillim here; BT Mo'ed Qaṭan 16b. To translate *mĕšunneh* 'different' as is the general practice would not convey the negative connotations required in the present context. For midrashim on Ps. 7:2 in which the simile 'different like an Ethiopian' has positive connotations see Midrash Tehillim here. Perhaps, even the authors of those midrashim may have intended to convey the sense 'black like an Ethiopian'. If so, the midrashim understood that "black is beautiful" even though the midrash quoted here by Rashi understood black to be synonymous with evil. Our rendering of *mĕšunneh* 'black, dark (of complexion)' is based upon Eccles. 8:1b: *ḥokmat 'ādām tā'îr pānāyw wĕʿoz pānāyw yĕšannē'* [MT, *yĕšunnē'*] "A person's knowledge makes his face light up while anger makes his face gloomy." On 'change the face' as an idiom meaning 'make the face dark, gloomy' in Biblical Heb., Biblical Aram., Ugar., and Akk. see Gruber, *Aspects*, pp. 358-62.

[8] With Zohory note that Rashi's source is BT Mo'ed Qaṭan 16b; cf. also Midrash Tehillim here.

[9] Here Rashi responds to the exegetical question, "To what does the demonstrative pronoun *zō't* 'THIS' (NJV renders 'SUCH THINGS') refer in v. 4a?"

[10] Similarly Breithaupt here.

[11] Cf. Deut. 25:9, 10.

[12] Cf. Midrash Tehillim here; cf. Maarsen here

[13] Heb. *yaḥzĕrû 'āḥarêkā,* which corresponds to Akk. saḥāru which corresponds semantically both to Biblical Heb. *sbb* 'gather about, surround' and to Eng. 'beg'; on Akk. *saḥāru* and Rabbinic Heb. *ḥāzar* see S. David Sperling, "Late Heb. *ḥzr* and Akk. *saḥāru,*" *JANES* 5 (1973), pp. 397-404.

[14] The last line is Rashi's paraphrase of v. 8b, q.v.

[15] In many editions of Rashi this comment is introduced by *dābār 'aḥēr* 'an alternative interpretation' [of v. 8b].

[16] Cf. *mišpāṭ,* lit., 'judgment', in the sense 'punishment' in Rashi's commentary on Ps. 5:4 and the verb *dûn,* cognate of Biblical Heb. *dîn,* in the sense 'find guilty' in Rashi's commentary on Ps. 6:11.

[17] If the words were taken to constitute a construct genitive chain; so, e.g., NJV, q.v.

[18] If the phrase be taken to be a noun followed by an attributive adjective.

[19] Rashi paraphrases the final clause, which in MT is *qaštô dārak* rather than Rashi's *yidrok qaštô.*

[20] Thus Rashi does not take sides here in the controversy as to whether Heb. *ḥibbēl* denotes 'conceive', 'be pregnant', 'travail' or 'give birth'. For the last mentioned view see Robert Gordis, *The Song of Songs and Lamentations,* rev. and augmented ed. (New York: Ktav, 1974), p. 73; NJV at Cant. 8:5 renders 'conceived'; contrast Samuel Rolles Driver and George

Buchanan Gray, *A Critical and Exegetical Commentary on the Book of Job*, ICC
(Edinburgh: T. & T. Clark, 1921), p. 315: "the verb means simply to be
pregnant with in Ca[nt]. 8⁵, Ps. 7¹⁵"; in his commentary on Cant. 8:5,
however, Rashi explains that *ḥibbĕlāh* means 'labor pains came upon her';
cf. *BDB*, p. 286.

²¹ See Midrash Tehillim here, and see Braude, *The Midrash on Psalms*,
vol. 1, pp. 110-111; vol. 2, p. 420, n. 40, and see Saul Lieberman, *Hellenism in Jewish Palestine* (New York: Jewish Theological Seminary, 1950), p.
12, n. 59; see also Yalqut Shim'oni here.

²² Here Rashi responds to the exegetical question, "What is the future
referred to by the future indicative verb 'I SHALL PRAISE'?"

PSALM VIII

1   ON THE GITTITH. [The *gittith* is] a musical instrument that comes from Gath where there were [craftsmen][1] available to produce it.[2] Our rabbis said that [the title 'ON THE GITTITH'] refers to Edom, which in the future will be trod like a winepress [*gath*] in accord with what is stated in the Bible, "I trod out a vintage alone" (Isa. 63:3).[3] However, the content of the psalm does not support that.

2a   HOW MAJESTIC IS YOUR NAME! More worthy than the power characteristic of those below.[4] But You in Your great humility.[5] Those below are not worthy that Your Presence should abide among them.

2b   YOU WHOSE SPLENDOR is worthy that You should place it[6] OVER THE HEAVENS, but You in Your humility You have STRENGTH.

3a   FROM THE MOUTHS OF the Levites and the priests, who are people who have grown up in filth,[7] and nursing babes.[8] *'ôlĕlîm* 'INFANTS' is a cognate of [the verb *'olaltî* 'I dirtied' in] "I dirtied my head in the dust" (Job. 16:15).[9] With reference to filth children are called *'ôlĕlîm.*[10]

3b   ON ACCOUNT OF YOUR FOES, [i.e.], to inform them that we are Your servants.

3c   TO PUT AN END TO the insults of ENEMY AND AVENGER, who say, "You [Israel] are no better than the rest of the nations.[11]

5   But as for me, when I see[12] YOUR HEAVENS.... I ask myself,[13] "WHAT IS MAN THAT YOU HAVE BEEN MINDFUL OF HIM...

6   THAT YOU HAVE MADE HIM LITTLE LESS... ?" [YOU MADE HIM LITTLE LESS THAN GOD] when You empowered Joshua to make the sun stand still[14] and to dry up the Jordan[15] and Moses to split the [Reed] Sea[16] and to ascend to heaven[17] and Elijah to revive the dead.[18]

8   *ṣōneh wa'ălāpîm* 'FLOCK AND KINE'. [This peculiar Hebrew expression is synonymous with the common Hebrew expression *ṣo'n ûbāqār* 'flock and herd'[19] as is demonstrated by the expression *šĕgar 'ălāpêkā* "the calving of your herd" (Deut.

7:13). There are many aggadic midrashim [on the phrase
FLOCK AND KINE], but they do not lend themselves to
be reconciled with the order of the Scripture verses.

PSALM VIII, NOTES
    [1] The word 'craftsmen' is missing in our ms.
    [2] *Mahberet Menahem*, p. 116, s.v. *gt*.
    [3] Midrash Tehillim here.
    [4] Cf. Midrash Tehillim here.
    [5] In most mss. and printed editions this phrase occurs only at the end
of the comment on v. 2b.
    [6] Rashi's substitution of a relative clause using the imperfect form of
the verb for MT's enigmatic imperative *tĕnāh* 'give' is shared by most of
the ancient versions and by many modern scholars; see *BH³* and commentaries.
    [7] Taking for granted that the root meaning of '*ôlĕlîm*.'infants' is 'dirtiers'
(see below in Rashi), Rashi responds here to the exegetical questions (1)
who, precisely are the infants from whose mouth the LORD is praised;
(2) why the designation 'dirtiers' applies specifically to them.
    [8] Heb. *yônĕqê šādayim*, lit., 'those who suck breasts'; the psalmist uses
the expression *yōnĕqîm* 'sucklings'.
    [9] See Rashi there; contrast Rashi's comment on Ps. 8:3 in his com-
mentary at BT Sotah 30b.
    [10] I.e., 'dirtiers', a designation derived from babies' constantly wetting
and dirtying their diapers. For the now preferred derivation of '*ôlēl* from a
root '*wl* 'to suck' see *BDB*, pp. 732a, 760b.
    [11] Cf. Midrash Tehillim here.
    [12] Here Rashi paraphrases the biblical text. While the biblical text has
kî'er'eh "when I shall see," Rashi writes *wa'ănî kĕše'ănî ro'eh*. Rashi's paraphrase intimates (1) that the biblical Hebrew imperfect may denote past,
future, or present; (2) that in Rashi's view the verb form in question denotes the present in our verse; and (3) that the present tense is expresseed
in Rabbinic-Medieval Heb. by the participle (as in Modern Hebrew).
    [13] Here Rashi supplies the *verbum dicendi* to introduce v. 5, which Rashi
understands to be a quotation; see *BGM*, p. 174; p. 350, n. 26.
    [14] Josh. 10:12-14.
    [15] Josh. 3:9-17.
    [16] Ex. 14:21, 26-29; 15:19; Ps. 106:9; 136:13; Neh. 9:11.
    [17] See Ex. 19:3a: "Moses went up to God"; Ex. 19:20: "Moses went up";
see also Ex. 24:12; etc.
    [18] 1 Kgs. 17:17-21.
    [19] Gen. 12:16; 20:14; 21:27; 24:35; Deut. 16:2; 1 Sam. 14:32; etc.

PSALM IX

1   *'almuth labben.* I read in the *masoret*[1] that it [*'almût*] is a single
word, for note that he [the *masoret*] listed it with[2] "He will
lead us *'almût*] 'evermore'" (Ps. 48:15). Early French Jewish
exegetes[3] and also Dunash[4] offered their respective interpretations, which are unacceptable to me. I read, however, in
Pesikta deRav Kahana that this text refers to Amalek and
Edom. [Hence we read in v. 6], "You blast the nations; You
destroy the wicked; You blot out their name forever."[5] I think,
however, that [the title] FOR THE LEADER. *'almût labbēn*
[means that] this poem refers to the eschatological era when
Israel's childhood and youth[6] will be renewed [*yitlabbēn*] and
when their virtue will be revealed and their victory will be
brought near, for Esau and his progeny will be wiped out.
[The philological basis for this interpretation is as
follows]:*'almût* [is a synonym of *yaldût* 'childhood'.][7] [The
word] *labbēn* is a form of [the infinitive] *lĕlabbēn* 'to renew'.[8]
However, Menahem [b. Saruq] interpreted *'almût labbēn* as
referring to a musical instrument whose name is *'almût*. [Ac-
cording to Menahem, therefore, *'almût*] is a form of the word
[*'ălāmôt*], which is used in this Book [of Psalms in the head-
ing] "on *alamoth*. A song" (Ps. 46:1).[9]

2b   ALL YOUR WONDERS [i.e.], the final redemption, which
is reckoned as the equivalent of all [the previous] miracles
just as it is stated in the Bible, "It will no longer be said,[10]['I
swear by the LORD who brought the Israelites out of the land
of Egypt']."[11]

5a   MY RIGHT AND CLAIM. There are in the Bible [numer-
ous examples of] precise synonyms juxtaposed. [Examples
include] *mišpāṭî wĕdînî* 'MY RIGHT AND MY CLAIM' (here);
"In heaven is my witness//and he who can testify for me is
on high" (Job. 16:19); "His bones are like tubes of bronze//
his limbs like iron rods" (Job. 40:18).[12]

5b   YOU PRESIDE ON THE BENCH[13] [i.e.], the chair of judgment.

6a   YOU BLAST NATIONS [i.e.], "Amalek, the first of nations"
(Num. 24:20).[14]

6b   YOU DESTROY THE WICKED, [i.e.], Esau.[15]

6c   YOU BLOT OUT THEIR NAME [in fulfillment of Your promise], "I will utterly blot out" (Ex. 17:14).[15]

7a   THE ENEMY ARE FINISHED, for[16] SWORDS ARE FOREVER. [I.e.], For SWORDS of hatred ARE FOREVER. Another equally plausible interpretation of[17] THE ENEMY ARE FINISHED—SWORDS ARE FOREVER [is the following]: That enemy, the SWORDS of whose hatred were FOREVER upon us, and this is the one of whom it is stated in the Bible, "And his fury stormed forever" (Am. 1:11); i.e., Esau.

7b   YOU HAVE TORN DOWN THEIR CITIES. [This refers to what is stated in the Bible], "Although you, Edom, say, 'We have been beaten down...'" (Mal. 1:4).[18]

7c   THEIR VERY NAMES ARE LOST at that time.[19]

8a   BUT THE LORD ABIDES FOREVER. His name will be whole and his throne will be whole as is suggested by [the expression] HIS THRONE (v. 8b). However, before he [Amalek] will have been blotted out it is written in the Bible, "For the hand [of Amalek] is against the thron'[20] of the LOR'"[20] (Ex. 17:16), [which is to say that] the thron' is defective and the name [of God] is defective.[21]

9   HE JUDGES THE WORLD WITH KINDNESS... GRACIOUSNESS.[22] Until the arrival of the end of days He will have been accustomed to judge them with mercy, [i.e.], according to the GRACIOUSNESS found in them. [Thus] He examines[23] them at night when they are sleeping [and thus removed] from [engaging in] transgressions.[24]

10a   MAY THE LORD BE A HAVEN FOR THE OPPRESSED in the eschatological era when His [judge's] bench will be set up for judgment MAY HE BE A HAVEN for Israel, who are oppressed.[25]

10b   FOR TIMES [lĕ'ittôt] IN THE TROUBLE[26] [i.e.], TIMES ['ittîm] OF TROUBLE.[27]

12   SING A HYMN TO THE LORD, WHO REIGNS IN [yōšēb] ZION. When He will have restored His reign [yĕšîbātô] they will thus sing to Him.[28]

13   HE REMEMBERS THEM [i.e.], the BLOOD, which was spilt in Israel.

14a   HAVE MERCY ON ME now in the Exile.[29]

14c   YOU WHO LIFT ME UP by means of Your redemption.

16   THE NATIONS SINK. This is the PRAISE, which I shall TELL (v. 15a).[30]

17   THE LORD HAS MADE HIMSELF KNOWN. All this [vv. 16-17] is the PRAISE (v. 15a). THE LORD HAS MADE HIMSELF KNOWN to people for He is the Ruler, and He governs, and He exacts vindication from His enemies, for HE WORKS JUDGMENT upon them. THE WICKED MAN IS SNARED. [I.e.], THE WICKED MAN has failed. HIGGAION 'thought'. We shall think [nehgeh] this.[31]

18   lis'ôlāh 'TO SHEOL'. R. Nehemiah said, "For any word which is in want of a lamed [indicating direction towards] as a prefix to it there has been provided[32] for it a [locative] hê as its suffix."[33] Examples include misraymāh' to Egypt' (Gen. 12:10, 11, 14; etc.); midbarāh 'to the wilderness (1 Kgs. 19:15; Isa. 16:1; etc.). They challenged him: "But here it is written, "LET THE WICKED RETURN lis'ôlāh [which, according to R. Nehemiah's grammatical rule, should mean 'to to Sheol', which is redundant]. Rabbi Abba b. Zabdi said, ["The apparent redundancy is Biblical Hebrew's way of indicating the great distance] 'to' the lowest level of Sheol."[34] Now what is the meaning of 'THEY WILL RETURN'? It is that after they will have left Gehinnom,[35] been judged and found guilty THEY WILL RETURN to the lowest level of Gehinnom.[36]

19a   NOT ALWAYS SHALL Israel THE NEEDY BE IGNORED without being rewarded for their having been subservient to HIM.[37]

19b   NOR THE HOPE OF THE AFFLICTED FOREVER LOST.

20a   RISE, O LORD! David prays to God [hammāqôm][38] that He should arise, i.e., He should hurry[39] to do this [which is attributed to God in vv. 18-19].[40]

20b   LET NOT Esau[41] HAVE POWER forever.

20c   IN YOUR PRESENCE because of the anger with which they angered You with respect to [the destruction of] Your Temple.

21a   FEAR [môreh]. [is related both etymologically and semantically to] marût 'lordship' and [semantically to] 'ôl 'yoke'. Another equally plausible interpretation is [that] môreh [is a synonym of] haślākāh 'casting' [and] a cognate of [the verb yārāh 'hurl' in] "He has hurled into the sea" (Ex. 15:4).[42]

21b   LET THE NATIONS KNOW that they[43] ARE MEN and not divinity that their might should prevail.

PSALM IX, NOTES

¹ With reference to the expression *ra'îtî* 'I read', found twice here in
Rashi's commentary on Ps. 9:1 see our discussion at Ps. 45, n. 13. Note
that the reading *"masoret"* is found in most of the medieval mss. of Rashi's
commentary here. A few mss. (Parma de Rossi 181/1; London Jews' College Montefiore 5,2; British Museum Harley 150) have the reading *"masoret
gĕdôlāh,"* i.e., *Masora Magna* (so Breithaupt here), which is the reading found
in current editions of the so-called Rabbinic Bible (*Miqra'ot Gedolot*) and in
Maarsen's edition where this reading is typical of his miscopying of Oxford ms. Oppenheim 34. Responding to his errant reading, Maarsen, following Ernst Ehrentrau, "Untersuchungen über die Entwicklung und den
Geist der Massora," *Jeschurun* 11 (1924), pp. 34-59; id., "Die Raschi-Stelle
Psalmen IX, 1," *Jeschurun* 11 (1924), pp. 515-520, notes that Rashi's comment on Ps. 9:1 constitutes an anomalous instance where a reference to
Masora Magna cannot be located in *Ochlah W'ochlah*, ed. Salomon Frensdorff
(Hanover: Hahn, 1864). Already in the first of his two studies in *Jeschurun*
11, p. 42, n. 3 Ehrentrau asked if it could really be fortuitous that those
cases Rashi cited as from *bammāsoret haggĕdôlāh* can all be located in the
work edited by Frensdorff while those cited as *bammāsoret* cannot. In the
later article Ehrentrau argued, therefore, that the correct reading here in
Rashi's commentary must be *bammāsoret* and not *bammāsoret haggĕdôlāh* and
that support for the former reading could be found in the early printed
editions of the Rabbinic Bible published at Salonika in 1515 and at Venice
in 1524. Ehrentrau intimated that the expanded term was an error introduced into late printed editions of Rashi's commentary here. We have noted
however, that both readings are found in medieval mss. It might, nevertheless appear that Ehrentrau's suggestions (1) that the reading *bammāsoret*
found in the majority of medieval mss. is the correct reading; and (2) that
it has a meaning distinct from "in the *Masorah Magna* " for the following
reasons: (1) it makes sense in the present context; (2) it finds support elsewhere. Sixty-three years after the publication of Ehrentrau's aforementioned
studies Prof. Shraga Abramson pointed out in "Yeš 'Em La-Miqra, La-
Masoret," *Lĕšone!nu* 50 (1986), pp. 31-32 [in Hebrew; the article actually
appeared in 1987] that throughout Rabbinic Heb. with the exception of
BT Pesahim 86b and as Rashi frequently explains *masoret* means "the
manner in which the Biblical text is written." Consequently, it would seem
plausible to suggest that in Rashi's commentary at Ps. 9:1 "I read in the
masoret" means "I read in a reliable ms. of the Book of Psalms." However,
this reasonable conclusion is to be rejected for two reasons: (1) the evidence
that elsewhere in Rashi's Bible commentaries the expression *bammāsoret*,
like the longer expression, refers to *Masorah Magna* (see Ps. 10:8; 80:3); (2)
the juxtaposition in Rashi's commentary here of the expression in question with the expression 'he listed it with' (on the meaning of which see
below, n. 3). Additional facts should be considered in advance of our conclusion as to the meaning of the assertion "I read in the *masoret"* in Rashi's
commentary here. According to the marginal *masorah* to the Petrograd ms.
B 19a of the Hebrew Bible both at Ps. 9:1 and at Ps. 48:15 the correct

reading in both cases is as two words 'al mût; so also *Die Massora Magna*, ed. S. Frensdorff (Hanover & Leipzig: Cohen & Risch, 1876), p. 141. However, the text of Petrograd ms. B 19a reads 'almût; at Ps. 9:1 and 'al-mût at Ps. 48:15. The divergence between the readings in Petrograd ms. B 19a and the marginal *masorah* to that ms. is symptomatic of the antiquity and authenticity of both traditions; similarly already *Minhat Shai* here. On the frequently observed phenomenon of the marginal masorah's contradicting the text of the ms. it accompanies see Alexander Sperber, "Problems of the Masorah," *HUCA* 17 (1943), pp. 336-338; 348-350; 358-360. Given the fact that both readings are attested in many mss. and ancient versions, it is reasonable to assume that Rashi could have seen the reading 'almût also in a collection similar to but not identical with *Ochlah W'ochlah*; see next note.

² Heb. *šeharê ḥibbēr lāh*. Cf. the use of this expression in Rashi's commentary at Ps. 42:9, which shows that when Rashi uses this expression with respect to *māsoret*, he refers to the systematized lists of peculiarities in the transmission of the Hebrew text of the Hebrew Bible, of which the most famous is *Ochlah W'ochlah*.

³ Heb. *pōtĕrîm;* see Menahem Baneth, "Les Poterim," *REJ* 125 (1966), pp. 21-33; id., *Rashi: Interpreter of the Biblical Letter*, pp. 8-9.

⁴ *Teshuvot Dunash*, p. 28.

⁵ PRK, ed. Mandelbaum, p. 43, lines 9-13.

⁶ The phrase "childhood and youth" is taken from Eccles. 11:10 (contrast NJV there: "youth and black hair"). See Rashi there for his reconciliation of the literal meaning 'blackness (of hair)' with the contextual meaning 'youth'; cf. Harold Louis Ginsberg, *Koheleth* (Tel Aviv & Jerusalem: Newman, 1961), p. 128 (in Hebrew).

⁷ Rashi thus takes 'almût to be the abstract noun formed from the concrete noun 'elem 'young man' attested in 1 Sam. 17:56; 20:22; cf. the feminine form 'almāh 'young woman' attested in Gen. 24: 43; Ex. 2:8; Isa. 7:14; Prov. 30:19; the feminine pl. 'ălamôt 'young women' attested in Ps. 46:1; 68:26; etc. and the abstract noun 'ălûmîm 'youth' attested in Isa. 54:4; Ps. 89:46; 90:8; etc. Following the Vulgate, which rendered 'almût labbēn "victori pro morte filii," i.e., "victory over the death of the son," ancient and medieval Christian exegetes saw here a reference to the resurrection of Jesus, whom they called 'the son of God'. Rashi attempts to defuse the weapon of Ps. 9 in the arsenal of Christian polemic by two means: (1) referring the psalm as a whole to the experience of collective Israel (see also Rashi at Ps. 22:2 and our discussion there); (2) demonstrating that there is a wide spectrum of legitimate scholarly opinion as to the meaning of the phrase in question, none of which suggests that it has anything to do with "death of the son". With reference to Rashi's anti-Christian polemic here see Hailperin, pp. 60-61; Shereshevsky, "Rashi and Christian Interpretations," *JQR*, n.s., 61 (1970-71), p. 78; id., *Rashi: the Man and His World*, p. 121.

⁸ I.e., the form *labbēn* is the *pi'el* infinitive construct without prefixed *lamed*.

⁹ *Mahberet Menahem*, p. 282, s.v. 'lm IV.

[10] The biblical text states, "They will no longer say...." Rashi's paraphrase points to the fact that in Biblical Heb. the passive is often expressed by the 3[d] pers. pl. active verb; see GKC #144f, g.

[11] See BT Berakot 12b. Our Rashi ms. does not quote the bracketed portion of the verse; I have supplied it for clarity.

[12] Note that Rashi's term "precise synonyms juxtaposed" embraces both synonymous parallelism in the two verses cited from Job and juxtaposition for intensification in Ps. 9:5. The Rabbinic source in Midrash Tehillim here states, *zeh 'eḥad miḥămîssāh dĕbarîm kĕpûlîm bammiqrā'* "This is one of five instances of duplication in the Bible." It appears that while the Rabbinic source limits duplication to five instances (Isa. 46:4; Ps. 9:5; Job. 16:19; 39:5; 40:18) Rashi regards the phenomenon as far more characteristic of biblical style than the Rabbinic source would lead us to believe. Rashi refers explicitly to synonymous parallelism in his commentary to BT Rosh ha-Shanah 18a (cited below in Ps. 33, n. 9); see also Rashi at Ps. 55:20 and our discussion there. Concerning Rashi's identification of juxtaposed synonyms not in parallelism see also Rashi at Ps. 55:14b. Contrast Gelles, pp. 99-105 and Kugel, p. 173 cited in our introduction, pp. 30-31.

[13] If *kissē'* here meant 'throne', i.e., *kissē' hammalĕkût* (Esth. 1:2; 5:10; 1 Ch. 22:10; etc.), the verb *yāšab*, lit., 'sit', would here mean 'be enthroned' (so NJV here). Rashi's perceptive comment to the effect that Ps. 9:5 refers not to a kingly throne but to the judge's bench suggests, therefore, that *yāšab* denotes that which the judge does upon his bench, i.e., 'preside'.

[14] Rashi's comment is taken from Midrash Tehillim here. NJV there renders "a leading nation." Rashi there, following T.O., understands 'the first of nations' to mean "He preceded all of them in fighting against Israel."

[15] Rashi's source here is Midrash Tehillim here.

[16] Heb. *kî*. Since Rashi does not insert this particle in his alternative interpretation of the verse, it is clear he does not here attest to a variant reading of the biblical text, which contains the missing conjunction. On the contrary, Rashi, like NJV, senses that the two halves of v. 7a constitute a *non sequitur*. Rashi attempts to solve the exegetical crux by suggesting that the reader is meant to supply the subordinate conjunction while NJV supplies dashes, q.v., which also suggest that a conjunction is wanting.

[17] Heb. *dābār 'aḥēr*. In Rabbinic literature this phrase links independent aggadic midrashim based on a single biblical text. It may also link independent halakic midrashim based on a single biblical text; see Kadushin, *The Rabbinic Mind*[3], pp. 71-72. Rashi employs this expression frequently in the Commentary on the Book of Psalms to link alternative exegeses of a single ambiguous biblical verse or expression.

[18] Cf. Midrash Tehillim here.

[19] Rashi here calls attention to the contrast between the use of the perfect form of the verb to express the past tense in v. 7 and the use of the imperfect to express the future tense in v. 8. In prose this phenomenon

would be less than noteworthy. In poetry, however, where both forms can express all tenses (see Rashi at Ps. 2:4) the phenomenon is worthy of note.

[20] Cf. Braude, *The Midrash on Psalms*, vol. 1, p. 142. The spelling of the words 'throne' and 'LORD' without the final letters is Braude's method of conveying in English translation the exegesis, which underlies the midrash here quoted, namely, that the words *ks* and YH in Ex. 17:16 represent defective forms of the word *ks'* 'throne' and YHWH, the ineffable name of God commonly represented in English translations of the Bible by 'the LORD', respectively.

[21] Rashi's source is Midrash Tehillim here; see also Rashi at Ex. 17:16.

[22] H. L. Ginsberg, "A Strand in the Cord of Hebraic Hymnody," *Eretz-Israel* 9 (1969), p. 46 translates Ps. 96:10 as follows: "Announce among the nations, 'YHWH has assumed kingship.' Truly, the world shall stand firm, it shall not totter; he will provide for the peoples with graciousness." Ginsberg explains his translation as follows: "'Provide for the peoples with graciousness'? Why not 'judge the peoples with equity', which is what the phrase is commonly supposed to mean? Because, firstly, in the latter case the world would not stand firm but would collapse, and heaven, earth, the sea and all it contains, the fields and all that are in them, and the very trees of the forest—or whatever survived of all these—would have cause not for jubilation (vv. 11-12) but for lamentation." [cf. Rashi at Gen. 1:2, s.v., 'God created'] Yehezkel Kaufmann, *History of the Israelite Religion* (4 vols.; Jerusalem: Bialik, 1963/Tel Aviv: Dvir, 1963), vol. 2, p. 722 (in Hebrew) explains that Heb. *šāpaṭ* means 'provide for' rather than 'judge in Ps. 7:9: 9:8-9; 67:5; 96:13; 98:9. While Rashi appears not to have contemplated Kaufmann's insight with respect to the latter verb, which is the key to Ginsberg's solution of the problem, Rashi's comment on our verse reveals most clearly (1) Rashi's sensitivity to the nuances of Heb. *ṣedeq* 'kindness' and *mêšārîm* 'graciousness' rediscovered by Kaufmann and Ginsberg; and (2) Rashi's realization that judgment is essentially incongruous with kindness and graciousness. See Rashi at Ps. 67:5; 96:13.

[23] Heb. *dān*, a cognate of Biblical Heb. *yādîn* 'HE JUDGES' here in v. 9 (Ginsberg in "A Strand in the Cord of Hebraic Hymnody," p. 46, following Kaufmann [see previous note] suggests the rendering 'he provides for').

[24] Rashi's source is Midrash Tehillim here.

[25] Rashi's source is Midrash Tehillim here.

[26] Literal rendering of the lemma. Note that the identical expression is found also in Ps. 10:1; the plural form *'ittôt* with a pronominal suffix is found in Ps. 31:16. Everywhere else the plural of *'ēt* 'appointed time' is *'ittîm*.

[27] Cf. NJV.

[28] Cf. Midrash Tehillim here.

[29] Here Rashi responds to the abrupt transition from the prophetic perfect in v. 13b to the imperative in v. 14.

[30] Rashi thus takes v. 16 as a quotation introduced by "I MIGHT TELL" in v. 15.

[31] Tempting as it might be render *nehgeh* 'We shall say' (see our discussion at Ps. 1:2 and 5:2) referring back to the PRAISE contained in vv. 16-17 and constituting with 'I MIGHT TELL' in v. 15a a kind of *inclusio* framing the PRAISE, Rashi's comment at 5:2 clearly indicates that he did not intend for us so to interpret the verb *nehgeh*.

[32] Impersonal 3^d pers. sing. employed as a passive; for such a usage in Biblical Heb. see NJV's treatment of Gen. 11:9; 16:14; 19:22; Ex. 15:23; etc.

[33] BT Yebamot 13b; JT Yebamot 1:6; cf. Midrash Tehillim here; for additional parallels see Zohory, p. 43.

[34] Cf. Midrash Tehillim here; for additional versions of the midrash see the notes in Midrash Tehillim, ed. Buber, here, and see Zohory, p. 43. On the grammatical interpretation contrast *GKC* #90e. For similar redundancy in Biblical Heb. cf. *lĕmērāḥôq* (2 Sam. 7:19; 2 Kgs. 19:25; etc.) and *lĕmin hayyôm* (Ex. 9:18; Deut. 4:23), in both of which two prepositions are employed instead of one. Ehrlich, *Mikrâ ki-Pheschutô*, Vol. 1, p. 5, n. 1 argues that the final *heh* in *lis'ôlāh* is simply the survival of an archaic genitive case ending.

[35] Here Rashi intimates that Rabbinic Heb. Gehinnom, which corresponds etymologically to NT Gehenna, is the functional equivalent of Biblical Heb. Sheol, the abode of all the dead; on the distinct nuances of these respective terms see Theodor H. Gaster, "Gehenna," *IDB*, vol. 2, pp. 361b-362b; id., "Dead, Abode of the," *IDB*, vol. 1, pp. 787a-788b.

[36] Rashi here utilizes the previously quoted midrash (see above n. 34) to attempt to account for the use of the verb *šwb* 'return', assuming that that verb must always denote going back to a place where one has been previously. As noted by William L. Holladay in his classic study, *The Root šûbh in the Old Testament* (Leiden: E. J. Brill, 1958), p. 53, when "there is evidence to the contrary," the verb in question need not refer to going back to "the initial point of departure"; concerning the use of the verb *šwb* in reference to going to a place where one has not been previously see the various commentaries on Ruth 1:6.

[37] Rashi's comment here is based upon Midrash Tehillim here.

[38] Just as in Hebrew Scripture God is referred to as both YHWH 'the LORD' and *'elohîm* 'God' (for additional biblical names and epithets of the deity see Bernhard W. Anderson, "God, Names of," *IDB*, vol. 2, pp. 407-417) so in Rabbinic literature and the literature derived therefrom (such as Rashi's commentaries) is God usually referred to as 'the Holy One Blessed be He' and frequently as *hammāqôm*, which probably means literally 'The Temple' and refers to God by reference to the place where He is enthroned just as from 1500 B.C.E. onward the Egyptian word *pr-ʿ* 'the great house', originally a designation of the royal palace came to designate the king of Egypt; hence Eng. pharaoh. Concerning Biblical Heb. *māqôm* 'temple' see John Skinner, *Genesis*, ICC (2^d ed.; Edinburgh: T. & T. Clark, 1930), p. 246; P. Kyle McCarter, Jr., *I Samuel*, AB, no. 8 (Garden City, N.Y.: Doubleday & Co., 1980), p. 142.

[39] Rashi's contention that the verb *qwm*, lit., 'arise', can denote 'hurry' accounts for the frequent use of this verb in the imperfect consecutive [*wayyāqom*] as an auxiliary verb meaning 'thereupon' (see Orlinsky, *Notes*, pp. 34-35; and see also index, s.v. *qum*), i.e., 'hurriedly, immediately' and for the use of the verb *mihēr*, lit., 'hurry' in the same sense in Gen. 24:18, 20 (see Orlinsky, *Notes*, p. 111).

[40] Since Rashi construes the verbs in vv. 18-19 as indicatives rather than jussives, he must now account for the abrupt transition from speaking about God in vv. 18-19 to a petition addressed to God in vv. 20-21.

[41] The biblical text reads here *'ĕnôš*, lit., 'a person, humankind' (hence NJV's "men"); Rashi, however, seems to interpret the parallelism MEN/ /NATIONS in v. 20 in light of his interpretation of the parallelism NA-TIONS//WICKED in v. 6 where, following Midrash Tehillim, he equates THE WICKED with Esau.

[42] Both the interpretation of *môreh* as a biform of *môrā'* 'fear' (so Ibn Ezra and Qimhi followed by NJV) and the first of the two interpretations suggested by Rashi are found in Midrash Tehillim here. Perusal of the lexicons and commentaries reveals that the meaning and etymology of *môreh* here in Ps. 9:21 is uncertain.

[43] Heb. *šehēm*, Rashi's paraphrase of the psalmist's *hēmmāh* 'THEY'.

1b DO YOU HIDE AT TIMES IN TROUBLE? [The transitive verb *taʿălîm* 'YOU HIDE' is ellipsis for] *taʿălîm ênêkā* 'You hide Your eyes'.[2] *lĕittôt baṣṣārāh* 'AT TIMES IN TROUBLE' means] *lĕittê haṣṣārāh* 'AT TIMES OF TROUBLE.[3]

2a *yidlaq* 'HOUNDS' [i.e.], *yirdop* 'pursues'. It is the same verb as is attested in "that you should pursue [*dālaqtā*] me" (Gen. 31:36).[4]

2b THEY ARE CAUGHT IN THE SCHEMES, which the wicked devise for them.[5]

3a THE WICKED CROWS. This refers to [what is stated in Ps. 10: 1]: WHY...DO YOU STAND ALOOF? while now the wicked Esau lauds himself for he achieves all HIS UN-BRIDLED LUSTS (v. 3b).

3c WHEN THE ROBBER [*bōṣēăʿ* BLESSED [*bērēk*], HE SCORNED THE LORD. [I.e.], when the robber [*gazlān*] [6] praised himself, thinking that although HE SCORNED THE LORD he will be safe. [The form] *bērēk* [7] has the same meaning as [the form] *bērēk* [8] It is a verb. You should know that if it were a noun the stress would be penultimate, [i.e.] on the first letter, and it would be pointed with a *pataḥ* [9] while this is pointed with a *qāmeṣ*,[10] and its stress is ultimate, [i.e.], on the *rêš*. Now do not be surprised about [the verb form] *bērēk*, that it is not vocalized *bērak*, for many words [containing the letter *r*]*êš* are so vocalized such as "The enemy blasphemed [*ḥērēp*] the LORD" (Ps. 74:18), which is not vocalized *ḥērap*.[11]

4a AS FOR THE WICKED, BECAUSE OF HIS ARRO-GANCE

4c ALL HIS SCHEMES tell[12] him, "The Holy One Blessed be He[13] DOES NOT CALL TO ACCOUNT anything that I may do for there is no justice."[14]

4d "THERE IS NO GOD" [corresponds in meaning to the Talmudic aphorism] "There is no Law, and there is no Judge."[15]

5a *yāḥîlû* 'THEY WILL PROSPER', [i.e.], *yaṣlîḥû* 'they will succeed'.[16] It is the same verb as is attested in[17] "Therefore his fortune will not prosper [*lōʾ yāḥîl*]" (Job. 20:21).

5b   YOUR JUDGMENTS ARE FAR BEYOND HIM. The JUDGMENTS consisting of Your punishments and disasters are far removed; [they are] BEYOND HIM in that he does not experience them.

5c   HE SNORTS AT ALL HIS FOES. By blowing wind he snorts at them so that they fall before him.

6   FROM GENERATION TO GENERATION, WHICH IS WITHOUT TROUBLE [means] "I shall not experience TROUBLE throughout my generations."

7   AND *tôk* 'FRAUD', a noun denoting an evil thought, which abides within him [*bĕtôkô*] continually.[18]

8c   HIS EYES SPY OUT YOUR BAND [*ḥêlĕkāh*]. [I.e.], THE EYES OF Esau like in wait FOR Israel, who are YOUR BAND. *lĕḥêlĕkāh* FOR YOUR BAND (here) [and] "YOUR BAND [*ḥêlĕkāh*]LEAVES IT FOR YOU" (v. 14d) are both [listed] in the *māsoret* among the words [in which] the pronominal suffix *kāh* is employed in place of the [conventional] pronominal suffix *kā*. Examples include *ûbĕkāh ûbĕʿammĕkā* "on you and on your people" (Ex. 7:29); *tĕbûnāh tinṣerekkāh* "Discernment will guard you" (Prov. 2:11); *kĕkol ʾăšer ṣiwwîtî ʾotākāh* "just as I have commanded you" (Ex. 29:35); *hanniṣṣebet ʿimmĕkāh* "who stood beside You" (1 Sam. 1:26). The *māsoret* informed us that *ḥêlĕkāh* has the same meaning as *ḥêlĕkā* [i.e.], *ḥêl šelĕkā* 'Your band'.[19]

10a   HE STOOPS, HE CROUCHES. Such is the way of the enemy that he puts down, lowers, and makes himself small so that he will not be noticed.

10b   AND *ḥelkāʾîm* FALL BECAUSE OF HIS MIGHT [*baʿăṣûmāyw*]. I read in the *Masorah Magna* that *ḥelkāʾîm* is one of fifteen [instances where] words are written as one word but are read as two words.[20] Examples include *bāgad*[21] "how propitious"[22] [in the verse] "Leah said,[23] *bĕgad* 'how propitious'" (Gen. 30:11); *ʾešdāt lāmô*[24] [which is read *ʾēš dāt lāmô*][25] (Deut. 33:2); *mallākem tĕdakkĕʾû*, which is read *mah lākem*... "what is it to you..." (Isa. 3:15).[26] The *ḥelkāʾîm* here is likewise [two words, meaning] *ḥēl nišbārîm* 'band of broken people'. [The rare noun] *kāʾîm* THE HAPLESS' is a cognate of [the participle *nikʾeh* 'crushed' in] "to hound to death...one crushed in spirit" (Ps. 109:16). Now if you should claim that the *nun* [in the word *nikʾeh* 'crushed' in Ps. 109:16] belongs to the root, [the phrase]

"because of causing the heart of the innocent to break
[*hakĕ'ôt*]" (Ezek. 13:22) provides evidence concerning it [that
it is not part of the root]. We have learned that the *nun* of
[the participle] *nik'eh* 'crushed' is like the *nun* of [the parti-
ciple] *nir'eh* 'appeared' (Gen. 12:7; 35:1) and like the *nun* of
[the participle] *nĕqallāh* 'light, trifling' (Jer. 6:14).[27] Thus the
meaning of it [v. 10b] is, "The army of the poor will be defeated by the wicked person's *'ăṣûmîm*, [i.e.], his hand gestures
and his winking." [Here in v. 10b the word *'ăṣûmāyw* 'his winking'] comes from the same root as [the noun *'ăṣûmāh* 'legal
argument'] in "Present your legal arguments" (Isa. 41:21)[28]
and [from the same root as the verb *'āṣam* 'wink'] in "and he
winks his eyes" (Isa. 33:15). [Assuming that the literal meaning of *ḥēl kā' îm* is, in fact, 'band of broken people', its idiomatic interpretation should be] 'band of poor people'. Another
equally plausible interpretation of *ba'ăṣûmāyw* is 'by means of
his warriors'. Rabbi Simon said, "The wicked person employs
in his army only warriors like himself in consonance with what
is stated in the Bible, 'And he commanded warriors, some of
the strongest warriors in his army to bind Shadrach,
Meshach,...'" (Dan. 3:20).[29]

13   WHY SHOULD THE WICKED MAN SCORN the Holy
One Blessed be He? Because HE THOUGHT YOU WILL
NOT CALL TO ACCOUNT.[30]

14a   YOU SEE what he is doing,[31] but You are silent,

14b   FOR AS FOR YOU, indeed it is Your way when YOU
TAKE NOTE OF MISCHIEF AND VEXATION

14c   TO GIVE WITH YOUR HAND. [I.e.], With Your power
You give a hand[32] to the wicked to succeed in their wickedness.

14d   YOUR BAND LEAVES IT FOR YOU. [I.e.], Israel, Your
people, who are YOUR BAND.

15b   AND EVIL MAN SO THAT WHEN YOU LOOK FOR
HIS WICKEDNESS YOU WILL FIND IT NO MORE. As
for the transgressors among Israel, when they see the wicked,
they leave for You the burden that You should execute judgment against the wicked.[33]

14e   YOU USED TO HELP THE ORPHAN in former times.

15a   O BREAK THE POWER OF THE WICKED AND EVIL
MAN

15b   SO THAT WHEN YOU LOOK FOR HIS WICKEDNESS

15c   YOU WILL FIND IT NO MORE. As for the transgressors among Israel when they see the wicked prospering, their heart leads them to do evil and to do wickedness, but once You have broken the arm of the wicked, if You come TO LOOK FOR the wickedness of the evil among Israel, You will not FIND it.

16   THE LORD WILL BE KING FOR EVER AND EVER when[34] GENTILES WILL HAVE LEFT HIS LAND.

18a   TO CHAMPION THE ORPHAN, [i.e.] to plead the cause of Israel, who are the ORPHANS AND THE DOWN-TRODDEN

18b   SO THAT Esau NO MORE

18c   TO TYRANNIZE HUMANITY [*'ĕnôš*], [i.e.], to grind up and to break up the weak [*'ĕnûšîm*][35] and the sick.

PSALM X, NOTES

[1] Our Rashi ms., like many other medieval Heb. mss. of the Book of Psalms and like the LXX and Vulgate, treats Pss. 9-10 as a single psalm and numbers them together as Ps. 9. However, the marginal numbering of the psalms skips the number 10 so that the psalm commonly designated Ps. 11 in the Hebrew tradition is so designated also in our Rashi ms. Modern commentators, q.v., generally agree that Pss. 9-10 were originally a single composition as evidenced by the alphabetical acrostic, which although incomplete, is carried through the two psalms, and the absence of a new title at Ps. 10:1.

[2] For the frequent *he'ĕlîm 'ayin* 'hide the eye', i.e., 'disregard', see Lev. 20:4; 1 Sam. 12:3; Isa. 1:15; Ezek. 22:26; Prov. 28:27; see also *he'ĕlîm 'ozen*, lit., 'hide the ear', i.e., 'turn a deaf ear' in Lam. 3:56; see BDB, p. 761a. Because, as Rashi indicates here, the verb *he'ĕlîm* is a transitive verb requiring a direct object, BH³ suggests emending *ta'ălîm* 'you hide (something)' to *tit'allēm* 'you hide yourself'. Dahood, here renders *ta'ălîm* "hide yourself" without comment. As Rashi and *BH³* both imply, the unemended text cannot convey this meaning.

[3] See our discussion at Ps. 9b. Note that the peculiar expression is a shared feature of Pss. 9-10, which our Rashi ms. treats as a single psalm; see n. 1 above.

[4] Rashi, following *Mahberet Menahem*, p. 125, distinguishes *dālaq* II 'hound, puruse' from *dālaq* I 'burn'; contrast *BDB*, p. 196a; *K-B³*, p. 214b.

[5] Here Rashi attempts to solve the problem of the biblical text's ambiguous use of personal pronouns and of pronominal prefixes and suffixes to the verb; cf. NJV margin. For an alternative solution see NJV: "MAY THEY BE CAUGHT IN THE SCHEMES THEY DEVISE." Rashi likewise attempts to determine the correct meaning in the present context of

the imperfect form of the verb *yittāpĕśû*, which may be construed as a present, a future, or a jussive. Rashi, followed by NJV margin, interprets the form as a present while NJV interprets it as a jussive.

⁶ Here Rashi substitutes the common Rabbinic Heb. term for 'robber' for the Biblical Heb. term, which is found also in Jer. 6:13; 8:10; Hab. 2:9; Prov. 1:19; 15:27. In his commentary at BT Bava Qama 94a Rashi cites Prov. 1:19 in support of his interpretation of Biblical Heb. *bōṣēaʿ*.

⁷ Transliteration reflects the vocalization found in our Rashi ms.; according to *BHS*³ the vocalization is *bērēk*.

⁸ According to Mandelkern, p. 237d the latter is the regular form of the verb 'he blessed' attested in Gen. 24:1, 35; 28:6; 49:28; etc. while the form *bērēk* is the pausal form found only twice—in Num. 23:20 and here in Ps. 10:3.

⁹ I.e., *pataḥ qāṭān*, which in Rashi's terminology denotes *e* as in Eng. 'bet', i.e., what contemporary terminology calls *seghol*; see Henry Englander, "Grammatical Elements and Terminology in Rashi's Biblical Commentaries, Part II—Rashi's Vowel Terminology," *HUCA* 12-13 (1937-38), pp. 505-521; id., "A Commentary on Rashi's Grammatical Comments," *HUCA* 17 (1942-43), p. 481.

¹⁰ I.e., *qāmeṣ qāṭān*. In Rashi's terminology *qāmeṣ qāṭān*. denotes *e* as in Eng. 'weigh', i.e., what contemporary terminology calls *ṣērê*; see Englander, *HUCA* 12-13, pp. 505-521.

¹¹ See *GKC* #22d.

¹² Our Rashi ms. reads *'ōmeret* 'she tells'; the context requires the reading *'ōmĕrôt* 'they tell' found in other Rashi mss.

¹³ Rashi supplies the subject of the verb.

¹⁴ Here Rashi treats the second clause as a quotation without verbum dicendi; cf. NJV: "The wicked, arrogant as he is, in all his scheming [thinks], 'He does not call to account....'" Note that while Rashi treats the final phrase 'ALL HIS SCHEMES' as the subject of the mentally supplied verbum dicendi, NJV, which makes 'THE WICKED' the subject of the mentally supplied verbum cogitandi 'thinks', treats 'ALL HIS SCHEMES' as an adverbial phrase modifying the missing verb; hence NJV's rendering "in all his scheming."

¹⁵ Sources of this proverb in Rabbinic literature include Midrash Tehillim here; Leviticus Rabbah 26:1; etc. The equation of the psalmist's words "THERE IS NO GOD" with the Aramaic proverb suggests that *'ĕlōhîm* 'GOD' is here taken to refer to the divine attribute of justice; for this convention in Rabbinic literature cf. Rashi at Gen. 1:1; 2:5; Ps. 56:5, 11.

¹⁶ So Rashi also at BT Berakot 7b; Megillah 6b.

¹⁷ Heb. *wĕdômeh lô*, which is the opposite of *ên lô dômeh*, which often designates an *hapax legomenon*; for discussion of the various nuances of these expressions see Frederick E. Greenspahn, "The Meaning of "Ein Lo Domeh and Similar Phrases in Medieval Biblical Exegesis," *AJSReview* 4 (1979), pp. 59-70.

[18] Rashi here attempts to account for the contextual meaning by equating *tôk* 'FRAUD' (so NJV) etymologically with *tôk* midst'; contrast *Mahberet Menahem*, p. 394, s.v. *tk*; see Rashi at Ps. 72:14.

[19] Ochlah W'ochlah, ed. Frensdorff, p. 94 #92.

[20] Ibid., p. 96 #99.

[21] Vocalization according to our Rashi ms. In the standard biblical text the *kethib* is *bĕgad*.

[22] The *qere* is *bā' gād* "Luck has come."

[23] So is the verse designated in *Ochlah W'ochlah*, ed. Frensdorff, p. 96 #99.

[24] Perhaps *mîmînô 'ĕšdāt lāmô* means "on the right side of them was [a place called] Eshdath"; cf. NJV.

[25] I.e., "a fiery law unto them"; cf. Rashi on Deut. 33:2; this interpretation is no longer tenable since it requires reading into one of the most archaic texts in Hebrew Scripture the Persian word loanword *dāt* 'law', which is first attested in the so-called Hebrew Scriptures in the Aramaic portions of Ezra (7:12, 14, 21, 26) as a designation of 'Torah'.

[26] See Rashi there.

[27] The *niphal* participle of the verb *qālal* 'be slight, trifling'; see *BDB*, p. 886.

[28] Rashi appears to suggest that the following semantic development takes place: *'āṣam* 'wink, blink (the eye)' > *'āṣûmāh* 'winking, blinking (the eye)' >*'āṣûmāh* 'legal argument conveyed by eye movements' > *'āṣûmāh, 'āṣûmôt* 'legal argument(s), case'. For numerous similar semantic developments in Biblical Heb. and in Akkadian see *passim* in Gruber, *Aspects*.

[29] See Midrash Tehillim here.

[30] Rashi here takes the two halves of the verse as question and answer. Contrast NJV, which treats the entire verse as a single question.

[31] Rashi construes the verse as a case of ellipsis, and he supplies the missing direct object of the verb 'YOU SEE'; NJV, q.v., attempts to solve the same problem by treating the transitive verb *rā'āh* as though it were an intransitive verb meaning 'look'.

[32] Rashi takes the psalmist's 'TO GIVE WITH YOUR HAND' as a double-entendre meaning both 'TO GIVE IS IN YOUR POWER' (similarly NJV) and 'TO GIVE A HAND', i.e., 'to help' (similarly Ibn Ezra).

[33] The clause "As for the transgressors...see the wicked" belongs to Rashi's comment on v. 15b-c, and it is repeated and completed below following the lemmas of vv. 15a-b-c. The clauses "they leave for You...against the wicked" are the continuation of Rashi's comment on v. 14b. The clauses in question have been combined and prefaced by the lemma of v. 15b in our Rashi ms. by scribal error.

[34] Rashi, following Midrash Tehillim here, suggests that v. 16b is a temporal clause modifying the noun *melek*, which Rashi, followed by NJV, treats as a verb meaning 'to be king'.

[35] Here Rashi appears to suggest that Heb. *'ĕnôš* 'human, humankind, humanity' is the singular of Heb. *'ĕnûšîm* 'weaklings'. Rashi takes the noun in question as the object of that infinitive.

PSALM XI

1c   HOW CAN YOU SAY TO ME, "FLEE..."? This is an allusion to "For they have driven me out today, so that I cannot have a share in the LORD'S possession" (1 Sam. 26:19), which refers to the fact that they ousted me [David, to whom the psalm is attributed in v. 1a] from the land [of Israel] to outside of the land [of Israel]. Here,

1b   however, he [David] says, "IN THE LORD I TAKE REFUGE" that He will enable me to return to have a share in His possession.

1c   HOW CAN YOU SAY? You drive ME away, [saying], "TAKE TO THE HILLS," [i.e.], "pass over to your mountain, you wandering bird, whom we have drive from every mountain like a wandering bird." The *kethib*[1] is *nûdû*,[2] for it is interpreted to refer also to Israel, to whom the Gentiles speak in the same vein.[3]

2a   FOR SEE, THE WICKED BEND THE BOW. [This refers to] Doeg and the informants of his generation who foment hatred between Saul and me [David]. THEY BEND their tongue, their treacherous BOW.[4]

2b   THEY SET THEIR ARROW ON THE STRING of the bow

2c   TO SHOOT under cover[5] AT THE UPRIGHT, [i.e.], David and the priests of Nob.

3a   WHEN THE FOUNDATIONS ARE DESTROYED. The priests of the LORD are virtuous people, who are the FOUNDATIONS of the world.[6]

3b   AS FOR THE VIRTUOUS ONE, WHAT DID HE DO? [I.e.], as for David, who did not sin, WHAT DID HE DO? In any case, you will bear guilt, and not I.

4a   THE LORD IS IN HIS HOLY TEMPLE.

4b   He who sees and examines your deeds, even though HIS lofty THRONE IS IN HEAVEN,

4c   THEY EYES of the LORD BEHOLD you on earth.

5a   THE LORD SEEKS OUT THE RIGHTEOUS. Thus if because I am smitten and pursued by you, you should congratulate yourselves, saying, "God has forsaken him" (Ps.

71:11), it is not true. On the contrary, it is the characteristic of the Holy One Blessed be He to trouble and to test the virtuous and not the wicked. This flax worker,[7] so long as He knows that His flax is soft, he beats upon it, but when it is not soft, he limits the pounding because it may become broken.[8]

5b   LOATHS [THE WICKED][9] so He hides from him the recompense of his iniquities for a long period of time, and then

6a   HE WILL RAIN DOWN UPON them in Gehinnom *paḥîm*, a biform of *pĕḥāmîm* 'coals'.[10] *zilʿāpôt* is a synonym of 'madness'[11]

7a   FOR THE LORD IS RIGHTEOUS; HE LOVES RIGHTEOUS DEEDS,

7b   and those who are THE UPRIGHT SHALL BEHOLD HIS FACE.[12]

2   However, our rabbis interpreted THE WICKED BEND THE BOW as a reference to Shebna and his band, and they interpreted

3a   WHEN THE FOUNDATIONS ARE DESTROYED [i.e., v. 3, as follows]: If THE FOUNDATIONS WERE DESTROYED by them, AS FOR THE VIRTUOUS ONE of the world, WHAT DID HE DO?[13] However, the syntax of the Bible verses is not congruent with the [latter] midrash.

PSALM XI, NOTES

[1] I.e., the version embodied in the text written in the unpointed manuscript scrolls [such scrolls of the Pentateuch and the Book of Esther are found in every synagogue; such scrolls of the prophetic books and the Five Megilloth are found in many synagogues] and in the body of the pointed mss. and printed editions as against the *qere*, which is both the marginal version in pointed texts and the version prescribed by *halakah* to be read aloud on all occasions.

[2] I.e., the imperative common plural; the *qere* is *nûdî* 'flee', which is imperative feminine singular.

[3] Rashi's source is Midrash Tehillim here.

[4] Rashi's treatment of BOW as a metaphor for 'lying tongue' is based upon Jer. 9:2. With Maarsen cf. Rashi there.

[5] Rashi's paraphrase of the psalmist's 'FROM THE SHADOWS'.

[6] With Maarsen cf. Midrash Tehillim here; see also BT Sanhedrin 26b and Rashi there; on the idea expressed here see Arthur Green, "The *Zaddik* as *Axis Mundi* in Later Judaism," *Journal of the American Academy of Religion* 45 (1977), pp. 327-47.

[7] Metaphor applied to God; for the source of the interpretation see next note.

⁸ With Zohory see Midrash Tehillim here; Genesis Rabbah 32:3; for additional parallels in Rabbinic literature see Zohory, p. 48.

⁹ Our Rashi ms. does not quote the bracketed portion of the verse; I have supplied it for clarity.

¹⁰ Cf. *BDB*, p. 809a.

¹¹ Both NJV and Rashi's commentary here according to Oxford ms. Oppenheim 34 interpret *ziťāpôt* to mean 'burning'; support for both views is to be found in *BDB*, p. 273a.

¹² Rashi suggests that the juxtaposition of vv. 7a and 7b-c intimates that the LORD'S granting an audience to the UPRIGHT is a logical consequence of the LORD's own RIGHTEOUSNESS.

¹³ Rashi refers to BT Sanhedrin 26a-b; see also Midrash Tehillim here. For Biblical references to Shebna see 2 Kgs. 18-19; Isa. 22:15; 36-37. Note that in Rabbinic literature "The Virtuous One of the World" is an epithet of God.

PSALM XII

1   ON THE SHEMINITH, [i.e.], a harp of eight strings.[1]

2   THE LOYAL HAVE VANISHED. All conspire against me, and they spy out the places where I hide, and they tell Saul, "Know, David is hiding among us" (Ps. 54:1).[2]

3c   WITH A HEART AND A HEART THEY SPEAK, i.e.], with two hearts. To me they exhibit friendship while hatred is concealed in their hearts.

5   BY [*lě*] OUR TONGUES WE SHALL PREVAIL [*nagbîr*]. [I.e.], We shall prevail [*nitgabbēr*] by means of [*bě*] OUR TONGUES.[3]

6a   BECAUSE [*mi-*] OF THE PLUNDERING OF THE POOR [i.e.], because of [*mēḥāmat*] [4] THE PLUNDERING OF THE POOR who are plundered by you such as the priests of Nob, my men and me,[5]

6b   and because of[4] THE GROANS OF THE NEEDY THE LORD SAYS, "NOW I SHALL ARISE to your help."[6]

6c   "I WILL PLACE IN SAFETY," HE TESTIFIES TO HIM. [I.e.], "I WILL PLACE them IN SAFETY," He tells concerning them.[7] [The verb] *yāpîaḥ* 'HE TESTIFIES' is a *verbum dicendi*. There are many examples of it in the Book of Proverbs (Prov. 6:19; 12:17; 14:5; 14:25; 19:5, 9), and in Habakkuk (Hab. 2:3) there is, "And there is one who gives testimony about the eschaton, and he does not lie."[8]

7a   THE PROMISES OF THE LORD ARE PURE PROMISES. They are so because He has the ability to fulfill them while the promises of people are not [valid] promises, for they [people] die, and they have not the ability to fulfill them. PURE [i.e.], clear and fulfilled. He does all that He promises; note that He promised me [David] vindication and kingship.

7b   SILVER PURGED. Note that they [THE PROMISES OF THE LORD] are like PURGED SILVER, which is manifest to the whole earth. *ba'ǎlîl* is a synonym of *gillûy* 'manifestly' in Mishnaic Hebrew: "whether it [the new moon] appeared manifestly or whether it did not appear manifestly..." (Mishnah Rosh ha-Shanah 1:5).[9]

7c   SEVENFOLD in their hearts. [10]

8a   YOU, O LORD, WILL KEEP THEM. Keep[11] it in their hearts.[12]

8b   PRESERVE THEM from this[13] GENERATION that they do not learn from their [this GENERATION's] behavior to be informers.[10] Another equally plausible interpretation [of v. 8 is the following]: KEEP THEM, [i.e.], those poor and impoverished who are persecuted FROM [being victimized by] THIS GENERATION, who are informers.

9a   ROUND ABOUT THE WICKED WALK CONTINU-ALLY to hide traps to ensnare me

9b   WHEN BASENESS [zullût] IS EXALTED AMONG MEN because of their jealousy in that their eye is jaundiced toward my greatness that I was taken from following the flock to be king.[14]

7c   SEVENFOLD. There is an aggadic midrash, which lends itself to being reconciled with the [present] context. [It reads as follows]: R. Joshua of Siknin [said] in the name of R. Levi, 'The children who were in the days of David before they had tasted the taste of sin used to know [how to expound] the Torah with forty-nine arguments in favor of each interpretation.'" This is the meaning of SEVENFOLD. [The midrash continues]: "David used to pray for them [those children], 'Master of the world, See how much Your Torah and YOUR PROMISE are clear and REFINED."[15]

9   This is the meaning of WHEN zullût IS EXALTED AMONG MEN: "when a man who is gluttonous ['îš hazzōlēl] is exalted in the eyes of others." This [comparison of David to a lowly type of person who achieves high status] is [similar to] the metaphor, which is employed elsewhere: "The stone that the builders rejected has become the chief cornerstone" (Ps. 118:22).[16] An aggadic midrash interprets it (Ps. 118:22) as a reference to Israel in the time to come when they will be exalted.[17]

PSALM XII, NOTES
   [1] See Rashi at Ps. 6:1.
   [2] See 1 Sam. 23:19-28; cf. BT Soṭah 48b.
   [3] Rashi's paraphrase suggests that the literal meaning of the clause may be otherwise; *BDB*, p. 149b renders, "We will give strength to our tongue." Alternatively, Rashi's comment may simply represent the equivalent of the psalmist's words in Rabbinic Heb.

[4] Rashi explains that the Biblical Heb. preposition *min*, which can have a variety of meanings, here means 'because of'.

[5] The order of the "the priests of Nob" and "me" are here reversed to satisfy the demands of English style, according to which the speaker always names himself/herself last in any enumeration.

[6] See 1 Sam. 22:9-19.

[7] Rashi here responds to the exegetical questions (1) whom will HE PLACE? (2) concerning whom does HE TESTIFY?

[8] Thus Rashi here anticipates Ehrlich, *Mikrâ ki-Pheschutô* 3 :450; Jacob Barth, *Etymologische Studien* (Berlin: H. Itzkowski, 1893), p. 24; and Mitchell Dahood, "Some Amibguous Texts in Isaias," *CBQ* 20 (1958), p. 47, n. 21, the latter in the light of Ugar. *yph* 'witness', in correctly understanding Heb. *yāpîāḥ* as a synonym of Heb '*ēd*. See Dennis Pardee, *yph* 'witness' in Hebrew and Ugaritic," *VT* 28 (1978), pp. 204-13. Note that Rashi's acceptance of the derivation of *yāpîāḥ* from the verbal root *pwḥ* 'blow' (see Rashi at Hab. 2:3) does not lead him astray as to its meaning in context.

[9] Rashi here applies to the exegesis of Ps. 12:7 the anonymous exegesis of the Mishnah passage found in BT Rosh ha-Shanah 21b: "What is the meaning of the term '*ālîl*? It is a synonym of 'manifestly'." This anonymous statement is followed in BT by Rabbi Abbahu's quoting Ps 12:7 in support of the anonymous exegesis of the Mishnah. Cf. JT Rosh ha-Shanah 1:5: "What is *ba'ālîl*? It is manifest [*mĕpûrsām*] just as you say (in Ps. 12:7), SILVER PURGED, MANIFEST TO THE WORLD, PURIFIED SEVEN TIMES." In light of the Mishnah passaged we may appreciate LXX's rendering of Heb. *ba'ālîl* by Gk. δοχιμιον 'demonstration, proof'. Moderns, who follow the Psalms Targum's equation of Heb.'*ālîl* with Aram. *kûrā*' 'crucible', readily admit that such a meaning for the Heb. word cannot be substantiated. See, *inter alia*, Dahood, *Psalms*, here; Thomas Kelly Cheyne, *The Book of Psalms*, 2 vols. (London: Kegan Paul, Trench, Trübner, 1904), 1:40-41; *BDB*, p. 760b.

[10] PRK, ed. Mandelbaum, p. 56.

[11] Rashi indicates here that the ambiguous imperfect is here synonymous with the imperative.

[12] The midrash reads, "Keep their Torah in their hearts."

[13] MT reads *zû*, which is normally a relative pronoun; Rashi substitutes for *zû* his interpretation of the latter in the present context, sc., *hazzeh* 'this'; Rashi's interpretation is followed by *BDB*, p. 262.

[14] The continuation of this comment is interrupted in our Rashi ms. by a further comment on v. 7c, which in other Rashi mss. precedes the above comment on v. 7c.

[15] PRK, ed. Mandelbaum, p. 56. The midrash states, however, "forty-nine arguments in favor of [the] purity [of the matter under investigation] and forty-nine arguments in favor of [the] impurity [of the matter under investigation]"; for similar expositions of our verse see apparatus to PRK there, and see Midrash Tehillim here.

[16] BT Pesaḥim 119a.

[17] See pasim in Midrash Tehillim at Ps. 118.

PSALM XIII[1]

2   [In this psalm the expression] 'HOW LONG' [is repeated] four times to correspond numerically to the four kingdoms,[2] and it [the rhetorical question 'HOW LONG?'] is asked on behalf of all Israel.[3]

4   LEST I SLEEP THE SLEEP OF DEATH [means LEST I die], for death is called 'sleep' [as in Jer. 51:39]. "They shall sleep eternal sleep."[4]

PSALM XIII, NOTES

[1] Our Rashi ms. treats Ps. 13 as though it were the continuation of Ps. 12: no space separates the comment on Ps. 13:2 from that on Ps. 12:9; the opening phrase of the psalm does not appear in large letters; nor is our Ps. 13 recognized in the marginal numeration, which recognizes our Ps. 12 as Ps. 12 and designates our Ps. 14 as Ps. 13. Since Ps. 13 is clearly set apart in the Psalter by the title FOR THE LEADER; A PSALM OF DAVID, the failure of our ms. to treat it as a separate composition arises not from the nature of the psalm but from the paucity of Rashi's comment thereon. In the same way many Rashi mss. misnumber Pss. 122, 129, 135 because of their having no commentary on Pss. 121, 128, 134.

[2] See Dan. 2:36-45, and see Rashi there.

[3] See Midrash Tehillim here.

[4] Cf. also Dan. 12:2.

PSALM XIV

1a THE BENIGHTED MAN THINKS.... David [here] prophesied concerning Nebuchadnezzar that in the future he would enter the Temple and destroy it without one of his troops objecting to his behavior.[1]

1b "THERE IS NO GOD" "so I shall ascend upon the back of a cloud" (Isa. 14:14).[2]

1c THEY ARE CORRUPT, THEY HAVE LUSTED EVIL WORK.[3] [The collective noun] 'ălīlāh 'EVIL WORK' [corresponds in meaning to the etymologically related plural noun] ma'ălālīm 'evil deeds'.[4]

3a ALL HAVE TURNED BAD.... None among his troops objects to his behavior.

3b ...FOUL. They have turned spoiled.

4 ARE THEY SO WITLESS...WHO DEVOUR MY PEOPLE? [I.e., WITLESS concerning their fate] insofar as it seemed to them as though they were eating bread, whose taste was that of sweet food.[5]

5a THERE THEY WILL BE SEIZED WITH FRIGHT when his [Nebuchadnezzar's] recompense will be paid to his son Belshazzar [through the latter's] experiencing FRIGHT in accord with what is stated in the Bible, "Then, as for the king, his countenance paled, his mind became confused, his thigh joints became slack, and his knees knocked each other" (Dan. 5:6).[6]

5b FOR GOD IS PRESENT IN THE GENERATION OF THE INNOCENT [e.g.], in the generation of Jeconiah, who were innocent people.[7]

6a YOU DERIDE THE COUNSEL OF THE POOR. You say that the counsel of Israel is folly in that they trust in the LORD, [for Israel says],

6b THAT THE LORD IS HIS REFUGE.[8]

7a However, the day will approach when HE WILL PROVIDE[9] FROM ZION THE VINDICATION OF ISRAEL in the future, and

7c then JACOB WILL EXULT....

PSALM XIV, NOTES

¹ Cf. Rashi at Ps. 53:1. Here Rashi responds to the exegetical question as to why the psalter contains at Ps. 14 and Ps. 53 two almost exact duplicates, in which the psalmist refers to THE BENIGHTED MAN, who THINKS, "THERE IS NO GOD." Rashi's answer is that the first of the two psalms refers to Nebuchadnezzar, who destroyed the First Temple while the latter refers to Titus, who destroyed the Second Temple. Sarna, "Psalms, Book of," *EJ* 13:1317 calls attention to the following additional instances of "psalm doublets": Ps. 18 = 2 Sam. 22; Ps. 31:2-4 = Ps 71:1-3; Ps. 40:14-18 = Ps. 70; Ps. 57:8-12 = Ps. 108:2-6; Ps. 60:7-14 = Ps. 108:7-14. The various midrashim in Midrash Tehillim at Ps. 14 and at Ps. 53 suggest a variety of villains spanning Biblical and ancient Jewish history as prototypes of the psalmist's BENIGHTED MAN, who THINKS, "THERE IS NO GOD."

² Rashi here points to the fact that the ruler of Babylon depicted in Isa. 14 displays the same arrogance attributed by the psalmist to the BENIGHTED MAN in Ps. 14:1; 53:2.

³ Ad hoc rendering of the lemma to reflect the interpretation presupposed by Rashi's comment. Note that if the verb *hit'îbû* is the *hiphil* of the verb *t'b* 'abominate', it means 'they behaved abominably'; combined, as it is here, with the direct object *'ălîlāh* 'WORK', it means 'they engaged in abominable activity'; cf. NJV's "Man's deeds are… loathsome." Our rendering of the lemma reflects, however, the assertion in other editions of Rashi here that the verb *hit'îbû* here is to be understand as though it were written *hit'îbû* 'they lusted'. With reference to the interchange of *'aleph* and *'ayin* presupposed by Rashi here cf. Am. 6:8 where *mětā'ēb 'ānokî* 'I loath' appears in synonymous parallelism with *śānē'tî* 'I hate'. There *mětā'ēb* is the *pi'el* participle of *t'b* 'loath', a biform of *t'b* ʿ abominate', which is attested in Deut. 7:26; 23:8; Ps. 119:163; etc. Heb *t'b* 'desire, long for' is attested three times, in the *qal* only, in Ps. 119:20, 40, 174.

⁴ For the former noun see also Ps. 66:5; for the latter noun see 1 Sam. 25:3.

⁵ Here Rashi alludes to a midrash attributed to Rabbah quoting R. Johanan at BT Sanhedrin 104b. This midrash takes *'ōkělê 'ammî*, which NJV here renders "who devour my people," to mean 'my people's foods'; hence it interprets *'ōkělê 'ammî 'ākělû leḥem* to mean, "They have eaten as bread My people's foods." Referring to Belshazzar's feast (Dan. 5:2-3), the midrash, quoted in many editions of Rashi here, asserts that whoever did not commit thievery against Israel did not taste a sweet taste in his food.

⁶ Rashi interprets the combination of facial expressions and body movements described here a symptoms of fear; contrast Gruber, *Aspects*, p. 360 for interpretation of the passage in question as a description of depression.

⁷ Rashi here refers to 2 Kgs. 24:14, q.v. In Rabbinic tradition 'blacksmith' and 'metalworker' there are epithets for Torah scholars. See BT Giṭṭin 88a; see also Rashi at 2 Kgs. 24:14; see also Ginzberg, *Legends of the Jews*, 4:286-87; 6:379-81, nn. 130-136.

[8] By treating v. 6b as an indirect quotation Rashi solves the exegetical dilemma of an apparent *non-sequitur* posed by the juxtaposition of vv. 6a-6b.

[9] Rashi treats *yittēn* as a future indicative, ignoring the appearance of *yittēn* here as part of the idiomatic expression *mî yittēn*, which is correctly rendered by NJV 'O that'; see *GKC* #151.

PSALM XV

3a   HE DID NOT SLANDER [*rāgal*]. This is the same verb as is attested in "He slandered [*wayĕraggēl*] your servant" (2 Sam. 19:28).

3c   AND HE DID NOT BEAR REPROACH FOR THE SAKE OF HIS RELATIVE. If his relative committed a transgression worthy of punishment, he punished him according to the law, AND HE DID NOT BEAR for him his REPROACH so that there be an excuse for one to reproach him saying, "Thus did so-and-so your relative transgress, but you covered up [for him]."

4a   FOR WHOM A CONTEMPTIBLE MAN IS ABHORRENT. He who is contemptible in his wickedness is abhorrent to the virtuous. Examples include [the virtuous] Hezekiah who dragged the bones of his [contemptible] father [Ahaz] in a contemptible manner.[1]

4c   HE TAKES AN OATH TO HURT himself, BUT HE DOES NOT CHANGE his oath. *A fortiori* he does not change it concerning something which is not to his disadvantage.

5b   NOR ACCEPTED A BRIBE AGAINST ['*al*] THE INNOCENT to declare him guilty in litigation by tampering with the verdict in his case. Moreover, our rabbis explained it [as follows]: NOR ACCEPTED A BRIBE ON BEHALF OF ['*al*] THE INNOCENT to declare him guiltless in his case. *A fortiori* he does not accept a bribe to tamper with the verdict.[2]

5c   HE SHALL NOT TOPPLE FOREVER. If HE TOPPLE, his toppling is not FOREVER, but he may topple and then arise.[3]

PSALM XV, NOTES

[1] Based on BT Sanhedrin 47a: FOR WHOM A CONTEMPTIBLE MAN IS ABHORRENT refers to Hezekiah King of Judah, who dragged the bones of his father on a bed of ropes." This midrash appears also verbatim in BT Makkot 24a and in Midrash Tehillim here.

[2] The two alternative interpretations derive from the ambiguity of the Heb. preposition '*al*. With reference to the second interpretation cf. Mekilta at Ex. 23:8 and Sifre Deut. at Deut. 16:19.

[3] Cf. the dictum attributed to R. Eleazar in BT Bava Meṣi'a 71a.

PSALM XVI

1   A *MICHTAM* OF DAVID. Our rabbis said, "[The title means
      'a poem] of David, who was *mak* 'meek' and *tam* 'unble-
      mished'[1]in that his wound [*makkātô*] was unblemished [*tammāh*]
      for he was born uncircumcised.'"[2] The biblical context is not
      in harmony with the *midrash*[3] here. There is a type of psalm[4]
      in which it is said "of David a *michtam*."[5] There one should
      interpret, "This song is by David, who was meek and unblem-
      ished, but here [in Ps. 16:1] where it is stated "a *michtam* of
      David" it is not proper so to interpret. Now I think that it
      [*michtam* in the present context] is one of the names of types
      of poetic styles, and there is a distinction among poetic styles.

2a   YOU SAY TO THE LORD, "YOU ARE MY LORD...."
      David said to the congregation of Israel,[6] "You must say[7] to
      the LORD, 'You are Lord, and You prevail over all who come
      against me.'"

2b   MY GOOD IS NOT INCUMBENT UPON YOU.[8] [I.e.],
      the favors, which You do for me are not incumbent upon You
      to reward me, for it is not because of my virtue that You fa-
      vor me.

3   THEY ARE FOR THE SAINTS WHO ARE IN THE
      EARTH. [Continuing the thought expressed in v. 2, Rashi
      explains that THEY, the favors, which You, LORD, do for
      me, the psalmist,] are for the sake of the [dead] saints[9] bur-
      ied in the earth,[10] who continually walked before You faith-
      fully. AND THE MIGHTY FOR WHOM IS ALL MY
      DESIRE. They are the mighty on whose behalf all my de-
      sires and all my needs are fulfilled.

4a   ...MAY HAVE MANY SORROWS. He [David] said all this
      [vv. 2b-4a] to the LORD. [V. 4a means], May there increase
      the sorrows of those who are disloyal to You, [and] who are
      zealous in[11] and devoted to the service of another god.

4b   I SHALL NOT POUR OUT libations[12] OF BLOOD. I shall
      not be like them[13] pouring blood on the altar[14] for idolatrous
      worship, nor[15] shall I utter the name of idolatry[16] with my
      lips.

5a   THE LORD IS MY ALLOTTED SHARE AND CUP. [I.e.], all my bounty is from Him.

5b   YOU CAST [*tômîk*] MY LOT.[17] You are He, who caused my hand to rest upon the better SHARE in consonance with what is stated in the Bible (in Deut. 30:19), "I have put before you life and death.... Choose life...." What the Bible says here may be compared to[18] a man who is devoted to one of his children so that he places his [that child's][19] hand over the better SHARE, [and he says], "Choose this one for yourself." *tômîk* [means] 'You lowered my hand upon the lot'.[20] This [verb form] is a cognate of [the verb *yimmak*[21] in] *yimmak hamměqāreh* "the ceiling sags" (Eccles. 10:18), which means 'it will be lowered'. Thus it is explained in Sifre.[22] For the sake of the [above] aggadic midrash it is possible also to analyze it [the form *tômîk*] as a cognate of [the gerund] *těmîkāh* 'holding' [i.e., from the verbal root *tmk*] as exemplified by "He took hold [*wayyitmok*] of his father's hand" (Gen. 48:17).[23]

6a   DELIGHTFUL COUNTRY HAS FALLEN TO MY LOT. Since the lot has fallen for me to belong to Your SHARE (v. 5a),[24] this is a DELIGHTFUL COUNTRY.

6b   INDEED FOR ME such AN ESTATE IS BEAUTIFUL.[25]

7a   I BLESS THE LORD. Up to this point David instructed[26] the congregation of Israel that it should say certain things, but now he says, "And I myself BLESS THE LORD WHO HAS GUIDED ME to choose life and to walk in His ways" (cf. Deut. 30:16-19).

7b   MY CONSCIENCE ADMONISHES ME AT NIGHT to love him. Our rabbis interpreted this as referring to Abraham our father, who learned Torah by himself before it was given [through Moses].[27] We,[28] however, must reconcile Bible verses with their contexts.[29]

8a   I SET THE LORD BEFORE ME CONTINUALLY. [I.e.], in all my deeds I have placed devotion to Him before my eyes. And why?

8b   SO THAT He will be continually[30] AT MY RIGHT HAND to help me[31] so that I SHALL NEVER BE SHAKEN.

9   SO MY HEART REJOICES....[32] because I am certain

10a   THAT YOU WILL NOT ABANDON ME TO SHEOL. For, indeed, with respect to the punishment[33] for the great transgression,[34] of which I was guilty, You announced to me the good news: "The LORD has indeed pardoned your sin" (2 Sam. 12:13). All the more so that You will not now abandon me so that I turn aside from You.

11a   YOU WILL TEACH ME THE PATH OF LIFE. [The verb *ôdî'ēnî*] is a future indicative[35] and not a modal imperfect expressing desire.[36]

11b   IN YOUR PRESENCE [IS PERFECT JOY].[37] [The] JOY, which is IN YOUR PRESENCE, is [that which is found] among the group of people which is [spiritually and ethically] near You.[38]

PSALM XVI, NOTES

[1]   BT Sotah 10b; Midrash Tehillim here.

[2]   Here Rashi combines two separate *midrashim* based on the Heb. word *miktām* According to the first *midrash, miktām* means *mak* and *tam*, i.e., 'meek' and 'unblemished'; according to the second *midrash*, which is introduced in BT Sotah 10b immediately after the former *midrash* by the formula *dābār 'āḥēr* 'another *midrash* [states]', *miktām* means not 'meek and unblemished' but *makkātô tammāh* 'his wound was unblemished' "for he was born uncircumcised." Rashi explains in his commentary there, "The place of circumcision, which is intended for a wound, was unblemished and whole, for it was unnecessary to remove it [the foreskin of the penis]." Rashi in his commentary on Ps. 16:1 ingeniously combines the two *midrashim*, the first of which speaks of David's unblemished character and the second of which speaks of David's virtue of having been born uncircumcised so that Rashi's own *midrash* makes David's unblemished character a consequence of his having been born circumcised. According to Avot deRabbi Nathan 2:12, the following thirteen biblical heroes were born circumcised: Job, Adam, Seth, Noah, Shem, Jacob, Joseph, Moses, Balaam, Samuel, David, Jeremiah, and Zerubbabel. See there for prooftexts. For additional references and discussion see Ginzberg, *Legends of the Jews*, vol. 5, p. 149, n. 51 and p. 267, n. 318. The equation of being born uncircumcised with being unblemished is reminiscent of R. Hoshaya's rationale for circumcision as the elimination of a blemish or defect in Genesis Rabbah 11:6: "Whatever was created in the first six days of Creation requires further preparation. For example, mustard seeds need sweetening, vetches need sweetening, wheat needs grinding; even man needs improvement."

[3]   Our Rashi ms. mistakenly reads *michtam* here.

[4]   There are four such psalms: Ps. 56; 57; 58; 59.

[5]   This he holds to be distinct from "a *michtam* of David" found only in Ps. 16 and 60.

[6]   By having David address himself to *keneset Yisrael* 'the congregation of Israel', which is feminine, Rashi accounts for the 2d pers. fem. sing. perfect verb *'āmartĕ* 'YOU SAY'. KJV, following the Targum, attempts to solve the same problem of the anomalous 2d pers. fem. sing. in a context of 1st

pers. sing. (referring to the male David) and 2ᵈ pers. masc. sing. (referring to God) by supplying 'O my soul' corresponding to Heb. *napšî*, which is also feminine, as antecedent of the pronominal suffix of the verb. Most modern translations and commentaries avoid the necessity of supplying a feminine antecedent by construing the form *'āmartĕ* as a defective, Phoenician-style spelling of *'āmartî* 'I said'; see Dahood, *Psalms* 1:187; *GKC* #44i and the examples cited there.

⁷ Here Rashi recognizes the precative perfect, i.e., the use of a perfect form of the verb as an imperative, which is now well documented from Ugaritic and Phoenician; this feature of Biblical Heb. was discussed at length in modern times by Moses Buttenweiser, "The Importance of Tenses for the Interpretation of the Psalms," in *Hebrew Union College Jubilee Volume* (Cincinnati: Hebrew Union College, 1925), pp. 89-111; id., *The Psalms Chronologically Treated with a New Translation* (Chicago: University of Chicago, 1938), pp. 18-25; see also Dahood, *Psalms*, 1:20.

⁸ Rendering of the lemma according to the interpretation presupposed by Rashi's comment. The interpretation of the preposition *'al* 'upon' as 'incumbent upon' is well-founded in biblical usage; see *BDB*, p. 753. Contrast NJV margin, which, like RSV's "I have no good apart from thee," adequately reflects the Targum, in which the word *bar* corresponds to Eng. 'but, apart from', but it is not an accurate rendering of the Heb. text, which lacks any expression meaning 'but, apart from' (cf. already the midrash attributed to R. Aha in Midrash Tehillim here). NJV, NEB, and Dahood prefer to join *ṭôbātî* 'MY GOOD' to the first half of the verse and to join *bal-'ālêkā* to v. 3. Rashi's interpretation makes this rearrangement unnecessary.

⁹ On *qĕdošîm* 'saints' as a term for the dead see Midrash Tehillim here; cf. also the similar use of the term *'ĕlohîm* 'gods' in 1 Sam. 28:13.

¹⁰ For this interpretation of *ba'āreṣ* 'in the earth' in Ps. 16:3 see Midrash Tehillim here; such a usage of Heb. *'ereṣ* 'earth' has been recognized in modern times by Dahood, *Psalms*, 1:106, q.v.

¹¹ Heb. *mĕhîrîm;* cf. *mĕhîr ṣedeq* 'zealous for equity' (so NJV) in Isa. 16:5.

¹² Rashi's paraphrase; the psalm has *niskêhem* 'THEIR LIBATIONS'.

¹³ Here Rashi interprets the pronominal suffix on *niskêhem* 'their libations' to refer to the devotees of the idolatrous gods; if, alternatively, the suffix were taken to refer to the gods, the suffix would lack a clear antecedent in the psalm. Dahood, *Psalms*, 1:88 interprets the suffix as a dative; hence a renders "libations to them," i.e., to the gods; see there, p. 127 on Ps. 20:3.

¹⁴ Lit., 'pouring the blood'; on this idiomatic usage see Mishnah Yoma 1:2.

¹⁵ Here Rashi, in paraphrasing substitutes the prosaic negative *lō'* for the rare, poetic (and characteristically Phoenician) *bal* found in this psalm.

¹⁶ While the psalm has THEIR NAMES, Rashi makes explicit to whom the name(s) belong(s).

¹⁷ Rendering of lemma according to the interpretation presupposed by Rashi's comment here; similarly Dahood, *Psalms*, 1:88: "You yourself cast

my lot." KJV's "Thou maintainest my lot" interprets *tômîk* as *qal* participle of the root *tmk* 'hold, support'; KJV's interpretation creates an anomaly since *gôrāl* is a stone lot, which is thrown; see *BDB*, p. 174a.

[18] This entire clause is expressed in Rashi's succint Heb. by the *kaph* of comparison.

[19] See Sifre, ed. Finkelstein, p. 121, line 6.

[20] I.e., You caused me to cast the lot. Thus Rashi here takes *tômîk* as a *hiphil* of *ymk*; see next note.

[21] So Dahood, *Psalms*, 1:89; he takes *ymk*, the root of *tômîk* as a biform of *mkk* 'sink, fall'.

[22] Rashi seems to refer to the passage found in Sifre, ed. Finkelstein, p. 120, lines 3-10. As noted by Maarsen here, Rashi does not quote the passage *verbatim*, nor is Rashi's analysis of the verb *tômîk* found in known additions of Sifre. Moreover, it is not cited in Finkelstein's critical apparatus to Sifre.

[23] Rashi suggests that the image suggested in Sifre of a loving father's guiding the hand of his beloved son as he cast the lot can shed light on Ps. 16:5 whether *tômîk* is taken to mean 'You cause casting (the lot)' or 'You hold (my hand while I cast the lot)'. However, as noted by Dahood (see above n. 21), *gôrāl* 'lot' must be the direct object of a verb of throwing *(mkk/ ymk)* rather than the object of a verb of holding *(tmk)*; *BDB*, p. 1069, s.v. *tmk* seem vaguely to sense this when they explain Ps. 16:5 as follows: "*thou dost grasp my lot* (i.e., take and cast it for me....)."

[24] I.e., Your share in the world, i.e., the people of Israel; cf. Deut. 4:20; Ibn Ezra on Deut. 4:19.

[25] Here Rashi writes out the second half of the verse almost *verbatim*; he interpolates the adjectival expression "such," and he substitutes the regular form *naḥălāh* 'estate' for the rare Phoenician-type form of the same noun, *naḥălāt*.

[26] Heb. *nibbā'* denominative verb derived from the noun *nābî'* 'prophet', i.e., one whose role is to instruct or admonish; for this nuance of the verb *nibbā'* in Biblical Heb. see Jer. 20:1; 25:13; 26:11, 18; see *BDB*, p. 612.

[27] Cf. the midrash attributed to R. Samuel b. Nahman in Midrash Tehillim here.

[28] Editorial "we," perhaps meaning "we Bible scholars," who are here distinguished from the creative writers responsible for midrashim; the latter he calls "Our rabbis"; for the idea that midrash is creative writing, which does not purport to be exegesis see Gruber, "The Midrash in Biblical Research," pp. 69-80.

[29] This idea is expressed in slightly different words in Rashi's commentary on Ex. 23:2 where he says, "I intend to reconcile it [the verse] with its specific characteristics according to its literal meaning." This sentence explains that one of Rashi's main purposes in his Bible commentaries was to reconcile anomalous expressions with their context in order to achieve greater understanding of both the expression and the context; on the latter statement of purpose and its parallels in Rashi's Bible commentaries see Kamin, *Rashi's Exegetical Categorization*, pp. 61-76.

[30] Heb. *tāmîd* 'ALWAYS' supplied by Rashi from v. 8a.

[31] Here Rashi indicates three things: (1) 'be at the right hand of' is an idiomatic expression meaning 'help'; see Ps. 110:5; 121:5; Eccles. 10:2; see Gaster, *MLC,* pp. 775-776; (2) the verse is elliptical; and (3) I SHALL NEVER BE SHAKEN is a consequence of God's 'being at my right hand'; contrast Dahood, *Psalms,* 1:86.

[32] Ellipsis dots here correspond to Rashi's *wĕgômēr* 'and it [the verse] finishes'.

[33] For *'āwôn* 'iniquity' in this rarer meaning 'punishment' see *BDB,* p. 731.

[34] The Bathsheba affair; see 2 Sam. 11-12; concerning the term "the great transgression" cf. W. L. Moran, "The Scandal of the Great Sin at Ugarit," *JNES* 18 (1959), pp. 280-81.

[35] *GKC* #107 calls this usage of the imperfect *futurum exactum,* i.e., 'future tense'; to Rashi's interpretation of the imperfect here contrast Midrash Tehillim here.

[36] On this usage of the Heb. imperfect see *GKC* #107 m-n.

[37] Rashi does not quote the bracketed portion of the verse. I have supplied it since Rashi's comment relates especially to this portion of the verse.

[38] Cf. PRK, ed. Mandelbaum, pp. 404-407.

PSALM XVII

2a   MAY VINDICATION COME FROM YOU. May the transgressions, of which I am guilty, for which I deserve to be punished by means of physical suffering, depart FROM YOU and may they not come before You in court.

2b   YOUR EYES WILL BEHOLD WHAT IS RIGHT. If I have to my credit[1] good deeds, MAY YOUR EYES LOOK upon them.

3a-b   YOU PROBED MY MIND, YOU HAVE VISITED ME AT NIGHT, [i.e.], at the evening hour with respect to the iniquity involving Bathsheba in accord with what is stated in the Bible (2 Sam. 11:2), "At the evening hour David arose...."

3c   YOU HAVE TESTED ME [*sĕraptanî* [I.e.], *nĕsîtanî*] 'You have put me to the test'.[2]

3d   YOU DID NOT FIND. [I.e.], You did not find[3] in me what You desired.[4]

3e   I DETERMINED THAT MY MOUTH SHOULD NOT TRANSGRESS. Should it again enter my mind to be tested[5] in Your presence, may MY MOUTH NOT TRANGRESS by saying again, "Probe me and try me" (Ps. 26:2) as I said previously in accord with what is stated in the Bible, "Probe me, O LORD, and try me" (Ps. 26:2), Now David said in the presence of the Holy One Blessed be He, "Why do they say 'the God of Abraham',[6] and they do not say, 'the God of David'?" He [the Holy One Blessed be He] said to him [to David], "I tested him with ten tests, and I found him unblemished." [Thereupon] he [David] said to Him, "Probe me and try me." Thus as it is found in [Babylonian Talmud] Tractate Sanhedrin (107a).[7]

4   AS FOR MAN'S DEALINGS IN ACCORD WITH THE COMMAND OF YOUR LIPS...

5   HOLDING MY FEET... Ever since ALL THE HUMAN DEALINGS, which I came to do, I HAVE KEPT IN VIEW for the sake of THE COMMAND OF YOUR LIPS THE WAYS[8] OF THE LAWLESS to turn aside from them so that I would not walk in them but would HOLD MY FEET con-

	tinually TO YOUR PATHS so that MY FEET would not[9] STUMBLE from them.
2b	MAY YOUR EYES BEHOLD WHAT IS RIGHT so that
2a	the VINDICATION WILL COME FROM YOU.
6b	THAT YOU WILL ANSWER ME, GOD. For I am certain[10] THAT YOU WILL ANSWER ME.
7	DISPLAY YOUR FAITHFULNESS...YOU WHO DE-LIVER WITH YOUR RIGHT HAND THOSE WHO SEEK REFUGE FROM ASSAILANTS [who assail] them.
8	...LIKE THE APPLE [OF YOUR EYE].[11] It is the black [spot], which is in the eye on which the light depends. Because of its blackness it is called *'īšôn*, a synonym of *ḥošek* 'darkness',[12] and the Holy One Blessed be He has provided for it [the pupil of the eye] a guard, [i.e.], the eyelids, which cover it continually.[13]
9a	THAT THEY DESPOIL ME.
9b	because of this that MY ENEMIES, who ENCIRCLE ME FOR A LIFE,[14] [i.e.], to take my life.
10a	WITH THEIR FAT THEY HAVE CLOSED. With their lard [*ḥēleb*], i.e., their fat [*šemen*], THEY HAVE CLOSED their hearts, and they have plastered over their eyes so as not]to see Your deeds (and so as not) to be in awe of You.
11a	AS FOR OUR FOOTSTEPS [*'aššurênû*] NOW THEY HAVE ENCIRCLED US. If our footsteps [*'ăqēbênû*][15] the enemies NOW HAVE ENCIRCLED US, and
11b	THEY SET THEIR EYES to infiltrate[16] THE LAND. Now it seems to me that David said this prayer after he had become guilty of the Uriah affair while Joab and Israel were in the land of the Ammonites laying siege to Rabbah (2 Sam. 11). David feared lest they [the Israelites] fail there on account of the transgression of which he was guilty and [lest] the Philistines and Moab and Edom and all of the land of Israel's evil neighbors who looked forward to the day of their [Israel's] demise might hear and attack them.
12	*yiksop* 'EAGER FOR' [means] *yaḥmod* 'he covets'; it is the same verb as is attested in *niksop niksaptā*[17] "indeed you were longing" (Gen. 31:30).[18]
13a	GO BEFORE[19] HIS [i.e.], the enemy's FACE.[20]
13b	CAUSE HIM TO STOOP.[21] [I.e.], bend his legs so that he will stoop and fall.

13c   RESCUE ME FROM all EVIL,[22] which is YOUR SWORD,[23] which You empower to exact punishment from those who are obligated to You.

14a   *mimĕtîm* YOUR HAND [i.e.], among those who die [*min hammētîm*] by YOUR HAND upon their beds. I prefer to be

14b   *mimĕtîm...mēḥeled* [i.e.], among those who die in old age after having been afflicted with a skin rash[24] [i.e.], *roilie* in O.F.[25] and among the virtuous, WHOSE SHARE is IN LIFE.

14c   BUT AS TO YOUR TREASURED ONES, FILL THEIR BELLIES. And among those whose stomachs[26] YOU FILL with "the good that You have in store[27] for those who fear You" (Ps. 31:20).

14e   SOMETHING TO LEAVE OVER [*yitrām*]. [I.e.], their properties, which they leave behind when they die.

15a   THEN because of Your kindness [*bĕṣidqātĕkā*] I WILL BEHOLD YOUR FACE. In the time to come, then I WILL BEHOLD YOUR FACE *bĕṣedeq* 'BECAUSE OF VIRTUE'. [I.e.], Dismiss from Your presence the charges against me (cf. v. 2), and take hold of the virtues [*haṣṣĕdāqôt*], which are to my credit, so that because of them I MAY BEHOLD YOUR FACE.

15b   LET ME BE FILLED WITH THE VISION OF YOU WHILE AWAKE. LET ME BE FILLED with seeing THE VISION OF YOU when the dead awaken from their slumber.[28]

PSALM XVII, NOTES

[1] Heb. *bĕyādî*, lit., 'in my hand'; when, however, *šebĕyādî*, lit., 'which is in my hand' refers to transgression, it means 'of which I am guilty'; see passim in Rashi's commentary on this psalm.

[2] Rashi here explains that the verb *ṣārap*, which usually refers to refining metal, is employed metaphorically in Ps. 17:3 to refer to putting people to a test.

[3] Rashi's paraphrase of the biblical text, which substitutes the standard negative particle *lō'* for the rare *bal* and employs the perfect form of the verb *māṣā'tā* to express the past tense.

[4] Here Rashi responds to the exegetical question, "What did You not find?" Rashi's interpretation is predicated upon his interpretation of v. 3b.

[5] Heb. *libḥôn*, lit., 'to test'

[6] Gen. 26:24; 28:13; 31:42; Ex. 3:6, 15, 16; 4:5; 1 Kgs. 18:36; and in the Rabbinic liturgy called "the eighteen benedictions"; see Birnbaum, *Daily Prayer Book*, [New York: Hebrew Publishing Co., 1949), p. 81.

[7] The mss. and the printed editions of Rashi state "Tractate Shabbat," which is an error; see Maarsen, p. 16, n. 12; Zohory, p. 64.

[8] Our Rashi ms. reads 'YOUR WAYS', which makes no sense in context.

[9] Here as at Ps. 17:3 Rashi substitutes the standard negative particle *lō'* " for the rare negative particle *bal* employed in the biblical text.

[10] Rashi here responds to the exegetical question, "Which of the many uses of the particle *kî* is reflected here?" Rashi, followed by KJV, JPS, RV, RSV, holds that *kî* here functions as a relative pronoun 'that' introducing a clause, which functions as the direct object of a verb of believing (cf. *BDB*, p. 471b). Other possible interpretations include "O that you would answer me" (Dahood, *Psalms* 1:92); "so that you will answer me" (Ehrlich, *Die Psalmen*, p. 30); "for thou wilt answer me" (NEB).

[11] Rashi does not quote the bracketed portion of the verse. I have supplied it for clarity.

[12] Rashi's apparent source is *Mahberet Menahem*, pp. 68-69, s.v. *'šwn*.

[13] Rashi here explains that the simile means that the psalmist here asks God to protect him just as God protects the pupil of the eye by providing eyelids.

[14] Heb. *běnepeš* rendered according to the interpretation presupposed by Rashi's commentary here; perhaps the original meaning of the clause is "encircle me at (my) neck"; on Heb. *nepeš* 'neck' see Mayer I. Gruber, "Heb. *da'ăbôn nepeš* 'dryness of throat': From Symptom to Literary Convention," *VT* 37 (1987), pp. 365-69 and the literature cited there.

[15] Here Rashi responds to the exegetical question, "What is the meaning of the noun *'aššurênû* here? Rashi's interpretation is followed by *BDB*, p. 81a, q.v.; NJV's rendering is supported by the parallelism at Ps. 17: 5; 40:3; 73:2; see Foster R. McCurley, Jr., "A Semantic Study of Anatomical Terms in Akkadian, Ugaritic, and Biblical Literature" (Ph.D. diss., Dropsie College, 1968), p. 95, n. 341.

[16] Heb. *lipšoṭ bě*; Rashi's interpretation of the psalmist's *linṭōt*, which NJV renders 'roaming over'.

[17] MT there reads *niksaptāh*; our Rashi ms. reads *niksaptā*.

[18] The rare verb *ksp* 'long for, covet' is attested also in Zeph. 2:1; Ps. 84:3; Job. 14:15.

[19] Heb. *qiddēm* 'go before' here in the nuance 'approach with hostility'; this usage is attested also in Ps. 18:6 (= 2 Sam. 22:6); 18:19 (=2 Sam. 22:19); 2 Kgs. 19:32 (= Isa. 37:33); Job. 30:27; other nuances of *qiddēm* 'go before' include 'receive favorably' as in Deut. 23:5; Isa. 21:14; Ps. 79:8; Neh. 13:2; and 'approach (God) in worship' as in Mic. 6:6; Ps. 88:14; 89:15; 95:2.

[20] Rashi responds to the exegetical question, "Whose face?"

[21] In late Heb. the verb *hikrîa'* may mean 'convince, win an argument, compromise'; see dictionaries; as Rashi intimates, in Biblical Heb. *hikrîa'* retains its primary meaning 'cause to stoop'; this verb is the *hiphil*-causative of the verb *kāra'* 'stoop', referrring to a posture of obeisance in Esth.

3:2-5; see Gruber, *Aspects*, pp. 171-172; cf. the Akkadian semantic equivalent of Heb. *hikrîaʿ*, sc., *šukmusu*.

[22] Rashi, followed by NJV, treats the noun *rāšāʿ* 'the wicked' as though it were the noun *rešaʿ* 'evil'; Rashi's comment, which follows, attempts to reconcile the equation of *rāšāʿ* 'the wicked (person/s)' with the inanimate object 'YOUR SWORD' by personifying the sword!

[23] Rashi takes YOUR SWORD as a noun in apposition to 'EVIL'; so also Vulgate; KJV; RV margin; RV; JPS, NEB, NJV, JB follow *GKC* #144m in taking 'YOUR SWORD' as an accusative of means 'with/by Your sword'.

[24] The apparent source of this midrash is Esther Rabbah 3:7 where it is asserted that precisely this is what happened to Rabbi Simeon b. Yohai and his son R. Eleazar; for parallels see Jacob Levy, *Neuhebräisches und Chaldäisches Wörterbuch*, rev. Heinrich Lebrecht Fleischer (4 vols.; Leipzig: Brockhaus, 1876-1889), vol. 2, p. 53a.

[25] From which is derived Modern French *rouille*. The O.F. word shares with Rabbinic Heb. *ḥalûdāh* the meaning 'rust' but not the meaning 'skin rash'; for literature concerning O.F. *roilie/roeille* see Levy, *Trésor de la langue des juifs français au moyen age*, p. 200.

[26] Here Rashi clarifies the meaning of Biblical Heb. *beṭen* by substituting the word *meʿayim*. In Biblical Heb. both words may designate either the uterus or the digestive organs. In Rabbinic Heb. *meʿayim* usually designates 'digestive tract' while *beṭen* is an infrequently attested synonym of *reḥem* 'uterus'; thus Rashi, who interprets *beten* in Ps. 17:4 to mean 'stomach', indicates this by substituting *meʿayim* in his commentary.

[27] Heb. *ṣāpantā*, from the same root as *ûṣĕpûnĕkā* 'BUT AS TO YOUR TREASURED ONES' in the biblical text.

[28] The biblical text may be taken to mean "Let me be satisfied from seeing your countenance while I am awake rather than in a dream"; cf. Num. 12:6-8 where Moses' intimacy with God is contrasted with the terms on which God converses with other prophets. Of the latter it is asserted there, "I shall make Myself known in the vision//I shall speak to him in the dream" (v. 6). Of Moses God says there, "I shall speak to him mouth to mouth, not in visions or riddles, and He will look upon the countenance of the LORD" (V. 8). The same term *tĕmûnāh* designates God's countenance in Num. 12:8 and in Ps. 17:15. Another plausible interpretation of our biblical text is "Let me be satisfied from seeing your countenance while I am yet alive, before it is too late; for this idea see also Job. 19:26, "Out of my flesh I want to see God"; see Tur-Sinai, *Job*, p. 306. KJV, RSV, NEB take *bĕhaqîṣ* to mean 'when I awake' rather than 'while I am awake'. Rashi, however, takes *bĕhaqîṣ* to mean 'when they awake', and he sees here a reference to the eschatological awakening of the dead from slumber, the metaphor for resurrection attested in Dan. 12:2. Rashi's interpretation seems to embody the view that sensory experience of God is largely limited to the primordial past and the eschatological future; for the latter view cf. Max Kadushin, *Worship and Ethics* (Evanston: Northwestern University Press, 1966), p. 217.

PSALM XVIII

1b   AFTER THE LORD HAD SAVED HIM.... [I.e.], when he had grown old and he had experienced all his troubles and he had been saved from them. AND FROM THE CLUTCHES OF SAUL. Was not Saul part of the group [of David's enemies referred to in the preceding phrase, "FROM THE HANDS OF ALL HIS ENEMIES"]? He was indeed, but[1] [he was excepted from the group] for he [Saul] was harsher to him [David] and pursued him more than all [the rest] of them.[2]

2   I ADORE YOU ['erḥoměkā] [i.e.], 'I love You ['e'ĕhoběkā]'. [Heb. rḥm 'love'][3] corresponds etymologically to the Aramaic verb with which we render into Aramaic [Heb.] wě'āhabtā 'You shall love' [sc.], wětirḥam (Targum Onkelos at Deut. 6:5).[4]

3   MY ROCK [salʻî] For You helped me at the Rock of Separation (see 1 Sam. 23:28) when I was pressed between Saul and his men [and] about to be captured in accord with what is stated in the Bible, "Saul and his men were trying to encircle David" (1 Sam. 23:25).[5] MY FORTRESS [ûměṣûdātî], a synonym of mibṣār 'fortification. MY ROCK [ṣûrî], a synonym of selaʻ 'rock'.[6] IN WHOM I SEEK REFUGE ['eḥĕseh [i.e.], abrier 'to take refuge' [in Old French].[7] [I.e.], 'I shall cover myself with His shade' in consonance with what is stated in the Bible, "And huddle against the rock for lack of shelter" (Job. 24: 8b) for the rocks are a covering and a shield for travellers from the winds and rain showers.

4a   ALL PRAISE! I CALLED ON THE LORD. With praises I shall pray to Him continually because I am confident that I shall be delivered from my enemies.[8]

5a   THERE SURROUNDED ME BANDS OF DEATH [i.e.], military detachments of enemies. The same usage [of the noun ḥebel 'band' to refer to a group of persons] is attested in "a band of prophets" (1 Sam. 10:5, 10).[9]

5b   TORRENTS OF BELIAL. This also is a term for military troops, who inundate like a stream.[10]

6a   BANDS OF SHEOL is a synonym of 'BANDS OF DEATH'

(v. 5a). [Targum Jonathan to 2 Sam. 22:6 renders 'BANDS OF DEATH' "troops of wicked people."

7   And as for me, what would I do IN MY DISTRESS?[11] I call[12] to THE LORD continually.

8   THEN THE EARTH ROCKED AND QUAKED... [In this verse the subordinate conjunction] *kî* is employed in the sense of *ka'ăšēr* 'when'. [Hence the verse means], "When He became angry,[13] so that He came to exact vengeance for His people and His servants from Pharaoh and his people, the earth rocked and quaked (v. 8a)."

9a   SMOKE WENT UP FROM HIS NOSTRILS. Likewise it is the manner of all anger [*hārôn 'ap*] to make smoke go up from[14] his nostrils.

10   HE BENT THE SKY AND CAME DOWN to pass through the land of Egypt.[15]

11b   GLIDING [*wayyēde'* means], 'HE FLEW' [*wayyā 'op*] (v. 11a) as is demonstrated by "As the eagle flies [*yid'eh*]" (Deut. 28:49).

12b   DARKNESS OF WATERS, which are in DENSE CLOUDS OF THE SKY, they are DARKNESS, which is AROUND HIM (12b). Lest you say that within the darkness there is no light a biblical verse intimates otherwise:

13   OUT OF THE BRILLIANCE, which is BEFORE HIM within His partition HAIL AND FIERY CLOUDS pierce and pass through HIS CLOUDS, which are AROUND HIM (12b). PASSED [*'āběrû*], [i.e.], *trépasant* 'having passed' [in Old French].[16] The hail disintegrated and passed over the Egyptians upon the Reed Sea.[17]

16a   THE OCEAN BED WAS EXPOSED[18]

16b   when all THE FOUNDATIONS OF THE EARTH were cleft for all the bodies of water in the world were cleft

16d   AT THE BLAST, [i.e.], at the blowing.[19]

17a   HE SENT FROM ON HIGH His angels to save Israel from the [Reed] Sea and from Egypt.

17b   [The verb] *yamšēnî* 'HE DREW ME OUT' is a verb referring to 'bringing forth' as is exemplified by "I drew him out [*měšîtîhû*] (Ex. 2:10).[20]

19   THEY OVERTOOK ME. My enemies were hurrying to overtake me to attack me ON THE DAY OF MY CALAMITY.

21a   ACCORDING TO MY MERIT [i.e.], my following You in
       the wilderness (cf. Jer. 2:2).

21b   *kĕbor-y[āday]* 'ACCORDING TO THE CLEANNESS OF
       [MY] H[ANDS],[21] a metaphor[22] for "clean... and pure of
       heart" (Ps. 24:4).

17a   Another equally plausible interpretation of HE SENT FROM
       ON HIGH, HE TOOK ME is that he [David][23] said it about
       himself with reference to the angel who came into the Rock
       of Separation to turn Saul away from him in accord with what
       is stated in the Bible, "An angel came to Saul..." (1 Sam.
       23:27).

21a   ACCORDING TO MY MERIT [i.e.], that I [David] did not
       kill him [Saul] when I cut the hem of his garment (cf. 1 Sam.
       24:5).

23   FOR I AM MINDFUL OF ALL HIS RULES. [I.e.], I have
       continually placed them on my heart (cf. Deut. 11:18) and
       before my eyes.

26a   WITH THE LOYAL, YOU DEAL LOYALLY. This is to
       say that it is indeed characteristic of Him to recompense
       measure for measure.

26-27 [The three adjectives] LOYAL, BLAMELESS, PURE refer
       respectively to the three patriarchs [Abraham, Isaac, and
       Jacob].[24] [WITH THE PURE,[25] i.e.], FAITHFUL.

27b   WITH THE PERVERSE refers to Pharaoh.

29a   IT IS YOU WHO LIGHT MY LAMP. When he [David]
       fought at night against the Amalekite army, which attacked
       Ziklag concerning which it is stated in the Bible, "David at-
       tacked them from before dawn until the evening of the next
       day" (1 Sam. 30:17).[26]

30a   WITH YOU, [i.e.], with reliance on You.

31b   TESTED [*ṣĕrûpāh*][27] [i.e.], *bĕḥûnāh* 'tried'. He promises, and
       He fulfills.

30b   WITH MY GOD I CAN SCALE A WALL. When he
       [David] came to fight against Jebus and he said, "Whoever
       slays a Jebusite...will become a chief and a prince..." (1 Ch.
       11:6), Joab brought a green cypress, and he ascended the wall,
       and he held fast to it [the cypress]. [Then] David said, "Let
       the righteous man [Joab] strike me..." (Ps. 141:5). The Holy
       One Blessed be He made it [the wall] short so that he [David]

was able to jump. [This midrash is found] in Midrash Tehillim.[28]

33b   WHO MADE MY PATH UNBLEMISHED. He removed[29] from MY PATH every sort of snare and stumbling block until it became safe and smooth.

34a   HE MAKES MY LEGS LIKE HINDS'. [The reason the psalmist says *'ayyālôt* 'HINDS' instead of *'ayyālîm* 'stags' (Cant. 2:9, 17; 8:14; Lam. 1:6) is that] the legs of the females stand up straighter than those of the males.[30]

35b   MY ARMS CAN BEND A BOW OF BRONZE. [The verb *wĕniḥătāh* 'CAN BEND'] is the same verb as is attested in "For Your arrows have struck" (Ps. 38:3). The *nun* is not a root letter of the word but like [the *nun* in] *niḥălû* "they were apportioned" (Josh. 14:1) [and like the *nun* in] *nitlû* "have been hanged" (Lam. 5:12).[31] [Thus our verse means]: "A brass bow was bent by my arms. David had brass bows hung up in his palace. When the kings of the Gentiles saw them, they would say to each other, "Do you think that David has the strength to draw these?" ["No," they would say]. "This [display of bows] is only for the purpose of frightening us." When he would hear them [speaking thus], he would draw them [the bows] in their presence.[32]

36   YOU HAVE MAGNIFIED YOUR HUMILITY TOWARD ME. You have magnified Your quality of HUMILITY so as to behave towards me with it.[33]

37a   YOU HAVE MADE WIDE MY STEPS BENEATH ME. Whoever makes wide his steps does not easily fall. In the same vein he [the Bible] says, "When you walk, your step will not be narrow" (Prov. 4:12a).

37b   *qarsûlay* 'MY FEET' are the legs from the ankles downward,[34] which are called *cheviles* [in Old French].[35]

41   YOU HAVE GIVEN ME THE NECK. They [MY ENEMIES] turn their neck[36] toward me, and they flee.

42a   THEY SHOUT to their idolatrous deity, BUT THERE IS NONE TO DELIVER, for it [their idolatrous deity] has not the capability [to deliver them].

42b   They go back, and they call UPON THE LORD, BUT HE DOES NOT ANSWER THEM.[37]

43b   I POURED THEM OUT[38] LIKE miry [*nārôq*] CLAY, which

is not thick. [The verb *'ărîqēm* 'I POURED THEM OUT']
is the same verb as is attested in "They were emptying
[*měrîqîm*]" (Gen. 42:35) [and in] "He has not been poured
[*hûrāq*] from vessel to vessel" (Jer. 48:11).[39]

44a YOU HAVE RESCUED ME FROM THE STRIFE OF
PEOPLE so that I shall not be punished for the sin of Israel
in perverting justice nor for making Israel serve [the king]
more than is permissible [according to the Torah].[40]

44b YOU HAVE SET ME AT THE HEAD OF NATIONS[41]
for whose [serving the king] there is no punishment.[42]

45a AT A MERE REPORT. Even if they are not in my presence but they hear a message delivered by an agent THEY
ARE SUBMISSIVE TO ME, [i.e.], they hearken to my discipline, and they hearken to my commands.

45b COWER BEFORE ME because of fear.

46a SHRIVEL [*yibbōlû*] [i.e.], 'wear out' [*yil'û*]. It is the same verb
[*nābēl* 'shrivel'] that is reflected in "You will surely shrivel"
(Ex. 18:18) [which T.O. renders into Aramaic] *mil'āh til'ē* "You
will surely wear out".

46b *weyahrĕgû* 'AND COME TREMBLING' is a verb expressive
of terror. Thus we render into Aramaic[43] "from rooms terror" (Deut. 32: 25) as *hargat mōtā'* 'agony of death'.[44] FROM
THEIR PRISONS.[45] Because of the afflictions of the prison
and jail wherein I inflict them.

47 [THE LORD],[46] who does for me all this [which is described
in v. 48] LIVES:

48a WHO HAS VINDICATED ME. [I.e.], He gives me the
strength to be avenged from my enemies.

48b *wayyadbēr* 'OVERTHREW'[47] [i.e.], 'He killed'. [The verb is]
a cognate of [the noun] *deber* 'plague'.[52] *tahtāy* 'UNDER ME'
[i.e.], in my place and in my stead as in the passage where it
is stated, "I give men in exchange for you" (Isa. 43:4) [where
tahtēkā, lit., 'under you', corresponds in meaning to *koprĕkā*
'ransom for you' in] "I have given Egypt as ransom for you"
(Isa. 43:3).

PSALM XVIII, NOTES

[1] In Rabbinic Heb. (including the dialect of Rashi) 'He was indeed,
but' is expressed by the single word *'ellā'*.

[2] Cf. Sifre Deuteronomy, ed. Finkelstein, p. 119.

[3] As pointed out in Mayer I. Gruber, "The Motherhood of God in Second Isaiah," *Revue Biblique* 90 (1983), p. 353, n. 6, "While Akkadian distinguishes between *ra'āmu* 'love' (from the root *r'm*) and *rêmu* 'have compassion' (from the root *rhm*), in Hebrew and Aramaic the two verbs coalesce as *rhm* 'love, have compassion'." Rashi here attempts to distinguish between the two nuances of the ambiguous Heb. and Aram. verb; the same distinction is found also in Jonah Ibn Janah, *Sepher Haschoraschim*, ed. Wlhelm Bacher (Berlin: M'kize Nirdamim, 1896), p. 477 (cited by Gruber, *Revue Biblique* 90, p. 353, n. 6); for an earlier source see next note.

[4] Rashi's apparent source for this observation is Midrash Tehillim here.

[5] Cf. Midrash Tehillim here.

[6] I.e., the uninflected form of the noun *sal'i* 'MY ROCK', which is found in the first part of the verse.

[7] I.e., 'to take refuge'; see Darmsteter, "Les Gloses," p. 82; cf. Rashi at 2 Sam. 22:3 and Darmsteter, "Les Gloses," *REJ* 54 (1907), p. 21; cf. Modern French *s'abriter*.

[8] Rashi here responds to the exegetical question as to why one should praise God before He has responded to the supplication.

[9] Our Rashi ms. reads "bands of prophets," which is nowhere attested in the Bible.

[10] Just as the 2 Sam. 22 recension of our psalm reads "breakers of Death" instead of "bands of Death," suggesting that the term is clearly a poetic synonym of "torrents of Belial," so does Rashi construe the two terms "bands of Death" and "torrents of Belial" as synonyms by attempting to demonstrate that both of them are metaphors for 'military troops'.

[11] The opening clause of v. 7 can be interpreted "In my distress I called on the LORD" (NJV). Rashi, however, divides this clause in the middle into a Talmudic-style question and answer.

[12] The biblical text reads *'eqrā'*, which can be interpreted as a past 'I called' (so NJV), a future, or a present; Rashi's paraphrase *'ănî qōrē'* reflects the last of these three possibilities.

[13] Rashi's point is that *kî hārāh lô* (NJV's 'BY HIS INDIGNATION, v. 8c), which Rashi treats as synonymous with *kî hārāh 'appô* 'when He became angry', is to be understood as an adverbial clause introducing vv. 8-16; contrast Gruber, *Aspects*, pp. 378-379.

[14] Rashi seems to suggest that the prefixed preposition *b* 'in' can be synonymous with *min* 'from'; for the recognition of this in modern times see Nahum M. Sarna, "The Interchangeability of the Prepositions *Beth* and *Min* in Biblical Hebrew," *JBL* 78 (1959), pp. 310-316; cf. Ziony Zevit, "The So-Called Interchangeability of the Prepositions *b, l* and *m(n)* in Northwest Semitic," *JANES* 7 (1975), pp. 103-112.

[15] Cf. Ex. 12:12; contrast Avot deRabbi Nathan, Chapter 34, which associates 2 Sam. 22:10 = Ps. 18:10 with the crossing of the Reed Sea.

[16] Darmsteter, "Les Gloses," *REJ* 54 (1908), p. 83.

[17] Rashi's source is Midrash Tehillim here.

[18] Our Rashi ms. reads with many medieval biblical mss. *'apqy ym*, lit., 'streams of the sea', which is the accepted reading at 2 Sam 22:16 and

which is also the reading presupposed by NJV's rendering "the ocean bed"; many moderns assume that the standard reading 'apqy mym 'channels of waters' (KJV) here at Ps. 18:16 is the result of improper word division and points to an original 'apqym ym, in which the final m of 'apqym is an enclitic mem; see Dahood, here.

[19] Rashi's source is Midrash Tehillim here.

[20] In his commentary at Ex. 2:10 Rashi explains that he differs from *Mahberet Menahem*, p. 246a in that the latter derives the verb yāmûš[û] 'it (they) will depart' (Josh. 1:8; Num. 14:44) and the verbs here referred to from a single biliteral root mš; Rashi, however, derives yāmûš from a biliteral root mš (in modern biblical lexicography the root is mwš] and the verbs cited here in Rashi's commentary from a triliteral root mšh [now known to be mšy]; see BDB, p. 559, s.v. mwš; p. 602, s.v. mšh; with reference to the nuances of mwš see Moshe Held, "Studies in Biblical Lexicography in the Light of Akkadian," in *Studies in Bible Dedicated to the Memory of U. Cassuto on the 100th Anniversary of his Birth* (Jerusalem: Magnes, 1987), pp. 114-26 (in Hebrew).

[21] Note that our Rashi ms. employs an abbreviation.

[22] Heb. lĕšôn; note that Rashi employs the term lāšôn to mean 'metaphor' also in his commentary at Ps. 23:2, 5; 31:11b; 45:5; 98:8; in his commentary at Ps. 12:9 Rashi employs the term dûgmā" to mean 'metaphor'.

[23] To whom the authorship of the psalm is attributed at v. 1.

[24] Rashi's comment here is based upon TJ to 2 Sam. 22:26-27; contrast Midrash Tehillim here; with Zohory, p. 70 cf. also BT Nedarim 32a.

[25] This lemma is missing in our Rashi ms.; it has been supplied here from other texts of Rashi's commentary.

[26] Rashi's source is Midrash Tehillim here.

[27] I.e., comparable to kesep ṣārûp 'refined silver'; for this metaphor applied to God's reliable promises see also Ps. 12:7; 119:140; Prov. 30:5.

[28] Midrash Tehillim at Ps. 18 #24.

[29] Our Rashi ms. reads by scribal error 'āsîr 'I shall remove' instead of hēsîr 'He removed'.

[30] Rashi's comment is based upon Midrash Tehillim here.

[31] I.e., the initial nun is the prefix of the niphal conjugation of the verb; apparently, Rashi derives the verb from a biliteral root ḥt; contrast BDB, p. 635b; K-B³, p. 653b, both of which take the plural form attested in Ps. 38:3 to be a niphal, the singular form found here to be a pi'el.

[32] Cf. Midrash Tehillim here.

[33] NJV treats the verb tarbēnî as a 3ᵈ pers. fem. sing. imperfect, whose subject is the feminine noun 'anwatĕkā 'YOUR CARE, CONDESCENSION' (see NJV margin) and whose direct object is 'ME' expressed by the pronominal suffix to the verb. Rashi, however, takes the verb tarbēnî as a 2ᵈ pers. masc. sing. imperfect addressed to God; he treats the noun 'anwatĕkā 'YOUR HUMILITY' as the direct object of the verb, and he takes the pronominal suffix as a dative; for such datives see GKC #117x.

[34] The expression 'from the ankles downward' follows the O.F. gloss in the Hebrew text of Rashi; it makes no sense in that position.

[35] I.e., *chevilles* in Modern French; see Darmsteter, "Les Gloses," *REJ* 55 (1908), p. 83; for the twenty-two instances of this O.F. gloss of Heb. *qarsûl* in Rashi's commentary on the Talmud see Catane, *Recueil*, p. 205.

[36] Rashi correctly relates the expression 'give me/him my/his enemy's neck' attested here in Ps. 18:41 (=2 Sam. 22:41) to the expression 'turn their neck toward their enemies' attested only in Josh. 7:8, 12. The former expression means 'repulse (them), bring about a (their) retreat' while the latter expression means 'retreat'. The functional equivalent of the former expression in Akk. is *irta nĕ'û/turrû* 'turn the (enemy's) chest' while the functional equivalent of the latter Heb. expression in Akk. is *arkāta suḫḫuru* 'turn the back'; see Foster R. McCurley, Jr., "A Semantic Study of Anatomical Terms in Akkadian, Ugaritic, and Biblical Hebrew" (Ph.D. diss., Dropsie College, 1968), pp. 187-89. The Eng. equivalent of *pānāh 'orep* 'retreat' is 'turn tail' (so NJV at Josh. 7:8, 12). The usage of Heb. *pānāh 'orep* 'turn the neck' attested in Josh. 7:8, 12 is to be distinguished from the homonymous *pānāh 'orep* 'turn the neck', i.e., 'ignore, disregard' attested in Jer. 2:27; 32:33; 2 Ch. 29:6, which is synonymous with *her'āh 'orep* 'show (them) the back of (his) neck' in Jer. 18:17. Akk. semantic equivalents of *pānāh 'orep* 'disregard' include *kišāda šabāsu, kišāda suḫḫuru*, and *kišāda nadû* while the antithetical posture of favor is described in Akk. as *kišāda turru* 'turn back (toward the object of favor) the front of the neck'; for these four Akk. expressions see *CAD*, K, p. 447. Examination of these expressions reveals that while Heb. *'orep* means 'back of the neck' Akk. *kišādu* means 'front of the neck'; Heb. *'orep* is therefore the lexical equivalent of Akk. *kutallu* rather than *kišādu*; see Edouard Dhorme, *L'emploi Métaphorique des noms de parties du corps en hébreu et en akkadien* (Paris: Geuthner, 1923), p. 95. Hence the Akk. expressions of antipathy which employ *kišādu* mean 'turn away (from the object of disfavor) the front of the neck' while the Heb. expressions of antipathy, which employ the word *'orep*, mean 'turn the back of the neck (toward the object of disfavor); hence also Heb. *pānāh 'orep* 'turn the back of the neck, retreat' corresponds to *arkāta suḫḫuru* 'turn the back'.

[37] Rashi's comment is based upon Midrash Tehillim here; for the idea cf. Rashi at Ps. 6:11.

[38] Heb. *'ărîqēm*, the reading in our Rashi ms. and in MT here; NJV's "I trod them flat" reflects the view generally accepted by biblical scholars that the *r* in *'ărîqēm*, in the MT here represents the misreading of an original *daleth* as in 2 Sam. 22:43: *'ădiqqēm* 'I ground them/stamped them' from the root *dqq*; see *BDB*, pp. 937-938; concerning the confusion of *d* and *r* in the MT see Friedrich Delitzsch, *Die Lese-und Schreibfehler im Alten Testament* (Leipzig & Berlin: Walter de Gruyter, 1920), pp. 105-07.

[39] Here Rashi follows *Mahberet Menahem*, p. 346.

[40] My bracketed explications of Rashi's enigmatic comment here are based upon his fuller, clearer comment at 2 Sam. 22:44; cf. Midrash Tehillim here.

[41] Heb. *gôyîm*, which Rashi understands to mean 'Gentiles'.

[42] See n. 40.

[43] I.e., Rabbinic Judaism in its official Aramaic version of the Pentateuch, Targum Onkelos.

[44] Cf. Midrash Tehillim here.

[45] Rendering of the lemma according to the understanding presupposed by Rashi's comment here; contrast NJV and NEB "strongholds"; KJV "close places"; Dahood, here, interprets Heb. *masgēr* "pericardium"; the latter view is found already in Midrash Tehillim here. Rashi's interpretation of *misgĕrôtêhem* as 'prisons' is supported by Isa. 42:7 where *masgēr* 'prison' is employed in synonymous parallelism with *bêt kele'* (= Akk. bīt kīli) 'jail': "Opening blind eyes [NJV margin remarks, "An idiom meaning 'freeing the imprisoned'; cf. (Isa.) 61:1], frees the prisoner from prison *(masgēr)*, those who sit in darkness from jail *(bêt kele')*." For *masgēr* 'jail, prison' see also Isa. 24:22 (so NJV there) and Ps. 142:8 (so NJV there).

[46] Rashi does not quote the bracketed portion of the verse; I have supplied it for clarity.

[47] Lemma rendered according to $K\text{-}B^3$, p. 201b, s.v. *dbr* I.

[48] Cf. Midrash Tehillim here.

PSALM XIX

2   THE HEAVENS DECLARE THE GLORY OF GOD. The poet himself explicated this statement [in vv. 4ff.]: THERE IS NO UTTERANCE, THERE ARE NO WORDS, [which is to say that] they [the heavens] do not speak with people except insofar as THEIR CIRCUIT[1] HAS GONE FORTH THROUGHOUT THE EARTH, and they [the heavens] give light to people. Therefore people DECLARE THE GLORY OF GOD, and they acknowledge and bless [Him] because of the luminaries.

3a   DAY TO DAY MAKES UTTERANCE. The work of Creation[2] is renewed from day to day: at evening the sun sets, and it rises in the morning. Therefore people utter words of praise. [DAY TO DAY itself MAKES UTTERANCE] by means of the days and the nights which teach people to praise and acknowledge [God].

5a   THROUGHOUT THE EARTH HAS GONE FORTH THEIR CIRCUIT [*qawwām*] [i.e.], the heavens, which are stretched out over the face of all the earth, and consequently

5b   THEIR WORDS ARE AT THE END OF THE WORLD, for all speak about the wonders which they see.

5c   HE, the Holy One Blessed be He, PLACED IN THEM, the heavens, A TENT FOR THE SUN,

6a   WHO IS LIKE A GROOM COMING FORTH FROM THE CHAMBER every morning. Now it is with reference to this that he [the poet] said, "THE HEAVENS DECLARE THE GLORY OF GOD" (v. 2a).

7b   AND HIS CIRCUIT [i.e.], the circuit of his [the sun's] circumambulation is from [one] end [of the sky] to the [other] end.

7c   NOTHING ESCAPES HIS HEAT. Were he [the sun] located in the lowest [of the seven] heaven[s], a person would not ESCAPE him because of his great heat.[3]

8   THE TEACHING OF THE LORD IS PERFECT. She also gives light like the sun in accord with what is stated at the end of the 9d stanza: MAKING THE EYES LIGHT UP, and

he [the Bible] says, "For the commandment is a lamp, the teaching is a light" (Prov. 6:23). Another equally plausible interpretation [of vv. 7-9 is as follows]:

7c NOTHING ESCAPES HIS HEAT on the Day of Judgment, "and the day that is coming will burn them" (Mal. 3:19), but

8a-b THE TEACHING OF THE LORD IS⁴ PERFECT, RE-NEWING LIFE so that she shields those who study her from that fire in accord with what is stated in the Bible, "To you who are devoted to me there shall arise [a sun of kindness and healing]" (Mal. 3:20).⁵

8c THE TESTIMONY OF THE LORD IS FAITHFUL. [I.e.], She [the Torah] is faithful to testify on behalf of those who study Her.

8b TURNING BACK THE SOUL. She [the Torah] turns him [who studies Torah] back from the paths of death to the paths of life.

9c LUCID, [i.e.], shining.

8-10 TEACHING [tôrāh], TESTIMONY ['ēdût], PRECEPTS [pĕqûdê], INSTRUCTION [miṣwat], FEAR [yir'at],⁶ JUDG-MENTS [mišpĕṭê] are six [terms for Torah], which correspond numerically to the six orders of the Mishnah.⁷

8d MAKING WISE THE SIMPLE [i.e.], giving wisdom to simpletons.

11d THAN THE HONEY [nopet]⁸ OF THE HONEYCOMB, i.e., than the honey [moteq]⁹ of the honeycomb.

12 IN OBEYING THEM¹⁰ THERE IS GREAT REWARD. I [the psalmist] have been careful about obeying them for the sake of "Your abundant good, which You have in store" (Ps. 31: 20).¹¹

13a WHO CAN BE AWARE OF ERRORS? I have been careful about them,¹⁰ but it is impossible to be so careful that I would not err in respect of them, so You

13b CLEAR ME FROM HIDDEN THINGS, which were hidden from me so that I did not know when I sinned in error.

14a AND FROM WILLFUL SINS [zēdîm] [i.e.], from zĕdônôt 'deliberate sins'.¹²

14c THEN I SHALL BE BLAMELESS. I shall be blameless.¹³ The sages asked [with reference to this assertion in this psalm of David], "What is David like?" [They answered], "Like a Samaritan who continually begs at doorways."¹⁴ Now they [the Samaritans] are more deceitful in this respect than all other people. [The Samaritan says], "Give me water to drink," a request which involves no monetary loss. Once he has drunk he says, "Here is a small onion." Once they have given him [the onion], he asks, "Is there an onion without salt?" Once they have given him [the salt], he says, "Give me a little bread so that the onion will not have a deleterious effect on me." In the same vein, David spoke first about errors (v. 13), and later about willful sins (v. 14a), and later about acts of rebellion.[15]

14d   OFFENSES [pĕšāʿy].[16] These are acts of rebellion by which someone intends to make someone else angry. Thus he [the Bible] says, "The king of Moab has rebelled [pāšaʿ] against me" (2 Kgs. 3:7).[17]

15   MAY...BE ACCEPTABLE, [i.e.], for persuasion to procure Your favor.[18]

PSALM XIX, NOTES

[1] Translation reflects Rashi's interpretation below; cf. KJV's "their line"; contrast NJV's "their voice," on which see marginal note to NJV; in support of the latter rendering see also Dahood, *Psalms*, 1:121; Barth, *Etymologische Studien*, pp. 29ff.; and cf. also Akk. *qu"û*

[2] Rabbinic Heb. *bĕrē'šît*, lit., 'in the beginning', designates "that which was made during the first six days of creation" (Kadushin, *Worship and Ethics*, p. 27); hence *maʿăśēh bĕrē'šît*, commonly rendered 'work of creation', should be rendered 'the making of that which was made during the first six days of creation'.

[3] Cf. BT Hagigah 12b.

[4] Rashi adds 3[d] pers. fem. sing. personal pronoun, which here as frequently in his dialect serves as copula.

[5] Our Rashi ms. does not quote this part of the verse; I have supplied it for clarity.

[6] This term is missing from the list in our Rashi ms.

[7] Cf. Midrash Tehillim here where a midrash attributed to R. Tanḥuma explicitly identifies each of the six terms with a specific order of the Mishnah.

[8] The rare Heb. *nopet* 'honey' corresponds etymologically to Akk. *nubtu*, which usually designates 'bees' honey'. As generally in Biblical Heb., Rabbinic Heb., and Akk., Ps. 19:11 distinguishes between *dĕbaš* (= Akk. *dišpu*) 'fig honey' and *nopet* 'bees' honey'; see next note.

[9] For Heb. *moteq* = Heb. *dĕbaš* 'honey' see Judg. 9:11: "But the fig tree replied, 'Have I stopped yielding my honey [*motqî*] and my sweet fruit that I should go and wave above the trees?'" Apparently, Rashi assumes that his reader would immediately identify *moteq* as 'honey' whether from the

honeycomb or produced from figs but that his reader would not know the meaning of *nopet*, which is attested only in Ps. 19:11; Prov. 5:3; 24:13; 27:7; Cant. 4:11.

[10] God's commandments.

[11] Cf. Tanḥuma, 'Eqeb.

[12] As noted in NJV margin, Heb. *zēdîm* can mean both 'willful sins' and 'corrupt men'. Rashi, followed here by NJV, holds that in the present context the word is synonymous with the cognate *zēdônôt* 'willful sins'.

[13] Here Rashi clarifies the stative verb *'eytām*, 1ˢᵗ pers. sing. imperfect of the verbal root *tmm*, by substituting the 1ˢᵗ pers. sing. imperfect of the verb 'to be' followed by the predicate adjective *tāmîm* 'blameless' from the same root as *'eytām*; on this verb form see *GKC* #67p. Note that in general Rashi's Heb., like Modern Heb., prefers the use of the verb 'to be' followed by a predicate adjective to Biblical Hebrew's use of stative verbs.

[14] See Lev. Rabbah 88:8; see also Midrash Tehillim here. It should be noted that Rabbinic Heb. *ḥizzēr 'al happětāḥîm* 'continually beg at doorways' exemplifies the semantic equivalent of Rabbinic Heb. *ḥzr* and Akk. *saḥāru* 'traverse'; see Sperling, "Late Hebrew *ḥzr* and Akkadian *saḥāru*," pp. 396-404; significantly Sperling does not discuss the expression 'continually beg at doorways'; for the Akk. equivalent of the latter see *MDP* 2, pl. 23, col. 6, lines 29-40 discussed in Gruber, *Aspects*, p. 46.

[15] See Midrash Tehillim here.

[16] While the biblical text employs the form *pešaʿ* 'offense' as a collective, the form found in our Rashi ms. is an abbreviation of the plural *pěšaʿîm*, which could not be written in full for lack of space on the line.

[17] Note that the noun *pešaʿ* 'offense' is derived from the verb *pāšaʿ* 'rebel'.

[18] Cf. Rashi's similar remarks concerning Heb. *rāṣôn* in his commentary at Lev. 19:5; Ps. 5:13; 145:16.

PSALM XX

2a MAY THE LORD ANSWER YOU IN TIME OF TROUBLE. This psalm [was composed] with reference to the fact that he [David] used to send Joab and all Israel to war while he himself used to remain in Jerusalem and pray for them as in the passage where it is stated, "It is better for you to support us from the town" (2 Sam. 18:3). "Were it not for David, Joab would not have been able to wage war."[1]

2b THE NAME OF JACOB'S GOD, who made a promise to him [Jacob] when he [Jacob] went to Haran and who kept His promise.[2] Therefore, it is stated, JACOB'S GOD.[3]

3 FROM HOLINESS [*miqqodeš*] [i.e.], from His holy Temple[4] where He is enshrined.[5]

4b APPROVE [*yĕdaššĕneh*] a verb referring to fat as is exemplified by "and they eat their fill and grow fat [*wĕdāšēn*] (Deut. 31:20). What it means is that He [God] will accept them[6] with pleasure as though they were "burnt offerings of fatlings" (Ps. 66:15).

4a-b YOUR MEAL OFFERINGS (4a)...AND YOUR BURNT OFFERINGS (4b) are [employed here as metaphors for] the prayers which you pray in war time.

6a LET US SING A HYMN TO YOU IN YOUR VICTORY. When the Holy One Blessed be He will have made you victorious, MAY WE all SING to the Holy One Blessed be He,

6b and in His NAME[7] ARRAYED BY STANDARDS, [i.e.], let us gather together, and let us do valiantly.[8]

7a NOW I KNOW. This [vv. 7ff.] is the hymn [*rinnāh*], which we will sing [*nĕrannēn*] NOW for the victory (cf. v. 6a), which came to Joab and Israel. I KNOW that God is pleased with me so that He answered me[9]

7b FROM HIS HEAVENLY SANCTUARY, for [God said], "Their [Israel's] victory is My victory."[10]

8a THEY [CALL] ON CHARIOTS. There are some nations that rely on their chariots, and there are some that rely ON their HORSES,

8b BUT WE OFFER INCENSE [*nazkîr*] IN THE NAME OF THE LORD. [The verb] *nazkîr* is a word referring to burning of incense and [by extension] prayer[11] as is exemplified by *mazkîr lĕbônāh* 'burns incense' (Isa. 66:3) and *'azkĕrātāh* 'its incense' (Lev. 2:2).[12]

9 and therefore, THEY COLLAPSE AND LIE FALLEN, BUT WE RALLY AND GATHER STRENGTH.

PSALM XX, NOTES

[1] Dictum attributed to R. Abba b. Kahana (late 3d century C.E.) in BT Sanhedrin 49a; Rashi explains there, "'Were it not for David', who used to occupy himself with [the study of] Torah, Joab would not have been able to wage war, but David's virtue helped Joab in David's wars." Interestingly, according to the Talmud passage the decisive Davidic virtue was study of Torah while Rashi's comment here on Ps. 20:2 suggests that the Davidic virtue which aided Joab was prayer.

[2] For the promise see Gen. 28:15: "Remember, I am with you: I will protect you wherever you go and will bring you back to this land. I will not leave you until I have done what I have promised you." For the fulfillment of the promise see Gen. 33:18.

[3] Rather than Abraham's God or Isaac's God; see Midrash Tehillim here.

[4] Other instances where *qodeš*, lit. 'holiness', means 'temple' include Ps. 24:3; 63:3; 68:25.

[5] If in Biblical Heb. the verb *šakan* 'dwell' when applied to God means 'to tabernacle' and it expresses the immanence of God (so Frank M. Cross, Jr., "The Priestly Tabernalce," in *Biblical Archaeologist Reader* [Chicago: Quadrangle Books, 1961], p. 226), in Rabbinic Heb. when applied to God it means 'to be enshrined' (from *miškān* 'shrine') or 'to be present in the shrine' (from Shekinah 'Divine Presence').

[6] Your prayers; see next comment.

[7] Here Rashi paraphrases; the biblical text reads, "IN THE NAME OF GOD."

[8] Both Rashi and NJV take nidgol as a denominative verb derived from the noun degel 'flag, standard' or 'military unit'; on these meanings of degel see Jacob Milgrom, *Numbers*, The JPS Torah Commentary (Philadelphia: Jewish Publication Society, 1990), p. 11.

[9] Rashi paraphrases; the biblical text reads, "HE WILL ANSWER HIM."

[10] Cf. Jer. 3:23.

[11] Rashi at Lev. 2:2 explains that "the handful [of a meal offering], which ascends to the Most High [is called *'azkārāh* 'reminder' because it] is the *zikkārôn* 'reminder' of the meal-offering through which its presenters are remembered for good and for [the LORD'S] satisfaction." Hence such an offering is tantamount to a prayer.

[12] It is well known that Ibn Janaḥ recognized in several places in the Bible a root *zkr* referring to "olfactory appreciation of incense and burnt offerings"; see Marvin H. Pope, *The Song of Songs*, AB, vol. 7C (Garden City, N.Y.: Doubleday, 1977), p. 304; Gordis, *Song of Songs and Lamentations,* p. 78. If in the *qal* the verb can mean 'smell, savor' as in Ps. 20:4, it should not be surprising to see the *hiphil* of the same verb meaning 'burn, offer incense', i.e., 'cause it to smell', attested in Ps. 20:8 and in Isa. 66:3; nor should it be surprising that from the same root is derived a noun *'azkārāh* 'incense' attested in Lev. 2:2.

PSALM XXI

2   THE KING[1] REJOICES IN YOUR STRENGTH. Our rabbis interpreted it as a reference to the king Messiah, but it is correct to interpret it as a reference to David himself as a retort to the Christians who found in it support for their erroneous beliefs.

3   *'areset* ('REQUEST')[2] is a *verbum dicendi*, and it is an *hapax legomenon*.

4a   YOU HAVE PROFFERED HIM BLESSINGS OF GOOD THINGS. Before I[3] asked You, You proffered me Your blessing through the agency of Nathan the prophet [who said in Your name], "I will raise up your offspring)..., and I will establish his royal throne forever" (2 Sam. 7:12-13).

4b   YOU HAVE SET UPON HIS HEAD A CROWN OF GOLD [as it is said in 2 Sam. 12:30]: "He took[4] the crown of their king, and it was [placed] on David's head."

5a   HE ASKED YOU FOR LIFE. When I[3] was fleeing out of the country to escape from Saul I continually prayed, "I shall walk before the LORD in the lands of the living" (Ps. 116:9).[5]

5b   YOU GAVE [it] TO HIM when You brought me[3] back to the land of Israel.

5c   A LONG LIFE for my[3] kingship, for You said, "I will establish his kingship[6] forever" (cf. 2 Sam. 7:13).

7   [The verb] *těhaddēhû* 'YOU GLADDENED HIM' is a cognate of [the noun] *hedwāh* 'gladness' (1 Ch. 16:27). WITH)...YOUR PRESENCE. [I.e.], in Paradise. Now our rabbis, who interpreted it as a reference to the king Messiah, cited as proof for the interpretation [Dan. 7:13]: "He approached the Ancient of Days, and they brought him before Him." Moreover, he [the Bible] says, "I will bring him near, that he may approach Me" (Jer. 30:21).[7]

8c   HE WILL NOT BE SHAKEN.

8a-b AND he trusts IN THE eternal[8] FAITHFULNESS OF THE MOST HIGH so that HE WILL NOT BE SHAKEN.[9]

9a   MAY YOUR HAND FIND ALL YOUR ENEMIES. Whatever plague of Your hand[10] that You can bring, bring upon Your enemies.

10b   AT THE TIME OF YOUR FACE [i.e.], at the time of Your anger.[11]

10c-d DESTROYS THEM like FIRE. This is a prayer.[12]

11   YOU WIPE THEIR OFFPSRING FROM THE EARTH. It is to the Holy One Blessed be He that he [the psalmist] says [this]. I.e., he prays[13] that He should make the offspring of the wicked Esau perish.

12a   FOR THEY SCHEMED AGAINST YOU. This refers to the wicked Titus, who thought that he killed God.[14]

12c   THEY WERE UNABLE to carry it out.[15]

13a   FOR YOU WILL MAKE THEM A SPOIL [šekem][16] in that You will make them a spoil [ḥēleq] when Israel will despoil [yĕhallĕqû] their wealth as it is stated in the Bible, "Her[17]...harlot's fee shall be...[for those who dwell before the LORD]" (Isa. 23:18).[18]

PSALM XXI, NOTES

[1] So NJV; the Hebrew text does not supply the definite article before 'KING'.

[2] So KJV.

[3] Throughout the psalm the king is referred to in the 3[d] pers. Since Rashi holds that the king here referred to is David, Rashi's paraphrase of the text has David, to whom the authorship of the psalm is attributed at Ps. 21:1, refer to himself in the 1st pers.

[4] NJV renders this active verb as a passive: "The crown was taken." On the impersonal use of the active voice corresponding to Eng. passive see Speiser, *Genesis*, p. 297, n. 3. JPS' rendering "And he took," assumes that the pronoun 'he' refers back to David in v. 29. Rashi finds in Ps. 21:4 an answer to the question as to who is the subject of the verb 'he took' in 2 Sam. 12:30, namely, God.

[5] Cf. Rashi there.

[6] Heb. *mamlaktô*; the text to which Rashi refers has *kissē' mamlaktô* as do other Rashi mss. here; most likely the reading in our ms. is the result of haplography.

[7] Midrash Tehillim here.

[8] Heb. *'ôlām*.

[9] The Massoretic accents suggest that the two halves of the verse together refer to the reciprocal relationship obtaining between the Davidic king and the LORD. The first half of the verse speaks of the king's reliance upon the LORD while the second half of the verse speaks of the LORD's FAITHFULNESS: "THROUGH THE FAITHFULNESS OF THE MOST HIGH [to the covenant He made with the Davidic dynasty] HE [the king] WILL NOT BE SHAKEN." Such an interpretation of the verse, which is reflected in NJV's rendering, requires positing two differ-

ent meanings of the preposition *b* in our verse: 'in' in the first clause; 'through, by virtue of' in the second clause. While KJV and NJV treat our verse as two independent clauses joined by the conjunctive *waw*, Rashi treats the verse as one independent clause whose predicate is TRUSTS and one dependent clause who predicate is WILL NOT BE SHAKEN. To indicate that the dependent clause functions as a noun, specifically the direct object of the verb TRUSTS, Rashi paraphrases supplying the relative particle *šĕ* 'that'.

[10] Rashi's substitution of the expression *makkat yādĕkā* 'plague of your hand' for the Bible's *yādĕkā* lit., 'Your hand', indicates that according to Rashi *yād*, lit., 'hand' here is not a metaphor for power but an extension of the idioms *yad YHWH*, lit., 'hand of the LORD' (Ex. 9:3); *yad 'ĕlôăh* 'hand of God' (Job. 19:21); *'eṣba' 'ĕlohîm*, lit., 'finger of God (Ex. 8:15), all of which mean 'plague'. Cf. Ugar. *yd ilm* and Akk. *qāt ili*, which, like these Heb. expressions, mean literally 'hand of god(s)', idiomatically, 'plague'.

[11] Note that *pānîm*, lit., 'face', denotes 'anger' also in Lam. 4:15 and 'sadness' in 1 Sam. 1:8; cf. Qimḥi; see (with Maarsen) also Rashi on Ps. 34:16; cf. the use of *'ap* 'face, nose, mouth' also in the extended meaning 'anger'; see Gruber, *Aspects*, pp. 550-553.

[12] Here Rashi indicates that the imperfect verb *yĕballĕ'ēm*, which could be taken as a future (KJV and RSV) or as a present (NJV) or as a jussive, is to be interpreted as a jussive.

[13] Here Rashi interprets the ambiguous imperfect *tĕ'ăbbēd* as a request; NJV interprets it as a present indicative; cf. n. 14.

[14] Here Rashi refers to the legend recorded in BT Gittin 56b: "He [Titus] took a sword, and he pierced the curtain [which hung at the entrance to the holy of holies]. A miracle was performed, namely, blood spurted forth. He [Titus] thought that he killed 'Himself'." Rashi in his commentary there explains that 'Himself' is an epithet of God. In my rendering of Rashi's commentary here I have substituted 'God' for 'Himself'. Note that while the Talmudic text expresses 'he thought' by *sābûr*, Rashi in his commentary here substitutes the Biblical Heb. equivalent *'āmar*. Note also that Rashi refers to the same legend below in his comment on Ps. 53:2.

[15] By supplying the infinitive finalis *la'ăśôtāh* 'to carry it out', Rashi intimates that the verse is elliptical insofar as in his view *bal-yûkālû* means simply 'THEY WERE UNABLE' leaving open the question 'UNABLE to do what?'

[16] Rashi holds that *šekem* here and in Gen. 48:2 and in Ps. 60:8 is synonymous with *ḥēleq*, lit., 'portion'; see Rashi there. It follows, therefore, from Rashi's use of the noun *ḥēleq* and the cognate verb *ḥilleq* in the meanings 'spoil' and 'despoil' respectively that in the present context he also interprets *šekem* to mean 'spoil'.

[17] I.e., Tyre's; see the context.

[18] I.e., Israel. Rashi does not quote the bracketed portion of the verse. I have supplied it for clarity.

1   ON [*'al*] AYYELETH HA-SHAHAR. [It is the] name of a musical instrument. Another equally plausible interpretation [of *'al* AYYELETH HA-SHAHAR] is "concerning [*'al*] the congregation of Israel, who is 'a loving doe' (Prov. 5:19),[1] 'that shines through like the dawn' (Cant. 6:10).[2] Our rabbis interpreted it as a reference to Esther.[3]

2b   WHY HAVE YOU ABANDONED ME? In the future she [the congregation of Israel is going into exile, and David composed this prayer with reference to the future [exile].[4]

2c-d   FAR FROM DELIVERING ME and from THE WORDS OF MY ROARING.[5]

3b   I CRY BY DAY. I cry[6] to You from day to day,[7] but You do not answer.[6]

4   BUT YOU ARE THE HOLY ONE, and[8] ENTHRONED to hear[9] THE PRAISES OF ISRAEL since primordial times.

7a   BUT I AM A WORM, LESS THAN HUMAN. He [the psalmist here] refers to Israel metaphorically as one person.

8   *yapṭîrû* [is a synonym of] *yiptěḥû* 'they will open'; it is from the same verbal root as is exemplified by [the noun *peṭer* 'opener' in the expression] *peṭer reḥem* "opener of the womb" (Ex. 13:12).

9   LET HIM COMMIT HIMSELF [*gol*] TO THE LORD. [The form *gol*] is from the same root as [the infinitive] *lāgôl*.[10] [The meaning of this verse is that] a person should turn over [*lěgôlēl*] his load and his burden to his Creator so that He will release him [from it].[11]

10a   *gôḥî* 'ONE WHO DRAWS ME FORTH',[12] [i.e.], who brings me out and who pulls me forth. It is a cognate of [the verb *yāgîaḥ* 'he draws forth' in Job. 40:23]: "He draws forth the Jordan...."

10b   MADE ME SECURE AT MY MOTHER'S BREAST.[13] You provided for a human breasts on which to rely[14] for sustenance.

11   UPON YOU WAS I CAST [*hošlaktî*] [i.e.], *nišlaktî* 'I was cast out[15] FROM THE WOMB as You say in the Bible, "carried since the womb" (Isa. 46:3). Since the tribes were born, You led them and guided them.[16]

13a   MANY BULLS. [A metaphor for] mighty kingdoms.

13b MIGHTY ONES OF BASHAN. They are also a term for bulls in Bashan, which were fat. ENCIRCLE ME [kittĕrûnî] [i.e.], surround me like a crown [keter], which encircles the head.[17]

14 A TEARING)...LION. [A metaphor for] Nebuchadnezzar.

15c LIKE WAX, [i.e.], tallow, which is liquefied by the heat of the fire.

16b malqôḥāy 'MY PALATE'. These are the ḥikkîm,[18] which are called palays [in O.F.].[19] [MY TONGUE CLEAVES TO MY PALATE because] when a person is sad no saliva is present in his mouth.[20]

16c TO THE DUST OF DEATH [i.e.], to the degradation[21] of dying. YOU COMMIT ME [i.e.] You sit me. [The verb tišpĕtēnî 'YOU COMMIT ME] is from the same root as [the gerund šĕpîtāh 'putting' in the expression] "putting the cauldron" (BT 'Avodah Zarah 12a) and [of the imperative šĕpôt in the expression] "put the pot [on the fire]" (2 Kgs. 4:38).[22]

17 LIKE LIONS)...MY HANDS AND FEET. [I.e., My enemies hurt my hands and feet] as though they had been crushed in the mouth of a lion. In the same vein Hezekiah said, "... like a lion, thus did he shatter all my bones" (Isa. 38:15).

18a I TAKE THE COUNT OF ALL MY BONES [i.e.], the pain of my limbs.

18b THEY LOOK ON)...rejoicing at my misfortune.

19b CASTING LOTS FOR MY GARMENTS. [I.e.], they despoil our property.

20b 'ĕyālûtî [i.e.], koḥî 'my strength'. It is a cognate of [the noun 'ĕyāl 'strength' in] "I became a man without strength" (Ps. 88:5), and it is a cognate of [the expression lĕ'ēl 'strength' in] "I have the strength" (Gen. 31:29).[23]

22 DELIVER ME FROM THE MOUTH OF THE LION just as YOU RESCUED ME[24] FROM THE HORNS OF THE WILD OXEN.[25] This [reference to WILD OXEN] is a metaphor for] the Amorite, "whose stature was like the cedars" (Am. 2:9) [i.e.], the thirty-one kings [listed in Josh. 12:9-24].[26]

23 THEN WILL I PROCLAIM YOUR FAME TO MY BRETHREN when all my assemblies are gathered together, and thus he [the psalmist] says to them:

24a YOU WHO FEAR THE LORD, PRAISE HIM! These [WHO FEAR THE LORD] are the proselytes[27] [as distinct

24b   from] ALL YOU OFFSPRING OF JACOB.

25b   THE PLEA OF THE LOWLY [i.e.], "the cry of the poor"
       (Job. 34: 28). Every [form of the verb] 'ănāyāh[28] in the Bible
       is a word referring to 'crying'. There is in addition the possi-
       bility of interpreting 'ĕnût [not as 'plea' but] as a synonym of
       'humiliation' as is exemplified by "to humble yourself [le'ānôt]
       before Me" (Ex. 10:3) for he [the lowly person] is humbled,
       and he prays before You.[29]

27a   THE LOWLY WILL EAT at the time of the Redemption
       in the Messianic Age.

27b   ALWAYS BE OF GOOD CHEER. He [the psalmist] said
       all this [vv. 24-27] before them [the assemblies alluded to in
       v. 23].

28   LET the Gentiles PAY HEED to the evil, which afflicted us.
       When they will have seen the good [which we will have ex-
       perienced in the Messianic Age], LET [them] TURN TO
       THE LORD.[30]

29   FOR KINGSHIP [will be] THE LORD'S when they will
       have seen that You have restored KINGSHIP and governance
       to Yourself.

30   ALL THE FAT PLACES OF THE EARTH SHALL EAT,
       AND THEY SHALL WORSHIP. Note that this is an in-
       verted Scripture,[31] [which is to be understood as though the
       word-order were as follows]: "The poor ate all the fat places
       of the earth, and they worshipped the LORD with praise and
       thanksgiving for the benefit [they received]." THE FAT
       PLACES OF THE EARTH [means] 'the goodness of the fat
       of the land'.

28b   THE ENDS OF THE EARTH will see all this [what is fore-
       told

28a   in v. 29], AND TURN TO THE LORD.

30b   ALL the dead of the Gentiles[32] SHALL KNEEL BEFORE
       HIM from the midst of Gehenna, but He will not show them
       mercy by resurrecting their souls from Gehenna.[33]

30c   HIS SOUL, [i.e., the soul] of each and everyone. HE DID
       NOT REVIVE, [i.e.], He will not revive.[34] Our rabbis inter-
       preted this verse [to mean] that before their death at the time
       when their soul is taken away the dying see the face of the
       Shekinah.[35]

31a   OFFSPRING SHALL SERVE HIM [i.e.], the OFFSPRING
       of Israel, who serve Him continually.

31b LET IT BE PROCLAIMED OF THE LORD TO A GEN-
ERATION. Invert the word order of the Scripture verse, and
then interpret it [as follows]:[36] LET IT BE PROCLAIMED
TO A later GENERATION for fame and for praise what He
has done for that progeny.

32a LET the earlier generations COME, AND LET THEM
TELL OF HIS KINDNESS TO PEOPLE YET TO BE
BORN FOR HE HAS DONE for them kindness.

PSALM XXII, NOTES

[1] In Prov. 5:19 "a loving doe" is one of a series of metaphors for a
loving wife; hence this metaphor is here applied to the congregation of
Israel, which here, as frequently in Rabbinic literature, is treated as the
consort, as it were, of the Holy One Blessed be He. Rashi's comment assumes that the literal meaning of 'al AYYELETH HA-SHAHAR is 'concerning the doe of the dawn'; cf. RSV's "according to the Hind of the
Dawn."

[2] Qimhi, who also prefers this interpretation, quotes it in the name of
"There are some who interpret."

[3] Midrash Tehillim here; Yalqut Shim'oni 2:566; 2:685.

[4] In the New Testament at Matt. 27:46 and Mk.15:34 Ps. 22:2a-b, "My
God, my God, why have You abandoned me," is quoted both in Heb. and
in Gk. by Jesus on the cross while Ps. 22:19 is treated as a prophecy fulfilled in Matt. 27:35; Mk. 15:24; Lk. 23:34; Jn. 19:24. It is characteristic
of Rashi to insist that psalms and other texts of the Heb. Bible, which the
Christians saw as prophecies concerning Jesus, are, in fact, prophecies
concerning Israel's suffering in the Exile at the hand of the Gentiles. With
reference to this tendency in Rashi see Erwin Isaac Jacob Rosenthal, "Anti-
Christian Polemic in Medieval Bible Commentaries," *JJS* 11 (1960), p. 125.

[5] Rashi (followed by NJV) takes the portion of the verse following the
caesura, "FAR FROM DELIVERING ME)...," as the continuation of the
question, "MY GOD, MY GOD, WHY HAVE YOU ABANDONED
ME?" This interpretation leaves the phrase "THE WORDS OF MY
ROARING" standing alone. Rashi (again followed by NJV) solves the
problem by supplying *ûmi* 'and from' between "FROM DELIVERING
ME" and the final clause.

[6] The biblical text expresses the present here by means of the so-called
imperfect, which can also be interpreted here as a future tense. Rashi's
paraphrasing in the late Heb. present tense eliminates the ambiguity. Note
that the form is feminine to refer to the congregation of Israel; see n. 1.

[7] The biblical text contrasts the adverbal *yômām* 'BY DAY' with the
adverbial *wĕlaylāh* 'AND BY NIGHT'. Rashi indicates, however, that the
adverbial *yômām* can mean not only 'by day' but also 'from day to day'; so
also *BDB*, p. 401.

[8] The Biblical text treats HOLY as in apposition to YOU and EN-
THRONED as the predicate of the sentence. Rashi, by supplying the conjunction 'and', indicates that he interprets HOLY and ENTHRONED as

two parts of a compound predicate. His supplying 'and' indicates that he believes that the psalmist employs asyndeton, i.e., the stylistic device of omitting the conjunction and leaving it to the reader to supply it mentally.

[9] Here Rashi responds to the exegetical question as to what is the syntactical relationship between ENTHRONED and ISRAEL'S PRAISES; for other solutions see Ibn Ezra and NJV.

[10] Rashi intimates that the root is *gll*, which means that the infinitive construct of the *qal* with prefixed *l* is *lāgōl*. Rashi, however, would have regarded the forms in question as forms of one of the fourteen biliteral roots *gl* listed in *Mahberet Menahem*, pp. 103-105.

[11] Midrash Tehillim here.

[12] Cf. *Mahberet Menahem*, p. 103.

[13] This verse could be taken to mean, "You were my source of security during infancy"; contrast Rashi, below.

[14] Heb. *liššā'ēn*, a contracted form of *lĕhiššā'ēn*, 'to lean'; cf. the use of the cognate *maš'ēn* 'stay, prop' to refer to sustenance in Isa. 3:1; see Gruber, *Aspects*, p. 568, n. 2. On contracted forms of the *niphal* infinitive see *GKC* #53q.

[15] Rashi employs the familiar *niphal* form of the verb to explain the psalmist's rare *hophal* form.

[16] Since Rashi's interpretation of Ps. 22 (see Rashi at v. 1) changes it from an individual lament to a community lament, the speaker's birth becomes the collective birth(s) of the founders of the Hebrew people.

[17] Cf. the discussion of circumambulation in Mayer I. Gruber, "Ten Dance-Derived Expressions in the Hebrew Bible," *Biblica* 62 (1981), pp. 331-32.

[18] Pl. of *hēk*; other Rashi mss. read here *hănîkayim*, which in Modern Heb. means 'gums'. Maarsen here points out, however, that Rashi in his commentary on BT Hullin 103b and BT 'Avodah Zarah 39b defines *hănîkayim*, as *hēk* 'palate'; in fact, the two terms are biforms; see *BDB*, p. 335a.

[19] Corresponding to Modern French *palais*, which is identical etymologically and semantically to Eng. 'palate'.

[20] See Shereshevsky, *Rashi: The Man and His World*, p. 183; p. 192, n. 76; see also Gruber, "Hebrew *da'ăbôn nepeš* 'dryness of throat': From Symptom to Literary Convention," pp. 365-369.

[21] Heb. *dike'ût*; this noun is unattested in Heb. before Gaonic times, and it is characteristically payyetanic; see Ben Yehudah, *Dict.* 2:935a.

[22] For Heb. *šāpat* 'put' see also Isa. 26:12; Ezek. 24:3; note that in 2 Kgs. 4:38; Ezek. 24:3; and BT 'Avodah Zarah 12a the verb *šāpat* refers specifically to 'put on the fire' while in Isa. 26:12 the verb has the more general meaning of 'put on'; cf. Ugar. cognate *ṭpd* 'put'.

[23] With Maarsen cf. *Mahberet Menahem*, pp. 42f., s.v. *'l* I; cf. also Rashi at Ex. 15:11.

[24] The Bible has two parallel clauses in which the psalmist asks, "DELIVER ME FROM THE MOUTH OF THE LION//RESCUE ME FROM THE HORNS OF THE WILD OXEN." The first of the two verbs

is in the imperative; the second in the precative perfect. On precative perfect in general see above, Ps. 16, n. 7. Because in the present instance Rashi does not interpret *'ănîtānî* as a precative, which would be an appropriate b-word for the imperative 'SAVE ME', he must account in some other way for the anomaly of an imperative in the first clause and a perfect in the second clause. Rashi solves this problem by supplying 'just as' between the two clauses. For *'ānāh*, lit., 'answer', in the sense 'deliver' in association with the verbal root *yš'* 'save' cf. Ps. 118: 21, "I thank You for You delivered me//and You became for me for salvation."

[25] The scientific name is *bos primigenius;* see W. Stewart McCullough, "Wild Ox," *IDB*, vol. 4, pp. 843-844; see also the entry *rě'ēm* in *EM* 7:296-297.

[26] So Breithaupt. The ingenious attempt of several scholars (see Maarsen here and the authorities cited there) to emend "thirty-one" to "another interpretation" is to be rejected. Those who emend assume that the reading "thirty-one" arose from a copyist's misinterpretation of ꝯ, which, it has been alleged, can represent either the numeral 31 or an abbreviation for *lāšôn 'aḥer(et)* 'another interpretation'. The scholars who devised the ingenious emendation forgot the enumeration of thirty-one Amorite (i.e., the aboriginal peoples of the land of Israel collectively in Am. 2:9; elsewhere they may be called Canaanite [see Judg. 1:1]) kings in Josh. 12:9-24. There is no support in the ms. tradition of our commentary for their emendation.

[27] So R. Samuel bar Nahmani in Midrash Tehillim here; Leviticus Rabbah 3:2. Rashi repeats this at Ps. 66:16; 115:11; 135:20 q.v.

[28] While it is modern practice generally to refer to a Heb. verb by the 3[d] pers. sing. perfect—in this case *'ānāh*—and to Eng. and Akk. verbs by the infinitive, Rashi's practice is generally to refer to a Heb. verb by citing the gerund—in this case *'ănāyāh*.

[29] Here in explaining v. 25 Rashi intimates that here *'ěnût* has the combined nuances of the two homonyms *'ānāh* I 'plead' and *'ānāh* II 'submit'. Presumably, the passive *ne'ěnāh* 'submit' is an extension of *'ānāh* II 'afflict'; cf. dictionaries.

[30] Here Rashi responds to the following exegetical questions: (1) Who are THE ENDS OF THE EARTH? (2) To what are they to PAY HEED? (3) Under what circumstances are they expected to TURN TO THE LORD?

[31] Heb. *miqrā' měsûrās;* i.e., a Scripture verse, whose word order does not reflect the syntax; on Rashi's treatment of this phenomenon see Shereshevsky, *Rashi: The Man and His World*, p. 97; for the treatment of this phenomenon in Rashi's Commentary on Psalms see also at Ps. 22:31; 33:14-15; 36:2; 39:6.

[32] Rashi's paraphrase of "THEY THAT GO DOWN IN THE DUST" (so NJV margin).

[33] This would seem to be the mirror image of Jesus' assertion in John 11:25: "I am the resurrection and the life: he that believeth in me, though he were dead, yet shall live."

[34] Rashi intimates that here the psalmist employs the perfect form of the verb to express future time. On this phenomenon, now called "prophetic perfect," see Driver, *Tenses* [3], pp. 18-21.

[35] Sifre Numbers, ed. Horovitz, p. 102.

[36] See n. 31, above.

PSALM XXIII

1a   A PSALM OF DAVID. Our rabbis said, "Wherever it is stated [in the titles of the psalms] 'a psalm of David'[1] [it means that] he [David] plays the harp and thereafter Shekinah[2] rests upon him." [The purpose of the] music [*mizmôr*] was to bring divine inspiration to David.[3] "Moreover," [our rabbis said], "every one [of the psalm titles] wherein it is stated, 'to[4] David a psalm'[5] [means that] Shekinah rested upon him, and afterwards he composed a song."[6]

1b   THE LORD IS MY SHEPHERD. [This metaphor means that] I am certain that

1c   I SHALL NOT LACK anything.[7]

2   IN ABODES OF GRASS [*binĕ'ôt dešeʾ*] [i.e.], in an abode of grasses [*bĕna'ăwāh dĕšaʾîm*].[8] Since he [the author of Ps. 23] began [the psalm] comparing his sustenance to the pasturage of cattle when he stated, "THE LORD IS MY SHEPHERD," the metaphor[9] "ABODES OF GRASS" is fitting.[10] David composed this psalm [when he was taking refuge] in the forest of Hereth (see 1 Sam. 22:5). It was called Hereth[11] because it had become as dry as pottery,[12] and the Holy One Blessed be He watered it with the lushness of the World to Come. [The source of this interpretation is] Midrash Tehillim [23:6].

3   HE RESTORES MY SOUL.[13] [I.e.], RESTORES to its former state my spirit, which was depressed by troubles and flight.

3a   IN RIGHT PATHS [i.e.], in straight paths[14] so that I should not fall into the hand of my enemies.

4a   IN A VALLEY OF BLACKNESS [i.e.], IN A VALLEY OF darkness. He [David] composed [this line] with reference to the Wilderness of Ziph (see 1 Sam. 23:14-15; cf. 1 Sam. 26:1; Ps. 54:1).[15] Every usage of the word *ṣalmāwet* 'blackness'is a synonym of *ḥošek* 'darkness'.[16] [Thus did] Dunash ben Labrat explain it.[17]

4c   YOUR ROD AND YOUR STAFF.[18] As for the sufferings I endured and the staff on which I rely [sc.], Your kindness, both of them WILL COMFORT ME in that they [the sufferings] will be for me [a means of] atoning for iniquity, and I am certain that

5a   YOU SPREAD A TABLE FOR ME. This is [a metaphor for] the kingship.[19]

5b   YOU ANNOINT MY HEAD WITH OIL. By Your decree I have already been annointed as king.

5c   MY DRINK IS ABUNDANT. A metaphor for[20] satiety.[21]

PSALM XXIII, NOTES

[1]   I.e., when the word order is *mizmôr lĕDāwîd* as it is in Ps. 3-6; 8-9; 12-15; 19-23; 29; 31; 38-39; 41; 51; 62-63; 65; 108; 140-141; 143 rather than *lĕDāwîd mizmôr* as it is in Pss. 24; 101; 109-110; 139.

[2]   Kadushin, *The Rabbinic Mind* [3], pp. 222-61 explains that in Rabbinic literature Shekinah is primarily a name for God; that this name is especially associated with the sense of God's nearness; that in many cases the term *Shekinah* refers to 'revelation of *Shekinah* ', which, in turn, may denote 'divine inspiration'; see below, n. 6.

[3]   Cf. also 1 Sam. 10:5, and contrast the view of prophetic inspiration presented by Kaufmann, *The Religion of Israel*, p. 50.

[4]   Both parts of the midrash are based on the observation that *lĕDāwîd* in any other context would most obviously mean 'to David', and both suggest that *lĕDāwîd* 'to David' be taken as ellipsis for "Divine inspiration came to David."

[5]   Heb. *lĕDāwîd mizmôr;* see also, n. 1.

[6]   The source of this midrash seems to be BT Pesahim 117a where we read as follows: "*LĕDāwîd mizmôr* intimates that Shekinah rested upon him, and afterwards he composed a song. *Mizmôr lĕDāwîd* intimates that he composed a song, and afterwards Shekinah rested upon him." Rashi in quoting this midrash here in the Psalms commentary makes the following changes: (1) he reverses the order of the explanations of the two biblical phrases; (2) in the explanation of *mizmôr lĕDāwîd* Rashi replaces 'composed a song' with 'plays on the harp'; (3) Rashi interpolates into the midrash an explanation of the word *mizmôr*, which includes the equation of Shekinah in the midrash with divine inspiration [Heb. *rûaḥ haqqodeš*]. It appears that Rashi made these changes for the following reasons: (1) Rashi could have cited the midrash at Ps. 3 where A PSALM OF DAVID is first attested in the Book of Psalms. Brilliant pedagogue that he was, Rashi chose to cite the midrash precisely at Ps. 23 where the reader sees for the first time in two adjacent psalms the two formulae—*mizmôr lĕDāwîd* in Ps. 23 and *lĕDāwîd mizmôr* in Ps. 24. Seeing the two distinct formulae in two adjacent psalms should motivate the reader to seek an explanation and to appreciate seeing one in Rashi's commentary precisely at this point. To make the midrash truly relevant to the biblical text at Ps. 23-24 Rashi presents the explana-

tions of the two formulae in the order in which they occur in Ps. 23:1 and 24:1 rather than in the order in which they occur in BT. (2) Rashi's second change in the midrash appears to indicate that he believes that the term *mizmôr* in the two formulae refers to the playing of an instrument rather than to the composing of the words of the psalm; he is supported both by the etymology of the word *mizmôr* and by the continuation of the text in BT; contrast Rashbam there. (3) Rashi's third change, the interpolation, seems to be meant to make the midrash and its relevance to the biblical formulae fully comprehensible.

[7] Assuming that we have here a case of ellipsis, Rashi supplies the implied direct object of the verb 'LACK'; similarly NJV; contrast KJV.

[8] Rashi's point here is that *ně'ôt* here as in Ps. 83:13 is a form of *nāweh* 'abode' rather than a form of *nôy* 'beauty'; see below on Ps. 93:5.

[9] Heb. *lěšôn*.

[10] Heb. *nāpal 'al*, a characteristic Gallicism in Rashi's Hebrew; see Banitt, *Rashi: Interpreter of the Biblical Letter*, p. 14, n. 37; see the discussion at Ps. 31:13.

[11] The midrash Rashi quotes here assumes that the name Hereth (Heb. *ḥeret*) is derived from the verb *ḥārāh* 'burn'; on this verb see Gruber, *Aspects*, pp. 491-492; but see also next note.

[12] Braude, *Midrash on Psalms*, vol. 2, p. 459, n. 12 suggests that this assertion involves a play on words involving the place-name *ḥeret* and the common noun *ḥeres*; note that the two words are homonyms in the late Ashkenazic speech.

[13] RSV, which corresponds to Rashi's understanding of the lemma.

[14] Note that JPS' "straight paths" follows Rashi's interpretation; contrast NJV's "right paths," which is equivalent to KJV-RSV's "paths of righteousness." The latter renderings assume that here the psalmist thanks God for guiding his moral behavior. Rashi's interpretation is more congruent with the context (vv. 2, 4), which speaks of God's guiding the physical rather than the moral paths of the psalmist.

[15] Midrash Tehillim here.

[16] Following Dunash (see below in Rashi, and see n. 17), Rashi sees Heb. *ṣalmāwet* as an abstract noun derived from the verbal root *ṣlm* 'be dark, be black' [which is well attested also in Akkadian and Arabic]. Dunash takes note of and accounts for the peculiar vocalization of the abstract ending as *āwet* rather than *ût*; see Dunash, p. 109. Dahood, here and Walter L. Michel, "ṢLMWT: 'Deep Darkness' or 'Shadow of Death',", *Biblical Research* 29 (1984), pp. 5-20 both try to revive the Septuagintal rendering "shadow of death" (LXX here) essentially because they see in the derivation from *ṣlm* a modern innovation without a basis in the exegetical tradition. In fact, not only were moderns anticipated by Dunash, who is followed by the venerable Rashi, but also Dunash was anticipated by LXX, which renders γνοφεράν 'darkness' at Job. 10:21. Cf. D. Winton Thomas, "*ṣalmāwet* in the Old Testament," *JSS* 7 (1962), pp. 191-200.

[17] *Teshuvot Dunash*, p. 109.

[18] In the psalm itself both the rod and the staff are the implements, and they are sources of comfort to the speaker. Rashi, following Midrash Tehillim (see next note), interprets them antithetically: the rod as a metaphor for the sufferings, which atone for sin; the staff as a metaphor for God's love.

[19] Cf. Midrash Tehillim here.

[20] Heb. *lĕšôn*.

[21] Cf. Midrash Tehillim here.

PSALM XXIV

1   THE LAND IS THE LORD'S [i.e.], the land of Israel.
     THE WORLD, [i.e.], the other lands.[1]

2   HE FOUNDED IT UPON SEAS, [AND HE ESTAB-
     LISHED IT UPON RIVERS].[2] [This verse alludes to the fact
     that] seven seas surround the land of Israel[3] and four rivers:
     Jordan, Yarmuk, Qarmiyon, and Pugah.[4]

3   WHO MAY ASCEND THE MOUNTAIN OF THE
     LORD? [The point of this question is that] even though all
     the world's people are His [as stated in v. 1] all are not wor-
     thy to approach Him except

4   HE WHO HAS CLEAN HANDS....

4b   WHO HAS NOT TAKEN HIS[5] SOUL IN VAIN, [i.e.],
     HAS NOT sworn IN VAIN by His Name and by HIS SOUL.
     We have found expression[s] referring to swearing employed
     with[6] [the noun] *nepeš* 'soul' as is attested in "the LORD of
     Hosts has sworn by His soul" (Jer. 51:14).

6   THIS ONE, whose deeds are such [as are described in vv.4-
     5] is[7] THE GENERATION OF THOSE WHO TURN TO
     HIM.

7   O GATES, LIFT UP YOUR HEADS. In the reign of
     Solomon my son when he [Solomon] will bring the Ark into
     the Holy of Holies and the gates will have stuck together he
     [Solomon] will have recited twenty-four psalms [*rĕnānôt*] with-
     out having been answered until he will have said, "Do not
     reject Your annointed one; remember the loyalty of Your
     servant David" (2 Ch. 6:42).[8]

7b   EVERLASTING DOORS, [i.e.], doors, whose holiness is
     everlasting.

PSALM XXIV, NOTES

    [1] Rashi, following Midrash Tehillim here, treats the two terms *'ereṣ* 'land,
earth' and *tēbel* 'dry land, world' as complimentary rather than synonymous and the parallelism as synthetic rather than synonymous. Such an
approach is exemplified in recent times by Kugel, *The Idea of Biblical Poetry*,
pp. 1-58; and Alter, *The Art of Biblical Poetry*, pp. 3-26. Nevertheless, the
Talmudic Rabbis and Rashi are criticized severely by Kugel, p. 173 and

Map to Psalm XXIV

by Gelles, *Peshat and Derash in the Exegesis of Rashi*, p. 101 for adopting just such an approach.

[2] Rashi does not quote the bracketed portion of the verse; I have supplied it for clarity.

[3] Rashi's comment here is based upon a midrash attributed to R. Johanan b. Napha (180-279 C.E.) in BT Bava Batra 74b (for parallels see Zohory, p. 87). The following are the seven seas according to the latter: the Sea of Tiberias [i.e., the Sea of Galilee]; the Sea of Sodom [i.e., the Dead Sea]; the Sea of [i.e., the Gulf of] Eilat [for the emended reading Eilat in place of the standard reading Heilat see Jesaias Press, "Beiträge zur historischen Geographie Palästinas," *MGWJ* 73 (1929), p. 53]; the Sea of Ulatha; the Sea of Sibki [i.e., the Samachonitis Sea]; the Aspamia Sea [i.e., the Banias]; and the Great Sea [i.e., the Mediterranean Sea]. See the accompanying map, which reflects the view of Press, "Beiträge," pp. 52-53 with respect to Ulatha as well as the view of Press, there, p. 52 that Banias (in Mishnah Parah 8:11 Panias or Pamias) in BT Bava Batra 74b refers to Lake Phialo or Phiala (Arab. *Birket Râm*), which, in the words of Joseph Schwarz, *A Descriptive Geography and Brief Historical Sketch of Palestine*, trans. Isaac Leeser (Philadelphia: A. Hart, 1850), p. 41, "is the actual source of the Jordan." However, Schwarz, pp. 41-48, rejects the basis in reality of the entire notion of seven seas surrounding the Land of Israel.

[4] Rashi's comment here is also based upon the midrash cited in n. 3. According to a medieval tradition the Qarmiyon and the Pugah correspond respectively to the Amanah and Pharpar of the Damscus reigion mentioned in 2 Kgs. 5:12; so also Hanoch Albeck, *Mishnah* (6 vols.; Jerusalem: Bialik/Tel Aviv: Dvir, 1958), 6:279 at Mishnah Parah 8:10 following 'Aruk, s.v. Qarmiyon (see Kohut, *Aruch Completum* 7:202a); so also Schwarz, pp. 53-54; for other views see Adolf Neubauer, *La Géographie du Talmud* (Paris: M. Levy,1868; reprint, Hildesheim: Georg Olms, 1967), p. 32; Press, "Beiträge," pp. 53-55; id., "Erwiderung," *MGWJ* 74 (1930), pp. 136-137; cf. M. Miesen, "Zür Geographie Palästinas," *MGWG* 74 (1930), pp. 135-36. See the accompanying map.

[5] This is the reading in our Rashi ms, and it is the reading adopted also in NJV margin and reflected in NRSV's gender neutral "their"; however, most extant texts read *napši* 'My life/soul'.

[6] Heb. *nōpēl 'al*, on which see Ps. 23, n. 10.

[7] Here Rashi responds to the exegetical question, "To what does the demonstrative pronoun 'THIS ONE' refer?" Also here as frequently Rashi employs the 3^{d} pers. personal pronoun as the copula.

[8] Rashi's comment here is based upon a midrash attributed to Rab Judah [b. Ezekiel] (d. 259 C.E.) quoting Rab (d. 247 C.E.) in BT Shabbat 30a.

PSALM XXV

1   I LIFT UP MY SOUL [i.e.], I direct my heart.

3   [...THE FAITHLESS] EMPTY-HANDED.[1]
[THE FAITHLESS are] the robbers and the plunderers, who cause the poor to dwell EMPTY-HANDED of their property. [This usage of EMPTY-HANDED] corresponds to the usage of [EMPTY-HANDED in] "Let me strip my enemies empty-handed" (Ps. 7:5).

7b   REMEMBER CONCERNING ME ACCORDING TO YOUR FAITHFULNESS, [i.e.], Remember FOR ME what is worthy of YOUR FAITHFULNESS, i.e., my good deeds.[2]

8a   GOOD AND UPRIGHT IS THE LORD, and He wants to acquit His creatures.

8b   THEREFORE HE SHOWS SINNERS THE WAY of repentance.[3]
Another equally plausible interpretation of HE SHOWS SINNERS [THE WAY is that He gives instructions] to manslayers, as it is stated in the Bible, "Prepare for yourself [the way]"[4] (Deut. 19:3),[5] [which means], "Asylum" was written [on a signpost][6] at an intersection.[7]

11a   FOR THE SAKE OF YOUR great[8] NAME,

11b   pardon[9] MY INIQUITY THOUGH IT BE GREAT.
It is appropriate for the Great [God][10] to pardon GREAT INIQUITY.[11]

12a   WHO is he[12] that[13] FEARS THE LORD

12b   HE SHALL BE SHOWN THE PATH, which He chose,[14] i.e., the moral path.

13   HIS SOUL SHALL LODGE IN PROSPERITY.
[I.e.], when he [who fears the LORD] lodges in the grave, HIS SOUL SHALL LODGE in prosperity.[15]

16b   FOR I AM ALONE, and the eye of the multitude is fixed upon me, and to them I AM ALONE.

16a   Therefore, TURN TO ME, HAVE MERCY ON ME for my prayer is necessary for the salvation of all Israel.[16]

18a   LOOK AT MY AFFLICTION AND SUFFERING,

18b   AND in deference to them FORGIVE ALL MY SINS.[17]

19   CRUEL HATRED [i.e.], unjustly.

5c   I BESEECH ALL OF TODAY,[18] this pre-eschatological
      era,[19] which is day for the Gentiles and night for Israel.[20]

6c   THEY ARE OLD AS TIME [i.e.], from the days of the first
      human,[21] to whom You said, "On the day on which you eat
      of it you will surely die" (Gen. 2:17). You gave him one of
      Your days, which is a thousand years [long].[22]

PSALM XXV, NOTES

[1]   So NJV. Rashi omits the bracketed portion of the verse, which I have
supplied for clarity. Note that according to NJV 'EMPTY-HANDED' is
an adverbial expression modifying the verb 'LET THEM BE DISAP-
POINTED' while according to Rashi this expression refers to the behavior of THE FAITHLESS toward their victims.

[2]   Similarly NJV, q.v.; contrast KJV: "Remember not the sins of my
youth, nor my transgressions: according to thy mercy remember thou me
for thy goodness' sake, O LORD." Here NJV follows Rashi while KJV
and most other English versions follow Qimhi, q.v.

[3]   Here Rashi responds to the exegetical question, "Which WAY?"

[4]   Rashi does not quote the bracketed portion of the verse; I have supplied it for clarity.

[5]   On the subject of the city of refuge in the Bible see Deut. 19; Num.
35; on this subject in the Mishnah see Makkoth, Chapter 3.

[6]   Bracketed portion supplied from Rashi's commentary on BT Makkoth
10b; see next note.

[7]   See BT Makkoth 10b. Rashi in his commentary there explains "was
written at an intersection" as follows: "Wherever there were two intersecting
roads, one of which [was] leading to the city of refuge, there was a post
set in the ground at that road, and on it was written 'Asylum'."

[8]   Rashi's interpolation of the adjective 'great' here in v. 11a anticipates
the midrash quoted at v. 11b.

[9]   Rashi paraphrases here substituting the imperative for the perfect
consecutive employed in the psalm.

[10] Supplied from Midrash Tehillim.

[11] Rashi here renders in concise Heb. the Aram. midrash attributed to
Rabbi Levi, a late 3[d] cent. C.E. Amora of Eretz-Israel in Midrash Tehillim
at Ps. 19:14.

[12] Heb. *mî hû'*, Rashi's paraphrase of the psalmist's *mî-zeh hā'îš* "WHO
IS THE MAN" (NJV renders "WHOEVER").

[13] Rashi here interpolates the definite article, which functions as a relative
particle.

[14] Rashi paraphrases using the perfect form of the verb in place of the
imperfect found in the biblical text, and he makes explicit what is unclear
in the Bible, namely, the subject of the verb 'HE SHALL CHOOSE',
namely, God.

[15] NJV, assuming that in Biblical Heb. *nepeš* denotes 'person', para-phrases: "He shall live a happy life." Rashi, however, assumes that here, as in late Heb., *nepeš* denotes 'soul' as distinct from 'body'. An anonymous midrash here in Midrash Tehillim interprets as follows: "HIS SOUL SHALL LODGE IN PROSPERITY in the grave." While Rashi's inter-pretation suggests that only the body will lodge in the grave while the soul will lodge in Paradise, the midrash suggests that the soul will also lodge in the grave. Note also that the biblical text expresses 'prosperity' by the masculine adjectival noun *ṭôb* while Rashi's Heb. employs the feminine form *ṭôbāh*.

[16] Rashi's comment here, which is based upon a midrash in Midrash Tehillim here, attempts to answer the question as to how David, to whom the psalm is attributed at v. 1, could call himself *yāḥîd* 'an only child' when according to 1 Ch. 2:15 David was the youngest of seven brothers. The midrash answers that in in his own family circle David was indeed one of a multitude but that as intercessor for Israel David was indeed *yāḥîd* 'alone'.

[17] Rashi here responds to the exegetical question, "What is the logical connection between the two requests in vv. 18a-b?"

[18] On the verb *qiwwāh* 'pray, beseech' see below at Ps. 27:14. 'ALL OF TODAY' is the literal interpretation of Heb. *kol-hayyôm*, which is presup-posed by the midrash Rashi quotes here. In Biblical Heb., however, *kol-hayyôm* is the normal way of expressing 'every day'; see *GKC* #127b,c; #117c; *BDB*, p. 400b; similarly *kol-ha'ādām* is the normal way of expressing in Bib-lical Heb. 'every man'; see *BDB*, p. 481b.

[19] Heb. *hā'ôlām hazzeh*, the opposite of *hā'ôlām habbā'*. The two terms are conventionally translated 'this world' and 'the world to come' based on the incorrect assumption that in these expressions '*ôlām* means 'world'. In fact, in these Rabbinic Heb. expressions as throughout Biblical Heb. '*ôlām* refers to a unit of time; cf. Kadushin, *The Rabbinic Mind* [3], p. 294.

[20] Day here being a metaphor for joy; night a metaphor for sadness. The source of this midrash is Midrash Tehillim here.

[21] I.e., Adam.

[22] This midrash, which is taken from Midrash Tehillim here, sees a concretization of God's love in the apparent contradiction between Gen. 2:17 and Gen. 5:5, which states, "All the days of Adam, which he lived, were nine hundred and thirty years. Then he died." Rather than assume that Gen. 5:5 means that God rescinded His decree, the midrash suggests that God found a way to practice both justice (by not rescinding the de-cree) and love (by prolonging Adam's life beyond the span of a twenty-four hour day). God did so, according to the midrash, by granting Adam one of God's own special days, which, according to Ps. 90:4, are a thou-sand years long. Adam's having lived, according to Gen. 5:5, nine hun-dred and thirty years points, therefore, to Adam's not having lived out the full day on which he ate of the forbidden fruit.

PSALM XXVI

1　JUDGE ME, O LORD.
Elsewhere, however, he [King David]¹ says, "Do not enter into judgment..." (Ps. 143:2). [The apparent contradiction is to be reconciled as follows]: David said, "When You are judging the wicked, JUDGE ME, for compared to the wicked I am virtuous. When, however, You are judging the virtuous, do not arraign me."²

4b　WITH HYPOCRITES [na'ǎlāmîm] [i.e.], those who cover up³ secretly doing their deeds.⁴

4c　I SHALL NOT COME [i.e.], I am not accustomed to come and to enter⁵ with them.⁶

6　IN INNOCENCE⁷ in that there is no robbery involved in the rites [miṣwôt] I perform. "A stolen palm frond [lulav] is invalid."⁸

7a　lašmiaʿ 'TO MAKE HEARD' is a biform of lěhašmiaʿ 'to make heard'.⁹

7b　[AND TELLING]¹⁰ ALL YOUR WONDERS.
This [verse refers to] Hallel [i.e., Pss. 113-118],¹¹ in which there is reference to the past and to the future and in which there is reference to [the war of] Gog [and Magog] and in which there is reference to the Messianic Age and in which there is reference to what is to happen in the future.¹²

12　MY FEET ARE ON LEVEL GROUND [mîšôr] [i.e.], in a just [yěšārāh].¹³ path.

PSALM XXVI, NOTES
¹ The author of Ps. 26 according to v. 1a and of Ps. 143 according to Ps. 143:1.
² Cf. Midrash Tehillim here.
³ Heb. hamměkassîm; other Rashi mss. read hanniknāsîm 'those who enter'.
⁴ Rashi notes that the literal meaning of na'ǎlāmîm is 'they hide themselves'; see dictionaries.
⁵ Cf. n. 3 above; note also that Rashi intimates that the imperfect form of the verb is here employed not to indicate the future 'I SHALL NOT COME' but to indicate habitual activity in the present: 'I am not accustomed to come'.

⁶ The persons mentioned in v.4b.

⁷ In Gruber, "Ten Dance-Derived Expressions," p. 331, n. 13 I stated, "The reference to palms washed in innocence reflects the idea...that God will not heed prayer or worship by those whose hands are defiled by guilt, an idea which derives its poignancy from the fact that ancient Israelites supplicated with palms spread apart..."; contrast Rashi; see next note.

⁸ Cf. Midrash Tehillim here; the only prescribed circumambulations of the altar known to Rabbinic Judaism take place on the festival of Tabernacles (Sukkot) when according to Mishnah Sukkah 4:5 the worshipper marches in procession around the altar with a citron and a palm frond (*lulav*) to the latter of which are bound three myrtle twigs and two willow branches (frequently the entire bouquet is referred to as *lulav* because of the prominence of the palm frond among the four plants). Hence the midrash which Rashi quotes here could not help but see in the second half of Ps. 26:6 a reference to the Sukkot processions. Therefore the midrash could not help but see in the first half of the verse a reminder of the halakah "a stolen *lulav* is invalid" (Mishnah Sukkah 3:1). Rashi's formulation, "There is no robbery involved in the rites I perform" is a restatement of the general principle, which BT Sukkah 30a sees expressed in the latter halakah, namely, that the attempt to fulfill a precept by means of a transgression is of no avail. This is to say that not only does the end not justify the means but also that in Rabbinic Judaism illegal means cannot possibly be used to fulfill any end no matter how lofty.

⁹ See *GKC* #53q.

¹⁰ Rashi does not quote the bracketed portion of the verse; I have supplied it for clarity.

¹¹ See *EJ* 7:1197-1199.

¹² Rashi's comment here is based on the midrash attributed to R. Abin in Leviticus Rabbah 30:5. There it is explained that the reference to the past is Ps. 114:1; the reference to Gog (i.e., the eschatological war referred to in Ezek. 38-39 and associated with the arrival in Jerusalem of Gog, the ruler of Magog; see *EJ* 7:691-693) in Ps. 117:10; the reference to the Messianic Age in Ps. 116:1; the reference to the future in Ps. 118:28. Rashi omits the reference in the midrash to the present generation (Ps. 115:1). While the midrash arranges the references according to the order of the chapters in Pss. 114-118, Rashi rearranges the references chronologically. "What is to happen in the future" refers to what is normally called *hāʿôlām habbāʾ*. 'the future [post-Messianic] era' commonly rendered 'the world to come'; with reference to our rendering 'the future era' cf. our remarks on *hāʿôlām habbāʾ* at Ps. 25, n. 19.

¹³ While most moderns follow Qimhi in understanding the verb 'āmĕdāh 'it stood' (NJV's "ARE") as a prophetic perfect referring to the psalmist's anticipated vindication, Rashi interprets it as a past tense belonging with vv. 1b; 4-7; 11a to the psalmist's declaration of innocence; hence while most moderns follow Qimhi in understanding *mîšôr* to mean 'a level place', on which the vindicated psalmist will stand to praise the LORD, Rashi takes it to denote the uprightness of the psalmist's behavior; note that *mîšôr*

and *yēšārāh* are cognates; note also that in our Rashi ms. the form *yšr* represents not the masculine adjective *yāšār* but an abbreviation for the longer feminine adjective *yĕšārāh*, for which there is not sufficient room on the line in our ms.

PSALM XXVII

3d IN THIS I TRUST [i.e.], in what he [the psalmist] said above [in v. lc], "THE LORD IS THE STRONGHOLD OF MY LIFE."[1]

4 TO FREQUENT HIS TEMPLE,[2] [i.e.], to appear[3] there each morning; so did Dunash [Ibn Labrat] explain [the meaning of the verb *lĕbaqqēr*].[4]

5a HE WILL SHELTER ME IN HIS PAVILION.
I am certain that HE WILL SHELTER ME in His Temple. We have learnt in Seder Olam[6] that this biblical verse was composed with reference to Joash son of Ahaziah, whose sister Jehosheba hid him in an upper chamber of the Holy of Holies in accord with what is stated in the Bible, "He stayed with her for six years, hidden in the House of the LORD " (2 Kgs. 11:3).[7]

5d RAISE ME HIGH UPON A ROCK [*ṣûr*].
He has put my feet upon a rock [*sela*].[8]

6 SACRIFICES OF SINGING [*tĕrû'āh*],[9] [i.e.], sacrifices over which they sing ['ōmĕrîm] a song.[10]

8a TO YOU MY HEART SAYS: 'SEEK MY FACE'."
[*lĕkā* 'to/for you' here means] *bišĕbîlĕkā* 'for you', [i.e.], 'in your behalf'.[11]
MY HEART says:[12] "SEEK all of you, Israel, My [i.e., the LORD's] face, and I [the LORD] shall hearken[13] to him [Israel]."

8b O, LORD, I SEEK YOUR FACE.

8a [The use of the expression] *lĕkā* ['to/for you' in the sense 'in your behalf'] corresponds to [the use of the prefixed preposition *lĕ* 'to/for' in the sense 'in behalf of' in] "Behold I am like your mouth for God" (Job. 33:6); "Will you argue for God?" (Job. 13:8), [i.e.], 'in His place'. Here [in Ps. 27:8a] also FOR YOU MY HEART SAID [means], "MY HEART came to me in Your place to say this ['SEEK MY FACE']."

9b DO NOT THRUST ASIDE. [I.e.], DO NOT cast down. [The verb *taṭ*[14] 'you thrust aside'] is the same verb as is attested in "He bent [*wayyēṭ*][15] the sky" (Ps. 18:10).

10a INDEED MY FATHER AND MY MOTHER ABAN-
DONED ME.

During the sexual intercourse [which resulted in King David's
being conceived] they [his parents] directed their attention
to their own pleasure. When they had achieved their pleasure,[16] he [the father] turned his face in one direction, and
she [the mother] turned her face in the other direction,[17]

10b BUT THE LORD GATHERED ME IN.[18]

The Holy One Blessed be He guards the semen and forms
the fetus.

12a TO THE WILL OF MY FOES, [i.e.], to the appetite of my
enemies so that their appetite is fulfilled through me.[19]

12b UNJUST ACCUSERS [i.e.], those who speak evil.[20]

13 HAD I NOT TRUSTED....

Were it not that I TRUSTED in the Holy One Blessed be
He, those [aforementioned in v. 12] FALSE WITNESSES
would have attacked me and put an end to me. As for [the
word] *lûlê*, it is dotted [to allude] to the midrash, which our
rabbis composed:[21] "I know that You will give the innocent
a reward in the world to come, but I do not know whether
or not I have a portion with them."[22]

14 [The repetition of the words 'LOOK TO THE LORD' at
the beginning and end of v. 14 means that] if your[23] prayer
is not accepted [by God], pray again.[24]

PSALM XXVII, NOTES

[1] Here Rashi responds to the exegetical question, "To what does the
demonstrative pronoun 'THIS' in v. 3[d] refer?" Rashi's answer is accepted
by Qimhi. Ibn Ezra suggests that the pronoun 'THIS' in v. 3[d] may, alternatively, refer to the psalmist's request set forth in v. 4. NJV interprets *bĕzō't*,
lit., 'IN THIS' as an adverbial expression meaning 'still'; so already Ehrlich,
Die Psalmen, p. 57; *BDB*, pp. 261b-262a, s.v. *zeh* #6; *K-B* [3], p. 254a; similarly, Dahood, here.

[2] So NJV; marginal note there adds: "Meaning of Heb. uncertain"; NEB
renders "and to seek him," but NEB margin adds the alternative translation, "and to pay my morning worship."

[3] Heb. *lērā'ôt*, the *niphal* infinitive construct of the verb 'to see', which
appears in the same sense in MT of Ex. 23:17: "Three times a year all
your males shall appear before the Sovereign, the LORD"; Ex. 34:23:
"Three times a year all your males shall appear before the Sovereign
LORD, the God of Israel"; Deut. 16:16: "Three times a year—on the Feast
of Unleavened Bread, on the Feast of Weeks, and on the Feast of Booths—
all your males shall appear before the LORD your God in the place that

He will choose. They shall not appear before the LORD empty-handed."
Granting that the passive form of the verb *rā'āh* 'see' is an 'emendation of
the scribes', who thought that the active expression 'see the face of the
LORD' was disrespectful to God (see commentaries on these verses), it
should be noted that the active expression is semantic equivalent of Akk.
pān šarri dagālu 'see the face of the king', which is an idiomatic expression
meaning 'serve the king' (see *CAD* D, pp. 23b-24a); from the latter idiom
is derived the title *dāgil pāni*, lit., 'he who sees (the king's) face', an idiomatic expression denoting 'subject, servant (of the king); the plural of the
latter Akk. title is rendered into Heb. as *rō'ê pěnê hammelek*, lit., 'they who
see the king's face', i.e., 'the king's personal attendants' (so Mordechai
Cogan and Hayim Tadmor, *II Kings*, AB, no. 11 [Garden City, N.Y.:
Doubleday & Co., 1988], p. 320, n. 19) in 2 Kgs. 25:19; Jer. 52:25; Esth.
1:14. Thus both the active form 'see the face of the LORD' and the alleged 'emendation of the scribes' 'appear before the LORD' are idioms
meaning 'serve the LORD by appearing periodically at His Temple'; hence
Rashi's usage here; cf. Mishnah Hagigah 2:7.

⁴ *Teshuvot Dunash*, p. 75. Dunash explains there that the infinitive *lěbaqqēr*
attested in Ps. 27:4 cannot be connected with the root *bqr* 'test, investi-
gate' attested in Lev. 13:36; 19:20 (contrast *Mahberet Menahem*, p. 89;
Rabbenu Tam in his *hakra-'ôt*, i.e., defenses of Menahem against Dunash;
see *Teshuvot Dunash Ben Labrat 'im Hakra-'ôt Rabbenu Tam*, ed. Z. Filipowski
[London & Edinburgh: Me'orerey Yeshenim 1855], p. 53). Dunash sees
lěbaqqēr as a denominative verb derived from the noun *boqer* 'morning',
and he holds that it means 'appear each morning'; similarly Dahood, here.
Ibn Ezra in his commentary here notes that the verb *biqqēr* 'to appear each
morning [*boqer*]' is to be compared to the verb *he'ěrîb* 'to appear every
evening ['*ereb*]' in 1 Sam. 17:16.

⁵ Heb. *šānînû*, which introduces a quotation from a Tannaitic source,
i.e., a text or tradition attributed to the period and the persons, who produced the Mishnah, i.e., c. 10-220 C.E.

⁶ Seder Olam, also called Seder Olam Rabbah is a history book, which,
according to R. Johanan b. Napha (d. 279 C.E.) in BT Yebamot 82b and
Niddah 46b, was composed by the Tanna R. Jose b. Halafta (see also BT
Shabbat 88a). This book, which is the basis of the chronology of the Rabbis and therefore of Rashi's Biblical and Talmudic chronology, is made
up of three divisions, each containing ten chapters. The first division deals
with the period from Creation to the Conquest of the Land of Israel by
Joshua; the second with the period from Joshua to the death of King
Zechariah (see 2 Kgs. 15:8-11); the third with the period from the death
of King Zechariah to the Bar Kochba rebellion. See previous note. See
Judah M. Rosenthal, "Seder Olam," *EJ* 14:1091-1093 for discussion and
bibliography. Note, however, that Rosenthal's assertion (there, p. 1092) that
the practice of dating from Creation, which is characteristic of Seder Olam,
is not otherwise attested prior to the 8th cent. C.E., has been disproved
by the 4ᵗʰ cent. C.E. dedicatory inscription belonging to the synagogue
attested at Susia in Judea. Concerning Seder Olam and its Tannaitic ori-

gin see now Chaim Milikowsky, "Seder Olam and Jewish Chronography in the Hellenistic and Roman Periods," *PAAJR* 52 (1985), pp. 115-139.

[7] Seder Olam, Chapter 18, q.v.

[8] Rashi explains that the noun *ṣûr*, which has a variety of meanings, here has the meaning 'rock'.

[9] The noun *těrû'āh* can denote (1) the blast of a trumpet or ram's horn (Num. 10:5ff; Lev. 25:9; etc.); (2) shouting (1 Sam. 4:5ff.; Job. 8:21); and (3) 'liturgical singing' (Ps. 33:3: 47:6); cf. *BDB*, pp. 929b-930a; Rashi's comment here proves that he assumes the noun is here employed in the latter sense; hence our rendering of the lemma.

[10] Rashi's comment here is based upon Tanḥuma, ed. Buber, Leviticus, p. 49, 'Emor #22.

[11] Heb. *bišelîḥûtěkā*.

[12] Rashi, followed by NJV, q.v., interprets the psalmist's perfect form of the verb *'āmar* as present in meaning; hence he paraphrases here employing the participle *'ōmēr*.

[13] Here Rashi employs the participle with future meaning.

[14] Short imperfect 2^d pers. masc. sing. *hiphil* of the verb *nāṭāh* 'incline, bend, stretch out, spread out'; cf. *BDB*, pp. 639b-641a; see next note.

[15] Imperfect-consecutive 3^d pers. masc. sing. *qal* of the verb *nāṭāh*; see previous note. The root is treated as *ṭ* I in *Mahberet Menahem*, p. 202, q.v.

[16] This comment is based upon a midrash found in Leviticus Rabbah 14:5. It appears that for reasons explained below Rashi rewrites the midrash. The text in Leviticus Rabbah employs the expression *'āśû ṣorkêhem* 'they fulfilled their needs' to express 'they achieved orgasm'. For numerous attestations of this idiom see Jastrow, Dict., p. 1271, s.v. *ṣorek*. Note that *'āśāh ṣorek* in the Heb. of Amoraic sources from Palestine corresponds to *gāmar* in the Heb. of the Mishnah and of BT. Rashi uses the expression *gāmar hǎna'āh* 'achieve pleasure' as an apt parallel to 'direct attention to pleasure' in the preceding clause of his adaptation of the midrash. Rashi thereby creates what should be called an "intention-fulfillment sequence". Moreover, to bring home the idea that the psalmist's both parents intended only to achieve their own pleasure Rashi uses the plural of the verb 'intend' while the midrash imputes the selfish intention only to King David's father, the fulfillment of the selfish pleasure to both. Rashi thereby breathes into the midrash a more egalitarian view of the two sexual partners. The midrash reads as follows: "'When a woman conceives...' (Lev. 12:2). This verse refers to what is written (in Ps. 51:7), 'Note that I was conceived through iniquity....' R. Aha said, 'Even the most pious of persons must of necessity have some iniquitous aspect. David said to the Holy One Blessed be He, "Lord of the universe, my father Jesse had no intention of fathering me. In fact, he intended [in having intercourse with my mother] only for his own pleasure. You must understand that it is so in that after having achieved their orgasms he [father] turns his face in one direction, and she [mother] turns her face in another direction. But You [God], take care of every drop [of semen] that is in it [the vagina, that it should not drip out and be lost!]." And it is with reference to this that David said, "My

father and my mother abandoned me, but the LORD gathered me in (Ps. 27:9).""""

[17] With reference to the idea that when the two sexual partners move away from each other and lie on their respective sides the likelihood of conception is lessened cf. the following advice to physicians concerning the treatment of infertility contained in J. Robert Wilson, Clayton T. Beecham, and Elsie Reid Carrington, *Obstetrics and Gynecology* (4th ed.; St. Louis, Mo.: C. V. Moshy, 1971), p. 152: "Not infrequently a woman may become pregnant soon after the initial visit [to the physician].... Such a favorable outcome early in the investigation may be credited to the helpful hints regarding the technique and timing of coitus.... Faulty sexual techniques can be corrected by discussing the entire act with both partners and suggesting necessary modifications. In order to be more certain that the semen remains in the posterior fornix and upper vagina, the woman should be instructed to maintain flexion of the thighs during and after intercourse, to remain supine for at least 30 minutes after the male ejaculation, and never to take a post coital douche."

[18] Rendering of the lemma according to the understanding presupposed by Rashi's comment; for the meaning of the verse in context see Gruber in *UF* 18 (1986), p. 143, n. 44.

[19] With Maarsen here cf. Rashi at Ps. 63:2; Prov. 23:2.

[20] Here Rashi is consistent with his assertion in his commentary on Ps. 12:6, q.v., that *yph* 'witness' is a verbum dicendi; note that Rashi's *dōḇĕrê ra'āh* 'those who speak evil' is the semantic equivalent of the Late Heb. Gk. loanword *qaṭēgôr* 'accuser, prosecuting attorney' (cf. Akk. *qāb lemutti* 'accuser' [lit., 'he who speaks of evil']); cf. also in Esth. 7:9 the opposite *dibbĕr ṭôb* 'defended' (lit., 'spoke good'), which corresponds to Akk. *damiqta qabû* 'to defend' and to the late Heb. Gk. loanword *sanêgôr* 'advocate, defense attorney'.

[21] Notwithstanding our acceptance throughout our translation of Rashi's Commentary on the Book of Psalms of the demonstration by Kamin, *Rashi's Exegetical Categorization*, pp. 136-39 that the expression *dārĕšû rabbôtênû* in Rashi's commentaries means simply 'Our rabbis interpreted', it appears that here Rashi employs the verb *dārĕšû* as a denominative verb meaning 'they composed a *midrash*'.

[22] The source of this midrash is BT Berakot 4a; with Zohory, p. 93 cf. also Midrash Tehillim here. This midrash takes for granted the idea that the six dots, three written above the word *lûlê* and three written below it express doubt. The midrash speaks of the doubt as to whether or not the psalmist has a portion in the life of the post-eschatological era. At an earlier stage the dots referred to a different doubt. Note that such dots expressing doubt belong neither to the vowel points nor to the Masoretic accents; these dots appear even in the unpointed biblical scrolls employed in the service of the synagogue. Such dots are found in fifteen places in the Hebrew Bible: ten in the Pentateuch (Gen. 16:5; 18:9; 19:33; 33:4; 37:12; Num. 3:39; 9:10; 21:30; 29:15; Deut. 29:28); four in the Books of the Prophets (2 Sam. 19:20; Isa. 44:9; Ezek. 41:20; 46:22); and once only in the

Hagiographa (here at Ps. 27:13). According to Avot deRabbi Nathan 34:5 the reason for these dots is as follows: "Ezra said, 'If Elijah the Prophet should appear and ask me, "Why did you write this [the word whose authenticity is doubtful]?" I shall say to him, "I have already placed dots over them [to indicate that they should be ignored]." Now should he say to me, "You have written properly," I shall remove the dots from them.'" For parallels to the latter account and for parallels to the phenomenon in the Hellenistic world see Lieberman, *Hellenism in Jewish Palestine*, pp. 38-46; see also Christian D. Ginsburg, *Introduction to the Massoretico-Critical Edition of the Hebrew Bible* (London: Trinitarian Bible Society, 1897; reprint, New York: Ktav, 1966), pp. 318-34; Romain Butin, *The Ten Nequdoth of the Torah* (Baltimore: J. H. Furst & Co., 1906; reprint, New York: Ktav, 1969); Israel Yeivin, *Introduction to the Tiberian Masorah*, trans. E. J. Revell, Society of Biblical Literature Masoretic Studies, ed. Harry M. Orlinsky, no. 5 (Missoula, Mt.: Scholars Press, 1980), pp. 44-46.

[23] The reading 'your prayer' is adopted from other editions of Rashi's commentary here; our Rashi ms. reads 'my prayer', which makes no sense in context.

[24] Rashi's comment here proves that he holds that Heb. *qiwwāh* in this context means 'pray'; cf. Akk. cognate *qu"û*; see *K-B*[3], pp. 1011b-1012b, s.v. *qwh* I.

PSALM XXVIII[1]

3   DO NOT DRAG ME OFF[2] WITH [i.e.], do not bring me[3] WITH THE WICKED.

7   AND WITH MY SONG I SHALL THANK HIM.
Now this is the thanksgiving hymn:[4]

8a   "THE LORD IS THE STRENGTH OF HIS PEOPLE"[5] [i.e.], of those who depend upon Him, and they are all the House of Israel[6]

8b   when[7] HE IS A STRONGHOLD FOR THE DELIVERANCE OF HIS ANNOINTED.

PSALM XXVIII, NOTES

[1] We noted at Ps. 13, n. 1 that Ps. 13 is treated in our Rashi ms. as part of Ps. 12; hence in our Rashi ms. Pss. 14-27 are numbered as Pss. 13-26 respectively; since the short comment on Ps. 28 is similarly appended to the comment on Ps. 27 (in our ms. Ps. 26), Ps. 29 is thus numbered in our ms. as Ps. 27.

[2] Lemma rendered according to NJV margin. RSV renders, "Take me not off." The latter translation equates the verb *māšak* 'pull, drag, draw' in the present context with *lāqaḥ* 'take' in the sense 'kill' in Jer. 15:15 and Job. 1:21; see Gruber, *Aspects*, pp. 507-508, and cf. William R. Taylor's comment on Ps. 28:3 in *IB* 4:152: "I.e., let me not suffer the violent end that befalls the godless, whom death drags off pitilessly like beasts caught in a net (cf. 10:9; 26:9; 49:14)." Note that *māšak* is attested in the sense 'drag off' also at Ps. 10:9; contrast Dahood here and NJV.

[3] I.e., to the same fate as THE WICKED AND EVILDOERS; cf. previous note; note that here Rashi employs the *hiphil hirgîl* in the sense 'cause to go'; this usage of Rabbinic Heb. *hirgîl* is to be distinguished from the homonymous *hirgîl* 'accustom'. In the latter sense *hirgîl* is a denominative verb derived from the participle *rāgîl* 'accustomed'; in the sense 'bring, cause to go' *hirgîl* is a denominative verb derived from the noun *regel* 'foot', and it is therefore analogous to Eng. 'peddle' derived from Lat. *pes* 'foot'. Generally, *hirgîl* 'accustom' is employed with the preposition *b* while *hirgîl* 'bring' is employed with the preposition *l* or with the accusative.

[4] Heb. *hôdayyāh*. Here as in Ps. 2:5, q.v., Rashi indicates that the following verse is to be understood as a quotation of the speaker referred to in the present verse.

[5] Note that the lemma here in our Rashi ms. supports the reading found in LXX and Saadiah (see NJV margin) against the standard Hebrew text of the verse, which reads, "THE LORD IS THEIR STRENGTH" (so NJV); see next note.

⁶ This comment appears to respond to the exegetical question, "Who are they who are referred to by the pronoun 'their' in the phrase 'THEIR STRENGTH'?" (see previous note); note that this question of Rashi's presupposes the standard Hebrew text of the verse and not the reading found in LXX, Saadiah, and the lemma of our Rashi ms.

⁷ Rashi here paraphrases the Bible's conjunctive *waw* by means of the expression *bĕ'ēt še* 'when', thereby indicating that the Bible's parataxis is to be understood as hypotaxis; on the rediscovery of this exegetical technique in modern times by NJV see Orlinsky, *Notes*, pp. 19-20.

PSALM XXIX

1b   *hābû* TO THE LORD.

[I.e.], Be prepared FOR THE LORD, and prepare for Him,[1] you SONS of the earth's powerful men.[2] It is on the basis of this clause that we are required to recite [the benediction] "patriarchs".[3]

1c   ASCRIBE TO THE LORD GLORY AND STRENGTH.

It is on the basis of this clause that we are required to recite [the benediction] "deeds of strength".[4]

2   ASCRIBE TO THE LORD THE GLORY OF HIS NAME.

This refers to [the benediction] "holiness of the Name".[5] This psalm[6] contains eighteen invocations of the Name of God.[7] Corresponding to them numerically[8] Sages[9] established [the] Eighteen Benedictions.[10]

3   THE VOICE OF THE LORD[11] WAS OVER THE WATERS at the Reed Sea [as stated in 2 Sam. 22:14], "the LORD thundered forth from heaven...."

4   THE VOICE OF THE LORD WAS WITH POWER.

At the time of the Giving of the Torah He decreased the volume of His voice in consideration of Israel's POWER in accord with what is stated in the Bible (in Ex. 19:19), "God replied to him[12] with a voice"[13] [i.e.], with Moses' voice.[14]

5   THE LORD'S THUNDER BREAKS CEDARS, [i.e.], the kings of the Gentiles as in the passages where it is stated, "the LORD thundered mightily against the Philistines..." (1 Sam. 7:10); "Truly,[15] Assyria shall fall because of the LORD's thunder..." (Isa. 30:31). [Your breaking the cedars, i.e., the kings of the Gentiles, took place] at the time of the Giving of the Torah [when You asked], "For what mortal [heard God's thunder][16]···and lived?" (Deut. 5:23). [The answer was]: You [Israel] heard, and you survived, but when the Gentiles hear they die.[17]

6   HE MADE the cedars and the mountains,[18] who came to hear the Giving of the Torah, SKIP LIKE A CALF. But when the Gentiles hear they die.[19] LEBANON AND SIRION are names of mountains.[20]

7   KINDLES FLAMES OF FIRE. Our rabbis explained that
    [each of] the [ten] locution[s] of the decalogue would come
    forth from His [the LORD'S] mouth and would be engraved
    on the [two] tablets [of stone] according to their [the word's
    written] form.[21]

8a CONVULSES THE WILDERNESS. [The verb *yāḥîl* 'CON-
    VULSES'] is a cognate of [the gerund *ḥîl* 'trembling' in the
    phrase] "trembling like that of a woman in labor" (Ps. 48:7).

8b THE LORD CONVULSES THE WILDERNESS OF
    KADESH. It [THE WILDERNESS OF KADESH] is the
    wilderness of Sinai just as our rabbis said in [BT] Tractate
    Shabbat [89a], "Five names are applied to it: the wilderness
    of Sinai,[22] the wilderness of Zin,[23] the wilderness of Kadesh,[24]
    the wilderness of Kedemoth,[25] the wilderness of Paran.[26] [It
    was called] the wilderness of Kadesh because therein [the
    people of] Israel were sanctified.[27]

9a THE LORD'S THUNDER WILL MAKES THE HINDS
    TREMBLE.[28]
    In the time to come He will frighten, and He will terrify the
    Gentiles, who are now standing firm like hinds as in the bib-
    lical passage where it is stated, "He made my feet like those
    of hinds" (Ps 18:34). Rabbi Phineas said, "'like those of rams'
    is not written here but rather 'like those of hinds' for the feet
    of the females stand more firmly than those of the males."[29]

9b AND STRIPPED FOREST BARE. [The verb *wayyeḥĕśop*] is
    a cognate of [the noun *maḥśop* 'exposure' in the phrase "ex-
    posure of the white" (Gen. 30:37). [AND STRIPPED FOR-
    ESTS BARE means that] He removed the bark from the trees
    of the forest, which is to say that He will strip them of their
    glory. [Note] that the Gentiles are compared to trees of the
    forest for it is stated in the Bible, "whose stature was like the
    cedars" (Am. 2:9).[30]

9c WHILE IN HIS TEMPLE, which will be built [in the future],
    ALL SAY, "GLORY!" [I.e.], all will praise [the divine] Name,
    and they will say:[31]

10a THE LORD SAT ENTHRONED alone in His greatness,

10b AND now also THE LORD SITS ENTHRONED, KING
    FOREVER.
    "As for idols, they shall vanish completely" (Isa. 2:18),

11a but to HIS PEOPLE HE WILL GRANT STRENGTH

11b   and the blessing of WELL-BEING.

[While I have explained vv. 9-10 as referring to the future], our rabbis explained it as referring to the Giving of the Torah, at the time of which the Gentiles became frightened and terrified so that they approached Balaam, and they asked him, "'What is the tumultuous thunder we have heard?'(1 Sam. 4:14). Is He [the LORD], perhaps, about to bring a flood (Gen. 6:17) upon the world?" He [Balaam] replied to them, "He [the LORD] already swore that He would not bring [another flood] (Gen. 8:21-22; 9:15). Rather, the tumultuous thunder you heard is the Holy One Blessed be He giving Torah to His people."[32]

PSALM XXIX, NOTES

[1] As Maarsen points out here, Rashi's interpretation of *hābû* (imperative pl. of the verb *yāhab* 'give, ascribe', cognate of Aram. *yĕhab* 'give') as 'prepare' is in consonance with Rashi's comment on Ex. 1:10: "Every occurrence of *hābāh* [long imperative singular of *yāhab*] is an expression referring to preparation and getting ready for something." Rashi thus suggests that in Ex. 1:10 *hābāh* is an auxiliary verb. He is correct, and this observation is valid also with regard to Gen. 11:3, 4, 7; 38:16. This observation is not correct, however, with reference to the remaining instances of *hābāh*, *hābû* where it is a transitive verb followed immediately by a direct object and where it means 'give, ascribe'. The instances of this latter usage in addition to all occurrences in Ps. 29 include Gen. 29:21; 30:1; 47:15; Judg. 1:15; Zech. 11:12; Ps. 96:7; 1 Ch. 16:28-29; etc. Unfortunately, modern biblical scholarship shares Rashi's tendency to overwork many a useful insight.

[2] In the psalm *bĕnê 'ēlîm*, lit., 'sons of gods' (hence NJV's "divine beings") are called upon to praise the LORD. Biblical theology in its oldest form, as in this, one of the oldest of the psalms, and as in Job. 1-2, conceives of the gods worshipped by Israel's ancient neighbors as creatures of the LORD, who serve as His courtiers. These *bĕnê 'ēlîm* correspond philologically to the Ugar. *bn ilm*, i.e., 'minor deities', who serve the major deities. Functionally the 'sons of gods' of the Hebrew Bible correspond to the angels or *pamalyā' šel maʿălāh* 'the heavenly entourage' in Rabbinic lore. In later times the term 'sons of gods' was avoided, apparently because this term would seem to imply recognition of a multiplicity of divinities who might challenge Israel's loyalty to the LORD; hence in the midrash to which Rashi here refers *bĕnê 'ēlîm* was taken to refer to *'ēlê 'āreṣ* 'the earth's powerful men', an expression attested in 2 Kgs. 24:15 and Ezek. 17:13. Note that in the latter expression *'ēlê* is the pl. construct of *'ayil* 'ram'. In the midrash to which Rashi refers (see next note) 'the earth's powerful men' is an epithet for the three patriarchs—Abraham, Isaac, and Jacob.

[3] According to the midrash quoted in BT Rosh ha-Shanah 32a and

BT Megillah 17b, the clause GIVE TO THE LORD SONS OF THE POWERFUL is the authority for the recitation of the first of the Eighteen Benedictions, which is called 'patriarchs' (see Birnbaum, *Daily Prayer Book*, p. 81 from "O Lord, open thou my lips" to p. 83 "Shield of Abraham"). As Rashi indicates in his commentaries on these two texts, the midrash construes GIVE as a transitive verb whose direct object, *běnê 'ēlîm* means 'members of the group of powerful men', i.e., the patriarchs; hence the entire clause GIVE TO THE LORD 'THE PATRIARCHS' means "Recite to the LORD the benediction called 'patriarchs'." Note that Rashi, who believes that in Biblical Heb. *hābāh* always means 'prepare' and that *běnê 'ēlîm* means 'descendants of powerful men' rather than 'members of the group of powerful men', does not believe that the midrash reflects the literal meaning of Ps. 29.

  ⁴ I.e., the second of the Eighteen Benedictions (see Birnbaum, *Daily Prayer Book*, p. 84 from "Thou, O Lord, art mighty forever" to "who revivest the dead") Rashi here again paraphrases BT Rosh ha-Shanah 32a; BT Megillah 17b. Note that in his paraphrasing the midrashim on each of the two clauses of v. 1 Rashi replaces BT's question and answer ("What is the Scriptural basis for our being obligated to recite the benediction… ? It is what is said in Scripture….") with a simple statement.

  ⁵ I.e., the third benediction of the Eighteen Benedictions (see Birnbaum, *Daily Prayer Book*, p. 86 from "Thou art holy" to "holy God"). Again Rashi paraphrases BT Rosh ha-Shanah 32a; BT Megillah 17b.

  ⁶ Heb. *mizmôr*.

  ⁷ The term here rendered 'invocation of the Name of God' is *hazkārāh*; pl. *hazkārôt*.

  ⁸ Heb. *kěnegdān*.

  ⁹ According to BT Berakot 32a these Sages were "the Men of the Great Assembly"; according to BT Megillah 17b they were "one hundred and twenty elders and among them a number of prophets"; according to Moses Maimonides, Mishneh Torah, Laws of Prayer 1:4 they were "Ezra and his legislature".

  ¹⁰ Heb. *Shemoneh Esreh*; see Birnbaum, *Daily Prayerbook*, pp. 82-96. Rashi's comment here is based upon the midrash attributed to R. Hillel the son of R. Samuel b. Nahmani in BT Berakot 28b.

  ¹¹ I.e., the LORD's thunder; cf. Ugar. *ql* 'thunder', and cf. Ex. 9:29: "the thunder [*haqqôlôt*] will cease, and the hail will be no more"; Ex. 9:33: "the thunder [*haqqôlôt*] ceased, and the hail and the rain did not fall to the earth." Note that Rashi in his comments on Ps. 29:3 and Ps. 29:5 anticipates this now generally accepted interpretation of Heb. *qôl*. In v. 4, however, for the sake of the midrash to which he alludes, Rashi takes *qôl* in its primary sense 'voice'.

  ¹² I.e., to Israel.

  ¹³ Heb. *běqôl*, which in context means 'in thunder'; so NJV there.

  ¹⁴ Rashi, following Tanḥuma Exodus, p. 70a, argues that if *běqôl*, lit., 'with voice', in Ex. 19:19 can mean 'with the voice of Moses' (so R. Simeon b. Pazzi in BT Berakot 45a), it follows that *bakkoăḥ*, lit., 'with/according

to the power' in Ps. 29:4 can mean 'according to the power of Israel', i.e., with no more volume than Israel can endure; cf. Mekilta, vol. 2, p. 223.

[15] Our Rashi ms. mistakenly reads *mî* 'who' instead of *kî* 'truly'.

[16] Rashi does not quote the bracketed portion of the verse; I have supplied it for clarity.

[17] Cf. Tanḥuma, Exodus, p. 69b.

[18] Rashi's suggestion that the accusative pl. suffix *ēm* in the word *wayyarqîdēm* 'HE MADE THEM SKIP' must refer both to the cedars mentioned in v. 5 and the mountains mentioned in v. 6 calls attention to the philological problem presented by this suffix. Since the publication of Harold Louis Ginsberg, "A Phoenician Hymn in the Psalter," *Atti del XIX Congresso Internationale degli Orientalisti [Rome, 1935]* (Rome: G. Bardi, 1938), pp. 472-476, it has been recognized that the verb should be vocalized *wayyarqēdma*, i.e., 'He made (him) skip' + enclitic *mem*, an archaic phenomenon, which has no apparent grammatical function in Biblical Heb. Thus the verse should be rendered, "He made Lebanon skip like a calf//and Sirion like a young wild ox" (cf. NJV). The Massoretic division of the verse, which derives from misconstruing the enclitic *mem* as the accusative pl. suffix *ēm*, makes the latter suffix in the first clause parallel to 'Lebanon and Sirion' in the second clause.

[19] This comment is duplicated here in our Rashi ms. from its proper place at the end of the comment on v. 5.

[20] Specifically Mt. Lubnan and Mt. Hermon.

[21] Cf. the midrash attributed to R. Akiva in Mekilta, vol. 2, p 266; this midrash presupposes the nuance 'voice' for Heb. *qôl*.

[22] Ex. 19:1,2; Lev. 7:38; Num. 3:4; 9:5; etc.

[23] Num. 13:21; 20:1; 27:14; etc.

[24] Num. 20:1,16; 3:36; Deut. 1:46; 32:51; etc.

[25] Deut. 2:26.

[26] Num. 10:12; 12:16; 13:3; etc.

[27] Note that in BT the midrash, there attributed to R. Jose the son of R. Hanina, a younger contemporary of R. Johanan b. Napha, provides an etiological etymology for each of the five names. Rashi here cites only the etymology of Kadesh as it is the only one relevant in the present context.

[28] Rendering of the lemma according to the interpretation presupposed by Rashi's comment here. According to Rashi's commentary on Deut. 32:18, *měholĕlekā* 'he who delivers you from the womb' (there), *yěholēl* (here in Ps. 29:9), and *ḥîl* 'trembling' (Ps. 48:7) are cognates. We may deduce from this assertion that Rashi holds that the primary meaning of the root *ḥîl* is 'tremble'. This view accounts for Rashi's interpretation of *yāḥîl* in Ps. 29:8 and of the polel form *yěholēl* here in Ps. 29:9. It follows from Rashi's view of the primary meaning of *ḥîl* 'tremble' that the association of *ḥîl* 'tremble' with a woman in labor yields a secondary meaning in the *qal* 'give birth'. Hence in the polel the verb can mean either (1) 'cause to tremble' (Ps. 29:9), causative of the primary meaning 'tremble', or (2) 'cause to give

birth, beget, bring forth from the womb' (Deut. 32:18), causative of the secondary meaning.

[29] Cf. Rashi's comment on Ps. 18:34 and our discussion there.

[30] I.e., the FOREST in Ps. 29:9 is, according to Rashi, a metaphor for 'the Gentiles'.

[31] Rashi construes v. 10 as a direct quotation without *verbum dicendi*; cf. Rashi at Ps. 2:2 and at Ps. 30:9-10.

[32] Rashi's comment here is based upon the midrash attributed to R. Eliezer of Modi'im (fl. 135 C.E.) in Mekilta, vol. 2, pp. 162-63.

PSALM XXX

1   A SONG FOR THE DEDICATION OF THE TEMPLE. [David, to whom the authorship is attributed at v. 1, composed it] so that the Levites should sing it at the dedication of the Temple.¹

2a   I EXTOL YOU, O LORD, FOR YOU LIFTED ME UP [*dillîtānî*], [i.e.], You elevated me [*higbahătānî*].²

2b   AND NOT LET REJOICE OVER ME MY ENEMIES, who were saying continually, "David has no portion in the World to Come." When, however, they saw that in deference to him the doors [of the Temple] opened for the Ark,³ all knew that the Holy One Blessed be He had granted pardon for that iniquity,⁴ and the faces of David's enemies became black like the sides of a pot.⁵

3c   AND YOU HEALED ME. This [healing] is [a metaphor for] forgiveness of iniquity; it is the same metaphor as is found in "...he will repent so that he will be healed" (Isa. 6:10).⁶

4b   FROM MY GOING DOWN INTO THE PIT, [i.e.], *mēridtî* 'from my going down' into Gehinnom [sc.], so that I would not descend into the pit.⁷

5a   O YOU FAITHFUL OF THE LORD, SING TO HIM about what He did for me, for You can rely on him to show you favor. Hence, even if you are in trouble, do not be afraid.

6a   FOR THERE IS A short (cf. Isa. 54:7) MOMENT IN HIS ANGER,   .

6b   and long LIFE [is to be achieved] by winning His favor,⁸ i.e.,⁹ by appeasing him.¹⁰

7a   IN MY WELL-BEING I THOUGHT. [I.e.], in my well-being¹¹ I continually thought¹²

7b   I SHALL NEVER¹³ BE SHAKEN, but the matter is not subject to my control, but rather it is subject to the control of the Holy One Blessed be He.

8a-b   IN showing me favor¹⁴ He established¹⁵ MY MOUNTAIN-LIKE QUALITY,¹⁶ [i.e.] my greatness, to be¹⁷ STRENGTH,

8c   but as soon as¹⁸ He hid His face from me¹⁹

8d   I WAS TERRIFIED,

9 and I CALLED TO YOU,[20] AND I MADE MY APPEAL
 continually, saying to You,[21]

10 "WHAT IS TO BE GAINED FROM MY DEATH... ?"
 and You heard my voice,[22]

12 and YOU TURNED MY LAMENT INTO DANCING.
 Our rabbis interpreted this entire psalm with reference to
 Mordecai and Esther and Haman in the Small Pesikta:[23]

7 Haman said, "WHEN I WAS UNTROUBLED I
 THOUGHT."

9a Esther said [from] "I CALLED TO YOU, O LORD..." up
 to

11b "BE MY HELP."

12 Mordecai and all[24] Israel said, "YOU TURNED MY
 LAMENT INTO DANCING."[25]

PSALM XXX, NOTES

[1] Both in Biblical and Rabbinic Heb. *bayit*, lit., 'house', without any qualifications may denote 'temple'; see dictionaries of Biblical and Rabbinic Heb.; cf. also Akk. *bītu;* Ugar. *bt.*

[2] Here Rashi's point is that the rare verb *dillāh* 'lift up' is a synonym of the well-known verb *higbîăh* 'elevate'.

[3] This is the same midrash to which Rashi refers at Ps. 24:7; the source is BT Shabbat 30a; cf. also Midrash Tehillim at Ps. 24:7; and see Rashi at Ps. 24:7.

[4] I.e., the Bathsheba affair; see 2 Sam. 11. Note that Rashi here takes it for granted here that David was guilty of adultery; contrast Rashi there.

[5] I.e., they blushed from embarrassment. Rashi here quotes the midrash verbatim.

[6] See Rashi there; cf. BT Megillah 17b; Tosafot at BT Rosh ha-Shanah 17b; cf. also NJV there: "And repent and save itself."

[7] Here Rashi makes four points (1) *yārĕdî* (so-called infinitive absolute + lst pers. sing. pronominal suffix) is synonymous with *ridtî* (so-called infinitive construct + lst pers. sing. pronominal suffix); (2) Biblical Heb. *bôr*, lit., 'pit' is employed here as a synonym of Biblical Heb. Sheol 'the netherworld', which is functionally equivalent to Rabbinic Heb. Gehinnom; (3) where Biblical Heb. uses an infinitive phrase *miyyārĕdî* = *mēridtî*, late Heb. prefers the use of a a subordinate clause; (4) the Biblical Heb. preposition *mi (= min)* can be the equivalent of the negative particle (see *BDB*, p. 583).

[8] Heb. *bĕharṣôtô*, Rashi's paraphrase of the psalmist's *rāṣôn*; see n. 14.

[9] Exegetical *waw*.

[10] Cf. Rashi's consistent treatment of *rāṣôn* at Ps. 5:13; 19:15; and see Banitt, *Rashi: Interpreter of the Biblical Letter*, p. 29.

[11] Here Rashi paraphrases substituting for the masculine form *šalwî* (unattested base form presumed to be *šelew* or *šālû*) the feminine form *šalwātî*,

which represents the frequently attested *šalwāh* + 1st pers. sing. pronominal suffix; see Mandelkern, p. 1173b.

¹² Here Rashi paraphrases substituting the past progressive for the psalmist's use of the so-called perfect and substituting a form of the verb *ḥāšab* in its modern sense 'think where the Bible expresses 'think' by a form of the verb *'āmar*.

¹³ Here Rashi substitutes the familiar negative particle *lō'* for the rare *bal*, which is employed in the biblical text.

¹⁴ Rashi's paraphrase; the biblical text has IN YOUR FAVOR; other Rashi mss. have "in His favor."

¹⁵ Rashi's paraphrase; the Bible has YOU ESTABLISHED.

¹⁶ So RSV.

¹⁷ By supplying the infinitive finalis of the verb 'to be' Rashi indicates here that he construes *'oz* as a noun employed as an objective complement (so KJV) rather than as a genitive following the noun *harěrî*. In the latter case the noun would function as an adjective meaning 'strong' modifying MY MOUNTAIN-LIKE QUALITY (so RSV); for other possible interpretations see Qimhi.

¹⁸ Here Rashi emphasizes the antithetic parallelism between 8a-b and 8c-d.

¹⁹ The Bible has YOU HID YOUR FACE.

²⁰ Rashi, followed by NJV, adds *waw*-conversive, and reverses the word order from the psalmist's TO YOU O LORD I CALL.

²¹ Rashi, followed by NJV, construes vv. 10ff. as a quotation.

²² Cf. v. 11a: HEAR, O LORD.

²³ Heb. Pesikta Zuta, commonly called Pesikta deRav Kahana (because the first named authority quoted therein is Rav Kahana; see PRK, ed. Mandelbaum, pp. xxii-xxiii), as distinct from the later and more extensive midrash compilation called Pesikta Rabbati, lit., 'the Large Pesikta'.

²⁴ This phrase is not found in PRK.

²⁵ PRK, ed. Mandelbaum, p. 145.

PSALM XXXI

6a INTO YOUR HAND I SHALL ENTRUST MY SPIRIT
always[1] because You[2]

6b REDEEMED ME from trouble.

7 THOSE WHO RELY ON EMPTY FOLLY
[i.e.], those who expect deliverance by the objects of idolatrous worship.

10 'ā šĕšāh 'WASTED', [i.e.], kāhătāh 'dimmed'; it is a cognate
of [the noun] 'ăšāšît 'lantern'. [The expression 'MY EYES
ARE WASTED' refers to the situation] in which a person
places a glass before his eyes to see something through the
glass, [and] the appearance of that object is not clear.[3]

11d MY LIMBS WASTE AWAY. [The verb 'āšĕšû 'they wasted
away'] is a a synonym of the verb rqb 'rot, decay, be eaten
by worms or moths'; [it is employed here to indicate that my
limbs were ravaged] as though a moth had eaten them.[4]

12a FROM ALL [mikkol] MY FOES [i.e.], by [mē'ēt][5] ALL MY
FOES.

12b I HAVE BECOME A REPROACH for derision AND TO
MY NEIGHBORS ESPECIALLY I am a reproach.[6]

12c A HORROR TO MY FRIENDS. They are horrified about
the things that happen to me.

13c AN OBJECT BEING LOST ['ōbēd] [i.e.], about to be lost.[7]
[In Biblical Heb.] the verb 'to lose'[8] is never employed with
reference to[9] the owner of the lost object so as to say 'He lost
it' [hû' 'ibbēd 'ōtāh]. Rather, [you say in Biblical Heb.], "the
lost object is lost from him," as you say [in the Bible], "which
may be lost from him" (Deut. 22:3);[10] "nor have you sought
lost objects" [ha'ōbĕdôt] (Ezek. 34:4).[11]

14a THE WHISPERINGS OF MANY [i.e.], the counsel of the
MANY. [The noun] dibbat 'WHISPERING' [means] parleïç
'talk, verbiage, gossip' [in Old French].[12] It is a cognate of[13]
[the participle dōbēb 'cause to whisper' in] "Causing the lips
of the sleeping to whisper" (Cant. 7:10);[14] and so is every attestation of dibbāh in the Bible.

14b   TERROR ON EVERY SIDE for they were frightening me
        and terrifying me.

14c   WHEN THEY SCHEME [i.e.], when they take counsel.[15]

16   MY TIMES[16] ARE IN YOUR HAND.
        The events,[17] which I experience are by Your command and
        in accord with Your decrees.

18a   LET ME NOT BE DISAPPOINTED WHEN I CALL YOU,
        After I HAVE CALLED YOU it would not be nice [if I were
        disappointed].[18]

18c   LET THEM BE SILENCED IN SHEOL.
        Let them be made silent and let them be stilled IN SHEOL.

19b   THAT SPEAK HAUGHTILY AGAINST THE RIGH-
        TEOUS,
        [i.e.], who say to Saul about me,[19] "David is out to do you
        harm" (1 Sam. 24:10).

20   HOW ABUNDANT IS THE GOOD.
        I know that in the eschatological era there is a good reward
        for Your devotees. Nevertheless, in this pre-eschatological
        era[20] in which the wicked encircle them [Your devotees] I
        pray that

21a   You hide them[21] IN YOUR FACE'S HIDING PLACE

21b   AGAINST SCHEMING MEN [i.e.], from bands of wicked
        people, who conspire together to harm them [Your devotees].

22   IN A BESIEGED CITY [i.e.] in Keilah when Saul said about
        me [David],[19] "He has been delivered [to me] by [his] com-
        ing to a town with gate and bars" (1 Sam. 23:7).

23a   I SAID IN MY HASTE [ḥopzî] When I left Keilah and I
        came to the wilderness of Maon and I was in a hurry [neḥpāz]
        to get away from Saul for he had overtaken me, and Saul and
        his men were surrounding me and my men to capture them,
        I SAID in my heart,[22]

23b   I HAVE BEEN SEVERED [nigzartî] [i.e.], 'I have been cut
        out' [nikrattî]. [The verb nigzartî 'I HAVE BEEN SEVERED']
        is a cognate of [the noun] garzen 'axe', which cuts down a
        tree. It is called garzen because of its 'severing' [gĕzêrātô]. Thus
        did Dunash [Ben Labrat] explain it.[23]

24b   THE LORD GUARDS THE LOYAL ['ĕmûnîm] [i.e.], those
        who believe in [ma'ămînîm bĕ] His deliverance and who rely
        upon Him.[24]

24c   'al-yeter 'UPON THE CORD' [is an idiom meaning] 'mea-
        sure for measure'; [this idiom refers to the fact that the punish-

ment] is directed toward him [the guilty party] like an arrow
UPON THE CORD of the bow. Alternatively, one can interpret 'UPON THE CORD' [as standing for the cliché] 'rope
for rope, line for line'.

PSALM XXXI, NOTES

¹ Maarsen points out here that Rashi supplies the adverb *tāmîd* 'always'
to indicate that the imperfect form of the verb is here employed to express
the future tense; contrast NJV, which renders the verb as a present.

² By supplying the subordinate conjunction *lĕpî* 'because' and the independent pronoun 'You', Rashi indicates that he interprets the perfect
form of the verb *pādîtāh* here as a past tense meaning 'YOU REDEEMED';
so KJV and RSV. Dahood, like Qimhi, construes the verb as a precative
perfect (on this phenomenon see our discussion at Ps. 16:2); NJV renders
both the imperfect verb in v. 6a and the perfect verb in v. 6b as a present
and thereby avoids the problem of sequence of tenses (future in v. 6a; past
in v. 6b), which Rashi's interpretation of the verbs creates and which his
treatment of v. 6b as a subordinate clause solves.

³ See the almost verbatim comment of Rashi on the same verb in a
similar context at Ps. 6:8, and see there also for Rashi's sources and our
discussion.

⁴ Rashi's suggestion that the verbal root *rqb* may refer both to physical debilitation and to being eaten by worms or moths' is supported by
Isa. 40:20; Hab. 3:16; Prov. 12:4; 14:30; and by Job. 13:28 respectively;
see also dictionaries of Biblical and Rabbinic Heb., s.v. *rqb*; Rashi's suggestion that the stative verb *'āšēš* 'waste away' is a cognate of the noun *'āš*
'moth' is derived from *Mahberet Menahem*, p. 293, which traces both to a
biliteral root *'š*; similarly *BDB*, p. 799b which traces both to the geminate
root *'tt*; *K-B³*, pp. 847-848 shows that Heb. *'āš* 'moth' is derived from the
Semitic root *'tt* while the Heb. *'šš* 'waste away' is derived from the Semitic
root *ǵtt*.

⁵ Here Rashi offers an interpretation of the ambiguous prefixed preposition *mi(n)*.

⁶ Most modern exegetes emend MT's *mĕ'ōd* 'ESPECIALLY' (which is
supported by LXX and the Vulgate) to *mā'ôr* (see Briggs, here; and see *BHS*,
here) in order to create three paralllel clauses: *hāyîtî ḥerpāh//wĕlišĕkēnay mā'ôr
//ûpaḥad limyuddā'āy* "I became a reproach//and to my neighbors a ter-
ror//and a horror to my friends." NJV's rendering, "I am the particular
butt of my neighbors, a horror to my friends," combines the first two clauses
and transposes 'to my neighbors' to the end of the combined clause. Rashi,
followed by KJV, treats the three clauses as a typical case of ellipsis in
biblical poetry, in which the verb 'I became' governs all three clauses and
in which the noun 'reproach' governs both the first and the second clauses;

⁷ Rashi interprets the participle as a present tense verb serving as the
predicate of a verbal clause while NJV interprets the participle as an attributive adjective modifying the noun 'OBJECT'.

[8] Heb. *lĕšôn 'ăbēdāh*; note that in this context the noun *lāšôn* in the construct referring to a specific verb in the genitive denotes 'the verb'; note also that while it is modern practice to refer to Heb. verbs using the 3^d pers. sing. masc. perfect just as it is customary to refer to Eng. verbs using the infinitive so it is Rashi's general practice to refer to verbal roots using the gerund.

[9] Heb. *kol...'ênô nôpēl 'al*; with Banitt, *Rashi: Interpreter of the Biblical Letter*, p. 14, n. 37 note that the expression here employed is a Gallicism derived from Fr. *cheoir* 'fall', hence, 'happen, apply, fit.' For this expression in Rashi's Commentary on the Book of Psalms see also at Ps. 16:1; 38:3; 45:8; 118:12; etc. Note also that our Rashi ms. here repeats by haplography "the verb 'to lose' and."

[10] NJV there renders "anything that your fellow loses"; Rashi here intimates that the Biblical usage is no less strange to his ears than it is to Modern English usage, which requires NJV to substitute a transitive verb whose subject is the owner and whose direct object is the 'lost object'

[11] This is the reading in our Rashi ms.; MT employs the singular *hā'ōbedet* 'the lost' (so NJV).

[12] Banitt, *Rashi: Interpreter of the Biblical Letter*, pp. 13, 46.

[13] Heb. *lĕšôn*.

[14] Similarly KJV, following Rashi.

[15] See Rashi at Ps. 2:2.

[16] Heb. *'ittôtāy*; see Rashi at Ps. 9:10; 10:1.

[17] Heb. *hā'ittîm*, lit., 'the appointed times'; see previous note.

[18] The bracketed portion of the comment is lacking in our Rashi ms.; I have supplied it from other versions of the commentary.

[19] David, to whom the authorship of Ps. 31 is attributed at v. 1.

[20] See our discussion of the expressions *ha'ôlām hazzeh, ha'ôlām habbā'* at Ps. 25, n. 19.

[21] Heb. *mastîrām*, lit., 'one who hides them', Rashi's paraphrase of the psalmist's *tastîrēm*, lit., 'YOU WILL HIDE THEM'.

[22] Rashi indicates by the addition of this expression that the verb *'āmar* here denotes 'to think' rather than 'to say'.

[23] *Teshuvot Dunash*, pp. 77-78; Dunash assumes that the verbal root and the noun are related by metathesis; his interpretation is found already in Midrash Tehillim here; so now also *K-B³*, p. 179b, s.v. *gzr* I; p. 194b, s.v. *grz*; NJV's rendering "I am thrust out" goes back to *Mahberet Menahem*, pp. 113-114.

[24] For the idea see Midrash Tehillim here.

PSALM XXXII

1a A MASKIL OF DAVID.

Sages said, "As for every psalm in which it is said, '*maskil*',[1] he [David] composed it with the aid of a ghostwriter.[2]

1b HAPPY IS HE WHOSE TRANSGRESSION IS FORGIVEN, [i.e.], he whose transgression the Holy One Blessed be He forgives

1c and whose sin He covers up.[3]

2a and WHOM He[4] DOES NOT HOLD GUILTY

2b and with the only condition that there should not be[5] IN HIS SPIRIT DECEIT, [which means] its being in his mind to return to his lewdness.[6]

3 AS LONG AS I SAID NOTHING rather than confess before You concerning my transgression, MY LIMBS WASTED AWAY because of my many groanings and sighs all day while I was preoccupied because of punishment.

4a FOR NIGHT AND DAY the fear of YOUR HAND, i.e.,[7] Your decrees,[8] was heavy[9] UPON ME.

4b MY VIGOR WANED. [*lěšaddî* 'MY VIGOR' means literally] 'my moisture' and likewise *lěšad haššāmen* (in Num. 11:8) [means] 'a moist oily cake'. Thus Dunash explained it.[10]

4c IN THE SUMMER DROUGHT. [I.e.], until the summer became dry like the summer aridity because of preoccupation with the heaviness of Your hand (see v. 4a) for I was preoccupied with my sins, and therefore

5a I DECLARE TO YOU MY SINS always. It [the imperfect form of the verb] is [employed here as] the present tense.

5b for I THOUGHT, "it is good that I SHOULD CONFESS MY TRANSGRESSIONS TO THE LORD."

5c Now that I have confessed and told Nathan the prophet my sin (2 Sam. 12:13a), YOU FORGAVE THE GUILT OF MY SIN in consonance with what is stated in the Bible, "The LORD has remitted your sin" (2 Sam. 12:13b).

6a AT A TIME WHEN YOU MAY BE FOUND [i.e.] when You make Yourself available to accept his prayer. When is this [time]? [The answer is]:[11]

6b   ONLY AT THE RUSHING OF MIGHTY WATERS so that[12] THEY WILL NOT OVERTAKE HIM [i.e.], so that he will not fall into the hand of the Gentiles, who are like a flood. Similarly we have found that when David prayed for this [that he not fall into the hand of the Gentiles], he said, "Let me fall[13] into the hands of the LORD, for His compassion is great, and let me not fall into the hands of men" (2 Sam. 14:14).

7a   YOU ARE A HIDING PLACE FOR ME[14] to hide in Your shade because of the fear of an enemy.

7c   JOYOUS SHOUTS OF [ronnê] DELIVERANCE [i.e.], a song of [rinnāh] rescue. [The imperfect form of the verb] tĕsobĕbēnî 'YOU SURROUND ME' is [employed here as] a present tense. [The clause means] "You have always surrounded me with THE JOYOUS SHOUTS OF DELIVERANCE," and thus You said to me:

8a   LET ME ENLIGHTEN YOU AND SHOW YOU,

8c   LET ME OFFER COUNSEL,

8d   [MY EYE IS ON YOU means], "I shall indicate to you with My eye what you shall do." [The verb] 'î'ăṣāh 'LET ME OFFER COUNSEL' is synonymous with [the verb qāraṣ 'wink' in the expression] qĕrîṣat 'ayin 'winking of an eye'[15] as is demonstrated by "He winked his eyes ['āṣāh 'ēnāyw] to plot mischief" in the Book of Proverbs (16:30).[16]

9a   BE NOT LIKE A HORSE OR MULE, which does not distinguish[17] between him who does him good and him who does him harm. When you put on his bridle, he closes his mouth, and he gnaws on his bridle. When you scrape him and curry him and adorn him with bit and bridle, he closes his mouth.[18] You are required to close, i.e., to shut his mouth and to restrain him with bit and bridle

9c   SO THAT HE WILL NOT APPROACH YOU, [i.e.], so that he will not approach you[19] to harm you when you are adorning him.

9b   WITH BIT AND BRIDLE HIS ORNAMENT ['edyô] TO CLOSE.
During his adornment when you are scraping him and currying him You must shut his mouth with bit and bridle so that he will not approach you. In Mishnaic Hebrew bĕlîmāh 'closing' is a synonym of masgēr 'shutting' [as in Tosefta

Bekorot 4:13], "[If] its mouth is closed [*bālûm*] or its feet are tied together [*mĕbûlāmôt*]..."[20]

PSALM XXXII, NOTES

[1] Pss. 32, 42, 44-45, 52-55, 74, 78, 88, 89, 142.

[2] This statement, which is repeated in Rashi's commentary at Ps. 88:1, is based upon a baraitha quoted in BT Pesaḥim 117a. Rashi explains in his commentary to BT there, "He [David] uttered [the basic idea], and the other person would fill in the details [*mĕpārēš*]." On the role of such a ghostwriter in the Babylonian Jewish academies in the Gaonic period see Caspar Levias, "Meturgeman," *JE* 8:521b. Note, however, that Levias and his Gaonic sources read those academies back into the Rabbinic period.

[3] Here Rashi paraphrases v. 1c replacing the Bible's passive constructions with active ones.

[4] Having made the Holy One Blessed be He the subject of the active verbs in his paraphrase of v. 1, Rashi does not find it necessary to quote the name of the LORD in v. 2.

[5] Rashi substitutes the imperfect construction *šellō' tihyeh* for the Bible's *'ên*, and he thereby indicates that in the present context *ên* expresses the future rather than the present.

[6] Lit., 'his vomit', which is employed here as in Isa. 28:8 as a metaphor for 'sin, lewdness'. Rashi's comment is based upon Midrash Tehillim here, which employs the simile found in Prov. 26:11.

[7] Explicative *waw*.

[8] Here Rashi clarifies the meaning of YOUR HAND AS 'the fear of Your decrees'; see above, Ps. 21:9a where Rashi interprets 'Your hand' as 'plague of Your hand'; see discussion there.

[9] The psalmist employs the stative verb *tikbad* 'she is heavy'. Rashi paraphrases using the verb 'to be' + the predicate adjective *kābēd* 'heavy'. Modern Heb. exhibits the same tendency as does Rashi's Heb. to replace Biblical Heb.'s stative verbs with the verb 'to be' + the predicate adjective.

[10] *Teshuvot Dunash*, p. 26.

[11] Rashi's point is that ONLY AT THE RUSHING OF MIGHTY WATERS stands in apposition to AT A TIME OF BEING FOUND; for alternative interpretations see the various translations and commentaries.

[12] Rashi supplies *'ăšēr* 'so that' to indicate that he regards THEY WILL NOT OVERTAKE HIM as a subordinate clause modifying the verb 'LET PRAY' rather than as the predicate of the noun WATERS; contrast NJV.

[13] So Rashi here; Heb. *'eplāh;* the biblical text has *niplāh* 'let us fall'.

[14] Lemma rendered according to RSV to bring out the paranomasia in Rashi's comment.

[15] Attested in Ps. 35:19; Prov. 6:13; 10:10, *qāraṣ 'ayin* always means 'look with malice' as does *'āṣāh 'ênayim*. The expression, which Rashi identifies here in Ps. 32:8 is a near homonym of the latter idiom. Note, however, that the expression employed in Prov. 16:30 refers to 'eyes' while the ex-

pression attested here in Ps. 32:8 refers to one 'eye'. Presumably, here, as frequently in the ancient Semitic languages, the two homonymous anatomical expressions derive from similar but culturally distinguished eye movements, one of which (referred to in Prov. 16:30) was understood to mean 'look with malice' while the other was understood to mean 'look with favor'. See Gruber, *Aspects*, pp. 19-21.

[16] See Rashi there.

[17] Rashi's paraphrase of the psalmist's *'ēn hābîn*, which NJV renders 'senseless'.

[18] Rashi's comment on v. 9 is based upon the midrash quoted in Midrash Tehillim here. Paraphrasing the midrash, Rashi imposes upon it his view that the verb *bālam* there is ellipsis for *bālam pîw* 'he closed his mouth'. The midrash itself reflects another meaning of the verb *bālam*, sc., 'kick'; see Braude, *The Midrash on Psalms*, vol. 1, p. 404.

[19] Here Rashi indicates by his paraphrase that the Bible's use of the negative *bal* followed by the infinitive is equivalent to late Heb. *šellō'* 'so that not' + the imperfect.

[20] Here Rashi, basing himself upon his comment at BT Hullin 107b, justifies his interpretation of the verb *bālam* in the midrash. For the correct reading of the text of the Tosefta, which is reflected in BT Bekorot 40b, see David Pardo, *Hasde David: Tosefet Qedushah* (Jerusalem: Frumkin, 1890), p. 75a.

PSALM XXXIII

2   WITH A HARP OF TEN [i.e.] of ten kinds of music.[1]

7a   LIKE A MOUND. [The word *nēd* 'MOUND' is] an expression referring to height. Accordingly, Onkelos rendered "they stood like a *nēd* 'mound'" (Ex. 15:8) into Aramaic [as follows]: *qᵉmô kᵉšûr* "they stood like a wall,"[2] and thus did Menahem interpret it.[3] [The word] *nēd* and [the word] *nō"d* 'bottle'[4] are not the same.

7b   STORES THE DEEPS[5] IN VAULTS. [I.e.], THE DEEPS [are] IN VAULTS under the earth.[6]

14b   *hišgîăḥ* 'HE GAZED' [i.e.], *hibbît* 'He looked'.[7]

15a   HE WHO FASHIONS TOGETHER THEIR HEART, [i.e.], the heart of all of them together.[8] Our rabbis interpreted it [v. 15] as referring back to [v. 14a so that vv. 14-15a would be understood as follows]: FROM HIS DWELLING-PLACE (v. 14a) GAZED (v. 14b) HE WHO FASHIONS TO-GETHER THEIR HEART (v. 15a).[9] They deduced [from here] that all of them are surveyed in one glance.[10]

PSALM XXXIII, NOTES

[1] Heb. *mînê nᵉˀîmāh*; apparently synonymous with *nîmîn* 'strings', the term Rashi employs at Ps. 6:1; 92:4; cf. Rashi at Isa. 17:11 and Maarsen's note there and here; cf. NJV here.

[2] So NJV there; contrast Rashi there.

[3] There is no such entry in known editions of Menahem's work; see *Mahberet Menahem*, p. 252; cf. *Mahberet Menahem*, ed. Fillipkowski, p. 121, n.229.

[4] Josh. 9:13; Judg. 4:19; Ps. 56:9; 119:83.

[5] I.e., the primeval waters [*tᵉhōm, tᵉhōmôt*], which covered everything before Creation; see Gen. 1:2; Ps. 104:3-9; Job. 38:8-11; etc.

[6] For the idea that since Creation the primeval waters have been placed under the earth forming the ground water or water table see Gen. 7:11; 8:2; 49:25; see also Rashi at Ps. 120; and see Theodor H. Gaster, "The Deep," *EJ* 5:1456-1457 and the literature cited there.

[7] Rashi here explains that the rare verb *hišgîăḥ*, which is attested only three times in the Hebrew Bible (Isa. 14:16; Ps. 33:14; Cant. 2:9) is a synonym of the commonly attested *hibbît*.

[8] Rashi here responds to the fact that the psalmist employs the sing. *lēb* 'heart' to refer to the several 'hearts' of several persons.

[9] Rashi interprets the statement attributed to R. Nahman b. Isaac (d. c. 356 C.E.) at BT Rosh ha-Shanah 18a as meaning that Ps. 33:14-15 is a case of inversion (*miqrā' mĕsûrās*). According to Rashi's interpretation, vv. 13 and 14 are synonymous main clauses while v. 15 is a relative clause modifying 'the LORD', who is the subject of the verbs in vv. 13 and 14. In fact, R. Nahman b. Isaac treats v. 15, WHO FASHIONS TOGETHER THEIR HEART//WHO DISCERNS ALL THEIR DOINGS, as ellipsis for "THE FASHIONER sees THEIR HEARTS TOGETHER//AND HE DISCERNS ALL THEIR DEEDS." According to Rashi in his commentary at BT Rosh ha-Shanah 18a, q.v., THE FASHIONER sees THEIR HEARTS TOGETHER (v. 15 is in synonymous parallelism with v. 14 [*wĕ'aqqĕrā' dilĕ'ēl minnēh qā' mĕhaddar*]. Note that the view attributed to R. Nahman b. Isaac in BT, the extension of that view in Rashi's commentary to BT, and the interpretation attributed here in Rashi's commentary to Ps. 33:15 to "our rabbis" are, in fact, three different and mutually exclusive interpretations of the syntax of Ps. 33:13-15. Cf. and contrast Maarsen's comment here.

[10] The phraseology is attributed to Rabbah b. Bar Hannah (c. 250-300 C.E.) quoting R. Johanan (b. Napha) [c. 180-279 C.E.] at BT Rosh ha-Shanah 18a. This statement is intended there as an explanation of Mishnah Rosh ha-Shanah 1:2, which employs Ps. 33:15 as a prooftext for its assertion, "At New Year all creatures pass before Him one by one."

PSALM XXXIV

1   WHEN HE FEIGNED MADNESS. [This is stated] with reference to what is stated in the Bible, "He scratched marks on the doors of the gate..." (1 Sam. 21:14b); "so he concealed his good sense from them" (1 Sam. 21:14a).
     IN THE PRESENCE OF ABIMELECH. All Philistine kings are thus called, and all Egyptian kings [are called] Pharaoh. Even though his name is Achish, he is called Abimelech.[1] An aggadic midrash [states] that he [Achish] was virtuous like Abimelech (in Gen. 20; 26) in that he [Achish] did not wish to kill him [David] although his people said to him, "Why, that's David, king of the land!" [The latter interpretation of the name Abimelech here at Ps. 34:1 is] in accord with what is stated in Midrash Tehillim.[2]

3a   MY SOUL MAKES ITS BOAST IN THE LORD.[3]
     [I.e.], I[1] brag and boast that I have such a patron to deliver [me] and to defend [me]. [The verb] tithallēl 'MAKES ITS BOAST' [corresponds in meaning to] se porvantera in O.F.[5]

3b   LET THE LOWLY HEAR the wonders that He did for me,[6] and as a consequence of that [hearing] may they [THE LOWLY] understand them [the wonders], AND REJOICE.[7]

5   MY TERRORS [mĕgûrôtay] is a synonym of [the commonly attested noun] paḥad 'fear'; it is a cognate of [the verb gûr 'be alarmed' in] "Moab was alarmed" (Num. 22:3).[8]

6   MEN LOOK TO HIM AND ARE RADIANT. All those who LOOK TO HIM in the midst of their trouble ARE RADIANT, i.e., their faces light up.[9]

9   COUNSEL [i.e.], speak.[10]

10   FEAR. [I.e.], Be fearful.[11] [The form yĕr'û 'FEAR'] is the imperative form of the verb.

11   [The verb] rāšû 'THEY DO LACK' is a verb referring to dallût 'poverty'.

15   SEEK [AMITY][12] in your place, AND PURSUE IT in another place.[13]

18   THEY, the righteous,[14] CRY OUT, AND THE LORD HEARS.

20   MANY EVILS THE RIGHTEOUS.[15]
     [I.e.], He [THE RIGHTEOUS] experiences many [harbēh] EVILS and fears, and he [THE RIGHTEOUS] is saved from all of them.[16]

21   HE, the Holy One Blessed be He,[17] PRESERVES ALL HIS[18] BONES.

22   The EVIL, which he does, PUTS TO DEATH the WICKED.
      tĕmôtēt 'PUTS TO DEATH' [is synonymous with] *tāmît* 'put to death'
      (Job. 5:2).[19]

23   [ALL WHO TAKE REFUGE IN HIM][20] SHALL NOT FEEL
      GUILTY.
      [I.e.], they will not feel sorry, saying, "We feel guilty [*'ašamnû*] that
      we took refuge in Him."[21]

PSALM XXXIV, NOTES

[1] According to 1 Sam. 21:14 David feigned madness in the presence
of King Achish of Gath. The historical books of the Bible do not mention
David's having feigned madness before any other king. It is universally
assumed, therefore, that Ps. 34:1 refers to the same incident that is recorded
in 1 Sam. 21. The exegetical problem, which Rashi seeks to solve here, is
why the same king is called Achish in 1 Sam. 21:14 and Abimelech here
in Ps. 34:1. Most modern commentators solve this problem by emending
Abimelech here to read "Achish". Rashi, whose suggestion is quoted by
Qimhi as an alternative interpretation, ingeniously suggests on the basis
of the parallel stories concerning Abraham and Sarah and Isaac and
Rebekah in Gen. 20 and 26 respectively that Abimelech is not a personal
name but rather the title of all Philistine kings. According to this explanation, Ps. 34:1 and 1 Sam. 21:14 do not contradict each other. The latter
refers to the king of Gath by his personal name; the former by his title.
Ibn Ezra and Qimhi offer another suggestion, namely, that Achish-
Abimelech is an example of a well-known phenomenon of biblical person-
alities who are known by more than one personal name. Examples include
Jacob-Israel; Jethro-Reuel-Hobab; Gideon-Jerubbaal; etc. The suggestion
put forward by Ibn Ezra and Qimhi appears in new dress in Dahood, *Psalms*,
1:205: "...it is quite possible that Abimelech was the Semitic name of the
king of Gath." Presumably, Dahood means that Achish is to be taken as
the king's Philistine name. On the origin of the name Achish see Joshua
Gutmann, "Achish," *EJ* 2:210-211.
[2] Note that Midrash Tehillim here states only, "He was called
Abimelech because he was virtuous like Abimelech."
[3] RSV's rendering of the lemma, which corresponds to the interpretation presupposed by Rashi's comment.
[4] Rashi here intimates that in Ps. 34:1 *napšî* 'MY SOUL' is employed
as periphrasis for the personal pronoun 'I'; so now NJV; see *BDB*, p. 660a.
[5] Cognate and semantic equivalent of Eng. 'to vaunt oneself', i.e., 'to
engage in vainglorious display of oneself'; see Levy, *Contribution*, #656.
[6] Here Rashi supplies the missing direct object of the verb 'HEAR',
without which the verse makes no sense.
[7] Here Rashi attempts to explain the logical connection between v. 3a
and v. 3b; cf. Ibn Ezra here.
[8] See *Mahberet Menahem*, p. 112, s.v. *gr* III.
[9] See *Mahberet Menahem*, p. 253, s.v. *nhr* II; note that Menahem there

already correctly understands *nhr* in Isa. 2:2; contrast KJV and RSV; see Gruber, *Aspects*, pp. 563-565; contrast Rashi at Isa. 2:2.

[10] Rashi here reflects the view of *Mahberet Menahem*, p. 199, s.v. *ṭʿm*, which distinguishes between *ṭʿm* I 'counsel' and *ṭʿm* II 'savour'; contrast NJV.

[11] Here as in Ps. 32:4, q.v., Rashi paraphrases an unfamiliar verb form by using the verb 'to be' + a well-known predicate adjective derived from the root of the unfamiliar verb form.

[12] So NJV; Heb. *šālôm*, commonly rendered 'peace'; note that our Rashi ms. does not quote this bracketed portion of the verse; I have supplied it for clarity.

[13] This midrash is attributed to the Palestinian Amora Hezekiah (early 3ᵈ cent. C.E.) in Perek Ha-Shalom, par. 4; see *The Minor Tractates of the Talmud*, ed. Abraham Cohen (2 vols.; London: Soncino, 1965), 2:598. The same midrash is attributed to the Tanna, R. Simeon b. Eleazar (2ᵈ cent. C.E.) in Avot deRabbi Nathan 12:5. This midrash seems to be inspired by the characteristic tendency of Rabbinic midrash to distinguish the nuances of words that are appear to be synonymous, in this case, 'seek' and 'pursue'.

[14] Rashi supplies the subject from v. 16.

[15] If, as is assumed by KJV, RSV, NJV, and Dahood, the meaning of these three words is MANY ARE THE MISFORTUNES OF THE RIGHTEOUS, then *rʿt* 'evils of, misfortunes of' must be vocalized as a plural construct *rēʿôt* rather than as in MT *rāʿôt*, which is the plural absolute. In the present context the latter form can function only as a participle, the predicate of the adjectival noun *rabbôt* 'MANY'. Hence the three words must be rendered MANY THINGS HARM THE RIGHTEOUS. Rashi, however, treats v. 20 as ellipsis for THE RIGHTEOUS experiences MANY EVILS.

[16] Here Rashi paraphrases v. 20b: THE LORD WILL SAVE HIM FROM THEM ALL.

[17] Here Rashi supplies the subject.

[18] I.e., the righteous person's.

[19] The biblical text employs the *polel* form of the root *mwt* 'to die'. Rashi supplies the synonymous *hiphil* form of the same root, which is more familiar not only to modern readers but also to readers in Rashi's time.

[20] Rashi does not quote the bracketed portion of the verse; I have supplied it for clarity.

[21] Rashi's comment here demonstrates that Rashi here has anticipated Jacob Milgrom, *Cult and Conscience: The Asham and the Priestly Doctrine of Repentance*, Studies in Judaism in Late Antiquity, vol. 18 (Leiden: E. J. Brill, 1976), p. 10 in interpreting Heb. *ʾšm* to mean 'feels guilt'.

PSALM XXXV

3   READY [THE SPEAR].[1]
     [I.e.], Arm yourself. AND CLOSE [ûsĕgor][2] AGAINST MY
     PURSUERS. [I.e.], Shield me from them like a partition.[3]

6   [LET THEIR PATH BE][1] DARK AND SLIPPERY.
     Both of them [DARK AND SLIPPERY] together so that their
     feet will slip in the slipperiness while the darkness will not allow
     them to watch out for the slipperiness; this is in consonance
     with what is stated in the Bible (in Jer. 23:12): "Therefore their
     path will become like slippery ground for them; they will be
     thrust into darkness, and they will fall into it."[4]

7b   THEY DUG FOR ME a pit to fall into it.[5]

8a   šo'āh. [I.e.], darkness.[6]

8b   HIS OWN NET, WHICH HE HID. Such is the normal
     practice to hide the net in straw or dirt so that one who passes
     over it will not sense it until he has been caught in it.

9   THEN SHALL I EXULT when I shall see their [my adver-
     saries'] fall.

10   ALL MY BONES will praise You[7] because of the fact that
     now[8]

11   MALICIOUS WITNESSES APPEAR... against me continu-
     ally.

13   MAY WHAT I PRAYED FOR HAPPEN TO ME.

14a I WALKED ABOUT AS THOUGH IT WERE MY
     FRIEND OR MY BROTHER.
     [I.e.], I WALKED ABOUT as if they were my brothers or
     my friends being sorry about their sorrow

14b LIKE MOURNING OF/FOR A MOTHER.
     [I.e.], like a son who mourns for his mother or like a mother
     who mourns for her son.[9]

15a BUT WHEN I LIMPED, THEY REJOICED, AND THEY
     GATHERED TOGETHER.
     When I limp[10] because I have suffered a wound, THEY RE-
     JOICED, AND THEY GATHERED TOGETHER.

15b nēkîm 'CRIPPLES' GATHERED TOGETHER. [I.e.], lame
     people. [The usage nēkîm 'cripples' is] in accordance with the

way in which we render [the name of Pharaoh] *Někōh* into
Aramaic as *hăgîrā'* 'Lame'.[11]

15c   THEY TORE, AND THEY DID NOT BLEED.[12]
       Had they torn my flesh, my blood would not flow to the
       ground when they were embarrassing me.[13]

16a   WITH THE HYPOCRISIES OF MOCKERS FOR A
       CAKE.
       For the hypocrisy of mockery—food and drink, which they
       hypocritically request that he should give them to eat and
16b   to drink THEY GNASH their teeth[14] AT ME.
       mā'ôg 'CAKE' is a term referring to food as is demonstrated
       by "[I swear] I have no cake [*mā'ôg*]"[15] (1 Kgs. 17:12) in the
       story of Elijah.

17a   HOW MUCH WILL YOU SEE?
       HOW MUCH patience[16] do You have to see all these [evils]?

17b   FROM THEIR *šo'āh* [i.e.], their darkness.[6]

19b   THEY LOOK ASKANCE. [I.e.], those who LOOK
       ASKANCE.[17]

20b   AGAINST THE QUIET ONES [*rigě'ê*] OF THE EARTH
       [i.e.], AGAINST the subdued OF THE EARTH. The same
       sense [of the root *rg'*] is illustrated by "Who quiets [*roga'*] the
       sea" (Isa. 51:15) and "My skin healed [*rāga'*]" (Job. 7:5). Thus
       Dunash explained [the meaning of the root in question].[18]

21   AHA, AHA is an exclamation of one who boasts to himself
       about his heart's desire.

23   WAKE, ROUSE YOURSELF, heavenly household, to ex-
       act MY CLAIM (23b) from my enemies.[19]

PSALM XXXV, NOTES
   [1] Rashi does not quote the bracketed portion of the verse; I have supplied it for clarity.
   [2] See next note.
   [3] This comment indicates that Rashi interprets *sĕgor* as the imperative
of the verb *sāgar* 'close'; similarly Ibn Ezra; so KJV. NJV, RSV, Dahood,
et al. follow Qimhi in interpreting *sĕgor* as a noun denoting a kind of weapon.
   [4] Cf. Rashi there.
   [5] By supplying the direct object, 'a pit to fall into it', Rashi indicates
that we have an instance of ellipsis. Most moderns eliminate the ellipsis
and the enigmatic *šahat rištām* 'PIT OF THEIR NET' from the first half
of the verse by transposing *šahat* 'PIT' to the second half of the verse; see
NJV and marginal note; contrast KJV, which follows Qimhi. M. Held, "Pits
and Pitfalls in Akkadian and Biblical Hebrew," *JANES* 5 (1973), p. 182,

n. 68 points out that Saadiah's Arabic rendering here also reflects a Hebrew text divergent from the problematic MT.

[6] Perhaps Rashi derives this interpretation from the juxtaposition of "a day of šo'āh and měšo'āh" with "a day of darkness and deep gloom, a day of densest clouds" in Zeph. 1:15; in his comment there, however, Rashi expresses the conventional view that šo'āh designates 'desolation'.

[7] The verb 'they will praise You' is Rashi's interpretation of the intent of the rhetorical question addressed to the LORD by ALL MY BONES in v. 10.

[8] Rashi intimates here that ALL MY BONES will praise (v. 10) is a continuation of v. 9, which refers to the time to come when the psalmist will have witnessed the fall of his enemies who now, at the time of the psalmist's plea, perpetrate the evils described in vv. 7, 11-12.

[9] Here Rashi points to the ambiguity of the Hebrew construct 'ăbel 'ēm, which can mean either 'mother's mourning (for someone else)' or '(someone else's) mourning for mother'. Similar to the enigma here are the enigmatic expressions in Mishnah Qiddushin 1:7 miṣwôt habbēn and miṣwôt hā'āb, lit., 'child's commandments' and 'parent's commandments' respectively. As is pointed out in BT Qiddushin 29a and 30b, the former expression can mean either 'commandments incumbent upon a child' or 'commandments performed upon a child' while the latter can mean either 'commandments incumbent upon a parent' or 'commandments performed upon a parent'. As is pointed out in BT Qiddushin 29a and 30b, the determination that in the context of Mishnah Qiddushin 1:7 the terms mean respectively 'commandments performed upon a child' and 'commandments performed upon a parent' derives not from grammar or syntax but from the larger cultural context of Mishnah Qiddushin 1:7.

[10] Rashi here as frequently paraphrases a temporal infinitive phrase by means of a temporal clause showing that the latter usage is preferred in Rabbinic and post-Rabbinic Heb. while the former is often the preferred functional equivalent in Biblical Heb.

[11] někēh, the construct of an unattested nākēh 'crippled', is attested in the Bible once in the expression někēh rûăḥ 'broken-hearted' in Isa. 66:2 and twice in the expression někēh raglayim 'crippled of feet' in 2 Sam. 4:4; 9:3. In none of these texts does TJ render ḥăgîrā' 'lame'. The following biblical texts refer to Pharaoh Neco II, who ruled 610-595 B.C.E.:2 Kgs. 23:29, 33, 34, 35; Jer. 46:2; 2 Ch. 35:20, 22; 36:4. TJ in 2 Kgs. and Jer. consistently treat the Pharaoh's name někōh (někô at Jer. 46:2) as though it were the Heb. word meaning 'crippled, lame', and it renders ḥăgîrā' 'lame'. It is to these passages in TJ that Rashi refers. The 8th or 9th century Targum to Chronicles published in today's Rabbinic Bibles also follows the example of TJ in the rendering of Neco's name. Rashi, however, was unaware of this Targum; hence he did not refer to it in his comment here.

[12] The exegetical problems in this portion of v. 15 are three: (1) what direct object is to be mentally supplied to the verb 'tear'; (2) what is the meaning of the verb dāmû.; (3) what is the relationship between the two ideas expressed by 'THEY TORE' and wělō' dāmû. The difficulties here

are immense; hence the interpretations are almost as numerous as the interpreters. The midrash, which Rashi quotes here, is attributed to Rava (d. 352 C.E.) at BT Bava Meṣiʿa and at BT Sanhedrin 107b.

[13] The expression, which I render here 'embarrass' means literally 'make the face pale'. The assumption behind the midrash is that the face of a person who has been embarrassed becomes pale because embarrassing someone causes the victim's blood to leave his body. This notion lent support to the Rabbinic contention that to embarrass a person is tantamount to bloodshed. According to the assumption of the midrash, King David had so frequently been shamed by his adversaries that he had no blood left. Hence, had his adversaries torn his flesh, they would have found that he did not bleed!

[14] The biblical text has the archaic form *śinnēmô*; Rashi substitutes the familiar form *śinnêhem*.

[15] Cf. the Modern Heb. cognate *ʿûgāh* 'cake'.

[16] Here Rashi responds to the exegetical question, "How much what?"

[17] Heb. *haqqōrĕṣîm ʿayin*; i.e., those whose winking denotes deceit; see Rashi at Prov. 6:13.

[18] As noted by Maarsen here, there is no discussion of such a root in *Teshuvot Dunash*; also, as noted by Maarsen here, Rashi must have meant to refer to *Mahberet Menahem*, p. 349, s.v. *rgm* III.

[19] With Zohory, p. 107 cf. the dictum of R. Johanan [b. Napha] in BT Sanhedrin 38b: "The Holy One Blessed be He does nothing without consulting the heavenly household [i.e., the angels]"; for parallels see Zohory, there. Rashi was inspired to assume that 23a is addressed to the angels since God is invoked only in the parallel clause 23b.

PSALM XXXVI

2   WHAT TRANSGRESSION SAYS TO THE WICKED IS IN MY HEART. Note that this is an inverted Scripture verse, [which should be understood as though the word-order were as follows]: There is IN MY HEART [knowledge][1] that the [personified] TRANSGRESSION, i.e.,[2] the evil inclination, says TO THE WICKED that there should be no

2b   FEAR OF GOD BEFORE HIS EYES.[3]

2a   The expression] 'IN MY HEART' refers to a person who says, "It seems to me."[4]

3a   FOR HE, the [personified] Transgression, distributed TO HIM enticements WITH HIS EYES so that the Holy One Blessed be

3b   He will FIND HIS INIQUITY TO HATE HIM.[6]

4b   HE WILL NOT CONSIDER DOING GOOD. [I.e.], He prevented himself[7] from CONSIDERING TO BETTER his behavior.[8]

5   HE IS SET ON A PATH OF NO GOOD. The Holy One Blessed be He set before him the path of good and the path of evil, and he chooses for himself A PATH OF NO GOOD.[9]

6   O LORD, YOUR FAITHFULNESS REACHES TO HEAVEN. Because of these wicked people You take away FAITHFULNESS from the lower regions,[10] and You elevate YOUR STEADFASTNESS TO THE SKY to remove it from people,[11] and

7a   YOUR BENEFICENCE IS dear among people[12] LIKE THE HIGH MOUNTAINS because of the behavior of the wicked, but

7b   YOUR JUSTICE comes to the world all the way to[13] THE GREAT DEEP.

7c   MAN ['ādām] AND BEAST YOU DELIVER, O LORD. You deliver people who are naked with respect to knowledge like Adam, and who make themselves like a beast with respect to humility.[14]

8a   HOW PRECIOUS IS YOUR FAITHFUL CARE. It is not worthwhile that it should be extended to these wicked people, but

8b   as for PEOPLE, who TAKE SHELTER IN THE SHADOW
        OF YOUR WINGS,

9   THEY FEAST ON THE RICH FARE....

12a   LET THE FOOT OF THE ARROGANT NOT GO WITH
        ME.

        [I.e.], LET THE [collective] FOOT of these wicked people
        NOT go with me[15] at the time of receiving reward lest their
        portion be with the virtuous.

12b   OR THE HAND OF THE WICKED DRIVE ME AWAY
        from my place when I come to possess a double portion,
        [namely], my portion and his portion in the good [land, i.e.,
        the land of Israel], in accord with what is stated in the Bible,
        "Therefore they will possess a double portion in their land"
        (Isa. 61:7). And then...

13a   THERE EVILDOERS WILL FALL.[16] There they will un-
        derstand their defeat,[17]

13b   and there THEY WILL BE THRUST DOWN,[16] and they
        will be[18] UNABLE TO RISE.

PSALM XXXVI, NOTES

    [1] See below, and cf. NJV.

    [2] Heb. *hû'*.

    [3] Similarly Qimhi; contrast Ibn Ezra, who comments as follows: "The
meaning is this: 'I think [*'eḥšōb*] IN MY HEART that TRANSGRESSION,
as it were, speaks [saying], "Evil man, fear not."' Therefore, GOD IS NOT
BEFORE HIS [the wicked man's] EYES." Thus while KJV and RSV take
'IN MY HEART' to refer to the place where TRANSGRESSION speaks
to the wicked, the three medieval commentators, followed by KJV, understand our verse to be a case of inversion, and they interpret 'IN MY
HEART' to mean 'I thought'. Rashi and Qimhi hold that all the remaining words in v. 2 tell what it was that the psalmist thought. They further
hold that the words of personified TRANSGRESSION are presented in
the form of indirect address. Thus they account for the reading 'HIS EYES'
rather than 'Your eyes'. Since Ibn Ezra presents the words of TRANS-
GRESSION as direct address, he must treat 'BEFORE HIS EYES' as the
comment of the psalmist himself concerning the wicked person to whom
TRANSGRESSION speaks. Ignoring MT's treatment of *paḥad 'ĕlōhîm* as
a single term 'fear of God', Ibn Ezra assigns the word 'fear' to the speech
of TRANSGRESSION and the words GOD BEFORE HIS EYES to the
psalmist narrator.

    [4] Hence NJV's "I know"; see previous note.

    [5] The literal meaning of v. 3 is FOR HE ENTICES HIM WITH HIS
EYES TO FIND HIS INIQUITY TO HATE. Rashi in his comment responds to the following exegetical problems presented by this text: (1) the

identification of the antecedents of the three personal pronouns HE, HIS, HIS; and (2) the identification of the object of the infinitive 'TO HATE'. NJV, q.v., following KJV, paraphrases v. 3.

[6] The biblical text employs the verb *heḥĕlîq* 'SPOKE SMOOTHLY' followed by the prepositional phrase *'ēlāyw* 'TO HIM' (cf. NJV's "BECAUSE ITS SPEECH IS SEDUCTIVE TO HIM"). In Biblical Heb. the verb employed here is an example of a non-causative *hiphil* of a root expressing "action in some particular direction"; see *GKC* #53f. In Rashi's Heb., however, the verb is treated as a causative *hiphil* requiring a direct object. Hence Rashi substitutes for the Bible's *heḥĕlîq* 'SPOKE SMOOTHLY' the expression *heḥĕlîq ḥălāqôt*, lit., 'distribute enticements'.

[7] Based on *Mahberet Menahem*, p. 169; see Maarsen here.

[8] Here as in the previous verse the Bible employs a non-causative *hiphil*, in this case *hēṭîb* 'DO GOOD'; see *GKC* #53f. Rashi, however, assuming that we have here a causative *hiphil*, treats the verb as ellipsis, and he supplies the direct object of the causative *hiphil hēṭîb* 'to better', sc., 'his behavior'.

[9] Cf. Deut. 30:15, 19; the parallel in Midrash Tehillim and Yalqut Shim'oni here refers not to Deut. 30 but to Prov. 2:13-14.

[10] I.e., the earth, the domain of people.

[11] Contrast Midrash Tehillim here.

[12] Here Rashi responds to the exegetical question, "In respect to what may it be said, 'YOUR BENEFICENCE IS LIKE THE HIGH MOUNTAINS'"?

[13] Heb. *'ad*.

[14] This interpretation is based upon a midrash attributed to Rab Judah b. Ezekiel (d. 299 C.E.) quoting Rab (d. 247 C.E.) at BT Hullin 5b. This interpretation treats the conjunctive *waw* (i.e., *û*) in the expression *'ādām ûbĕhēmāh*, lit., 'MAN AND BEAST', as an explicative *waw* so that the Heb. expression means 'a person who is (like) a beast'.

[15] While the biblical text employs a verb with a pronominal suffix, Rashi paraphrases employing a verb followed by a prepositional phrase.

[16] Rendering of the lemma according to the interpretation presupposed by Rashi, who construes the verb as a prophetic perfect.

[17] Heb *mappālātām*, a cognate of the verb *npl* 'fall'; note the paranomasia in Rashi's comment.

[18] Rashi's paraphrase employing the future reminds us that he construes all the perfect verbs in v. 13 as prophetic perfects, i.e., perfects which refer to future events as having already taken place; on this phenomenon in Biblical Heb. see *GKC* #106n.

PSALM XXXVII

1a DO NOT COMPETE WITH EVILDOERS.[1]
He [the psalmist] admonishes Israel that they should not
COMPETE with the success of EVIL DOERS by behaving
in accord with their behavior. [The verb *tithar* 'YOU COM-
PETE'] is the same verb as that which is attested in "How
can you compete [*tĕtaḥăreh*] with horses" (Jer. 12:5) by running at their pace? [The verb *tithar* corresponds in meaning
to] *aatir* 'compete, contend' in Old French.[2]

1b DO NOT BE ENVIOUS OF WRONGDOERS so as to DO
WRONG like them.[3]

3a TRUST IN THE LORD, and do not say, "If I do not rob
and steal and covet the wealth of others, how shall I make a
living?"

3b AND DO GOOD, and then You will abide in the land for a
long time.[4]

3c AND you will GRAZE[5] ON FAITHFULNESS.
You will eat, i.e., You will make a living as a reward for the
faithfulness with which You believed in the Holy One Blessed
be He by relying upon Him and by doing good.

4 DELIGHT IN THE LORD. [I.e.], Delight in dainties[6]
through the support of the Holy One Blessed be He.

5 TURN TOWARD THE LORD.
Turn to Him all your requests for daily needs.[7]

7a BE PATIENT FOR THE LORD [i.e.], wait for His deliverance. [The verb *dwm* 'BE PATIENT'] is the same verb as
that which is attested in the story of Jonathan, "If they say
to us, 'Wait' [*dômû*]" (1 Sam. 14:9).[8]

7b *wĕhithôlēl* 'TRUST' is a cognate of [the noun] *tôḥelet* 'hope'
(Prov. 13:12 etc.).[9]

7c DO NOT COMPETE[1] thinking,[10] "I shall do evil like him,
and I shall succeed like him."

8a GIVE UP ANGER, ABANDON FURY.
[I.e.], GIVE UP doing evil so that you will not experience
[divine] ANGER. AND ABANDON behavior, which causes
you to experience the FURY of the Holy One Blessed be He.

9a   FOR AS FOR EVIL MEN, whom you now see succeeding, they WILL BE CUT OFF.

10a   A LITTLE LONGER. When you wait A LITTLE LONGER you will see that THERE WILL BE NO WICKED MAN.

10b   YOU WILL LOOK UPON HIS PLACE. When you look upon[11] the place where he was,

10c   HE WILL BE GONE, for he died, and he perished.[12]

14   THE WICKED DRAW [*pātěhû*] THEIR SWORDS.
       THE WICKED of their own initiative begin conflict and war.[13]

16   BETTER IS A SMALL NUMBER FOR THE VIRTUOUS.
       [I.e.], BETTER are A SMALL NUMBER of people who go [to the aid of the virtuous people][14]

16b   THAN A MULTITUDE OF WICKED PEOPLE,[15] [i.e.], Amraphel and his allies, all of whose multitudes they [Abraham and his allies] succeeded in killing.[16]

18a   THE LORD IS CONCERNED FOR THE DAYS OF THE BLAMELESS.
       He is familiar with their behavior.

18b   THEIR PORTION, i.e., their receiving a reward from him LASTS FOREVER.

20   *kîqar kārîm*[17] [i.e.], 'like the light of a morning cloud, which appears at dawn and shines upon the expanses of the plain.[18] *kārîm* [means] 'plain'. It is the same word, which is attested [in the singular] in "a wide plain" [*kar nirḥāb*] (Isa. 30:23). [The word *yěqar* is the same word as is attested in] *'ādām bîqār* "a man in honor" (Ps. 49:13, 21) [and which is attested in the plural] *yěqārôt* "thick clouds" (Zech. 14:6).[19] Some, however, interpret *kîqar kārîm* "like the honor give to [*kikěbôd*][20] sheep" whom they fatten for the slaughter.[21]

21b   THE RIGHTEOUS IS GENEROUS AND KEEPS GIVING. [This refers to] the Holy One Blessed be He, who is RIGHTEOUS AND GENEROUS with His own wealth AND KEEPS GIVING to the one who lends to the other what he has stolen from him.[22]

22a   THOSE BLESSED BY HIM, the world's Virtuous One, SHALL INHERIT THE LAND.

23   THE STEPS OF A MAN [*geber*] [i.e.], he who is a champion [*gibbôr*] with respect to devotion to the Holy One Blessed be He.

24   HE WILL NOT BE CAST DOWN.
        [I.e.], he will not be hurled away so as to become abandoned
        [cf. v. 25].

25   I HAVE BEEN YOUNG [AND AM NOW OLD].[23]
        The prince of the world[24] authored it [this verse] for David
        was not so old.[25]

26a   HE, the virtuous person, IS ALWAYS GENEROUS to the
        poor AND LENDS to them.

26b   AND HIS SEED [wĕzar‘ô] [i.e.], whatever he has sown for
        charity ultimately is FOR A BLESSING.

30a   THE MOUTH OF THE RIGHTEOUS first CONSIDERS
        in his heart WISDOM to see the penalty the Torah has pre-
        scribed for every thing,

30b   AND afterwards HIS TONGUE SPEAKS WHAT IS
        RIGHT.[26]

31b   HIS FOOTSTEPS DO NOT FALTER.
        [I.e.], his steps do not slip.

35b   ûmit’arēh ‘WELL-ROOTED’ [i.e.] maśrîś "who had struck
        roots" (Job. 5:3). It is a cognate of [the infinitive ‘ārôt ‘rooted’
        in] "Whatever is rooted by the Nile" (Isa. 19:7).[27] Moreover,
        in Mishnaic Hebrew there are many [attestations of the ver-
        bal root in question. E.g.], a tree [a branch] "of which is
        broken off and it is attached [ûmĕ‘ôrāh] by its bark" (Mishnah
        ‘Uqṣin 3:8 and cf. passim there).[28] LIKE A ROBUST NA-
        TIVE TREE, [i.e.], like one of the natives of the country,
        who are rooted [therein] and are full of wealth.

37a   MARK THE BLAMELESS.
        Look at the behavior of the blameless[29] to learn from their
        deeds.

37b   FOR THERE IS A FUTURE FOR THE MAN OF INTEG-
        RITY.
        Though he may not have a [happy] past, he will have a
        [happy] FUTURE.

38   However, [as for] TRANSGRESSORS (38a) and WICKED
        PEOPLE (38b) they are CUT OFF (38b) and UTTERLY DE-
        STROYED (38a).

PSALM XXXVII, NOTES
    [1] Rendering of the lemma according to the understanding presupposed
by Rashi's comment; according to this view the verb tithar is the qal imperfect of the verb thr ‘compete’; so also Qimhi.

[2] See Darmsteter, "Les Gloses," *REJ* 56 (1908), p. 10; *REJ* 54 (1907), p. 222; see also Greenberg, *Foreign Words*, p. 120.

[3] Cf. BT Megillah 6b.

[4] Heb. *wĕ'az tiškôn*. Here Rashi paraphrases the third clause of the verse *šĕkon-'ereṣ* 'ABIDE IN THE LAND'. The form *šĕkon* can be construed either as an imperative or as an infinitive construct. If, as seems most plausible, the form is taken as an imperative, the verse consists of four imperatives: TRUST IN THE LORD, DO GOOD, ABIDE IN THE LAND, and REMAIN LOYAL. The rewards for carrying out these imperatives are set forth in v. 4 just as the rewards for carrying out the imperatives of v. 5 are set forth in v. 6. Rashi's paraphrase indicates that he construes *šĕkon* here as an infinitive construct employed to indicate the result of the behavior called for by the first two imperatives.

[5] Heb. *wĕtir'eh*; Rashi's paraphrase of the psalmist's imperative *ûrĕ'ēh*

[6] Heb. *tit'addēn*. The latter verb is attested in the Bible only in Neh. 9:25. In Rabbinic Heb. the *hitpa'el* forms of both *'ng* and *'dn* are frequently attested both in the sense 'be rejuvenated' and 'delight in dainties'; see Jastrow, *Dict.*, pp. 1044-1045; pp. 1091-1092.

[7] Rashi, following Midrash Tehillim here, substitutes a transitive pilpel imperative *galgēl* for the psalmist's *qal* imperative *gôl*. Interpreting v. 5 as meaning 'pray', Rashi makes explicit what is implicit in 'pray', i.e., request for daily needs, the content of the middle thirteen sections of the thrice-daily recited Amidah (see Birnbaum, *Daily Prayer Book*, pp. 85-90; see the discussion in Kadushin, *Worship and Ethics*, p. 107).

[8] So also Qimhi; contrast *Mahberet Menahem*, p. 126, s.v. *dm* II (followed by *BDB*, p. 198a, s.v. *dmm* I, *K-B³*, p. 217, s.v. *dmm* I), which does not distinguish between *dm* 'be silent' and *dm* 'wait'.

[9] I.e., a derivative of the verb *yhl* 'wait' (*BDB*, pp. 403-404), which appears in *Mahberet Menahem*, p. 175 as *hl* XII; Qimhi, in his commentary here distinguishes between the meaning of the verb *wĕhithôlēl*, which is related to that of the noun *tôhelet* and the root of our verb, which for Qimhi, followed by modern dictionaries of Biblical Heb., is *hwl* I 'whirl' (*BDB*, p. 297b).

[10] Heb. *lômar*, lit., 'saying'.

[11] Here Rashi paraphrases the psalmist's *wĕhitbônantā* by means of the verb *wĕtistakkēl* thus substituting the imperfect of a verb regularly used to mean 'look' in Late Heb. for the perfect consecutive of a verb which means 'look' only rarely even in Biblical Heb.

[12] Here Rashi reflects the view (by no means unanimous) that THE WICKED, unlike the virtuous, not only die but also lose their immortality; see Rashi at Deut. 33:6 following BT Sanhedrin 92a; Qimhi at Ezek. 18:21. The idea that personal immortality is denied the wicked is to be distinguished from the teaching of Avicenna reflected in Rashi's commentary at Ps. 49:11 that the development of one's intellectual capacity is a necessary prerequisite for achievement of immortality.

[13] Here Rashi responds to the exegetical question as to why the drawing of the sword, elsewhere referred to by the verb *šālap* (e.g., Judg. 3:22;

8:10 etc.), should here be referred to by the verb *pātaḥ* 'open', which often has the connotation 'begin' in Rabbinic Heb. (see dictionaries).

[14] The bracketed clause is not found in our Rashi ms.; it is supplied for clarity from other editions of Rashi's commentary on this verse.

[15] Rashi takes *ṣaddîq* 'THE VIRTUOUS PERSON' as a collective noun referring to VIRTUOUS PEOPLE in general. The adjectival noun *mĕʿaṭ* 'A SMALL NUMBER' can refer to 'A SMALL NUMBER of people' (so Rashi) or to 'A SMALL NUMBER of worldly possessions' (so Eng. versions). The noun *hāmôn* can denote 'wealth' (Isa. 60:5; Ezek. 29:19; Eccles. 5:9), 'tumult' (1 Sam. 14:19; 2 Sam. 18:29), and 'multitude' whether of persons (Judg. 4:7; Ezek. 39:11) or of things (1 Ch. 29:16; 2 Ch. 31:10). Rashi here understands *hāmôn* to mean 'a multitude of people' while NJV here understands *hāmôn* to mean 'abundance of wealth'; cf. *BDB*, p. 242.

[16] Rashi's comment is based upon Tanḥuma, ed. Buber, Lek Leka #7, which, in turn, is based upon Gen. 14; for additional Rabbinic parallels see Zohory, p. 111.

[17] Transliteration of the Heb. lemma, which is the basis of Rashi's discussion.

[18] Rashi's comment appears to be based upon the midrash attributed to R. Ishmael in Yalqut Shim'oni here.

[19] This observation is also based upon the midrash attributed to R. Ishmael in Yalqut Shim'oni here.

[20] Our Rashi ms. reads here by scribal error *kibĕkôr* 'like the firstborn.

[21] This interpretation is attributed to R. Phineas in Yalqut Shim'oni here.

[22] Cf. PRK, p. 424.

[23] Our Rashi ms. does not quote the bracketed portion of the verse; I have supplied it for clarity.

[24] As Rashi explains in his commentary on BT Yebamot 16b, "the prince of the world" is the name of an angel; similarly Rashi in his commentary on BT Hullin 60a; on angels in Rabbinic thinking in general and in Rashi's commentary in particular see our discussion at Ps. 29, n. 2; 49, n. 48; 50, n. 11; concerning the possible identification of "the prince of the world" with the angel Metatron in Hebrew liturgical poetry see Tosafot to BT Hullin 60a, s.v. "This verse."

[25] BT Yebamot 16b; note that here as at Ps. 45:2; Judg. 5:31; Ezek. 1:2-3 Rashi, in this case following BT, anticipates the modern critical view that the content of some chapters of Hebrew Scripture requires them to be the product of multiple authorship; see also BT Hullin 60a with reference to the non-Davidic and non-divine (but rather angelic) authorship of Ps. 104:31.

[26] Since NJV here accepts Ginsberg's demonstration that the verb *hāgāh* always means 'utter' and never means 'think, consider' (see our discussion at Ps. 1, n. 12), it follows that the two clauses of v. 30 represent an instance of synonymous parallelism: "THE MOUTH OF THE RIGHTEOUS UTTERS WISDOM// AND HIS TONGUE SPEAKS WHAT IS RIGHT." Since Rashi, however, assumes that *hāgāh* always means 'think, consider' (see our discussion at Ps. 1, n. 12), Rashi is forced to treat the

two clauses of v. 30 as synthetic parallelism. The addition of the temporal adverb 'afterwards', Rashi's implied interpretation of the psalmist's conjunctive *waw*, eliminates the apparent non-sequitur.

[27] *Mahberet Menahem* traces the two forms to a common root '*r* VII; contrast *BDB*, p. 788; *K-B³*, pp. 834-835, which trace them to the verb '*ārāh* I 'to be naked' (*Mahberet Menahem*, p. 290, '*r* V).

[28] With Zohory see also BT Hullin 128b-129a.

[29] Heb. *tĕmîmîm*; Rashi thus paraphrases in the plural the psalmist's employment of the singular *tām* 'BLAMELESS' as a collective.

PSALM XXXVIII

1 A PSALM OF DAVID. TO BRING TO REMEMBRANCE [i.e.], to be recited in time of trouble TO BRING TO REMEM-BRANCE Israel's trouble before the Holy One Blessed be He. He [King David] composed it on behalf of all Israel.

3a WERE AIMED [*niḥătû*] [i.e.], 'were thrown'. The verb *ḥt*[1] is employed with reference to[2] the bending[3] of a bow. In accordance with this usage is "can bend a bow of bronze" (Ps. 18:35). Now the nun is not part of the root in the word [*niḥătû*], for if it were so, he [the psalmist here in Ps. 38:3] would have had to say *ninḥătû* [instead of *niḥătû bî*].[4]

3b *wattinḥat* 'SHE HAS FALLEN' is a synonym of *wattērēd* 'she descended'.[5] Now in this instance the nun is a root letter in the word.

4 *mětom* 'SOUNDNESS' [i.e.], *tĕmîmût* 'blemishlessness'; *anterin* in [O.F.].[6]

5 *yikbĕdû* 'THEY ARE HEAVY' [i.e.], *kĕbēdîm* 'heavy'.[7]

7 *na'ăwêtî* 'I AM BENT' is a cognate of [the noun *'awwît* 'convulsion' in the Rabbinic Heb. expression] *'ōḥăzattô 'awwît* 'he gets a convulsion'.[8] [The noun corresponds in meaning to] *estordison*[9] 'confusion' in O.F.[10]

8 MY KIDNEYS ARE FULL OF INSIGNIFICANCE.[11] [I.e.], In my thoughts[12] I am insignificant in my own eyes.

9 *nĕpûgôtî* 'I AM BENUMBED' [i.e.], I have been weakened [*neḥlaptî*]. [The verb *nĕpûgôtî*] is from the same root as is[13] [the verb in] *wayyāpog libbô* "His heart went numb" (Gen. 45: 26) [and the noun *hăpûgôt* 'respite' in] *mē'ēn hăpûgôt* "without respite" (Lam. 3:49).

10 [YOU ARE AWARE OF][14] ALL MY DESIRES. [I.e], You know all my needs.

11 COMPLETELY SURROUNDED [*sĕharḥar*] [i.e.], encircled by anguish.[15] Now this [word *sĕharḥar*] belongs to [the category of] words [featuring] reduplicated [syllables][16] such as *yĕraqraq* 'very green' (Lev. 13:49); *'ădamdām* 'very red' (Lev. 13:49);[17] *sĕgalgal* 'very round';[18] *ḥomarmārû* 'they have become very distressed' (Lam. 1:20).[19]

12a [MY FRIENDS AND COMPANIONS][14] STAND BACK FROM MY AFFLICTION. When those who seem to be my FRIENDS when it is pleasant for them see that I suffer AFFLICTION, they do not stand by me during my difficulty, but THEY STAND BACK, and they do not help me.

12b THOSE WHO ARE CLOSE TO ME [i.e.], those who make themselves appear close.[20]

13a THEY SEEK.[21] They seek traps for me.[22]

13c   *yehgû* THEY CONSIDER'[23] [i.e.], 'they think'.[24]
14   BUT I AM LIKE A DEAF MAN.
       [The people of] Israel hear the insults directed at them by the
       Gentiles, but they do not respond. Why? [The answer is to be found
       in v. 16]:
16   FOR IT IS FOR YOU THAT I WAIT that You should redeem
       me and that You should save me from them.[25]
17   FOR I FEAR THEY WILL REJOICE OVER ME.
       Therefore [*lĕkak*],[26] we[27] are silent, for we think to ourselves,[28] "If
       we answer them with harsh words, perhaps they will see our de-
       feat and REJOICE over us WHEN our FOOT GIVES WAY, and
       they will VAUNT THEMSELVES AGAINST us, saying, 'Were
       you not gloating over your victory?'"
18a   FOR I AM ON THE VERGE OF COLLAPSE. Therefore we are
       anxious LEST THEY REJOICE over us (v. 17) for we are
       experienced in suffering, and we are always ready for defeat.[29]
18b   MY PAIN IS BEFORE ME. I am ready to suffer[30] ALWAYS.
19a   I ACKNOWLEDGE MY INIQUITY.
       My heart acknowledges to me MY INIQUITY, and therefore,
19b   I AM FEARFUL, i.e., afraid, OVER MY SIN that it should not
       cause me COLLAPSE (v. 18a) and PAIN (v. 18b).
20   [MY ENEMIES][14] HAVE GROWN STRONG WITH VITAL-
       ITY.
       They strengthen their VITALITY in peace and happiness.
21   FOR PURSUING GOOD [i.e.], FOR our adherence to the Holy
       One Blessed be He and His commandments.

PSALM XXXVIII, NOTES
  [1] See Rashi and our discussion at Ps. 18:35.
  [2] Heb. *nōpēl bĕ*; concerning this Gallicism in Rashi's Hebrew see the
discussion at Ps. 31:13.
  [3] Heb. *yĕriat*, lit., 'shooting of'; the rendering 'bending' is required both
by English usage, according to which a bow is bent, an arrow is shot, and
by the present context in Rashi's commentary, which refers to bows.
  [4] See the extensive discussion concerning the significance of Rashi's
comment here within the context of Rashi's view of the weak verb in Biblical Heb. in Henry Englander, "Rashi's View of the Weak, 'ayin-'ayin, and
pe-nun Roots," pp. 419-422.
  [5] The latter form is attested eight times in the Hebrew Bible: (Gen.
24:16, 45; Ex. 2:5; 1 Sam. 25:23; 2 Kgs. 1:10, 12; Ruth 3:6; Lam. 1:9)
while the form *wattinḥat* is found only here at Ps. 38:3.
  [6] I.e., 'whole, perfect'; note that O.F. *anterin* lies behind Modern French
entier and Eng. 'entire'; see Greenberg, *Foreign Words*, p. 187; Darmsteter,
"Les Gloses," *REJ* 56 (1908), p. 70.
  [7] Here as frequently in his commentaries (see, e.g., at Ps. 32:4; 34:10)
Rashi explains the meaning of the imperfect of a stative verb by employ-

ing a synonymous participle from the same root; see our discussion at the above citations.

⁸ Lit., 'a convulsion gets him'; cf. *'ăhāzanî haššābaṣ*, lit., 'agony has gotten me' in 2 Sam. 1:9; for Rabbinic Heb. *'ōḥāzattô 'awwît* 'he gets a convulsion' see BT Giṭṭin 9a; Hullin 60b. Note, however, that in Rashi's commentary to both of those texts the O.F. gloss is *cranpe*, i.e., Eng. 'cramp' while in most mss. and printed texts of Rashi's commentary here the O.F. gloss is *estordison* 'confusion'; see next note.

⁹ This is the generally accepted reading of the gloss here; see Greenberg, *Foreign Words*, p. 187; note, however, that the reading in our Rashi ms., *'agrôpîśôn*, appears to represent a conflation of *cranpe* and *estordison;* see previous note.

¹⁰ See Levy, *Contribution* #430.

¹¹ Rendering of the lemma according to the view presupposed by Rashi's comment; according to this view, which goes back to Rava (299-352 C.E.) in BT Shabbat 31b, the word *kesel* can denote 'kidney', which, in Rabbinic psycho-physiology can serve as the functional equivalent of the 'mind'; see our discussion at Ps. 49, n. 30. In fact the word *kesel* denotes 'sinew'; see Moshe Held, "Studies in Comparative Semitic Lexicography," in *Studies in Honor of Benno Landsberger on his Seventy-Fifth Birthday April 21, 1965*, ed. Hans G. Güterbock and Thorkild Jacobsen, Assyriological Studies, no. 16 (Chicago: University of Chicago Press, 1965), p. 402.

¹² This interpretation follows logically from Rashi's assumption that the noun *kesel* here denotes 'kidney'; see previous note.

¹³ Heb. *lĕšôn.*

¹⁴ Rashi does not quote the bracketed portion of the verse; I have supplied it for clarity.

¹⁵ Rashi makes the same comment at BT Giṭṭin 70a. There, however, the word for anguish is *dĕ'āgāh* while here it is *yāgôn*. Rashi's comment in both places indicates that according to him the primary meaning of *shr*, which is the root of *shrhr*, is 'circumambulate'; cf. Akkadian cognate *saḥāru* and cf. Sperling, "Late Hebrew *ḥzr* and Akkadian *saḥāru*," pp. 397-404.

¹⁶ For nouns with reduplicated syllables see *GKC* #84ᵇ k-m; for verbs with reduplicated syllables see there #55d-g.

¹⁷ According to Rashi at Lev. 13:49 the forms of the names of the colors which feature reduplication denote the most intense form of the color while according to Ibn Ezra there the forms featuring reduplication denote a less intense form of the color; see the extensive discussion in Athalya Brenner, *Colour Terms in the Old Testament*, JSOT Supplement Series, no. 21 (Sheffield: JSOT Press, 1982), pp. 106-110; contrast Rashi at Ps. 68:14.

¹⁸ As noted by Maarsen here, this example is unattested in the Bible, but it is well known in Rabbinic Heb. as in BT Shabbat 31a in the narrative concerning the Gentile who asks Hillel, "Why do Babylonians have very round heads?" Note that while *shrhr* may well be a form of the root *shr* and that while *'ădamdām* is certainly a more (or less) intense form of *'ādom* and *yĕraqraq* a more (or less) intense form of *yāroq*, the adjective *sĕgalgal*

cannot be demonstrated to derive from a root *sgl*; see the discussion in Ben Yehuda, *Dict.*, vol. 8, pp. 3955-3956.

[19] See Gordis, *The Song of Songs and Lamentations*, p. 159.

[20] NJV renders *qĕrôbay* "my kinsmen". For *qārôb* as an adjective 'related by kinship' (always employed with the preposition *'el* or *lĕ*) see Lev. 21:2, 3; 25:25; Num. 27:11; Ruth 2:20. In Ps. 15:3 and Job. 19:14, as here at Ps. 38:12, *qārôb*, lit., 'one who is near', is employed in parallelism with nouns designating companions. Qimhi explains here that *qārôb* denotes 'one who is close' whether through business or as neighbors or as relatives, and he stresses that our verse is an example of synonymous parallelism. Rashi also appears to conclude from the parallelism "x STAND BACK FROM MY AFFLICTION//y STAND FAR OFF" that *qĕrôbay* here is a synonym of *'ōhăbay* 'MY FRIENDS'. Since, therefore, *'ōhăbay* here means "those who seem to be my friends but who in fact are not", it follows that the synonymous *qĕrôbay* must likewise mean "those who make themselves appear close but who in fact are not."

[21] Our Rashi ms. reads here *wayĕbaqqĕšû*, a reading which is found in many other medieval Bible mss. and which is preferred by BHS here; NJV's rendering 'LAY TRAPS' reflects the standard reading *wayĕnaqĕšû*; see next note.

[22] Rashi's comment seems to support the standard reading *wayĕnaqĕšû mĕbaqšê napšî* "Those who seek my life (i.e., to kill me) set traps for me."

[23] Rendering of the lemma according to the understanding of the verb *hāgāh* presupposed by Rashi's comment and confirmed by Rashi's treatment of the verb elsewhere (see our discussion at Ps. 1, n. 12; see also at Ps. 37, n. 26).

[24] Heb. *yahšĕbû*.

[25] With Zohory cf. BT Shabbat 88b; for parallels see Zohory, p. 114.

[26] By paraphrasing the Bible's *kî* as *lĕkak* 'therefore', Rashi indicates that in the present context *kî* is a subordinate conjunction rather than an asseverative meaning 'indeed'; concerning the various nuances of *kî* in Biblical Heb. see lexicons; see Muilenberg, "The Linguistic and Rhetorical Usages of the Particle *kî* in the Old Testament," pp. 135-160; Aejmelaeus, "Function and Interpretation of *kî* in Biblical Hebrew," pp. 193-209 and the extensive literature cited there; see also Rashi's *responsum* concerning the nuances of the particle *kî*, above, pp. 94–105.

[27] Rashi construes the psalmist's first person singular throughout Ps. 38 as referring to personified Israel. He thereby transforms Ps. 38 from an individual lament to a community lament; see Rashi at v. 1.

[28] Lit., 'we say in our hearts', a well known idiom in Rashi's Heb. denoting 'think'.

[29] The latter two clauses paraphrase v. 18b.

[30] This must be Rashi's meaning in light of (1) Rashi's paraphrase of v. 18b in his comment on v. 18a; and (2) the meaning of *bā' 'al* lit., 'came upon' throughout Rashi's Commentary on Psalms (see Ps. 35:15; 37:8; 39:2; 40:16; 73:1,7,16,18; 80:1), sc., 'experience, suffer'. The literal meaning of Rashi's comment here is, "It is ready to come upon me."

PSALM XXXIX

1   FOR JEDUTHUN. The name of a person. [He was] one of the singers [who performed liturgical music before the Ark in the City of David in the days of David according to 1 Ch. 16:41].[1] There was also a musical instrument whose name was *jeduthun*.[2] An aggadic midrash [states that the expression JEDUTHUN in psalm titles] refers to the judgments [*haddātôt*], i.e., the troublesome decrees, which were decreed against[3] Israel.[4]

2   I RESOLVED I WOULD WATCH MY STEP....
As for us,[5] it was our intention[6] to watch ourselves amidst all the troubles we experience so that we neither question nor speak harshly against God's justice even though the wicked people who are before us are making trouble for us.

3a   We were[7] DUMB, SILENT many days, and we even were
3b   STILL WITH RESPECT TO GOOD [i.e.], even with respect to words of Torah because of the fear of them [our adversaries],
3c   AND as a result our[7] PAIN WAS INTENSE, and we trembled, and in our silence our[7]
4a   MIND arose[8] WITHIN us,[7]
4b   and in our thought[9] it was aflame[10] within us like FIRE, and that is what was causing us
4c   to SPEAK before You WITH our TONGUE.[11]
The following [verse] is what we were saying:[12]
5a   TELL us, O LORD, our TERM [i.e.], how long we shall be in trouble
5c   so that we may KNOW when we shall be FINISHED with it.[13]
6a   LOOK, MY DAYS are measured HANDBREATHS.
[I.e.], a person's DAYS are numbered. Just as an object, which is measured in handbreaths [is limited in size] so are a person's days limited [in number].[14]
6b   Our[7] SPAN, i.e., our old age, IS AS NOTHING IN YOUR SIGHT.

[The Biblical Heb. noun] *ḥeled* 'SPAN' is a cognate of [the Rabbinic Heb. noun] *ḥălûdāh* 'rust'[15] [which means] *roilie* [in O.F.].[16]

6c   ALL...EVERY MAN. [This verse is another instance of inversion, and it is to be understood as follows]: AS FOR EVERY MAN, his days and his status[17] ARE VAPOR.

7a   ALAS IN A SHADOW [*bĕṣelem*], [i.e.], in darkness. Dunash explained that it [*ṣelem* in this usage is a homonym of *ṣelem* 'image' and] a cognate of *ṣalmāwet* 'darkness'.[18]

7b   ALAS VAPOR is[19] all their bustle and pride.[20]

7c   HE HEAPS UP grain[21] in the field all the days of the harvest, NOT KNOWING WHO WILL GATHER it into the house, for perhaps he will die before the ingathering.

8   AND NOW WHAT DO I WISH? [I.e.], What is the request which I request and beseech[22] of You?

9   It is only that You DELIVER ME FROM MY TRANSGRESSIONS, and MAKE ME NOT THE BUTT OF THE BENIGHTED Esau. Bring also upon him [Esau] afflictions and pains so that he will not be able to say to me, "You suffer, but as for us, we do not suffer." Now this prayer caused the bringing of punishments in the form of diseases upon the Gentiles.[23]

10b   FOR IT IS YOUR DOING that You have made us endure more trouble than all the Gentiles.

11   FROM THE FEAR OF YOUR HAND, [i.e.], from the fear of Your plagues.[24] [The noun] *tigrat* 'FEAR OF' is a cognate of [the verb *wayyāgor* 'was alarmed' in] "Moab was alarmed" (Num. 22:3). The taw is a preformative[25] in the word [*tigrāh* 'fear'] as is [the prefixed taw in each of the following words]: *tĕnûbāh* 'produce' (Isa. 27:6); *tĕlunnāh* 'murmuring'[26] *tĕqûmāh* 'ability to stand up' (Lev. 26:37), *tĕḥinnāh* 'supplication for favor' (1 Kgs. 8:38 = 2 Ch. 6:29), 'favor' (Josh. 11:20; Ez. 9:8).[27]

12a   WITH PUNISHMENTS, which are written in the Torah for our iniquities, with which we offended You, You punished us.[28]

12b   CONSUMING LIKE A MOTH WHAT HE TREASURES. You made our flesh deteriorate like a garment, which it [a moth][29] ate. WHAT HE TREASURES, [i.e.], his [a person's own] flesh is what he treasures.[30]

14 LOOK AWAY FROM ME. [I.e.], Withhold Your hand[31] from striking me. AND LET ME RECOVER, [i.e.], let me regain my strength.[32]

PSALM XXXIX, NOTES

[1] For the source see Rashi's *Introduction to the Psalter*.

[2] In 1 Ch. 16:41; 25:1, 3, 6; 2 Ch. 5:12; 35:15 Jeduthun is juxtaposed with personal names; hence it also would seem to be a personal name. In Ps. 39:1; 62:1; 77:1, however, jeduthun seems to be the name of a musical instrument. Similarly it has been debated whether Heb. *māhôl* denotes 'dance' or a musical instrument and whether Ugar. *mrqdm* denotes 'dancers' or 'castinets' since both these terms are found juxtaposed with terms for musical instruments; see the discussion in Gruber, "Ten Dance-Derived Expressions in the Hebrew Bible," pp. 343-344.

[3] Heb. *'al*. Here is a rare instance in our Rashi ms. where a letter (here the *'ayin* has been omitted and then entered above the line.

[4] For the source see Rashi's *Introduction to the Psalter*.

[5] Here as in Ps. 38 Rashi treats the psalmist's first person utterances as the words of personified Israel. Hence he paraphrases the psalmist's 'I' as we, the psalmist's 'MY' as 'our', etc.

[6] *hāyāh bĕlibbēnû*, lit., 'it was in our heart' (cf. Ps. 36:2), Rashi's paraphrase, which indicates that he interprets *'āmartî*, lit., 'I said', to mean 'I thought'; cf. NJV's "I resolved."

[7] See above, n. 5.

[8] Heb. *qām*; the psalm text reads *ham* 'was hot'; hence NJV's "My mind was in a rage"; perhaps the reading *qām* is simply a scribal error for *ham*.

[9] On Rashi's paraphrasing the psalmist's 1st pers. sing. pronominal suffixes as 1st pers. pl. see above, n. 5. Following *Mahberet Menahem*, p. 134, Rashi holds that the noun *hăgîg*, which is attested only here and in Ps. 5:2, is derived from the same root as *hegyôn* (here in Rashi's paraphrase of the psalm; for biblical attestations see the discussion at Ps. 1:2, above); see the discussion in Dahood, *Psalms*, here; see also above at Ps. 5:2.

[10] Here Rashi employs the masc. sing. participle, which could also be interpreted as a present while the psalmist employs the 3d pers. fem. sing. imperfect; I have translated using the past tense because all the other verbs in vv. 2-4 are past tense verbs.

[11] Regardless of whether the noun *hăgîg* and the verb *hāgāh* are cognates, once it is recognized that *hăgîg* means 'murmuring' (so *BDB*, p. 211b) the synonymous parallelism in v. 4 should be obvious: MY HEART WAS AFLAMED WITHIN ME WHEN I MURMURED//A FIRE BURNED (WHEN) I SPOKE WITH MY TONGUE. Since Rashi construes *hăgîg* as a cognate of *hāgāh*, which he wrongly interprets to mean 'think' (see discussion at Ps. 1:2), he must account for the logical relationship between the thought referred to in the first two thirds of v. 4 and the speech referred to in the final third of the verse. This is the purpose of his comment here.

[12] RSV and NJV also treat v. 5a as a quotation.

[13] The literal meaning of the verse is as follows: TELL ME, O LORD, MY END, AND AS FOR THE MEASURE OF MY DAYS, WHAT IS IT? LET ME KNOW HOW FLEETING I AM. The noun *qiṣṣî* 'MY END' here means 'the appointed time for the end of my life' just as *qiṣṣô*, lit., 'his end' means 'the appointed time for the end of his life' in the Medieval Hebrew hymn "Unetaneh Toqef" (see Philip Birnbaum, *High Holyday Prayer Book* [New York: Hebrew Publishing Co., 1951], p. 361 where *qiṣṣô*, is rendered 'a timely end'); this usage of Heb. *qēṣ* corresponds to Phoenician *'ēt* 'appointed time for the end of my life' in *KAI* 14:2. When Rashi reads into our psalm the personification of persecuted Israel, *qēṣ* can no longer mean 'the appointed time for the end of an individual's life'. Hence he construes *qēṣ* here to mean 'span of time allotted' as in the Passover Haggadah where *ḥiśśēb 'et-haqqēṣ* means 'He deducted from the amount [*ḥeśbôn*] of the (originally) allotted span of time' (see *The Passover Haggadah*, ed. Nahum N. Glatzer, rev. ed. [New York: Schocken Books, 1969], p. 30 and n. 3 there). The latter midrash seeks to account for the discrepancy between the four hundred years originally allotted to Israel's enslavement in Egypt according to Gen. 15:13 and the mere two hundred and ten years of actual enslavement according to Rabbinic tradition (see Rashi at Gen. 15:13); cf. Josephus, Antiquities, ii, xv, 2 for the similar tradition of two hundred and fifteen years of enslavement and Josephus' attempt to reconcile this tradition with Gen. 15:13. Note that in Ps. 39:5 itself *hādēl* 'FLEETING' (so NJV) refers to the temporality of the psalmist's earthly existence while in Rashi's paraphrase the same adjective in the plural, which we render 'FINISHED', refers to the temporariness (in the long view) of Israel's suffering.

[14] Cf. *Mahberet Menahem*, p. 200.

[15] See Mishnah Kelim 13:5; Tosefta Tohorot 3:4; etc.

[16] I.e., Modern French *rouille*; see Darmsteter, "Les Gloses françaises de Raschi dans la Bible," *REJ* 56 (1908), p. 71; see the discussion at Ps. 17, n. 25.

[17] Heb. *maṣṣābô*, a cognate of the participle which means 'ENDURES' in the psalm verse.

[18] *Teshuvot Dunash*, p. 109; see discussion at Ps. 23:4.

[19] Here Rashi employs the personal pronoun *hû* as copula, thus making the noun 'VAPOR' the subject of a nominal sentence; see next note.

[20] NJV follows Rashi in paraphrasing this clause as a nominal sentence: "mere futility is his hustle and bustle." RSV's "Surely for nought are they in turmoil" is a literal rendering of the clause.

[21] Contrast Qimhi and NJV, who interpret our verse as a reference to the gathering of monetary wealth.

[22] Here Rashi paraphrases by means of the participle *mĕyaḥēl* 'beseech' the psalmist's cognate noun *tôḥaltî* 'MY SUPPLICATION'.

[23] This comment is based upon the midrashim in Genesis Rabbah 88:1. The thesis of these midrashim is that Jews suffer for their sins during the present pre-eschatological era so that they should not have to suffer in the

post-eschatological era (commonly called "the world to come") and that
the Gentiles who will be punished in the post-eschatological era are free
from suffering during the present pre-eschatological era (commonly called
"this world"). This thesis is apparently contradicted by the reality that
Gentiles do indeed suffer disease in this world. This latter fact is accounted
for by the midrashim at Genesis Rabbah 88:1 as the consequence of God's
hearkening to the prayer of Israel in Ps. 39:9 as interpreted in the midrashim
attributed to R. Hama b. R. Haninah (3ᵈ cent. Palestinian Amora) and R.
Samuel b. Nahman (late 3ᵈ and early 4ᵗʰ cent. Palestinian Amora). The
content of this prayer as interpreted by these sages is found in Rash's comment here. The conviction that God hearkened to this prayer reconciles,
according to Rashi and the midrashim, the apparent contradiction between
the thesis outlined above and the reality of disease among the Gentiles.

²⁴ On 'hand' (of God) as an idiom for 'plague' in Biblical Heb. and
Rashi's understanding of this see above at Ps. 21:9a; 32:4.

²⁵ Heb. yĕsôd nōpēl; see discussion at Ps. 119:5.

²⁶ This is the only one of the four examples given here, which is not
attested in the Bible in the form in which Rashi quotes it here. For the
plural of this noun see Ex. 16:12; Num. 14:27; 17:20.

²⁷ On taw preformative nouns in general see GKC #85p-r.

²⁸ Rashi responds here to the exegetical question, "WITH which PUN-
ISHMENTS?"

²⁹ The bracketed expression is missing in our Rashi ms.

³⁰ With Maarsen cf. Job. 2:2 for the same idea. Note that Rashi in his
comment paraphrases the psalmist's masculine form of the noun by means
of the feminine form.

³¹ See above, v. 11.

³² Here Rashi explains the meaning of a rare Heb. word by means of a
more common one.

PSALM XL

2a I TRULY PRAYED TO THE LORD in Egypt.[1] Now this psalm, [like Pss. 38-39, was composed] on behalf of all Israel.

2b HE INCLINED TOWARD ME His ear.[2]

3a OUT OF THE PIT OF TUMULT,[3] [i.e.], OUT OF the imprisonment[4] of Egypt and OUT OF THE TUMULT of their roaring.

3b THE SLIMY CLAY, [i.e.], from the [Reed] Sea.[5]
    [The word] hayyāwēn[6] 'SLIME' is a synonym of repeš [7] 'mire'; [it means] fanjos 'mud' in O.F.[8]

3d STEADIED [kônēn], [i.e.], he directed [hēkîn].[9]
    'ăšūrāy 'MY LEGS',[10] [i.e.], ṣᵉʿāday 'my footsteps'.[11]

4   A NEW SONG, [i.e.], the Song at the Sea (Ex. 15:1-19).[12]

5   OR TO FOLLOWERS OF [wᵉśāṭê] FALSEHOOD, [i.e.], those who turn aside [haśśōṭîm] from the path of virtue toward the falsehood of idolatry.

6b YOUR WONDERS AND YOUR PLANS FOR US. For our sake You created Your world; for us You divided the [Reed] Sea;[13] and You made PLANS in advance to benefit us. [E.g.], You delayed us in the wilderness forty years, and [it was] because of the Amorites, who had cut down the trees and destroyed their country when they heard that Israel were coming forth from Egypt to possess their land.[14]

6c NONE CAN EQUAL YOU.
    No king or deliverer is to be compared to Him [God].

6c LET ME TELL, AND LET ME SPEAK.
    If I were[15] to tell and to speak,

6d THEY ARE MORE THAN CAN BE TOLD.

7a,c YOU DID NOT ASK FOR...BURNT OFFERING AND SIN OFFERING
    at the time of the Giving of the Torah.[16] [This verse] is in accord with what is stated in the Bible, "Now if you will truly hearken to My voice" (Ex. 19:5).[17]

7b YOU OPENED FOR ME [MY EARS].[18] [I.e.], You made them hollow for hearing.

8a THEN, at the time of the Giving of the Torah,[19] I SAID, to You,

8b SEE, I HAVE ENTERED into the bond of Your covenant[20] [by saying], "We will do and obey" (Ex. 24:7). Now this fact

8d-e IS WRITTEN ABOUT ME as testimony IN A SCROLL DOCUMENT,[28] [i.e.], in the Torah of Moses.[21]

9   YOUR TEACHING IS IN MY INMOST PARTS.

10a   I PROCLAIMED [YOUR] RIGHTEOUSNESS, [i.e.], even at the
        Well (see Num. 21:17-18a), the Song of Deborah (Judg. 5:1-31a).[22]

10b   I DID NOT WITHHOLD [*'eklā'*] [i.e.], I did not hold back [*'emnā'*]
        [The verb *kāla'* 'withhold'] is the same verb as is attested in. "The
        rain…was withheld" (Gen. 8:2) [and in v. 12 of the present psalm],
        "YOU WILL NOT WITHHOLD," [which means]."Do not hold
        back."

12   WILL PROTECT ME, [i.e.], will guard me.[23]

13   ENVELOPED, [i.e.], encircled.[24]

15   TO DESTROY IT, [i.e.], to put and end to it. [The root of *lispôtāh*
        'TO DESTROY IT'] is identical with that with which we render
        into Aramaic "Until all that generation had come to an end [*tom*]"
        (Num. 32:13; Deut. 2:14): *'ad děsap.*[25]

16   LET THOSE… BE DESOLATE. [I.e.], Let them ask.
        BECAUSE OF THEIR EMBARRASSMENT. When they have
        received THEIR EMBARRASSMENT BECAUSE OF everything
        in the [same] measure that they dished it out and in the [same]
        way that they went against me. [The expression] *'al 'ēqeb* 'BECAUSE
        OF' [means literally] *en mes treces*[26] 'in my footsteps' in O.F WHO
        SAY OVER ME [*lî*] "AHA!".[I.e.], WHO SAY concerning me
        [*bišěbîlî*],[27] "AHA!".[I.e.], when trouble is experienced [by the Jews],
        they rejoice in our calamity.

18a   Every attestation of POOR AND NEEDY in the Book of Psalms
        (Ps. 35:10; 37:14; 40:18; 70:6; 74:21; 86:1; 109:16, 22) is a meta-
        phor for Israel.

18b   MAY HE THINK OF ME. May He give attention to me, think-
        ing of my poverty and my neediness so as to deliver me.

PSALM XL, NOTES
   [1] This interpretation is consistent with Rashi's interpretation of vv. 3-
4; q.v.
   [2] Perceiving that the verb *wayyēṭ* is transitive, Rashi, taking the usage
as ellipsis, supplies the missing direct object; cf. *BDB*, p. 641a concerning
Hos. 11:4.
   [3] Rendering of the lemma according to RSV margin, which corresponds
to the interpretation presupposed by Rashi's comment here. Note that while
KJV, RSV, NJV and others treat *bôr ša'ôn* as a construct genitive, Rashi
(see below) treats the two nouns as the compound object of the preposition *mi-*'OUT OF'.
   [4] The interpretation of *bôr* 'PIT' as a metaphor for enslavement derives from the use of *bôr* to designate 'prison' in Gen. 41:14; Ex.12:29; Jer.
37:16; 38:6-11, 13; Zech. 9:11.
   [5] When the deep water of the Reed Sea was made to stand as walls

on either side of the people of Israel (Ex. 14:23, 29), the floor of the sea, which but a moment before had been covered by the deep water, was SLIMY CLAY.

⁶ Attested only here and in Ps. 69:3.

⁷ Isa. 57:20.

⁸ See Levy, *Contribution* #454.

⁹ While Biblical Heb. employs the *polel* of the root *kwn* 'be firm' (see *BDB*, p. 465) and its passive, the *polal* (Ps. 37:23), as well as the *hiphil* (Jer. 10:23; Ps. 119:33; Prov. 16:9) to refer to God's directing aright the steps of people, Rabbinic Heb., followed by Rashi's Heb. and Modern Heb., generally avoids the *polel* and *polal and* employs the corresponding *hiphil*. Hence Rashi here translates the Biblical expression into the corresponding Rabbinic Heb. expression, which would be more familiar to his readers.

¹⁰ So NJV; see Dahood, *Psalms*, 1:95, n. 5.

¹¹ So *BDB*, p. 81a.

¹² Contrast Midrash Tehillim here, followed by Qimhi. They assume that the speaker is King David while Rashi holds that the speaker is personified Israel; see Rashi at v. 2a.

¹³ Up to this point Rashi has explicated 'YOUR WONDERS'; from here on Rashi will explain 'YOUR PLANS'. Rashi's midrashic distinction suggests that a non-midrashic interpretation of the verse requires treatment of 'YOUR WONDERS AND YOUR PLANS' as an hendiadys meaning 'Your wondrous plans'.

¹⁴ The source of this midrashic account of the forty years in the wilderness as a benefit rather than as a punishment (contrast Num. 14:26-45) must be Mekilta, vol. 1, pp. 171-172; see also Mekilta deRashbi, p. 45; so already Maarsen here. Rashi cites the same midrash at Ps. 68:11.

¹⁵ Lit., 'If I came'.

¹⁶ Here Rashi responds to the exegetical question, "When was it that YOU DID NOT ASK?"

¹⁷ Other editions of Rashi quote also Jer. 7:22; q.v.; see also Am. 5:15; 1 Sam. 15:22.

¹⁸ Literal rendering of the lemma, which reflects the understanding presupposed by Rashi's comment; note that Rashi does not quote the bracketed portion of the verse. Rashi assumes that in the expression *kārāh 'ozen* 'open the ear', which is attested only here at Ps. 40:7, the verb *kārāh* 'dig' (see dictionaries) means 'hollow out', i.e., remove the excess ear wax, which interferes with a person's understanding. It appears that an ear so stuffed with excess ear wax that neither hearing nor understanding can take place is referred to both as *kābĕdāh* 'heavy, laden (with wax)' (Isa. 59:1) and *hikbîdû* 'they were laden (with wax)' (Zech. 7:11); cf. Isa. 6:10, "Make his ears heavy (with wax)." Jer. 6:10 speaks of those who are incapable of heeding the word of the LORD because "their ear is uncircumcised." It is reasonable to suggest that this expression derives from a description of a person whose hearing was temporarily impaired because the outer ear was covered over with ear wax just as the expression 'uncircumcised of flesh' (Ezek. 44:7)

derives from the description of a man or boy whose prepuce is covered over by the foreskin.

[19] Here Rashi responds to the exegetical question, "When?"

[20] The expression *māsoret habběrît* 'bond of the covenant' is attested in the Bible only at Ezek. 20:37.

[21] The term 'Torah of Moses' (commonly 'Law of Moses' in Bible translations) is found in the Bible in Josh. 8:31, 32; 23:6; 1 Kgs. 2:3; 2 Kgs. 14:6; 23:25; Mal. 3:22; Dan. 9:11, 13; Ez. 3:2; 7:6; Neh. 8:1; 2 Ch. 23:18; 30:16. For its significance in the Josh. Kgs., and Mal. verses see commentaries. All agree that in the hagiographa verses the term refers, as it does here in Rashi, to the Pentateuch.

[22] Rashi points out in his commentary on Judg. 5:31 that the portion of the verse following the caesura, "And the land was tranquil forty years," does not belóng to the Song of Deborah.

[23] Here Rashi notes that the less frequently attested verb *nāṣar* 'keep, guard, protect' is synonymous with the more frequently attested verb *šāmar*.

[24] The verb *'āpap*, 'envelop' is attested in only five places in the Bible: 2 Sam. 22:5; Jonah 2:6; Ps. 18:5; 40:13; 116:3. It is not surprising, therefore, that Rashi finds it necessary to explain that it is a synonym of the common verb *sābab* 'encircle'; on the nuances of the latter verb see Gruber, "Ten Dance-Derived Expressions in the Bible," pp. 331-335.

[25] Rashi here quotes Targum Onkelos, the Babylonian Talmud's official Aramaic rendering of the Pentateuch (see BT Megillah 3a; BT Qiddushin 49a); hence Rashi says here, "with which *we* render into Aramaic," i.e., in accord with the officially accepted Aramaic rendering. The root is *spy* 'end', which Rashi, following Menahem, would regard as *sp*.

[26] I.e., Eng. 'tracks'; see Rashi also at Ps. 56:7; 70:4; 78:20; 119:33; see also Banitt, *Rashi: Interpreter of the Biblical Letter*, p. 33.

[27] Here Rashi indicates that the preposition *lě*, whose common meaning is 'to', is employed in Ps. 40:16 in the sense 'concerning'; similarly NJV, q.v.

PSALM XLI

2a [THOUGHTFUL]¹ OF THE WRETCHED, [i.e.], a sick person, by visiting him. [This interpretation of the word *dāl* 'THE WRETCHED'] is in consonance with what is stated in the Bible in the Amnon narrative, "Why are you so *dal*² i.e., 'sick'] (2 Sam. 13:4).

2b IN BAD TIMES. I.e., Gehinnom. Now what is his reward in this [pre-eschatological] era?³ [It is the following]:

3 THE LORD WILL GUARD HIM, [i.e.], him who visits him [the sick], and who deals kindly with him [the sick].⁴

4a ON HIS SICKBED. When he⁵ too gets sick, He WILL SUSTAIN HIM. Now what is the meaning of 'ON HIS SICKBED'? It means a patient's seventh day [of illness] when he is extremely sick. Thus it is explained in Aggadath Tehillim.⁶

4b YOU TURN OVER HIS WHOLE BED DURING HIS ILLNESS.
Even when his illness is severe for him so that his place of rest and relaxation is turned over.⁷

5 I SAID, "O LORD, HAVE MERCY ON ME."
As for me, I have no kind⁸ visitors, and when I cry out on account of my illness and say,⁹ "O LORD, HAVE MERCY ON ME...,"

6a MY ENEMIES rejoice over me, and they say an EVIL thing OF ME:

6b "WHEN WILL HE DIE... ?"¹⁰

7a HE SPEAKS FALSELY. [I.e.], he makes himself appear as though he empathizes, but while he sits in my presence

7b HIS MIND STORES UP EVIL thoughts for him:¹¹

7c what evil HE WILL SPEAK¹² when he leaves, and when HE GOES OUT, SPEAKS it.¹³

8b CONCERNING ME THEY THINK something, which is EVIL¹⁴ FOR ME. Now what is the thought?¹⁵ [It is]:

9a "MAY SOMETHING BANEFUL FLOW IN HIM."
[I.e.], may all the wicked deeds, which he has done, FLOW, i.e., be poured into his body.

9b *wĕhô'îl* 'insofar as' [is the meaning of] *'ăšēr*. "HE'LL NOT

ARISE FROM HIS BED AGAIN." Thus they[16] curse[17] me.[18]

10c MADE BIG AGAINST ME A TRAP ['*āqēb*],[2] Ḳi.e.], 'ambush' [*ma'ărāb*].[19] [The word '*āqēb* 'trap, ambush'] is the same word as is attested in "and his ambush on the west side of the city..." (Josh. 8:13).[20]

11 When You have mercy on me and You let me rise again[21]

12 I shall KNOW[22] THAT YOU ARE PLEASED WITH ME when[23] MY ENEMY CANNOT SHOUT a shout of joy OVER ME.

13 Let me see that YOU SUPPORTED[24] ME BECAUSE OF MY INTEGRITY.

14 BLESSED IS THE LORD....[25]
So shall I bless You when I shall have recovered from my illness.

PSALM XLI, NOTES

[1] Rashi does not quote the bracketed portion of the verse; I have supplied it for clarity.

[2] In MT the word order is *kākāh dal;* in our Rashi ms. it is *dal kākāh*.

[3] See Ps. 25, n. 23.

[4] Cf. Midrash Tehillim here; BT Nedarim 40a.

[5] I.e., he who is praised in vv. 2-3.

[6] See Midrash Tehillim here. There, however, the reading is 'fourth day'. The midrash is inspired by the realization that '*ereś dawwāy* 'SICKBED' means literally 'bed of the habitually sick' and not simply 'bed of the sick', which would be '*ereś dāweh*. The form *dawwāy* is an "intensified participle of the active verb." The doubling of the second root consonant indicates "a longer continuation of the state" (*GKC* #84). Hence the midrash suggests that from the fourth day of the illness onward the patient is no longer considered *dāweh* 'sick' but *dawwāy* 'habitually sick'. Rashi, perhaps following a different version of the midrash, holds that one goes from being 'sick' to 'habitually sick' on the seventh day of the affliction.

[7] In Rabbinic literature a person who is severely sick is spoken of as having his/her bed turned over. Hence God's mitigation of the illness is described by the psalmist as turning over the bed (again) so that it is now right side up. Note that NJV here understands the verb *hpk* 'turn over, transform' in the abstract rather than in the physical sense.

[8] Heb. *lĕṭôbāh*; cf. Rashi's comment on v. 3.

[9] Here Rashi intimates that he interprets the perfect verb '*āmartî* 'I SAID' (so NJV) as present in meaning.

[10] Rashi in his comment on vv. 5-6 solves the problem of the apparent non-sequitur in vv. 5-6a by treating v. 6a as the main clause, v. 5a as a temporal clause modifying the ver" *yō'mĕrû* 'THEY SAY', and v. 6b as a quotation following the verb 'THEY SAY'. Rashi also indicates that the

expression *yō'mĕrû ra' lî* 'THEY SAY EVIL OF ME' is a *double entendre*. Hence, in commenting on v. 6a Rashi interprets it both as an idiom meaning 'they rejoice over me' and literally, 'they say evil about me'.

[11] The biblical text here has *lô* 'FOR HIM'; Rashi explicates, *lĕaṣmô* 'for himself'.

[12] Literal interpretation of the imperfect *yĕdabbēr* presupposed by Rashi's comment; NJV renders it as a present 'HE SPEAKS THEN'.

[13] Rashi, following Midrash Tehillim here, takes v. 7c, *yēṣē' lahûṣ yĕdabbēr* as a *double entendre;* hence here as in his comment on v. 6a Rashi interprets the clause twice, once according to each of the two meanings he finds therein.

[14] Rashi here indicates that the feminine adjective *rā'āh* (NJV renders "the worst") is an adjectival noun functioning as the direct object of the verb 'THEY THINK'.

[15] Rashi's point here is that v. 9 is a quotation introduced by the verb 'THEY THINK' in v. 8b.

[16] Those spoken about in vv. 6-8.

[17] Our Rashi ms. reads *mitqallĕlîm* 'they curse themselves'; most likely the latter reading is a scribal error for *mĕqallĕlîm* 'they curse', the reading found in other editions of Rashi commentary here.

[18] I.e., the psalmist.

[19] See Banitt, *Rashi: Interpreter of the Biblical Letter*, pp. 33, 99-100.

[20] Qimhi, followed by KJV and RSV, takes *'āqēb* 'heel' in Ps. 41:10 to be a form of the word 'heel'.

[21] Rashi's paraphrase of v. 11, a request, as a response to the exegetical question arising from v. 12, "When SHALL I KNOW THIS?"

[22] Rashi's paraphrase of the psalmist's perfect.

[23] Rashi indicates that here Biblical Heb. *kî* means *ka'ăšer* 'when'.

[24] In the present context the perfect verb *tāmaktā*, lit., 'YOU SUPPORTED', can be construed either as a prophetic perfect thanking God in advance for hearkening to the supplication contained in vv. 11-12, or as a precative perfect voicing a request (on the precative perfect in Biblical Heb. see the discussion at Ps. 16:2). Rashi here indicates that he construes the verb as a precative perfect.

[25] Ps. 41:14 is not a part of Ps. 41 but the doxology, which concludes the first of the five books into which the psalter is divided (for the doxologies at the end of Books Two, Three, and Four respectively see Ps. 72:18-19; 89:53; 106:48; see commentaries. Rashi, however, indicates by his comment here that he construes v. 14 as part of Ps. 41.

PSALM XLII

1   BY THE SONS OF KORAH, "Assir and Elkanah and Abiasaph" (Ex. 6:24). They were originally part of their father's conspiracy, but at the time of the revolt they disassociated themselves.[1] When all those who were around them were swallowed up when the earth opened its mouth, their place remained in the earth's mouth in accord with what is stated in the Bible, "The sons of Korah did not die" (Num. 26:11). It was there [in the earth's mouth] that they sang a hymn of thanksgiving and [from there that] they ascended, and it was there that they composed these [eleven] psalms [attributed to them: Pss. 42; 44-49; 84; 85; 87; 88].[2] Divine inspiration rested upon them, and they prophesied concerning the Exiles and concerning the destruction of the Temple and concerning the kingship of the Davidic dynasty.[3]

2   AS THE STAG SHE CRIES FOR WATERCOURSES. The verb *'ārag* 'cry' is employed with reference to[4] the voice of the hind just as the verb *nāham* 'roar' is employed for a lion, *šîqûq* 'growling' for a bear, *gā'āh* 'moo' for bulls, and *ṣipṣûp* 'chirping' for birds.[5] Our rabbis said, "This hind is the kindest of the wild animals for when the wild animals are thirsty for water they assemble in her presence so that she should look imploringly to Heaven. What does she do? She digs a hole (cf. Eccles. 10:8), and she puts her head into it,[6] and she cries [*gō'āh*],[7] and the Holy One Blessed be He has mercy upon her so that the Abyss sends up water for her sake."[8] AS THE STAG SHE CRIES.[9] It is not stated, "As the hind[10] SHE CRIES" but "AS THE STAG." Scripture spoke in a combination of the masculine and the feminine [grammatical forms to intimate the following]: The male cries [*'ôrēg*] concerning the matter of the water as we have explained. As for the female, when she squats[11] to give birth [and] her womb contracts so that she screams, the Holy One Blessed be He has mercy upon her, and he summons for her a snake, which strikes at her abdomen so that her womb opens up.[12]

3b   O WHEN WILL I COME TO APPEAR BEFORE GOD[13]

by ascending [to Jerusalem] for the festival?[14] Now he [the psalmist] prophesied here concerning the destruction of the Temple,[15] and the utterance three times, "WHY SO DOWN-CAST?" (Ps. 42:6, 12; 43:5)[16] corresponds numerically to the three kingdoms that will in the future [17] put an end to the Temple Service. [In each instance] Israel cry out [to God], and they are redeemed from the kingdom of Babylon, of Greece, and of Edom [respectively].[18]

3a   MY SOUL THIRSTS. Israel says[19] this during the Babylonian Exile.

4   MY TEARS HAVE BEEN...FOOD. From here we learn that sorrow takes away a person's appetite so that he does not desire to eat. In the same vein he [the Bible] says concerning Hannah, "She wept and would not eat" (1 Sam. 1:7).[20]

5a   LET ME RECALL THESE THINGS..., i.e.,

5c   WHEN I WALKED WITH THE CROWD [sāk]. This is what I remember[21] with my soul pouring itself out[22] when I remember the festival pilgrimages [to Jerusalem] when I used to walk with a throng of people[23] moving with them[24]

5d   TO THE HOUSE OF GOD.[25]

[The word] sāk [can be] a synonym of ḥešbôn 'sum'.[26] [The word] sāk [can also be] a synonym of 'a wall of people'.[27] [The word] sāk [can also be] a synonym of ṣabbîm 'litters' (Isa. 66:20) and 'eglôt ṣāb 'litter wagons' (Num. 7:3).[28] [As for the verb 'eddaddēm 'I MOVED WITH THEM'],[29] it is the same verb as is attested in mědaddîn 'ăgālîm ûsěyāḥîn....wěhā'iššâh mědaddâh 'et-běnâh "[On the Sabbath] they may make calves and foals walk...and the mother may make her son walk" (Mishnah Shabbat 18:2).[30] Now this word ['eddaddēm] serves as [a synonym of the] two words 'eddaddeh 'immāhem 'I move with them' just as [in] "They were unable dabběrô 'to speak with him' lěšālôm 'peacebly'" (Gen. 37:6) [dabběrô lěšālôm is a synonym of] dabbēr 'immô běšālôm.[31]

5e   THE THRONG CELEBRATES A FESTIVAL [means] that they [THE THRONG] were going to celebrate a festival [lāḥōg].[32] Now an aggadic midrash [states that] ḥôgēg is a Greek loanword, for they [the Greeks] call a pool of water ḥôgěgîn.[33] Now it was on the basis of this [interpretation].that the poet [Eliezer ha-Kalir] wrote 'ōṣēm hāmôn ḥôgēg wěšôṭēp kannōhār "the tremendous throng celebrating the festival and the river-like flood (of people)."[34]

6a   [The verb] *tištôḥăḥî* 'DOWNCAST' is the same verb as is attested in "We lie prostrate [*šāḥāh*] in the dust" (Ps. 44:26). Now, as for [the verb] *šḥ*,[35] when it is employed in the *mitpaʿel* conjugation,[36] the *taw* [of the *mitpaʿel* prefix] is placed between the word's root letters[37] according to the manner of every word whose first root letter is *shin*.[38]

6c   HAVE HOPE, [i.e.], wait expectantly for Redemption.

7   I REMEMBER YOU SINCE THE LAND OF JORDAN, [i.e.], since what You did for us at the Jordan [River] and the mountains of Hermon.[39] After all the provocation with which we had provoked Your anger at Shittim (Num. 25:1-9) You dried up the Jordan [River] for us [so that we could cross it] (Josh. 3-4).[40] SINCE MOUNT MIZAR, [i.e.], Mt. Sinai,[41] which is small[42] compared to the rest of the mountains. After we had provoked Your anger thereon by the golden calf episode You forgave us our iniquities, and You accompanied us.[43.]I recall all these things in my Exile, in which You withhold benefitting me and Your punishments are newly devised against me one after another.

8a   ABYSS TO ABYSS. [I.e.], one trouble summons her colleague[44]

8b   AT THE SOUND OF YOUR WATERSPOUTS, which shower upon me punishments like flooding water until

8c   ALL YOUR BREAKERS AND BILLOWS HAVE SWEPT OVER ME.[45]
[The word] *mišbārêkā* 'YOUR BREAKERS' is a synonym of [*gallê*] *hayyām* "[waves of][46] the sea" (Isa. 48:18). [They are called 'breakers' because] its [the sea's] billows ascend upward, they break, and they fall.[47]

9a   BY DAY MAY THE LORD VOUCHSAFE HIS FAITHFUL CARE
May the light of redemption come, and MAY THE LORD VOUCHSAFE to us HIS FAITHFUL CARE.

9b   AT NIGHT, [i.e.], in the darkness of exile and trouble. MAY *šîrōh* BE WITH ME. [I.e.], may His abiding be with us. [The word] *šîrōh* is a synonym of 'abiding' [*ḥănāyāh*]. Hence we render [Heb.] *wayyiḥan* "He encamped" (Gen. 26:17).by Aramaic *ûšĕrā'* "He encamped."[48] I learned this [that *šîrōh* here in Ps. 42:9 is a cognate of Aram. *šĕrā'* 'abide'] from the Massorah Magna,[49] which listed this [the word *šîrōh* with the word *šîrōh* 'his song' in] "His song[s] were one thousand and five" (1 Kgs. 5:12) in the alphabetical list of homonyms. It [the Massorah Magna] taught me that this [word *šîrōh* in Ps. 42:9] is not a form of the word *šîr* 'song'. However, an aggadic midrash interprets it as a form of the word *šîr* 'song', and it interprets it as follows: Israel say to the Holy One Blessed be He, "Remember for us what You did for us in Egypt. You commanded us for that day, the day before Passover, and we observed it, and on that night we sang to You a hymn [*šîrāh*], the Hallel [Pss. 113-118]. Now, however, I [the congregation of Israel][50] observe many commandments, but You do not redeem me.[51] Therefore,

10   I SAY TO GOD, MY ROCK, WHY HAVE YOU FOR-
     GOTTEN ME....

11   BY MURDER OF MY BONES MY FOES REVILED ME.
     It is so caught in my bones how much my foes are reviling
     me that it seems as though they are killing me.[52]

PSALM XLII, NOTES

[1]   See Numbers Rabbah 18:8. The two assertions: (1) that Korah's sons were originally part of their father's conspiracy; and (2) that Korah's sons repented and disassociated themselves from the conspiracy solve two exegetical problems. The assertion, "The sons of Korah did not die" (Num. 26:11) intimates that at the time when the conspirators were executed by an act of God (Num. 16:31-35; 26:9-10) the sons of Korah were not part of the revolt. Since, however, there is no earlier reference to Assir, Elkanah, and Abiasaph's disassociation from the conspiracy, Rabbinic tradition accounts for the important place, which Korah's sons occupy in the Book of Psalms and in 1 Ch. 9:19 as a reminder of the value of repentance. See Midrash Tehillim at Ps. 45:1 #4.

[2]   Cf. the *baraitha* in BT Sanhedrin 110a; Numbers Rabbah 18:20: "A place was set up for them in Gehenna." Rashi here at Ps. 42 does not speak as he does in his commentary on Num. 26:11, following the *baraitha*, of Gehenna. Instead, he distinguishes here between the earth's ingestion ("The earth opened its mouth" [Num. 16:31a]) and the earth's digestion ("it swallowed them...." [Num. 16:31b]). According to Rashi here at Ps. 42:1, Korah's three sons were among the conspirators whom the earth ingested. Because they repented at the time of the rebellion, the earth did not swallow them.

[3]   If it be assumed that the sons of Korah refer to Moses' three contemporaries—Assir, Elkanah, and Abiasaph—the question arises as to how the Korahite psalms can refer to the Exiles (Ps. 44:12; 85:2; and see below in Rashi's commentary for additional references), the Davidic dynasty (Ps. 45), and the destruction of the Temple (Ps. 87). 1 Ch. 9:19 suggests

that those who were known in the monarchic period as Korahites were indeed descendants of Abiasaph and his brothers. Since, therefore, the only "sons of Korah" known to the Bible are Moses' contemporaries, the only way to account for their knowledge of post-Mosaic events is to assume that they possessed the gift of prophecy. See passim in Midrash Tehillim on the Korahite psalms.

⁴ Heb. *nōpēl 'al*, a Gallicism, derived from O.F. *cheoir* 'fall, happen, apply, fit'; see Banitt, *Rashi: Interpreter of the Biblical Letter*, p. 14, n. 37.

⁵ Rashi's source is *Teshuvot Dunash*, p. 31. For *nāham* 'roar' of lions see Isa. 5:29; Prov. 19:12; 20:2; 28:15. The verb *šāqaq* 'growl' is used of a bear only in Prov. 28:15; *gā'āh* 'moo' is attested only in 1 Sam. 6:12 (of a cow) and Job. 6:5 (of a bull); *ṣipṣēp* is attested in the sense 'chirp' (of a bird) only in Isa. 10:14. In Isa. 38:14 the same verb means 'neigh' (of a horse) while in Isa. 8:19 and 29:14 it is used of the wound made by the ghosts of the dead.

⁶ Cf. George Cansdale, *All the Animals of the Bible Lands* (Grand Rapids: Zondervan, 1970), pp. 90-92.

⁷ The same verb, which, according to Rashi's previous comment, characteristically refers to the sound made by oxen.

⁸ Rashi's source is Midrash Tehillim on Ps. 22:1 #14.

⁹ Literal rendering of the lemma presupposed by Rashi's comment; note that in the Hebrew text of the psalm here we have a masculine noun with a feminine verb.

¹⁰ I.e., the feminine noun with the feminine verb; note that our Rashi ms. has the reading *kě 'ayyālôt* 'as hinds', most likely a scribal error for *kě 'ayyelet* 'as the hind'.

¹¹ See Gruber, *Aspects*, p. 324, n. 2.

¹² Cf. almost verbatim the midrash in Yalqut Shim'oni here.

¹³ So Massoretic vocalization. The consonantal text means, "AND LET ME SEE THE FACE OF GOD," which is an idiomatic expression meaning, "Let me serve God at His Temple." The same idiom, with the tetragrammaton instead of the generic name 'God', occurs elsewhere only in Ex. 23:15, 17; 34:20, 23; Deut. 16:4, 16. In all these cases the expression refers to assembling at the LORD'S sanctuary for the three festivals of Passover, Shavuot (also called in English Weeks or Pentacost), and Sukkot (also called in English Booths or Tabernacles). Cf. Rashi's comment here. With reference to Heb. *rā'āh pānîm* 'see the face' in the sense 'serve' cf. Akk. *ina pān dagālu*; see *CAD*, D, pp. 23b-24a; note also that the latter expression is the source of the title 'those who see the king's face', i.e., 'the king's most intimate servants' in 2 Kgs. 25:19; Jer. 52:25; Esth. 1:14.

¹⁴ See previous note.

¹⁵ Therefore he speaks longingly of attendance at the Temple.

¹⁶ This midrash of unknown origin assumes that Pss. 42-43 of the now standard editions of the Bible constitute "a single lyric consisting of three stanzas, each of which is followed by a refrain (xlii, 5, 11, xliii, 5)" (so Dahood, *Psalms*, 1:255; and so most modern commentaries). Note that Pss. 42-43 are treated as a single psalm also in Midrash Tehillim, q.v., and in

many mss. of the Book of Psalms (see *BH³* at Ps. 43:1) and so also in our ms. of Rashi's Commentary on Psalms; see Ps. 43, n. 1 and Ps. 44, n. 1.

[17] I.e., the future from the perspective of Korah's sons who were contemporaries of Moses.

[18] The Babylonian kingdom put an end to the Temple Service in 586 B.C.E. The Temple Service was restored in accord with the Edict of Cyrus (Ez. 1:1-4) in 538 B.C.E. (Ez. 3:1-7). The Greek kingdom refers to the kingdom of Antiochus IV, which profaned the Temple in 168 B.C.E. The Temple Service was restored by Judah Maccabee in 165 B.C.E. Edom in Rashi's comment here refers to both the Roman Empire, which put an end to the Temple Service in 70 C.E., and Christendom, to whom the Jews in Rashi's time and place remained subjugated. "They are redeemed" here in Rashi's comment is a prophetic present. Rashi intimates that just as the Temple Service was restored after having been abolished by the Babylonians and after having been abolished by the Greeks so will it be restored soon after having been abolished by Edom. Rashi intimates that the millenium during which the Temple was not restored from 70 C.E. to his own day is no different from the three years during which it was suspended under the Greeks and the forty-eight year period during which it was suspended under the Babylonians. All three suspensions were revealed to the sons of Korah. As the two came to an end in due course so, Rashi intimates, the present suspension of the Temple Service will come to an end in due time.

[19] The verb is feminine to indicate that the speaker personifies *kĕnesset Yiśra'ēl* 'the congregation of Israel', which is feminine in gender.

[20] Rashi's source is Midrash Tehillim here.

[21] Rashi's paraphrase of v. 5a.

[22] Rashi's paraphrase of v. 5b.

[23] Rashi's paraphrase of v. 5c.

[24] Rashi's paraphrase of v. 5d.

[25] Having given the general sense of the portion of v. 5, which concludes with the phrase "TO THE HOUSE OF GOD," Rashi will now proceed to discuss the possible meanings of the noun *sāk* and the verb *'eddaddēm* Then he will attempt to show that the interpretation of these words as 'crowd' and 'move' (so now also NJV) is justified not only contextually but also etymologically.

[26] This meaning, which is not attested in the Bible, but which is known in Rabbinic, Medieval and Modern Heb. (see Ben Yehuda, *Dict.*, vol. 8, pp. 4033-4035), could be used to justify Rashi's understanding of *sāk* in Ps. 42:5 as 'a throng of people', i.e., 'a large sum of people'.

[27] Assuming that *sāk* is a cognate of the verb *sākak* 'overshadow, screen'; see *BDB*, p. 696 for the verb and its cognates. According to this second possible etymology *sāk* still designates 'a throng of people'.

[28] Like the second suggestion, this third suggested etymology means that *sāk* is derived from the verb *sākak* 'cover'. Note, however, that while according to Rashi's first two suggestions *sāk in* Ps. 42:5 denotes 'a throng of people', according to the third, *sāk* denotes 'litter wagon(s) full of people'.

Note also that *sāk* in Rashi's third sense is attested nowhere else in either Biblical or post-Biblical Heb.

29 Lemma omitted in our Rashi ms by scribal error.

30 The verb *dādāh* 'walk, proceed' is attested in the Bible only twice—here at Ps. 42:5 and once again in Isa. 38:15—both times in the *hitpaʿel*; see Mandelkern, p. 291b. In the two attestations in Mishnah Shabbat 18:2 cited here by Rashi, the verb appears in the causative *piʿel*; see dictionaries of Rabbinic Heb. Note that here in the Mishnah as twice only in the Bible (Isa. 45:10; 49:15) the noun *'iššāh*, lit., 'woman', means specifically 'mother'.

31 Rashi appears to assume that his contemporaries would not recognize a Heb. verb or infinitive with a pronominal suffix expressing the object of a preposition. Therefore, he explains the meaning of *'eddaddēm* by paraphrasing as verb followed by a preposition + pronominal suffix, *'eddaddeh ʿimmāhem* just as would a teacher in Modern Israel where the spoken dialect does not normally employ the contracted form. After dealing with the meaning of the word, Rashi returns to explain the grammatical phenomenon of verb or infinitive + pronominal suffix expressing the object of a preposition. On the latter phenomenon see *GKC* #57-60. Note that Rashi the master pedagogue does not digress from his main point, the meaning of the word *'eddaddēm*, to discuss the pronominal suffix *ēm*. He returns to the latter bit of grammatical *minutiae* only after dealing fully with the main point. All who would teach Hebrew Scripture and Heb. philology would do well to follow Rashi's example. In passing Rashi notes that while Medieval (and Modern) Heb. expresses 'peaceably' by *bĕšālôm*, Gen. 37:6 employs the expression *lĕšālôm*. In Biblical Heb. either expression can be used; for examples of both see Mandelkern, pp. 1182-1183. Contrast the distinction between the two expression drawn by R. Abin the Levite in BT Berakot 64a. He contends that the former expression is used when the destination is death, the latter when the destination is a temporal one.

32 In all three of its attestations in the Hebrew Bible—Zech. 14:16, 18, 19—the infinitive *lāḥōg* can only mean 'to celebrate (the festival of Sukkot)'. Rashi here asserts that the participle *ḥōgēg* in Ps. 42:5c also means 'celebrate a festival'. As Rashi indicates, however, this interpretation, which is supported by his exegesis of vv. 3 and 5a-b, is open to question; see previous note.

33 The midrash is found in Midrash Tehillim here. While Rashi uses the midrash simply to present another interpretation of the word *ḥōgēg* in Ps. 42:5, the midrash has another purpose, namely, to praise Israel for their faithfulness in observing the festival pilgrimages. Hence the midrash states, "What is the meaning of 'THE THRONG *ḥōgēg*'? It [the word *ḥōgeg*]Ǧ is a Greek loanword [derived from] *'ḥōgîm* of water' [i.e., aqueducts]. Just as aqueducts had no limit [as to the amount of water that could flow through them] so did Israel have no limit [as to their numbers] when they were going on pilgrimage [to Jerusalem] for the festival." The Greek word is ἀγωγός; see Krauss, *Lehnwörter*, pt. 2, p.249.

[34] In his Yoṣer (liturgical poems for the Morning [i.e., Shaharit] Service) for Shabbat Shekalim (i.e., the Sabbath which precedes or coincides with the New Moon of Adar [in a leap year Second Adar]; for the text of the hymn in question see *Otzar Ha-Tefillot* (2 vols.; Vilna: Romm, 1928), vol. 2, p. 154.

[35] Rashi, following Menahem Ibn Saruq, treats both geminates such as *šḥḥ* and hollow verbs such as *šwḥ* as biliteral roots.

[36] We would say *hitpaʿel*; see Englander, "Grammatical Elements and Terminology in Rashi's Biblical Commentaries," *HUCA* 11 (1936), p. 388, n. 157. Englander, "A Commentary on Rashi's Grammatical Comments," *HUCA* 17 (1942-43), p. 482 insists that *šāḥāḥ* 'she is prostrate', the root of which is *šwḥ*, is not a cognate of *tištôḥăḥî*, which is *šḥḥ;* so *BDB*, pp. 1001, 1005. Rashi could not help but treat them as cognates derived from a biliteral root *šḥ;* see previous note.

[37] Remember that Rashi considers the root in question biliteral; see nn. 35, 36.

[38] See *GKC* #19n; #54b.

[39] Here Rashi interprets the psalmist's 'HERMONIM' as referring to an entire mountain range (contrast NJV's rendering "Hermon"). On this mountain range, which is frequently referred to in the Bible simply as "Mt. Hermon" (Deut. 3:8; 4:48; Josh. 11:17; 12:1,.5; 13:5, 11) see Michael Avi-Yonah and Efraim Orni, "Hermon, Mount," *EJ* 8:373-375.

[40] The source of this midrash is Midrash Tehillim here. As for why Israel should be especially grateful that despite what had happened at Shittim (Num. 25:1-9) God dried up the Jordan for Israel, note that Israel's last stopping place before crossing the Jordan was Shittim (Josh. 3:1). Presumably, Israel's passing a second time through Shittim would, as it were, remind God of what had happened there previously. God's recalling those events would, presumably, justify His not letting Israel cross the Jordan River.

[41] See Yalqut Shimʿoni here. Mount Mizar is mentioned only once in the entire Bible, here at Ps. 42:7. The midrash here follows the midrashic tendency to identify the unknown and infrequent personal or place name with a known and frequent personal or place name.

[42] Heb. *ṣāʿîr* (= Akk. *ṣeḥru* 'small'), cognate of the proper name Mizar (Heb. *miṣʿār*).

[43] Note that the final clause of Rashi's comment here is a paraphrase in the indicative of the request Moses makes in Ex. 34:9.

[44] Note that Rashi here treats 'ABYSS' as a metaphor for 'trouble' and that he anticipates his interpretation of v. 8 in his final comment on v. 7c.

[45] Note that v. 8c is found verbatim also in Jonah 2:4b.

[46] The bracketed expression is omitted from our Rashi ms. by scribal error.

[47] Cf. the discussion of the semantic equivalent *dky* 'wave' in Ps. 93:3 in Harold R. (Chaim) Cohen, *Biblical Hapax Legomena in the Light of Akkadian and Ugaritic*, SBL Dissertation Series, no. 37 (Missoula Montana: Scholars Press, 1978), pp. 25-26.

[48] Rashi refers to the rendering in Targum Onkelos, which is Rabbinic Judaism's official Aramaic translation of the Pentateuch; see BT Megillah 3a; Qiddushin 49a.

[49] *Ochlah W'ochlah*, ed. Frensdorff, p. 64.

[50] Heb. *kĕneset Yiśrā'ēl*, which is feminine; hence the verb. 'keep' is also feminine.

[51] Cf. Midrash Tehillim here.

[52] Rashi responds here to the exegetical question, "What is meant by 'MURDER OF MY BONES'?"

PSALM XLIII[1]

1b   FROM AN UNKIND NATION. That is Edom, for Esau[2] dwelt among two virtuous peoples but did not learn from their behavior.[3]

1a   JUDGE ME. [I.e.], Vindicate me.[4]

3   SEND FORTH YOUR LIGHT AND YOUR TRUTH.
[YOUR LIGHT is a metaphor for] the king Messiah, who is referred to metaphorically as light in accord with what is stated in the Bible, "I prepared a lamp for my Messiah" (Ps. 132:17). [YOUR TRUTH is a metaphor for] Elijah the Prophet, who is true, a truthful prophet.[5]

4   ...TO...TO GOD, the Holy One Blessed be He,[6] who is MY DELIGHT, MY JOY.[7]

PSALM XLIII, NOTES

[1] The comment on Ps. 43 is treated in our Rashi ms. as the continuation of the comment on Ps. 42 because, as Rashi indicates in his comment on Ps. 42:3b, q.v., Rashi regards Ps. 42-43 as a single psalm. Since the short comment on Ps. 13 is appended in our ms. to the comment on Ps. 12 and since the short comment on Ps. 28 is appended to the comment on Ps. 27, Ps. 44 is numbered in our ms. as Ps. 41;see our discussion at Ps. 13, n. 1 and at Ps. 28, n. 1.

[2] The progenitor of Edom (Gen. 36:1-9; Deut. 2:3); see next note.

[3] This comment is based upon the midrash on Ob. 1:1 attributed to R. Isaac, a 3^d cent. C.E. Palestinian Amora, in BT Sanhedrin 39b. R. Isaac refers to "the wicked Esau, who lived with two virtuous people but did not learn from their behavior." Rashi in his commentary there explains that the 'two virtuous people' were Esau's mother Rebekah and his father Isaac. Both in R. Isaac's midrash and in Rashi's use of it here in his commentary on Ps. 43:1 Edom the nation and Esau the progenitor of that nation are treated as one. Treating Esau and Edom as one is an example of the Rabbinic notion of corporate personality. See Kadushin, *The Rabbinic Mind*[3], pp. 82, 218; id., *Organic Thinking* (New York: Bloch, 1938), pp. 10-11; p. 268, n. 31. For Rashi, Edom read into the prayer of collective Israel in Ps. 42-43 probably refers to Christendom. See M. Seligsohn, "Edom, Idumea," *JE* 5:41.

[4] The exegetical problem here is to determine the appropriate nuance of the verb *šāpaṭ*, which can mean 'govern' (Isa. 33:22), 'judge impartially' (Gen. 16:5; Ps. 82:1), 'punish' (Ex. 6:6; Ezek. 7:3, 8; Ob. 1:21), 'deliver' (Judg. 3:10), as well as 'vindicate' (1 Sam. 24:16; 2 Sam. 18:19); see dictionaries; see also Banitt, *Rashi: Interpreter of the Biblical Letter*, pp. 32-33.

⁵ The midrashim in Midrash Tehillim here identify Elijah with the LIGHT and the Davidic Messiah with the TRUTH using other prooftexts.

⁶ Here Rashi indicates that Biblical Heb. *'ēl*, which can mean also 'a (foreign) god' (Ps. 44:21; 81:10), here designates 'the Holy One Blessed be He', i.e., 'God'. Just as Rashi, following Talmudic tradition, uses the title 'the Holy One Blessed be He' so would modern Orthodox Jews say 'Ha-Shem', lit., 'the [divine] Name' and so would modern Christian Bible scholars say 'Yahweh'.

⁷ The biblical text employs apposition. Rashi clarifies the relationship of 'MY DELIGHT, MY JOY' to 'GOD' by making 'MY DELIGHT, MY JOY' the predicate of a relative clause modifying 'GOD'.

PSALM XLIV[1]

2a   WITH OUR EARS WE HAVE HEARD. Here you learn that the sons of Korah [to whom this psalm is attributed in v. 1] were speaking on behalf of these generations, who come after them, for were [it] on their own behalf [that they spoke], it would not have been appropriate for them to say,

2b   "OUR FATHERS HAVE TOLD US," for in fact they [the sons of Korah] themselves saw the miracles of the wilderness,[2] of the [crossing of the Reed] Sea [on dry land],[3] of the [crossing of the] Jordan [River on dry land],[4] and the wars of Joshua.[5] Thus is it [our verse] explained in Aggadath Tillim [sic].[6]

3c   YOU BROUGHT MISFORTUNE ON PEOPLES. You brought misfortune[7] on seven great peoples,[8] and You drove them out[7] before us, and You with Your hand and Your might

3a-b   DISPLACED them from their land, and YOU PLANTED our ancestors therein.[9]

5   DECREE VICTORIES FOR JACOB even now.

6   WE TRAMPLE [*nābûs*] OUR ADVERSARIES. [I.e.], we tread upon [*nirmôs*] our enemies.[10] [The verb *nābûs*] is from the same root as [the participle *mitbôseset* 'wallowing' in Ezek. 16:6], "wallowing in your blood" [and the participle *bôsîm* 'tramping' in Zech. 10:5], "They shall be like warriors tramping through the mud of the streets."

10   YET YOU HAVE REJECTED AND DISGRACED US. Even now that YOU HAVE REJECTED us AND DISGRACED US, we

9   PRAISE YOUR NAME UNCEASINGLY.[11]

11a   YOU MAKE US RETREAT. [The imperfect verb *tĕšîbēnû*, which could serve in Biblical Heb. as a past, a present, or a future] is a present [in this context].[12]

11b   PLUNDERED FOR THEMSELVES. [I.e.], "They have despoiled" our properties "each one for himself" (Num. 31:53).

20a   *kî* YOU CAST US DOWN INTO A PLACE OF JACKALS. This *kî* serves as a synonym of *ka'ǎšer* 'when'[14]. [Vv. 20-22 therefore mean]: Even when You threw us down "into[15] a land of desert and pit" (Jer. 2:6), the wilderness, THE PLACE OF JACKALS,[16]

20b   and You covered us[7] IN BLACKNESS [ṣalmāwet], [i.e.], 'darkness' [hošek],[17] nevertheless,

21   IF WE FORGOT THE NAME OF OUR GOD,

22   He WILL SEARCH IT OUT, FOR HE KNOWS THE SECRETS....

23b   AS SHEEP OF SLAUGHTER, [i.e.], AS SHEEP for slaughter.[18]

PSALM XLIV, NOTES

[1] In our Rashi ms. this psalm is designated as Ps. 41; see Ps. 43, n. 1.

[2] For these miracles see Deut. 8:2-4.

[3] Ex. 14:15-21.

[4] Josh. 3-4.

[5] Josh. 6-12.

[6] Cf. Midrash Tehillim here.

[7] The psalmist employs an imperfect form of the verb to express the past tense; Rashi paraphrases using the perfect form of the same verb.

[8] See Deut. 7:1, the only complete list in the entire Pentateuch of 'the seven nations', which lived in the land of Israel before Israel returned from Egypt under the leadership of Joshua. Deut. 7:1's reference to these people as 'seven nations' becomes standard in Rabbinic literature.

[9] Cf. Midrash Tehillim here.

[10] Here Rashi explains that the verbal root bws, which is attested fifteen times in the Bible is synonymous with the verbal root rms, which is attested twenty-seven times in the Bible. Rashi also explains here that qām 'foe' is a synonym of the more familiar 'ōyēb 'enemy'.

[11] Rashi, ignoring the SELAH at the end of v. 9, treats vv. 9-10 as a single sentence in which v. 10 is a subordinate clause and v. 9 the main clause. To do so he must construe the particle 'ap at the beginning of v. 10 not as 'YET' (NJV) but as 'ap 'im 'even though'. For the various meanings of Biblical Heb. 'ap see dictionaries.

[12] See the discussion at Ps. 1:3 above.

[13] Rashi here uses Num. 31:53 to clarify the realia behind Ps. 44:11. In both verses the direct object is missing. Therefore, Rashi supplies it in quoting from Num. 31:53.

[14] On the various meanings of Biblical Heb. kî see Antoon Schoors, "The Particle kî, " pp. 240-76; Aejmelaeus, "Function and Interpretation of kî in Biblical Hebrew," pp. 193-209; and the literature cited by Aejmelaeus, especially James Muilenberg, "The Linguistic and Rhetorical Usages of the Particle kî in the Old Testament," pp. 135-60; see also Rashi's responsum concerning the nuances of the particle kî, above, pp. 94–105.

[15] In Jer. 2:6 the prefixed preposition b means 'in, through'; in Rashi's comment on Ps. 44:20 the same preposition means 'into'.

¹⁶ Cf. Jer. 10:22; 49:33; Mal. 1:3. Note that while NJV takes the word *tannîm* in our verse to be a biform of the singular noun *tannîn*. sea monster' (on the latter noun see now Chaim (Harold) Cohen, "The Other Meaning of Biblical Hebrew *tannîn* 'Snake' or 'Crocodile'," in *H. M. Gevaryahu Festschrift*, ed. Ben-Zion Lurie and Shmuel Avramsky [Jerusalem: Israel Society for Biblical Research, 1989], pp. 75-81 [in Hebrew]) Rashi takes the word *tannîm* here as elsewhere in the Hebrew Bible (e.g., Isa. 34:13; 35:7; 43:20; etc.) to be a plural noun meaning 'jackals'. Ironically, just as MT at Ezek. 32:2 employs the form *tannîm* to denote 'crocodile' or 'sea monster' so does our Rashi ms. employ here the form *tannîn* to denote 'jackals'.

¹⁷ Here Rashi reminds us of what he has demonstrated at Ps. 23:3, q.v. (see also Rashi at Ps. 39:7, s.v. *ṣelem*), that *ṣalmāwet* means 'darkness'.

¹⁸ Rashi, following the practice of Late Heb. and Late Aram., substitutes a preposition for the construct genitive. Also he indicates here that the feminine form *ṭibḥāh*, which is attested only here in Ps. 44:23 and in Jer. 12:13 (and with a pronominal suffix also at 1 Sam. 25:11), is synonymous with the frequently attested masculine form *ṭebaḥ* 'slaughter'.

PSALM XLV

1   FOR LILIES.[1] [I.e.], it was in honor of Torah scholars [that] they [the sons of Korah] composed this song, for they [Torah scholars] are soft like LILIES and comely like LILIES, and like LILIES they make good deeds blossom.[2] [The term] MASKIL [in the title means that this psalm was written for the sons of Korah] by a ghost-writer.[3] A LOVE [yĕdîdôt] SONG, [i.e.] a love ['ăhûbîm] SONG,[4] A SONG in praise of them [the LILIES, i.e., the Torah scholars],[5] to endear them to ordinary people and to endear their [the LILIES, i.e., the scholars'] Torah to them [ordinary people].

2a   MY HEART IS ASTIR. Thus the poet began his song.[6] [The poet means], "MY HEART motivated within me GRACIOUS WORDS[7] in praise of you, Torah scholars. [The verb] rāḥaš is a *verbum movendi* and so is every form of [the verbs] šîrûṣ 'creeping' and riḥûš 'rustling'.[8]

2b   I SAY MY WORKS FOR[9] THE KING.
[The expression 'MY WORKS' refers to] this song, which I composed, i.e., I worked it out.[10]
I SAY it [this song] FOR[9] one who is worthy of being king, in accord with what is stated in the Bible, "By virtue of me [personified Wisdom] kings shall reign" (Prov. 8:15).[11]

2c   MY TONGUE is glib with songs like the PEN OF AN EXPERT SCRIBE.[12]
I read[13] in R. Moses the Interpreter's book[14] [that the word] māhîr 'ready'[15] [means] 'expert'[16] in Arabic.[17]

3a   YOU [Torah scholars respectively][18] ARE FAIRER THAN[19] ALL MEN, who occupy themselves with a temporal occupation. Why?

3b   Because[20] YOUR SPEECH IS ENDOWED WITH GRACE to render legal decisions correctly.

3c   THEREFORE [GOD] BLESSED YOU [FOREVER][21] in accord with what is stated in the Bible, "May the LORD grant strength to His people" (Ps. 29:11a).[22] And what is his [the Torah scholar's] reward? [It is that] "The LORD will bless His people with well-being" (Ps. 29:11b).[23]

4a   GIRD YOUR SWORD UPON YOUR THIGH to wage the
      war of Torah.[24] Now it [the metaphorical SWORD] is
4b   YOUR SPLENDOR AND GLORY.[25]
5a   [RIDE][21] UPON A WORD OF TRUTH to render legal de-
      cisions properly and to enjoy the MEEKness of[26] JUSTICE.
5b   AND LET HER INSTRUCT YOU.
      [As for the exegetical question as to what is the subject of the
      verb wĕtôrĕkā 'LET HER INSTRUCT YOU', the answer is
      as follows]: As for the Torah, which is[27] the WORD OF
      TRUTH, with which you occupy yourself, she will teach you
      military strategy for YOUR RIGHT HAND to perform
      AWESOME DEEDS. Since he [the psalmist] referred to the
      study of Torah by the metaphor of war, it is appropriate with
      reference to it[28] [the study of Torah, to employ] the expres-
      sion yāmîn 'RIGHT HAND', which is prepared [mĕyummenet][29]
      to wage war.

6a   YOUR ARROWS, SHARPENED,
6c   THE BREAST OF THE KINGS ENEMIES. Note that this
      verse is a case of inversion.[30] We have found that students
      [of Torah] are called arrows, for it is stated in the Bible, "Like
      arrows in the hand of a warrior are sons born to a man in
      his youth" (Ps. 127:4).[31] Moreover, Torah scholars who ar-
      gue with each other about the halakah are called each other's
      temporary enemies in accord with what is stated in the Bible,
      "They[32] shall not be put to shame when they contend with
      the enemy in the gate" (Ps. 127:5).[33]
6b   PEOPLES FALL AT YOUR FEET.[34] As a reward for
      [Israel's studying] Torah the Gentiles will fall at Israel's feet.
7a   YOUR DIVINE SEAT [IS EVERLASTING].[21] [I.e.], your
      seat as a judicial officer[35] forever and ever. [The use of the
      term 'ĕlohîm 'god' to designate judicial authority is] in accord
      with what is stated in the Bible, "I shall make you [Moses]
      'ĕlohîm 'judge' over Pharaoh" (Ex. 7:1). Now why [is this so,
      that YOUR JUDICIAL BENCH IS EVERLASTING]?[36]
7b   [It is so] because YOUR ROYAL SCEPTER IS A SCEP-
      TER OF EQUITY,[37] which means that your judicial deci-
      sions are reliable, and you are fit to rule.
8   CHOSEN TO ANOINT YOU WITH OIL OF GLAD-
      NESS.
      The expression 'anointing with oil' can be employed in con-

nection with any expression denoting 'promotion to office'
as is the case with kings.[38]

9b,   MYRRH AND ALOES AND CASSIA [qĕṣî'ôt]. We render
      [Heb.] qiddāh (Ex. 30:24; Ezek. 27:10) by Aram. qĕṣî'ātā' 'cas-
      sia'.[39]

9a   ALL YOUR ROBES [bigĕdotêkā] [The assertion, "ALL YOUR
      ROBES ARE MYRRH..." means], "All your garments
      [bĕgādêkā][40] give off a fragrance like the fragrance of spices."[41]
      A midrash based upon it ["ALL YOUR ROBES ARE
      MYRRH..."] IS "ALL bigĕdotêkā, i.e.,[42] Your sins [sêrhônêkā][43]
      are wiped away so that they give off a sweet fragrance."[44]

9c   AMONG IVORY PALACES FROM ME THEY MADE
      YOU REJOICE.
      Palaces which are AMONG the best IVORY PALACES,
      [i.e.], the palaces,[45] which have been prepared for you in
      Paradise to make you rejoice in them.
      FROM ME THEY MADE YOU REJOICE. [I.e., palaces],
      which are from me[46] [and] which pay your reward, MADE
      YOU REJOICE.

10a   ROYAL PRINCESSES will be visiting you in accord with
      what is stated in the Bible, "Their queens will be your
      wetnurses" (Isa. 49:23).[47] byqqĕrôtêkā. [In this word] the [let-
      ter] qoph is pointed with a daghesh [forte to indicate doubling
      of the letter qoph] because it is a form of [the word] biqqûr
      'visit' even though a yod is written before it [the qoph].[48] I read[13]
      in Rav Saadiah's Treatise on Vocalization[49] [that] this word
      [byqrwtyk] is listed in the same category as [the word mĕšyssāh
      'spoiler' in] "Who was it gave over Jacob to despoilment?"
      (Isa. 42:24), which is spelled with a yod while the samek is
      pointed with a daghesh [forte to indicate doubling of the letter
      samek].[50]

10b   šēgal 'THE CONSORT' [means] queen.[51] [THE CONSORT
      STANDS AT YOUR RIGHT HAND means], "Your wife
      shall stand[52] AT YOUR RIGHT HAND IN GOLD OF
      OPHIR."

11a   TAKE HEED, LASS,[53] AND NOTE. TAKE HEED, Con-
      gregation of Israel, AND NOTE the path of virtue.

11b   INCLINE YOUR EAR to the Torah

11c   FORGET YOUR PEOPLE, [i.e.], the Gentiles among whom
      you were raised, AND YOUR FATHER'S HOUSE, [i.e.],

the idolatry,[54] which your ancestors worshipped across the
River [Euphrates].[55]

12   AND THE KING WILL DESIRE YOUR BEAUTY. Now,
      if you will do accordingly,[56] THE KING, [i.e.], the Holy One
      Blessed be He, WILL DESIRE the beauty of your deeds.[57]

13   O TYRIAN LASS....WILL COURT YOUR FAVOR
      WITH GIFTS. Now as a reward for this[58] you will be privi-
      leged that the wicked Esau[59] will bring you tribute payments[60]
      and gifts. Those [who will one day court your favor] are they
      who are presently THE WEALTHIEST PEOPLE.[61]

14   GOODS OF ALL SORTS. THE ROYAL PRINCESS....
      This verse refers to what is stated in the Bible, "They shall
      bring all your brothers... [as an offering][21]. (Isa. 66:20).[62] As
      for those upon whom all honor[63] depends, and they are the
      King's entourage, who behaved chastely, now their garments
      are more distinguished looking than the gold woven garments
      of high priests.[64]

15a   IN[65] EMBROIDERED GARMENTS SHE WILL BE
      BROUGHT TO THE KING. In embroidered garments[66]
      they will bring them[67] as tribute[68] to the King [who reigns]
      over the whole earth.

15b   MAIDENS IN HER TRAIN, HER COMPANIONS.
      [This means that people] from the Gentiles will run after
      them[67] in accord with what is stated in the Bible, "They will
      take hold of the corner of a Jew's garment...[69] saying, 'Let
      us go with you, for we have heard that God is with you.'"
      (Zech. 8:23).

15c   ARE PRESENTED TO YOU. It is to the Holy One Blessed
      be He that the psalmist addressed this.[70]

17   SUCCEED YOUR ANCESTORS....
      He [the psalmist] addressed this to each and every Israelite.

18   I COMMEMORATE YOUR FAME.
      The psalmist addressed this to the Holy One Blessed be He.[71]

PSALM XLV, NOTES
    [1] Rendering of the lemma according to the interpretation presupposed
by Rashi's comment; cf. RSV: "according to lilies."
    [2] In Canticles Rabbah on Cant. 2:1-2 there is a series of midrashim,
in which the speaker who says in Cant. 2:1, "I am a rose of Sharon//a
lily of the valleys" is said to be either the people of Israel, the wilderness
(Isa. 35:1; 41:9), or the land of Israel. Time and again it is asserted in these

midrashim, q.v., that one of the bases of comparison is that he or she, who
is compared to a rose//a lily, makes good deeds blossom. In a midrash
quoted in Tanḥuma B, p. 2b, n. 8 it is asserted that "lilies" at Cant. 7:3 is
a metaphor for 'Sages', i.e., 'Torah scholars'. Likewise, in a midrash attributed to R. Giddal quoting Rav at BT Shabbat 30b, lilies in Cant. 5:13
is taken to refer to persons who study Torah. Maarsen cites here the latter two midrashim, but he does not mention the midrash found in Canticles Rabbah. He remarks that he was unable to identify Rashi's source
here. The reason for this may well be that Rashi here is not quoting a
specific midrash, but he is creating a new midrash from two ideas found
in Rabbinic literature. The first of these is the assertion that the common
feature of roses//lilies and a valued group or entity is that both produce
blossoms, the latter's blossoms being good deeds. The second idea is that
lilies is a metaphor for Torah scholars. As intimated in BT Shabbat 30b,
this idea may have been suggested by the aural and visual similarity of Heb.
šošānāh 'lily' and the verb šānāh 'to study Tannaitic traditions'.

³ See the discussion at Ps. 32:1.

⁴ Here Rashi explains the meaning of an infrequently attested root by
means of one which is attested more frequently. Note that the noun yĕdîdôt
'love' occurs only twice in the Bible, here at Ps. 45:1 and again at Ps. 84:2.
Note that the abstract noun 'ăhûbîm is the same kind of abstract noun represented by nĕ'ûrîm 'youth' (Isa. 54:6; Ps. 127:4 and frequently with pronominal suffixes) and zĕqēnîm 'old age' (Gen. 21:2, 7; 37:3; 44:20). On this
type of noun see GKC #124d. Note that while the form 'ăhûbîm is unattested in the Bible, the synonymous 'ăhăbîm is attested in Hos. 8:9; Prov.
5:19; 7:18.

⁵ See above.

⁶ Rashi's comment here, like his comments at Judg. 5:31 and Ezek.
1:1 is source-critical. He indicates that Ps. 45:1, the psalm title, is not from
the same pen as the psalm itself, which begins at v. 2. See introduction,
p. 129, n. 9.

⁷ So NJV; Heb. dābār ṭôb, lit., 'a kind word' (cf. Esth. 7:9), which seems
to be the near semantic equivalent of Akk. amat damiqti, lit., 'word of goodness', which is employed as the functional equivalent of Gk. συνηγορία
(> late Heb. sanēgoriyāh 'advocacy of another's cause').

⁸ The modern scholarly convention is to refer to Biblical Heb. verbs
by the 3ᵈ pers. sing. perf. of the qal if the verb is attested in the qal. Here
Rashi, however, refers to two verbs, which are indeed attested in the qal,
by the pi'el participle.

⁹ Heb. prefixed preposition lĕ can also mean 'to'; Rashi's exegesis requires that here it be interpreted to mean 'for'; on the various nuances of
this preposition see dictionaries.

¹⁰ Rashi explains that ma'ăśay, lit., 'my works', here means 'my song'
since the verb ăśāh 'make, do, work out', can mean also yāsad 'compose'.

¹¹ Rashi's comment here reflects the midrash embedded in the tale
concerning R. Huna, R. Hisda, and Genibah at BT Gittin 62a. According to this tale, rabbis, i.e., Torah scholars, are called kings because of what

is stated in Prov. 8:15, which can mean that kings are persons who embody *ḥokmāh* 'wisdom, sagacity'. Since the Mishnaic Heb. equivalent of Amoraic Heb. *rabbānān* 'our rabbis' is *ḥăkāmîm* 'sages, wise men', i.e., 'those who embody *ḥokmāh*, it follows that rabbis are people who embody *ḥokmāh*. Now since both kings and rabbis *are* 'people who embody *ḥokmāh*' and since persons or things that are equal to the same thing are equal to each other, it follows that rabbis, i.e., Torah scholars, can indeed be called kings.

[12] Rashi clarifies the metaphor by paraphrasing it as a simile.

[13] Heb. *rā'îtî*, lit., 'I saw', refers again and again in Rashi's Heb. to reading silently (see Rashi also at Ps. 9:1; 10:10; 60:4; 70:1). Heb. *qārā'tî*, lit., 'I called, declaimed', which is employed in Modern Heb. to mean 'I read (even silently)', seems to be reserved in Rashi's language for 'reading aloud'.

[14] Heb. *bysôdô šel R. Mošeh haddaršān*. It is widely assumed on the basis of this cliché by which Rashi introduces information gleaned from R. Moses' the Interpreter's book that the book in question was called *Yesod*, i.e., *Foundation* (see Liber, *Rashi*, p. 110). It is true that in Biblical Heb. the noun *yěsôd* means 'foundation, base' and that it is derived from the verb *yāsad* 'establish, found, fix'; see *BDB*, pp. 413b-414a. In Rashi's commentaries, however, the verb *yāsad* means 'compose, author, write'. Hence the noun *yěsôdô* is employed in Rashi's commentaries to mean 'his work, his book, his composition'. Note also that while in Modern Heb. and in Yiddish the term *daršān*. may denote a 'preacher of sermons', there is no evidence for such a usage of the term in Rashi's Heb. On the contrary, in Rashi's Commentary on the Book of Psalms R. Moses the Interpreter (!) is usually cited as a source of philological minutiae. See introduction, p. 3, n. 14

[15] KJV; JPS.

[16] So now NJV.

[17] On the references to Arabic in Rashi's Commentary on the Book of Psalms see below at Ps. 60:4.

[18] See Rashi at v. 1.

[19] Rashi's placing of his comment after *mibběnê 'ādām* indicates that he, followed now by NJV, interprets the prefixed preposition mi(n) to mean 'than' rather than 'among' (= RSV's 'of'). According to Rashi, therefore, *yāpyāpîtā min* means 'You are more beautiful than' rather than 'You are the most beautiful of'. It should be pointed out that Rashi's interpretation of the verb here is inconsistent with the view he expresses unequivocally at Lev. 13:49, s.v. *yěraqraq* that reduplication expresses the superlative.

[20] By this question and answer Rashi indicates that the first two clauses of v. 3 constitute an example of synthetic parallelism.

[21] Rashi does not quote the bracketed portion of this clause; I have supplied it for clarity.

[22] According to this comment the people of God is not all Israel but only Torah scholars.

[23] Rashi intimates here that the two parallel clauses in Ps. 29:11a-b represent synthetic rather than synonymous parallelism.

[24] In Rabbinic literature scholarly debate is correctly perceived to resemble war. See BT Megillah 15b; Hagigah 14a; Sanhedrin 42a, 93b, 111b.

Hence the midrash quoted here by Rashi has no difficulty seeing a reference to a sword in a hymn allegedly addressed to Torah scholars collectively.

[25] Rashi here attempts to solve the exegetical *crux* presented by the phrase YOUR SPLENDOR AND GLORY following the *caesura*. RSV renders "in your glory and majesty," treating the phrase as an adverb modifying the verb 'GIRD'.

[26] MT reads *wěʾaněwāh-ṣedeq*, lit., 'AND MEEKNESS-TRUTH'; RSV margin, like Rashi, takes this expression to be the same in meaning as *wěʾaněwat-ṣedeq* 'meekness of truth'; contrast NJV's "and meekness and right."

[27] Here Rashi employs the explicative *waw*.

[28] Heb. *nōpēl bô*.

[29] Note the play on words.

[30] So now NJV here; on the recognition of this phenomenon in Rashi's Bible commentaries see Rashi at Ps. 17:7; 22:30; 22:31; 33:14-15; 36:2; Shereshevsky, "Inversions in Rashi's Commentary," pp. 263-68; id., *Rashi: The Man and His World*, pp. 92-99.

[31] Rashi has not, in fact, demonstrated that 'arrows' can designate 'students' but only that 'arrows' can designate *bānîm*, lit., 'sons, children'. It is accepted, however, in Rabbinic exegesis that *bānîm* 'sons' can designate 'students of Torah'. Rashi here at Ps. 45:6 apparently takes it for granted that the reader understands the latter point. Hence, he appears to assume that the reader will draw from the demonstration that 'arrows' can designate *bānîm* the conclusion that 'arrows' can designate 'Torah scholars', who are called *bānîm*.

[32] The antecedent in Ps. 127 is "sons born to a man in his youth."

[33] The source of this midrash may be the *baraitha* at BT Qiddushin 31a-b.

[34] On 'fall at the feet' as a symbolic act signifying obeisance and as a metaphor for military defeat see Gruber, *Aspects*, pp. 187-257.

[35] Rashi, following Ex. 2:14 employs the expression *śar wěšōpēṭ*, lit., 'prince and judge' as an hendiadys designating 'judicial official' (contrast Orlinsky, *Notes*, p. 100). Moreover, Rashi here indicates that the two words *kisăʾkā ʾělōhîm* are to be taken here as a construct genitive meaning 'Your divine throne' (similarly NJV; RSV) rather than as a noun subject followed by a vocative (RSV margin's "Your throne, O God"). Moreover, Rashi indicates that since *kissēʾ* 'seat' is not modified here by *malěkût* 'kingship' but by *ʾělōhîm* the expression *kissēʾ ʾělōhîm* is not a metaphor for kingship but a metaphor for judicial authority. Note that Rashi does not cite any prooftext to demonstrate that *ʾělōhîm* can denote 'judge'. He takes it for granted that this is an established fact. This notion, which is reflected in T.O. at Ex. 21:6; 22:17; etc. probably derives from the appearance of *ʾělōhîm* 'God' in such expressions as 'go to God' (Ex. 22:8), which, like its Akk. equivalent in the Code of Hammurapi, is an idiom meaning 'go to a court of law'.

[36] By intimating that the second half of the verse answers a question about the first half of the verse, Rashi indicates that the parallelism is synthetic rather than synonymous; see above, nn. 20, 23.

[37] So NJV. Note that the scepter or mace, a symbol of the sovereignty of both royalty and legislative bodies to this day, was originally a weapon of judicial punishment like the modern police officer's "night stick". Cf. Mayer I. Gruber, "Scepter," *EJ* 14:935.

[38] Cf. Rashi at Ps. 105:15 and our extensive discussion there.

[39] 'We render' here means 'We Jews in our canonical Aramaic translations of the Pentateuch and the Prophets, which are Targum Onkelos and Targum Jonathan respectively'; see Rashi at Ps. 40:15, n. 25.

[40] By means of this paraphrase Rashi intimates that the form *bigĕdotêkā* found only here at Ps. 45:9 is the plural (with added pronominal suffix) of an unattested *bigdāh*, the hypothetical feminine biform of the masculine noun *beged* 'garment'.

[41] So also NJV and RSV. This, however, is not what the verse says. The verse metaphorically compares garments and spices, implying that as pleasant as are ALOES etc. to the smell so are the garments in question pleasing to the sight and (perhaps) the touch.

[42] Explicative *waw*.

[43] Note that the noun *sêrāḥôn* has the literal meaning 'stench' and the extended meaning 'offense, mischief'; see Jastrow, *Dict.*, pp. 987b-988a.

[44] This midrash, which is attributed to R. Johanan [b. Napha] in JT Pe'ah 1:1, treats the anomalous form *bigĕdotêkā* as defective spelling for *bĕgîdôtêkā* 'your treacheries'; with reference to the idea expressed by this midrash cf. the contention in Isa. 1:18 that repentance turns red sins white.

[45] Note that Rashi refers to the heavenly palaces using the fem. pl. form *hêkālôt* while the psalm speaks of earthly palaces using the masc. pl. construct form *hêkĕlê*.

[46] Rashi, like LXX and Ibn Ezra, interprets the word *minnî* as a short form of the preposition *mimmennî* (so *GKC* #103i); NJV, following Qimhi, takes the word *minnî* as a short form of the word *minnîm* 'lutes' otherwise attested only in Ps. 150:4 (see Rashi there).

[47] By means of this prooftext Rashi demonstrates that his interpretation of Ps. 45:10a fits the cultural context of biblical eschatology. In the following comment Rashi will try to justify his interpretation linguistically.

[48] The *yod* could be taken to indicate that in the word *byqqĕrôtêkā* the letter *bet* is a preposition followed by a noun derived from the root *yqr* 'be precious, be honored'. Hence RSV renders "are among your ladies of honor"; similarly NJV's "are your favorites". The latter interpreters ignore the doubling of the *qoph*, however.

[49] Henry Malter, *Saadiah Gaon: His Life and Works* (Philadelphia: JPS, 1921), p. 141, n. 303 conjectures that the work referred to here by Rashi is part of *Kutub al-Lugal*, i.e., *Books on Language*. Malter also notes there, p. 140, n. 297 that Saadiah himself refers to this work in his commentary on the *Sepher Yeṣirah* both by the aforementioned title and as *The Book of the Daghesh and the Raphe*. Samuel A. Poznański, "Who is the Rav Saadiah Mentioned by the French Bible Commentators?" *Ha-Goren* 9 (1923), 69 (in Hebrew) conjectures that Rashi in fact made use of a copy of the Arabic original of Saadiah's *Books on Language* since Rashi's ignorance of Arabic

would not have prevented him from noting that in it Saadiah juxtaposed the Hebrew words *byqrwtyk* and *mšsyh*.

[50] Here Rashi seems to say that in Saadiah's treatise the word is spelled *mšsyh*. and is vocalized *mĕšîssāh*. Note that in our editions of the Bible (so-called MT) there is a *Kethib-Qere* variant. The Kethib is *mšwsh* while the Qere is *mĕšîssāh*. Saadiah here, according to the testimony of Rashi, attests to a variant text in which *w* is replaced by *y* and the consonantal text is vocalized *mĕšîssāh*. Rashi's point is that the anomalous *plene* spelling *mšysh* in Saadiah's testimony to Isa. 42:24 proves that the first *yod* in *byqrwtk* can indeed be taken as anomalous *plene* writing of *byqqĕrôtêkā*, whose root letters are *bqr* and not *yqr*.

[51] Here Rashi correctly interprets Heb. *šēgāl*, which is a loanword from Akk. *ša ekalli*, lit., 'of the palace', which is employed in Akk. to mean 'the queen, the principal wife of the king'; see H. Gevariahu, *"šēgāl," EM* 7:522-524. Ibn Ezra and Qimhi here, like LXX at Neh. 2:6, fall victim to the eytmological fallacy in explaining *šēgāl* as a derivative of the verb *šgl* 'engage in coitus with' (Deut. 28:30; Isa. 13:16; Jer. 3:2; Zech. 14:2).

[52] Rashi clarifies the meaning of the ambiguous Biblical Heb. perf. *niṣĕbāh*, lit., 'she stood' by paraphrasing in the *hitpaʿel* future *tityaṣṣēb*.

[53] Vss. 3-10 are addressed to a man, whom Rashi, following various midrashim, takes to be a personification of Torah scholars collectively. Vss. 11-17 are addressed to *bat* 'LASS'. Rashi here deals midrashically with the exegetical question, "Who is she?"

[54] This comment may reflect the realization that Heb. *bayit*, lit., 'house', can mean 'temple'. Examples of this usage include 2 Sam. 7:13; 1 Kgs. 5:17; Hag. 2:9.

[55] I.e., in Mesopotamia from where Abraham came to Canaan. See Gen. 11:31; 12:5; 24:4, 10; Josh. 24:2-3; with Zohory, p. 136 note that this comment is influenced by Genesis Rabbah 39:1.

[56] As advised in v. 11.

[57] This comment convincingly suggests that contra NJV the verb *wĕyitāʾw* should be rendered as a subordinate clause 'so that he will desire' rather than as an independent clause, 'and let him be arouse'. On subordinate clauses introduced by *waw*-conjunctive see Orlinsky, *Notes*, pp. 19-20.

[58] That in accord with v. 11 you, Israel, look to the path of virtue, incline your ear to the Torah, and cease to emulate the Gentiles in order to achieve material success.

[59] Maarsen here suggests that "the wicked Esau" here is a midrashic exegesis of *ṣor* in the biblical text. While NJV renders *bat ṣor* 'Tyrian lass', Rashi, according to Maarsen, treats *bat* 'LASS' as the person addressed and *ṣor* as the subject of the predicate 'WILL COURT YOUR FAVOR'. Moreover, according to Maarsen, Rashi here treats the consonants *ṣr* not as representing the proper noun Tyre but as the common noun *ṣār* 'enemy', of whom Esau is paradigmatic. Cf. PRK, ed. Mandelbaum, p. 133, lines 1-2.

[60] Heb. *'eškārîm*. This noun is twice attested in the Bible only in the singular *'eškār* meaning 'tribute' in Ezek. 27:15 and Ps. 27:10. This noun is a

loanword from Akk. *iškaru*, which denotes a kind of tax. See Mayer I. Gruber, "Akkadian Influences in the Book of Ezekiel," (M.A. Essay, Columbia University, 1970), pp. 12-13.

[61] In other words, do not seek now to achieve success by assimilation. If you can wait patiently, you will see the day when the now successful Gentiles will seek to court the favor of Israel.

[62] Rashi here intimates that like NJV he construes *kol-kĕbûdāh* (NJV's "GOODS OF ALL SORTS") to denote 'tribute'.

[63] Heb. *kol-kābôd*, a second and alternative interpretation of the psalmist's *kol-kĕbûdāh*.

[64] Rashi here deals with three exegetical problems. First, he seeks to determine the meaning of the prefixed preposition *mi(n)* in the expression *mimmišbĕṣôt zāhāb*. The preposition in question can mean, *inter alia*, 'from' or 'more than'; contrast the various translations, whose disparate renderings demonstrate the existence of an exegetical *crux*. Second, Rashi seeks to determine the meaning of *mišbĕṣôt zāhāb*, which has been rendered variously as 'golden mountings' (NJV); 'golden embroidery' (RSV), etc. He determines that the Heb. expression in question is a technical term for the vestments of the Jewish high priest in the days of the First and Second Temples. Hence he understands the elliptical verse as follows: ALL GLORY TO HER [whose] ATTIRE IS MORE [distinguished] THAN HIGH PRIESTLY GARMENTS. Rashi explains here in his commentary that she, who is praised in v. 14, is *kĕnēsiyyāh šel melek* 'the King's entourage', i.e., 'the LORD'S entourage', the Jews.

[65] Ibn Ezra remarks in his commentary on this verse that the preposition *lĕ* here is synonymous with the preposition *bĕ* 'in'; so RSV; see next note.

[66] Rashi here intimates that he holds that *lĕ* in the biblical text here corresponds to *bĕ* 'in'; see previous note.

[67] I.e., the Jews, whom THE ROYAL PRINCESS personifies.

[68] Here Rashi intimates that the implied subject of the verb *tûbal* 'SHE WILL BE BROUGHT' is not 'THE ROYAL PRINCESS' (v. 14) but 'offering' found in Isa. 66:20 and quoted in Rashi's exegesis of Ps. 45:14.

[69] The ellipsis dots in our translation correspond to the expression *wĕgô*, an abbreviation for *wĕgômēr* 'and it [the verse continues and] concludes' in our Rashi ms. Since our Rashi ms. does quote all the remainder of the verse the expression *wĕgô* and our ellipsis dots are superfluous. Apparently, the scribe responsible for our ms. copied the expression from an early ms., which did not quote the rest of Zech. 8:23 even though he himself did see fit to copy out the rest of the latter verse.

[70] In vv. 11-13 the 'LASS', who personifies Israel, is addressed in the 2d pers. sing. In vv. 14-15b the 'LASS' is spoken about in the 3d pers. sing. In v. 17, according to Rashi, Israel is addressed in the 2d pers. sing. masc. Hence the essential exegetical problem in v. 15c is to determine who is being addressed *lāk* 'to you'. The latter form can be either 2d pers. sing. fem. or 2d pers. sing. masc. pausal. Rashi opts for the latter interpretation.

[71] The exegetical problem Rashi addresses here is that in v. 17 the psalmist addresses Israel collectively in the 2^d pers. sing. while here in v. 18 he addresses God in the 2^d pers. sing. NJV solves this exegetical problem by printing v. 18 as a separate stanza.

PSALM XLVI

1 ON *ALAMOTH*. [This term '*ălāmôt*] is the name of a musical instrument in [the Book of] Chronicles (1 Ch. 15:20).[1]

2 WHEN HE MAKES THE EARTH REEL in the time to come concerning which it is stated in the Bible, "The earth will wear out like a garment" (Isa. 51:6). When the sons of Korah[2] saw [the miracle][3] that was done for them in that all who were around them were swallowed up while they remained standing in [mid]-air, with prophetic inspiration they told Israel that in the future there will be done for them [i.e., for all Israel] something like this miracle [done for the sons of Korah].[4]

4a They [the sons of Korah] said, "ITS WATERS [RAGE AND FOAM]."[5] [I.e.], they [ITS WATERS] drive away dung and clay and mud[6] according to their nature.[7]

4b MOUNTAINS WILL QUAKE BEFORE HIS MAJESTY, [i.e.], that of the Holy One Blessed be He, who is mentioned at the beginning of the psalm.[8]

5 THERE IS A RIVER, the river of Paradise.[9]

6 BY DAYBREAK, [i.e.], before the time set for Redemption.[10]

10 CONSIGNING WAGONS TO THE FLAMES. [I.e.], the war chariots of the Gentiles.

PSALM XLVI, NOTES

 [1] Cf. Rashi at Ps. 9:1.

 [2] To whom the psalm is attributed at v. 1.

 [3] Heb. *nēs;* this word is missing from our Rashi ms. For the correct understanding of Rabbinic Heb. *nēs* see Kadushin, *The Rabbinic Mind*[3], pp. 152-167.

 [4] The source of this midrash is Midrash Tehillim here.

 [5] Rashi does not quote the bracketed portion of the verse; I have supplied it for clarity.

 [6] Cf. Isa. 57:20: "But the wicked are like the troubled sea, which cannot rest, whose waters toss up mire and mud."

 [7] Heb. *kĕmišpāṭām.*

 [8] Note that Rashi calls v. 2, the first word of which is GOD, "the beginning of the psalm." His view is accepted by modern scholars, who hold that v. 1 is an appended title from the pen of someone other than the author of the psalm; see Otto Eissfeldt, *The Old Testament: An Introduction*, trans.

Peter Ackroyd (New York: Harper & Row, 1965), p. 451. Note that NEB omits these titles.

[9] Cf. Louis Ginzberg, *Legends of the Jews*, vol. 5, pp. 14-15, 126.

[10] Cf. Midrash Tehillim here.

PSALM XLVII[1]

1   THRUST DOWN THE PALM.[2] [I.e.], Pledge to each other
to RAISE A JOYOUS SHOUT FOR GOD.

4   HE SUBJUGATES [*yadbēr*] PEOPLES INSTEAD OF US.
[The verb *yadbēr* means], 'He will distribute pestilence [*deber*][3]
among the Gentiles instead of us so that His anger may cool
off through them while we are saved in accord with what is
stated in the Bible, "I give Egypt as a ransom for you... "
(Isa 43:3).

5   HE CHOSE [OUR HERITAGE][4] FOR US, and He will
return us into it, and then

6   He will be exalted[5] MIDST ACCLAMATION..., THE
BLASTS OF THE HORN [*shofar*], which we will blow in His
presence during the song accompanying burnt offerings and
peace offerings (cf. Num. 10:10), and we shall say,[6]

7a   "...SING TO GOD...."

9a   GOD REIGNS OVER ALL[7] NATIONS. This is what all
will say.[8]

9b   [GOD][4] IS SEATED ON HIS HOLY THRONE.
Now [when the Gentiles will have said this], the [divine]
throne is whole,[9] and the power [of the Holy One Blessed
be He] is triumphant, and they [people] will declare that

10a   THE GREAT OF THE PEOPLES ARE GATHERED TO-
GETHER at His City,[10] who have volunteered themselves[11]
for the slaughter, i.e., to be killed for the sanctification of His
Name.[12]

10b   THE PEOPLE OF THE GOD OF ABRAHAM, who was
the first volunteer, the first of the proselytes.[13] Now [in the
future time described in vv. 5-10] it is known[14]
THAT GOD'S ARE THE SHIELDS OF THE EARTH.
[I.e.], He has the ability to shield those who seek refuge in
Him (cf. Ps. 18:31 = 2 Sam. 22:31).

PSALM XLVII, NOTES
  [1] In our Rashi ms. the comments on Pss. 46-48 are grouped together
and numbered collectively as the comments on Ps. 43; see above at Ps. 13,
n. 1 and at Ps. 28, n. 1 for the explanation as to why our Ps. 45 is num-

bered in our Rashi ms. as Ps. 42, and see above at Ps. 43, n. 1 for the explanation as to why our Ps. 43 is treated by Rashi as the continuation of our Ps. 42, which is numbered in our Rashi ms. as Ps. 40. It follows from the aforementioned observations that our Ps. 49 will be numbered in our Rashi ms. as Ps. 44; see there.

² NJV, RSV and other modern translations follow LXX and Vulgate in understanding the expression *tāqaʿ kap* to mean 'clap palm(s)', i.e., 'applaud', a well-known *gestus* of worship among many Protestant denominations. In fact, such a *gestus* of worship is referred to in Biblical Heb. by the expression *māḥāʾ kappayim* 'clap the palms' in Isa. 55:12; Ps. 98:8 (see Rashi there); see also *māḥāʾ yād* 'clap hand' a *gestus* of joyous exultation at the defeat of one's enemy in Ezek. 25:6. Here, however, Rashi points out that in all its other attestations *tāqaʿ kap* (Nah. 3:19; Prov. 6:1; 17:18; 22:26), like *tāqaʿ yād* in Job. 17:3, is a *gestus* of pledging surety. Hence Rashi deduces that also in Ps. 47:2 *tāqaʿ kap* must mean 'pledge surety'. The nature of the *gestus* described by *tāqaʿ kap* may be deduced from the other uses of *tāqaʿ* and from other biblical expressions meaning 'pledge surety', which involve the hand or palm. With objects other than musical instruments the verb *tāqaʾ* means 'thrust, drive in, lower'. Typical is Judg. 16:14: "And she pinned in with a peg...." Other hand-gesture derived expressions in Biblical Heb. meaning 'pledge surety' are *nātan yād taḥat* 'put hand under' (1 Ch. 29:24) and *śām yād taḥat yerek* 'put hand under thigh' (Gen. 24:9; 47:29). But the usual meaning of *tāqaʿ* 'thrust, drive in, lower' and these other expressions suggest that *tāqaʿ kap* in the sense 'pledge surety' derives from a legal *gestus* of lowering the hand/palm. See Leslie R. Freedman, "Studies in Cuneiform Legal Terminology with Special Reference to West Semitic Parallels" (Ph.D. diss., Columbia University, 1977), pp. 9-33; 106-48.

³ Rashi takes *hidbîr* to be a denominative verb derived from the noun *deber* 'pestilence'; *Mahberet Menahem*, p. 119 takes *hidbîr* to mean 'lead'; see Rashi at Ps. 18:48.

⁴ Rashi does not quote the bracketed portion of the verse; I have supplied it for clarity.

⁵ Here Rashi paraphrases the Bible's *weʿālāh*, a perfect-consecutive verb meaning 'He will be exalted' (cf. NJV's "ascends"), by employing the imperfect, the form of the verb, which Rabbinic Heb. normally employs to express the future. Also, here as in Ps. 46:11 and elsewhere Rashi expresses the stative by means of the *hitpaʿel* where Biblical Heb. employs the *qal*.

⁶ Rashi here calls attention to the fact that here the psalmist abruptly switches from a narrative about God and Israel to a song of praise. Rashi construes this song (v. 7) as a quotation without *verbum dicendi* of the hymn to be recited in the future era depicted in vv. 4-6.

⁷ The lemma in our Rashi ms. adds here the word *kol-*, which is absent from the standard Heb. text (so-called MT) of our psalm. For other ancient and medieval witnesses to the textual tradition reflected here see *BHS* here.

[8] In his comment on v. 6 Rashi noted that vv. 7-8 are what the Jews will sing in the time to come. They will ask all peoples to praise God. Rashi suggests that the Gentiles' liturgical response is found in v. 9.

[9] See PRK, ed. Mandelbaum, p. 53; see also Rashi at Ex. 17:16.

[10] Jerusalem.

[11] Heb. *hitnaddĕbû*, a play on the word *nĕdîbîm* 'GREAT'.

[12] I.e., for martyrdom.

[13] See BT Sukkah 49b.

[14] This clause seems to supply an answer to the exegetical question, "What is the meaning of the particle *kî* 'for, that' in v. 10b?" Rashi opts for the meaning 'that'; Dahood interprets *kî* here as an emphatic particle meaning 'truly' while NJV renders 'for'.

PSALM XLVIII[1]

2   IN THE CITY OF OUR GOD.
In the time to come when He will have rebuilt His City [Jerusalem], He will be for them[2] GREAT AND...ACCLAIMED.

3a   FAIR-CRESTED, [i.e.], a city, which is a fair crest [*nôp*].[3]
It is the same word as is found in[4] [the Rabbinic Heb. expression] *nôp šel 'îlān* 'crest of a tree'.[5] Another equally plausible interpretation [of the word *nôp*] is 'beautiful bride',[6] for, in fact, in the cities of the [Aegean] Sea they call a bride *nynphe*.[7]

3b   JOY OF ALL THE EARTH. And what is her joy? [The answer is]

3d   *yarkětê ṣāpôn* [8] [i.e.], "the side [*yerek*][9] of the altar towards the North [*ṣāpôn*]" (Lev. 1:11) where sin offerings and guilt offerings are slaughtered.[10] Whoever is sorry about his sins brings [to the aforementioned location] his sin offering or his guilt offering,[11] and he receives expiation, and he departs from there happy. Thus by virtue of the sacrifices happiness[12] comes into the world.[13]

4   HAS MADE HIMSELF KNOWN AS A HAVEN. When He will be manifest therein[14] in the time to come, this is what people will say.

5a   THE KINGS JOINED FORCES to fight against her [Jerusalem] in the war of Gog and Magog.[15]

5b   THEY ADVANCED TOGETHER to war.

6   THEY SAW the Holy One Blessed be He go forth to fight against those nations.

8b   IN AN EASTERLY GALE.
This is an expression denoting punishment, for by means of it the Holy One Blessed be He exacts punishment from the wicked, as for example, where it is stated in the Bible, "The LORD drove back the sea by means of an easterly gale..." (Ex. 14:21). Likewise, with reference to Tyre, "An easterly gale wrecked you at sea" (Ezek. 27:26); [another illustration of 'easterly gale' as instrument of divine punishment is the fol-

lowing]: "I shall scatter them in the face of the enemy as does an easterly gale" (Jer. 18:17).[16]

8a   SHIPS OF TARSHISH. They are neighbors of Tyre.[17] [Alternatively], it [TARSHISH] is Africa,[18] and it [is reached] via Edom.[19]

9   THE LIKES OF WHAT WE HEARD [in] the speeches of consolation from the mouths of the prophets WE HAVE NOW WITNESSED.

10a   *dimmînû*, O GOD, YOUR LOYALTY.
[After telling us in vv. 4-9 what people will say in the time to come, here in v. 10] the prophet[20] turns again in prayer to the Holy One Blessed be He, and he says, "*dimmînû*," i.e.,[21] *qiwwînû* 'We beseech'[22] YOUR LOYALTY that we may

10b   experience this Your vindication IN YOUR TEMPLE.

11   LIKE YOUR FAME...SO IS YOUR PRAISE. When YOUR FAME is great SO IS YOUR PRAISE [great] in the mouth of all.

12   BECAUSE OF YOUR JUDGMENTS when You will execute justice among the Gentiles.[23]

13   [The imperatives in this verse are addressed to] the people of Zion,[24] you who rebuild her.
COUNT ITS TOWERS. [The verb *sappĕrû* 'COUNT'] is a verb referring to enumeration [*minyān*].[25] [It means] 'Know how many towers are appropriate for her'.

14a   OF ITS RAMPARTS [*lĕḥêlāh*], [i.e.], of its wall. [The word *ḥêl*] is the same word as is attested in[4] [the phrase] *ḥêl wĕḥômāh* "rampart and wall" (Lam. 2:8).

14b   *passĕgû*[26] HER PALACES. [This means] make tall her palaces. [The verb *passĕgû*] is a cognate of [the noun *pisgāh* in the phrase *'aśdot happisgāh* "slopes of Pisgah" (Deut. 3:17), [which we render into Aramaic as] *rāmātā'* "the heights".[27]

14c   THAT YOU MAY RECOUNT her heights and her beauty TO THE GENERATION which follows you.[28]

15   [HE WILL LEAD US *'al-mût*][29] as does a person who guides his small child.[30]

PSALM XLVIII, NOTES
[1] See Ps. 47, n. 1.
[2] I.e., the Gentiles; cf. Midrash Tehillim here. Other texts of Rashi's Commentary read here 'for her', i.e., Jerusalem, rather than 'for them'.
[3] This word is an *hapax legomenon* in Biblical Heb.

⁴ Heb. *lěšôn*.

⁵ See, e.g., Mishnah 'Erubin 10:8; Makkot 2:7.

⁶ Our translation here adopts the reading *kallāh šel yôpî* found here in many texts of Rashi's commentary; the expression *kělîlat yôpî* 'a perfect beauty' found in our Rashi ms. is taken from Ezek. 27:3 and Lam. 2:15. The scribe responsible for our Rashi ms. probably thought of the latter expression here because in Lam. 2:15 it is juxtaposed with the phrase "joy of all the earth, which is found also immediately below in Ps. 48:3b.

⁷ This observation is attributed to the Palestinian Amora R. Simeon b. Lakish (3ᵈ cent. C.E.) in BT Rosh ha-Shanah 26a, where the relevance of this observation to the exegesis of Ps. 48:3 is noted. Cf. also Exodus Rabbah 36:2, where the phrase "in the cities of the Sea" is replaced by "in Greek." On these and parallel texts see Krauss, *Lehnwörter*, vol. 2, pp. 361-62. On Gk. νύμφη see Liddell and Scott, pp. 1012-1013.

⁸ Literally, "uttermost Zaphon"; NJV renders "summit of Zaphon." By placing "uttermost Zaphon" in apposition to "Mount Zion" the psalmist declares that the latter represents for the religion of Israel what Zaphon represents in the pre-Mosaic literary heritage of the Canaanite-speaking peoples (Hebrew, of course, is a Canaanite dialect; cf. Isa. 19:18). Cf. Dahood, *Psalms*, vol. 1, pp. 289-290. Dahood assumes there that Zaphon is Mt. Cassius, the ancient Syrian equivalent of the Greek Olympus. However, Harold Louis Ginsberg, "Reflexes of Sargon in Isaiah After 715 B.C.E.," *JAOS* 88 (1968), p. 51, n. 26 argues most convincingly that not Zaphon but Lallu is the Canaanite Olympus while Zaphon both in the Bible (e.g., Isa. 14:13; Job. 26:7) and in Ugaritic designates 'heaven'. Hence, what the psalmist asserts here is that the earthly Jerusalem is the heavenly city. Cf. Jon D. Levenson, *Sinai and Zion* (San Francisco: Harper & Row, 1986), pp. 111-137. Rashi, attempting to say something significant about our verse, without the benefit of Ugaritic, which came to light only in 1929 C.E., makes use of a midrash; see n. 13.

⁹ Concerning the comparison of *yarkětê* 'uttermost parts of' and *yerek* 'side of' see now Dahood, *Psalms*, vol. 1, p. 290 at Ps. 48:3.

¹⁰ See Lev. 1:11; 6:25; 7:2; Mishnah Zebaḥim 5:1.

¹¹ For the distinction between sin offering and guilt offering see Milgrom, *Cult and Conscience* (Leiden: E. J. Brill, 1976).

¹² Heb. *ṭôbāh* = Akk. *ṭubbātu* 'happiness'.

¹³ Rashi's source here is Midrash Tehillim here.

¹⁴ In Biblical Heb. the verb *šākan* is generally understood to mean 'settle down, abide, dwell' (*BDB*, p. 1014b). Cross, "The Priestly Tabernacle," pp. 224-227 argues most convincingly that when applied to God in the Bible the verb *šākan* is to be understood as a denominative verb derived from the noun *miškān* 'tent'. In this usage the verb, which Cross renders 'to tent', refers to God's accompanying His people in their travels. The sense of God's nearness, which is conveyed in Biblical Heb., according to Cross, by the verb *šākan* 'to tent' is conveyed in Rabbinic Heb. by the noun *Shekinah* 'the Divine Presence'; on the latter see Kadushin, *The Rabbinic Mind*³, pp. 225-228. In Rashi's comment here at Ps. 48:4 the verb *šākan*

appears to be employed not as a denominative verb derived from *miškān* but rather as a denominative verb derived secondarily from the Rabbinic Heb. noun *Shekinah*, i.e., 'God's nearness'; hence our rendering 'be manifest'.

[15] In Ezek. 38-39, q.v., Gog is the ruler of Meshech in the land of Magog, who leads the attack upon Jerusalem, which will lead to the eschatological war, which will culminate in universal recognition of the sovereignty of the LORD and the restoration of the fortunes of the House of Israel in the land of Israel. In Rabbinic literature this eschatological war is called "the war of Gog and Magog"; cf. the entries "Gog" and "Magog" in *The Illustrated Dictionary and Concordance of the Bible*, ed. Geoffrey Wigoder (New York: Macmillan, 1986), pp. 403, 645.

[16] Rashi's noting that in the Bible an easterly gale is a *means* by which God exacts punishment should lend support to the view that the correct reading in Jer. 18:17 is not *kĕrûăḥ qādîm* "as does an easterly gale" but *bĕrûăḥ qādîm* "by means of an easterly gale." Note that Rashi's suggestion is taken from Mekilta to Ex. 14:21 (see Mekilta, vol. 1, p. 230), which attests to the reading *bĕrûăḥ* at Jer. 18:17; on the latter see *BH³* and *BHS* and the various critical commentaries.

[17] I.e., "SHIPS OF TARSHISH means 'ships of the Mediterranean Sea'. In his commentaries at Isa. 2:16; 23:1; 60:9; Ezek. 27:12 and Jonah 1:3 Rashi states unequivocally that Tarshish is the name of a sea. Rashi's suggestion here at Ps. 48:8 that Tarshish ships are neighbors of Tyre, which in antiquity was an island in the Mediterranean off the Lebanese coast (see Ezek. 27:2, 4), is supported by Jonah 1:3, which speaks of sailing to Tarshish via the port of Jaffa. In his commentary at 1 Kgs. 10:22, however, Rashi renders *'ŏnî Taršîš* (NJV following KJV renders 'Tarshish fleet') *sĕpînat 'Aprîqā'* 'ship of Africa'. In offering two different interpretations of Tarshish in the Latter and Former Prophets respectively Rashi follows TJ. TJ at Isa. 2:16; 23:1; 60:9; Ezek. 27:12, 25; 38:13; and Jonah 1:3 renders the proper name 'Tarshish' by the Aram. common noun *yamā'* 'the sea'. However, TJ renders *'ŏnî Taršîš* at 1 Kgs. 10:22 and *'ŏniyyôt Taršîš* at 1 Kgs. 2:49 by Aram. *sĕpînat 'Aprîqā'* 'an African ship'; see below, nn. 18,19.

[18] It appears that here in Ps. 48:8 Rashi offers two alternative interpretations of Tarshish for three reasons: (1) each of these is suggested elsewhere by the authoritative TJ; (2) Rashi possessed no authoritative Psalms Targum, which could have determined for him the appropriate rendering of Tarshish as did TJ in the other passages (see Rashi at 1 Kgs. 10:19 and at BT Megillah 21b; see on this point Berliner, "Beiträge," p. 29; Englander, "Rashi as Bible Exegete and Grammarian," pp. 344-345); (3) both readings are equally plausible in the context of Ps. 48:8.

[19] Rashi's astute observation that Africa in TJ to 1 Kgs. 10:22; 22:49 must denote East Africa, which is reached directly via Edom, is based on two parallel passages in the historical books of the Bible. 1 Ch. 9:21 states, "For the king [Solomon] had ships going to Tarshish" while the parallel account i 1 Kgs. 9:26 states, "King Solomon made a fleet at Ezion-Geber, which is near Eiloth on the shore of the Red Sea in the land of Edom."

Moshe Eilat, "Tarshish," *EM* 8:942 contends, however, that the reading "Tarshish" in MT at 1 Ch. 9:21; 20:36-37 is a scribal error for "Ophir" of 1 Kgs. 10:11. If so, the equation of Tarshish with a location in East Africa rather than a location on the Mediterranean lacks historical foundation.

²⁰ Insofar as the psalmist in vv. 4-9 describes the future fulfillment of prophecies of consolation, Rashi is justified in calling him a prophet. Concerning the claim of Ibn Ezra and other medieval Jewish exegetes that the psalms are prophetic writings see Uriel Simon, *Four Approaches to the Book of Psalms: From Saadya Gaon to Abraham Ibn Ezra* (Ramat-Gan: Bar-Ilan University Press, 1982) [in Hebrew].

²¹ Exegetical *waw*.

²² Similarly Qimhi and Arnold B. Ehrlich, *Die Psalmen* (Berlin: M. Poppelauer, 1905), p. 108. If Rashi and the latter authorities are correct, the present verse employs a homonym of the widely attested Heb. verb *dimmāh* 'compare, imagine' (see lexicons). Interestingly Cheyne, *The Book of Psalms*, vol. 1, p. 214 suggests doubtfully that a reading *qiwwînû* may lie behind LXX's ὑπελάβομεν; in fact, LXX's rendering most likely reflects the same interpretation of MT's *dimmînû*, as is found in Vulgate, Ibn Ezra, KJV, and now also in NJV. On *qiwwînû* in the sense 'beseech' see Rashi at Ps. 27:14.

²³ Perhaps this remark reflects the sufferings of the Jews at the hands of the Christians at the time of the First Crusade (1095-1099); for the view that Rashi's commentaries may, in fact, refer to those sufferings see Shershevsky, *Rashi: The Man and His World*, pp. 241-43.

²⁴ Heb. *běnê ṣiyyôn*, lit., 'sons of Zion', which may call to mind *bônê ṣiyyôn* 'builders of Zion'; cf. the interpretation of *bānayik* 'your sons' in Isa. 54:13 as *bōnāyik* 'your builders' attributed to R. Elazar quoting R. Haninah in BT Berakot 64a and quoted in Birnbaum, *Daily Prayer Book*, pp. 409-411.

²⁵ Rashi points here to the exegetical difficulty that elsewhere the *piᶜel* of the root *s-p-r* denotes not 'count' but 'recount, narrate' while 'count (numbers)' is expressed by the *qal*; cf. *BDB*, pp. 707b-708a. The standard modern commentaries are silent on this point. Perhaps the unusual use of the *piᶜel* here is meant to denote 'count repeatedly'. On the use of the *piᶜel* to indicate repetition see *GKC* #52f. Note that English 'recount', the usual rendering of *sippēr*, can also mean both 'tell' and 'count again'.

²⁶ This verb is an *hapax legomenon* of uncertain meaning; see dictionaries, and see previous note.

²⁷ In T.O. to Deut. 3:17. As noted by Maarsen, Rashi's entire exegesis of v. 14b, including the demonstration from T.O., is found verbatim in Midrash Tehillim here.

²⁸ Rashi, followed here by KJV, clarifies the meaning of the phrase *lědôr 'aḥărôn*, which otherwise might be wrongly interpreted to mean 'the last generation'; cf. the discussion of *'aḥărît hayyāmîm* 'days to come' (Gen. 49:1) in Speiser, *Genesis*, p. 364 and in Orlinsky, *Notes*, p. 141; contrast NJV here: "a future age."

²⁹ Our Rashi ms. does not quote the lemma.

[30] Maarsen suggests here that this exegesis rests upon the equation of the psalmist's 'al-mût with Rabbinic Heb. 'alîmût = zĕrîzût 'urgency' in JT Megillah 2:4; Moʿed Qaṭan 3:7, quoted in Yalqut Shimʿoni here. In fact, the explicit interpretation of the psalmist's 'al-mût as a synonym of lĕʾāṭ 'slowly' found in many Rashi mss. here, suggests that Rashi rejects that exegesis.

1 *ḥeled* 'THE WORLD'. I.e.,[1] 'the earth', [which is called *ḥeled*] because it is old and rusty [*ḥălûdāh*],[2] *roeille* in O.F.[3] Our rabbis explained[4] [that the earth is called *ḥeled*] because because of the *ḥălûdāh*] 'mole',[5] which is on the land but not in the sea, for our rabbis taught [in a *baraitha*], "Everything that is on land is in the sea except for the mole"[6]

3a ALSO SONS OF A PERSON [*běnê 'ādām*]. [While v. 2 is addressed to 'ALL YOU PEOPLES', i.e., all of humankind, v. 3a is addressed specifically to Israel, i.e.], the sons of Abraham, who is called "the greatest person [*'ādām*] among the giants" (Josh. 14: 15),[7] [i.e., among] the sons of Ishmael (Gen. 25:12-18) and the sons of Keturah (Gen. 25:1-4).[8]

3b ALSO SONS OF A MAN [*běnê 'îš*],[9] the sons of Noah who is called "virtuous *'îš* 'man'" (Gen. 6:9).[10]

4b MY THOUGHT IS FULL OF INSIGHT. As for the thoughts of my heart,[11] they are insights.

5a I SHALL INCLINE MY EAR TO THE PROVERB, to words of [Torah],[12] which is called "the ancient proverb" (1 Sam. 24:14).[13]

5b SET FORTH to you TO THE MUSIC OF A LYRE riddles.[14] Now this is the riddle:

6a WHY must I fear[15] IN TIME OF TROUBLE when the punishment you ordain[16] is meted out? [The answer to this riddle is as follows]: Because of

6b THE INIQUITY OF MY HEELS ENCIRCLES ME. [I.e.], iniquities, which I trample with MY HEELS because I make light of them, for in my eyes they are minor sins, testify against me in court.[17] All the moreso do the Gentiles who rely on faith [make light of iniquities, which will ultimately testify against them in God's court of justice].[18]

7 [As for MEN WHO TRUST IN THEIR RICHES],[19] what profit is there in their wealth? Is it not true that

8 A BROTHER is NOT able to redeem[15] his brother with his money, for if [people] are coming to redeem each one his brother,

9   THE PRICE [*pidyôn*] will go up[20] more than any form of capital. Therefore, perforce, he CEASES FOREVER to redeem him[21]

10   so that he might live ETERNALLY AND NEVER SEE THE GRAVE.[22]

11a   FOR ONE SEES THAT THE WISE DIE, and they are not saved from death. Therefore, perforce, HE CEASES (v. 9) to toil and to exert himself for the REDEMPTION [*pidyôn*] (v. 9) of his brother.

11c   THEIR WEALTH [*ḥêlām*], [i.e.], their money [*māmônām*].

11a-b With respect to THE WISE reference is made to dying [*mîtāh*][23] while with respect to THE FOOLISH AND IGNORANT reference is made to perishing ['*ăbîdāh*][24] because [when the FOOLISH AND IGNORANT die] the body and the soul perish.[25]

12a   THEIR HEART[26] [SAYS THAT] THEIR HOUSES ARE FOREVER.
     [I.e.], their plans are to build for themselves houses that will last forever.

12c   THEY CALL BY THEIR NAMES[27] their houses,[28] which they build so that they will be for them a memorial, as is exemplified by "He named the city after his son Enoch" (Gen. 4:17); Antiochus built Antioch; Seleucus built Seleucia.[29]

14a   [*kesel* 'FOLLY'][30] is a synonym of[31] *sĕtût* 'foolishness'.[32]

14b   AFTER THEM WITH THEIR MOUTHS THEY WILL SPEAK.
     I.e., those who come AFTER THEM[33] [i.e., after the fools described in vv. 7-14b] will speak about them, and they will recount WITH THEIR MOUTHS what happened to the afore-mentioned. [The verb] *yirṣû*, [whose normal meaning is 'they will be pleased'],[34] is [here] a verb referring to discourse [*harṣā'at dĕbārîm*].[35] However, our rabbis explained[36] [v. 14 as follows]:

14a   SUCH IS THE FATE of the wicked: their end is to perish. But THEY HAVE *kesel* 'KIDNEY', [i.e.], THEY HAVE fat on their *kĕsālîm*, and it [the fat] covers up their kidneys so that they [their kidneys] do not counsel them [the wicked] to turn away from their evil.[37] Now lest you say that it [their evil] is unknown to them,[38] for they forget that their fate is to die, [the latter half of] the verse is an intimation that one is to conclude otherwise:

14b   WHAT IS AFTER THEM WITH THEIR MOUTHS
      THEY SPEAK,[39]
      which is to say that the day of their fate [yôm 'aḥărîtām] is con-
      tinually IN THEIR MOUTHS, and they are not afraid of
      it.

15   LIKE A FLOCK THEY ARE SET FOR SHEOL.
      Just as a flock is gathered into a sheepfold so are they SET
      FOR SHEOL.
      The pointing of the taw [in the verb šattû 'THEY ARE SET']
      with a daghesh [forte] is an alternative to [writing the word with]
      a second taw [as follows]: "šutĕtû 'THEY WERE SET' FOR
      SHEOL," [i.e.], into the foundations [šĕtôtêāh] of SHEOL,
      [i.e.], to the lowest level [thereof]. In the same way [that the
      verb šattû here in Ps. 49:15 is a cognate of the noun šātôt 'foun-
      dations' in Isa. 19:10 and Ps. 11:3] so is [the verb šattû 'they
      set' in Ps. 73:9]: "They set their mouths against their
      mouth,"[40] i.e., their slander.

15b   DEATH SHALL FEED ON THEM. [I.e.], the angel of
      death[41] will devour them. Now do not question the usage of
      [a verb referring to] 'eating' [to denote 'dying'], for we have
      found the same thing elsewhere in the Bible: "Death's first-
      born will consume his children" (Job. 18:13).[42]

15c   THE UPRIGHT SHALL RULE OVER THEM[43] AT DAY-
      BREAK, [i.e.], at the time of [eschatological] Redemption
      when the morning of THE UPRIGHT will dawn, and they
      [THE UPRIGHT] will rule[44] over them [the wicked] in ac-
      cord with what is stated in the Bible, "You shall trample the
      wicked to a pulp" (Mal. 3:21).[45]

15d   AND THEIR FORM IS TO WASTE AWAY SHEOL.
      [This verse's assertion that] the form[46] of the wicked will waste
      away SHEOL [intimates that] Gehinnom[47] will disappear, but
      they will not disappear.

15e   TILL ITS HABITATION[48] BE GONE so that they will no
      longer have a dwelling [maddôr]. The Holy One Blessed be
      He will take out[49] the sun from its case so that it will burn
      them in accord with what is stated in the Bible, "The day
      that comes shall burn them up" (Mal. 3:19).

16a   HOWEVER, GOD WILL REDEEM MY SOUL.
      But as for me, since I inclined MY EAR TO THE PROV-
      ERB (v. 5a), GOD WILL REDEEM MY SOUL so that I
      shall not go down to Sheol,

16b   FOR HE WILL TAKE ME while I live to walk in His ways.
19a   THOUGH HE CONGRATULATES HIMSELF IN HIS
      LIFETIME.
      The wicked CONGRATULATES HIMSELF IN HIS LIFE-
      TIME, saying, "May it be well with you, O my self. May no
      evil befall you."[50] However, other people do not say of him
      such a thing.
19b   THEY MUST ADMIT THAT YOU DID WELL BY
      YOURSELF.
      But as for you [the reader of Ps. 49], if you heed my words,
      all people WILL ADMIT THAT YOU DO GOOD FOR
      YOURSELF by straightening out your behavior.
20   YOU WILL APPROACH THE GENERATION OF HIS
      [THE WICKED PERSON'S] ANCESTORS. When you will
      have completed your days and you will have died, YOU
      WILL APPROACH, and you will see THE GENERATION
      of the wicked people being punished in Gehinnom, who
20b   WILL NEVER SEE DAYLIGHT AGAIN.[51]
21   MAN DOES NOT UNDERSTAND HONOR. The path to
      [eternal] life is presented to him so that if he takes it, indeed
      he will be honored,[52] but he does not understand what is good.

PSALM XLIX, NOTES,
   [1] Heb. *hû'*.
   [2] Cf. Midrash Tehillim here, and cf. Rashi at Ps. 17:4; 39:6.
   [3] So Rashi also at Ps. 17:14; 39:6; see our discussion there.
   [4] See JT Shabbat 14:1 where the view here attributed to "our rabbis"
is attributed to R. Aha quoting R. Abbahu; this interpretation is quoted
also in Yalqut Shim'oni here; cf. Rashi's comment on R. Zeira's exegesis
of Ps. 49:2 at BT Hullin 127a. Note that both the first of Rashi's two exegeses of the word *heled*, which is presented anonymously, and the second,
which is attributed to "our rabbis," both derive from Rabbinic midrash.
It has been shown, however, by Berliner, "Beiträge zur Geschichte der
Raschi Commentare," p. 26 and confirmed by Kamin, *Rashi's Exegetical
Categorization*, p. 140 that the expression *rabbôtênû* 'our rabbis (explained)'
is used generally to identify a view stemming from BT and to set it apart
from a rabbinic source of lesser standing.
   [5] The feminine noun *huldāh* is amply attested in Rabbinic Heb.; it is
unattested in Biblical Heb. with the possible exception of the feminine
proper name Huldah (2 Kgs.22:14 = 2 Ch. 34:22). The masculine form
of the noun *holed* 'mole' is attested in the Bible only at Lev. 11:29.
   [6] BT Hullin 127a; for parallels see Saul Lieberman, *Tosefta Ki-Fshuṭah*,
Order Zeraim, pt. 2 (New York: Jewish Theological Seminary of America,
1955), pp. 652-653.

⁷ The entire verse reads as follows: "The name of Hebron was formerly 'the city of 'Arba'. He [*'Arba'*] was the greatest among the giants"; so Qimhi there; see also Rashi there; similarly NJV. The midrash quoted here by Rashi presupposes the notion that the proper name 'Arba' is an epithet of Abraham. See, e.g., *Midrash Haggadol on the Pentateuch: Genesis*, ed. Mordechai Margulies (Jerusalem: Mosad Harav Kook, 1947), p. 375, lines 5-8 (in Hebrew); for additional sources see Menahem M. Kasher, *Torah Shelemah: Genesis*, vol. 4 (New York: American Biblical Encyclopedia Society, 1951), pp. 919-920 (in Hebrew).

⁸ Cf. Midrash Tehillim here.

⁹ In some contexts the Heb. noun *'ādām* can denote 'person', whether male or female (Gen. 1:26-27; 5:1-2; Lev. 1:2; etc.) while *'îš* often means 'man' to the exclusion of 'woman' (Gen. 2:23-24; 7:2). Elsewhere *'îš* can denote 'person', either male or female (Lev. 19:3, 11; Num. 21:9; Ps. 1:1). Ehrlich, *Die Psalmen*, p. 109 holds that intrinsically *běnê 'ādām* and *běnê 'îš* are synonymous. However, the twice repeated 'ALSO' suggests that here in Ps. 49:3 the second expression is not synonymous with the first and that the parallelism is synthetic rather than synonymous. Hence Rashi is justified on stylistic grounds in distinguishing between the two groups of persons.

¹⁰ Rashi's source is Midrash Tehillim here. According to this midrash the *běnê 'ādām* being the Abrahamites, are the higher status group while the Noahides, i.e., the Gentiles, are the lower status group; so also according to the midrash immediately following in Midrash Tehillim, which interprets *běnê 'îš* as 'the members of the seventy nations', i.e., the Gentiles.

¹¹ Rashi here, as in Ps. 2:1; 9:17; 19:15; 37:30, falls into the trap he prepared for himself at Ps. 1:2 where he noted correctly that the verb *hāgāh* and its noun derivative *higgāyôn* always refer to a function of the *lēb*. Failing to draw the correct conclusion that *lēb* as the seat of *higgāyôn* 'uttering' must denote 'throat, the organ of speech' (see Ginsberg, "Lexicographical Notes," p. 80 cited at Ps. 1:2 above), Rashi concludes that *higgāyôn* as the function of the *lēb* 'mind, seat of thought' must denote 'thought'. Hence he interprets *hāgût libbî* here at Ps. 49:4 as meaning *maḥšěbôt libbî* 'the thoughts of my heart'; contrast NJV.

¹² The bracketed word is missing from our Rashi ms. by haplography; I have supplied it from other Rashi texts.

¹³ Cf. Rashi there; the source of this interpretation is Midrash Tehillim here.

¹⁴ Heb. *ḥiddôt*, a paraphrase of the psalmist's *ḥiddātî* 'MY RIDDLE' (so RSV), which NJV correctly renders 'my lesson' (see Chaim [Harold R.] Cohen, "Some Overlooked Akkadian Evidence Concerning the Etymology and Meaning of the Biblical Term *māšāl*," in *Bible Studies—Y.M. Grintz in Memoriam* [Tel Aviv: Tel Aviv University, 1982], p. 373 [in Hebrew] for demonstration that Heb. *ḥiddāh* is the semantic and etymological equivalent of Akk. *ḥittu* 'saying'). Our rendering reflects the interpretation presupposed by Rashi's comment.

[15] Rashi's paraphrase selects the nuance of the ambiguous Heb. imperfect, which is appropriate in this context.

[16] Heb. *dînêkā*, lit., 'your punishments'.

[17] Cf. Tanḥuma at Deut. 17:12; Yalqut Shim'oni at Ps. 49:6.

[18] Here Rashi directly attacks the Pauline doctrine expressed in NT Galatians 2:16: "Knowing that a man is not justified by the works of the law, but by the faith of Jesus Christ, even we have believed in Jesus Christ, that we might be justified by the faith of Christ and not by the works of the law; for by the works of the law shall no flesh be justified"; for the NT doctrine in question see also Romans 1:17; Galatians 3:11; and Hebrews 10:38-39.

[19] Our Rashi ms. does not quote the lemma.

[20] Heb. *yityaqqēr*; here as frequently Rashi paraphrases a Biblical Heb. *qal*-stative using the *hitpa'el*.

[21] Rashi responds here to two exegetical questions: (1) What is the subject of the verb *wěḥādal* 'he will cease, stop'? and (2) What is the direct object of this verb?

[22] Rashi turns into a statement the psalmist's rhetorical question, "SHALL HE LIVE ETERNALLY AND NEVER SEE THE GRAVE?"

[23] Rashi refers to the verb *yāmûtû* 'THEY DIE' (v. 11a).

[24] Rashi refers to the verb *yō'bēdû* 'THEY PERISH' (v. 11b).

[25] Rashi here seems to reflect the teaching of the Persian Muslim philosopher Avicenna (980-1037 C.E.). The latter taught that at death "the soul separates [from the body] to exist eternally as an individual. Souls that have lead pure lives and have actualized their [intellectual] potentialities continue in eternal bliss, contemplating the celestial principles. The imperfect souls, tarnished by the body, continue in eternal torment, vainly seeking their bodies, which once were the instruments of their perfection" (so Michael E. Marmura, "Avicenna," *Encyclopedia of Philosophy*, 1:228). Rashi's comment here may be the earliest Hebrew source to incorporate Avicenna's teaching, whose impact on Maimonides (1135-1205) is well known. See the latter's commentary on Mishnah Sanhedrin 10:1. Shlomo Pines, "Avicenna," *EJ* 3:957 notes, "The influence of Avicenna on Jewish philosophy remains largely to be studied."

[26] Heb. *qirbām*; RSV margin renders 'their inward (thought)'; contrast NJV and RSV, which, following LXX and Peshitta emend *qirbām* to *qibrām* 'THEIR GRAVE'. The emended text is the basis of a midrash in Midrash Tehillim here, q.v.

[27] The exegetical problem faced by Rashi here is to supply the direct object of the verb *qārē'û* 'THEY CALLED'.

[28] By stating *'et bātêhem*, i.e., the sign of the definite direct object followed by the noun 'their houses', Rashi emphasizes that he is solving the exegetical problem identified in n. 31.

[29] Cf. Midrash Tehillim at Ps. 9:7 #8; cf. also Genesis Rabbah 23:1. Rashi following the latter midrash, cites biblical and Hellenistic illustrations of the phenomenon described in Ps. 49:12, as interpreted by Rashi. A modern commentator would want to add also examples from the pre-

Hellenistic Near East, such as Azitawaddia (*KAI* 26) and Dur-Sharrukin (=Sargon's fortress), and, perhaps, some twentieth century examples such as Leningrad and Stalingrad.

[30] Lemma is absent from our Rashi ms., which has only a blank space here; our rendering is taken from KJV, which reflects the interpretation presupposed by Rashi's comment here. RSV's rendering "foolish self-confidence" is a compromise between KJV's rendering and the interpretation 'self-confidence' defended in Briggs, vol. 1, p. 410 and reflected also in NJV here; for another view see Dahood, *Psalms*, vol. 1, pp. 299-300. Held, "Studies in Comparative Semitic Lexicography," pp. 401-406 has shown that (1) the Heb. noun *kesel* means primarily 'sinew, tendon' and, by extension, 'inner strength, confidence'; and (2) the noun is unrelated to the verb *kāsal* 'be foolish' (Jer. 10:8), from which is derived the noun *kĕsîl*.

[31] Interpreting *lî* (='to me') in our Rashi ms. as a scribal error for *l*, the abbreviation for *lĕšôn*; on the meanings of the latter exegetical term in Rashi's Bible commentaries see introduction, pp. 141–146.

[32] See *Mahberet Menahem*, p. 219.

[33] Here Rashi justifiably takes *'aḥărêhem* to be a substantive meaning literally 'their followers', rather than a preposition meaning 'after them'. Without Rashi's interpretation of *aḥărêhem* v. 14b would contain a predicate with no subject.

[34] So NJV also here.

[35] The latter usage of the verb *rāṣāh* is unattested in Biblical Heb. but amply attested from Tannaitic Heb. onward; for references see Jastrow, *Dict.*, p. 1493b.

[36] Here as in Rashi's comment on v. 2 "our rabbis explained" introduces a citation from BT; cf. n. 4 above.

[37] Rava in BT Shabbat 31b understands *kesel* to mean 'kidney'. The latter organ is in Rabbinic psycho-physiology the functional equivalent of Freud's super-ego or of common Eng. 'conscience'. Rashi adds here from his commentary on BT the explanatory clauses, "and it covers up *kilyôtām*... from their evil."

[38] Lit., 'a matter forgotten by them'. Rashi in BT Shabbat 31a explains that this means, "Lest you assume that they did evil unintentionally...."

[39] Rava's question in BT is, "Will you perhaps say that it is forgotten by them? The verse is an intimation from which one is to conclude otherwise: WHAT IS AFTER THEM WITH THEIR MOUTHS THEY SPEAK." Rav here, like Rashi in the latter's own interpretation (above), takes *'aḥărêhem* to be a noun. While Rashi took this noun to be the subject of v. 14b, Rava took it to be the direct object. Note that Rashi's interpretation of the verb *yirṣû* goes back at least to Rava.

[40] Rashi's point seems to be that while *šātû* without doubled *taw* means simply 'put, place', the anomalous *šattû* (Ps. 49:15; 73:9), which can be either passive (Ps. 49) or active (Ps. 73), refers specifically to placing an object down in Sheol or up in heaven. It seems to him plausible, therefore, that the twice-attested *šattû* is a cognate of the twice-attested *šātôt* 'foundations'.

[41] Contrast Eng. versions, which see here a reference to Death personified. Dahood (here) feels that the imagery is elucidated by the Ugaritic text *UT* 51 (= *CTA* 4= *KTU* 1.4): VIII; 15-18, where it is said, "Minor deities, do not approach Môt [= Ugaritic deity of summer drought, whose name is the etymological equivalent of Heb. *māwet* 'death'] lest he treat you like a lamb in his mouth"; my rendering; cf. H. L. Ginsberg's rendering in *ANET*[3], p. 135b; contrast Dahood's rendering in his commentary here at Ps. 49:15. Just as Dahood sees here in Ps. 49:15 a reference to a Canaanite deity so does Rashi see here "the angel of death," an important figure in Rabbinic and post-Rabbinic Jewish theology. Interestingly, Dahood's remark, no less than Rashi's comment, is eisegesis in that it attempts to bring to bear upon the biblical text, by free association, an idea, which belongs to a different conceptual world. The Ugaritic myth refers to a major deity named Mot, who belongs to a pantheon; Rashi refers to Rabbinic angelology; the psalmist, on the other hand, seems to refer to an event or process, death, personified. Perhaps, however, one can link the three usages of the word *môt/māwet* as follows: in Ugaritic literature the word designates a god; in biblical literature the divine powers of Canaanite religion have been reduced to the level of creatures, who serve the will of the one God; in Rabbinic literature these creatures become 'angels'; cf. our discussion of *běnê 'ēlîm* 'divine beings' at Ps. 29, n. 2. This genetic relationship seems to be suggested by Rashi's comment here. Moreover, Rabbinic Judaism's transformation of what had once been the gods of the Canaanites into 'angels' is analogous to Christianity's transformation of local deities into saints; on the latter phenomenon see Gordon Jennings Laing, *Survivals of Roman Religion* (New York: Cooper Square Publishers, 1931), pp. 8-15. Interestingly, the treatment of what had once been Canaanite deities as 'angels' in Rabbinic Judaism (as reflected in Rashi's comment here) and the treatment of pagan deities as saints in Christianity are probably the correct and analogies for the understanding of the frequent references to Canaanite deities alongside of the one supreme creator God in the Hebrew Bible; for a summary of attempts to understand this phenomeon without the utilization of these analogies see Jon D. Levenson, *Creation and the Persistence of Evil* (San Francisco: Harper & Row, 1988).

[42] Rendering based on Rashi at Job. 18:13, where Rashi equates 'Death's firstborn' with the angel of death. Marvin Pope, *Job*, AB, vol. 15 (3[d] ed.; Garden City, N.Y.: Doubleday & Co., 1973), p. 135 discusses 'Death's firstborn' in light of the Ugaritic texts; however, as Pope admits, not only do the Ugaritic texts not attest to Mot's firstborn but also they offer no information whatsoever concerning any offspring of that deity! See previous note.

[43] Heb. *bām*; our Rashi ms. has here the scribal error *šām* 'there'.

[44] Our Rashi ms. reads *bôdîm*, a scribal error for *rôdîm*.

[45] Cf. Midrash Tehillim here.

[46] Here Rashi substitutes the familiar feminine form of the noun *ṣûrātām* 'their form' for the anomalous *ṣûrām* in the *qeri* of MT here at Ps. 49:15; cf. Mandelkern, p. 993d.

⁴⁷ Gehinnom here functions as Rabbinic Judaism's near counterpart to SHEOL; on the distinction that should be drawn between NT Gehenna [= Rabbinic and post-Rabbinic Heb. Gehinnom], "the place or state of the final punishment of the wicked" and Biblical Heb. Sheol [= NT Hades in Acts 2:27, 31; Rev. 20:13-14], "the abode of all the dead in general" see Werner E. Lemke, "Gehenna," in *Harper's Bible Dictionary*, p. 335; see also below, n. 51.

⁴⁸ This misinterpretation of *zĕbûl* at 1 Kgs. 8:13 = 2 Ch. 6:2; Isa. 63:15; Hab. 3:11 goes back to LXX; See Samuel E. Loewenstamm, "*zĕbûl*," *EM* 2:907-908; see now Victor (Avigdor) Hurowitz, *I Have Built You an Exalted House*, JSOT Supplement Series, no. 115 (Sheffield: JSOT Press, 1992), p. 285.

⁴⁹ Heb. *môṣî'*, lit., 'takes out'.

⁵⁰ Cf. Deut. 29:18.

⁵¹ I.e., they will not live again. It is reasonable for the psalmist to speak of the dead as not seeing light, for in his world-view the domain of the dead is a subterranean world called Sheol. Rashi reads in here the view first expressed in Dan. 12 that it is only the wicked who will remain in Sheol in the eschaton when the virtuous will arise from their graves and again see the light. Thus here as in his comment on v. 15d Rashi equates Biblical Heb. Sheol with late Heb. Gehinnom; see above, n. 47.

⁵² As noted by Maarsen here, *nikbād* 'honored' here is Rashi's paraphrase into standard Heb. of the psalmist's rare in Heb. and characteristically Aram. *yĕqār* 'honor'.

PSALM L

1a GOD, GOD, THE LORD,[1] [i.e.], THE LORD God,[2] whose name is THE LORD [i.e., YHWH].

1b SPOKE AND SUMMONED THE WORLD, and He

2 APPEARED FROM ZION, which is AN ADORNMENT OF BEAUTY. *miklal* 'ADORNMENT' is a noun.[3] [It corresponds semantically to] *parement* 'adornment' in O.F.[4] [Here] the future redemption has been prophesied.[5]

3 AND LET HIM NOT BE SILENT concerning the blood of His devotees, which has been spilt.

4a LET HIM SUMMON THE HEAVENS to punish the heavenly princes of the Gentiles,[6]

4b AND THE EARTH to punish the kings of the earth.

4c TO DEFEND [*lādîn*] HIS PEOPLE, [i.e.], to avenge HIS PEOPLE It is the same usage of the verb [*dîn*] as is attested in "For he will defend [*yādîn*] His people, and He will avenge the blood of His devotees" (Deut. 32:36a +43b).[7]

5a BRING IN MY DEVOTEES, which is to say that in addition [to the summons described in v. 4] LET HIM SUMMON (v. 4a) the heavens and the earth to BRING IN to Him the Exiles in accord with what is stated in the Bible, "Awake, O north wind, Come O south wind!" (Cant. 4:16).[8]

5b WHO MADE A COVENANT WITH ME OVER SACRIFICE insofar as they received the Torah with the accompaniment of a covenant [ceremony] and a sacrifice in accord with what is stated in the Bible, "This is the blood of the covenant that He makes..." (Ex. 24:8).

8a I CENSURE YOU NOT FOR YOUR SACRIFICES. If you do not offer Me sacrifices

8b AND if YOUR BURNT-OFFERINGS are not[9] MADE TO ME DAILY, I pay no attention to that.

9a I SHALL NOT ACCEPT A BULL FROM YOUR ESTATE [for] they are not yours but Mine.

9b FROM YOUR PENS. [The word *miklĕʾôtêkā* 'YOUR PENS'] designates a shed for the flock. It is the same word as is attested in "He cut off from the pen [*miklā'*][10] the flock" (Hab. 3:17).

10b BEHEMOTH ON A THOUSAND MOUNTAINS.
This [*Behemoth*] is the one put aside for the eschatological banquet. [He is called BEAST[11] ON A THOUSAND MOUNTAINS because] he is the one who consumes the vegetation on a thousand mountains per day while they [the vegetation] grow back each and every day [anew].[12]

11b THE CREATURES [*zîz*] OF THE FIELD, [i.e.], the creeping things of the field.[13] [They are called *zîz*] because they move [*zāzîm*] from place to place. [I.e., *zîz* is the semantic equivalent of] *esmouvement* in O.F.[14] WITH ME [means], "I know all of them."[15]

13 SHALL I EAT THE FLESH [of *'abbîrîm*]? i.e.,[16] 'bulls'.[17] [The meaning of this rhetorical question is as follows]: I did not tell you to present a sacrifice, for I need for Myself not food but satisfaction, for I said, "Let us do His will."[18]

14a OFFER TO THE LORD CONFESSION.[19]
[I.e.], make confession concerning your behavior, and return to Me.[20] This is the sacrifice in which I delight.

19b AND YOKE [YOUR TONGUE][21] TO DECEIT.
You make deceit a habit with you by speaking evil. This is the sacrifice in which I delight.[22]

14b Thereafter PAY YOUR VOWS TO THE MOST HIGH for [only] then will they be favorably accepted.

16c AND MOUTH THE TERMS OF MY COVENANT, [i.e.], My Torah.

18b AND YOU ARE PLEASED WITH HIM. [I.e.], you are pleased to walk with him.

20b THE SON OF YOUR MOTHER with whom you have no just quarrel, for he does not share with you an inheritance.[23] *dopî* 'DEFAMATION', [i.e.] a word of disparagement to push him aside; it is a cognate of [the verb] *yehdāpennû* "if he push him" (Num. 35:20).[24]

21b YOU WOULD FANCY, [i.e.], You thought that I WAS LIKE YOU reconciling Myself to your evil behavior.

23a HE WHO SACRIFICES CONFESSION.[25]
As for him who offers Me a sacrifice of repentance and confession of his sins, he HONORS ME.

23b   AND AS FOR HIM WHO MAKES A PATH, [i.e.], him
who returns to me wholeheartedly AND MAKES A PATH[26]
for sinners to return to Me

23c   I WILL SHOW HIM great SALVATION.[27]

PSALM L, NOTES

[1] Literal rendering of the lemma found in JPS; note that throughout
NJV and other standard Eng. translations of the Bible from KJV onward
the words LORD and GOD printed in capitals represent the Tetragrammaton, i.e., the Heb. four letter proper name of God read according to
the vowel signs in the traditional Heb. text as *'ădonāy* 'Lord' and *'ĕlohîm*
'God' respectively; see Leo G. Perdue, "Names of God in the Old Testament," in *Harper's Bible Dictionary*, pp. 685-687.

[2] Heb. *YHWH hā'ĕlohîm*, which is attested in 1 Sam. 6:20; 1 Kgs. 18:37;
Neh. 9:7; 1 Ch. 22:1, 2; other mss. of Rashi's commentary read here *'ĕlohê
hā'ĕlohîm* 'the supreme God', which is attested in Deut. 10:17 (cf. Ps. 136:2).
According to the latter reading, which is found in the Rabbinic Bibles and
in Maarsen's editon, Rashi asserts here that *'ēl ĕlohîm* 'God, God', which is
attested here in Ps. 50:1 and also twice in Josh. 22:2, once in Ps. 62:2 and
twice in Ps. 77:2, is synonymous with 'the supreme God'. Dahood, here
at Ps. 50:1, presents the same assertion as a new interpretation discovered
by D. N. Freedman!

[3] Here Rashi's point is that the initial *mem* of *miklal* represents the
preformative element in a noun of the *maqtal* class of nouns and not the
prefixed preposition *mi(n)* followed by a noun *kĕlal;* contrast Briggs, here.

[4] So also in Modern French; on the gloss see Darmsteter, *REJ* 56 (1908),
71.

[5] Jerusalem, having been destroyed by the Roman legions and not
having been rebuilt as a Jewish city when Rashi wrote his commentary,
can only be described as 'AN ADORNMENT OF BEAUTY' with respect
to the 'future (from Rashi's perspective) Redemption'.

[6] With Zohory cf. Mekilta, vol. 2, p. 20. Both the latter midrash and
Rashi's comment here share the Rabbinic notion that each of the (seventy)
nations of the world is governed by a heavenly prince. These heavenly
princes or angels are conceived as creatures of God and members of God's
royal court. The idea that God permits the (seventy) nations of the world
to adore their respective princes but insists that Israel deal directly with
God is adumbrated in Deut. 4:19 and in the Septuagintal reading of Deut.
33:8: "...He fixed the boundaries of peoples in relation to the number of
the divine beings." On the *bĕnê 'ēl* 'divine beings' in Heb. Scripture and
their correspondence both to the 'gods' of Canaanite religion and the 'angels, heavenly princes' of Rabbinic Judaism see our discussion at Ps. 29,
n. 2; Ps. 49, n. 41.

[7] Note that there is no such Scripture verse. Rashi combines the initial clause of Deut. 32:37 and the middle clause of Deut. 32:43. Apparently, Rashi sees in the latter clause the means by which there is achieved

the end spoken of in the former clause. Note also that 'His devotees' here renders Heb. *'ăbādāyw* while in Ps. 50:5a 'MY DEVOTEES' renders Heb. *ḥăsîdāy.*

[8] Cf. Canticles Rabbah 4:16.

[9] By understanding the negative particle *lō'* as governing both clauses (for this phenomenon see below, v. 9, and see *GKC* #152a), Rashi sees the two clauses as synonymous and affirming that God is not concerned with whether or not one offers Him sacrifices. As noted by Ibn Ezra here, this idea is in consonance with Jer. 7:22. The only viable alternative is to understand the verse as follows: "I CENSURE YOU NOT FOR YOUR SACRIFICES, for YOUR BURNT OFFERINGS ARE MADE TO ME DAILY." This latter rendering construes the verse as synthetic parallelism. The idea expressed by this rendering, namely, that the only reason why God does not censure you concerning your sacrifices is that you are punctilious about them, is at odds with the rest of the psalm. NJV'S "I CENSURE YOU NOT FOR YOUR SACRIFICES AND YOUR BURNT-OFFERINGS MADE TO ME DAILY" is at odds with the entire context, in which the psalmist, speaking in the name of God, does precisely that.

[10] *Sic* in our Rashi ms.; in MT of Hab. 3:17 the word is spelled with final *āh* rather than with final *ā'*.

[11] Contrast NJV's "THE BEASTS" [plural]. The midrash Rashi quotes assumes that *běhēmōt* here as in Job represents a Phoenician-type feminine singular like *ḥokmōt* in Prov. 9:1; see our discussion in Gruber, *Aspects*, p. 527, n. 1.

[12] Cf. Ginzberg, *Legends of the Jews*, vol. 5, p. 49, n. 141.

[13] In Biblical Heb. the expression is either *remeś* 'creeping thing' (Gen. 6:7; 7:23; etc.) or *remeś hā'ădāmāh* 'creeping thing of the earth' (Gen. 1:25; 6:20).

[14] I.e., 'moving about'; cf. Darmsteter, *REJ* 56 (1908), 71; cf. Modern French *émouvent.*

[15] Rashi here intimates that the two halves of v. 11 constitute noun-verb synonymous parallelism; on this phenomenon see Daniel Grossberg, "Noun/Verb Parallelism: Syntactic or Asyntactic," *JBL* 99 (1980), 481-488.

[16] Explicative *waw.*

[17] So also Rashi at Ps. 22:13.

[18] Cf. Jer. 7:22-23.

[19] From v. 8 through v. 13 the psalmist, speaking in the name of God, has downplayed the value of sacrificial worship. Hence NJV's rendering of v. 14a, "Sacrifice a thank offering to God," seems incongruous in its context. Heb. *tôdāh* can, however, mean 'confession', 'thanksgiving choir', 'thanksgiving', as well as 'thank offering' (see *BDB*, pp. 392-393). Rashi's interpretation seems more congruent with the context of our verse; contrast Ibn Ezra.

[20] I.e., 'repent'.

[21] Rashi does not quote the bracketed portion of the verse; I have supplied it for clarity.

[22] Our Rashi ms. repeats here this clause, which is the final clause of the comment on v. 14a.

[23] In Biblical and in Ugaritic poetry 'mother's son' is the poetic synonym of 'brother'; see Moshe Held, "Additional Pairs of Words in Synonymous Parallelism in Biblical Hebrew and in Ugaritic," Lěšonē!nu 18 (1953), 146; p. 151, n. 31; id., "The Action-Result (Factitive-Passive Sequence of Identical Verbs in Biblical Hebrew and Ugaritic," JBL 84 (1965), 275; p. 281, n. 58. Rashi here at Ps. 50:2 takes 'THE SON OF YOUR MOTHER' not as a poetic synonym of 'brother' in v. 20a but as a qualification of 'brother'. Since in Rabbinic halakah inheritance is normally from the father to his sons and not from the mother (see Mishnah Baba Batra 8:1 and BT ad loc, Rashi takes it for granted that the division of the inheritance is a just cause for controversy between brothers who are sons of the same father. However, to pick a quarrel with half-brothers who have only a mother in common and with whom one is not required to share a paternal estate is, in the view of Rashi here, either foolish or deliberately wicked.

[24] Maarsen in his note here raises the question as to whether the comparison is indeed to yehdāpennû in Num. 35:20 or to yehdĕpuhû in Job. 18:18, which is cited by Mahberet Menahem, p. 130, s.v. dp. In fact, both quotations employ the same verb hādap 'push', which is unrelated etymologically to dopî.

[25] See above, n. 24.

[26] For the idea cf. Ps. 51:15.

[27] Rashi's paraphrase of the psalmist's "THE SALVATION OF GOD" supports the view that rûāḥ 'ĕlohîm 'wind of God' (Gen. 1:2) and 'ēš 'ĕlohîm 'fire of God' (Job. 1:16) mean 'mighty wind' and 'mighty fire' respectively; for this view see Robert Gordis, The Book of Job (New York: Jewish Theological Seminary of America, 1978), p. 16; W. Gunther Plaut, Genesis: A Modern Commentary, trans. into Heb. by Aviv Meltzer (Jerusalem: Hebrew Union College, 1988), p. 8; contrast Orlinsky, Notes, p. 55.

PSALM LI

3a HAVE MERCY UPON ME.[1]

5b MY SIN IS BEFORE ME [*negdî*] CONTINUALLY.
    Insofar as I am regretful and concerned about it, it seems to
    me as though it is before me [*lĕpānay*] every hour.

6a AGAINST YOU ALONE HAVE I SINNED.
    Therefore, it is in Your power to forgive. Even with respect
    to what I did to Uriah[2] I SINNED only AGAINST YOU,
    who warned against the thing.[3]

6c SO THAT YOU WILL BE RIGHT IN WHAT YOU SAY.
    I had the strength to overcome my lust. However [I did not
    overcome it] so that people would not say, "The servant pre-
    vailed over his master." In fact, I said to You, "Probe me
    and try me" (Ps. 26:2), and You probed me and I was found
    wanting. Thus YOU WILL BE RIGHT and not I.[4]
    Another equally plausible interpretation of SO THAT YOU
    WILL BE RIGHT IN WHAT YOU SAY [is the following]:
    If You pardon me, YOU WILL BE RIGHT in Your sen-
    tence[5] before all the wicked who are unrepentant so that
    they will not be able to say, "Had he repented, we would not
    have been rewarded."[6]

7   INDEED I WAS BORN WITH INIQUITY. So how can I
    not sin?
    Moreover, the essential act of creating me was by means of
    sexual intercourse, through which there come about many
    iniquities.[7] Another equally plausible interpretation [of v. 7
    is as follows]: The essential act of creating me was through
    the agency of male and female [a merism for 'people'], all of
    whom are full of sin.[8] There are midrashim on this verse,
    but they are incongruent[9] with the subject matter being dis-
    cussed in this psalm.

8a INDEED YOU DESIRE TRUTH. Hence I hereby admit
    the truth, [namely], that I sinned. IN THE *ṭuḥôt*. These
    [*ṭuḥôt*] are the kidneys,[10] which [are called *ṭuḥôt* because] they
    are smooth.[11]

8b AND IN A HIDDEN PLACE [*sātûm*] TEACH ME WIS-
    DOM.

[I.e.], and in the heart, which is HIDDEN [*sātûm*], teach me the WISDOM of confessing.[12]

9   PURGE ME WITH HYSSOP as does one who purifies a leper[13] or one defiled by the dead.[14]

14a   GIVE BACK TO ME THE JOY OF YOUR DELIVER-ANCE [i.e.], prophetic inspiration,[15] which has departed from me.

14b   [The adjective] *nĕdîbāh* [in the phrase *rûăḥ nĕdîbāh* 'VIGOR-OUS SPIRIT'] is a synonym of *qĕṣînût* 'nobility'.[16]

15   I WILL TEACH TRANSGRESSORS YOUR WAYS. They will learn from me, and THEY WILL REPENT if they see that You forgive me.

16   SAVE ME FROM BLOODGUILT so that I not die by the sword as punishment for Uriah whom I killed.[17]

17   O LORD, OPEN MY LIPS. Pardon me so that I shall have an opportunity[18] to DECLARE YOUR PRAISE.

18   YOU DO NOT WANT ME TO BRING SACRIFICES. For if You WANT, I shall give it to You.[19]

20   MAY IT PLEASE YOU to build the Temple within her [Jerusalem] during the days of Solomon my son.[20]

PSALM LI, NOTES

[1] Heb. *ḥonnēnî*, which serves as the psalm title in our Rashi ms.

[2] Rashi does not comment on the first four verses of this psalm. However, in his comment on v. 6 Rashi attempts to understand the psalm in light of the attribution at v. 2: WHEN NATHAN THE PROPHET CAME TO HIM AFTER HE HAD CONSORTED WITH BATH-SHEBA (contrast NJV's rendering "come to Bathsheba"). For the account of David's adultery with Bathsheba, the attempted cover-up, and David's arranging for Uriah to fall in battle agains the Ammonites see 2 Sam. 11:2-27. For the account of Nathan's rebuking David, the latter's acknowledging his guilt, and the LORD's forgiveness see 2 Sam. 12:1-13. By asserting that Ps. 51:6a accurately describes the extent of David's guilt both with respect to his having committed adultery with Uriah's wife Bathsheba and with respect to his having arranged for Uriah to be killed, Rashi underscores the fact that in halakah both adultery and murder are essentially crimes against God. Moreover, to the extent that God's Torah governs interpersonal relations, even the offenses against the person of Uriah—taking his wife and taking his life—are first and foremost sins against God. Concerning the biblical roots of the view of the law here alluded to by Rashi see Moshe Greenberg, "Some Postulates of Biblical Criminal Law," in *Yehezkel Kaufmann Jubilee Volume*, ed. M. Haran (Jerusalem: Magnes, 1960), p. 11-12; see also Shalom M. Paul, *Studies in the Book*

of the Covenant in the Light of Cuneiform and Biblical Law, VTS 18 (Leiden: E. J. Brill, 1970), p. 37, nn. 4-6.

³ For the warnings see Ex. 20:13 = Deut. 5:17.

⁴ Here Rashi translates into Heb. an Aram. midrash attributed to Rava (299-352 C.E.) at BT Sanhedrin 107a; see n. 6 below.

⁵ Heb. *bĕdînĕkā*.

⁶ The source of this midrash is Midrash Tehillim here. The exegetical difficulty, which inspires both of the midrashim quoted by Rashi here, is that the subordinate conjunction *lĕma'an* usually means 'in order that' and introduces a purpose clause. Such a meaning of the clause introduced by *lĕma'an* in Ps. 51:6 seems to be incompatible with the preceding two clauses (v. 6a-b), "AGAINST YOU ALONE HAVE I SINNED AND DONE WHAT IS EVIL IN YOUR SIGHT." The first midrash makes v. 6c explain the purpose of what is stated in v. 6a-b while the second midrash makes v. 6c explain the purpose of what is stated in vv. 3-4. An alternative solution of the exegetical difficulty is to assume that here in Ps. 51:6 as in Am. 2:7; Ps. 68:24; Prov. 2:20 and elsewhere "*lĕma'an* expresses consequence rather than purpose" (Dahood at Ps. 51:6).

⁷ This interpretation suggests not that sexual intercourse is in itself an evil, an idea to which Ps. 51:7 can, indeed, lend itself, but that it is an act fraught with spiritual danger because of the many grave offenses, which can be accomplished only through sex relations: adultery, incest, coitus during the woman's menses, bestiality, homosexuality (Lev. 18), coitus interruptus (see Gen. 38:9 and commentaries including Rashi); and rape (2 Sam. 13:14).

⁸ Similarly Dahood here: "All men have a congenital tendency toward evil; this doctrine finds expression in Gen. 8:21; 1 Kgs. 8:46; Job. 4:17; 14:4; 15:14; 25:4; Prov. 20:9"; cf. Briggs, here.

⁹ Heb. *'ēnān mityaśśĕbîn*; on this important exegetical term in Rashi's Bible commentaries see Kamin, *Rashi's Exegetical Categorization*, pp. 60; 209-262; Gelles, pp. 14, 144-146.

¹⁰ I.e., the organ of thought in Jer. 11:20; 17:10; 20:12. In Ps. 16:7, however, the kidneys function as the conscience.

¹¹ Rashi here takes *ṭuḥôt* 'kidneys' to be a cognate of *ṭîaḥ* 'whitewash', which is used to make walls 'smooth' (cf. Ezek. 13:12); contrast *Mahberet Menahem*, p. 196; concerning *ṭuḥôt* see Pope, *Job*, p. 302.

¹² Rashi correctly senses that the two words *ṭuḥôt* and *sātûm* must be poetic parallels. Hence, if the former means 'kidneys', which, as noted above (n. 10) are treated frequently in the Bible as the seat of thinking, the latter must also designate an organ of thought. For *lēb* 'heart' in association with 'kidneys' see the verses from Jeremiah cited in n. 10 above.

¹³ See Lev. 14:4, 6, 49, 51, 52.

¹⁴ See Num. 19:6, 18.

¹⁵ Lit., "the Holy Spirit," which is mentioned explicitly in v. 13b, "Take not away from me Your Holy Spirit," and which is alluded to in v. 14b, "Let a vigorous spirit sustain me." Rashi's exegesis of v. 14a derives

from a midrash attributed to R. Judah b. Ezekiel quoting Rav at BT Yoma 22b and BT Sanhedrin 107a.

[16] Rashi (here followed by NJV) thus implicitly rejects the alternative interpretation of *rûaḥ nĕdîbāh* as 'willing spirit' (KJV, RSV, NEB). Moreover, Rashi implies that the verb *nādab* 'be willing' and the noun *nĕdîbîm* 'nobles' are derived from homonymous roots. Rashi's point seems to be that in v. 14b the psalmist is not asking for the gift of submissiveness but once again for the gift of prophetic inspiration, here called 'NOBLE SPIRIT'.

[17] See Midrash Samuel, p. 25b; see also above, n. 2. Note that Rashi does not attempt to whitewash either David's adultery or his attempted cover-up; see Rashi also at Ps. 30:2b; contrast Rashi at 2 Sam. 11.

[18] Heb. *pitḥôn peh*, lit., 'opening of the mouth', employed here by Rashi as a pun on v.17.

[19] Cf. v. 18b.

[20] Here Rashi paraphrases v. 21a in the light of v. 21b. At the same time he deals with the exegetical question as to how can King David, to whom the psalm is attributed in vv. 1-2, ask for the building of Jerusalem. The answer Rashi gives is that the psalm is not post-Exilic but pre-Solomonic; cf. Rashi at Ps. 24; 30; etc.

PSALM LII

3a   WHY DO YOU BOAST, i.e.,[1] brag OF THE EVIL, which you do, you THE WARRIOR, in [the study of] Torah?[2]

3b   GOD'S FAITHFULNESS IS EVERY DAY[3] saving whoever is pursued by you.[4] Another equally plausible interpretation of GOD'S FAITHFULNESS IS EVERY DAY [is the following]: "Had he [Abimelech] not given me [bread] would not others have given [it] to me?"[5]

4b   [Biblical Heb.] *mĕluṭṭāš* 'SHARPENED' [corresponds in meaning to Rabbinic Heb.] *mĕḥuddād* 'sharpened'.[6] WORKS TREACHEROUSLY [like a razor which] cuts the flesh along with the hair.[7]

7   [The verb] *wĕyissāḥăkā* 'AND PLUCK YOU' [means] *wĕyaʿăqorĕkā* 'and He will uproot you'.[8] [The verb] *wĕšērĕšĕkā* 'AND ROOT YOU OUT' [means] 'he will root out[9] after you to uproot all the roots'. [The privative *piʿel* denominative verb *šēreš* 'uproot', derived from the noun *šoreš* 'root' corresponds semantically to] *ésraçiner* 'uproot' in O.F.[10]

8b   THEY WILL JIBE AT HIM. Now this [which follows in v. 9] is the jibe, which they will utter AT HIM:[11]

9a   "HERE, this is THE FELLOW, who did not make[12] the Holy One Blessed be He his trust.[13] See what happened to him."

9c   HE RELIED UPON HIS MISCHIEF[14] [i.e.], he strengthened himself[15] in his wickedness.

10   BUT AS FOR ME, the [heretefore] pursued, now I shall be through Your power LIKE A THRIVING OLIVE TREE through my son [Solomon] and through my son's sons [who will be] IN THE TEMPLE OF the Holy One Blessed be He.[16]

11   FOR YOU HAVE DONE [i.e.], when You will have done[17] this for me. He [the psalmist] addressed this verse to the Holy One Blessed be He.[18]

PSALM LII, NOTES
  [1] Exegetical *waw*.

² Rashi's comment here is based upon a midrash attributed to R. Isaac, a 3ᵈ generation Amora from Palestine, at BT Sanhedrin 106b.

³ Heb. *kol-hayyôm*, which according to NJV margin means, "all the day" (emphasis mine). In fact *kol-hayyôm* 'every day' here at Ps. 52:3 and at Gen. 6:5; Isa. 28:24; 65:2; Jer. 20:8; Ps. 86:3; Prov. 23:17; etc. corresponds syntactically to such expressions as *kol-hā'ādām* 'all persons' (Gen. 7:21; Num. 12:3; 16:29; 1 Kgs. 5:11), *kol-hā'îš* 'all men' (2 Sam. 15:2), *kol-habbēn* 'all sons' (Ex. 1:22) and the like; see *GKC* #127b; contrast *kol-hayyôm hahû'* 'all that day' in Ex. 10:13; Num. 11:32; 1 Sam. 19:24.

⁴ Rashi, following Midrash Tehillim here, understands vv. 3-7 as being addressed to Doeg the Edomite; this exegesis is based upon v. 2 of the psalm; cf. 1 Sam. 22:9-10.

⁵ Cf. Midrash Tehillim here.

⁶ Attested in the *pu'al* only here but in the *qal* meaning 'to sharpen' at 1 Sam. 13:20, the verb *lāṭaš* means 'to draw (a sword)' at Ps. 7:13 (see Rashi there) while at Job. 16:9 it means 'to stab'. The verb *ḥdd* 'to be sharpened' appears in the *qal*-stative in Hab. 1:8 and three times in the *huphal* in Ezek. 21:14-16; the *pu'al* participle *mĕḥuddād*, which is familiar to speakers of Modern Heb., is typical of Rabbinic Heb.; see dictionaries of Rabbinic Heb.

⁷ Maarsen notes here that Qimhi clarifies this simile. Qimhi explains in his commentary here that just as a sharpened razor, with which a person intends to cut a little bit but which cuts a great deal, deceives its user so did Doeg, whose tongue uttered a few words, which did much harm, deceive David.

⁸ Here Rashi uses the verb *'āqar*, which is frequently attested in both Biblical and Rabbinic Heb., to explain the rare synonym *nāsaḥ;* the latter verb is attested only four times in the Heb. Bible (Deut. 28:63; Ps. 52:7; Prov. 2:22; 15:25).

⁹ Here Rashi paraphrases in the future imperfect the psalmist's perfect consecutive form.

¹⁰ Elsewhere Rashi glosses Heb *šērēš* by the synonymous O.F. *desraçiner;* see Banitt, *Rashi: Interpreter of the Biblical Letter*, pp. 67-68; Catane, *Recueil* #1023.

¹¹ Rashi's point is that v. 9 is a quotation (so NJV) and that the verb *yišḥāqû* is the *verbum dicendi* introducing the quotation.

¹² The psalmist employs the so-called imperfect to express the past tense; Rashi paraphrases, using the perfect, which serves as the past-tense form in Rabbinic and post-Rabbinic Heb.

¹³ Rashi here paraphrases the biblical text, substituting for the psalmist's 'GOD' the Rabbinic 'the Holy One Blessed be He' and for the psalmist's *mā'ûzô* 'HIS REFUGE' *mibṭāḥô* 'his trust'.

¹⁴ Rashi, Qimhi, and Ibn Ezra all pass over in silence the play on words: DID NOT MAKE GOD HIS REFUGE [*mā'ûzô*]...; HE TOOK REFUGE [*yā'oz*] IN HIS MISCHIEF.

¹⁵ Heb. *hitgabbēr;* this interpretation assumes that the verb *yā'oz* is a a cognate of the noun *'oz* 'strength' (so Mandelkern, p. 839) rather than a

cognate of the verb meaning 'take or seek refuge' (so *BDB*, p. 731b); see previous note.

[16] The psalm itself says, BUT I AM LIKE A THRIVING OLIVE TREE IN GOD'S TEMPLE. Contrast NJV's 'GOD'S HOUSE', which ignores the truth that Heb. *bayit* (= Akk. *bītu)* must be rendered according to context as 'dynasty, temple, palace, house' (cf. Orlinsky, *Notes*, p. 25). Rabbinic exegesis sees in 'GOD'S TEMPLE' here a reference to the Jerusalem Temple built by King Solomon. Such a reference in a psalm attributed to King David can, in Rabbinic exegesis, refer to David's anticipation of the Temple to be built by his son Solomon (see 2 Sam. 7); see above at Ps. 24; 30; 51; see below at Ps. 122.

[17] Rashi's point is that the psalmist, confident that God will deliver him from his present troubles, speaks of his future vindication as though it had already been realized. This attitude is a well-known and frequently discussed feature of Biblical psalms of lament. Hence, when the psalmist says in v. 11, I SHALL PRAISE YOU FOREVER, FOR YOU HAVE DONE, the psalmist means, "I SHALL PRAISE YOU FOREVER when You will have acted."

[18] Here Rashi calls attention to the abrupt switch from speaking about God in the third person in v. 10 to addressing God in the second person in v. 11.

PSALM LIII

1   ON MAHALATH, the name of a musical instrument.[1] Another equally plausible interpretation [of 'al māḥălat] is 'with
reference to ['al] Israel's illness [maḥālāh] when the Temple
will have been destroyed. He [David][2] previously composed
another psalm like this one, "THE BENIGHTED MAN
THINKS, 'THERE IS NO GOD'" (Ps. 14:1b = Ps. 53:2a):[3]
the [other] one (Ps. 14) with reference to the destruction of
the first [Temple] and this (Ps. 53) with reference to Titus in
the [time of the destruction of the] Second Temple.[4]

2   THE BENIGHTED MAN THOUGHT, 'GOD IS NO
MORE'. [This is stated with reference to Titus] when he
tore the curtain [separating the Holy of Holies from the rest
of the Temple] and his sword dripped with blood. He
[Titus] thought he killed [God] Himself.[5]

4a   EVERYONE IS DROSS [sāg] [The particple sāg] is a cognate of [the plural noun] sîgîm 'dross'.[6]

4d   NOT EVEN ONE among all his [Titus'] army, who protests
against him.

5   IN FACT[7] one must know[8] concerning THOSE WHO DE-
VOUR MY PEOPLE[9] like a repast of BREAD AND DO
NOT INVOKE GOD that their fate is that

6a   THERE[10] THEY will[11] BE SEIZED WITH FRIGHT in
the time to come.

6b   This [FRIGHT] WAS NOT like the former FRIGHT,
which befell Belshazzar (Dan. 5),[12]

6c   FOR in this [post-Second Temple] Redemption the Holy
One Blessed be He WILL HAVE SCATTERED THE
BONES OF YOUR BESIEGERS [i.e.], those who are be-
sieging you, O Jerusalem,[13] in accord with what is stated in
the Bible, "His flesh will rot..." (Zech. 14:12).

6d   YOU [i.e.], You, O LORD,[14] HAVE PUT TO SHAME my
enemies[15]

6e   for You rejected them.[16]

PSALM LIII, NOTES
    [1] This interpretation derives from *Mahberet Menahem*, p. 116, s.v. *gat*;

contrast NJV margin: "Meaning of Heb. unknown."

   [2] To whom this psalm is attributed in v. 1.

   [3] On duplicate psalms in general see Ps. 14, n. 1.

   [4] For the source of this midrash see Ps. 14, n. 1.

   [5] See BT Giṭṭ in 56b and Rashi's comment there.

   [6] If so, *kullô sāg* should mean "EVERYONE IS DROSS" (so NJV). Rashi's apparent source is Midrash Tehillim. Dahood, here renders *sāg* 'miscreant', assuming that in the Northern dialect of the Elohistic Ps. 53 *sāg* is the semantic equivalent of *sār* in the Southern dialect of the Yahwistic Ps. 14:3; cf. Briggs at Ps. 14.

   [7] Heb. *hălō'* rendered as an asseverative particle to reflect the interpretation presupposed by Rashi's comment here; contrast NJV's treatment of *hălō'* as an interrogative particle and of v. 5 as a question; for other instances in Biblical Heb. where *hălō'* may be taken as an asseverative particle see Orlinsky, *Notes*, pp. 95, 120, 126, 249; Dahood, *Psalms*, vol. 2, p. 24, n. 2 and the extensive literature cited there.

   [8] Rashi's paraphrase of the psalmist's *yādĕ'û* 'THEY MUST KNOW'.

   [9] Our Rashi ms. employs the singular; the biblical text and other versions of the commentary employ the plural, which is preferable here since the following clauses refer back to THOSE WHO DEVOUR MY PEOPLE using plural verbs.

   [10] For *šām* 'there' as the place of judgment after death see Job. 1:21; 3:17; Eccles. 9:10; for parallels in Gk. and Egyptian see Pope, *Job*, p. 16 at Job. 1:21.

   [11] Rashi paraphrases employing the imperfect to express the future; the biblical text employs a prophetic perfect; hence NJV employs the Eng. future tense.

   [12] V. 6a means literally, "THERE WAS NO FEAR." NJV renders "Never was there such a fright," noting in the margin, "Meaning of Heb. uncertain." Rashi is justified in seeing this clause as contrasting Titus' fear with that of Belshazzar since the parallel verse in Ps. 14 (v. 5) does not contain this clause; see Rashi and our discussion there.

   [13] Here Rashi answers the exegetical question, "Who is being addressed in v. 6b?"

   [14] By adding the words "You, O LORD" following the lemma *hĕbîšotāh* 'YOU HAVE PUT TO SHAME' Rashi intimates that while in the abrupt switch from 3[d] pers. masc. sing. to 2[d] pers. fem. sing. in v. 6c Jerusalem is addressed, here in v. 6d it is God who is addressed in the 2[d] pers. sing

   [15] Rashi supplies the unstated direct object of the verb 'YOU HAVE PUT TO SHAME'; contrast NJV, which assumes that the implied direct object is 'YOUR BESIEGERS' (v. 6c)

   [16] Paraphrasing v. 6e and avoiding the abrupt change of persons from 2[d] to 3[d] pers. in addressing (and referring to) God, which is characteristic of both biblical psalmody and Rabbinic liturgy. On this phenomenon in Rabbinic liturgy see Kadushin, *The Rabbinic Mind* [3], p. 267. Note that until recently many biblical scholars thought that all such abrupt changes

reflected not the psychology of religion but ancient interpolation; not surprisingly, the latter view was adopted also to explain the appearance of the phenomenon in Rabbinic liturgy; see Arthur Spanier, "Zur Formengeschichte des altjüdischen Gebetes," *MGWJ* 78 (1934), pp. 438-447.

PSALM LIV

3b   BY YOUR POWER JUDGE ME [*tĕdînēnî*] [i.e.], vindicate
      me.[1] This verse reflects the same nuance [of the verb *dîn* 'to
      judge'] as is reflected in[2] "For the LORD will vindicate
      [*yādîn*] His people" (Deut. 32:36).

7a   *lĕśōrĕrāy* 'OF MY WATCHFUL FOES' [means] *lĕʾōyĕnāy* 'of
      those who look upon me with enmity'.[3] [The participle *śōrēr*]
      is a cognate of [the verb *ʾăśûrennû* 'I shall look upon him' in]
      "I shall look upon him but not close up" (Num. 24:17).

7b   BY YOUR FAITHFULNESS
      Insofar as You are faithful and You promised to exact pun-
      ishment from slanderers and murderers, therefore DE-
      STROY THEM.[4]

PSALM LIV, NOTES

[1] So now RSV; NJV; etc.

[2] Heb. *kĕmô*.

[3] Heb. *śōrĕray* 'my enemies' is attested four more times in the Bible, all
in the Book of Psalms: 5:9; 27:11; 56:3; 59:11, and the biform *śûrāy* is attested once in Ps. 92:12. The participle *ʾōyēn* 'one who looks with enmity',
which Rashi rightly regards as the semantic equivalent of *śōrēr* is attested
only once in the Bible, in 1 Sam. 18:9. Rashi, however, appears to assume
that his reader would be more familiar with *ʾōyēn* than with *śōrēr*. The obvious explanation is that the verbal root of the former expression is well-
attested in Rabbinic Heb. while the verbal root of the latter is unknown
in Rabbinic Heb. *Mahberet Menahem*, p. 368, s.v. *śr* VI presents the semantic equivalence of *śōrēr* and *ʾōyēn* only as a possibility. He does not treat
śōrēr and *ʾăśûrennû* as cognates.

[4] Rashi's comment here seems to be inspired by (a) Sifra at Lev.
19:16, which juxtaposes precisely the Heb. terms for slander and murder
employed here; and (b) Sifra at Lev. 18:1, which interprets "I am the
LORD" (passim in Lev. 18-19) to mean, "I AM full of compassion; I AM
a judge in exacting punishment, and I AM faithful to pay a reward"; cf.
Rashi at Lev. 19:16.

PSALM LV

3   I SHALL MOURN [*'ārîd*] IN MY SADNESS [*běśîḥî*].
    [I.e.], I shall grieve [*'et'ônēn*][1] in my sorrow [*běṣa'ǎrî*].[2] [The verb *'ārîd* 'I SHALL MOURN'] is a cognate of [the noun *měrûdî* 'my mourning' in] "my affliction and my mourning"[3] (Lam. 3:19) [and of the verb *wěyāradtî* 'I shall mourn' in] "and I shall mourn upon the mountains" (Judg. 11:37).[4]

4c FOR THEY BRING EVIL UPON ME. Doeg and Ahito- phel impute to me iniquities to prove that I am worthy of death, and they make [the shedding of] my blood legiti- ·mate.[5]

5   *yāḥîl* 'IS CONVULSED' [i.e.], *yid'ag* 'is concerned'.

8   SURELY, I WOULD...FAR OFF....

9a I[6] WOULD SOON FIND ME A REFUGE.
    If I had wings I would flee FAR OFF[7] and hasten to save myself[8]

9b FROM the hands of them, who are like THE SWEEPING WIND,
    which uproots trees. [The participle *so'āh* 'SWEEPING'] is a cognate of [the verb *wayyassa'* 'He uprooted' in] "He up- roots... like a tree" (Job. 19:10).[9]

10b CONFUSE [*pallag*] THEIR SPEECH. Separate them so that no person will understand[10] THEIR SPEECH.[11]

10c FOR I SEE LAWLESSNESS AND STRIFE done by them.[12]

11 DAY AND NIGHT THEY ENCIRCLE IT.
    [The compound subject of this clause is] STRIFE (v. 10c) and EVIL (v. 11b).

12a *hawwôt* [i.e.], *šeber* 'destruction'.[13]

12b FRAUD AND DECEIT, a synonym of 'overreaching'[14]

13a IT IS NOT AN ENEMY WHO REVILES ME.
    So long as I live I CAN BEAR my revilement with which you revile me for you are a person who is great in [knowl- edge of] the Torah.[15]

14a A MAN [*'ěnôš*] LIKE MY WORTH [i.e.], a man [*'îš*] impor- tant like me.

14b *mĕyûdā'î* 'MY FRIEND' is a synonym of *'allûpî* 'MY COM-
PANION';[16] it is a cognate of [the verb *wā'ēdā'ăkā* 'I have
known you' in] "I have known you by name" (Ex. 33:17),
[which we render into Aram. by][17] *wĕrabbîtāk* 'I exalted
you'.[18]

15a WHO TOGETHER we used to[19] TAKE SWEET COUN-
SEL[20] in the Torah.[21]

15b IN GOD'S HOUSE we used to[21] WALK ABOUT *bĕrāgeš*
[i.e.], among a multitude.[22] IN GOD'S HOUSE [i.e.], in the
houses of study.[23]

16a DEATH AGAINST THEM. [I.e.], May the Holy One
Blessed be He INCITE against them the Angel of Death.[24]
yaššî [means] *yĕsaksēk* 'he will stir up' (Isa. 9:10) [and] *massît*
'entice' (Jer. 43:3; 2 Ch. 32: 11). It is the same verb as is attested in "He [the snake] enticed me [*hiššî'anî*], and I ate"
(Gen. 3:13).

16c IN THE PLACE OF THEIR SOJOURN [*bimĕgûrām*] [i.e.],
bimĕlônām 'in the place of their lodging'.[25]

18 EVENING, MORNING, AND NOON [refer to] *shaḥarit*
'the morning prayer, *'arevit* 'the evening prayer', and *minḥah*
'the afternoon prayer', [the] three [daily] prayers [pre-
scribed by *halakah*].[26]

19a FROM THE BATTLE AGAINST ME [i.e.] from the war I
experience.[27]

19b FOR THE SAKE OF MULTITUDES.... [I.e.], FOR this
He did for me for the sake of[28] the multitudes, who were of
help to me by praying for me[29] in accord with what is stated
in the Bible, "All Israel and Judah loved David" (1 Sam.
18:16).

20a GOD HEARS the prayer of those [aforementioned] multitudes,

20b AND the King, who is ENTHRONED IN THE EAST
ANSWERED THEM.[30]

20c BECAUSE THERE ARE NO PASSINGS FOR THEM,
[i.e.], for those [aforementioned] wicked people, who are
pursuing me [the psalmist]. [THERE ARE NO PASSINGS
FOR THEM means that] they do not think of[31] the day of
their passing [i.e.], they are not in awe of the day of death.

21 HE SENT FORTH HIS HANDS.[32] This [person, who
SENT FORTH HIS HANDS], is the villain, Ahitophel.[33]

AGAINST HIS ALLY [bišlomāyw] [i.e.], against someone who was at peace [šālēm] with him.[34]

22   ḥālĕqû 'THEY WERE SLIPPERY'[35] is a cognate of [the noun] ḥălaqlaqqôt 'slipperiness' (Ps. 35:6). [The noun maḥămā'ot[36] in the phrase] maḥămā'ot pîw is a cognate of [the noun] ḥem'āh 'butter', and the initial mem is a preformative[37] like the mem of ma'ăśēr 'tithe' (Gen. 14:20; Num. 18:21, 26) and the mem of mar'eh 'appearance' (Gen. 12:11; 24:16; etc.) and the [initial] mem of ma'ămar 'word' (Esth. 1:15; 2:20; 9:32). ûqĕrob-libbô [means] 'And his thinking [wĕlibbô] is about war.[38] AND THEY WERE pĕtîḥôt. Menahem [Ibn Saruq] interpreted [this noun as] a synonym of ḥărābôt 'swords'.[39] I, however, think that it is a word meaning 'curse' in Aramaic in accord with what we read [in the Babylonian Talmud, Rosh ha-Shanah 31b]: "Amemar wrote out a curse [pĕtîḥā'] against her." Now that [kind of curse is [called] 'a writ of excommunication'.

23   yĕhabĕkā [means] maśśa'ăkā 'your burden'.[40]
[As for v. 23, CAST YOUR BURDEN ON THE LORD AND HE WILL SUSTAIN YOU; HE WILL NEVER LET THE RIGHTEOUS MAN COLLAPSE, in which suddenly someone is spoken to about God after vv. 2-21, in which the psalmist addresses God (vv. 1-12; 16) or his treacherous friend (vv. 13-15) or speaks about God (vv. 17-20)], prophetic inspiration responds to him [the psalmist] with these words. yĕkalkĕlekā 'HE WILL SUSTAIN YOU' [means] 'He will bear your burden'. It is a cognate of [the noun] kilkûl 'support, sustenance', [which is] rendered into Aramaic in the Targum of Jon[athan] son of Uzziel[41] as mĕsobar 'sustenance'.[42] môṭ 'COLLAPSE' [i.e.] 'slipping of foot'.

PSALM LV, NOTES
    [1] KJV here follows Rashi and renders "I mourn."
    [2] As noted by Maarsen here, so Rashi also in his comment at BT Sanhedrin 70a on Prov. 23:29.
    [3] RSV emends mĕrûdî to mĕrôrî 'my bitterness' while RSV margin renders MT's mĕrûdî 'my wandering', construing the noun as a derivative of a verbal root rwd 'wander'; cf. NJV's rendering 'ārîd "I AM TOSSED ABOUT," which also assumes derivation from the latter root (see BDB, p. 923b).
    [4] NJV renders according to the context 'lament'; however, NJV's marginal note suggest that this nuance of the verb yārad 'descend' derives

from the symbolic act of descending a hill or mountain in mourning reflected in Isa. 15:3; this suggestion echoes Rashi's comment at Judg. 11:37. Ehrlich, *Mikrâ ki-Pheschutô*, vol. 2, p. 76 argues that *wěyāradtî* in Judg. 11:37 is a scribal error for an original *wěradtî*. While Ehrlich derives the latter form from an Arab. root meaning 'to wander' (see above n. 3), Rashi's comment here at Ps. 55:3 leads us to suggest that indeed the correct reading at Judg. 11:37 is *wěradtî* but that the common root of *'ārîd* (Ps. 55:3), *měrûdî* (Lam. 3:19), and *wěradtî* (Judg. 11:37) is *rwd* 'to mourn'.

[5] Rashi's comment here is based upon the midrash attributed to R. Samuel in Midrash Tehillim at Ps. 3:3 #5/6.

[6] The reading "LET HIM SOON FIND ME A REFUGE" in our Rashi ms. probably represents a scribal error.

[7] In Biblical Heb. "I WOULD FLEE FAR OFF" is expressed by the imperfect form of the *hiphil* of the verb *rhq* 'to be far' followed by the infinitive construct (without prefixed *lamed* of the verb *ndd* 'to flee'. In Rashi's Heb. the same sentence is expressed by the perfect of the verb 'to be' followed by the *hiphil* participle of the verb *rhq* to be far' followed by the infinitive construct (with prefixed *lamed*) of the verb *nûd* 'to wander'.

[8] Rashi's paraphrase of v. 9a.

[9] Since Rashi, following Menahem, treats so-called *lamed-he* verbs such as *sa'āh* 'sweep' and *pe-nun* verbs such as *nāsa'* 'uproot' as biliteral roots (see Englander, *HUCA* 7 [1930], 399-437; *HUCA* 11 [1936], 367-389), it is understandable that Rashi here, following Menahem, would not distinguish between these two roots. Like *Mahberet Menahem*, p. 268, s.v. *s'*, Rashi treats them as a single root meaning 'uproot'.

[10] For this nuance of the verb *šāma'* cf., e.g., Isa. 33:19.

[11] Rashi's comment here responds to the exegetical question as to how the verb *pālag*, whose basic meaning is 'divide, separate' can be employed in a secondary meaning 'confuse'.

[12] In v. 10a the psalmist speaks of 'THEIR SPEECH'; it is not clear to whose speech the psalmist refers. In v. 10b the psalmist speaks of 'LAWLESSNESS AND STRIFE'. Apparently, vv. 10a-b constitute a non-sequitur. Rashi solves the latter problem while supplying an answer to the question raised with respect to v. 10a. He does so by supplying the words *'al yādām* 'by them', suggesting that the 'LAWLESSNESS' is brought about by the persons, to whose 'SPEECH' the psalmist refers in v. 10a.

[13] Rashi's comment is based on *Mahberet Menahem*, p. 136, s.v. *hy* II; similarly Qimhi here: 'destruction and evil'; similarly *BDB*, p. 217b; RSV 'ruin'; similarly Briggs, here; for another approach see Zorell, p. 187; Dahood, *Psalms*, vol. 2, p. 13 at Ps. 52:4 and NJV here, which renders 'malice'; KJV already renders 'wickedness'.

[14] Concerning *'ônā'āh* 'overreaching' in Rabbinic lore see Kadushin, *Worship and Ethics*, pp. 207-209. Note that many editions of Rashi's commentary here have instead of the equation of Biblical Heb. *mirmāh* 'DECEIT' with 'overreaching' the equation of Biblical Heb. *tôk* with Heb. *makkāh* 'wound', which is found in Rashi's commentary again at Ps. 72:14;

the latter equation is accepted in *BDB*, p. 1067b; contrast Qimhi, followed by NJV, which understands *tôk* as a noun meaning 'fraud'.

[15] With Zohory, p. 155 note that Rashi's comment here is based on the midrash attributed to R. Nahman at Midrash Tehillim at Ps. 55 #1 and the last of the midrashim in Midrash Tehillim at Ps. 3:3 #4-5.

[16] The word with which it is juxtaposed in this verse. Thus Rashi here reaffirms the observation made in his comment at Ps. 9:5: "In the Bible precise synonyms are juxtaposed"; see our discussion there, and contrast the arguments of Gelles and Kugel there cited.

[17] The bracketed portion of the comment is missing from our Rashi ms.

[18] So T.O. there; note that the expression *mĕtargĕmînān* 'we render into Aram.' refers to the renderings found in Rabbinic Judaism's *official* Targums, sc., T.O. on the Pentateuch and TJ on the Prophets; see above at Ps. 40, n. 25; Ps. 42, n. 48. Note also that when Rashi refers to the rendering in T.O. of a Pentateuchal verse he is discussing or to the rendering in TJ of a Prophetic verse he is discussing Rashi employs the expression *targûmô* 'its rendering in the [official] Targum'; this expression is never found in Rashi's commentary with respect to verses from the psalter because Rashi was unaware of any Targum on the Book of Psalms; concerning the latter observation see Ps. 48, n. 18.

[19] Here Rashi intimates that the psalmist has employed the imperfect form of the verb to express the past progressive.

[20] Rendering of the lemmas according to the interpretation presupposed by Rashi's comment; so, under the influence of Rashi, KJV and JPS.

[21] Cf. Midrash Tehillim on the previous verse.

[22] Similarly Ibn Ezra and Qimhi and so KJV, RSV, et al.; contrast Rashi at BT Yoma 24b. There Rashi interprets *regeš* here in Ps. 55:15b not as a word meaning 'multitude' but as a word meaning the loud voice of a multitude. NJV renders "together."

[23] As we noted at Ps. 52, n. 16 Biblical Heb. *bêt 'ĕlohîm*, lit., 'God's House', should normally be rendered idiomatically as 'God's Temple'; here, however, Rashi alludes to the Rabbinic view that institutions of Torah learning are also temples of God by virtue of the conviction that study of Torah is a form of worship; on the latter conviction see Kadushin, *The Rabbinic Mind*[3], p. 213.

[24] Here as in Ps. 49:15, q.v., the Bible speaks of personified Death, and Rashi sees a reference to the Rabbinic 'Angel of Death' while recent commentators see a reference to the Canaanite deity Mot.

[25] It appears that by this comment Rashi wishes to emphasize that the psalmist here calls the earthly abode of the wicked *māgûr*, lit., 'place of sojourning', i.e., a temporary abode rather than *môšab*, lit., 'place of dwelling'; cf. the comment of the Passover Haggadah on the verb *wayyāgor* 'he sojourned' at Deut. 26:5; see Glatzer, *Passover Haggadah*, pp. 32-33.

[26] According to R. Samuel [b. Nahmani] at Midrash Tehillim here, Ps. 55:18 is the scriptural prooftext for the three daily prayer services said to

have been instituted by the patriarchs—Abraham, Isaac, and Jacob, respectively. The midrash explains that King David said [in composing Ps. 55:18], "Insofar as the fathers of the world prescribed them [the three prayer services], I also SHALL PRAY EVENING, AND MORNING, AND AT NOON."

[27] Here Rashi, followed by most commentators, asserts that *miqqĕrob* means 'from the battle'. Obadiah Sforno (1475-1550) realized, however, that *qĕrob* here can represent the infinitive construct of the verb *qārab* 'approach'. According to Sforno, therefore, vv. 19-20 mean, "He safely redeemed my life from [those who were] approaching me. Indeed many were against me." For *'immādî* 'against me' see Job. 6:4a; see *BDB*, p. 767; contrast Rashi.

[28] Rashi here renders the prefixed preposition of *bĕrabbîm* by means of *bišĕbîl* 'for the sake of'; contrast KJV and RSV, which ignore the preposition.

[29] Cf. Midrash Tehillim here.

[30] In this brilliant comment Rashi construes v. 20a up to and not including Selah 'Pause' as synonymous parallelism, in which *yišma'* 'HE HEARS' and *wĕya'ănēm* 'HE ANSWERS THEM' (contrast NJV's 'humbles') both refer to God's response to the prayers of David's multitude of devotees on behalf of their beloved monarch; see Rashi on v. 19. Now if the verbs *yišma'* and *wĕya'ănēm* are synonymous, Rashi must find in the second clause a synonym for *'ēl*, i.e., another divine name or epithet. This Rashi finds in *yōšēb qedem*, for Rashi here anticipates Samuel R. Driver, *The Books of Joel and Amos*, CB (Cambridge: Cambridge University Press, 1897), p. 132 by almost ten centuries, and he takes *yōšēb* here (as in Am. 1:5, 8) as ellipsis for *yōšēb 'al kissē'* 'he who is enthroned on the throne' (= Akk. *āšib parakki*), i.e., 'the king'. See Mayer I. Gruber, "The Many Faces of Hebrew *nāśā' pānîm*," *ZAW* 95 (1983), p. 257, n. 25. The question remains as to whether Rashi here understands *yōšēb qedem* to mean 'He who is enthroned in the East' (i.e., at Jerusalem; so Ibn Ezra here) or 'He who is enthroned of old' (so Qimhi followed by RSV, NJV). Rashi's treatment of this verse should put to rest the claim of Gelles, p. 101 that "Rashi fail[ed] to take note of the existence of *parallelismus membrorum*."

[31] Reading with other editions of Rashi's commentary here *'ēn nōtĕnîm libbām 'el*; the reading in our Rashi ms. *'ēn nōtĕnîm lāhem 'el*, lit., 'they do not give themselves [a thought] of' may represent either an elliptical means of expressing the same idea or simply a scribal error by which *libbām* 'their heart, their thought' became *lāhem* 'to themselves'.

[32] Gesture-derived expression meaning 'to harm' (so NJV here); see Paul Humbert, "Etendre la main," *VT* 12 (1962), pp. 383-395.

[33] Based on Midrash Tehillim here; see next note.

[34] Based on Midrash Tehillim here. Ps. 55:4, 21 aptly describes the behavior of a fifth columnist such as Ahitophel, King David's advisor, who became a secret agent on behalf of Absalom's underground. Ahitophel's behavior is described in 2 Sam. 15-17. The difference be-

tween a midrash and an illustration or a parallel is that a midrash asserts that in fact King David, to whom Ps. 55 is attributed at Ps. 55:1, refers specifically to Ahitophel in vv. 4, 21.

[35] Based on Rashi's comment here; cf. Rashi at Ps. 35:6; contrast NJV: 'smoother'. Aside from the argument advanced by Rashi at Ps. 35:6, his interpretation here at Ps. 55:22 seems to be supported by his comparison to butter in v. 22b.

[36] Modern Heb. writers took *maḥămā'ôt* to be the plural of a supposed *maḥămā'āh* 'compliment'; hence the use of the latter noun and its supposed plural in the sense 'compliment(s) in contemporary Heb. speech and letters; see Ben Yehudah, Dict., vol. 6, pp. 2917-2918; Ya'aqov Canaani, *Ozar Ha-Lashon Ha-'Ivrit*, vol. 9 (Jerusalem & Tel Aviv: Massada, 1968), p. 2788.

[37] On the significance of the expression *yĕsôd nōpēl* in Rashi's grammatical terminology see the discussion at Ps. 119:5. Here Rashi's point is that contra *Mahberet Menahem*, p. 178, s.v., *ḥm* III (followed by Qimhi, KJV, NJV; so also Midrash Tehillim here), the initial *mem* of *maḥămā'ot* is not a form of the preposition *mi(n)* 'more than'. Instead, Rashi asserts, *maḥămā'ot* is a *maqtal* noun synonymous with the segholate noun *ḥem'āh* 'butter' in the same way that *malbûš* (Zeph. 1:8) is a synonym of *lĕbûš* (Job. 24:7) 'garment'. *BDB*, p. 563a notes that to render 'more than butter' one must change MT's vocalization. Rashi's interpretation of *maḥămā'ot* as a synonym of *ḥem'āh* 'butter' indicates his awareness that in Biblical Heb. (as is the case also in Phoenician) the suffix *ot* can be feminine singular as well as plural; on the latter phenomenon see Gruber, *Aspects*, p. 527, n. 1; Dahood, *Psalms*, vol. 2, p. 37.

[38] Here as in v. 19 Rashi, followed by NJV, takes *qĕrob* to be a form of the noun *qĕrāb* 'battle'.

[39] *Mahberet Menahem*, p.306, s.v., *ptḥ* III; so NJV.

[40] With Zohory, p. 158 cf. BT Rosh ha-Shanah 26b; Midrash Tehillim here.

[41] Rabbinic Judaism's official Aramaic translation of the Prophetic Books (Joshua, Judges, Samuel, Kings, Isaiah, Jeremiah, Ezekiel, and The Book of the Twelve [Minor] Prophets); see BT Megillah 21b; see above, n. 18.

[42] Examples of TJ's rendering Heb. *klkl* by Aram. *sbr* include 2 Sam. 20:3; 1 Kgs. 18:13; Zech. 11:16. Note, however, that at Gen. 47:12 T.O. renders Heb. *kilkēl* by Aram. *zān* 'sustain'.

PSALM LVI

1   [*'al*]¹ THE SILENT DOVE AMONG THE FAR OFF.²
He [King David]³ composed [this psalm] with reference to
[*'al*]⁴ himself, for he was far away [*rāḥôq*]⁵ from the land of
Israel [sojourning] with Achish, and Golitah's brothers
asked Achish's permission to kill him in accord with what is
stated in the Bible, ["The courtiers of Achish said to him],
'Why, that's David, king of the land!'" (1 Sam. 21:12). Now
he [David] was [behaving] among them [the Philistines of
Gath] like a silent dove.⁶

2   MEN PERSECUTE ME [*šĕ'āpanî 'ĕnôš*] [i.e.], they seek to
swallow me; *goloser* 'desire passionately' in O.F.⁷ [The verb
šā'ap, which appears here in the form *šĕ'āpanî* 'HE PANTS
AFTER ME'] is the same verb as is attested in *šā'ăpāh rûăḥ*
"She pants after the wind" (Jer.2: 24).⁸

3   HEAVEN [*mārôm*] [i.e.], the Holy One Blessed be He who is
[enthroned in]⁹ *mārôm* ¹⁰

5   WHEN¹¹ GOD I SHALL PRAISE HIS WORD. [I.e.],
even when He comes against me with the attribute of justice,
I SHALL PRAISE HIS WORD, and I shall trust (cf. vv. 4,
5b) in Him.¹²

6   EVERY DAY THEY CONTINUALLY SADDEN MY
WORDS.
Those who pursue me sadden me until all the words of my
mouth are sadness and crying [*sĕʿāqāh*].

7a   THEY PLOT, THEY LIE IN AMBUSH. They are lying in
wait by¹³ spending the night in the place to which they hope
that I will go,

7b   and they WATCH¹⁴ MY FOOTSTEPS [*'ăqēbay*] [i.e.], *treces*
in O.F.¹⁵ in order to spy me out and to bring to that place
those who are in pursuit of me. [In] all of this [vv. 2, 6-7] he
[David] was complaining about the wicked among Israel,
who were lying in ambush against him and because of the
fear of whom he fled to Achish. *yāgûrû* [means] *yālînû* 'they
spend the night'¹⁶; *yiṣpônû* [means] *yeʾerĕbû* 'they will lie in
wait'. [THEY HOPED MY DEATH]¹⁷ corresponds in

meaning to THEY HOPED for MY DEATH. When they know and they hope[18] [concerning the] way in which I go.[19]

8   TO ESCAPE BY MEANS OF EVIL.

[They hope][20] to find[21] escape [*haṣṣālāh*] by means of evil and transgression and wickedness. *pallēṭ* is synonymous with *lĕpallēṭ* 'to escape'.[22] They anticipate people telling them to kill me.

9a   YOU KEEP COUNT OF MY WANDERINGS.

You know the number of the places to which I have fled.

9b   Put MY TEARS INTO your FLASK[23] so that they may be preserved before You. IS IT NOT IN YOUR ACCOUNT-ING. Indeed, put it into Your numerical record by counting it among the rest of my troubles.

11   OF GOD I BOAST; OF THE LORD I BOAST.

[The point of the two clauses, one employing the generic name GOD, the other employing the tetragrammaton, is that] I SHALL BOAST concerning divine Justice and concerning divine Love.[24]

14   IN THE LIGHT OF LIFE is a metaphor for the land of Is-rael.[25]

PSALM LVI, NOTES

[1] Rashi does not quote the bracketed portion of the verse; I have supplied it for clarity.

[2] Lemma rendered according to Franz Delitzsch, *The Psalms*, vol. 2, p. 166. This interpretation coincides with the one which underlies the midrash, which Rashi quotes here; see below. Dahood, here conjectures that "according to 'The Dove...'" means "to be sung to the tune of the song called 'The Dove'...." Cf. the practice of designating by name the tunes to which hymns are sung in present-day Christian hymnals.

[3] To whom the psalm is attributed in the continuation of v. 1.

[4] Here Rashi answers the exegetical question, "What is the meaning of the preposition '*al* here?" Contrast Dahood, whose view is cited in n. 2; contrast also NJV's 'on', which appears to assume, on the analogy of Ps. 5:1; 6:1; 8:1 that JONATH-ELEM REHOKIM is the name of a musical instrument.

[5] Here the midrash accounts for David's referring to himself in Ps. 56:1 as among the REHOKIM 'far off'. Rashi's comment is based upon the midrash attributed to R. Phineas (a late 4th cent. C.E. Palestinian Amora) in Midrash Tehillim here.

[6] This comment, which is based on the continuation of the midrash cited in the previous note, accounts for David's referring to. himself in Ps. 56:1 as a SILENT DOVE. The midrash is justified in seeing this as a fit-

ting metaphor to describe David's silence, which is alluded to in 1 Sam. 21:13-14; q.v. There it is noted that David 'took to heart' the words of Achish's servant and that David reacted first by feigning an epileptic seizure (v. 13; see for this interpretation of David's behavior Roland Kenneth Harrison, "Disease," in *International Standard Bible Encyclopedia*, ed. Geoffrey William Bromiley [4 vols.; Grand Rapids: Eerdmans,1979], vol. 1, p. 956) and soon thereafter by fleeing. Since the passage, which describes in great detail David's thoughts and actions, does not mention David's having said even a word, it is reasonable to deduce from that passage that David was silent.

[7] Levy, *Contribution*, #37, s.v. *agulusement*; #491, s.v. *goroç*; see also Breithaupt here.

[8] So Dahood, here. RSV's 'trample' is based upon LXX, which construes *šeʾāpanî* as a form of the homonym *šāʾap* 'to crash'; see *BDB*, p. 983b.

[9] Heb. *yōšēb* supplied from other editions of Rashi's commentary here; presumably, it is missing from our Rashi ms. by haplography; on the nuance of this Heb. participle see our discussion at Ps. 55:20.

[10] The psalmist's use of the noun *mārôm* 'Heaven' as an epithet of God is the perfect analogy to the Rabbinic Heb. divine epithet *šāmayim*, lit., 'Heaven(s)' and to the Rabbinic Heb. divine epithet *hammāqôm*, lit., 'The Temple', which derives from another locale where God is also 'enthroned'. For *māqôm* in Biblical Heb. in the sense 'temple' see Deut. 12:11; 1 Sam. 7:16; Jer. 7:3 and passim. The erroneous view that in Rabbinic Heb. *hammāqôm* means 'The Omnipresent' probably derives from the dictum attributed to R. Jose b. Halafta at Gen. Rabbah 68:9: "The world is not His Place, but He is the Place of the world," which, in fact, *presupposes* and explains eisegetically the use of *māqôm* as an epithet of God.

[11] This rendering of the prefixed preposition *bĕ*, lit., 'in', reflects Rashi's eisegesis. The correct exegesis of vv. 4-5a is reflected in NJV's "When I am afraid, I trust in You, in God, whose word I praise."

[12] Rashi here seems to take for granted that his readers know the established rule in Rabbinic exegesis that the generic divine name *ʾĕlohîm* 'God' refers to divine justice while the tetragrammaton refers to divine love. Hence *bēʾlohîm* can be seen to mean, "Even when He is *ʾĕlohîm*, i.e., Justice." Contrast the midrash attributed to R. Nehorai in Midrash Tehillim here; the latter midrash explicitly asks and replies to the question, "What is the difference in meaning between 'IN GOD' and 'IN THE LORD'?" Cf. below, n. 24.

[13] Heb. *wĕ* here interpreted as exegetical *waw*.

[14] Here Rashi's paraphrase substitutes the participle *šōmĕrîm* for the psalmist's imperfect *yišmĕrû*; this substitution reflects the fact that the participle and the imperfect express the present in Rabbinic and Biblical Heb. respectively.

[15] I.e., Eng. 'tracks'. The same O.F. gloss of Heb *ʿeqeb* is found in Rashi also at Ps. 40:16; 70:4; 77:20; 119:33; see Ps. 40, n. 26.

[16] This means that *yāgûrû* here is a form of *BDB*'s *gwr* I 'sojourn' rather than a form of *BDB*'s *gwr* II 'stir up strife, quarrel'. Contrast NJV's "THEY PLOT". KJV'S rendering "They gather themselves together" assumes derivation from a secondary meaning of *BDB*'s *gwr* I; see *BDB*, pp. 157b-158b; contrast *Mahberet Menahem*, pp. 111-112, which treats *gr* 'sojourn' and *gr* 'gather' as two distinct roots.

[17] Lemma, which is missing from our Rashi ms., probably by haplography, supplied from other editions of Rashi's commentary.

[18] Rashi's paraphrase substitutes a participle for the psalmist's perfect *qiwwû*.

[19] Our Rashi ms. reads by scribal error 'he goes'.

[20] Bracketed portion of Rashi's comment supplied for clarity from other editions of Rashi's commentary here.

[21] The letters למו, which appear before the word למצוא 'to find' in our Rashi ms. here probably represent dittography of the first three letters of the latter word.

[22] Contrast NJV's "Cast them out for their evil." The latter rendering assumes that *pallēṭ* is an imperative while Rashi understands it to be an infinitive construct; cf. Rashi at Ps. 77:11.

[23] Rashi paraphrases using the short imperative *śîm* instead of the psalmist's archaic long imperative *śîmāh*. Likewise, he expresses 'in Your flesh' by two words *běnō'd šellěkā* instead of the psalmist's *běnō'děkā*.

[24] Cf. Qimhi and Midrash Tehillim. The idea is that the generic term 'God' refers especially to God's Justice while the tetragrammaton refers especially to God's Love; cf. Rashi at v. 5 above and at Gen. 2:4b.

[25] Rashi's comment here is based upon Midrash Tehillim here.

PSALM LVII

1   FOR THE LEADER. DO NOT DESTROY.
David so named this psalm because David was about to die,
and he composed this psalm, saying, "DO NOT DE-
STROY me, O LORD."

2a   HAVE MERCY ON ME…HAVE MERCY ON ME.
[The point of the repetitive parallelism is] HAVE MERCY
ON ME so that I shall not kill and so that I shall not be
killed.[1]

2d   UNTIL DANGER PASSES [i.e.] until the evil[2] shall pass.

4b   THE REPROACH OF MY PERSECUTOR. HE WILL
DELIVER ME (4a) from THE REPROACH OF MY PER-
SECUTOR, who plans to swallow me.[3]

5   AS FOR ME, AMONG THE LIONS [i.e.], Abner and
Amasa, who were lions in [their knowledge of the] Torah
but who did not protest against [the behavior of] Saul.[4] LET
ME LIE DOWN THE FLAMING. [I.e.], LET ME LIE
DOWN among [*bě*] THE FLAMING [i.e.], among [*bên*] the
Ziphites, who are inflamed over [their] evil inclination and
slander.[4]

6a   EXALT YOURSELF OVER THE HEAVENS.
[I.e.], Remove Yourself from the lower realms, which are
not worthy that You should be present among them,

6b   and OVER ALL THE EARTH may You be glorified for
this.[5]

7b   The enemy[6] MADE A TRAP FOR ME.

7d   THEY FELL INTO IT. Their ultimate punishment is to fall
into it.[7]

8   MY HEART IS FIRM. [This is repeated twice[8] to indicate
that I am] loyal to You while experiencing divine Justice and
while experiencing divine Love..[9]

9a   AWAKE, O MY GLORY [*kěbôdî*], so that I not sleep until
the third hour as is the glory of other kings.[10]

9b   AWAKE, O HARP AND LYRE. [I.e.], Wake[11] me up, you
HARP AND the LYRE hung over my bed pointed to the
North so that when midnight arrives a northerly wind blows
upon it so that David gets up and studies Torah.

9c   LET ME WAKE UP THE DAWN. I wake up the dawn; the dawn does not awaken me.[12]

PSALM LVII, NOTES

[1] Rashi's comment is based on Midrash Tehillim here; cf. Rashi's comments at Ps. 56:5, 11.

[2] Rashi suggests here that the rare Biblical Heb. noun *hawwôt* is a synonym of the well-known noun *rāʿāh* 'evil'.

[3] Cf. Rashi at Ps. 56:2.

[4] See Leviticus Rabbah 26:2; cf. Midrash Tehillim at Ps. 7 #7; for additional parallels see Zohory, p. 161.

[5] Rashi's comment is based on Midrash Tehillim Ps. 7 #7; for additional parallels see Zohory, p. 162.

[6] Rashi supplies the missing subject.

[7] THE PIT THEY DUG FOR ME (v. 7c); for the idea see Ps. 7:16; Prov. 26:27; Eccles. 10:8.

[8] Cf. Rashi at v. 2.

[9] Cf. Rashi and Midrash Tehillim at Ps. 56:5, 11.

[10] *Mishnah of Rabbi Eliezer*, ed. H. G. Enelow (New York: Bloch, 1933), p. 127a; see also Midrash Tehillim here.

[11] The psalmist employs an intransitive verb; Rashi substitutes a transitive verb.

[12] Based on Midrash Tehillim here; for additional parallels see Zohory, p. 163.

PSALM LVIII

1   A MICHTAM. A type of song.¹

2a   IS JUSTICE REALLY SILENT [*'ēlem*]? YOU SPEAK.
David composed this psalm because he came to the encampment where Saul was sleeping (1 Sam. 26:5-7), "and he took the spear and the jar" (1 Sam. 26:12), and he went away, and he called out, "Will you not answer Abner?" (1 Sam. 26:14), which is to say, "Are you not now obligated to prove to Saul and to show him that he was pursuing me without cause? For had I wanted to do so, I could have killed him." Thus did he [David] say in [this] his song: "Has JUSTICE REALLY gone silent [*ne'ĕlam*] from your mouths?"² [*tĕdabbērûn* 'YOU SPEAK' means] that you were under obligation to speak.

2b   WITH EQUITY [means] You were under obligation to execute the justice³ of which 'YOU SPEAK' (v. 2a).

3   EVEN IN THE HEART YOU DEVISE EVILS.
And not only that [with which David charges Abner & Co. in v. 2] but⁴ in your hearts you plan evil to do wrong and thievery.⁵ [The plural noun] *'ôlôt* 'EVILS' is a biform of *'ăwôlôt* 'evils'.⁶ [The latter plural form of sing. *'āwel* 'evil'] corresponds to the way in which there is formed from [the singular noun] *šôr* 'bull' [the plural] *šĕwārîm* 'bulls' and from [the singular noun] *'îr* 'city' [the plural noun] *'ăyārîm* 'cities' [attested in] "They had thirty cities" (Judg. 10:4), which is a form of [the noun] *'îr* 'city', i.e.,⁷ *qiryāh* 'city'.⁸ IN THE LAND YOU WEIGH OUT THE LAWLESSNESS OF YOUR HANDS. Within⁹ THE LAND you make the LAWLESSNESS of your hands¹⁰ tip the scales for it is very weighty.

4   THE WICKED WERE TURNED ASIDE [*zôrû*] FROM THE WOMB.
From their mother's they are made estranged [*na'ăśîm zārîm*] from the Holy One Blessed be He as was Esau: "The sons struggled with each other within her" (Gen. 25:22).¹¹ [The verb *zôrû* is a biform of the verb] *nāzôrû* 'turned, estranged'

(Isa. 1:4; Ezek. 14:5). It belongs to the same morphological class as do [the verb *šômmû* in] *šômmû šāmayim* "Be appalled, O heavens" (Jer. 2:12); [the verb *robbû* in] *wayĕmārăruhû wārobbû* "They embittered him, and they became enemies" (Gen. 49:23);[12] [and the verb *rômmû* in] *rômmû mĕʿat* "They are exalted for a while" (Job. 24:24). All of these [verbs] are plural passives.[13]

5a   THEY HAVE VENOM.

They have[14] venom [*ʾeres*][15] for killing people LIKE the venom of A SNAKE.

5b   LIKE A DEAF VIPER that STOPS ITS EAR.

As for the snake, when it grows old it becomes deaf in one of its ears, and HE STOPS the other [EAR] with dirt so that he will not hear the charm when the snake-charmer charms him so that he will do no harm.[16]

6a   SO AS NOT TO HEAR....

[This verse] is joined [by the relative particle *ʾăšer* 'SO AS'] to the previous verse [to convey the following meaning]: He stops HIS EAR so that HE WILL NOT HEAR THE VOICE OF his CHARMERS,

6b   MUTTERER OF SPELLS [i.e.], one who knows how to charm snakes.

7   *maltĕʿôt* 'FANGS', [i.e.], the inner teeth, which are called *maisseles* 'molars' [in O.F.].[17]

8b   LET HIM, the Holy One Blessed be He,[18] AIM HIS ARROWS at them so that[19] THEY BE CUT DOWN.

9   *šabbĕlûl*. Some interpret it as [O.F.] *limace* 'slug';[20] and some interpret it as [O.F.] *maisseles* 'molars';[21] and some interpret it as a cognate of *šibbolet mayim* 'flood of water' (Ps. 69:16).[22] *temes* [*yahălok*][23] [i.e.], 'melting away [*nāmēs*] as it moves [*wĕhôlēk*].[24] [The word] *temes* is a substantive, and the [letter] *taw* therein is a preformative[25] like the *taw* of [the noun *tebel* 'incest' in] *tebel ʿāśû* "They committed incest" (Lev. 20:12).[26] The falling of an *ʾešet*,[27] [which is called] in O.F. *talpe*[28] 'mole', which has no eyes. It is [the Biblical Heb.] *tinšemet* 'mole' (Lev. 11:30), which we render into Aram. *ʾašûtāʾ* 'mole';[29] so did our Rabbis interpret it [*ʾešet*],[30] but some interpret it "a woman's stillbirth".[31]

10a   BEFORE YOUR THORNS UNDERSTAND BRAMBLEHOOD.

[It means that] BEFORE soft thorns know to be hard brambles [i.e.], before the children of the wicked will have grown up.[32]

10b BOTH LIVING AND IN WRATH.[33]

I.e., in might and in strength and in WRATH the Holy One Blessed be He will whirl them away.[34] *ḥay* 'LIVING' is an expression referring to *gĕbûrāh* 'might'

12a HUMANKIND WILL SAY, "INDEED THERE IS A RE-WARD FOR THE VIRTUOUS."

I.e., Then people[35] will say, "Certainly there are rewards and the payment of a wage for the behavior of the virtuous, for the Holy One Blessed be He vindicates them."

12b THERE IS GOD; [He is] judge [*dayyān*] [and he] judges [*šōpēṭ*][36] the wicked ON EARTH.

PSALM LVIII, NOTES,

[1] Cf. Rashi at Ps. 16:1.

[2] Here Rashi, following Midrash Tehillim here, paraphrases v. 2a. This interpretation takes *'ēlem* as an adjective derived from the verb *'lm* 'be silent'; so also Ibn Ezra quoting R. Moses Ibn Gikatilla; and so already Aquila; see also Mandelkern, p. 98a.

[3] Interpreting *tišpĕṭû*, like *tĕdabbērûn* as a command; NJV takes both as questions.

[4] Heb. *wĕlō' 'ôd 'ellā';* this interpretation of the psalmist's ambiguous *'ap* is in consonance with meaning #2 in *BDB*, p. 65a, i.e., 'the more so' while NJV's passing over the word in silence suggests that NJV interprets the word according to meaning #2 in *BDB*, p. 64b, i.e., 'also, yea'.

[5] Heb. *ḥāmās;* rendering based on Rashi's comments at Ps. 71:4; Isa. 1:17.

[6] Rashi's point is that *'ōlōt* is an anomalous pl. form of the sing. noun *'āwel* 'evil'.

[7] Explicative *waw*.

[8] Rashi's point is that the unusual form of the pl. of the noun *'îr* 'city' might be mistaken for the pl. of the noun *'ayir* 'ass'; see Rashi at Judg. 10:4; and see J. Alberto Soggin, *Judges*, Old Testament Library (Philadelphia: Westminster, 1981), p. 196.

[9] Heb. *bĕtôk;* Rashi's explication of the nuance of the psalmist's ambiguous prefixed preposition *bā*.

[10] Following the Masoretic pointing and accents, Rashi makes it clear that the expression ' OF YOUR HANDS' is periphrasis for the possessive pronoun 'Your'.

[11] Cf. Midrash Tehillim here; Gen. Rabbah 63:6.

[12] Rendering based upon Rashi's comment there.

[13] Englander, "Grammatical Elements and Terminology in Rashi,"

HUCA 11 (1936), p. 393 notes that *lĕšôn niphal* in Rashi's Bible commentaries is not synonymous with "belonging to the *niphal* conjugation'. For example, *niphal* is characterized by Rashi as *lĕšôn hitpāʿēl*, i.e., 'reflexive'. If in Rashi's language *hitpāʿēl* can designate a non-*hitpāʿēl* conjugation reflexive (see Englander, there, n. 42), it should not be surprising that *lĕšôn nipʿălû* in Rashi's language can designate non-*niphal* passives. In fact, Rashi here at Ps. 58:4 has collected four examples of the *qal*-passive of hollow verbs; see Rashi also at Gen. 49:23. On the *qal*-passive see Jakob Barth, "Das passive Qal und seine Participien," in *Jubelschrift zum Siebzigsten Geburtstag des Dr. Israel Hildesheimer* (Berlin: Engel, 1890), pp. 145-133; *HG*, pt. 2 #15.

[14] Here Rashi responds to the exegetical question, "Does *lāmô* mean 'their [venom]' (so NJV following KJV) or 'they have [venom]'?"

[15] Here Rashi indicates that 'venom', which is called *ʾereś* in Medieval and Modern Heb., is called *ḥēmāh* in Biblical Heb. On the forms of this word and its Semitic cognates see Gruber, *Aspects*, pp. 200; 483; 513-516; 520-528; 531-532; 534-535; 537-538; 542-543; 545; 547-552.

[16] Rashi's comment here is full of the dry humor that is of the essence of the midrashic imagination. Surely, the original intent of v. 5b is to say that it is a characteristic of the wicked person to stuff the ears so as not to hear moral instruction. With earplugs in place the auditory capacity of the wicked person is comparable to that of a deaf viper; cf. Qimhi here; cf. Midrash Tehillim here. However, a hyperliteral reading of the verse raises at least two questions: 1) If the viper is deaf, why does he stop up his ear? 2) Why does he stop up his (one) ear and not both ears? Rashi's comment begins where the obvious answers to both of these questions leave off. These answers are 1) He is deaf in only one ear; 2) therefore, in order not to hear he needs to stop up the other ear.

[17] With reference to the O.F. gloss, its meaning and its proper spelling in Heb. ש''רילישמ and in Latin script (*meselers*) see Catane, *Recueil* #68, #2319, #2322, #2332. With reference to Heb. *malṭāʾôt* see dictionaries and commentaries.

[18] Here Rashi answers the exegetical question, "Who is the subject of the verb 'LET HIM AIM'?" For alternative answers see Alexander Francis Kirkpatrick, *The Book of Psalms*, CB (Cambridge: Cambridge University Press, 1902) p. 329.

[19] Rashi paraphrases the psalmist's *kĕmô* by means of the expression *kĕdê še* 'so that'.

[20] So Rashi in his commentary at BT Shabbat 77b; contrast Rashi at BT Moʿed Qaṭan 6b where he glosses Heb. *šabbĕlûl* with O.F. *limaçon* 'snail'; on these respective glosses see Catane, *Recueil* #290, #1026; for the distinction between the two see also there #1082; note that the two nouns preserve their respective meanings in Modern French; see dictionaries. For the interpretation of *šabbĕlûl* in Ps. 58:9 as 'snail' (or 'slug') see also Midrash Tehillim here.

[21] This inappropriate gloss is the product of scribal error, specifically contamination from Rashi's comment on v. 7.

[22] *Mahberet Menahem*, p. 372, s.v. *šbl* I.

[23] Our Rashi ms. does not quote the bracketed portion of the verse; I have supplied it for clarity.

[24] Similarly NJV; so Rashi at BT Mo'ed Qaṭan 6b.

[25] Heb. *yĕsôd nōpēl*; see discussion at Ps. 39:11; 55:22; 119:5.

[26] See also *GKC* #85p, which renders *temes* "a melting away"; note, however, that while for *GKC* the root is *mss*, for Rashi, following *Mahberet Menahem*, p. 242, the root is *ms*.

[27] Rendering of the lemma on the basis of Rashi's commentary on BT Mo'ed Qaṭan 6b; this interpretation also goes back to Midrash Tehillim here.

[28] From this is derived Modern French *taupe*; on O.F. *talpe* see Levy, *Contribution* #760.

[29] Similarly Rashi at Lev. 11:30; cf. Rashi at BT Mo'ed Qaṭan 6b; Midrash Tehillim and Psalms Targum here. Here again, Rashi's citing T.O. on Lev. 11:30 rather than the Psalms Targum here proves that the latter Targum was unknown to Rashi; see above Ps. 48, n. 18; Ps. 55, n. 18; on the interpretation of Biblical Heb. *tinšemet* at Lev. 11:30 contrast *BDB*, p. 675b: "lizard or chameleon."

[30] Assuming that Heb. *'ešet* in Ps. 58:9 is an *hapax legomenon* and a cognate of Aram. *'ašûtā'* 'mole'; with Zohory, p. 166 see Midrash Tehillim here; BT Mo'ed Qaṭan 6b; JT Mo'ed Qaṭan 1:4.

[31] So now NJV, q.v. In light of Baneth, "Les Poterim," pp. 27-28; id., *Rashi: Interpreter of the Biblical Letter*, pp. 8-9 and passim, s.v. *ptr*, it is reasonable to suggest that while both interpretations can be found in Midrash Tehillim here Rashi's use of the expression *wĕyēš pōtĕrîm* with respect to the latter interpretation marks it as the one endorsed by his immediate forbears in Northern France.

[32] First Rashi explains the literal meaning of the verse. Then he explains that this verse embodies three metaphors: (1) thorns becoming brambles is a metaphor for growing up; (2) thorns are a metaphor for the children of the wicked; and (3) brambles are a metaphor for the wicked.

[33] KJV's rendering of the lemma has been adopted because of its proximity to Rashi's interpretation; contrast Gruber, *Aspects*, p. 492.

[34] Here Rashi substitutes late Heb. *yĕsa'ărēm* for the archaic *yiš'ārennû*.

[35] Rashi substitutes the Rabbinic Heb. pl. *bĕriyyôt* 'people' for the psalmist's collective *'ādām* 'HUMANKIND'.

[36] The psalmist says, "INDEED THERE IS GOD JUDGING ON EARTH." Rashi's comment suggest that the participle *šōpĕṭîm* 'JUDGING', which can be construed as an attributive adjective modifying *'ĕlohîm* 'GOD', functions here both as a noun 'judge' in apposition with 'GOD' and as a verb 'to judge', the predicate of which 'GOD' is the subject.

PSALM LIX A[1]

1   DO NOT DESTROY. He [David][2] thus titled the psalm because he was close to death, i.e., to being destroyed, and he was pleading for mercy for this reason. THEY WATCHED HIS HOUSE (cf. 1 Sam. 19:11) when Michal told them [Saul's messengers] that he [David] was sick (1 Sam. 19:14) when [in fact] she had spirited him away during the night (1 Sam. 19:11-13).[3]

4b   THEY SOJOURN[4] WITH ME. [I.e.], they spend the night in my house to watch over me.

5a   FOR NO GUILT. [I.e.], I did not sin against them. THEY ARE PREPARED. They are readied to kill [me].

6c   BESTIR YOURSELF TO BRING ALL NATIONS [gôyîm] TO ACCOUNT. When the Gentiles [gôyîm] are judged, judge these wicked [Israelite] people [who pursue the psalmist], and

6d   HAVE NO MERCY on them.

7a   THEY RETURN EACH EVENING.
It is not enough for them what they have done during the day, but also THEY RETURN EACH EVENING to their evil behavior of watching that I not flee and leave the city. Now, what did they do during the day?

8a   LOOK, every day THEY RAVE WITH THEIR MOUTHS to pass on to Saul information about me.

8b   SWORDS ARE ON THEIR LIPS, and they think,[5] "WHO HEARS?"

9a   BUT YOU, O LORD, who

9c   MOCK ALL THE NATIONS,

9b   LAUGH also at these wicked people.[6]

PSALM LIX, NOTES
  [1] In our Rashi ms. Ps. 59, vv. 1-9 is numbered as Ps. 55. The reasons for the difference of 4 in the numbering of the psalms between our printed editions and our Rashi ms. are as follows: our Rashi ms. treats our Pss. 12 and 13 as a single psalm; it treats Pss. 27 and 28 as a single psalm; and it treats Pss. 42-44 as a single psalm. As we have noted above in connection with those psalms, the scribe responsible for our Rashi ms. (or the scribal tradition he followed) combined the comments on our Pss. 12 and 13; 27

and 28; 43 and 44 because in each instance the latter comment was extremely short. However, the treatment of our Ps. 42 and 43 as a single psalm reflects Rashi's adherence to the reasonable view that these constitute in fact a single poem. On the other hand, our Rashi ms. treats our Ps 59:1-9 and our Ps. 59:10-18 as two separate compositions, numbered respectively as Ps. 55 and Ps. 56. For the recognition of a division of our Ps. 59 into stanzas precisely where our Rashi ms. separates its Pss. 55 and 56 see NJV.

[2] To whom the authorship of the psalm is attributed in v. 1.

[3] Cf. Midrash Tehillim here.

[4] Heb. *yāgûrû*; here as at Ps. 56:7, q.v., NJV, following *BDB*, p. 158b derives the verb *yāgûrû* from *BDB* 's *gwr* II 'lie in wait; Rashi, here as at Ps. 56:7, treats the verb *yāgûrû* as a derivative of *BDB* 's *gwr* I 'sojourn'; note that *Mahberet Menahem* cites neither of these attestations in his discussion of the homonymous biliteral roots *gr*.

[5] Lit., 'they say in their heart'; Rashi, followed by NJV, supplies missing verbum dicendi before virtual quotation; see Gordis, *BGM*, p. 350, n. 26.

[6] Without sayng so explicitly, Rashi treats v. 9 as an example of inversion, i.e., a Scripture verse, whose word order does not reflect the syntax; on Rashi's treatment of this phenomenon see Ps. 22, n. 31; Ps. 45, n. 30; Ps. 93, n. 11. Thus he treats the final clause of the verse, "YOU MOCK ALL THE NATIONS," as an adjectival relative clause modifying 'BUT YOU'. Moreover, Rashi treats *tiśḥaq* 'YOU LAUGH' as a precative. Finally, it should be noted that here in his comment on v. 9 as in his comment on v. 6 Rashi distinguishes between the wicked of Israel and the wicked Gentiles; cf. Dahood, *Psalms*, vol. 2, p. 67: "An awareness that two different categories of foes are the target of the psalmist's invective facilitates an appreciation of the lament's structure and metaphors."

PSALM LIX B[1]

10   HIS STRENGTH, LET ME WAIT FOR YOU.
      [It means], THE STRENGTH ['uzzô] and the might of my
      mighty enemy being upon me, LET ME WAIT FOR YOU,
      i.e., let me look forward to [your] delivering me from him.[2]

11a   WILL GREET ME.
      [I.e.], He will send His aid to greet me before the power of
      my enemies will prevail over me.

11b   HE WILL LET ME SEE WITH RESPECT TO MY EN-
      EMIES what I desire to see.

12a   DO NOT KILL THEM, for this is not a punishment which
      is remembered

12b   LEST MY PEOPLE BE UNMINDFUL of it, for all the
      dead are forgotten. Instead,

12c   REMOVE THEM from their wealth so that they will be
      poor people. This is a punishment that will be remembered
      for a long time.

13a-b THE SIN of their mouth is[4] THE WORD OF THEIR
      LIPS.[5]
      The poor people, who are pursued by them,

13c   are trapped[6] BY THEIR PRIDE

13d   because of[7] THE IMPRECATIONS AND LIES, which
      they utter.[8]

14a   PUT AN END TO them[9] in Your FURY, King [and]
      Judge,

14b   THAT IT MAY BE KNOWN THAT You RULE OVER
      JACOB.[10]

15   THEY RETURN AT EVENING. [This verse is the]
      continuation of the earlier verse, They speak[11] THE SIN
      OF THEIR MOUTH during the day (v. 13), and AT
      EVENING they return[12] to ambush those who have re-
      ported on them.[13]

16   THEY WANDER IN SEARCH OF FOOD all night as do
      dogs.[14] If they have not had their fill [during the day],[15] then
      let them go to sleep having had their fill so that they sleep.

17   BUT AS FOR ME, when I shall have escaped from them,

IN THE MORNING I SHALL SING OF YOUR STRENGTH.[16]

PSALM LIX B NOTES

[1] See above, Ps. 59 A, n. 1.

[2] Similarly KJV. NJV and RSV, on the other hand, adopt a variant reading of the Heb. text, which substitutes *'uzzî* 'MY STRENGTH', an epithet of God, for the dangling 'HIS STRENGTH' of the standard Heb. text. Rashi ingeniously turns the dangling noun into a nominative absolute.

[3] Here Rashi indicates that the psalmist's archaic *pîmô* 'OF THEIR MOUTH' is the equivalent of late Heb. *šel pîhem*.

[4] Heb. *hû'*, the 3ᵈ pers. sing. masculine personal pronoun employed here, as frequently in Rashi's Heb., as the copula.

[5] Here Rashi's point is that the phrase 'THE WORD OF THEIR LIPS' is employed in apposition with the phrase 'THE SIN OF THEIR MOUTH'. Rashi's comment here reinforces our contention at Ps. 9:5 that Rashi does indeed recognize the use in the Bible of synonymous expressions both in juxtaposition and in parallelism and further shows that Gelles, p. 102 has drawn the wrong conclusions from Rashi's comment there.

[6] Rashi construes the imperfect verb *wĕyillākĕdû* as present in meaning. Hence he paraphrases with the participle *nilkādîm*. He assumes that the subject of the verb is 'the victims of the treacherous behavior of the wicked'. Qimhi, followed by KJV, NJV, et al., takes *wĕyillākĕdû* as a jussive, "Let them be trapped," and he understands the subject of the verb to be 'the wicked'.

[7] Here Rashi understands the prefixed preposition *mē* (= *min*) in the word *ûmē'ālāh* (NJV renders "and by the imprecations") to mean *mippĕnê* 'because of'. For this meaning of Biblical Heb. *mē* [*min*] see *BDB*, p. 579b.

[8] Here Rashi indicates that the imperfect verb *yĕsappĕrû* here functions as a relative clause (cf. *GKC* #155f) and that it is present in meaning.

[9] Here Rashi, followed by NJV, supplies the direct object of the imperative *kallēh* 'PUT AN END TO'.

[10] It is well known that in Rabbinic exegesis the generic term *'ĕlohîm* 'God' refers specifically to God as Judge (see, e.g., Rashi at Ps. 56:5, 11 and at Gen. 2:4). Moreover, it is accepted that in the liturgical benediction [berakah] the expression *'ĕlohênû* 'our God' constitutes a reference to God's kingship (see Tosafot to BT Berakot 40b, s.v. *'ĕlohênû*). It appears, therefore, that Rashi treats v. 14 as an instance of inversion (on this phenomenon see Ps. 59:9 and our discussion there), which is to say that the word order does not reflect the syntax. He understands *'ĕlohîm* in v. 14b as a vocative meaning 'O King [and] Judge', whose syntactic place is in v. 14a. He holds that the immediate continuation of the clause beginning with 'THEY KNOW THAT' (NJV renders "that it may be known") is the participle *mōšēl*, which Rashi understands to mean 'You rule'.

[11] Heb. *hēm mĕdabbĕrîm;* Rashi's paraphrase of the psalmist's 'THE WORD OF THEIR LIPS'.

[12] Rashi paraphrases the psalmist's imperfect verb with a participle to indicate that here the psalmist has employed the imperfect to convey the present tense.

[13] Rashi's point is that in vv. 13 and 15 the psalmist describes the behavior of the wicked while v. 14 is a parenthetical prayer of petition in which the psalmist asks God to do away with the wicked.

[14] Rashi's point is that v. 16 is a continuation of the simile found in v. 15; note that this simile occurs also in v. 7.

[15] The bracketed phrase, which is not found in our Rashi ms., is supplied from other editions of Rashi's commentary here.

[16] Rashi's arrangement of the clauses indicate that he treats v. 17 as a case of inversion (see above n. 10); contrast MT: BUT I WILL SING OF YOUR STRENGTH//IN THE MORNING I SHALL EXTOL YOUR FAITHFULNESS.

PSALM LX

1 ON [*'al*] SHUSHAN EDUTH. A MICHTAM OF DAVID (TO BE TAUGHT).

[It means] A MICHTAM OF DAVID concerning [*'al*] the testimony of the Sanhedrin, who have been compared to a lily [*šôšānāh*], for it is stated in the Bible, "Your naval is like a round goblet...hedged about with lilies" (Cant. 7:3).[1] [The expression 'TO BE TAUGHT' alludes to the following]: When he [King David] is in need [of advice] they [the Sanhedrin] should instruct him as to what he should do. [For example], when he fought against Aram he sent Joab against them. They asked him [Joab], "Are you [the Israelites] not the descendants of Jacob? What happened, then, to the oath he [Jacob] swore to Laban upon 'this mound' (see Gen. 31: 43-54)?" Now Joab did not know how to reply. He went to David, [and] he told David, "This is what the Arameans said to me." They went to inquire of the Sanhedrin. They [the Sanhedrin] asked them [David and Joab], "Did not they [the Arameans] violate the oath first? In fact, it is stated in the Bible, 'From Aram has Balak brought me, Moab's king from the hills....' Moreover, Cushan-rishathaim was an Aramean" (see Judg. 3:7-11).[2]

2 JOAB RETURNED AND DEFEATED EDOM....[3]

[As for the contradiction between the figure twelve thousand recorded here in Ps. 60:2 and the figure] "eighteen thousand" recorded in the Book of Kings[4] and in the Book of Chronicles [it can be explained as follows]: Abishai killed in the first [Edomite] campaign [six thousand],[6] and Joab [killed another] twelve thousand when he was returning from fighting against Aram.[7]

2a *bĕhaṣṣôtô* 'WHEN HE FOUGHT' is an example of the same verb as is attested in "When they agitated [*bĕhaṣṣôtām*] against the LORD" (Num. 26:9).

3a YOU HAVE REJECTED US, YOU HAVE MADE A BREACH IN US. [Here the psalmist refers to the fact that] during the period of the judges we [the Israelites] suffered many troubles from the enemies surrounding us.

3b   '*ānaptā* 'YOU HAVE BEEN ANGRY' [i.e.] *qāṣaptā* 'You were wroth'[8] at us.

3c   From now on[9] return[10] TO US in your reconciliation.[11]

4a   YOU HAVE MADE our[12] LAND QUAKE for us by means of many invading armies.

4b   *pĕṣamtāh* 'YOU HAVE TORN IT OPEN' [i.e.], *šābartāh* 'You have broken it [*'ôtāh*]. Now I read in Dunash's book[13] that it [the verb *pṣm*] is [typically] Arabic,[14] but he [Dunash] did not explain its meaning [there]. However, in the work of[15] R. Moses the Interpreter,[16] he [R. Moses] explained that it [the verb *pṣm*] is a verb referring to 'tearing', and he presented evidence for the [aforementioned] interpretation [from the fact that in] *wĕqāraʿ lô ḥallônāy* "and he cuts out windows for it"[17] (Jer. 22:14) [the verb] is rendered into Aramaic [by TJ] *ûpaṣêm*.. However, I hold that [the Aram. expression] *ûpaṣêm*. by means of which Jonathan [b. Uzziel] rendered [Heb. *wĕqāraʿ*] into Aram. is a verb referring to the setting up of a window[18] [as it is also] in all openings, which have *pĕṣîmîm* 'bonds for frames'.[19]

4c   MEND [*rĕpāh*] ITS FISSURES. [The imperative *rĕpāh* 'MEND'] is a cognate of [the late Heb. noun] *rĕpûʾāh* 'healing, medicine'[20] even though it [the imperative *rĕpāh*] is written with a *hê* [rather than with an *'aleph* as is the noun *rĕpûʾāh*]. Many words behave in this manner.[21]

4d   FOR IT IS COLLAPSING [*māṭāh*], a verb referring to *šĕplût* 'being or becoming low'.

5   *yayin tarʿēlāh*[22] [i.e., wine] that stops up the heart and veils it. [The verb] *rʿl* [from which is derived the adjective *tarʿēlāh*] is a verb referring to veiling as is exemplified by [the verb form *horʿālû* 'they were veiled' in] "and the cypress trees were veiled" (Nah. 2:4).[23] and in Mishnaic Heb. [the participle *rāʿûl* 'veiled' in] *mĕdiyôt rĕʿûlôt* "Median Jewesses [go forth] veiled" (Mishnah Shabbat 6:6).[24]

6a   YOU HAVE GIVEN[25] YOUR DEVOTEES *nēs* [i.e.], *nisyônôt* 'trials'[26] consisting of many troubles

6b   *lĕhitnôsēs* [i.e.], to be tested[27] by them as to whether they can abide in [their] devotion to You.

6c   FOR THE SAKE OF GLORIFYING [*qošeṭ*] [i.e.], to glorify [*leqaššēṭ*] Your attributes in the world so that when You do them a favor, the Gentiles will not question You. On the contrary, they will glorify Your judicial decisions[28] by saying, "Appropriately He favored them, for they stood by Him despite many trials."[29]

7a MIGHT BE RESCUED [i.e.], might be delivered from harm.

7b DELIVER WITH YOUR RIGHT HAND, which You turned back when their enemies prevailed over them,[30] AND ANSWER ME, for if You ANSWER ME, those on whose behalf I [King David][31] am fighting MIGHT BE RESCUED (v. 7a).

8a HE SWORE[22] BY HIS HOLINESS that I [David] would be king over them.

8b LET ME EXULT in His victory.

8c LET ME DIVIDE UP [’aḥallĕqāh] THE BOOTY [šĕkem]. [I.e.], I shall give them[33] as their properties a portion of the properties of their enemies.[34]

8d AND MEASURE THE VALLEY OF SUKKOTH. As for this SUKKOTH, I do not know from which nation it [was conquered by Israel]. I do know, [however], where is [the location of the] Sukkoth, to which Israel came when they were journeying from Rameses (Ex. 12:37).[35]

9a GILEAD [AND MANASSEH][36] ARE MINE to rule over them.[37]

9c MY SCEPTER [i.e.], my officials.

10a MOAB WOULD BE MY WASHBASIN in that I shall wash in them as in a bronze basin which is prepared for washing therein.

10b [naʿălî] [i.e.], masgēr šellî ‘my lock’.[38]

10c BECOME ASSOCIATED WITH ME, O PHILISTIA! [I.e.], Join yourself[39] to my government. [David found it necessary to issue this call], for Gath belongs to Philistia and likewise Gaza, [both of] which David conquered.

11a WHO WILL BRING ME NOW TO THE BASTION? If you do not watch over me and help me with respect to the fortresses of Edom (see v. 11b), WHO WILL BRING ME, and

11b WHO WILL LEAD ME against them.[40]

12b wĕlōʾ tēṣēʾ [means] wĕʾênĕkā yôṣēʾ ‘You do not march’.[41]

14 yābûs ‘tread down’ [means] yirmos ‘TRAMPLE’.

PSALM LX, NOTES
  1 See Midrash Tehillim here.

² With Zohory see Midrash Tanḥuma at Deut. 1:6; Midrash Tehillim here; Genesis Rabbah 74:13.

³ The verbs are reversed in our Rashi ms.

⁴ Referring here to 2 Sam. 8:13, Rashi, like Jerome, and unlike the Rabbinic tradition at BT Bava Batra 14b-15a, appears to designate our Book[s] of [1-2] Samuel along with our Book[s] of [1-2] Kings as "The Book of Kings".

⁵ 1 Ch. 18:12.

⁶ The bracketed expression is missing from our Rashi ms. and is supplied from other editions of Rashi's commentary here.

⁷ Here Rashi also responds to the exegetical question, "What is the meaning of 'RETURNED AND DEFEATED'?" Rashi intimates that he correctly construes the expression as an hendiadys meaning, 'defeated again'. This philologically correct exegesis provides the basis for the resolution of the apparent contradiction between the figures provided in Ps. 60:2 and the historical books respectively.

⁸ On these two verbs see Gruber, *Aspects*, p. 553 and p. 547 respectively.

⁹ By means of this adverbial expression Rashi attempts to smooth the psalmist's abrupt transition from the perfect employed as a past tense to the imperfect employed as a command.

¹⁰ Following Midrash Tehillim here, Rashi suggests that the psalmist's request, "RESTORE US" means "RESTORE US to your favor by Your turning back to us from Your anger."

¹¹ Heb. *birĕṣônĕkā*; with respect to our rendering see the discussion of Rashi's consistent treatment of the word *rāṣôn* 'reconciliation' in Banitt, *Rashi: Interpreter of the Biblical Letter*, p. 29.

¹² The biblical text reads *'āreṣ* '(the) earth, (the) land', which can refer to the world at large or to a specific body of land. In the context of Ps. 60 the word probably refers to 'our land', i.e., 'the land of Israel'; Rashi makes this explicit.

¹³ I.e., *Teshuvot Dunash*, pp. 88-92. Note that in Rashi's expression *dibrê Dunaš*, lit., 'the words of Dunash', as in Biblical Heb. *dibrê Yirmiyāhû* (Jer. 1:1) and *dibrê 'Amôs* (Am. 1:1), the word *dibrê*, lit., 'the words of', means 'the book of'.

¹⁴ On Rashi's references to Arabic cognates—all taken from Dunash Ibn Labraṭ or R. Moses the Interpreter—see Simon Eppenstein, "Les comparisons de l'Hebreu avec l'Arabe chez les exegetes du nord de la France," *REJ* 47 (1903), pp. 47-56. References to Arabic in Rashi's commentary on Psalms are found at Ps. 45:2; 60:4; 68:17; 74:6.

¹⁵ Heb. *bysôdô šel*; see the discussion in the introduction, p. 7, n. 14.

¹⁶ Traditionally, R. Moshe ha-Darshan, and in Eng., Rabbi Moses the Preacher; since *dāraš* in Rashi's Heb. usually means 'interpret' and never means 'give a sermon' (see Kamin, *Rashi's Exegetical Categorization*, pp. 136-157) and since R. Moses was neither a Yiddish-speaking itinerant preacher of the early twentieth century nor a Southern Baptist clergyman the traditional renderings must be eliminated.

¹⁷ So RSV, whose rendering is in harmony with the view of R. Moses.

[18] So NEB at Jer. 22:14; note that in our Rashi ms. the scribe has inverted the order of the words *tiqqûn* and *hallôn*, and he has corrected the word order by the supralinear numerals א and ב over the words to be read first and second respectively.

[19] See Jastrow, *Dict.*, p. 1205a.

[20] In Biblical Heb. the noun *rĕpû'āh* is unattested. Instead we find at Jer. 30:13; 46:11; Ezek. 30:21 the characteristically Phoenician form *rĕpû'ôt* 'remedy, healing' while at Prov. 3:8 we find *rip'ût* 'medicine, drug'. The latter form is morphologically and semantically equivalent to Canaanite *ripūtu* 'healing' mentioned in the 14th cent. B.C.E. El-Amarna Letter #269, line 17.

[21] I.e., the letters *'aleph* and *hê* interchange in various forms of the same root. For additional examples of the phenomenon of final *hê* forms of verbs, whose third radical is *'aleph* see *GKC* #75pp. Rashi's comment suggests not only that Rashi considers the final *'aleph* of the verb *rāpā'* 'get well' (Isa. 6:10) to be a root letter but also that he considers *'aleph* to be the third radical of the imperative *rĕpāh* here at Ps. 60:4. Contrast *Mahberet Menahem*, pp. 345, 355, which distinguishes between the triliteral *rp'* (Ex. 15:26; Prov. 3:8) and the biliteral *rp* (2 Kgs. 2:22; Jer. 8:11; Ezek. 47:12), both of which refer to 'healing'; contrast Englander, "A Commentary on Rashi's Grammatical Comments," p. 484.

[22] I.e., 'poison wine'; for extensive discussion of these and related expressions in Biblical Heb. see Gruber, *Aspects*, p. 530, n. 2; contrast NJV's "wine that makes us reel" and NJV margin: "a bitter draft".

[23] So Rashi there, q.v.

[24] This is the established reading in Rashi here and at Nah. 2:4. However, Rashi's comment on the Mishnah at BT Shabbat 65a presupposes the accepted reading in the Mishnah: "Arabian Jewesses go forth wrapped while Median Jewesses [go forth] with cloaks looped up over their shoulders." Note, however, that there is some evidence for the deletion of "go forth" in the first clause; see Saul Lieberman, *Hayerushalmi Kiphshuto* (Jerusalem: Darom, 1934), p. 111.

[25] This is the sense of the perfect required in the present context by Rashi's interpretation (for Rashi's midrashic source see below, n. 29); contrast NJV, which interprets the verb as a precative perfect.

[26] Rashi, following a midrash (see below, n. 29), takes *nēs* here to be a short form of the word *nissāyôn* 'trial'; contrast NJV, which understands *nēs* here in its usual meaning in Biblical Heb., 'banner' (see dictionaries).

[27] Rashi's understanding of the denominative verb *lĕhitnôsēs* follows logically from his understanding of the noun *nēs* (see previous note and see below, n. 29), from which the verb is derived. Similarly, NJV, which takes *nēs* to mean 'banner', takes the verb to mean 'rally around'.

[28] Heb. *rîbêkā* 'Your judicial decisions' (cf. Biblical Heb. semantic equivalent *šĕpāṭîm* in Ex. 12:12) here refers to the sufferings of Israel, which are interpreted by this term to be concretizations of God's Justice.

[29] Rashi's comment on v. 6 is based upon a midrash found in Genesis Rabbah 55:1; see also Yalqut Shim'oni, vol. 2 #777.

[30] It is often said that disaster falls because of *hastārat pānîm,* i.e., God's hiding His face. Here Rashi suggests a similar idea, which might be conceptualized as *hašābat yād,* i.e., God's turning away His hand. While the former metaphor refers to God's apparent display of unconcern; the latter idea seems to refer to God's apparent physical uninvolvement.

[31] To whom the psalm is attributed at v. 1.

[32] Heb. *dibbēr,* lit., 'He spoke'; for the divine oath in question see Ps. 89:36; 2 Sam. 7:9-16.

[33] Those on whose behalf King David is doing battle, namely, the virtuous among Israel; cf. Rashi at v. 7b.

[34] This comment seems to embody Rashi's interpretation of *šĕkem* as 'booty'; cf. Rashi at Ps. 21:13; contrast NJV here.

[35] See Rashi there.

[36] Rashi does not quote the bracketed portion of the verse; I have supplied it for clarity.

[37] Here Rashi answers the exegetical question, "In what sense may King David say of Gilead and Manasseh, 'They are mine'?"

[38] Contrast Rashi on the near duplicate Ps. 108:10; contrast also *Mahberet Menahem,* p. 257, which distinguishes between *n'l* I 'shoe' and *n'l* II 'lock' [*masgēr*].

[39] Heb. *hithabbĕrî.* Rashi here understands the verb *hitro'a'* as a denominative verb derived from the noun *rēa'* 'friend'; contrast NJV, which treats the verb as a form of the verb *hērîa'* 'shout' (cf. Midrash Tehillim here).

[40] Rashi takes *mî* in 11a and in 11b as the interrogative pronoun 'who'. NJV, on the other hand, takes the clauses introduced by *mî* as volitive subjunctives; on the latter usage see *GKC* #151a, d.

[41] So NJV; here Rashi indicates that the psalmist employs the imperfect form of the verb to convey the present tense.

PSALM LXI

3   FROM THE END OF THE EARTH even though I am far
     from my men, whom I [King David]¹ send to war against
     my enemies. I CALL TO YOU WHEN MY HEART IS
     FAINT because of them. Now about what do I call to you?
     [The answer is] that YOU LEAD ME TO A ROCK that is
     higher² and stronger THAN I.

5   O THAT I MIGHT DWELL IN YOUR TENT FOREVER.
     [I.e.], Benefit me in the pre-eschatological era and in the escha-
     tological era.³

6b   YOU HAVE GIVEN THE INHERITANCE OF YOUR DE-
     VOTEES.
     [It means that] through my agency You have returned the cities
     of their inheritance.⁴

7a   ADD DAYS TO THE DAYS OF THE KING.
     If it had been decreed for me to die as a youth, add⁵ DAYS TO
     my days so that my years will be seventy years

7b   LIKE the years of EVERY GENERATION.⁶

8a   MAY HE [i.e.], the king, DWELL IN GOD'S PRESENCE
     FOREVER.

8b   May KINDNESS AND FAITHFULNESS, in which he engages,
     be summoned to GUARD HIM. [The imperative] *man* [refers to]
     hazmānāh 'summoning' as does [the imperfect consecutive of the
     same root *mn*⁷ 'summon' in] "The LORD summoned [*wayĕman*] a
     gourd" (Jonah 4:6).⁸

9   SO [*kēn*] I WILL SING HYMNS TO YOUR NAME.
     [I.e.], Just as You are kind to me so [*kak*] I WILL SING HYMNS
     TO YOUR NAME so that I will be fulfilling MY VOWS DAY
     AFTER DAY.

PSALM LXI, NOTES
¹ To whom the psalm is attributed at v. 1.
² Here Rashi substitutes a late Heb. relative clause *šehû' rām* for the
psalmist's use of a stative verb in the imperfect, *yārûm*, to express the same
syntactic relationship; on the Biblical usage see *GKC* #155f.
³ Rashi's comment here is based upon the midrash attributed to Rav
Judah b. Ezekiel in the name of Rav in BT Yebamot 96b; Bekorot 31b;
Midrash Shmuel 19.
⁴ The exegetical question raised by v. 6 is, "To whom is it that YOU

HAVE GIVEN THE INHERITANCE OF YOUR DEVOTEES?" Rashi's comment suggests that the answer is that by means of the wars of King David You gave back to Your devotees the cities alotted to them, which had been usurped by the Philistines, Jebusites, Canaanites and other peoples.

[5] Here Rashi substitutes the imperative for the psalmist's imperfect.

[6] See Midrash Tehillim at Ps. 92 #10; Genesis Rabbah 19:14; cf. Ps. 90:10 and Rashi's commentary there.

[7] *Mahberet Menahem*, p. 242; *K-B³*, p. 567 traces it to a triliteral root *mnw* or *mny*.

[8] Cf. Midrash Tehillim here; so now also NJV.

PSALM LXII

1   ON JEDUTHUN, the name of a musical instrument.[1] An aggadic midrash [states, however, that '*al Yĕdûtûn* means] "referring to the judgments, which are imposed upon Israel through the agency of their enemies."[2]

2   MY SOUL WAITS QUIETLY [*dûmiyyāh*]. [The latter participle] is derived from the same verbal root as is attested in [the imperative *dôm* 'be patient' in] "Be patient and wait for the LORD" (Ps. 37:7).

3   I SHALL NOT TOPPLE *rabbāh*[4] [i.e.], great topplings.[3] An aggadic midrash [states, however, that] *rabbāh* is [a name for] Gehinnom.[4]

4a   ATTACK [*tĕhôtĕtû*]. Menahem [Ibn Saruq] interpreted it [the verb *tĕhôtĕtû*] as from the same root as [the imperative *hĕtāyû* 'attack' in] "Attack the food" (Jer. 12:9) [and of the verb *wayyēte'* 'he attacked' in] "The heads of the people attacked" (Deut. 33:21).[5] HOW LONG WILL YOU ATTACK A MAN? It seems to me, however, that one should interpret it [the verb *tĕhôtĕtû*] as a cognate of [the noun] *hawwôt* 'destruction' and that [the] *hê* [and the second] *taw* should be [regarded as part of the] root.[6] Just as there is formed from [the root] *mt* [the noun] *māwet* 'death' so [is there formed] from [the root] *ht*[7] [the singular noun] *hawwat*.[8] Now the plural is *hawwôt*, and it [sing. absolute *hawwāh*; construct sing. *hawwat*; plural *hawwôt*] is a word referring to 'design for destruction and deceit'.[9]

4b   AS THOUGH HE WERE A LEANING WALL, which is about to fall on people.

5a   FROM HIS RANK.
       Since you are afraid of the man lest he become king and give you your due, you LAID PLANS[10] TO TOPPLE upon him the evil.

5c   IN THE MOUTH[11] of each and every one of them[12] THEY BLESS

5d   WHILE INWARDLY THEY CURSE. SELAH.

10a   MEN ARE MERE BREATH.

So do not be afraid of them since

9b   the Holy One Blessed be He IS OUR REFUGE.

10b   PLACED ON A SCALE.

If they [MEN and BREATH (v. 10a)] came TO BE PLACED ON A SCALE, they [MEN] and BREATH (v. 10a) would be equal [in weight]. This is its literal meaning. A midrash based upon it[13] [relates our verse] to the subject of married couples.[14]

11c   IF WEALTH BEARS FRUIT.

[It means that] if you see wicked people whose money prospers and grows, PAY IT NO MIND. *ḥêl* 'WEALTH' [means] *māmôn* 'money'.[15] *yānûb* 'BEARS FRUIT' [means] 'sprouts' [*yiṣmaḥ*]; it is a cognate of [the noun] *tĕnûbāh* 'fruit' (Isa. 27:6).[16]

12a   ONE THING GOD HAS SPOKEN, out of which

12b   TWO THINGS HAVE I HEARD.[17]

Now what are these 'TWO THINGS'? [The answer is that the first of these 'TWO THINGS' is the following]:

12c   THAT Yours is the MIGHT

13b-c   to reward[18] EACH MAN ACCORDING TO HIS DEEDS.

The second [of these 'TWO THINGS' is the following]:

13a   For KINDNESS [*ḥesed*] IS YOURS.

Now from which of the divine utterances have we heard them [these two things]? [The answer is], From the second divine utterance of the decalogue. We have heard from it that the Holy One Blessed be He visits guilt and shows kindness, for [therein] it is said, "visiting the guilt of the parents..." (Ex. 20:5-6). Therefore I am certain that He will pay a good reward to the virtuous and punishment to the wicked. I learned this [exegesis of vv. 12-13] from the work of Rabbi Moses the Interpreter.[19] Our rabbis, however, found support for it[20] [the idea that a single divine utterance conveys two meanings] in [the fact that] "Remember [the Sabbath]" (Ex. 20:8) and "Observe [the Sabbath] (Deut. 5:12) were uttered in a single divine utterance [of the decalogue].[21]

13a   [Now as for] AND KINDNESS IS YOURS, O LORD, what is the KINDNESS? [It is]

13b   THAT YOU REWARD EACH MAN ACCORDING TO HIS DEEDS

and not strictly [ACCORDING TO] HIS DEEDS but [according to] a small part of them in accord with what is stated in the Bible, "For You...have been forbearing [punishing us] less than our iniquity [deserves]" (Ezra 9:13). This is the way it [Ps. 62:13] is interpreted in Aggadat Tehillim.[22.] However, it is proper to interpret it[23] [as follows]: FOR KINDNESS IS YOURS in that you have the power to reward EACH MAN ACCORDING TO HIS DEEDS.[26]

PSALM LXII, NOTES

[1] *Mahberet Menahem*, p. 116, s.v. *gt*; p. 282, s.v. 'lm IV; see Rashi at Ps. 5:1 and our discussion there.

[2] See Rashi's Introduction to the Psalter and Rashi at Ps. 5:1; 39:1; 77:1; for the sources see our discussion at Rashi's Introduction, n. 24.

[3] Heb. *môṭôt gĕdôlôt*; other Rashi mss. have the synonymous reading *môṭôt rabbôt*. This interpretation is defended by Qimhi; similarly Delitzsch, vol. 2, p. 206 Briggs, vol. 2, p. 71; the latter, like Ehrlich, *Psalms*, p. 141 regards the word *rabbāh* as a late addition to the verse.

[4] Midrash Tehillim here; similarly but independently Dahood, here, q.v.

[5] *Mahberet Menahem*, p. 135, s.v. *hg*.

[6] Contrast *BDB*, p. 223b, which treats our verb as an *hapax legomenon* derived from Arab. *hwt* 'shout at, threaten'.

[7] On Rashi's treatment of hollow verbs in general see Englander, "Rashi's View of the Weak, *'ayin-'ayin*, and *pe-nun* Roots," pp. 434-435.

[8] In all three of its occurrences in this form—Mic. 7:3; Prov. 10:3; 11:6—the noun seems to mean 'destructive design'.

[9] The plural of the noun does seem to have this meaning in Ps. 5:10; 55:12; however, at Ps. 38:13; 52:4; 91:3; Prov. 17:4; and Job. 6:30 the plural seems to denote 'deceitful utterance'.

[10] Here Rashi paraphrases the psalmist's 'THEY LAID PLANS' (NJV: "They lay plans").

[11] Heb. *bĕpîw*, lit., 'in his mouth'.

[12] Here Rashi responds to the exegetical question, "In the mouth of whom?" Rashi's answer is that both the singular and the plural in v. 5 refer to unnamed wicked persons, who are here spoken of both individually and collectively.

[13] On double interpretations employing the terminology *pĕšûṭô-midrāšô* see Kamin, *Rashi's Exegetical Categorization*, pp. 158-208.

[14] Rashi here refers to Leviticus Rabbah 29:8, q.v.

[15] So LXX; Ibn Ezra and Qimhi; and so KJV; contrast NJV, which follows the Vulgate. *BDB*, p. 298b, s.v., *hayil*, treats 'might' and 'wealth' as nuances of a single word; so also *K-B³*, pp. 298-299.

[16] *Mahberet Menahem*, p. 251 derives both the verb and the noun from a biliteral root *nb* meaning *'ômeṣ* 'strength'.

[17] It has been argued that the parallelism of ascending numbers x// x+1 proves that the two parallel clauses are synonymous (see our discussion at Ps. 91:7 and see Wolgang M. W. Roth, "The Numerical Sequence

x/x+1 in the Old Testament," *VT* 12 [1962], pp. 300-311). If so, both clauses assert that the smallest unit of divine speech contains twice the amount of information conveyed by the comparable unit of human speech. According to Rashi's comment here, however, the two clauses constitute contrasting parallelism, and they contrast human perception with divine communication.

[18] Heb. *lĕšallēm*; Rashi's paraphrase of the psalmist's 'YOU REWARD'; Rashi's paraphrase is adopted by NJV here.

[19] On this work see Rashi and our discussion at Ps. 45:2; Ps. 60:4.

[20] Heb. *dārĕšûhû*. Generally in Rashi's Bible commentaries *dārĕšû rabbôtênû* means simply 'our rabbis interpreted' (see Kamin, *Rashi's Exegetical Categorization*, pp. 136-139 and passim in our translation of Rashi's Commentary on Psalms) and the direct object of the verb is the verse under discussion. Here, however, the accusative pronominal suffix *hû* ' it' refers not to a biblical text but to an idea which, as Rashi here informs us, has been found in a variety of biblical texts; hence our rendering here. For another rare example of the verb *dārĕšû* in Rashi's Commentary on Psalms in a sense other than 'they interpreted (the biblical verse)' see Rashi at Ps. 27:13 and our discussion there.

[21] The source of this midrash is Mekilta, vol. 2, p. 252. On Rabbinic Heb. *dibbûr* 'divine utterance' see Mayer I. Gruber, "The Change in the Name of the Decalogue," *Beth Mikra* 26 (1981-82), pp. 16-21 (in Hebrew).

[22] I.e., Midrash Tehillim here.

[23] Heb *lĕpôtrô*; on the various nuances of the verb *pātar* in Rashi's biblical commentaries see Baneth, "Les Poterim," pp. 21-33.

[24] I.e., YOUR KINDNESS consists in Your not exercising Your power to reward EACH MAN ACCORDING TO HIS DEEDS. This interpretation derives exegetically the same idea that the previously quoted midrash derives eisegetically. Assuming, as he does throughout his discussion of Ps. 62:13 that the word *ḥesed* means 'kindness' rather than 'faithfulness' (so NJV), Rashi here responds to the exegetical question, "What KINDNESS can possibly be expressed when YOU REWARD EACH MAN ACCORDING TO HIS DEEDS?"

PSALM LXIII

1   IN THE DESERT OF JUDAH fleeing from Saul.[1]

2b   MY BODY YEARNS [*kāmah*] FOR YOU. [The verb *kāmah* is] a verb referring to desire, and it is an *hapax legomenon*.[2]

2c   IN A PARCHED LAND [i.e.], in the desert.

3a   *kēn* I BEHELD YOU IN THE SANCTUARY.... [The particle *kēn* here] corresponds in meaning to[3] *ka'ăšēr* 'just as'.[4] [The idea expressed in vv. 2-3 is the following]: I was thirsting (v. 2a)

3b   TO SEE YOUR MIGHT AND YOUR GLORY just aṣ I BEHELD YOU IN THE Temple [i.e.], the Tabernacle of Shiloh. Let my soul (see v. 2c) swear[6] by the visions of YOUR MIGHT AND YOUR GLORY.

9b   YOUR RIGHT HAND SUPPORTS ME so that I will not fall.

10   THOSE enemies of mine, WHO SEEK TO DESTROY MY LIFE. They ambush me on a dark day so that I will not notice them.

11   MAY THEY THROW HIM OUT [*yaggîrûhû*] BY MEANS OF THE SWORD. [The verb *yaggîrûhû*] is a cognate of [the gerund] *gĕrîrāh* 'pulling out, dragging'[7] as is [the participle *muggārîm* 'dragged' in] "dragged down a cliff" (Mic. 1:4) [and the noun *gār* 'water source' in] "He stops up the stream at the water source" (Job. 28:4).[8]

12a BUT THE KING SHALL REJOICE. He [King David][9] used to say [this] about himself, for, in fact, he had already been annointed [long before he fled from Saul to the Judean desert].[10]

12b ALL WHO SWEAR BY HIM SHALL EXULT. [It means that] when they will have seen that You will have saved me [from Saul], all who cleave to You and who swear by Your Name SHALL EXULT.

12c WHEN...IS STOPPED [*yissākēr*], [i.e.], 'is closed' [*yissātēm*]; it is the same verb as is attested in "The fountains of the deep...were stopped up" (Gen. 8:2).

PSALM LXIII, NOTES

[1] With Dahood, here see 1 Sam. 22:5; 23:14-15; cf. Midrash Tehillim here.

[2] Heb. *wĕ'ên lô dimyôn*. Note, however, the distinction drawn between *hapax legomenon* and such expressions as *wĕ'ên lô dimyôn* 'it has no cognate' in the Medieval Jewish Bible commentators and grammarians by Green-spahn, "The Meaning of *'Ein Lo Domeh* and Similar Phrases in Medieval Biblical Exegesis," pp. 59-70.

[3] Heb. *kĕmô*.

4 Cf. *BDB*, p. 486a.

[5] Heb. *kĕderek šĕ*.

[6] See below, v. 12b.

[7] Well-attested in Rabbinic Heb. (see Jastrow, *Dict.*, p. 269a) as also in Modern Heb., the gerund is unattested in Biblical Heb.

[8] I.e., at the place from where the water is naturally flowing or being dragged out; see *Mahberet Menahem*, pp. 111-112, s.v. *gr* II; contrast other exegetes of Job. 28:4.

[9] To whom the psalm is attributed at v. 1.

[10] See 1 Sam. 16:13; assuming that the imperfect here expresses the future tense, Rashi responds here to the exegetical question as to why the psalmist speaks here of future rather than present rejoicing.

PSALM LXIV

2a HEAR MY VOICE, O GOD, WHEN I PLEAD.
As for this psalm, the authors of [the various midrashim found in] Aggadat Tehillim [on this psalm] interpreted it as referring to Daniel, who was thrown into a lions' den (see Dan. 6:17).[1] The entire content of the psalm is very much in harmony with the *aggadah*.[2] David foresaw by means of prophetic inspiration everything that would happen to him [Daniel], and he [David] prayed for him [Daniel], for Daniel was a descendant of his, for it is stated in the Bible, "And some of your descendants...whom you will beget... will be eunuchs in the palace of the king of Babylon" (Isa. 39:7; cf. 2 Kgs. 20:18). These [unnamed descendants] were [in fact] Daniel, Hananiah, Mishael, and Azariah (Dan. 1:6).

2b FROM THE ENEMY'S TERROR. These [enemies] are the satraps, who took counsel against him [Daniel], for it is stated in the Bible, "Then the ministers and the satraps sought to find fault with Daniel..." (Dan. 6:5).

3b FROM A CROWD OF [*mērigšat*][3] EVILDOERS. [These people are called *rigšat* 'A CROWD OF'] because they crowd together [*mitraggěšîm*][4] to plot his [Daniel's] death, for it is written in the Bible, "They went together [*'argîšú*][5] to the king" (Dan. 6:7).

4b THEY AIM THEIR ARROWS, i.e.,[6] their slander.

5a TO SHOOT FROM HIDING with their arrows.

6b THEY SPEAK [*yěsappěrú*] TO CONCEAL TRAPS.
[I.e.], They speak [*yědabběrú*][7] to the king cunningly hidden words, which even the king does not understand. Why were they doing this? [The answer is]: For they were intending TO CONCEAL TRAPS, by which he [Daniel] would be caught when they said to Darius, "'All the ministers of the kingdom have advised...establishing a royal ordinance' (Dan. 6:8a) that no person should recite any prayer to any deity except you [Darius] for thirty days."[8]

7a THEY SEARCH FOR [*yaḥpěśú*] PLOTS [*'ōlōt*].
[I.e.], They seek [*měbaqqěšîm*][9] plots [*'ălîlôt*].[10] [What is said

about Daniel here in Ps. 64:7a][11] corresponds to what is stated in the Bible, "They sought to find fault with Daniel" (Dan. 6:5).

7b   *ṭāmĕnû* 'THEY HAVE CONCEALED'[12] in their heart, and they did not reveal the search [*hopeś*][13] of the plots SEARCHED [*mĕḥuppāś*] by them OR[14] their INWARD thoughts OR[14] the depth of their heart.[15] EACH and every one[16] ONE INSIDE HIM [i.e.], everyone concealed the plot.

8   GOD SHALL SHOOT THEM [i.e.], shoot them[17] into a lions' den in accord with what is written in the Bible, "The king commanded, and they brought these men, who had slandered Daniel, and they were cast into the lions' den" (Dan. 6:25a).

9a   THEIR TONGUE SHALL BE THEIR DOWNFALL.
    [I.e.], The defeat, with which they [Darius' ministers] had intended to defeat them [the Jews] was turned back upon them [as follows]: THEIR TONGUES BOUNCED AROUND in their heads so as to wag their heads

9b   so that ALL WHO SEE THEM should laugh at them.

11a   THE RIGHTEOUS [i.e.], Daniel, SHALL REJOICE.

11c   LET ALL THE UPRIGHT IN HEART PRAISE THEMSELVES
    for their uprightness, and let them laud themselves for they are certain that the Holy One Blessed be He is at their assistance.

PSALM LXIV, NOTES
    [1] See Midrash Tehillim here.
    [2] For the definition of the terms *midrash* and *aggadah* see our introduction, (p. 128, n. 4).
    [3] Note that NJV here reflects the interpretation of the root *r-g-š* found in Rashi at Ps. 2:1; see also Rashi at Ps. 55:15.
    [4] Rashi here responds to the exegetical question, "What is the meaning of *rigšaṭ*?"
    [5] This is the reading in our Rashi ms.; *BHS* reads *hargîšû*. Concerning the meaning of this word see the extensive discussion in Louis F. Hartman and Alexander A. Di Lella, *The Book of Daniel*, AB, no. 23 (Garden City, N.Y.: Doubleday, 1978), p. 194 at Dan. 6:7.
    [6] Heb. *hû'*.
    [7] Here Rashi paraphrases the less frequently attested verb employed by the psalmist with a more well known synonym.
    [8] Rashi quotes the first part of the verse in the original Aramaic; this portion is indicated by the single quotation marks ('...') within the larger

quotation. Rashi translates the second part of the verse into Hebrew. Moreover, while according to Dan. 6:8b the proposed decree was to enjoin every person from making any request of any god or of any person for thirty days, Rashi in his commentary here omits the phrase "or of any person."

[9] In his paraphrase Rashi indicates that in v. 7 the psalmist employs the imperfect form of the verb to express the present.

[10] Here Rashi intimates that the noun 'ōlōt 'malice' here at Ps. 64:7 (see also Ps. 58:3, and with Harold Louis Ginsberg, *The Legend of King Keret*, BASOR Supplementary Studies, nos. 2-3 [New Haven: American Schools of Oriental Research, 1946], p. 49 followed by Dahood at Ps. 58:3 cf. Ugar. *g!lt* 'malice' in *CTA* 16 [=*KTU* 1.16], vi, lines 32-33) is synonymous with the more common 'ălîlāh 'plot' attested in Deut. 22:14, 17; Ps. 141:4; etc. and frequently in late Heb.

[11] See Rashi at v. 2a.

[12] It is well known that Rashi here attests to a reading ṭāmĕnû 'THEY HAVE CONCEALED', which, although supported by many medieval mss. of the Hebrew Bible (see *BHS* here) and adopted now by NJV, is at variance with the commonly accepted reading tamĕnû 'THEY HAVE ACCOMPLISHED' (see NJV margin) known to Ibn Ezra and Qimhi. See *Minḥat Shai* ad loc. Englander, "Grammatical Elements and Terminology in Rashi," *HUCA* 15 (1939), pp. 426-29 discusses twenty instances where Rashi quotes a variant text of the Bible. Jacob Reifmann, "Notes on Rashi's Commentary," *Beth Ha-Talmud* 5 (1886), p. 56 (in Hebrew) cites in addition to Ps. 64:7 also Isa. 47:2 and Jer. 33:3 as instances where Rashi quotes a text of the Bible, which deviates from the one commonly called MT; see also Maarsen here.

[13] Rashi's paraphrase of the psalmist's ḥēpeś.

[14] Heb. *waw* cojunctive.

[15] Rashi's paraphrase of the psalmist's 'A DEEP HEART', which NJV renders, "his secret thoughts".

[16] Rashi conveys this by repeating the word 'îš, which by itself would mean 'each one'; see *GKC* #123c.

[17] Rashi paraphrases the biblical *yōrēm*, which represents verb + accusative pronominal suffix by means of *yōreh 'ōtām*, which represents verb + independent accusative pronoun. Apparently, Rashi assumes that his readers, like native speakers of Modern Hebrew, need to have the archaic form explained by the later form.

PSALM LXV

2   FOR YOU SILENCE [*dumiyyāh*] IS PRAISE.
Silence [*šětîqāh*]¹ is PRAISE FOR YOU because there is no
end to Your praise, and whoever multiplies Your praise only,
so to speak, detracts [from your praise].²
O GOD IN ZION [i.e.], GOD, who is present [*haššōkēn*]³
among them.⁴
Another equally plausible interpretation of FOR YOU SI-
LENCE IS PRAISE, O GOD IN ZION: The fact that You
were silent [*dômamtā*], i.e.,⁵ [that] You kept quiet [*heḥerastā*],
about what Your enemies did IN ZION IS PRAISE, for You
have the capability of taking vengeance, but You forbear.⁶

5   HAPPY IS THE MAN WHOM YOU CHOOSE AND
BRING NEAR who⁷ WILL DWELL in⁸ YOUR COURTS.

6   ANSWER US WITH VICTORY THROUGH AWESOME
DEEDS.
[I.e.], ANSWER US by doing AWESOME DEEDS against
the Gentiles.

8   STILLS [*mašbîaḥ*] [i.e.], *mašpîl* 'puts down'. The same usage
[of the verb *hišbîaḥ*] is reflected in "But a sagacious person
puts it back down" (Prov. 29:11).⁹

9b   THE COMINGS FORTH OF¹⁰ MORNING AND OF
EVENING. YOU MAKE SHOUT to You Your creatures,¹¹
WHO LIVE AT the ENDS OF THE EARTH (v. 9a). In the
morning [they say, "Praised are You, O LORD], Maker of
the heavenly lights,"¹² and in the evening [they say, "Praised
are You, O LORD] who brings on the evenings."¹³

10a   YOU TAKE CARE OF [*pāqadtā*] THE EARTH [AND IR-
RIGATE IT].¹⁴ [It means that] when You wish to benefit it
[the earth, You take care of [*pōqēd*] THE EARTH and irrigate it.¹⁵

10b   YOU ENRICH IT GREATLY [i.e.], You enrich it greatly.¹⁶

10c   With¹⁷ Your CHANNEL,¹⁸ which is FULL OF WATER, and

10d   YOU PROVIDE GRAIN FOR those who live at the ends
of the earth (v. 9a);¹⁹

10e   for so do You prepare it.²⁰

11a   As for *tĕlāmêăh* 'HER FURROWS', these are the rows made
        by the plough. *rawweh* 'SATURATING' corresponds in mean-
        ing to *lĕrawwēh* 'to saturate'.[21] [The clause] *naḥēt* ITS RIDGES
        corresponds in meaning to *lĕnaḥēt*[22] ITS RIDGES [i.e.], to
        leave ITS RIDGES to provide satisfaction[23] for people.

11b   YOU SOFTEN IT [*tĕmogĕgennāh*] WITH SHOWERS of rain.
        [The verb] *tĕmogĕgennāh* is a verb referring to softening.[24]

12a   YOU CROWN THE YEAR WITH YOUR BOUNTY, and
        by means of the rains You crown with every favor the year,
        which You wish to favor.

12b   YOUR PATHS. These are the heavens, which are the dust
        of Your feet. *yirʿăpûn* 'IS DISTILLED' [i.e.], 'they drip'
        [*yēṭîpûn*].[25] *dāšen* 'FATNESS' [i.e.], *šūmān* 'fat'.[26]

13   The heavens DRIP into THE PASTURELANDS.

14a   THE MEADOWS ARE CLOTHED WITH FLOCKS.
        [I.e.], The Sharon and the[27] Arabah will dress themselves from
        the flocks, which come to graze upon the FATNESS (v. 12b),
        which the rain made to sprout.

14b   THE VALLEYS MANTLED WITH GRAIN by the rain,
        and then

14c   the people[28] RAISE A SHOUT and[29] BREAK INTO
        SONG.

PSALM LXV, NOTES

[1] The first exegetical question to which Rashi responds in his commentary on Ps. 65 is "What is the meaning of *dumiyyāh* ?" Rashi here takes
this noun to be a derivative of Menahem Ibn Saruq's *dm* II (= *BDB*'s *dmm*
I) 'be silent'; see *Mahberet Menahem*, p. 126; *BDB*, p. 198b. NJV follows the
first of two suggestions proferred by Ibn Ezra, namely, that *dumiyyāh* is
derived from the verb *dāmāh* 'be like'. Ibn Ezra's second suggestion, namely,
that the noun *dumiyyāh* derives from the verb *dāmāh* 'wait' is followed by
Qimhi and KJV.
[2] Rashi's comment here appears to be based upon the dictum attributed to R. Jacob of the village of Nehoria in JT Berakot 9:1 and in Midrash
Tehillim here; with Zohory, p. 177 cf. also BT Megillah 18a and Midrash
Tehillim at Ps. 19 #2.
[3] Treating *škn* as a denominative verb derived from the Rabbinic Heb.
noun Shekinah; see our discussion at Ps. 48, n. 14.
[4] I.e., 'among those who dwell in Zion'; other editions of Rashi's commentary here read with the psalmist 'IN ZION'.
[5] Explicative *waw*.
[6] Rashi's source is Midrash Tehillim here. Unquestionably, in Rabbinic
Heb. *'orek 'ap* is a synonym of *'erek 'appayim* 'forbearance'; contrast my in-

terpretation of Biblical Heb. *'orek 'ap* in Gruber, *Aspects*, pp. 506-507.

[7] Rashi's Heb. dialect requires him to supply the relative pronoun *'ǎšēr* while Biblical Heb. uses only a verb in place of the entire relative clause; see *GKC* #155f.

[8] Biblical Heb. employs here the locative accusative; Rashi's Heb., like English, requires the preposition 'in'; see *GKC* #117bb.

[9] See Rashi there; cf. *Mahberet Menahem*, p. 372, s.v. *šbḥ* II 'break'; see also *BDB*, p. 986, s.v. *šābaḥ* I 'soothe, still'.

[10] The psalmist most likely means by *môṣā'ê boqer wāʿereb* 'the places from which morning and evening emanate respectively', i.e., east and west; cf. Phoenician *môṣā' šamš* 'east', lit., 'the place from which the sun comes forth' in *KAI* 26 A, 4-5; cf. Biblical Heb. *môṣā'* 'the place of [the sun's] coming forth', i.e., 'the east', in Ps. 75:7; see also in Ps. 19:7, "for at the end of the earth is the place of its [the sun's] going forth." If, in fact, *môṣā'ê* here in v. 9b refers to east and west, the two halves of the verse repeat the same idea in different words, namely, that God is adored both in the east and in the west; cf. Mal. 1:11; Ps. 113:3. Rashi, however, prefers to see Ps. 65:9 as an example of synthetic rather than synonymous parallelism. Hence he takes 'THE COMINGS FORTH...' as a phrase in apposition with 'SIGNS' (end of v. 9a). Rashi's reading of the first half of the verse suggests that the observation of celestial phenomena such as the sunrise and the sunset serves as a stimulus to worship [*yir'āh*; cf. NJV's "are awed"]. The second half of the verse suggests that by means of these stimuli—the coming forth of the morning and the coming forth of the evening—God makes people pray. Rashi's insightful comment on the phenomenology of prayer in Judaism anticipates that of Kadushin, *Worship and Ethics*, p. 95.

[11] *běriyyôtêkā*, i.e., 'Your people'.

[12] Cf. Birnbaum, *Daily Prayer Book*, p. 73.

[13] Ibid., p. 191.

[14] Rashi does not quote the bracketed portion of the verse; I have supplied it for clarity.

[15] Apparently the appearance of the verbs 'YOU TAKE CARE' and 'YOU IRRIGATE' in the perfect and the imperfect with *waw*-consecutive respectively suggests to Rashi that the former verb is to be construed as a subordinate clause, the latter as the main clause of the sentence.

[16] Here Rashi substitutes the Rabbinic Heb. present for the ambiguous Biblical Heb. imperfect and the frequently attested adverb *harbēh* for the adverbial noun *rabbat*.

[17] Rashi is here echoed by NJV, q.v.

[18] Rashi's paraphrase of the psalmist's 'CHANNEL OF GOD'.

[19] By supplying this phrase from v. 9a Rashi replies to the question posed by the expression *děgānām* 'THEIR GRAIN', namely, "Whose grain?" Moreover, Rashi treats the pronominal suffix on *děgānām* as an anticipatory pronominal suffix. On this phenomenon see Gordis, The *Song of Songs and Lamentations*, p. 23, n. 81.

[20] NJV's rendering, q.v., follows Rashi's paraphrase.

[21] Rashi's point is that *rawwēh* here should not be construed as an imperative but as an infinitive construct; so also NJV. The form *rawwēh* could be taken either way; the form *lěrawwēh* can only be the infinitive construct.

[22] Just as according to Rashi and NJV *rawwēh* is the infinitive construct and not the imperative so also here they take *naḥēt* to be, like the form *lěnnaḥēt*, infinitive construct and not imperative.

[23] Unlike Ibn Ezra and Qimhi, who are followed by NJV, who take the form *naḥēt* to be the *pi'el* infinitive of the verb *nḥt* 'descend', Rashi understands the inifinitive *naḥēt* to be a denominative verb derived from the noun *naḥat* 'quietness, rest'; so also *BDB*, p. 629a.

[24] See *Mahberet Menahem*, p. 236, s.v. *mg*.

[25] See Rashi at Deut. 32:2; the spelling *yyṭp* in our Rashi ms. suggests the hiphil of a biliteral root *ṭp* (see *Mahberet Menahem*, p. 200, s.v. *ṭp* I, and see Rashi at Ex. 1:20, s.v. *wayyêṭeb*); today the accepted derivation is from the triliteral root *nṭp*; see dictionaries.

[26] The relatively rare Biblical Heb. noun *dešen* (the pausal form is *dāšen*) is here said to correspond in meaning to the widely attested Rabbinic Heb. noun *šûmān*; Rashi's comment here probably derives from *Mahberet Menahem*, p. 133, s.v. *dšn* I.

[27] Our Rashi ms. here has the scribal error *mimma'ărabāh*, which means literally 'from westwardly'; that it makes no sense is the prima facie evidence that no commentator intended such a reading where other texts of Rashi's commentary, followed here by our translation, read *wěhā'ărābāh*.

[28] Rashi supplies the missing subject of the clause.

[29] Rashi subsitutes conjunctive *waw* for the psalmist's *'ap*, which can mean either 'and/also' or 'yea/ the more so' (see *BDB*, pp. 64-65).

PSALM LXVI

2a RAISE A SHOUT FOR GOD, ALL THE EARTH.[1]

5b WHO IS HELD IN AWE FOR HIS ACTS.
[I.e.], let him be held in awe BY MEN lest He find in them
[some] transgression, for all their deeds are known to Him.

6 HE TURNED THE SEA INTO DRY LAND [refers to the]
Reed Sea (cf. Ex. 14:21).

7c LET THEM NOT BE HIGH [ʾal-yārûmû] [i.e.], LET THEM
NOT be high-handed.

8a O PEOPLES, BLESS OUR GOD because of His wonders.

9a For He GRANTED US[2] LIFE among you during the Exile
so that you are incapable of destroying us.

10 YOU HAVE TRIED US by means of great suffering.

11b *mûʿāqāh* 'TRAMMELS' is a synonym of *masgēr*,[3] i.e.,[4] *kebel*
'fetter', which [is called *mûʿāqāh* because it] compresses [*mēʿîq*],[5]
i.e.,[4] presses [*mēṣîq*].[6]

12 YOU HAVE LET MEN RIDE OVER US [refers to Your
having let ride over us] the kings of each and every nation.[7]

13a I SHALL ENTER YOUR TEMPLE[8] [means that] when You
will have built the Sanctuary[9]

13b We shall PAY our VOWS [which we vowed][10] during the
Exile.[11]

15 *mēḥîm* 'FATLINGS' [i.e.], *šěmēnîm* 'fatlings'.[12] It is a cognate
of [the noun] *môaḥ* 'fat' (Job. 21:24).[13]

16 ALL GOD-FEARING MEN. These are the proseyltes, who
will have undergone conversion.[14]

17a I CALLED TO HIM WITH MY MOUTH [refers to the fact
that] when we were in exile we CALLED upon Him, and
we told of His exaltedness with our tongues.[15]

17b *wěrômam* 'HE WAS GLORIFIED' corresponds in meaning to
[late Heb.] *wěnitrômam*.[16]

18 HAD I AN EVIL THOUGHT IN MY MIND....
[This verse means that] He [God] has not dealt with us in
accord with our sins. [On the contrary] He has dealt with us
as though He does not see and as though He does not hear
(cf. v. 18b) THE EVIL THOUGHT which is IN our
MINDs.[17]

19   'ākēn [means] Truly one should know.[18]
20   WHO HAS NOT TURNED AWAY MY PRAYER from His
      Presence nor turned away HIS FAITHFUL CARE FROM
      ME.[19]

PSALM LXVI, NOTES,

[1] While v. 2a serves in our Rashi ms. as the distinctive heading of the
psalm, Rashi's commentary begins at v. 5b, q.v.

[2] Heb. napšēnû; lit., 'our persons' (pl.); note that this reading found in
our Rashi ms. is a well-known variant of the standard napšēnû, lit., 'our
person' (sing.); see BHS.

[3] Note, however, that in each of its other attestations in the Bible—
Isa. 24:22; 42:7; Ps. 142:8—Rashi interprets masgēr as 'prison'.

[4] Explicative waw.

[5] The verbal root 'ûq 'compress' is attested only twice in the Hebrew
Bible, both occurrences in Am. 2:13; note that Rashi's explanation of the
noun mûʿāqāh is shared by BDB, p. 734b.

[6] Here Rashi alludes to the fact that the rare in Biblical Heb. ʿûq is
the Aram. cognate of Heb. ṣûq and that the Targums employ the verbal
rot 'ûq to render the Heb. verbal root ṣûq at Isa. 29:2; 51:13 and elsewhere.

[7] Contrary to the impression which Maarsen (followed by Zohory, pp.
179-180) gives in his note here, the most that Rashi's comment here has
in common with the midrash quoted in Pesikta deRab Kahana, ed. Buber,
p. 43b (= PRK, ed. Mandelbaum, vol. 1, p. 81, line 4) and that quoted in
Pesikta Rabbati, p. 67a is the quotation of Ps. 66:12.

[8] Heb. bêtĕkā, lit., 'Your House' (so NJV); see Ps. 30, n. 1.

[9] Heb. bêt hammiqdāš; this comment shows that Rashi takes it for granted
that bêtĕkā in v. 13a means 'YOUR TEMPLE' (see previous note).

[10] The bracketed portion of the comment is missing in our Rashi ms.

[11] In vv. 1-12 the psalmist speaks in the 1st pers. pl. while from v. 13 to
the end of the psalm he speaks in the 1st pers. sing. Hence a number of
modern exegetes have contended that Ps. 66 was originally two independent psalms—the first a communal hymn of praise to God, the second an
individual's hymn of thanksgiving; for a summary of views and their ex-
ponents see Dahood, Briggs, and other standard commentaries. By transposing all the 1st pers. sing. verbs of vv. 13-20 into the 1st pers. pl., Rashi
anticipates those modern exegetes who see in the individual of vv. 13-20
a personification of the community of Israel; see, e.g., William R. Taylor
in IB, vol. 4, p. 343.

[12] So NJV, KJV, RSV, Dahood, et al.

[13] Cf. Rashi at Job. 21:24; on Heb. môaḥ and its Ugaritic cognate mḫ
see Gruber, Aspects, pp. 389, 394.

[14] See Rashi at Ps. 115:11 and our discussion there.

[15] Here Rashi paraphrases v. 17b: "HE WAS GLORIFIED UNDER
MY TONGUE" (Rashi's interpretation; see below).

[16] Rashi's point is that here the polal conjugation rômam functions as a

passive rather than as a factitive; similarly Qimhi here and *BDB*, p. 927a.

[17] With Maarsen here cf. the midrash on our verse at BT Qiddushin 40a; on v. 18 itself see the next note.

[18] As noted by Maarsen here, this interpretation of *'ākēn* appears verbatim in Rashi at 1 Sam. 15:32 and at Jer. 3:23. Karl Budde, "Brief Communications," *JBL* 40 (1921), p. 40, n. 1 emends v. 18a, *'āwen 'im rā'îtî bĕlibbî* "AS FOR INIQUITY, HAD I SEEN IT IN MY HEART" to read *'āmartî 'āwen bĕlibbî* "I THOUGHT EVIL IN MY HEART". This emendation assumes that original *'mrty* was misread in antiquity as *'m r<' y>ty* and that original *'ny* was misread either as *'nw > 'wn* or as *'yn > 'wn*. For the well-attested phenomena, which underlie the conjectural emendation see Friedrich Delitzsch, *Lese-und Schreibfehler*, #3-5; #103. Better still is *BH³*'s emendation *'ănî 'āmartî bĕlibbî* "I thought." With this latter reading the direct object of the verb 'I thought' is v. 18b, "THE LORD WILL NOT HEARKEN." As Budde sensed, the two vv. 18-19 then constitute an example of the pair *'āmartî...'ākēn* 'I had thought...contrary to what I had thought'. This pair is attested at Isa. 49:4; Jer. 3:19-20; Zeph. 3:7; Ps. 31:23; 82:6-7; Job. 32:7. It should be observed that "Budde's brilliant discovery" (so Dahood, *Psalms*, vol. 2, p. 270 at Ps. 82:6) set forth in *JBL* 40 (1921), pp. 39-41 has been anticipated by Rashi's grandson, R. Samuel b. Meir (Rashbam) in his commentary at Ex. 2:14 where he explains that *'ākēn* means *lō' kĕmô šehāyîtî sābûr* "Not as I had thought."

[19] Rashi's point is that the verb and the negative particle found in the first half of the verse govern also the second half of the verse.

PSALM LXVII[1]

2a   MAY GOD BE GRACIOUS TO US AND BLESS US.
2b   MAY HE MAKE HIS FACE SHINE by exhibiting a smil-
      ing face[2] by giving dew and rain.[3]
3   THAT YOUR WAY BE KNOWN ON EARTH.
      [I.e.], may they[4] know[5] that it is characteristic of You to ben-
      efit [Your people],[6] and for this
4   MAY THEY[7] PRAISE YOU, and
5   MAY THEY EXULT AND SHOUT FOR JOY
      FOR YOU JUDGE the world[8] WITH EQUITY [*bĕmîšôr*]
      [i.e.], *lizĕkût* 'for acquittal'.[9]

PSALM LXVII, NOTES
   [1] This psalm is so numbered in current additions of the Hebrew Scriptures; in our Rashi ms. it is numbered Ps. 64. The reasons for this discrepancy are explained in Ps. 43, n. 1. Note that Rashi's commentary on this
psalm is missing from ms. Oxford Bodleian Ms. Can. Or. 60 where the
scribe states, "This psalm, however, has no [Rashi] commentary at all."
Likewise, Oxford Bodleian Ms. Opp. Add. Fol. 24 contains no commentary, and the scribe states, "This psalm, however, has no [Rashi] commentary." In Oxford Bodleian Ms. Opp. Add. 4to 52 the comment on Ps. 67
precedes that on Ps. 66; however the initial comment on Ps. 67:1 there
actually refers to Ps. 66:1. Likewise, in Ms. Firkovitch I/15 the comment
on Ps. 67:1 appears between the comment on Ps. 65 and the comment on
Ps. 66, which is followed by the quotation of Ps. 67:2, which, in turn, is
followed by the comment on Ps. 67:3-5 known from most of the medieval
mss. including Vienna 220. These facts suggest that just as there is a clear
and widely attested manuscript tradition that no Rashi commentary on Ps.
121 and 134 (see our remarks there, and see also our remarks at Ps. 128,
n. 1) has been preserved and just as the commentary on most of the other
psalms has been preserved by all the medieval mss. without significant variants
so are there two important traditions as to whether or not Rashi's Commentary on Psalms should contain a commentary on Ps. 67. Moreover,
these facts demonstrate that when the standard printed editions of Rashi's
Bible commentaries contain material not found in some of the best mss.,
such additional materials are not the invention of the editors of the printed
editions; they also belong to the manuscript tradition(s) of Rashi's Bible
commentaries.
   [2] Cf. Gruber, *Aspects*, pp. 561-562.
   [3] Maarsen here points out that Rashi here interprets v. 2 in light of v.

7, which equates God's blessing with the land's yielding her produce. The verse is similarly interpreted by Ginsberg, "A Strand in the Cord of Hebraic Hymnody," pp. 46-47; contrast Sifre Numbers #41.

[4] I.e., the Gentiles; the biblical text states *'ammîm* 'PEOPLES'.

[5] Rashi's paraphrase, which employs the jussive *yēdĕ'û* intimates that the psalmist's infinitive construct *lāda'at* is here employed as an infinitve consecutive, which is to say that it is to be understand as though it were a verb of the same form as those preceding it, which, in this case, are the jussives in v. 2.

[6] The bracketed portion of the comment is not found in our Rashi ms. although it appears in other editions of Rashi here. The comment is based upon Midrash Tehillim here. Note that, as pointed out by Ginsberg, "A Strand in the Cord of Hebraic Hymnody," pp. 46-47, Ps. 67 speaks of the peoples of the world's rejoicing because God provides for them with kindness. Rashi and his sources in Midrash Tehillim were responding to the same exegetical difficulty confronted by Ginsberg following Kaufmann, *History of the Israelite Religion*, vol. 2, pp. 721-723 (in Hebrew), namely, that if Ps. 67 speaks of God's *judging* peoples with *equity* wherein is the cause for rejoicing? Failing to see that the verb *šāpaṭ* 'judge' can also mean 'provide for', Rashi and his sources read into Ps. 67 the idea found for the first time in Isa. 42:10-17, namely, that the cause of the Gentiles' joy is their having come to learn about God as a result of their perceiving the special favor He has done for Israel.

[7] *lĕ'ummîm* 'NATIONS', i.e., the Gentiles.

[8] Heb. *hā'ōlām*, Rashi's paraphrase of the psalmist's *'ammîm* 'THE PEOPLES'.

[9] Here Rashi has fully anticipated Ginsberg's remarks concerning *mîšôr* in "A Strand in the Cord of Hebraic Hymnody," pp. 46-47.

PSALM LXVIII

2   GOD WILL ARISE, AND[1] HIS ENEMIES [i.e.], Esau and his ilk,[2] WILL BE SCATTERED.

3   *kĕhindōp* 'AS IS DISPERSED' [i.e.], *kĕhitnaddēp* 'as is dispersed'.[3] [The entire clause, "DISPERSE...AS IS DISPERSED", means]. "Just as SMOKE is dispersed so DISPERSE them."[4]

4b   THEY SHALL BE JUBILANT WITH JOY.
Now this is the jubilation and the joy, i.e.,[5] they will thus proclaim:[6]

5a   "SING TO GOD...."

5b   *sollû* 'EXTOL' is a verb referring to praise. The same usage [of the verb *sll*][7] is reflected in "It [wisdom] shall not be praised [*lō' tĕsulleh*] in comparison to fine gold of Ophir" (Job. 28:16)[8] [and in] "who are praised [*hamĕsulla'îm*] in comparison to gold" (Lam. 4:2).[8]

5c   BY YAH HIS NAME [i.e.], by His Name, which is Yah, a name referring to fear [*yir'āh*] in accord with the way in which we render it into Aramaic [in T.O. at Ex. 15:2 where we employ Aram.] *dĕḥîlā'* 'Fear' [in translating into Aramaic the name Yah in the phrase] "my might and praise of Yah."[9] The same usage is reflected in "upon the throne of Yah" (Ex. 17:16), and the same usage is reflected in "For in Yah...you have an everlasting Rock" (Isa. 26:4), [which is rendered into Aram. by TJ as follows]: "Look! Thus you will become mighty, through the word of 'Fear' [*dĕḥîlā'*], Who is mighty forever." Now the poet [who composed Ps. 68] said [in juxtaposition] "praise Him,"[10] "fear Him,"[11] and "EXULT" (v. 5d). Now this [juxtaposition of exultation and fear] corresponds to what is said elsewhere, "Exult in trembling" (Ps. 2:11).[12]

6   FATHER OF ORPHANS. This [part of the psalm beginning with v. 6] is the hymn of praise, which you[13] will sing to Him [sc.], the entire content [from v. 6] to the end of the psalm [v. 36]. [God is called] FATHER OF ORPHANS because He became Father to Israel, who are orphans, for it is stated in the Bible, "We have become orphans, fatherless" (Lam. 5:3). [God is called] CHAMPION OF WIDOWS because he

championed the cause of Israel, of whom it is stated in the Bible, "She became like a widow" (Lam. 1:1).[14]

7a GOD RESTORES THE LONELY TO THEIR HOMES.
As for Israel, who were scattered, He gathered them together, each one from his place of exile, and he RESTORED them safely TO THEIR HOMES, and [he restored them to being] a complete community.[15]

7b SETS FREE [môṣî'] THE IMPRISONED SAFE AND SOUND.[16]
[I.e.], He set free[17] Israel from Egypt in a month which is appropriate [kāšēr][18] for travelers [to go forth insofar as at that time of the year] there is neither extreme heat nor extreme cold.[19]

7c WHILE THE REBELLIOUS Egyptians MUST LIVE IN A PARCHED LAND. [I.e.], Their land remained dry and arid.

9c AS FOR THIS SINAI, it also trembled[20] BECAUSE OF THE LORD,[21] THE GOD OF ISRAEL.

10a YOU RELEASED A BOUNTIFUL RAIN.
In addition to the aforementioned: if we[22] were in need of rain you released,[23] i.e.,[24] You continually poured[25] upon us bountiful rains.

10b WHEN YOUR INHERITANCE [nahǎlātěkā] LANGUISHED, YOU SUSTAINED IT.
[I.e.], when YOUR INHERITANCE [i.e.], Your land, was languishing, i.e.,[24] it was thirsty for rain, YOU SUSTAINED it.[27]

11a YOUR ASSEMBLY DWELLS THERE.
The usage [of the noun ḥayyāh in the sense 'assembly'] is attested also in "The Philistines had gathered in force [laḥayyāh]" (2 Sam. 23:11).[28] Another equally plausible explanation [of the meaning of the noun ḥayyāh in v. 11a is that] the Congregation of Israel is designated the Holy One Blessed be He's domesticated beast and His wild beast [ḥayyātô].

11b IN YOUR KINDNESS YOU PROVIDE.
[This refers to the fact that] when Israel came forth from Egypt, You made them go about in the desert for forty years because the Canaanites had suddenly[29] cut down the [fruit] trees [of the land of Israel so that Israel would find no sustenance and thereby perish]. Since, however, the Israelites went into the desert [instead of entering the land of Israel], they

[the Canaanites] thereupon repaired everything.[30]

12a   THE LORD GIVES A WORD.

12b   THE WOMEN WHO BRING GOOD NEWS are[31] A
VAST ARMY.
Again He will be heard announcing in a loud voice to the
armies of the many nations. Now what is the utterance? [It
is the words contained in vv. 13-14]:

13a   MAY THE KINGS OF THE ARMIES of the nations
SURELY BE REMOVED [*yiddodûn yiddodûn*].
[I.e.], may they be removed [*yitnodĕdû*],[32] i.e., may they be
thrown out of the land of Israel,

13b   AND MAY the Congregation of Israel, who is [the metaphori-
cal] HOUSEWIFE,[33] DIVIDE their SPOIL in accord with
what is stated in the Bible, "Her profits and her harlot's fees
[shall be consecrated to the LORD]" (Isa. 23:18).[34]

14   IF YOU LIE DOWN AMONG THE SHEEPFOLDS....
All of this [i.e., not only v. 13 but also v. 14] He will say to
them.[35] [V. 14 means that] if you were lying within the borders [of the land of Israel] and you enjoyed pleasures, then
you [the people of Israel] are My

14b   DOVE [i.e.], my Congregation, WHOSE WINGS are[36]
SHEATHED IN SILVER....
Now what is the [metaphorical] SILVER and the [metaphori-
cal] GOLD? [They are constituted by what is stated in the
following verse]:

15a   WHEN THE ALMIGHTY SPREAD OUT.
[I.e.], when the Holy One Blessed be He will have spread
out[37] before them [THE KINGS] his Torah

15b   THROUGH WHICH[38] THE KINGS are made snowy white.
[An equally plausible interpetation of v. 15b is the following]:
THEREIN[39] [i.e.], in a "land of deepest gloom" (Job.
10:21b).[40]

14b   Then HER WINGS were[36] SHEATHED IN SILVER, [i.e.],
the [metaphorical] silver, i.e., the preciousness of Torah and
commandments.
WINGS OF [*kanĕpê*] A DOVE [i.e.], *plumes* in O.F.[41] *wĕ'ebrôtêāh*
'ITS PINIONS' [i.e.], 'its wings [*kĕnāpêāh*] with which they
fly'.[42] *byraqraq ḥārûṣ* 'IN FINE GOLD'. Dunash ben Labraṭ
explained that *ḥārûṣ* is [another word for] gold, and therefore the psalmist juxtaposed it with SILVER. Now the *yĕraqraq*

ḥārûṣ is the gold, which is imported [to the land of Israel] from Havilah[43] and from Ethiopia. [It is] very very fine gold. It is neither yellow nor red, and therefore it is called *yĕraqraq*, reflecting the same grammatical form as is exemplified by [the adjective *'ădamdām* 'pink' in the expression] *lābān 'ădamdām* 'white streaked with pink' (Lev. 13:42), which is neither white nor red. Therefore, it [the final syllable of the adjective] is reduplicated [to produce forms such as] *yĕraqraq* [and] *'ădamdām*[44]

15a   KINGS. These are [a metaphor for] Torah scholars, for it is stated in the Bible, "Through me[45] kings reign" (Prov. 8:15). [The infinitve] *bĕpārēś* 'WHEN HE SPREAD OUT' is a cognate of [the verb *ûpārĕśû* 'and they shall spread out' in] "And they shall spread out the cloth" (Deut. 22:17), [which means that] "they should make the matter as clear as a new cloth."[46]

16a   MOUNTAIN OF GOD, MOUNT BASHAN.
[This verse answers the question as to] where did HE SPREAD it OUT? (v. 15a) [The answer is] at Mount Sinai, which is THE MOUNTAIN OF GOD, near Bashan in Transjordan.[47]

16b   MOUNT GABNUNIM [i.e.], a mountain unique among the mountains. GABNUNIM is a synonym for mountains.[48] Any tall object can be called *gāb* 'height'. [Mount Sinai is called MOUNT GABNUNIM] because of its height. [That any tall object can be called *gāb*] is demonstrated by "You built for yourself a high place [*gāb*] (Ezek. 16:24).[49]

17a   WHY ARE YOU HOSTILE?
All of this [v. 17] is [another quotation] introduced by "THE LORD GIVES A WORD" (v. 12). In addition [to vv. 13-14] He will say to them, "WHY *teraṣṣĕdûn*, MOUNTAINS [*gabnûnîm*]?" [which means], WHY do you lie in ambush, Tall Mountains, to destroy

17b   THE MOUNTAIN, which GOD DESIRED AS HIS DWELLING,
i.e.,[50] the Temple Mountain.

17c   MOREOVER, He[51] WILL ABIDE there FOREVER. Its sanctity is permanent.[52] Once it was selected for His enthronement [the] Shekinah no longer abided elsewhere.[53]

17a   *teraṣṣĕdûn*. I read in the work by R. Moses the Interpreter[54] [that the verbal root] *rṣd* means[55] *mĕ'ārēb* 'lie in ambush' in

Arabic.[56] Menahem, however, interpreted [the verb] *teraṣṣĕdûn* as a cognate of *tirqĕdûn* 'you dance'.[57] The latter etymology is congruent with this [i.e., our aforementioned] interpretation of the text.[58]

18a GOD'S CHARIOTS ARE TWO MYRIADS....
This also is [a quotation] introduced by "THE LORD GIVES A WORD. THE WOMEN WHO BRING NEWS...." [The purpose of v. 18 is] to make mention of the endearment [in which God holds] His people,[59] [which endearment is exemplified by the fact that] even when GOD'S CHARIOT was revealed [there were] TWO MYRIADS[60] of thousands[61] of persons at ease [*ša'ănānîm*],[62] [i.e.], *šĕnûnîm* 'whetted beings' [which means] 'sharp angels',[63]

18b and THE LORD[64] was among them.[65]

18c At SINAI IN THE HOLY PLACE, there also[66]

19a YOU WENT UP, you, the prince of My people, Moses son of Amram,[67] and YOU TOOK CAPTIVE the Torah,[68] and YOU RECEIVED TRIBUTE from those on high to give them to human beings.[69]

19b EVEN THE REBELLIOUS ALSO, THAT THE LORD MAY DWELL.
[I.e], Moreover, in addition you [Moses] brought it about that the Holy One Blessed be He DWELLS [*šākēn*][70] in the Tabernacle [*miškān*] among a people, who had been REBELLIOUS and insubordinate and provoking Him to anger.[71]

20a BLESSED IS THE LORD. This [section of the psalm, beginning with v. 20 and concluding with v. 22] is part of the hymn [*šîr*] referred to above [in v. 5a where it is said], "SING TO GOD."[72]

20b HE WILL GIVE US A BURDEN.[73]
[I.e.], He will give us great deliverance full of a burden as much as we can bear.[74]

21a GOD IS FOR US...OF DELIVERANCE.
God is a deliverer,

21b AND before Him there are many ESCAPES [i.e.], kinds of death.[75] ESCAPES [i.e.], paths TO DEATH.[76]

22a HOWEVER, He does not give them to us, but He WILL SMASH with them THE HEADS OF HIS ENEMIES.

22b THE HAIRY CROWN [i.e.], THE CROWN of Esau, "a hairy man" (Gen. 27:11),[77] who continually WALKS ABOUT

IN HIS GUILT and does not repent of his evil.[78]

23 THE LORD SAID, "I WILL RETRIEVE FROM BASHAN...," for indeed He promised to retrieve us from among the "mighty ones of Bashan" (Ps. 22:13b) "and from the coastlands" (Isa. 11:11).[79]

24a THAT YOUR FEET MAY WADE [timḥaṣ] THROUGH BLOOD.
When "HE WILL SMASH THE HEADS OF the enemy" (v. 22), our feet will be submerged [bôqěʿôt in blood. [The clause] timḥaṣ [THROUGH BLOOD] is synonymous with 'be submerged [bōqēaʿ] within the blood' as is demonstrated by "His neck was submerged [māḥăṣāh], and it passed through" (Judg. 5:26).[80] [The verb bāqaʿ] is the same verb as is attested in wědāgěrāh ûbāqěʿāh [81] "and shall brood and hatch" (Isa. 34:15). [In the meaning 'be submerged'] it [the verb bqʿ] is [typically] Mishnaic Heb. [as exemplified by the following: "Those who came on festival pilgrimage to Jerusalem used to be submerged [hāyû bōqěʿîm] in blood up to their ankles" (Tosefta ʿEduyot 3:2).[82] Another equally plausible interpretation of timḥaṣ [here in Ps. 68:24a] is [that it is the name of] a utensil by means of which wine is drawn out of the wine-pit; it is called maḥaṣ 'ladle' in [BT] Tractate ʿAvodah Zarah [74b].[83]

24b AS FOR THE TONGUE OF YOUR DOGS, FROM the blood of the ENEMIES ITS PORTION [minnēhû]. [I.e.], May its sustenance be [FROM the blood of the ENEMIES]. [The noun mān 'PORTION' here attested] is the same noun attested in what we say [in the Babylonian Talmud], "What is the meaning of this [word] mān? It is a term referring to food, for it is written in the Bible, 'who assigned [minnāh] your food...' (Dan. 1:10)" [BT Sukkah 39b].[84]

25 THEY SAW YOUR PROCESSIONS, O GOD.
[I.e.], You are pleased to deliver these people [i.e., Israel], because when THEY SAW YOUR PROCESSIONS when You were sanctified at the [Reed] Sea,

26a SINGERS MARCHED IN FRONT to sing before You the Song at the Sea (= Ex. 15:1-19),

26b and BEHIND them the INSTRUMENTALISTS. These were the angels.[85]

26c AMIDST MAIDENS PLAYING TIMBRELS along with Miriam, "who took the timbrel in her hand" (Ex. 15:20),[86]

and her servant girls,[87] and they sang their hymn of praise.

27 IN ASSEMBLIES BLESS GOD…FROM THE FOUN-
TAIN OF ISRAEL. [This seemingly enigmatic verse refers
to the fact] that even fetuses sang the hymn from within their
mothers' wombs.[88]

28a THERE IS LITTLE BENJAMIN THEIR RULER, who is
made ruler over them.[89] [The unusually vocalized form] *rōdēm*
corresponds in meaning to *rōdām* 'their ruler'.[90] Now it is from
THERE that he [the tribe of Benjamin] became worthy to
be their [all the tribes of Israel's] king[91] because he was the
first to descend into the [Reed] Sea. In the same vein, Samuel
told Saul, "You make look small to yourself, but you are the
head of the tribes of Israel" (1 Sam. 15:17), which Jonathan
[b. Uzziel] rendered into Aramaic [as follows]: "The tribe of
Benjamin passed through the [Reed] Sea ahead of all the
other tribes."[92]

28b THE PRINCES OF JUDAH ARE THE SOURCE OF
THEIR BEING STONED.[93] [This happens as follows]: They
[the Judahites] are jealous of them [the Benjaminites], so they
[the Judahites] throw stones [at the Benjaminites] and so [do]

28c THE PRINCES OF ZEBULUN AND NAPHTALI, and thus
he [Judah] said to him [Benjamin]:

29 …GOD ORDAINED STRENGTH.
Another equally plausible interpretation of *rigmātām*[94] is [that
it is a biform of] *riqmātām* 'their embroidered [garments]'
(Ezek. 26:16), [which is] a synonym of *'argāmān* 'purple-[dyed
wool]' (e.g., Ex. 25: 4). So did Menahem construe it.[95]

29b DISPLAY STRENGTH ['*ûzzāh*], O GOD.
Now the psalmist returns to his prayer, in which he prayed,
"MAY GOD ARISE, AND MAY HIS ENEMIES BE SCAT-
TERED" (v. 2). DISPLAY STRENGTH, O GOD. I.e., Make
Yourself strong,

29c YOU, who[96] DID FOR US all these things [recounted in vv.
6-28].

30a and FROM YOUR TEMPLE ABOVE JERUSALEM.…
Now since the KINGS (v. 30b) will see the glory of YOUR
TEMPLE, which is ABOVE JERUSALEM

30b MAY THEY BRING YOU gift [*dôrôn*] and TRIBUTE.

31a BLAST THE BEAST OF THE MARSH [*qāneh*], i.e., Esau,

who has been compared to a wild boar, which dwells among the reeds.[97]

31b **THE HERD OF BULLS AMONG THE PEOPLES, THE CALVES.**
Until "they became fat and sleek" (Jer. 5:28; cf. Deut. 32:15) they were like oxen[98] [i.e.], BULLS among the other nations, who, by comparison to them [Israel], are only calves.[99]

31c **THEY COME CRINGING WITH PIECES [bĕraṣṣê] OF SILVER.**
They are not reconciled [mitraṣṣîm] with any person unless he [the latter person] appeases them [mĕraṣṣeh] with money.[100]

31d **HE SCATTERED[101] PEOPLES.**
[I.e.], they scattered the tribes. [The use of Biblical Heb. 'ammîm, lit., 'peoples' to mean 'tribes'] corresponds to what you [the reader of the Bible] read "Lover indeed of peoples ['ammîm]" (Deut. 33:3) [which means, "with an additional love He loved the tribes"].[102]

31e **WHO** always **DELIGHT IN WARS** [i.e.], who delight in fighting against us.

32a **TRIBUTE-BEARERS [ḥašmannîm] SHALL COME,** and then, when You destroy Esau and King Messiah arises, they will bring You gifts **FROM EGYPT** and from **CUSH.**
Menahem interpreted ḥašmannîm as the name of a country. [To be precise: Menahem states], "ḥašmannîm are the inhabitants of Hashmonah (Num. 33:29) [which is] the name of a country."[103] However, the French Jewish exegetes[104] interpret it [the hypothetical singular ḥašman from which, presumably, is derived the plural ḥašmannîm attested only here at Ps. 68:32] as a synonym of [the late Heb. Gk. loanword] dôrôn 'gift'.[105]

33b **SING TO GOD** for He showed His greatness by redeeming[106] His people.

34b hēn yittēn [i.e.], hēn nōtēn 'LOOK! HE GIVES.[107]
Now our rabbis interpreted the entire psalm up to "BLESSED IS THE LORD EVERY DAY" (v.20) as a reference to the Giving of the Torah, "IN WHICH YOUR TRIBE DWELLS" (v. 11). As for me, I cannot reconcile myself to saying that "THEY DWELL THERE" (v. 11) is an expression suggesting that they [the tribes of Israel] were settled down by virtue of the Torah.[108] Moreover, as for "THE MOUNTAIN GOD DESIRED FOR HIS ENTHRONE-

MENT" (v. 17b), I cannot reconcile myself to interpreting it as a reference to Mt. Sinai,[109] for, in fact, He did not DESIRE it [Mt. Sinai] FOR HIS ENTHRONEMENT nor for abiding there[110] forever. Here, however, it is written about it [the unnamed holy place], "HE SHALL ABIDE THERE FOREVER" (v. 17c). Likewise, they [mis]-interpreted "KINGS OF THE ARMIES [malĕkê şĕbā'ôt]" (v. 13a) as "all the angels of the hosts" [kol-mal'ăkê şĕbā'ôt].[111] This, however, is not the meaning of the biblical text.

36 YOU ARE HELD IN AWE, O GOD, BECAUSE OF YOUR TEMPLES. Because You destroyed it [the Temple] they will hold You in awe, for people will say, "If He did not show deference to His Temple, how much the more so [will he not show deference] to the wicked among the Gentiles."

PSALM LXVIII, NOTES

[1] The addition of the conjunctive *waw* here in our Rashi ms., which is not found in standard editions of the Hebrew Bible, is shared by many medieval mss. of the Hebrew Bible, and it is witnessed also by LXX, the Peshitta, and Jerome (see *BHS* here).

[2] Cf. Genesis Rabbah 65:14; 66:7.

[3] Rashi's paraphrase of the anomalous Biblical Heb. *kĕhindōp* by the unequivocally passive Rabbinic Heb. *hitpa'el* suggests that he interprets the unusual Biblical Heb. form as a *niphal* passive; so also *BDB*, p. 623b; $K\text{-}B^3$, p. 637a, *BHS*, and others suggest revocalization of the Biblical Heb. form as a regular *niphal* infinitive with prefixed particle *kĕhinnādēp*.

4 Similarly NJV, RSV, and others.

[5] Explicative *waw*.

[6] Rashi's point is that in the present context the verb *yāśîśû* 'THEY SHALL BE JUBILANT' is a *verbum dicendi* and that this verb introduces a quotation, which begins with v. 5a and concludes at the end of v. 36; see Rashi at v. 6.

[7] For Rashi, following *Mahberet Menahem*, p. 265, the root is *sl*.

[8] See Rashi there; contrast *Mahberet Menahem*, p. 265, which separates *sl* IV 'evaluate, compare' attested in Job. 28:16; Lam 4:2, from *sl* V 'extol'.

[9] Rendering based on T.O. there; contrast Rashi there, and contrast NJV.

[10] Heb. *šibbĕḥû lĕpānāyw*, lit., 'Praise before Him', Rashi's paraphrase of the psalmist's *sollû* 'Extol'.

[11] Heb. *gûrû mippānāyw*, Rashi's paraphrase of his interpretation of *bĕYāh* (see above).

[12] See there.

[13] I.e., you, who were addressed in the imperative plural in v. 5, *šîrû*.

[14] Rashi's comment appears to be based on Midrash Tehillim here.

[15] Rashi's comment appears to be based upon Lamentations Rabbah Petihta 29.

[16] NJV's and NEB's "safe and sound" is based on Rashi's interpretation (see below), which is clearly based on an attempt to relate the *hapax legomenon bakkošārôt* to late Heb. *kāšēr* 'be fitting, appropriate' found in the Bible only in Eccles. 2:21; 4:4; 5:10; 10:10; 11:6; and Esth. 8:5 and frequently in Rabbinic Heb. Ibn Ezra, followed by Qimhi, sees in *košārôt* a term for 'fetters' derived from the root *qšr* 'bind' with the initial *k* representing an original *q*. Recent scholarship has seen here a reference to the Canaanite goddesses of birth known to us from Ugarit as k<u>t</u>rt; see *K-B*[3], p. 446a and the extensive literature cited there.

[17] Rashi intimates here that the participle, which is employed in Rabbinic and later Heb. as a present tense form, here in Ps. 68:7 expresses the past tense. On this usage of the participle in Biblical Heb. see Bendavid, *Biblical Hebrew and Rabbinic Hebrew*, vol. 2, pp. 545-547 (in Hebrew); see also the discussion in BT Berakot 38a.

[18] See above, n. 16, and see below, n. 19.

[19] The source of Rashi's comment here is Mekilta, vol. 1, pp. 139-140.

[20] Here Rashi intimates the following: (1) v. 9 is composed of three parallel clauses; (2) the verb found in the first clause (*rāʿăšāh* 'TREMBLED') governs also the third clause; (3) the conjuction *'ap* 'also' at the beginning of the second clause is to be supplied mentally also at the beginning of the third clause.

[21] Here our Rashi ms. has the anomalous reading y^yy, which stands for the tetragrammaton, i.e., 'THE LORD' while the commonly attested reading in the psalm here is *'ĕlohîm* 'God'.

[22] Our Rashi ms. reads 'they were in need', which makes no sense in context; hence we have adopted the reading 'we...' from other editions of Rashi's commentary.

[23] By paraphrasing using the perfect form of the verb Rashi points to the fact that the psalmist has employed the imperfect to express the past tense; this common feature of Biblical Heb. and Ugaritic has spawned a variety of scholarly theories; see, *inter alia*, "Symposium: The *yiqtol* in Biblical Hebrew," *Hebrew Studies* 29 (1988), pp. 7-42.

[24] Explicative *waw*.

[25] Heb. *wĕhiṭṭaltā*; for this usage of the *hiphil* of the verb *nāṭal* 'take' in Rabbinic Heb. see Mishnah Giṭṭin 5:9.

[26] Here Rashi indicates that where Rabbinic (and so also Modern) Heb. uses a temporal clause introduced by *kĕše* 'when', Biblical Heb. can use a verb in the perfect introduced by *waw*-conjunctive; see *GKC* #164a-b; see also Orlinsky, *Notes*, p. 22 for the rediscovery of Rashi's technique of rendering intelligible this kind of Biblical Heb. temporal clause.

[27] Our Rashi ms. reads *'ōtān* 'them', which makes no sense in this context; other editions of Rashi here read *'ōtāh* 'it'. Here as at Ps. 64:8 Rashi substitutes for a Biblical Heb. verb containing an accusative pronominal

suffix a verb followed by the independent accusative pronoun; see our remarks there.

[28] Cf. Rashi there. Dahood finds support for a similar interpretation of *ḥayyāṯěkā* 'your family' in 2 Sam. 23:13 where *ḥayyat Pělištîm* corresponds to *maḥăneh Pělištîm* 'a camp of Philistines' in 1 Ch. 11:15. Moreover, Dahood equates the rare Heb. *ḥayyāh* 'family' with Ugar. *ḥwt* 'house, dynasty, realm.

[29] Heb. *'āmědû*, lit., 'they arose', is employed here as an auxiliary verb meaning 'thereupon, immediately, suddenly' like the Biblical Heb. counterpart *qwm*; concerning the use of late Heb. *qwm* as the equivalent of classical Biblical Heb. *'md* see Eduard Yechezkel Kutscher, *A History of the Hebrew Language*, ed. Raphael Kutscher (Leiden: E. J. Brill/Jerusalem: Magnes, 1982), p. 84; on Biblical Heb. *qwm* as an auxiliary verb employed in the sense here attributed to *'md* see Orlinsky, *Notes*, pp. 34-35.

[30] The same *aggadah* is quoted in Rashi at Ps. 40:6, q.v.

[31] Heb. ' is the abbreviation for Heb. *hēn*, the 3[d] pers. fem. pl. personal pronoun, which here, as frequently in Rashi's Heb., serves as the copula; note that Rashi's interpreation of v. 12b as a nominal sentence in which 'A VAST ARMY' is the predicate nominative is reflected in NJV.

[32] Rashi's clarification of this expression, which follows, demonstrates that he interprets neither the psalmist's *yiddodûn* nor the paraphrase *yitnodědû* found in Ps. 64:9 (see Rashi there) as an active verb; contrast the various modern commentaries and dictionaries.

[33] Heb. *něwat bayit*; cf. NJV's "housewives"; this interpretation goes back to LXX, the Old Latin, and the Vulgate.

[34] Rashi does not quote the bracketed portion of the text from Isa.; I have supplied it for clarity.

[35] See Rashi at v. 12.

[36] The standard Heb. text of the psalm employs the form *nehpāh* 'SHEATHED', which can be read as the singular of either the perfect or the participle; since the subject 'WINGS', of which the form in question is the predicate, is plural *BHS* suggests emending to *nehpōt*, which is the plural of the participle. Rashi here substitutes the plural of the perfect *nehpû* suggesting that the singular is to be understood as a plural. Dahood, here resolves the apparent anomaly by suggesting that the form *nehpāh* may be a dual.

[37] Here Rashi substitutes a temporal clause for the psalmist's infinitive construct, and he employs a verb in the perfect in the sense of an Eng. future perfect.

[38] The psalmist writes *bāh*; Rashi paraphrases this in late Heb. as *'ăšer bāh*.

[39] Heb. *bāh*; an alternative interpretation of Biblical Heb. *bāh*; cf. previous note.

[40] Here Rashi suggests that ZALMON is an abstract noun meaning 'blackness', derived from the root *ṣlm* 'be black', from which, according to Rashi, is derived *ṣalmāwet* 'blackness' in Job. 10:21b and elsewhere; on the latter noun see Rashi and our discussion at Ps. 23:4; 39:7; 44:20.

[41] I.e., 'feathers' (so also *plumes* in Modern French); see Rashi at BT Hullin 56b; and see Catane, *Recueil* #372; 2161; contrast NJV: "wings of".

[42] NJV's rendering, q.v., treats the two clauses as synonymous parallelism employing the fixed pairs 'wings/pinions'; 'silver/gold'. Rashi, however, assumes rightly that silver and gold are not synonymous and that *kanĕpê* 'feathers of' (see previous note) cannot be synonymous with *'ebrôtêāh* 'her wings, pinions'. Hence he interprets the two clauses as synthetic parallelism, in which the first clause asserts that the feathers of the bird's head and body are silver-plated while the second clause asserts that the wings are gold-plated. Rashi intimates that while in his Heb. *kānāp* is the regular word for 'wing', in Biblical Heb. it can mean simply 'feather'.

[43] See Gruber, "Havilah," *EJ* 7:1493-1494.

[44] This entire comment is taken almost verbatim from *Teshuvot Dunash*, pp. 41-42. According to Dunash, reduplicated color adjectives refer to pale colors; so also Ibn Ezra at Lev. 13:49; contrast Rashi there and at Ps. 38:11, and see our discussion at Ps. 38:11. Dunash's suggestion here that *yĕraqraq* is to yellow and red as *'ădamdām* 'pink' is to red and white implies that for him *yĕraqraq* means 'orange'.

[45] In Rabbinic exegesis the personified Wisdom of Prov. 8:15 is the Torah.

[46] Similarly Rashi there. Finkelstein in his edition of Sifre Deuteronomy, p. 269 notes that this midrash is not an authentic element in the textual tradition of the Sifre.

[47] I.e., Mount Sinai is here called Mount Bashan because of its proximity to Bashan in Transjordan.

[48] In our Rashi ms. the scribe has inadvertently inserted the next clause of the commentary in the middle of this clause. We have restored the correct order in our translation.

[49] In other editions of Rashi's commentary here the order of these clauses differs.

[50] Heb. *hû'*.

[51] Rashi here substitutes the personal pronoun where the biblical text employs the tetragrammaton.

[52] I.e., the Temple Mountain's sanctity, unlike that of Mount Sinai, which was temporary; see Mishnah Zebaḥim 14:7-8.

[53] This comment treats the verb *šākan* 'dwell' as a denominative verb derived from the noun Shekinah 'Divine Presence'; see above at Ps. 48, n. 14.

[54] See above at Ps. 45:2; 60:4.

[55] Heb. *hû'*, lit., 'it (is)'.

[56] Similarly *BDB*, p. 952b.

[57] *Mahberet Menahem*, p. 355. This assertion would assume that both Heb. *rqd* and Heb. *rṣd* derive from proto-Semitic *rḍd* just as Heb. *mḥq* and Heb. *mḥṣ* derive from proto-Semitic *mḥḍ*; on the latter see *K-B³*, p. 541a, s.v. *mḥṣ*, p. 541b, s.v. *mḥq*. However, there is abundant evidence that Heb. *rqd* derives from common Semitic *rqd*; hence Menahem's brilliant suggestion is to be rejected.

[58] According to Rashi at v. 17a, God asks the Gentiles why they disturb the Temple Mountain. In light of Ps. 29 where the LORD's sovereignty over the forces of nature is expressed in terms of His causing Lebanon and Sirion to dance, Rashi is correct in pointing out that the general sense of Ps. 68:17a is the same regardless of which etymology of the verb *rṣd* is preferred.

[59] Our Rashi ms. has here the scribal error *'aṣmô* 'Himself' instead of *'ammô* 'His people'.

[60] This interpretation of Heb. *ribbôtayim*, which is reflected in Midrash Tehillim here, has been confirmed by Ugaritic; see Dahood here.

[61] MT here reads *'alpê* "THOUSANDS OF"; Rashi substitutes *'ălāpîm* 'thousands'.

[62] Heb. *ša'ănānîm* 'persons at ease' is attested in Am. 6:1; Zech. 1:15; Ps. 123:4; the singular *ša'ănān* 'person at ease' is found in one important medieval Heb. ms. of the Bible (see *BHS* here). Other editions of Rashi's commentary read here with the standard Heb. text of Ps. 68:18 *šin'ān*. It is now widely accepted that the word is a cognate of Ugar. tĆnn 'archer'; see Dahood, here and the literature cited there. According to this interpretation, *šin'ān* here should designate the extraterrestrial beings, who accompany the divine chariot. Rashi, following the Rabbinic exegesis reflected in Midrash Tehillim, so interpreted the word; hence his interpretation 'angels' (similarly Psalms Targum here). Following Midrash Tehillim, Rashi, not unlike the moderns referred to above, sought to justify his interpretation not only contextually but also etymologically; hence the suggestion taken over from Midrash Tehillim that *šin'ān* is a collective noun derived from the verb *šānan* 'sharpen' (see Ps. 64:4; 140:4).

[63] Our Rashi ms. has the scribal error *mělākîm* 'kings' instead of *mal'ākîm* 'angels'.

[64] Heb. yʸy, which is the way in which our, Rashi ms. indicates the tetragrammaton, which is commonly represented in English versions by 'THE LORD'; the standard Heb. text has instead the epithet *'ădonāy*, which is commonly rendered "the Lord".

[65] Rashi paraphrases the psalmist's *bām* by *běnêhem*.

[66] Rashi's addition of these two words indicate that he rejects MT's verse division according to which "AT SINAI IN THE HOLY PLACE" belongs with what precedes it. The various modern commentators engage in verbal acrobatics attempting to find the syntactic connection between v. 18c and v. 18a. Rashi simply attaches v. 18c to v. 19.

[67] Here Rashi, following Midrash Tehillim, answers the exegetical question, "Who is addressed in v. 19?"

[68] Rashi's brief comment here is based on Midrash Tehillim here.

[69] Based on Midrash Tehillim here; contrast NJV's "having received tribute of men" (emphasis mine); Rashi paraphrases MT's *bā'ādām* by *liběnê 'ādām*.

[70] Cf. v. 17b above.

[71] Rashi's comment here is based on Midrash Tehillim here.

[72] William F. Albright, "A Catalogue of Early Hebrew Lyric Poems (Psalm 68)," *HUCA* 23, pt. 1 (1950-51), pp. 1-39 analyzed our psalm as thirty-three psalm titles. Dahood, here, saw it as a triumphal hymn. Rashi sees in this psalm scattered references both to a hymn addressed to God and to a divine utterance. Throughout his commentary on this psalm Rashi calls the reader's attention to each of these two elements, and he thereby suggests that the reader may want to separate and reconstruct these two elements.

[73] This rendering reflects Rashi's understanding of the verb *yaʿămos*; this interpretation is found also in BT Sanhedrin 100a; Midrash Tehillim here, the Psalms Targum, and Ibn Ezra's commentary here; this interpretation is reflected also in KJV's "loadeth us *with benefits*"; contrast NJV's "He supports us", i.e., "He will bear our burden." Dahood's contention that such a rendering requires us to reject MT's vocalization and to revocalize the verb as a privative *piʿel* clarifies the exegetical difficulty, which inspires the interpretation adopted by Rashi.

[74] Cf. the Rabbinic sources cited in the previous note.

[75] Cf. BT Berakot 8a.

[76] Contrast NJV's "escape from death," which goes back to LXX and the Vulgate.

[77] This interpretation of the synonymous parallelism in v. 22a-b HEAD OF HIS ENEMIES//HAIRY CROWN is consistent with Rashi's comment on v. 2.

[78] Here Rashi seems to anticipate Speiser's recognition of the durative *hitpaʿel*. See Ephraim Avigdor Speiser, "The Durative Hithpaʿel: A tan Form," in *Oriental and Biblical Studies: Collected Writings of E. A. Speiser*, ed. J. J. Finkelstein and Moshe Greenberg (Philadelphia: University of Pennsylvania Press, 1967), pp. 506-514.

[79] Rashi sees in our verse's reference to "BASHAN" and "THE DEPTHS OF THE SEA" literary allusions to images found elsewhere in the Bible and which refer to Israel's being oppressed by the Gentiles and to Israel's being in Exile respectively. Albright, followed by Dahood (see Dahood, here), likewise sees here literary allusions to the well-known pair Serpent//Sea in Canaanite mythology.

[80] Our rendering of the second part of the quotation is based on Rashi's comment at Judg. 5:26; note that the interpretation of the first part of the quotation advocated by Rashi here differs from the one he presents in his commentary at Judg. 5:26.

[81] This is the word order found in our Rashi ms.; it is the reverse of the word order found in the Bible at Isa. 34:15. NJV there likewise reverses the Hebrew word order for 'hatch and brood' is an instance of *hysteron proteron*, i.e., the employment in literature of a word order which is the reverse of the order, which is known from experience; for additional examples of this rhetorical device see Gordis, *Job,* p. 149 at Job. 14:10.

[82] Quoted also in BT Menaḥot 103b; for additional parallels and variant readings see Lieberman, *Tosefta Ki-Fshuta: Order Moʿed*, pt. 4, p. 565 to Tosefta Pasḥa' 4:12, line 77.

[83] For additional references to the latter noun in Rabbinic Heb. see dictionaries. Rashi assumes that from the single root *mḥṣ* 'to be submerged' there can be formed two synonymous noun forms, one without any preformative and one with preformative *t*. This assumption is confirmed by the existence of such pairs of nouns as *gĕmûl* and *tagmûl* 'benefit' and *lĕbûš* and *tilbošet* 'clothing'; etc.

[84] Rashi here, following BT Sukkah 39b, contends that the verb *minnāh* and its cognates refer not simply to apportioning but specifically to 'apportioning portions of food'. Hence *minnēhû* at Ps. 68:24b must mean 'his livelihood'. While it is clear that in Ps. 68:24b the psalmist asks God to have dogs devour the blood of his enemies, the contention that *minnāh* means 'give out food' cannot be sustained in the light of Jon. 2:1; 4:6-8; Ps. 61:8; Job. 7:3; 1 Ch. 9:29, in none of which are the objects (or persons) primarily comestibles. With Maarsen note that Rashi here quotes Dan. 1:10 in accord with MT and not in accord with BT there.

[85] Rashi's comment here is based upon Midrash Tanḥuma, ed. Buber, Beshallaḥ #13; our Rashi ms. contains here the scribal error *hammĕlākîm* 'the kings' instead of *hammal'ākîm* 'the angels'.

[86] Rashi here paraphrases Ex. 15:20 employing the perfect form of the verb *lāqĕḥāh* 'she took' instead of the imperfect consecutive.

[87] Contrast Ex. 15:20, which speaks not of "her servant girls' but of "all the women"; Midrash Tehillim here quotes Ex. 15:20 verbatim.

[88] Rashi's comment is based upon Midrash Tehillim here. This midrash takes it for granted that Heb. *māqôr*, lit., 'FOUNTAIN' can denote 'uterus' as, in fact, this word does in Lev. 12:7; 20:18; Prov. 5:18.

[89] Rashi here responds to the exegetical question, "What is the meaning of the peculiar form *rōdēm*?" Rashi's answer is reflected in NJV's "who rules them."

[90] Similarly Mandelkern, p. 1076b; Delitzsch, vol. 2, p. 266.

[91] Saul, the first king of Israel was from the tribe of Benjamin, the youngest (see, e.g., Gen. 43:29) and the smallest of the tribes (1 Sam. 9:21).

[92] Maarsen here, following Weiss, "The Life of R. Salomon b. Isaac," p. 69, n. 20 sees Rashi's reference here to TJ at 1 Sam. 15:17, where reference could have been made to the Psalms Targum on Ps. 68:28a, as evidence that Rashi did not know the Psalms Targum found in our Rabbinic Bibles; cf. our remarks at Ps. 48, n. 18; 55, n. 18; 58, n. 29. Note also that Rashi here cites a version of TJ, which deviates both from that found in the standard printed editions and from the versions represented in the text and apparatus of Alexander Sperber, *The Bible in Aramaic, vol. II: The Former Prophets According to Targum Jonathan* (Leiden: E. J. Brill, 1959), p. 123.

[93] Ad hoc translation intended to reflect the interpretation presupposed by Rashi's comment here; contrast NJV's "who commanded them." The latter rendering relates Heb. *rigmātām* to the familiar Ugar. verb *rgm* 'say, command' while Rashi here relates the Heb. noun in question to the familiar Biblical Heb. verb *rgm* 'to stone'.

[94] Previously interpreted by Rashi to mean 'their being stoned' (see previous note).

[95] Neither of these assertions about *rigmātām* is found in *Mahberet Menahem*, p. 349, s.v. *rgm*. On the contrary, Menahem explains there that *regem* in Zech. 7:2 and *rigmātām* in Ps. 68:28 means *lahăqātām* 'their entourage'. See Maarsen here and notes to *Mahberet Menahem*, ed. Fillipowski, p. 162. Interestingly, the interpretation, which Rashi here attributes to *Mahberet Menahem* is found already in Jerome's *Juxta Hebraeos*.

[96] Heb. *'ăšēr*, the classical (Jerusalem dialect) equivalent of the psalmist's rare (Northern Heb. dialect) relative pronoun *zû*, which is attested fifteen times in the Hebrew Bible (see *K-B³*, p. 255a); see, e.g., Ex. 15:13, 16; Ps. 9:16; 10:2; etc.

[97] Rashi's source is Midrash Tehillim here.

[98] Our ms. reads *kpyrm* 'lions', which is clearly a scribal error for *kprym* 'like oxen'.

[99] Cf. BT Pesaḥim 118b.

[100] Rashi's source is Midrash Tehillim here.

[101] Our Rashi ms. reads *pizzēr*; contrast MT's *bizzar*, which is commonly held to be a biform of the 3^d pers. sing. perfect *pizzēr* 'he scattered'; see Ibn Ezra and Qimhi, and note with the latter authorities that *bzr* as a biform of *pzr* is found in Biblical Heb. also in Dan. 11:24.

[102] So Rashi there following T.O. there.

[103] *Mahberet Menahem*, p. 192.

[104] Heb. *wĕhappōtĕrîm*; see Baneth, "Les Poterim," p. 27; id., *Rashi: Interpreter of the Biblical Letter*, p. 8.

[105] Such an interpretation is reflected already in Midrash Tehillim here, q.v.

[106] Heb. *wĕgā'al*, lit., 'and He redeemed'. Here in Rashi's Heb. as frequently in Biblical Heb., the conjunctive *waw* introduces a subordinate clause; on this phenomenon in Biblical Heb. and its proper translation into idiomatic English see Orlinsky, *Notes*, pp. 19-20; Speiser, *Genesis*, pp. lxvi-lxvii.

[107] Cf. RSV's "Lo, He gives"; Rashi's point is that the psalmist here employs the imperfect form of the verb to indicate present time.

[108] Contrast R. Hiyya at BT 'Erubin 54a.

[109] Contrast Midrash Tehillim here.

[110] Heb. *liškôn bô*; see above, n. 53.

[111] Rashi here agrees with R. Judan quoting R. Aibo in PRK, ed. Mandelbaum, p. 84, line 3, and he disagrees with Midrash Tehillim here. In fact, both interpretations derive from variant readings in the textual tradition; see *BHS*.

PSALM LXIX

1   ON ['*al*] LILIES.
[It means] on behalf of ['*al*] Israel, who are lilies [Heb. *shoshanim*] "among the thorns" (see Cant. 2:2) in that the thorns pierce them.[1] [The preposition '*al* 'on behalf of' refers to the fact that] he [the psalmist] prayed on their behalf ['*ălêhem*].

2b   FOR THE WATERS [a metaphor for] the Gentiles.

3a   INTO THE SLIMY [*bywēn*] DEEP [*měṣûlāh*] [i.e.], *babbôṣ* "in the mire" (Jer. 38:22), i.e., in the mud of THE DEEP.

3d   THE FLOOD [*wěšibbolet*] of water; i.e.,[2] the strong current of the river; *fil* in Old French.[3]

4b   IS DRY [*niḥar*] [i.e.], *yābēš* 'it was dry'. [The verb *niḥar*] is a cognate of [the verb *ḥārāh* 'it was dried out' in] "[My bone] dried out from the heat" (Job. 30:30).

4c   MY EYES FAIL. Every extended anticipation[4] is called [in Biblical Heb.] *kilyôn 'ênayim* 'failure of the eyes' as is exemplified by "[Your eyes] fail with longing for them" (Deut. 28:32);[5] "consuming the eyes" (Lev. 26:16);[6] "but the eyes of the wicked shall fail" (Job. 11:20).[5]

5d   MY FALSE ENEMIES hate me[7] because I do not chase after their falsehood to adopt their error.

5e   THEN I SHALL RESTORE [WHAT I HAVE NOT STOLEN].[8]
When they[9] gather themselves to attack me,[10] I bribe them with money, which I HAVE NOT STOLEN from them.[11]

7   LET THOSE WHO LOOK TO YOU NOT BE DISAPPOINTED ON MY ACCOUNT. [I.e.], do not let me into their [my enemies'] hand lest THOSE WHO LOOK TO YOU BE DISAPPOINTED at what happens to me so that they will ask, "Did it not thus happen to someone who used to LOOK to the Holy One Blessed be He?"

9   TO MY BROTHERS [i.e.], to Esau.[12]

10   JEALOUSY WITH RESPECT TO YOUR TEMPLE.[13]
When they [Israel's enemies] saw the endearment with which You [God] treated him [Israel] while YOUR TEMPLE was standing, they became JEALOUS of me [Israel personified

by the psalmist].

11b [WHEN I WEPT AND FASTED],[14] I WAS REVILED FOR IT.

[It means that] because I weep and pray and fast[15] they make fun of me.

14a AS FOR ME, MAY MY PRAYER COME TO YOU....

[I.e.], may MY PRAYER be

14b AT A FAVORABLE MOMENT.

16c *we'al-te'ețar* 'LET...NOT CLOSE OVER ME' [i.e.], Let THE MOUTH OF THE PIT (v. 16d) of trouble [i.e.], this alien woman,[16] who opens her mouth to swallow me, not close ['*al-tisgôr*] OVER ME. [The verb] *te'ețar* is a cognate of [the adjective] '*ițțēr* 'restricted' in the expression] 'restricted as to the use of his right hand' [i.e.], 'closed with respect to his right hand so that he does not use it [i.e., 'lefthanded' (Judg. 3:15; 20:16)].[17]

19 COME NEAR TO MY SOUL[18] *gĕ'ālāh* [i.e.], *gĕ'al 'ôtāh* 'redeem her'.[19]

21b *wā'ānûšāh* 'LET ME BE IN DESPAIR'. [Etymologically *wā'ānûšāh* is related to hypothetical] *wā'ānûš* 'I am in despair';[23] it corresponds in meaning to [hypothetical] *wĕ'ehleh* 'let me be sick'. [The verb *wā'ānûšāh*] is a cognate of [the participle *'ānûšāh* 'incurable' in] "Her wounds are incurable" (Mic. 1:9), and it is a cognate of [the verb *wayyē'ānaš* 'he became very sick' in] "...the child [of Bathsheba][20]...became very sick" (2 Sam. 12:15). Now if you should ask, "How is it possible that this '*aleph* [in the word *wā'ānûšāh*] serves as a root letter and serves [also] as the first pers. sing. prefix?"[21] [my answer is that] this is the general rule with respect to any verb[22] whose initial root letter is *aleph* as, for example, [the verb *wā'ōhab* 'I loved' in] "I loved Jacob" (Mal. 1:2); [the verb *'āhēb* 'I love' in] "Those who love me I love" (Prov. 8:17). Note that each of these forms [of the verb *'hb* 'love'] corresponds in meaning to [hypothetical] *w"hb* [with double '*aleph* contracted to single '*aleph*], and likewise [the verb *'āsēp* 'I will sweep away' in] "I will sweep everything away" (Zeph. 1:2) corresponds in meaning to [hypothetical] *"sp*.

21c TO CONDOLE.

[I HOPED] that friends would come TO CONDOLE me and to comfort me.

22 FOR MY FOOD [*běbārûtî*] [i.e.], *bisĕ'ûdātî* 'for my meal'.[23]
    [The noun *bārût* 'food'] is a cognate of [the verb *'ebrāh* 'may
    I eat' in] "Please let my sister Tamar come...so that I may
    eat from her hand" (2 Sam. 13:6).[24]

23b AND FOR PEACE.
    When they hope FOR PEACE, in fact their PEACE will be
    turned into A SNARE.

27a FOR this people,[25] WHOM You[26] HAVE STRUCK, THEY
    PERSECUTE. [This means], You [God] got a little bit an-
    gry, and they [the Gentiles] furthered the disaster.[27]

27b DURING THE PAIN OF YOUR FALLEN ONES THEY
    CONTINUALLY RECITE their words taking counsel, "Let
    us destroy them 'while they are in pain'" (Gen. 34:25).

32a AND MAY IT, my praises TO THE LORD BE MORE
    PLEASING THAN A BULL [*šôr par*].[28]
    [This expression *šôr par*, lit., 'bull steer'] refers to the bull [*šôr*],
    which Adam sacrificed, and which was created with its [full]
    stature and [sexual] desire.[29] On the very day on which it
    was created he [Adam] sacrificed it, for a bull on the day of
    its birth is called *šôr* 'bull' in accord with what is stated in
    the Bible, "a bull or a sheep or a goat when it is born" (Lev.
    22:27). [This means that] on that very day it seemed to be a
    three-year-old steer [*par*].[30]

32b WITH HORNS AND HOOVES. [This word order refers
    to the fact that] his horns preceded his hooves, for he was
    created with his [full] stature and with his horns, and his head
    came out of the earth first. The earth bore him in the man-
    ner in which all are born [head first].[31] Consequently, his
    horns preceded his feet.[32]

PSALM LXIX, NOTES
    [1] Cf. Rashi at Ps. 80:1. The source of the midrash quoted here is Can-
ticles Rabbah at Cant. 2:2. With Maarsen cf. also the commentary of Joseph Hammeqanne, ed. Chaim Oppenheim in *Beth Talmud* 3 (1883), p. 46:
"Note that while the biblical simile 'like a lily among the thorns' means
'Your beauty is outstanding just as a lily stands out for its beauty among
the thorns,' the midrash reinterprets the simile to mean 'You are a help-
less victim among armed enemies.'"
    [2] Heb. *hû'*.
    [3] While our Rashi ms. usually designates Old French glosses by the
abbreviation *bl*, which we render by the abbreviation O.F., here we find
the Heb. term *bela'az* 'in Old French' spelled out in its entirety.

⁴ For this expression see Prov. 13:12. Note that Rashi and other medieval commentaries and most moderns take Heb. *kālû 'ênayim* to mean 'the eye wore out', i.e., the eyes lost their capacity to see because of eyestrain brought on by prolonged looking in anxious but unfulfilled expectation. Contrast Gruber, *Aspects*, pp. 390-399, where it is demonstrated that *kālû 'ênayim*, lit., 'the eyes emptied', refers to the profuse crying, which is a symptom of acute depression.

⁵ KJV.

⁶ Cf. KJV.

⁷ Heb. *śōně'îm 'ôtî*, Rashi's paraphrase of the psalmist's *śōně'ay* in v. 5b; see our remarks at Ps. 64, n. 17.

⁸Rashi does not quote the bracketed portion of the verse; I have supplied it for clarity. Our Rashi ms. contains the scribal error *yāšîb* 'he will restore' instead of *'āšîb* 'I shall restore'.

⁹ 'MY FALSE ENEMIES' (v. 5d, q.v.).

¹⁰ Heb. *'ālay*, lit., 'against me'.

¹¹ Here Rashi responds to two exegetical questions: (1) What shall I restore? and (2) How can one restore what one has not stolen?

¹² Rashi treats the psalmist here as a personification of the people of Israel collectively. Israel collectively are an extension of the person of Jacob the patriarch. Christendom, segements of which have been known to treat the Jews as less than human, is regarded in Medieval Hebrew thinking as the collective extension of Esau, the twin brother of Jacob (see Gen. 25:25-26). Rashi's comment here suggests that whatever quarrels have arisen between Jewry and Christendom are, therefore, a family squabble. Like many a domestic argument to this day, the controversy is rooted in the failure of the siblings to treat each other as children of the same parents.

¹³ Concerning Heb. *bayit*, lit., 'house' (see NJV here), in the sense 'temple' see Ps. 30:1; 66:13 and our remarks there.

¹⁴ Rashi does not quote the bracketed portion of the verse; I have supplied it for clarity.

¹⁵ Rashi, followed here by NJV, q.v., takes the psalmist's *wā'ebkeh baṣṣôm napšî*, lit., "I WEPT AMIDST AFFLICTION OF MY PERSON", to mean 'I WEPT, AND I FASTED'.

¹⁶ The Heb. words here translated "trouble...alien woman" are *ṣārāh nokriyyāh*. In Prov. 23:27b the three words *bě'ēr ṣārāh nokriyyāh* constitute a nominal sentence which can mean "An alien woman is a narrow well" (see NJV and NJV margin there). The three words could also be rendered "An alien woman is a well/pit of trouble." The latter interpretation is the basis of Rashi's assertion here that *bě'ēr pîāh* 'THE MOUTH OF THE PIT' (Ps. 69:16c), which could also be interpreted to mean 'the well/pit, which is her mouth', refers to the metaphor contained in Prov. 23:27b.

¹⁷ The source of this remark is *Mahberet Menahem*, p. 37; this etymology is accepted by *BDB*, p. 32a.

¹⁸ Periphrasis for the personal pronoun; hence NJV's rendering "me."

¹⁹ Here as at v. 5d (see n. 7) Rashi finds it necessary to translate for his readers Biblical Heb. verbal forms with accusative pronominal suffixes into

the corresponding late Heb. forms with detached accusative pronouns (the latter being forms of the accusative particle *"et* with the appropriate pronominal suffixes).

²⁰ Normally in our translation square brackets indicate expressions not found in Rashi's commentary, which I have supplied for clarification of the meaning. Here, however, it is Rashi, who quoting the two widely separated expressions 'the child' and 'he became sick' from 2 Sam. 12:15, modifies the noun 'the child' with his own adjectival expression "of Bathsheba."

²¹ Cf. Englander, "A Commentary on Rashi's Grammatical Comments," p. 484.

²² Heb. *têbāh*, which normally means 'word' in Rashi's commentary. Here, however, it can only mean 'verb'. When, however, Rashi notes that a given word is a verb rather than some other part of speech, his term for 'verb' is *lĕšōn pāʿal*; see Englander, "Grammatical Elements and Terminology in Rashi II," p. 389.

²³ The noun *bārût* occurs only here in Biblical Heb. Rashi, contending that it means 'meal' (cf. RSV and Dahood, 'food'), equates it with the common Rabbinic Heb. term for 'meal', *sĕʿûdāh*.

²⁴ Rashi here follows *Mahberet Menahem*, p. 89, s.v. *br* VI.

²⁵ I.e., Israel. Note that Rashi, by adding the expression 'this people', clarifies the meaning in this context of the relative pronoun *ʾăšer* 'whom'. Note also, however, that if, contrary to Rashi, the psalmist here is not a personification of Israel but either some unknown personage or 'everyman', the meaning of *ʾăšer* will be 'he/she whom'.

²⁶ Rashi supplies here the independent personal pronoun 'You', which is found in the biblical text not here but immediately after *kî* 'FOR'. Note also that Rashi's inserting the accusative particle *ʾet* immediately after *kî* may reflect a variant reading rather than an interpretation (see the ancient versions cited in *BHS*); conversely the ancient versions cited in *BHS*, which apparently reflect such a variant reading, may in fact demonstrate the exegetical necessity of treating *ʾăšer* as the direct object of the verb 'YOU HAVE STRUCK'.

²⁷ Based on Zech. 1:15: "For I was only angry a little, but they [the Gentiles] overdid the punishment."

²⁸ The first exegetical question, with which Rashi will deal in his comment here, is "Why does the psalmist employ two synonymous terms *šōr* and *par* to mean 'bull' when one would have been sufficient?" Note that the Masoretic accents treat the two nouns as belonging together at the end of v. 32a.

²⁹ Based on a midrash attributed to R. Joshua b. Levi in BT Hullin 60a. This comment suggests that either of the terms alone might have alluded either to a male bovine of any age or to an adult male bovine; the two terms together suggest unequivocally both male bovine and adult male.

³⁰ Cf. Mishnah Parah 1:2.

³¹ The idea that the animals presented to Adam in Gen. 2:19-20 emerged from the earth as do the young of animals from the womb is inspired by

Gen. 1:24: "God said, 'Let the earth bring forth every kind of living creature: cattle, creeping things, and wild beasts of every kind.' And it was so."

[32] Based on a midrash attributed to Rab Judah [b. Ezekiel] in BT Hullin 60a.

PSALM LXX

1   FOR THE LEADER. OF DAVID. LEHAZKIR.
[LEHAZKIR 'to call on, invoke'] is an expression referring to prayer as is demonstrated by "But we call on [*nazkîr*] the name of the LORD our God" (Ps. 20:8) and likewise [by the verse] in [1] Chronicles [16:4], "...to invoke and to praise... the LORD...."[1] I read in Midrash Tillim [*sic*][2] [that David may be] compared to a king who became angry at his flock so that he tore down the sheepfold, and he turned out the flock and the shepherd. Some time later he brought back the flock, and he rebuilt the sheepfold, but he did not remember [*lō' hizkîr*] the shepherd.[3] The shepherd said, "Look! The flock has been returned, and the sheepfold has been rebuilt, but as for me, I am not remembered [*lō' múzkār*]. In the same way it is stated above [in the previous psalm], "For God will deliver Zion" (Ps. 69:36a), "and those who cherish His name shall dwell there" (Ps. 69:37b). Look! The sheepfold has been rebuilt,[4] and the flock has been gathered in, but the shepherd has not been remembered [*lō' nizkar*]. Therefore, it is stated (here in Ps. 70:1-2), TO REMIND [*lĕhazkîr*] (v. 1) GOD (v. 2) OF DAVID (v. 1)[5] THAT HE SHOULD SAVE ME (v. 2).[6]

4a   MAY THEY RETURN[7] UPON THEIR SHAMEFUL FOOTSTEP
measure for measure as they did to me.[8] UPON THE FOOTSTEP [*'al 'eqeb*] [i.e.], 'on the very same path' [i.e., O.F.] *enses treces* 'the same tracks'.[9]

4b   THOSE WHO SAY OF ME [*lî*][10] [i.e.], concerning me [*'ālay*].[11] "AHA! AHA!" is an exclamation of joy upon one's[12] seeing one's[12] enemy[13] [suffer] in accord with one's[12] desire.[14]

6b   HASTEN TO ME to help.[15]

PSALM LXX, NOTES
    [1] MT there reads *úlĕhazkîr* while the established reading in Rashi's commentary here is *lĕhazkîr*. In fact, while Rashi's manner of citing the verse from 1 Ch. clearly informs us that he calls attention here precisely

to those words in 1 Ch. 16:4, which support his thesis with respect to *lĕhazkîr* in Ps. 70:1, it cannot be cited in support of the notion that Rashi here witnesses to a version of 1 Ch. 16:4 lacking the conjunctive *waw* of *ûlĕhazkîr*.

[2] Heb. *tylym*. Elsewhere (Ps. 44:2; 86:2, 3) Rashi seems to refer to Midrash Tehillim as Aggadat Tehillim.

[3] The order of the last two clauses is reversed in our Rashi ms.

[4] Rashi, following Midrash Tehillim here, uses the rebuilt sheepfold as a metaphor for the rebuilt Zion, i.e., Jerusalem, and the gathering in of the flock as a metaphor for the ingathering of the exiled people of Israel in the land of Israel.

[5] In Rashi's Heb. this expression appears at the head of the clause as it does in the biblical text; to express the meaning, which Rashi here attaches to vv. 1-2, English syntax requires the word order we have adopted.

[6] Contrast Midrash Tehillim, which simply quotes Ps. 70:1, "FOR THE LEADER, OF DAVID, FOR BRINGING TO MIND." Rashi, however, ignoring the verse division, which separates the caption "OF DAVID FOR BRINGING TO MIND" (v. 1) from v. 2a, "O GOD, TO SAVE ME," reads these phrases as one sentence. Thereby Rashi constructs a more intelligible ending to the midrash.

[7] Note that Ps. 70 is an almost verbatim duplicate of Ps. 40:14-18. On duplicate psalms in general see our remarks at Ps. 14, n. 1. While here the verb is *yāšûbû* 'MAY THEY RETURN' at Ps. 40:16 the verb is *yāšommû* 'Let them be desolate'.

[8] In his commentary at Ps. 40:16 Rashi expresses the same thought less concisely.

[9] While Rashi does not seem to feel it necessary to comment on very much of Ps. 70, seeing that most of it is found in Ps. 40:14-18, on which he comments extensively ad loc, Rashi seems to feel compelled again and again to supply the O.F. gloss *trece* 'track, footstep' wherever Heb. *'eqeb* does not mean 'heel'; see Banitt, *Rashi: Interpreter of the Biblical Letter*, p. 33; and see Rashi at Ps. 40:16; 56:7; etc.

[10] This word is not found in the standard Hebrew text followed by NJV; the variant reading, to which Rashi attests here, is found in many medieval mss. and ancient translations (see *BHS* here) and in the standard text at Ps. 40:16.

[11] Here, as in his comment at Ps. 40:16, Rashi indicates the precise nuance of the ambiguous Biblical Heb. *lî*.

[12] Lit., 'his'.

[13] Heb. *birĕ'ôtô bĕ'oyĕbô*. Note that Heb. *rā'āh bĕ*, lit., 'see upon' is an idiomatic expression meaning 'look upon with evil intent'; cf. *BDB*, p. 908a.

[14] See *Mahberet Menahem*, p. 34, s.v. *'aḥ* III.

[15] Here Rashi responds to the exegetical question, "HASTEN TO ME for what?"

PSALM LXXI

1   I SEEK REFUGE IN YOU, O LORD

3b   TO COME CONTINUALLY into that HABITATION to be delivered therein from the pursuer.[1]

3c   YOU COMMANDED TO SAVE ME. [To the exegetical question, "Whom DID YOU COMMAND TO SAVE ME?" Rashi replies]: Many times You SAVED me through Your messengers.

4   *wĕḥōmēṣ* 'AND THE LAWLESS' is a cognate of [Rabbinic Heb.] *ḥōmēs* 'robber',[2] and so is [the passive participle *ḥāmōṣ* 'the robbed' in Isa. 1:17], "compensate[3] the *ḥāmōṣ* " [i.e.], *nigzāl* 'the robbed'.

6b   YOU ARE *gōzî* [i.e.], He who delivered me from the womb. YOU ARE He who brings me out and makes me pass through. [The participle *gōzî*] is a cognate of [the verb *wayyagoz* 'he brought out' in Num. 11:31], "He brought out quails from the sea," and it is a cognate of [the participle *gāz* 'it goes out' in Ps. 90:10], "...for it goes out quickly, and we fly."[4]

7   I HAVE BEEN A PORTENT TO MANY.[5]
Many saw my troubles, and they were concerned lest there happen to them something like my trouble, lest I might be an omen ['*ôt*] concerning them [so that they would say], "As it happened to this person so may it happen to us." [What is said here in Ps. 71:7] is in accord with what is stated [elsewhere] in the Bible, "Ezekiel will be for you [as an omen and][6] as a portent" (Ezek. 24:24).

9   IN OLD AGE. [I.e.], if I have grown old in sins, which is to say that I have sinned a great deal.

10a   FOR MY ENEMIES SAID *li* 'OF ME' [i.e.], ENEMIES SAID '*ālay* 'about me'[7]

10b   THEY TOOK COUNSEL TOGETHER.

11   SAYING, "GOD HAS FORSAKEN HIM." We are not subject to punishment for our actions against him ['*ālāyw*], for he has already stumbled through transgression."[8]

14a   AS FOR ME, I WILL HOPE ALWAYS for Your deliverance, and when You will have delivered me

14b   I shall add[9] TO ALL THE PRAISE OF YOU.

15   I DO NOT KNOW THE NUMBERS of the kindnesses and the deliverances, which You have done for me.[10]

16   I COME to thank and to praise YOUR MIGHTY ACTS.[11]

19a[12] YOUR MIGHTY ACTS TO ALL WHO ARE TO COME. [I.e.], TO EVERYONE who MAY COME to me I SHALL PROCLAIM (v. 18b) YOUR MIGHTY ACTS.

19b   YOUR BENEFICENCE, which is HIGH AS THE HEAVENS, O GOD. The two verses (19a-19b)[13] are joined to "I SHALL PROCLAIM YOUR STRENGTH TO THE NEXT GENERATION" (v. 18b).[14]

23   MY LIPS SHALL BE JUBILANT with the song of the harp's melody when[15]

22!   I WILL SING A HYMN TO YOU with a harp.[16]

PSALM LXXI, NOTES

[1] RSV, following Qimhi, takes ṣûr māʿôn in v. 3a as a construct genitive chain meaning 'a rock of refuge'; this interpretation of the literal meaning lies behind NJV's idiomatic rendering "a sheltering rock," which assumes that a construct genitive chain in Biblical Heb. and other ancient Semitic languages is the functional equivalent of attributive adjective and noun in Modern English. Rashi's use of the late Heb. demonstrative 'ôtāh 'that', i.e., 'the aforementioned', to describe māʿôn suggests that for him as for Qimhi ṣûr māʿôn means 'rock of habitation'. This means that the infinitive lābô' has no object. Rashi suggests that the reader supply the indirect object 'into it' referring back to māʿôn; so KJV: "Be thou my strong habitation, whereunto I may continually resort."

[2] Note that 'rob' is a common meaning of the verb ḥāmas in Rabbinic Heb. In Biblical Heb., however, ḥāmas means 'oppress'. Hence Dahood, here in seeking to render ḥōmēs 'robber' argues against ḥōmēs being a cognate of Biblical Heb. ḥōmēs 'oppressor' (Prov. 8:36) and in favor of its being a cognate of Akk. ḥamāsu 'despoil, rob'. For Rabbinic Heb. ḥōmēs 'robber' see BT Giṭṭin 49b; Sanhedrin 38a; etc.

[3] Rendering based on Rashi there.

[4] See Rashi there where also citing Num. 11:31 Rashi argues that the verb gz denotes haʿăbārāh 'causing to pass (through)'; so Mahberet Menahem, p. 102, s.v. gz II. It appears that for Rashi not only is gôzî synonymous with môṣîʾî 'he who brings me out and maʿăbîrî 'he who makes me pass through' but also that the two expressions môṣîʾî and maʿăbîrî employed here in this context are synonymous.

[5] Rendering of the lemma according to RSV, which reflects the interpretation presupposed by Rashi's comment here.

[6] Bracketed portion of the quotation is Rashi's interpolation.

⁷ Here Rashi answers the exegetical question, "What is the meaning of the preposition *lě* ?" His answer is that in the present context it must mean *'al* 'about, concerning'; so RSV.

⁸ Here Rashi paraphrases v. 11b, "CHASE HIM AND CATCH HIM, FOR NO ONE WILL SAVE HIM."

⁹ Here Rashi substitutes the imperfect *'ôsîp* 'I shall add' for the psalmist's perfect + *waw*-consecutive, which is Biblical Heb.'s preferred means of expressing the future in a main clause; the form, which Rashi supplies, is the normal equivalent in Rabbinic Heb. as in Modern Heb.

¹⁰ Here Rashi answers the exegetical question, "NUMBERS of what?" For alternative answers to this question see KJV and RSV. Dahood renders simply, "I knew no numbers."

¹¹ The exegetical difficulty here is to determine the syntactic relationship between the verb 'I SHALL COME' and the prepositional phrase *bigĕbûrôtêkā* 'IN/WITH/CONCERNING YOUR MIGHTY DEEDS'. Rashi, followed by NJV, q.v., assumes that we have here a case of ellipsis. Contrast RSV and KJV. Dahood prefers to solve the problem by understanding *bigĕbûrôtêkā* to mean 'into Your Temple'; see Dahood, *Psalms*, vol. 2, p. 175.

¹² So NJV; *BHS* takes this as v. 18c.

¹³ Rashi's comment suggests that he, like *BHS*, regards NJV's v. 19a as 18c; otherwise it makes no sense for him to refer to 19a and 19b as "two verses".

¹⁴ Rashi's point is that YOUR MIGHTY ACTS TO ALL WHO ARE TO COME (v. 19a), YOUR BENEFICENCE, which is HIGH AS THE HEAVENS, O GOD (v. 19b), and YOUR STRENGTH TO THE NEXT GENERATION (v. 18b) are all elements of the compound direct object of the verb I SHALL PROCLAIM (v. 18b).

¹⁵ Heb. *kěše*, Rashi's interpretation of the psalmist's ambiguous *kî*.

¹⁶ Supplied from v. 22b; Rashi suggests that v. 23b, "I WILL SING TO YOU" is ellipsis for "I WILL SING TO YOU WITH THE HARP" (v. 22b).

PSALM LXXII

1   OF SOLOMON.

He [King David]¹ prayed this prayer *'al* 'concerning'²
Solomon his son when he foresaw by means of prophetic inspiration that in the future he [Solomon] would request
from the Holy One Blessed be He a heart to discern and to
understand justice (cf. 1 Kgs. 3:9).

YOUR JUDGMENTS, [i.e.], Your laws [*dînêkā*], which are
taught [*šĕnûyôt*] ³ in the Torah.

YOUR JUSTICE [*ṣidqātĕkā*] so as to justify the sentence.⁴

Both THE KING and THE KING'S SON refer to
Solomon.⁵ An alternative interpretation is [as follows]: [EN-
DOW]⁶ THE KING WITH YOUR JUDGMENTS
[means] "May the afflictions run their course with me, and
do kindness [*ṣĕdāqāh*] so that there will be well-being in his
time."⁷

3a   LET THE MOUNTAINS PRODUCE WELL-BEING in
his time FOR THE PEOPLE. Now what is the WELL-BE-
ING that the mountains produce? [The answer is as fol-
lows]: When they produce fruit, people are not selfish. Each
person invites his neighbor under his vine and under his fig
tree.⁸

3b   AND THE HILLS WITH KINDNESS [*ṣĕdāqāh*].

[It means], AND THE HILLS will produce well-being for
them,⁹ WELL-BEING as recompense for the KINDNESS
that will be done.¹⁰ An alternative interpretation of 'THE
MOUNTAINS LIFT UP' [is as follows]: MOUNTAINS (in
v. 3a) is [a metaphor for] princes, and so is HILLS (v. 3b). It
is the same metaphor which is employed in what is stated in
the Bible, "I shall lift up my eyes toward the mountains" (Ps.
121:1).¹¹

5   THEY SHALL FEAR YOU WITH THE SUN.

When he [King Solomon] will enjoy well-being and the
princes will bring him gifts and give him taxes, then THEY
SHALL FEAR YOU WITH THE SUN. [I.e.], then they
will arise early to their [morning] prayers at sunrise.

BEFORE THE MOON. [means that] they will make the
evening prayer early before the night without neglect of the
afternoon [*minḥāh*] prayer.[12] Another interpretation of LET
THEM FEAR YOU AS LONG AS THE SUN SHINES is
[as follows]: From me [King David] may Israel learn to fear
You all the days of the sun and the moon.
GENERATIONS ON END. AND BEFORE THE MOON
[i.e.], while the moon exists,[13] and they are before it.[14]
There are many [occurrences] in Mishnaic Hebrew [of a
similar expression, which also means 'while it exists', sc.]
bipĕnê habbayit 'while the Temple exists' and *šellō' bipĕnê
habbayit* 'while the Temple is non-existent'.[15] *dôr dôrîm* 'GEN-
ERATIONS ON END' means *lĕ'ôlām* 'forever'.

6a   LET HIM BE LIKE RAIN THAT FALLS ON A MOWN
FIELD.
[I.e.], LET his word[16] DESCEND upon Your people and
into their hearts LIKE RAIN, which descends upon the
mown herbage, which is in need of the rains after they have
mowed it, in accord with what is stated in the Bible, "It was
the latter growth after the king's mowings" (Am. 7:1b).[17]

6b   *zarzîp 'āreṣ* 'DOWNPOUR ON THE GROUND'. [As for
the term *zarzîp*], it is the word for *ṭippîm* 'drops' in Aramaic.
[For example], in [BT] Tractate Yoma (87a) [we read],
"Drops [*zarzîpê*] of water were touching [his head]."[18]

7a   THAT THE RIGHTEOUS MAY FLOURISH IN HIS
TIME. [THE RIGHTEOUS here means] Israel [collec-
tively].

7b   AND MAY ABUNDANT WELL-BEING flourish in his
time (v. 7a).[19]

7c   [TILL THE MOON IS NO MORE means] may this well-
being (v.7b) be long, until there is no world. Now all of this
prayer [of King David on behalf of King Solomon] was fulfilled except for this request (v. 7c). [The latter request was
not fulfilled] because Solomon sinned. His [King Solomon's]
sovereignty [over all the tribes] was not continued for the
sovereignty [over all the tribes] was given to David on condition: "If your descendants keep my covenant" (cf. 1 Kgs.
2:4).[20] Israel FLOURISHed IN HIS TIME (v. 7a) in accord
with what is stated in the Bible, "Judah and Israel were as
numerous as the sand of the sea" (cf. 1 Kgs. 4:20), AND

there was ABUNDANCE of WELL-BEING (v. 7b) in accord with what is stated in the Bible, "Judah and Israel dwelt securely, each person under his vine...all the days of Solomon" (1 Kgs. 5:5).

8a   LET HIM RULE FROM SEA TO SEA [i.e.], all of the land of Israel from the Reed Sea to the Philistine Sea.[21]

8b   FROM THE RIVER TO THE ENDS OF THE EARTH, "For he [Solomon] controlled the whole region west of the Euphrates..." (1 Kgs. 5:4).

9   ṣiyyîm 'groups of princes'. [This interpretation of ṣiyyîm as meaning 'groups' is] in accord with the manner in which we[22] render into Aramaic wĕṣîm miyyad Kittîm,[23] sc. wĕṣî'an yistarḥan.... "and groups turned away...."

10a   LET KINGS OF TARSHISH AND THE ISLANDS PAY TRIBUTE.
       [This request of King David on behalf of King Solomon finds its fulfillment in 1 Kgs. 10:22-23]: "For the king [Solomon] had a Tarshish fleet on the sea.... Once every three years the Tarshish fleet came in....

10b   KINGS OF SHEBA. [This request of King David on behalf of King Solomon finds its fulfillment in the famous visit of] the Queen of Sheba (1 Kgs. 10:1-13). 'eškar [means] dôrôn 'gift'.[24]

11   LET ALL NATIONS SERVE HIM. [This request of King David on behalf of King Solomon finds its fulfillment in the following]: The whole world[25] were bringing[26] "tribute to King Solomon" (1 Kgs. 5:1) [in accord with what is stated in the Bible in 1 Kgs. 10:25]: "And each one would bring his tribute."

14a   FROM FRAUD [tôk] AND LAWLESSNESS [ḥāmās] [i.e.], FROM makkôt 'plagues'[27] AND FROM gezel 'thievery'.[28] HE REDEEMS THEM by means of the justice and charity[29] that He does among them.

15a   SO LET HIM [i.e.], Solomon,[30] LIVE.
       AND MAY HE [i.e.], the Holy One Blessed be He,[31] GIVE HIM SOME OF THE GOLD OF SHEBA. And so it [King David's prayer on behalf of King Solomon] was [fulfilled], for it is written in the Bible, "[... I also grant you...] both wealth and honor so that none can compare with you..." (1 Kgs. 3:13).

15b-c LET PRAYERS FOR HIM BE SAID ALWAYS [BLESS-
INGS ON HIM
INVOKED AT ALL TIMES].³² The prayer and the blessing are synonymous.³³ When the Holy One Blessed be He
says to a person, "May you be blessed" (Deut. 7:14), it is an
expression referring to prayer.³⁴

16a *pissat-bar* 'ABUNDANCE OF GRAIN'. [In this expression
the construct *pissat* 'ABUNDANCE OF' is a cognate of
[Mishnaic Heb. *pissāyôn* 'spreading (of a leprous spot)'
[Mishnah Nega'im 1:3, 5 and passim], [and it means] *tosepet*
'addition' and *ribbûy* 'abundance'.³⁵ However, our rabbis interpreted it [*pas*] as a synonym of *glûsqā'ôt* 'loaves of white
bread'³⁶ for [being eaten in] the Messianic Era³⁷ and the
entire psalm as referring to the Messiah.³⁸ An alternative interpretation of *pissat-bar* is [that *pissat*] is a synonym of *rāṣôn*
'favor' [and] a cognate of *piyyûs* 'conciliation'. [The phrase
pissat-bar 'FAVOR OF GRAIN' refers to the fact that people
are conciliated and favored by the Holy One Blessed be He
when He gives them peace and sustenance in the world.

16b LET ITS FRUIT THRIVE LIKE THE FOREST OF
LEBANON.
[*piryô*, lit., 'ITS FRUIT" here means] grains of wheat as large
as the fruit of trees [i.e.], as large as the kidneys of a large
bull,³⁹ which [grains of wheat] were in the time of Simeon b.
Shetah.⁴⁰

16c AND LET THEM, Israel,⁴¹ SPROUT UP FROM THE
CITY,
Jerusalem,⁴² LIKE COUNTRY GRASS.

17a MAY HIS [i.e.], Solomon's⁴³ NAME BE remembered⁴⁴
FOREVER⁴⁵
with his wealth and with his wisdom.

17b WHILE THE SUN LASTS, MAY HIS NAME *yinnôm*.
[I.e.], all the days of the sun may HIS NAME be exalted.
[The *niphal* verb] *yinnôm* is a word referring to kingship and
authority. It is a cognate of [the noun *mānôn* 'lord' in] "his
end is that he will be the lord" (Prov. 29:21);⁴⁶ [and of]
ûlĕnînî "and against my inheritor" (Gen. 21:23) [in which
progeny is designated *nîn* 'inheritor' because *nîn* is] one who
exercises control [*šālîṭ*] over the property of others. [Hence
in Ps. 74:8] "They resolved, *nînām* altogether" [means]

476   RASHI'S COMMENTARY ON PSALMS IN ENGLISH WITH NOTES

"Their kings altogether [thought]."[47]

17c   LET MEN INVOKE HIS BLESSEDNESS UPON THEM-
SELVES. [I.e.], a person will say[48] to his child, "Be wise and
rich like Solomon."[49]

18   BLESSED BY THE LORD IS THE DOER OF GREAT
WONDERS.[50]

[This is said] with reference to fire descending from heaven
through the agency of Solomon my [i.e., the psalmist's]
son.[51]

20   END OF[52] THE PRAYERS OF DAVID SON OF
JESSE.[53]

Our rabbis interpreted[54] kollû [as an abbreviation so that v.
20 means] "kol-ēllû [55] 'all of these' are THE PRAYERS OF
DAVID"[56] so as to subsume under the name of David the
entire book, even that portion which Korah and [the rest of
the] ten elders composed.[57] The reason that [the entire book
is here at Ps. 72:20 attributed to King David] is that he is
called "the sweet singer of Israel" (2 Sam. 23:1).[58] One
ought, however, to interpret kollû [here] as a synonym of
nistayyĕmû 'there have been brought to an end'. [Moreover,
the verb form kollû] is an example of the same grammatical
form as are [the verbs in rommû mĕʿaṭ "They are exalted a
little while" (Job. 24:24) [and] šommû šāmayim "Be exalted, O
heavens" (Jer. 2:12).[59] Now, if this be so [that our verse
states, THE PRAYERS OF DAVID SON OF JESSE
HAVE BEEN BROUGHT TO AN END], why was the
psalm [72] not written in its [proper] place [at the end of the
psalter]? [The answer is that] "There is no chronological
order in the Book [of Psalms]."[60] Moreover, it makes sense
to suppose that he [King David] composed it [Ps. 72] in his
old age when he made Solomon his son king [in his stead]
(see 1 Kgs. 1:28-39).

PSALM LXXII, NOTES

[1]   See also Rashi at Ps. 127:1; similarly, Ibn Ezra. Note that Rashi, unlike
Saadiah Gaon (see Simon, Four Approaches to the Book of Psalms, pp. 24-27),
is not committed a priori to the exclusively Davidic authorship of the psalter.
On the contrary, half of Rashi's introduction to the Book of Psalms (and
see also Rashi at Ps. 72:20, below) is the rabbinic dictum that attributes
the authorship of the psalms to eleven poets including David. Solomon,
however, is not one of these eleven poets.

² For *lĕ* 'of' = '*al* 'concerning, for' see Rashi at Ps. 71:10.

³ Perhaps the participle *šĕnûyôt* 'taught, recited' is employed here instead of the participle *kĕtûbîm* 'written' to hint that King David here refers to the Oral Torah, which is transmitted by oral recitation; on the various meanings of 'Oral Torah' see Mayer I. Gruber, "The Mishnah as Oral Torah: a Reconsideration," *Journal for the Study of Judaism* 15 (1984), pp. 112-122.

⁴ The Rabbinic Heb. idiom *ṣiddûq haddîn* corresponds semantically to Eng. 'theodicy' and refers to submission to divine dispensation such as the death of a loved one by the recital of an appropriate berakah or Scripture verse; see Jastrow, *Dict.*, p. 1263.

⁵ The two expressions are employed here in synonymous parallelism.

⁶ Rashi does not quote the bracketed portion of the verse; I have supplied it for clarity.

⁷ The second interpretation, which is based upon a midrash in Midrash Tehillim here, differs from the former in two respects: (1) It takes KING and KING'S SON as antithetical rather than as synonymous expressions; (2) it takes *mišpāṭêkā* 'YOUR JUDGMENTS' and *ṣĕdāqāh* as antithetical concepts as they are in Rabbinic Heb. rather than as synonyms meaning 'justice' as they are in Biblical Heb. Concerning *ṣĕdāqāh* 'kindness' in Rabbinic Heb. see Kadushin, *The Rabbinic Mind³*, p. 297; see also Avi Hurvitz, "The Biblical Roots of a Talmudic Term: The Early History of the Concept *ṣĕdāqāh* [= charity, alms]," in *Studies in Language*, nos. 2-3 (Jerusalem: Institute of Jewish Studies, 1987), pp. 155-160 (in Hebrew).

⁸ Rashi's comment is based upon a midrash in Midrash Tehillim here.

⁹ Here the midrash correctly perceives that 'THE HILLS' is a b-word, i.e., a fixed poetic parallel, for 'THE MOUNTAINS'. Hence v. 3b must be synonymous with v. 3c. Since, apparently, this is not the case, the midrash assumes that v. 3b is an example of ellipsis and that the phrase WITH KINDNESS (v. 3c) must modify the verb PRODUCE, which is written only in v. 3a but is understood in v. 3b as well.

¹⁰ Rashi's comment is based upon a midrash in Midrash Tehillim here.

¹¹ With Tanḥuma Toledot 14 cf. Zech. 4:7.

¹² Contrast Midrash Tehillim here, and see Maarsen's comment.

¹³ Here Rashi, followed by NJV, q.v., explains that the expression *lipĕnê x* means 'while x exists'; this comment is to be understood in light of Rashi's comments on '*al-pĕnê* and '*el-pānāyw* at Gen. 11:28 and Deut. 7:10 respectively; see our discussion at Ps. 92, n. 7.

¹⁴ Here Rashi attempts to account for the meaning of the idiomatic expression *lipĕnê x* 'while x exists' by reference to the literal meaning of *lipĕnê* 'before'.

¹⁵ Examples include Mishnah Hullin 5:1; 6:1; 7:1; 10:1; 11:1.

¹⁶ Here Rashi supplies the missing subject of the verb *yērēd* 'MAY IT DESCEND'. Rashi holds that the pronominal prefix refers to the royal word of Solomon.

¹⁷ JPS rendering adopted because of its congruence with Rashi's comment here.

[18] Cf. Qimhi here.

[19] By his additions to v. 7b from v. 7a Rashi intimates that in his view "MAY THE RIGHTEOUS FLOURISH" and "AND ABUNDANT WELL-BEING" are parallel clauses, in the second of which there is ellipsis since the verb found in v. 7a governs also the subject of v. 7b.

[20] The text there, followed by many editions of Rashi here, reads, *yišměrû darkām* "watch their behavior".

[21] Term for the Southeastern Mediterranean Sea found in the Bible only in Ex. 23:31.

[22] I.e., the Jews collectively since their Aramaic rendering follows T.O., which is designated Jewry's official Aramaic version of the Pentateuch in BT Megillah 3a; Qiddushin 49b.

[23] Num. 24:24; Rashi in his commentary there interprets *ṣîm* to mean 'ships'. There he supports this interpretation by citing Isa. 33:21 and its rendering in TJ (which is designated Jewry's official Aramaic version of the Books of the Prophets in BT Megillah 3a).

[24] Biblical Heb. *'eškar* 'tribute' is attested only at Ezek. 27:15 and Ps. 72:10. Today it is generally taken to be a loanword derived from Akk. *iškaru* 'tax'; see Gruber, "Akkadian Influences in the Book of Ezekiel," pp. 12-13. Maarsen here states that the source of Rashi's equation of rare Biblical Heb. *'eškar* with the late Heb. Gk. loanword *dôrôn* derives from *Mahberet Menahem*, s.v. *'eškar*. This is incorrect. What Menahem states (there, p. 69) is the following: "It is a synonym of *šay* 'gift' (Isa. 18:7; Ps. 68:30; 76:12), and it is a synonym of *minḥāh* 'tribute' (1 Kgs. 5:1; etc.) and of *těšûrāh* 'gratuity' (1 Sam. 9:7)."

[25] Rashi's paraphrase alludes to the fact that 1 Kgs. 5:1 uses the merism "from the Euphrates [to] Philistia and on to the border of Egypt" to designate 'the whole world'. The verse continues, "they were presenting tribute and serving Solomon" (my own literal rendering). Perhaps this verse is the source of Rashi's equating 'serving' in Ps. 72:11b with 'bringing (tribute)'.

[26] Heb. *měbî'îm*, a paraphrase of *maggîšîm* 'presenting' in 1 Kgs. 5:1.

[27] See Rashi at Ps. 55:12 and the discussion there.

[28] Concerning *ḥāmās* 'stealing' see Rashi's treatment of *ḥōmēṣ* 'thief' at Ps. 71:4 and our discussion there.

[29] Heb. *mišpāṭ* and *ṣědāqāh* cf. n. 7.

[30] Here Rashi answers the exegetical question, "Who is the object of the verb 'LET HIM LIVE'?"

[31] Here Rashi answers the exegetical question, "Who is the subject of the verb 'MAY HE GIVE'?"

[32] Rashi does not quote the bracketed portion of the verse; I have supplied it for clarity.

[33] Here Rashi demonstrates his awareness that clauses 15b and 15c constitute an instance of synonymous parallelism.

[34] Having argued that the poetic structure intimates that *těpillāh* and *běrākāh* are synonymous, Rashi adds a lexical proof, citing a verse, Deut. 7:14, in which *bārûk* 'blessed' refers to *těpillāh* 'prayer'.

[35] Contrast *Mahberet Menahem*, p. 304, s.v. *pas*. Note that Menahem does not invoke the Mishnaic Heb. cognate spelled with samek but the Biblical Heb. cognate of *pissāyôn*, sc. the verb *pāśāh* spelled with *śin*. Note also that Menahem is less than enthusiastic.

[36] See Israel W. Slotki, *The Babylonian Talmud: Kethuboth Translated into English* (London: Soncino Press, 1936), p. 270, n. 11 at BT Ketubbot 111b.

[37] As we saw at Ps. 2:2, Rashi uses sound philology to show that Messianic interpretations of the psalms are not exegesis but eisegesis. Thereby he defuses such midrashim, rendering them useless in the Christian attempt to prove that the Hebrew Bible refers to Jesus of Nazareth. For the midrash in question see BT Ketubbot 111b and BT Shabbat 30b. Note that the midrash does not employ the term "King Messiah" or "Messianic Era" but only *'ātîdāh* 'in the future'.

[38] See Midrash Tehillim at Ps. 72:1 #3; 72:16 #6; 72:8 #5.

[39] The latter simile is taken from an anonymous midrash on *ḥēleb kilyôt ḥiṭṭāh* "the kidney fat of wheat" (Deut. 32:14) at BT Ketubbot 111b.

[40] Rashi here explains that the previously referred to midrash refers to the following tradition recorded in Sifra Behukotay 1 and in Leviticus Rabbah 35:10 (ed. Margulies, vol. 4, p. 829): "It happened during the time of [his sister] Queen Salome [the widow of King Alexander Jannaeus; he ruled 103-76 B.C.E.; she ruled 76-67 B.C.E.] that it used to rain from one Sabbath Eve to the next Sabbath Eve until the grains of wheat were [as big] as kidneys, the grains of barley [as big] as olive pits, and the lentils [as big] as golden dinars...."

[41] Here Rashi responds to the exegetical question, "Who is the subject of the verb 'LET THEM SPROUT'?"

[42] Here Rashi responds to the exegetical question, "What city?"

[43] Here Rashi answers the exegetical question, "Whose name?" Rashi's answer is consistent with the approach he adopts in v. 1, q.v.

[44] The exegetical problem is that we have in this verse a copulative verb 'LET IT BE', a subject 'HIS NAME', and an adverb 'FOREVER'. Rashi supplies the missing predicate adjective 'remembered'.

[45] Heb. *lĕ'ôlām*.

[46] Our rendering of Prov. 29:21 reflects Rashi's interpretation of that verse in his commentary there; contrast the completely opposite interpretation of the proverb in the commentary by Joseph Qimhi, which is attributed to Ibn Ezra in the Rabbinic Bible ad loc.

[47] I.e., *nînām* means 'their kings'; cf. BT Megillah 10b.

[48] Heb. *'ōmēr*, lit., 'he is saying'.

[49] Cf Rashi at Gen. 12:3; cf. also Speiser there.

[50] Rendering of the lemma reflects Rashi's interpretation, according to which *bārûk* YHWH is the subject and 'DOER OF GREAT WONDERS' is the predicate of a nominal sentence. Contrast KJV, NJV, and other English versions, which follow Ibn Ezra in treating 'DOER OF GREAT WONDERS' as a phrase in apposition with 'THE LORD, THE GOD OF ISRAEL'.

[51] Here Rashi refers to Solomon's having offered sacrifices at the dedication of the Temple (1 Kgs. 8:5). He assumes that here, as at Moses' dedication of the Tabernacle (Lev. 9:24), the fire which consumed the sacrifices "came forth from before the LORD."

[52] Heb *kāllû*; see below.

[53] Our Rashi ms. treats Ps. 72:20, the colophon of the second of the five books into which the Psalter is divided in MT, as a separate Ps. 70 following Ps. 69, which is commonly designated Ps. 72 in current editions, and preceding Ps. 71, which is commonly designated Ps. 73 in current editions.

[54] Kamin, *Rashi's Exegetical Categorization*, pp. 136-157 demonstrates that in Rashi's commentaries the expression *rabbôtênû dārěšû* means simply "Our rabbis interpreted" and does not designate the interpretation which follows as eisegetical or errant. The use of the root *drš* to designate errant interpretations begins with Rashi's grandson, R. Samuel b. Meir. Here, however, what marks the interpretation introduced by *rabbôtênû dārěšû* as in Rashi's view errant is the expression, which follows, sc., *wěyēš liptôr* "However, one ought to interpret (as follows)."

[55] Lest the reader assume that the recognition of an abbreviation in the Bible immediately classifies this rabbinic interpretation of Ps. 72:20 as eisegetical, it should be noted that modern critical scholarship has correctly identified abbreviations in Jer. 7:4 where *hmh*, which is pointed in MT as *hēmmāh* 'they', is most likely an abbreviation for *hammāqôm hazzeh* 'this Place' (so *BH³* and *BHS* ad loc) and at Prov. 1:10 where *'l-tb'*, which is pointed in MT as *'al-tōbē'* 'Do not be willing', is most likely an abbreviation for *'al-tēlēk bědderek 'ittām* "Do not go in the path with them" (cf. Prov. 1:15; so *BH³* ad loc); concerning other examples of abbreviations in the Hebrew Bible and extensive bibliography see Godfrey R. Driver, "Abbreviations in the Massoretic Text," *Textus* 1 (1960), pp. 112-131; id., "Once Again Abbreviations," *Textus* 4 (1964), pp. 76-94.

[56] An anonymous midrash in Midrash Tehillim here presents this interpretation as a solution to the exegetical difficulty presented by the interpretation of v. 20 as "The prayers of David, the son of Jesse, are ended" (RSV). The difficulty is, "Were the remainder [of the psalms, i.e, Ps. 73-150] not prayers of David son of Jesse?"

[57] In a midrash attributed to R. Meir at BT Pesaḥim 117a the interpretation of *kollû* as an abbreviation for *kol-'ellû* 'all of these' is used to prove that David wrote the entire Book of Psalms. Rashi here notes that R. Meir's view is at variance with the view set forth in BT Bava Batra 15a, according to which King David composed the psalter along with ten elders. It is the latter view, which Rashi adopts in his introduction to the psalter, q.v. It should be noted that the view adopted by Saadiah Gaon, namely, that the entire psalter is Davidic, is not at variance, as it were, with "the rabbinic view" but in accord with one rabbinic view, that of R. Meir, and therefore in opposition to another rabbinic view. Contrast Simon, *Four Approaches to the Book of Psalms*, pp. 24-27.

[58] Here Rashi attempts to find a basis in the Bible for the view of R.

Meir, which appears, at least to Rashi, to contradict the evidence of the psalter itself.

[59] For Rashi as for Menahem the verbs currently understood to belong to the classes *lamed-yod* (such as *kly* 'to be finished'), *'ayin-waw* (such as *rām* 'he is exalted; infin. *rûm* 'to be exalted') and our geminate verbs such as *šāmam* 'to be appalled') are all regarded as biliteral roots. See Englander, "Rashi's View of the Weak, *'ayin-'ayin* and *pe-nun* Roots," p. 415. It appears, however, contrary to Maarsen, that Rashi is pointing not only to the derivation of *kollû* from a biliteral root *kl* but also to the existence of a variety of forms of such roots in which there is a gemination of the second root consonant following a long vowel. In view of his rendering *kollû* by Rabbinic Heb. *nistayyĕmû*, which is a *nitpaʿel*-passive, and in view of his comparison of *kollû* to *šommû* and *rommû*, which he lists as [*qal*-] passives at Ps. 58:4, it is reasonable to conclude that Rashi here is intimating that *kollû* here is a *qal*-passive and that he is attempting thereby to account for the gemination of the *lamed*. *BHS* prefers not to account for this gemination and to emend MT to read *kālû* 'they ended' rather than *kollû* 'they were brought to an end'. *B-L* #45z notes that *kollû* is so pointed in MT because the Tiberian Massoretes regarded it as a *pual*. It should be remembered that the Tiberian Massoretes regard all *qal*-passives as *pual*. See discussion at Ps. 58:4, and see *HG*, pt. 2 #15.

[60] Cf. the cliché, "There is no chronological order in the Torah," which while frequently invoked by Rashi in his Bible commentaries is found in BT only at Pesaḥim 6b where it is attributed to R. Menashia b. Taḥlipha quoting Rav (d. 247 C.E.).

PSALM LXXIII

1   A PSALM OF ASAPH.

GOD IS TRULY GOOD TO ISRAEL. It is because the content of this psalm speaks about the troubles, which Israel experiences that he [the psalmist] began it in this manner. This is its meaning [i.e., the meaning of v. 1]: Even though I cry out against and question Israel's sufferings, I know that the Holy One Blessed be He is good to them and that it is for their good that He makes them suffer so as to earn the life of the post-eschatological era.[1]

2   AS FOR ME, before I thought about this,[2] MY FEET HAD ALMOST STRAYED, and MY STEPS WERE...LED OFF COURSE so as to turn away from God.

3   FOR I ENVIED THE WANTON [i.e.] those who are disturbed in their behavior,[3] when I saw their well-being.

4a   FOR THEIR ARE NO BANDS IN THEIR DEATH.
[The word *ḥarṣubbôt* 'BANDS'] is a word referring to 'binding' ['*ăsîrāh*] as is exemplified by "to unlock *ḥarṣubbôt* of wickedness" (Isa. 58:6),[4] [in which the word denotes] the fetters, in which they [the wicked affluent in Isa. 58] bind the poor. Here there is no suffering even[5] IN THEIR DEATH. Those among them who die, die

4b   while they are STRONG AS A PORTICO [i.e.], without suffering.[6]
Our rabbis interpreted it [the expression *ḥrṣbt*] as an acronym[7] [so that *'ēn ḥrṣbt* means] "THERE ARE NONE *ḥărēdîm* 'afraid' and *'ăṣēbîm* 'nervous' *miyyôm* 'because of the day of' *mîtāh* 'death'.[8]
Another equally plausible interpretation [of *ḥrṣbt* as an acronym is the following: *'ēn ḥrṣbt* means] that the HolyOne Blessed be He DOES NOT *mĕ'aḥēr* 'hinder' *ṣibyônām* 'their desire'.[9]

3   THE WANTON [*hôlĕlîm*] [i.e.], the mixed up [*mĕ'urbābîm*]; [the participle *hôlĕlîm*] is a cognate of [the participle *māhûl* 'mixed' in] "Your wine is mixed with water" (Isa. 1:22).[10]

6a   SO PRIDE ADORNS THEIR NECKS.

Because they do not suffer punishments arrogance has give them[11] [the ability] to be extremely haughty.[12]

6b ROBBERY ENWRAPS THEM AS A MANTLE.[13]

The ROBBERY which they do makes them fat, and it enwraps their genitals and their buttocks with thick masses of fat and flesh.[14]

7a FAT SHUTS OUT THEIR EYES.

Because of the abundance of fat their eyes protrude; [conversely], as for every person who is thin, his eyes are sunken.[15]

7b WISHES SURPASS THE HEART.[16]

More than their heart looks forward and hopes and anticipates, they experience [irrational] desires.[17] [These irrational desires] SURPASS in their reach the desire oftheir heart.[18]

8a THEY SCOFF at their friends.[19]

8b AND THEY SPEAK IN AN EVIL MANNER OF OPPRESSION

[i.e], of oppressing the poor.[20]

8c FROM ON HIGH THEY SPEAK in the manner of Pharaoh and Sennacherib and Nebuchadnezzar. Pharaoh said, "Who is the LORD [that I should heed His voice][21]?" (Ex. 5:2). Sennacherib [said], "Who is there among all the gods of the countries [who saved their country from me][21]?" (Isa. 36:20). Nebuchadnezzar [said], "I will mount the back of a cloud" (Isa. 14:14).[22] It is to this [that the psalmist refers when he says,

9 THEY SET THEIR MOUTHS AGAINST HEAVEN.[23]

10a THEREFORE HIS PEOPLE RETURN HITHER.

Because His people see that "the way of the wicked prospers" (Jer. 12:1), they return to the way of the wicked by adopting their behavior.[24]

hălôm 'HITHER' is the same word as is attested in "Who brought you hither?" (Judg. 18:3); [it means] *pōh* 'here'.

10b AND WATERS OF A FULL[25] ARE SQUEEZED TO THEM.

Now, as for the waters of a FULL stream, these are words of Torah. These are regarded BY THEM as a juice, and they look upon it with contempt.[26]

11 They say,[27] "HOW COULD GOD KNOW?"

[I.e.], HOW can we say that the Holy One Blessed be He has knowledge and that His Torah is Truth?

12   LOOK, they are[28] THE WICKED, and they transgress His Torah, and note that they are[28] the TRANQUIL OF THE WORLD,[29] and they multiply power and wealth.

[The construct adjectival noun *šalěwê* 'TRANQUIL OF' in the phrase] TRANQUIL OF THE WORLD is a cognate of [the noun] *šalěwāh* 'tranquility'.[30] *hiśgû* 'AMASSED' [i.e.], *higdîlû* 'multiplied'.[31] Now Menahem [b. Jacob Ibn Saruq] explained *yāšûb 'ammô hǎlôm* (v. 10a) [as follows]: "The wicked will return to pound [*lahǎlôm*] the Holy One Blessed be He's people." Now I learned the former [interpretation of v. 10a set forth above] from the words of R. Meir the son of R. Isaac, the prayer leader, may the memory of the virtuous be for a blessing.[32]

13   IT WAS FOR NOTHING THAT I KEPT MY HEART PURE.

All of this [v. 13] is a continuation of [the characterization of the wicked in v. 11],[33] "THEY WILL SAY, 'HOW COULD GOD KNOW?'" They [the wicked] also say, "IT WAS FOR NOTHING, i.e.,[34] for no reward do we observe His commandments

14a   SEEING THAT we are[35] CONSTANTLY AFFLICTED."

14b   AND MY PUNISHMENT. It appears that continually from morning to morning[36] new troubles are devised.[37]

15a   HAD I DECIDED, "LET ME TELL AS."

[I.e.], Asaph[38] said, "Had I thought[39] to TELL all AS it is" [i.e.], all that His people say about this:[40]

15b   I SHOULD HAVE BEEN FALSE TO THE CIRCLE OF YOUR DISCIPLES. [I.e.], All of them are faithless and wicked people.

16a   SO I APPLIED MYSELF TO UNDERSTAND THIS [namely], what is the attribute of the Holy One Blessed be He [which I experienced?] Indeed,

16b   IT WAS INJUSTICE IN MY EYES.

[I.e.], it seemed to me that this attribute was for me [INJUSTICE] and not justice.[41]

17   UNTIL I came[42] TO GOD'S SANCTUARY, which is in Jerusalem,[43] and I saw what happened to Sennacherib,[44] and then I understood[45] the FATE of the wicked, which is annihilation, and then I thought:

18a All the good fortune, which they experience is SMOOTH-NESS, with which the Holy One Blessed be He smooths out their path so that it should be easy and smooth so that they will not consider returning to Him; hence they perish. HOWEVER, WITH SMOOTHNESS YOU MADE FOR THEM ALL the goodness, which they experience, for look, their end is [that]

18b YOU MAKE THEM FALL THROUGH BLANDISH-MENTS.

19 BY TERRORS [i.e.], by demons.[46]

20a LIKE A DREAM WITHOUT AWAKENING [mēhāqîṣ] [i.e.], like a sleep without end [qēṣ], which is permanent sleep. Such did they [Sennacherib's troops] experience: "The LORD's angel went forth, and he slew in the Assyrian camp..." (Isa. 37:36).

20b O LORD, IN THE CITY [bāʿîr] YOU TREATED THEIR IMAGE WITH CONTEMPT. There in Jerusalem where they did evil their IMAGE-like-ness[47] was treated with contempt in that all of them were burnt.[48]

21a WHEN MY HEART HAD SOURED. Before I saw by means of prophetic inspiration this defeat [of Sennacherib],[49] MY HEART was souring because of the "way of the wicked," which "prospered" (Jer. 12:1).

21b I was PIERCED THROUGH[50] in MY KIDNEYS. [The verb 'eštônān 'I WAS PIERCED'] is a cognate of [the participle šānûn 'sharpened' in the expression] "sharpened sword" Prov. 25:18).[51] Now when it [the root in question] is conjugated in the hitpaʿel,[52] the taw [of the prefix of the hitpaʿel is placed in the midst of the root [letters] of the word, according to the manner of every word whose initial root letter is shin.[53]

22 AS FOR ME, I was A DOLT, and I did not KNOW[54] what was the attribute [of God I was experiencing],[55] and I was like a beast[6] TOWARD YOU.

23a Moreover, AS FOR ME, even though I saw all this [injustice described in vv. 2-14] I was ALWAYS WITH YOU, i.e.,[57] I did not budge from devotion to You.

23b YOU HELD MY RIGHT HAND to keep me in devotion to You when my feet were about to stray from Your paths.

[This is] in consonance with what he [the psalmist] said above [in v. 2], "MY STEPS WERE NEARLY OFF COURSE."

24a   *tanḥēnî* 'YOU GUIDED ME', [i.e.], *niḥîtanî* 'You guided me'.[58]

24a   AFTER HONOR YOU TOOK ME. After You bestowed upon Sennacherib the honor, which You apportioned to him, YOU TOOK ME toward You. The [disjunctive Massoretic] accent *rĕbîaʿ* [over the word 'AFTER'] separates [the word] 'AFTER' [from what follows] so as to interpret it as referring to what precedes it. You produced wondrous signs for Israel, and You destroyed Sennacherib.[59]

25   WHOM ELSE HAVE I IN HEAVEN?
[Have I] some angel whom I have chosen[60] for myself for a god? Of course not. [I have chosen] You alone.

26   MY FLESH *kālāh* [i.e.], MY FLESH AND MY HEART are desirous of You. [The verb *kālāh*] is a verb referring to desire as is exemplified by "My soul longs for [*kālĕtāh*] Your deliverance" (Ps. 119:81a).[61]

27b   WHO ARE UNTRUE TO YOU [i.e.], whoever separates himself from You.[62]

28b   YOUR MESSAGES[63] [i.e.], Your dispatches [i.e.], the divine inspiration, which enters me to say it.

PSALM LXXIII, NOTES

[1] Cf. Midrash Tehillim here.

[2] Namely, the idea expressed in v. 1 and in the midrash thereon; the source is Midrash Tehillim here.

[3] For this interpretation of *hōlĕlîm* see also with Maarsen Rashi at Isa. 1:22 where Rashi quotes Midrash Koheleth Rabbah at Eccles. 2:2: see also PRK, ed. Mandelbaum, pp. 385-88.

[4] See *Mahberet Menahem*, p. 189.

[5] In my translation I have moved the word *'ap* 'even' from the beginning of the sentence to here.

[6] Rashi's simile represents his interpretation of the psalmist's *ûbārî' 'ûlām* as a metaphor; contrast NJV'S "Their body is healthy"; for other possible interpretations see Ibn Ezra ad loc.

[7] Heb. *lĕśôn nôṭarîqôn;* on abbreviations in the Bible and in Rabbinic exegesis see my discussion at Ps. 72:20.

[8] See BT Shabbat 31b and Rashi's comment there.

[9] Midrash Tehillim here.

[10] I.e., Rashi derives both words from a biliteral root *hl* meaning 'mix'; contrast *Mahberet Menahem*, p. 140.

[11] Heb. *he'ĕnîqātām*. This *hiphil* verb is attested in Biblical Heb. only at Deut. 15:14. Rashi's use of this verb here suggests that for him—as also for *BDB*, p. 778b; *K-B³*, p. 812b; an d Mandelkern, p. 905a—this verb is a cognate of the *qal 'ănāqtēmô* 'SHE ADORNED HIM' here at Ps. 73:6a. The latter verb is most likely, as *BDB* and *K-B³* hold, a denominative verb derived from the noun *'ănāq* 'necklace' (Judg. 8:26; Prov. 1:9; Cant. 4:9). However, the verb *he'ĕnîq* 'bestow' is better derived from a homonymous root *'nq*; so *Mahberet Menahem*, p. 286. The alternative is to accept *BDB*'s far-fetched interpretation of Deut. 15:14: "Thou shalt make a rich necklace for him from thy flock and from thy granary and from they winepresses."

[12] Lit., 'to raise up haughtiness above their necks'. Here again Rashi refers to the basic meaning of *'ănāqtēmô* 'she put (it) upon their necks'.

[13] Rendering of the lemma based upon Rashi's understanding of the noun *ḥāmās* and its cognates at Ps. 71:4 and Isa. 1:17.

[14] This comment means that Rashi understands the literal meaning of the verse as follows: *ya'ătop šît ḥāmās lāmô* "ROBBERY ENWRAPS GENITALIA FOR MEN." Rashi takes the word *šît* neither as a noun meaning 'mantle' (so NJV; KJV; NEB; Briggs; RSV; Dahood) nor as a participle meaning 'putting' (Psalms Targum). Instead, following *Mahberet Menahem*, p. 370, Rashi takes *šît* as a biform of *šēt* 'genitalia' attested in 2 Sam. 10:4 and Isa. 20:4. Hence Rashi's comment here: *šĕtôtêhem wĕ'agĕbôtêhem*, which means literally, "their genitals and their buttocks"; similarly Breithaupt, here.

[15] Based upon Midrash Tehillim here; see Midrash Tehillim, ed. Buber, p. 167b, n. 15.

[16] This literal translation of the lemma, which treats the three words *'ābĕrû maskiyyôt lēbāb* as respectfully verb, subject, and direct object, reflects Rashi's interpretation. Note that *maśkît* in the sense 'imagination' (*BDB*, p. 917) or 'fancy' (NJV here at Ps. 73:7) is attested only here at Ps. 73:7 and at Prov. 18:11. *K-B*, p. 517a labels this meaning of the word 'doubtful'.

[17] According to Rashi, our verse contrasts rational expectation, whose seat is the *lēbāb*, lit., 'heart', a functional equivalent of Eng. 'mind' with the boundless requests of 'desire', which is the functional equivalent of of the Freudian id.

[18] The source is Midrash Tehillim here.

[19] Rashi responds to the exegetical question, "At whom do they scoff?"

[20] Rashi's comment here reflects his observation in his comment on Lev. 19:13 following Sifra that the verb *'šq* refers specifically to withholding of the wages of a salaried employee; contrast Orlinsky, *Notes*, p. 209.

[21] Rashi does not quote the bracketed portion of the verse; I have supplied it for clarity.

[22] Rashi, followed by many moderns, here asserts that the Babylonian king quoted in Isa. 14:14 is Nebuchadnezzar II of Babylonia (605-562 B.C.E.) because of Isa. 13:1, which designates Isa. 13:2-14:27 as "the Babylonian pronouncement." Ginsberg, "Reflexes of Sargon in Isaiah

After 715 B.C.E.," pp. 49-53 shows that Isaiah intends for Isa. 14:14 to represent the words of his own contemporary, Sargon II of Assyria (722-705 B.C.E.), who was king of both Assyria and Babylonia; cf. Kaufmann, *History of the Israelite Religion*, vol. 6-7, p. 223.

[23] Rashi's comment at v. 8c seems to be inspired by the midrash in Midrash Tehillim at v. 9; q.v.

[24] Heb. *le'ĕḥoz bĕdarĕkêhem*, lit., 'to grasp onto their paths'; contrast Job. 17:9, "The virtuous person grasps his own path."

[25] The obvious exegetical problem is to identify the appropriate noun modified by this adjective. Hence, KJV, following Ibn Ezra, supplies 'cup'. Rashi, following Ps. 65:10 (cf. Maarsen here) supplies *peleg* 'stream'. Dahood, on the other hand, takes *mālē'* as an adjectival noun 'the full one', employed here as a synonym for 'the ocean'.

[26] Rashi assumes that 'TO THEM' in v. 10b refers to the same wicked people to whom the psalmist has been referring since v. 4. Here at v. 10b he notes that while they are objectively [i.e., from the psalmist's perspective] 'WATERS OF A FULL stream', a well-known metaphor for Torah in Rabbinic literature (see Mekilta, vol. 2, pp. 89-90), they are 'TO THEM', i.e., to the wicked, something 'WRUNG OUT' (KJV). Rashi explains (1) that 'TO THEM' means *bĕ'ênêhem* 'in their eyes'; (2) that *yimmāṣû* 'SQUEEZED, WRUNG OUT' means 'made into *tamṣit*, i.e., 'a juice squeezed out from a fruit'; and (3) that the Torah is to the wicked not a primary, God-given substance but a material extracted by human hands from pre-existing material. In other words, according to Rashi, Ps. 73:10b tells us that the cause of the difference between the wicked and the virtuous is that the former do not believe in God-given Torah while the latter do believe. Rashi's plausible interpretation of v. 10b attempts to discover the less than obvious syntactic relationship between the words, the meaning of which can be established without doubt.

[27] Heb. *wĕ'ōmĕrîm*; Rashi's paraphrase of the psalmist's *we'āmĕrû* 'they will say'.

[28] Rashi supplies the 3[d] pers. masc. pl. pronoun *hēm*, lit., 'they', which here, as frequently in late Heb., is employed in the sense of the Eng. copula 'are'; see the discussion in our introduction above, pp. 137–139.

[29] Rendering of the lemma assumes that Rashi understands *'ôlām* here in its late Heb. sense 'world'; on the latter development see Kadushin, *The Rabbinic Mind*[3], pp. 293-95; that Rashi so understands *'ôlām* here is supported by the paraphrase *šalĕwîm bā'ôlām* 'tranquil in the world' found in other Rashi mss. here.

[30] See Ps. 122:7; Prov. 17:1; etc.

[31] Similarly *Mahberet Menahem*, p. 360, s.v. *śg* I. Note that where standard Biblical Heb. employs the root *gdl* 'be(come) big', Aram. employs *śg'* or *rby*. Here at Ps. 73:12 we have a Semitic root, which is rare but not unknown in Biblical Heb. but frequent in Aram.

[32] The latter is best known as the author of the liturgical poem "Akdamut" chanted responsively in Ashkenazi synagogues on Shavuot (see Birnbaum, *Daily Prayer Book*, pp. 647-53); for biographical details and

bibliography see Abraham David, "Meir ben Isaac Sheliaḥ Zibbur," *EJ* 11:1255.

[33] Rashi notes correctly that v. 13 expresses the point of view of the wicked rather than that of the psalmist; see vv. 1, 15. On the other hand, throughout the psalm the point of view of the wicked is expressed in the plural while that of the psalmist is couched in the singular. Hence Rashi finds it necessary to state explicitly that v. 13 expresses in the singular the point of view of the wicked collectively. Contrast Ibn Ezra, who takes v. 13 as an expression of the point of view of the psalmist.

[34] Heb. *wĕ*, the exegetical *waw*; see Dahood here.

[35] Rashi paraphrases substituting plural for singular because of his view that vv. 13-14 expresses in the singular the point of view of the wicked, which elsewhere in the psalm is couched in the plural; see above, n. 33.

[36] Heb. *mibboqer labboqer*, Rashi's interpretation of the psalmist's *labbĕqārîm* 'BY THE MORNINGS'; NJV, following Rashi, renders "each morning".

[37] The exegetical difficulty to which Rashi responds here is, in the words of Dahood here, "the need of a verb in this sentence position."

[38] The psalmist, to whom Ps. 73 is attributed at v. 1.

[39] Lit., "Had I said in my heart"; Rashi here intimates that here in Ps. 73:15 and elsewhere in Biblical Heb. *'āmar* 'say' can mean 'think'; so NJV: "Had I decided."

[40] The exegetical problem confronted here by Rashi is the identification of the object of the preposition *kĕmô* like, as'; see the various commentaries. Ehrlich, *Die Psalmen*, p. 172 adopts the same approach as does Rashi, namely, to take v. 15b as the object of the preposition.

[41] Rashi's point is that in Judaism suffering is normally interpreted as God's Justice. See Mishnah Berakot 9:2: "...and over bad news one is supposed to say 'Blessed [are You, O LORD, our God, King of the world], the Faithful Judge'"; see Birnbaum, *Daily Prayer Book*, p. 777.

[42] The psalmist here employs the imperfect *'ābô'*. Rashi clarifies the past meaning of this imperfect in its context by paraphrasing *'ad-'ābô'* by means of the perfect *'ad-'ăšer bā'tî*

[43] Since the psalmist writes *miqdĕšê 'ēl* 'SANCTUARIES OF GOD', it is not unequivocal that he is employing plural majestatis to refer to Solomon's Temple; hence Rashi's eisegetical note to the latter effect.

[44] Here Rashi refers to the events described in 2 Kgs. 18:13-19:37; Isa. 36-37; 2 Ch. 32:1-23.

[45] Rashi's paraphrase *hēbantî* indicates that the psalmist employs the imperfect *'ābînāh* as a preterite.

[46] Heb. *šēdîm*; so Rashi on the sing. *ballāhāh* 'terror' at Isa. 17:14 and on the plural again at Job. 18:11. In his comment on Ezek. 26:21 Rashi intimates that this interpretation is taken over from the *pōtĕrîm* 'the French Jewish exegetes who preceded Rashi'; see the discussion at Ps. 68:32 and the literature cited there.

[47] Rashi takes 'THEIR IMAGE' to refer to their 'image-likeness' (Gen.

1:26-27), i.e., 'their bodies'.

[48] This comment is based upon a midrash found in Exodus Rabbah 18:5. This midrash is, in part, a response to an exegetical question, which arises with respect to Isa. 10:16b: "Under its [Assyria's] glory shall burn a burning like that of fire." The exegetical question is, "What is the meaning of 'under his glory'?" The midrash answers, "He [God] burnt their [the Assyrians'] from inside [their clothing], and he left their clothing outside [their cremated bodies]. The glory of a person is his clothing." This midrash is quoted also in Qimhi's comment on 2 Kgs. 19:35.

[49] See Rashi's exegesis of v. 20.

[50] The psalmist employs the verb *'eštōnān* in past meaning. To indicate this Rashi could have paraphrased *hištōnanti* (see nn. 42 and 45 above). However, to indicate that the verb is stative in meaning, Rashi paraphrases using the verb 'to be' + a participle.

[51] The complete phrase there is "like a club, a sword, a sharpened arrow"; so NJV. Rashi here supports a view, which is rejected by *Mahberet Menahem*, p. 68, s.v. *'eštōnān*.

[52] Heb. *ūkěšěhû' mitpā'ēl*.

[53] See *Mahberet Menahem*, p. 67, s.v. *'eštolāl û*.

[54] The psalmist says, *wě'ānî-ba'ar wělō' 'ēdā'*, lit., "NOW AS FOR ME, BEING A FOOL, I DO NOT/DID NOT KNOW." Here we have a casus pendens followed by a negative followed by a verb in the imperfect, which can be present, future or past in meaning. Rashi's paraphrase understands v. 22 as two independent clauses in the past tense joined by a coordinate conjunction.

[55] I.e., whether justice or injustice; see Rashi at v. 16 above and the discussion there.

[56] Rashi, for the sake of clarity, turns the psalmist's metaphor into a simile. Moreover, Rashi's paraphrase indicates that he understands MT's *běhēmôt* not as a feminine plural but as a singular as in Job. 12:7; 40:15. It is now know that *běhēmôt* in all these three cases is a Phoenician-type feminine singular; see Dahood, here; see Pope at Job. 12:7; 40:15.

[57] Exegetical *waw*.

[58] Here Rashi's point is simply that *tanḥēnî* is an imperfect employed to express the past; hence he supplies the corresponding perfect form of the verb.

[59] See Rashi at vv. 17-21 above.

[60] Our Rashi ms. reads by scribal error *bḥrt* 'you chose' instead of *bḥrty* 'I have chosen'.

[61] Similarly *Mahberet Menahem*, p. 214, s.v. *kl* VI.

[62] Cf. *Mahberet Menahem*, p. 155, s.v. *zn* V.

[63] MT's *malăkôtěkā* could be taken to mean simply 'YOUR WORKS' (KJV; NJV; et al.). Rashi, however, perceiving that etymologically the word means 'message' (cf. Heb. *mal'āk* 'messenger' and the verbal root *l'k* 'send' frequently attested in Ugaritic), sees here an explicit reference to the divine inspiration he mentions in connection with vv. 21ff.

1b WHY, O GOD, DO YOU FOREVER REJECT US
DO YOU FUME IN ANGER. [The source of this expression is the fact that] as for whoever is angry, smoke comes
out of his nostrils.[1]

2a YOU MADE LONG AGO [i.e.], before the creation of the
world, in accord with what is stated in the Bible, "You have
been our refuge in every generation, before the mountains
came into being" (Ps. 90:1-2).

2c WHERE YOU DWELL.[2] This is an unusual usage[3] [of the
word _zeh_].[4] It is a cognate of[5] [the relative pronoun _zû_ in] _zû_
ḥāṭā'nû lô "against whom we sinned" (Isa. 42:24), and note
that it [the relative clause _zeh šākantā bô_ 'WHERE YOU
DWELL'] corresponds in meaning to[6] [standard Heb.] _'ăšer_
šākantā bô "in which You dwell."[7]

3 LIFT UP YOUR FEET [_pĕ'āmêkā_] FOR A TUMULT
[_lĕmaššu'ôt_], a word referring to destruction; it is a cognate of
[the noun] _še'iyyāh_ 'ruins' (Isa. 24:12); and it is a cognate of
[the verb _tiššā'eh_ 'lies waste' in] "lies waste and desolte" (Isa.
6:11).[8] [V. 3a means], Raise up Your rhythm [_pĕ'îmôtêkā_] and
Your terrors so that they will be for Your enemies FOR A
PERPETUAL TUMULT because of all the evil, which the
enemy perpetrated in the Temple. Thus did Menahem treat
it [_pa'am_ 'foot'] as a cognate of [the verb _p'm_ 'agitate' in]
"His spirit was agitated" (Gen. 41:8).[9]

4a YOUR MEETING PLACES.[10]
These [MEETING PLACES] is [a term for] the Temple,
with respect to which it is stated in the Bible, "There I will
meet with you" (Ex. 25:22).[11]

4b THEY SET UP THEIR OWN SIGNS AS SIGNS.
When they became powerful enough to destroy it [the
Temple], then THEY SET UP for themselves their
divinatory signs,[12] which are true SIGNS.[13] Now what are
the forms of divination [alluded to here]? [They are, of
course, the following]: "He [Nebuchadnezzar] has shaken
arrows, consulted teraphim..." (Ezek. 21:26).[14]

5   HE IS KNOWN WHEN[15] HE IS BRINGING AXES ON
     HIGH INTO A THICKET OF TREES.
     The enemy became known, for when he was striking at the
     gates of the Temple, he was BRINGING his blows ON
     HIGH against Heaven. On what basis did he [the enemy]
     know this? [He knew this] for he saw that the tree entangles
     and grabs hold of the axes and swallows them in consonance
     with what our rabbis said, "One gate of Jerusalem swal-
     lowed all of them."[16] [As for the term *sĕbak* 'THICKET' in
     the phrase] 'AXES INTO A THICKET OF TREES', it is
     the same word as is attested in "caught in the thicket" (Gen.
     22:13). [The phrase in its entirety means that] the tree [was]
     entangling them [the axes], and they [the axes were] becom-
     ing entangled in them [the trees].

6   BUT NOW,[17] even though he [Nebuchadnezzar] saw that
     it would be difficult [for him to fight], he did not restrain
     himself from breaking down all its entrances and all its
     gates.[18]

6a   [The subject of the verb] 'THEY HACKED AWAY' [is]
     'the enemies'.

6b   BY MEANS OF *kaśśîl* [19] AND BY MEANS OF *kĕlappôt*.[20]
     These are carpenters' tools of destruction. [Note that in Jer.
     46:22], "They shall come against you[21] with axes," Jonathan
     b. Uzziel rendered [*ubĕqardummôt* 'with axes'] into Aram. by
     ubĕkaśśîlîn.[22] [The hapax legomenon] *kĕlappôt*. is [typically]
     Arabic.[23] Thus did Dunash explain that it is one of the car-
     penters' tools.[24]

8a   THEIR LEADERS[25] THOUGHT TOGETHER.
     [I.e.], All their rulers,[26] the earlier as well as the later, had
     one thought. [The word] *nînām* 'THEIR LEADERS'
     [means] *môšlêhem* 'their rulers. Cognate to it are [the verb
     yinnôn 'may it be exalted' in] "May His Name be exalted"
     (Ps. 72:17b) and [the noun *mānôn* 'ruler' in] "His latter one
     will be a ruler" (Prov. 29:21).[27] The earlier [rulers] and the
     later [rulers] [had one thought,[28] namely], to attack[29] Israel's
     patron[30] so that afterwards they [the Gentiles] will attack
     them [Israel].[31] You may understand that it is so because

8b   THEY BURNT ALL THE TEMPLES[32] OF THE
     LORD,[33] which were IN THE LAND.
     [*môʿădê* YHWH 'TEMPLES OF THE LORD' means liter-

ally] His meeting places.[34] [Moreover, v. 8b refers to the fact that] the Philistines destroyed Shiloh;[35] Nebuchadnezzar destroyed the First Temple;[36] and the Romans destroyed the Second Temple.[37]

9a   SIGNS FOR US, which You promised through Your prophets,
WE HAVE NOT SEEN, and we do not see them during the long time[38] that we are in Exile. [Here] Asaph[39] has prophesied concerning the period of the Exile.

9b   *'ad-māh*[40] 'HOW LONG' [is synonymous with] *'ad mātay*[41] 'how long!' [Both exclamations are ellipsis for "How long] shall we be in this trouble?"

11b DRAW IT OUT OF YOUR BOSOM.
gārēš 'drive out' is a synonym of *kallēh* 'DRAW OUT'[42] [as is demonstrated by the juxtaposition in] *kālāh gārēš yĕgārēš* "drawing out he will surely drive out" (Ex. 11:1).[43]

12   O GOD, MY KING FROM OF OLD.
Are You not our deliverance from aforetime?[44]

13b THE HEADS OF THE MONSTERS. These [MONSTERS] are [a metaphor for] Egyptians, who are called 'monsters' in accord with what is stated in the Bible, "[Pharaoh king of Egypt], the mighty monster sprawling in his channels" (Ezek. 29:3).[45]

14a THE HEADS OF LEVIATHAN. Pharaoh is so called in accord with what is stated in the Bible, "The LORD will punish with His...cruel sword Leviathan the Elusive Serpent" (Isa. 27:1).

14b YOU GAVE HIM AS FOOD TO A PEOPLE FOR *ṣiyyîm*. [I.e.], You gave[46] their[47] wealth TO the PEOPLE of Israel[48] for consumption of it.[49] *lĕṣiyyîm*. [i.e.], 'for groups', i.e., the troops whom You brought out [of Egypt].[50] *ṣiyyîm*. [means] *ṣîôt* 'groups' in accord with the way in which Onkelos rendered into Aramaic [the word *wĕṣîm* in] "*wĕṣîm* from the quarter of Kittim" (Num. 24:24) [namely], *wĕṣi'ān* 'and groups'.[51]

15a YOU CLEFT SPRINGS from the rock.[52]

15b YOU DRIED UP the Jordan, which is a MIGHTY river.[53]

16a THE DAY IS YOURS.
[THE DAY here is a metaphor for] the Redemption of Israel.

THE NIGHT ALSO.
Your people were in the troubles of the NIGHT.[54]

16b   IT WAS YOU WHO SET IN PLACE THE ORB and light.

17a   YOU FIXED THE BOUNDARIES OF their LAND with every benefit.[55]

17b   SUMMER AND WINTER—YOU MADE THEM. Note that this is a reference to[56] "He keeps for our benefit the weeks appointed for harvest" (Jer. 5:24).[57] [It means that] You have not changed the rules of the calendar on them.

18   REMEMBER THIS: The ENEMY that BLASPHEMED You when it destroyed us.

19a   DO NOT DELIVER TO THE WILD BEAST[58] [i.e.], to the battalions of the Gentiles. Now [the use of the term 'WILD BEAST' as a metaphor for Gentiles who ruthlessly attack Israel] is similar to [the simile in] "The Philistines gathered together like a wild beast" (2 Sam. 23:11).[59]
YOUR TURTLEDOVE.
[The Biblical Heb. form] *tôrĕkā* [corresponds in meaning to late Heb.] *tôr šelĕkā* 'Your turtledove'.[60] [This word *tôr* is the same word as [is attested in the plural in the phrase "turtle-doves and young pigeons" (Lev. 1:14; 5:7, 11; etc. As for this turtledove, when the male dies, his mate does not pair with another male. Similarly, Israel have not swapped You for another deity even though You were far from them so that she was like a widow.[61]

19b   [The unusual expression] *ḥayyat 'ăniyyêkā* [means] *nepeš 'ăniyyêkā* 'the life of Your poor'.[62]

20a   LOOK TO THE COVENANT, which You made with our ancestors.

20b   HAUNTS OF LAWLESSNESS. *nĕwēh ḥāmās* 'haunt of LAWLESSNESS'[63] is an expression denoting a dwelling place.

21   LET NOT THE DOWNTRODDEN TURN AWAY from You[64] DISAPPOINTED with respect to his prayer.[65]

22   *ḥerpātĕkā* 'THAT YOU ARE BLASPHEMED' [i.e.], *gid-dûpĕkā* 'Your being reviled'.[66]

PSALM LXXIV, NOTES
   [1] Similarly Rashi at Ps. 18:9; see Gruber, *Aspects*, pp. 510-13.

² The lemma in our Rashi ms. consists of the two words *šākantā bô*.

³ Heb. *tiqqûn hallāšôn hû*'; see Rashi at Ex. 14:28, and see Breithaupt here.

⁴ Which is normally not a relative pronoun but a demonstrative pronoun.

⁵ Heb. *kĕmô*.

⁶ Heb. *kĕmô*.

⁷ For discussion of *zeh* and *zû* as relative pronouns see *GKC* #138g.

⁸ *Mahberet Menahem*, p. 359, s.v. *š'* II.

⁹ *Mahberet Menahem*, p. 305, s.v. *p'm* II. Menahem treats the verb *p'm* 'move', from which he derives *pĕ'āmêkā* in Ps. 74:3, as distinct from *p'm* III 'foot' attested in Ps. 58:11; Cant. 7:2; etc. *K-B*³, pp. 896-98 now recognizes maximally two roots—a verbal root *p'm* 'move', and a primary noun *p'm* meaning "foot, time, hammer, etc."

¹⁰ Heb. *mô'ădêkā*; Dahood renders 'assembly' (cf. KJV) based on Ugar. *m'd* and Phoenician *mw'd*. RSV renders 'thy holy place' based on Heb. *'ohel mô'ēd* (commonly rendered 'tent of meeting'), a standard designation of the portable tent sanctuary passim in Ex. 29; 40; Lev. 4; Num. 4; etc.

¹¹ In the previous note it was pointed out that the English versions have seen fit to choose between a functional rendering of *mô'ădêkā* 'Your sanctuary' and one based on the derivation of the noun from the root *w'd* 'meet, assemble'. Rashi correctly sees in Ex. 25:22 a way to reconcile the two alternatives as follows: The Temple is designated a Meeting Place because it is the placed where God and Moses are to meet.

¹² Here Rashi responds to the exegetical question, "What kind of signs did they set up?" Qimhi follows Rashi in understanding "THEY SET UP THEIR SIGNS" to mean 'they engaged in divination'. KJV, McCullough (*IB*, vol. 4, p. 394), and Dahood see here a reference to military standards. Rashi's interpretation derives from Midrash Tehillim here.

¹³ Here Rashi responds to the exegetical question, "What is the syntactic relationship of 'SIGNS' to the rest of v. 4b?" KJV and RSV render "for signs," thereby treating the noun 'SIGNS' as an indirect object of the verb 'THEY SET UP'. Rashi, on the other hand, treats 'SIGNS' as a nominal sentence, "[They are] SIGNS," functioning as a relative clause modifying the noun 'THEIR SIGNS'. Rashi here alludes to the fact that in Rabbinic Heb. 'they are signs' and 'they are true signs' are synonymous. Note that NJV reflects Rashi's exegesis.

¹⁴ On these forms of divination see J. S. Wright, "Divination," in *The Illustrated Bible Dictionary*, ed. James Dixon Douglas (3 vols.; Leicester, Eng.: Inter-Varsity, 1980), vol. 1, pp. 391-392.

¹⁵ Heb. *kĕ*.

¹⁶ Rashi's apparent source is BT Sanhedrin 96b; the latter source employs the word *daššā'* 'entrance, doorway' while Rashi employs here the word *tar'ā'* 'gate'.

¹⁷ Heb. *wĕ'attāh*; in MT, however, it is written defectively *w't*.

¹⁸ This clause reflects Rashi's exegesis of v. 6a-b. He interprets *pittûhêāh* to mean 'her entrances'; contrast KJV, RSV, and NJV: "its carved work."

Rashi's treatment of this noun is shared in antiquity by LXX and Symmachus and in modern times by Dahood.

[19] KJV: "axes."

[20] KJV: "hammers"; see below, n. 24.

[21] This reading found in our Rashi ms. is found also in many other medieval Heb. mss. of the Book of Psalms (so *BHS* here); NJV's rendering "her" reflects the standard Heb. text.

[22] This may suggest that in Heb. where the same noun *kaššîl* is a *hapax legomenon* attested only at Ps. 74:6 the noun likewise means 'axe'; so KJV.

[23] On Rashi's Arabic etymologies see the discussion at Ps. 60, n. 14.

[24] *Teshuvot Dunash*, p. 56.

[25] Heb. *nînām*; see next note.

[26] I.e., the rulers of the Gentiles; Heb. *mōšĕlêhem*. Rashi's interpretation of *nînām* here is consistent with his comment on *yinnôn* at Ps. 72:17; q.v. Contrast NJV's "Let us destroy them," which reflects Qimhi's treatment of *nînām* as a form of the verb *yānāh* 'destroy, afflict'; so *BDB*, p. 413a. A midrash at Midrash Tehillim here takes *nînām* here to mean 'their progeny'; the latter interpretation assumes that the word is a form of the word *nîn* 'progeny' attested at Gen. 21:23; Isa. 14:22; etc.; so *K-B*[3], p. 615a.

[27] *Ad hoc* rendering of Prov. 29:21b to reflect the interpretation presupposed by Rashi's comment here.

[28] See Rashi's comment on v. 8a above.

[29] Heb. *lĕhizdawwēg*; see Jastrow *Dict.*, p. 383b, s.v. *zāwag*.

[30] Heb. *paṭrôn*, a loanword derived from Gk. πάτρων = Lat. patronus, from which is derived Eng. 'patron'. See Krauss, *Lehnwörter*, pt. 2, pp. 438-39. In the present context "Israel's patron" means God.

[31] Contrast the midrashim at Midrash Tehillim here, which see the attack on Israel as coming before the attack on the God of Israel; Rashi's comment is based in part on the words attributed to Gog and Magog in Midrash Tehillim at Ps. 2 #4.

[32] Heb. *mô'ădê*, the pl. construct of the word whose singular in v. 4 Rashi rightly interprets to mean 'Temple'.

[33] MT reads 'God'; our Rashi ms. reads yᵉy, which represents the tetragrammaton commonly rendered 'THE LORD'.

[34] See Rashi at v. 4, and see above, nn. 10 and 11; see also Midrash Tehillim here.

[35] This is nowhere stated in the Bible. It can, however, be inferred from the fact that when the Ark of the Covenant was retunred to Israel by the Philistines it was not brought back to Shiloh. Apparently, between the events described in 1 Sam. 4 and those described in 1 Sam. 5-6 Shiloh was captured and raised. The only explicit references to the destruction of Shiloh in the Hebrew Bible are at Jer. 7:12, 14; 26:6, 9; Ps. 78:60. Presumably, Shiloh was destroyed c. 1050 B.C.E.

[36] 2 Kgs. 25:9; 2 Ch. 36:19; the date was 7 Ab 586 B.C.E.

[37] The date was 9 Ab 70 C.E.; see Mishnah Ta'anit 4:6.

[38] Heb. *bĕyāmîm rabbîm*, lit., 'in many days'.

[39] To whom the psalm is attributed at v. 1.

⁴⁰ This expression is attested also in Ps. 79:5 and Ps. 89:47.

⁴¹ Attested twenty-nine times in the Hebrew Bible, this expression is commonly compared to the etymologically equivalent Akk. *adi māti* and to Lat. *quousque*, both of which are commonly said to mean 'Enough!'; for list of occurrences of *'ad mātay* in the Hebrew Bible see Mandelkern, p. 707c-d; for comparison with the Akk. and Lat. expressions see the various modern commentaries on the various passages.

⁴² Our scribe meant to say, "*kalleh* [the word found in Ps. 74:11b] is a synonym of *gārēš*."

⁴³ Cf. NJV: "He will drive you out of here one and all"; from Rashi's comment at Ps. 9:5 it should be more than clear that Rashi holds that synonyms occur both in parallel clauses and juxtaposed in the same clause. Here Rashi acknowledges that juxtaposition of words can be used to demonstrate that they are synonyms; contrast the claims of Gelles, pp. 99-105; Kugel, p. 173.

⁴⁴ In this comment Rashi answers four exegetical questions: (1) What is the syntactic function of 'GOD' in v. 12? (2) What is the syntactic function of 'MY KING'? (3) What is the syntactic function of 'FROM OF OLD'? and (4) What is the syntactic function of v. 12b? KJV takes 'AND GOD' as the subject of a nominal sentence, whose predicate nominative is 'MY KING OF OLD' Hence KJV construes v. 12b as an adjectival participial phrase modifying 'MY KING OF OLD'. RSV takes 'GOD' as the subject but 'MY KING' as a noun in apposition with 'GOD' and 'FROM OF OLD' and v. 12b as the compound predicate adjective. Rashi, however, takes 'AND GOD MY KING' as a vocative referring to the understood subject 'You', v. 12b as the predicate nominative, and 'FROM OF OLD' (v. 12a) as an adverb modifying the copula.

⁴⁵ Rashi infers from Ezek. 29:3 where Pharaoh, the ruler of Egypt, is addressed as "the mighty monster," that ordinary Egyptians are just plain monsters.

⁴⁶ By substituting the perfect Rashi indicates that the psalmist employs the imperfect form of the verb as a preterite.

⁴⁷ According to Rashi, this means "Egypt's"; see Ex. 11:2; 12:35-36.

⁴⁸ Here Rashi answers the exegetical question, "What people?"

⁴⁹ Having taken 'YOU GAVE HIM' to refer to the bestowal on Israel of Egypt's wealth, Rashi has no choice but to take *lĕma'ăkāl*, lit., 'AS FOOD' in the secondary sense 'for consumption'.

⁵⁰ The Israelites who left Egypt are referred to as 'troops' in Num. 33:1; see also passim in Num.

⁵¹ Similarly Rashi at Ps. 72:9; contrast Rashi at Num. 24:24. It is not necessary to assume that Rashi has changed his mind about the meaning of *ṣî* between the time he completed his commentary on Num. 24:24 and the time he wrote the commentary on Pss. 72 and 74 (on the relative dating of these commentaries see Introduction, pp. 4, 7–9). In his commentary at Ps. 72:9 and Ps. 74:14 Rashi does not invoke the meaning of the noun *ṣiyyîm* at Num. 24:24 but only the meaning of the term there according to T.O. Rashi's point here is that the latter's rendering of the noun

there at Num. 24:24 is the correct rendering of the noun *ṣiyyîm* at Ps. 74:14b.

⁵² Rashi intimates that v. 15a exhibits an ellipsis: "YOU CLEFT A SPRING." A spring, he suggests, cannot be cleft; a rock can be cleft so that ground water emerges in a spring as recorded in Isa. 48:21b, "He cleaved the rock and water gushed forth"; for the idea cf. Ex. 17:6; Deut. 8:15; Ps. 78:15-16; 114:8; Job. 28:10. It is quite possible, however, that there is no ellipsis here at Ps. 74:15 since the verb *bāqa'* 'cleave' is frequently employed with a body of water as its object in referring to the parting of the waters of the Reed Sea; see Ex. 14:16; Ps. 78:13; Neh. 9:11. Moreover, the verb *bāqa'* 'cleave' is used with reference to the gushing forth of subterranean water in Gen. 7:11. It appears, therefore, that Rashi's treatment of Ps. 74:15a as ellipsis is not required by the vocabulary. It seems that Rashi is motivated by the contrasting parallelism in v. 15. In the second half of the verse the object is 'RIVERS' and the verb denotes 'DRY UP'. We have already seen that *bāqa'* 'cleave' with 'spring' as an object refers to the sudden appearance on the surface of ground water. Apparently, taking these factors into account, Rashi sees in v. 15a a reference to God's making water appear where there was none and in v. 15b a reference to the appearance of dry land where previously there was only water; see Qimhi here.

⁵³ By means of his paraphrase *nahar* Rashi intimates what Qimhi states explicitly, namely, that if v. 15b refers to the drying up of the Jordan (Josh. 4), then *naharôt* there must be a singular noun, albeit plural construct in form. On such nouns in Biblical Heb. see above at Ps. 73:22. If, contra Rashi, Ps. 74:13-14 is interpreted as a series of cosmogonic reminiscences rather than as references to events in the history of Israel, then the two halves of v. 15 may both be interpreted as references to God's victory over rebellious water sources. In v. 15a God's victory over rebellious springs employs the same verb *bāqa'* 'split' used in the Reed Sea tradition (see previous note) to mean 'cause to dry up'. The cosmogonic interpretation eliminates the need to construe *naharôt* in v. 15b as a singular. Rashi's reinterpretation of cosmogonic references as references to events in the history of Israel is anticipated by the author of Ps. 114, who transforms the Canaanite fixed pair *ym//nhr* "Sea//River" into "Sea//Jordan" (Ps. 114:3, 5). Here at Ps. 74:15b the transformation turns the Jordan into "a mighty river."

⁵⁴ Just as Rashi takes 'THE DAY' in v. 16a as a metaphor for Redemption so does he taken 'THE NIGHT' in v. 16b as a metaphor for the Exile.

⁵⁵ In the context of this psalm, which speaks about the LORD's role in cosmogony, "YOU FIXED ALL THE BOUNDARIES OF THE EARTH" means "You set the earth apart from the sky and the water"; for the same idea see Gen. 1:6-10; Ps. 104:9. In Rashi's reinterpretation of "YOU FIXED ALL THE BOUNDARIES" as a reference to Israelite history, Heb. *gĕbûlôt*, lit., 'boundaries' (so at Deut. 19:14), is taken in its secondary sense 'territory' (so at Mal. 1:4), and *'āreṣ*, lit., 'land, earth', is

taken not in the secondary sense 'world' but in the sense 'land (of Israel)';
for the latter exegesis see also Rashi at Ps. 24:1.

[56] Heb. *dûgmat*.

[57] Rashi, for whom *yāṣar* 'he made' and *nāṣar* 'he kept' are both derived
from homonymous biliteral roots *ṣr* (see *Maḥberet Menaḥem*, pp. 324-25),
appears to take *yāṣartā* in Ps. 74:17b as a form of *ṣr* 'keep' rather than as
a form of *ṣr* 'make'.

[58] Rashi does not comment here on the appearance of a feminine singular noun not in the construct state ending in *at*; contrast Ibn Ezra and
Qimhi; on this rare but not unknown phenomenon see *GKC* #80f.

[59] Similarly NJV's "in force"; cf. KJV's "as a troop"; see Rashi there;
contrast Gersonides, who takes *ḥayyāh* there to be a biform of *miḥyāh* 'sustenance'; in his comment at Ps. 68:11 Rashi seems to take *ḥayyāh* at 2
Sam. 23:11 to be a place name.

[60] Here Rashi responds to the exegetical question, "Is *tôrĕkā* a noun
with pronominal possessive suffix, or is it a verb with accusative suffix
corresponding in meaning to *wĕtorekkā* 'and let her instruct you' at Job.
12:7-8?" Rashi opts for the former view while Dahood here opts for the
latter interpretation. The gemination of the *k* in the verb form at Job.
12:7-8 is the product of the assimilation of the energic *nun*.

[61] With Maarsen and Zohory note that Rashi's source is Canticles
Rabbah 1:63.

[62] McCullough, *IB*, vol. 4, p. 398 argues that *ḥayyat* must be emended
to *ḥayyê* to have this meaning. Qimhi, however, shows in his commentary
here that the equation of *ḥayyāh* and *nepeš* is supported by Job. 33:20 where
the nouns *ḥayyātô* and *napšô* appear in synonymous parallelism.

[63] By interpreting pl. construct *nĕ'ôt* by means of sing. construct *nĕwēh*,
Rashi indicates that *nĕ'ôt* is related etymologically to *nāweh* 'dwelling place'
rather than to *nā'eh* 'pretty'; see Rashi at Ps. 83:13; 93:5.

[64] Answering the exegetical question, "NOT TURN AWAY from
whom or from what?"

[65] Answering the exegetical question, "DISAPPOINTED with respect
to what?"

[66] The two nouns *ḥerpāh* 'blasphemy' and *giddûpîm* 'reviling' appear in
synonymous parallelism in Zeph. 2:8. The two verbs *ḥērēp* and *giddēp* are
juxtaposed in 2 Kgs. 19:22 = Isa. 37:23; Ps. 44:17. The nouns *ḥerpāh*
ûgĕdûpāh 'blasphemy and reviling' are juxtaposed at Ezek. 5:15. The word
order is always *ḥrp-gdp*. This word order suggests that in Biblical Heb. *ḥrp*
is relatively more well known while *gdp* is the rarer, more literary root.
However, Rashi's tendency to explain *ḥrp* as meaning *gdp* here at Ps.
74:22 as also at Ps. 31:12 and Joel 2:17 suggests that in Rashi's Heb. *gdp*
is the more familiar and *ḥrp* the rarer word.

PSALM LXXV

1   FOR THE LEADER. DO NOT DESTROY[1] Israel.

2a   WE PRAISE YOU, O GOD, for good fortune.

2b   WE PRAISE YOU also for ill fortune.[2]

2c   AND YOUR NAME IS NEAR in our mouths continually.[3]

2d   Our generations[4] HAVE TOLD OF YOUR WONDROUS DEEDS continually.

3a   WHEN I TAKE A HOLIDAY [i.e.], when we[5] have a holiday,[6] we do not engage in vulgarity and levity as do all the [other] nations.[7] [Instead],

3b   I WILL GIVE JUDGMENT EQUITABLY. [I.e.], we take heed to praise You and to laud You by mentioning some aspect of the event commemorated on that day.[8]

4a   EARTH AND ALL ITS INHABITANTS DISSOLVE. At the time of the Giving of the Torah when EARTH AND ALL ITS INHABITANTS were DISSOLVING because of the condition that You made with them at the time of Creation that if they [Israel] would not accept the Torah, they [the EARTH AND ALL ITS INHABITANTS] would return to chaos.[9]

4b   IT IS I, Your people Israel,[10] WHO ESTABLISHED ITS PILLARS when I said, "We will faithfully do" (Ex. 24:7).[11]

5   TO hōlĕlîm [i.e.], to the wicked,[12] who are mixed up.[13]

7   FOR NEITHER FROM THE PLACE OF THE COMING FORTH of the sun NOR FROM THE PLACE OF its SETTING[14] nor from the deserts[15] to which you dispatch expeditions in order to make more money—not through any of these is one to achieve stature.[16]

8a   FOR GOD METES OUT justice[17] for all the evil, which you have done.

8b   HE BRINGS DOWN ONE MAN, HE LIFTS UP ANOTHER. HE BRINGS DOWN the exalted, and HE LIFTS UP the lowly.[18]

9a   THERE IS A CUP of debilitation[19] IN His[20] HAND.

9b   AND THE WINE ḥāmar [i.e.], ḥāzāq ' is strong';[21] [it means] vinose in Old French.[22]

9c   FULL OF MIXED WINE.
        [I.e.], the cup is FULL OF[23] mixed wine for pouring,[24] i.e.,[25]
        for giving all the nations to drink.[26]

9d   FROM THIS HE POURS.
        From this cup He will pour and distribute drink for them.
        [The verb *wayyāgēr* 'HE POURED'] is a cognate of [the par-
        ticiple *muggārîm* 'poured out' in] "poured out down a slope"
        (Mic. 1:4).[27]

10   AS FOR ME, I WILL DECLARE FOREVER [i.e.], hence-
        forth,[28]
        His vengeance and His might.[29]

11a   ALL THE HORNS OF THE WICKED [i.e.], of the
        wicked Esau,[30]
        I WILL CUT them in accord with what is stated in the
        Bible, "I will wreak My vengeance on Edom[31] through My
        people Israel" (Ezek. 25:14). Israel will cut off Esau's horn,

11b   and then[32] THE HORNS OF THE RIGHTEOUS [i.e.],
        the world's righteous, Israel, who are the glory of the Holy
        One Blessed be He, WILL BE LIFTED UP.[33]

PSALM LXXV, NOTES
   [1] NJV follows KJV in treating *'al-tašḥēt* in the title as an obscure, un-
translatable musical term. Rashi, followed by RSV, understands the
expression to be a negative imperative. The exegetical difficulty which
remains and with which Rashi deals here is to supply an appropriate direct object of the transitive verb 'DESTROY'; see Midrash Tehillim here.
   [2] Rashi, like Midrash Tehillim, sees in the repetitive parallelism a reminder of Mishnah Berakot 9:2, which prescribes a benediction to be recited upon hearing good news and another benediction to be recited upon
hearing bad news; for these benedictions see also Birnbaum, *Daily Prayer
Book*, p. 777.
   [3] Rashi, following Midrash Tehillim, responds to the exegetical question, "In what way IS YOUR NAME NEAR?"
   [4] Here Rashi supplies the missing subject. NJV supplies 'men' while
Ibn Ezra supplies 'the prophets'. For other solutions requiring a different
vocalization see LXX; Peshitta; Dahood. Qimhi takes the verb *sippĕrû* as
a prophetic perfect meaning "They [Israel and the Gentiles who will have
experienced the Redemption] will tell...."
   [5] Rashi substitution of 1st pers. pl. for the psalmist's 1st pers. sing. suggests that the psalmist personifies Israel.
   [6] Heb. *yôm ṭôb*. Note that in Biblical Heb. 'holiday' is most frequently
expressed by *mô'ēd* as here or by *ḥag*. In Rabbinic Heb. the most common
expression is *yôm ṭôb*.

[7] Cf. PRK, ed. Mandelbaum, p. 422, line 6-p. 423, line 4.

[8] See BT Shabbat 24a.

[9] Rashi's comment is based on Midrash Tehillim here.

[10] It is obvious that God is addressed in v. 2. It is equally obvious that in vv. 8-10 God is spoken about by the psalmist. The exegetical question to which Rashi responds here at v. 4b is "Who is the speaker?" Ibn Ezra and Qimhi both comment here, dibĕrê hammĕśôrēr "the words of the psalmist." We have noted at v. 3, n. 8 that Rashi sees the psalmist as a personification of Israel. Hence Rashi explains here that I, the psalmist, is "Your people Israel." Contrast, inter alia, Sforno, Rogerson and McKay, Weiser, and NJV, all of whom hold that the speaker here is God.

[11] From the same midrash to which Rashi alludes in his comment at v. 4a; see n. 9.

[12] NJV renders "wanton men"; KJV "fools"; RSV "the boastful" while Qimhi and Sforno understand hōlĕlîm to mean 'the frivolous'. A glance at the variety of disparate interpretations should suffice for an appreciation of the seriousness of the exegetical question facing Rashi here.

[13] Cf. Rashi's comment on hōlĕlîm at Ps. 73:3; see discussion there, and see also Rashi at Eccles. 10:13.

[14] NJV correctly renders môṣā', lit., 'place of coming forth', as 'east' and ma'ărāb, lit., 'place of setting', as 'west'. The exegetical difficulty is that môṣā' is attested in this sense in Biblical Heb. only here. Elsewhere in Biblical Heb. môṣā' means either 'source' (1 Kgs. 10:28 = 2 Ch. 1:16; Job. 28:1), usually 'water source' (2 Kgs. 2:21; Isa. 58:11; etc.) or 'utterance' (Num. 30:13; Deut. 23:24; etc.). Rashi's reconstruction of the longer expression môṣā' haššemeš 'the place of the coming forth of the sun', from which undoubtedly môṣā' in the sense 'east' is derived, is confirmed by the 8th cent. B.C.E. Phoenician inscription of Azitawadda discovered at Karatepe in 1946 C.E. There in KAI 26:4-6 'from the east to the west' is expressed by lmmṣ' šmš w'd mb'y, lit., "from the going forth of the sun unto its coming home." Rashi's attaching a feminine pronominal suffix to ma'ărab shows that Rashi correctly derives ma'ărāb in the sense 'west' from a hypothetical ma'ărab šemeš 'the place of the sun's setting' to which one may compare the synonymous mĕbô' haššemeš in Deut. 11:30; Josh. 1:4; etc. Rashi's ma'ărābāh is the semantic equivalent of Phoenician mb'y as well as of Heb. mĕbô'ô in Mal. 1:11; Ps. 50:1; 113:3.

[15] Rashi's paraphrase of the psalmist's "OR FROM THE DESERT"; cf. NJV's rendering "or the wilderness."

[16] Here Rashi, following R. Abba (late 3d cent.-early 4th cent. C.E. Babylonian Amora, who settled in Palestine; see Yizhaq Dov Gilat "Abba [Ba]," EJ 1:30) in Midrash Tanḥuma, ed. Buber, Maṭṭot #9:43, takes the word hārîm as an infinitive construct employed as ellipsis for hārîm qeren, lit., 'lifting up of the head/horn', which is employed in vv. 5b and 6a in the sense 'be arrogant'; on the idiom hērîm qeren see below, n. 33. Alternatively, the three words wĕlo' mimmidbar hārîm can be taken to mean 'nor form the mountainous wilderness'; so LXX; Vulgate; Jerome. This interpretation is supported by the majority of Heb. mss., which point mdbr as a

construct with *pataḥ* in the final syllable rather than as an independent noun with *qameṣ* in the final syllable. Ibn Ezra explains that "mountainous wilderness" refers to "the South"; hence KJV's rendering of *wĕlō' mimmidbar hārîm* "nor from the South". Briggs, *BH*³, and Weiser emend *wĕlō' mimmidbar umēhārîm* "neither from the wilderness nor from the mountains."

[17] The participle *šōpēṭ* could be taken as a predicate noun. Hence KJV's "But God is the judge." Since Rashi takes *šōpēṭ* as the simple predicate of a verbal sentence, he must supply the direct object of this verb *šōpēṭ* 'HE METES OUT'; cf. RSV: "But it is God who executes judgment"; similarly NJV.

[18] For this idea see Ps. 18:28; 147:6; Prov. 29:23; Job. 5:11 (on which see Gruber, *Aspects*, p. 128, n. 1).

[19] Heb. *hattarĕʾēlāh* 'poison'. See Gruber, *Aspects*, pp. 513-537 on the poison draught as a form of judicial punishment in the Hebrew Bible. The rendering 'debilitation' reflects Rashi's comment on *kōs hattarĕʾēlāh* in Isa. 51:22.

[20] Rashi's paraphrase; the biblical text reads "IN THE LORD'S HAND."

[21] This interpretation of *ḥāmar* is based on Midrash Tehillim here. The anonymous comment there appears to take the verb *ḥāmar* 'be strong' as the etymon of the Rabbinic Heb. adjective *ḥāmûr* 'strong, heavy'.

[22] Rashi at Deut. 32:14 offers three alternative interpretations of *ḥāmer* 'wine' there; one of these is that *ḥāmer* there is an adjectival noun corresponding in meaning to vernacular *vinose*, which, he says, means 'lauded for its taste'.

[23] Here Rashi responds to the exegetical question, "What is the syntactic function of the participle *mālē'*?" NJV's "wine fully mixed" assumes that *mālē'* functions here as an adjective modifying the noun *mesek*; so also RSV. Rashi, followed by Qimhi, takes *mālē'* as a stative verb whose subject is *kōs* 'CUP'. E. Wiesenberg, "A Note on *mizzeh* in Psalm lxxv 9," *VT* 4 (1954), p. 434 notes that *kōs* in Biblical Heb. is a feminine noun. If so, *mālē'* cannot be the predicate of a clause referring to *kōs* 'cup'. For evidence that *kōs* is feminine see Ps. 23:5; Lam. 4:21. In both Ugaritic and Rabbinic Heb., however, *kōs* is masculine. The Ugar. evidence consists of the expression *ksm ṭlṭm* "thirty cups" in UT 35:19. Were the noun feminine, we would expect to see *kst* instead of *ksm*. For Rabbinic Heb. *kōs* as a masc. noun see passim in Mishnah Pesahim 10. While the Rabbinic evidence in itself does not justify Rashi's treatment of *kōs* in Ps. 75:9 as masc., the Ugar. evidence suggests that Rashi may be correct and that he is not simply reading the Bible as though it were written in Rabbinic Heb.

[24] Here Rashi recognizes both that Biblical Heb. *mesek* 'mixed wine' is the etymological and semantic equivalent of Rabbinic Heb. *mezeg* and that late Heb. *māzag*, lit., 'mix', takes on the meaning 'pour'; see Rashi at Isa. 19:14; Gruber, *Aspects*, p. 529, n. 1; p. 530, n. 1.

[25] Exegetical *waw*.

[26] The psalmist refers to "ALL THE WICKED OF THE EARTH" (v.

9b). Rashi equates these persons with those people to whom the poison draught is to be administered according to Jer. 25:15; see also Jer. 49:12; Obad. 1:16.

[27] See also *Mahberet Menahem*, p. 111, s.v. *gr* II.

[28] Rashi here responds to the exegetical question, "What is the meaning of *lĕ῾ôlām*? Does it mean 'to the world' as it can mean only in late Heb., or does it mean 'forever' as in Biblical Heb.?"

[29] Here Rashi supplies the missing direct object of the verb 'I WILL DECLARE'.

[30] For Esau as the quintessentially wicked person see Rashi at Ps. 58:4.

[31] The descendants of Esau; see Gen. 36.

[32] By the addition of this word Rashi intimates that the parallelism is synthetic rather than antithetic, that the degradation of Esau and the exaltation of Israel are sequential rather than simultaneous, that Israel's security depends upon the subjugation of his adversaries.

[33] The expression *hĕrîm qeren*, lit., 'lift up the horn', is often used to mean 'lift up the head', referring to postures of joy, pride, or arrogance; see above, n. 16; see also Gruber, *Aspects*, p. 354, n. 1; pp. 605-606. Hence 'cut off the horns' serves as a metaphor for 'degrade' while 'exalt the horns of PN' serves as a metaphor for 'exalt the status of PN'.

1   FOR THE LEADER; WITH INSTRUMENTAL MUSIC.
2   GOD HAS MADE HIMSELF KNOWN IN JUDAH.
4   THERE HE BROKE THE ARROWS OF THE BOW of Sennacherib and his troops.[1] [As for] rišĕpê qāšet 'THE AR-ROWS OF THE BOW' [the element rišĕpê in] rišĕpê qāšet 'THE ARROWS OF THE BOW' is not the same word [as the element rišpê in] rišpê 'ēš 'sparks'[2] (Cant. 8:6), [3] for the expression rišpê 'ēš is not employed with reference to a bow. Moreover, the form attested here (in Ps. 76:4) exhibits the spirantized form [of the letter p] while rišpê 'ēš exhibits the plosive form [of the letter p].[4] Now [the element rišĕpê in] rišĕpê qāšet is a form of [the word rešep in] ûlĕḥumê rešep "consumed by an arrow"[5] (Deut. 32:24), which we render into Aramaic as 'ôp 'flying',[6] and in the same vein [it is stated in Job. 5:7], "the sons of Resheph ascend 'to fly [ʿûp]." The latter [expression bĕnê rešep] is also a synonym of arrows [ḥiṣṣîm], which fly in accord with what is stated in the Bible (in Ps. 91:15), "or the arrow that flies by day." [Hence], THERE HE BROKE rišĕpê qāšet [means, "THERE HE BROKE] arrows, which the bow sends flying."
5a   YOU ARE nāʾôr, GLORIOUS.
      [The adjective] nāʾôr is a cognate of [the verb niʾēr 'spurn' in][7] "He spurned His Temple" (Lam. 2:7); "You spurned the covenant with Your servant" (Ps. 89:40). [Hence, YOU ARE nāʾôr means that You] repudiate Your enemies and Your foes, and You sweep them away from the world. He is called nāʾôr 'spurning' in respect of His deeds just as [He is called] ḥannûn (Ex. 22:26; Joel 2:13; Jon. 4:2; etc.) and raḥûm 'merciful'[8] (Ex. 34:6; Deut. 4:31; Ps. 78:38; etc.), qannōʾ wĕnōqēm 'passionate and avenging' (Nah. 1:2) [respectively] because He is ḥōnēn 'dispensing grace' (Ps. 37:21, 26; etc.), and He is mĕraḥēm 'dispensing mercy'[9] (Ps. 116:5), and He is mĕqannē' 'passionate' (Num. 11:29) and He is nōqēm 'avenging' (Ps. 99:8).[10]
5b   MORE MAJESTIC THAN THE MOUNTAINS OF PREY.

[I.e.], stronger than preying giants, who are tall as mountains,[11] but in Your presence their power is not noticed.

6a ’eštôlělû 'WERE DESPOILED' [corresponds in meaning to] hisštôlělû. [There appears here the prefix ’aleph instead of the prefix he"[12] in the perfect of the hitpa‘el] just as in "Afterward, Ahaziahu ’ethabbar with Jehoshaphat" (2 Ch. 20:35)[13] [where the latter verb] corresponds in meaning to hithabbēr 'entered into a partnership'.[14] [The verb form] ’eštôlělû is derived from the same root[15] as [that from which is derived the noun šôlāl in] "He brings counselors[16] to šôlāl " (Job. 12:17), and this [noun šôlāl] is a synonym of mišgeh 'error' and a cognate of[17] [Aram.] šālû 'fault' (Dan. 6:5). [The verb ’eštôlělû means] 'they err like fools'. Now the taw is placed in the hitpa‘el conjugation in the middle of the verb as is the case with any verb whose first root letter is shin.[18]

6b THEY SLEPT [nāmû] THEIR SLEEP [šěnātām]. [I.e.], they dozed off [nirděmû] into sleep. [The verb nāmû 'THEY SLEPT'] is a cognate of [the noun] těnûmāh[19] 'slumber'.[20]

6c COULD NOT FIND THEIR HANDS, i.e.,[21] their strength, when You came to exact punishment from them.

7 HE LAY STUNNED AND CHARIOT AND HORSE. The wāw of wěrekeb 'AND CHARIOT' is lexically insignificant just as in "And these are the children of Zibeon: and Aiah [wě’ayyāh] and Anah" (Gen. 36:24) the wāw of wě’ayyāh is lexically insignificant.[22]

8 EVER SINCE YOUR ANGER. I.e., from the time when You became angry.

9 IN HEAVEN YOU PRONOUNCED SENTENCE. When Isaiah prophesied concerning the punishment of Sennacherib, and it [the prophecy] was fulfilled with respect to him [Sennacherib], THE LAND of Israel, which WAS AFRAID of him [Sennacherib] and of his troops, then CALMED DOWN.[23]

10a AS GOD ROSE TO EXECUTE JUDGMENT [i.e.] to execute JUDGMENT against His enemies.

10b TO DELIVER Hezekiah and the people associated with him.[24]

11a FOR HUMAN ANGER PRAISES YOU. The anger of the wicked causes people to thank the Holy One Blessed be He [as follows]: When they [the wicked] display their anger so

that the Holy One Blessed be He punishes them, all praise
Him, and they themselves praise Him when they see that
their anger is inconsequential, as we have found in respect
of Nebuchadnezzar: When he threw Hananiah, Mishael,
and Azariah into the fiery furnace, what is stated there in
the Bible? [It is stated], "May the name of [the great]^{25} God
be blessed..." (Dan. 2:20).^{26}

11b   AND THEREBY *taḥgor* THE REST OF THE ANGER.
[I.e.], You delay, and You hinder. [I.e.], the rest of the nations are delayed, and they are prevented from displaying
their arrogance and their anger. [The verb] *taḥgor* is a word
referring to delay in Mishnaic Hebrew [as in the following
baraitha]: "A cut made by a knife is large enough so that it
may stop [*šetaḥgor*] a finger nail."^{27} I heard it said in the
name of R. Eliezer Ha-Gaon, the son of R. Isaac^{28} that he
was wont to use this biblical verse [Ps. 76:11] as proof for
[the meaning of the verb *taḥgor*] in that *baraitha*.^{29} There is
another way to explain this use of [the verb] *ḥăgîrāh* in accord with its usual literal meaning [i.e.], as "a verb referring
to binding".^{30} [If so], its [our verse's] meaning is, "It is fitting for You to gird on anger and to enwrap Yourself in jealousy, for Yours are power and ability." Now the meaning of
this [usage of the noun] *šě'ērît* 'THE LAST BIT' is that since
human anger is insignificant, all the belts of anger have remained in Your domain.

12a   MAKE VOWS AND PAY Your vows.^{31}

12b   ALL WHO ARE AROUND HIM [i.e.], who experience
this deliverance,^{32} and so they did^{33} in accord with what is
stated in the Bible (in Isa. 19:18), "There shall be in Egypt
five cities speaking the language of Canaan and swearing
loyalty to the LORD of Hosts...."^{34}

12c   SHALL BRING TRIBUTE TO THE AWESOME ONE.
Why? Because when He so desires,

13   HE CURBS THE haughty^{35} SPIRIT OF PRINCES, i.e.,
He will lessen their arrogance. *yibṣor* 'HE WILL CURB'
[means] *yěmāʿēt* 'He will decrease' just as [does the same verb
in] "It will not be diminished from them" (Gen. 11:6).^{36} This
entire psalm refers to the fall of Sennacherib, for we have
found no enemy falling at Jerusalem except for him.

PSALM LXXVI NOTES

[1] See below at v. 12, n. 33.

[2] Literally, 'arrows of fire'; note that the arrow is the symbol of the Canaanite god of pestilence, Resheph; hence rešep comes to mean 'arrow'; see the literature cited in the next note.

[3] Rashi most likely adopts the distinction from *Mahberet Menahem*, p. 356, s.v. ršp. Moses Ibn Gikatilla, quoted by Ibn Ezra here, holds that rišpê 'ēš 'sparks' and rišĕpê qāšet 'arrows of the bow' are one and the same. This view is generally accepted today. Hence RSV renders "flashing arrows'; NJV "fiery arrows of the bow"; see Pope, *Song of Songs*, p. 670, s.v. "darts"; Samuel E. Loewenstamm, "Rešep" *EM* 7:437-441 (in Hebrew); Diethelm Conrad,"Der Gott Reschef," *ZAW* 83 (1971), pp. 157-183; Willaim J. Fulco, *The Canaanite God Rešep*, American Oriental Series, Essay 8 (New Haven: American Oriental Society, 1976), p. 60; Yigal Yadin, "New Gleanings on Resheph from Ugarit," in *Biblical and Related Studies Presented to Samuel Iwry*, ed. Ann Kort and Scot Morschauer (Winona Lake, Indiana: Eisenbrauns, 1985), pp. 259-274.

[4] So also Qimhi here.

[5] *Ad hoc* rendering based on Rashi's intimation here that rešep is a synonym of ḥēṣ 'arrow' everywhere except in Cant. 8:6; cf. Gruber, *Aspects*, p. 521: "consumed by pestilence". Note, however, that in his comment at Deut. 32:24 Rashi interprets ûlĕḥumê rešep to mean "attacked by demons". The latter interpretation assumes that rešep means 'demon', and it finds support in Job. 5:7.

[6] Here Rashi refers to Targum Onkelos at Deut. 32:24, wĕ'akîlê 'ôp "consumed by a flying [arrow]".

[7] Qimhi rejects this etymology of nā'ôr as incorrect, and he cites as correct the interpretation of nā'ôr as a *niphal* participle of the root n'r 'be bright'; hence NJV's rendering "resplendent"; KJV's and RSV's "glorious".

[8] Or 'full of love'; see discussion in Gruber, "The Motherhood of God in Second Isaiah," p. 353, n. 6; S. David Sperling, "Biblical rḥm I and rḥm II," *JANES* 19 (1989), pp. 149-159; see also David Kimhi, *Sefer Ha-Shorashim*, ed. J. H. R. Biesenthal and F. Lebrecht (Berlin: G. Bethge, 1947), p. 350b, s.v. rḥm.

[9] Or 'loving'; see the literature cited in the previous note.

[10] Rashi's assertion that nā'ôr belongs to the same class of adjectives as do ḥannûn, raḥûm, and qannō' means that Rashi here anticipates Barth's assigning nā'ôr to the qaṭṭûl class of intransitive adjectives derived from the perfect stem of the verb. See Jakob Barth, *Die Nominalbildung semitischen Sprachen* (2ᵈ ed.; Leipzig: J. C. Hinrichs, 1894) p. 53. This means that the long vowel under the initial nun of nā'ôr is compensation for the doubling of the second letter of the root, which in this case is 'aleph, which cannot be doubled. Rashi's intimation that nā'ôr is a qaṭṭûl adjective is, therefore, to be distinguished from the view referred to by Ibn Ezra and Qimhi and explicitly rejected by the latter, which sees nā'ôr as an example of what Barth calls the qāṭûl class of intransitive adjectives derived from the per-

fect of stative verbs whose thematic vowel is o. See Barth, *Nominalbildung*, p. 13. Qimhi cites as examples of the latter class of adjectives *gādôl* 'big' and *qārôb* 'near'. Rashi, like Barth (p. 53) with respect to *raḥûm*, construes *nā'ôr* as belonging to a class of adjectives, which are grammatically passive but functionally active. On this and related phenomena see Chomsky, *David Kimhi's Hebrew Grammar*, p. 365, n. 642. Englander, "A Commentary on Rashi's Grammatical Comments," p. 485b passes over Rashi's comment on Ps. 76:5 in silence.

[11] Here Rashi construes MOUNTAINS OF PREY as a metaphor. NJV's "ON THE MOUNTAINS OF PREY" presupposes emending the initial mem of *mēharĕre ṭārep* to *bĕ* 'in, on'.

[12] It is generally accepted that these two perfect hitpa'el forms with initial *'aleph* rather than initial *he'* are Aramaisms. See *B-L*, pp. 351, 439; Max Wagner, *Die lexikalischen und grammatikalischen Aramaismen im alttestamentlichen Hebräisch*, BZAW, no. 96 (Berlin: Topelmann, 1966), pp. 136-137. It should be pointed out, however, that the preference for *'aleph* over *he'* is less a characteristic of Aramaic vs. Hebrew than a characteristic of Eastern (Mesopotamian) vs. Western (Palestinian) dialects of both Hebrew and Aramaic. For example, BT spells Akiba *'qyb'* while JT spells Akiba *'qybh*.

[13] Our Rashi ms. reverses the order of the names; the biblical text reads, "Jehoshaphat *'etḥabbar* with Ahaziah."

[14] The assertion that Jehoshaphat of Judah and Ahaziah of Israel formed "a trading syndicate" is contradicted by 1 Kgs. 22:50. See the summary of views in Jacob M. Myers, *II Chronicles*, AB, vol. 13 (Garden City, N.Y.: Doubleday, 1965), p. 114, n. 35; pp. 116-117.

[15] This is an *ad hoc* rendering of both the participle *nigzar* 'it is derived' and of the noun *gizrāh* 'root'. See Englander, "Rashi's View of the Weak, *'ayin-'ayin*, and *pe-nun* Roots," pp. 408-409; id., "Grammatical Elements and Terminology in Rashi," pp. 405-408.

[16] Jer. 18:18 (see also Ezek. 7:26) shows that *'ēṣāh* 'counsel' is the quintessential business of the sage; our verse, correctly understood by Rashi here and in his comment at Job. 12:17, says simply that God, as author and owner of all that is, including both wisdom and error (Job. 12:16), has the wherewithal to transform the sage—the quintessential counselor—into a fool who gives bad advice; see also Job. 12:20 where *ṭa'am* is the etymological and semantic equivalent of Akk. *ṭēmu* 'understanding'.

[17] Since Rashi employs the term *lĕšôn* to mean both 'synonym of' and 'cognate of', he can say that *šôlāl* is *lĕšôn mišgeh wĕšālû*.

[18] I.e., following the first root letter as an infix rather than as part of the prefix as is normally the case; see *GKC* #19n; 54b; see Rashi at Ps. 73:21 and n. 53 there.

[19] Contra Maarsen here, *Mahberet Menahem*, s.v. *nm*, is not the source of Rashi's comment here.

[20] *tĕnûmāh* 'slumber' is attested as a b-word for *šēnāh* 'sleep' in Ps. 132:4; Prov. 6:4 while pl. *tĕnûmôt* 'slumber' is attested as a b-word for pl. *šēnôt*

'sleep' at Prov. 6:10; 24:33; *těnûmôt* appears to be a b-word for *tardēmāh* 'dozing' at Job. 33:15.

[21] Rashi employs exegetical *waw* to show that here HANDS is employed as a metaphor for strength.

[22] Heb. *ṭěpēlāh*. Rashi here follows Dunash Ibn Labrat, *Teshuvot Dunash*, p. 23. The latter was challenged by Menahem b. Jacob Ibn Saruq, Ibn Janah, Profirat Duran, et al.; see Profirat Duran, *Ma'aseh Ephod*, cap. 13, reprinted also in *Mahberet Menahem*, ed. Filipowski, p. 76. The Rabbinic and Medieval Heb. adjective *ṭěpēlāh*. appears to be the etymological and semantic equivalent of Biblical Heb. *tāpēl* 'tasteless'. On the latter adjective see Rashi at Job. 6:6 and Lam. 2:4. The use of this adjective to mean 'lexically insignificant' corresponds to Gersonides' use of the expression *wěṭa'ămô*, lit., 'and its taste is', to mean 'its meaning is'; see passim in Gersonides' commentaries on the Pentateuch and Job. In his comment on Gen. 36:24 Rashi employs the term *wāw yětêrāh* 'superfluous *wāw*'. Rashi's comments at Gen. 36:24 and here at Ps. 76:7 belie the popular notion that Rashi finds meaning in every insignificant feature of the Biblical text.

[23] On the midrashic source of Rashi's comment here see below, n. 33. The midrash answers the following exegetical questions: (1) which SENTENCE? (2) which LAND WAS AFRAID? (3) how could it have CALMED DOWN? Failure to reckon with Rashi's insight that WAS AFRAID and CALMED DOWN must be sequential rather than simultaneous, KJV and RSV render "the earth feared, and was still"; cf. also NJV's 'the earth was numbed with fright". The assertion that the SENTENCE referred to an event, which took place at a specific time in the land of Israel requires that *'ereṣ* 'the land/the world' must denote 'the land [of Israel]' rather than 'the world'.

[24] Here Rashi substitutes for the psalmist's ALL THE LOWLY OF THE EARTH a reference to specific historical persons.

[25] This adjective added in our Rashi ms. is not found in the biblical text here quoted.

[26] This is the biblical prooftext cited also in the standard printings of Rashi's commentary here. Other mss. and Maarsen's edition, however, quote here Dan. 3:28, q.v., which is more appropriate in the present context, which attempts to answer the exegetical question, "How does human anger lead to the praise of God?"; contrast the midrash attributed to R. Levi in JT Ma'aserot 3:4.

[27] Cf. the slightly different wording of the baraitha in BT Berakot 37b: "Now how large is a cut? It is large enough so that it may stop a finger nail."

[28] Also called Eliezer the Great and Eliezer b. Isaac of Worms; fl. 11th cent. C.E. A disciple of Rabbenu Gershom, he headed the *yeshivah* at Mainz, where he taught Isaac b. Judah, who was Rashi's teacher.

[29] Heb. *Mishnah*. In my paper, "Deciphering Rashi: the Case of the term *lashon*," presented at the International Meeting of the Society of Biblical Literature in Jerusalem (August 1986) I argued, *inter alia*, that in

Rashi's Hebrew *leshon Mishnah* designates early Rabbinic, i.e., Tannaitic Hebrew represented by Mishnah, Tosefta, Baraitha, Tannaitic midrashim, while *leshon 'aggadah* designates later Rabbinic, i.e., Amoraic Hebrew as exemplified by the Amoraic midrashim and the Amoraic Hebrew passages in the Talmuds. Subsequently, the late Prof. Pinchas Peli kindly shared with me a letter addressed to him in October 1968 by the late Prof. Saul Lieberman in which the latter already demonstrates that *leshon Mishnah* in the Hebrew of Rashi and the Tosafists means Tannaitic Hebrew, such as "the dialect of baraitha as opposed to the Amoraic dialect." Hence it should not be surprsing that here also Rashi employs the term *Mishnah* to designate a *baraitha.*

[30] *Mahberet Menahem*, p. 168, s.v. *ḥgr.*

[31] Here Rashi supplies the missing direct object of the verbs VOW and PAY.

[32] Answering the exegetical question, "What is the meaning of ALL WHO ARE AROUND HIM?"

[33] As pointed out by Maarsen here, Rashi alludes here to a midrash quoted in extenso in Rashi at Isa. 19:18. According to this midrash, which Rashi attributes to Seder Olam [chapter 23], Isaiah's prophecy was already fulfilled when in reaction to the disastrous plague at Lachish (2 Kgs. 19:35) Sennacherib disbanded his army. The Egyptian recruits "accepted the kingship of Heaven," and returning home they built an altar to the LORD in Egypt in accord with Isa. 19:20. See Dov Ber Ratner, ed., *Seder Olam Rabbah* (New York: Talmudical Research Institute, 1966), p. 194, nn. 42ff.

[34] In the context of Isa. 19 this verse expresses an eschatologcal hope that the hallmarks of the Israelite way of life, to wit, the use of Hebrew as a spoken language and recognition of the LORD of Hosts as God, will be widespread in Egypt.

[35] Rashi's supplying the adjective 'haughty' intimates that in Ps. 76:13 SPIRIT (Heb. *rûăḥ*) by itself refers to haughtiness but that this usage is not self-understood.

[36] Contrast Rashi at Gen. 11:6.

PSALM LXXVII

1   CONCERNING ['al] JEDUTHUN [i.e.], CONCERNING the judgments [haddātôt wĕhaddînîn, i.e., the tribulations], which Israel experiences.[1]

3a   MY HAND [i.e.], my wound.[2]

3b   BY NIGHT IT FLOWS OUT.
During the Exile, which is like NIGHT,[3] its [the wound's][4] moisture and its bitterness FLOWS OUT,
WITHOUT RESPITE. I.e.,[5] its flow does not dissipate.[6]

4a   LET ME RECALL, O GOD, the kindness, which He was accustomed to do for me when He was favorably disposed toward me.[7]

4b   LET ME SPEAK of those kindnesses and favors,

4c   AND LET MY SPIRIT BE OVERWHELMED. [The verb hit'aṭṭēp 'to be overwhelmed' means] pasmer 'to faint' in O.F.[8]

5a   YOU GRASPED THE šĕmûrôt OF MY EYES.[9]
[The noun] šĕmûrôt is a biform of [the noun 'ašmûrôt 'vigils' in the phrase] 'ašmûrôt laylāh 'night vigils'.[10] [Here the psalmist alludes to the fact that normally] when a person wakes up from his sleep, his mind is set at ease, and his [happy] mood returns to him, but I [the psalmist][11] am not so during the night of Exile.[12] My eyes are continually stuck together[13] like those of a sleeping person, [and I am] impervious of heart because of the troubles I experience.[14]

5b   My mood is overwrought,[15] but we are not an instrument of divine revelation.[16]

6   MY THOUGHTS TURN TO DAYS OF OLD, recalling the kindnesses, which You performed with our ancestors.

7a   DURING THE NIGHT LET ME RECALL MY SINGING.
During this Exile, which is like night,[17] I recall my songs, which I used to sing in the Temple.[18]

7b   I COMMUNE WITH MYSELF. [I.e.], I consider.

7c   MY SPIRIT INQUIRES,[19]
"What, in fact, is the attribute of the Holy One Blessed be He?" And I ask,[20]

8 "WILL THE LORD REJECT FOREVER?"

9a HAS HIS FAITHFULNESS DISAPPEARED [*he'āpēs*]?
[I.e.], Is it possible that it was used up?[21]

9b WILL HIS PROMISE BE UNFULFILLED?
[The psalmist here refers to] an ancient decree that He
[God] would never again turn away from His anger.[22]

10a HAS GOD FORGOTTEN to be pitying.[23]
[The form] *ḥannôt* 'HOW TO PITY' is the same grammatical
form as is represented by[24] [the forms] *'ăśôt* 'to do'[25]
[and] *rĕ'ôt* 'to see'.[26] Another equally plausible interpretation
of *ḥannôt* is [that it functions not as an *infinitive finalis* meaning 'to pity' but as a gerund meaning] pitying.[27]

10b HAS HE IN ANGER STIFLED HIS COMPASSION?

11a AND I SAID, "THIS IS TO FRIGHTEN ME."
My thoughts say to me,[28] "This [my suffering] is strictly for
the purpose of instilling in me fright, i.e.,[29] to make me
afraid so that I will return to Him.[30]
[The form] *ḥallôtî* corresponds in meaning to *lĕhallôt*[31] 'for
frightening me'. It is a cognate of *ḥôlî* 'sickness' and *ḥîl* 'terror'.[32]

11b THE RIGHT HAND OF THE MOST HIGH HAS
CHANGED.
[I SAID][33] that THE RIGHT HAND OF THE MOST
HIGH, which had been "glorious in power" (Ex. 15:6a) has
been changed[34] so that now "He has withdrawn His right
hand" (Lam. 2:3).

13 I THOUGHT[35] ABOUT ALL YOUR WORKS, which
You have already done for us.

14 YOUR WAYS ARE HOLINESS.
Your characteristic attribute is to hallow Your Name in the
world by executing punishment against the wicked.[36]

17 THE WATERS SAW YOU...AND WERE CONVULSED
when You were revealed at the [Reed] Sea.

18a CLOUDS ['*ābôt*] STREAMED WATER.
[I.e.], clouds [*šĕḥāqîm*] dripped a stream of thick ['*ăbîm*] water.[37]

18c *ḥăṣāṣêkā* 'YOUR STONES' is a form of the word *ḥāṣāṣ*
'gravel' (Prov. 20:17; Lam. 3:16);[38] it is a cognate of [the
noun *mĕḥaṣĕṣîm* 'chisels' in] "chisels[39] among the watering

places" (Judg. 5:11).

19   IN A WHEEL. As in a wheel.[40]

YOUR THUNDER WAS IN A WHEEL[41] at the [Reed] Sea to confound the Egyptian camp.[42]

20c   YOUR TRACKS COULD NOT BE SEEN.

Footsteps are not discerned upon water.

'iqqĕbôtêkā[43] 'YOUR TRACKS' [means] *treces* [= Eng. 'tracks'] [in Old French].[44]

PSALM LXXVII, NOTES

[1] The immediate source may be Midrash Tehillim here; see also Rashi at Ps. 39:1; 62:1; for the source of this midrash see Rashi's Introduction, n. 24.

[2] Heb. *makkātî*; for the background of this interpretation see Rashi at Ps. 21:9 and our discussion there; see also Rashi at Ps. 81:15. Rashi's interpretation of Ps. 77:3 is reflected in KJV's "My sore ran in the night, and ceased not."

[3] Here Rashi intimates that 'NIGHT' here at Ps. 77:3 is a metaphor for 'Exile'; cf. Rashi at Ps. 74:16.

[4] So Breithaupt.

[5] Explicative *waw*.

[6] We construe the reading *tāmîd* 'continually' found in our Rashi ms. as scribal error for *tāmîr*; concerning the latter reading see the discussion in Breithaupt and in Maarsen here.

[7] Here Rashi supplies the missing direct object of the transitive verb *'ezkĕrāh* 'LET ME RECALL'.

[8] See Levy, *Contribution*, #784.

[9] The form is attested only here. Most moderns interpret *šĕmûrôt 'ênāy* to mean 'my eyelids'; see Briggs; RSV; NEB; NJV. Rashi's interpretation was anticipated by Symmachus and Aquila. Note, however, that despite Rashi's etymological comment here, Rashi's running commentary on the verse is much more compatible with the interpretation 'eyelids'.

[10] The precise phrase *'ašmûrôt laylāh* is unattested in the Bible. The phrase *'ašmûrāh ballaylāh* 'watch in the night' is found in Ps. 90:4. Moreover, the term *'ašmûrôt* clearly designates divisions of the night in Judg. 7:19; Ps. 63:7; 119:148; and Lam. 2:19.

[11] Who personifies Israel.

[12] See above, at v. 3

[13] So that I cannot open my eyes.

[14] Rashi sees in the psalmist's assertion that God has grasped his eyelids so that he cannot see (see n. 9 above) a metaphor for the absence of prophetic revelation in the Exile; see nn. 15, 16.

[15] Rashi's paraphrase of the biblical text alludes to the fact that everywhere else in the Bible the verb *pā'am* 'to be overwrought' is employed with the noun *rûăḥ* 'mood'. He suggests that *nip'amtî* 'I WAS OVER-

WROUGHT' means *pāʿămāh rûḥî* 'My mood is overwrought'. By so doing, Rashi equates the psalmist's [=Israel's] despair at the absence of prophetic revelation with Pharaoh's despair at being unable to interpret his dreams in Gen. 41:8, where it is stated that when Pharaoh awoke from his dreams *wattippāʿēm rûḥô* "his mood was overwrought."

[16] In keeping with his understanding of the basic idea of the verse (see n. 14), Rashi takes *wĕlōʾ ʾădabbēr*, lit., "I DO NOT SPEAK" (cf. NJV's "I cannot speak") as an allusion to the absence of *dibbûr* "the revelation of God in the form of a locution" (Kadushin, *A Conceptual Approach to the Mekhilta*, p. 36), i.e., 'prophecy'. The implication of the verse, as construed by Rashi, is that divine revelation would calm Israel's disturbed mood just as Joseph's dream interpretation calmed Pharaoh's disturbed mood.

[17] Cf. Rashi at v. 3 and at v. 4.

[18] Rashi's source is the midrash attributed to R. Judah b. R. Simeon in PRK, ed. Mandelbaum, pp. 281-83.

[19] By his paraphrase Rashi intimates that the long imperfect *ʾāśîḥāh* 'LET ME COMMUNE' and the imperfect with *waw*-conversive *wayĕḥappēś* 'AND HE INQUIRED' are both employed in Ps. 77:7 to express the present.

[20] Rashi's added *verbum dicendi* expresses most clearly what the psalmist sought to convey by means of the circumlocution "MY SPIRIT INQUIRED."

[21] Rashi clarifies the meaning of the rare stative verb *ʾāpēs* 'to disappear'.

[22] Cf. PRK, ed. Mandelbaum, p. 282.

[23] Rashi paraphrases employing the infinitive of the verb 'to be' followed by the *polel* participle in place of the psalmist's rare usage, which Rashi discusses immediately below.

[24] Heb. *lĕśôn;* other mss. of Rashi's commentary employ the synonymous *kĕmô;* cf. the discussion of these expressions in our introduction, pp. 140–146.

[25] Gen. 2:4; Ps.109:16; etc.

[26] Ex. 10:28, 29; Num. 35:23; 1 Sam. 17:28. Rashi's point here is that the form *ḥannôt,* which is attested only here, is, like the frequently attested *ʿăśôt and rĕʾôt,* an infinitive construct. The double *nun* would seem to reflect the geminate root *ḥnn*; however, Jakob Barth, *Wurzeluntersuchungen* (Leipzig: J.C. Hinrichs, 1902), p. 21 argues that the root is not *ḥnn* but *ḥnh,* which is to say, in contemporary terms, *ḥny*; so also GKC #67r; HG, p. 135, n. f. For Rashi, however, our *ḥnn* and our *ḥny* are subsumed under the homonymous biliteral roots *ḥn;* cf. *Maḥberet Menaḥem,* p. 181.

[27] Rashi here proposes not an alternative to his earlier grammatical comment but a slight modification of his earlier comment on the meaning of the form in question.

[28] Here Rashi answers the exegetical question, "To whom did the psalmist say this?" Rashi's answer intimates that here the verb *ʾāmar,* lit., 'to say', is employed in the nuance 'to think'.

[29] Explicative *waw* employed before a familiar verb form used to explain a less familiar verb form, which is alleged to be cognate to the noun Rashi interprets here.

[30] Cf. PRK, ed. Mandelbaum, p. 283.

[31] Rashi's point is that the infinitve construct without the prefixed *lamed* here functions as a gerund just as it would with the prefixed *lamed*.

[32] Mandelkern lists these nouns under the distinct roots *ḥlh* (p. 395) and *ḥwl* (p. 374) respectively; so *BDB*, pp. 317, 296; *K-B³*, pp. 303, 298. Rashi, however, derives both nouns from a single biliteral root *ḥl*; contrast *Mahberet Menahem*, p. 174, which treats the two nouns as derivatives of the homonymous biliteral roots *ḥl* V and *ḥl* VI respectively.

[33] I supply the verb 'I SAID' from v. 11a as required by Rashi's prefacing v. 11b with the relative particle *'ăšēr*, which implies that v. 11b belongs to the speech introduced by the verb 'I SAID' in v. 11a.

[34] Heb. *ništannēt; nitpaʿel* participle of the verb *šānāh* 'change', the *qal* infinitive construct of which appears in v. 11b.

[35] Heb. *wĕhāgîtî;* here rendered according to Rashi's understanding of the meaning of the verb *hāgāh;* see Rashi at Ps. 1:2 and our discussion there. Our Rashi ms. reads by haplography *whgyt* 'You thought' instead of *whgyty* 'I THOUGHT'.

[36] Cf. Isa. 5:16: "And the LORD of Hosts is exalted by judgment, The Holy God proved holy by retribution."

[37] This comment seems to attempt to answer the exegetical question as to why in Hebrew clouds are called, *inter alia*, *ʿābôt*, lit., 'thicks'; contrast *Mahberet Menahem*, p. 274, which treats *ʿb* 'cloud' as distinct from *ʿb* 'be thick'; so also *BDB*, which derives *ʿāb* 'cloud' from a root *ʿwb* (*BDB*, p. 727f.), which is distinct from the verb *ʿābāh* 'to be thick' (*BDB*, p. 716a).

[38] *Mahberet Menahem*, p. 185, s.v. *ḥṣ* II.

[39] So the Middle High German gloss *kisel* in the printed edition of Rashi's commentary at Judg. 5:11.

[40] Rashi, followed by NJV, converts the psalmist's metaphor into a simile.

[41] Cf. Rashi's previous comment, and see previous note.

[42] Cf. Ex. 14:24.

[43] So MT; our Rashi ms. reads, however, *ʿăqēbôtēkā*.

[44] Concerning this gloss see Rashi at Gen. 49:19; Jer. 13:22; Ps. 40:16; 56:7; 70:4; 119:33; Cant. 1:8.

PSALM LXXVIII

1a-b A MASKIL OF ASAPH. GIVE EAR, MY PEOPLE, TO MY TEACHING.[1]

2 LET ME EXPOUND AN APHORISM OF MY MOUTH. These are words of Torah.[2]

4 WE WILL NOT WITHHOLD THEM FROM THEIR CHILDREN.[3] [I.e], we also WILL NOT WITHHOLD FROM THEIR, our fathers'[4] CHILDREN, by not informing them of what THEY [OUR FATHERS][5] TOLD US (v. 3).

7 *kislām* 'THEIR CONFIDENCE'[6] [i.e.], *tôḥāltām* 'their hope'.[7] The same usage of the word [*kesel*] is found in "Did I make gold my confidence?" (Job. 31:24).

8 LIKE THEIR FATHERS, who were in Egypt and in the wilderness.[8]

9a THE EPHRAIMITE, who left Egypt by violent means[9] before the appointed time,[10] and they relied upon their own prowess and upon their weaponry,[11] and the end result of their behavior was

9c that they HAD TO TURN BACK IN THE DAY OF BATTLE as it is explained in the Book of Chronicles, "The men of Gath, born in the land, killed them"[12] (1 Ch. 7:21).

9b *rômê* [i.e.], 'casting and throwing' [BOWS]. [The construct pl. *rômê*] is a cognate of [the verb *rāmāh* 'hurl' in] *rāmāh bayyām* "He hurled...into the sea" (Ex. 15:1b).[13]

12 HE PERFORMED MARVELS IN THE SIGHT OF THEIR FATHERS. Afterwards, when the appointed time[14] arrived, they also WENT ON SINNING AGAINST HIM (v. 17) as he [the psalmist] concludes further on.
IN THE SIGHT OF THEIR FATHERS [means that] Abraham, Isaac, and Jacob came to the [Reed] Sea, and the Holy One Blessed be He showed them how He would redeem their descendants.[15]

13 LIKE A WALL [*nôd*] [i.e.], "a tall heap,"[16] in consonance with the way we render into Aramaic [the noun *nôd* 'wall' in] "They stood like a wall" (Ex. 15:6) [sc.], *kĕšûr* 'like a wall'.[17]

15a HE SPLIT ROCKS. [Here the psalmist refers to] "You shall strike the rock..." (Ex. 17:6).

15b HE GAVE THEM DRINK WITHIN[18] THE MIGHTY ABYSS. [It means that] even when they were within [bĕtôk] the [Reed] Sea, whose waters are salty, He provided for them springs of sweet water within [bĕtôk] the abyss.[19]

16b AND HE MADE TO DESCEND LIKE THE RIVERS WATERS, which were flowing from the well, and the [twelve tribal] princes[20] were making ridges with their staffs so that the waters were following after them toward the encampment of each and every tribe. [This interpretation is] in accord with what is stated in the Bible (in Num. 21:18), "with maces, with their own staffs," as it is expounded in Forty-Nine Rules.[21]

17b DEFYING [lamĕrôt] [i.e.], 'provoking' [lĕhaqnît.].[22] It is the same verb as is attested in "You were mamrîm 'defiant'" (Deut.9:7).[23]

20 šĕ'ēr 'FLESH'. [I.e.], bāśār 'meat'.[24]

21b FIRE BROKE OUT AGAINST JACOB. [The verb niśśĕqāh 'IT BROKE OUT'] is the same verb as [the verb wĕhiśśîqû 'and they shall kindle' in] "And they shall make fire, and they shall kindle" (Ezek. 39:9), which is a verb referring to kindling and burning.[25] [This verse] corresponds to what is written in the Torah, "A fire of the LORD broke out [wattib'ar] against them" (Num. 11:1).

25a A HUMAN ATE BREAD OF 'abbîrîm [i.e.], angels' bread.[26] Another equally plausible interpretation of [BREAD OF 'abbîrîm is that] 'abbîrîm is [a biform of] 'ēbārîm 'limbs' [and that the manna was called 'bread of limbs'] because it was [totally] absorbed by the limbs [of the body] so that they [the wilderness generation of Israel] were not required to use the organs of elimination.[27]

26 HE SET THE EAST WIND MOVING. [Here the psalmist refers to what is narrated in Num. 11:31], "A wind...started up, brought quail...."

30a lō' zārû FROM THEIR CRAVING. [I.e.], they did not become estranged [zārîm] FROM THEIR CRAVING when they had achieved all THEIR CRAVING.

30b THE FOOD WAS STILL IN THEIR MOUTHS [refers to] "The meat was still between their teeth, not yet chewed,

when the anger of the LORD blazed forth against the
people" (Num. 11:33).[28] Another equally plausible interpretation of *lō' zārû* (v. 30a) is [the following]: They had not yet
been separated FROM THEIR CRAVING when they experienced the trouble and the punishment.[29]

31   AND THE YOUTH OF [*băḥûrê*] ISRAEL [i.e.], the choic-
est [*nibḥārîm*] among them.
"*wĕhā'sapsup* among them" (Num. 11:4) are the elders,[30] for
[concerning the elders] it is stated in the Bible, "Gather for
Me ['*espāh-lî*] seventy men [of the elders of Israel]" (Num.
11:16).[31]

34   WHEN HE STRUCK THEM, THEY TURNED TO
HIM....
This [apparent repentance] was also not in honesty; it was
only deceitful speech (v. 36a):

36b   THEY LIED TO HIM WITH THEIR WORDS.

37a   THEIR HEART, unlike their mouth, WAS INCON-
STANT TOWARD HIM,

38a   BUT nevertheless,[32] HE BEING MERCIFUL to them and
even wiping away[33] their INIQUITY continually, did not
DESTROY them.[34]

38b   AND HE WAS FREQUENT—many times—TO TURN
HIS ANGER from them,[35] and even when He exacted punishment[36] from them,

38c   HE did NOT STIR UP[37] against them ALL HIS VE-
NOM[38] but only a very little.[39]

39   [FOR HE REMEMBERED THAT THEY WERE BUT
FLESH, A PASSING BREATH THAT DOES NOT RE-
TURN].[40] [The verse means that] since[41] He remembered[42]
THAT THEY WERE FLESH and that the evil inclination
is embedded in their hearts and that this [evil inclination] is
A SPIRIT THAT DEPARTS when they [humans] die, and
that that SPIRT WILL NOT RETURN to them in the future era, [for] when they experience resurrection, the evil
inclination will not have dominion over them. It is [theologi-
cally] untenable to interpret A SPIRIT THAT DEPARTS
BUT DOES NOT RETURN [to mean] 'their SPIRIT OF
LIFE, which is in them',[43] for if you so interpret, you deny
[the dogma of] the resurrection of the dead. Thus it is
pointed out in Aggadat Tehillim.[44]

40 HOW MANY times[45] DID THEY DEFY HIM continually[46] IN THE WILDERNESS?

41 *hitwû*. [This is] a verb referring to [making] a sign as is demonstrated by *wehitwîtā tāw* "You shall make the sign of a *taw*"
(Ezek. 9:4).[47] Now a sign is an expression referring to a portent and a testing. [This is to say that *hitwû* means], "They
sought from Him a symbol and a sign" [as in Ex. 17:7]: "Is
the LORD present among us or not?"

45 [HE SENT...A FROG],[40] AND IT DESTROYED THEM.
[I.e.], they [the frogs] castrated them [the Egyptians].[48]

47b BY MEANS OF *ḥănāmal*. [This is] the name of [a kind of]
locust.[49] However, a midrash based upon it [takes *baḥănāmal*
not as 'by means of a locust' but as an abbreviation of the
sentence] *bā' ḥān ûmāl* "he came, he camped, and he cut
down."[50] [This abbreviation means that] it cut down the
herbage and the grass, and it consumed them.

48a HE GAVE THEIR BEASTS OVER TO HAIL.
When the HAIL began to fall (see Ex. 9:22-23), the Egyptian would attempt to hide his flock in the house, but the
HAIL became a sort of barrier in front of him. Then the
Egyptian would slaughter it [his sheep] and place it on his
shoulder to carry it home to eat it. Then a bird would come
and take it away from him. Now this is [what is referred to
in the second half of the verse]:

48b THEIR CATTLE TO THE RESHEPHS [i.e.], to the birds
as is demonstrated by "The young *reshephs* go high to fly"
(Job. 5:7).[51] This [interpretation of *lārĕšāpîm* 'TO THE
RESHEPHS'] is a midrash based upon it. However, according to its literal meaning, *lārĕšāpîm* [here at Ps. 78:48b] refers
to *rišpê 'ēš* 'fiery darts' (Cant. 8:6)[52] in consonace with what
is written (in Ex. 9:24), "...fire flashing amidst the hail."

50a HE CLEARED A PATH FOR HIS ANGER. Even though
the plagues were sent in anger, they performed only the service for which they were sent. What they were commanded
to kill they killed but not every [living thing, for] they [the
plagues] walked [only] in their own paths.[53]

50c THEIR LIVES [*ḥayyātām*] [i.e.], their bodies [*gûpām*].

55a HE EXPELLED...BEFORE THEM seven nations.[54]

55c IN THEIR [i.e.], the Gentiles'[55] TENTS.

56 YET THEY DEFIANTLY TESTED [GOD, MOST

HIGH][56] in the period of the judges.

57   LIKE A TREACHEROUS BOW, which does not deliver the arrow to the target designated by the archer.[57]

61   HE LET HIS MIGHT GO INTO CAPTIVITY. [I.e.], He handed over the Ark and the tablets [of the decalogue] to the Philistines.[58]

63a   FIRE CONSUMED THEIR YOUNG MEN. [This refers to] the fire of His [God's] anger.

63c   THEY WERE NOT SUNG A NUPTIAL SONG. [I.e.], they [THEIR MAIDENS] were not led into the palanquin and the bridal chamber because the young men [whom they were supposed to marry] died in the war.[59] [The verb] hullālû 'THEY WERE SUNG A NUPTIAL SONG' is a cognate of [the noun] hillûlā' 'wedding' in Aramaic. Our rabbis interpreted it [v. 63] as referring to Nadab and Abihu.[60] I am not intellectually satisfied so to interpret it, because, look, he [the psalmist] already began [in v. 60 to refer to] the Tabernacle of Shiloh.[61]

64a   THEIR PRIESTS FELL BY THE SWORD. [The priests referred to here are] Hophni and Phineas (1 Sam. 4:17).

64b   AND THEIR WIDOWS COULD NOT WEEP.[62] Even the widows were not allowed to mourn him for, in fact, she [the wife of Phineas] also died on the day of the report [concerning the capture of the Ark and the death of Eli and Phineas] in accord with what is stated in the Bible, "She squatted, and she gave birth,[63] for she experienced her uterine contractions" (1 Sam. 4:19).[64]

65b   SHAKING OFF [mitrônēn], [i.e.] awakening and regaining strength like a warrior waking up from his wine. [The participle] mitrônēn is a cognate of [the gerund] rinnāh 'joyful song' (Isa. 14:7; 44:23; Ps. 30:6; 42:5; 47:2; 118:15; etc.).

66   HE STRUCK HIS FOES IN THE BACK. [I.e., He afflicted them with] afflictions of the buttocks, i.e., hemorrhoids,[65] and this is for them a shameful insult[66] for all time.[67]

67   HE REJECTED THE TABERNACLE OF JOSEPH. This is Shiloh, which is in the territory of Joseph.[68]

69   HE BUILT HIS SANCTUARY LIKE THE HEAVENS. [The parallelism LIKE THE HEAVENS/LIKE THE EARTH suggests that the psalmist means] like the heavens

and the earth, concerning which mention is made in the Bible of two hands, for it is stated in the Bible, "The sanctuary, O LORD, which Your hands established" (Ex. 15:17). An equally plausible interpretation of LIKE THE HEAVENS/LIKE THE EARTH HE ESTABLISHED IT is that just as they [the heavens and the earth] have no replacement so does the Temple have no replacement for providing an abode for the Divine Presence.[69]

70   FROM THE SHEEPFOLDS [*miklĕ'ōt ṣō'n*] [i.e.], from the sheds of [*dîrê*] the flock. [The feminine plural construct *miklĕ'ōt*] is a form of the same noun as is attested in the singular in "Sheep have vanished from the fold" (Hab. 3:17).

71   FROM MINDING THE NURSING EWES. For when he was shepherding the nursing flock for his father he was kind. Hence he would lead out the kids first, and he would feed them the uppermost parts of the grass, which are soft. After them he would lead out the rams, who eat the middle parts of the grass, and afterwards he would lead out the old ewes, who eat the roots. The Holy One Blessed be He remarked, "This man is fit to shepherd My people."[70]

PSALM LXXVIII, NOTES

[1] In our Rashi ms. this line serves as the title of the psalm, which is designated in the margin as Ps. 76.

[2] Here Rashi alludes to the assertion in Midrash Tehillim that psalms and wisdom literature no less than the Pentateuch and the Prophets constitute Torah. For additional literature on this Rabbinic attitude see Mayer I. Gruber, "The Meaning of *'ōrāyĕtā'* in the Babylonian Talmud," *Hebrew Studies* 22 (1981), p. 32, n. 22.

[3] *BH*[3] suggests the emendation *bānênû* 'our children'. Dahood, here, responding to the same exegetical difficulty, namely, that the members of the generation following the psalmist's are called not 'our children' but 'THEIR (i.e., our fathers'; see v. 3) CHILDREN', argues that *bānîm* here means 'grandchildren'.

[4] Rashi's response to the exegetical difficulty discussed in the previous note.

[5] Rashi does not quote the bracketed portion of the verse. I have supplied it for clarity.

[6] See Held, "Studies in Comparative Semitic Lexicography," p. 403.

[7] Cf. *Mahberet Menahem*, p. 219, s.v. *ksl* I.

[8] Cf. Yalqut Shim'oni, pt. 1 #242; pt. 2 #819.

[9] Heb. *bizĕrôā'*, lit., 'by arm'.

[10] Heb. *lipĕnê haqqēṣ*. Note that here as in Rashi at Ps. 46:6; 78:12; 130:6, Rabbinic Heb. *qēṣ* corresponds in meaning to Biblical Heb. and

Phoenician *'ēt* and to Biblical Heb. *mô'ēd* 'appointed time'; this meaning of *qēṣ* is attested also in Biblical Heb. in Hab. 2:3, q.v.

[11] Lit., 'their arrows'.

[12] The sons of Ephraim; cf. Rashi at Ex. 15:14. The source of the midrash quoted by Rashi both here at Ps. 78:9 and there at Ex. 15:14 is Mekilta at Ex. 15:14. By asserting that the sons of Ephraim left Egypt by violent means in advance of the canonical Exodus described in the Pentateuch (Ex. 1-15) and alluded to in the Prophets (Jer. 2:6; Hos. 12:14; Am. 9:7), the midrash solves the exegetial difficulty presented by the Book of Chronicles' portrayal of the sons of Ephraim living in the land of Israel without benefit of the Exodus. On the absence of the Exodus in the ideology of the Book of Chronicles see Sara Japhet, *The Ideology of the Book of Chronicles and Its Place in Biblical Thought* (Jerusalem: Bialik, 1977), pp. 319-333 (in Hebrew); for modern attempts to reconcile 1 Ch. 7:21 with the Exodus tradition see there, p. 320, n. 383; for the rabbinic traditions, which respond to this exegetical problem see Gerald J. Blidstein, "The Ephraimite Exodus: A Re-Evaluation," *Jerusalem Studies in Jewish Thought* 5 (1986), pp. 1-13 (in Hebrew). Note that the midrash Rashi quotes at Ps. 78:9 anticipates the modern historians, who hold that there was more than one Exodus from Egypt; see, *inter alia*, Kevin G. O'Connell, "Exodus," in *Harper's Bible Dictionary*, ed. Paul J. Achtemeier (San Francisco: Harper & Row, 1986), pp. 288-291.

[13] Both forms are listed in most mss. of *Mahberet Menahem* under *rm* IV, which corresponds to *BDB*, p. 941 *rāmāh* I 'cast, shoot'.

[14] Heb. *qēṣ*; see above, n. 10.

[15] The source of this midrash is Gen. Rabbah 92:2. This midrash is inspired by the fact that in Rabbinic literature the noun *'abot*, lit., 'fathers', usually designates not simply 'ancestors' but specifically the three patriarchs—Abraham, Isaac, and Jacob.

[16] Cf. Rashi at Ex. 15:8.

[17] T.O. at Ex. 15:8.

[18] As noted by Maarsen here, following *Minhat Shay*, Rashi here relies on a biblical text, which reads *bitĕhômôt* rather than the generally accepted reading *kittĕhômôt*. The latter reading accounts for KJV's "as if from the mighty abyss." Rashi's reading is supported by many medieval mss.; see *BH³*. Perhaps the best reading would be *mittĕhômôt rabbāh* 'from the mighty abyss'. It is reasonable to assume that an original *mem* could have been misread as *bet* in the paleo-Hebrew script while the *bet*, in turn, was readily confused with *kaph* in the square script. Alternatively, original *bitĕhômôt* may itself mean 'from the abyss' if we accept the view of Sarna, "The Interchangeability of the Prepositions *Beth* and *Mem* in Biblical Hebrew," pp. 310-316. However, Rashi's remarks here show that he understood *bitĕhômôt* to mean 'in the abyss'.

[19] Cf. Mekilta, ed. Lauterbach, vol. 1, p. 225, lines 27-31; Midrash Tehillim at Ps. 114 #7; both employ as prooftexts Ps. 78:16. Maarsen here notes that Rashi differs from the Rabbinic sources in his use of *bitĕhômôt* 'in the abyss' as a prooftext.

[20] Heb. *hannĕśî'îm*; cf. Num. 7:10ff.

[21] In his commentary at Ex. 26:5 Rashi refers to the Baraitha of Forty-Nine Rules while in his commentary at Ex. 27:6 he refers to the "Mishnah of Forty-Nine". Benjamin Weiss, "Mishnat ha-Middot," *EJ* 12:109 and Yitzhak Dov Gilat, "Baraita de-Melekhet ha-Mishkan," *EJ* 4:193-194 follow Louis Ginzberg, "Baraitha of Forty-Nine Rules," *JE* 2:517-518 in distinguishing between the aggadic midrash referred to here (see also Rashi at 1 Kgs. 7:16, 18, 28) and Mishnat ha-Middot, the work designated by Gandz, following Steinschneider, as "the first Hebrew Geometry written about 150 C.E." (so Solomon Gandz, "Studies in the History of Mathematics from Hebrew and Arabic Sources," *HUCA* 6 [1929], p. 263; contrast Gandz, there, pp. 271-272; id., *The Mishnat Ha-Middot* [Berlin: Springer, 1932], p. 2).

[22] Here Rashi explains the meaning of a verb frequently attested in Biblical Heb. by means of a verb, which enters the language only in late Rabbinic Heb. Apparently, he assumes that his readers will readily understand *hiqnîṭ* but will be at a loss at comprehending *mārāh*.

[23] Moreover, both the infinitive construct *lamĕrôt* and the participle *mamrîm* are *hiphil* forms of the verb *mārāh* 'defy, rebel'; see Mandelkern, p. 702d; *GKC* #53q.

[24] So NJV; see *Mahberet Menahem*, p. 372, s.v. *ŝ'r* III; Mekilta at Ex. 21:10.

[25] Similarly *Mahberet Menahem*, p. 368, s.v. *ŝq* I.

[26] The literal meaning of *'abbîr* is 'mighty one'; hence NJV's "a hero's meal". The interpretation adopted by Rashi, which is found in several midrashim in Midrash Tehillim here and in the Psalms Targum, is found already in LXX and Vulgate here.

[27] According to R. Simeon b. Laqish (3[d] cent. C.E.) at Midrash Tehillim here, the manna was called 'bread of *'abbîrîm*' because when eating it the Israelites were like the angels in that they did not have to urinate or defecate. For him the two interpretations of *'abbîrîm* are not contradictory but complimentary. Rashi's source seems to be a *baraitha* in BT Yoma 75b where the former interpretation is attributed to R. Aqiba, the latter one to R. Ishmael.

[28] By substituting Num. 11:33 for the parallel version here at Ps. 78:31, Rashi reminds us that Num. 31 and Ps. 78 tell the same story almost verbatim.

[29] According to the latter interpretation, vv. 30a and 30b are synonymous, and both serve as temporal clauses modifying the verb *'ālāh* 'FLARED UP' in v. 31. According to the former interpretation, v. 30a is not synonymous with v. 30b. On the contrary, v. 30a concludes the thought of v. 29 while v. 30b introduces a new thought; contrast Maarsen here.

[30] In his commentary at Num. 11:4, Rashi interprets "mixed multitude"; so *BDB*, *K-B*[3], et al. In Numbers Rabbah 15:19 the two interpretations are attributed to R. Simeon b. Abba (3[d] century Amora) and R. Simeon b. Manasia (2[d]-3[d] century Tanna). In Tanḥuma, Beha'aloteka 16 the two views are attributed to R. Samuel b. Nahmani (late 3[d]-early 4th

century Amora) and R. Nehemiah (2^d cent. Tanna).

³¹ The latter interpretation assumes that the noun *'āsapsup* derives from the verb *'sp* 'gather' and denotes 'those who were gathered'.

³² Heb. *wĕ'ap 'al pî kēn*, which represents Rashi's interpretation of the conjunctive *waw* at the beginning of v. 38 as a subordinate conjunction.

³³ See Baruch A. Levine, "Kippurim," *EI* 9 (1969), pp. 88-95 (in Hebrew).

³⁴ Here Rashi intimates that the Biblical Heb. imperfect may function, *inter alia*, both as a present and as a preterite; see Rashi at Ps. 1:3. Hence he paraphrases *yĕkappēr* as a present progressive and *lō' yašḥît* as a preterite.

³⁵ Answering the exegetical question, "TO TURN AWAY from what/whom?"

³⁶ As noted by Rashi, the following clause suggests that indeed God did stir up a little of His anger. V. 38b, however, states that He turned away His anger. Here Rashi attempts to resolve the apparent contradiction.

³⁷ Again Rashi's paraphrase intimates that here the Biblical Heb. imperfect is employed as a preterite.

³⁸ Cf. Gruber, *Aspects*, p. 550.

³⁹ Cf. the midrash attributed to R. Judah b. Simeon in Midrash Tehillim here.

⁴⁰ Rashi does not quote the bracketed text; I have supplied it for clarity.

⁴¹ Heb. *lĕpî še;* ancticipating NJV, Rashi interprets the so-called conversive *waw* as a subordinative conjunction.

⁴² The psalmist employs imperfect with *waw* -conversive; Rashi paraphrases with perfect *zākar.*

⁴³ I.e., breath, *elan vital*, or soul.

⁴⁴ I.e., Midrash Tehillim here, which suggests that those who deny the Rabbinic dogma of the Resurrection of the Dead employ Ps. 78:39 as a prooftext.

⁴⁵ Biblical Heb. *kammāh* 'HOW MANY?' may refer to units of time or of matter; Rashi points out that here the reference is to time.

⁴⁶ With Maarsen cf. Rashi at v. 37 above.

⁴⁷ Cf. *Mahberet Menahem*, p. 393, s.v. *taw;* for other interpretations of *hitĕwû* in Ps. 78:41 see Midrash Tehillim here.

⁴⁸ The source of this midrash, which responds imaginatively to the exegetical question, "How did frogs destroy them?" is Midrash Tehillim here; q.v.

⁴⁹ The precise meaning of this *hapax legomenon* is yet to be established; see dictionaries.

⁵⁰ This midrash is attributed to R. Johanan [b. Napha] in Midrash Tehillim here.

⁵¹ Up to this point Rashi's comments on v. 48 derive from Midrash Tehillim here, #14.

[52] See Pope, *Song of Songs*, p. 670; see also the discussion at Ps. 76:4, above.

[53] With Zohory cf. Midrash Tehillim here; Exodus Rabbah 10:1.

[54] The psalmist simply states *gôyîm* 'NATIONS'. Rashi answers the exegetical question, "Who were the only Gentiles whom God expelled from the land of Israel to make possible the settlement of the people of Israel there?" The only biblical source for the Rabbinic practice of referring to the Canaanites as 'seven nations' is Deut. 7:1; see also Josh. 3:10; 24:11.

[55] The exegetical difficulty confronted by Rashi here is the ambiguity of the pronominal suffix 'THEIR'; Rashi's solution is now accepted by NJV.

[56] Rashi does not quoted the bracketed portion; I have supplied it for clarity.

[57] Cf. Rashi at Ps. 52:4.

[58] So NJV, whose marginal note seems to suggest that they follow Ibn Ezra in assuming that 'HIS MIGHT' here at Ps. 78:61 must designate the Ark since the latter is called 'the Ark of Your might' at Ps. 132:8. The tragedy referred to by Rashi here is described in 1 Sam. 4:11ff.

[59] Rashi, followed by NJV, suggests that "they were not sung a nuptial song" is *pars pro toto* meaning "They did not get married."

[60] Midrash Tehillim here.

[61] Rashi's point is that the midrash ignores the clear chronological arrangement of Ps. 78.

[62] On Heb. *bkh* 'weep, cry' in the extended meaning 'mourn' see Gruber, *Aspects*, pp. 402-410.

[63] On the Ugaritic parallel to Heb. *wattikra' wattēled* 'she squatted, and she gave birth', *tqtnṣ wtld*, see Gruber, *Aspects*, p. 324, n. 2.

[64] The prooftext, to which Rashi refers, is actually found in the following verse, v. 20: "As she lay dying, the women attending her said, 'Do not be afraid, for you have borne a son.' But she did not respond or pay heed."

[65] So also Psalms Targum here.

[66] Heb. *ḥerpat giddûp*, a construct genitive, which means literally, 'a shame of an insult'.

[67] Here Rashi paraphrases v. 66b: "DEALING THEM LASTING DISGRACE." The midrash, which is reflected both in Rashi's comment and in the Psalms Targum, is inspired by the assumption that our verse is a case of synonymous parallelism. "He afflicted them with hemorrhoids" answers the exegetical question, "What is both an affliction in the buttocks and a cause of shame?'

[68] With Maarsen cf. BT Zebaḥim 118a.

[69] Cf. Rashi at Hos. 11:9. Contrast Paul in 2 Corinthians 6:16. The latter asserts, "You [the Christian community] are the temple of the living God...."

[70] Rashi's source is the midrash attributed to R. Joshua the Priest in Midrash Tehillim here.

PSALM LXXIX

1a [A PSALM OF][1] ASAPH. O GOD, HEATHENS HAVE ENTERED YOUR DOMAIN.

1b INTO HEAPS.[2] Now why [the superscription] PSALM? It is [in fact] a lament. However, since it is stated in the Bible, "The LORD emptied out His venom" (Lam. 4:11a), upon what did He empty it out? [The answer is found in the third clause of Lam. 4:11]: "He kindled a fire in Zion...." It [Ps. 79] is A PSALM, i.e.,[3] a [joyful] song [in celebration of the fact] that he poured out His venom (cf. Lam. 4:11a) on the wood and on the stones [of Zion; see Lam. 4:11], and He did not wreak destruction upon His children.[4]

2c THE FLESH OF YOUR FAITHFUL.[5] [Why are the victims of Your wrath called FAITHFUL?] Were they not wicked people? [Indeed, they were]. However, since they accepted their punishment, they are, in fact, YOUR [i.e., God's] FAITHFUL.[6] In the same vein He[7] says, "lest your brother be degraded before your eyes" (Deut. 25:3) [which implies that] as soon as he [the culprit] has been flogged, he is [considered] your brother. Thus it is explained in the *aggadah*.[8]

4 *wĕqeles* 'AND DERISION' is a synonym of 'speaking calumny'.[9] It corresponds in meaning to *lĕmāšāl* 'a paradigm [of deserved suffering]'[10] (Deut. 28:37; 1 Kgs. 9:7; Jer. 24:9; Ps. 69:12; 2 Ch. 7:20).

5 *'ad-māh*[11] 'HOW LONG' [is synonymous with] *'ad-mātay* [lit.], 'how long?'[12]
    te'ĕnap[13] 'WILL YOU BE ANGRY?' [I.e.], *tiqṣop*[14] 'will You be wroth?'
    qinā'tĕkā 'YOUR INDIGNATION' [i.e.], Your anger, with which You are inflamed [*mĕqannē'*] to be avenged. [The noun *qinā'tĕkā* 'YOUR INDIGNATION'] is a cognate of [the adjective *qannā'* 'impassioned' in the expression] "impassioned God" (Ex. 20:5; 34:14; Deut. 4:24; 5:9; 6:15). [It means] *emprenement* 'frenzy, excitement, state of being inflamed' in O.F.[15]

11   *hôtēr* 'REPRIEVE'. [I.e.], Let out [*pĕtaḥ*] prisoners. [The *hiphil* imperative *hôtēr* is a form of the verb, whose *hiphil* imperfect consecutive is attested in] "He sent an agent, and [through this agent] he granted him [the prisoner] a reprieve" (Ps. 105:20).[16]

bĕnê tĕmûtāh[17] 'THOSE CONDEMNED TO DEATH'. [I.e.], sons of her who is killed for Your sake.

tĕmûtāh [is the semantic equivalent of] *enmorinde* 'dying' in O.F., and there is an example of it[18] in Rabbinic Hebrew: "It is better that Israelites should eat the flesh of *tĕmûtôt* ritually slaughtered than that they should eat the flesh of *tĕmûtôt*, which died a natural death." Now our Rabbis explained [that *tĕmûtāh* in the latter quotation] in [BT] Tractate Qiddushin [21b-22a] [designates] the flesh of an animal in danger of dying naturally, which was ritually slaughtered.[19]

PSALM LXXIX, NOTES

[1] Rashi does not quote the bracketed portion of the verse. I have supplied it since Rashi's comment deals with it.

[2] So Rashi at Mic. 1:6; cf. KJV here.

[3] Here Rashi employs exegetical *waw*.

[4] The exegetical question and the answer seem to be taken from Lamentations Rabbah 4:15; similarly Midrash Tehillim here. Rashi quotes this midrash also in his commentary at BT Qiddushin 31b, s.v. "It so happened"; see also Tosafot there.

[5] Heb. *ḥasîdêkā*; KJV and JPS render 'Your saints'

[6] For the idea that wicked persons, who accept the punishment due them, are virtuous see the dictum attributed to Judah b. Tabbai in Mishnah Avot 1:8.

[7] I.e., God, the author of Scripture, or 'the Bible'.

[8] The apparent source is Midrash Tehillim here.

[9] Cf. Rashi at Hab. 1:10.

[10] Cf. Rashi at Deut. 28:37.

[11] Attested also in Ps. 4:3; 89:47.

[12] Complete list of attestations in Mandlekern, p. 707c-d, s.v. *mātay*; another synonym is *'ad-'ānāh* attested in Ex. 16:28; Num. 14:11 (2); Josh. 18:3; Jer. 47:6; Hab. 1:2; Ps. 13:2 (2), 3 (2); 62:4; Job. 18:2; 19:2 and the biform *'ad-'ān* found only in Job. 8:2. All these expressions correspond semantically to Akk *adi māti* and to Lat. *quousque*, which mean 'Enough!'

[13] On the etymology and meaning of this verb see Gruber, *Aspects*, pp. 552-553.

[14] On the etymology and meaning of this verb see Gruber, *Aspects*, p. 520, n. 1; p. 547, n. 1.

[15] Banitt, *Rashi: Interpreter of the Biblical Letter*, p. 28; see also Darmsteter,

"Les Gloses" *REJ* 56 (1908), p. 72; 53 (1907), p. 176, n. 6; 54 (1907), pp. 3, 5, 6, 9, 216.

[16] See Rashi and Qimhi there. For Rashi, following *Mahberet Menahem*, p. 396 the forms *hôtēr* (Ps. 79:11), *mattîr* (Ps. 146:7), and *wayyattîrēhû* (Ps. 105:20) all derive from biliteral root(s) tr. *BDB*, p. 684a derives the latter two forms from the verb *nātar* III 'be free', be loose', but it treats *hôtēr* under the verb *yātar* 'remain over' in *BDB*, p. 45b. *K-B*[3], pp. 695-696 derives all three forms from *nātar* III 'tear away'; hence it emends *hôtēr* at Ps. 79:11 to *hattēr;* so already Ehrlich, *Die Psalmen*, p. 193; cf. *BDB*, p. 45b. Other Rashi mss. here cite *mattîr* (Ps. 146:7) as a cognate of *hôtēr*.

[17] Lit., 'sons of dying'.

[18] The word *těmûtāh*, which is unattested in Biblical Heb. outside of Ps. 79:11 and its near doublet, Ps. 102:21.

[19] Other mss. of Rashi read *ûpērûšô* 'Now its meaning is' in place of our ms.' 'Now our Rabbis explained'; in fact, it is Rashi in his commentary at BT Qiddushin 21b who explains that *těmûtāh* there corresponds in meaning to the common expression *mesukkenet* 'an animal in danger of dying naturally' (see, e.g., Mishnah Hullin 2:6); cf. Levy, *Neuhebräisches und chaldäisches Wörterbuch*, vol. 4, pp. 650-651, s.v. *těmûtāh*.

PSALM LXXX

1　ON[1] *SHOSHANIM; EDUTH.* OF ASAPH. A PSALM. It is
A PSALM of testimony [EDUTH], for in it he [the psalmist
Asaph] hinted at three Exiles, and he prayed concerning
them. In fact, it is stated three times in this psalm, "RE-
STORE US...SHOW YOUR FAVOR SO THAT WE
MAY BE DELIVERED" (vv. 4, 8, 20). In it [this psalm] he
[the psalmist] hinted to him [Israel] concerning three troubles that they would experience in the future at the hands of
the Aramean kings, for it is stated in the Bible [that] in the
era of [the dynasty of] Jehu,[2] "for the king of Aram had decimated them and trampled them like the dust under his feet"
(2 Kgs. 13:7).

2a　SHEPHERD OF ISRAEL [i.e.], their leader and their
sustainer.

2b　JOSEPH. All Israel are called by the name of Joseph because he provided for them during the famine.[3]

2c　[God is addressed as] ENTHRONED ON THE CHERU-
BIM in accord with what is stated in the Bible, "There [be-
tween the two cherubim] I will meet with you" (Ex. 25:22).
APPEAR. [I.e.], Show Your strength.

3a　AT THE HEAD OF EPHRAIM, BENJAMIN, AND
MANASSEH!
When Israel needed Your help even though they were
wicked

3b　and unworthy ROUSE YOUR MIGHT. Why?

3c　AND FOR YOU FOR HELP FOR US.
'FOR YOU' [*lĕkā*] [i.e.], 'it is incumbent upon You' ["*ālêkā*]
to help us, both the innocent and the guilty just as it was said
to Moses, "Seeing, I have seen..." (Ex. 3:7). Why are there
these two mentions of 'seeing'? [The answer is that] I [God]
see that in the future they will provoke Me to anger; nevertheless I have taken note of their suffering because of the
oath that I swore to Abraham, Isaac, and Jacob.[4] [The mention of] EPHRAIM [in v. 3a] refers to the war against Aram
when he [Ben-hadad, king of Aram] besieged Samaria, and

he sent messengers to Ahab [saying], "Your wives and your children are mine; your silver and your gold are mine" (cf. 1 Kgs. 20:3). [The mention of] MANASSEH [in v. 3] refers to the era of Jehoash son of Jehoahaz concerning which it is stated in the Bible, "for He [the LORD] saw the suffering of Israel" (cf. 2 Kgs. 13:4; Ex. 3:7), "for the king of Aram had decimated them" (2 Kgs. 13:7). Moreover, he [Jehoash] defeated him [Ben-hadad son of Hazael, king of Aram] in war three times, as it is stated in the Bible, "Three times Jehoash defeated him, and he recovered the towns of Israel" (2 Kgs. 13:25). [The mention of] BENJAMIN [in v. 3] refers to the era of Ahasuerus when Mordecai and Esther were in danger and the entire generation was dependent upon them.

3c AND FOR YOU FOR HELP FOR US. This [word *ûlĕkāh*] is not a form of the verb *hălîkāh* 'walking'[5] Rather it is a biform of *ûlĕkā* 'and for you'. Moreover thus it is [listed] in the *masoret*[6] together with *ûlĕkāh 'ēpô'* "for you now" (Gen. 27:37) in the story of Jacob; "for you the report of the bad news is not a source of reward" (2 Sam. 18:22); "for you is the vestment; be a chief over us" (Isa. 3:6).[7]

4 RESTORE US from the Babylonian Exile where Mordecai was.[8]

5b HOW LONG WILL YOU BE WRATHFUL by means of the troubles [at the hands of] the Greek kings,[9] who greatly afflicted Israel?

6a YOU HAVE FED THEM TEARS AS THEIR DAILY BREAD in Egypt,

6b AND YOU MADE THEM DRINK A THIRD [*šāliš*][10] OF TEARS in Babylonia where they [the Jews] were [in Exile] seventy years,[11] which is A THIRD of [the] 210 [years] of [enslavement] in Egypt.[12] I learned this [interpretation of 'A THIRD' here at Ps. 80:6] from the book by Rabbi Moses the Interpreter.[13] However, one ought to explain ['A THIRD' here at Ps. 80:6 as a reference to the Greek kings;[14] they are called collectively 'A THIRD'] because the Greek kingdom was the third trouble [which Israel experienced]. Now if you should say [that] it [the Greek kingdom] was the fourth [trouble rather than the third] insofar as Persia and the Medes preceded [Greece and followed Babylonia], [I shall counter as follows]: The entire seventy years of

Babylonia is only a single Exile.[15] Now Menahem [Ibn Saruq] interpreted *šālîš* as the name of a drinking vessel, and in the same vein he interpreted [the noun *šālîš* in] "And He meted earth's dust with a *šālîš*." (Isa. 40:12).[16] Our rabbis interpreted it ['A THIRD'] as a reference to three tears, which Esau shed,[17] with reference to which it is stated in the Bible, "He cried a cry" (Gen. 27:34)—that is one [cry]. [The attributive adjective] 'great' [modifying 'cry' there]—that is two; 'and bitter' [the second attributive adjective there also modifying 'cry']—that is three. Now because of them [the three cryings] he merited living by his sword as it is stated in the Bible, "If you will be remorseful[18]..." (Gen. 27:40).

7a   YOU SET US[19] AT STRIFE. You set[20] us AT STRIFE WITH OUR NEIGHBORS, who strove with us.

7b   OUR ENEMIES, the Greeks.

8   RESTORE US...SO THAT WE MAY BE DELIVERED[21] from the Greeks.

9a   YOU PLUCKED...FROM EGYPT. Again[22] he [the psalmist] referred to the Roman[23] Exile. [The] VINE is [a metaphor for] Israel,[24] whom You plucked up [*hissaʿtā*][25] FROM EGYPT. [I.e.], You uprooted them from there. [The long imperfect verb *tassiaʿ* 'YOU PLUCKED'] is the same verb as is attested in [the short imperfect consecutive in] "He plucked up [*wayyassaʿ*] my hope like a tree" (Job. 19:10).[26]

9b   Afterwards You expelled[27] seven NATIONS,[28] and You planted[27] Israel in their land.

10a   YOU REMOVED BEFORE HER.[29]

10b   IT TOOK DEEP ROOT [*wattašrēš šorāšêāh*] [i.e.], *hišrîšāh šorāšêāh* "it took deep root".[30]

11b   ITS BOUGHS covered[31] MIGHTY CEDARS.
        MIGHTY CEDARS [*ʾarzê ʾēl*] [i.e.], 'strong cedars' [*ʾărāzîm ḥăzāqîm*],[32] a metaphor for[33] "powerful kings" (Ps. 136:18).[34]

12a   SHE SENT HER BRANCHES TO THE SEA.
        She sent[35] her head ornaments. [*qĕṣîrêāh* 'HER BRANCHES'] is the same word as is attested in "and it will produce a branch" (Job. 14:9).[36] [The expression 'TO THE SEA' refers to the fact that] her [the land of Israel's] boundary was UP TO the Great [i.e., the Mediterranean] SEA.

12b   AND HER BOUGHS[37] TO THE RIVER. [This refers to

the fact that] the breadth of the land of Israel is "from the [Sinai] Desert to the River"[38] [i.e.], the Euphrates River.[39]

13a   WHY DID YOU BREACH ITS, that vineyard's WALL

13b   SO THAT EVERY PASSERBY PLUCKS ITS FRUIT [i.e.], ALL who came picked her fruit. [The verb *'ārāh* 'pluck' attested here] is the same verb as is attested in "I have plucked my myrrh" (Cant. 5:1) and likewise in Mishnaic Heb. *mĕlō' hā'ôreh wĕsallô* "the space occupied by the fruit-picker and his basket" (Mishnah Shebi'it 1:2).[40]

14a   A BOAR FROM A FOREST GNAWS AT IT.

[The verb *yĕkarsĕmennāh* 'HE GNAWS AT IT'] is the same verb as is attested in "As for a field...if ants gnaw at it" in Mishnaic Hebrew (Mishnah Pe'ah 2:7),[41] and it is a verb referring to 'stripping off'.[42] *miyyā'ar* 'FROM A FOREST'. [In the Masoretic text] the [letter] *'ayin* is suspended in it [the word *miyyā'ar*]. [This phenomenon suggests that] when Israel have been innocent, their enemies have become like the beast of the Nile [*hayĕ'or*], which lacks the strength [to survive] on land; when, however, punishment is decreed against them [Israel], it [the Nile beast] becomes strong like the forest animal, which destroys and kills.[43]

As for A BOAR FROM A FOREST, this is a metaphor for Esau, for it is written in the Bible, "It devours and it crushes, and what is left it tramples with its foot" (Dan. 7:7). Moreover, it [the pig] has some of the identifying marks of purity[44] just as Esau has the merit of the patriarchs.[45]

14b   *wĕzîz śāday* 'AND CREATURES OF THE FIELD' [i.e.], "every creeping thing of the ground" (Gen. 1:25; 6:20). Why is it called *zîz* ? [It is called *zîz*] because it moves [*zāz*] and eats them and goes away.[46]

yir'ennāh 'FEEDS ON IT' [i.e.] *rō'eh 'ālêāh* 'it grazes upon her'[47] [the vine][48] [and] its branches, and it consumes them.

16a   THE STOCK, WHICH YOUR RIGHT HAND PLANTED [i.e., the vine (v, 9)], which is established and settled, WHICH YOUR RIGHT HAND PLANTED. [The noun] *kannāh* 'STOCK' is a cognate of [the noun *kannekā* 'your post' attested in] "and he will restore you to your post" (Gen. 40:13).[49]

16b   AND OVER THE SON YOU ADOPTED FOR YOURSELF [i.e.]

OVER Esau, who was dear to his father, who used to call him "my son" (Gen. 27:1, 37), YOU ADOPTED FOR YOURSELF the vine (v. 9) Jacob in accord with what is stated in the Bible, "You shall serve your brother" (Gen. 27:40).

17a   And now she [the vine, i.e., Israel] IS BURNT BY FIRE AND CUT DOWN. [The verb from which is derived the passive participle *kĕsûḥāh* 'CUT DOWN'] is the semantic equivalent of [the verb *zāmar* 'prune' in] *lō' tizmôr* "You shall not prune" (Lev. 25:4), [which Targum Onkelos renders into Aramaic by] *lā' tiksāḥ* "You shall not cut down."[50]

17b   PERISHING. They are continually perishing[51] BEFORE YOUR ANGRY BLAST, i.e., Your anger.

18a   MAY YOUR HAND[52] BE UPON YOUR RIGHT HAND MAN [i.e.], upon Esau,[53] who is about to collect payment from him [i.e., Israel].[54]

18b   THE ONE YOU HAVE TAKEN AS YOUR OWN so that his "abode" will be "among the fat places of the earth" (Gen. 27:39).[55]

19a   LET US NOT TURN AWAY FROM YOU. [I.e.], Do not cause us to be TURNed AWAY FROM YOU.

19b   REVIVE US from the Exile so that we may call to mind Your kindness and Your might,

19c   AND then WE WILL INVOKE YOUR NAME.

20   O LORD, GOD OF HOSTS. Here [in this third occurrence of the refrain found in vv. 4, 8, 20] there are mentioned three names of God [LORD, GOD, HOSTS] while in the middle [version of the refrain at v. 8] there are two names of God [GOD, HOSTS] and in the first [version of the refrain at v. 4] there is one name of God. Each [version of the refrain is worded] according to the intensity of the [respective] exiles, the suffering, and the redemption.

PSALM LXXX, NOTES

[1] Heb. *'al;* so our Rashi ms. and many medieval Heb. Bible mss. (see *BHS* here); however, the normative reading in the Heb. text of the Bible here is *'el* 'TO'.

[2] Specifically during the seventeen-year reign of Jehoahaz son of Jehu.

[3] Here Rashi responds to the exegetical question as to why Israel and Joseph are in synonymous parallelism here in v. 2. Modern Biblical scholarship answers this same exegetical question by suggesting that this

"psalm was composed in the Northern Kingdom destroyed in 721 B.C.E." (Dahood here) and that the pair Israel/Joseph refers to the Northern Kingdom (cf. Dahood here), in which the dominant tribes— Ephraim and Manasseh (cf. v. 3)—traced their ancestry to Joseph (cf. Gen. 41:51-52; Ezek. 37:15-22).

⁴ Rashi's comment appears to be based upon Tanḥuma Shemot #20; cf. Exodus Rabbah 3:3. The midrash Rashi quotes here seeks a moral in the apparently redundant use of two forms of the same verb—infinitive absolute followed by a finite verb. In fact, this usage is employed for emphasis, and it means, "Indeed I have seen"; see *GKC* #113.

⁵ I.e., contra KJV, NJV, Dahood, et al., the form *ûlĕkāh* does not represent the *waw*-conjunctive followed by the long imperative *lĕkāh* 'go' from the verbal root *hlk* 'go'.

⁶ See *Ochlah W'ochlah*, ed. Frensdorff, p. 247; on the significance of the term 'in the *masoret*' see the discussion at Ps. 9, n. 1.

⁷ Contrast Rashi's division of the clause in his comment at Isa. 3:7.

⁸ See above at v. 1; see below, n. 21.

⁹ The Ptolemies and the Seleucids. For the history of the period in question see Victor Tcherikover, *Hellenistic Civilization and the Jews* (Philadelphia: Jewish Publication Society, 1959).

¹⁰ Dahood, here suggests the rendering 'bronze bowl' derived from Ugar. *ṭlṭ* 'bronze'. NJV at Isa. 40:12c suggests that *šālîš* 'third' may mean "a third of an ephah"; cf. Rabbinic Heb. *rĕbî'ît*, lit., 'a fourth', constantly employed to mean 'one fourth of a log'; cf. Modern Israeli Heb. *qîlô*, lit., 'thousand', employed to mean 'one kilogram'. The suggestions of both Dahood and NJV make it clear that Heb. *šālîš* refers both in Isa. 40:12 and in Ps. 80:6 to a vessel for weighing out and serving both solids and liquids. See below in Rashi.

¹¹ Jer. 25:11; 29:10. In fact, there were only fifty-nine years from the Exile of Jehoiachin (597 B.C.E.) to the Edict of Cyrus (538 B.C.E.; forty-eight from the destruction of the First Temple (586 B.C.E.) to the Edict of Cyrus; see Rashi at Ezra 1:1.

¹² The Rabbinic tradition that contra Gen. 15:13 and Ex. 12:40 the Israelites' sojourn in Egypt was only two hundred and ten years is found in Seder Olam, Chapter 3. Josephus, Antiquities 2.15.2 preserves an alternate tradition of two hundred and fifteen years of enslavement in Egypt. See the discussion in Samuel R. Driver, *The Book of Exodus*, CB (Cambridge: Cambridge University Press, 1911), pp. 101-102 at Ex. 12:40, and see Rashi at Gen. 15:13.

¹³ For references to this source in Rashi's Commentary on the Book of Psalms see also at Ps. 45:2; 60:4; 62:13; 68:17.

¹⁴ See above, at v. 5.

¹⁵ Rashi at Ezra 1:1 explains that the seventy years (sic.) from the destruction of the First Temple (586 B.C.E.) to the renewal of the work of the building of the Second Temple in the second year of Darius I (520 B.C.E.) embraces the periods of the Persian and Median kingdoms.

¹⁶ So also Rashi at Isa. 40:12; the source is *Mahberet Menahem*, p. 382,

s.v. *šlš* III; Maarsen's assertion that this interpretation is absent from *Mahberet Menahem* is an error.

[17] Rashi's source for this statement is Midrash Tehillim here; see also Yalqut Shim'oni here.

[18] So Rashi at Gen. 27:40.

[19] Heb. *těšîmēnû*, the imperfect form of the verb, which, in Biblical Heb. can be past, present or future in meaning; see next note.

[20] Rashi's paraphrase, using detached pronouns for the subject and object. His use of the perfect *śām* indicates that Rashi here interprets the imperfect as past in meaning.

[21] See the comments on the refrain,"RESTORE US...SHOW YOUR FAVOR SO THAT WE MAY BE DELIVERED" (vv. 4, 8, 20) in Rashi at vv. 1, 4, 20.

[22] Heb. *ḥāzar wě*, lit., 'he returned and', a use of hendiadys, which is characteristic of Rabbinic Heb. and of the Heb. of Rashi and Rashbam. Modern Heb. would use an adverbial expression such as *šûb* or the colloquial *'ôd happa'am* 'again'.

[23] The reading Arameans in the printed editions is undoubtedly an emendation of the Christian censors, who took 'Romans' as an uncomplimentary reference to themselves; see N. Porges, "Censorship of Hebrew Books," *JE* 3:642-50.

[24] Rashi's source is the midrash on Gen. 40:9-10 attributed to R. Jeremiah b. Abba at BT Hullin 82a where our verse is employed as a prooftext in support of the contention that 'vine' in Gen. 40:9-10 is a symbol of Israel; similarly Dahood, here.

[25] Rashi's point is that the imperfect *tassîa'* functions here as a preterite; so now also NJV, q.v.

[26] Here Rashi asserts and then attempts to demonstrate that the *hiphil* of the verb *ns'* (according to *Mahberet Menahem*, p. 268 the root is *s'*) can mean 'uproot'; see now Gordis, *Job*, p. 51 at Job. 4:21.

[27] The biblical text employs the imperfect form of the verb as a preterite; Rashi paraphrases employing the perfect.

[28] See Deut. 7:1-5.

[29] I.e., before the vine, which symbolizes Israel; lemma rendered according to the understanding presupposed by Rashi's comment.

[30] Rashi clarifies the meaning of the imperfect consecutive by paraphrasing in the perfect.

[31] In v. 11a the verb *kossû* is *qal* passive meaning 'they were covered'; Rashi, followed by NJV construes the verse as an example of synonymous chiastic parallelism in which the verb found only in the first clause governs also the second clause, which means "BY ITS BOWS [were covered] MIGHTY CEDARS." Rashi here paraphrases this awkward construction employing the active verb 'covered' as the predicate of the noun subject 'ITS BOWS'.

[32] Lit., 'cedars of greatness'; better than Rashi's interpretation would be 'towering cedars' (so Dahood here); cf. *harěrê 'ēl* 'tall mountains' at Ps. 36:7, and see Dahood there. Note that there as here Rashi interprets *'ēl* as

referring to greatness of strength rather than to greatness of height.

[33] Heb. kĕmô.

[34] There in Ps. 136:18 the reference is to the kings of Canaan-Transjordan, of whom Sihon and Og are singled out in vv. 19-20 there; see Rashi and our comment at Ps. 118:17, below.

[35] Here Rashi equates the (to his readers) less familiar imperfect consecutive pi'el with the more familiar perfect of the qal.

[36] Rashi here follows Mahberet Menahem, p. 338 in distinguishing between qṣr II 'reap, harvest' and qṣr III 'branch'; cf. BDB, p. 849b; K-B³, p. 1049a, s.v. qāṣîr II.

[37] Heb. yônqôtêāh, a synonym of qĕṣîrêāh; see Mahberet Menahem, p. 158a; K-B³, p. 1049a.

[38] Ex. 23:31.

[39] Just as from the perspective of the land of Israel the desert par execellence is the Sinai Desert, which gives its name to the fourth book of the Pentateuch, Bemmidbar "In the [Sinai] Desert," so is the Mediterranean the sea par excellence and the Euphrates the river par excellence. For references to the latter as simply "the River" see, e.g., Josh. 24:2 and passim; Jer. 2:18; Neh. 2:7; etc.

[40] With Maarsen see Rashbam at BT Bava Batra 82b.

[41] The source of this observation is Teshuvot Dunash, p. 55; contrast Mahberet Menahem, p. 223, s.v. krś; see the discussion in Cohen, Biblical Hapax Legomena, p. 21.

[42] Heb. nĕtîqāh; see Cohen, Biblical Hapax Legomena, p. 20.

[43] Cf. Midrash Tehillim here; Avot deRabbi Nathan 34; all three versions of the midrash take it for granted that the Masoretic suspended 'ayin attests to an unresolved question as to whether the correct reading is with 'aleph or with 'ayin.

[44] The pig has cloven hooves, but it is not a ruminant (see Lev. 11:7; Deut. 14:8); similarly, Esau is a descendant of both Abraham and Isaac, but just as the pig is not kosher so is Esau not Israel.

[45] Cf. the first of the two midrashim attributed to R. Phineas and R. Hilkiah quoting R. Simon in Midrash Tehillim at Ps. 80 #6.

[46] Similarly, Dahood renders wĕzîz śādāy "and what moves in the field"; contrast K-B³, p. 257a.

[47] Generally in Biblical Heb. the verb rā'āh is either intransitive meaning 'graze' or transitive meaning 'shepherd'. Rarely, as here, the verb is transitive, meaning 'graze upon'; hence Rashi's comment, which also informs us that here the imperfect form of the verb is present in meaning; see BDB, pp. 944b-945a, s.v. rā'āh I.

[48] The antecedent of the accusative plural suffix is again the 'VINE', i.e., Israel, first mentioned in v. 9.

[49] Cf. Mahberet Menahem, p. 217, s.v. kn VII; Teshuvot Dunash, pp. 92-93; cf. also Qimhi here.

[50] In Rashi's almost verbatim comment on kĕsûḥîm 'cut down' at Isa. 33:12, Rashi employs the expression kĕmô in place of lĕšôn 'a semantic equivalent of' indicating that in Rashi's commentaries the two expressions

kĕmô and *lĕšôn* are often interchangeable; see the discussion in our introduction, pp. 140–146.

[51] As noted by Maarsen here, the exegetical question addressed here by Rashi is "What is the meaning of the imperfect form of the verb here?" Rashi, followed by NJV, contends that it is present progressive in meaning; Qimhi here interprets it as a preterite while RSV takes it as a jussive.

[52] Here as at Ps. 21:9; 39:11 Rashi takes "Your [i.e., God's metaphorical] hand" to mean 'plague, affliction'; see the discussion at Ps. 21:9. NJV here at Ps. 80:18 takes 'YOUR HAND' to be a metaphor for 'Your help'. Note, however, that the latter usage of 'hand' is confined to Ezra-Neh. and Ch.; see *BDB*, p. 390a. Not surprisingly, each of these two interpretations of *yādĕkā* here at Ps. 80:18 inspires midrashim found in Midrash Tehillim here; q.v.

[53] So Midrash Tehillim here.

[54] See Gen. 27:40, which T.O. interprets as follows: "...when his [Jacob's] descendants transgress the laws of the Torah, you shall remove his [Jacob's] yoke from upon your [Esau's] neck."

[55] I.e., Esau; see Midrash Tehillim here.

PSALM LXXXI

1　FOR THE LEADER; ON THE GITTITH, a musical instrument which comes from Gath.[1]

3b　THE MELODIOUS LYRE AND HARP. R. Hiyya b. Abba[2] says, *nebel* 'HARP' and *kinnôr* 'LYRE' are one and the same. R. Simeon says, "They differ from each other in the number of their base and treble strings."[3] Now why is it called *nebel*? Because it puts to shame [*mĕnabbēl*] all other kinds of musical [instruments].[4]

2　SOUND THE SHOFAR[5] on the New Year.[6]

4a　ON THE NEW MOON [*baḥodeš*] [i.e.], at the renewal [*ḥiddûš*] of the moon.[7]

4b　AT THE *kesse'*, [8] the day appointed, prepared and fixed for it. In the same vein "He will come home at the *kesse'*" (Prov. 7:20) [i.e.], at the appointed time which has been fixed.[9]

5　FOR IT [*hû'*] IS A LAW FOR ISRAEL from the Holy One Blessed be He to blow the shofar on the New Year, and that [*hû'*] is the Holy One Blessed be He's day of JUDGMENT.[10]

6a　HE MADE IT A TESTIMONY CONCERNING JOSEPH[11] [because] Joseph got out of prison on the New Year.[12]

6c　I UNDERSTOOD A LANGUAGE THAT I HAD NOT KNOWN.
It is explained in [BT] Tractate Soṭah [36b] that [the angel] Gabriel taught him [Joseph] seventy languages.[13]

7b　FREED FROM THE CAULDRON [*middûd*] [i.e.], from servile labor, [sc.], cooking [with] pots as is the habit of slaves. [The noun 'CAULDRON' in the expression *middûd* 'FROM THE CAULDRON' [means] *qĕdērāh* 'pot'. It is the same noun as is reflected in "He shall thrust it into the pan or into the *dûd* 'cauldron'" (1 Sam. 2:14).[14]

8a　IN DISTRESS YOU CALLED AND I RESCUED YOU. All of you[15] CALLED from the DISTRESS of the slavery of "the burdens of Egypt" (Ex. 6:6, 7), AND I RESCUED you.[16]

8b   I ANSWERED YOU IN SECRET THUNDER.
You called me in secret [i.e.], privately, but I answered you[17] WITH the sound of THUNDER. I made known My might and My awesomeness publicly.[18]

8c   I TESTED YOU AT THE WATERS OF MERIBAH even though the knowledge that in the future You would rebel AT THE WATERS OF MERIBAH was revealed to me. Thus it is expounded in the Mekilta.[19] However, it seems that according to its literal meaning
I SHALL ANSWER YOU IN SECRET THUNDER is something like "And it shall be that He who responds with fire" (1 Kgs. 18:24). [I.e.] I SHALL RESPOND to the extent that You were in need. What is the meaning of 'hiding you in thunder'? [It means] that I hid you on a day of thunder and trouble.

9   HEAR, MY PEOPLE. After I have done all this for you, it is proper that you should hearken to Me.

11c   OPEN YOUR MOUTH WIDE to ask from Me all your heart's desires.

11d   AND I WILL FILL IT. As much as you will ask I WILL FILL.

13   ACCORDING TO THE VISION OF THEIR HEART [i.e.], according to the perception of their eyes. [The noun šĕrîrût 'vision'] is a cognate of [the participle] šōrēr 'watching' in] because of those who watch me" (Ps. 5:9).[20]

14   IF ONLY MY PEOPLE WOULD LISTEN TO ME. [I.e.], if they were still wanting to turn back to Me and to hearken to Me,[21]

15a   THEN I WOULD SUBDUE THEIR ENEMIES AT ONCE.
[I.e.], in a short while I would SUBDUE My ENEMIES.[22]

15b   I SHALL REMOVE MY HAND.
[I.e.], I SHALL REMOVE My plague[23] from you to inflict it upon your enemies, and then

16a   THOSE WHO HATE THE LORD SHALL COWER BEFORE HIM,

16b   AND THE APPOINTED TIME for their punishment SHALL BE ETERNAL.

17a   HE FED HIM [i.e.], Israel

17b   AND FROM THE ROCK He sated them[24] WITH

HONEY when they walked in His ways in accord with what is stated in the Bible, "He fed him honey from the crag" (Deut. 32:13).

PSALM LXXXI, NOTES

¹ Similarly Rashi at Ps. 8:1; see n. 2 there.

² Our Rashi ms. contains the dittography R. Hiyya b. R. Hiyya b. Abba.

³ Rashi's source is Midrash Tehillim here; I have closely followed Braude, vol. 2, p. 54 in rendering the final clause.

⁴ This comment is taken almost verbatim from an unattributed midrash in Midrash Tehillim here.

⁵ Heb. *hārî'û*, which is so employed in BT Ta'anit 16b and passim in Rabbinic Heb.; rendering of the lemma reflects the interpretation presupposed by Rashi's comment.

⁶ Cf. BT Rosh ha-Shanah 31b and Rashi there.

⁷ I.e., the new moon. The exegetical question here addressed by Rashi is which of the two meanings of Biblical Heb. *hodeš*, "new moon" or "month" is appropriate in the present context. LXX, Rabbinic exegesis (BT Beṣah 16a; Rosh ha-Shanah 8a-b; 34a) and modern biblical lexicography agree that here the word means 'new moon' as it does in other cases where the word refers to a specific day; see Deut. 16:1; 1 Sam. 20:5; 2 Kgs. 4:23; etc.; see dictionaries.

⁸ Spelling of the word *kesse'* reflects the spelling found in our Rashi ms. KJV renders "at the appointed time"; RSV renders "at the full moon"; LXX "on an auspicious day"; Ibn Ezra comments, "the new moon on which the moon is hidden [*yitkasseh*]"; the latter interpretation assumes that the words *hodeš* and *kesse'* are synonyms; this view goes back to the Talmudic sources cited in n. 7. KJV's rendering derives from Rashi; see below. The renderings of RSV and NJV "at/on the full moon" go back to Aquila, Symmachus, and Jerome. Modern scholars have found support for this view in the Phoenician text *KAI* 43, l. 12: [*bhd*]*šm wbks'm yrh md yrh 'd 'lm* "[at the new moo]ns and at the full moons, from month to month forever," in Syriac *kēsā'* 'full moon', and in the Ugaritic text RS 24.271 (see *Ugaritica* V, p. 583) where in a list of deities such as *dgn wb'l* "Dagon and Baal" (l. 4) we find in 1.6 *yrh w ksa* "Moon and *kesse'*." For a survey of modern views see Yitzhak Avishur, *Phoenician Inscriptions and the Bible* (2 vols.; Jerusalem: E. Rubenstein, 1979), vol. 1, pp. 141-42 (in Hebrew).

⁹ Rashi similarly cites Ps. 81:4 in his commentary on Prov. 7:20. The source of the view Rashi expresses in both places is *Mahberet Menahem*, p. 218, s.v. *ks* I. This view is reflected also in the comment of Rashi's grandson Rabbenu Tam in Tosaphot at BT Beṣah 16a: "*kesseh* is a synonym of 'appointed time' as is reflected in 'He will come home at the *kesse'* " (Prov. 7:20)."

¹⁰ While NJV, following Ibn Ezra, takes *hoq* 'LAW' and *mišpāṭ* 'RUL-

ING' (our rendering 'judgment' reflects the interpretation presupposed by Rashi's comment) as synonyms referring to the injunction 'BLOW THE SHOFAR' (v. 4), Rashi interprets only *ḥoq* as referring to this injunction.

[11] Rendering of the lemma in accord with Rashi's interpretation. The Northern Israelite psalmist, here as at Ps. 77:16; 80:2, employs Joseph as a designation for the people of Israel collectively. Hence the correct rendering is Dahood's "As a command he imposed it on Joseph when he went from the land of Egypt"; cf. also Harold Louis Ginsberg, *The Israelian Heritage of Judaism* (New York: Jewish Theological Seminary of America, 1982), p. 50.

[12] The sources of Rashi's comment are BT Rosh ha-Shanah 10b and Midrash Tehillim here. Unquestionably, both midrashim are inspired by our verse, which, contrary to the intent of the psalmist (see n. 11), was construed as a reference to the personage named Joseph in Gen. 41:14. Rashi's comment here suggests that just as Passover commemorates the Exodus and Shavuot the Giving of the Torah so does New Year commemorate the liberation of Joseph from prison (that this event took place on the first day of the year is suggested by Gen. 41:1; apparently Pharaoh dreamed on the last night of the old year; Joseph was summoned the next day, which was New Year). For a similar historicizing tendency see the account of the origin of the Day of Atonement in the Book of Jubilees 34:18-20.

[13] In Rabbinic lore "[the] seventy languages" means "all languages". The unattributed aggadah tells us that the Egyptian populace took it for granted that a person fit to be viceroy of Egypt should know all languages. For a similar assertion concerning the members of the Sanhedrin see BT Sanhedrin 17a. The aggadah at BT Soṭah 36b goes on to tell that the angel Gabriel helped Joseph respond to the challenge by teaching him the seventy languages. Rashi uses this aggadah to provide the Sitz im Leben for Joseph's assertion, "I UNDERSTOOD A LANGUAGE THAT I HAD NOT KNOWN."

[14] As noted by Maarsen here, Rashi's source is *Mahberet Menahem*, p. 123, s.v. *dûd* II; see also Midrash Tehillim here. Menahem himself questions the equation of *dûd* in Ps. 81:7 with *dûd* 'cooking pot' in 1 Sam. 2:14; 2 Ch.35:13; etc.; see *Mahberet Menahem*, p. 123, s.v. *dûd* III 'basket'. Moshe Held, "The Root *zbl/sbl* in Akkadian, Ugaritic, and Biblical Hebrew," *JAOS* 88 (1968), p. 94 points out that here in Ps. 81:7 *dûd* is employed as a synonym of *sebel* (found also in 1 Kgs. 11:28; Neh. 4:11) = Akk. *tupšukku* = Akk. *kudurru*, which refers to the basket laden with clay for the making of bricks for the royal building projects. Just as 'to enslave' or 'to impose forced labor' is expressed in Akkadian as 'I imposed (the carrying of) the basket' (see Held, there, p. 95) so does our psalm refer to emancipation from slavery as "his hands are free from the basket" (so Held, there, p. 94); cf. Ibn Ezra. Qimhi wrongly surmised that the psalmist here referred to the labor of making cauldrons. For illustration of the corveé basket from 7th cent. B.C.E. Mesopotamia see ANEP[2] #124. Note that Rashi correctly understood that 'to be free from the *dûd* is to be free from

servile labor; see also Midrash Tehillim here. He erred in not identifying correctly the specific activity from which the idiom is derived.

[15] The psalmist has the LORD address Israel collectively in the 2[d] pers. masc. sing. Rashi's paraphrase emphasizes the fact that the LORD here addresses all Israel.

[16] Rashi substitutes the plural for the psalmist's 2[d] pers. masc. sing.

[17] Rashi employs the perfect 'innîtîkā to indicate that the psalmist employs the imperfect 'e'enĕkā as a preterite.

[18] Rashi, following Abba Saul (mid 2[d] cent. C.E.) in Mekilta, vol. 2, p. 196, lines 58-60, treats v. 8 as an instance of miqrā' mĕsûrās 'inversion'. Hence, while according to the Masoretic accents bĕsēter ra'am is a construct genitive meaning "in the secrecy of thunder," Rashi treats bĕsēter 'in secrecy' as an adverbial phrase modifying 'YOU CALLED' in v. 8a and bĕ...ra'am 'with thunder' as an adverbial phrase modifying 'I ANSWERED YOU' in v. 8b. Note that Qimhi here quotes the views of Rashi and Ibn Ezra without naming his sources. The exegetical difficulty to which Rashi, following Abba Saul, responds here is the obvious contradiction of bĕsēter 'in secrecy' and ra'am 'thunder'.

[19] Cf. Mekilta, vol. 2, pp. 196-97.

[20] In his comment on šĕrîrût libbî at Deut. 29:18 Rashi also asserts that the noun šĕrîrût is a cognate of the verb šwr 'perceive' (for Rashi the root is šr; cf. Mahberet Menahem, p. 368) citing 'ăšûrennû "I shall perceive him" (Num. 24:17). Moreover, he explains that šĕrîrût libbî means "what my heart sees to do." Thus, according to Rashi, šĕrîrût lēb is synonymous with mar'eh 'ênayim, lit., 'seeing of the eyes', which means 'superficiality' (see Isa. 11:3). Rashi, however, is incorrect, for šôrĕrāy at Ps. 5:9 and 'ăšûrennû at Num. 24:17 derive from a triliteral root šwr 'see, perceive' while the element šĕrîrût in the expression šĕrîrût lēb 'stubbornness' derives from a root šrr 'be hard', which is amply attested in Aramaic and in Rabbinic Heb.; see BDB, p. 1057; cf. Ibn Ezra and Qimhi here at Ps. 81:13.

[21] Cf. BT Avodah Zarah 5a and Rashi there; see Maarsen's comment here.

[22] In addition to reversing the word order Rashi responds to the exegetical difficulty presented by the fact that kim'at 'AT ONCE' usually means 'almost, hardly, just' while here it means 'quickly' as also at Job. 32:22; see BDB, p. 590.

[23] For Rashi's treatment of yād 'hand' as a metaphor for makkāh 'plague' see Rashi at Ps. 21:9; 39:11; 77:3; 80:18; see the discussion at Ps. 21:9, n. 10.

[24] The psalmist employs the first person quoting God; Rashi paraphrases in the 3[d] pers., speaking about God.

PSALM LXXXII

1   GOD STANDS IN THE DIVINE ASSEMBLY to see that they judge fairly.[1]
Now as for you, O judges,[2]

2   HOW LONG WILL YOU JUDGE PERVERSELY?

3   VINDICATE [THE LOWLY AND THE POOR].[3]
If he is innocent in his court case, do not subvert his verdict in order to show partiality to the wicked (cf. v. 2b).

5   THEY, the judges who pervert justice,[4]
NEITHER KNOW NOR UNDERSTAND that it is because of this crime that THEY GO ABOUT IN DARKNESS, and that it is for this reason that THE FOUNDATIONS OF THE EARTH TOTTER.[5]

6   YOU FOR DIVINE BEINGS[6] [i.e.], angels.[7]
When I gave the Torah to Israel I gave it to you so that the angel of death would have no dominion over you.

7a   BUT YOU SHALL DIE AS DID the first MAN insofar as you have acted perversely like him.[8]

7b   Indeed, FALL LIKE ANY of the primevals,[9] who died.[10]
A midrash aggadah [interprets], "LIKE ANY heavenly PRINCE" in accord with what is stated in the Bible, "The LORD will punish the host of heaven in heaven" (Isa. 24:21).[11]

8   ARISE, O GOD for judgment. It is in Your power.[12]

PSALM LXXXII, NOTES

[1] The continuation of the verse, "AMONG THE DIVINE BEINGS HE PRONOUNCES JUDGMENT," makes it clear that 'THE DIVINE ASSEMBLY' is, *inter alia*, a judicial body; cf. Midrash Tehillim here. Rashi here responds to the exegetical question, "Why is it that 'GOD STANDS IN' this court of justice?"

[2] Here Rashi calls attention to the fact that the psalmist has abruptly switched from speaking about God in the 3[d] pers. sing. to addressing the judges in Israel's law courts; see Rashi at v. 8, below.

[3] Rashi does not quote the bracketed portion of the verse. I have supplied it for clarity.

[4] The psalmist switches abruptly from addressing the judges in the 2[d] pers. pl. (vv. 2-4) to a description of the judges in the 3[d] pers. pl. (v. 5). It

is less than obvious who is being described here. Briggs here holds that v. 5 is a description of the fate of the victims of the injustice referred to in v. 2. Kirkpatrick, like Rashi and Ibn Ezra, holds that v. 5 describes the culprits.

⁵ Noting that the verbs *yādaʿ* 'know' and *yābîn* 'understand' are transitive, Rashi understands the final two clauses of v. 5 as noun clauses functioning as the compound direct object of the compound predicate "THEY NEITHER KNOW NOR UNDERSTAND." He indicates that these clauses so function by supplying the particle *'ēt*, which is the sign of the direct object. According to Rashi's interpretation, "THEY GO ABOUT IN DARKNESS" refers to the punishment of eternal damnation to be meted out to the wicked judges; see Ps. 49:20. Alternatively, "THEY GO ABOUT IN DARKNESS" can be taken as an independent clause synonymous with the first two, and 'DARKNESS' can be taken as a metaphor for 'ignorance'; cf. Eccles. 2:14.

⁶ Heb. *'ĕlohîm.*

⁷ See also Rashi at Ps. 8:6; other attestations of *'ĕlohîm* meaning 'angel' include Gen. 32:2, 28; see *BDB*, p. 43.

⁸ Rashi's comment on vv. 6-7 is taken almost verbatim from an unattributed baraitha (i.e., a Tannaitic, i.e., Mishnaic era dictum, which is not found in the Mishnah itself) in BT Avodah Zarah 5a. According to this baraitha, just as Adam (in Rabbinic literature always *'ādām hārī'šôn* 'the first man'; see Kadushin, *Worship and Ethics*, p. 267, n. 85) was to have lived forever had he not transgressed the one commandment he was given, sc., not to eat of the fruit of the tree of knowledge, so was Israel upon accepting the Torah, granted immortality. However, since they, like Adam, transgressed, they, like Adam, must die. Note that our Rashi ms. errantly reverses the order of the words *tĕmûtûn* 'YOU SHALL DIE' and *hārī'šôn* 'the first'; our scribe has called attention by supralinear numerals (א = 1; ב = 2) to the correct word order.

⁹ Heb. *rī'šônîm*, Rashi's paraphrase of the psalmist's *śārîm* 'PRINCES'; in other editions of Rashi's commentary here the adjective *rī'šônîm* follows and modifies the noun *śārîm.*

¹⁰ Jacob b. Zvi Hirsch of Mir suggests in his supercommentary 'Ateret Zvi that Rashi here summarizes the following midrash found in Sifre Deuteronomy at Deut. 32:2: "What is the meaning of 'You shall fall like one of the princes'? R. Judah [b. Ilai] said, '[It means] either like Adam or like Eve'." Neither Finkelstein's text nor his apparatus has this midrash; see Sifre Deuteronomy, ed. Finkelstein, p. 341, ll. 3-4.

¹¹ The source of this midrash is Midrash Tehillim here. Jacob b. Zvi Hirsch of Mir in his commentary *'Ateret Zvi* here points out that the first interpretation, whose source Rashi does not cite, treats vv. 7a-b as synonymous parallelism while the second midrash treats vv. 7a-b as synthetic parallelism.

¹² Rashi's paraphrase of "JUDGE THE EARTH, FOR ALL THE NATIONS ARE YOUR POSSESSION" (v. 8b-c).

PSALM LXXXIII

2   O GOD, DO NOT BE SILENT.
[I.e.], Do not react with silence to our oppression with which our enemies are oppressing us.

6b   THEY HAVE MADE AN ALLIANCE AGAINST YOU.
[This][1] counsel (see v. 6a) is specifically[2] against You[3] in order to cause Your Name to be forgotten, for You are not 'their God' but only 'our God' [i.e.], 'the God of Israel' (Ex. 5:1; 32:27; Josh. 7:13, 19, 20; Jer. 7:3, 21; etc.). Now once "ISRAEL'S NAME WILL BE MENTIONED NO MORE" (v. 5b) Your Great Name will likewise not be remembered.[4]

9a   ASSYRIA TOO [i.e.], even Assyria, which belonged to the rest of the nations [but concerning whom] it is stated in the Bible, "From that land Assyria departed" (Gen. 10:11), [which refers to the fact that] Assyria disassociated himself from the scheme of the generation of the separation.[5] Here [in Ps. 83:9, however, it is pointed out that] he joined them [the other nations] in [doing] evil.[6]
Another equally plausible interpretation of 'ASSYRIA TOO' is [the following]: This [nation] TOO, which at its inception chose [to do] good deeds[7] in that they [the Assyrians] separated themselves from the counsel of Nimrod,[8] even he[9] [Assyria] went back to being wicked. Therefore, he joined with them in destroying Your Temple. [The source of this latter interpretation is] Genesis Rabbah.[10]

9b   THEY GIVE SUPPORT....
All these [nations listed in vv. 7a-9a] gave help to our neighbors Moab and Ammon and Amalek to attack us.

10   DEAL WITH THEM AS YOU DID WITH MIDIAN at the hands of Gideon (Judges 6-8),
WITH SISERA at the hands of Barak (Judges 4-5).

11a   WHO WERE DESTROYED AT EN-DOR.
I do not know which of the wars was there [whether] Gideon's[11] or Barak's.[12]

11b   WHO BECAME DUNG [*domen*] FOR THE FIELD [i.e.], *zĕbel mĕpúzar* 'scattered manure'; [so] Jonathan [b. Uzziel] rendered [the word *domen* 'dung' in his Aramaic version of the Prophets (2 Kgs. 9:37; Jer. 8:2; 9:21; 16:4; 25:33)].[13]

13 WHO SAID. [The antecedent of the relative pronoun 'WHO' is] these nations mentioned above (in vv. 7-9): Edom and the Ishmaelites and all their allies.[14]

"LET US TAKE AS OUR POSSESSION."

What is the direct object [of the verb]?[15] [The answer is] 'God's Temple'.[16]

14 MAKE THEM LIKE THISTLEDOWN, LIKE STUBBLE DRIVEN BY THE WIND. Now what is THISTLEDOWN [*galgal* ? It is the tops of thistles of the field, which are called *cardons* 'thistles' in O.F.[17] When the winter arrives they become detached and removed automatically, and they open up slowly so that the part which is detached assumes the appearance of the rim of the wheel of a wagon, and the wind carries it away.[18]

16b WITH YOUR STORM [i.e.], *torbèyllon* 'whirlwind' in O.F.[19]

PSALM LXXXIII, NOTES

[1] The bracketed expression is not found in our Rashi ms.; it is supplied from other editions of the commentary.

[2] Heb. *'ēnāh 'ellā'*, lit., 'only'; our Rashi ms. omits the *'ellā'* by haplography; we have supplied it from other texts of the commentary.

[3] This comment appears to be based upon Midrash Tehillim here.

[4] Cf. Midrash Tehillim here.

[5] The latter midrash on Gen. 10:11 is found in Genesis Rabbah 37:4. Rashi here employs that midrash to supply an answer to the exegetical question, "Why does the psalmist employ the emphatic conjunction *gam* 'TOO' (= Rabbinic Heb. *'ap*) expressing surprise with respect to Assyria?"

[6] Cf. Genesis Rabbah 37:4.

[7] Heb. *ma'ăśîm;* our Rashi ms. reads by scribal error *ma'ăśērîm* 'tithes'.

[8] For the tradition that it was Nimrod who instigated the building of the Tower of Babel see Rashi also at BT 'Avodah Zarah 53b, s.v. 'House of Nimrod'; see also *Midrash Hag-gadol*, ed. S. Schechter (Cambridge: Cambridge University Press, 1902), pp. 183-184.

[9] Heb. *'ap hû';* Rashi's paraphrase of the psalmist's *gam;* see above, n. 5.

[10] Cf. Genesis Rabbah 37:4.

[11] So Ibn Ezra here. Jacob b. Zvi Hirsch of Mir in his supercommentary *'Atteret Zvi* suggests that Gideon may have been a native of En-dor since Gideon belonged to the tribe of Manasseh (Judg. 6:15) and En-dor was in the territory of Manasseh (Josh. 17:11).

[12] Jacob b. Zvi Hirsch of Mir in his supercommentary *'Atteret Zvi* notes

that [Joseph] Ibn Yaḥya (1494-1514) [in his Commentary on the Five Scrolls and the Hagiographa (Bologna: The Partners, 1538)] points out that En-dor is in the vicinity of Taanach and Megiddo (Josh. 17:11), which figure prominently in the Song of Deborah (Judg. 5:9); so now recently Othniel Margalith, "Dor and En-dor," *ZAW* 97 (1985), pp. 109-111. Modern commentators are perplexed as much as was Rashi concerning the association of En-dor with either Gideon or Barak; hence the common tendency is to emend En-dor in Ps. 83:11 to En-Harod in light of Judg. 7:1; see *BHS* here; Briggs, vol. 2, p. 221.

[13] Rashi's *zēbel mĕpûzar* is a Hebraization of TJ's *zēbal mĕbuddar*.

[14] Contrast Midrash Tehillim here, which assigns the quotation in v. 13 to the persons named in v. 12.

[15] Heb. *'et mah?*

[16] Which is called in Ps. 83:13 *nĕ'ôt 'ĕlohim*, which Rashi interprets to mean 'GOD'S ABODE' (see Rashi at Ps. 93:5), i.e., 'the Temple'; contrast NJV's "the meadows of God".

[17] The Modern French equivalent is *chardons;* see Greenberg, *Foreign Words*, p. 194.

[18] Rashi here responds to the exegetical question, "Why is THISTLE-DOWN (so NJV and NEB) called in Heb. *galgal* 'wheel' (cf. RSV margin's 'tumbleweed')?" Rashi's description corresponds to that commonly given for *Gundelia tournefortii*, one of the most common of the thirty or more species of tumbleweeds found in the land of Israel; see *Flora and Fauna of the Bible*, Helps for Translators (2[d] ed.; London: United Bible Societies, 1980), p. 187; see also Immanuel Löw, *Die Flora der Juden* (4 vols.; Vienna: R. Löwit, 1924-1934), 1: 413-415; see also Rashi at Isa. 17:13.

[19] The Modern French equivalent is *tourbillon;* cf. Eng. turbulence; see Greenberg, *Foreign Words*, p. 194.

PSALM LXXXIV

2   HOW [*mah*] LOVELY ARE YOUR TABERNACLES. [I.e.], How much [*kammāh*]¹ loved and liked ARE YOUR TABERNACLES.

3a   *niksĕpāh* 'LONGS' [i.e.], *neḥmĕdāh* 'desires'.² *kālĕtāh* 'YEARNS FOR' [i.e.], *nit'awwĕtāh* 'thirsts for'³.... [The verb *kālĕtāh*] is the same verb as is attested in "David's soul yearned⁴ to die⁵ because of Absalom" (cf. 2 Sam. 13:39) THE COURTS OF THE LORD, for they have been destroyed. He [the psalmist] composed it [this psalm] with reference to the Exile.⁶

3b   MY HEART AND MY FLESH WILL SING. [I.e.], they will pray about this [Exile].

4   EVEN A SPARROW HAS FOUND A HOME. [This refers to the fact that] birds made their nests in its [the Temple's]⁷ ruins. However, [according to] a midrash aggadah [this psalm] refers to [the Temple] when it was standing, and the SPARROW is a metaphor for the Congregation of Israel, who put her fledglings there.⁸

5a   PRAISES BELONG TO⁹ him who makes the effort to dwell¹⁰ IN YOUR TEMPLE,

5b   THEY FOREVER PRAISE YOU therein.¹¹

6a   WHO FINDS REFUGE IN YOU. [I.e.], who made You the REFUGE in which he trusts.

6b   HIGHWAYS ARE IN THEIR HEARTS. [I.e.], in his heart he imagines the HIGHWAYS of his behavior to straighten out his beahvior.

7a   THOSE WHO PASS ['ōbĕrê] THROUGH THE VALLEY [bĕ'emeq] OF WEEPING [bākā'] [i.e.], those who transgress [hā'ōbĕrîm 'al] Your Law and who are therefore in the deepest part [bĕ'ōmĕqāh] of Gehinnom engaged in weeping [bekî] and wailing.

7b   THEY MAKE IT INTO A SPRING with their tears.¹²

7c   Also¹³ THE TEACHER [môreh] CLOTHES [US] WITH BLESSINGS. [I.e.], they bless and thank Him,¹⁴ and they say, "He judged us fairly, and His verdict is just, and HE CLOTHED us WITH BLESSINGS, TEACHING [*môreh*] us to walk in the way of goodness, but we did not heed Him."[15]

8a   THEY GO FROM RAMPART TO RAMPART. [I.e.], Those people who are mentioned above, "THOSE WHO DWELL IN YOUR HOUSE" (v. 5a), who have "HIGHWAYS IN THEIR HEARTS" (v. 6b), SHALL GO FROM RAMPART TO RAMPART [i.e.], from the house of study to the synagogue.[16]

8b   AND HE [i.e.], their army, i.e.,[17] their 'TROOP',[18] WILL APPEAR BEFORE the Holy One Blessed be He IN ZION.

9b   HEAR MY PRAYER concerning building Your Temple.

10a   OUR SHIELD. It is [a metaphor for] the Temple, which shields us.

10b   LOOK UPON THE FACE OF David[19] YOUR AN-NOINTED, and take note of his deeds of lovingkindness and of his effort, which he exerted and expended for the building of it [the Temple referred to in v. 10a].[20]

11a   BETTER ONE DAY IN YOUR COURTS and that one should die the following day THAN to live elsewhere[21] A THOUSAND.

11b   I WOULD RATHER A THOUSAND TIMES[22] STAND AT THE THRESHHOLD [i.e.], to stand guard [*lišqōd*] at the threshhold [*sap*][23] and by the doorposts

11c   THAN DWELL IN THE TENTS OF THE WICKED [i.e.], THAN to be dwelling IN THE TENTS OF Esau[24] so as to cleave to them.

12   FOR...SUN AND SHIELD. One should interpret 'SUN' [here] literally.[25] Midrash Tehillim, however, interprets it as a synonym of 'wall'.[26]

PSALM LXXXIV, NOTES

   [1] Rashi clarifies the meaning in context of the ambiguous interrogative particle *mah*.

   [2] The rare verb *ksp* 'long for' is attested in this active meaning both in the *qal* (Ps. 17:12; Job. 14:15) and in the *niphal* (Gen. 31:30 and here at Ps. 84:3). Rashi notes correctly that in the present context the verb *ksp* is synonymous with the more well-known verb *ḥmd* 'desire'; with Maarsen cf. Rashi and Targum Onkelos at Gen. 31:30. However, contrary to the impression Rashi creates here, the *niphal* of the latter verb means 'to be desirable' while 'to desire' is conveyed by the *qal* and the *piʿel* of the verb *ḥmd*.

³ Rashi probably means only to say that the rare anatomical expression *kālĕtāh napšî* attested only here and in Ps. 119:81 means 'I covet'; so *Mahberet Menahem*, p. 214, s.v. *kl* VI. The fact that the *hitpaʻel* of the root *'wy* 'desire' is used to refer to thirst in 2 Sam. 23:15 (= 1 Ch. 11:17), "David was thirsty [*wayyit'awweh*], and he said, 'Would that someone would give me a drink of water from the well of Bethlehem, which is near the gate'," suggests that *kālĕtāh napšî* 'I covet' may originally have meant 'I thirst'. The literal meaning of this expression would be 'my throat is emptied out of its moisture'. On Heb. *kālāh* 'empty out' see Gruber, *Aspects*, pp. 390-99; for *nepeš* meaning 'throat' see Lorenz Dürr, "Hebr. *näpäš* = akk. *napištu* = Gurgel, Kehle," *ZAW* 43 (1925), pp. 262-69; Gruber, "Hebrew *da'ăbon nepeš* 'dryness of throat'," pp. 365-69.

⁴ Our Rashi ms. reads *wattekal nepeš Dāwîd*; similarly, 4QSamᵃ reads *wattekal rûăh Dāwîd*; so also some LXX mss.; contrast the standard Hebrew text: *wattekal Dāwîd*, in which a feminine singular verb serves as the predicate of a masculine singular noun subject.

⁵ Heb. *lāṣē't*, lit., 'to depart'.

⁶ Answering the exegetical question as to why does the psalmist LONG FOR and YEARN FOR the Temple and why does he not put an end to his longing by going there, Rashi concludes that the *Sitz im Leben* of Ps. 84 is the Babylonian Exile (586-538 B.C.E.).

⁷ Cf. Lam. 5:18.

⁸ See Midrash Tehillim here.

⁹ Rendering of the lemma *'ašrê* according to Rashi's interpretation of the word *'ašrê* in his commentary at Ps. 1:1, q.v.; see also below, n. 11.

¹⁰ Rashi's interpretation of the psalmist's 'THOSE WHO DWELL'.

¹¹ If the word *'ašrê* is interpreted here as it is by Rashi at Ps. 1:1 (see there, and see above, n. 9), Ps. 84:5 means that those who receive God's praise will add to His praises.

¹² With Zohory cf. Midrash Tehillim here and Exodus Rabbah 7:3.

¹³ Heb. *wĕ'ap*, which is Rashi's paraphrase of the psalmist's *gam* 'ALSO'.

¹⁴ Lit., 'His Name'.

¹⁵ Rashi's source is Midrash Tehillim here.

¹⁶ The reading "from the synagogue to the house of study" found in Ms. JTS L 778 and Ms. Leiden Scaliger 1 is congruent not only with Rashi's source in Midrash Tehillim here and in BT Berakot 64a but also with the normative rabbinic idea that study of Torah is a higher level of divine service than is prayer; see, e.g., BT Shabbat 10a; cf. Maarsen, p. 84, n. 12.

¹⁷ Explicative *waw*.

¹⁸ This comment incorporates an alternative interpretation of the noun *hayil* 'TROOP', which was previously assumed to mean 'rampart'.

¹⁹ By means of this historicizing gloss Rashi subtly undermines the Christian interpretation of *mĕšîhekā* 'OF YOUR ANNOINTED ONE' as a reference to Jesus; contrast the Messianic interpretation attributed to R. Phineas the priest in Midrash Tehillim here, and note that LXX and

Vulgate render Heb. *mĕšîḥekā* here cristou sou and christi tui respectively; cf. Rashi's treatment of the noun *māšîăḥ* 'annointed one, king' at Ps. 2:2; 105:15.

[20] See 1 Ch. 22.

[21] Followed by Qimhi; NJV.

[22] Note that our Rashi ms. here interpolates the word *'elep* 'A THOU-SAND TIMES' from v. 11a.

[23] The treatment of the verb *histôpēp* as a denominative verb derived from the noun *sap* 'threshhold' goes back to *Mahberet Menahem*, p. 269, s.v. *sp* III; it is accepted by Qimhi, and it finds its way, probably via the latter, into *BDB*, p. 706; *K-B³*, p. 722 and NJV; but see Alan Robinson, "Three Suggested Interpretations in Ps. LXXXIV," *VT* 24 (1974), pp. 380-81.

[24] This comment reflects both (1) the idea met with in Rashi's commentary at Ps. 9:6; 109:2 that Esau is the quintessential embodiment of wickedness; and (2) the lesson to Rashi's own contemporaries that as comfortable as are the tents of Esau-Edom, i.e., European Christendom, the Jew's proper home is in the Middle Eastern country, whose capital is Jerusalem!

[25] This interpretation of the word *šemeš* 'SUN', which is found in NJV, requires the interpretation of the entire clause as a metaphor.

[26] This interpretation of the word *šemeš*, which is followed also by NJV margin, sees the word *šemeš* here as a biform of the noun *šimšāh* 'battlement', which is attested only in Isa. 54:12 (see Rashi there). This interpretation also requires that the entire clause be taken as a metaphor. It is to be preferred to the interpretation 'sun' because the metaphor 'You are a battlement' is congruent with the metaphor 'YOU ARE A SHIELD'. The interpretation of *šemeš* under discussion is presented by Rashi in his comment on our verse in his commentary on BT Sukkah 10a. Jacob Reifmann, "Various Studies on the Psalms Targum," pt. 2, *Beth Ha-Talmud* 2 (1882), p. 222 (in Hebrew) notes that the exegesis in question is reflected in the Targum's *šûr rām* "a high wall". If, as Maarsen has argued (*Parshandatha*, vol. 3, p. VIII), Rashi wrote his commentary on the psalter toward the end of his life after having written his Talmud commentaries, it is reasonable to conclude that here in his comment on Ps. 84:12 Rashi is emphasizing his rejection of the exegesis he had earlier adopted in his commentary at BT Sukkah 10a. It has been noted frequently (see Maarsen and Zohory) that the exegesis Rashi cites here in the name of Midrash Tehillim is absent from current editions of Midrash Tehillim.

PSALM LXXXV

2   YOU HAVE FAVORED YOUR LAND if YOU HAVE RESTORED JACOB'S FORTUNE.[1]

3   YOU HAVE FORGIVEN YOUR PEOPLE'S INIQUITY, and[2] YOU HAVE PARDONED THEIR SIN, and[2]

4a   YOU HAVE WITHDRAWN from them ALL YOUR ANGER, and[2]

4b   YOU HAVE TURNED Yourself[3] AWAY FROM YOUR RAGE.

Then YOU FAVORED YOUR LAND (v. 2). Now so long as You do not do this YOUR LAND, i.e.,[4] Your world, is not favored.[5]

5   RETURN US [šûbēnû] [means] "You return [šûb], and cause us to return [hăšîbēnû].[6]

7   SURELY YOU WILL ultimately REVIVE US AGAIN, for indeed You have so promised us through the agency of Your prophet.[7]

9a   LET ME HEAR WHAT [GOD, THE LORD],[8] WILL SPEAK.

[I.e.], Let me be privileged[9] to hear what the Holy One Blessed be He WILL SPEAK

9b   when[10] HE WILL PROMISE WELL-BEING TO HIS PEOPLE.

9d   MAY THEY NOT TURN TO FOLLY [lĕkislāh] [i.e.], lišṭût 'to foolishness'[11] [i.e.], to sinning against Him.

11a   KINDNESS AND TRUTH MET when Israel were people who speak [the] TRUTH. [When Israel will again be such people] KINDNESS from heaven (cf. v. 12) will MEET with them.

11b   JUSTICE [sedeq] AND WELL-BEING KISS.

The charity [haṣṣĕdāqāh][12] which Israel used to perform and the WELL-BEING from the Holy One Blessed be He will kiss each other, which is to say that the end result of charity is well-being.[13]

12a   TRUTH SPRINGS UP FROM THE EARTH.

When Israel used to act truthfully,

12b   then they would look down from heaven[14] upon the deeds of charity which they used to perform on earth.

13   He[15] ALSO BESTOWS HIS BOUNTY, [i.e.], "He will open... His bounteous store, the heavens, to provide rain" (Deut. 28:12) so that our land will yield its produce.

14   [CHARITY GOES BEFORE HIM][8] AS HE PUTS HIS FEET TO THE ROAD [derek]. [I.e.], the Holy One Blessed be He PUTS CHARITY[16] into the manner[17] in which he relates to His children.[18]

PSALM LXXXV, NOTES

[1] Rather than construing vv. 2a-b as two clauses in synthetic parallelism, Rashi construes them as independent and dependent clauses respectively. With Maarsen cf. Rashi at Deut. 32:43.

[2] By supplying the coordinate conjunction, Rashi intimates that the several expressions employed in vv. 3-4 are not poetic synonyms but expressions referring to successive steps in God's manifestation of His forgiveness.

[3] Here Rashi supplies a direct object for the transitive verb hešíbótā.

[4] Explicative waw.

[5] While Dahood, following Buttenweiser, construes vv. 2-4 as a series of precative perfects petitioning the LORD's favor, Rashi takes vv. 2-4 as a reminder to the LORD of His past favors as a prelude to the petitioning of His favor in vv. 5-8; similarly Ibn Ezra. Qimhi, however, followed by NJV, takes the perfects in vv. 2-4 as prophetic.

[6] Here Rashi intimates that the qal of the verb šwb 'return' is here to be understood simultaneously both as an intransitive verb and as a causative; the latter usage of the verb in question is attested, inter alia, in v. 2, q.v.

[7] See Ezek. 37.

[8] Our Rashi ms. does not quote the bracketed portion of the verse; I have supplied it for clarity.

[9] Construing Heb. 'ezkeh as a cohortative like the psalmist's 'ešmĕ'āh 'LET ME HEAR'.

[10] Heb. kĕše, which is Rashi's unequivocal interpretation of the psalmist's ambiguous kî, which NJV leaves untranslated.

[11] With Maarsen cf. Rashi at Ps. 49:14. Rashi here explains a rare Biblical Heb. expression by using one which is completely unknown in Biblical Heb. but frequently attested in Rabbinic Heb.

[12] Rashi construes Biblical Heb. ṣedeq 'JUSTICE' in the sense of Rabbinic Heb. ṣĕdāqāh 'charity'; see below, nn. 16, 18.

[13] Heb. šālôm, which KJV and JPS consistently rendered 'peace'; see Orlinsky, Notes, p. 228.

[14] Rashi's paraphrase of v. 12b substitutes a pl. active verb for the sing. passive of the biblical text.

[15] Heb. *zeh*, lit., 'This One', which is Rashi's paraphrase of the psalmist's 'THE LORD'.

[16] Heb. *ṣedeq* 'JUSTICE', which Rashi, here as in v. 11b, construes in the sense of Rabbinic Heb. *ṣĕdāqāh* 'charity'; see above, n. 2, and see below, n. 18.

[17] *bĕdarĕkê pĕʿāmāyw*, lit., 'into the paths of His feet', a phrase based upon *lĕderek peʿāmāyw* 'HIS FEET TO THE ROAD' in v. 14.

[18] This interpretation of v. 14 as a prayer of petition requires that *ṣedeq* here not be rendered 'justice' but 'charity, kindness', which is the normal meaning of the feminine form *ṣĕdāqāh* in Rabbinic Heb. (see Kadushin, *The Rabbinic Mind*[3], pp. 297-98) and of *ṣedeq* in Biblical Heb. at Ps. 96:13; on the latter see Ginsberg, "A Strand in the Cord of Hebraic Hymnody," p. 46; see also Hurvitz, "The Biblical Roots of a Talmudic Term: The Early History of the Concept *ṣĕdāqāh*," pp. 155-60.

PSALM LXXXVI

1   A PRAYER OF DAVID. INCLINE YOUR EAR.

2   FOR I AM STEADFAST for I hear my being reviled and my being scorned, and I have the wherewithal to take revenge, but I am silent. Thus it [is interpreted] in Aggadat Tillim.[1] An equally plausible interpretation is [that which] our rabbis interpreted in [BT] Berakot [4a]: "AM I not STEADFAST? All the kings of the east [and the west] are enthroned in their glory before me while as for me, my hands are stained with blood, with [aborted] foetus and with placenta... [in order to declare a woman pure for her husband]."[2]

3   ALL DAY LONG [i.e.], all [during] the Exile, which is [bright as] DAY for the Gentiles and [dark as] NIGHT for Israel. Thus it is interpreted in Aggadat Tillim.[3]

4   I LIFT UP MY SOUL [i.e.], I shall direct my heart.[4]

8b   AND THERE ARE NO DEEDS LIKE YOURS. [Mortal kings build the lower stories of a building first and the upper stories later, but You are] the One who builds the upper stories first.[5]

10b   AND PERFORM WONDERS, YOU ALONE.
Before the angels were created[6] the heavens and the earth were created. Therefore,

9a   ALL THE NATIONS YOU HAVE MADE

9c   WILL PAY HONOR TO YOUR NAME.

13   FROM THE DEEPEST PART OF SHEOL.
It is customary for adulterers to be put into the deepest part of Sheol, and it is from there that You saved me, for Nathan said to me, "Also the LORD has pardoned your sin; you shall not die" (2 Sam. 12:13).[7]

14a   ARROGANT MEN HAVE ARISEN AGAINST ME. [King David here refers to] Doeg[8] and Ahitophel.[9]

14c   THEY ARE NOT MINDFUL OF YOU. [I.e.], They [Doeg and Ahitophel] did not remember what they had seen [namely], that Samuel annointed me by Your decree.[10]

16c   THE SON OF YOUR MAIDSERVANT.

[The significance of this metaphor is that] the son of a maid-servant debases himself before his master more than does a purchased slave, because the son of a maidservant is a homeborn slave,[11] who has grown up in the lap of his master.[12]

17a   SHOW ME A SIGN OF YOUR FAVOR so that it will be known to others that You have forgiven me,

17b   THAT MY ENEMIES MAY SEE the sign AND BE FRUS-TRATED.

However, the Holy One Blessed be He did not heed [this request so as] to show the sign during his [King David's] lifetime but rather in the lifetime of Solomon his son when the gates [of the Temple] stuck to each other and would not open until he [King Solomon] said, "Do not reject Your annointed one; remember the loyalty of Your servant David" (2 Ch. 6:42).[13]

PSALM LXXXVI, NOTES

[1] I.e., Midrash Tehillim, which is referred to in Rashi's Commentary on the Book of Psalms as Aggadat Tillim also at Ps. 44:2 and at Ps. 86:3.

[2] Rashi omits the bracketed portion. I have supplied it for clarity from BT Berakot 4a. The midrash cited here reflects the rabbinic tendency to portray biblical heroes as rabbis who answered questions on ritual law.

[3] I.e., in Midrash Tehillim here (see above, n. 1); note that in Midrash Tehillim instead of the phrase *kol-haggālût* 'all the Exile' the phrase is *hā'ôlām hazzeh* 'this era'.

[4] I.e., Biblical Heb. *nepeš* in Ps. 86:4, like Heb. *lēb* in Eccles. 9:1, 3 and throughout Rabbinic Heb., corresponds to Eng. 'mind, psyche'; hence, according to Rashi, *nāśā' nepeš* means 'direct the mind'; alternatively, *nepeš* here may refer to the organ of speech as in 1 Sam. 1:15; Ps. 42:5; Job. 24:12; cf. Qimhi here; for *nāśā' nepeš* see also Hos. 4:8; Ps. 143:8.

[5] The source of this midrash is Midrash Tehillim here, from which I have supplied the bracketed portion, without which the quotation is incomprehensible unless Rashi assumes that quoting the punch line is sufficient to bring to the mind of the readers the entire midrash. The prooftext is Gen. 1:1: "God created the heavens and [then] the earth."

[6] I.e., when You, God, were truly ALONE, for the angels were not created until the second day of Creation; see Rashi at Gen. 1:5.

[7] Cf. Midrash Tehillim here; note that the sin of which King David, the author of Ps. 86 according to Ps. 86:1, was pardoned in 2 Sam. 12 was adultery. The exegetical question to which the midrash responds is, "Why THE DEEPEST PART OF SHEOL?" Note that here as also in his commentary at Ps. 24:7; 30:2 (see also Rashi at Ps. 51) Rashi takes it

for granted that King David was guilty of adultery; contrast Rashi at 2 Sam. 11.

[8] See 1 Sam. 21-22, and see below, n. 10.

[9] See 2 Sam. 15-17, and see below, n. 10.

[10] Rashi's source is Midrash Tehillim here; for the decree in question see 1 Sam. 16:12. With reference to Heb. *pîkā*, lit., 'your mouth', i.e., 'Your decree', cf. Akk. *pû* 'decree'; see the discussion in S. David Sperling, "Gen. 41:40: A New Interpretation," *JANES* 10 (1978), p. 119.

[11] Heb. *yĕlîd bayit*; see, *inter alia*, Gen. 14:14; 17:13, 23; Jer. 2:14; on the latter see Moshe Held, "Rhetorical Questions in Ugaritic and Biblical Hebrew," *EI* 9 (1969), 76, n. 42 where it is pointed out that Heb. *yĕlîd bayit* is the etymological and semantic equivalent of Akk. *wilid bītim*, which means 'slave'.

[12] Rashi's source here is Midrash Tehillim at Ps. 116:16; with Maarsen cf. Rashi at Ps. 116:16.

[13] The source of this midrash is BT Shabbat 30a; note that this midrash is quoted in Rashi's Commentary on the Book of Psalms also at Ps. 24:7; 30:2.

PSALM LXXXVII

1   OF THE KORAHITES. A PSALM. A SONG.
     ITS COMPOSITION[1] WAS IN REFERENCE TO [*bĕ*]
     THE HOLY MOUNTAINS. As for the COMPOSITION
     of this psalm, the psalmist composed it with reference to [*'al*]
     Mount Zion and Jerusalem.[2]

3a   GLORIOUS THINGS WERE SPOKEN IN YOU.
     As for you, O Jerusalem, glorious words were spoken in you
     out of the mouth of the Holy One Blessed be He. Now what
     are the GLORIOUS THINGS?

3b   [They are] that you are THE CITY OF GOD. *SELAH*.[3]

4a   I MENTION RAHAB AND BABYLON AMONG
     THOSE WHO ACKNOWLEDGE ME. In addition he [the
     psalmist] said this about you [Jerusalem]: "I MENTION
     Egypt[4] AND BABYLON above THOSE WHO AC-
     KNOWLEDGE ME by bringing them[5] as an offering in
     accord with what is stated in the Bible, "Out of all the na-
     tions they shall bring all your brothers...as an offering to the
     LORD..." (Isa. 66:20).[6]

4b   HERE ARE PHILISTIA AND TYRE ALONG WITH
     ETHIOPIA.
     They also, like Egypt and Babylon, will direct their attention
     to ask and to remember concerning each one,

4c   "THIS ONE WAS BORN THERE" [i.e.], this one was
     from a family of persons born in Zion, in accord with what
     is stated in the Bible, "You shall be picked up one by one"
     (Isa. 27:12).[7]

5a   AND TO ZION IT SHALL BE SAID,

5b   EVERY MAN WAS BORN THERE. [I.e.], when they[8]
     bring them [the Israelites returning from Exile] "as an offer-
     ing" (Isa. 66:20), TO ZION IT SHALL BE SAID concern-
     ing each one,[9] "This one is from among those [who were
     born here but who] went into Exile from you [personified
     Jerusalem] and from their kin."[10]

5c   HE WILL ESTABLISH HER ON HIGH.
     The Holy One Blessed be He WILL ESTABLISH HER

[Jerusalem] higher than all [other] cities.[11]

6a   THE LORD WILL INSCRIBE IN THE REGISTER OF PEOPLES.

This [verse is] a case of inversion.[12] Indeed, [the word] [SE]LAH, which is written[13] at the end of it refers to the first part of it [so that v. 6a should be understood as follows]: THE LORD WILL INSCRIBE IN THE REGISTER OF PEOPLES. *SELAH,* [14] which is to say:

In the future when the Holy One Blessed be He will record the Gentiles for anathema,[15] He will count all the Israelites who have been assimilated among them and even those who have been forcibly converted, and He will liberate them [the Israelites] from among them [the Gentiles], and He will say,

6b   "THIS ONE WAS BORN to[16] those who went into Exile from Zion," and He will choose for Himself even these.[17]

Now it is with reference to this [ingathering of assimilated and converted Jews] that Isaiah said, "'And from them likewise I shall take for priests and for Levites,'[18] said the LORD" (Isa. 66:21). [This means that] from the nations who bring them [the exiled Israelites] as an offering (see Isa. 66:20) I shall take those who are assimilated among them. Now there will be [among those Israelites] priests and Levites who are not known [among humankind to be priests and Levites]; however, to Me they are revealed [as being priests and Levites even though they themselves are unaware of their priestly or Levitical or even Israelite origin], "said the LORD" (Isa. 66:21).[19] Now where in the Bible did the LORD say [such a thing]? [He said such a thing in Deut. 29:28]: "The hidden things belong to the LORD our God."[20]

7a   PEOPLE WILL SING; LIKEWISE PEOPLE WILL DANCE

because of this [referred to in v. 6].

7b   ALL MY SPRINGS [i.e.], "all my inward parts" (Ps. 103:1)[21] [will sing] OF YOU [i.e.], of Your salvation.[22] [The noun *ḥōlĕlîm* 'DANCERS' in the expression] 'AND DANCERS ALIKE' is a cognate of [the noun] *mĕḥōlôt* 'dances' (Judg. 21:21).[23]

PSALM LXXXVII, NOTES

¹ Heb. *yĕsûdātô*, which Rashi interprets in the light of late Heb. *yāsad* 'compose, write, author' (see above at Ps. 42:1, 5; 45:1; 57:1; see also, introduction, p. 7, n. 14); similarly Ibn Ezra and Qimhi; contrast KJV: "His foundation *is* in the holy mountains"; the latter follows verbatim Vulgate's "fundamenta ejus in montibus sanctis"; so also LXX; similarly Jerome and NJV.

² Qimhi explains that the plural 'mountains' may refer to the two mountains, Mt. Zion and Mt. Moriah.

³ Similarly Ibn Ezra; contrast NJV: "Glorious things are spoken of you, O city of God." The latter rendering echoes Qimhi's interpretation.

⁴ Here Rashi intimates that RAHAB in Ps. 87:4 is "a poetic term for Egypt"; so now NJV at Ps. 87:4. NJV there finds support for this interpretation in Isa. 30:7: "For Egypt's help is worthless and empty, therefore I have called her 'Rahab who sits still'"; so RSV; contrast NJV; see also Gaster, *MLC*, p. 768, and Dahood here. 'Rahab' means literally 'the proud one'; see Rashi at Isa. 30:7; hence the application of this epithet to the mythical sea monster in Isa. 51:9; Ps. 89:11; Job. 9:13; 26:12; cf. also *marhēbāh* 'the arrogant city' in Isa. 14:4 according to IQIs^a and LXX.

⁵ I.e., the Israelites, from Exile back to Jerusalem.

⁶ Cf. Midrash Tehillim here.

⁷ Cf. BT Ketubot 75a.

⁸ The nations mentioned in v. 4; see Rashi there.

⁹ Heb. *kol-'eḥad wĕ'eḥad*, is Rashi's paraphrase of the psalmist's *'îš wĕ'îš* (v. 5).

¹⁰ Heb. *ûmittôlĕdôtêhem*, which Breithaupt renders *de illorum (Israelitarum) generationibus*; for Heb. *tôlĕdôt* 'kin' cf. Aram. *tôldûtā* 'kinship', on which see Jastrow, *Dict.*, p. 1653.

¹¹ For the idea see Rashi at Deut. 17:8; for a history of religions perspective on this idea see Robert L. Cohn, *The Shape of Sacred Space* (Chico, California: Scholars Press, 1981), pp. 63-74; Levenson, *Sinai & Zion*, p. 175.

¹² On this phenomenon in Rashi's Bible commentaries see Shereshevsky, "Inversions in Rashi's Commentary," id., *Rashi: The Man and His World*, pp. 92-99; and see Rashi at Ps. 45:6, and see our discussion there.

¹³ Heb. *hā'āmûr*, lit., 'which is stated'.

¹⁴ Rashi takes it for granted that Selah means 'Pause'; note that the first syllable of the word SELAH is omitted by haplography from our Rashi ms.

¹⁵ Heb. *lĕdērā'ôn*, which is attested in the Bible only at Isa. 66:24; Dan. 12:2.

¹⁶ Eng. idioms requires 'born to'; Heb. *mē* means lit., 'from'.

¹⁷ Those who were born abroad to assimilated and converted Jews in addition to those who were themselves born in Zion but were carried away as captives. Contrast the psalmist, who speaks not of Jews but of all peoples' adopting Jerusalem as their native city and of God's adopting all people as citizens of Jerusalem.

[18] This is the reading in our Rashi ms.; such a reading is found also in many other medieval Heb. Bible mss.

[19] With reference to Rashi's comment at Isa. 66:21 see Maarsen there and here. Rashi's comment here, which is a conflation of several midrashim in Midrash Tehillim here, brilliantly solves the apparent contradiction between Trito-Isaiah's universalism, which appears to contemplate proselytes' becoming priests and Levites, and Rabbinic *halakah*, according to which proselytes may not even marry priests (see Maimonides, Mishneh Torah, Laws of Forbidden Intercourse 18:1, 3; see also Qimhi at Isa. 66:21).

[20] Rashi's comment here is based on the midrash attributed to R. Phineas the priest at Midrash Tehillim here.

[21] Heb. *qĕrābay*.

[22] With Maarsen here cf. Canticles Rabbah at Cant. 1:4.

[23] Cf. Gruber, "Ten Dance-Derived Expressions in the Hebrew Bible," pp. 341-45.

PSALM LXXXVIII

1   FOR THE LEADER; ON ['AL] *MAHALATH LEANNOTH.*
     [The latter three Hebrew words, which can be rendered lit-
     erally, "concerning sickness to be endured," suggest that this
     psalm was composed] *'al* 'in response to' lovesickness (Cant.
     2:5) and suffering with which she [Israel] was made to en-
     dure during the punishments of the Exile.
     OF HEMAN THE EZRAHITE.[1] He was [one of the sons
     of Zerah son of] Judah as he was listed in [1] Chronicles
     (2:6): "The sons of Zerah: Zimri, Ethan, Heman, Darda,
     and Calcol, five in all,"[2] and they were great sages in accord
     with what is stated in the Bible, "Solomon" (1 Kgs. 5:10)
     "was wiser than all...the sons of Mahol" (1 Kgs. 5:11).[3]
     They composed psalms, and they [their psalms] were in-
     clude in the Book of Psalms; therefore they were named "the
     sons of Mahol".[4]
     A *MASKIL.* Wherever [in the Bible] it is stated, *'MASKIL',*[5]
     it [the psalm was composed] with the aid of a ghost writer[6]
     in the following manner: The prophet[7] would have the ghost
     writer present with him so that when he would experience
     [prophetic] inspiration, he [the prophet/psalmist] would tell
     the content of the prophecy to the ghost writer, and the lat-
     ter would give literary expresssion to it.

2   BY DAY I CRY OUT and also BY NIGHT I stand[8] BE-
     FORE YOU.[9]

4   FOR I AM SATED WITH MISFORTUNE. He [the
     psalmist] says this concerning the Congregation of Israel.[10]

5   *'ēn 'ĕyāl.* [I.e.], *'ēn koăḥ* 'has no strength'. [The noun *'ĕyāl*
     'strength' is] a cognate of [the abstract noun *'ĕyālût* 'strength'
     found in] "My strength, hasten to my aid" (Ps. 22:20).[11]

6   FREE AMONG [*bĕ*] THE DEAD. Here I am among [*bên*][12]
     THE DEAD. FREE from the world and finished [*wĕkal-
     lēh*].[13] [THE DEAD are called] FREE[14] because they are
     FREE from the world.[15]
     AND CUT OFF BY YOUR HAND. [I.e.], by means of
     Your plagues THEY WERE CUT OFF from the world.[16]

7   AT THE BOTTOM OF THE PIT. This is [a metaphor
     for] the Exile.

8a   *sāmĕkāh* 'LIES HEAVY'. [I.e.], *nišʿănāh* 'leans' UPON ME.

8b   YOU AFFLICT ME WITH ALL YOUR BREAKERS.
      SELAH.
      mišbārîm 'BREAKERS' is a synonym of 'waves of the sea'.[17]
      As for every eruption of Your anger, in all of them YOU
      AFFLICT them[18] continually.[19]

9a   YOU MAKE ME ABHORRENT TO THEM.
      As for the Gentiles, in whose eyes I was important,[20] I am
      now abominable[20] to them.[21]

9b   SHUT IN [i.e.], imprisoned and I am unable to leave.[22]

11a   DO YOU WORK WONDERS FOR THE DEAD?
      [I.e.], for the wicked, who are termed DEAD even while
      they are alive,[23] for them do you not perform[24] miracles?

11b   DO THE SHADES RISE TO PRAISE YOU?
      [It means], WILL the Gentiles, who were negligent[25] with
      respect to Your service and with respect to Your Torah,
      RISE and PRAISE YOU? [This clause is to be understood]
      as a question.[26]

12a   IS YOUR FAITHFUL CARE RECOUNTED IN THE
      GRAVE?
      [I.e.], if we die at the hand of our enemies, shall be be able
      to recount Your praise IN THE GRAVE?

16a   TURNED OVER [*minnoʿar*]...AND NEAR DEATH.
      [I.e.], dying from being turned over [*mittôk tišnoq*].[27] [The
      gerund *noʿar*] is from the same verbal root as is reflected in
      "The LORD turned over Egypt" (Ex. 14:27).

16b   YOUR TERRORS. *'āpûnāh*, [I.e., I, the Congregation of
      Israel, am] confident and rational [although] Your terror[28]
      is in my heart. [The feminine adjective] *'āpûnāh* 'confident'
      is a cognate of [the word *'open* found in] "a pronouncement
      spoken *'al 'opnāyw* " (Prov. 25: 11b) [i.e.], *'al mĕkônāyw* 'upon
      its bases [in fact and in logic]'.[29]

19b   AND MY COMPANIONS OUT OF MY SIGHT.[30]
      I was made absent, i.e.,[31] I ceased being among them.[32]

PSALM LXXXVIII, NOTES

   [1] He is mentioned in the psalter only here, but see 1 Ch. 6:18; 15:17,
19; 16:41-42; 25:1, 4-6; 2 Ch. 5:12; 29:14; 35:15. Rashi's identification in
his commentary here and in his commentary at 1 Kgs. 5:11 of Heman the
psalmist with Heman the sage mentioned in 1 Kgs. 5:11 (cf. 1 Ch. 2:6)
derives from PRK, ed. Mandelbaum, p. 61.

[2] In the standard Heb. text of 1 Ch. 2:6 the penultimate name is Calcol, and the last name is Dara; the form Darda is known from some medieval Heb. mss. of 1 Ch. and from 1 Kgs. 5:11.

[3] Rashi here omits in his citation the names of the five sages, the second of whom is Heman.

[4] Alternatively, *běnê māḥôl* may mean "members of the guild of dance musicians"; see "Mahol," in *Illustrated Dictionary and Concordance of the Bible*, p. 646.

[5] See above, Ps. 32:1, n. 1.

[6] Similarly Rashi at Ps. 32:1; cf. also Rashi at Ps. 45:1; for the source and discusssion see Ps. 32:1, n. 2.

[7] For the idea that psalmody is included in prophecy, from which it follows that a psalmist should be designated a prophet, see Midrash Tehillim 90:4: "R. Levi taught in the name of R. Hanina: 'The eleven psalms, which Moses composed, are set down in the books of the prophets.'" The eleven psalms are Pss. 90-100; see Midrash Tehillim at Ps. 90:3, and see Rashi at Ps. 90:1.

[8] Heb. *'ănî nākôn.*

[9] Rashi understands *yôm* 'BY DAY' and *ballaylāh* 'BY NIGHT' as poetic parallels introducing two synonymous clauses, both of which mean 'I pray'; for this pair cf. Ps. 42:9; 77:3; 121:6. Seeing that the second clause lacks a verb, he takes 'BEFORE YOU' as ellipsis for 'I am standing BEFORE YOU'. Hereby Rashi intimates that 'stand before the LORD' is a posture of prayer-derived idiom for 'pray' synonymous with *ṣā'aq* 'cry out'; so now Gruber, *Aspects*, p. 150 referring to Jer. 18:20; Ps. 106:30-31. Rashi's explication of this ellipsis, which is methodologically identical with the manner in which the masters of Ugaritology restore a broken cuneiform tablet, should put to rest the notion that Rashi failed to understand the nature of Biblical parallelism (contrast Kugel, p. 173; Gelles, p. 101); contrast NJV, which follows Ibn Ezra's exegesis.

[10] Following Midrash Tehillim at v. 2, Rashi conceives of the speaker as a personification of collective Israel. Thereby he transforms Ps. 88 from a lament of the individual to a lament of the community.

[11] See Rashi at Ps. 22:20. Maarsen's suggestion here that Rashi's source is *Mahberet Menahem*, s.v. *'el* I (pp. 42-43) is incorrect; the likely source is *Mahberet Menahem*, s.v. *'yl* II (p. 39).

[12] Here Rashi, followed by NJV, asserts that in the present context the preposition *bě*, lit., 'in', means 'among'; see also *BDB*, p. 88a.

[13] Ephraim Zalman Margalioth, *Shem Ephraim* (Munkacz: Kahn, 1913) here suggests emending *wěkalleh* to *kěmô ḥălālîm* 'like the fallen'. There seems, however, to be no basis in the manuscript tradition of Rashi's commentary for such a restoration here.

[14] See also Job. 3:19.

[15] With Breithaupt here cf. the dictum attributed to R. Johanan [b. Napha] in BT Niddah 61b: "The meaning of FREE AMONG THE DEAD (Ps. 88:6) is [as follows]: Once a person is dead he is made free of

obligations [*miṣwôt*]"; cf. the almost verbatim quotation at BT Shabbat 30b; 151b.

[16] For *yad* 'hand' as a metaphor for *makkāh* 'plague' in Rashi's commentary on the psalter see Rashi at Ps. 21:9; 39:11; 77:3; 80:18; 81:15; and see discussion at Ps. 21:9, n. 10; for the ambiguity of the preposition *mi(n)*, which can mean, *inter alia*, 'by' as well as 'from', see *BDB*, p. 579.

[17] With Maarsen see Rashi's explanation at Jonah 2:4.

[18] I.e., all Israel, personified by the psalmist who speaks in the 1st pers. sing.

[19] With Maarsen note that Rashi alludes here to the assertion of R. Eliezer b. Jehozadaq in BT 'Erubin 54a that *Selah* means 'continually'.

[20] Both adjectives are feminine since they refer to the Congregation of Israel; see Rashi at v. 4.

[21] Rashi's paraphrase points to the fact that the psalmist's archaic *lāmô* is the equivalent of Classical Heb. *lāhem* 'to them'.

[22] Rashi's paraphrase of the psalmist's I DO NOT GO OUT.

[23] The source is a *baraitha* in BT Berakot 18b, which attributes this idea to Sifra deBe Rab; this dictum is unattested, however, in current editions of the Sifra.

[24] Rashi's paraphrase substitutes the Rabbinic Heb. present tense for the psalmist's imperfect.

[25] Rashi fully appreciates the fact that vv. 11a-b contain two parallel clauses in which *mētîm* 'DEAD' and *rĕpā'îm* 'SHADES' are synonyms. Where Rashi differs from modern interpreters is in his assumption that both terms function here as metaphors for 'wicked Gentiles'. Note that the Rabbinic Heb. idiom *rippē' yādayim*, lit., 'slacken the hands', i.e., 'be negligent', corresponds semantically to Akk. *aḫa nadû*. The etymology of Heb. *rĕpā'îm* here quoted by Rashi derives from BT Ketubbot 111b; cf. Rashi at Isa. 26:14.

[26] Rashi is correct in seeing a question in v. 11b; this verse is an example of the stylistic device known as the double rhetorical question identified by Rashi in his commentary at Jer. 14:22; 23:20; Job. 27:10; on the double rhetorical question see Yitzhak Avishur, "Patterns of the Double and the Triple Question in the Bible and in Ugaritic," in *Zer Li'Gevurot*, ed. B. Z. Luria (Jerusalem: Kiryat Sefer, 1973), pp. 421-464 (in Hebrew); id., "The Triple Question in the Book of Jeremiah," *Beth Mikra* 45 (1971), pp. 152-170 (in Hebrew); Eliezra Herzog, "The Triple Rhetorical Argument in the Latter Prophets" (Ph.D. diss., Jewish Theological Seminary of America, 1991); Held, "Rhetorical Questions in Ugaritic and Biblical Hebrew," pp. 71-79.

[27] Maarsen here points out that Rashi here and at Ex. 14:27 follows T.O.'s interpretation of the verb *ni'ēr* at Ex. 14:27.

[28] See Rashi at Prov. 25:11.

[29] See the discussion of this comment in Kamin, *Rashi's Exegetical Categorization*, pp. 71-72.

[30] Maarsen here points out that Rashi's comment here presupposes the pointing *maḥšāk* 'absence' rather than MT's *maḥšāk* 'darkness'. *BH*³ pre-

fers the reading *maḥśāk,* which is supported by many Heb. mss., Jerome, and Peshitta.

[31] Explicative *waw.*

[32] Heb. *neḥdaltî mēhem;* note that in Biblical Heb. *ḥādal* 'cease' is employed in the *qal* and *hophal;* never in the *niphal.*

PSALM LXXXIX

1   A MASKIL OF ETHAN THE EZRAHITE.[1] However,
He also is one of five brothers who were poets.[1] However,
our rabbis interpreted it [the name Ethan the Ezrahite] as
[an epithet of] Abraham our patriarch. [According to this
interpretation, Abraham is called Ethan the Ezrahite] because of [the biblical verse], "Who has roused from the
East?" (Isa. 41:2).[2]

2b   I WILL PROCLAIM YOUR FAITHFULNESS WITH
MY MOUTH.
As for You, of whom I know that You keep Your promise
and fulfill Your commitments.

3a   FOR I SAID, "'ôlām ḥesed yibbāneh."[3]
[I.e.], I thought[4] that the world will be built on Your loyalty
and [that] IN THE HEAVENS YOU ESTABLISH YOUR
FAITHFULNESS. [This means] that it [YOUR FAITH-
FULNESS] will be established and fulfilled. Now, what is
the FAITHFULNESS [i.e., the promise, here referred to]?
[It is] the same promise, which You promised to David
through the agency of Nathan the prophet, saying,

4a   "I HAVE MADE A COVENANT WITH MY CHOSEN
ONE

5a   to ESTABLISH his PROGENY FOREVER."[5]

6a   AND THE HEAVENS WILL ACKNOWLEDGE YOUR
WONDERS, O LORD, if You will[6] keep Your promise.

6b   YOUR FAITHFULNESS, TOO [i.e.], the faithfulness of
Your promises THEY WILL ACKNOWLEDGE (v. 6a)[7] IN
THE ASSEMBLY OF HOLY BEINGS [i.e.], in the great
ASSEMBLY of angels.[8]

10b   běśô' gallāyw 'WHEN ITS WAVES SURGE' [i.e.], běhinnāśē'
gallāyw 'when its waves surge'.[9]
YOU STILL THEM [těšabběḥēm] [i.e.], tašpîlēm 'You put
them down'. Now the same root [šbḥ 'still, put down'] is attested in "A dullard vents all his rage, but a wise man calms
it down" (Prov. 29:11), and it is attested in "who stills the
raging seas" (Ps. 65:8).[10]

11   RAHAB. [This is an epithet of] Egypt.[11]

16a   WHO KNOW THE SOUND OF THE SHOFAR, around which they arrange [the recitation of] verses proclaiming the kingship of God, verses proclaiming God's mindfulness, and verses proclaiming the significance of the shofar.[12]

18   THROUGH YOUR FAVOR [i.e.], when You are pleased with them [i.e., Israel].[13] [The noun *rāṣôn* 'FAVOR' means] *apaiement* 'appeasement' in Old French.[14]

20a   TO YOUR FAITHFUL ONES [i.e.], Nathan the prophet and Gad the seer.[15]

20b   I HAVE PROVIDED my HELP for David[16] to help him continually.

23   NO ENEMY SHALL OPPRESS HIM.
[I.e., THE ENEMY] will not prevail over him so as to behave[17] toward him as a creditor [*nōšeh*].[18]

28   I WILL APPOINT HIM FIRST-BORN. [This is simply a metaphor for] I WILL MAKE HIM great.[19]

33a   I WILL PUNISH THEIR TRANSGRESSION WITH THE ROD.
This is what Nathan the prophet said about Solomon, "When he commits iniquity, I shall chasten him with the rod of people" (2 Sam. 7:14b). This [prophecy] refers to Rezon the son of Eliada, who arose as his adversary.[20] "And with plagues inflicted by humans" (2 Sam. 7:14c).[21] This [prophecy] refers to Asmodeus. [The reason that the plagues inflicted by Asmodeus are attributed in 2 Sam. 7:14c and in Ps. 89:33b to *běnê 'ādām* 'humans'] is that the demons were children of Adam.[22]

36   I SHALL NOT BE FALSE TO DAVID. [The verb *kzb*] is the same verb as is attested in "whose waters do not fail" (Isa. 58:11), [which is rendered] *failyant* 'failing' [in Old French].[23]

38   AN ENDURING WITNESS IN THE SKY.
[It means that] the moon and the sun are witnesses for him [King David] in that as long as they exist his dynasty will exist in accord with Jeremiah, who said, "If you could break My covenant with the day and My covenant with the night... only then could My covenant with David be broken" (Jer. 33:20-21).

39   YET YOU HAVE REJECTED.

You dealt strictly with his [King David's] descendants, taking account of their iniquity, with respect to which YOU REJECTED them, and You spurned[24] them in the reign of Zedekiah.[25]

40   YOU HAVE REPUDIATED [i.e.], You cancelled.[26]

41a   ALL HIS DEFENSES, which he [King David] built in Jerusalem.[27]

41b   HIS STRONGHOLDS [i.e.], the Temple Mountain[28] and the stronghold of Zion.[29]

44a   YOU HAVE TURNED BACK ['ap-tāšîb] THE BLADE [ṣûr] OF HIS SWORD [ḥarbô].
You turned back [hăšēbôtā 'āḥôr],[30] i.e.,[31] You turned over [hāpaktā] the sharp part of his sword. [The noun ṣûr 'BLADE' and the noun ḥarbô 'SWORD'] are the same as [the two words found in the plural in the expression ḥarěbôt ṣûrîm 'sharp knives' (Josh. 5:2),[32] and [the root of the noun ṣûr 'BLADE'] is likewise reflected in "No weapon sharpened [for use] against you shall succeed" (Isa. 54:17).[33]

44b   AND HAVE NOT SUSTAINED HIM [i.e.], You did not help him stand up[34] so that he would not fall.

45a   YOU HAVE BROUGHT TO AN END HIS SPLENDOR[miṭṭěhorô], [i.e.], zěrîḥātô 'his shining'; it is a cognate of ṣāhŏrāyim 'noon'[35] (Isa. 16:3; Jer. 20:16; etc.), which we render into Aramaic by ṭěhărā' (so TJ at Isa. 16:3; Jer. 20:16); and it is a cognate of [Heb. ṭohar 'brightness' in] "and like the very sky in respect of brightness" (Ex. 24:10).

45b   AND YOU HAVE HURLED [miggartāh] TO THE GROUND.
[I.e.], You have cast down, and You have lowered. Every verb referring to being lowered is [rendered into Aramaic] in Targum Jonathan by [the verb] měgar.[36]

48a   I REMEMBER WHAT IS AGE [i.e.], how elderly I am.[37] [In other words], Are not my few days [short] enough for You in that You [will] exact punishment from me at my death [which is] a few days [off]?[38]

48b   WHY [SHOULD YOU HAVE CREATED EVERY MAN][39] IN VAIN [šāwě']? [This question is to be interpreted as an assertion meaning] lěhinnām for nought', i.e.,[40] lěhebel 'for no purpose' YOU CREATED EVERY MAN.

51b   THAT I HAVE BORNE IN MY BOSOM MANY

PEOPLES. During the Exile I [Israel, personified by the psalmist], bear their suffering and their burden.[41]

52 AT THE HEELS [i.e.], at the time of[42] the King Messiah. Now it [the use of the expression '*iqqěbôt*, lit., 'heels of' to mean 'time of'] is [typically] Mishnaic Hebrew [as is exemplified by the apothegm], "On the heels of the Messiah arrogance will increase" (Mishnah Soṭah 9:15).[43]

53 BLESSED IS THE LORD FOREVER[44] in respect of all the salvation that He has done for us.

PSALM LXXXIX, NOTES

[1] In 1 Kgs. 5:11 Ethan the Ezrahite appears as one of the four *běnê māḥôl*, which can mean either "son of Mahol" (so NJV) or "members of the guild of composers of dance music" (so apparently Rashi here); in 1 Ch. 2:6 it is written, "The sons of Zerah: Zimri, Ethan, Heman, Calcol, and Dara, five in all." Note that Zimri is the only of these names not found in the list of the four in 1 Kgs. 5:11, and that Dara of 1 Ch. 2:6 appears to be a variant of Darda found in 1 Kgs. 5:11. Rashi here suggests that Ethan the Ezrahite is to be added to the list of the ten poets who contributed compositions to the psalter quoted in Rashi's Introduction to the Book of Psalms, q.v. Note, however, that this suggestion is not original with Rashi; it is found in BT Baba Batra 15a in the form of an anonymous challenge spoken in Aramaic to the Tannaitic tradition (BT Baba Batra 15a; see also Midrash Tehillim at Ps. 1:1) that the psalter contains the compositions of only ten poets.

[2] Rashi here takes it for granted that Isa. 41:2, "Who has roused ṣedeq from the East?" refers to God's having summoned Abraham (Gen. 12:1ff.) from Ur of the Chaldeans (Gen. 11:31; 15:7; Neh. 9:7) that he might pursue ṣedeq 'justice' (see Gen. 18:19); see Rashi at Isa. 41:2. Modern commentators prefer the view of Ibn Ezra that the verse refers to God's summoning Cyrus to conquer Babylon. Assuming that *mimmizrah* 'from the East' refers to Abraham, Rav at BT Bava Batra 15a asserts that Ethan the Ezrahite here in Ps. 89:1 must be Abraham. Apparently, Rav reasons that since 'she (the sun) arises from the East' is expressed in Heb. by *tizrah*, Heb. *'ezrah* must mean "I (who) arise from the East."

[3] While NJV construes Biblical Heb. *'ôlām* as an adverbial expression meaning 'forever', Rashi interprets *'ôlām* here according to its additional meaning in Rabbinic Heb., 'world'; on *'ôlām* in Rabbinic Heb. see Kadushin, *The Rabbinic Mind*[3], pp. 293-95.

[4] Rashi notes correctly that in the present context Biblical Heb. *'āmar*, lit., 'say', means 'think'.

[5] Rashi paraphrases the psalmist's 2d pers. masc. sing. pronominal suffix employing the 3d pers. masc. sing.

[6] Heb. *'im hāyîtā*, lit., 'if You were, employed here in the sense of an Indo-European subjunctive.

[7] Rashi's point is that 'YOUR WONDERS' (v. 6a) and 'YOUR FAITHFULNESS' (v. 6b) constitute the compound direct object of the verb 'THEY WILL ACKNOWLEDGE' in v. 6a.

[8] See v. 8.

[9] Here Rashi's point is that the rare *qal* infinitive construct is synonymous with the more frequently attested *niphal* infinitive; similarly Ps. 24:9 employs the *qal* imperative of the verb *nāśā'* where the context would seem to call for the *niphal* imperative; on the latter anomaly see Held, "The Action-Result (Factitive-Passive) Sequence," p. 276, n. 8 and the literature cited there.

[10] See above, Ps. 65:8, n. 9.

[11] In fact, Rahab here is an epithet of the Sea Monster; see Gaster, *Thespis*, pp. 446-50. However, it is true that in Isa. 30:7 and in Ps. 87:4 Rahab is indeed an epithet of Egypt; see Rashi at Ps. 87:4. For a possible explanation of the latter usage as deriving from the former see Nahum M. Sarna, "Rahab," *EM* 7:329.

[12] See Birnbaum, *High Holyday Prayer Book*, pp. 377-394; see the discussion in Mishnah Rosh ha-Shanah 4:5-6.

[13] So already Breithaupt.

[14] See our discussion of this O.F. gloss at Ps. 5, n. 7.

[15] Rashi here and both Rashi and Tosafot at BT 'Avodah Zarah 20b attest to the plural reading *laḥăsîdêkā* 'TO YOUR FAITHFUL ONES', which is found in current editions of MT. This latter reading is supported also by LXX and Vulgate. However, various midrashim found in BT Avodah Zarah and Yalqut Shim'oni here attest to the reading *laḥăsîdēkā* 'TO YOUR FAITHFUL ONE' (singular), which they interpret to refer to David; so now Dahood here. Qimhi here also assumes the singular form, which he interprets as a reference to the prophet Samuel (see 1 Sam. 16:1ff.). Ibn Ezra, who reads "Your faithful ones," interprets this as a reference to "the psalmists such as Heman and Ethan, who were called prophets and seers." The latter assertion finds support in 1 Ch. 25:1, 5. The latter assertion is to be understood against the background of Ibn Ezra's conviction that the psalter is not simply a book of prayers addressed to God but rather a collection of prophetic utterances. On this view and its history see Simon, *Four Approaches to the Book of Psalms*, pp. 168-69 and passim (in Hebrew). NJV margin suggests that 'THE FAITH-FUL ONE spoken to IN A VISION must be Nathan the prophet and that the VISION is recorded both in Ps. 89:4-5 and in 2 Sam. 7:1-17. The plural reading *laḥăsîdêkā* requires Rashi to include the other prophet, who was active when David was King of Israel in Jerusalem, sc., Gad (see 1 Sam. 22:5; 2 Sam. 24; 1 Ch. 21; 29). Cf. Briggs here.

[16] Rashi hereby intimates that the psalmist's 'WARRIOR' is a reference to David.

[17] Lit., 'be'.

[18] As noted by Maarsen here, Rashi's interpretation of the meaning of the verb *yaśśî'* follows *Maḥberet Menaḥem*, p. 359, s.v. *ś'* III. This line of exegesis, which is followed also by Moses Ibn Gikatilla (quoted in Ibn

Ezra here), Qimhi, and *BDB*, p. 673b, s.v. *nš'* I, is reflected already in LXX. For possible derivation of the verb *yaššî'* from *BDB*'s *nš'* II 'beguile, deceive' see Ibn Ezra and Briggs here.

[19] My explication of Rashi's comment is based on a comparison of Rashi's similar remarks at Ex. 4:22; 12:30; Deut. 33:17, which are cited in Maarsen's comment here.

[20] Rashi's exegesis is based upon an anonymous comment in Tanḥuma, ed. Buber, Bereshit #26, which sees here a reference to 1 Kgs. 11:23, q.v. Rashi employs the verb *'āmad* in its late Heb. sense 'arose', which is equivalent to classical Biblical Heb. *qām*, which is employed in the *hiphil* with God as subject and Rezon as direct object in 1 Kgs. 11:23. Concerning Rezon see "Rezon" in *EM* 7:343-44 (in Hebrew).

[21] The latter phrase is paraphrased as follows in Ps. 89:33b: "Their iniquity with plagues."

[22] In Rashi's language, as always in Rabbinic Heb. 'Adam' is *'ādām hāri'šôn* 'the first man'. Here Rashi alludes to a midrash found in Tanḥuma, ed. Buber, Bereshit #26. The latter midrash contends that during the period of one hundred and thirty years (Gen. 5:3) that intervened between the tragic death of Abel (Gen. 4:8) and the birth of Seth (Gen. 4:25) Adam eschewed sexual contact with Eve. However, spirits did have intercourse with him so that he fathered demons. Cf. parallels in BT 'Erubin 18b; Gen. Rabbah 20:24; for additional parallels see Theodor-Albeck ed. of Gen. Rabbah there and Tanḥuma, ed. Buber, Bereshit #26, n. 225. These midrashim reflect recognition of both (1) the physiological fact that an adult male who eschews all sexual activity will experience periodic nocturnal emissions of semen; and (2) the folk belief that these emissions occur because the sleeping man is having intercourse with demons. Moroever, Rashi's comment is inspired by the recognition (see Tanḥuma, ed. Buber, there) that the noun *nega'*, which means 'plague, affliction' in 2 Sam. 7:14; Ps. 89:33 means 'demon' in Ps. 91:10. This assertion is lent plausibility by the demonstration that Ps. 91 in its entirety is an incantation recited to drive away demons; on the latter idea see Gaster, *MLC*, pp. 769-771; 851, n. 1.

[23] See Rashi also at Ps. 116:11, and see the discussion there.

[24] Rashi paraphrases the psalmist's imperfect as a perfect, indicating that the psalmist has employed the imperfect form of the verb as a preterite.

[25] Our Rashi ms. reads Hezekiah with supralineal correction of the first two consonants *h, z* to *z, d*, yielding the correct reading, Zedekiah. Rashi here refers to the events described in 2 Kgs. 24:12-25:7. These events took place during the years 597-586 B.C.E. Note, however, that the status of Jehoiachin, the exiled King of Judah, was exalted in 561 B.C.E.; see 2 Kgs. 25:27-30.

[26] So Rashi also at Lam. 2:7 where Ps. 89:40 is cited as proof.

[27] See 2 Sam. 5:9; 1 Ch. 11:8.

[28] See 2 Sam. 24:18-25; 1 Ch. 21:18-22:19.

[29] See 2 Sam. 5:7-9; 1 Ch. 11:7-8.

[30] By means of this paraphrase Rashi intimates that here the psalmist employs the imperfect form of the verb as a preterite.

[31] Note the explicative *waw*.

[32] Rendering of *ḥarĕbôt ṣûrîm* based on Rashi there. Rashi, who finds support also in TJ, sees the two words *ḥarĕbôt* and *ṣûrîm* as synonymous meaning 'swords, blades', the juxtaposition of which suggests intensity; for the latter phenomenon cf. Speiser, *Genesis*, p. 156, n. 20 concerning *rōbeh qaššāt*, lit., 'bowman, archer' (Gen. 21:20), which Speiser renders "a skilled bowman"; contrast NJV and RSV at Josh. 5:2: "flint knives".

[33] Rendering of Isa. 54:17 based on Rashi's commentary there, q.v. Moderns follow Qimhi in treating *yûṣar* there as *qal* passive of *yṣr* 'fashion'; hence NJV renders: "No weapon formed against you...."

[34] Paraphrasing a form of classical Heb. *qwm* by its standard equivalent in late Heb., *ʿmd*.

[35] The common root is proto-Semitic (and Arab. and Ugar.; see Gordon, UT #19.1048) *ẓhr*. Proto-Semitic *ẓ* consistently appears as *ṣ* in standard classical (Jerusalem dialect) Hebrew and as *ṭ* in common Aramaic (see Sabatino Moscati, *An Introduction to the Comparative Grammar of the Semitic Languages* [Wiesbaden: Harrassowitz, 1969], p. 29); see *K-B*[3], p. 946a, s.v. *ṣāhŏrayim*; p. 354a, s.v. *ṭāhôr*.

[36] Rashi's point is that the verb *mgr* appears only twice in the Hebrew Bible—once in the *qal* passive *pāʿûl* participle in Ezek. 21:17 and again here in Ps. 89:45 in the *piʿel* perfect; the meaning of the verb, which is called for by the context here, sc., 'hurl, cast down', is well established for the root *mgr* in Targumic Aramaic; note that the view attributed to Rashi in Mandelkern, p. 657c, s.v. *mgr* is supported by Rashi at Ezek. 21:17 but contradicted by Rashi here at Ps. 89:45.

[37] Lit., "how much old age I have."

[38] The implication of v. 48a is that the psalmist asks God to cease and desist from afflicting him (her) and to give the psalmist a brief respite during the limited time the psalmist still has to live.

[39] Rashi does not quote the bracketed portion of the verse; I have supplied it for clarity.

[40] Explicative *waw*.

[41] Cf. Ex. 1:11; Isa. 53:4.

[42] Heb. *sôpê* lit., 'ends of'; cf. the semantic equivalent *qēṣ*, lit., 'end', which means secondarily 'appointed time'; on the latter meaning of Heb. *qēṣ* see Rashi at Ps. 78:9, 12.

[43] Most likely the Mishnaic apothegm was inspired by Ps. 89:52 and reflects the interpretation of *māšîaḥ* here as a reference to the eschatological Messiah of Roman period and later Judaism; contrast Rashi's correct and purposeful exegesis of the word *māšîaḥ* in his commentary at Ps. 2:1; 84:10; 105:15.

[44] This verse does not properly belong to Ps. 89. It is a doxology, which closes the third of the five books, into which the Book of Psalms is divided; see modern commentaries; on this point Rashi is silent here; contrast Qimhi here.

PSALM XC (90)

1a **A PRAYER OF MOSES, THE MAN OF GOD.**
As for the eleven psalms [Ps. 90-100] from this one up to [but not including] "Of David, A Psalm" (Ps. 101:1), Moses composed all of them. Corresponding to them numerically he [Moses] composed eleven blessings for eleven tribes in "This is the blessing" (Deut. 33).[1]

1b **YOU HAVE BEEN OUR REFUGE** [mā'ôn] [i.e.], mādôr 'dwelling place'[2] and mānôs 'a place of refuge',[3] to which one can flee.[4]
YOU HAVE BEEN...[IN EVERY GENERATION][5] [i.e.], from aforetime,[6] for **YOU WERE IN EXISTENCE** before everything.

2a **BEFORE THE MOUNTAINS WERE BORN** [i.e.], created, and

2b before[7] You brought forth[8] **THE EARTH AND THE WORLD.**

2c **FROM** first **ERA TO** last **ERA YOU ARE GOD.**[9]

3a **YOU RETURN MAN** ['ĕnôš] **TO DUST** [dakkā'].
You make a person ['ādām] endure sufferings until You turn him into being weak and about to die.[10]

3b **YOU TELL HIM** by means of sufferings,[11] **"RETURN YOU MORTALS** from your wicked behavior."[12]

4a **FOR IN YOUR SIGHT A THOUSAND YEARS....**
When [the creation of] repentance first entered Your mind, You considered it affirmatively; hence You created it. The years were in need of it [repentance] because [the days of][13] humans were many because **A THOUSAND YEARS IN YOUR SIGHT** were only a passing, i.e., fleeting, day, and [very] little of the night [was] with it [that almost thousand year day]. [The proof of this last assertion is] that You told the first man,[14] "Indeed, on the day on which you eat of it you shall surely die" (Gen. 2:17). Now he [Adam] lived "930 years" (Gen. 5:5). It follows that a thousand years add up to a full day, and a little of the night was with it.[15]

4b   LIKE YESTERDAY, which has already past.[16]

5   YOU FLOODED THEM; THEY WILL BE [EXPERI-
       ENCING] SLEEP.
       Now You have snatched away the aforementioned
       YEARS,[17] and You have brought them to a few days, which
       are only like slumber because two generations are seventy
       years as it is explained toward the end of the stanza:[18] "THE
       SPAN OF OUR LIFE IS SEVENTY YEARS" (v. 10). Now
       these [SEVENTY YEARS] are regarded as constituting a
       single sleep in accord with what is stated in the Bible,
       "When the LORD brought back Zion's exile, we were like
       dreamers" (Ps. 126: 1),[19] and [this] is stated with reference
       to the seventy years of the Babylonian Exile.[20]
       [The verb] zĕramtām 'YOU FLOODED THEM' is a verb
       referring to flooding; it is a cognate of [the noun zerem
       'flood' in] zerem mayim "a flood of water" (Hab. 3:10).

5b   AT DAYBREAK IT PASSES AWAY LIKE GRASS.
       Whatever is born at night dies AT DAYBREAK at the end
       of the time of sleeping, and if

6a   AT DAYBREAK IT FLOURISHES, [but] immediately IT
       PASSES AWAY,

6c   and by sunset IT WITHERS AND DRIES UP.[21]
       Now what is the reason [for humans' temporality]?

7   [It is] THAT[22] WE ARE CONSUMED BY YOUR AN-
       GER..., and because of all this

8a   YOU HAVE SET OUR INIQUITIES BEFORE YOU

8b   and[23] 'ălûmēnû.
       You have put the sin of our youth

8c   IN THE LIGHT OF YOUR FACE [i.e.], opposite You, to
       look at them. [The noun] 'ălûmēnû [means] nĕûrēnû 'our
       youth'; it is a cognate of [the noun 'elem 'young man' in]
       "Whose son is this young man?" (1 Sam. 17:56).

9a   HAVE PASSED IN YOUR WRATH.
       [I.e.], they have been removed, and they have passed, and
       they have gone their way IN YOUR WRATH.

9b   LIKE AN UTTERANCE [hegeh] [i.e.], like a pronounce-
       ment [dibbûr], which is quickly concluded.[24]

10a   THE DAYS OF OUR LIFE ARE BECAUSE OF THEM
       SEVENTY YEARS. [I.e.], THEY DAYS OF OUR LIFE
       because of these our iniquities (v. 8a) and because of these

the sins of our youth (v. 8b) ARE SEVENTY YEARS.[25]

10b AND IF THERE BE EXTENSIONS [bigĕbûrôt].
AND IF his days extend [gābĕrû][26] greatly, EIGHTY YEARS.

10c AND THEIR PRIDE IS TROUBLE AND SORROW.
As for all the greatness and power, which a person has during these [seventy] years, they are only TROUBLE AND SORROW. Now why is this?
[It is] BECAUSE[27] THEY PASS BY [i.e.], for, in fact,
IT PASSES BY QUICKLY, AND WE FLY AWAY [i.e.],
in a quick transition[28] we fly, i.e.,[29] we die. [The word] gāz is a word referring to transition; it is a cognate of [the verb nāgôzû 'they are over' in] "They are over and gone" (Nah. 1:12) and likewise [of the verb wayyāgoz 'it brought across' in] "It brought quails from across the sea" (Num. 11:31).

11a WHO CAN KNOW YOUR FURIOUS ANGER?
In such a few days as these [described in v. 10] who can acquire for himself a heart to know YOUR FURIOUS ANGER and to fear You?

11b But as for You, YOUR WRATH MATCHES THE FEAR OF YOU.
Just as You are fearsome so is YOUR WRATH harsh in exacting punishment from sinners.

12a HE TAUGHT [hôdaʿ] [30] US TO COUNT OUR DAYS RIGHTLY when in the beginning HE MADE KNOWN [hôdaʿ] in the world the number of our long days. Since we live many days, we can acquire a HEART,[31]

12b AND WE SHALL BRING into them[32] A HEART OF WISDOM. wĕnābî' 'AND WE SHALL BRING' is a verb referring to bringing.[33]

12a An alternative interpretation of "kēn [34] HE TAUGHT US TO COUNT" is "[HE TAUGHT US TO COUNT] 70 years." [This exegesis interprets the word kēn[37] numerically as follows]: the numerical value [of the letters k = 20 and n = 50] adds up to 70.

13a TURN, O LORD, from Your anger

13c AND REPENT [i.e.], think a kind thought,[35] TOWARDS YOUR SERVANTS.

14a SATISFY US AT DAYBREAK WITH YOUR STEADFAST LOVE [i.e.], on the day of redemption and vindication, which is [called] DAYBREAK and light with respect to the night of trouble and sighing [which precedes it].[36]

14b THAT WE MAY SING FOR JOY ALL OUR DAYS, i.e., throughout all the troubles, which we have endured, during these OUR DAYS.

15a GIVE US JOY in the days of the Messiah
ACCORDING TO the number of THE DAYS YOU HAVE AFFLICTED US in the Exile,[37]

15b and according to the number of THE YEARS that WE HAVE SUFFERED MISFORTUNE.

17a THE FAVOR OF THE LORD OUR GOD [i.e.], His *Shekinah* [38] and His consolation.

17b PROSPER AMONG US THE WORK OF OUR HANDS. [The verb *kônĕnāh*] is an imperative; [the form] *kônĕnāh* is the same grammatical form as is represented by *šômĕrāh* 'keep' (Ps. 25:20; 86:2; 1 Ch. 29:18) and *šŏpĕṭāh* 'judge' (Ps. 82:8; Lam. 3:59).[39]

17c PROSPER IT [*kônĕnēhû*] [i.e.], *kônēn 'ôtô* ' Prosper it'.[40]
Now [Moses[41] says] twice, "Prosper it" and " Prosper the work of our hands" (vv. 17b, 17c) [because once][42] refers to the building of the Tabernacle, in which he [Moses][41] blessed Israel and prayed that the Shekinah might abide among THE WORK of their HANDS in the Tabernalce and once [in a prayer] that there should be a blessing upon THE WORK OF THEIR HANDS.[43]

PSALM XC, NOTES
[1] Cf. the various midrashim in Midrash Tehillim at Ps. 90 #3.
[2] So KJV, following Ibn Ezra. Note that while the verbal root *dwr* 'dwell' is amply attested in Biblical Heb., the noun, which is widely attested in Mishnaic Heb., is unattested in the Bible.
[3] So NJV, following Qimhi; for the noun *mānôs* see, *inter alia*, Ps. 59:17; 142:5.
[4] Lit., "a place of fleeing to go there."
[5] The bracketed portion of the lemma is not quoted in our Rashi ms.; I have supplied it for clarity from other editions of Rashi's commentary here.
[6] Heb. *mēʿôlām*.
[7] By repeating the word *bĕṭerem* 'BEFORE', Rashi makes it clear that the adverb modifies both the verb *yullādû* 'THEY WERE BORN' and the verb *wattĕḥôlēl* 'YOU BROUGHT FORTH'; so also Ibn Ezra and Qimhi, and so KJV and NJV; and so already LXX and Vulgate.

[8] Characteristically, Rashi paraphrases, substituting a perfect for the imperfect consecutive.

[9] Rendering of the lemma, which reflects Rashi's interpretation, which understands Biblical Heb. *'ôlām* according to its primary meaning 'era' as in the Rabbinic Heb. expressions *hā'ôlām hazzeh* 'this (pre-eschatological) era' and *hā'ôlām habbā'* 'the coming (i.e., post-eschatological) era'; on the latter expressions see the discussion at Ps. 25, n. 19.

[10] Taking *dakkā'* to mean 'beaten, crushed'; similarly KJV: "destruction"; so *K-B³*, p. 212; *BDB*, p. 194; cf. *Mahberet Menahem*, pp. 130-31, s.v. *dk*; the latter, however, does not cite the present attestation.

[11] Rashi here responds to the exegetical question, "How does God convey His message?"

[12] Here Rashi answers the exegetical question, "From what should they return?" Contrast Ibn Ezra, whose comment, "to the dust from which you were taken" (cf. Gen. 3:19), answers a different exegetical question, sc., "To what should they return?"

[13] The bracketed expression is not found in our Rashi ms., but it is found in other editions of Rashi's commentary here.

[14] I.e., Adam; see Ps. 89, n. 22, and see the discussion in Kadushin, *Worship and Ethics*, p. 267, n. 85.

[15] Cf. Genesis Rabbah 19:14.

[16] Rashi's paraphrase points to the fact that Biblical Heb. *kî* here corresponds in meaning to Rabbinic Heb. *še* and to the fact that the Biblical Heb. imperfect *ya'ăbor* is here employed as a preterite.

[17] See v. 4a. Here Rashi attempts to identify the noun antecedent referred to by the accusative pronominal suffix *am* of the the verb *zĕramtām* 'YOU FLOODED THEM'.

[18] Heb. *'inyān*. Rashi refers here to a thought unit consisting of vv. 1-12, in which the psalmist contrasts the temporality of humans with the eternality of God.

[19] Our rendering follows Rashi's comment there.

[20] Rabbinic tradition is acutely aware of the fact that the time span from the destruction of the First Temple in 586 B.C.E. to the Edict of Cyrus in 538 B.C.E. is slightly more than half the seventy years of exile posited by Dan. 9:2 on the basis of Jer. 29:10. To complete the span of seventy years Seder Olam Rabbah, Chapter 27 proposes a variety of starting points prior to 586 B.C.E. and a variety of points of termination later than the Edict of Cyrus.

[21] Rashi's comment seems to treat vv. 5b-6 as repetititve parallelism: AT DAYBREAK IT PASSES AWAY LIKE GRASS//AT DAYBREAK IT FLOURISHES, BUT IT WILL PASS AWAY//IN THE EVENING IT WILL WITHER, AND IT WILL DRY UP. Rashi's exegesis presupposes the following questions, which arise from his construing vv. 5b-6 as an example of repetitive parallelism dealing with a single subject, 'humankind', here referred to by impersonal 3[d] pers. masc. sing. verbs, both imperfect and perfect consecutive: (1) Who dies AT DAYBREAK? (2) If it dies AT DAYBREAK, how can it flourish AT DAYBREAK? (3) If it sur-

vives the morning, what then? Rashi's answer is that humans in general live considerably less than the seventy years, which are represented in Ps. 90:5-6 by the twenty-four hour period from sunset to sunset. Rashi observes that those rare individuals who do survive the proverbial night will have died by the following sunset.

[22] Heb. *kî*, which NJV renders 'So'.

[23] Rashi adds here *wĕ'et* indicating that *'ăwonotênû* 'OUR INIQUITIES' and *'ălûmênû* 'THE SIN OF OUR YOUTH' (so Rashi at v. 8b) are compound direct objects of the verb *šattā* 'YOU HAVE SET' and that vv. 8a-b constitute an instance of synonymous parallelism.

[24] Note, with Maarsen, that this explanation of the noun *hegeh* is taken from *Mahberet Menahem*, p. 134. Note also that Rashi's comment here at Ps. 90:9 is a rare instance where Rashi attributes to a derivative of the verb *hāgāh* the meaning 'speak' rather than the meaning 'think'; see our discussion at Ps. 1:2.

[25] Assuming that the word *bāhem* in v. 10a means 'BECAUSE OF THEM' (see previous note), Rashi explains that the antecedents of the pronoun 'THEM' are to be found in v. 8.

[26] Our Rashi ms. contains the scribal error *gārĕmû* 'they caused'.

[27] Heb. *kî*.

[28] Rashi's interpretation of the adverbial expression *gāz* is taken from *Mahberet Menahem*, p. 102. Menahem there uses the term *ma'ăbar* 'transition' while Rashi here employs the unusual cognate *'ĕbarat* (so is it vocalized in our Rashi ms., which only vocalizes highly unusual forms).

[29] Explicative *waw*.

[30] Rashi takes the verb *hôda'* to be a 3[d] pers. masc. sing. perfect; contrast Ibn Ezra and moderns, including NJV, who take *hôda'* to be the imperative 'teach us'; so already *Mahberet Menahem*, p. 130.

[31] See v. 12b, and see Rashi at v. 11a.

[32] Here Rashi answers the exegetical question, "Where SHALL WE BRING?"

[33] As noted by Maarsen here, Rashi's point is that the word *nābî'* here is not to be construed as the noun denoting 'prophet'; contrast BT Bava Batra 12a where *wĕnābî' lĕbab ḥokmāh* is interpreted as a nominal sentence meaning, "A prophet is a wise heart."

[34] Previously interpreted to mean 'RIGHTLY'; see above.

[35] With Maarsen here, note that Rashi here summarizes his observation at Gen. 6:6; Ex. 32:12 that *niḥam* 'repent' means 'think differently, change one's mind'.

[36] Cf. Ps. 30:6.

[37] Cf. Midrash Tehillim here.

[38] Cf. Midrash Tehillim; note that in Rashi's language as in Rabbinic Heb. Shekinah refers to the sense of the nearness of God; see Kadushin, *The Rabbinic Mind* [3], pp. 225-228.

[39] I.e., long imperative; see *GKC* #48i.

[40] Rashi's point is that the form *kônĕnēhû* consists of the short impera-

tive *kônēn* 'prosper' and the accusative pronominal suffix *ēhû*; on the latter suffix see *GKC* #58d; #58i, n. 2.

[41] To whom the authorship of Ps. 90 is attributed in v. 1.

[42] The bracketed expression is not found in our Rashi ms.

[43] As noted by Maarsen here, Rashi here quotes the same midrash to which Rashi refers in his commentary at Ex. 39:43 and at BT Shebu'ot 15b, s.v. "a song against plagues". In all those places it is asserted that Ps. 90:17 is the blessing referred to in Ex. 39:43 and that it means, "May the Shekinah abide among the works of your hands." Maarsen remarks here that Rashi's thrice-quoted midrash is "a different version" from that which is found in Sifra, Shemini de Miluim 15; Sifre Numbers, ed. Horovitz, p. 191, lines 1-15 and Seder Olam Rabbah, Chapter 6. In fact, the various rabbinic texts present three major versions as follows: (1) According to Tosefta Menahot 7:8 and according to Sifra, quoting R. Meir, Moses' blessing referred to in Ex. 39:43 consisted of Deut. 1:11, to which the people responded with the words of Ps. 90:17. (2) According to Tanhuma Pequde #11, quoting R. Meir and according to Sifre Numbers and Seder Olam Rabbah, not quoting R. Meir, Moses' blessing consisted of "May it be [the divine] Will that the *Shekinah* abide among the works of your hands," to which the people responded with Ps. 90:17, which means, "May the Shekinah abide among the works of your hands." See the discussion in S. Lieberman, *Tosefeth Rishonim*, pt. 2 (Jerusalem: Bamberger & Wahrmann, 1938), p. 253. (3) The Numbers Rabbah version is reflected in Rashi's commentaries at Ex. 39:43 and BT Shebu'ot 15b where Rashi attributes this midrash to Sifra. Unique to Rashi at Ps. 90:17 is the suggestion that the repetition of the imperative 'PROSPER' here refers to Moses' having asked in Ex. 39:43 for two distinct blessings.

PSALM XCI (91)

1a   HE WHO DWELLS IN THE SECRET PLACE OF THE
MOST HIGH [refers to] the Holy One Blessed be He, who
DWELLS IN THE SECRET PLACE of the heavens.[1] Another equally plausible interpretation is [as follows]: "As for
him who takes refuge IN THE SECRET PLACE of the
wings of the Divine Presence,[2]

1b   he ABIDES IN His [God's] SHADE, for the Holy One
Blessed be He takes care of him". Note that in this psalm
Moses our Rabbi[3] summons people to take refuge under the
wings of the Divine Presence. Shaddai is an epithet referring
to strength.[4]
[The word *ṣēl* 'shade' in] IN THE SHADE OF THE AL-
MIGHTY is the same word as is found in "I delight to sit in
his shade"
(Cant. 2:3).

2   I SAY OF THE LORD that He is MY REFUGE. Now why
shall I say this?

3   [The answer is supplied in v. 3]: FOR HE WILL SAVE
YOU [i.e.], every person, FROM THE FOWLER'S TRAP.

4a   *bĕ'ebrātô* 'WITH HIS PINION'; [The noun *'ebrāh* 'PINION'
means] *kānāp* 'wing'.[5]
yāsek[6] 'HE WILL COVER' [i.e.], *yĕsokēk* 'He will cover'.[7]

4b   YOU WILL FIND REFUGE. [I.e.], you will find cover.

4c   AN ENCIRCLING [SHIELD][8] is a shield, which surrounds
the person close to one's four sides.[9] [The participle] *sōḥērāh*
'ENCIRCLING' is a cognate of [Aramaic] *sĕḥor sĕḥor* [the
expression by means of which TJ renders Heb. *sābîb sābîb*
'around (and) around' in Ezek. 37:2; 40:5 and passim]
'around (and) around'.

5a   YOU NEED NOT FEAR...if you trust in Him.

5b   THE ARROW THAT FLIES [i.e.], a demon that flies
about like an arrow.[10]

6   *deber* 'PLAGUE'...*qeṭeb* 'SCOURGE' are the names of [dis-
tinct] demons, one of which [*deber* 'PLAGUE'] wreaks havoc
during the night and one of which [*qeṭeb* 'SCOURGE']
wreaks havoc at noon.[11] *yāšûd* 'RAVAGES' [i.e.], *yĕšōdēd* 'destroys'.[12]

7a   MAY FALL [*yippol*] AT YOUR SIDE. [The verb *yippol*, lit.,
      'it may fall'] refers here to *hănāyāh* 'being located'; the same
      usage is found in "He shall be located [*nāpāl*] alongside all of
      his brothers" (Gen. 25:18).[13]
      AT YOUR SIDE [i.e.], at your left side,[14] there may be lo-
      cated A THOUSAND demons.

7c   BUT NOT one of them[15] SHALL REACH YOU to wreak
      havoc.

8b   *wĕsillûmat* 'THE PUNISHMENT' [i.e.], *kilāyôn* 'the elimina-
      tion'. Now why is it [that YOU WILL SEE this]?

9a   [The reason is] BECAUSE YOU said, "THE LORD is MY
      REFUGE."
      Note that this [v. 9a] is an elliptical Bible verse.[16]

9b   YOU MADE THE MOST HIGH YOUR HAVEN [i.e.],
      YOU MADE the Holy One Blessed be He the refuge of
      your trust.

10a   WILL NOT BEFALL [*lō' tĕ'unneh*] [i.e.], there will not hap-
      pen [*lō' tiqreh*]. Now [the rare verb *'n*][17] is the same verb as
      is attested in "and God caused him to happen [*'innāh*] into
      his hand" (Ex. 21:13).[18]

12   LEST YOU BE HURT [*tiggōp*] [i.e.], lest you slip
      [*tikkāšēl*].[19] Likewise, every form of the verb root exemplified
      by the gerund *nĕgîpāh* 'hurting' is the semantic equivalent of
      O.F. *açoper* 'to be hurt'.[20]

PSALM XCI, NOTES

[1] The exegesis Rashi adopts here is reflected in numerous midrashim
found in Midrash Tehillim here. NJV's "O you who dwell in the shelter of
the Most High" reflects Qimhi's exegesis while KJV's "He that dwelleth
in the secret place of the Most High" follows LXX and Vulgate.

[2] Heb. *Shekinah*; see the discussion at Ps. 90, n. 38.

[3] For the attribution of Ps. 91 to Moses see Rashi at Ps. 90:1.

[4] See the extensive discussion in Abraham Ibn Ezra's commentaries
at Ex. 6:2 where this interpretation is attributed to Samuel ha-Nagid (993-
1056 C.E.). At Gen. 17:1, however, Rashi interprets *šadday* to mean
"whose [*še*] is enough [*day*]." In his commentary at Ex. 6:2 Ibn Ezra attributes the latter interpretation to Saadiah Gaon (892-942 C.E.).

[5] See *Mahberet Menahem*, p. 22.

[6] So MT; our Rashi ms., however, reads *yysk*.

[7] Rashi assumes that for his readers the *polel* form of the root *skk*
'cover' (Rashi, following *Mahberet Menahem*, pp. 263-64, would have construed the root as *sk)* will be more comprehensible than the synonymous
hiphil form found in the biblical text.

⁸ Our Rashi ms. omits the bracketed portion of the lemma; following other editions of Rashi's commentary, I have supplied it for clarity.

⁹ At Ps. 5:13 Rashi remarks similarly concerning ṣinnāh 'shield' without the addition of wĕsōḥērāh 'which encircles'.

¹⁰ Cf. the midrash attributed to R. Berechiah in Midrash Tehillim here; see the discussion at Ps. 76:4.

¹¹ With Maarsen cf. Midrash Tehillim here; BT Pesaḥim 11b; Rashi at Job. 3:4.

¹² Rashi assumes that the *polel* form of the verb will be more comprehensible to his readers that the synonymous *qal*.

¹³ Rashi makes the same observation at Gen. 25:18 where he cites also Judg. 7:12, q.v., and at BT Yebamot 24b where he comments on Isa. 54:15.

¹⁴ Rashi assumes that the parallelism YOUR SIDE//YOUR RIGHT is antithetic; so also NJV and Dahood. This interpretation of the parallelism runs counter to the evidence that 'THOUSAND//TEN THOUSAND' is a fixed pair meaning 'very many'. If 'THOUSAND//TEN THOUSAND' are to be treated as synonyms so must 'YOUR SIDE' be treated as a synonym of 'YOUR RIGHT'. See, *inter alia*, Stanley Gevirtz, *Patterns in the Early Poetry of Israel* (2^d ed.; Chicago: University of Chicago Press, 1973), p. 16; Menahem Haran, "Biblical Studies," *Tarbiz* 39 (1969), p. 110 (in Hebrew) and the literature cited there. Nevertheless, the interpretation adopted by Rashi, Dahood, NJV and others should be of interest to those who believe that translations of God's word should afford equal time to the left-handed and should avoid anti-sinistral language.

¹⁵ Rashi supplies the missing subject of the 3^d pers. sing. imperfect verb *yiggāš* 'IT SHALL REACH'.

¹⁶ Rashi refers to the absence of a *verbum dicendi* before the quotation, and he supplies the verb *'āmartā* 'you said'. Rashi's most plausible interpretation suggests that the psalmist in v. 1 affirms his own reliance upon God while in vv. 3-13 the psalmist recommends the same reliance to an unnamed addressee, and the psalmist describes the positive rewards of the addressee's adoption of the psalmist's stance summarized in vv. 2, 9: "THE LORD IS MY REFUGE." For numerous examples of quotations not introduced by *verbum dicendi* see *BGM*, pp. 169-89.

¹⁷ *Mahberet Menahem*, p. 50, s.v. *'n* IV, holds that the verb refers to 'plotting'. The most up-to-date lexicography recognizes here a triliteral root *'ny* meaning 'happen'; see *K-B*³, p. 68a, s.v. *'nh* III.

¹⁸ Contrast Rashi at Ex. 21:13 where Rashi contends that the verb in question means 'summon' or 'prepare' [*zimmēn*].

¹⁹ In his commentary at BT Shabbat 109a Rashi explains that *mî šennāgĕpāh yādô* means *nikšĕlāh wĕlāqĕṭāh* 'it slipped, and it was hurt'; he notes further that the root *ngp* attested in the baraitha is the same root as is attested here in Ps. 91:12 and in the expression *dam maggĕpātāh* 'blood of her injury' in Mishnah Makshirin 6:8.

²⁰ See Catane, *Recuiel* #2040; see below at Ps. 109, n. 11.

PSALM XCII

1 A PSALM. A SONG; FOR THE SABBATH DAY. [I.e.], A SONG of Levites FOR THE SABBATH DAY, which they chant on Sabbaths.[1] It deals with the subject of the future era,[2] which is wholly Sabbath.[3]

3a TO PROCLAIM YOUR STEADFAST LOVE AT DAYBREAK [i.e.], at the time of the Redemption.[4]

3b YOUR FAITHFULNESS EACH NIGHT. While the trouble of the Exile is still [with us] one is to have faith in You that You will keep Your promise. All of this is beautiful and GOOD (v. 2a).

4 WITH A TEN [i.e.], with a ten-stringed lyre.[5]

7 A BRUTISH MAN CANNOT KNOW what is stated below.[6]

8 WHEN THE WICKED SPROUT LIKE GRASS he [A BRUTISH MAN] does not know that their sprouting is only for the purpose of their being permanently destroyed, for "He requites his enemies" to their faces[7] by destroying them[8] (Deut. 7:10).[9]

9 BUT YOU ARE EXALTED. In all Your judicial decrees You have the upper hand insofar as all people justify to themselves Your decree.[10]

11b I AM SOAKED IN FRESHENING OIL.
[I.e], I AM SOAKED IN THE OIL of rulership.[11] [The verb] *ballotî* 'I AM SOAKED' is a cognate of [the passive participle *bālûl* 'soaked' in] "soaked in oil" (Ex. 29:40; Lev. 14:21; Num. 15:9).[12]

12a OF MY WATCHFUL FOES [*běšûrāy*] [i.e.], of those who look upon me with enmity [*bě'ôyyěnay*]. [The participle *šûrāy* 'MY WATCHFUL FOES'] is a biform of *šorěrāy* 'my watchful foes' (Ps. 5:9).[13]

12b OF [*bě*] THE WICKED [*měrē'îm*] WHO BESET ME, [i.e.], of ['al] the bad people [*rěšā'îm*] WHO BESET ME I HEAR from behind the curtain[14] so they will not succeed in doing away with us, for I heard the following:

13a THE RIGHTEOUS BLOOM LIKE A DATE-PALM....

[THE RIGHTEOUS PERSON is] LIKE A DATE-PALM in producing fruit,[15]

13b   AND LIKE A CEDAR in that its trunk grows new shoots.[16]

14   PLANTED will be the righteous people[17] IN THE HOUSE OF THE LORD.

15a   *yĕnûbûn* 'THEY WILL GROW' [i.e.], *yiṣmĕḥû* 'they will sprout'.[18]

15b   THEY WILL BE OLEAGINOUS [*dĕšēnîm*] [i.e.], *šĕmēnîm* 'fat',[19] and then

16   they will ATTEST[20] THAT THE LORD IS UPRIGHT, MY ROCK....

PSALM XCII, NOTES

[1] Here Rashi suggests that Ps. 92 is designated "A SONG FOR THE SABBATH DAY" because of its being chanted on the weekly Sabbath by the Levites as it was in the period of the Second Temple; see Mishnah Tamid 7:1. The midrash upon which Rashi's comment is based is found, *inter alia*, in PRE 19 and Avot deRabbi Nathan 1.

[2] I.e., the post-eschatological era; on this rendering of Heb. *hāʿōlām habbāʾ* see our discussion at Ps. 25:5.

[3] Mishnah Tamid 7:1; see the discussion at BT Rosh ha-Shanah 31a. Rashi, following Mishnah Tamid, has juxtaposed two alternative interpretations of the prefixed preposition *lĕ* in the phrase *lĕyôm haššabbāt*; according to the first of the two interpretations *lĕ* means 'for' while according to the second interpretation *lĕ* means 'concerning, about' (see *BDB*, p. 512b); other midrashim interpret *lĕ* to mean 'by' as in the frequent *lĕdāwid mizmôr* 'A Psalm of David'; so is the preposition *lĕ* of *lĕyôm haššabbāt* interpreted in the liturgical poem "To the God who rested from all His works of Creation" in the Sabbath Morning Service; see Birnbaum, *Daily Prayer Book*, pp. 340-41; cf. the midrash attributed to R. Simeon in Yalqut Shim'oni here; the same midrash appears anonymously in Midrash Tehillim here.

[4] With reference to the interpretation of DAYBREAK as a metaphor for redemption and NIGHT as a metaphor for exile see Rashi also at Ps. 86:3.

[5] Cf. the midrash attributed to R. Judah quoting R. Ilai in Midrash Tehillim at Ps. 81:3.

[6] Answering the exegetical question, "To what does the demonstrative pronoun 'THIS' at the end of v. 7b refer?"

[7] Heb. *ʿal pĕnêhem*. Here Rashi paraphrases the biblical text, which reads *ʾel pānāwy* 'to his face'. Just as Rashi's paraphrase emends sing. *ʾel pānāwy* to match the plural 'HIS ENEMIES' so does *BHS*, following several medieval Heb. mss., read *lĕśonĕʾô* 'to his enemy' to match the singular 'TO HIS FACE'. Moreover, Rashi's substitution of *ʿal* for *ʾel* is anticipated by the Samaritan recension of Deut.; see below, n. 9.

⁸ Heb. *lĕha'ăbîdām*. Here again Rashi paraphrases the biblical text, which reads *lĕha'ăbîdô* "by destroying him"; this latter aspect of Rashi's treatment of Deut. 7:10 here in his commentary on Ps. 92:8 is followed by NJV at Deut. 7:10. The apparent incongruity found in MT has, however, been explained as Scripture's deliberate attempt to refer separately to each and every individual enemy of the LORD: see *GKC* #145l; Driver, *Deut.*, p. 102.

⁹ Rashi in his commentary at Deut. 7:10 and at Gen. 11:28 equates the idiom *'el pānāwy* of Deut. 7 with *'al pānāwy* of Gen. 11, and he interprets both to mean 'during his lifetime'; Ehrlich, followed by NJV only at Deut. 7 (see Orlinsky, *Notes*, p. 248) interprets the idiom to mean 'instantly'.

¹⁰ Midrash Tehillim here notes that R. Berechiah interpreted the words "BUT YOU ARE EXALTED, O LORD, FOR ALL TIME" to mean "You have the upper hand FOR ALL TIME." Rashi's suggestion that God's having the upper hand is demonstrated particularly by people's justification to themselves of His decrees, i.e., responding to the death of a loved one by reciting the benediction, "Praised are You...the True Judge" (see Rashi also at Ps. 101:1; for the benediction see Birnbaum, *Daily Prayer Book*, p. 777) was probably inspired by the fact that in Midrash Tehillim R. Berechiah's comment is followed immediately by a midrash attributed to R. Judah b. Palya. The latter begins his remarks on v. 9 by quoting Job. 1:21, which is functionally equivalent to the benediction in question.

¹¹ With Maarsen note that this midrash appears in Aramaic in Midrash Samuel 19:6.

¹² Cf. *Mahberet Menahem*, p. 84, s.v. *bl* IV.

¹³ See Rashi at Ps. 5:9; see *Mahberet Menahem*, p. 368, s.v. *šr* VI.

¹⁴ Throughout Rabbinic and post-Rabbinic literature "to hear from behind the curtain" means "with God's help to become privy to secret information."

¹⁵ The exegetical question, "How is the virtuous person comparable to the palm tree?" and the answer Rashi supplies are found in Midrash Tehillim here; for numerous other answers see Midrash Tehillim here.

¹⁶ The exegetical question, "How is the virtuous person comparable to the cedar?" and the answer Rashi supplies are found in Midrash Tehillim here.

¹⁷ Here Rashi answers the exegetical question, "What will be PLANTED IN THE HOUSE OF THE LORD?" He precludes the possibility that it is A DATE-PALM TREE and a CEDAR TREE that will be planted there. Asserting that it is virtuous people, who will be PLANTED there, Rashi intimates that v. 11 is a case of ellipsis in that the commentator and reader must supply the subject and the copula for this sentence, which contains only a participle employed as a predicate adjective and an adverbial phrase 'IN THE HOUSE OF THE LORD' modifying that participle.

[18] Rashi equates the relatively rare verb *nwb* 'grow' with the relatively common verb *ṣmḥ* 'sprout' also at Ps. 62:11, q.v.

[19] Again Rashi explains a relatively rare Heb. word by means of a common one.

[20] Here Rashi intimates that the infinitive construct *lĕhaggîd* 'ATTEST-ING' is employed as an infinitive consecutive, i.e., in place of a finite verb in the same construction as the previous verb, in this case the imperfect employed as a future, 'THEY WILL BE'; on this usage of the infinitive see *GKC* #114p.

PSALM XCIII

1a THE LORD IS KING, HE IS ROBED IN GRANDEUR. They will say this in the time to come.[1]

1b THE WORLD STANDS FIRM. [I.e.], the earth will rejoice when He becomes King.

3 RIVERS RAISED [THEIR VOICE].[2] This is an idiom for outcry and complaint.[3] [The verse expresses metaphorically]: As for You, O LORD, Look at the Gentiles who inundate [You] like rivers. Having raised their voice, they murmur, and continually they raise high their very deepest water sources to display arrogance toward You.[4]

4a ABOVE [*mi-*] THE THUNDER OF THE MANY WATERS. Every form of [the verb] *tômîk* 'You cast' (Ps. 16:5) and of [the noun] *dakkā'* 'beaten,crushed' (Ps. 90:3) is a word referring to depth and lowliness.[5] I [the psalmist] knew that MORE THAN [*mi-*] THE THUNDER OF THE MANY WATERS, which murmur against us[6]

4b and more than the majesty of THE BREAKERS OF this SEA

4c IS THE LORD MAJESTIC ON HIGH, and Your power prevails over them.

5 YOUR TESTIMONIES, which Your prophets testified and promised CONCERNING YOUR TEMPLE, which is[7] THE SACRED ABODE,[8] ARE VERY TRUSTWORTHY. [The expressions] CONCERNING YOUR TEMPLE and FOR MANY DAYS[9] [intimate that] he [Israel] looks forward to them [the fulfillment of YOUR TESTIMONIES], and [that] even though MANY DAYS have elapsed,[10] they [YOUR TESTIMONIES] ARE VERY TRUSTWORTHY.[11] *na'ăwāh* 'ABODE' is a cognate of [the construct noun *nĕ'ôt* in the phrase] *nĕ'ôt 'ĕlohîm* 'God's abode'(Ps. 83:13)[12] [and of the noun] *nāweh* 'abode' (Ex. 15: 13; Isa. 27:10; 33:20; 34:13; Jer. 50:7; etc.). You should know that no [other] attestation of *n'wh* in the Bible treats the *'aleph* as a consonant because they [the other attestations of *n'wh* Jer. 6:2; Ps. 33:1; Ps. 147:1; Prov. 17:6; 19:10; Cant.

1:5; 2:14; 4:3; 6:4] are words referring to[13] 'beauty', but this [*n'wh* 'abode' here at Ps. 93:5] treats the *'aleph* as a consonant.[14]

PSALM XCIII, NOTES

[1] Rashi here responds to the exegetical question, "What is the situation in life, in which this exclamation would be appropriate?" According to a midrash quoted in BT Rosh ha-Shanah 31a, Ps. 93 is designated the psalm for the sixth day of the week (see also Mishnah Tamid 7:4) because it was on the sixth day of Creation that God "completed His work and became King over them." According to R. Hanina in Midrash Tehillim here, the situation in life, which called forth Ps. 93 was the victory over Pharaoh at the Red Sea. Mowinckel introduced the view now widely taken for granted by scholars that psalms containing the exclamation, "The LORD is King" were composed for the symbolic enthronement of God at the Israelite New Year; see Elmer A. Leslie, *The Psalms* (New York: Abingdon, 1949), pp. 73-77. Rashi here suggests that the assertion that God is King of the world will be appropriate only in the time to come when all people will have accepted His sovereignty.

[2] Literal meaning of the lemma to which Rashi responds; note that Rashi does not quote the bracketed portion of the verse; I have supplied it for clarity.

[3] Examples of the expression 'he/she raised his/her voice' referring to outcry or complaint include Gen. 21:16; Gen. 27:38; 29:11; 1 Sam. 24:17; 2 Sam. 3:32.

[4] Cf. Midrash Tehillim at Ps. 93:7.

[5] Here Rashi suggests that *dokyām* in v. 3 is a cognate of *dakkā'* 'lowly' (Isa. 57:15; Ps. 90:3; in the plural construct form *dakkĕ'ê* at Ps. 34:19); hence Rashi's paraphrase *'imqê nibĕkêhem* 'their very deepest water sources' in his comment at v. 3; NJV, following the parallelism interprets the *hapax legomenon dokyām* to be a synonym of *qôlām* 'their thunder'; hence NJV's rendering "its pounding".

[6] As per Rashi at v. 3, these bodies of water are here understood to be metaphors for 'the Gentiles'.

[7] Rashi here intimates that *na'ăwāh qodeš* 'THE SACRED ABODE' is an appositive of *bêtĕkā* 'YOUR TEMPLE'.

[8] Lit., 'abode of holiness'; however, ancient Semitic languages including Rabbinic Heb. frequently use a construct genitive chain as the equivalent of a noun followed by an attributive adjective; see *GKC* #128p; well-known examples in Rabbinic Heb. are 'land of holiness' for 'holy land'; 'the Sabbath of Your holiness' for 'your holy Sabbath' and 'the Scriptures of Your holiness' for 'Your Holy Scriptures'.

[9] Interpretation of *lĕ'orek yāmîm* presupposed by Rashi's comment; NJV renders idiomatically, "for all times".

[10] Note that in Heb. *lĕ'orek* 'for many' and the verb *'ārĕkû* 'many elapsed' are related etymologically.

¹¹ Without saying so explicitly, Rashi indicates by his rearrangement of the word order that he regards v. 5 as a case of *miqrā' měsûrās*, i.e., inversion, which is to say a verse whose word order, for poetic reasons obscures the syntactic relationship of the words. According to Rashi's reconstruction, the author of Ps. 93:5 adopted the following wordorder: YOUR TESTIMONIES (subject of sentence); ARE TRUSTWORTHY (verb); VERY (adverb modifying verb); CONCERNING YOUR TEMPLE (adjective phrase modifying the subject YOUR TESTIMONIES), THE SACRED ABODE (phrase in apposition to YOUR TEMPLE); FOR MANY DAYS (adverbial phrase modifying the verb ARE TRUSTWORTHY).

¹² So does Rashi render there; contrast NJV: "meadows of God".

¹³ Heb. *lěšôn*, which in this context, may also mean 'cognates of'.

¹⁴ The brilliant insight that in Ps. 93:5 is to be distinguished from *n'wh* in all other passages because the former is the only instance of *n'wh* with consonantal *'aleph* derives from the Massoretes; for Massoretic sources and for the explanation of the Massoretic terminology, which is the basis of our rendering of Rashi's comment here see Elias Levita, *Massoreth Ha-Massoreth*, ed. and trans. by Christian David Ginsburg (London: Longmans, Green, Reader and Dyer, 1867; repr. New York: Ktav, 1968), p. 170. On consonantal and non-consonantal (quiescent) *'aleph* see *GKC* #23.

PSALM XCIV

1a GOD OF RETRIBUTION, LORD.
Show and reveal to them Your retribution.[1]

4   UTTER INSOLENT SPEECH [*yit'amměrû*] [i.e.] *yištabběḥû* 'vaunt themselves' [The verb *'āmar* II, a homonym of *'āmar* II 'say'][2] is the same verb as is attested in *he'ěmārtā* 'You bestowed praise' (Deut. 26:17).[3]

8a TAKE HEED, YOU MOST BRUTISH. The Gentiles are the world's fools.[4]

9   SHALL HE WHO IMPLANTS THE EAR... ? [I.e.], Is it possible that the Holy One Blessed be He, who IMPLANTed THE EAR WILL NOT HEAR the outcry of His people and its [that people's] sufferings?[5]

10 SHALL HE NOT PUNISH? [I.e.], He will discipline you for this.

11 THE LORD KNOWS your THOUGHTS, which you are thinking [namely], to aggrandize yourselves by means of the crown of kingship, [and He knows] THAT THEY ARE FUTILITY.

12 PRAISED IS THE MAN. [I.e.]. PRAISED[6] are the virtuous people,[7] who are oppressed by you provided that they will be busy with Torah and commandments.[8]

13 TO GIVE HIM TRANQUILITY FROM DAYS OF MISFORTUNE, i.e., FROM THE DAYS of the punishment in Gehinnom[9] UNTIL they see that A PIT IS DUG FOR THE WICKED.[10]

15a JUDGMENT SHALL AGAIN ACCORD WITH JUSTICE so that they [the punishments] will be justified from their [the culprits'] standpoint,

15b AND... AFTER the carrying out of sentence ALL THE UPRIGHT will be gathered together so that they may collect their rewards.[11]

17 *dûmāh* 'SILENCE' is [a biform of] *dumiyyāh* 'silent' (Ps. 39:3).[12]

16b WHO WILL STAND UP FOR ME?
[I.e.], Whose merit will awaken [compassion] for us among these evildoing Gentiles?

20   SHALL THE SEAT OF INJUSTICE BE YOUR PART-
        NER?
        |I.e.], Can there be compared to You the Gentile kingdoms,
        which FRAME statues and molten objects of MISCHIEF
        BY STATUE [i.e.], for a STATUE so that their [idolatrous]
        worship is for them a STATUTE?[13]

21a   THEY BAND TOGETHER [yagoddû]. [I.e.], they shall be
        gathered as bands [gĕdûdîm][14] TO DO AWAY WITH [i.e.],
        to kill, Israel[15]

21b   THEY CONDEMN, [i.e.], they make them subject to pun-
        ishment by means of a judgment in court in order to kill
        them.[16]

23   'ônām 'THEIR EVIL', [i.e.], their violent behavior; it is the
        same word as is attested in "He reserves [the punishment of]
        his evil for his [the wicked person's] children" (Job. 21:19).

PSALM XCIV, NOTES
   [1] To which reference is made when the psalmist in v. 1a-b twice addresses the LORD as 'GOD OF RETRIBUTION'.
   [2] So *Mahberet Menahem*, p. 48.
   [3] In his commentary at Deut. 26:17 Rashi states emphatically that
heˁĕmartā (there) and *heˀĕmîrĕkā* (Deut. 26:18) are both words concerning
whose meaning "there is no Scriptural witness." Current editions of
Rashi's commentary on Deuteronomy append the following gloss: "I
found a witness, and it [the verb twice attested in Deut. 26:17-18] is an
expression referring to beauty; it is the same verb as is attested in "ALL
EVILDOERS VAUNT THEMSELVES" (Ps. 94:4). This gloss is absent
from the best mss.; see Chavel, *ad loc.*; concerning the expression 'I found'
in Rashi's Bible commentaries see our introduction, pp. 158–161. It appears that when Rashi wrote his commentary on Deut. 26 he did not accept the view that *ˀmr* in Deut. 26:17-18 and in Ps. 94:4 is the same root.
By the time Rashi composed his commentaries on BT Berakot 6a and
Hagigah 3a, q.v., Rashi had changed his mind and come to believe that
there is attested both in Deut. 26:17-18 and in Ps. 94:4 a verb *ˀmr*, which
means 'praise'. Still later, Rashi incorporated this view in his commentary
here. On the relative dating of Rashi's Pentateuch, Talmud, and Psalms
commentaries see our introduction, pp. 7–9.
   [4] In the present context the Gentiles in question are the idolators as
well as the atheists and agnostics, who fail to acknowledge the Holy One
Blessed be He as both Creator and Supreme Judge. Rashi's comment
here is inspired by two *aggadot* found in BT Avodah Zarah 2b-3a, q.v., in
which Gentiles' non-observance of the precepts of the Torah is attributed
to foolishness; for the similar notion that idolatry is the result of misun-
derstanding cf. Isa. 44:18-20.

⁵ In its original biblical context the rhetorical question *hălō' yišmă'* 'SHALL HE NOT HEAR?' means that the LORD perceives the misbehavior of the wicked. Rashi's supplying the direct object "the outcry of His people" suggests that he reads into *hălō' yišmă'* the nuance 'heed'. This eisgesis is made possible by the ambiguity of Heb. *šama'*; on the latter see Gruber, "The Midrash in Biblical Research," pp. 69-80.

⁶ Interpreting *'ašrê* in accord with Rashi at Ps. 1:1, q.v.; note that since the midrash upon which Rashi bases his comment here refers to the plight of a Job-like innocent sufferer, therefore, while 'THE MAN' in question may be "praised," it is equally clear that unless he be demented, he has little cause to be "happy"!

⁷ Here Rashi calls our attention to the fact that biblical psalmody often says 'the man'—usually Heb. *hā'îš*, here Heb. *haggeber*—when the intent is 'people'; see also Ps. 34:9; 40:5; 52:9; 127:5.

⁸ As noted by Maarsen, Rashi's comment here is based upon Midrash Tanḥuma, ed. Buber, Miqqēṣ 16.

⁹ Rashi here sees in Ps. 94:13 a summary of the Rabbinic doctrine of "chastisements of love," i.e., that sufferings experienced while alive can, as it were, be credited to a person's account when one is called to account after one's death. This doctrine is expressed most eloquently by Moses Nahmanides in "The Gate of Retribution," in *Collected Writings of Nahmanides,* ed. Chaim Chavel (Jerusalem: Mosad Harav Kook, 1963), pp. 264-320 (in Heb.)

¹⁰ The literal meaning of v. 13 is that the virtuous is absolved of experiencing misfortune "WHILE ['ad] A PIT IS DUG FOR THE WICKED." Rashi transforms this half-truth, which is reminiscent of the wisdom of Job's friends, into a statement of the Rabbinic doctrine that such simple justice is achieved not in this life but only after death.

¹¹ With Maarsen cf. the midrash attributed to Samuel the Little in Midrash Tehillim here.

¹² So apparently *Mahberet Menahem,* p. 126, s.v. *dm* 11; *K-B*³, p. 208a; *BDB,* p. 189; Zorell, p. 169b; contrast Dahood, here.

¹³ Contrast Deut. 4:19, which suggests that it was the LORD, who apportioned to the Gentiles the worship of the hosts of heaven.

¹⁴ Cf. *Mahberet Menahem,* p. 99, s.v. *gd* I.

¹⁵ The psalmist writes *ṣaddîq* 'THE RIGHTEOUS'. Here as throughout the psalm Rashi transforms the unnamed victims into suffering Israel.

¹⁶ Maarsen notes that the verb *hiršîă'* 'cause one to be convicted' is so used also in Deut. 25:1; it should be added that Rashi so interprets it also there.

PSALM XCV

1   COME LET US SING UNTO THE LORD.

4   *wĕtōʿapôt* 'PEAKS' is a word referring to height;[1] [and it is a cognate of the participle][2] *mĕʿôpēp* 'flying' (Isa. 14:19; 30:6).[3]

6   *nibrĕkāh* 'LET US KNEEL' is the same verb as is attested in "He made the camels kneel down" (Gen. 24:11).[4]

7   O, IF YOU WOULD BUT HEED HIS CHARGE THIS DAY.

9   TRIED ME THOUGH THEY HAD SEEN MY DEEDS. [I.e.], THEY TRIED ME for no reason, for THEY HAD already SEEN MY DEEDS.

10   FORTY YEARS *ʾāqût* WITH THAT GENERATION. [I.e.], I argued [*qāṭĕtî*][5] with them [i.e.], I contended with them. [The verb *ʾāqût*] is the same verb as is attested in "I argued with myself" [*nāqĕṭāh napšî*] (Job. 10:1).[6]

    FORTY YEARS so as [almost] to kill them in the desert, for[7] I thought, [8] "THEY ARE SENSELESS."

11   TO MY RESTING-PLACE [i.e.], to the land of Israel and to Jerusalem, which I [God] have named 'RESTING PLACE' as it is stated in the Bible, "This is My resting-place forever" (Ps. 132:14).[9]

PSALM XCV, NOTES

[1] Cf. T.O. and Rashi at Num. 23:22.

[2] Bracketed text supplied from other editions of Rashi's commentary here.

[3] So Rashi also at Num. 23:22. By equating the roots of *tōʿăpôt* and of *mĕʿôpēp*, Rashi asserts that Menahem's *ʿp* I and *ʿp* VI (see *Mahberet Menahem*, p. 287) are not homonymous but identical. Once Biblical lexicography traced both *tōʿăpôt* and *mĕʿôpēp* to triliteral roots, the root of the former had to be *yʿp* the root of the later *ʿwp*; for the former see, e.g., *BDB*, p. 419.

[4] Rashi, following *Mahberet Menahem*, p. 90 distinguishes *brk* I 'kneel', which is attested only in Gen. 24:11; Ps. 95:6; and 2 Ch. 6:13 and which is a denominative verb derived from the noun *berek* 'knee' as is Eng. 'kneel' from 'knee' from the frequently attested *brk* II 'bless'; cf. Gruber, *Aspects*, p. 171.

[5] MT reads *ʾāqût*. By substituting the perfect *qāṭĕtî*, Rashi calls our attention to the psalmist's use of an imperfect as a preterite.

⁶ So also Midrash Tehillim here and *Mahberet Menahem*, p. 329, s.v. *qṭ* I.

⁷ Heb. *kî*; Rashi's interpretation of the psalmist's conjunctive *waw* as a subordinate conjunction 'for' anticipates the remarks found in Orlinsky, *Notes*, pp. 19-20.

⁸ Heb. *'āmartî*; here again Rashi's paraphrase calls attention to the psalmist's use of an imperfect to express the preterite.

⁹ Rashi's source is Midrash Tehillim here.

PSALM XCVI

1   SING TO THE LORD A NEW SONG.

7a ASCRIBE TO THE LORD, O FAMILIES OF THE
    PEOPLES.
    Now what is it that you should give[1] to Him? [The answer
    to this question is given in v. 7b]:
    ASCRIBE TO THE LORD GLORY AND STRENGTH.[2]

10a "THE LORD IS KING." "Peoples tremble" (Ps. 99:1) This
    song will be [sung] in the time to come.[3]

10c HE JUDGES THE PEOPLES WITH EQUITY [i.e.],
    those [peoples] for whom He "will make pure speech" (Zeph.
    3:9),[4] WITH EQUITY [mēšārîm] [i.e.], charitably.[5]

11 LET THE SEA THUNDER to shout at the first.

12 ALL THE TREES OF THE FORESTS [are a metaphor
    for] all the rulers of the Gentiles.[6]

PSALM XCVI, NOTES
    [1] So KJV. Note that this correct interpretation of the imperative *hābû*
'give, render' is at variance with what Rashi suggests at Ps. 29:1, q.v.
    [2] Pointing out that the direct object of the imperative 'ASCRIBE' is
missing from v. 7a but supplied in v. 7b, Rashi thereby summarizes
Rashbam's observation in his commentary at Ex. 15:6 that in staircase
parallelism "the first half [of the verse] does not complete its message before the latter half arrives and repeats it and completes its message." Berliner, *Raschi*, pp. ix-x demonstrated that Rashi learned about staircase
parallelism from his grandson, Rashbam, and that he revised his comment upon Ex. 15:6 to reflect the lesson he learned from Rashbam. Moreover, Bodleian ms. 271 and Vienna ms. 32 of the comments of the
Tosaphists on the Pentateuch state at Gen. 49:22 that Rashi named the
stylistic phenomenon in question for his grandson, Rashbam; see our discussion in our introduction, pp. 7–9.
    [3] Cf. Yalkut ha-Mekiri here.
    [4] This obscure expression in Zeph. 3:9 refers both in its biblical con-
text and in Rabbinic exegesis to idolators' renouncing idolatry and accepting the LORD as God; see BT A.Z. 24a; JT A.Z. 2:1; etc. The
association of 'clear language' with acceptance of the LORD as King appears to derive from the perception that the polytheistic Gentiles speak
strange languages, which sound to Hebrew ears like gibberish; see Isa.
33:19; Jer. 5:15; Ezek. 3:5-6. Zephaniah's "pure language" is therefore
the same as "the lip of Canaan" in Isa. 20:18, i.e., Hebrew, the language

of Holy Writ. Zeph. 3:9 suggests, therefore, that in the time to come the decree of Gen. 11:7 will be rescinded.

⁵ Heb. *bizĕkût;* cf. the interpretation of *zĕkût* in Rashi's and in Maimonides' commentaries on Mishnah Avot 1:6. Rashi here anticipates Ginsberg, "A Strand in the Cord of Hebraic Hymnody," p. 46b; "Why not [render] 'judge the people with equity', which is what the phrase is commonly supposed to mean? Because, firstly, in the latter case the world would not stand firm but would collapse..."; to the latter remark cf. Midrash Tehillim here: "The Gentiles are judged by Him only *bĕmîšôr* 'with equity', and when they have nothing [in the way of a virtuous record] on which to rely, they perish."

⁶ Cf. Rashi also at Isa. 10:33; Ps. 29:5, 9.

PSALM XCVII

1a   THE LORD IS KING. [The verb *mālak* 'IS KING' is a prophetic perfect describing a state of affairs, which will be realized] when He [the LORD] will have taken away the sovereign power from Esau and his progeny.[1]

1b   LET THE EARTH EXULT. This refers to what Ezekiel said: "When the whole earth rejoices, I [the LORD] will make you a desolation" (Ezek. 35:14). It was concerning Esau that it was so prophesied.[2]

4a   HIS BOLTS OF LIGHTNING [*bĕrāqāyw*] [i.e.], *zahărûrîn* 'flashes of lightning'.[3] [[The word *bĕrāqāyw*] is a form of the same word [*bārāq* 'lightning'] as is attested in "It has been polished in order that it may have lightning" (Ezek. 21:15).

4b   *wattāḥēl* 'AND TREMBLED' is a cognate of [the gerund *ḥîl* 'trembling' in] "trembling like that of a woman in labour" (Ps. 48:7).[4]

5   *kaddônag* 'LIKE WAX' [i.e.], *kĕšaʿăwāh* 'like wax'.[5]

7   WHO PRIDE THEMSELVES [i.e.], who glorify themselves in idolatry.[6]

8   YOUR JUDGMENTS [i.e.], Your vengeance.[7]

11   LIGHT IS SOWN FOR THE VIRTUOUS. [The psalmist refers to] a literal 'sowing', which is being prepared to sprout for them.[8]

PSALM XCVII, NOTES

[1] Similarly Rashi at Ps. 96:10a. Here Rashi's source is Midrash Tehillim here.

[2] Cf. Rashi's almost verbatim comment at Ezek. 35:14; cf. Midrash Tehillim here and at Ps. 95:1. Note that while in Ezek. 35 Esau refers to the ancient Transjordanian Kingdom of Edom, whose progenitor was Jacob's brother Esau, for Rashi as for many Medieval Hebrew writers Esau and Edom are epithets for the Christian kingdoms, which ruled over the Jews in Central Europe; see Max Seligsohn, "Edom," *JE* 5:41.

[3] Rashi assumes that his readers will not know the meaning of Biblical Heb. *bārāq* 'lightning'. The word *zahărûr*, a loanword in Medieval Heb. from Babylonian Jewish Aramaic *zahărûraʾ* 'red light, glare, reflex' (so Jastrow, *Dict.*, p. 382b) is employed by Rashi to explain *bārāq* also at Ps. 135:7, q.v.; see Ben Yehuda, *Dict.*, vol. 3, p. 1300.

[4] See Rashi there.

⁵ So Rashi also at Mic. 1:4 and Ps. 22:15, q.v. Rashi here explains a rare Biblical Heb. word by reference to a common Mishnaic Heb. word.

⁶ Rashi's *ba'ăbôdāh zārāh* "in idolatry" paraphrases the psalmist's *bā'ĕlîlîm* "IN IDOLS".

⁷ With Maarsen note that Rashi at Ex. 28:15 and Isa. 32:7 points out that Heb. *mišpāṭ* has at least four other meanings, depending on the context; see also Banitt, *Rashi: Interpreter of the Biblical Letter*.

⁸ In light of Maarsen's suggestion that we examine Midrash Tehillim here it appears that Rashi may refer here to the midrash there, according to which the light created on the first day of Creation (Gen. 1:3-4) and which is distinct from the light of the sun created on the fourth day (Gen. 1:14-19) was stored away for the benefit of the virtuous in the time to come.

PSALM XCVIII

1 SING TO THE LORD [A NEW SONG].[1]
All these [instances of the expression "a new song," i.e., Isa. 42:10; Ps. 33:3; 40:4; 96:1; 98:1; 144:9;149:1] refer to the future.[2]

8a LET THE RIVERS CLAP THEIR HANDS.
The prophets[3] spoke metaphorically.[4] [The psalmist here does] not [mean], "Would that the RIVERS had HANDS." [LET THE RIVERS CLAP THEIR HANDS] is rather a metaphor for happiness and joy.[5]

PSALM XCVIII, NOTES
   [1] Rashi does not quote the bracketed portion of the verse. I have supplied it since Rashi's comment on v. 1 refers specifically to the bracketed expression.
   [2] I.e., eschatological time. The source of Rashi's comment is Midrash Tehillim here; contrast Rashi at Ps. 40:4.
   [3] For the designation of the psalmists as prophets see Rashi at Ps. 42:1; 46:2; 48:10; 64:2: 73:21.
   [4] Lit., in a language that the ear comprehends. The continuation of Rashi's comment here demonstrates that Rashi's expresion here means 'metaphorically'.
   [5] Cf. Midrash Tehillim here, which quotes R. Nehemiah to the effect that reference is made to physical rather than metaphorical clapping and also to the effect that the clapping in question is a *gestus* of joy.

PSALM XCIX

1a   THE LORD IS KING
PEOPLES TREMBLE refers to the War of Gog and
Magog[1] when PEOPLE WILL TREMBLE in consonance
with what is stated in the Bible, "Now this shall be the affliction..." (Zech. 14:12).[2]

1b   *tānûṭ* 'QUAKES' is a cognate of [the verb *nāṭāyû* 'strayed' in]
"My feet strayed" (Ps. 73:2).[3]

4a   'MIGHTY KING' [i.e., v. 4a] is a continuation of the previous verse [as follows]:[4]

3-4   THEY PRAISE YOUR NAME, namely, 'MIGHTY
KING, WHO LOVES JUSTICE'.

4b   IT WAS YOU WHO ESTABLISHED EQUITY [*mēšārîm*,
i.e.], compromise and the making [of peace][5] between
people. YOU ESTABLISHED [*mēšārîm* 'charitableness'][6]
when You said [in the Torah], "If you should see your
enemy's donkey prostrate [under its burden...you must
surely help him]" (Ex. 23:5);[7] "If you encounter your
enemy's bull [or his donkey wandering, surely you must return it to him]" (Ex. 23:4).[8] Now who can see his enemy extend him a favor and not feel prompted to embrace him and
to kiss him. [This midrash is taken from] Tanḥuma.[9]

7a   HE SPOKE TO THEM IN A PILLAR OF CLOUD. [Lest
you think that HE did so only to Moses and Aaron mentioned in v. 6a, it should be pointed out that He did so] also
to Samuel [mentioned in v. 6b], and it is in reference to this
that it is stated in the Bible, "'Is the seer here?' 'He is here,'
the women exclaimed'" (I Sam 9: 11-12). You will see the
cloud situated over his doorway in acccord with what you
read in the Bible, "And he is here when there is the cloud"
(Num. 9:20).[10]

7b   THEY OBEYED HIS DECREES, THE LAW, which[11] HE
GAVE THEM.

8a   YOU WERE A GOD FORGIVING Israel's iniquities[12]
lāhem 'FOR THEM' [i.e.], *bišěbîlām* 'on their behalf'.[13]

8b   BUT YOU EXACTED RETRIBUTION FOR THEIR

MISDEEDS. Moses and Aaron were punished for [their failure to affirm the holiness of God at Meribah (Num. 20:2-13) when they said], "Listen, you rebels" (Num. 20:10). Samuel [was likewise punished] because he failed to train his sons in moral behavior; [therefore] he died young.[14]

9b   FOR THE LORD OUR GOD IS HOLY. He is hallowed in the world because He is very exacting with respect to the virtuous. In the same vein the Bible says, "He will be hallowed through My honor" (Ex. 29:43).[15]

PSALM XCIX, NOTES

[1] Both the Jewish and the Christian traditions envisage a world war's taking place at the end of days before the arrival of the Messianic Era. In Christianity the last battle is called Armageddon. In Jewish tradition it is called the War of Gog and Magog on the basis of Ezek. 38-39, which refers to the leader of the forces of evil as Gog, who emanates from the land of Magog.

[2] For the notion that Zech. 14 refers to the same eschatological war as is described in Ezek. 38-39 (see previous note) see Rashi at BT Megillah 31a, and cf. the various modern commentaries.

[3] Rashi here is wrong. The verb *tānûṭ* is a 3[d] pers. sing. fem. imperfect of the root *nwṭ* 'shake, quake' (cf. *BDB*, p. 630a) while the verb *nāṭāyû* is a rare example in the Bible of the way a 3[d] pers. pl. perfect of a *lamed-yod* root would appear had not final *ayû* generally been contracted to *û*; see *B-L* #57. The same verb appears with *ayû* contracted to *û* in Isa. 45:12 where the form is *nāṭû*. Because Rashi, following Menahem, treated all weak verbs as biliteral roots he was tempted to trace *tānûṭ* and *nāṭāyû* to a common root *nṭ*. *Maḥberet Menahem* does not treat this root at all.

[4] Contrast Ibn Ezra for whom 'MIGHTY KING' is an epithet by which the LORD is addressed in v. 4.

[5] The bracketed portion is missing by haplography from our Rashi ms.

[6] See Rashi at Ps. 96:10 and our discussion there.

[7] Rashi here at Ps. 99:4 does not quote the entire verse. I have supplied for clarity the end of the verse rendered according to Rashi at Ex. 23:5.

[8] Again I have supplied for clarity the portion of the verse, which Rashi does not quote here at Ps. 99:4.

[9] The midrash, which Rashi here attributes to Midrash Tanḥuma is similar but not identical to a midrash found in the several extant recensions of Midrash Tanhuma at Ex. 21:1 and in Midrash Tehillim at Ps. 99:4. In those midrashim it is explained that 'YOU ESTABLISHED CHARITABLENESS' when You said...'help him'... (Ex. 23:5) because God's requiring enemies to help each other leads to their mutual appreciation and socializing, which, in turn, lead them to friendship.

[10] Had we known this midrash only from Rashi's commentary, it would appear that the author of our midrash noted correctly that *yēš* 'there is' has the nuance 'he is home' in 1 Sam. 9:12 and that the imaginative author of the midrash reads this nuance into Num. 9:20 where the contextual meaning of *wěyēš 'ăšer yihyeh heʿānān* is "Whenever there shall be the cloud". However, a glance at Rashi's apparent source, a midrash attributed to R. Judan in Midrash Shmuel 13:8 and PRK, ed. Mandelbaum, pp. 70-71 shows that the latter deduced from Num. 9:20 that *yēš* means 'cloud'.

[11] Rashi, followed by KJV (in italics) and by RSV but not by NJV, makes it clear that 'HE GAVE THEM' is a relative clause modifying 'LAW', which is part of the compound direct object of the verb 'OBEYED'.

[12] Here Rashi supplies the direct object of the participle FORGIVING. and he thereby intimates that the verse is an example of ellipsis.

[13] The expression *lāhem* 'TO/FOR THEM' could refer either to Israel's iniquities or to Israel. Rashi here indicates that he rejects the former interpretation and accepts the latter.

[14] This comment presupposes our knowing that according to Seder Olam Rabbah, Chapter 13, Samuel lived "only fifty-two years"; see commentaries there for explanation of this assertion, and note that in JT Berakot 4:1 R. Levi, who likewise presupposes Samuel's short lifespan, explains the latter as a consequence of Hannah's having prayed too much (1 Sam. 1:12).

[15] As Rashi explains in his comment at Ex. 29:43, the contextual meaning of *wěniqdāš bikěbodî* is "It [the Tabernacle] shall be hallowed by means of the Shekinah's abiding there." There Rashi points to the fact that Biblical Heb. *kābôd* 'Glory' in Ex. 29:43 is the functional equivalent of Rabbinic Heb. *Shekinah* (concerning *Shekinah* as a physical manifestation of God see Kadushin, *The Rabbinic Mind*[3], pp. 222-261). Rashi in his commentary at Ex. 29:43 appends to the aforementioned comment a paraphrase of a midrash found in BT Zebaḥim 115b, which Rashi summarizes here at Ps. 99:9: "'honor' (Ex. 29:43) [i.e.], through My honored people."

PSALM C

1   A PSALM FOR *tôdāh* [i.e.], for *hôdāyāh* 'thanksgiving', to be
     sung during [the presentation of] sacrifices of *tôdāh*
     'THANKSGIVING'.[1]
2   SERVE THE LORD WITH GLADNESS. Now why to
     such an extent should we serve the LORD? The answer is
     found in v. 4]:
4   ACKNOWLEDGE THAT THE LORD IS GOD, who will
     pay you the reward for Your service. However, those who
     serve idolatry do not have to SERVE WITH GLADNESS
     because they are not paid a reward.
3   HE MADE US, AND NOT WE [i.e.], when we were not
     [yet] in the world.[2]
4   *bĕtôdāh* [i.e.]. *bĕhôdāyāh* 'with thanksgiving'.
5c   HIS FAITHFULNESS [i.e.], the promise, which he prom-
     ised abides FOR ALL GENERATIONS. He is faithful with
     respect to [His] promise.

PSALM C, NOTES
   [1] So RSV and so NJV margin; contrast NJV. Here Rashi responds to
two exegetical questions. The first question is, "What is the meaning of
tôdāh?" The second is, "What is the meaning of *mizmôr lĕtôdāh?*" In answer
to the first question Rashi contends that Biblical Heb. *tôdāh*, which can
correspond in meaning either to Rabbinic Heb. *hôdā'āh* 'confession' (so
NJV at Ezra 10:11) or to Rabbinic Heb. *hôdāyāh* 'thanksgiving' (so NJV at
Ps. 26:7), here means 'thanksgiving'. In answer to the second question
Rashi contends that just as "A psalm, a song for the Sabbath Day" (Ps.
92:1) designates a psalm sung by the Levites during sacrificial worship on
the Sabbath in the Temple so does "A PSALM FOR *tôdāh* " designate a
psalm sung during the presentation of the type of sacrifice called *zebah*
tôdāh 'sacrifice of thanksgiving'; for the latter term see Lev. 7:12; 22:29;
Ps. 116:17; for the plural *zibĕhê tôdāh* as in Rashi here see Ps. 107:22; for
the designation of such offerings simply as *tôdāh* as posited here by Rashi
see Lev. 7:12; Jer. 17:26; 33:11; Ps. 50:14, 23.
   [2] Rashi here interprets the *kethib wĕlō'*, lit., 'AND NOT', rather than
the *qere wĕlô* 'AND HIS'. At Ps. 139:16 where *kethib* and *qere* present the
very same pair of variants as here Rashi interprets both *kethib* and *qere*.
Here Rashi interprets the conjunctive *waw* as a subordinate conjunction
meaning 'when'; see Rashi at Ps. 95:10 and our comment there.

PSALM CI

1a   OF DAVID. A PSALM.

1b   LET ME SING OF KINDNESS[1] AND JUSTICE.
When You show me kindness, I shall praise You, "Praised [are You, O LORD our God, King of the world], who is kind and does kindness," and when You show me justice, I shall sing, "Praised [are You, O LORD our God, King of the world], the reliable Judge."[2] In either case,

1c   I WILL CHANT A HYMN TO YOU, O LORD.[3]

2a   I WILL STUDY [i.e.], I shall give heed, concerning[4] THE WAY OF the BLAMELESS.

2b   WHEN SHALL I ATTAIN the straight way for walking in it continually?[5]

2c   I SHALL WALK CONTINUALLY IN MY BLAMELESS-NESS OF HEART even WITHIN MY HOUSE privately[6] as well as publicly.

3   [The abstract noun] *sēṭim* 'CROOKEDNESS' is a cognate of [the verb *tiśṭeh* 'she goes astray' in] "if his wife go astray" (Num. 5:12);[7] [it means] "turning aside from the [proper] path"; *destoltes* 'deviations' in O.F.[8]

4b   I WILL KNOW NOTHING OF EVIL. I shall neither love nor have any acquaintance with[9] any EVIL thing.[10]

5   I CANNOT ENDURE [THE HAUGHTY AND THE PROUD MAN][11] that he should become my friend lest I learn from his [wrong] behavior.[12]

8a   EACH MORNING I WILL DESTROY....
[I.e.], Every day I shall GET RID OF (8b) a few of those who are deserving of the death penalty.[13]

PSALM CI, NOTES

[1] Heb. *ḥesed*. NJV's rendering "faithfulness" sees *ḥesed.* and *mišpāṭ* 'justice' as synonyms and reflects the observations of Nelson Glueck, *Hesed in the Bible*, trans. Alfred Gottschalk (Cincinnati: HUC Press, 1967). However, the midrash, which Rashi quotes here, sees *ḥesed.* not as a synonym of justice but as its opposite, sc., 'kindness', as generally in Rabbinic Heb. Moreover, Felix Asensio, *Misericordia et Veritas* (Rome: Universitatis Gregorianae, 1949), p. 137 argues that in Biblical Heb. as well *ḥesed.* often denotes 'gift, grace, benevolence'; see Gerald A. Larue's introduction to

Glueck, *Hesed*, p. 13. Note that Dahood's rendering "love and justice" is in consonance with Rashi but at odds with Dahood's acceptance in his commentary here of Glueck's thesis.

² See Mishnah Berakot 9:2; see Birnbaum, *Daily Prayer Book*, p. 777.

³ Similarly Midrash Tehillim here, q.v.

⁴ The psalmist employs the prefixed preposition *bĕ*, lit., 'in'; Rashi's paraphrase *'al* clarifies the meaning.

⁵ Rashi here responds to two exegetical questions: (1) "What is the grammatical form of the verb *tābô'* : is it 2ᵈ pers. sing. masc. 'you will come' or is it 3ᵈ pers. sing. fem., 'she will come'?" (2) "Who/what is the subject of the verb *tābô'?*" LXX, Vulgate, and Qimhi, followed by KJV, RSV, Dahood, NEB, and many others, understand the verb to be 2ᵈ pers. sing. masc., and they understand the entire clause *mātay tābô' 'ēlāy* as a question, "O when wilt thou come unto me" (KJV) addressed to God. Rashi and Ibn Ezra, followed by Sforno, Ehrlich (see his extensive discussion here), and NJV, interpret *tābô'* as 3ᵈ pers. sing. fem. 'she will come', and they understand 'WAY OF THE BLAMELESS' in v.2a as the antecedent of the pronominal suffix 'she'. Rashi's interpretation is to be preferred to that of Qimhi et al. because it alone makes sense of the several clauses of v. 2 both in relationship to each other and in relationship to vv. 1 and 3. Rashi's interpretation suggests that the psalmist precedes from praising the divine attributes of love and justice (v.1) to learning about human virtue (v.2a) to desiring to embody human virtue (v.2b) to becoming an exemplar of human virtue (vv.2c-8). Contrast Dahood here.

⁶ Heb. *bĕhaṣnēa̅*; the meaning of this expresion is demonstrated by the contrast *bĕhaṣnēa̅ kĕmô bĕparhesyā'* "privately well as publicly." In Biblical Heb. the infinitive *haṣnēa̅* occurs only once in Micah 6:8 where it means 'modestly' (but see NJV margin); in Rabbinic Heb. *haṣnēa̅* means 'chastity'; see Jastrow, *Dict.*, p. 364a.

⁷ In recognizing that the *s* of *sēṭîm* is identical with the *ś* of the verb *śāṭāh* 'go astray', Rashi follows *Mahberet Menahem*, p. 363, s.v. *śṭ*. Note that in Rabbinic Heb. as here at Ps. 101:3 the root in question is always written with *s*. The spelling of the root with *s* here at Ps. 101:3 suggests that our psalm belongs to late Biblical Heb.; see Kutscher, A *History of the Hebrew Language*, p. 14.

⁸ See Catane, *Recueil* #1569; note that in other editions of Rashi's commentary here the reading is *destolemant*; see J. Greenberg, *Foreign Words in the Bible Commentary of Rashi*, p. 195.

⁹ Rashi here points to the fact that Heb. *yāda'* 'know' has a wide variety of connotations, and he provides readers of his commentary with the nuances appropriate to the present context; see *BDB*, pp. 393-395.

¹⁰ Rashi intimates here that *ra'* 'evil' in Ps. 101:4 is an adjectival noun.

¹¹ Rashi does not quote the bracketed portion of the verse. I have supplied it for clarity.

¹² Rashi here answers two exegetical questions: (1) "What about him is it that I CANNOT ENDURE?" and (2) "Why is it that I CANNOT ENDURE HIM?"

[13] The psalmist says, "EACH MORNING I WILL DESTROY ALL THE WICKED OF THE LAND SO TO RID THE CITY OF THE LORD OF ALL EVILDOERS." Rashi responds to the exegetical question, "Why must our psalmist destroy 'ALL THE WICKED' 'EACH MORNING'?" Rashi explains that in order to destroy ALL the psalmist intends to destroy a few each morning.

PSALM CII

1 A PRAYER OF THE LOWLY MAN WHEN HE IS FAINT [*kî yaʿăṭōp*][1] [i.e.] *bĕhitʿaṭṭēp napšô bĕṣārāh* 'when his neck was bent over because of sorrow'.[2]

4 *nihārû* 'ARE CHARRED'. The [prefixed] *nun* [in the word *nihārû* is a servile letter[3] like the *nun* [s] in *naʿăśû* 'they were made' (Lev. 18:30; Isa. 46:10; Ps. 33:6; Neh. 5:18); *niqqĕbû* 'they were called' (Num. 11:17; Ezra 8:20; 1 Ch. 12:31; 16:41; etc.).[4] Moreover, this verb is a verb referring to dryness as is demonstrated by "My bones are dried up [*ḥārāh*] by the heat" (Job. 30:30); "The bellows are dried up [*nāhar*]"[6] (Jer. 6:29).

7a 'A GREAT OWL' [*liq'at*] is the name of a kind of bird.[7]

7b AN OWL [*kôs*] AMONG THE RUINS is the name of a kind of bird; [it is found in the list of non-kosher birds]: "the little owl [*hakkôs*], the cormorant..." (Lev. 11:17).[8] 'RUINS' [i.e.], 'deserts'. I AM LIKE A GREAT OWL IN THE WILDERNESS. So are we [the Jews] wandering continually from our own place [the land of Israel] to go about in the Exile.

8 *śāqadtî* I CONSIDERED [i.e.], I thought about myself:[9] "Here I am[10] LIKE A LONE BIRD UPON A ROOF sitting by himself without a mate. *bôdēd* 'LONE' [means] 'sitting alone'.[11]

9b *mĕhôlālay* 'MY DERIDERS' [i.e.], 'those who make fun of me'; [the participle *mĕhôlālay*] is a cognate of *hôlēlôt* 'foolishness' (Koh. 1: 17).[12]

9c USE MY NAME TO CURSE.[13] Having "seen my misfortune" (cf. Num. 11:I5), they USE MY NAME TO CURSE, saying, "If it should not happen to me as it happened to Israel, may He [God] do thus to me as He did to Israel."[14]

10 MIXED [MY DRINK][15] WITH CRYING. [I.e.], *māzagtî* 'I mixed [it]'[16] with tears.[17]

11b FOR YOU first LIFTED ME UP, i.e.,[18] You exalted me, but now[19] YOU CAST ME DOWN from heaven to earth. Now had You not first LIFTED ME UP, my reproach would not have been so very great.

12   LIKE A LENGTHENING SHADOW at eventide[20] when the shadows lengthen so that in the darkness the shadows are not perceived but they gradually vanish.

13a   BUT YOU, O LORD, who ['ăšer] [21] ARE ENTHRONED FOREVER, "and swore" to us "by Your name" (cf. Ex. 32:13). Now just as You exist [FOREVER] so are You obligated to maintain our existence in like manner.

14   YOU WILL SURELY ARISE AND TAKE PITY ON ZION, FOR IT IS TIME TO BE GRACIOUS TO HER, for thus did You promise: "[For the LORD will vindicate His people...] when He sees that their might is gone..." (Deut. 32:36);[22] so look: "their might is gone."

15   YOUR SERVANTS TAKE DELIGHT IN [i.e.], they love, ITS STONES, AND CHERISH ITS DUST. Now an aggadic midrash [states that] when Jeconiah and his Exile went forth [from Jerusalem in 597 B.C.E.; see 2 Kgs. 24:12-16; 2 Ch. 36:9-10] they took with them some of the stones of Jerusalem and [some of] its dust in order to build a synagogue there in Babylon.[23]

16   THE NATIONS WILL FEAR Your Name[24] when You deliver Your people.

18   hā'ar'ār [i.e.], 'he who cries out'; [the noun 'ar'ār is a cognate of the verb yē'ō'ērû 'they will cry out' in] "they shall cry out a cry of destruction" (Isa. 15:5).[25] An alternative interpretation of 'ar'ār is 'destroyed and devastated'; [if so, the noun 'ar'ār is] a cognate of the verb 'ārû 'ārû "Destroy, destroy" (Ps. 137:7).[26]

19a   MAY THIS BE WRITTEN DOWN. Those who experience the deliverance will say this: "MAY THIS deliverance BE WRITTEN DOWN in order to tell of it TO A COMING GENERATION."

19b   A CREATED PEOPLE [i.e.], A PEOPLE that became a new creation by virtue of going out from slavery to freedom, from darkness to light.[27]

20   BEHOLDS THE EARTH [in order to gaze][28] upon the affliction of His people.

21   tĕmûtāh 'DEATH' [i.e.], "sick [unto death]";[29] enmorinde 'dying' in O.F.[30]

24   HE DRAINED... IN MID-COURSE. He [the psalmist] reverts to his previous complaint, [sc.], YOU LIFTED ME

UP; THEN YOU CAST ME DOWN (v. 11); MY DAYS
ARE LIKE A LENGTHENING SHADOW (v. 12) [when
he says], "My enemy[31] DRAINED MY STRENGTH IN
MID-COURSE."

25   I SAY to the LORD,[32] "You are MY GOD;[33] DO NOT
TAKE ME AWAY IN THE MIDST OF MY DAYS."
[I.e.], Do not remove us in order to destroy us[34] from off the
earth[35] by the hand of our enemies IN THE MIDST OF
our[36] DAYS. Now what are[37] "our DAYS"? [They are]

25b   all the days of YOU, WHOSE YEARS GO ON FOR GEN-
ERATIONS ON END [which] You promised to maintain
our existence before You in consonance with what is written
toward the end of the psalm: "AND YOUR YEARS
NEVER END" (v. 28b), "AND the PROGENY of Your
devotees WILL ENDURE BEFORE IN YOUR PRES-
ENCE" (v. 29b).

26   *lĕpānîm* 'OF OLD'[38] [i.e.], from the beginning.

27c   YOU CHANGE THEM LIKE CLOTHING [i.e.], as a
person turns over his garment to remove it.

28a   BUT YOU ARE THE SAME.[39] [I.e.], YOU ARE THE
SAME, who continues to exist.[40]

PSALM CII, NOTES

[1] Note that Rashi at Lam. 2:11 glosses *bĕ'āṭēp* with O.F. *pasmer* 'to
faint'; see Rashi at Jonah 2:8.

[2] Here and in his comment on Ps. 102:1 in BT 'Avodah Zarah 7b,
Rashi anticipates Lienhard Delekat, "Zum hebräischen Wörterbuch," *VT*
14 (1964), pp. 33-35 in recognizing that the starting point for arriving at
an understanding of Heb. *'ṭp* is the appearance of this verb primarily in
anatomical expressions involving *lēb* 'heart, chest'; *nepeš* 'neck'; and *rûaḥ*
'breath'. Moreover, anticipating the method developed in Gruber, *Aspects,*
Rashi here notes that the anatomical expressions, which are the key to
uncovering the meaning of the verb *'ṭp*, describe physical manifestations
of *ṣārāh* 'sorrow'. Rashi at Isa. 57:16 proves that Rashi understood *'ṭp* to
mean 'to bend over' while *Mahberet Menahem*, p. 92, s.v. *bt* IV proves that
Rashi, who leaned heavily on Menahem, should have been aware of the
primary meaning of Heb. *nepeš*, sc., 'neck', long before Dürr, "Hebr. *nāpāš*
= akk. *napištu* = Gurgel, Kehle."

[3] So Englander, "A Commentary on Rashi's Grammatical Comments," p. 486.

[4] The verb *niḥārû* and the verbs to which Rashi compares it are all 3d
pers. pl. perfect *niphal* forms of verbs which the latest Biblical Heb. grammar derives from *lamed-yod* roots. For Rashi, as for Menahem, all of these

are biliteral roots. Since a reasonably intelligent reader of Rashi's commentary who has not mastered the esoteric features of Heb. grammar, might in each instance assume that the prefixed *nun* is the first letter of a triliteral root, Rashi informs him/her otherwise.

[5] See *Mahberet Menahem*, p. 187, s.v. *ḥr* IV; cf. Gruber, *Aspects*, pp. 491-492.

[6] Here Rashi, following *Mahberet Menahem*, p.187, errs as does Qimhi following Rashi at Jer. 6:29. Were this verb the singular of *niḥărû*, i.e., 3[d] pers. sing. perfect *niphal* of the root *ḥry*, it would be vocalized *niḥar;* in fact, *nāḥar* is the 3[d] pers. sing. perfect *qal* of the root *nḥr* 'snort'; see John Arthur Thompson, *The Book of Jeremiah*, NIC (Grand Rapids: Eerdmans, 1980), p. 265; *BDB*, p. 637b.

[7] Rashi here treats the initial *lamed* as part of the name of this bird species. Since, however, *q't* is attested as the name of a species of bird in Lev. 11:18; Deut. 14:17; Isa. 34:11; Zeph. 2:14, it would appear that Heb. *lq't* here at Ps. 102:7 represents the prefixed preposition *lĕ* 'to, unto' + *qā'āt;* for the identification of the latter see next note.

[8] For the identification of the eight species of owls mentioned in the Heb. Bible see George Soper Cansdale, *All the Animals of the Bible Lands* (Grand Rapids: Zondervan, 1970), pp. 147-149 and the literature cited there; see also Virginia C. Holmgren, *Bird Walk Through the Bible* (New York: Seabury, 1972), pp. 56-61; 68-73.

[9] Contrast NJV and RSV: "I lie awake." In Ps. 127:1 Rashi interprets *šôqēd* as synonymous with *ṣōpeh* 'look'. In fact, the rendering of *šqd* 'consider, be perspicacious' is most appropriate also in Isa. 29:20; Jer. 1:12; 31:28; 44:27; Dan. 9:14.

[10] Heb. *hinĕnî;* paraphrase of the psalmist's AND I HAVE BECOME; similarly NJV.

[11] This expression describes Jerusalem after her people have been exiled in Lam. 1:1 and personified Israel after he has been devastated in Lam. 3:28; see also Jer. 15:17.

[12] For definition of *hôlēlôt* see Rashi there; cf. Rashi at Ps. 5:6; 73:3; 76:5.

[13] NJV, which reflects Rashi's exegesis; similarly RSV; contrast KJV: "they...are sworn against me," which is a literal rendering of Heb. *bî nišbĕ'û.*

[14] This comment on 'CURSE BY MY NAME' is a mirror image of Rashi's comment on "may they bless themselves by your name" at Gen. 12:3.

[15] Rashi does not quote the bracketed portion of the verse. I have supplied it for clarity.

[16] Here Rashi's point is that Biblical Heb. *māsak* is the etymological and semantic equivalent of Rabbinic Heb. *māzag;* see Gruber, *Aspects*, p. 529, n. 1; see Rashi at BT 'Avodah Zarah 58b.

[17] Heb. *bekî* 'CRYING' may denote "weeping, wailing, lamentation, [or] mourning"; so Gruber, *Aspects*, p. 411. Rashi here selects the nuance appropriate to the present context.

[18] Explicative *waw*.

[19] Rashi intimates that the *waw* conversive in *wattašlîkēnu* means much more than simply 'and'.

[20] With Maarsen cf. Jer. 6:4.

[21] Rashi intimates that what follows is a relative clause.

[22] Rashi does not quote here the bracketed portion of the quotation. I have supplied it for clarity.

[23] At BT Megillah 29a where Abbaye asserts that the *Shekinah* is present at the synagogue of Shaf-weyathib in Nehardea, Rashi comments: "Jeconiah and his circle built it from stones and dust, which they brought with them when they were exiled in order to fulfill what is stated in the Bible, 'YOUR SERVANTS DELIGHT IN ITS STONES, AND CHERISH ITS DUST' (Ps. 102:15)."' So also Rashi at BT 'Avodah Zarah 43b. For extensive bibliography concerning this legend, which appears to originate with the Letter of Sherira Gaon (c. 906-1006 C.E.), pt. 3, chapter 1, see Maarsen here and see also notes to Soncino Talmud at the passages cited.

[24] Rashi here paraphrases the psalmist's THE NAME OF THE LORD.

[25] Rashi at Isa. 15:5 treats the latter verb as a cognate of Aram. *'r'r* 'shout' in TJ at Isa. 16:10; note, however, that Rashi there refers to a version of TJ, which is otherwise unattested; see Sperber, *The Bible in Aramaic*, *ad loc.*

[26] Dahood at Ps. 102:18, following K-B^3, p. 738a, derives both from a quadraliteral root *'r'r*, which they regard as a biform of *'rh* 'lay bare'.

[27] The source of these latter expressions for the Exodus is Mishnah Pesahim 10:5.

[28] Bracketed expression supplied from other editions of Rashi's commentary; note that the expression *rā'āh bĕ'ŏnî* 'gaze upon the affliction of' is found in Gen. 29:32; 1 Sam. 1:11.

[29] Bracketed expression supplied from other editions of Rashi's commentary; cf. KJV at 2 Kgs. 20:1 = Isa. 38:1; cf. 2 Ch. 32:24.

[30] See the discussion at Ps. 79:11.

[31] Here Rashi supplies the missing subject of the verb *'innāh* 'HE DRAINED'.

[32] Here Rashi supplies the missing addressee.

[33] While KJV, RSV, NJV take *'ēlî* 'MY GOD' as a vocative, Rashi construes 'MY GOD' as ellipsis for the nominal sentence, which he reconstructs.

[34] Heb. *lĕhašmîdēnû* occurs in the Bible only at Deut. 1:27.

[35] Rashi here employs the expression *min hā'ădāmāh* "from the earth" (Gen. 2:7, 9, 19; 4:10, 11; 5:29) in the sense of *mē'al pĕnê hā'ădāmāh* "from off the face of the earth" in Gen. 6:7; 7:4, 8; Ex. 32:12; Deut. 6:15; 28:21, 63; etc.

[36] Here again Rashi sees the psalmist, who writes "MY DAYS," as a personification of the people Israel; see Rashi at v. 13.

³⁷ The 3^d pers. plural pronoun *hēm*, lit., 'they', serves as the copula; see the discussion in our introduction, p. 139.

³⁸ Our Rashi ms. reads by scribal error *lipnêhem* 'BEFORE THEM'.

³⁹ NJV. As Maarsen notes, Rashi's comment indicates that he also understands Heb. *hû'* in this sense; for this meaning of Heb. *hû'* see Gordis, *Job* at Job. 3:19.

⁴⁰ Taking *'ōmēd wĕ* as an auxilliary verb meaning 'continues to'; alternatively, Rashi's comment may be rendered "who abides and exists."

PSALM CIII

1 BLESS THE LORD, O MY SOUL. Here there are five [occurrences of the expression] "Bless [the LORD, O my soul]" (Ps. 103:1, 2, 22; 104:1, 35) corresponding numerically to five worlds in which a person dwells in accord with what our Rabbis stated in [Babylonian Talmud] Tractate Berakot [p. 10a]: "One who dwells in one's mother's womb sings a hymn of praise;[1] one who nurses at one's mother's breast sings a hymn of praise";[1] and likewise [all of them[2] cited in BT there sing their appropriate hymns of praise].[3]

5 YOUR YOUTH IS RENEWED LIKE THE EAGLE'S, i.e., just like eagle, which molts every year.[4] Now there is an aggadic midrash concerning a species of eagle, which when it becomes aged returns [to its youth].[5]

7 HE MADE KNOWN HIS WAYS TO MOSES.

14b HE IS MINDFUL THAT WE ARE DUST. He is MINDFUL, and He has not forgotten that WE ARE DUST, and He knows that

14a AS FOR A HUMAN, HIS DAYS ARE LIKE THOSE OF GRASS....

16 A WIND PASSES BY [i.e.], a mortal disease.[6]

19 RULED [mašālāh] [i.e.], 'rules' [môšelet].[7]

22a ALL HIS WORKS, which are[8]

22b IN ALL PLACES wherein there is HIS DOMINION.

PSALM CIII, NOTES
[1] Our Rashi ms. adds 'at the Sea'.
[2] This phrase is missing in our Rashi ms.
[3] Rashi cites only the first and third of the five worlds referred to in BT Berakot 10a by R. Johanan [b. Napha] quoting R. Simeon b. Yohai. Note that while Rashi speaks of "five worlds in which a person dwells" the Talmudic source refers to five psalms composed by "David who lived in five worlds." Interestingly, precisely here where Rashi explicitly cites his source we see that he has completely rewritten it. The other three worlds are 1) when he emerged from the womb; 2) when he saw the downfall of the wicked; and 3) when he looked upon the day of death.
[4] Lit., "is renewed each year [with respect to the feathers of] its wings and [the rest of its] plumage."

⁵ The bracketed phrase is missing from our Rashi ms. Maarsen and Zohory suggest that Rashi alludes to Genesis Rabbah 19:5; for parallels from the classical world and from the medieval Christian world see Gaster, *MLC* #277; with Maarsen cf. also Qimhi quoting Saadiah here.

⁶ Rashi thus takes 'WIND' here as a metaphor.

⁷ Rashi's point is that the Biblical Heb. perfect *māšālāh*, the pausal form corresponding in meaning to the regular form of the perfect, *māšĕlāh*, which can mean 'she ruled', here functions as a present meaning 'she rules'.

⁸ By adding this phrase, Rashi indicates that he regards the two halves of v. 22 not as synthetic parallelism, in which 'IN ALL PLACES' would serve as an adverbial phrase modifying the verb 'BLESS', but as synonymous parallelism, in which 'PLACES wherein there is HIS DOMINION' functions as b-word to 'ALL HIS WORKS'.

PSALM CIV

1   BLESS...O MY SOUL.

2a   HE WEARS LIGHT LIKE A GARMENT [i.e.], HE
      WEARS THE LIGHT of the sky as A GARMENT.

4a   HE MAKES HIS ANGELS WINDS [i.e.], HE MAKES the
      WINDS His agents.[1]

6a   AS FOR THE ABYSS, YOU COVERED IT AS WITH A
      GARMENT.
      This an example of the same [comparison][2] which is em-
      ployed in another place, "When I made the cloud his[3] gar-
      ment..." (Job..38:9). ABYSS [těhôm], i.e.,[4] Sea.

6b   WATERS STAND ABOVE THE MOUNTAINS.
      [This verse refers to the fact that the] ocean is higher than
      all [the rest of] the world, [and it] STANDS ABOVE THE
      MOUNTAINS. In the same vein He [the Bible] says, "He
      summons the waters of the sea, and He pours them out upon
      the surface of the earth" (Am. 5:8; 9:6). "Pouring" means
      'from above to below'.[5]

7a   THEY FLED AT YOUR BLAST [i.e.], when You said,
      "Let the water...be gathered" (Gen. 1:9),[6] and it was

7b   AT that SOUND [that] THEY RUSHED AWAY, and they
      gathered together

8   AT THE PLACE, which YOU ESTABLISHED FOR
      THEM.

9   YOU SET for them[8] BOUNDS [i.e.], the sand,[9] which sur-
      rounds their shore.

12a   THE BIRDS OF THE SKY DWELL UPON THEM [i.e.],
      upon the springs [mentioned in v. 10].

12b   AMONG 'opā'îm 'FOLIAGE' [i.e.], the branches of trees; it
      is the same word as is found in "And its foliage [wě'opyēh]
      was beautiful" (Dan. 4:18).

14   YOU MAKE THE GRASS GROW....

15a   WINE, that[10] CHEERS THE HEARTS OF MEN. The lat-
      ter also[10] He brings forth[11] OUT OF THE EARTH (v. 14c).

15b   and oil[12] with which[13] TO MAKE THE FACE SHINE

15c   AND BREAD, that[14] SUSTAINS MAN'S LIFE.

16   THE TREES OF THE LORD in the Garden of Eden.[15]

17   WHERE BIRDS MAKE THEIR NESTS, i.e., Israel, who are called 'birds'.[16] [The verb] *yĕqannĕnû* 'MAKE THEIR NESTS' is a cognate of [the noun *qēn* 'nest' in the phrase] *qan-ṣippor* "bird's nest" (Deut. 22:6).[17]

18a   THE HIGH MOUNTAINS He created[18] FOR WILD GOATS.

18b   *maḥseh* 'REFUGE'. Every cognate of [the noun] *maḥseh* is a word referring to shade and hiding place, in which a person can take cover from rain and from water;[19] *abriement* in O.F.[20]

19a   TO MARK THE SEASONS [i.e.], to count by it times and festivals.[21]

19b   THE SUN KNOWS WHEN TO SET [*mĕbô'ô*], but the moon does not KNOW WHEN TO SET [*mĕbô'ô*]. There are times when it comes [*bā'*] late; there are times when it comes [*bā'*] early. [22]

20   YOU BRING ON DARKNESS, AND IT BECOMES NIGHT. Every day[23] You darken [*ma'ărîb*] [24] the sun so that it becomes night,

20b   WHEN ALL THE BEASTS OF THE FORESTS STIR.

22a   WHEN THE SUN RISES, THEY COME HOME to their hiding places so that they are hidden from people.

23   and then[25] every[26] PERSON GOES OUT TO ONE'S WORK.

24   *qinyānêkā* 'YOUR POSSESSIONS'. [The word *qinyān* corresponds in meaning to and is related etymologically to] *miqneh* 'property' (Ezek. 38:12; Job. 1:10; 36:33); *qinyānêkā* means] *qinyan šelĕkā* 'Your property'; it is a cognate of [the active participle *qôneh* 'owner' in] "owner of heavens and earth" (Gen. 14:19); [and of the passive participle *qānúy* 'possessed' in] "*Everything* possessed on your behalf" (BT Nedarim 35a).[27]

25   *ûrĕḥab yādayim* 'AND WIDE OF HANDS', i.e., WIDE of area;[28] *larjes* in O.F.[29]

26b   TO SPORT WITH three hours a day. Thus did our Rabbis say in [Babylonian Talmud] Tractate 'Avodah Zarah [p. 3b],[30] and so is it explained in the Book of Job [40:29]: "Will you play with him as with a bird?"[31]

29   *tôsep rûḥām* 'YOU TAKE AWAY THEIR BREATH'. [The

verb *tôsēp* 'YOU TAKE AWAY' is] a verb referring to destruction as is demonstrated by "they have come to an end
[*sāpû*]: they are finished [*tammû*] " (Ps. 73:19).[32]

30 YOU SEND BACK YOUR BREATH at the resurrection of
the dead.[33]

32 HE TOUCHES THE MOUNTAINS, AND THEY
SMOKE as it is explained with respect to Sinai: "Now
Mount Sinai was all in smoke" (Ex. 19:18).

33 WHILE I STILL AM, i.e., WHILE I AM STILL alive.[34]

35 MAY SINNERS *ḥaṭṭā'îm* DISAPPEAR. [*ḥaṭṭā'îm* means]
ḥōṭē'îm 'sinners'.[35]

PSALM CIV, NOTES

[1] Here Rashi answers two exegetical questions: (1) Which of the two
nouns is the direct object, and which is the objective complement? (2)
Does *mala'kāyw*, lit., 'His messengers, His angels', designate extraterrestrial beings, i.e., 'angels', or any sort of messengers? Rashi's answers to
these questions are accepted by RSV and NJV; contrast KJV, which gives
the alternate answer to each of these questions, and therefore renders,
"Who maketh his angels spirits."

[2] Note that Rashi correctly compares a simile found in Ps. 104:6 with
a metaphor found in Job. 38:9.

[3] As noted by Rashi there, the pronominal suffix refers to the primeval sea, called there *yām* 'Sea' but here *tĕhôm* 'ABYSS'; see Rashi's next
comment.

[4] Heb. *hû'*.

[5] Rashi's comment is a conflation of three dicta, one attributed to R.
Abbahu, another to R. Eliezer b. Menaham, and the third unattributed,
in Genesis Rabbah 23:7. With the continuation of Genesis Rabbah there
cf. Rashi at Am. 5:8; 9:6.

[6] With Maarsen cf. Yalkut ha-Mekiri at Ps. 93 #12; Genesis Rabbah
5:1.

[7] Rashi paraphrases employing the standard Heb. relative particle
'ăšēr to clarify the meaning of the psalmist's rare *zeh* 'which', which is so
employed also in Ps. 74:2; 104:26; see Dahood at Ps. 74:2.

[8] I.e., the primeval waters.

[9] With Maarsen cf. Jer. 5:22.

[10] The two exegetical questions posed by v. 15a are (1) What is the
syntactic function of 'AND WINE'? and (2) What/ who is the subject of
the verb 'CHEERS'? Rashi, followed by KJV, RSV, NJV, construes
'AND WINE' as part of the compound object of the infinitive *lĕhôṣî'* 'TO
BRING FORTH' in v. 14a (the other element in this compound object is
leḥem 'BREAD'; see Ibn Ezra here) and the verb 'CHEERS' as the predicate of an adjectival relative clause modifying 'WINE'. Contrast LXX

and Vulgate, which take 'AND WINE' as the subject of an independent clause, whose predicate is 'CHEERS'.

[11] Rashi, like Ibn Ezra, construes the infinitive *lĕhôṣî'* as an infinitive consecutive referring to the activity of the subject of the previous clause, sc., God. Contrast Qimhi, KJV, RSV, NJV, which follow LXX and Vulgate in interpreting *lĕhôṣî'* as infinitive finalis, whose subject is *hā'ādām* 'MAN, HUMANKIND' in v.14b.

[12] Ignoring the prefixed preposition *mē* 'from, more than', Rashi, followed by NJV, construes wine, oil, bread (v. 15) as the compound objects of the infinitive *lĕhôṣî'* (v. 14c). Ehrlich arrives at the same sense by construing the initial *m* of *mšmn* as dittography of the final *m* of *pānîm* 'FACE'. Contrast the verbal acrobatics of Qimhi and Dahood.

[13] Here Rashi, followed by NJV, indicates that the infinitive phrase functions as a purpose clause.

[14] Here Rashi, followed by NJV and KJV, indicates that the clause introduced by the verb 'SUSTAINS' functions as a relative clause modifying 'BREAD' and that the grammatical subject is the implied relative pronoun 'that'.

[15] With Maarsen see the various midrashim at Genesis Rabbah 15:1; see also Midrash Tehillim here. Rashi here attempts to answer the exegetical question as to which trees are preeminently 'THE TREES OF THE LORD'. Assuming that the genitive phrase "OF THE LORD" connotes possession, Rashi suggests that our verse refers to the "tree of knowledge" (Gen. 2:9; 3:1-19) and the "tree of life" (Gen. 2:9; 3:22-24). Alternatively. "OF THE LORD" here, like "of God" in the expressions "wind of God" (Gen. 1:2) and "fire of God" (Job. I:16) may denote simply 'great, tremendous'. Indeed, "tremendous trees" is an appropriate designation for 'CEDARS OF LEBANON' (Ps. 104:16b); so Qimhi; cf. Briggs.

[16] Rashi takes 'BIRDS' as a metaphor; see Rashi at Ps. 84:4; contrast Midrash Tehillim here.

[17] In fact, the verb *qinnēn* 'make a nest' is a denominative verb derived from the noun *qēn* 'nest'; see dictionaries.

[18] By supplying the verb 'He created', Rashi suggests that 'THE HIGH MOUNTAINS' is part of the compound direct object of the verb *'āśāh* 'HE MADE' in v. 19. Contrast NJV's "are".

[19] Cf. Rashi at Ps. 118:8.

[20] I.e., 'cover, refuge'; see Levy, *Contribution* #13.

[21] See Rashi at Gen. 1:14.

[22] The latter statement is taken from BT R.H. 25a where a *baraitha* reports it as a formula, which Rabban Gamaliel [II] had inherited "from my paternal grandfather's house." The midrash, which sees in Ps. 104:19b a prooftext for Rabban Gamaliel's dictum is attributed to R. Johanan [b. Napha] at BT R.H. 25a. In the context of BT R.H. 25a the expression "the moon comes" refers to the first appearance of the new moon.

[23] Maarsen suggests that the phrase "every day" provides Rashi's answer to the exegetical question, "Why does the psalmist employ the im-

perfect form of the verb?" According to Maarsen, the imperfect here refers to habitual uncompleted action; for discussion of this usage of the imperfect see Driver, *Tenses* [3], pp. 38-39; Rashi at Ex. 15:1.

[24] Here Rashi's comment lends support to those who relate Heb. *'ereb* 'evening' to Akk. *erēpu* 'become dark' rather than to *erēbu* 'enter'. See the discussion in *CAD*, E, pp. 279-80; contrast *AHW*. p. 233b; *K-B*[3], pp. 830-831.

[25] Rashi., followed by NJV, hereby indicates that what is described in v. 23 follows both sequentially and logically upon what is described in v. 22.

[26] Rashi thus indicates that *'ādām* 'PERSON' is here employed as a collective.

[27] As suggested by Maarsen, Rashi follows Menahem in failing to distinguish between *qānāh* in the nuance 'create' (Gen. 14:19; Ps. 104:24; Prov. 8:22) and *qānāh* in the sense 'acquire'. *Mahberet Menahem*, p. 330 lists under *qn* III instances, which can mean only 'acquire'; under *qn* II he lists both instances which mean 'acquire' and instances which mean 'create'; contrast Moshe Held, "Studies in Biblical Homonyms in the Light of Akkadian," *JANES* 3 (1970-71), p. 47, n. 1.

[28] Maarsen surmises here that Rashi's interpretation of the idiom WIDE OF HANDS is based upon Rashi's observation at Deut. 24:14 following T.O. that Heb. *yād*, lit., 'hand', can mean 'place'. More likely, Rashi's comment here at Ps. 104:25 is based upon his observation in his commentary at Gen. 34:21 that the use of the anatomical expression 'wide of hands' with reference to places represents the application to them of an apt description of a person who is generous, i.e., his/her hands are opened wide to bestow benefits.

[29] I.e., 'large' in Modern French and in Eng.

[30] According to Rav Judah [b. Ezekiel] quoting Rav in BT 'Avodah Zarah 3b, this activity takes place during the last three daylight hours of every twelve hour period of daylight.

[31] This rhetorical question belongs to the series of such questions in Job. 40:25-41:26, in which the LORD asks Job if the latter thinks that he, like the LORD, could prevail over Leviathan? With respect to the mythological creature called Leviathan (= Ugar. *lôtān)* see Umberto Cassuto, "Leviathan," *EM* 4:485-486 (in Hebrew).

[32] Rendering of the two verbs at Ps. 73:19 is taken from Briggs, vol. 2, p. 146. With Maarsen cf. *Mahberet Menahem*, p. 269, s.v. *sp* II.

[33] With Maarsen cf. Midrash Tehillim here.

[34] So KJV, RSV, NJV.

[35] So now NJV. In fact, Rashi misleads his readers, for *ḥōṭĕʾîm* means literally 'people who miss the mark', i.e., 'people who err' while *ḥaṭṭāʾîm* means literally 'people who habitually miss the mark'. Maarsen, however, suggests that Rashi's point is to distinguish *ḥaṭṭāʾîm* 'habitual sinners' from *ḥāṭāʾîm* 'sins', which is identical in its spelling to the form found here.

PSALM CV

1a-b PRAISE THE LORD; CALL ON HIS NAME.

1c *'ălîlôtāwy* 'HIS DEEDS' [i.e.], *ma'ălālāyw* 'His deeds'.[1]

3 PRAISE YOURSELVES THROUGH HIS HOLY NAME. [I.e.], yourselves in the majesty of HIS HOLY NAME in that you have a patron like Him. PRAISE YOURSELVES [means] *porvantez* [*vous*] in O.F.[2]

8b THE WORD HE COMMANDED FOR A THOUSAND GENERATIONS [i.e.], the Torah,[3] which He commanded that it should be made known at the end of a thousand generations, but He saw that the world cannot exist without Torah so He subtracted from them [the thousand] nine hundred and seventy-four generations.[4] However, one ought to interpret it [the word *dābār*] according to its contextual meaning:[5] HE IS MINDFUL concerning Israel[6] OF HIS COVENANT (8a), which HE COMMANDED, i.e., He promised[7] to keep for them FOR A THOUSAND GENERATIONS (8b) in accord with what is stated in the Bible, "Who keeps His gracious covenant to the thousandth generation of those who love Him and keep His commandments" (Deut. 7:9).

11 SAYING, "TO YOU I WILL GIVE.... This [promise] is the covenant, which He made for them.[8]

13 WANDERING FROM NATION TO NATION. Abraham sojourned in the land of the Philistines (Gen. 21:34) and in Egypt (Gen. 12:10-20) and in the land of Canaan (Gen. 13:12; 16:3),and so did Isaac (Gen. 26:1; 31:18), and so did Jacob (Gen. 37:1; 46:5) All of them went from one place of exile to another.[9]

14b HE REPROVED KINGS ON THEIR ACCOUNT. [E.g.], "But the LORD afflicted Pharaoh" (Gen. 12:17); and likewise, "For the LORD had closed fast [every womb] of [the household of][10] Abimelech" (Gen. 20:18).

15 MY ANNOINTED ONES [*měšîḥāy*] [i.e.], My persons of high status. Every [form of the verbal root represented by the gerund] *měšîḥāh* 'annointing' is a word referring to political power and high status.[11]

16a HE CALLED DOWN A FAMINE in order to cause them to go into exile to Egypt.[12]

16b *matṭeh leḥem* 'STAFF OF BREAD' [i.e.], *misʿan leḥem* 'prop of bread' (Isa. 3:1).

17 HE SENT AHEAD OF HIM[13] A MAN, JOSEPH, who had been SOLD INTO SLAVERY there.

18b AN IRON COLLAR WAS PUT ON HIS NECK. R. Huna b. Idi said, "She [Potiphar's wife] put an iron pendule [*širtûăʿ*] under his chin so that if he should lower his face [to avoid looking at her] the pendule would strike him."[14]

19a UNTIL HIS DECREE WAS FULFILLED [i.e., the decree] of the Holy One Blessed be that He should fulfill His decree so that it should come about that Israel would descend into Egypt.[15]

19b THE DECREE OF THE LORD PURGED HIM.
It tested Joseph, who, having been put on trial, overcame his lust for the wife of his overlord, and because of her he was made to suffer when he was PURGED by suffering when he was put in jail.[16]

20a THE KING of Egypt SENT his agents TO HAVE HIM FREED.

20b THE RULER OF NATIONS, i.e.,[17] Pharaoh,[18] RELEASED HIM.

22a [TO BIND][19] THE SOUL. This expression ['to bind the soul'] is an idiom referring to affection as is [the semantic parallel] "Jonathan's soul was tied [*niqšĕrāh*] to the soul of David" (1 Sam. 18:1). [The entire infinitive phrase 'TO BIND THE SOUL OF HIS PRINCES' means that] when he [Joseph] interpreted the dream [of Pharaoh] all of them [the PRINCES] liked him [Joseph].[20]

24 [VERY][22] FRUITFUL. [I.e.], He made them fruitful, and He made them multiply.[23]

28b THEY DID NOT DEFY HIS WORD [refers to the fact that] the plagues [referred to in vv. 27-36; cf. Ex. 7:14-12:30; Ps. 78:44-51], concerning which He commanded, came in accord with His commands, and they did not alter His decree.[24]

40 HE ASKED, AND HE BROUGHT QUAIL. Israel ASKED for meat, AND the Holy One Blessed be He[26] BROUGHT quails.[27]

41   THEY FLOWED IN THE PARCHED LAND, A
      STREAM. [I.e.], STREAMs FLOWED[28] from the well[29]
      "in a land of drought and darkness" (Jer. 2:6).

42   The Holy One Blessed be He, MINDFUL OF HIS SA-
      CRED PROMISE,[30] which was with[31] HIS SERVANT
      ABRAHAM, whom He had promised,[32] "And in the end
      they shall go forth with great wealth" (Gen. 15:14); "and
      they shall return here in the fourth generation" (Gen. 15:16).

PSALM CV, NOTES

[1] The two synonymous nouns derived from the root '*ll* 'to do' exem-
plify the principle established by Samuel b. Meir in his commentary on
'*ônāh* 'dwelling' at Ex. 21:10, q.v., that there are many examples of pairs
of synonymous nouns derived from the same root, in which one of the
pair has the prefix *m* while the other does not.

[2] Cognate to Eng. 'vaunt yourselves'; the bracketed portion of the
gloss is not found in our Rashi ms.

[3] In its context *dābār* 'WORD' means 'the promise' (so NJV) as it does
also at 1 Sam. 1:23; 1 Kgs. 6:12; 8:26; see below. The midrash, which
Rashi quotes here, reads into *dābār* another of its meanings, sc., 'law',
which is exemplified by Ex. 12:24; 15:2; 19:4; etc. (see Mayer I. Gruber,
"The Change in the Name of the Decalogue," *Beit Mikra* 26 (1981-82), pp.
17-18 (in Hebrew); id., "The Mishnah as Oral Torah: a Reconsideration," *JSJ* 15 (1984), p. 116, n. 19). It is this nuance of *dābār* which the
midrash here correctly equates with the common meaning of *tôrāh* in
Rabbinic literature, i.e., 'Law'.

[4] Rashi's comment is based on the midrash at Midrash Tehillim here,
which is attributed to R. Levi quoting R. Samuel b. Nahmani (fl. late 3[d]
cent. C.E.-early 4th cent. C.E.). This midrash explains that Ps. 105:8
means that the Torah was to have been given to the thousandth generation of humankind. The midrash accounts for the discrepancy between
this assertion and the observation that the Torah was given at the end of
only twenty-six generations from Adam to Moses by suggesting that nine
hundred and seventy generations of potential descendants of "the generation of the flood" perished when Noah's contemporaries were wiped out.
For the idea that the death of a person includes the death of his/her potential descendants see Mishnah Sanhedrin 4:5.

[5] Kamin, *Rashi's Exegetical Characterization*, pp. 57-130 observes that in
Rashi's commentary on the Pentateuch *pěšûṭô* means only 'its literal meaning' and never 'its contextual meaning'. Nevertheless, the present context
allows of no other meaning for *pěšûṭo* than 'contextual meaning'. The literal or primary meaning of *dābār* is 'word'; see dictionaries.

[6] Rashi brings this phrase up from v. 10b.

[7] By treating 'HE COMMANDED' as the predicate of a relative
clause modifying 'HIS COVENANT', Rashi intimates that *dābār*, lit.,

'word', is a synonym of 'COVENANT'. By interpreting 'HE COM-
MANDED' to mean 'He promised', Rashi intimates that the synonyms
'COVENANT'// 'WORD' both denote a divine promise to Israel.

[8] The use of *lāhem* 'for them' rather than *'ittām* 'with them' points up
the fact that, as Rashi emphasizes here, covenant in Ps. 105 as in Genesis
is not a contract between God and Israel but a promise by God to Israel
to give the people of Israel the land of Israel forever.

[9] Lit., "They went into exile [*gālû*] from resident alienship to resident
alienship"; our Rashi ms. has the anomalous reading *gārû*, which could be
taken as a denominative verb meaning 'they had the status of resident
aliens [*gērîm*].

[10] Bracketed portions of the quotation are omitted in our Rashi ms.;
I have supplied them for clarity.

[11] Note the offhand, matter-of-fact way in which Rashi defuses the
term 'MY ANNOINTED ONES', which LXX and Vulgate render 'my
christs'. Contrast Rashi's detailed comment and our remarks at Ps. 2:2.
Contrast Midrash Tehillim here: "...MY ANNOINTED ONES. These
are the patriarchs. AND MY PROPHETS.... These are the matriarchs,
who were prophetesses...." Cf. the latter comment and Rashi's not quoting it with St. Jerome's homily no. 31 on our verse in *The Homilies of Saint
Jerome*, vol. 1, trans. Marie Liguori Ewald (Washington: Catholic University of America, 1964), p. 232: "'Touch not my annointed, and to my
prophets do no harm.' The psalmist is speaking of the patriarchs themselves. Shame on the Jews, therefore, who say that unless one is annointed
with the royal unguent, he cannot be called 'the annointed'. They say that
our Lord is not the Christ because He was not annointed with the kingly
ointments, but before the law, the patriarchs had not been annointed with
royal unguent, yet are called 'the annointed'. The annointed, moreover,
are those whom the Holy Spirit annoints; hence, our Lord is justly called
the Christ. This they deny and in so doing go counter to the Sacred Scriptures." John Mason Neale and Richard Frederick Littledale, *A Commentary
on the Psalms from Primitive and Mediaeval Writers and from the Various Office
Books and Hymns*, vol. 3 (London: Joseph Masters, 1874), pp. 350-351 show
that Jerome's interpretation of Ps. 105:15 is normative in ancient and
medieval Christian exegesis. Note that Rashi avoids the contextual interpretation and provides a purely philological note in order to undermine
the use of Ps. 105:15 in Christian polemic against Judaism.

[12] Midrash Tehillim here.

[13] Heb. *lĕpānāyw*, i.e., ahead of Israel collectively; MT reads *lipnêhem*
'AHEAD OF THEM'.

[14] Tanḥuma Vayesheb 8; cf. Genesis Rabbah 87:11.

[15] With Zohory cf. Midrash Tehillim here.

[16] According to Qimhi, the contextual meaning of v. 19b is that by divine fiat Joseph was released from prison. Qimhi suggests that by saying
THE DECREE PURGED HIM the psalmist compares liberation from
jail to the purging from silver of base metals alloyed with it. According to
Ibn Ezra, the DECREE OF THE LORD refers to the correct interpreta-

tion of Pharaoh's dreams, which God revealed to Joseph. For other interprstations see the various commentaries. The abundance of different interpretations derives from the ambiguity of both Heb. *'imrāh* 'WORD, DECREE' and Heb. *ṣĕrāpātĕhû* 'IT PURGED HIM'.

[17] *hû*".

[18] This comment reveals very clearly that Rashi correctly understands v. 20 as a case of synonymous parallelism, in which (1) the synonymous pairs are *melek//mōšēl* *'ammîm* KING//RULER OF NATIONS and *wayattirēhû//wayepattĕḥēhû* AND HE HAD HIM FREED//AND HE RELEASED HIM; and (2) the verb *šālaḥ* 'HE SENT' located only in the first half of the verse is to be understood as part of the combined predicate of both KING and RULER OF NATIONS, both of which refer to Pharaoh. See Alter, *The Art of Biblical Poetry*, p. 25. With Rashi's treatment of the synonymous parallelism here contrast Kugel, *The Idea of Biblical Poetry*, p. 173: "Rashi (1040-1105) is, in general, scrupulous in reading B [i.e., the second of two parallel verses or parts of verses] as distinct over against A." See our discussion above, pp. 150–154.

[19] Our Rashi ms. does not quote the bracketed portion of the lemma, which I have rendered according to KJV. Note that NJV's "to discipline" follows RSV in reading with LXX, Peshitta, and Jerome *lysr* instead of MT's *l'sr*.

[20] For the idea which Rashi finds in Ps. 105:22 see Gen. 41:37. Rashi's interpretation is convincing in that it treats 'BIND THE SOUL' as semantic equivalent of Eng. 'capture the heart'.

[21] Rashi supplies the subject of the verb.

[22] Rashi does not quote the bracketed portion of the verse. I have supplied it for clarity.

[23] Rashi's point is not only that *wayeper* 'HE MADE FRUITFUL' is the imperfect consecutive corresponding to the *hiphil* perfect *hiprāh* 'HE MADE FRUITFUL' but also that Ps. 105:24 describes God's fulfillment of the promise that He made at Gen. 17:20; Lev. 26:9, "I shall make you fruitful, and I shall make you multiply"; cf. also Gen. 17:6; 48:4.

[24] Similarly, several midrashim in *Yalkut ha-Mekiri* here. The exegetical question to which they respond is "What is the grammatical subject of *wĕlō' mārû* 'THEY DID NOT DEFY'. They suggest that the grammatical subject should be HIS SIGNS...HIS WONDERS (v. 27), and DARKNESS (v. 28a). Ibn Ezra, followed by Qimhi, suggests that the subject may be Moses and Aaron (v. 26). Briggs, at a loss as to the subject of the predicate *wĕlō' mārû*, suggests that v. 28b is "a glossator's assertion that at this period, in distinction from that covered by [Ps.] 106, the people did not rebel against Yahweh, but were faithful to him."

[25] See Ex. 16:11-13; Num. 11:31-34, and see next note.

[26] The subject of most of the 3[d] pers. sing. verbs in vv. 8-44 is 'THE LORD OUR GOD' (v. 7); hence it is necessary for Rashi to point out that the subject of v. 40a is Israel while the subject of v. 40b is again 'the Holy One Blessed be He'. At v. 40a KJV supplies the subject "The people" while NJV and RSV following numerous modern commentators,

supported by LXX and Jerome, emend to "they asked" in v. 40a, thus making it clear that the subject is Israel, who are referred to in the plural in vv. 37-38.

[27] The biblical text uses the collective *śĕlāw* as at Ex. 16:13; Num. 11:32. Rashi's substitution of the plural (so also KJV and RSV) found only at Num. 11:31 suggests that Rashi assumes that the latter form would be more familiar to his readers.

[28] Rashi suggests that the apparently singular noun *nāhār* 'STREAM' is in fact a collective noun; hence it may govern a plural verb (cf. *GKC* #145) and be understood to mean 'streams'.

[29] I.e., the well opened up when HE OPENED A ROCK (v. 41a); cf. Ex. 17:6; Num. 20:2-13; 21:16-17; Deut. 8:15; Ps. 114:8.

[30] Lit., 'HIS SACRED WORD'; see discussion in nn. 3, 7 above; see also n. 32 below.

[31] This paraphrase *'ăšer hāyāh 'im* indicates that Rashi interprets the particle *'et* here in the sense 'with' and not as the sign of the definite accusative; moreover the expression 'which was with' applied to 'HIS SACRED WORD' reinforces Rashi's treatment of 'HIS WORD' in v. 8b as a synonym of 'HIS COVENANT' in v. 8a.

[32] This clause proves that Rashi understands *dĕbar qodšô* 'HIS HOLY WORD' to mean "His sacred promise".

PSALM CVI

1   HALLELUJAH.

2   WHO CAN TELL THE MIGHTY ACTS OF THE LORD.[1]

4   WITH FAVOR TO YOUR PEOPLE [i.e.], when You show favor to YOUR PEOPLE.

7c   BUT REBELLED AT THE SEA.
They were people of little faith.[2] [Hence], they said, "Just as we are ascending from this side [of the sea] so are the Egyptians ascending from [the] opposite side[3] so that they will pursue us." Thereupon[4] the Holy One Blessed be He gestured to the Sea so that it [the Sea] vomited them up onto the dry land.[5] Then "Israel saw Egypt dead on the shore of the sea" (Ex. 14:30). Therefore, "they[6] had faith in the LORD" (Ex. 14:31). However, at the beginning they did not have faith.[7]

13b   THEY WOULD NOT WAIT TO LEARN HIS PLAN.
[I.e.], they did not pray to him.[8]

14   THEY WERE SEIZED WITH CRAVING. [This refers to their saying], "Who will feed us meat?" (Num. 11:4).[9]

15b   THEN MADE THEM WASTE AWAY. [This refers to what is stated in the Pentateuch], "The LORD was angry with the people [so the LORD struck the people with a very severe plague]" (Num. 11:33).[10]

16   THEY PROVOKED THE JEALOUSY OF MOSES. [I.e.], they made him angry. [The use of the verb *wayĕqanĕ'û* to mean 'they provoked jealousy' rather than 'they were jealous'][11] is the same usage as is reflected in "They incensed Me [*qinĕ'ûnî*] with no-gods" (Deut. 32:21).

18   A FIRE BLAZED AMONG them, "and it consumed...the people who were offering the incense" (Num. 16:35).

20   THAT FEEDS ON GRASS. There is nothing more abominable nor more disgusting than a BULL when he FEEDS ON GRASS, for he discharges a great deal of excrement, and he is soiled with it.[12]

24   THEY REJECTED THE DESIRABLE LAND.

This refers to the commissioning of the spies [of whom it is said], "They spread" (cf. Num. 13:32)[13] "calumny concerning the land" (Num. 14:36).

26 SO HE RAISED HIS HAND in oath.[14]

27 AND TO OVERTHROW THEIR SEED AMONG THE NATIONS.

From that moment there was decreed against them the destruction of the Temple, for since they wept on the eve of the ninth of Av, the Holy One Blessed be He said, "They engaged in unwarranted weeping. Therefore I shall establish for them [on that evening][15] weeping for generations."[16]

33a BECAUSE THEY, Moses and Aaron, REBELLED AGAINST HIM. This refers to [the passage where Moses and Aaron say]: "Listen, you rebels" (Num. 20:10).[17]

33b HE MADE A PRONOUNCEMENT WITH HIS LIPS [i.e.], an oath:[18] "Therefore you shall not lead this congregation" (Num. 20:12).

34 In the days of Joshua THEY DID NOT DESTROY THE NATIONS AS THE LORD HAD COMMANDED THEM,[19] "You shall not let a soul remain alive" (Deut. 20:16) [and] "They shall not remain in your land" (Ex. 23:33),[20] but they [the Israelites] allowed them [the Canaanites] to dwell among them as "slaves to do forced labor" (Josh. 16:10).[21]

41 HE HANDED THEM [the Israelites] OVER TO THE NATIONS in the days of the judges [in the period intervening] between judges; for example, Eglon and Cushan-rishathaim;[22] Sisera,[23] the Philistines,[24] and Midian.[25]

43c AND SO THEY WERE BROUGHT LOW [wayyāmokkû] BY THEIR INIQUITY. [I.e.], they were made lowly [šĕpēlîm][26] BY THEIR INIQUITY.

47 DELIVER THEM[27] also now,[28] O LORD OUR GOD.

PSALM CVI, NOTES

[1] These two quotations from vv.1-2 serve as the title of Ps. 106 (numbered Ps. 104 in our Rashi ms.; see our discussion at Ps. 72, n. 53; Ps. 117, n. 1) in our Rashi ms. Rashi's commentary on this psalm commences at v. 4.

[2] Rashi adapts this from BT Pesaḥim 118b: "For Rav Huna (d. 296 C.E.) said, 'Israel who were in that generation were people of little faith.'"

[3] Rashi takes this verbatim from BT Pesaḥim 118b where "And they

said, 'Just as...from [the] opposite side'" is part of a midrash on Ps. 106:7c attributed to Rabbah b. Mari.

[4] Heb. 'ad še.

[5] Here in Rashi's version of the midrash, God gestured, and personified Sea acted in response to the divine gesture. The version attributed to Rabbah b. Mari at BT Pesaḥim 118b records a dialogue between the Holy One Blessed be He and śar šel yām, lit., 'Prince of Sea', i.e., the numen or angel, whom God has placed in charge of the Sea. Concerning Rabbinic Judaism's transformation of Canaanite deities such as Mot 'Personified, deified Death' and Yam 'Personified, deified Sea' into angels and the implications of this transformation for understanding biblical monotheism see our discussion at Ps. 49, n. 41.

[6] The Israelites.

[7] Utilizing materials drawn primarily from BT Pesaḥim 118b, Rashi presents a resolution of the contradiction between "They had faith in the LORD" (Ex. 14:31) and "THEY REBELLED AT THE SEA" (Ps. 106:7c).

[8] Heb. lō' qiwwû; my rendering of Rashi here reflects the correct interpretation of Heb. qiwwāh 'pray' in Rashi at Ps. 27:14. With Maarsen cf. Rashi's comment here to Mahberet Menahem, p. 186, s.v. ḥk I.

[9] Rashi's suggestion that Ps. 106:14 refers to the event described in Num. 11:4 is most appropriate since both texts contain the Hebrew expression, which means literally, "They craved a craving."

[10] Rashi does not quote the bracketed portion of the verse. However, it is the bracketed portion of the verse that corresponds to Ps. 106:15. Had Dahood, q.v., following Rashi, compared our verse to Num. 11:33, q.v., he would not have seen the need to construe our verse as synonymous parallelism.

[11] Contrast KJV, RSV, NJV, who follow Ibn Ezra and Qimhi.

[12] Cf. Midrash Tehillim here; Mekilta, vol. 1, p. 249.

[13] Rashi here employs perfect with waw conjunctive; at Num. 13:32 MT employs imperfect with waw consecutive while at Num. 14:36 the infinitive is employed.

[14] Rashi, followed by NJV, notes that in the present context Heb. nāśā' yād 'raise the hand' describes a gesture accompanying oath taking, in which one points the right hand in the direction of the LORD's heavenly throne. See Rashi also at Deut. 32:40; see Gruber, Aspects, p. 33.

[15] Bracketed phrase found in Tanḥuma (see next note) but absent from BT and from Rashi here.

[16] Rashi's comment here is taken almost verbatim from Tanḥuma, ed. Buber at Num. 14:1; similarly Rabbah quoting R. Johanan b. Napha in BT Ta'anit 29a where the claim of Mishnah Ta'anit 4:6 that "on the ninth of Ab it was decreed that our ancestors should not enter the land [of Israel]" is justified.

[17] Rashi's interpretation, which is also accepted by David Qimhi, q.v., is to be rejected for it fails to reckon with the fact that the implied subject of all the 3[d] pers. plural verbs from v. 12 on is "the Israelites". The cor-

rect interpretation, sc., "THEY, the Israelites, REBELLED AGAINST HIM" [i.e.], Moses, is attributed by David Qimhi to his father Joseph (c. 1105-1170).

[18] Rashi observes correctly that elsewhere the expression 'pronounce [bt'] with the lips' (Lev. 5:4 [twice]; Num. 30:7-9) always refers to an oath or a vow. Moreover, his conclusion that this must be the case also here must have been reinforced by the midrash in Tanhuma at Ex. 6:6 and quoted by Rashi at Num. 20:12, which claims that Num. 20:12 constitutes an oath sworn by the LORD because it is introduced by lākēn 'therefore'.

[19] Whether 'ăšēr 'āmar YHWH lāhem is rendered "concerning whom the LORD commanded them" (KJV) or "of whom the LORD said" (LXX) the clause inspires the exegetical question "Where did the LORD command this?" Rashi's answer is Deut. 20:16; Ex. 23:33. RSV-NJV's "as the LORD commanded them" presupposes emending 'ăšēr to ka'ăšēr.

[20] See also Deut. 7:1-2, 16. Note that Ps. 106:34 reflects both (a) the view peculiar to Deuteronomy, that the Israelites were required to annihilate the Canaanites in order to avoid the risk of religious contamination [see G. von Rad, Deuteronomy: A Commentary, OTL (Philadelphia: Westminster, 1966), p. 133]; and (b) the view of Judges 1:21, 27-36 that in fact the Israelites did no such thing (see the various modern commentaries on Ps. 106).

[21] RSV; cf. Judges 1:30.

[22] According to Judg. 3:8-10 the judge Othniel delivered Israel from Cushan-rishathaim, to whom Israel had been subject for eight years. According to Judg. 3:11, "the land" then "had peace for forty years" until the death of Othniel. Thereupon, the Israelites again fell into sin. They were punished for this by being subject to King Eglon of Moab for eighteen years until they were again delivered by the judge Ehud. Then "the land was tranquil for eighty years" (Judg. 3:12-30).

[23] Whose subjugation of Israel took place between the death of Ehud (Judg. 4:1) and the appearance of Deborah, Barak and Jael (Judg. 4:4-5:31).

[24] During the forty years following the death of the judge Abdon (Judg. 12:15-13:1) and the triumph of Samson (Judg. 13:2-16:31).

[25] According to Judg. 5:31, Jael's triumph over Sisera was followed by forty years of tranquility. These were followed by seven years during which Israel was subject to Midian until the triumph of the judge Gideon (Judg. 6:1-8:28).

[26] Cf. Held, "Pits and Pitfalls in Akkadian and Biblical Hebrew," p. 189: "Indeed a perusal of mkk in Hebrew and Aramaic reveals that the latter is a synonym of špl...." Anticipating Held, Rashi here sees in the rare mkk [for Rashi as for Mahberet Menahem, p. 239 the root was mk] a synonym of the common špl.

[27] Probably a scribal error in our Rashi ms.; MT reads "DELIVER US."

[28] Here Rashi points to the fact that in contrast to the "historical poem" in vv. 7-46, v. 47 is a "prayer for help" (so Dahood). As Rashi in-

timates by means of his two-word interpolation, the psalmist's enumeration of the LORD's past kindnesses and acts of forbearance is a more than subtle suggestion that the LORD should also help Israel *now*.

PSALM CVII

1   GIVE THANKS TO THE LORD, FOR HE IS GOOD[1]
       [is what]

2   THE REDEEMED OF THE LORD WILL SAY[2] when He
       will have redeemed them[3] FROM ADVERSITY.

4   [WHO][4] LOST THEIR WAY IN THE WILDERNESS.
       Now as for people who travel in deserts, they also must give
       thanks,[5] for often they LOSE their way, and they are

5   HUNGRY and THIRSTY (v. 5a), AND HE BROUGHT
       THEM (v. 30; cf. v. 7, 'HE SHOWED THEM'), i.e., He
       will lead them. Therefore,

8   THEY SHOULD THANK THE LORD FOR HIS KIND-
       NESS.

10   PEOPLE   WHO   DWELL   IN   DARKNESS   AND
       GLOOM.[6]
       Also persons imprisoned in jail must give thanks when they
       leave their prisons.[7]

11   BECAUSE THEY DEFIED THE WORD OF GOD.
       [This verse teaches that] a person experiences suffering only
       as a consequence of one's sin.[8]

16   FOR HE SHATTERED GATES OF BRONZE, which
       were locked in front of them.

17   FOOLS WHO SUFFERED FOR THEIR SINFUL WAY
       AND FOR THEIR INIQUITIES by diseases, which consti-
       tute punishments. They also are among those who must give
       thanks. There are distinguishing marks[9] in this chapter,[10]
       and they are to be interpreted as a substitute for [the par-
       ticles] *'ak* 'howbeit' and *raq* 'only' to indicate a limitation,
       which is to say that if persons entreat [God][11] before the
       passing of sentence, their appeal is granted; [if they en-
       treat][12] after the passing of sentence, their appeal is not
       granted.[13]

27   *yāḥoggû* is a verb referring to destruction,[14] and the same ver-
       bal root is exemplified by [the construct plural noun *ḥagwê*
       'clefts of' in] "in the clefts of the rock"[15] (Cant. 2:14), and the
       same verbal root is exemplified by [the noun *ḥoggā'* 'fear of

destruction' in] "The land of Judah will be for Egypt a source of fear of destruction" (Isa. 19:17).[16]

30   THEY REJOICED WHEN THEY, the waves,[17] QUIET-ED DOWN. *mĕḥôz* 'PORT' is a synonym of *gĕbûl* 'boundary', and Menahem treated it as a cognate of [the noun *ḥāzût* 'border' in] "Your border[18] with Sheol [will not endure; When the sweeping flood passes through, You shall be its victims]" (Isa. 28:18).[19] [There the meaning of "Our[20] border with Sheol" is] "Our[20] boundary so that it [Sheol] will not enter into our territories." The same verbal root is attested in [the noun *mĕḥĕzāh* in the expression] *mĕḥĕzāh mûl mĕḥĕzāh* "window opposite window" (1 Kgs. 7:4-5).[21]

33   HE TURNS THE RIVERS INTO A WILDERNESS. [I.e.], He turns the Gentiles' habitations into ruins.

34   INTO A SALT MARSH to be like a salty land in not producing fruit.

35   HE TURNS THE WILDERNESS INTO POOLS. [I.e.], He turns a destroyed habitation into a built-up place; thereby He restores it to its former state.

39   AFTER THEY HAD BEEN FEW AND CRUSHED. [I.e.], formerly they were few and crushed[22] BY OPPRESSION, MISERY, AND SORROW.

41b   AND HE MAKES FAMILIES LIKE A FLOCK. [I.e.], with respect to the NEEDY (v. 41a), HE MAKES FAMILIES of his progeny numerous LIKE A FLOCK.[23]

42b   *qāpĕṣāh* 'SHE WILL SHUT' [i.e.], *sātĕmāh* 'she will close';[24] [the verb *qāpĕṣāh* 'she will shut'] is the same verb as is attested in "Do not shut [*tiqpōṣ*] your hand" (Deut. 15:7).

PSALM CVII, NOTES

[1]   Rendering of the lemma reflecting Rashi's interpretation of the verb *hôdāh* 'give thanks' at Ps. 100:1, 4, and what is more important, Rashi's interpretation of this verb in his commentary at Ps. 107:4-17.

[2]   Rendering of the lemma according to the interpretation presupposed by Rashi's comment. The exegetical question, to which Rashi responds here is "What is it that 'THOSE REDEEMED BY THE LORD WILL SAY'?" Ibn Ezra supplies less succinctly the same answer; similarly, KJV, RSV, NJV.

[3]   Rashi's paraphrase employing the imperfect *kĕšeyipdēm* as a future perfect suggests that Rashi construes the psalmist's *gĕ'ālām* as a prophetic perfect; see Driver, *Tenses*[3], #14.

[4]   Heb. *'ăšĕr;* I have brought it down from v. 2b in accord with Rashi's

interpretation of v. 4 as in apposition with v. 2b.

⁵ In BT Berakot 54b Rav Judah [b. Ezekiel] quotes Rav: "There are four [types of people] who must give thanks. [These are] people who have travelled at sea; people who have travelled through deserts; a person who was sick and who recovered; and a person who was confined in prison and who was set free." In BT there this statement is followed by a *midrash halakah* (on this term see our introduction, p. 128), which employs Ps. 107:23-31, 4-8, 17-21, 10-15, respectively as prooftexts. Rashi utilizes both Rav's assertion and the *midrash halakah* to elucidate Ps. 107:4, 10, 17. Note that Rav's assertion is accepted as legally binding in Maimonides, Mishneh Torah, Laws of Blessings 10:8; Shulhan Aruk, Orah Hayyim 219:1; see Birnbaum, *Daily Prayer Book*, pp. 123-124.

⁶ Literal rendering of the lemma in which the noun *ṣalmāwet* is rendered 'gloom' following RSV; see Rashi at Ps. 23:4; 39:7; 44:20.

⁷ Rashi's correct interpretation of v. 10a in light of v. 10b following BT Berakot 54b (see n. 6), "BOUND IN CRUEL IRONS," should put to rest the false notions (a) that Rashi "failed to take note of the existence of *parallelismus membrorum*" (Gelles, p. 101) and (b) that "it is therefore altogether doubtful whether the Rabbis possessed any notion of the literary device called *parallelismus membrorum*" (Gelles, p. 99). For the idea that prisoners dwell in unlit, windowless chambers see also Isa. 42:7.

⁸ Cf. the dictum of R. Ammi at BT Shabbat 55a-b: "There is no death without sin, and there is no suffering without iniquity." Ibn Ezra here, q.v., softens this from "only" to "in many cases". The hyperbolic statement of Rashi here is at odds with Isa. 53; Job. 42 and with BT's making the latter teaching canonical in BT Berakot 5b.

⁹ Heb. *sîmāniyyôt;* the term is taken from the *baraitha* in BT R.H. 17b where it designates the seven inverted *nuns* which are supposed to be written in the right margin of vv. 21, 22, 23, 24, 25, 26, 40. The same term is employed in a *baraitha* found in Avot deRabbi Nathan 34:4 and in BT Shabbat 115a where it designates the two inverted *nuns* which appear in the Torah scroll before and after Num. 10:35-36. See below, n. 13. For history of the "distinguishing marks" and various terms used to designate them see Aron Dotan, "Masorah," *EJ* 16:1408, s.v. "isolated letters".

¹⁰ Heb. *pārāšāh.*

¹¹ Heb. *ṣāʿăqû,* lit., 'they cried out'; note that in Rabbinic Heb. the protasis of a conditional sentence characteristically employs the perfect form of the verb while in Biblical Heb. the imperfect is used.

¹² Rashi omits the bracketed clause as self-understood; I have supplied it for clarity from the *baraitha.*

¹³ Rashi's source is the *baraitha* at BT R.H. 17b. Characteristically, Rashi does not quote it verbatim.

¹⁴ So Rashi also at Isa. 19:17; Cant. 2:14 (Rosenthal in his notes to Rashi's commentary at Cant. 2:14 wrongly cites *Mahberet Menahem,* s.v. *hgw* as Rashi's source for this assertion); contrast Ibn Ezra and Qimhi, who follow *Mahberet Menahem,* p. 168 in identifying our verb with the common Heb. verb *hgg* (for Menahem the root is *hg*) 'circumambulate'; on the

latter see Gruber, "Ten Dance-Derived Expressions," pp. 329-330.

[15] KJV; RSV.

[16] *Ad hoc* rendering of Isa. 19:17 based on Rashi there; cf. NJV: "And the land of Judah shall also be the dread of the Egyptians."

[17] Rashi supplies the subject of the verb 'THEY QUIETED DOWN' from v. 29b.

[18] Heb. *ḥāzûtĕkem*, which is the reading in MT at Isa. 28:18 and in many editions of Rashi's commentary here; our ms. reads, however, *mahazûtēnû* 'our border'; see below, n. 23.

[19] I have supplied the remainder of the verse from NJV so that the contextual support for Menahem's interpretation may be seen; see *Mahberet Menahem*, p. 171, s.v. *ḥz* II. NJV at Isa. 28:18 follows Rashi there in treating *ḥāzôt* as a cognate of *ḥōzeh* 'pact' (Isa. 28:15). Modern Biblical Heb. lexicography understands *mĕḥôz* as the construct of a noun *māḥôz* 'harbor', which is the same as Aram. *māḥôzā'* and Akk. *māḥāzu* 'port, harbor'; see Cohen, *Biblical Hapax Legomena*, p. 70, n. 127. The identification of Heb. *māḥôz* with Akk. *māḥāzu*, which means literally 'place of grasping' from the root *'ḥz* invalidates Rashi's attempt at Job. 8:17 to relate our noun to a verb *ḥāzāh*.

[20] *Sic*; see n. 18.

[21] MT reads there *ûmûl mĕḥēzāh 'el mĕḥēzāh*.

[22] Here Rashi characteristically substitutes the verb 'to be' followed by predicate adjectives for the Bible's stative verbs.

[23] Rashi's point here is to show how elements of the first half of the verse correspond to elements in the second half and complement them; cf. n. 7 above.

[24] I take both the psalmist's *qāpĕṣāh* and Rashi's gloss *sātĕmāh* as prophetic perfects; cf. the paraphrase *wĕ'ôlātāh tiqpoṣ-pîāh* "and wickedness shall shut its mouth" in the High Holy Day prayer *Ubeken* in Birnbaum, *High Holyday Prayer Book*, p. 33.

PSALM CVIII[1]

2a   MY HEART IS FIRM, O GOD.
[I.e.], MY HEART is loyal to You.[2]

2b   "ALSO MY SOUL [*'ap-kĕbôdî*]." "ALSO MY SOUL" is what I sing to You.[3] Another equally plausible interpretation of *'ap-kĕbôdî* is "even [*'ap*] according to my honor [*kĕbôdî*] I shall not refrain from singing to You, and I shall not give myself honor.[4]

3b   I AWAKEN THE DAWN. It is the practice of other kings that dawn awakens them, but I[5] awaken the dawn, for I arise at midnight when HARP AND LYRE (v. 3a) awaken me. [This interpretation is] in accord with what our rabbis said: "A lyre was hung above King David's bed. Whenever midnight arrived, the north wind would blow upon it so that it would play automatically [thereby awakening King David before dawn so that he in turn would awaken the dawn].[6]

5   HIGHER THAN THE HEAVENS. Another text [i.e., the parallel at Ps. 57:11][7] states, "as high as heaven." Our rabbis explained that here (at Ps. 108:5) the psalmist refers to people who behave as they ought without any ulterior motive while there (Ps. 57:11) the psalmist refers to people who behave as they ought out of an ulterior motive.[8]

7   ANSWER ME,[5] for all Your people, i.e.,[9] THOSE WHOM YOU LOVE, depend on me.[10]

8a   GOD PROMISED BY HIS HOLINESS[11] that I would be king and that the time would come when I WOULD EXULT[12] in His promise.

8b   I WOULD...DIVIDE UP the land of my enemies, SHECHEM [Heb. *šekem*], as a portion for Israel. [The noun *šekem* is not a place-name but a common noun meaning 'portion']; it is the same noun as is reflected in "one portion [*šekem*] more than to your brothers" (Gen. 48:22).[13] THE VALLEY OF SUKKOTH.

10a   MOAB WOULD BE MY WASHBASIN, i.e., my vassals and my servants, [who serve me] as does an implement of which persons make use.[14]

10b   ON EDOM I WOULD CAST MY SHOE [i.e.], my service, so that their kings would put my shoes[15] on my feet.

10c   I WOULD RAISE A SHOUT [i.e.], I lift up (my) voice to
make them afraid of me.

11a   WHO WILL BRING ME to the Messianic Era to stretch
forth a hand agasint Esau and against the cities of Egypt?
[The answer is]:[16]

11b   HE WHO LED ME already against EDOM when I slew
eighteen thousand of them in the Valley of Salt (see 2 Sam.
8:13).[17]

PSALM CVIII, NOTES

[1] With Qimhi note that vv. 2-6 are a virtual doublet of Ps. 57:8-12 and
that vv. 7-14 are a virtual doublet of Ps. 60:7-14. Like modern commentators, Rashi largely confines himself here to commenting on the variants
found in Ps. 108, which are not found in Ps. 57; 60.

[2] So Rashi also at Ps. 57:8.

[3] Rashi's two points here are (1) that in v. 2b the verb '*āšîrāh* means "I
sing" rather than "Let me sing" or "I shall sing"; and (2) that the phrase
'*ap-kĕbôdî* 'ALSO MY SOUL' constitutes a quotation following the *verba
dicendi* '*āšîrāh wĕ*'*azammĕrāh* 'I WILL SING, AND I WILL CHANT A
HYMN'. This interpretation is supported by Ps. 57:8, q.v.

[4] Cf. Midrash Tehillim #2 here; cf. KJV: "even with my glory."

[5] I.e., King David, to whom the authorship of this psalm is attributed
at Ps. 108:1.

[6] Cf. Rashi at Ps. 57:9 and our discussion there.

[7] See n. 1, above.

[8] Rashi's comment is taken almost verbatim from Rava (299-352
C.E.) in BT Pesaḥim 50b. The latter suggests that the variants '*ad* (Ps. 57)
and *mē*'*al* (Ps. 108) where one would have expected the identical reading
point to the truth of the dictum attributed to Rav Judah quoting Rav: "...
for from [behaving as one ought] with an ulterior motive develops [be-
having as one ought] without an ulterior motive."

[9] Exegetical *waw*.

[10] Rashi attempts to explain the logical connection between v. 7a and
v. 7b; Rashi's solution is further elucidated by his comment on the parallel (see n. 1 above) at Ps. 60:6.

[11] Rendering of the lemma according to NJV margin; cf. Ps. 105:42
and our discussion at Ps. 105:8; see also Ps. 89:4, 36.

[12] With Maarsen cf. Rashi at Ps. 60:8.

[13] So NJV there; see Rashi there and at Ps. 21:13; 60:8.

[14] Rashi notes that 'WASHBASIN' is a metaphor, and he explains the
metaphor; cf. the similarly gross metaphors applied to themselves by
Pharaoh's Canaanite vassals in the Amarna letters; with reference to our
rendering cf. Breithaupt.

¹⁵ Rashi substitutes Rabbinic Heb. *min'al* 'shoe' for its Biblical Heb. cognate and synonym *na'al*, which is used again in Modern Heb.

¹⁶ Here Rashi anticipates Kugel, *The Idea of Biblical Poetry*, p. 7 in suggesting that the two halves of a verse of biblical poetry may constitute a question and answer.

¹⁷ The parallel passage in 1 Ch. 18:12 attributes this feat not to David himself but to Abshai son of Zeruiah; but see v. 13 there; Ps. 60:2, q.v., gives a different numerical figure. Rashi's comments here and at Ps. 60:2 attest to the correct reading "Edom" in 2 Sam. 8:13 rather than "Aram" as in most printed editions of the Bible; see *BH* ^{3,} *BHS* and NJV there.

PSALM CIX

1   O GOD.
This was composed on behalf of all Israel.[1]

2   FOR THE MOUTH OF THE WICKED [i.e.], Esau.[2]

4   BECAUSE OF MY LOVE for You THEY ACCUSE ME, BUT I AM PRAYER. I.e.,[3] I PRAY to You continually.[4]

7   WHEN HE IS JUDGED in Your presence MAY HE EMERGE from Your judgment GUILTY, i.e.,[3] liable.

8   HIS POSITION [i.e.], his exalted status; *provostie* [in O.F].[5]

10b AND THEY WILL ASK CONTINUALLY, AND THEY WILL SEEK BECAUSE OF THEIR DISASTERS. [I.e.], because of the rumor of disaster[6] that spread concerning them, all will ask concerning them, "What happened to So-and so and So-and-so?"[7]
'AND THEY WILL SEEK' means 'others [WILL SEEK]', for it is pointed with a short *qāmeṣ*.[8] Likewise, 'AND THEY WILL ASK' of others, means that others will ask[9] concerning them. There is in addition the possibility of interpreting [the verb] *wěśi'ēlû* as an intensive form [of the verb meaning] that they will be begging at doorways.[10]

11   MAY the lender SEIZE [*yěnaqqēś*] ALL HIS POSSESSIONS.
May THE CREDITOR SEIZE ALL that he has. Now the verb *mitnaqqēś* is fittingly employed with reference to a person who makes an effort continually and enthusiastically to do something, i.e., he is agitated and he knocks about; it is the same usage [of the verbal root *nqś*], which is attested in "and his knees knocked [*nāqśān*] together" (Dan. 5:6); it is the same usage, which is attested in "Beware of being lured [*těnaqqēś*] after them" (Deut. 12:30). Here [in Ps. 109:11] also the lender [*hannóqēś*] will enthusiastically move about and go in search of someone else's money.
MAY HIS CREDITOR SEIZE ALL HIS POSSESSIONS [means], "HIS CREDITOR should approach and touch ALL that he has." [The verb *yěnaqqēś* corresponds in meaning to] *soit açoper* in O.F.[11] [The verse means] "May[12] the

legal claim[13] of the CREDITOR strike at and rest upon[14] ALL his money." Now this [creditor] is Jacob, who acts as a creditor toward Esau, for it is stated in the Bible, "The elder shall serve the younger" (Gen. 25:23).

14a   INIQUITY WITH RESPECT TO HIS ANCESTORS.[15] [I.e.], INIQUITY, which he [Esau] committed with respect to ['al] his ancestors, sc.,[16] Abraham [his grandfather], from whose life he took away five years.[17] and his father [Isaac], in whom he caused blindness.[18]

14b   DO NOT BLOT OUT THE SIN WITH RESPECT TO HIS MOTHER when he destroyed her womb[19] and he concealed from people the day of her burial so that they would not curse her because Esau had come forth from her belly. [This assertion] is in accord with what is stated in the Bible, "Deborah, Rebekah's wetnurse died...; so it was named *Allon* weeping" (Gen. 35:8);[20] in Greek 'another' is called *allon*.[21] [Now the mourning for Deborah is called "another weeping"] because Jacob had another mourning[22] besides that for Deborah, for his mother died, and they concealed[23] her death.[24]

15a   MAY THE LORD BE AWARE OF these iniquities ALWAYS

15b   AND CAUSE THEIR [i.e., Esau' and his chieftans'][25] NAMES TO BE CUT OFF FROM THE EARTH.

16a   BECAUSE HE WAS NOT MINDED TO ACT KINDLY by taking part in the mourning for his father[26] like Jacob, who prepared lentil stew (Gen. 25:29, 34)[27] to condole Isaac. [We know that the lentil stew was, in fact, prepared for the meal of condolence following the burial of Abraham] for on that same day Abraham died.[28]

16b   THE POOR MAN [i.e.], Israel.[29]

17a   HE LOVED THE CURSE [i.e.], the curse of the Holy One Blessed be He, whom he denied.

19a   LET IT, the curse (see v. 18), BE an enwrapment LIKE A CLOAK.[30]

19b   AND FOR A GIRDLE [i.e.], 'a belt';[31] it is the same noun as is attested in "he untightened the girdle[32] of the mighty" (Job. 12:21), [which means] "he opened the waistband[33] of the strong."[34]

23a   LIKE A LENGTHENING SHADOW at eventide.

23b   I AM SHAKEN. [This is] an expression referring to bewil-
derment [tašnûq] and confusion [ṭērûp] and stupefaction
['ōṭem].
LIKE THE LOCUST in that it wanders about [seemingly]
confused.[35]

Psalm CIX, Notes

[1] Here, as frequently, Rashi, by seeing the psalmist as a personification of all Israel, transforms a psalm, which moderns, following Gunkel,
classify as an individual lament, into a community lament.

[2] See Rashi also at Ps. 9:6; 84:11.

[3] Explicative waw.

[4] Here Rashi supplies a most plausible answer to the exegetical question, "What does it mean to be 'PRAYER' personified?" Most moderns
emend 'I AM A PRAYER' out of existence.

[5] I.e., administrative function, charge'; see Levy, Contribution #101;
our Rashi ms. reads by metathesis provotsie.

[6] Heb. mittôk qôl ḥorĕbāh, which is Rashi's interpretation of the psalmist's mĕḥorbôtêhem 'BECAUSE OF THEIR DISASTERS'.

[7] Unlike Rashi, who holds that "people in general" are the subject of
the compound predicate, "THEY WILL ASK CONTINUALLY, AND
THEY WILL SEEK," KJV, RSV, NJV follow Ibn Ezra and Qimhi in
treating 'HIS CHILDREN' (v. 10a) as the subject. KJV and NJV are required, therefore, to follow Ibn Ezra and Qimhi in supplying 'bread' as
the direct object of the two verbs. NJV also follows Ibn Ezra and Qimhi
in interpreting mĕḥorbôtêhem to mean "from their hovels" (similarly KJV),
an adverbial expression modifying the compound predicate and referring
to the dwelling places of the wicked person's children. The interpretation
suggested by Ibn Ezra and Qimhi goes back to LXX and Vulgate while
Rashi's interpretation appears to be sui generis.

[8] As noted in Englander, "Grammatical Elements and Terminology
in Rashi," p. 428 this vocalization is not found in what was in Englander's
time the standard Hebrew text; it is, however, found in the Leningrad
ms., which forms the basis of BH[3], BHS, and several Israeli editions of the
Hebrew Bible.

[9] Here Rashi's point is that the form wĕsi'ēlû is perfect consecutive,
i.e., future in meaning.

[10] So NJV; see above, n. 7.

[11] I.e., Modern French achopper, i.e., 'stumble'; see Rashi at Ps. 91:12;
Jer. 13:16; see Darmstetter, "Les Gloses Françaises de Raschi dans la
Bible," REJ 54 (1907), p. 222, n. 5.

[12] Heb. yĕhî; here Rashi interprets the verb yĕnaššēq as a jussive; so
NJV.

[13] Heb. mišpāṭ.

[14] Heb. nōqēš wĕniš'ān 'al. This hendiadys employs the more frequently
attested qal of the verb nqš, which the psalmist employs in the pi'el. Rashi's

use of the participle *nis'ān* intimates that he interprets the *pi'el* as durative, implying that the psalmist means to say not only that the object of his imprecation should be attacked but also that the attack should be unrelenting.

[15] Heb. *'āwôn 'ăbotāyw* could also be rendered "iniquity of his ancestors" (so KJV, RSV, NJV). The ambiguity of the Heb. construct, which makes possible these two alternative interpretations is discussed at length in BT Qiddushin 29a, 30b with reference to Mishnah Qiddushin 1:7.

[16] Heb. *lĕ*.

[17] I.e., the five years difference between the longer lifespan of Isaac, who lived 180 years (Gen. 35:28) and the shorter lifespan of Abraham, who lived only 175 years (Gen. 25:7); see PRK, ed. Mandelbaum, p. 37; Tanḥuma Ki Teṣe #4; for additional references to this midrash see the notes in PRK there.

[18] See Gen. 27:1, and cf. Rashi there. The source of the midrash quoted here is PRK, ed. Mandelbaum, p. 38; for additional sources see notes there.

[19] In PRK, ed. Mandelbaum, p. 39 it is explained that the sin he (Esau) committed with respect to his mother was that "when he came forth from his mother's womb he cut her uterus so that she could not [again] give birth. This is the event about which it is written (in Am. 1:11), 'Because he [Edom!] pursued his brother with the sword *wĕšiḥēt rahămāyw* "and he destroyed his mother's womb".'" For the variety of modern attempts to solve the *cruces* at Am. 1:11 see, in addition to the standard commentaries, Robert Gordis, "Studies in the Book of Amos," in *American Academy for Jewish Research Jubilee Volume* (2 vols.; Jerusalem: American Academy for Jewish Research, 1980), vol. 1, pp. 210-211; see also Shalom M. Paul, *Amos*, Hermeneia (Minneapolis: Fortress, 1991), pp. 64-66.

[20] See Rashi there.

[21] Gk. = ἄλλον is the masc. sing. accusative while = ἄλλος is the masc. sing. nominative; see dictionaries.

[22] On words, whose primary sense is 'weep', meaning 'mourn' in Heb., Akk., and Ugar., as well as in Modern European languages see Gruber, *Aspects*, pp. 402-434.

[23] In the midrash upon which Rashi's comment is based it is the verses of the Bible that did the concealing by not revealing the facts, which Rabbinic midrash succeeded in uncovering; for Rashi's source see the next note.

[24] Rashi's source is PRK, ed. Mandelbaum, p. 40; for additional references to this midrash see notes in PRK, ed. Mandelbaum, there; cf. Rashi at Gen. 35:8.

[25] See Gen. 36:40-43; see RSV and NEB there.

[26] As noted by Maarsen, Rashi here interprets *ḥesed* 'KINDNESS' in light of Gen. 47:29. There the hendiadys *ḥesed wĕ'emet* 'kindness and truth' corresponds in meaning to late Heb. *ḥesed šel 'emet* 'true kindness,' which, on the basis of Gen. 47:29, q.v., is usually taken to refer to the kindness

we perform by burying and mourning the dead, who cannot repay us. See Rashi there.

[27] The first of these verses mentions only *nāzîd* 'stew' (cf. Rashi there); the second specifies "lentil stew."

[28] Rashi's source, a *baraitha* in BT Bava Batra 16b, explains why lentil stew is served at the meal following a funeral; cf. Rashi at Gen. 25:30; see also Genesis Rabbah 63:11.

[29] The psalmist may well refer to his own suffering at the hand of some unnamed enemy; for Rashi's interpretation see above, n. 1.

[30] Heb. *ma'ăṭeh kĕbeged*, Rashi's paraphrase of the psalmist's "LIKE THE CLOAK HE WRAPS."

[31] Heb. *ḥăgorāh*, which is attested in the Bible at Gen. 3:7; 2 Sam. 18:11; 1 Kgs. 2:5; 2 Kgs. 3:21; Isa. 3:24, is the Modern Heb. term for 'belt'.

[32] Heb. *mĕzîăḥ*, the construct of *mēzaḥ*, which is attested only at Ps. 109:19b and at Isa. 23:10.

[33] Heb. *'ēzôr*, the most frequently attested term for 'belt' in Biblical Heb., is found in 2 Kgs. 1:8; Isa. 5:27; 11:5; Ezek. 23:15; Job. 12:18; and eight times in Jer. 13:1-11.

[34] Similarly Rashi at Job. 12: 21.

[35] Contrast Prov. 30:27: "The locusts have no king; yet they all march in formation" (NJV), but see Nah. 3:17; Tosefta Shabbat 12:5, and see Jacob Palmoni, "*'arbeh*," *EM* 1:525.

PSALM CX—INTERPRETATION A

1b **THE LORD**[1] **SAID TO MY LORD.**[2] Our rabbis interpreted[3] [MY LORD] as a reference to Abraham, our father,[4] and I shall interpret it in accord with their words, for everyone called him 'lord' [as in] "lord, hear us"[5] (Gen. 23:11, 15); "hear me,[6] lord" (Gen. 23:6).[7]

1c **SIT AT MY RIGHT HAND.** [I.e.], wait for My deliverance, "and wait for the LORD" (Ps 37:7). *yĕšîbāh* 'sitting' means[8] *'ăqîbāh* 'waiting',[9] and in the same vein He [i.e., God, the author of the Pentateuch] says, "You waited [*wattēšĕbû*] at Kadesh many days" (Deut. 1:46).

AT MY RIGHT HAND means 'FOR deliverance by means of MY RIGHT HAND.[10]

1d **WHILE I MAKE YOUR ENEMIES**, Amraphel and his allies (Gen. 14:1).[11]

2a **THE LORD WILL STRETCH FORTH...YOUR MIGHTY SCEPTER.**

[The noun] *maṭṭeh* 'SCEPTER' is a synonym of *miš'ān* 'prop' as is demonstrated by "every *maṭṭeh* 'staff' of bread" (Ps. 105:16)[12] [i.e.], rations.

[THE LORD WILL SEND FORTH FROM ZION].[13] When you return from the war with your men exhausted from the pursuit [of the enemy],[14] the Holy One Blessed be He will have sent[15] Melchizedek, the king of Salem to "bring out bread and wine" (Gen. 14:18).

2b **HOLD SWAY** in war **OVER YOUR ENEMIES** confidently.

3a **YOUR PEOPLE COME FORWARD WILLINGLY ON YOUR DAY OF BATTLE.** [I.e], when you gather a military force to pursue them [i.e., Amraphel and his allies; see Gen. 14:14], your people and your friends will volunteer themselves[16] to go forth to battle with you in accord with what we find in the Bible, "He [Abraham] armed his trained men[17] born in his house" (Gen. 14:14) and no more. However, Aner and Eshkol and Mamre (see Gen. 14:24) volunteered themselves on their own initiative to follow him in aid of him.[18]

3b   IN MAJESTIC HOLINESS FROM THE WOMB *mišěḥār*
'LET DOWN'.[19] You will have this by virtue of the HOLY
majesty, which was yours from your mother's womb in that
"he [Abraham] recognized [who was] his Creator at three
years of age."[20]

FROM THE WOMB *mišěḥār* 'LET DOWN' [i.e.], since
you came down from the womb. [The expression *mišěḥār*] is
related etymologically to [the expression in the Mishnah],
"They may let down [*maššilîn*] fruit by way of a trap-door
[on a festival]" (Mishnah Beṣah 5:1) where there is someone[21] who reads in that Mishnah *mašḥîrîn*.

3c   YOURS IS THE DEW OF YOUR YOUTH.

The proper manner in which you behaved in YOUR
YOUTH will be regarded as [THE DEW OF] YOUR
YOUTH.[22] It will be a pleasant feature OF YOURS like
DEW, which is pleasant and comfortable.[23]

4a   THE LORD HAS SWORN AND WILL NOT RELENT.

Since he [Abraham] was anxious because of the populations
whom he killed [during the war against the invading kings;
see Gen. 14:15, 17], he was told, "Fear not, Abraham"
(Gen. 15:1);[24] HE WILL NOT RENEGE on the favor,
which He promised to You.[25]

4b   YOU ARE A PRIEST FOREVER BECAUSE OF THE
WORD OF MELCHIZEDEK. The priesthood and kingship will issue from you so that your descendants will become the heirs of your [eighth] ancestor Shem (see Gen.
11:10-27) with respect to priesthood and kingship, which
were granted to him.[26] [The final *yod* in the word] *dibrātî*
'WORD' is superfluous [final] *yod*[27] as in [the adjective
rabbātî 'great' in] "great with people" (Lam. 1:1).

BECAUSE OF THE WORD OF MELCHIZEDEK
[means] BECAUSE OF the decree of[28] MELCHIZEDEK.

4c   YOU ARE A PRIEST. Among the connotations of *kōhēn*
'PRIEST' are 'high' status' and 'authority' as reflected in
"and David's sons were priests" (2 Sam. 8:18).[29]

5a   THE LORD,[30] who was[31] AT YOUR RIGHT HAND in[32]
the war (Gen. 14),

5b   CRUSHED IN THE DAY OF HIS ANGER the four kings
(see Gen. 14:1, 17) KINGS.

6a   It is He who[33] WORKS JUDGMENT UPON THE NA-

TIONS, HEAPING UP BODIES. This verse refers to the prediction associated with the Covenant Between the Pieces where he [Abraham] was told concerning Egypt, "I will execute judgment upon the nation they shall serve" (Gen. 15:14). *mālē' gĕwiyyôt* 'HEAPING UP BODIES' [refers to] gathering corpses. [The participle] *mālē'* is a word referring to gathering [*'ăsîpāh*] as is demonstrated by "gathered together [*mālē'*] they called after you" (Jer. 12:6); "over which is assembled a gathering of shepherds" (Isa. 31:4); "they gather together against me" (Job. 16:10).[34] Now where did he WORK JUDGMENT HEAPING UP BODIES? [He did so in the instance described in] "Egypt dead on the shore of the sea" (Ex. 14:30).

6b HE CRUSHED HEAD UPON A GREAT COUNTRY. This is the same idiom as is found in the prophecy of Habakkuk: "You crushed the head of an evil house" (Hab. 3:13), i.e., the head of Pharaoh, who was head, i.e., ruler,[35] over a country greater and more important than all the [other] countries, for it is stated in the Bible, "The ruler of nations[36] released him"[37] (Ps. 105:20). [Pharaoh is so designated in Ps. 105:20] because all the nations were subservient to the government of Egypt.[38]

7a [WHO] DRANK FROM A STREAM BY THE ROAD [i.e.], the Nile River.[39] As it walked by the road, his [i.e., Pharaoh's] nation used to drink, and it did not require rain water.

7b THEREFORE HE HOLDS HIS HEAD HIGH. THEREFORE he [the nation of Egypt] used to HOLD HIS HEAD HIGH and boast, "The Nile is mine, and I made it" (Ezek. 29:9).[40]

PSALM CX—INTERPRETATION A, NOTES
[1] YHWH, the tetragrammaton.
[2] *la'ădonî* 'to my sovereign'.
[3] Heb. *rabbôtēnû dārĕšû*; see Kamin, *Rashi's Exegetical Categorization*, pp. 136-139; see Ps. 2, n. 2.
[4] Cf. the various *midrashim* in Midrash Tehillim here.
[5] MT reads "hear me".
[6] MT reads "hear us".
[7] Cf. Midrash Tanḥuma Vayera' #5; Tanḥuma, ed. Buber Hayye Sarah #1.
[8] Heb. *'ēn... 'ellā'*; the usage is eisegetical here because in the present

context *šēb,* lit., 'sit', means 'be enthroned' rather than 'wait' as it does in Lev. 13:46; Lam. 3:28; and passim in Rabbinic literature.

[9] Rashi's source is Midrash Tehillim here. The latter source cites Targum Onkelos at Num. 22:19 in support of the suggested interpretation of *yĕšîbāh.*

[10] With reference to 'RIGHT HAND' as a metaphor for deliverance cf. the similar use of 'arm' in Isa. 53:1.

[11] Cf. Midrash Tehillim here.

[12] Which corresponds to "every prop of [*miš'ān*] of bread" in Isa. 3:2; with Maarsen cf. Rashi at Lev. 26:26; see also Rashi at Ps. 105:16.

[13] Rashi does not quoted the bracketed lemma; I have supplied it for clarity.

[14] Lit., 'exhausted and pursuing'.

[15] Since the previous clause employs the future *kĕšĕtāšûb* 'when you return', the verb *šālaḥ,* lit., 'He sent' must be taken as a prophetic perfect and rendered into Eng. as future perfect.

[16] Heb. *yitnaddĕbu,* cognate of the psalmist's *nĕdābôt,* lit., 'FREEWILL OFFERINGS', which NJV renders 'WILLINGLY'.

[17] Rendering follows Rashi at Gen. 14:14.

[18] The idea that Aner, Eshkol, and Mamre are not to be identified with "his trained men" (Gen. 14:14) seems to derive from a reasonable close reading of Gen. 14:24, which distinguishes "my servants" (a synonym of "those born in my house"; see Held, "Rhetorical Questions in Ugaritic and Biblical Hebrew," p. 76, n. 42) from "the men who went with me, Aner, Eshkol, and Mamre." This close reading is at odds with the interpretation found in PRE Chapter 27, which is cited by Maarsen as Rashi's source here.

[19] NJV, following the ancient versions, Ibn Ezra, and Qimhi, renders "from the dawn"; such an interpretation requires revocalization of *mišĕḥār* to *miššaḥar;* Rashi's unusual approach echoes the Masoretic vocalization and calls the reader's attention to a *crux interpretum.*

[20] In Tanḥuma, ed. Buber, Lek Leka #33 this assertion is attributed to R. Aha quoting R. Hanina, who notes that the numerical equivalent of the word *'ēqeb* 'inasmuch as' in "inasmuch as Abraham obeyed Me" (Gen. 26:5) is 172, which is three years less than Abraham's total lifespan of 175 years (Gen. 25:7). R. Haninah deduces that the three years' difference between the two figures represents the years during which Abraham did not "recognize his Creator".

[21] According to BT Beṣah 35b, the correct reading is the subject of a dispute between Rab Judah [b. Ezekiel] and R. Nathan.

[22] Here Rashi answers the exegetical question, "What aspect of YOURS is it that will be so regarded?"

[23] Here Rashi explains the metaphor.

[24] *Sic;* MT, however, reads "Abram".

[25] With Maarsen cf. Rashi at Gen. 15:1. As noted by Maarsen, the source of the idea that Gen. 15:1 refers to Abraham's anxiety about his killing the four kings is Genesis Rabbah 44:4. There we find three alter-

native explanations of this anxiety: (1) Abraham's concern that he may have killed innocent people; (2) the possibility of reprisal from the victims' sons; (3) the possibility that by being saved from death in battle in the preeschatological era Abraham forfeited his portion in the life of the posteschatological era.

[26] See BT Nedarim 32b where Melchizedek is said to be another name for Shem son of Noah; see commentary of R. Nissim b. Reuben of Gerona (14th cent. C.E.) *ad loc.*; see also Max Seligsohn, "Shem in Rabbinical Literature," *JE* 11:261-262.

[27] I.e., a final *yod*, which has no grammatical function in the grammar of standard Biblical Heb.; see below at Ps. 113, n. 5.

[28] For Heb. *dābār* 'word' meaning 'decree' see *děbar hammelek* 'the king's decree' in Esth. 1:12, 17; 2:8; 4:3; 8:17; 9:1.

[29] Rashi there follows TJ's rendering *rabrěbîn* 'officers'; so also Qimhi there, who calls attention to a midrash attributed to Rava (299-352 C.E.) in BT Nedarim 62a. According to the latter midrash, King David's sons were called "priests" because they were "disciples of the wise," i.e., experts in Torah-lore, by virtue of which they were entitled to status and power.

[30] The reading in MT is *'dny*, an epithet of God, not the proper name *YHWH*; in our Rashi ms., however, the reading is y[y]y, which stands for the tetragrammaton, *YHWH*.

[31] Here Rashi attempts to answer the exegetical question, "What is the syntactic function of the phrase 'AT YOUR RIGHT HAND'?" He suggests that this phrase is ellipsis for an entire relative clause, "who was AT YOUR RIGHT HAND in the war." Note that 'to be at the right hand of someone' is an idiomatic expression meaning 'to be someone's ally or helper'; cf. Akk. *ana idi* PN *alāku;* see Gruber, *Aspects,* p. 72, n. 4; see Ps. 80:18; 121:5. KJV at Ps. 80:18 seems to be the source of Eng. "your right hand man".

[32] The preposition is missing from our Rashi ms.

[33] Heb. *hû';* concerning this usage of the Heb. personal pronoun cf. Gordis, *Job* at Job. 3:19. By suggesting that the relative clause in v. 5a refers back to events alluded to in vv. 1-4, i.e., the events described in Gen. 14, Rashi construes v. 5a as the transition between vv. 1-4, which refer to the past, and vv. 5b-7, which refer to the future.

[34] See Rashi there.

[35] Taking *rō'š* to mean literally 'head, top' and *bêt* to mean literally 'house', NJV suggests that MT means "smash the roof of the house of evil" or that *bêt* must be emended to *běnê* 'sons of' so that the clause would mean "crush the heads of men of evil." Recognizing the idiomatic use of *rō'š* 'head' to mean 'ruler' (see Judg. 11:8, 9; Ezek. 38:2, 3; 39:1; etc.) and of *bêt* 'house of' to mean 'nation of' (see, e.g., "House of Israel" in Jer. 48:13; Ps. 115:10), Rashi brilliantly concludes that *māḥaṣ rō'š* 'crush head' is an idiom denoting military victory over the ruler of a nation, a meaning which makes sense in both Ps. 110:6 and Hab. 3:13.

[36] Pharaoh.

[37] Joseph.

[38] Rashi's source for this notion could be Ezek. 29-32.

[39] Heb. *hnhr;* our Rashi ms. reads by haplography *hhr.*

[40] Our ms. reads "I made myself." On the idea that the land of Israel's dependence on heaven-sent rain taught the people of Israel humbly to depend on the providence and grace of God see Martin Buber, *Israel and Palestine,* trans. Stanley Goodman (London: East & West Library, 1952), pp. 24-29; 39-47.

PSALM CX—INTERPRETATION B

Alternatively, one may interpret the psalm with reference to David.[1]

1b   THE LORD[2] SAID concerning the activities of Saul, MY LORD[3]
       when I [David][4] was in flight from him (see 1 Sam. 18-31).

1c   SIT AT MY RIGHT HAND. [I.e.], Pause and wait for My deliverance.[5]

1b   *la'ǎdonî* [lit.], 'TO MY LORD' [means] *'al 'ǎdonî* 'for my lord' just as "Pharaoh will say *libĕnê Yisrā'ēl* 'to the Israelites' (Ex. 14:3) [means "Pharaoh will say of the Israelites" (NJV) and just as] "The men of the place asked *lĕ'ištô* 'to his wife'" (Gen. 26:7) [means "The men of the place asked about his wife" (cf. NJV) and just as] "Say to me, 'He is my brother'" (Gen. 20:13) [means "Say of me, 'He is my brother'"].[6]

2a   THE LORD WILL STRETCH FORTH FROM ZION YOUR MIGHTY SCEPTER [i.e.], the good deeds, which are accumulated to your credit. Another equally plausible interpretation [of v. 2] is "You will again reign in Zion, and there HE WILL SEND to you a MIGHTY SCEPTER, and then you will

2b   HOLD SWAY OVER YOUR ENEMIES."

3a   YOUR PEOPLE COME FORWARD WILLINGLY ON YOUR DAY OF BATTLE. [I.e.], the people of Israel will volunteer themselves[7] ON THE DAY when you achieve victory[8] as it is explained in [1] Chronicles (12) that people joined him from each and every tribe (1 Ch. 12:1-17), "when he was going to Ziklag" (1 Ch.12:21): "some Manassites went over to" him... (1 Ch. 12:20); "of the Gadites...to follow David..." (1 Ch. 12:9).

3b   IN MAJESTIC HOLINESS [FROM THE WOMB].[9] [I.e.], because of the majesty of the holiness, which was yours from your youth.

3c   YOURS IS THE DEW OF YOUR YOUTH.
       The nice childhood and the beautiful adolescence, which were yours, will be for you like the DEW, which is pleasant

and sweet, and it will profit you by making you successful.

4a   THE LORD HAS SWORN...that kingship would be yours forever.

4b   YOU ARE A PRIEST FOREVER. Now [in] which of the priesthoods? A priesthood, which is higher in status than the priesthood of Melchizedek, and this refers to the priest-hood,[10] which is[11] kingship, which is higher in status than the high priesthood, for it [kingship] is [acquired] at the price of thirty qualifications.[12]

4c   'al dibrātî MELCHIZEDEK [means] above[13] the decree of[14] MELCHIZEDEK, who was "priest of God the Most High" (Gen. 14: 18). Now if you should ask, "Was he not also king?" (see Gen. 14:18)[15] [I would reply as follows]: "King-ship over Gentiles is not regarded as the equivalent of king-ship with respect to Israel."

5a   THE LORD[16] will be continually[17] AT YOUR RIGHT HAND to save you.

5b   Who[18] CRUSHED IN THE DAY OF HIS ANGER KINGS, who fought against Abraham (Gen. 14:1, 17), Joshua (Josh. 10-11), and Barak (Judg. 4:22).

6   HE WORKS JUDGMENT UPON THE NATIONS, HEAPING UP BODIES. And He [who defended Israel in times past as related in v. 5b], again in the time of your [King David's][19] descendant Hezekiah WILL WORK JUDGMENT UPON Sennacherib's troops.

6b   [mālē' gĕwiyyôt 'HEAPING UP BODIES' means] gathering corpses.[20]

6c   ['HE CRUSHED HEAD UPON A GREAT COUNTRY' means] He smashed[21] Sennacherib, who was the HEAD of Nineveh and Assyria, which was A GREAT COUNTRY.[22]

7a   who DRINKS FROM THE STREAM ON HIS WAY. Note that he drinks, for he is proud that his troops have drunk from the waters of the Jordan in accord with what is stated in the Bible, "It is I who have drawn and drunk wa-ter. I have dried up with the soles of my feet..." (Isa. 37:25).

7b   THEREFORE HE HOLDS HIS HEAD HIGH. He [Sennacherib] used to laud himself and take pride in his high position.

7a   An alternative interpretation of HE DRINKS FROM THE STREAM

ON HIS WAY is [that] it [the STREAM] is a deadly poison, which is [administered in the form of] the customary drink of the whole world. David [here in Ps. 110:7a] prophesied concerning him [Sennacherib] that he would die for his wickedness.

7b *'al-kēn yārîm rō'š*, i.e., "because of ['al] him[23] who[*'ăšēr*] HOLDS HIS HEAD HIGH, i.e., because he used to HOLD HIS HEAD HIGH.

PSALM CX—INTERPRETATION B, NOTES

[1] Rather than Abraham as in Interpretation A.

[2] See Interpretation A, n. 1.

[3] See Interpretatin A, n. 2

[4] To whom the psalm is attributed in v. 1a.

[5] See Interpretation A, above.

[6] For Interpretation A Rashi understood the prefixed preposition *lĕ* in v. 1 in its most frequent sense, 'to'; interpretation B calls for the less frequent sense 'concerning'; hence Rashi must prove that such a usage of the preposition is indeed attested. Concerning the various nuances of the preposition in question see dictionaries.

[7] See Interpretation A, n. 16.

[8] Heb. *ḥayil*, which could mean 'battle' (so NJV); I render it 'victory' in accord with Rash's suggestion here that this noun is ellipsis for the idiom *'āśāh ḥayil*, lit., 'do battle', which means 'achieve victory'.

[9] The bracketed portion of the lemma is not quoted in our Rashi ms.; I have supplied it for clarity.

[10] See Rashi at Ps. 110:4c, Interpretation A.

[11] The construct, normally rendered 'priesthood of', here expresses 'priesthood, which is'; cf. *GKC* #130e.

[12] With Maarsen note that Mishnah Avot 6:6 states that there are thirty prerequisites for royalty but only twenty-four for the [high] priesthood. Philip Blackman, *Mishnayoth* (6 vols.; London: Mishna Press, 1954), vol. 4, pp. 544-546 spells out and explicates the thirty and the twenty-four.

[13] Contrast the meaning of the Heb. preposition *'al* suggested here with the one suggested in Interpretation A.

[14] So also in Interpretation A.

[15] If so, the assertion that David as king is of higher status than Melchizedek as priest (see above, at v. 4b) would be invalidated.

[16] See Interpretation A, n. 30.

[17] Contrast Interpretation A.

[18] In Interpretation A 'THE LORD' (v. 5a) is treated as the subject of the verb 'HE CRUSHES' (v. 5b) while 'AT YOUR RIGHT HAND' (v. 5a) is treated as part of an elliptical relative clause modifying 'THE LORD'. In Interpretation B 'THE LORD' (v. 5a) is treated as the subject

of a nominal sentence, whose predicate is 'AT YOUR RIGHT HAND' while v. 5b is construed as a relative clause modifying 'THE LORD'.

[19] See above, n. 4.

[20] So Rashi also in Interpretation A, q.v.

[21] Heb. *wayyimḥaṣ;* the biblical text employs the synonymous *māḥaṣ.*

[22] Rashi's interpretation of the idioms here is identical with the one he presents in Interpretation A; the only difference between the two interpretations of v. 6 is in the identification of the alleged historical allusions.

[23] Rashi's alternative interpretation of the particle *kēn* in the phrase *'al-kēn,* which is normally taken to mean 'THEREFORE'.

PSALM CXI

1   HALLELUJAH. I PRAISE THE LORD WITH ALL MY HEART.[1]

4a   HE MADE A MEMORIAL TO HIS WONDERS.
[I.e.], He established for Israel Sabbaths and festivals and com-mandments, and He wrote in them [in the fourth of the command-ments of the Decalogue in Deut. 5:15], "Remember that you were a slave in Egypt."[2]

4b   [The reason HE MADE A MEMORIAL TO HIS WONDERS is] because He IS GRACIOUS AND COMPASSIONATE[3] to His children, and He delights in the virtuous.[4]

5   *ṭerep.* [I.e.], *māzôn* 'food'.[5]

6a   HE REVEALED TO HIS PEOPLE HIS POWERFUL WORKS.
[The apparent non-sequitur created by the juxtaposition of v. 6a with v. 6b, which states, HE GAVE THEM THE TERRITORY OF (OTHER) NATIONS, suggests that] when HE GAVE THEM [the Israelites] THE TERRITORY OF (OTHER) NATIONS, then He made known to them His power and His might. Moreover, Midrash Tanḥuma [states]: "He [God] wrote for Israel the Book of Genesis in order to inform them that the land [of Israel] is His and that He has the authority to settle in it whomever He wishes and to uproot them and to settle others [in it]. Hence the Gentiles should not be able to say to Israel, 'You are robbers for you took away the land of the seven nations.'"[6]

8   WELL-FOUNDED are HIS PRECEPTS (v. 7b) on an eternal[7] foundation.[8] They are supported by punishments and warnings, and the biblical passages are arranged in a specific order, which is for[9] teaching *midrash halakah,*[10] and it is with reference to this that Solomon said, "His legs are marble pillars" (Cant. 5:15).[11]

PSALM CXI, NOTES

[1] Our ms. employs the opening verse of the psalm as a title, the equivalent of our designation, "Psalm CXI". In the margin of our ms. the chapter is designated Ps. 109.

[2] Qimhi refers to an almost verbatim interpretation as *derash*, i.e., eisegesis.

[3] Vv. 4a-4b are an apparent *non sequitur*; Rashi, however, suggests here that v. 4b functions as an adverbial clause modifying HE MADE A ME-MORIAL in v. 4a.

[4] Here Rashi responds to the exegetical question, "With respect to whom is God's being GRACIOUS AND COMPASSIONATE manifest?"

[5] So now NJV; with Maarsen note that Rashi's likely source is *Mahberet Menahem*, which distinguishes between *ṭrp* I, a verbal root meaning 'snatch' whose noun derivative means 'prey' and *ṭrp* II, a noun meaning 'human food'; contrast *BDB*, p. 383, according to which the latter usage is a late development from the former.

[6] See Midrash Tanḥuma, ed. Buber, vol. 1, p. 4a; see also Rashi at Gen. 1:1 and the remarks of Chavel there.

[7] Heb. '*ad*, a reference to *lā'ad* 'FOR ALL ETERNITY' in v. 8.

[8] Heb. *semek* from the same root as *sĕmûkîm* 'WELL-FOUNDED'. See n. 10.

[9] Our rendering of Rashi's exegetical *waw*; see above, p. 139.

[10] In BT Yebamot 4a Rabbi Elazar [b. Pedat] uses our verse, THEY ARE *sĕmûkîm* 'JUXTAPOSED' FOREVER as proof of the idea that derivation of *halakah* on the basis of the juxtaposition of biblical passages is part of the divine law itself.

[11] Cf. Canticles Rabbah 5:14.

PSALM CXII

1 HALLELUJAH. HAPPY IS THE MAN.

2b A GENERATION OF UPRIGHT MEN, whose DESCEN-
DANTS WILL BE (2a) BLESSED.[1]

4a A LIGHT AROSE [*zāraḥ*] IN THE DARKNESS. [The
verb *zāraḥ* 'AROSE' is here employed] in the sense of *hizrîāḥ*
'He [God] raised up'.[2] [According to] a midrash based upon
it [v. 4a] He [God] Himself, as it were, became for them A
LIGHT in accord with what is stated in the Bible, "The
LORD is my light and my help" (Ps. 27:1).

5a ALL GOES WELL WITH THE MAN WHO LENDS
GENEROUSLY....
I.e., HE IS GENEROUS to poor people in that HE LENDS
to them without stinting[3] by saying, "I have not the wherewithal,"

5b and HIS THINGS, which are necessary for him [i.e., the
poor person] with respect to food, drink, and clothing He
supplies[4] WITH EQUITY, i.e.,[5] moderation,[6] so that he[5] is
sparing of his resources; [alternatively] *yĕkalkēl dĕbārāyw* [may
mean] "he [the lender] manages his belongings.[7]

7b HIS HEART IS FIRM. [I.e.], HIS HEART is loyal to his
Creator.

8 HIS HEART IS RESOLUTE [*sāmûk*]. [I.e.], it leans on and
trusts in the Holy One Blessed be He.

10 WHEN THE WICKED PERSON SEES [the success of the
philanthropist who gaves away his/her money], *wĕkāʿas*,
[which is] a verb, which corresponds in meaning to *wĕyikʿas*
'then he will be angry'; therefore the [first] half of it is
pointed with *qāmeṣ* [i.e., long *ā*] and the [second] half of it
with *pataḥ* [i.e., short *a*], and its accent is on the final syllable.[8]

PSALM CXII, NOTES
 [1] Anticipating NJV, Rashi takes vv. 2a-b as two parallel clauses, the
subject of both of which is 'HIS DESCENDANTS' and the simple predicate of both of which is 'HE WILL BE'. Moreover, Rashi takes the verb

yĕborāk 'HE WILL BE BLESSED' as the predicate of a relative clause modifying 'UPRIGHT MEN'.

[2] Rashi's interpretation of 'LIGHT' as the direct object of a verb whose subject is 'THE LORD' is supported by v. 4b, which is a list of adjectives describing the subject of that verb, i.e., 'the LORD'; cf. NJV margin.

[3] See Jastrow, *Dict.*, p. 318a, s.v. *diqdēq*.

[4] Heb. *mĕkalkēl*, a paraphrase of the psalmist's *yĕkalkēl*, which NJV renders 'CONDUCTS (AFFAIRS)'; see below, n. 7.

[5] Explicative *waw*.

[6] Heb. *bĕmiddāh*.

[7] Similarly NJV, q.v. According to the first interpretation the verb *kilkēl* means 'supply, sustain' as is generally the case in Biblical Heb.; see *BDB*, p. 465a; the second interpretation assumes that *kilkēl* 'supply, sustain' may have the extended meaning of 'manage, govern'; cf. the same extended meaning of the semantic equivalent *pirnēs* in Rashi's commentary at Ruth 1:1. According to the first interpretation the pronominal suffix of *dĕbārāyw* 'HIS THINGS' is taken to refer to each of the poor persons who are the objects of the beneficence of 'THE MAN WHO LENDS GENEROUSLY'. According to the second interpretation the pronominal suffix refers to 'THE MAN WHO LENDS GENEROUSLY'. Both interpretations see in v. 5b a limitation on the generosity of the philanthropist. While the first interpretation confines this idea to the word *bĕmišpāṭ* 'WITH EQUITY', the second interpretation sees this idea as the point of the entire clause. Rashi makes the same point in his comment on Ps. 112:5 in his commentary on BT Hullin 84b.

[8] The Massorah of the Leningrad Ms. of the Bible reproduced in *BHS* anticipates Rashi here; the text of the ms. reproduced there reads, however, *wĕkāʾās;* the long vowel in the final accented syllable according to that ms. can be accounted for by noting the disjunctive accent, which calls for a pausal form of the verb with *qāmeṣ* rather than *pataḥ* in the final syllable.

PSALM CXIII

1   HALLELUJAH. O SERVANTS OF THE LORD GIVE
     PRAISE.

5a   WHO IS LIKE THE LORD OUR GOD...IN HEAVEN
     AND ON THE EARTH?[1] that He will

5b   ASCEND[2] TO BE ENTHRONED[3] AND DESCEND[4] TO
     SEE? [The forms] *magbîhî* 'ASCENDS' (v. 5), *mašpîlî* 'DE-
     SCENDS' (v. 6), *měqîmî* 'RAISES' (v. 7), *lĕhôšîbî* 'TO SET'
     (v. 8), and *môšîbî* 'SETS' (v. 9) all contain superfluous final
     yod.[5]

9   THE CHILDLESS WOMAN [*'ăqeret habbayit*][6] is [a meta-
     phor for] Zion, who is like a barren woman [*'ăqārāh*]. [The
     participle *môšîbî* 'HE SETS' refers to the fact that] He will
     set her [*yošîbennāh*] [7] A HAPPY MOTHER OF CHILDREN
     "for Zion will have travailed; she will indeed have given
     birth to her children" (Isa. 66:8).

PSALM CXIII, NOTES

[1] By quoting vv. 5-6 in this manner, i.e., all of v. 5 up to the *caesura*
followed immediately by all of v. 6 after the *caesura*, Rashi intimates that
vv. 5-6 together constitute a *miqrā' měsûrās*, i.e., an instance of inversion,
i.e., a verse, which for stylistic reasons employs a word order, which ob-
scures the syntactic relationship of the words; similarly Ehrlich, *Die
Psalmen*, p. 286. Hermann Gunkel, *Die Psalmen* (5th ed.; Göttingen:
Vandenhoeck & Ruprecht, 1968), pp. 492-93 (and others cited there) and
BH[3] emend the text so that the order of the clauses is 5a-6a-5b-6a. Qimhi
suggests two alternative interpretations of vv. 5-6: (1) WHO IS LIKE
THE LORD OUR GOD, FOR IT IS HE WHO ASCENDS above all
the other deities TO BE ENTHRONED, AND HE DESCENDS TO
LOOK AT the lowly whether they are IN THE HEAVENS or ON THE
EARTH; and (2) WHO IS LIKE THE LORD OUR GOD WHO AS-
CENDS TO BE ENTHRONED IN THE HEAVENS AND WHO DE-
SCENDS TO LOOK UPON THE EARTH. Interestingly, NJV is
uninfluenced here either by the critical commentators who emend the
word order or by the medieval commentators who assume a case of inversion. Instead, NJV follows KJV, LXX and Vulgate in rendering the
clauses according to their word order in *textus receptus*. Briggs, vol. 2, p.
389, makes sense of the word order of *textus receptus* as follows: "*He who
stoopeth to look*. From the supreme heights He stoopeth, in order to look
through all the regions below—namely, *In the heavens*], for He is conceived

as above the heavens; *and in all the earth,* beneath the heavens." For the idea that the LORD is indeed enthroned *above* the heavens see Ps. 113:4b; 57:6, 12; 108:6. On *miqrā' měsûrās* in Rashi's exegesis see Rashi at Ps. 17:7; 22:30, 31; 36:2; 93:5; etc.

² Rashi here uses the regular form *magbîăh* rather than the irregular form with superfluous final *yod, magbîhî,* which is employed in the biblical text; see his next comment. On the use of the so-called "inwardly transitive *hiphil* exemplified by *magbîăh* 'ascending' (lit., 'making oneself high') and *maśpîl* 'descending' (lit., 'making oneself low') see *GKC* #53d.

³ For Heb. *yāšab* 'be enthroned' see Gruber, "The Many Faces of Hebrew *nāśā' pānîm* 'lift up the face'," p. 257, n. 25; similarly, NJV, here.

⁴ Rashi here uses the regular form *maśpîl* rather than the irregular form with superfluous final *yod, maśpîlî* employed in the biblical text; see n. 2.

⁵ I.e., a final *yod*, which, according to Rashi, has no grammatical function in Biblical Heb. According to *Mahberet Menahem,* p. 109, s.v. *gnb,* the final *yod* is added for metrical reasons; similarly, Briggs, vol. 2, p. 390. For other views see Chomsky, *David Kimhi's Hebrew Grammar,* p. 81, n. 111. Most modern scholars see in the participles and nouns with superfluous final *yod* forms peculiar to a Heb. dialect, in which the genitive case of the substantive is indicated as in Ugaritic, Akkadian, Classical Arabic and perhaps Standard Phoenician (see Harold Louis Ginsberg, "The Northwest Semitic Languages," in *The World History of the Jewish People,* vol. 2, ed. B. Mazar [Tel Aviv; Massada, 1970], p. 109) by final *i*; see Dahood, here.

⁶ On the use of *'ăqeret habbayit,* lit., 'the home's barren woman' in Rabbinic Heb. to mean 'housewife' see David Marcus, "Some Antiphrastic Euphemisms for a Blind Person in Akkadian and Other Semitic Languages," *JAOS* 100 (1980), p. 307.

⁷ On the use of the participle in Biblical Heb. to express either the past, present or future tense see *GKC* #116 n, o, p.

PSALM CXIV

1a WHEN ISRAEL WENT FORTH FROM EGYPT.

1b FROM A PEOPLE OF STRANGE SPEECH [*lōʿēz*] [i.e.], a people of another language,[1] which is not the holy tongue.[2] [As for the word *lōʿēz*], its cognate[3] is [the word *nōʿāz* in Isa. 33:19], "No more shall you see the barbarian folk ['*am nōāz*], the people of speech too obscure...." Now [as for my contention that *lʿz* and *nʿz*, which appear to be distinct roots, are indeed cognates, note that the letters] *nun* and *lamed* are interchangeable[4] as is exemplified by *niškāh* 'room, chamber' (Neh. 13:7), which is [a biform of] *liškāh* 'room, chamber'[5] (Neh. 13:4, 5, 8, etc.) in the Book of Ezra.[6]

2 JUDAH BECAME HIS HOLY ONE. He [the LORD] took Judah for His lot, His territory, and His holiness,[7] and they, in turn, hallowed His Name by descending into the [Reed] Sea in accord with what we have learned in the *aggadah:* This verse refers to the fact that Nahshon [prince of the tribe of Judah] jumped [before all the other tribal princes] into the [Reed] Sea, and he said, "I shall descend first," in accord with what is stated in the Bible, "As for the princes of Judah, their heap of stones" (Ps.68:28b).[8] Now it is with reference to this [*event*] that it is stated [here in v. 2], "JUDAH BECAME HIS HOLY ONE."

3a JORDAN RAN BACKWARD for all the primeval waters were split.[9]

7 *ḥûlî hāʾāreṣ*[10] [i.e.], *ha-mĕḥôlēl ʾet hāʾāreṣ* 'He who gives birth to the earth'.[11] Now it [the form *ḥûlî*] contains a superfluous *yod* like the *yod* of *hammagbîhî lāšābet* "He who ascends to be enthroned" (Ps. 113:5b) and [like the

9a superfluous *yod* of] *hahōpkî* 'WHO TURNED'.

9b [The expression *lĕmaʿyĕnô* 'INTO A FOUNTAIN' in v. 9b], 'INTO A FOUNTAIN OF WATER' [contains] a superfluous [final] *waw* like [the superfluous final *waw* in the form *wĕḥayĕtô* 'and the animal' in the phrase] "and the animal of the forest" (Ps. 50:10; 104:11, 20). [Hence the form *lĕmaʿyĕnô* means the same thing as] *lĕmaʿayan* 'into a fountain'.

PSALM CXIV, NOTES

[1] Heb. *śĕpat 'aḥēr*, lit., 'lip of another'; on the use of the construct genitive construction in the Semitic languages as periphrasis for noun + attributive adjective see *GKC* #128 o-p.

[2] Rashi treats the feminine noun *śāpāh* 'lip, language' as a masculine noun.

[3] Heb. *ḥăbērô*, lit., 'his friend'; similarly, Ibn Ezra designates a word which appears to have no cognate as *'ēn lô rēaʿ*, lit., 'he has no friend'; see Greenspahn, "The Meaning of "Ein Lo Domeh and Similar Phrases in Medieval Biblical Exegesis," pp. 62-63.

[4] Cf. Moscati, *An Introduction to the Comparative Grammar of the Semitic Languages,* #8.26; on interchanging consonants in Heb. see Rashi on Lev. 19:16.

[5] The observation that *liškāh* and *niškāh* are biforms is found already in *Mahberet Menahem*, p. 259, s.v. *niškāh*. Rashi, however, adds here the general principle, which accounts for these biforms.

[6] In the English Bible the books of Ezra and Nehemiah are counted as two separate books among the thirty-nine books of the Old Testament. In the twenty-four book Hebrew Bible or Tanakh of the Jews the two books are counted as one which is called Ezra just as First and Second Samuel are considered one book (and so also 1-2 Kings and so also 1-2 Chronicles) and just as the twelve minor prophets are counted as a single book called "The Twelve".

[7] Here Rashi treats the *segholate* noun *qodeš* 'HOLINESS', which can mean 'temple, sanctuary' (see NJV margin here, and see Ps. 134:2) as a synonym of the gerund *qĕdûšāh* 'holiness'.

[8] Ps. 114:2 seems to say that it was at the Exodus that the LORD selected the territory of Judah as the site for the Temple. Rashi here alludes to the midrash found in Midrash Tehillim here (see also Mekilta, vol. 1, pp. 232-234). According to this midrash, when the Israelites arrived at the Reed Sea, each of the tribes wanted to demonstrate its faith in the LORD by being the first to jump into the sea before the waters had yet parted. The several tribes fought each other, first verbally and later by throwing stones at each other. Judah prevailed over the others, and the LORD rewarded the tribe of Judah by establishing the Temple within his territory and by selecting one of his families, the House of David, to be the ruling dynasty. The midrash seems to have been inspired by Ps. 68:28, which it understood as follows: "There [at the Reed Sea] Benjamin the youngest is their ruler, the princes of Judah are with their pile of stones [and so are] the princes of Zebulun, [and so are] the princes of Naphtali." The midrash suggests that *rdm* 'is their ruler' be taken as an abbreviation for *rad yam* 'he descended into the sea'. Thus understood, the verse suggests that when Benjamin had already descended into the sea and thereby had seemed to have won for himself the site of the sanctuary (Shiloh) and the royal family (the dynasty of Saul), Judah with his pile of stones prevailed. Perhaps, there is here also a reading back into the pre-Conquest period of

the story of David's prevailing over Saul because of his victory over Goliath with a pile of stones!

⁹ By employing sea/Jordan in synonymous parallelism the author of Ps. 114 has appropriated for the events of Israel's history the fixed pair Sea//River, which belongs to Canaanite cosmogony. The midrash, to which Rashi alludes here (see Mekilta, vol. 1, pp. 231-232) shares with the psalmist the conviction that the events of Israel's history are of cosmic significance.

¹⁰ By not translating the lemma we treat it in the manner presupposed by Rashi's comment here, i.e., as an enigma; note also that our Rashi ms. prefaces the word 'āreṣ with definite article, not found in the Masoretic Text.

¹¹ Rashi suggests that while in vv. 5-6 we have a question, "Why are you dancing?" v. 7 supplies the answer, "Because of the LORD, the Creator of the earth...." In his commentary at Ex. 1:15 notes that frequently the same verbal root may be employed in the identical meaning in the *qal* and in the intensive (*pi'el* or *hiphil*) conjugation. On the basis of this principle Rashi here asserts that the *qal* of the verb *ḥwl*, which often means 'travail, give birth' (Isa. 54:1; 66:8) can also mean 'beget, father'; in fact, this is true of the *qal* of the verb *yld* (see dictionaries); contrast *Mahberet Menahem*, p. 175.

PSALM CXV

1   NOT TO US,[1] O LORD, NOT TO US.
Help us[2] neither on our behalf nor in consideration of the virtue[3] of our deeds, BUT TO YOUR NAME GIVE GLORY so that they

2   NOT[4] SAY, "WHERE...IS THEIR GOD?"

7   BUT CANNOT TOUCH. [The verb *yĕmišûn* 'TOUCH'] is the same verb as is attested in *yĕmûšēnî*[5] *'ābî* "my father touches me" (Gen. 27:12).[6]

11   O YOU WHO FEAR THE LORD. These are the proselytes.[7]

PSALM CXV, NOTES

[1] So NJV; Rashi's comment indicates that Rashi interprets the amibuous *lānû* to mean both 'to us' and 'for us' simultaneously.

[2] The idiom *'āśāh 'im* 'help', lit., 'do with' may be derived from Biblical and Rabbinic Heb. 'do (something) with'; on the latter expression in Biblical Heb. see *BDB*, p. 794a.

[3] For this Rabbinic Heb. usage see Jastrow, *Dict.*, p. 626b.

[4] By paraphrasing *lāmmāh* by the phrase *kĕdê šellō'* 'so that...not' Rashi indicates his anticipation of *K-B*³, p. 523a and of Dahood here who translates 'lest' and of NJV, which renders 'let not' here and at Ex. 32:12.

[5] Our Rashi ms. quotes the verb in *plene* spelling; contrast MT of Gen. 27:12 where the spelling is defective.

[6] While *BDB*, p. 558a and *K-B*³, p. 532a posit a biform root *mwš* /*myš*, Rashi here posits the biliteral root *mš*; on Rashi's positing biliteral roots see Englander, "Rashi's View of the Weak, *'ayin-'ayin* and *pe-nun* Roots," pp. 417-425, and see passim in our notes.

[7] With Zohory, p. 320 note that the likely source of this assertion is Midrash Tehillim at Ps. 22:24; with Zohory there see also Mekhilta, vol. 3, pp. 140-141; Leviticus Rabbah 3:2.

PSALM CXVI

1   I LOVED THAT THE LORD WILL HEAR
[I.e.], I desired that the LORD should hear my voice.

2   AND IN MY DAYS I CALLED.
[I.e.], In my days of trouble I called to Him, but in my days of redemption I forgot him.[1]

3   BANDS OF DEATH.
[I.e.], groups of enemies seeking to kill me.
BANDS OF DEATH (here at Ps. 116:3) [corresponds to] "bands of Sheol" (in Ps. 18:5).[2] [*mēṣārê* SHEOL[3] means][4] 'the borders of Sheol'.

9   IN THE LANDS OF THE LIVING.
[I.e.], the land of Israel from which my pursuers drove me in the days of Saul and against whose will I returned.

10a   I BELIEVED WHEN I SPOKE.
[I.e.], I BELIEVED what Ziba said about Mephibosheth [when I spoke to Ziba, saying, "Behold, all that belongs to Mephibosheth is yours" (2 Sam. 16:4)].[5]

10b   I RESPONDED [*ʿānîtî*] GREATLY.
[I.e.], I had spoken harshly, and I apologized [*naʿănêtî*] to you.[6]

11   I THOUGHT IN MY HASTE to flee from the presence of Absalom, "EVERY MAN IS A LIAR and a betrayer of his friend," for I saw my son seek to kill me, and all Israel were repaying me evil for good. Therefore I BELIEVED Ziba (see v. 10a), and I thought, "Even Mephibosheth is a liar and he is betraying me." Every form of the root *kzb* refers to loss of faith in that in which one had trusted. [It is the semantic equivalent of Old French] *failyant*,[7] as is demonstrated by "whose waters do not fail" (Isa. 58:11). Some, however, explain it [our verse as follows]: I THOUGHT IN MY HASTE at the Rock of Controversy when Saul and his men were encircling me and my men in order to seize me, and with reference to which it is stated in the Bible, "David was hastening to go" (1 Sam 23:30), EVERY PERSON IS A LIAR. The Prophet Samuel who is reliable as a prophet,

even he is a LIAR, for he annointed me king.[8]

14   *negdāh nā' lĕkol 'ammô*. [I.e.], *neged kol 'ammô* "in the presence
of all His people".[9]

15   IS GRIEVOUS IN THE LORD'S SIGHT. The Holy One
Blessed be He showed me that it is a hard and serious matter in His sight to let His devotees die. *hammāwĕtāh* [is a form
of the noun] *māwet* 'death'. It is an example of the same
grammatical form [of the noun as is exemplified by the
nouns] *habbayĕtāh* 'homeward' (Gen. 39:23), *haḥûṣāh* 'street-
ward' (Gen. 39:29).[10]

16a   YOUR SERVANT, THE SON OF YOUR MAIDSER-
VANT.
[David's point is that] one raised up to be a servant is not to
be compared to a servant purchased from the market
place.[11]

16b   YOU HAVE UNDONE THE CORDS THAT BOUND
ME.
You have removed from my neck "thongs and bars of a
yoke" (Jer. 27:2).

17   A THANK OFFERING.[12] Sacrifices of thanks for the wonders You did for me.

18   MY VOWS. The sacrifices I vowed.

19   *bĕtôkēkî* is synonymous with *bĕtôk* 'in the midst of'.[13]

PSALM CXVI, NOTES
[1] With Maarsen and Zohory cf. Tanḥuma Jethro 16; Tanḥuma
Niṣabim 1.
[2] Other Rashi mss. read here: "[As for the expressions], BANDS OF
DEATH (here), "bands of Sheol" (Ps. 18:5), they are all synonymous with
'groups' as is exemplified by [the expression] "band of prophets" (1 Sam.
10:5). Quite possibly, the scribe of our ms. intended this entire comment
and omitted the greater portion of it through error.
[3] NJV renders "the torments of Sheol"; note that *mēṣar* 'torment' (Ps.
118:5) and *mēṣar* 'border, straits' are treated as nuances of a single noun
both in *BDB*, p. 865a and in Jastrow, *Dict.*, p. 828a; if this be so, the semantic equivalent in English is indeed 'strait, straits'; see English dictionaries.
[4] The lemma is missing from our ms.; we have supplied it from other
mss.
[5] The bracketed portion of Rashi's comment is not found in our ms.;
we have supplied it from other mss.
[6] On this usage of *na'ănêtî* in Rabbinic Heb. see Jastrow, *Dict.*, p.
1093b.

⁷ As noted by Banitt, *Rashi: Interpreter of the Biblical Letter,* p. 60, both Heb. *kōzēb* and O.F. *failyant* can mean 'treacherous' but have the root meaning 'failing'.

⁸ The first of Rashi's two alternative suggestions as to the situation in life, which accounts for David's having said, WHEN I SPOKE I BE-LIEVED THAT EVERY PERSON IS A LIAR, derives from the assertion of Rav in BT Shabbat 56a; the second, introduced by the formula, "Some, however, explain it," is taken from Midrash Tehillim 18:7.

⁹ Here Rashi intimates that the following have no grammatical or lexical significance: (1) the suffix *āh* on the word *negdāh,* which he equates with the regular *neged* 'before'; (2) the particle *nā'* placed between the preposition and the object of the preposition; and (3) the additional preposition *lĕ* following *negdāh nā'.* Dahood, here, suggests that "the extended form" of the preposition *neged* employed here at Ps. 116:14 "is doubtless used for metrical purposes."

¹⁰ Rashi here intimates that the form *hammāwĕtāh* represents the noun *māwet* with prefixed definite article and final locative *heh.* Hence Rashi is saying that v. 15 means "It is difficult in the eyes of the LORD that his devotees are 'deathward', i.e., mortal."

¹¹ The source of this comment is Midrash Tehillim here. The latter midrash puts into King David's mouth a popular proverb to the effect that born slaves are more reliable than persons who were raised for other work and subsequently sold into slavery; the implication is that devotees of God, who are also called *'ăbādîm* 'slaves, servants' are also most reliable when they have been born into a religious environment.

¹² See our n. 1 on Rashi's commentary at Ps. 100:1.

¹³ So NJV; so also Dahood, here; q.v.; other Rashi mss. read, "*bĕtôkēkî* is synonymous with *bĕtôkēk* 'in the midst of you'"; cf. NJV margin.

PSALM CXVII[1]

1   PRAISE THE LORD, ALL YOU NATIONS.[2]

2a   FOR GREAT IS HIS STEADFAST LOVE TOWARD US, which is to say [PRAISE THE LORD, ALL YOU NATIONS; EXTOL HIM, ALL YOU PEOPLES] (v. 1) even though it is[3] we, Israel, toward whom HIS STEADFAST LOVE IS GREAT.

2b   THE FAITHFULNESS OF THE LORD ENDURES FOREVER for He has kept His promise, which He promised the patriarchs.[4]

PSALM CXVIII:1-4[5]

1 PRAISE THE LORD.
2 LET ISRAEL DECLARE, [*"kî*[6] HIS STEADFAST LOVE
   IS ETERNAL"][7] because[8] HIS STEADFAST LOVE IS
   ETERNAL.

PSALM CXVII AND PSALM CXVIII:1-4, NOTES

[1] Since the short comment on Ps. 13 is appended in our Rashi ms. to
the comment on Ps. 12 and since the short comment on Ps. 28 is appended
to the comment on Ps. 27 and since Rashi treats Ps. 42-43 as a single psalm,
the numbering in our Rashi ms. of all the psalms from Ps. 44 through Ps.
71 is exactly three numbers lower than the chapter numbers found in standard
Jewish and Protestant Bibles (see Ps. 43, n. 1). We noted in Ps. 72, n. 53
that our Rashi ms. treats Ps. 72:20, which is the colophon of the second of
the five books into which the psalter is divided in MT, as a separate Ps. 70,
following Ps. 69, which is commonly designated Ps. 72 in standard Jewish
and Protestant Bibles. Consequently, the number in our Rashi ms. of all
the psalms from Ps. 73 through Ps. 117 is exactly two numbers lower than
the chapter numbers found in standard Jewish and Protestant Bibles. Hence
the shortest chapter in the Bible, Ps. 117, is numbered in our Rashi ms. as
Ps. 115. Note, however, that in our Rashi ms. there is appended to the
short comment on Ps. 117 (Ps. 115 in our ms.) a comment on Ps. 118:1-
2. Since our Rashi ms. skips from #115 to #117 in its marginal numbering of the psalms, it is reasonable to conclude that the scribe who prepared
our ms. understood that our Ps. 118:1-4 constitutes a separate Ps., which
he would have counted as Ps. 116. The treatment of Ps. 118:1-4 as a separate composition is found in other medieval mss. as well and is reflected in
its treatment in the Jewish liturgy. The unique treatment of these four verses
in Jewish liturgy is that after each of these is sung aloud by the cantor the
congregation responds aloud and in unison with Ps. 118:1 (see Birnbaum,
Daily Prayer Book, p. 571). The more common practice in Jewish liturgy is
for the cantor to repeat aloud what has already been said silently by the
members of the congregation. Concerning Ps. 118:1-4 see below, n. 5.

[2] This line serves as the psalm title in our Rashi ms.; Rashi's first comment on this psalm is appended to v. 2 and notes that in the light of v. 2
v. 1 seems to make no sense; contrast Midrash Tehillim here, which attempts to make very good sense of the apparent *non sequitur*.

[3] Heb. *wĕ'ap kî*, which is both (1) Rashi's interpretation of the psalmist's ambiguous *kî*, which NJV renders "for"; (2) Rashi's way of calling
attention to the *non sequitur* cited in n. 2.

[4] Rashi's source is Midrash Tehillim here; cf. Ps. 105:8-11.

[5] Since our Rashi ms. skips #116 in the numbering of the psalms and numbers Ps. 117 as Ps. 115 and Ps. 118:5-25 as Ps. 117, it is reasonable to conclude that the scribe who produced our Rashi ms. saw in Ps. 118:1-4 a separate psalm, #116.

[6] See below, n. 8.

[7] Rashi does not quote the bracketed portion of the verse; I have supplied it for clarity.

[8] Heb. *lĕpî še,* which suggests both (1) a response to the exegetical question, "Why should Israel declare, 'HIS STEADFAST LOVE IS FOREVER'?" and (2) an answer to the exegetical question, "What is the meaning of the particle *kî* in the present context?"

PSALM CXVIII:5-25[1]—INTERPRETATION A

5a   IN DISTRESS I CALLED ON THE LORD

5b   HE ANSWERED ME WITH GREAT ENLARGEMENT
      [*bmrḥb*]. [I.e.], HE ANSWERED ME in consideration of the
      fact that [*bmh*] I was a virtuous person so that he brought me
      out of DISTRESS into RELIEF [*mrḥb*]. Now like it [*bmrḥb*
      in that *bmrḥb* is an abbreviation for *bmh mrḥb*] is *'šr...b'š*
      "which catches fire" (Judg. 15:14), [which stands for the
      fact] that fire [*š'š*] comes down [*yrd*] from heaven and simi-
      larly *"nk bstr r'm* "I answered you in secret thunder" (Ps.
      81:8b) [is an abbreviation for] "I shall hide you [*'styrk*] from
      the thunder [*mn hr'm*]."[2]

8   IT IS BETTER TO TAKE REFUGE [*laḥăsôt*] IN THE
      LORD.
      ḥissāyôn 'taking refuge' means 'hiding in the shade',[3] and it is
      a small matter. However, 'TRUST' (v. 8b) is a sound matter
      and a strong support. Nevertheless, TO TAKE REFUGE
      IN THE LORD is BETTER than trusting in people.[4]

10a   ALL THE NATIONS HAVE BESET ME refers to the wars
      of Gog and Magog[5] in which all the nations will be there in
      accord with what is stated in the Bible, "For I will gather all
      the nations to Jerusalem for the war" (Zech. 14:2).[6]

10b   *'ămîlam* 'I WILL CUT THEM DOWN'[7] [i.e.], I shall cut
      them off.[8] [The verb *'ămîlam*] is a cognate of [the verb *yĕmôlēl*
      'it is cut down' in Ps. 90:6 where we read] *yĕmôlēl wĕyābēš* "It
      is cut down, and it withers."[9]

12b   THEY SHALL BE EXTINGUISHED LIKE BURNING
      THORNS. Every form of [the verb whose gerund is] *dĕ'îkāh*
      'extinguishing' refers to jumping and leaping; it[10] hurries to
      be torn loose and drawn away from its place. Therefore, it is
      employed with[11] the noun 'fire' and with the noun 'water' as
      is exemplified by *nid'ăkû mimmĕqômām* "They vanish from
      their place"[12] (Job. 6:17) and likewise *yāmāy nid'ākû*[13] "My
      days vanished" (Job. 17:1) and likewise *wĕnērô 'ālāyw yid'āk*
      "his lamp [which is] over him is removed"[14] (Job. 18:6).
      [The leaping referred to by the verb *dā'ak*] refers to the man-

ner of the flame, which separates itself from the wick and ascends upward when it is extinguished.[15]

13   YOU, my enemy, Esau,[16] PRESSED ME HARD.

14   THE STRENGTH AND THE MIGHT OF THE LORD, AND IT BECAME VINDICATION FOR ME.

[The form] '*ōzî* 'THE STRENGTH' [contains] superfluous final *yod*, for we find '*zy* vocalized with a *ḥaṭēp-qāmeṣ* [i.e., short *o*] rather than *šûrûq (û)* only in three places in the Bible where it is written juxtaposed with *wĕzimrat* 'THE MIGHT' (Ex. 15:2; Isa. 12:1; Ps. 118:14). Unquestionably, *wĕzimrat* is the *nomen regens* of the divine name [YAH, i.e., THE LORD], and you may not interpret it as though it were "and my *zimrāh*."[17] Now do not be surprised by [the construction] *wayehî lî liyšû'āh* 'AND IT BECAME VINDICATION FOR ME' [in which the predicate is separated from the subject by the conjunction 'AND' and] that he [the psalmist] did not say *hāyāh lî liyšû'āh* 'became VINDICATION FOR ME', for there are many [constructions] like these in the Bible [such as] "And he paid no heed to the word of the LORD, and he abandoned [*wayya'ăzōb*] his slaves and his livestock in the field" (Ex. 9:21). [There instead of writing 'and he abandoned'] He [the divine author of Exodus] could have written, 'he abandoned' ['*āzab*].[18]

15a THE JOYOUS SHOUTS OF DELIVERANCE will be in the future[19] IN THE TENTS OF THE RIGHTEOUS. Now what is the JOYOUS SHOUT OF DELIVERANCE?

15b [It is] "THE RIGHT HAND OF THE LORD IS TRIUMPHANT."

16a They will shout, "THE RIGHT HAND OF THE LORD IS EXALTED."[20]

17   I, the Congregation of Israel, SHALL NOT DIE a permanent death like the rest of the nations, BUT I SHALL LIVE....[21]

18   PUNISHED ME SEVERELY in Exile, and there all my iniquities were expiated, BUT HE DID NOT HAND ME OVER TO DEATH.

19   OPEN THE GATES OF RIGHTEOUSNESS FOR ME. Now these are THE GATES OF RIGHTEOUSNESS:

20   THE GATEWAY of the Temple, which is TO THE

LORD. THE RIGHTEOUS SHALL ENTER
THROUGH IT, and there

21   I SHALL PRAISE YOU, FOR YOU HAVE ANSWERED
ME from Exile.

22   THE STONE THAT THE BUILDERS REJECTED is [a
metaphor for] a people that was lowly among the nations.

23   "THIS IS THE LORD'S DOING." So shall all say.

PSALM CXVIII:5-25—INTERPRETATION A, NOTES

[1] In our Rashi ms. Ps. 118:5-25 is counted as Ps. 117; see the discussion at Ps. 117, n. 1. With *BHS* at Ps. 118:5 and at Ps. 118:26 note that the treatment of Ps. 118:25 as a composition distinct from Ps. 118:1-4 and from Ps. 118:26-29 as in our Rashi ms. is found also in many other medieval Bible mss. Note, however, that Rashi's comment at Ps. 118:17 in PSALM 118 INTERPRETATION B, below, demonstrates that for him Ps. 118:17 and vv. 26-29 belong to a single composition.

[2] Cf. Rashi's comment at Ps. 72:20; 78:47.

[3] Cf. the use of the verb *ḥāsāh* in Judg. 9:15.

[4] By calling attention to the primary meanings of the two verbs *ḥsh* and *bṭḥ*, Rashi emphasizes that our verse is hyperbolic. As an hyperbolic proverb the verse has the typical hyperbolic proverb formula well-known in both Biblical and Rabbinic literature: *ṭôb 'x" m'y"* "better is 'x' than 'y'"; on this type of proverb see Graham S. Ogden, "The 'Better'-Proverb (Tôb-Spruch), Rhetorical Criticism, and Qoheleth," *JBL* 96 (1977), pp. 489-505 and the literature cited there.

[5] See Ps. 2, n. 4.

[6] For equation of the war spoken of in Zech. 14 with the eschatological war associated with the names of Gog and Magog in Ezek. 38-39 see BT Megillah 31a and Rashi there.

[7] Marginal note in NJV: "Meaning of *'amilam* in this and the following two verses uncertain."

[8] Heb. *'akrîtām*; see *Mahberet Menahem*, p. 240, s.v., *ml* I.

[9] Cf. KJV: "...it is cut down, and withereth"; contrast NJV.

[10] The subject of our verb; whatever that subject may be.

[11] Heb. *nōpēl 'al*; see the discussion in our introduction, p. 138, n. 9.

[12] Cf. NJV: "They disappear where they are."

[13] MT reads *niz'ākû*; Rashi and most other interpreters treat the latter *hapax legomenon* as a cognate of the verb under discussion here.

[14] This rendering is required by Rashi's interpretation; if *dā'ak* means literally 'be extinguished, go out', then Job. 18:6 should be rendered, "His lamp, which is over him, goes out."

[15] Banitt, *Rashi: Interpreter of the Biblical Letter*, pp. 14, 39 shows that Rashi treats Heb. *dā'ak* as the semantic equivalent of O.F. *terzalier*, which is, as pointed out by Banitt, there, p. 39, "a metathetic compound" of two distinct verbs, *tresaler* 'pass over' and *tressaillir* 'jump up, get over'. Such an

approach made it unnecessary for Rashi to assume two homonymous roots d^ck.

[16] The interpolations, "my enemy, Esau," constitute Rashi's response to the exegetical question, "To whom does the psalmist address himself in v. 13?"; for a variety of possible answers including Esau see Midrash Tehillim here.

[17] The latter interpretation is accepted by KJV and NJV; with Maarsen note that Rashi here briefly summarizes his lengthy explanation given in his commentary at Ex. 15:2.

[18] On the interchangeability of the forms in question in Biblical Heb. see, *inter alia*, Anson F. Rainey, "The Ancient Hebrew Prefix Conjugation in the Light of Amarna Canaanite," *Hebrew Studies* 27 (1986), pp. 4-19.

[19] Usually, a nominal sentence is assumed to refer to present time; since v. 15 describes a time of joy at variance with the present state of affairs described in vv. 5-14, Rashi suggests that v. 15 refers to the future.

[20] Thus Rashi intimates that vv. 15b-16 constitute a quotation.

[21] While Christians argue that Jews and other non-Christians experience permanent death unless they accept Jesus as their savior (see, e.g., NT Romans 8), Rashi here argues that it is the Jews, who by adhering to their ancestral faith overcome death and find immortality.

PSALM CXVIII—INTERPRETATION B[1]

17   One ought to interpret the entire psalm from "I SHALL NOT DIE BUT LIVE" with reference to David himself.

18a   [Thus]: THE LORD PUNISHED ME SEVERELY for the Bathsheba affair with punishments such as "He shall pay for the lamb four times over" (2 Sam. 12:6). In fact, David suffered from leprosy for six months.[2]

18b   BUT HE DID NOT HAND ME OVER TO DEATH is in accord with what is stated in the Bible, "The LORD has remitted your sin; you shall not die" (2 Sam. 12:13).

19   OPEN THE GATES OF RIGHTEOUSNESS FOR ME. Now what are 'THE GATES OF RIGHTEOUSNESS'? [They are] the gates of synagogues and houses of study, which are 'THE LORD'S' (v. 20a) and through which THE RIGHTEOUS enter (cf. v. 20b)

21   I PRAISE YOU, FOR YOU HAVE ANSWERED ME. From here on [vv. 21-29] David, Samuel, Jesse, and David's brothers [each composed [their respective verses] as it is explained in [the tenth chapter of BT Pesaḥim, which is called after its opening words] "Eves of Passovers".[3] Whoever composed one [of the verses in question] did not compose another.

Psalm CXVIII—Interpretation B, Notes

[1] This comment of Rashi on Ps. 118:17-29, which is treated in our Rashi ms. as part of Rashi's comment on Ps. 118:26-29, proves that Rashi did not recognize Ps. 118:26 as the beginning of distinct composition as did the scribe responsible for our Rashi ms.; see below, Ps. 118:26-29, n. 1.

[2] BT Yoma 22b.

[3] Rashi refers to the interpretation attributed to R. Samuel b. Nahmani, quoting R. Johanan in BT Pesaḥim 119a, q.v. According to this interpretation, David composed v. 21; Jesse v. 22; David's brothers v. 23; Samuel v. 24; David's brothers v. 25a; David v. 25b; Jesse v. 26a; Samuel v. 26b; all of them v. 27a-b; Samuel v. 27c; David v. 28a; all of them v. 28b.

PSALM CXVIII: 26-29[1]

26a MAY HE WHO ENTERS BE BLESSED IN THE NAME
OF THE LORD.
They shall say this to those who present first fruits and to
those who come to Jerusalem on festival pilgrimages.[2]

26b *bēraknûkem* 'WE BLESS YOU' [i.e.], *bēraknû 'etĕkem* 'we bless
you'.[3]

27c TIE UP THE FESTAL OFFERING. As for the [animals
for] sacrifices and festival offerings, which they used to buy
and inspect for blemishes, they would tie [them] to the legs
of their beds UNTIL they could bring them into the Temple
court to the HORNS OF THE ALTAR.[4]

PSALM CXVIII: 26-29, NOTES

[1] Our Rashi ms., like many other medieval Heb. Bible mss. (see *BHS*
at Ps. 118:26), treats Ps. 118:26-29 as a distinct psalm, which is numbered
Ps. 118 (see above at Ps. 117, n. 1; Ps. 118:5-25, n. 1). Consequently, the
numbering of the psalms from Ps. 118:26 through Ps. 134 follows the
numbering found in standard Jewish and Protestant Bibles. Note that in
Jewish liturgy Ps. 118:26-29 is treated as a distinct unit. It is recited by
each worshipper silently, and each verse is repeated twice; see Birnbaum,
Daily Prayer Book, p. 573.

[2] With Zohory cf. Midrash Tehillim here and BT Hagigah 26b.

[3] Apparently Rashi assumes that verbal forms with both subject and
object suffixes might be incomprehensible to his readers; Rashi's explanation corresponds to the reading in 4QPs[b].

[4] With Zohory cf. PRK, ed. Mandelbaum, p. 106. Note that Rashi's
comment is a response to two exegetical questions: (1) To what is one to
BIND THE FESTAL OFFERING? (2) What is the meaning of the preposition *'ad* in v. 27c? According to NJV, the latter preposition means 'to',
and the 'binding' is "to the horns of the altar."

PSALM CXIX

1   PRAISEWORTHY ARE THOSE WHO ARE BLAME-
         LESS WITH RESPECT TO BEHAVIOR.[1]

3a   THEY HAVE DONE NO WRONG. Praiseworthy[2] are the
         righteous if all this [behavior described in vv. 1-2] is [found]
         in them.[3]

3b   BUT HAVE FOLLOWED HIS WAYS. Even though
         THEY HAVE DONE NO WRONG (v. 3), their praisewor-
         thiness [*šibḥām*][4] is not complete unless they HAVE FOL-
         LOWED HIS WAYS. Similarly, Scripture says, "Shun evil
         and do good" (Ps. 34:15). [I.e.], even though you shun evil,
         all is not complete unless you do good. [This comment is a]
         midrash aggadah.[5]

5a   *'aḥălay* THAT MY WAYS WERE FIRM. [In the word]
         'aḥălay[6] [the initial] *'aleph* is a formative letter[7] in the word
         which from time to time drops out[8] like the [initial] *'aleph*
         which is in [the noun *'aḥăwātî* 'my declaration' in] "...my
         declaration is in your ears" (Job. 13:17)[9] and the [initial]
         'aleph of [the noun *'āsûk* ' jug' in] "jug of oil" (2 Kgs. 4:2).[10]
         [Hence] *'aḥălay* [means] *tĕpillôtay* 'my prayers', [and the
         clause as a whole means] "These [my prayers] are 'THAT
         MY WAYS WERE FIRM.'"[11] The same word is found in
         "my lord's requests before the prophet" (2 Kgs. 5:3)[12] [i.e.],
         "my lord's need is to pray that he may come before the
         prophet, who is in Samaria." The meaning of [Heb.] *'aḥlîyôt*
         'wishes'[13] is *suhet*[14] 'wish' in Old French, like that of a person
         who says, "Would that I were rich; would that I were wise."

11   IN MY HEART I HID.[15] I did not let it leave [MY
         HEART] to be forgotten by me.

16   I TAKE DELIGHT[16] [i.e.], I occupy myself.[17] [The verb
         'eśta'ăśā' 'I TAKE DELIGHT'] is from the same root as[18]
         [the verb in] "A man will busy himself [*yiś'eh*] with his
         Maker" (Isa. 17:7) and "Let them not busy themselves [*wĕ'al-
         yiś'û*] with false promises" (Ex. 5:9).[19]

17a   GRANT YOUR SERVANT something[20]

17b   so THAT I MAY LIVE by means of it. [I.e.], GRANT Your
         kindness.[21]

18b   WONDERS FROM YOUR TORAH [i.e., things], which are not explicitly stated therein.

19a   I AM ONLY A SOJOURNER IN THE LAND. [I.e.]. The days of my life are few.

19b   DO NOT HIDE FROM ME the wonders of YOUR COMMANDMENTS, which are hidden lest I be unable to fulfill them.

18b   WONDERS FROM YOUR TORAH [i.e., things], which are not explicitly stated therein.[22]

20   MY SOUL IS CONSUMED. My soul breaks apart because of desire [ta'ǎwāh].[23] [The verb gārĕsāh 'she is consumed'] is a cognate of [the noun geres 'grits' in the phrase] gereś karmel "grits of the fresh ear" (Lev. 2:14) and [in the phrase] "some of the grits and oil" (Lev. 2:16). Menahem (b. Jacob Ibn Saruq) treated the expression lĕta'ǎbāh [24] as a cognate of [the participle mĕtā'ēb 'destroying' in] "I [shall] destroy the Pride of Jacob" (Am. 6: 8).[25] Both of these [the expression lĕta'ǎbāh and the participle mĕtā'ēb] refer to[26] destruction [šeber].[27]

22   TAKE AWAY[28] FROM ME. [The verb gōl 'TAKE AWAY'] refers to[26] gilgûl 'rolling away' as is exemplified by [the verb wayyāgel 'he rolled away' in Gen. 29:10], "He rolled away the stone."

23   ...SPEAK AGAINST ME. [YOUR SERVANT STUDIES YOUR LAWS].[29] [The meaning of this apparent non sequitur is that] even though[30] the kings of the Gentiles[31] mock me because I am occupied with the Torah,

24   [...YOUR DECREES ARE][29] MY DELIGHT [i.e.], my occupation.

25   REVIVE ME IN ACCORDANCE WITH YOUR WORD. Just as You promised me [32] kindness through Nathan the prophet.[33]

26   I HAVE DECLARED to You MY WAY [i.e.] my needs and my sins,[34] with respect to which You have responded to me.[35]

28   MY SOUL MELTS [dālĕpāh] [i.e.], 'drips',[36] i.e., it disappears gradually.[37]

33   I WILL OBSERVE THEM 'ēqeb.[38]
       I shall watch it[39] in all of its paths and in the footsteps of its tracks. The meaning of 'ǎqēbîm 'footprints, traces' is treces in OF.[40]

38a FULFILL YOUR PROMISE ['*imrātĕkā*, lit., 'your speech'], which You promised[41] TO YOUR SERVANT.

38b WHICH IS FOR THOSE WHO WORSHIP YOU. [I.e., Fulfill Your promise] so that I and my progeny will be reverers of Your Name, for it was on this condition that You promised me, "If your descendants will watch their behavior...[there shall never cease to be one of your people on the throne of Israel]" (1 Kgs. 2:4).[42]

39a REMOVE THE TAUNT. Pardon me for that sin [with Bathsheba][43] so that my enemies will no longer be able to taunt me with it.

39b FOR YOUR RULES ARE GOOD, and I already take it upon myself to make fourfold compensation for the [proverbial] ewe (cf. 2 Sam. 12:6).[44]

41b MAY...YOUR DELIVERANCE reach me[45]

41c LIKE YOUR PROMISE [*kĕ'imrātĕkā*, lit., 'like Your speech'], which You promised.[46]

43a DO NOT UTTERLY TAKE THE TRUTH AWAY FROM MY MOUTH. [I.e.], Do not separate THE TRUTH FROM MY MOUTH. [The verb *taṣṣēl* 'You will take away'] is from the same root as[47] [the verb *wayyaṣṣēl* 'He took away' in Gen. 31:9], "God took away your father's livestock...."

43b *yiḥāltî* 'I PUT MY HOPE' [means] *qiwwîtî* 'I hoped'.[48]

45a I WILL WALK ABOUT AT EASE [i.e.], in *halakah*[49] [which is] spread among Israel.[50]

45b I TURNED TO [*dārastî*] [i.e.], 'I sought' [*biqqaštî*] [51]

49 REMEMBER YOUR WORD, which You promised[52] through the prophet Nathan TO YOUR SERVANT.

52a [I REMEMBER] YOUR RULES OF OLD, that You inflict punishments but turn from Your anger and forgive,[53]

52b AND therefore I FIND COMFORT IN THEM.

54 IN THE HOUSE OF MY FEAR [i.e.], IN THE HOUSE of my anxiety. [The noun *mĕgûrāy* 'MY FEAR' is a biform of the noun *māgôr* 'terror' attested in] "terror on every side" (Jer. 5:25) [and of the verb *wayyagor* 'he was alarmed' in] "Moab was alarmed" (Num. 22:3).

55 I REMEMBERED AT NIGHT [i.e.], in time of trouble and tribulation.[54]

56   THIS HAS BEEN FOR ME a crown which fit me, a testimony FOR ME and for [those of] my progeny who [will be] fit to rule as a reward FOR the fact that I HAVE OBSERVED YOUR PRECEPTS
So did the Sages of Israel explain it (in BT 'Avodah Zarah 44a).[55]

59a   I HAVE CONSIDERED MY WAYS. [I.e.], I considered the loss to be incurred through observing a commandment against its reward and the reward of transgression against the loss to be incurred thereby.[56] Therefore,

59b   I HAVE TURNED BACK TO YOUR DECREES, for I saw that it is the best [way] of them all.

61a   BANDS OF WICKED PEOPLE PREYED UPON ME. [I.e.], Groups[7]
of wicked people despoiled me. [The verb ʽiwwĕdûnî 'PREYED UPON ME'] is a cognate of [the noun ʽad 'prey' in Gen. 49:27], yōʼkal ʽad "He devours prey."[58] Thus did Menahem construe it,[59] but it is preferable to explain it as a cognate of ʽôd 'in addition' as in ʽôd zeh mĕdabbēr "There came in addition this narrator" (Job. 1:16, 17), which is to say that [ʽiwwĕdûnî means] "They came in addition, and they became more numerous than me."

67a   BEFORE I DECLAIMED.[60] BY MEANS OF YOUR COMMANDMENTS (v. 66) [i.e.], before I recited them[61] in the study houses I WENT ASTRAY, with respect to them, i.e., I sinned.

67b   BUT NOW that I have been HUMBLED[62] with respect to them I KEEP Your Torah,[63] for the study of Torah [hammidraš] teaches me to turn away from sin. Therefore I request of You,[64]

66   TEACH ME GOOD SENSE AND KNOWLEDGE.

67   [The verb ʼeʽĕneh 'I DECLAIMED' in] 'BEFORE I DECLAIMED' is a verb referring to reciting and studying in the Study House. It is from the same root as [the verb taʽan 'she shall declare' in Ps. 119:172], "My tongue shall declare Your promise," and also [the participle ʽôneh 'reciter' in Mal. 2:12], "May the LORD cut off from the man who does it alert [ʽēr] and reciter [ʽôneh] from the tents of Jacob..." [which means], alert among the sages and reciter among the disciples.[65]

69 ACCUSED ME [*tāpĕlû*] FALSELY. [I.e.], they fabricated CONCERNING ME FALSELY, and from the same root is "And You would fabricate [*wattiṭpol*] concerning my guilt" (Job. 14:17).[66]

71a IT WAS GOOD FOR ME THAT I WAS HUMBLED.... It was GOOD in my eyes when I was enduring sufferings, i.e., I WAS HUMBLED

71b SO THAT I might turn away from evil behavior and that I might observe YOUR LAWS.

74 THOSE WHO FEAR YOU WILL SEE ME favorably, AND THEY WILL REJOICE, for their reward will be like my reward, for after all I am one of THOSE WHO FEAR YOU, and "I hope for Your word" (Ps. 119:81).

75 RIGHTLY HAVE YOU HUMBLED ME. [I.e.], justly HAVE YOU HUMBLED ME.

78 ...FOR THEY HAVE WRONGED ME WITHOUT CAUSE. [I.e.], For no reason they accused me.

81 *kālĕtāh* 'USED UP' it ['*ōtāh*].[67]

82 MY EYES WERE USED UP. They were gazing continually until they were used up.[68]

83 LIKE A WATER-SKIN DRIED IN SMOKE. Like a leather bag, which dries up as a result of smoke.

86 THEY PERSECUTED ME WITHOUT CAUSE. [I.e.], For no reason [*laššāwĕ*][69] my enemies PERSECUTED ME.

96 FOR EVERY COMPLETION [i.e.] for the conclusion of everything there is a TERMINUS [*qēṣ*] and a boundary, but with respect to Your commandments there is no TERMINUS or boundary for their completion.

99a FROM ALL MY TEACHERS I GAINED INSIGHT.[70] From each one I have learned a little.

99b CONVERSATION FOR ME. All my conversation was about them.[71]

101 I KEPT [*kālī'tî*] MY FEET. [I.e.], I withheld. [The verb *kālī'tî* 'I KEPT' is] a cognate of [the verb in 1 Sam. 25:33], "Today You kept me [*kĕlitinî*] from incurring blood guilt."[72]

103 PLEASING [*nimlĕṣû*] [i.e.], *nimtĕqû* 'were sweet'[73]

105 YOUR WORD IS A LAMP TO MY FEET. When I am about to render a decision in ritual law, I look into Your Torah, and it keeps me away from what is forbidden just as a lighted lamp saves a person from pitfalls.[74]

107a   *naʿănêtî* 'I AM AFFLICTED' [means] 'I became humble ['*ānî*] and meek'. It is the same root as is reflected in [the verb *wĕʾānāh* 'be humbled' in Hos. 5:5], "Israel's arrogance shall be humbled before Him," the Aramaic Targum [of which] is *wĕyimʾak* 'it shall be lowered';[75] and it is the same root as is reflected in [the infinitive *lēʿănôt* 'to humble oneself' in Ex. 10:3], "to humble yourself before Me." Now "a humble person ['*ānî*] is regarded as dead."[76] Therefore,

107b   REVIVE ME IN ACCORDANCE WITH YOUR WORD.

108   MY MOUTH'S FREEWILL OFFERINGS [i.e.], the words of appeasement, which my mouth bestows upon You. Every cognate of the word *nĕdābāh* 'freewill offering' is an expression referring to appeasement.

109a   MY LIFE IS ALWAYS IN MY PALMS. [I.e.], Many times I was exposed to dangers, in many dangers close to dying,

109b   AND nevertheless,[77] I DO NOT NEGLECT YOUR TEACHING.

112   TO THE UTMOST [*ēqeb*] FOREVER. [I.e.], on their paths and on their trails.[78]

113   I HATE MEN OF DIVIDED HEART [*sēʿăpîm*]. [The latter means] 'those who think evil thoughts'. It is derived from the same root as [the noun *sēʿippay* 'my thoughts' in Job. 20:2], "In truth, my thoughts urge me to answer,"[79] and [the noun *sēʿippîm* 'opinions' in 1 Kgs. 18:21], "between two opinions."[80] Now when you vocalize *sēʿippîm*, it is the noun denoting 'thought', but when you vocalize *sēʿăpîm*, [81] it refers to 'those who think it' [the thought].

117b   AND I WILL MUSE UPON YOUR LAWS. [The verb *wĕʾeśʿāh*] is a cognate of [the verb in Ex. 5:9], "Let them not pay attention to deceitful promises."[82] An equally plausible exegesis is that [the verb] *wĕʾeśʿāh* 'AND I WILL MUSE' refers to telling and repeating as is reflected in our rendering [the noun *wĕlišnînāh* 'and for a byword' in] "for a proverb and for a byword" (Deut. 28:37) by Aramaic *ûlĕšôʿîn* 'and for a byword'.[83]

118   *sālîtā* 'YOU WALK OVER'. [I.e.], 'You trampled'; [i.e.], You made them into a trampling-place. It is the same verb as is attested in "He walked over [*sillāh*] all my heroes" (Lam. 1:15).[84]

120a [The verb] *sāmar* is a cognate of [the verb *tĕsammēr* 'causes to stand up' in Job. 4:15], "It [the wind in Job. 4:15a][85] makes the hair of my flesh stand up."[86] The verb refers to a person whose hairs stood up, [which is called] *harizer* in O.F.[87]

120b I AM IN AWE OF YOUR RULINGS [i.e.], of the punishments arising from your verdicts.[88]

122a GUARANTEE [*'ărob*] YOUR DEVOTEE. [The verb *'ărob*] refers to saving;[89] [it means] *garantis* in O.F.[90] [The verse means] "Be a guarantor for me against evil."

123 FOR YOUR PROMISE OF VICTORY [*lĕ'imrat ṣidqekā*, lit., 'Your word of vindication'] [i.e.], the promise which You promised me.[91]

126a IT IS A TIME TO ACT FOR THE LORD.... This verse is a continuation of the immediately preceding verse [in which the psalmist asks], GIVE ME UNDERSTANDING THAT I MIGHT KNOW YOUR DECREES to understand what is a TIME TO ACT for Your sake.[92]

126b so that[93] those who HAVE VIOLATED YOUR TEACHING may act in order to find favor and forgiveness. Find (it) for them, and let me do (it) also for all my sins.[94] Our rabbis, however, deduced from it[95] that it is proper to transgress God's laws[96] in order to make a hedge and a fence for Israel as is exemplified by Gideon (Judg. 6:24-32) and by Elijah at Mt. Carmel (1 Kgs. 18), who sacrificed at high places.[97] In addition, I have seen it [Ps. 119:126] explained in the *aggadah* [as follows]: "Whoever does his Torah [study] at appointed times violates the covenant, for a person is supposed to be toiling in the [study of] Torah all the hours of the day."[98]

127 RIGHTLY [*'al-kēn*] DO I LOVE.... [I.e.], Because [*'al-'ăšēr*] I LOVE YOUR COMMANDMENTS it is proper that You teach me what I should do "at a favorable moment" (Ps. 69:14) so that "You will receive me favorably" (Gen. 33:10). There are many [attestations of the expression] *'al-kēn* [which elsewhere means 'therefore'],[99] whose meaning is 'because' [*'al-'ăšēr*]. Examples include "For because seeing your face" (Gen. 33:10); "For because you know where we should camp in the wilderness" (Num. 10:31); "because of the gain he made" they perish[100] (Isa. 15:7).[101]

128   I DECLARE ALL YOUR PRECEPTS TO BE JUST.[102] ALL PRECEPTS [i.e.], everything, which You have commanded in Your Torah, I DECLARE TO BE JUST. [I.e.], they [God's precepts] are just in my eyes, and I said of them that they are just. For this I am worthy that You should show me favor and that You should pardon me..

129a YOUR DECREES ARE WONDROUS. [I.e.], YOUR DECREES ARE hidden from and wondrous for people [which refers to the fact that] there are easy precepts, the reward for [the observance of] which You have made large such as [the precept of] sending away [the mother bird from] the nest [when collecting the eggs] (Deut. 22:6-7).[103]

129b RIGHTLY DO I OBSERVE THEM—all of them, for it has not been made known "which will prosper" (Eccl. 11:6).[104]

130a THE OPENING [pētaḥ] OF YOUR WORDS ENLIGHTENS [i.e.], the beginning of Your words enlightened the heart of Israel, for You are He who does

130b GRANT UNDERSTANDING TO THE SIMPLE. When You said, "I the the LORD am your God who brought you out [of the land of Egypt]"[105] (Ex. 20:2), You made known to them the kindness You had done for them when You ransomed them "from the house of bondage" (Ex. 20:2) so that they should know that You are their Sovereign so that they would accept Your sovereignty and Your divinity. Afterwards, You made Your divinity singular for them [when You said], "You shall have no [other gods besides Me]" (Ex. 20:3).[105] Afterwards, You decreed Your decrees [in the remaining eight commandments of the decalogue]. An equally plausible midrash [based on the same literal interpretation of pētaḥ as 'opening, beginning' reads as follows]: THE OPENING OF YOUR WORDS ENLIGHTENS [refers to] the beginning of Your words in the Creation, "Let there be light" (Gen. 1:3) [while the juxtaposition in Ps. 119:130 of this reference to Gen. 1:3 with the words] GRANTS UNDERSTANDING TO THE SIMPLE [teaches us that] from there [Gen. 1:3] they will understand everything, and they will open up [yiptĕḥû, a cognate of the noun pētaḥ] words of Torah. [This last midrash is found in] Tanḥuma.[106]

131   wā'eš'āpāh 'I PANT' is a verb denoting 'swallowing'.[107] It

comes from the same root as [the verb *šā'ăpāh* 'she swallowed' in Jer. 2:24], "She swallows the wind...."

134 REDEEM ME FROM BEING WRONGED BY MAN [i.e.], from the evil inclination, which perverts [*hā'ôšēq*] people from the proper path.[108]

139 I AM CONSUMED WITH MY RAGE [*qin'ātî*]. The zealousness [*haqqin'āh*], with which I am zealous for your Name because of those who forget your words CONSUMES me as it makes me angry at them.

148a EACH WATCH.[109] [The end of the first] half of the night is [the same as the end of] two watches.[110] According, however, to him who opines that it [the end of the first half of the night] is three watches,[111] you must say, "At night David used to get out of his bed at the [end of the] first third of the night, and he would busy himself with [the study of] the Torah until midnight in accordance with what is stated [here in Ps. 119:148b], AS I MEDITATE ON YOUR PROMISE. From midnight onward he used to busy himself with songs and praises in accordance with what is stated (in Ps. 119:62), "I arise at midnight to praise You."[112]

149b PRESERVE ME, AS IS YOUR RULE by means of Your Torah and by means of Your commandments, which guide[113] the days of my life.

150 THOSE WHO PURSUE INTRIGUE DRAW NEAR. [This verse speaks about] a sinners' council following the counsel of their sins and drawing far away from Your Torah to draw near to the counsel of their sins.[114]

151 YOU, O LORD, ARE NEAR to these far-away people who draw far away from Your Torah. [I.e., YOU ARE NEAR] if they turn away from their [evil] way.[115]

152a I KNOW FROM YOUR TESTIMONIES [*mĕ'ēdōtêkā*] OF OLD [*qedem*]. [I.e.], before [*qodem*] the event happened I knew it from YOUR TESTIMONIES [*mĕ'ēdōtêkā*]: [E.g.], before they [the people of Israel] inherited the land [of Israel], You commanded them concerning the first fruits, heave-offerings, and tithes, and before You gave them rest from their enemies, You commanded them, "When the LORD gives you rest..." (Deut. 25:19), to install a king, to wipe out Amalek, and to build the Temple.[116]

152b THAT YOU HAVE ESTABLISHED THEM FOREVER

[*lĕ'ôlām*]. THAT on the basis of things which are yet to be at the end of the world [*lĕsôp hā'ôlām*][117] YOU HAVE ESTAB-LISHED (v. 152b) YOUR DECREES (v. 152a).[118]

160   THE BEGINNING OF YOUR WORD IS TRUTH. The latter part of Your word proved concerning the beginning [thereof] that it is TRUTH, for when the Gentiles heard, "I [the LORD am Your God...]; You shall have [no other gods besides Me]; You shall not swear [falsely]..." (Ex. 20:2-7), they said, "It is all for His benefit and for His honor." When, however, they heard, "Honor [your father and your mother]; You shall not murder; You shall not commit adul-tery..." (Ex. 20:12ff.) they acknowledged concerning THE BEGINNING OF YOUR WORD that it is TRUTH.[119]

162   I REJOICE OVER YOUR PROMISE [*'imrātĕkā*] [i.e.], over Your promise [*habtāḥātĕkā*], which You promised me.[120] Another equally plausible interpretation [of the literal mean-ing] of '*al 'imrātĕkā* 'CONCERNING YOUR UTTER-ANCE' is, "[I REJOICE] concerning one of Your enigmatic utterances [*'imrôtêkā*] when I understand it." Our rabbis in-terpreted it as a reference to circumcision: When David was in the bathhouse and saw himself without fringes (see Num. 15:37-41) and without *tefillin*[121] and without [a scroll of the] Torah, he said, "Woe unto me that I am naked of all pre-cepts." When, however, he glanced at his circumcision, he rejoiced, and when he exited he said, "I REJOICE OVER circumcision,[122] which was originally given with a form of the verb '*saying*' and not with a form of the verb '*speaking*' as it is stated (in Gen. 17:9), 'God said [*wayyō'mer*] to Abraham, "As for You, keep My covenant."'"[123]

164a SEVEN TIMES EACH DAY. In the Morning Service [I re-cite] two benedictions[124] before the 'Reading of the Shema'[125] and one after it,[126] and in the Evening Service [I recite] two [benedictions] before it[127] and two after it.[128]

164b FOR YOUR JUST RULES [i.e.], over the 'Reading of the Shema', which is *dibrê tôrāh* 'laws of Torah'.[129]

166   I HOPE [*śibbartî*] [i.e.], *hoḥaltî* 'I WAIT'.

168b ALL MY WAYS [*kol-dĕrākay*] ARE BEFORE YOU. [I.e.], You know all my behavior [*kol-dĕrākay*].

169b GRANT ME UNDERSTANDING ACCORDING TO YOUR WORD. [I.e.], GRANT ME UNDERSTANDING

of the laws of Your Torah[130] according to their meaning in
halakah and according to their literal meaning.

171   SHALL POUR FORTH PRAISE. [I.e.], they will speak.
172   MY TONGUE SHALL DECLARE [*ta'an*]. Every [attesta-
tion of the root whose gerund is] *'ăniyyāh* 'declaring' is an expression referring to a loud voice.[131]

PSALM CXIX, NOTES
   [1] Rendering of v. 1, which serves in our Rashi ms. as the title of Ps.
119, according to the understanding presupposed by Rashi's comment on
v. 3; Rashi's commentary on this psalm begins with v. 3.
   [2] Translation of *'aśrê* based upon Rashi's understanding of *'aśrê* at Ps.
1:1; q.v.
   [3] Here Rashi intimates that he construes all of vv. 2-3a as a single
nominal sentence of which the word *'aśrê* 'praiseworthy' is the subject, and
everything else is the compound predicate.
   [4] This remark supports our contention that Rashi here at Ps. 119:1 as
at Ps. 1:1 interprets *'aśrê* to mean 'praiseworthy'.
   [5] Cf. the saying attributed to R. Ze'era at Midrash Tehillim 1:7.
   [6] NJV and other English translations follow LXX and Vulgate in interpreting Heb. *'ahălay* as an interjection 'would that'. Rashi follows
Menahem and anticipates Ehrlich, *Mikra ki-Pheschuto*, 2:343 at 2 Kgs. 5:3
in construing *'ahălay* here as a noun + pronominal suffix meaning 'my
prayer'; see *Mahberet Menahem*, p. 36; the view that *'ahălay* is a noun meaning 'my prayer' is shared by Ibn Janah, *Sepher Haschoraschim*, p. 22; Ibn
Ezra in his commentary on Ps. 119:5 and in his commentary on 2 Kgs.
5:3. Qimhi follows Rashi and Menahem in interpreting *'ahălay* as a noun
meaning 'my prayer(s)', but, like Rashi at 2 Kgs. 5:3, he accepts the view,
which Menahem specifically rejects, that *'ahălay* is a cognate of the verb
wayĕhal in the expression *wayĕhal Mošeh* 'Moses beseeched' in Ex. 32:11.
Menahem points out correctly that it is not the verb *hillāh*, which means
'beseech' but the idiom *hillāh pĕnê*, which means 'beseech'. Umberto
Cassuto, "Daniel e le spighe: Un episodio della tavola I D di Ras
Shamra," *Orientalia*, n.s., 8 (1939), pp. 238-243 took for granted that Heb.
'ahălay is an interjection meaning 'would that', and he assumed that this is
the meaning of Ugar. *'ahl* in I D (*CTA* 19 II= *KTU* 1.19), lines 64 and 71.
Subsequently, Dahood here and *K-B³*, p. 33b find in Ugar. *'hl* support for
the interpretation of Heb. *'ahălay* as an interjection. However, the interpretation of Ugar. *'hl* as an interjection requires translators of the lines in
question to supply in brackets a missing *verbum dicendi*. See translations of
Gaster and Driver; and cf. Ginsberg's and Coogan's treatment of the
words following *'hl* as quotations. *Mirabile dictu*, the missing verb in the
two Ugaritic lines should have the same precise meaning in its context as
the Medieval Heb. verb *'hl*, which is the most likely etymon of Biblical
Heb. *'ahălay* 'wish, entreaty'. Moreover, Ugar. *'hl* lends itself to being interpreted as a 3[d] pers. sing. of the perfect of a root *'hl*, which would be

vocalized *'aḥala* and rendered 'he asked'; contrast Baruch Margalit, *The Ugaritic Poem of Aqhat* (Berlin & New York: Walter de Gruyter, 1989), pp. 392-393. Concerning Medieval Heb. *'ḥl* 'beseech' and the Modern Heb. development from it of *'iḥēl* 'wish someone (well)' see Ben Yehuda, *Dict.*, vol. 1, p. 151.

[7] Heb. *yĕsôd*. Englander, in his "Grammatical Elements and Terminology in Rashi's Biblical Commentaries, pt. I," pp. 371-383 demonstrates that throughout Rashi's Bible commentaries *yĕsôd nōpēl* means 'non-root letter' and that *yĕsôd*, which scholars had previously misunderstood to mean 'root letter' means 'formative letter', i.e., a grammatically significant consonant, which is neither a root letter nor a preposition nor a pronominal prefix or suffix. On Rashi's terms for 'root letter' see above at Ps. 42:6.

[8] Englander in his "Grammatical Elements and Terminology in Rashi's Biblical Commentaries, Pt. I," pp. 371-383 shows (1) that Rashi believes in biconsonantal and uniconsonantal roots; and (2) that Rashi holds that no consonant, which drops out in any form of the word can belong to the root. Hence, a letter which is neither a preposition nor a pronominal suffix or prefix but which is found in all forms of the root is called variously *yĕsôd nōpēl battêbāh* 'a dropping-out formative letter in the word' (Rashi on Ps. 39:11), *yĕsôd nōpēl* 'dropping-out formative letter' (Rashi on Isa. 11:8), or, as here, "a formative consonant in the word, which from time to time drops out from it".

[9] According to *BDB*, p. 296a *'aḥăwāh* 'declaration', attested only in Job. 13:17, is a noun derived from the verb *ḥiwwāh* 'tell, declare'.

[10] According to *BDB*, p. 692 *'āsûk* 'jug' is a noun derived from the verb *sāk* (root *swk)* 'pour, annoint'.

[11] Rashi here construes v. 5a as a nominal sentence whose subject is *'aḥălay* 'my prayers' and whose predicate is the noun clause *yikkonû dĕrākāy* 'WOULD THAT MY WAYS WERE FIRM', whose verb is a jussive; the 3[d] pers. fem. pl. pronoun *hēn* functions here as frequently in Rashi's Heb. as the copula.

[12] Rendering based on Rashi's interpretation there.

[13] According to Maarsen, *Parshandatha*, vol. 3, p. xii *'aḥăliyôt* is one of six words in Medieval Heb. first attested in Rashi's Commentary on Psalms. According to Ben Yehuda, *Dict.*, vol. 1, p. 151b *'aḥăliyôt* 'wishes' is the plural; the singular is *'aḥălît* 'wish'. Related to this noun are Medieval Heb. *'iḥēl* 'beseech, express a wish' and Modern Heb. *'iḥēl* 'wish somebody (something)'; see above, n. 6.

[14] Corresponding to Modern French *souhait* 'wish'; See Darmsteter, "Les Gloses Françaises de Raschi dans la Bible," *REJ* 56 (1908), p. 74.

[15] Heb. *ṣāpantî*, lit., 'I hid'. Rashi's comment responds to the exegetical question, "How did the psalmist hide God's promise?"

[16] Heb. *'eśta'ăśā '*.

[17] Heb. *'eṯ'asseq*.

[18] Heb. *kĕmô*.

[19] Similarly NJV there; for *dābār* 'promise' see Rashi at Ps. 119:25, 49.

²⁰ Here Rashi intimates that the verb *gāmal* 'grant' is transitive and that therefore the reader must supply the direct object in our text, which, being an example of ellipsis, does not spell out the direct object. Other examples of *gāmal* 'grant' where the direct object must be supplied mentally include Ps. 13:6; 116:7. In 1 Sam. 24:18 the direct object of our verb is *tôbāh* 'kindness'. In Prov. 3:12 the object is *tôb wĕlō'-ra'* 'kindness rather than unkindness' while in Gen. 50:15, 17; Isa. 3:9; Ps. 7:5; Prov. 3:30 the direct object is 'unkindness'; see next note.

²¹ According to Rashi *gāmal 'al* 'grant (kindness) unto' is synonymous with the Rabbinic Heb. idiom *gāmal ḥesed* 'grant kindness'. This idiom is unattested in Biblical Heb. where we find instead either *gāmal (ha-) ṭôb(āh)* [see previous note for attestations] or *'āśāh ḥesed*, lit., 'do kindness', which is attested in Gen. 19:19; 21:23; 24:12, 14; Ex. 20:6; etc.

²² This comment is repeated here in our Rashi ms. by dittography.

²³ Rashi here intimates that in Biblical Heb. *b* and *w* are interchangeable as, in fact, they are in several modern Semitic languages and in Akkadian. See Moscati #8.9; cf. *GKC* #19o. Hence Rashi regards *ta'ăbāh*, which is attested only here in Ps. 119:20, as a cognate of the frequently attested *ta'ăwāh* 'desire'. *BDB*, p. 16b and Mandelkern, p. 22a treat *ta'ăwāh* as a noun derived from the verb *'wh* 'desire'. *BDB*, p. 1060a and Mandelkern, p. 1238c treat *ta'ăbāh* as a noun derived from the verb *t'b* 'desire', which is attested only in Ps. 19:40 and Ps. 119:174; see below.

²⁴ Rendered "with longing" in NJV here.

²⁵ So *Mahberet Menahem*, p. 396, s.v. *t'b*. Menahem's interpretation of the participle *mĕtā'ēb* in Am. 6:8 is shared by Ibn Ezra in his commentary there. Rashi, however, in his commentary there follows TJ in understanding the root *t'b* in Am. 6:8 as a biform of *t'b* 'despise'. The interchange of the consonants *'aleph* and *'ayin* is attested also in *g'l* 'reject', a biform of *g'l* (Lev. 26:43; Jer. 14:19; etc.) and distinct from *g'l* 'redeem' (Ex. 6:6; Lev. 25:25; etc.); see dictionaries. Qimhi, however, in his commentary on Am. 6:8 suggests that *t'b* 'despise and *t'b* 'desire' are examples of the phenomenon, which in modern times has been described by Robert Gordis, "Studies in Roots of Contrasted Meanings," *JQR*, n.s., 27 (1936), pp. 33-58.

²⁶ Heb. *lĕšôn*.

²⁷ Similarly *Mahberet Menahem*, p. 396, referring to *tā'abtî* in Ps. 119:174; and *mĕtā'ēb* in Am. 6:8.

²⁸ Our Rashi ms. reads *gôl*, which supports the conjectural emendation proposed in *BHS*; the standard Heb. text reads *gal*.

²⁹ Rashi does not quote the bracketed portion of the verse, but it is necessary to have this portion of the verse in mind in order to understand Rashi's comment on this verse.

³⁰ Heb. *'ap 'al pî*, which is Rashi's interpretation of the psalmist's *gam*; so now NJV: "though".

³¹ I.e., the princes referred to in v. 23.

³² Rashi here intimates that in this verse *dābār*, lit., 'word', means 'promise'. Other attestations of *dābār* meaning 'promise' include Josh.

21:43; 23:14; Num. 30:3; etc.; cf. *BDB*, p. 182a; see above, n. 19.

[33] 2 Sam. 7:8-16.

[34] Rashi here takes *derek*, lit., 'WAY', to mean both 'needs' and 'sin'. For *derek* meaning 'needs' see Isa. 56:11; 57:18; 58:13. For *derek* meaning 'sin' see Isa. 66:3; Hos. 4:9; 12:3; Prov. 7:25; 14:14.

[35] The Bible employs imperfect with *waw*-consecutive *watta'ănēnî* 'AND YOU HAVE ANSWERED ME'. Rashi paraphrases using the independent personal pronoun *'attāh* 'You' followed by the perfect *'ănîtanî* 'You responded to me'.

[36] Cf. *Mahberet Menahem*, p. 126, s.v. *dlp*.

[37] Rashi here intimates that the psalmist has employed a *qal*-perfect, which is present progressive in meaing.

[38] The primary meaning of Heb. *'āqēb* is 'heel' of a person (Gen. 3:15; 25:26) or of an animal (Gen. 49:17; Judges 5:22). On Semitic cognates see McCurley, p. 55 and p. 96, nn. 346-347. Secondarily, the plural *'ăqēbîm* means 'tracks, steps' or 'footprints' (Ps. 56:7; 77:20; 89:52; Cant. 1:8); so McCurley, p. 96, n. 346. Similar to this nuance of *'qb*, which, according to Rashi, is attested here in Ps. 119:33, is the use of Heb. *regel* 'foot' (Gen. 18:4; 19:2; Ex. 3:5; etc.) to denote 'footstep' (Deut. 33:14; 1 Sam. 2:9; 1 Kgs. 14:6; etc.) and the use of Heb. *pa'am* 'foot' (2 Kgs. 19:24 = Isa. 37:25; Isa. 26:6; Cant. 7:2) in the secondary sense 'footstep' at Ps. 17:5; 57:7; 74:3; 85:14; 119:133. The verb *'āqab* 'supplant' (Gen. 27:36; Hos. 12:4; etc.) is a denominative verb derived from the noun *'āqēb* 'footstep', and it means literally, 'walk in the footsteps of'; cf. Dhorme, *L'emploi*, p. 160. From this verb in turn is derived the preposition *'ēqeb* 'because, following in the footsteps of' (Gen. 22:18; Num. 14:24; Deut. 17:12; etc.), the noun *'ēqeb* 'reward' (lit., 'that which follows'; Ps. 19:12) and the adverb *'ēqeb* 'diligently (following the footsteps)'. It is this last usage of *'ēqeb*, which is attested here in Ps. 119:33; contrast Rashi; contrast also *BDB*, p. 784b: "to the end" and NJV's "Meaning of Heb. uncertain." Similar to the verb, adverb, and preposition derived from *'āqēb* 'heel' are those derived from *regel* 'foot'; see *BDB*, pp. 919b-920, s.v. *regel*; for adverbs and prepositions derived from anatomical terms see McCurley, pp. 230-244.

[39] Heb. *'ešmĕrennāh*, a form attested at the head of v. 34b. Rashi appears to assume that the reader of Psalms in his day would find this form readily comprehensible but the synonymous *'eṣrennāh* attested here in Ps.119:33 incomprehensible.

[40] This O.F. gloss of Heb. *'ēqeb* is found in Rashi also at Gen. 49:19; Ps. 40:16; 56:7; etc.; see Banitt, *Rashi: Interpreter of the Biblical Letter*, p. 33.

[41] This adjective phrase informs us that *'imrātĕkā*, lit., 'Your speech', here means 'Your promise', as seen now by NJV; see *BDB*, p. 57a; cf. the synonymous usage of *dābār* 'word' in v. 25 and Rashi's treatment of it there.

[42] Rashi does not quote the bracketed portion of the verse. I have supplied it for clarity.

[43] So Maarsen, whose interpretation is confirmed by Rashi's comment

on v. 39b and by the usage of the expression 'that iniquity' to refer to David's affair with Bathsheba also in Rashi's comment on Ps. 30:2; see nn. 4-6 there.

[44] Here Rashi alludes to the fact that according to Ex. 21:37, "If a person steals a bull or a sheep and slaughters or sells it, he shall pay compensation of five bulls for the bull and four sheep for the sheep"; according to Mishnah Bava Qama 7:1 this anomalous rule concerning what might today be called punitive damages is limited to the instances mentioned in the biblical verse.

[45] Here Rashi intimates that our verse is an example of ellipsis insofar as v. 41b has no verb, which Rashi supplies on the basis of v. 41a.

[46] Hence NJV's idiomatic rendering, "as You have promised"; see Rashi and our discussion at v. 38 above.

[47] Heb. kĕmô.

[48] As we have noted at, Ps. 27, n. 24, Heb. qiwwāh can mean either 'pray' or 'hope'.

[49] In Rabbinic Heb. halakah, lit., 'walking', denotes Talmudic law, individually and collectively; note the play on words.

[50] Behind NJV's idiomatic "at ease" is Heb. bārĕḥābāh, lit., 'in the broad place'. Heb. rḥbh 'broad place' corresponds to Targumic Aram. rwḥ; see Jastrow, Dict., pp. 1456-1457. Hence Heb. rĕḥābāh brings to Rashi's mind the verb rwḥ 'spread'. Hence the association in Ps. 119:45 of 'walking in' (from the same Heb. root as halakah) and 'broad places' brings to Rashi's mind the dictum in Tosefta Sanhedrin 7:1, "From there halakah spreads forth [rôwaḥat] among Israel." Note also that Rashi glosses the rare in Rabbinic Heb. verb rwḥ by the more well-known Rabbinic Heb. synonym pšṭ.

[51] Rashi here renders literally according to context, and he does not connect Biblical Heb. dārašti 'I searched', whose object here is piqqûdêkā 'Your precepts' with its Rabbinic Heb. cognates midrash, beth midrash, etc.

[52] See above, nn. 19, 32, 41.

[53] Rashi here attempts to explain the apparent non sequitur that in the first half of the verse the psalmist tells us that he never forgets God's mišpāṭîm, which can mean 'punishments' as well as 'RULES' (see dictionaries, and see Banitt, Rashi: Interpreter of the Biblical Letter, pp. 32-33), while in the second half of the verse the psalmist declares, "I FIND COMFORT." Rashi thus explains that it is precisely what the psalmist remembers about God's punishments that is consolation, namely, that the punishments are short-lived.

[54] Rashi holds that laylāh 'night' in Ps. 119:55 is a metaphor for ṣārāh 'trouble' and for 'ăpēlāh. The latter term is employed in Biblical Heb. (Deut. 28:29; Joel 2:2; Zeph. 1:15) to denote 'darkness'. In Rabbinic Heb., however, this term is used metaphorically to denote 'mental anguish, tribulation' (see Jastrow, Dict., p. 103). Rashi seems to use it in this latter sense here in the commentary.

[55] The psalmist's 'THIS HAS BEEN FOR ME' inspires the exegetical

question, 'THIS HAS BEEN *what* FOR ME?" NJV supplies the answer, 'MY LOT'. For Rashi's response to the exegetical crux see below.

[56] Rashi's formulation here is taken directly from Mishnah Avot 2:1; the connection between the idea expressed there and our psalm verse is found in Leviticus Rabbah 35:1; the connection was probably fostered by the occurrence of the verb *ḥiššēb* 'consider' both in Mishnah Avot there and in Ps. 119:59.

[57] Cf. Rashi on Ps. 116:3.

[58] So Qimhi; Ibn Janah, *Sepher Haschoraschim*, p. 358 finds support for this view in the fact that the Targumic Aram. equivalent of Heb. *šālāl* 'spoil' is *'ădā'āh*. Ibn Janah (there, p. 358), following Hayug (John W. Nutt, ed., *Two Treatises on Verbs Containing Feeble or Double Letters* by R. Jehudah Hayug of Fez [London: & Berlin: Asher & Co., 1870], p. 50) cites the clause *'āz ḥullaq 'ad-šālāl* "Then spoil-booty will be distributed" (Isa. 33:23). It appears that in this clause the rare *'ad* 'spoil' is glossed by the familiar *šālāl* 'booty' just as in Isa. 51:22 the *hapax legomenon qubba'at* 'chalice' is glossed by *kôs* 'cup' and just as in Jonah 2:4 *mĕṣûlāh* 'the deep' is glossed by *bilĕbab yammîm* 'in the seas'; on the latter two glosses see Cohen, *Biblical Hapax Legomena in the Light of Akkadian and Ugaritic*, p. 85, n. 200.

[59] *Mahberet Menaḥem*, p. 277, s.v. *'d* III; the latter finds support for this view in the fact that Targumic Aramaic's equivalent of Heb. *šālāl* booty' is *'ădā'āh*.

[60] Rashi assumes that we have here a form of the verb *'ānāh* 'declaim' (*'ānāh* IV in *BDB*, p. 777). Here in his first comment on v. 67 Rashi intimates that he holds that the psalmist has made use of the literary device called in Arabic *talḥin*, i.e., the use of a word which has two distinct meanings (here 'declaim' and 'be punished') in order "to bring both meanings simultaneously to the consciousness of the reader, who derives a delicate aesthetic pleasure from the instantaneous recognition of both meanings" (Gordis, *BGM*, p. 167). Hence Rashi's paraphrase of *ṭerem 'e'ĕneh...wĕ'attāh* as *ṭerem... wĕ'attāh miššena'ănêtî* "Before I recited them...but now that I have been punished."

[61] *ḥāgîtî bāhem.*

[62] Here Rashi treats *'e'ĕneh* as a preterite of *'ānāh* III; see above, n. 60.

[63] Rashi's paraphrase of the psalmist's *'imrātĕkā* 'YOUR WORD'.

[64] Here Rashi intimates that v. 66 is a dependent clause functioning as an adverb modifying the verb *šāmartî* in v. 67.

[65] Clearly *'ēr wĕ'ōneh* in Mal. 2:12 is a merism meaning 'all progeny'; hence TJ renders "son or grandson". Ibn Ezra sensed that TJ's rendering was a guess based on the context, which cannot be substantiated by known etymologies of the two nouns. Vulgate reflects the Rabbinic tradition that equates *'ēr* with Lat. *magister* (= Heb. *ḥākām* 'sage') and *'ōneh* with Lat. *discipulus* (= Heb. *talmîd* 'disciple'). In his commentary on the Talmud (BT Shabbat 55b; Sanhedrin 82a) Rashi seeks to justify the equation etymologically. The sage is called *'ēr* 'alert' because of the sharpness of his mind reflected in his teachings while the disciple is called *'ōneh* 'reciter' because he merely repeats what he has heard from the sage. If so, the

mark of a sage is his originality! One might ask why Rashi has chosen the midrash on Mal. 2:12 rather than Job. 3:1 or Deut. 27:14 to demonstrate that *'ōneh* can mean 'declaim'; see Rashi on those verses, and cf. modern translations and commentaries. It seems that Rashi was justified in invoking the midrash on Mal. 2:2 as proof since this midrash, like Ps. 119, employs the verb in a study of Torah context. The midrash is attributed to Rav in BT Shabbat 55b, Sanhedrin 82a, to Rabbi in Sifra Aḥare 13:4.

[66] So *Mahberet Menahem*, p. 201.

[67] Rashi here indicates that he holds that *kālāh* here is a transitive verb, which requires the direct object 'it'; he intimates also that the verse is an example of ellipsis.

[68] Concerning the expressions *kālĕtāh 'ayin* 'the eye was used up', *kālû 'ênayim* 'the eyes were used up' see Gruber, *Aspects*, pp. 386-400.

[69] Rashi here alludes to the synonymity of the two expresions *šeqer* 'falsehood' and *šāwĕ'* ' vanity' exemplified by the Ex. and Deut. versions of the decalogue respectively. In Ex. 20:13 a 'false witness' is called *'ēd šeqer* while in Deut. 5:17 he is called *'ēd šāwĕ'*. Moreover, Rashi intimates here that just as *šāwĕ'*, whose primary meaning is 'vanity, for no reason' can be used to mean 'falsehood' in Deut. 5:17 so can *šeqer*, whose primary meaning is 'falsehood' be employed in Ps. 119:86 to mean 'for no reason'.

[70] Rashi's interpretation of the lemma; Rashi's comment demonstrates that he, like Ben Zoma in Mishnah Avot 4:1 and the several midrashim in Midrash Tehillim on Ps. 119:43, interprets the prefixed preposition *min* in the sense 'from'; most modern translations, however, follow LXX, Vulgate and Ibn Ezra, in interpreting the prefixed preposition *min* in *mikkol* to mean 'than'; on the various meanings of Heb. *min* see dictionaries.

[71] I.e., YOUR [God's] DECREES.

[72] According to Mandelkern, p. 559 and *BDB*, p. 476 the root is *k-l-'* 'shut up, restrain, withhold', and this is distinct from the verb *kālāh* 'use up, empty' discussed in nn. 67-68 above. For recognition that *kālī'tî* 'I withheld' here in Ps. 119:101 is a cognate of *kĕlitinî* 'You kept me from' in 1 Sam. 25:33 see *BDB* (there) and Mandelkern (there); see *Mahberet Menahem*, p. 214, s.v., *kl* VII.

[73] Rashi correctly deduces from the parallelism "How *nimlĕṣû* to my palate Your words//more than honey to my mouth" that the *hapax legomenon nimlĕṣû* is semantic equivalent of **nimtĕqû*, which is 3d pers. pl. niphal perfect of the verb *mātaq* 'be sweet', which is attested in the Bible only in *qal* and *hiphil*. KJV, following Rashi, renders, "How sweet are thy words unto my taste! *yea sweeter* than honey to my mouth!" Similarly RSV; NEB; Ehrlich; JB; contrast *BDB*, p. 576b.

[74] The midrashim at Midrash Tehillim on Ps. 27:2 and on Ps. 119:44 see in our verse a reference to David the potential sinner being saved from sin. For David the *poseq*, i.e., one who renders decisions in *halakah*, see BT Berakot 4a.

[75] Cognate of Heb. *mwk* attested in Lev. 25:25, 35, 39, 47; 27:8; for

another possible attestation of this root in Heb. see above at Ps. 16:5.

[76] BT Nedarim 41a.

[77] By the addition of this expression Rashi seeks to explain the apparent *non sequitur* in this verse; perhaps the psalmist employs the conjunctive *waw* in precisely this meaning; see Orlinsky, *Notes*, pp. 19-20; NJV here omits the conjunction altogether.

[78] Rashi takes *'ēqeb* to mean 'in the footsteps of, following'; see above, n. 38.

[79] In his commentary there Rashi explains that *sĕʿippay* means *maḥšĕbôtay* 'my thoughts'.

[80] In his commentary there Rashi explains that *sĕʿippîm* means *maḥăšābôt* 'thoughts'.

[81] MT vocalizes the *s* with *ṣērē*, i.e., *ē* while our Rashi ms. vocalizes with *seghol*, i.e., *e*.

[82] See Rashi's comment on v. 16 above.

[83] When Rashi says, "our rendering...by Aramaic...," he refers to the interpretation given to a given word or expression in the Hebrew Scriptures by either of the two Aramaic translations of the Scriptures, which the Babylonian Talmud regards as canonical. These are Targum Onkelos (T.O.) on the Pentateuch and Targum Jonathan (TJ) on the Early and Later Prophets. For the canonicity of these Targums see BT Megillah 3a; Qiddushin 49a; see also our discussion at Ps. 40, n. 25; Ps. 42, n. 48; Ps. 45, n.42; Ps. 48, n. 18; Ps. 55, n. 18; Ps. 58, n. 29; Ps. 68, n. 92.

[84] So *Mahberet Menahem*, p. 265, s.v. *sl* III; contrast the standard Eng. rendering 'reject'.

[85] So Rashi in his commentary there.

[86] Gordis, *Job*, p. 49 points out, following Rashi and others, that in the *pi'el* the verb is transitive (Job. 4:15) while in the *qal* it is intransitive (Ps. 119:120).

[87] With Darmsteter, "Les Gloses Françaises de Raschi dans la Bible," *REJ* 56 (1908), p. 74 cf. Modern French *se herisse*; see also Rashi at Jer. 51:27 and Darmsteter, "Les Gloses Françaises de Raschi dans la Bible," *REJ* 54 (1908), p. 227.

[88] On the ambiguity of Heb. *mišpāṭ* 'ruling' see, with Maarsen, Rashi at Isa. 32:7; on Rashi's comment there see Banitt, *Rashi: Interpreter of the Biblical Letter*, pp. 15, 32, 101.

[89] See also Rashi at Isa. 38:14.

[90] The etymon of Eng. 'guarantee'; see Greenberg, *Foreign Words in the Bible Commentary of Rashi*, p. 197.

[91] Cf. vv. 38, 41, above.

[92] Heb. *lišmekā*, lit., 'for Your Name', which is periphrasis for 'for You'; here Rashi paraphrases in the 2[d] person the psalmist's reference to God in the 3[d] person.

[93] His addition of *'ēk* 'so that' is Rashi's answer to the exegetical question as to the syntactical relationship between the two clauses; Rashi thus takes v. 126b as an adverbial purpose clause modifying the verb 'GIVE ME UNDERSTANDING' in v. 126a.

⁹⁴ Rashi has here presented his view of the literal meaning of the verse; he will now summarize two midrashim based on the verse.

⁹⁵ Heb. *dārĕšû mimmenû.* In this expression the verb *dāraš* means 'deduce', and it refers to a teaching inspired by the verse itself. On the verse serving as a stimulus for midrashic creativity see Kadushin, *The Rabbinic Mind³*, pp. 113-117. The use of the verb *dāraš* here attested is to be distinguished from the more common *dārĕšû* 'they interpreted', which in Rashi's commentaries can refer either to literal or midrashic interpretation; on this common usage see Kamin, *Rashi's Exegetical Categorization*, pp. 136-139.

⁹⁶ On the expression *dibrê tôrāh* 'God's laws' see Mayer I. Gruber, "The Mishnah as Oral Torah: A Reconsideration," pp. 116-117.

⁹⁷ Cf. Leviticus Rabbah 22:6.

⁹⁸ See JT Berakot 9:5; and see parallels cited by Zohory, p. 340; contrast Mishnah Avot 1:15. Note that in our Rashi ms. the word order "hours of the day" is reversed and corrected by supralinear dots, a single dot indicating word #1, two dots indicating word #2.

⁹⁹ E.g., Ex. 16:29; 20:11; for additional references see *BDB*, p. 487, s.v. *'al-kēn.*

¹⁰⁰ Heb. *'ābĕdû,* which is Rashi's paraphrase of Isaiah's *upĕqûdātām* "their punishments'.

¹⁰¹ NJV accepts Rashi's interpretation of *'al-kēn* in Gen. 33:10 and Num. 10:31 but not at Isa. 15:7. In his commentary on Num. 10:31 Rashi cites also Gen. 38:26, "For it is because I did not give her (in marriage) to my son Shelah"; Gen. 19:8, "Do not do anything to these men because they have come under the shelter of my roof."

¹⁰² Lemma rendered according to NJV margin, which follows Rashi in taking *yiššartî* here to be a declarative *pi'el* derived from the verb *y-š-r* 'to be just, straight'.

¹⁰³ According to Deut. 22:6-7 the reward is 'longevity'.

¹⁰⁴ Cf. Mishnah Avot 2:1; BT Hullin 142a; Tanḥuma Ki Teṣe #2; Rashi at Deut. 22:7.

¹⁰⁵ Rashi does not quote the bracketed portion of the citation; I have supplied it for clarity.

¹⁰⁶ Tanḥuma Vayaqhel 6 (pp. 129-130); Tanḥuma, ed. S. Buber, Exodus, pp. 123-124.

¹⁰⁷ Similarly Qimhi.

¹⁰⁸ Qimhi, takes *'ōṣeq 'ādām,* lit., 'human wrongdoing' to refer to the wrong likely to be done to the psalmist by others while Rashi takes 'human wrongdoing' to refer to the pitfalls into which the psalmist fears his human nature may lead him.

¹⁰⁹ This division of the night, i.e., the period from sunset to sunrise, into watches is reflected also in Ex. 14:24; Judg. 7:19; 1 Sam. 11:11; Ps. 63:6; 90:4; Lam 2:19. According to a *baraitha* quoted in BT Berakot 3b, Rabbi Nathan and Rabbi Judah the Patriarch disagreed as to whether the night is divided into three watches (R. Nathan) or four (Rabbi Judah the Patriarch). Max Landsberg, "Night," *JE* 9:304a holds that the threefold

division of the night goes back to the Bible while the fourfold division is of Roman origin. The first of the three watches is mentioned in Lam. 2:19; the middle watch in Judg. 7:19; the third in Ex. 14:24 and 1 Sam. 11:11.

[110] According to the view of Rabbi Judah the Patriarch; see previous note.

[111] I.e., Rabbi Nathan; see n. 106.

[112] Cf. BT Berakot 3b; with Maarsen and Zohory see also Midrash Tehillim 57:4 and Lamentations Rabbati 2:27.

[113] Following Maarsen, *hnhn't* is emended to *hnhgt*.

[114] Note the chiastic structure of the verse: verb-substantive//substantive verb: THERE DREW NEAR THOSE WHO PURSUE INTRIGUE//FROM YOUR TORAH THEY DREW FAR. This structure suggests that the verbs *qārĕbû* 'they drew near' and *rāḥāqû* 'they drew far' are antithetical. Hence, Rashi explains that the drawing near is to the antithesis of 'YOUR TORAH', from which, according to the verse, "THOSE WHO PURSUE INTRIGUE...DREW FAR"; cf. Ps. 1; contrast NJV.

[115] V. 150 talks about the righteous and the wicked while v. 151 talks about God's tender loving care. Perhaps the only reason for the juxtaposition of these two ideas is that both verses begin with forms of the root *q-r-b* chosen to fill out the alphabetical acrostic. Rashi, however, suggests a connection between the content of the two verses.

[116] Cf. BT Sanhedrin 20b.

[117] Kadushin, *Rabbinic Mind* [3], pp. 293-295 notes that in both Biblical and Rabbinic Heb. *ʿôlām* may refer to 'periods of time'; in Rabbinic Heb. *ʿôlām* has the added meaning of 'world; hence while the psalmist here employs *lĕ ʿôlām* to mean 'indefinitely, forever' the midrash here quoted reads into v. 152 the Rabbinic usage of *ʿôlām*.

[118] Here as in his comment on v. 152a Rashi interprets *ʿēdōtêkā* to mean 'testimonies' (contrast NJV's "decrees"); Rashi's point is that the empirical evidence for the reliability of God's eschatological promises will only be established when eschatological concepts will have become, in Kadushin's words (*Rabbinic Mind*[3], p. 364), like "value-concepts in general," "experiential concepts" rather than beliefs.

[119] In BT Qiddushin 31a the Babylonian Amora Rava (d. 352 C.E.) employs Ps. 119:60 as a proof-text for the notion that when the decalogue was first spoken by the divine voice at Mt. Sinai to all humankind the Gentiles' immediate reaction to the duties to God (commandments 1-4) was, "It is His own honor that He seeks." Rava remarks there, "Does THE BEGINNING OF YOUR WORD IS TRUTH [mean that] THE BEGINNING OF YOUR WORD but not the end of Your word is truth? [No.] Rather [what it means is that] from the end of Your word [commandments 5-10 of the decalogue] it is seen that THE BEGINNING OF YOUR WORD IS TRUTH."

[120] Rashi, followed here by NJV, understands *'imrāh*, lit., 'utterance' to mean specifically 'promise'; similarly does Rashi understand *dābār* in v. 25; see above, nn. 19, 32.

[121] Concerning the Jewish ritual objects called tefillin in Hebrew sources and phylacteries in the New Testament see Louis Isaac Rabinowitz, "Tefillin," *EJ* 15:898-904; David A. Glatt and Jeffrey H. Tigay, "Phylacteries," *Harper's Bible Dictionary*, pp. 795-796.

[122] Rashi here combines part of a midrash attributed to Rabbi Meir at Midrash Tehillim 6:1 (a variant of the same midrash is found in BT Menaḥot 43b) with the assertion of Rabban Simeon b. Gamaliel (BT Shabbat 130a) and of Rabbi Judah b. Ilai (BT Megillah 16b) that Ps. 119:162 refers to circumcision.

[123] With Maarsen see Rashi also at BT Megillah 16b.

[124] I.e., the benediction beginning "Blessed art thou...who formest light" and concluding "Blessed art thou...Creator of the lights" (Birnbaum, *Daily Prayer Book*, pp. 71-74) and the benediction beginning "With a great love" and concluding "Blessed art thou...who hast graciously chosen thy people Israel" (Birnbaum, *Daily Prayer Book*, pp. 74-76).

[125] The three biblical passages—Deut. 6:4-9; Deut. 11:13-21; Num. 15:37-41—beginning "Hear, O Israel" and concluding "I am the Lord your God"; see Birnbaum, *Daily Prayer Book*, pp. 75-78.

[126] The benediction beginning "True and certain" and concluding "Blessed art thou...who hast redeemed Israel"; see Birnbaum, *Daily Prayer Book*, pp. 77-82.

[127] I.e., the two paragraphs beginning respectively "Blessed art thou, Lord our God" and "Thou hast loved" see Birnbaum, *Daily Prayer Book*, p. 192.

[128] I.e., the benediction beginning "True and trustworthy" and concluding "Blessed art thou, O Lord, who hast redeemed Israel" (see Birnbaum, *Daily Prayer Book*, p. 196) and the benediction beginning "Grant, Lord our God" and concluding "Blessed art thou, O Lord, who guardest thy people Israel forever" (see Birnbaum, *Daily Prayer Book*, p. 198); the Talmudic source for the liturgical structure referred to here is Mishnah Berakot 1:4; the source for the use of Ps. 119:164 as a proof-text in support of that Mishnah is Midrash Tehillim 6:1.

[129] Here Rashi alludes to the fact that *dibrê tôrāh*, lit., 'words of Torah', usually means 'laws of Torah'; see above, n. 96.

[130] Heb. *dibrê tôrāh*; see previous note.

[131] Cf. nn. 60, 65; cf. *Mahberet Menahem*, p. 284, s.v. 'n II.

PSALM CXX

1   A SONG OF THE STEPS, which the Levites should sing while standing on the fifteen steps, which descend from the court of Israel to the court of the women.[1] Now there are here fifteen psalms, which belong to the genre 'A SONG OF THE STEPS'.[2] Now our rabbis said that David composed them in order to raise up the water table [*hattĕhôm*] as it is explained in [BT] Tractate Sukkah [53a-b].[3]

2   FROM TREACHEROUS LIPS. [This expression is a metaphor for] the descendants of Esau,[4] who hunt down people by means of their mouths with malicious slander.[5]

3a WHAT WILL HE, the Holy One Blessed be He,[6] GIVE YOU?

3b AND WHAT WILL HE ADD TO YOU? [The answer is that He will give you *šĕmîrôt* 'care', i.e., barriers. Hence you [the human tongue (v. 3c)] are located [*nĕtûnāh*] [7] behind a double barrier.[8]

4a [You are like][9] A WARRIOR'S SHARP ARROWS, and therefore you kill [victims] in a distant place as does an arrow.[10]

4b WITH HOT COALS OF BROOM-WOOD. When charcoals made of any other kind of wood are extinguished on the surface, they are extinguished on the inside [as well], but as for these [COALS OF BROOM-WOOD], when they are extinguished on the surface, they are not extinguished within.[11]

3a An alternative interpretation of 'WHAT WILL HE GIVE YOU?' is 'WHAT IS the Holy One Blessed be He ultimately going to decree as punishment for you? [The answer is]

4   WARRIOR'S ARROWS...WITH COALS OF BROOM-WOOD [i.e.], arrow from above and Gehinnom from below.[12]

5   WOE IS ME. The Congregation of Israel said, "I have already been afflicted in many places of exile. For example,[13] I SOJOURNED IN MESHECH with the Japhethites during the Persian Empire." [The connection of Japhethites

with Meshech is found in Gen. 10:2: "The Japhethies are...]
and Greece... and Meshech."[14]

7   I AM AT PEACE with them, BUT WHEN I SPEAK to
them ['ălêhem] peace, THEY come to fight against me.[15]

PSALM CXX, NOTES

[1] Cf. Mishnah Sukkah 5:4; Middot 2:5; the latter source notes that the steps in question were circular; for pictorial illustrations see "Temple," *EJ* 15:961-962. As noted by Maarsen here, the Mishnah does not say that the Levites sung Ps. 120-134 while standing on the steps. It only states that the number of these psalms corresponds to the number of steps on which they sang.

[2] Ps. 120-134.

[3] There R. Johanan [b. Napha] states that when King David dug the cisterns from which the water was drawn for pouring on the altar, the personified Abyss [Heb. *těhôm*] "arose and threatened to submerge the world." David thereupon wrote the Name of the LORD upon a shard, which he threw into the Abyss so that the Abyss descended 16,000 cubits [i.e, c. 24,000 feet; c. 7315 meters]. Noting that "the nearer it [the water table] is to the earth [i.e., ground level], the better can the earth be irrigated," King David sang the fifteen [SONGS OF THE] STEPS. The Abyss [i.e., the water table] responded by ascending 15,000 cubits [note the multiple of 15, the number of the SONGS OF THE STEPS!] and remaining 1,000 cubits [i.e., 1500 feet; 475 meters] below the surface.

[4] Cf. the midrash in Midrash Tehillim here, which identifies slander as a characteristic vice of "the wicked kingdom," i.e., Rome, i.e., Edom, i.e, the descendants of Esau.

[5] Cf. the midrash quoted by Rashi at Gen. 25:28: "*kî-ṣayid běpîw* 'FOR THERE WAS HUNTING BY MEANS OF HIS MOUTH....' BY MEANS OF THE MOUTH of Esau, who used to hunt him, i.e., deceive him [Isaac] by means of his [Esau's] words." The source of this midrash is Genesis Rabbah 63:10.

[6] Here Rashi supplies the missing subject of the verb *yittēn;* contrast NJV, which interprets the verb as an impersonal 3[d] pers. employed as a passive.

[7] Rashi's paraphrase of the verb *yittēn* 'he will give'; see previous note.

[8] Rashi's comment here is based upon the midrash attributed to R. Jose b. Zimra, an Amora of the land of Israel (1st half of 3[d] cent. C.E.) at BT 'Arakin 15b and Rashi's comment there. Like NJV, q.v., the midrash assumes that the two questions in vv. 3a-b are addressed to 'DECEITFUL TONGUE' (v. 3c). According to R. Jose b. Zimra, the double barrier consists of flesh, i.e., the cheeks and bone, i.e., the teeth; see Leo Jung, *'Arakin Translated into English*, The Babylonian Talmud, ed. I. Epstein (London: Soncino,1960), p. 86, n. 13.

[9] I have supplied three words for clarity; see next note.

[10] Rashi's interpretation of v. 4a as a metaphor applied to and ad-

dressed to 'DECEITFUL TONGUE' (v. 3c) is based upon a midrash in Midrash Tehillim here. The midrash explains that the tongue is like an arrow and unlike a sword in that having been let loose it cannot be withdrawn even if its owner should change his/her mind; see also Genesis Rabbah 98:19.

[11] Rashi's source is the anonymous midrash at Genesis Rabbah 98:19.

[12] Based upon a midrash attributed to R. Hisda quoting Mar Uqba in BT 'Arakin 15b, Rashi's comment here suggests that v. 4 is not a series of metaphors applied to 'DECEITFUL TONGUE' but the answer to the LORD's query to 'DECEITFUL TONGUE'. In the midrash the Holy One Blessed be He proposes to "the prince of Gehinnom" that the two of them cooperate in punishing 'DECEITFUL TONGUE'. The midrash explains that 'A WARRIOR'S ARROWS' mean 'ARROWS of the Holy One Blessed be He' since the LORD is compared to a warrior in Isa. 42:13, q.v. The midrash also explains that COALS refers to Gehinnom.

[13] Heb. hēn; paraphrase of the psalmist's kî.

[14] The identification of Meshech with Persia is at variance with the midrash at BT Yoma 10a cited by Maarsen and by Zohory as Rashi's source for this comment; contrast also Qimhi and the Psalms Targum here.

[15] Here Rashi paraphrases the psalmist's "THEY ARE FOR WAR"; similarly LXX and Vulgate; contrast Qimhi: "I AM PEACE in my mouth, AND WHEN I SPEAK peace to them [' ălêhem], THEY speak OF WAR.

PSALM CXXI

1   A SONG FOR ASCENTS.
     I TURN MY EYES TO THE MOUNTAINS.[1]

Psalm CXXI, Notes

[1] Our Rashi ms., like most mss. of Rashi's Commentary on the Book
of Psalms, records no Rashi commentary on Ps. 121. Like many Rashi mss.,
our Rashi ms. records the number of the psalm and the opening lines; see
the discussion of this phenomenon above, p. 159. The following mss. of
Rashi's Commentary on the Book of Psalms contain a commentary on Ps.
121: Berlin 140; Florence Plut. 3.8; British Library Harley 150 (where it
is introduced by the expression "I found," on which see the discussion in
our introduction. Leipzig B.H. fol. 4; Leiden Scal. 1; Oxford Bodleian Can.
Or. 60; Oxford Bodleian Opp. Add. 4to 52; Paris 111; Paris 161; Rostock
32; JTS L 781 as do the standard Rabbinic Bibles. The current editions
of the Rabbinic Bible here have Rashi misquote BT Hagigah Chapter 2
when he means to quote the commentary of Tosafot at BT Hagigah 13a
to the effect that the payyetan Eleazar ha-Kallir was the son of the 2^d cent.
C.E. Tanna R. Simeon b. Yoḥai. The comment in those editions clearly
represents the attempt of various scribes to elucidate with notes in parentheses the following comment, which is found in the famous Second Rabbinic Bible, vol. 4 (Venice: Bomberg, 1525; repr., Jerusalem: Makor, 1972):
I [the scribe responsible for the Rashi ms. copied out in the Second Rabbinic Bible] found [the following comment; my doing so places me in a
dialogic relationship of one-upmanship vis-à-vis the scribes responsible for
the more reliable medieval mss., who say, "I did not find"]: A SONG FOR
THE STEPS. He [the ancient editor of the Book of Psalms] hinted in the
second psalm [in the series Ps. 120; 122-134] at the steps which ascend
for the virtuous in the eschatological era from under the Tree of Life [Gen.
3:24] to the [divine] Throne of Glory [in heaven] in accord with what is
taught in Sifre [i.e., Sifre Deuteronomy, ed. Finkelstein, p. 105, lines 5-
6]: "A song of the steps" [so Pss. 120; 122-134] is not written here [at Ps.
121:1] but rather "A SONG FOR THE STEPS." [The latter title] is in
honor of Him who [i.e., God] in the eschatological era will provide steps
for the virtuous in the eschatological era. Now it is this that [Eleazar] ha-
Qaliri [referred to] when he wrote, "and from under them thirty steps one
atop another all the way to the Throne of Glory they [the souls] fly and
ascend melodiously singing SONG OF THE STEPS." For Eleazar ha-
Kallir's liturgical poem with English translation see David A. De Sola, *The
Festival Prayers According to the Ritual of the German and Polish Jews: Vol. VI: Service
for the Feast of Tabernacles* (London: P. Vallentine, 1881), p. 217. For more
than a millenium this poem formed part of the service for the second day

of the festival of Tabernacles (Sukkot). It is now generally accepted that Eleazar ha-Kallir lived in the land of Israel in the 7th cent. C.E. See "Kallir, Eleazar", *EJ* 10:713-715.

PSALM CXXII

1 A SONG OF ASCENTS.
I REJOICED WHEN THEY SAID TO ME ["WE ARE
GOING TO THE HOUSE OF THE LORD"].[1]
I [King David][2] heard that people [were] saying, "When will
that old man die so that Solomon his son may become king
and build the Temple?" and I [was] happy.[3]

2 OUR FEET STOOD in war[4] in every place for the sake of
[*bišĕbîl*][5] YOUR GATES, within which people learn Torah,
O JERUSALEM.

3a JERUSALEM BUILT UP. When Solomon my son will have
built the Temple within her she [Jerusalem] will be BUILT
UP by virtue of the Divine Presence, the Temple, the Ark,
and the altar.

3b LIKE A CITY, WHICH IS ASSOCIATED WITH HER
[i.e.], like Shiloh, for Scripture compared them [Jerusalem
and Shiloh] to each other, for it is stated in the Bible, "to
the rest and to the inheritance" (Deut. 12:9),[6] [which is traditionally interpreted as follows]: "Rest" refers to Shiloh;
"inheritance" refers to Jerusalem.[7] However, our rabbis said
that [our verse alludes to the fact that] there is A JERUSA-
LEM BUILT UP in Heaven, and in the future the terrestrial
Jerusalem will be like her.[8]

4a TO WHICH[9] TRIBES WENT UP.
At Shiloh,[10] to which[11] TRIBES WENT UP when they
WENT UP from Egypt when the Tabernacle was set up with-
in her.

4b THE TRIBES OF YAH, which [epithet] is
TESTIMONY ON BEHALF OF ISRAEL, [which TES-
TIMONY was necessary] because the Gentiles were habitually casting aspersions upon them when they left Egypt; they
[the Gentiles were habitually] saying about them "that they
were bastards," and they [were] saying, "If the Egyptians
exercised control over their [the Israelites'] bodies all the more
so [must the Egyptians have exercised control] over their [the
Israelites'] wives!" [Hence] the Holy One Blessed be He said,

"I testify concerning them [the children born to the Israelite women in Egypt] that they are the children of their fathers [i.e., of the Israelite husbands of the Israelite women; they are not the offspring of the Israelite women's alleged forced cohabitation with their Egyptian overlords." Hence] He [the Holy One Blessed be He] put His Name upon them [by calling them] "ha-Reuben-y, ha-Simeon-y..." (Num. 26:7) [with prefixed *heh* and suffixed *yod*]; He added to them [the two letters of the divine name YaH] one at each end of [their original names Reuben, Simeon, etc.] so that this name YAH IS TESTIMONY ON BEHALF OF ISRAEL.[12]

5a   FOR THERE THE THRONES OF JUDGMENT STOOD. FOR also in Jerusalem the Divine Presence will be manifest, and there they will sit on them [THE THRONES OF JUDGMENT] to judge the Gentiles.

5b   THRONES OF THE HOUSE OF DAVID, i.e.,[13] royal[14] THRONES OF THE HOUSE OF DAVID.

6   PRAY FOR THE WELL-BEING OF JERUSALEM, and say to her,[15] "MAY THOSE WHO LOVE YOU BE AT PEACE,

7a   AND MAY THEIR BE WELL-BEING WITHIN YOUR RAMPARTS."

8   FOR THE SAKE OF MY KIN, Israel, AND FRIENDS, even I, King David, PRAY FOR YOUR WELL-BEING.

PSALM CXXII, NOTES

[1] Rashi does not quote the bracketed portion of the verse; I have supplied it for clarity.

[2] To whom the psalm is attributed in v. 1.

[3] Rashi's comment here is based upon a midrash attributed to R. Joshua b. Levi (Amora of the Land of Israel in the first half of the 3[d] cent. C.E.) at BT Makkot 10a. This midrash is inspired by the exegetical question, "How could King David to whom this psalm is attributed in v. 1, say that he rejoiced when people said, 'WE ARE GOING TO THE LORD'S TEMPLE,' seeing that the Temple was not built until the eleventh year after the death of King David (see 1 Kgs. 6:38)?"

[4] Rashi, following the midrash attributed to R. Joshua b. Levi at BT Makkot 10a, takes 'FEET STOOD' as an idiom meaning 'wage war'; support for such an interpretation of the expression may be found in Zech. 14:4.

[5] Contrast R. Joshua b. Levi (BT Makkot 10a), who interprets *biše'ārayik* to mean "by virtue of YOUR GATES." Both he and Rashi take advan-

tage of the ambiguity of the prefixed preposition *bĕ* in Biblical Heb.; contrast NJV: "inside your gates."

⁶ KJV.

⁷ So Rashi at Deut. 12:9; his source is Sifre Deut. there; so also Tosefta Zebaḥim 13:20; BT Zebaḥim 119a. Deut. 12:9 explains to the Israelites, who are about to enter the Land of Israel, that they are permitted to offer sacrifice to the LORD in places other than the Jerusalem Temple ("the place which the LORD your God will choose," Deut. 12:18) "because you have not yet come to the alotted haven" (NJV at Deut. 12:9). Not taking the two expressions "rest" and "inheritance" as hendiadys, *midrash halakah* sees here a prooftext for the idea expounded in Mishnah Zebaḥim 14:6, 8 that Shiloh served in the period of the judges as the exclusive sanctuary of the LORD just as according to Deuteronomy Jerusalem was so to serve from the time of the building of Solomon's Temple.

⁸ Rashi's comment is based upon a midrash attributed to R. Johanan [b. Napha] at BT Ta'anit 5a.

⁹ Heb. *šeššām* consists of the relative particle *še*, which is characteristic of late Biblical Heb. and of Rabbinic Heb., and the adverb *šām* 'there'; see below, n. 11.

¹⁰ Rashi takes v. 4 as an adjectival relative clause modifying "A CITY WHICH IS ASSOCIATED WITH HER" (v. 3b), i.e., Shiloh; see Rashi at v. 3b.

¹¹ Heb. *"ăšēr šām*; here, ironically, Rashi replaces the psalmist's typically late Heb. *še* with classical Biblical Heb. *'ăšēr*; on the relative pronoun in earlier and later Heb. see Kutscher, *A History of the Hebrew Language* # 45; #206.

¹² Cf. Rashi at Num. 26:5; cf. the midrash attributed to R. Huna quoting R. Idi in Canticles Rabbah at Cant. 4:12; cf. also Yalqut Shim'oni at Num. 26:5. The reading la-Reuben-y; la-Simeon-y (see 1 Ch. 27:16) found in our Rashi ms. here are inappropriate in the present context.

¹³ Explicative *waw*.

¹⁴ By adding this modifier, Rashi suggests that the two usages of 'THRONES' constitute synthetic parallelism rather than repetitive parallelism.

¹⁵ Rashi, anticipating a methodology expounded by Gordis, "Quotations as a Literary Usage in Biblical, Oriental and Rabbinic Literature," pp. 157-219, recognizes that v. 6b is a quotation before which the reader must supply a *verbum dicendi*.

PSALM CXXIII

1   A SONG OF ASCENTS. TO YOU ENTHRONED
[*hayyošĕbî*] IN HEAVEN I TURN MY EYES. [The final *yôd*
in the word *hayyošĕbî* is [a final] superfluous *yôd*.[1]

4b   THE SCORN OF THE COMPLACENT [i.e.], THE
SCORN of the COMPLACENT Gentiles.[2]

4a,c   We had our fill of[3] CONTEMPT (4c), with which they
showed contempt for THE VALLEY OF THE DOVES,
which is [an epithet of] Jerusalem.[4] *lĕga'ăyônîm* 'OF THE
HAUGHTY'[5] is written in the Bible as a single word, but it
is to be read as two words:[6] [*lige'ê yônîm* 'TO THE VALLEYS
OF THE DOVES'].

PSALM CXXIII, NOTES

[1] See the discussion at Ps. 113:5.

[2] Rashi's paraphrase converts this text with the definite article at the
beginning of a construct genitive chain into Standard Biblical Heb., in which
the definite article is attached only to the second element in a construct
genitive chain; concerning the anomalous construction in MT here see
Dahood here, and see C. H. Gordon, "Azitawadd's Phoenician Inscription," *JNES* 8 (1949), p. 112.

[3] Heb. *śāba'nû*; Rashi's paraphrase of the psalmist's periphrastic, "OUR
THROAT HAS HAD FOR IT ITS FILL"; Rashi's paraphrase is echoed
in NJV's idiomatic rendering, q.v.

[4] With Maarsen cf. the midrash on Isa. 60:8 attributed to Rabbah in
BT Bava Batra 75b. There the return of the exiled Jews to rebuilt Jerusalem is compared to the return of doves to their cotes.

[5] Vocalization of the *kethib* follows BH[3].

[6] For the list of fifteen such cases in the Hebrew Bible see Oklah
W'ochlah, ed. Frensdorff #99; see Rashi also at Ps. 10:10; 55:16.

PSALM CXXIV

1   A SONG OF ASCENTS.
     WERE IT NOT FOR THE LORD, WHO WAS ON OUR
     SIDE.

3b   IN THEIR BURNING RAGE AGAINST US.
     The grammatical form exemplified by *baḥărôt* 'in burning' is
     the same grammatical form as is exemplified by[1] *baʿăśôt* 'when
     they handled' (Ezek. 23:21).[2]

4b   *naḥlāh* 'DISEASE' is a cognate and a synonym of *ḥŏlî* 'sick-
     ness.'[3]

5   WE[4] escaped from them LIKE A BIRD, which ESCAPED
     FROM THE FOWLER'S TRAP.

Psalm CXXIV, Notes

[1]   The entire clause up to and including the word 'by' is expressed in
Rashi's Heb. by the two words *baḥărôt kĕmô;* with reference to the nuances
of *kĕmô* in Rashi's exegetical terminology see above, pp. 140–141.

[2]   Apparently, Rashi felt that these two instances of the infinitive construct preceded by the prefixed preposition *bĕ* would be especially confus-
ing to the beginning reader of Biblical Heb. In both cases the prefixed
preposition is vocalized with *pataḥ* (i.e., *a*) rather than with shewa mobile
because of the rule that two shewa mobile may not appear in adjoining
syllables; see Jacob Weingreen, *A Practical Grammar for Classical Hebrew* (2ᵈ
ed.; Oxford: Clarendon, 1959), pp. 8-11. Rashi correctly sensed that without
benefit of Weingreen's essay on the subject the reader might parse the two
forms as feminine plural nouns preceded by *ba* (preposition meaning 'in'
+ definite article) meaning 'in the'.

[3]   Such a noun derived from the very same root *ḥly*, from which is derived the noun *ḥŏlî* 'sickness' (Deut. 7:15; 28:61; Isa. 53:3; etc.) is attested
in Isa. 17:11; this noun *naḥălāh* is a *niphal* participle of the root *ḥly*; see BDB,
p. 317b; K-B³, p. 650, s.v. *naḥălāh* II. G. R. Driver, "Isaiah I-XXXIX:
Textual and Linguistic Problems," *JSS* 13 (1968), p. 45, followed by NEB,
renders the latter noun "wasting disease". However, the context proves that
the homonym *naḥlāh* here at Ps. 124:4 is simply the masculine noun *naḥal*
'stream' with the addition of paragogic *heh*; cf. *GKC* #90f; so already Qimḥi
here following a suggestion of Ibn Ezra here; the interpretation of *naḥlāh*
here as 'stream' goes back to LXX and Vulgate.

[4]   Heb. *napšēnû*, lit., 'our soul' (so KJV), employed as periphrasis for the
personal pronoun; see BDB, p. 660.

PSALM CXXV

1   A SONG OF ASCENTS.
     THOSE WHO TRUST IN THE LORD ARE LIKE
     MOUNT ZION.
     THOSE WHO TRUST IN THE LORD cannot be moved
     just like MOUNT ZION, which CANNOT BE MOVED.

2   For just as[1] JERUSALEM, HILLS ENFOLD IT, so does the
     Holy One Blessed be He[2] ENFOLD HIS PEOPLE.

3a-b THE SCEPTER OF THE WICKED SHALL NEVER
     REST [UPON THE LAND ALOTTED TO THE RIGH-
     TEOUS],[3] for the Holy One Blessed be He will not allow
     the government[4] OF THE WICKED to REST UPON THE
     RIGHTEOUS

3c   THAT THE RIGHTEOUS be wary of[5] SETTING THEIR
     HAND TO WRONGDOING.

5a   BUT THOSE WHO IN THEIR CROOKEDNESS ACT
     CORRUPTLY toward people by devising slanderous accu-
     sations,

5b   LET THE LORD MAKE THEM GO THE WAY OF
     EVILDOERS.

PSALM CXXV, NOTES

[1] Rashi's *kî ka'ăšer...kēn* "For just as...so" represents Rashi's interpretation of the *waw*-conjunctive at the beginning of v. 2b as comparative *waw*;
on this phenomenon see K-B³, p. 248a; see Prov. 25:25; Eccles. 7:1; see
GKC #161a. Moreover, Rashi suggests here that v. 2 is like v. 1 in that it
compares the LORD to Jerusalem.

[2] Rashi's paraphrase of the psalmist's 'THE LORD'.

[3] Rashi does not quote the bracketed portion of the verse; I have supplied it for clarity.

[4] Here Rashi intimates that *šēbeṭ* 'SCEPTER OF' is a metaphor for
memšelet 'government of'.

[5] Expansion and explication of the psalmist's negative *lō'*.

PSALM CXXVI

1 A SONG OF ASCENTS.
WHEN THE LORD RESTORES THE CAPTIVITY[1] OF
ZION from the Babylonian exile, we shall be[2] LIKE
DREAMERS.

4b LIKE WATERCOURSES IN THE NEGEB.
[I.e.], LIKE WATERCOURSES full of water in a parched
land, which provide it [the land] with moisture, so will we
become thriving when You restore OUR CAPTIVITY (v.
4a).[3]

5a THEY WHO SOW, in which arid land [do so] IN TEARS
because they are anxious lest it [what THEY SOW] not
sprout.

5b THEY reap[4] WITH SONGS OF JOY because of the watercourses full of water when they [the waters] are made to
flow therein.

6a HE GOES ALONG WEEPING....
So do Israel sow virtue before the Holy One Blessed be He
IN TEARS (v. 5a) in the Exile, but

5b THEY SHALL REAP it WITH SONGS OF JOY when You
pay their wage[5] in the future.

PSALM CXXVI, NOTES

  [1] The interpretation of the noun *šbyt* as 'captivity' was commonly accepted until the discovery of the 8th cent. B.C.E. Aramaic treaties from
Sephire; see Dahood, here.

  [2] Rashi's substitution of the imperfect form of the verb for the psalmist's
perfect intimates that Rashi, like many moderns, including Duhm and
Gunkel, interprets *hāyînû* as a prophetic perfect.

  [3] The *qere*, which is quoted in our Rashi ms. is *šĕbûtēnu*, which can only
mean 'our fortunes'; so NJV; however, the *kethib* is *šĕbîtēnu*, which Rashi
understood to mean 'our captivity'; see above, n. 1.

  [4] Rashi's paraphrase employing the participle where the psalmist employs the imperfect, which may be understood as denoting the future as
in Rashi's final comment on this psalm; see below.

  [5] This metaphor for restoration of Israel from exile is derived from Isa.
40:10; 62:11.

PSALM CXXVII

1a   A SONG OF ASCENTS.

FOR SOLOMON,[1] which David composed with reference to Solomon, for he [David] foresaw by means of prophetic inspiration that in the future he [Solomon] would build the Temple and [that] on that same day he [Solomon] would marry Pharaoh's daughter (see 1 Kgs. 3:1), and with reference to this deed it is stated in the Bible, "This city has aroused My anger and My wrath from the day it was built..." (Jer. 32:31).[2] Therefore, he [David] composed this psalm [asking Solomon], "Why, my son, should you build [the Temple] and turn aside from the Omnipresent?"[3] Insofar as He does not delight in it,[4]

1c   ITS BUILDERS LABOR IN VAIN ON IT.

1e   THE WATCHMAN KEEPS VIGIL IN VAIN. [I.e.], for no profit does the WATCHMAN watch.[5]

2a   IN VAIN DO YOU, the craftsmen, who RISE UP EARLY and who STAY UP LATE at their work, earning their living through pain and exertion [i.e.], through

2b   BREAD OF ANXIETY [i.e., bread earned] as a result of toil.

2c   INDEED,[6] MAY the Holy One Blessed be He[7] GIVE to him who banishes sleep from his eyes in order to study Torah. TO HIS BELOVED SLEEP[8] [i. e.], to one who banishes sleep from his eyes.[9]

3a   NOTE THAT A GIFT FROM THE LORD to whom [i.e.], to the aforementioned type of person, ARE CHILDREN, for he has disciples whom he trains, who are to whom like children.[10]

3b   THE FRUIT OF THE WOMB, HIS REWARD. [I.e.], THE REWARD IS THE FRUIT of the Torah, which is within him [bĕlibbô], for it is stated in the Bible, "It is good that you store them inside you [bebiṭnekā]" (Prov. 22:18).[11]

4a   LIKE ARROWS IN THE HAND OF A WARRIOR for fighting his enemies with them

4b   ARE SONS BORN TO A MAN IN HIS YOUTH [i.e.], the disciples, whom a person trains during one's youth.[12]

5a THE LAUDATIONS OF THE MAN WHO FILLED HIS QUIVER WITH THEM[13] [i.e.], with the aforementioned types of arrows. *'ašpāh* is the case for the arrows, which is called cuyvre in O.F.[14]

5b THEY SHALL NOT BE PUT TO SHAME WHEN THEY CONTEND WITH HIS[15] ENEMY IN THE GATE. Torah scholars who prove each other wrong with respect to halakah seem like mutual enemies.

PSALM CXXVII, NOTES

[1] Rendering of the ambiguous prefixed preposition *lě* reflects Rashi's interpretation, which is followed by KJV. The rendering "of Solomon" (RSV; NJV) suggests Solomonic authorship, which is at variance with Rashi's attribution of all the SONGS OF ASCENTS to David in his commentary at Ps. 120:1, q.v.; hence the need to account for Ps. 127's having been written by David but for Solomon; see below in Rashi.

[2] With Maarsen cf. Seder Olam, chapter 15; BT Niddah 70b; Leviticus Rabbah 12:5; with Zohory see also Rashi at 1 Kgs. 3:3.

[3] Traditional English rendering of Rabbinic Heb. *ha-Māqôm*, lit., "The Place," an epithet of God, probably derived from the designation of the place of God's enthronement on earth, Jerusalem in general, and the Temple in particular as "The Place" (see Deut. 12:14; 17:10; Jer. 7:14; etc.) just as in Rabbinic Heb. the divine epithet "the Heavens" is derived from the conception that God is enthroned in the sky (cf. Ps. 2:4; 103:19;123:1; etc.). See Kadushin, *The Rabbinic Mind*[3], pp. 204-205. The midrash here quoted is best appreciated when it is realized that *ha-Māqôm*, traditionally rendered "The Omnipresent," is an epithet derived from a designation of "The Temple". If so, the author of the midrash has David ask Solomon, "Why have you rejected the true Temple, which is God Himself, by building your Temple?"

[4] Cf. Isa. 1:11; Hos. 6:6; 1 Sam. 15:22.

[5] Here Rashi substitutes more familiar expressions for the psalmist's less familiar ones.

[6] Interpreting Heb. *kēn* as an emphatic; cf. Rashi at Ex. 1:12.

[7] Rashi supplies the implied subject.

[8] RSV's rendering of the lemma, which reflects Rashi's interpretation.

[9] Cf. BT Ketubbot 62a and Rashi's comment on our verse there; cf. also Midrash Tehillim here.

[10] With Maarsen cf. the midrash based on Isa. 8:18 at Leviticus Rabbah 11:7; and JT Sanhedrin 10:2; see also Rashi at BT Qiddushin 30b; contrast the midrash found in Midrash Tehillim here, BT Shabbat 152a and elsewhere (see Aaron Hyman, *Torah Hakketubah Wehammesurah* [3 vols.; Tel Aviv: Dvir, 1965], vol. 3, p. 59). The latter midrash suggests that the reward of virtue is to father sons rather than daughters; Rashi, who fathered

three daughters but no sons, suggests instead that the reward of virtue is not biological children but spiritual progeny, i.e., disciples.

[11] With Maarsen cf. the midrash on Prov. 22:18 attributed to R. Ammi at BT 'Erbuin 54a.

[12] See Rashi at BT Qiddushin 30b, s.v. "sons of one's youth."

[13] Rendering of the opening word *'aśrê* based upon Rashi at Ps. 1:1.

[14] I.e., Eng. 'quiver'; see Levy, *Contribution* #269; see also J. Greenberg, *Foreign Words in the Bible Commentary of Rashi*, p. 197.

[15] Literal rendering of the Heb.; contrast NJV's rendering 'the'. The switch from singular (v. 5a) to plural (v. 5b) and back to singular 'HIS' leads RSV to translate all the forms in this verse in the singular. Rashi's comment alludes to the possibility that the psalmist deliberately refers to several people, whom he treats as individuals.

[16] Rashi's source seems to be the midrash attributed to R. Hiyya b. Abba in BT Qiddushin 30a.

PSALM CXXVIII

1   A SONG OF ASCENTS.
      HAPPY ARE ALL WHO FEAR THE LORD.[1]

PSALM CXXVIII, NOTES

[1] Our Rashi ms., like most mss. of Rashi's Commentary on the Book of Psalms, supplies no Rashi commentary on Ps. 128. Like many other Rashi mss., our ms. supplies the number and the opening lines. The scribes responsible for Oxford Bodleian ms. Can Or. 60 and Oxford Opp. Add. Fol. 24 explain that they have supplied the opening lines and the numbers of Pss. 67, 121, 128, and 134, for which they were unable to find any Rashi commentary, so as not to lose count of the number of psalms. See our discussion of this phenomenon above, p. 160. Seven Rashi mss. (Florence Plut. 3.8; JTS L 781; Leiden Scaliger 1; Leipzig B.H. fol. 4; London Harley 150; Oxford Bodleian Opp. Add. 4° 52; Rostock 32) all have a one line comment on Ps. 128:6. While Ps. 128:6 is rendered in NJV, "and live to see your children's children. May all be well with Israel," the author of the one line comment in the aforementioned Rashi mss., clearly interpreted the verse as follows: "SEEING SONS OF YOUR SONS IS PEACE FOR ISRAEL." The comment reads as follows: "...SONS OF YOUR SONS. If they have inherited an estate without a woman having need of a brother-in-law [to perform levirate marriage or to release her from levirate marriage; see Deut. 25:5-10], then there IS PEACE in the world." Typically, London Harley ms. 151 prefaces and follows this one line comment with the expresion "I found," on which see the discussion in our introduction. The Commentary of Rashi on the Book of Psalms contained in the Rothschild ms. now designated Israel Museum 180/51/1, like most mss. of Rashi's Commentary on the Book of Psalms, contains no comment on either Ps. 121 or on Ps. 134. However, at Ps. 128 it presents a series of short comments on vv. 3-4, which do not appear elsewhere in the manuscript tradition of Rashi's Commentary on the Book of Psalms. Oxford Boldeian ms. 107/1 contains the following: "A SONG OF ASCENTS. HAPPY ARE ALL WHO FEAR THE LORD (1a); YOU SHALL BE HAPPY AND YOU SHALL PROSPER (2b). [I.e.], YOU SHALL BE HAPPY in the preeschatological era, AND YOU SHALL PROSPER in the posteschatological era; and thus did our rabbis interpret it [see Mishnah Avot 4:1]. AND...PEACE [šālôm] UPON ISRAEL (6b); PEACE is to be understood according to its literal meaning...." Note that the long comment found in the standard editions of the Rabbinic Bible, which I did

not find in any of the mss. I was able to examine (see above, pp. 158–164) concludes with an expanded version of the comment on v. 6 found in seven mss. cited above. Ms. Parma de Rossi 551 supplies at Ps. 128 a long comment taken from the Commentary on the Book of Psalms by Abraham Ibn Ezra.

PSALM CXXIX

1   A SONG OF ASCENTS.
     SINCE MY YOUTH THEY HAVE OFTEN ASSAILED
     ME.

3   THEY MADE LONG FURROWS. [The noun *ma'ănîtām*
     'their furrow'] is a synonym of[1] *telem* 'furrow' (Job. 39:10); it
     is the same noun as is attested in "within a space about half
     a furrow long [in] an acre of land" in [the Book of 1] Samuel
     [14:14].[2]

6b   THAT FADES BEFORE [*qadmat*] IT CAN BE PULLED UP.
     [I.e.], THAT before [*qodem*][3] they pull it up, i.e.,[4] they de-
     tach it from its place, IT HAS FADED.[6]

7b   NOR *ḥiṣnô* FOR THE GATHERER OF SHEAVES.[7] [The
'   noun *ḥiṣnô*] is the same noun as is attested in "They will bring
     your sons in [their] arm" (Isa. 49:22); [it means] *ésèle* in Old
     French.[8] It is likewise attested in "I likewise shook out *ḥoṣnî*
     'my sleeve'"[9] (Neh. 5:13).

PSALM CXXIX, NOTES
   [1] Heb. *hû'*.
   [2] With Maarsen cf. *Mahberet Menahem*, p. 285, s.v. *'n* X; Rashi at Hos.
10:4; see also Rashi at 1 Sam. 14:14; see now K-B³, p. 581b.
   [3] Rashi paraphrases a rare Biblical Heb. expression by means of its
common cognate in Rabbinic Heb.
   [4] Exegetical *waw*.
   [5] Biblical Heb. *šālap* 'draw out' means 'pluck out, detach, pull up (grass)'
only here; hence Rashi clarifies its nuance by equating it with the regular
Rabbinic Heb. verb *tālaš* 'detach', which is completely unattested in Biblical Heb.
   [6] Heb. *yābēš* 'it is dried out'.
   [7] Rendering of the lemma to reflect Rashi's understanding. The Old
French gloss shows that Rashi interprets *ḥoṣen* as an anatomical term in
all of its attestations. M. Malul, "Also I shook out my sleeve," *Beth Mikra*
31 (1986), pp. 17-22 (in Hebrew) demonstrates that 'hem' is the most appropriate rendering in all three instances.
   [8] Old French *ésèle*, from which is derived Modern French *aiselle* 'arm-
pit', glosses Heb. *ḥoṣen* also in Rashi at Isa. 49:22; Heb. *'aṣṣilôt yādêkā* 'your
armpits' in Rashi at Jer. 38:12 and Heb. *'aṣṣîlê yāday* 'my arm joints' in
Rashi at Ezek. 13:18 (on the latter verse see Moshe Greenberg, *Ezekiel
1-20*, AB, vol. 22 [Garden City, N.Y.: Doubleday, 1981]).
   [9] I.e., the portion(s) of the garment through which one puts the arm(s);
cf. Ibn Ezra ad loc.

PSALM CXXX

1 A SONG OF ASCENTS. OUT OF THE DEPTHS.[1]

4a YOUR IS THE POWER TO FORGIVE.
   [I.e.], You have not given permission to an agent to forgive.[2]
   This assertion is congruent with what is stated elsewhere in
   the Bible, "For he [the angel; see Ex. 23:20-23] will not pardon your offenses" (Ex. 23:21).[3]

4b SO THAT YOU MAY BE HELD IN AWE because of the
   fact that a person should not rely on forgiveness by anyone
   other than [the LORD].

6a-b I AM MORE EAGER FOR THE LORD[4] THAN
   WATCHMEN FOR THE MORNING. Note that I belong
   to those who look forward to the Redemption [of Israel].[5]

6c WATCHMEN FOR THE MORNING.
   They continually look forward from one watch to another.[6]

Psalm CXXX, Notes

[1] While v. 1 serves in our Rashi ms. as the distinctive heading of the
psalm, Rashi's commentary on this psalm begins at v. 4a, q.v.

[2] This assertion is clearly meant to show that there is no basis in
Hebrew Scripture for the assertion in the New Testament that Jesus
also can forgive sins; see, e.g., Mark 2:5-12; Acts 5:31.

[3] With Maarsen cf. Tanḥuma and Tanḥuma, ed. Buber at Ex.
23:21; see also Rashi there.

[4] The epithet 'ădonāy; not the tetragrammaton.

[5] With Maarsen cf. Rashi at Ps. 92:3; there Rashi treats "morning" as a metaphor for Redemption and "nights" as a metaphor for
Exile.

[6] Heb. qēṣ 'aḥar qēṣ; see the discussion of late Heb. qēṣ at Ps. 78,
n. 10. In applying this expression to the metaphor at hand Rashi
alludes to the three or four watches (i.e., changing of the guards or
shifts of guard-duty) atop the city walls in Tannaitic times; see
Mishnah Berakot 1:1 and BT Berakot 3a-b.

PSALM CXXXI

1   A SONG OF ASCENTS.
    O LORD, MY HEART IS NOT PROUD.
2a I HAVE TAUGHT MYSELF TO BE QUIET AND CON-
    TENTED [by leaning] on You LIKE A BABY [gāmûl] who
    is enabled to lean[1]
2b UPON ITS MOTHER. [Here the passive participle] gāmûl
    means 'nursling'.[2]
2c LIKE A BABY [gāmûl] IS MY SOUL UPON ME.[3] [I.e.],
    MY SOUL within me is [i.e., feels] toward You like a
    nursling at its mother's breast.[4]

PSALM CXXXI, NOTES

   [1] Heb. šehû' nātûn, lit., 'who is placed'.
   [2] Maarsen notes that everywhere else Rashi interprets gāmûl to mean
'weaned from its mother's breast'; see Rashi at Gen. 21:8; Isa. 28:9; and
so also NJV here. However, Rashi here anticipates the observation of
William R. Taylor in IB, vol. 4, pp. 683-684: "The word...means, lit.,
'finished' or 'completed' and may imply either 'weaned' or 'nursed'. But
a weaned child is not ipso facto a tranquil child. The figure is that of a
child which after being suckled is composed."
   [3] Rendering of the lemma according to the understanding presupposed by Rashi's comment.
   [4] Rashi's interpretation emphasizes the maternal simile applied to
God, which has been rediscovered in recent times by Phyllis Trible, God
and the Rhetoric of Sexuality (Philadelphia: Fortress, 1978), p. 70, n. 2.

PSALM CXXXII

1   A SONG OF ASCENTS.
HIS EXTREME SELF-DENIAL ['unnôtô] [i.e.], his self-af-
fliction, with which he exerted and labored to find for You a
Place.¹

5   UNTIL I FIND A PLACE [i.e.], UNTIL I know where will
be the Place of His Sanctuary.

6a   IN EPHRATH [i.e.], in the most important and excellent
Place. [The noun EPHRATH is not to be taken as a proper
noun]; it is a cognate of [the adjective ephrathite in] "son of
Tohu, son of Zuph, an ephrathite" (1 Sam. 1:1), which
means 'important, of noble descent'.² Another equally plausible interpretation of "WE HEARD IT IN EPHRATH" is
["WE HEARD IT] in the Book by Joshua," who came from
Ephraim (Num. 13:8) that he [Joshua] says with respect to
all the tribal boundaries, "the boundary curved" (Josh. 15:9,
11; 18:14), but here [with respect to Jerusalem] he [Joshua]
says, "The boundary ran up and" struck "the...flank of the
Jebusites...Jerusalem" (Josh. 15:8), which means that Jerusalem is higher than all the [other] places, and she is worthy of
the Temple, for it is stated in the Bible, "You shall arise, and
you shall ascend to the Place" (Deut. 17:8), which intimates
that the Temple is higher than the entire land of Israel.³
Thus⁴ is [this verse] interpreted in [BT] Zebaḥim [54b].⁵

6b   WE CAME UPON IT IN THE REGION OF JAAR,⁶ i.e.,
in the territory of Benjamin, who has been compared to a
beast of the forest [Heb. JAAR], for it is stated in the Bible,
"Benjamin is a ravenous wolf."⁷

7a   LET US GO TO HIS TABERNACLES there.⁸

10b   DO NOT REJECT YOUR KING⁹ [i.e.], Solomon, when
he comes to install the Ark therein.¹⁰

12b   AND THIS MY TESTIMONY I TEACH THEM.
[I.e.], THIS, which ['ăšer] I TEACH THEM.¹¹

15   ṣêdāh 'ITS STORE OF FOOD' [i.e.], mĕzônāh 'her food'.¹²

18b   yāṣîṣ 'shall sparkle' [i.e.], 'shall shine'. [The verb yāṣîṣ] is a
cognate of [the noun noṣĕṣîm 'sparkle' in] "and their sparkle
was like the luster of burnished bronze" (Ezek. 1:7).¹³

PSALM CXXXII, NOTES

¹ Heb. *māqôm*; see below, v. 5.

² Rashi's comment on Heb. *'eprat* here and at 1 Sam. 1:1 and again at Ruth 1:2 is, as noted by Shabbetai Bass (1641-1718) in his supercommentary Siphete Hakamim 'Lips of the Wise' on Rashi's comment on Ruth 1:2, based upon the series of midrashim in Leviticus Rabbah 1:3. These midrashim are inspired by the realization that the term cannot mean Ephraimite (so NJV at 1 Sam. 1:1) since David, who is called "the son of an Ephrathite" (1 Sam. 17:12) was from the tribe of Judah as were Mahlon and Chilion, who are called Ephrathites at Ruth 1:2 and since Elkanah, who is called an Ephrathite in 1 Sam. 1:1 was a Levite according to 1 Ch. 6:12. On the ambiguity of the term in question see *Harper's Bible Dictionary*, ed. Paul J. Achtemeier (San Francisco: Harper & Row, 1985), pp. 273-274, s.v. "Ephraimite," "Ephrathite," "Ephrathah".

³ Sifre Deut. there; BT Qiddushin 69a; Sanhedrin 87a; Zebaḥim 54b; quoted by Rashi at Deut. 17:8; for history of religions perspectives on the idea see Cohn, *The Shape of Sacred Space*; Levenson, *Sinai & Zion*.

⁴ Referring to the equation of EPHRATH with "The Book of/by Joshua".

⁵ The tractate, which is nowadays called Zebaḥim 'Sacrifices', is called by Rashi, following BT Zebaḥim 45a and Bava Meṣi'a 109b, *šĕḥiṭat qodāšîm* 'Slaughtering of Consecrated Animals'.

⁶ With William R. Taylor in *IB*, vol. 4, p. 686 note that 'REGION OF JAAR' is "a poetic variant of the region of Kiriath-jearim (cf. 2 Sam. 6:2-12; 1 Ch. 13:1-14)."

⁷ Cf. BT Zebaḥim 54b.

⁸ By adding this word Rashi makes explicit the connection between this exclamation and vv. 5-6.

⁹ Heb. *māšîăḥ*; see Rashi at Ps. 2:2.

¹⁰ See Rashi at Ps. 24:7.

¹¹ Since Rashi, following the Masoretic vocalization *zô*, interprets *zw* as the fem. sing. demonstrative adjective 'THIS' referring to *'ēdôtî* 'MY TESTIMONY' (see our discussion at Ps. 119, n. 118), he must supply the relative particle *'ăšĕr* 'which' between *zw* and 'I TEACH THEM'; so also Qimhi and so already LXX and Vulgate. NEB and NJV, following KJV and RSV, appear to agree with Dahood's revocalization of *zw* as the archaic poetic relative particle *zû* 'that, which'.

¹² Here Rashi explains that the typically Biblical Heb. term is synonymous with the typically Rabbinic, which occurs in the Bible only at Gen. 45:23 and 2 Ch. 11:23.

¹³ NJV, which clearly derives both the plural noun *noṣĕṣîm* 'sparkle' and the imperfect verb *yāṣîṣ* from a triliteral root *nṣṣ*; Rashi, on the other hand, must have taken both forms as derivates from a biliteral root *ṣṣ*; for Rashi's view of roots, which are today recognized as containing an initial

n see Englander, "Rashi's View of the Weak, *'ayin-'ayin* and *pe-nun* Roots," pp. 417-425; contrast *Mahberet Menahem*, which derives the noun from a biliteral root *nṣ* (see there, p. 258) and the verb from a monoliteral root *ṣ* (see there, p. 323).

PSALM CXXXIII

1   A SONG OF ASCENTS.
HOW GOOD AND HOW PLEASANT IT IS THAT BROTHERS DWELL TOGETHER. When the Holy One Blessed be He will DWELL in the Temple, the people of Israel [will be] called BROTHERS and friends.[1]

2   LIKE FINE OIL, with which the sons of Aaron the priest were annointed (Ex. 30:22-33; Lev. 8:12), RUNNING DOWN from his head and his BEARD to the collar [*pî rō'š*] of his robe, for the beard lies over the collar of [*pî*] the robe.[2]

3   So [*kēn*] pleasant is THE DEW OF HERMON, which is high above the mountains of Zion. Now the dew from Hermon runs down upon the mountains of Zion. As is annointing oil for high status[3] so is Mount Zion with respect to glory and honor for Israel. As is FINE OIL (v. 1) so [*kēn*] is THE DEW OF HERMON. As is this so is this. [The use of two repeated comparative *kaph*'s here in vv. 2-3, LIKE FINE OIL...LIKE THE DEW OF HERMON] is the same usage as is attested in "And it will be like the people like the priest" (Hos. 4:9) [which means, "the people shall fare like the priests"].[4]

1   However, our rabbis interpreted THAT BROTHERS DWELL as a reference to Moses and Aaron in connection with the subject of sacrilege with respect to annointing oil; [on that basis they interpreted] the entire psalm in [BT] Tractate Horayot [12a].[5] However, in the language of the Pentateuch and of the Prophets and the Writings[6] there are "metaphor and simile, the words of the wise and their riddles" (Prov. 1:6).[7] Moreover, the correct interpretation of [the superscription] A SONG OF ASCENTS is [that] it [Ps. 133] was composed in honor of the Temple.[8]

PSALM CXXXIII, NOTES
   [1] Cf. Rashi at Ps. 122:8.
   [2] Here Rashi explains the realia presupposed by the simile "IT [THAT BROTHERS DWELL TOGETHER, v. 1b] IS LIKE FINE OIL ON THE HEAD RUNNING DOWN ONTO THE BEARD, THE

BEARD OF AARON [the fine oil] THAT COMES DOWN OVER
THE COLLAR OF HIS ROBE" (v. 2). Rashi suggests that in Ps. 133:2
Heb. *'al* 'ON, OVER' has the meaning 'to', which is more clearly expressed by Heb. *'el*. He notes that the term *pî* 'mouth of' means *pî rōš*, lit.,
'head opening', i.e., 'collar' (cf. Dahood, here). Moreover, he suggests that
the fem. pl. *middôtāyw* 'his garments' (KJV) refers to the priestly robe (so
NJV), which is called *kuttonet* 'tunic' in Ex. 28:39, 40; 29:5, 8; Lev. 8:7;
etc. Concerning *middôt* see Dahood here.

3 Cf. Rashi at Ps. 105:15.

4 NJV there; so Rashi there; to Rashi's description of the syntactic
usage in question cf. Ibn Ezra and Qimhi at Hos. 4:9; *GKC* #161.

5 According to Tannaitic tradition recorded there, when the annointing oil dripped from Aaron's head to his beard, Moses feared that he
might have committed sacrilege by pouring on too much oil. A heavenly
voice reassured Moses that he was guiltless. Aaron, fearing that he might
be guilty of the offense in question, was told by a heavenly voice: "HOW
GOOD AND HOW PLEASANT IT IS THAT BROTHERS DWELL
TOGETHER [which is to say that] just as Moses is not guilty of sacrilege
so are you not guilty of sacrilege."

6 Heb. *qabbālāh*; concerning the desgination in Rabbinic literature of
the Prophets and the Writings, i.e., the last nineteen books of Hebrew
Scripture, as distinct from the Pentateuch, as *qabbālāh* see Norman M.
Bronznick, "Qabbalah as a Metonym for the Prophets and Hagiographa,"
HUCA 38 (1967), pp. 285-295.

7 Granted that the literal meaning of *'aḥîm* is 'brothers' and that a literal interpretation of 'brothers' in a context referring to Aaron would support the view of Ps. 133 found in BT Horayot 12a, Rashi holds that the
author of Ps. 133 employed *'aḥîm* metaphorically as explained above. My
rendering of the terms *māšāl* 'metaphor' and *mĕlîṣāh* 'simile' reflect Rashi's
understanding of the verse both in the present context and in his commentary at Prov. 1:6.

8 See Rashi at Ps. 120:1.

PSALM CXXXIV

1   A SONG OF ASCENTS.
     NOW BLESS THE LORD.[1]

Psalm CXXXIV, Notes
   [1] Our Rashi ms., like most mss. of Rashi's Commentary on the Book of Psalms and like the printed Rabbinic Bible, contains no commentary on Ps. 134. Ms. Rostock 32 contains the following one line comment on Ps. 134: "Now our rabbis interpreted (it) with reference to the priests when they ascend the dais [to bless the people]." The only other ms. of Rashi's Commentary on Psalms, which contains a comment on Ps. 134, Oxford Bodleian 107/1 provides the following comment:

A SONG OF ASCENTS. This was composed with reference to the Temple. It is stated, "LIFT UP YOUR HANDS TOWARD THE SANCTUARY [*qodeš*]" (v. 2a). [The use of the term *qodeš* to refer to the Temple] is in consonance with what is written (in Ex. 28:29, 35; Lev. 16:2, 3, 16, 20, 33; etc.) *haqqodeš* "the sanctuary". [LIFT UP YOUR HANDS refers to the fact that the priests] pronounce the blessing with raised palms. Now some explain that when the high priest pronounced the blessing he would not lift his hands higher than the frontlet [Heb. *ṣîṣ;* see Ex. 28:36; 39:30; Lev. 8:9] on which is written 'Holy to the LORD' (additions). MAY THE LORD BLESS YOU FROM ZION (v. 3) [teaches] that blessing also comes from Zion, for it is stated in the Bible, "MAY THE LORD BLESS YOU FROM ZION." [This interpretation is from] R. Tanhuma (additions).

Concerning the significance of the expression "additions" here see our introduction, pp. 161–162.

1   HALLELUJAH. PRAISE THE NAME OF THE LORD.

7b   HE MAKES *bĕrāqîm*[1] FOR THE RAIN. They [*bĕrāqîm*] are the sky's flashes of lightning,[2] which gleam [*mabrîqîm*] and glow before the rain;[3] they are called esloide [i.e., 'lightning' in Old French].[4]

7b   *môṣē'* is a form of the verb *mĕṣî'āh* 'finding',[5] which is to say that ["*môṣē'* THE WIND FROM HIS VAULTS" means], "He [the LORD] established VAULTS where they [WINDS] are available[6] for Him to send them on His [various] errand[s]."

9   *bĕtôkēkî* is synonymous with *bĕtôkēk* 'in your midst'.[7]

13   O LORD, YOUR NAME ENDURES FOREVER.
     As were Your greatness and Your authority back then[8] so be it now, and so be Your ability to punish and to avenge us.

14a FOR THE LORD WILL CHAMPION HIS PEOPLE.
     [I.e.], He will exact judgment on your behalf[9] from their enemies.

14b *yitneḥām*[9] [i.e.], *yit'aššēt* 'reconsider'.[10]

20b YOU WHO FEAR THE LORD are the proselytes.[11]

PSALM CXXXV, NOTES

[1] NJV renders 'LIGHTNING'; so Rashi, q.v.

[2] See Rashi at Ps. 97:4.

[3] This expression represents Rashi's interpretation of the psalmist's 'FOR THE RAIN' as alluding to the idea expressed in Modern French by *trainée de lumière avant la pluie*, sc., that lightning precedes the rain; see next note.

[4] See Levy, *Contribution* #56.

[5] All moderns agree with Qimhi in construing *môṣē'* as a biform of *môṣî'* "He brings forth" (KJV), the *hiphil* participle of the verb *yāṣā'* 'exit, go forth'; see *GKC* #53o; Bauer & Leander, p. 443. The latter interpretation goes back to LXX and Vulgate. Note also that while moderns refer to a Biblical Heb. verb by its 3d pers. masc. sing. perfect or its infinitive, Rashi usually refers to a verb by its gerund as here.

[6] Heb. *mĕṣûyîm*, the pl. of the passive participle of the verb *māṣā'* 'find'.

[7] I.e., Rashi construes the final *yôd* of *bĕtôkēkî* as superfluous final *yôd*; on this phenomenon see Rashi at Ps. 113:5; cf. NJV margin "against you".

⁸ In the days of Moses and Joshua alluded to in vv. 8-12.

⁹ Heb. *mišpĕtêkem;* on the ambiguity of the Heb. root *špṭ* and of its semantic equivalent *dyn* employed here by the psalmist see Rashi at Isa. 32:7.

¹⁰ This rendering of the verb *yit'aššēt,* which is found in Biblical Heb. only at Jonah 1:6, is supported both by the context in Jonah and by Rashi's interpretation of *yitneḥām* (here and also at Num. 23:19; Deut. 32:36) in his commentary at Gen. 6:6, s.v. *wayyinaḥēm* 'He regretted'. Rashi is correct in noting in his commentary at Jonah 1:6 and concerning the Aram. cogante *'ăšît* in his commentary at Dan. 6:4 that the verb means 'think'. For the history of the nuance 'take (favorable) thought for' see George M. Landes, "Linguistic Criteria and the Date of the Book of Jonah," *EI* 16 (1982), pp. 155-156.

¹¹ Concerning the source of this assertion see above, Ps. 22, n. 27; 115, n. 7; see also Ps. 66:16.

PSALM CXXXVI

1   PRAISE THE LORD; FOR HE IS GOOD,
FOR HIS KINDNESS IS FOREVER.[1]
Twenty-six [repetitions of] FOR HIS KINDNESS IS FOR-
EVER are mentioned in this psalm. They correspond numerically to twenty-six generations [from Adam to Moses]
during which the world [$h\bar{a}$'$\bar{o}l\bar{a}m$] was without [the Giving of
the] Torah [through Moses; see Ex. 18-20], and it contin-
ued to exist by virtue of HIS, the Holy One Blessed be He's
KINDNESS.[2]

PSALM CXXXVI, NOTES

[1] Rendering of the lemma to reflect the interpretation of *ḥesed* 'KIND-
NESS' reflected in Rashi's commentary here; see also Rashi at Ps. 101:1.

[2] Cf. Rabbi Joshua b. Levi (Palestinian Amora of the 1st half of the 3d
cent. C.E.) in BT Pesaḥim 118a; see also Numbers Rabbah 12:12. This
comment treats the word *ôlām* as a *double entendre*, which it is in Rabbinic
Heb. where it can refer to both units of time, in this case twenty-six generations, and 'the world'; see Kadushin, *The Rabbinic Mind*[3], pp. 293-294.

PSALM CXXXVII

1   BY THE RIVERS OF BABYLON, THERE WE SAT when we descended into Exile.

3a   [FOR OUR CAPTORS ASKED US THERE FOR SONGS].[1]
     I.e., Nebuchadnezzar asked them to sing for him as they [the Levites] used to sing upon the [Levites'] podium.[2]

2   UPON ʿărābîm WITHIN IT [i.e.], ʿărĕbê-naḥal 'willows of the brook' (Lev. 23:40; Job. 40:22).[3]

3b   wĕtôlālênû śimḥāh [designates] types of musical instruments; [they are so designated] because people hang them up; thus did Menahem [b. Jacob ibn Saruq] explain wĕtôlālênû śimḥāh [to mean] wĕtôlālênû of joy.[4] However, one ought to interpret wĕtôlālênû "our enemies, who deride us and make fun and treat us like fools";[5] it is a cognate of [the participle mĕhôlālāy 'my deriders' in] "My deriders use my name to curse" (Ps. 102:9b).[6]

4   HOW CAN WE SING? It is not stated, "We shall not sing" but rather "HOW CAN WE SING?" [which] intimates that [in response to the Babylonians' request in v. 2, "SING FOR US..."] the Levites immediately[7] mangled their thumbs with their teeth. Therefore, it is stated, "HOW CAN WE SING while our thumbs are mangled?"[8] Isaac.[9] HOW.[10]

5   ...FORGET YOU.... The Congregation of Israel says this.[11]

6   IF I DO NOT RAISE UP JERUSALEM to the memory of the mourning of her destruction. [I.e.], I SHALL ARISE to recall them above all my joy.

7   STRIP IT STRIP IT [ʿārû ʿārû] is a verb referring to destruction; the same verb is attested in "Babylon's broad wall will surely be razed" (Jer. 51:58);[12] and the same verb is attested in "razing[13] it from foundation [to top]" (Hab. 3:13).[14] It [the verb ʿr 'raise'] is employed only with reference to an object which can be uprooted from the earth.

PSALM CXXXVII, NOTES

[1] Neither the printed editions nor the mss. call attention to the fact that Rashi skips from discussing v. 1 to discussing v. 3a and back to v. 2 and then again to v. 3b. However, the content of the second part of Rashi's comment, following the quotation of v. 1, clearly explains the meaning of v. 3a; hence our supplying the bracketed lemma and hence our interpretation of the initial *waw* as explicative, 'I.e.'.

[2] Midrash Tehillim here; Pesikta Rabbati 31:4.

[3] Rashi here anticipates the moderns, who hold that throughout the Bible the plant name *'ărābîm* designates the *Populus euphraitica*, whose common name in Eng. is "Euphrates aspen". For description and discussion see Harold N. Moldenke and Alma L. Moldenke, *Plants of the Bible* (Waltham, Mass.: Chronica Botanica, 1952), p. 183; for pictorial illustration see Noga Hareuveni, *Nature in our Biblical Heritage*, trans. Helen Frenkley (Kiryat Ono, Israel: Neot Kedumim, 1980), p. 79; see the discussion in Jehuda Feliks, "Willow," *EJ* 16:517-518 and the literature cited there.

[4] Maarsen here, following *Mahberet Menahem*, ed. Fillipowski, p. 184, n. 364, points out that Menahem does not actually say this. Note, however, that in *Mahberet Menahem*, p. 394 the author insists that his four entries, p. 394, s.v. *tl* represent distinct nuances of *yĕsôd 'eḥād* 'a single root'. The fourth nuance refers to hanging of movable objects; these are *telyĕkā* 'your sword' [so Rashi at Gen. 27:3]; the verb *tālînû* 'we hung up' [our lyres] (Ps. 137:2); and *wĕtôlālênû* (Ps. 137:3; this example is cited in many but not all mss. of *Mahberet Menahem*; see critical apparatus there, p. 394, l. 19). Rashi suggests in his commentary at Gen. 27:3 that *telyĕkā* 'your sword' is so designated "for it is customary to hang it up." Apparently, Rashi's observations both at Gen. 27:3 and here derive from a close reading of *Mahberet Menahem*, s.v. *tl*; cf. Qimhi here.

[5] Taking *maṣṭîm* as *hiphil* participle of the root *šṭy* 'to be foolish'.

[6] See Rashi there.

[7] Rabbinic Heb. *'āmĕdû*, lit., 'they arose', employed here, as frequently in Rabbinic Heb., as an auxiliary verb like Biblical Heb. *qām*; on the latter usage see Orlinsky, Notes, pp. 34-35.

[8] Cf. Pesikta Rabbati 31:4; Midrash Tehillim here.

[9] Rashi attributes the preceding midrash to R. Isaac, who is, perhaps, R. Isaac b. Tablai, to whom it is attributed at Midrash Tehillim here. The latter source seems, however, to present a conflation of midrashim attributed to R. Isaac b. Tablai in Pesikta Rabbati 28:3 and midrashim recorded anonymously in Pesikta Rabbati 31:4.

[10] This word is repeated by dittography in our Rashi ms. from v. 4, above.

[11] Rashi here calls attention to the psalmist's abrupt shift from quoting the words of the exiled Jews in Babylonia in vv. 1-4 in 1st pers. pl. to quoting personified Israel in 1st pers. sing. in vv. 5-6.

[12] Heb. *'ar'ēr tit'ar'ar*, which *BDB*, p. 792b derives from a root *'rr* II 'strip oneself' while *BDB*, p. 788b derives *'ārû* at Ps. 137:7 and *'ārôt* at

Hab. 3:13 from the verb *'ārāh* 'be naked, bare'. Rashi indicates below that he traced all three to a common biliteral root *'r*. *Mahberet Menahem*, p. 290 traces both *'ārû* at Ps. 137:7 and *'ārôt* at Hab. 3:13 to a common root *'r* V.; but he is silent concerning the forms found in Jer. 51:58. With Maarsen, note that the comparison of *'ārû* in Ps. 137:7 with *'ar'ēr* in Jer. 51:58 goes back to R. Abba b. Kahana (late 3^d cent. Palestinian Amora) in Midrash Tehillim here.

¹³ Heb. *'ārôt;* see previous note.

¹⁴ Rashi does not quote the bracketed portion of the verse; I have supplied it for clarity.

PSALM CXXXVIII

1a   OF DAVID. I SING TO YOU WITH ALL MY HEART.

1b   BEFORE *'ĕlohîm* [i.e.], in the presence of[1] princes.[2]

2   BECAUSE YOU HAVE EXALTED YOUR WORD MORE THAN ALL YOUR NAME. [I.e.], YOUR NAME[3] is "Lord of power"[4] and "Passionate and Avenging" (Nah. 1:2). Yet YOU HAVE EXALTED YOUR WORD, i.e., Your promise of Your beneficence and Your kindness MORE THAN ALL YOUR NAME. In other words, [Your promise is that] You forego [the exercise of] Your attributes of justice, and [You] forgive us.

3b   *tarhîbēnî*[5] [i.e.], *higdaltanî* 'You have exalted me'.[6]

4b   FOR [*kî*] THEY HAVE HEARD THE WORDS YOU SPOKE.
     [I.e.], when[6] THE HEARD THE WORDS YOU SPOKE [sc.], "You shall not murder; you shall not commit adultery" (Ex. 20:13; Deut. 5:16), they acknowledged [*hôdû*][8] concerning "I the LORD am your God" and "You shall have no other gods" (Ex. 20:2-3; Deut. 5:6) that it was worthwhile to make them accept the yoke of His kingdom first and afterwards that He should make all His decrees.[9]

6   *yĕyēdā'* [means] *yĕyassēr* "He will discipline" (Deut. 8:5); it is the same nuance [of the verb *yāda'* 'know'] that it reflected in "He punished [*wayyoda'*] the people of Succoth with them" (Judg. 8:16).[10]

8a   THE LORD WILL SETTLE ACCOUNTS FOR ME.
     [I.e.], He will agree[11] to my requests.

8c   THE WORK OF YOUR HANDS [i.e.], the Temple, of which it is stated in the Bible, "Your hands established" (Ex. 15:17).[12]

PSALM CXXXVIII, NOTES

[1] Heb. *lĕ'ênê*, lit., 'to the eyes of'; paraphrase of the psalmist's *neged* 'BEFORE'.

[2] Heb. *śārîm*. With Maarsen note that Rashi here bases his interpretation on Midrash Tehillim here, which states, "BEFORE *'ĕlohîm* [means] BEFORE Sanhedrin [which is called *'ĕlohîm*], for it is stated in the Bible,

"You shall not curse *'ĕlohîm*" (Ex. 23:27), [i.e., "You shall not curse the judges"; so Targum Onkelos there; cf. Rashi there and BT Sanhedrin 66a]. Note that here as in Ps. 29:1, Rashi, following the Rabbinic tradition, denies the existence of gods alongside of God; hence, any biblical verse, which might be construed as referring to such divine beings, must be interpreted as referring to mortals; see our discussion at Ps. 29, n. 2 and at Ps. 49, n. 48.

³ I.e., God's essence or nature.

⁴ Heb. *ba'al gĕbûrôt*, an epithet found in the second benediction of the so-called amidah; see Birnbaum, *Daily Prayer Book*, p. 84.

⁵ Vocalization reflects plene ready found in our Rashi ms.

⁶ So Vulgate; cf. *Mahberet Menahem*, p. 350, according to which all occurrences of the root *rhb* refer to *memšālāh* 'political power'. Rashi here intimates that the verb *tarhîbēnî* is an imperfect employed as a preterite.

⁷ Rashi indicates that here the ambiguous Biblical Heb. *kî*, which NJV renders 'FOR', has the meaning of Rabbinic Heb. *keše* 'when'.

⁸ Rashi here intimates that in v. 4 the psalmist employs the imperfect verb *yôdûkā* as a preterite.

⁹ Cf. the midrash attributed to R. Phineas at Numbers Rabbah 8:3, and contrast the midrash attributed to Ullah Rabbah at BT Qiddushin 31a.

¹⁰ Rashi's comment is based upon *Mahberet Menahem*, p. 130, s.v. *dᶜ* III; see Rashi at Ps. 74:5. This interpretation treats the two halves of v. 6 as antithetic parallelism.

¹¹ Rashi, followed by NJV attributes to the verb *gāmar* 'conclude' the precise nuance of Eng. 'conclude' in such expressions as 'conclude an agreement' and 'conclude a treaty; cf. Rabbinic Heb. *nimnû wĕgāmĕrû* 'they [their votes] were counted, and they agreed' in Mishnah Yadayim 4:1, 3.

¹² In his commentary at Ex. 15:17, Rashi, following Midrash Tehillim at Ps. 139:5, notes that while the world is described as being made, as it were, with one divine Hand (Isa. 48:13), the Temple was/will be made, as it were, with two divine Hands. Hence 'THE WORK OF YOUR HANDS' in Ps. 138:8c must allude to the Temple rather than to the created world!

PSALM CXXXIX

1 OF DAVID. A PSALM.
   O LORD, YOU HAVE EXAMINED ME AND KNOW ME.

2a YOU DISCERN TO MAKE ME A COMPANION [*lěrē'î*] FROM AFAR.
   [I.e.], YOU DISCERN FROM AFAR to draw me to Your companionship [*rē'ûtěkā*], i.e., Your endearment.
   TO MAKE ME A COMPANION [i.e.], *lěhabběrēnî 'ēlêkā* 'to make me a friend to You'.[1]

3a YOU SURROUNDED [*zērîtā*] MY PATH ['*orḥî*] AND MY LYING DOWN. [I.e.], You have drawn a boundary around my road [*darkî*] and my dwelling and my [place of] lying down[2] so that I cannot do anything without Your knowledge. [The verb *zērîtā*] is a cognate of [the noun *zēr* 'moulding' in] "a gold moulding around it" (Ex. 25:24); thus did Menahem construe it.[3] Our rabbis, however, interpreted it [the verb *zērîtā*] as a reference to the fertilized ovum, for the child is fashioned from the purest part of it.[4] Now as for the meaning of *zērîtā*, it is the same verb as is attested in "Sulphur is strewn [*yězoreh*] upon his home" (Job. 18:15), and it is the same verb as is attested in [Rabbinic Heb.] "*zôreh* 'winnows' (the grain) to remove the chaff, which is in it."[5]

3b ARE FAMILIAR WITH [*hiskantā*][6] [i.e.], 'You have learned'.[7]

5a YOU HEDGE ME BEFORE AND BEHIND [i.e.], face and back.[8]

5b *kapěkā* 'YOUR PRESSURE' [i.e.], '*apěkā*, i.e., 'Your domination';[9] *destrayt* in Old French.[10]

6 IT IS BEYOND...KNOWLEDGE....
   It is covered and hidden FROM ME.

7b A place to FLEE FROM YOUR PRESENCE.[11]

9a I SHALL TAKE THE WING OF THE DAWNSTAR.
   [I.e.], If I could TAKE[12] for myself wings like this DAWNSTAR, which shines briefly from one end of the earth to the

other, I would likewise fly hurriedly until[13]

9b   I COME TO REST ON THE WESTERN HORIZON.

11a   IF I SAY, "SURELY DARKNESS WILL COVER ME...."
        [I.e.], If[14] I said,[15] "I shall be hidden in darkness, and the
        darkness will make darkness over me so that You cannot see
        me...." [The verb] *yěšupēnî* 'IT WILL COVER ME' is a cog-
        nate of [the noun] *nešep*.[16]

11b   AND NIGHT *'ôr* OVER ME. [I.e.], AND may the NIGHT
        be [*yěhî*] a source of darkness[17] before me. This [word] *'ôr* is
        a synonym of *'ōpel* 'darkness' (Ps. 11:2; 91:6; Job. 30:26;
        etc.).[18] It is the same verbal root as is attested in *yāpîṣ 'ănan*
        'ōrô "a cloud spreads His darkness" (Job. 37:11)[19] as well as
        in "all stars of darkness" (Ps. 148:3)[20] as well as in "He made
        dark [*wayyā'er*] the night" (Ex. 14:20).[21]

12a   EVEN there I have no escape, for DARKNESS IS NOT
        DARK FOR YOU.

12c   LIKE DARKNESS LIKE LIGHT.
        [I.e.], to You both of them are the same.

13a   MY KIDNEYS, which think all my thoughts.[22]

13b   *těsukkēnî* [i.e.] *těsokěkēnî* 'You covered me'.[23]

15b   I WAS MADE IN A HIDDEN PLACE by means of inter-
        course.

15c   IN THE RECESSES OF THE EARTH [i.e.], in the lowest
        [of the three] compartment[s] of my mother's womb.[24]

16a   MY UNFORMED LIMBS and my shape and my final form
        before I was born. I.e., YOUR EYES SAW [ME] before I
        came into the world.

16b   THEY WERE ALL RECORDED IN YOUR BOOK. I.e.,
        all who, like me are formed from dust,[25] they and I alike
        were all together revealed to You before being created.[26]

16c   DAYS THEY WERE FORMED AND NOT [*wělō'*] ONE
        IN THEM.
        [I.e.], All the deeds of humankind and its destiny were re-
        vealed to You as though they had already been formed even
        though not even one of them was yet living and even though
        not one of them was yet in the world. Now these are the
        wonders of the works of our God and the characteristic of
        the divine power [namely], that the things to take place in
        the future are revealed to Him before they sprout (cf. Gen.
        2:5) and the things to come before they come to pass. In the

same vein He says, "Before I created you in the womb I selected you..." (Jer. 1:5). [Additions].[27]

16a   YOUR EYES SAW MY EMBRYO [golmî].
[I.e.], as soon as You created the world YOUR EYES SAW
THE EMBRYOS OF [golmê] the future generations.[26]

16b   IN YOUR BOOK [i.e.], "The Book of the Generations of
Humankind" (Gen. 5:1), which You showed to the first human [Adam].[28] [The imperfect form of the verb] yikkātēbû
[here corresponds in meaning to the perfect form of the
verb] niktēbû 'they were recorded'.

16c   DAYS THEY WERE FORMED AND NOT ONE IN
THEM.
[I.e], They were going to be created in the future at the end
of many DAYS, BUT NOT ONE of them was yet created
IN THEM [i.e., in those early days].[29] This is its [v. 16c's]
meaning according to the consonantal text.[30] However, according to the manner in which it is traditionally read,[31] wĕlô
'AND FOR HIMSELF'[32] its [v. 16c's] meaning is as follows:
DAYS WERE FORMED. He [the LORD] showed him
[the first human] DAYS to be created in the future; He
separated ONE from them, the Sabbath Day.[33] An equally
plausible interpretation [of FOR HIMSELF ONE] is [the
following]: "This is the Day of Atonement [which is set
aside] for forgiveness."[34]

17a   NOW TO ME HOW DEAR [yāqĕrû] ARE YOUR
FRIENDS [rē'ēkā].[35] [Here] the Congregation of Israel says,
"HOW honored [nikbĕdû][36] in the eyes of the Holy One
Blessed be He[37] are the virtuous people in every generation."

17b   AND HOW NUMEROUS THEIR HEADS [i.e.], the sum
of their numbers. [The use of the noun rō'š 'head' to mean
'number'] is the same idiomatic usage as is attested in
"When you count" (Ex. 30:12).[38]

18a   I COUNT THEM [i.e.], if I come to count the quality of
their good deeds, THEY EXCEED THE GRAINS OF
SAND.

18b   I AM AT THE END, BUT I AM STILL WITH YOU.
[I.e.], Look! I have now come to the end of the generations,
which You apportioned from then [since Creation, alluded
to in v. 16] until today, and until this generation [which is]

WITH YOU, i.e., in the fear of You. I[39] have not turned aside from [following] after You.

19a   IF YOU WOULD ONLY SLAY [THE WICKED],[40] would that YOU WOULD ONLY SLAY THE WICKED Esau.[41]

20a   WHO SAY, "YOU," FOR INTRIGUE, i.e., they invoke Your Name in connection with their evil designs, and they ascribe Your divinity to idols.

20b   nāśû" is an alternate spelling of nāśĕ'û 'they took' IN VAIN.[42] [The verset as a whole means], "Your enemies took Your Name IN VAIN."[43] [The noun] 'ārêkā [corresponds in meaning to] 'ôyĕbêkā 'your enemies'.[44]

24a   IF I HAVE VEXATIOUS WAYS [i.e.], IF I HAVE a vexatious WAY, i.e., their mischief.[45]

PSALM CXXXIX, NOTES

[1] Rashi construes lĕrē'î as pi'el infinitive of the verbal root of the noun rēā' 'companion, neighbor' with 1st pers. sing. accusative pronominal suffix; the verb is attested in the pi'el in Judg. 14:21, in the hithpa'el in Prov. 22:24, and in the qal in Jer. 22:22; Ps. 37:3; Prov. 13:20; 15:14; 28:7; 29:3. Contrast NJV, RSV, KJV, all of which follow Ibn Ezra in construing lĕrē'î as prefixed preposition lĕ + a noun cognate of ra'ăyôn meaning 'thought' + 1st pers. sing. possessive pronominal suffix; see below at v. 17a.

[2] Rashi paraphrases substituting common words for the psalmist's rare words. E.g., he substitutes for the rare root rb' the more common cogante rbṣ. Note that both roots derive from proto-Semitic rbḍ; see BDB, p. 918, s.v. rb' II; rbṣ. The fact that outside of Ps. 139:3 Biblical Heb. rb' always refers to sexual intercourse (cf. Heb. škb 'lay') may have inspired the midrash to which Rashi refers below.

[3] Mahberet Menahem, p. 159, s.v. zr V.

[4] Rashi here refers to the midrash attributed to R. Hanina b. Papa in BT Niddah 31a. The latter assumes that the ṭippat tašmîš, lit., 'drop produced at intercourse' contains genetic material contributed by both the male and the female sexual partners. R. Hanina b. Papa (late 3d cent. Palestinian Amora) asserts that Ps. 139:3 alludes to the Holy One Blessed be He's selecting only the best parts of the genetic material; see Rashi there.

[5] This portion of Rashi's comment is based upon the baraitha attributed to the School of Ishmael in BT Niddah 31a immediately after the midrash attributed to R. Hanina b. Papa. For elucidation of these midrashim in relation to Ps. 139:3 see Rashi there; see also Midrash Tehillim here.

[6] This is the reading in our Rashi ms.; MT, however, has the unusual plene reading *hiskantāh*.

[7] So all ancients and moderns as required by the context.

[8] With Maarsen cf. Midrash Tehillim here.

[9] Rashi correctly understands that *kapekā* here connotes 'Your domination'. He errs, however, in that rather than interpret *kapekā* as 'Your palm(s)' employed as a metaphor for 'Your domination', Rashi takes *kap* here as a form of the noun *'ekep* 'pressure', which is attested only in Job. 33:7; see Rashi there; see also *Mahberet Menahem*, p. 6, line 24.

[10] The form reflected in our ms. is a dialectical form of the more common destreynt, which corresponds etymologically and semantically to Eng. 'distraint'; moreoever, the term corresponds semantically to Biblical Heb. *'ekep* 'pressure' (see previous note); see J. Greenberg, *Foreign Words in the Bible Commentary of Rashi*, p. 303, n. 584; Levy, *Contribution* #304.

[11] A paraphrase of v. 7b, "WHERE CAN I FLEE FROM YOUR PRESENCE?" Rashi employs the adverbial phrase to explain v. 9.

[12] Rashi treats the imperfect verb *'eśśā"* as a subjunctive introduced by *"im* 'if' in v. 8a; so already LXX, Vulgate, and so now NJV, q.v.

[13] Here Rashi answers two exegetical questions: (1) Why the wings of *śahar* 'DAWNSTAR'? (2) What is the syntactic relationship of the two halves of v. 9? To the first question Rashi replies that DAWNSTAR's wings propel the psalmist quickly from East to West. To the second question he replies that the two halves of v. 9 represent the protasis and apodosis of a conditional sentence. Moreover, while NJV, KJV, and RSV follow Ibn Ezra in understanding v. 9a as expressing the psalmist's desire to hitch a ride on personified DAWNSTAR, Rashi, like LXX, understands 'WINGS OF DAWNSTAR' as a metaphor denoting "wings like dawnstar".

[14] Rashi points out that v. 11a, like all the verses beginning with v. 8a, is a conditional sentence; see n. 12.

[15] Here Rashi substitutes a perfect for the psalmist's imperfect with *waw*-consecutive.

[16] So *Mahberet Menahem*, p. 366, s.v. *śp* II; the latter understands *nešep* to mean *'aśmûrāh* 'watch', i.e., 'subdivision of the night according to guard-duty'. Hence the verb *yĕšupēnî* refers, according to Menahem followed by Rashi, to being protected by a cover of darkness. *BDB*, p. 676a treats *nešep* 'twilight' as a noun derived from a triliteral root *nšp* while *BDB*, p. 1003 derives *yĕšupēnî* from a triliteral root *šwp*. Ibn Ezra, *BDB*, p. 1003 and NJV accept both the unlikelihood of our verb's being a cognate of the noun *nešep* and the likelihood that Rashi's interpretation of the meaning makes perfect sense in context.

[17] Heb. *ma'ăpîl*, a biform of the participle *ma'ăpēl*, which is attested in Josh. 24:7.

[18] Cf. *Mahberet Menahem*, p. 58, s.v. *'r* V; see Rashi at Ps. 148:3; Ibn Ezra here holds that *'ôr* here is the familiar noun meaning 'light'; so already LXX and Vulgate, and so KJV, RSV, NJV.

[19] Cited in *Mahberet Menahem*, p. 58, s.v. *'r* V.

[20] See our discussion there; with Maarsen cf. BT Pesaḥim 2a; contrast NJV's "all bright stars."

[21] Cited in *Mahberet Menahem*, p. 58, s.v. *"r* V; contrast Rashi there.

[22] I.e., the kidneys are, as it were, in biblical psychology a possible seat of the thought processes; see Ps. 7:10; 16:7; 26:2; 73:21; Jer. 12:2.

[23] The latter form, albeit with *ś* rather than *s*, is attested in Job. 10:11. While the form *tĕsukkēnî* demonstrates assimilation of the second and third letters of the root *skk,* the form *tĕśokĕkēnî* demonstrates dissimilation. Rashi assumes that his readers would more readily recognized and understand the latter form.

[24] See BT Niddah 31a and Rashi's commentary there.

[25] I.e., all humankind; see Gen. 2:7.

[26] Rashi's comment here is based upon the midrash attributed to R. Simeon b. Lakish (3[d] cent. C.E.) quoting R. Eleazar b. Azariah (late 1st cent. C.E.) in Pesikta Rabbati #23.

[27] The designation here in our Rashi ms. of the first of the two series of comments on v. 16 as *tô[sāpôt]* should demonstrate beyond a shadow of doubt that the appearance of comments, which are so designated, in the printed editions of Rashi's Bible commentaries are not the invention of the printers but belong to the manuscript tradition of Rashi's Bible commentaries long before the first printed editions; see also our discussion at Ps. 134, n. 1, and see our introduction, pp. 161–162.

[28] Rashi's comment here is based on the continuation of the midrash cited in n. 26.

[29] Rashi notes that here, as frequently in Biblical Heb., the so-called imperfect form of the verb, which is employed in Medieval and Modern Heb. to express the future tense, is employed as a preterite.

[30] Heb. *hammāsoret šekkātûb*; cf. Rabbinic Heb. *māsoret* 'consonantal text' in BT Pesahim 86b; Sukkah 6b; Megillah 3a; Qiddushin 18b; Nedarim 37b; Sanhedrin 4a (twice); 6b (three times); Makkot 7b (twice); Zebahim 37b (four times); 38a; Keritot 17b. In the terminology of the medieval Massoretes this term *māsoret* is replaced by *kethib*; for the use of the latter term already in Amoraic sources see Robert Gordis, *The Biblical Text in the Making*, p. LII, n. 69. Here at Ps. 139:16c as in Ps. 100:3 the *kethib* is *wĕlō"* 'AND NOT' while the *qere* is *wĕlō'* 'AND TO/FOR HIM'.

[31] Heb. *hammiqrā' šehû' niqrā'*; cf. Rabbinic Heb. *miqrā'* 'traditional reading'; see the sources cited in n. 30; the Rabbinic term corresponds in meaning to the medieval massoretic term *qere;* on the latter term see passim in Gordis, *The Biblical Text in the Making.*

[32] Rather than *wĕlō'* 'AND NOT'.

[33] Here Rashi explains the meaning of the phrase *wĕlō' 'eḥād* 'AND FOR HIM ONE'. The two interpretations of v. 16c are based upon a series of midrashim in Pesikta Rabbati #23.

[34] In Pesikta Rabbati #23 the latter view is attributed to R. Levi; the former view to R. Isaac.

[35] Rendering of the lemma according to the understanding presup-

posed by Rashi's comment. NJV, RSV, KJV, following Ibn Ezra, render
rēʿĕkā 'Your thoughts' assuming that here as in v. 2 we have a noun *rʿy*,
which is a cognate of the noun *raʿăyôn* 'thought, idea'. Rashi, like LXX
and Vulgate, sees here the well known noun *rēăʿ* 'companion'; cf. Rashi at
v. 2 above.

[36] Here Rashi paraphrases rare Biblical Heb. but standard Aram. *yqr*
by its standard Biblical Heb. equivalent *kbd*.

[37] Rashi's interpretation of the psalmist's 'TO ME'.

[38] Just as it is deduced from the use of the idiom 'go to God' (Ex. 21:6;
22:7), i.e., 'go to court' that Heb. *ʾĕlohîm* 'God' can mean 'judges' (see
Rashi at Ex. 22:7; etc.) so is it deduced here from the idiom 'lift up the
head', i.e., 'take account of' that *rōʾš*, lit., 'head', means 'number'. Rashi's
source here is *Mahberet Menahem*, p. 347, s.v. *rʾš* II. On the idiom *nāśāʾ rōʾš*
'count' see E. A. Speiser, "Census and Ritual Expiation in Mari and Israel," in *Oriental and Biblical Studies: Collected Writings of E. A Speiser*, ed. J. J.
Finkelstein and M. Greenberg (Philadelphia: University of Pennsylvania
Press, 1967), pp. 177-178.

[39] I.e., personified Israel; see Rashi at v. 17a.

[40] Rashi does not quote the bracketed portion of the verse. I have supplied it for clarity.

[41] For Esau as the quintessentially wicked personality see Rashi at Ps.
9:6; 109:2; 140:5.

[42] So *BDB*, p. 669b; the latter reading is attested in 11QPsᵃ.

[43] I.e., *ʾnāśûʾ* IN VAIN' = *ʾnāśĕʾû* IN VAIN' is ellipsis for "they took
Your Name in vain" (cf. Ex. 20:7; Deut. 5:11).

[44] Rashi's source is *Mahberet Menahem*, p. 290, s.v. *ʿr* IV; so also Ibn
Ezra; KJV; RSV; NJV; cf. *BDB*, p. 786, s.v. *ʿr* II.

[45] First Rashi clarifies the meaning of the noun *ʿōṣeb*, lit., 'VEXA-
TION', which is employed here as an adjective modifying the noun *derek*
'WAY' (for the grammatical usage in question see *GKC* #128p), by employing as an adjective the cognate participle *mĕʿaṣṣĕbāh*; then Rashi explains that 'a vexatious way' means *qilqûl* 'mischief'; note Rashi's use of
the explicative *waw*, here rendered 'i.e.'.

PSALM CXL

1   FOR THE LEADER....

2   RESCUE ME...FROM EVIL MEN.[1]

3b THEY WILL SOJOURN[2] WARS.[3]
    [I.e.], there will be WARS in the places of their sojourn, i.e.,
    in their settlements. *'akšûb* [i.e.], *'akkābîš* [4] [i.e.], *érinée* 'spider'
    in O.F.[5]

6a-b WITH ROPES THEY. SPREAD OUT A NET. The man-
    ner of [using]
    a NET is to tie a long ROPE at the top of it; now, as for the
    hunter, when he sees the birds located under the NET, he
    pulls the ROPE so that the NET falls upon the birds.
    ALONG THE WAY [means] near my paths and my feet.[6]
    [The preposition] *lĕyad* 'ALONG' [means] *'ēṣel* 'near'; it is
    the semantic equivalent of [*'el-yad*, lit., 'at hand' in] "Look,
    Joab's field is next to mine [*'el-yādî*]" (2 Sam. 14:30).[7]

9a THE DESIRES OF THE WICKED [i.e.], the wicked
    Esau.[8]

9b DO NOT LET HIS PLAN [*zĕmāmô*] PROSPER. [I.e.] DO
    NOT let his design succeed.[9]

9c THEY WILL BE PROUD. [I.e.], for [*kî*] they will become
    arrogant [*yitgā'û*]. However our rabbis interpreted *zĕmāmô* as
    a [noun] synonym of [the noun] *resen* 'muzzle' (Isa. 30:28;
    Ps. 32:9; Job. 30:11; 41:5) such as that which muzzles [*haz-
    zōmēm*] the mouth of a camel,[10] and it is [typically] Mishnaic
    Hebrew.[11] [According to the latter interpretation of *zĕmāmô*]
    'al tāpēq [which was understood above to mean 'DO NOT
    LET PROSPER', must be understood to mean] DO NOT
    remove [*'al tôṣî'*][12] [the aforementioned muzzle] from his
    cheeks.[13]

10 MAY THE HEADS OF THOSE WHO BESET ME...
    MISCHIEF.
    As for the brigade composed of the numerous troops[14] of
    Esau, who plan to lead me away from You,[15] MAY THE
    MISCHIEF OF THEIR LIPS COVER THEM.[16]

11a COALS of Gehinnom.[17]

11b MAY THEY BE CAST INTO PITS [*mahămorôt*] NEVER
     TO RISE AGAIN. INTO *mahămorôt* [means] 'into wars and
     strife'; it is a cognate of [the participle *mamrîm* 'rebelling' in]
     "You were rebelling" (Deut. 9:24).[18]

12a MAN OF TONGUE, i.e., Esau, "for there was hunting by
     means of his mouth" (Gen. 25:28). [I.e.], he [Esau] hunted
     him [Isaac] by means of his mouth.[19]

12b LET THE EVIL, which he[20] does CAPTURE HIM.

13   I KNOW THAT ultimately THE LORD WILL DO JUS-
     TICE with[21] THE POOR by avenging His servants.[22]

14   ONLY, may He do it speedily so that[23] RIGHTEOUS
     MEN WILL PRAISE His[24] NAME.

PSALM CXL, NOTES

[1] These quotations from vv. 1-2 serve as the distinctive heading of this
psalm in our Rashi ms. However, Rashi's commentary on this psalm begins with v. 3b, q.v.

[2] Heb. *yāgûrû*; rendering according to the interpretation presupposed
by Rashi's comment; contrast NJV's "they plot"; Dahood's "they plan".
Many moderns revocalize as *yĕgārû* from the verb *gārāh* 'stir up strife' (see
William R. Taylor in *IB*, vol. 5, p. 710; K-B[3], p. 177b, s.v. *gwr* II; *BDB*, p.
158b, s.v. *gwr* II), agreeing that the Masoretic vocalization supports
Rashi's interpretation.

[3] According to Rashi's interpretation the noun WARS is a locative
accusative serving as the direct object of the verb SOJOURN.

[4] Rashi, like the Psalms Targum, takes the *hapax legomenon* ʾkšwb to be
a biform of ʾkbyš, which is attested in Isa. 59:5; Job. 8:14; so NJV. The
two forms are seen to be related by metathesis (cf. the biforms *śmlh* and
ślmh, both of which mean 'garment') and the interchange of *w* and *y*,
which are often indistinguishable in Qumran mss. 11QPs[a] reads here
ʾakbyš. KJV, RSV, and Dahood follow LXX and Vulgate in treating ʾaksûb
as a distinct lexeme noting a kind of snake; this view is supported by the
parallelism. Ibn Ezra, q.v., refuses to commit himself either way.

[5] I.e., Modern French arraignée.

[6] *Mahberet Menahem*, p. 276, s.v. ʾgl V notes that the noun *maʿăgal* refers
to *nĕtîb* 'a path' in Isa. 26:7; Prov. 4:26; 5:6. See also Rashi at Ps. 23:3; cf.
NJV.

[7] With Maarsen cf. Rashi at Ex. 2:5.

[8] For Esau as the wicked person par excellence see Rashi also at Ps.
9:6; 109:2; 139:19a; etc. As Maarsen suggests, here Rashi may have in
mind the midrash on our verse in BT Megillah 6b-7a.

[9] Here Rashi paraphrases substituting well-known words for less familiar words; for the ambiguity of the psalmist's vocabulary here see below in Rashi.

[10] See Gen. Rabbah 75:9; BT Megillah 6a-b.

[11] See Mishnah Terumot 9:3: *lō' zōmēm 'et habbĕhēmāh* "he fails to muzzle the beast"; Rashi, followed by Ben Yehuda, *Dict.*, p. 1354, associates the verb *zāmam* 'muzzle' especially with the camel, probably because of the famous midrash in Gen. Rabbah 59:11, quoted in Rashi at Gen. 24:10.

[12] Both treatments of Biblical Heb. *pwq* have their advocates in modern times; see *BDB*, p. 807b; *K-B³*, p. 869b.

[13] See Rashi at BT Megillah 6a; cf. Qimhi here.

[14] With Maarsen note that Rashi here, as at Ps. 139:17, takes *rō'š* 'head' to mean *ḥešbôn* 'sum, number'; see Rashi and our discussion at Ps. 139:17.

[15] The *hiphil* participle *mĕsibbāy* 'THOSE WHO BESET ME' means literally 'those who surround me'; it denotes persons who conspire against the psalmist; for this usage of the verbal root *sābab*, lit., 'encircle', and the synonymous *hiqqîp* see Gruber, "Ten Dance-Derived Expressions in the Hebrew Bible," p. 335, n. 30. Rashi, however, attaches to the participle a meaning 'lead away, transfer', which is indeed attested for the *hiphil* of the verb *sbb* (for Rashi, following *Mahberet Menahem*, p. 261, the root is *sb*) in 2 Sam. 3:12; 1 Ch. 12:23; etc.

[16] Here Rashi substitutes the standard Biblical Heb. pronominal suffixes for the rare, archaic, poetic ones employed by the psalmist here.

[17] Here Rashi responds to the exegetical question, "Which COALS?"

[18] The latter form is a *hiphil* participle of the root *mry* 'rebel' while the pl. noun *mahmorôt*, whose root is *hmr*, means 'pits' as do its Ugar. and late Heb. cognates; see *K-B³*, pp. 524, 598. Rashi, apparently, traced both forms to a biliteral root *mr*.

[19] In his commentary at Gen. 25:28 Rashi points out that the contextual meaning of *kî ṣayid bĕpîw* is "when/for game was in his mouth" (cf. NJV margin there); however, Rashi there also cites the midrash alluded to here; the source of this midrash is Gen. Rabbah 63:10. Note that this midrash is inspired by the ambiguity of the pronoun in the phrase "in his mouth," which, apart from its immediate context, may refer either to Isaac's mouth or to Esau's mouth.

[20] Heb. *'îš ḥāmās* 'THE LAWLESS MAN'; Rashi here responds to the exegetical question, "Which EVIL?" so NJV.

[21] Heb. *'im;* here employed in the sense of 'with respect to'; the psalmist employs a double accusative.

[22] The latter phrase is based upon Ps. 79:10.

[23] Rashi responds to the abrupt transition from petition (vv. 2-13) to praise (v. 14), and he suggests that the particle *'ak* 'however' (so *Mahberet Menahem*, p. 42) supplies this transition. NJV leaves the particle untranslated.

[24] Rashi here paraphrases the psalmist's 'YOUR NAME'.

PSALM CXLI

1   I CALL YOU O LORD, HASTEN.

2   *mas'at kappay* 'THE LIFTING UP OF MY PALMS',[1] i.e., that I raise up[2] MY PALMS toward You.

3a   SET A GUARD OVER MY MOUTH when I pray to You so that 1 will speak pure words, which will be a means of reconciliation.[3]

3b   *dal śĕpātāy* 'THE DOOR OF MY LIPS',[4] i.e.,[5] 'the upper lip'.[6]

4c   WITH MEN [*'et 'īšīm*] [i.e.], 'with people' [*'im 'ănāšīm*].[7]

4d   LET ME NOT FEAST ON THEIR DAINTIES. [I.e.], I shall not be present[8] at their meal.

5a   LET THE RIGHTEOUS PERSON STRIKE ME IN LOYALTY, AND LET HIM REPROVE ME. [I.e.], I prefer that an authentic and virtuous prophet REPROVE ME, i.e., chastise me, for all his strokes,[9] i.e., his chastisements,[10] are [manifestations of] KINDNESS.[11]

5b   LET MY HEAD NOT REFUSE SUCH CHOICE OIL, i.e., the [annointing] oil of kingship, which was poured on my head, as it is stated in the Bible, "You annointed my head with oil" (Ps. 23:5). [The entire clause, however, is a metaphor, which means], May He NOT remove[12] MY HEAD from the reproof of a virtuous person so that [I] go and eat (cf. v. 4d) WITH EVILDOERS (v. 4c).

5c   FOR SO LONG AS MY PRAYER [i.e.] so[13] LONG AS MY PRAYER is in my mouth, note that it is for the detriment of EVILDOERS (v. 4c)[14] so that I do not stumble on their account.

6a   MAY THEIR JUDGES SLIP ON THE ROCK, for these peoples' judges and leaders[15] SLIPPED from the path of virtue into the path of the evil inclination and the stone heart,[16] which is hard as a ROCK.[17]

6b   FOR THEY HEARD my pleasant utterances, which I utter concerning the commandments of the Holy One Blessed be He, but they do not turn back from [their evil][18] path. Our rabbis in the Baraitha of Sifre interpreted it [v. 6] as a reference to Moses and Aaron, who died because of [their sin with respect to] the rock (see Num. 20:7-13).[19] I, however, am unable to interpret the verse so that its second part and its first part make sense together. However, one can almost interpret it in a manner that its various parts will fit together by saying that these [latter day] persons [mentioned in v. 6b] are comparable with respect to [their] stubbornness to those persons [i.e.], Moses and Aaron, who died because of them [the Israelites who provoked Moses and Aaron] for these [latter day] persons also HEAR MY SWEET WORDS, but they do not repent.

7a   AS WHEN ONE CLEAVES trees[20] AND BREAKS UP THE EARTH

7b   so[21] OUR BONES ARE SCATTERED so as to reach the door of death[22] because of the EVIL DEEDS (v. 5c) of sinners. *pôlēăḥ* 'CLEAVES' is a verb referring to *biqqûaʿ* 'splitting'; it is the same verb as is attested in "He pierced [*yĕpallaḥ*] my kidneys" (Job. 16:13).

8a   MY EYES ARE FIXED UPON YOU. [This verse] is a continuation of earlier verses, [namely]: "SET A GUARD OVER MY MOUTH" (v. 3); "LET MY MIND NOT TURN..." (v. 4); "MY EYES ARE FIXED UPON YOU" (v.8).[23]

8b   DO NOT LET MY PERSON FALL FROM YOUR PRESENCE.[15] [The verb *taʿar* 'let her fall'] is the same verb as is attested in "She dropped [*wattaʿar*] her jar into the trough" (Gen. 24:20).[24]

10   LET THE WICKED PEOPLE FALL INTO HIS NETS.[15] [I.e.], Let the wicked person himself fall INTO HIS NETS, which he spreads at my feet.[25]

PSALM CXLI, NOTES

[1]   I.e. 'my supplication'; see Gruber, *Aspects*, pp. 39-40.

[2]   Rashi's point is that *masʿat* is a gerund derived from the verb *nsʾ*; cf. *GKC* #45e; 74h.

[3]   Heb. *lĕrāṣôn*; see Rashi at Gen. 33:10; Lev. 19:5; 22:19; Ps. 5:13; 19:15; 145:15; and see Banitt, *Rashi: Interpreter of the Biblical Letter*, p. 29.

[4]   NJV's rendering follows Ibn Ezra; *BDB*, p. 194b; *K-B³*, p. 212b, all of whom assume that Heb. *dal* here is a biform of Heb. *delet* 'door' attested elsewhere; with *BDB*, *K-B³*, and Dahood here note that the short form without the feminine ending is found in Phoenician and in Punic; with

Ibn Ezra and Dahood cf. the semantic equivalent *pitḥê pîkā* "gates of your mouth" in Mic. 7:5.

⁵ Heb. *hî'*.

⁶ While the authorities cited in n. 5 seek to understand the expression *dal śĕpātāy* by determining the etymology of *dal*, which leads to the literal translation, "the door of my lips" (NJV), Rashi treats the expression as an anatomical term, for which he provides an idiomatic explanation. Rashi's explanation makes sense insofar as lips do not have doors, and his interpretation inspires one to look forward to finding the semantic equivalent in an as yet unearthed text from the ancient Semitic world.

⁷ Here Rashi informs us (a) that the equivocal *'et*, which may function either as a preposition meaning 'with' (*'et* II in *BDB*, p. 85b) or the sign of the definite direct object (*'et* I in *BDB*, p. 84b), is employed in the former sense in the present context; (b) that *'iśîm*, the rare plural of *'iś* 'man' attested only in Isa. 53:3; Ps. 141:4; and Prov. 8:4, is synonymous with the regularly attested form *'ănāśîm*.

⁸ Rabbinic Heb. *mêsēb*, which may mean either 'recline (at the dinner table)' or 'sit around (the table)'; see dictionaries of Rabbinic Heb.

⁹ Heb. *mahălumôt*; attested in the Bible only in Prov. 18:6; 19:29, this noun is derived from the verb *ḥlm* 'strike' employed earlier in the verse.

¹⁰ Cognizant of the fact that *mahălumôt* designates "blows on the body" in Prov. 18:6; 19:29 (*BDB*, p. 240b), Rashi points out that the verb *ḥlm* here in Ps. 141:5 is employed metaphorically to refer to discipline.

¹¹ Heb *ḥesed*, which NJV renders "LOYALTY"; see the discussion at Ps. 101, n. 1

¹² Heb. *yāsîr*, which is Rashi's interpretation of the psalmist's verb *yānî*; with Maarsen see Rashi at Num. 32:7 apropos of the evidence that Rashi read here *yānî"* note that *Mahberet Menahem*, p. 250 derives the verb from a biliteral root *n"*.

¹³ Heb. *kol*; Rashi's interpolation suggests that he construes the psalmist's *'ôd* 'LONG AS' as a variation on *kol-'ôd...bî* "so long as...in me" (Job. 27:3).

¹⁴ Here Rashi paraphrases the psalmist's *bĕra'ôtêhem*, which NJV renders "against their [the EVILDOERS of v. 4; so marginal note in NJV] evil deeds." While Rashi and Ibn Ezra, followed by KJV, interpret *rā'ôt* as 'bad things' that should happen to the EVILDOERS, NJV and RSV interpret *rā'ôt* to mean 'bad things' done by the EVILDOERS; contrast Rashi at v. 7, below.

¹⁵ Heb. *dayyānêhem ûmanhîgêhem*, which points to the fact that Biblical Heb. *śôpēṭ* may denote 'ruler' as well as 'judge'; see *BDB*, p. 1047a.

¹⁶ This expresion, which derives from Ezek. 11:19; 36:26, denotes stubbornness and insensitivity.

¹⁷ I.e., may their own insensitivity be the cause of their downfall.

¹⁸ The bracketed expression is missing from our Rashi ms.; I have supplied it for clarity from other editions of Rashi's commentary here.

¹⁹ See Sifre Deut. at Deut. 3:23; the designation *baraitha* refers to the

fact that Sifre is regarded by Rashi, following the Babylonian Talmud, as extra-Mishnaic Tannaitic literature.

[20] Rashi supplies a direct object for the transitive verb 'CLEAVES'.

[21] Heb. *kēn*; Rashi here reminds his readers that the two halves of v. 7 constitute a comparison.

[22] Rashi's paraphrase of the psalmist's 'THE MOUTH OF SHEOL', which suggests that Rashi may have been inspired by Ps. 6:6 where Sheol is b-word, i.e., poetic synonym of *māwet* 'death'.

[23] I.e., vv. 1-4 and v. 8 together express a single thought, "Help me because I am dependent upon You," while vv. 5-7, which refer to the psalmist's troubles and the sources of those troubles, constitute a digression.

[24] See Rashi there; see also *Mahberet Menahem*, p. 290, s.v. 'r II; see BDB, p. 788b, s.v. *'ārāh*.

[25] Rashi responds to the fact that in MT the subject and the verb are both in the plural while the pronominal suffix attached to the noun 'NETS' is singular; Rashi suggests that the latter noun refers to the individual nets prepared by the individual wicked persons; for the idea cf. Ps. 7:16; Prov. 26:27; 28:10; Eccles. 10:8; see also Esth. 7:10.

PSALM CXLII

1   A MASKIL OF DAVID WHILE HE WAS IN THE CAVE
when he cut off "the corner of Saul's cloak" (1 Sam. 24:4-5).

4b   YOU KNOW MY · COURSE [i.e.], how many traps
[*môqĕšîm*] there are in it.[1]

5b   I HAVE NO FRIEND.
[I.e.], there is no one among all of Saul's intimate associates,[2] who might prevent him [from injuring me].

8c   THROUGH ME [*bî*] VIRTUOUS PEOPLE WILL
CROWN [*yaktîrû*].
[I.e.], for my sake [*bišĕbîlî*] VIRTUOUS PEOPLE WILL
CROWN You [i.e., God], and they will praise[3] YOUR
NAME insofar as You support Your devotees.[4]

PSALM CXLII, NOTES

[1] Rashi alludes here to v. 4d, "THEY HAVE LAID A TRAP [*paḥ*]."
For *paḥ* 'trap' and *môqĕšîm* 'traps' in synonymous parallelism see Ps. 140:6.

[2] Heb. *mĕšārĕtāyw*, lit., 'his servants'.

[3] Here Rashi paraphrases v. 8b.

[4] The psalmist, like the authors of many of the Akkadian prayers called *nîš qāti* 'lifting of the hand' and like Moses in Ex. 32:12-13 and Num. 14:13-19, attempts to tell God that it is worth God's while to help him out. It will be, as it were, good public relations for God. What is less obvious in the original is made more forceful in Rashi's paraphrase.

PSALM CXLIII

1a A PSALM OF DAVID. O LORD, HEAR MY PRAYER.

1b ...AS YOU ARE FAITHFUL by being faithful to[1] the promise, which You promised.

3 MY FOE HOUNDED ME. I.e., if I have sinned against You, note that I have [already] been punished. This psalm was composed on behalf of all Israel.[2]

5 I THOUGHT OF THE DAYS OF OLD when You performed for us many wonders.[3]

4b yištômēm 'NUMBED' is a verb referring to silent wonder;[4] it is the same verb as is attested in "And for seven days I sat there stunned [mašmîm] among them" (Ezek. 3:15c);[5] "and Tamar remained stunned" (2 Sam. 13:20).[6]

6 IN THIRSTY EARTH[7] during the Exile.[8]

7 MY SPIRIT IS USED UP.

A person who desires something very much but does not achieve it is referred to by the expressions kilyôn 'ênayim 'used up of eyes' and kilyôn rûaḥ 'used up of spirit.[9]

8 IN THE MORNING [i.e.], when Redemption sprouts.[10]

9b I COVER UP[11] TO YOU.

[I.e.], I cover up[12] my troubles from all people, telling them [only] TO YOU.[13]

PSALM CXLIII, NOTES

[1] Heb. lĕha'ămîn; lit., 'by making faithful'; i.e., 'fulfilling'; this literal use of the hiphil of the verb 'mn is most peculiar since in both Biblical and Rabbinic Heb. the hiphil of the verb 'mn normally means 'rely upon, believe in'; see dictionaries. Our rendering of the infinitive is the only one, which will make sense in the present context.

[2] Here as in numerous places in the psalter, Rashi transforms an individual lament into a community lament by conceiving of the suffering psalmist as a personification of the Jewish people or as a spokesperson on their behalf; see, e.g., Ps. 6; 22.

[3] Heb. nissîm; traditionally, 'miracles'; on the nuances of nēs 'wonder, miracle' in Rabbinic Heb. see Kadushin, The Rabbinic Mind³, pp. 152-167.

[4] I take as an hendiadys Rashi's 'ôṭem wĕtimmāhôn, lit., 'closing [of the lips; cf. Prov. 17:28] and wonder'; similarly Rashi at Isa. 59:16; for this interpretation of the verb see now M. Greenberg, Ezekiel 1-20, p. 17; con-

trast Rashi at Isa. 52:14 where the interpretation in question is not applicable.

[5] *BDB*, pp. 1030-1031 construes the two forms as respectively *hithpolel* and *polel* forms of the verb *šāmēm* 'be desolated, appalled'.

[6] Cf. M. Lohfink, "Enthielten die im Alten Testament bezeugten Klageriten eine Phase des Schweigens?" *VT* 12 (1962), pp. 267-269.

[7] Heb. *b'rṣ;* contrast MT's *k'rṣ* 'LIKE THIRSTY EARTH'; see Maarsen here.

[8] In the present context *napšī*, traditionally 'my soul', could be taken as periphrasis for the personal pronoun 'I' or in its primary sense 'my throat', which became hoarse from crying out to God for help, which was slow in coming. Rashi here adopts the former interpretation. Since Rashi declares in his comment at v. 3 that the "I" of the psalm is Israel collectively, Rashi is justified in suggesting that v. 6 refers to Israel's collective suffering in exile.

[9] Anticipating Gruber, *Aspects*, Rashi treats the anatomical expressions as idioms. While Gruber, *Aspects*, pp. 386-399 understands both of these idioms as denoting sadness, Rashi, like most exegetes (see Gruber, *Aspects*, pp. 391-393), takes both as idioms denoting longing; hence Modern Heb. *kilyôn 'ênayim* 'longing'. Rashi, seeing that both expressions are idioms, ignores their literal meaning. Gruber, noting that both are anatomical expressions, seeks in human behavior an interpretation of the idioms that accounts also for their literal meanings.

[10] Taking 'MORNING' as a metaphor for 'beginning of Redemption' just as 'night' is often taken as a metaphor for 'Exile' and 'day' a metaphor for 'Redemption'; with Maarsen see Rashi at Ps. 74:16; 92:3.

[11] Heb. *kissîtî;* see next note.

[12] By employing the participle, Rashi intimates that the psalmist here employs the lst pers. sing. of the so-called perfect to express the present tense; on the latter phenomenon in Biblical Heb. see Rashi at Gen. 14:22; *HG*, vol. 2 #6e.

[13] Taking v. 9b as an instance of ellipsis, Rashi supplies the missing direct object of the verb *kissîtî* and thereby attempts to solve a famous crux interpretum; cf. the various modern commentaries.

PSALM CXLIV

1 OF DAVID. BLESSED IS THE LORD...WHO TRAINS....

2 *hārôdēd* PEOPLES¹ UNDER ME [i.e.], *hārôqaʼ*,² i.e., 'spreads out' [*šôtēăḥ*] MY PEOPLE so that it can lie down in its place. [The idiom *rôdēd ʻammî*] corresponds semantically to "he spreads out [*šôtēăḥ*] nations" (Job. 12:13),³ [which means] 'he enlarges them'. The verb *rdd* is the verb employed in Targumic Aramaic for rendering *rôqaʻ* as when we render [Heb.] *wayĕraqqĕʼû* "they stretched out" (Ex. 39:3) [by means of Aram.] *wayĕraddîdû*.⁴ Some, however, interpret *hārôdēd ʻammîm taḥtāy* to mean "who weakens nations under me."⁵ However, in an accurate edition of the biblical text the reading is *ʻammî* 'MY PEOPLE' [rather than *ʻammîm* 'PEOPLES'], and the marginal note of the masorah thereon is "In three places⁶ the seemingly correct reading⁷ is *ʻammîm*, but in fact the correct reading⁸ is *ʻammî* 'MY PEOPLE'.⁹ Now, as for the word *taḥtāy* 'UNDER ME', there is a marginal note of the masorah thereon, [which states], "Read *taḥtāyw* 'under Him'."¹⁰

3 WHAT IS MAN [i.e.], Who are Esau and Ishmael to You that You care about them so as to increase their eminence?¹¹

7 *pĕṣēnî* 'RESCUE ME' [means here literally], 'let me out', and it is a verb referring to 'rescuing' [*haṣṣālāh*] as is exemplified by [its use in] "who rescue [*happôṣeh*] His servant David" (Ps. 144:10).¹²

10 WHO GIVE VICTORY TO KINGS refers to "the Rock of Separation" (1 Sam. 23:28) where when David was about to be captured by Saul "an angel came and told Saul, 'Come quickly'" (1 Sam. 23:27). [Thereby] He [the LORD] saved Saul from being a murderer and David from being killed.¹³

11 *pĕṣēnî wĕhaṣṣîlēnî* 'RESCUE ME, AND RESCUE ME'¹⁴ [which is redundant; the redundancy suggests the following idea]: Just as You rescued [David] then so [please] now RESCUE ME [i.e.],

12a US [Israel], WHOSE SONS now..., i.e., for[15] now this gen-
     eration is worthy.
     OUR SONS ARE LIKE SAPLINGS, which are free of
     blemish; so are they [OUR SONS] clean of sin.[16]

12c OUR DAUGHTERS are pleasingly tall in stature
     LIKE PILLARS of a stone house, whose stone PILLARS
     are aligned each one parallel to the other as it ascends so
     that the PILLARS are straight.

12d CARVED FOR THE STRUCTURE OF THE TEMPLE.
     [I.e., OUR DAUGHTERS are] praised by the mouths of
     those who see them, for they [who see OUR DAUGH-
     TERS] compare them to the high STRUCTURE OF THE
     TEMPLE.[17]
     Our rabbis, however, interpreted OUR DAUGHTERS
     ARE LIKE CORNERSTONES [to mean], "they are filled
     with sexual desire as the CORNERS of the altar are full of
     blood, but they have intercourse only with their hus-
     bands."[18]

13a mězāwênû ARE FULL, i.e., zāwiyyôt 'the corners'[19] of our
     storehouses ['ôṣārôt] are "FULL of all good things" (Deut.
     6:11).

13b SUPPLYING PRODUCE OF ALL KINDS [mizzan 'el-zān]
     [i.e.], food [māzôn] from year to year.[20] [The expression
     mizzan 'el-zān [means] "from the time of the ingathering of
     this year's harvest until the season of the ingathering of the
     following year's harvest." [The term] zan [means] gouvernail
     'food, provisions' [in O.F.].[21]

13c NUMBER THOUSANDS, EVEN MYRIADS.
     [I.e.], they gave birth by thousands and by myriads.

14   OUR CATTLE ['allûpênû] ARE WELL CARED FOR.
     [I.e., 'allûpîm, i.e.], the prominent among us ARE CARED
     FOR by those who are less prominent than they because the
     less prominent heed [the counsel of] the prominent, and
     consequently THERE IS NO BREACHING among us.[22]
     AND NO SORTIE [i.e.], NO evil rumor GOES OUT far
     away.
     AND NO WAILING [i.e.], NO sound of the tumult of war.

15   THESE ARE THE LAUDATIONS OF THE PEOPLE
     WHO HAS IT SO[23] [i.e.], WHO HAS all this bounty.

Psalm CXLIV, Notes

[1] Heb. *'ammîm; sic*; for other witnesses to this reading found here in our Rashi ms. see NJV margin, and see *BHS*; note that in his commentary below Rashi discusses the two readings *'ammîm* 'PEOPLES' and *'ammî* 'MY PEOPLE' (the standard reading).

[2] Rashi suggests that the *qal* participle of the verb *rāqa'* is the semantic equivalent of the *qal* participle of the verb *rādad*. According to *BDB*, pp. 921b, 955b, the primary meaning of both of them is 'beat out'; see next note.

[3] Here Rashi notes that the specific nuance of the verb *rāqa'*, which is here shared by the verb *rādad*, is 'spread out', which is normally expressed in Rabbinic Heb. by the verb *šāṭaḥ*; on the latter see *BDB*, pp. 1008-1009.

[4] So T. O. there; note that Rashi there equates both the Heb. verb and its Aram. equivalent with Old French *estendre*, i.e., 'extend'.

[5] Rashi here may be referring to the traditional oral rendering of the Bible into Old French, whose errors Rashi sought to correct (see Banitt, *Rashi: Interpreter of the Biblical Letter*, p. 8) much as many modern commentaries seek to correct the hitherto canonical KJV. The interpretation here rejected by Rashi is shared by Jerome, Peshitta, and the Psalms Targum. Here again it should be noted that Rashi does not attribute the rejected view to the Psalms Targum printed in the Rabbinic Bibles because, as noted previously (see our discussion at Ps. 48, n. 18; Ps. 55, n. 18; 58, n. 29; 68, n. 92) Rashi did not know of that Targum.

[6] The three instances are 2 Sam. 22:48; Ps. 18:48; 144:2; see *Minhat Shai* here.

[7] Heb. *sĕbîrîn*; for the various views on *sĕbîrîn* see Gordis, *The Biblical Text in the Making*, pp. 26-27.

[8] Heb. *qĕrāyîn*.

[9] Here Rashi's quotation of the masoretic note corresponds to the masoretic note in the Leningrad ms., which forms the basis of BHS, q.v.; note, however, that while the latter ms. employs the abbreviations *sbr* and *wqr*, Rashi's commentary here spells out the terms.

[10] Rendering of the expression *qĕrê* follows Gordis, *The Biblical Text in the Making*, p. 7, n. 1. With Maarsen here, *Minhat Shai* et al. note that such a masoretic note is unattested in extant mss. and printed editions of the Hebrew Bible. However, the reading, without a masoretic note, is attested in a number of Heb. mss.; see *BHS*.

[11] Rashi's comment makes explicit the universalism implicit in the psalmist's use of the word *'ādām*, a generic term, which means both 'human being' and 'humankind'. Rashi's comment reminds his readers that despite their frequent mistreatment of the Jews, Esau (i.e., Christendom) and Ishmael (i.e., the Arab and Islamic world) belong with Israel to the family of *'ādām*, who are the object of God's loving concern.

[12] So NJV there; Rashi's source is *Mahberet Menahem*, p. 306, s.v. *pṣ* II.

[13] Rashi's source is the midrash attributed to R. Eliezer in Midrash Tehillim at Ps. 18:3.

[14] Rendering of the lemma according to the understanding presupposed by Rashi's comment; see Rashi at v. 7; see also the discussion of the implications of this exegesis in our introduction, p. 184.

[15] So NJV, q.v.

[16] With Maarsen cf. the midrash attributed to R. Zutra b. Tobiah quoting Rav in BT Pesaḥim 87a.

[17] Rashi contends that in context the simile refers to the pyshical beauty of the young Israelite women.

[18] Rashi here quotes the continuation of the midrash cited in n. 16. This midrash suggests (1) that the Jewish ideal is that women no less than men should be passionately desirous of sexual pleasure; (2) that there is no virtue in being uninterested in sex; (3) that there is great virtue in having sexual desire but seeking to fulfill it only within the marital bond.

[19] Rashi's view of *mzw* as a cognate of the noun *zāwît* 'corner, cornerstone, pillar' follows *Mahberet Menahem*, p. 152, which seems to trace both to a root *zwy*. Rashi's comment here stresses the paranomastic aspect of vv. 12-13. Rashi's treatment is echoed by Mandelkern, p. 352a, s.v. *zāwît*; contrast *BDB*, p. 265a, s.v. *māzû*; contrast *K-B*[3], p. 535a, s.v. *māzû*.

[20] Here Rashi follows *Mahberet Menahem*, p. 155, s.v. *zn* I in taking *zn* as a cognate of the noun *māzôn* 'sustenance'.

[21] In our Rashi ms. the final *l* of this word is omitted. Perhaps our ms. copied this word exactly as it appeared in an earlier ms., in which, in fact, the word appeared at the end of the line and was therefore abbreviated. Note that the O.F. word employed here is the semantic equivalent of Heb. *kalkālāh* 'sustenance', which defines *zan* in *Mahberet Menahem*, p. 155.

[22] I.e., so long as the followers and leaders each know their respective places there is no social conflict. Rashi's comment is based upon the midrash attributed to R. Johanan (b. Napha) in Ruth Rabbah Proem #6. This midrash construes *'allûpênû* here as a form of the noun *'allûp* (Gen. 36:15ff.) rather than as a form of the noun *'elep* 'bull'; while the context would appear to support the latter interpretation (so, e.g., NJV's "our cattle"), the masoretic vocalization militates against this view; hence Dahood, here revocalizes *'alpēnû*.

[23] Rendering of the lemma reflecting Rashi's interpretation of the expression *'ašrê* in his commentary at Ps. 1:1; 119:1.

PSALM CXLV

1   A SONG OF PRAISE. OF DAVID.

4   ONE GENERATION SHALL LAUD YOUR WORKS
    TO ANOTHER, and also as for me,[1]

5   THE GLORIOUS MAJESTY OF YOUR SPLEN-
    DOR...WILL I RECITE.

6a One generation to another (v. 4)[2] SHALL TALK OF THE
    MIGHT OF YOUR AWESOME DEEDS, AND also as for
    me,[1]

6b I WILL RECOUNT YOUR GREATNESS.

7   One generation to another (v. 4)[2] SHALL CELEBRATE
    YOUR ABUNDANT GOODNESS.

11 THEY SHALL SPEAK to each other[3] OF YOUR MIGHT,
    saying, "It is proper for us

12 TO MAKE HIS MIGHTY ACTS KNOWN AMONG
    MEN AND THE MAJESTIC GLORY OF HIS, the Holy
    One Blessed be He's, KINGSHIP."[4]

16b HE PROVIDES [*maśbĭăʿ*] FOR EVERY LIVING THING
    FAVOR. To the extent adequate for its sustenance[5] HE
    PROVIDES His kindness and His favor and His blessing.[6]
    rāṣôn 'FAVOR' [means] *apaiment* 'reconciliation' [in O.F.].[7]

21 MY MOUTH SHALL UTTER THE PRAISE OF THE
    LORD, AND also[1] ALL FLESH SHALL BLESS HIS
    HOLY NAME.[8]

PSALM CXLV, NOTES

[1] Rashi calls our attention to the psalmist's speaking in the parallel versets of vv. 4, 6, 21 alternately in the first person expressing the psalmist's own desire to praise the LORD and in the 3[d] pers. expressing the hope that others will do so. It should likewise be observed that in vv. 1-2, 7, 10, 11, 13, 15, 16 the psalmist addresses the LORD while in vv. 3, 8, 9, 12, 14, 17, 18, 19, 20 the psalmist speaks about the LORD; cf. Adele Berlin, "The Rhetoric of Psalm 145," in *Biblical and Related Studies Presented to Samuel Iwry*, ed. Ann Kurt and Scott Morschauer (Winona Lake, Indiana: Eisenbrauns, 1985), p. 21.

[2] Rashi supplies from v. 4a the unnamed subject of the 3[d] pers. pl. verbs in vv. 6ff.

[3] Here Rashi follow through on what was pointed out in n. 2, and

thereby he supplies an answer to the exegetical question raised in v. 11b by 'THEY SHALL SPEAK', namely, "To whom?"

[4] Construing v. 12 as a quotation of the words the psalmist wants one generation to say to another, Rashi supplies the *verbum dicendi lē'mor* 'saying' and the clause, "It is proper for us," which transforms v. 12 into a quotation.

[5] Here Rashi notes that the participle *maśbîă‘* means literally "PROVIDES *śoba'* 'satisfication'".

[6] Since Rashi construes the participle *maśbîă‘* as containing within itself both verb and direct object, he must construe *rāṣôn* 'FAVOR' as an additional part of a compound direct object. Here Rashi explains the meaning of this element of the direct object.

[7] See the discussion of this frequent Old French gloss at Ps. 5, n. 7.

[8] Rashi adds the particle *'et*, the sign of the definite direct object before 'HIS HOLY NAME'.

PSALM CXLVI

1   HALLELUJAH. PRAISE THE LORD, O MY SOUL!

2   WHILE I EXIST [i.e.], WHILE I AM STILL alive.

4   *'eštônôtāyw* [i.e.], *maḥšĕbôtāyw* 'his plans'.[1]

5   PRAISED IS HE WHOSE HELP IS THE GOD OF JACOB,[2] whom the Holy One Blessed be He promised, "Remember, I am with you: I will protect you...and I will bring you back [to this land]"[3] (Gen. 28:15). Now why is he praised? [He is praised] because He [THE GOD OF JACOB IS],

6a   MAKER OF HEAVEN AND EARTH, THE SEA....
Now since everything is His, He is capable of protecting him [the person described in v. 5] on sea and on land. However, a mortal king, although he can protect on land cannot protect him at sea.[4]

6c   HE KEEPS TRUTH [*'ĕmet*] FOREVER.
[I.e.], to the end of many generations He fulfills, and HE KEEPS the truth of His promise.

9b   *yĕ'oddēd* 'HE GIVES COURAGE' is a verb referring to strength.

10   THE LORD SHALL REIGN FOREVER.
[I.e.], He will establish His kingdom at the time of the Redemption of His children [i.e., Israel].[6]

PSALM CXLVI, NOTES

[1] *Mahberet Menahem*, p. 294, s.v. *'št* I; see *BDB*, p. 799b; *K-B*[3], p. 850b; so also NJV, q.v.

[2] Rendering of the lemma according to the understanding presupposed by Rashi's comment; concerning Rashi's interpretation of the expression *'ašrê* 'PRAISED IS' see our discussion at Ps. 1:1; 119:1.

[3] Rashi does not quote the bracketed portion of the verse; I have supplied it for clarity.

[4] With Zohory cf. JT Berakot 9:1.

[5] Rashi here attempts to call attention both to the contextual meaning of *'ĕmet* here, i.e., 'promise' and the common meaning of *'ĕmet* in late Heb., i.e., 'truth'.

[6] R. Jose the Galilean (2[d] cent. C.E.) explains in Mekilta, vol. 2, p. 80 that the imperfect *yimlok* 'HE WILL REIGN' refers to the future while the noun *melek* '(He is) King' would have implied that He reigns 'even now in the preeschatological age'.

PSALM CXLVII

1   HALLELUJAH. IT IS GOOD TO CHANT HYMNS TO
     OUR GOD.
     [I.e.], IT IS GOOD to chant hymns[1] to Him.[2]

9a   THE BEASTS THEIR FOOD [*laḥmāh*] [i.e.], their feed.[3]

9b   TO THE RAVEN'S BROOD. Our rabbis explained that
     he [THE RAVEN] is cruel to his BROOD, but the Holy
     One Blessed be He has compassion for them so that he pro-
     vides for them mosquitoes, which enter their mouths from
     their excrement.[4]

10   HE, the Holy One Blessed be He,[5] DOES NOT PRIZE
     THE STRENGTH OF HORSES, NOR VALUE the swift-
     ness of the running of THE THIGHS OF MEN.

16   *kĕpor* 'FROST'; [i.e.], *gĕlîdā'* 'frost' [in Aramaic].[6]

14   THE FAT OF WHEAT [i.e.], the best [i.e.] fat[7] WHEAT.

17a HE TOSSES DOWN HAIL LIKE CRUMBS [*kĕpittîm*].
     The water freezes and becomes many broken pieces.[8] Now
     a midrash aggadah [states], "*kĕpittîm* 'ACCORDING TO
     THE CRUMBS' [i.e.], everything in accord with the capac-
     ity of the people; [e.g.], as for the poor person, in accord
     with his lack of clothing, He [God] makes it easier for him.[9]

17b WHO CAN ENDURE [HIS ICY COLD][10] without becom-
     ing frozen by the COLD?

18a HE ISSUES A COMMAND—IT MELTS THEM [i.e.],
     the aforementioned hailstones.[11]

18b HE MAKES HIS west WIND BLOW to melt the ice so that
     THE WATERS FLOW.[12]

PSALM CXLVII, NOTES

[1] Heb. *lĕzammēr*, the most familiar form of the infinitive construct to
Rashi's readers both in the commentator's lifetime and now; the psalmist
employs the rarer form *zammĕrāh*; on this and like forms see *GKC* #52p;
cf. *GKC* #45d.

[2] Rashi's point is that *'ĕlohênû* 'OUR GOD' should be construed as the
indirect object of the infinitive *zammĕrāh* 'TO CHANT HYMNS'; so KJV;
RSV; NJV; et al.; *BHS* notes that one medieval ms. supplies the prefixed
preposition *lĕ*.

[3] Just as the nouns *'okel* and *ma'ăkal* 'food (of persons), feed (of ani-

mals)' are derived from the verb *'ākal* 'eat' so is *lehem* 'food' derived from
the verb *lāham* 'eat' (Ps. 141:4; Prov. 4:17; 9:5; 23:1, 6). However, while
ma'ăkal may designate any and all food of both humans and other creatures, *lehem* usually means specifically 'bread'. Hence, Rashi finds it necessary to point out that here *lehem* retains its primary meaning 'food'.

[4] Cf. Rashi at BT 'Erubin 22a; Leviticus Rabbah 19:1; Rashi at Job.
38:41. Contrast Holmgren, *Bird Walk Through the Bible*, pp. 146-147: "Anyone who watched ravens would soon learn that these birds are loyal and
considerate mates and devoted parents. You will also learn that young
raven nestlings squawk for food with louder and longer cries than almost
any other species you could name, so they were the example that came
almost immediately to mind when the writers of Job 38:41 and
Psalm 147:7-9 wanted to call up a reminder of how God the Father provides for all small wildlings, giving each its food—not with his own hand
but by providing parent ravens as he does almost all wild parents, beast
or bird—with the instincts to choose the food best suited to infant needs,
to bring such food again and again as long as the opened beaks and lifted
voices reveal hunger's need." PRE, quoted in Elijah Schochet, *Animal Life
in Jewish Tradition* (New Yok: Ktav, 1984), p. 145 suggests a compromise
between the two views of the raven: "The parent raven is negligent in
caring for her young, presumably because she fails to recognize them as
their own owing to the fact that the young birds are born with white
feathers. God therefore personally provides food for the fledglings by
causing maggots to spring forth from their excrement. The baby birds are
sustained for several days until such time as their feathers turn black and
they become recognizable to their parents, who then proceed to care for
their needs." Sylvia Bruce Wilmore, *Crows, Jays, Ravens, and their Relatives*
(Middlebury, Vt.: Paul S. Eriksson, 1977), p. 152 notes that the view that
ravens are insensitive parents is reflected also in the German epithet
Rabenmutter applied to a cruel mother and in the English expression "an
unkindness of ravens." She suggests that the notion that ravens do not
feed their young may derive from the fact that "after the initial brooding
of the young [which lasts for twenty days; see there] the parents roost
away from the nest." She points out, however, that the fledglings remain
in the nest for a total of six to six and a half weeks. Apropos of Rashi's
comment here one should note that Tony Angell, *Ravens, Crows, Magpies
and Jays* (Seattle and London: University of Washington Press, 1978), p.
35 points out that when carrion is unavailable ravens eat dung!

[5] Rashi reminds his readers that the antecedent of the 3[d] pers. sing.
pronominal prefix of the verb *yehpāṣ* 'HE PRIZES' here at v. 10 is 'THE
LORD' in v. 7.

[6] See T.O. at Gen. 31:40; Psalms Targum here; the Heb. form *gālîd* is
attested in the Mishnah 'Ohalot 8:5; Miqwa'ot 7:1; in many other mss. of
Rashi's Commentary on Ps. 147:16 Heb. *kĕpor* is glossed not by Aram.
gālîd but by the Old French equivalent geleé.

[7] Here Rashi equates the psalmist's *hēleb* 'FAT' with the more common *šemen* 'fat'; cf. Rashi at Deut. 32:14.

⁸ Biblical Heb. *pittîm* (Lev. 2:6; 6:14; Ps. 147:17) means 'crumbs' while the Rabbinic Heb. biform *pĕtîtîm* means 'broken pieces'. The repetition of the same plural noun in Rabbinic Heb. means 'many'.

⁹ I was no more successful than the authors of previous studies on Rashi's Commentary on Psalms in locating the source of this midrash.

¹⁰ Rashi does not quote the bracketed portion of the verse; I have supplied it for clarity.

¹¹ See above, v. 17.

¹² With Maarsen contrast the Tannaitic source quoted in BT Bava Batra 25b, which attributes frost to the west wind and melting of frost to the east wind.

PSALM CXLVIII

1   HALLELUJAH.

3   BRIGHT STARS [i.e.], STARS of night.[1]

6b   HE GAVE A BOUNDARY between them [*bāhem*] [so that] one of them[2] should function during the day and the other one should function during the night.

6c   SO THAT IT WOULD NOT TRANSGRESS the aforementioned BOUNDARY.[3]

7   *tanînîm* 'SEA MONSTERS' [designates] gigantic fish.[4]

8a   FIRE AND HAIL; *glace* in O.F.[5] AND SMOKE, a dark[6] cloud, which is called *brüine* 'fog' [in O.F.].[7]

8b   STORM WIND THAT EXECUTES HIS COMMAND, i.e., His commission. Our rabbis said that these things [the divine agents enumerated in vv. 7-8] were originally hidden away in Heaven, but David came along and brought them down to earth becasue they were various kinds of punishments, and it was not seemly that they should be found in the dwelling place of the Holy One Blessed be He.[8]

PSALM CXLVIII, NOTES

[1] See Rashi at Ps. 139:11 where he argues that in several places in the Bible including Ps. 139:11; 148:3 there is a root *'wr*, which denotes 'darkness' rather than 'light'; cf. *Mahberet Menahem*, p. 48, s.v. *'r* V.

[2] I.e., SUN AND MOON; see v. 3a.

[3] Rendering of the lemma to reflect Rashi's interpretation; note that Rashi treats *ḥoq* 'BOUNDARY' as the direct object of both the verb *nātan* 'HE GAVE' and the verb *ya'ăbor* 'IT WOULD TRANSGRESS'. Most interpreters follow LXX, Vulgate, and Qimhi in taking *ḥoq* as the direct object of the verb *nātan* but as the subject of the verb *ya'ăbor*; hence NJV's "establishing an order that shall never change."

[4] With Maarsen note that this is Rashi's interpretation of the contextual meaning of *hattanînîm* also at Gen. 1:21; the discovery of the Ugaritic tablets has shown, however, that the *aggadah* referred to by Rashi at Gen. 1:21 correctly understands *tanîn* as a synonym of Leviathan.

[5] I.e., 'ice'; see Catane, *Recueil*, #10, 190, 1612.

[6] Heb. *šō'āh*, on which see Rashi at Ps. 35:8 (cf. Maarsen here).

[7] I.e., Modern French brume; see Darmsteter, "Les gloses françaises de Raschi dan la Bible," *REJ* 56 (1908), p. 76, nn. 1-2; J. Greenberg,

Foreign Words in the Bible Commentary of Rashi, p. 198.

    [8] As noted by Maarsen here, Rashi's comment here is based upon the midrash attributed to Rab Judah quoting Rab in BT Hagigah 12b.

PSALM CXLIX

1   HALLELUJAH. SING TO THE LORD A NEW SONG.

6a   WITH PAEANS TO GOD IN THEIR THROATS, and these same are like TWO-EDGED SWORDS IN THEIR HANDS.[1]

8   WITH SHACKLES [*ziqqîm*] [i.e.], chains.[2]

9   THE JUDGMENT, WHICH IS WRITTEN [i.e.], "I shall wreak My vengeance on Edom…" (Ezek. 25:14). Now should you say, "Ezekiel was not yet born when David composed this [psalm],"

[I would respond], "David [here in Ps. 149:9] prophesied concerning the eschatological redemption. Therefore, when the eschaton will have arrived, this JUDGEMENT will already have been WRITTEN a long time."[3]

PSALM CXLIX, NOTES

[1] Rashi thus intimates that the two halves of the verse constitute synonymous parallelism, in which the same idea is referred to employing different words; on Rashi's recognition of synonymous parallelism see our discussion in our introduction, pp. 150–154.

[2] Heb. *šaršĕrôt*; Rashi explains the strictly Biblical Heb. term by reference to a term, which is found frequently in both Biblical and Rabbinic Heb.

[3] Cf. Midrash Tehillim at Ps. 150:1.

PSALM CL

1   HALLELUJAH. PRAISE GOD IN HIS SANCTUARY.

4   WITH *minnîm* AND *'ûgāb*.[2] These are [the names of] musical instruments.[1]

5a   *ṣilṣĕlê-šāma'*[2] [i.e.], cymbals [*mĕṣiltayim*][2] that make a loud noise. [The word] *šāma'* is a substantive; it is the same word, which appears elsewhere with the vocalization *šēma'*,[3] but because of the caesura it is vocalized with *qāmeṣ gādôl* [i.e., *ā* rather than *ē* in the first syllable],[4] and therefore[5] its accent is penultimate [i.e.], under the *shin* [rather than the *'ayin*].[6] PSALMS IS COMPLETED. PRAISE TO THE SUPREME GOD.[7]

PSALM CL, NOTES

[1] *Mahberet Menahem*, p. 242, s.v. *mn* VII argues that "according to the context they [*minnîm*] are stringed instruments"; at p. 276, s.v. *'gb* I he states that *'ûgāb* is "a musical instrument."

[2] Rashi here asserts what *Mahberet Menahem*, p. 318, s.v. *ṣl* II offers only as a possibility, namely, that the name of the musical instrument twice designated by the plural construct *ṣilṣĕlê* in Ps. 150:5 may be a cognate of *mĕṣiltayim* 'cymbals' frequently attested in 1-2 Ch. (see Mandelkern, p. 996c) as well as in Ezra 3:10; Neh. 12:27. The plural absolute of the former, sc., *ṣelṣĕlîm* is attested in 2 Sam. 6:5.

[3] This form is attested in the meaning "rumor, report" in Gen. 29:13; Ex. 23:1; 1 Kgs. 10:1; etc.

[4] Cf. *GKC* #93.

[5] Because it is a segholate noun rather than the verb *šāma'* 'he heard'.

[6] As is the case with respect to the verb *šāma'* 'he heard'.

[7] Many other Rashi mss. conclude with similar formulae; these formulae, like the opening formula, "And may He who dwells among Proverbs" (see above in *Rashi's Introduction to the Psalter*, p. 165) are from the pens of the respective scribes.

BIBLIOGRAPHY

I. BIBLE TEXTS AND TRANSLATIONS

Hebrew

Kennicott, Benjamin. *Vetus Testamentum Hebraicum cum Variis Lectionibus.* 2 vols. Oxford: Clarendon Press, 1776-1780.

Kittel, D. Rudolph, ed. *Biblia Hebraica.* 3^d ed. Stuttgart: Württemburg Bibelanstalt for the American Bible Society, 1959.

Opher, Yosef, ed. *Jerusalem Crown: The Bible of the Hebrew University of Jerusalem,* Jerusalem: Ben-Zvi, 2000.

Rudolph, Wilhelm, and Hans Peter Rüger. *Biblia Hebraica Stuttgartensia* 2^d ed. Stuttgart: Deutsche Bibelgesellschaft, 1983.

Greek

Rahlfs, Alfred, ed. *Septuaginta.* 2 vols. in one. Stuttgart: Deutsche Bibelgesellschaft, 1979.

Latin

Biblia Sacra Juxta Vulgatam Clementinam. Rome: Typis Societatis S. Joannis Evang., 1956.

Aramaic

Grossfeld, Bernard. *The Targum Onkelos to Leviticus and the Targum Onkelos to Numbers.* Translated with Apparatus and Notes. The Aramaic Bible, vol. 8. Edited by Martin McNamara. Wilmington, Del.: Michael Glazier, 1988.

————. *The Targum Onkelos to Deuteronomy.* Translated with Apparatus and Notes. The Aramaic Bible, vol. 9. Edited by Martin McNamara. Wilmington, Del.: Michael Glazier, 1988.

Sperber, Alexander. *The Bible in Aramaic.* 4 vols. Leiden: E. J. Brill, 1959-1973.

English

The Authorized Version, Commonly called the King James Version, 1611.

Good News Bible. New York: American Bible Society, 1976.

The Holy Bible: The New Revised Standard Version. Oxford & New York: Oxford University Press, 1989.

Margolis, Max L., ed. *The Holy Scriptures.* Philadelphia: Jewish Publication Society, 1917.

The New English Bible: The Old Testament. Oxford: Oxford University Press, 1970; Cambridge: Cambridge University Press, 1970.

The Revised Standard Version of the Bible. New York, Edinburgh, and Toronto: Thomas Nelson & Sons, 1952.

Tanakh: A New Translation of The Holy Scriptures According to the Traditional Hebrew Text. Philadelphia: Jewish Publication Society, 1985.

II. Rabbinic Literature

Avot de-Rabbi Nathan

Neusner, Jacob. *The Fathers According to Rabbi Nathan: An Analytical Translation.* Brown Judaic Studies, no. 114. Atlanta: Scholars Press, 1986.

Saldarini, Anthony J. *The Fathers According to Rabbi Nathan (Abot de Rabbi Nathan) Version B: A Translation and Commentary.* Studies in Judaism in Late Antiquity, vol. 11. Leiden: E. J. Brill, 1975.

Schechter, Solomon, ed. *Aboth deRabbi Nathan.* Vienna: Mordechai Knopfelmacher, 1887.

Mishnah

Mishnah. 7 vols. Vilna: Romm: 1887-1909 (in Hebrew).

Albeck, Hanoch, ed. *Mishnah.* 6 vols. Jerusalem: Bialik/Tel Aviv: Dvir, 1958 (in Hebrew).

Blackman, Philip. *Mishnayoth.* 6 vols. London: Mishna Press, 1954.

Neusner, Jacob, trans. *The Mishnah.* New Haven and London: Yale University Press, 1988.

Seder Olam

Milikowsky, Chaim Joseph. "Seder Olam: A Rabbinic Chronology." 2 vols. vol. 1: Introduction; vol. 2: Text and Translation [and critical apparatus]. Ph.D. diss., Yale University, 1981.

Ratner, Dov Ber. ed. *Seder Olam Rabbah.* New York: Talmudical Research Institute, 1966.

Tosefta

Lieberman, Saul, ed. *The Tosefta.* 4 vols. New York: Jewish Theological Seminary of America, 1955-1988.

Neusner, Jacob, trans. *The Tosefta Translated from the Hebrew with a New Introduction.* 2 vols. Peabody, Mass.: Hendrickson, 2002.

Talmuds

Texts

Babylonian Talmud. Editio Princeps. 42 vols. Venice: Bomberg, 1520-1523.

Babylonian Talmud. 22 vols. Vilna: Romm, 1880-1886.

Malter, Henry, ed. *The Treatise Ta'anith of the Babylonian Talmud Critically Edited on the Basis of Twenty-four Manuscripts, Quotations by Old Authorities and Early Editions, and Provided with Notes Containing the Critical Apparatus.* New York: American Academy for Jewish Research, 1930 (in Hebrew).

Na'eh, Baruch, ed. *Gemara Shelemah: Tractate Pesahim from the Babylonian Talmud.* Jerusalem: Torah Shelemah Institute, 1960 (in Hebrew).

Porush, Hillel, ed. *The Babylonian Talmud with Variant Readings: Tractate Gittin (II).* Jerusalem: Yad Harav Herzog/Instiute for the Complete Israeli Talmud, 2000 (in Hebrew).

Translations

Epstein, Isidore, ed. *The Babylonian Talmud in English*. 6 vols. in 34. London: Soncino, 1938.
Neusner, Jacob. *The Talmud of Babylonia: An American Translation*. 36 vols. Brown Judaic Studies. Atlanta: Scholars Press, 1984-2000.

Jerusalem Talmud

Text

Sussman, Yaacov, ed. *Talmud Yerushalmi According to Ms. Or. 4720 (Scal. 3) of the Leiden University Library with Restorations and Corrections and Introduction*. Jerusalem: Academy of the Hebrew Language, 2001.

Translation

Neusner, Jacob. *The Talmud of the Land of Israel: A Preliminary Translation and Explanation*. Chicago Studies in the History of Judaism. 35 vols. Chicago & London: University of Chicago Press, 1982.

Minor Tractates of the Talmud

Cohen, Abraham, ed. *The Minor Tractates of the Talmud*. 2 vols. London: Soncino Press, 1965.

Midrashim

Texts

Buber, Solomon, ed. *Midrasch Tehillim (Schocher Tob)*. Vilña: Romm, 1891.
———. *Midrash Shmuel*. Cracow: Joseph Fischer, 1893.
———. *Midrash Tanḥuma*. 2 vols. Vilna: Romm, 1885.
———. *Pesikta de Rav Kahana*. 2^d ed. Vilna: Romm, 1925.
———. *Yalkut ha-Mekiri on the Book of Psalms*. Berdichev: Hayyim Joseph Sheftel, 1900.
Enelow, Hyman G., ed. *The Mishnah of Rabbi Eliezer*. New York: Bloch, 1933.
Epstein, Jacob Nahum, ed. *Mekilta deRabbi Sim'on b. Jochai*. Edited and Completed by Ezra Zion Melamed. Jerusalem: Mekize Nirdamim, 1955.
Finkelstein, Louis, ed. *Sifre on Deuteronomy*. Berlin: Gesellschaft zur Förderung der Wissenschaft des Judentums, 1939; reprint, New York: Jewish Theological Seminary of America, 1969.
———. *Sifra on Leviticus*. 4 vols. New York: Jewish Theological Seminary of America, 1983-1991.
Friedman [= Ish Shalom], Meir. *Pesikta Rabbati*. Vienna: By the editor, 1880.
Horovitz, Hayyim S., ed. *Sifre ad Numeros*. Leipzig: Foch, 1917.
Jellinek, Adolf. *Bet ha-Midrash*. 2^d ed. 6 vols. Jerusalem: Bamberger & Wahrmann, 1938.
Kensky, Allan David. "Midrash Tanhuma Shmot: A Critical Edition of 'Midrash Tanhuma Shmot' (standard edition) through Beshallah, based on Manuscripts and Early Editions with an Introduction and Commenrary." Ph.D. diss., New York: Jewish Theological Seminary of America, 1990.

Kern Ulmer, Rivka. *Pesikqta Rabbati: A Synoptic Edition of Pesiqta Rabbati Based Upon All Extant Manuscripts and the Editio Princeps.*
   vol. 1. University of South Florida Studies in the History of Judaism, no. 155. Atlanta: Scholars Press, 1997.
   vol. 2. University of South Florida Studies in the History of Judaism, no. 200. Atlanta: Scholars Press, 1999.
   vol. 3. Studies in Judaism. Lanham, Md.: University Press of America, 2002.
Lauterbach, Jacob Z., ed. and trans. *Mekilta de-Rabbi Ishmael.* 3 vols. Philadelphia: Jewish Publication Society, 1933.
Lieberman, Saul, ed. *Midrash Debarim Rabbah.* 2^d ed. Jerusalem: Wahrmann Books, 1964.
Mandelbaum, Bernard, ed. *Pesikta de Rav Kahana.* 2^d augmented ed. 2 vols. New York: Jewish Theological Seminary of America, 1987.
Margulies, Mordecai, ed. *Midrash Haggadol on the Pentateuch: Genesis.* Jerusalem: Mossad Harav Kook, 1947.
———. *Midrash Wayyikra Rabbah.* 5 vols. Jerusalem: Louis M. & Minnie Epstein Fund of the American Academy of Jewish Research, 1953-1960.
———. *Midrash Rabbah on the Torah and the Megilloth.* 2 vols. Vilna: Romm, 1938.
———. *Midrash Tanḥuma.* Warsaw: Avraham Kahana, 1907.
———. *Pirke deRabbi Eliezer.* Jerusalem: Eshkol, 1983.
Schechter, Solomon, ed. *Midrash Hag-gadol on Genesis.* Cambridge: Cambridge University Press, 1902.
Shinan, Avigdor, ed. *Midrash Rabbah, Shemot, Chapters 1-14: A Critical Edition Based on a Jerusalem Manuscript with Variants, Commentary and Introduction.* Jerusalem: Dvir, 1984.
Theodor, Julius, ed. *Bereschit Rabbah mit kritischen Apparat und Kommentar,* 2^d printing with additions and corrections by Ch. Albeck. 3 vols. Jerusalem: Wahrmann, 1965.
Yalqut Shim'oni. 2 vols. New York & Berlin: Choreb, 1926.

Translations

Braude, William Gordon, trans. *The Midrash on Psalms.* 2 vols. Yale Judaica Series, vol. 13. New Haven: Yale University Press, 1959.
———. *Pesikta Rabbati.* Yale Judaica Series, vol. 18. 2 vols. New Haven: Yale University Press, 1968.
Freedman, Harry, and Maurice Simon. *Midrash Rabbah Translated into English.* 10 vols. London: Soncino, 1939.
Friedlander, Gerald. *Pirke Rabbi Eliezer According to the Text of the Manuscript Belonging to Abraham Epstein of Vienna Translated and Annotated with Introduction and Indices.* London: Kegan Paul, Trench, Trübner, 1916.
Neusner, Jacob. *Esther Rabbah I: An Analytical Translation.* Brown Judaic Studies, no. 182. Atlanta: Scholars Press, 1989.
———. *Genesis Rabbah: The Judaic Commentary to the Book of Genesis: A New American Translation.* Brown Judaic Studies, nos. 104-106. 3 vols. Atlanta: Scholars Press, 1985.
———. *Judaism and Scripture: The Evidence of Leviticus Rabbah.* Chicago Studies in the History of Judaism. Chicago & London: University of Chicago Press, 1986.
———. *Lamentations Rabbah: An Analytical Translation.* Brown Judaic Studies, no. 193. Atlanta: Scholars Press, 1989.

————. *Mekhilta According to Rabbi Ishmael: An Analytical Translation.* Brown Judaic Studies, nos. 148 and 154. 2 vols. Atlanta: Scholars Press, 1988.

————. *Pesiqta deRab Kahana: An Analytical Translation.* Brown Judaic Studies, nos. 122-123. Atlanta: Scholars Press, 1987-1988.

————. *Sifra: An Analytical Translation.* Brown Judaic Studies, nos. 138-140. 3 vols. Atlanta: Scholars Press, 1988.

————. *Sifre to Numbers. An American Translation. and Explanation.* Brown Judaic Studies, no. 118. Atlanta: Scholars Press, 1986.

————. *Sifre to Deuteronomy. An Analytical Translation.* Brown Judaic Studies, no. 98. Atlanta: Scholars Press, 1987.

————. *Song of Songs Rabbah: An Analytical Translation.* Brown Judaic Studies, nos. 197-198. 2 vols. Atlanta: Scholars Press, 1989.

Townsend, John T. *Midrash Tanhuma.(S. Buber Recension), vol. 1: Genesis.* Hoboken, N.J.: Ktav, 1989.

————. *Midrash Tanhuma. (S. Buber Recension), vol. 2: Exodus and Leviticus.* Hoboken, N.J.: Ktav, 1997.

III. Jewish Liturgy

Birnbaum, Philip. *Daily Prayer Book.* New York: Hebrew Publishing Co., 1949.

————. *High Holyday Prayer Book.* New York: Hebrew Publishing Co., 1951.

De Sola, David A., trans. *The Festival Prayers According to the Ritual of the German and Polish Jews.* 6 vols. London: P. Vallentine, 1881.

Glatzer, Nahum N., ed. *The Passover Haggadah.* rev. ed. New York: Schocken Books, 1969.

Goldschmidt, Daniel. *Seder Ha-Selihot According to the Lithuanian Rite.* Jerusalem: Mossad Harav Kook, 1965 (in Hebrew).

Hedegard, David, ed. *Seder R. Amram Gaon, Part I.* Lund: Lindstedt, 1951.

Kronholm, Tryggve, ed. *Seder R. Amram Gaon, Part II.* Lund: CWK Gleerup, 1974.

Lavon, Yaakov, trans. *The Complete ArtScroll Selichos.* Edited with a Commentary by Avie Gold. ArtScroll Mesorah Series. Edited by Meir Zlotowitz and Nosson Scherman. New York: Mesorah Publications, 1996.

Otzar Ha-Tefillot. 2 vols. Vilna: Romm, 1928 (in Hebrew).

Rosenfeld, Abraham. *The Authorised Selichot for the Whole Year.* London: n.p., 1969.

Sluçki, Mordecai, ed. *Azharot leHag ha-Shavuot leRabbenu Elijah ha-Zaken.* Warsaw: Halter, 1900.

IV. Halakic Codes

Jacob ben Asher (d. 1340). Arba'ah Turim.

Joseph Qaro (1488-1575). Shulhan Aruk.

Moses ben Jacob of Couci (13th cent.). Sepher Mitzvot Gadol.

Moses Maimonides (1135-1204). Mishneh Torah.

V. Dictionaries, Grammars, and Concordances

Banitt, ed. *Le Glossaire de Bâle.* 2 vols. Jerusalem: Israel Academy of Sciences & Humanities, 1972.

————. *Le Glossaire de Leipzig.* 2 vols. Jerusalem: Israel Academy of Sciences & Humanities, 1998.

Bauer, Hans, and Pontus Leander. *Historische Grammatik der hebräischen Sprache des Alten Testamentes.* Hildesheim: G. Olms, 1962.

Ben Yehuda, Eliezer. *A Complete Dictionary of Ancient and Modern Hebrew*. 17 vols. New York & London: Thomas Yoseloff, 1945-1959.

Bergstrasser, Gotthelf. *Hebräische Grammatik*. 2 vols. Leipzig: F.C.W. Vogel, 1919-1929.

Brown, Francis, Samuel Rolles Driver, and Charles A. Briggs, *A Hebrew and English Lexicon of the Old Testament*. corrected impression. Oxford: Clarendon Press, 1952.

Canaani, Ya'aqov. *Ozar Ha-Lashon Ha'Ivrit*. 18 vols. Jerusalem & Tel Aviv: Massada, 1960-1989.

Chomsky, William, ed and trans. *David Kimhi's Hebrew Grammar*. New York: Bloch Publishing Co., for the Dropsie College for Hebrew and Cognate Learning, 1952.

Dunash Ben Labrat. *Teshubot de Dunash Ben Labrat*. Edición critica y traducción española de Angel Sáenz-Badillos. Granada: Universidad de Granada; Salamanca: Universidad Pontificia de Salamanca, 1980.

————. *Sepher Teshuvot Dunash Ben Labrat 'im Hakrā'ôt Rabbenu Tam*. Edited by H. Fillipowski. London and Edinburgh: Me'orerey Yeshenim, 1851.

Even-Shoshan, Abraham. *Ha-Millon Ha-Hadash*. 3 vols. Jerusalem: Kiryat Sepher, 1970 (in Hebrew).

Gesenius, Wilhelm. *Gesenius' Hebrew Grammar*. Edited by E. Kautzsch. 2^d Eng. ed. revised by A. E. Cowley. Oxford: Clarendon Press, 1910.

Hyman, Aaron. *Torah Hakketubah Wehammesurah*. 3 vols. Tel Aviv: Dvir, 1965.

Ibn Janah, Jonah. *Sepher Haschoraschim*. Edited by Wilhelm Bacher. Berlin: M'kize Nirdamim, 1896.

Jastrow, Marcus. *A Dictionary of the Targumim, the Talmud Babli and Yerushalmi, and the Midrashic Literature*. 2 vols. New York and Berlin: Verlag Choreb, 1926; London: Shapiro, Vallentine & Co., 1926.

Kimhi, David. *Radicum Liber* (= *Sepher ha-Shorashim*). Edited by J. H. R. Biesenthal and F. Lebrecht. Berlin: G. Bethge, 1847.

Koehler, Ludwig, and Walter Baumgartner, *Lexikon in Veteris Testamenti Libros*. Leiden: E. J. Brill, 1953.

Koehler, Ludwig, and Walter Baumgartner. *Hebräisches und Aramäisches Lexikon zum Alten Testament*. 3^d ed. 5 vols. Leiden: E. J. Brill, 1953-1990.

Kohut, Alexander, ed. *Aruch Completum*. Vienna & Berlin: Menorah, 1926.

Levy, Jacob. *Neuhebräisches und chaldäisches Wörterbuch*. Revised by Heinrich Lebrecht Fleischer. 4 vols. Leipzig: Brockhaus, 1876-1889.

————. *Wörterbuch über die Talmudim und Midrashim*. Edited by Heinrich Lebrecht Fleischer. 2^d ed. Edited by Lazarus Goldschmidt. 4 vols. Berlin and Vienna: Harz, 1924.

Liddell, Henry George, and Robert Scott. *A Greek-English Lexicon*. 9th ed. Revised and augmented by Henry Stuart Jones with the assistance of Roderick McKenzie and with the cooperation of many scholars, with a revised supplement. Oxford: Clarendon Press, 1996.

Mandelkern, Solomon. *Veteris Testamenti Concordantiae Hebraicae atque Chaldaicae*. Leipzig: Veit et Comp., 1896.

Menahem Ben Saruq. *Mahberet*. Edición critica y traducción española de Angel Sáenz-Badillos. Granada: University of Granada, 1986.

————. *Sepher Mahberet Menahem*. ed. H. Fillipowski. Edinburgh: Me'orerey Yeshenim, 1854.

Oppenheim, A. Leo, ed. *The Assyrian Dictionary of the Oriental Institute of the University of Chicago*. Chicago: Oriental Institute, 1956-; Glückstadt: J. J. Augustin, 1956-.

Soden, Wolfram von. *Akkadisches Handwörterbuch.* 3 vols. Wiesbaden: Harrassowitz, 1965-1981.

Sokoloff, Michael. *A Dictionary of Jewish Babylonian Aramaic of the Talmudic and Geonic Periods.* Ramat-Gan: Bar-Ilan University Press, 2002.

————. *A Dictionary of Jewish Palestinian Aramaic of the Byzantine Period.* 2^d ed. Ramat-Gan: Bar-Ilan University Press, 2002.

Weingreen, Jacob. *A Practical Grammar for Classical Hebrew.* 2^d ed. Oxford: Clarendon Press, 1959.

VI. Texts, Studies, and Commentaries

Abecassis, Deborah. "Reconstructing Rashi's Commentary on Genesis from Citations in the Torah Commentaries of the Tosafot." Ph.D. diss., Montreal: McGill University, 1999.

Abraham b. David of Posquières. *Temim De'im.* Lemberg: Herz Grossman, 1812.

Abramson, Shraga. "Yesh 'Em La-Miqra, La-Masoret." *Lěšonénu* 50 (1986), pp. 31-36 (in Hebrew).

Adler, Marcus Nathan, ed. *The Itinerary of Benjamin of Tudela.* London: H. Frowde, 1907.

Aejmelaeus, Anneli. "The Function and Interpretation of *ki* in Biblical Hebrew." *Journal of Biblical Literature* 105 (1986), pp. 193-209.

Agus, Irving. *Rabbi Meir of Rothenburg.* 2 vols. Philadelphia: Dropsie College, 1947.

————. *Urban Civilization in Pre-Crusade Europe.* 2 vols. New York: Yeshiva University Press, 1965.

————. *The Heroic Age of Franco-German Jewry.* New York: Yeshiva University Press, 1969.

Ahl, Sally. "Epistolary Texts from Ugarit: Structural and Lexical Correspondences in Epistles in Akkadian and Ugaritic." Ph.D. diss., Brandeis University, 1973.

Ahrend, Moshe, ed. *The Commentary of Rabbi Yosef Qara on the Book of Job.* Jerusalem: Mossad Harav Kook, 1989 (in Hebrew).

Albright, William F. "A Catalogue of Early Hebrew Lyric Poems (Psalm LXVIII)." *Hebrew Union College Annual* 23 (1950-51), pp. 1-39.

Allen, Leslie C. *Psalms 101-150.* Word Biblical Commentary, vol. 21. Waco, Texas: Word Books, 1983.

Allony, Nehemya. *The Scansion of Medieval Hebrew Poetry: Dunash, Yehuda Halevi and Abraham Ibn Ezra.* Jerusalem: Mahbarot Lesifrut & Mossad Harav Kook, 1951 (in Hebrew).

Alter, Robert. *The Art of Biblical Poetry.* New York: Basic Books, 1985.

Anderson, Bernhard. W. "God, Names of." *Interpreter's Dictionary of the Bible* 2: 407-417.

Angell, Tony. *Ravens, Crows, Magpies, and Jays.* Seattle & London: University of Washington Press, 1978.

Aptowitzer, Victor. "Deux problèmes d'histoire littéraire." *Revue des Etudes Juives* 55 (1908), pp. 84-95.

————. *Introductio ad Sefer Rabiah.* Jerusalem: Mekize Nirdamim, 1938.

"Concerning the History of Rashi's Commenary on the Talmud." In *Sefer Rashi*, pp. 286-321. Edited by Yehudah Leib Ha-Kohen Fishman Maimon. Jerusalem: Mossad Harav Kook, 1941.

Aquin, Louis Henry. *Scholia Rabi Salomonis Jarchi in librum Esther.* Paris: Blaise, 1622.

Artz, Frederick B. *The Mind of the Middle Ages*. 3ᵈ ed. rev. New York: Alfred A. Knopf, 1966.

Arzt, Max. *Justice and Mercy*. New York: Holt, Rinehart & Winston, 1963.

Asensio, Felix. *Misericorida et Veritas*. Rome: Universitatis Gregorianae, 1948.

Assad, Thomas. "FitzGerald, Edward." In *Encylopedia Americana* [1991 edition], vol. 11, p. 339.

Assaf, Simḥah. "Slaves and the Slave Trade Among Jews in the Middle Ages." In *Be-Ohaley Ya'akov*, pp. 223-256. Edited by Simhah Assaf. Jerusalem: Mossad Harav Kook, 1943 (in Hebrew).

Auld, A. Graeme. "What Was the Main Source of the Book of Chronicles?" In *The Chronicler as Author: Studies in Text and Texture*, pp. 91-99. Edited by M. Patrick Graham and Steven L. McKenzie. Journal for the Study of the Old Testament Supplement Series, no. 263. Sheffield: Sheffield Academic Press, 1999.

Avinery, Isaac. *Heichal Rashi*. rev. ed. 2 vols. Jerusalem: Mossad Harav Kook, 1979-1985.

Avishur, Yitzhak. "Addenda to the Expanded Colon in Ugaritic and Biblical Verse." *Ugarit Forschungen* 4 (1972), pp. 1-10.

———. *Phoenician Inscriptions and the Bible*. 2 vols. Jerusalem: E. Rubenstein, 1979 (in Hebrew).

Avi-Yonah, Michael, and Efraim Orni. "Hermon, Mount." *Encyclopaedia Judaica* 8:373-375.

Awerbuch, Marianne. *Christlich-jüdische Begegnung im Zeitalter Frühscholastik*. Munich: Kaiser, 1980.

Azulai, Hayyim Joseph David. *Shaar Yoseph Hay on Tractate Horayot*. Leghorn: A. Santini & Co., 1756 (in Hebrew).

———. *The Names of the Great Ones*. vol. 1. Leghorn: G. Falorni, 1774; vol. 2. Leghorn: A. I. Castello & E. Sahadun, 1784 (in Hebrew).

———. *Va'ad La Hakamim*. Leghorn: A. I. Castello & E. Sahadun, 1796.

———. *The Names of the Great Ones*. Edited by Yizhaq Isaac Benjacob. Vilna: Romm, 1852 (in Hebrew).

———. *Birke Yoseph*. Vienna: Adalberte della Torre, 1859.

Bacher, Wilhelm. "Raschi." In *Jahrbuch für Geschichte und Literatur*, 1906, pp 86-106.

Baer, Yitzhak. "Rashi and the Historical Reality of His Time." *Tarbiz* 20 (1949), pp. 320-332 (in Hebrew).

Baker, David W. "Further Examples of the *Waw Explicativum*." *Vetus Testamentum* 30 (1980), pp. 129-136.

Baker, Joshua, and W. Ernest Nicholson. *The Commentary of Rabbi David Kimhi on Psalms CXX-CL*. Cambridge: Cambridge University Press, 1973.

Ballaban, Steven. "The Enigma of the Lost Second Temple Literature: Routes of Recovery." Ph.D. diss., Cincinnati: Hebrew Union College-Jewish Institute of Religion, 1994.

Bandstra, Barry. "The Syntax of the Particle 'KY' in Biblical Hebrew and Ugaritic." Ph.D. diss., Yale University, 1982.

Baneth, Menahem. "Les Poterim." *Revue des Etudes Juives* 125 (1966), pp. 21-33.

Banitt [= Baneth], Menahem. "Rashi's Commentary to Scripture and Vernacular Translations." In *Benjamin de Vries Memorial Volume*, pp. 252-267. Edited by Ezra Zion Melamed. Tel Aviv: Tel Aviv Research Authority & Stichting Fronika Sanders Fonds, 1968.

———. *Rashi: Interpreter of the Biblical Letter*. Tel Aviv: Chaim Rosenberg School of Jewish Studies, 1985.

Bar-El, Joseph. *Sefer Pitronot Rashi*. Tel Aviv: Payprus, 1992.

Baron, Salo W. "Rashi and the Community of Troyes." In *Rashi Anniversary Volume*, pp. 47-71. Edited by H. L. Ginsberg. New York: American Academy for Jewish Research, 1941.

Barth, Jakob. "Das passive Qal und seine Participien." In *Jubelschrift zum Siebzigsten Geburtstag des Dr. Israel Hildesheimer*, pp. 145-153. Berlin: Engel, 1890.

———. *Etymologische Studien zum semitischen insbesondere zum hebräischen Lexicon*. Berlin: Itzkowski, 1893.

———. *Die Nominalbildung semitischen Sprachen*. 2^d ed. Leipzig: J. C. Hinrichs, 1894.

———. *Wurzeluntersuchungen*. Leipzig: J. C. Hinrichs, 1921.

Bass, Shabbetai (1641-1718). *Siphete Hakamim*. Supercommentary on Rashi's Commentary on the Pentateuch and the Five Megilloth. Found in *Miqra'ot Gedolot*.

Beattie, D. R. G. *Jewish Exegesis of the Book of Ruth*. Journal for the Study of the Old Testament, Supplement Series, no. 2. Sheffield: JSOT Press, 1977.

Becker, Dan. *The Risāla of Judah ben Quraysh: A Critical Edition*. Texts and Studies in the Hebrew Language and Related Subjects, vol. 7. Tel-Aviv: Tel-Aviv University, 1984.

Beinart, Haim. "Denia." *Encyclopaedia Judaica* 5:1534-1535.

Beit-Arié, Malachi. "The Relationship Between Early Hebrew Printing and Handwritten Books: Attachment or Detachment." *Scripta Hierosolymitana* 29 (1989), pp. 1-26.

Bendavid, Abba. *Biblical and Rabbinic Hebrew*. rev. ed. 2 vols. Tel Aviv: Dvir, 1967-1971 (in Hebrew).

Berlin, Adele. *The Dynamics of Biblical Parallelism*. Bloomington: University of Indiana Press, 1985.

———. "The Rhetoric of Psalm 145." In *Biblical and Related Studies Presented to Samuel Iwry*, pp. 17-22. Edited by Ann Kort and Scott Murschauer. Winona Lake, Ind.: Eisenbrauns, 1985.

Berliner, Abraham. "Analeketen zu dem Raschi-Commentare." *Monatsschrift für die Wissenschaft des Judentums* 12 (1863), pp. 393-398.

———. *Raschii (Salomonis Isaacidis) in Pentateuchum Commentarius*. Berlin: By the author, 1866.

———. "Beiträge zur Geschichte der Raschi Kommentare." *Jahresbericht des Rabbiner-Seminars zu Berlin für 1901/1902*, pp. 1-48.

———. *Raschi: Der Kommentar des Salomo b. Isak über den Pentateuch*. 2^d ed. Frankfurt am Main: J. Kaufmann, 1905 (in Hebrew).

Blenkinsopp, Joseph L. *Prophecy and Canon*. Notre Dame: University of Notre Dame Press, 1977.

———. *A History of Prophecy in Israel*. Philadelphia: Westminster, 1983.

Blidstein, Gerald J. "The Ephraimite Exodus: A Re-Evaluation." *Jerusalem Studies in Jewish Thought* 5 (1986), pp. 1-13 (in Hebrew).

Bloch, Joshua. "Rashi: The Great Expounder of the Bible and Talmud." In *Rashi: His Teaching and Personality*, pp. 49-61. Edited by Simon Federbusch. New York: Cultural Division of the World Jewish Congress, 1958.

Blondheim, David S. "Liste des Manuscrits des commentaires bibliques de Raschi." *Revue des Etudes Juives* 91 (1931), pp. 71-101; 155-174.

Blumenfield, Samuel M. *Master of Troyes: A Study of Rashi the Educator*. New York: Behrman House for the Jewish Institute of Religion, 1946.

Boureaux, Alain. *The Lord's First Night: The Myth of the Droit de Cuissage*. Translated from French by Lydia G. Cochrane. Chicago: University of Chicago Press, 1998.

Boyarin, Daniel. Review of *A Manual of Babylonian Jewish Aramaic*, by David
  Marcus. In *Journal of Near Eastern Studies* 42 (1983), pp. 297-298.
———. *Carnal Israel*. Berkeley: University of California Press, 1993.
Brenner, Athalya. *Colour Terms in the Old Testament*. Journal for the Study of the
  Old Testament Supplement Series, no. 21. Sheffield: JSOT Press, 1982.
Breithaupt, Johann Friedrich, ed. and trans. *R. Salomonis Jarchi, Commentarius
  Hebraicus*. 2 vols. Gotha: Schalii, 1710-1713.
Breuer, Mordechai. "Toward the Investigation of the Typology of Western
  Yeshivot in the Middle Ages." In *Studies in the History of Jewish Society in the
  Middle Ages and in the Modern Period*, pp. 45-55. Edited by E. Etkes and Y.
  Salmon. Jerusalem: Magnes, 1980 (in Hebrew).
Briggs, Charles Augustus, and Emilie Grace Briggs. *A Critical and Exegetical Com-
  mentary on the Book of Psalms*. International Criticial Commentary. 2 vols.
  Edinburgh: T. & T. Clark, 1906-07.
Brin, Gershon. "Studies in R. Judah the Pious' Exegesis to the Pentateuch."
  Te'udah 3 (1983), pp. 224-225 (in Hebrew).
Brongers, Hendrik Antonie. "Alternative Interpretationen des sogennanten waw
  copulativum." *Zeitschrift für die alttestamentliche Wissenshcaft* 90 (1978), pp. 273-
  277.
Bronznick, Norman W. "Qabblah as a Metonym for the Prophets and Hagio-
  grapha." *Hebrew Union College Annual* 38 (1967), pp. 285-295.
Buber, Martin. *Israel and Palestine*. Translated by Stanley Goodman. London: East
  & West Library, 1952.
Bücher, Karl. *Die Bevölkerung von Frankfurt am Main im XIV. und XV. Jahrhundert*.
  Tübingen: H. Laupp, 1886.
Budde, Karl. "Brief Communications." *Journal of Biblical Literature* 40 (1921), pp.
  39-41.
Butin, Romain François. *The Ten Nequdot of the Torah*. Baltimore: J. H. Furst & Co,
  1906; reprint, New York: Ktav, 1969.
Buttenweiser, Moses. "The Importance of the Tenses for the Interpretation of the
  Psalms." In *Hebrew Union College Jubilee Volume*, pp. 89-111. Cincinnati: He-
  brew Union College, 1925.
———. *The Psalms Chronologically Treated with a New Translation*. Chicago: Univer-
  sity of Chicago Press, 1938.
Buttrick, George Arthur, ed. *Interpreter's Bible*. 12 vols. New York and Nashville:
  Abingdon, 1955.
Cansdale, George Soper. *All the Animals of the Bible Lands*. Grand Rapids: Zonder-
  van, 1970.
Cantera y Burgos, Francisco. *El judio Salmantino Abraham Zacut; notas para la historia
  de la astronomia en la España medieva*. Madrid: Bermejo, 1931.
Carroll, Robert P. "Razed Temple and Shattered Vessels." *JSOT* 75 (1997), pp.
  93-106
Cassuto, Umberto. "Daniel e le spighe: un episodio della tavolla I D dei Ras
  Shamra." *Orientalia*, new series, 8 (1939), pp. 238-243.
———. "Leviathan." *Encyclopedia Miqra'it* 4:485-486 (in Hebrew).
Catane, Mochè. *Recueil des Glosses*. 2^{d} ed. Jerusalem: Gitler Bros., 1988.
———. *Ozar ha-La'azim*. Jerusalem: Gitler Bros., 1990 (in Hebrew).
———. *La Vie en France au XIe siècle d'après les écrits de Rachi*. Jerusalem: Editions
  Gallia, 1994.
Cavigneaux, Antoine. "Lexikalische Listen." *Reallexikon der Assyriologie* 6: 608-641.
Chavel, Chaim Dov, ed. *The Torah Commentaries of Rabbenu Moses b. Nahman*. 2 vols.
  Jerusalem: Mossad Harav Kook, 1959 (in Hebrew).

————. *The Commentaries of Rashi on the Torah*. Jerusalem: Mossad Harav Kook, 1983 (in Hebrew).

Chazan, Robert. *Medieval Jewry in Northern France: A Political and Social History*. Baltimore & London: Johns Hopkins University Press, 1973.

Cheyne, Thomas Kelly. *The Book of Psalms*. 2 vols. London: Kegan Paul, Trench, Trübner & Co., 1904.

Chomsky, William. "Some Traditional Principles in Biblical Exegesis." In *Essays on the Occasion of the Seventieth Anniversary of the Dropsie University*, p. 133-37. Edited by Abraham I. Katsh and Leon Nemoy. Philadelphia: Dropsie University, 1979.

Chones, Simon Moses. *Toledot HaPoskim*. Warsaw: F. Baumritter,1910.

Civil, Miguel. "Lexicography." In *Sumerological Studies in Honor of Thorkild Jacobsen on His Seventieth Birthday*, pp. 123-157. Assyriological Studies, no. 20. Chicago & London: University of Chicago Press, 1975.

Cogan, Mordechai, and Hayim Tadmor. *II Kings*. Anchor Bible, vol. 11. Garden City, N. Y.: Doubleday & Co., 1988.

Cohen, Chaim (Harold). "Studies in Early Israelite Poetry I: An Unrecognized Case of Three-Line Staircase Parallelism in the Song of the Sea." *Journal of the Ancient Near Eastern Society* 7 (1975), pp. 13-17.

————. *Biblical Hapax Legomena in the Light of Akkadian and Ugaritic*. Society of Biblical Literature Dissertation Series, no. 37. Missoula, Montana: Scholars Press, 1978.

————. "Some Overlooked Akkadian Evidence Concerning the Etymology and Meaning of the Biblical Term *māšāl*." In *Bible Studies—Y.M. Grintz Memorial Volume*, pp. 315-324. Tel Aviv: Tel Aviv University, 1982 (in Hebrew).

———— "The Other Meaning of Biblical Hebrew *tannîn* 'snake or crocodile'." In *H. M. Y. Gevaryahu Festschrift*, pt. 2, pp. 75-81. Edited by Ben-Zion Lurie and Shmuel Avramsky. Jerusalem: Israel Society for Biblical Research, 1989 (in Hebrew).

————. "Jewish Medieval Commentary on the Book of Genesis and Modern Biblical Philology, Part I: Gen 1-18." *Jewish Quarterly Review*, new series, 81 (1990), pp. 1-11.

Cohen, Gerson D., ed. *A Critical Edition With a Translation and Notes of the Book of Tradition (Sefer Ha-Qabbalah) by Abraham Ibn Daud*. Philadelphia: Jewish Publication Society, 1967.

Cohen, Menachem, ed. *Mikra'ot Gedolot 'Haketer'*. Ramat-Gan: Bar-Ilan University Press, 1992-.

Cohn, Robert. *The Shape of Sacred Space*. Chico, Calif.: Scholars Press, 1981.

Conforte, David. *Liber Kore ha-Dorot*. Edited by David Cassel. Berlin: A. Asher, 1846.

Conrad, Diethelm. "Das Gott Reschef." *Zeitschrift für die alttestamentliche Wissenschaft* 83 (1971), pp. 157-183.

Craigie, Peter C. *Psalms 1-50*. Word Biblical Commentary, vol. 19. Waco Texas: Word Books, 1983.

Cross, Frank Moore, Jr. "The Priestly Tabernacle." In *Biblical Archaeologist Reader*, pp. 201-228. Chicago: Quadrangle Books, 1961.

Dahood, Mitchell. "Some Ambiguous Terms in Isaias." *Catholic Biblical Quarterly* 20 (1958), pp. 41-49.

————. *Psalms*. 3 vols. Anchor Bible, vols. 16-17A. Garden City, N.Y.: Doubleday & Co., 1965-1968.

Dan, Joseph. "Rashi and the Merkabah." In *Rashi 1040-1990: Homage à Ephraim . . E. Urbach*, pp. 259-264. Edited by Gabrielle Sed-Rajna. Paris: Editions du Cerf, 1993.

Darmsteter, Arsène. "Les Gloses Françaises de Raschi dans la Bible." *Revue des Etudes Juives* 53 (1907), pp. 161-193; 54 (1908), pp. 1-34; 205-235; 55 (1908), pp. 72-83; 56 (1908), pp. 70-98.

Darom, Avraham, ed. *The Complete Commentary on the Psalms by David Qimhi*. Jerusalem: Mossad Harav Kook, 1979 (in Hebrew).

David, Abraham. "Meir ben Isaac Sheliaḥ Zibbur." *Encyclopaedia Judaica* 11:1255.

David, Yonah. *Lexicon of Epithets in Hebrew Liturgical Poetry*. Jerusalem: Rubin Mass, 2001 (in Hebrew).

Delano Smith, Catherine, and Mayer I. Gruber. "Rashi's Legacy: Maps of the Holy Land." *The Map Collector*, no. 59 (summer 1992), pp. 30-35.

Delekat, Lienhard. "Zum hebräischen Wörterbuch." *Vetus Testamentum* 14 (1964), pp. 33-35.

Delitzsch, Franz. *Biblical Commentary on the Psalms*. 2^d ed. Translated by Francis Bolton. 3 vols. Edinburgh: T. & T. Clark, 1871.

Delitzsch, Friedrich. *Die Lese- und Schreibfehler im Alten Testament*. Leipzig & Berlin: Walter de Gruyter, 1920.

Dhorme, Edouard. *L'emploi Métaphorique des noms de parties du corps en hébreu et en akkadien*. Paris: Geuthner, 1923.

Dietrich, Manfried, Oswald Loretz, and Joaquín Sanmartín. *The Cuneiform Alphabetic Texts from Ugarit, Ras Ibn Hani and Other Places. (KTU: second, enlarged edition)*. Münster: Ugarit-Verlag, 1995.

Dinur, Benzion. *Israel in the Diaspora*. 2 vols. 2^d ed. Tel Aviv: Dvir/Jerusalem: Bialik Institute, 1958.

Dönner, Herbert, and Wolfgang Röllig. *Kanaanäische und Aramäische Inschriften*. 2^d ed. 3 vols. Wiesbaden: Harrassowitz, 1968.

Doron, Pinchas. *The Mystery of Creation According to Rashi: A New Translation and Interpretation of Rashi on Gen. 1-VI*. New York: Ktav, 1982.

Dotan, Aron. "Masorah." *Encyclopaedia Judaica* 16:1401-1482.

Driver, Godfrey R. "Abbreviations in the Massoretic Text." *Textus* 1 (1960), pp. 112-131.

———. "Once Again Abbreviations." *Textus* 4 (1964), pp. 76-94.

———. "Isaiah I-XXXIX: Textual and Linguistic Problems." *Journal of Semitic Studies* 13 (1968), pp. 36-57.

Driver, Samuel R. *A Treatise on the Use of the Tenses in Hebrew*. 3^d ed. Oxford: Clarendon Press, 1892.

———. *The Books of Joel and Amos*. Cambridge Bible for Schools and Colleges. Cambridge: Cambridge University Press, 1897.

———. *A Critical and Exegetical Commentary on Deuteronomy*. 3^d ed. International Criticial Commentary. Edinburgh: T. & T. Clark, 1902.

Dubarle, Andre Marie. *Judith: Formes et sens des diverses traditions*. 2 vols. Rome: Institut Biblique Pontifical, 1966.

Dürr, Lorenz. "Hebr. *näpäš* = akk. *napištu* = Gurgel, Kehle." *Zeitschrift für die alttestamentliche Wissenschaft* 43 (1925), pp. 262-269.

Ehrentrau, Ernst. "Untersuchungen über die Entwicklung und den Geist der Massora." *Jeschurun* 11 (1924), pp. 34-59.

———. "Die Raschi-Stelle Psalmes IX,1." *Jeschurun* 11 (1924), pp. 515-520.

Ehrlich, Arnold B. *Mikrâ kî-Pheschutô*. 3 vols. Berlin: H. Itzkowski, 1899- 1901.

———. *Die Psalmen*. Berlin: M. Poppelauer, 1905.

Eilat, Moshe. "Tarshish." *Encyclopedia Miqra'it* 8:942.

Eissfeldt, Otto. *The Old Testament: An Introduction*. Translated by Peter Ackroyd. New York: Harper & Row, 1965.

Elfenbein, Israel. *Responsa Rashi*. New York: Shulsinger, 1943.

———. "Rashi in His Responsa." In *Rashi: His Teachings and Personality*, pp. 63-98. Edited by Simon Federbusch. New York: Cultural Division of the World Jewish Congress, 1958.

Elbogen, Ismar. *Jewish Liturgy: A Comprehensive History*. Translated by Raymond P. Scheindlin. Philadelphia: Jewish Publication Society/New York: Jewish Theological Seminary of America, 1993.

Elijah ben Isaac of Carcassone (13th cent.). *Sefer Assufot*. Edited with Critical Notes by Abraham Isaac Dziubas. London: J. Noroditsky, 1941; reprint, Jerusalem: n.p.,1970.

Encyclopaedia Judaica. S.v. "Kallir Eleazar."

Encyclopaedia Judaica. S.v. "Temple."

Encyclopedia Americana, 1991 ed. S.v. ""'Rubaaíyát of Omar Khayyam."

Englander, Henry A. "Rashi's View of the Weak, 'ayin-'ayin and pe-nun Roots." *Hebrew Union College Annual* 7 (1930), pp. 399-437.

———."Grammatical Elements and Terminology in Rashi's Biblical Commentaries, Part I." *Hebrew Union College Annual* 11 (1936), pp. 387-429.

———."Grammatical Elements and Terminology in Rashi's Biblical Commentaries, Part II—Rashi's Vowel Terminology." *Hebrew Union College Annual* 12-13 (1937-1938), pp. 505-521.

———. "Grammatical Elements and Terminology in Rashi." *Hebrew Union College Annual* 14 (1939), pp. 367-429.

———."Rashi as Bible Exegete and Grammarian." *CCAR Yearbook* 50 (1940), pp. 342-359.

———. "A Commentary on Rashi's Grammatical Comments." *Hebrew Union College Annual* 17 (1942-43), pp. 427-498.

Eppenstein, Simon. "Les Comparisons de l'Hebreu avec l'Arabe chez les exegetes du nord de la France." *Revue des Etudes Juives* 47 (1903), pp. 47-56.

———. "Studien über Joseph ben Simeon Kara als Exeget." *Jahrbuch der Jüdisch-Literarischen Gesellschaft* 4 (1906), pp. 238-268.

Epstein, Abraham. *Moses ha-Darschan aus Narbonne*. Vienna: Alkalay, 1891.

Epstein, Abraham, ed. "Rabbi Samuel b. Meir's Commentary on 'Avodah Zarah." *Ozar Tob* (= hebräische Beilage zum *Magazin für die Wissenschaft des Judentums*) 14 (1887), pp. 1-7 (in Hebrew).

Epstein, Jacob Nahum. "L'auteur du commentaire des chroniques." *Revue des Etudes Juives* 58 (1909), pp. 189-199.

———. "The Commentary on Horayot Attributed to Rashi." *Tarbiz* 3 (1932), pp. 218-225 (in Hebrew).

———. "The Commentaries of R. Jehudah ben Nathan and the Commentaries of Worms." *Tarbiz* 4 (1932), pp. 11-34; 153-192 (in Hebrew).

Faur, José. "The Legal Thinking of Tosafot: An Historical Approach." *Dine Yisrael* 43 (1975), pp. xliii-lxxii.

———. "A Crisis of Categories: Kabbalah and the Rise of Apostasy in Spain." In *The Jews of Spain and the Expulsion of 1492*, pp. 42-45. Edited by Moshe Lazar and Stephen Haliczer. Henry J. Leir Library of Sephardica. Lancaster, Cal.: Labyrinthos, 1997.

Feinstein, Moshe. *Igrot Moshe: Yoreh De'ah*, Part III. Bnei Braq, n.p., 1981.

Feliks, Jehuda. "Willows." *Encyclopaedia Judaica* 16:517-518.

Finkelstein, Louis. *Jewish Self Government in the Middle Ages*. 2[d] printing. New York: Feldheim, 1964.

Fitzmyer, Joseph A. "Some Notes on Aramaic Epistolography." *Journal of Biblical Literature* 93 (1974), pp. 201-225.

Fleischer, Ezra. "Solomon ben Judah ha-Bavli." *Encyclopaedia Judaica* 15:124.

Flora and Fauna of the Bible. Helps for Translators. 2^d ed. London: United Bible Societies, 1980.

Florsheim, Yoel. *Rashi on the Bible in His Commentary on the Talmud.* 3 vols. Jerusalem: Rubin Mass, 1981-1991 (in Hebrew).

———. "Rashi's Commentary on Mo'ed Katan." *Tarbiz* 51 (1982), pp. 421-444 (in Hebrew).

———. "Concerning Rashi's Biblical Exegesis." *Sinai* 59 (1996), pp. 71-76 (in Hebrew).

———. "More Concerning Rashi's Commentary on Tractate Mo'ed Qatan." *Sinai* 63 (2000), pp. 174-181 (in Hebrew).

Fraenkel, Jonah. "Rashi's Commentary on the Babylonian Talmud." *Encyclopaedia Judaica* 13:1564.

———. *Rashi's Methodology in His Exegesis of the Babylonian Talmud.* 2^d ed. Jerusalem: Magnes, 1980 (in Hebrew).

Freedman, Leslie R. "Studies in Cuneiform Legal Terminology with Special Reference to West Semitic Parallels." Ph.D. diss., Columbia University, 1977.

Freimann, Aron. "Manuscript Supercommentaries on Rashi's Commentary on the Pentateuch." In *Rashi Anniversary Volume,* pp. 73-114. Edited by H. L. Ginsberg. New York: American Academy for Jewish Research, 1941.

Freimann, Jacob. *Siddur Rashi.* Berlin: Mekize Nirdamim, 1911.

Frensdorff, Salomon, ed. *Ochlah W'ochlah.* Hanover: Hahn, 1864

———. *Die Massora Magna.* Hanover & Leipzig: Cohen & Risch, 1876.

Friedman, Shamma. "Rashi's Talmudic Commentaries and the Nature of the Revisions and Recensions." In *Rashi Studies,* pp. 147-75. Edited by Zvi Arie Steinfeld. Ramat-Gan: Bar-Ilan University Press, 1993 (in Hebrew).

Frisch, Amos. *"wĕ'anĕtāh."* *Tarbiz* 69 (2000), pp. 445-447. (in Hebrew).

Fudeman, Kirsten. "Father-, Mother-, Other Tongue" (forthcoming).

Fulco, William J. *The Canaanite God Rešep.* American Oriental Series, Essay, no. 8. New Haven: American Oriental Society, 1976.

Galatzer-Levy, Robert M., and Mayer I. Gruber, "What an Affect Means: A Quasi-Experiment About Disgust." *Annual of Psychoanalysis* 20 (1992), pp. 69-92.

Gandz, Solomon. "Studies in the History of Mathematics from Hebrew and Arabic Sources." *Hebrew Union College Annual* 6 (1929), pp. 247-276.

———. *Mishnat Ha-Middot.* Berlin: Springer, 1932.

Gaster, Theodor H. *Thespis.* rev. ed. Garden City, N.Y.: Doubleday & Co., 1961; reprint, New York: Harper & Row: Harper Torchbooks, 1966.

———. "Gehenna." *Interpreter's Dictionary of the Bible* 2:361-362.

———. *Myth, Legend, and Custom in the Old Testament.* New York and Evanston: Harper & Row, 1969.

———. "The Deep." *Encyclopaedia Judaica* 5:1456-1457.

Geiger, Abraham. *Parschandatha: Die nordfranzösische Exegetschule.* Leipzig: Leopold Schnauss, 1855.

Gelles, Benjamin J. *Peshat and Derash in the Exegesis of Rashi.* Etudes sur le Judaïsme médiéval, vol. 9. Leiden: E. J. Brill, 1981.

Gevaryahu, Haim M. Y. *"šēgāl."* *Encyclopedia Miqra'it* 7:522-524.

Gevirtz, Stanley. *Patterns in the Early Poetry of Israel.* 2^d ed. Chicago: University of Chicago Press, 1973.

Geyer, John B. "Twisting Tiamat's Tail: A Mythological Interpretation of Isaiah XIII 5 and 8." *Vetus Testamentum* 37 (1987), pp. 164-179.

Gilat, Yizhaq Dov. "Abba [Ba]." *Encyclopaedia Judaica* 1:30.

————. "Baraita de-Melekhet ha-Mishkan." *Encyclopaedia Judaica* 4:193-194.

Ginsberg, Harold Louis. "A Phoenician Hymn in the Psalter." In *Atti del XIX Congresso Internationale degli Orientalisti (Rome1935)*, pp. 472-476. Rome: Tipografia del Senato, 1938.

————. *The Legend of King Keret.* BASOR Supplementary Series, nos. 2-3. New Haven: American Schools of Oriental Research, 1946.

————. *Koheleth.* Tel Aviv and Jerusalem: M. Newman, 1961 (in Hebrew).

————. "Lexicographical Notes." In *Hebräische Wörtforschung*, pp. 71-82. Supplements to Vetus Testamentum, vol. 16. Leiden: E. J. Brill, 1967.

————. "Reflexes of Sargon in Isaiah After 715 B.C.E." *Journal of the American Oriental Society* 88 (1968), pp. 49-53.

————. "A Strand in the Cord of Hebraic Hymnody." *Eretz-Israel* 9 (1969), pp. 45-50.

————. "Job the Patient and Job the Impatient." *Congress Volume: Rome 1968*, pp. 88-111. Supplements to Vetus Testamentum, vol. 17. Leiden: E. J. Brill, 1969.

————. "The Northwest Semitic Languages." In *The World History of the Jewish People*, vol. 2, pp. 102-124. Edited by Benjamin Mazar. New Brunswick, N.J.: Rutgers University Press, 1970.

————. *The Israelian Heritage of Judaism.* New York: Jewish Theological Seminary of America, 1982.

Ginzberg, Louis. "Baraitha of Forty-Nine Rules." *Jewish Encyclopedia* 2:517-518.

————. "Cherethithes." *Jewish Encyclopedia* 4:116.

————. *Geonica.* 2 vols. New York: Jewish Theological Seminary of America, 1909.

————. *Legends of the Jews.* 7 vols. Philadelphia: Jewish Publication Society, 1913-1938.

Ginsburg, Christian David. *Introduction to the Massoretico-Critical Edition of the Hebrew Bible.* London: Trinitarian Bible Society, 1897; reprint, New York.: Ktav, 1966.

Glatt, David A., and Jeffrey H. Tigay. "Phylacteries." In *Harper's Bible Dictionary*, pp. 795-796. Edited by Paul J. Achtemeier. San Francisco: Harper & Row, 1985.

Glueck, Nelson. *Hesed in the Bible.* Translated by Alfred Gottschalk. Cincinnati: Hebrew Union College Press, 1967.

Golb, Norman. *Spertus College of Judaica Yemenite Mansucripts: An Illustrated Catalogue.* Chicago: Spertus College of Judaica Press, 1972.

————. *History and Culture of the Jews of Rouen in the Middle Ages.* Tel Aviv: Dvir, 1976 (in Hebrew).

————. *The Jews in Medieval Normandy.* Cambridge: Cambridge University Press, 1998.

Goldschmidt, Daniel. *On Jewish Liturgy.* Jerusalem: Magnes, 1980 (in Hebrew).

Goodblatt, David M. *Rabbinic Instruction in Sassanian Babylonia.* Studies in Judaism in Late Antiquty, vol. 9. Leiden: E. J. Brill, 1970.

————. "The Beruriah Traditions." *Journal of Jewish Studies* 26 (1975), pp. 68-86.

Gordis, Robert. "Studies in Roots of Contrasted Meanings." *Jewish Quarterly Review*, new series, 27 (1936), pp. 33-58.

————. "Quotations as a Literary Usage in Biblical, Oriental, and Rabbinic Literature." *Hebrew Union College Annual* 22 (1949), pp. 157-219.

————. *The Book of God and Man*. Chicago & London: University of Chicago Press, 1966.

————. *The Biblical Text in the Making*. augmented edition. New York: Ktav, 1971.

————. *The Song of Songs and Lamentations*. rev. and augmented ed. New York: Ktav, 1974.

————. *The Book of Job*. New York: Jewish Theological Seminary of America, 1978.

————. "Studies in the Book of Amos." In *American Academy for Jewish Research Jubilee Volume*, vol. 1, pp. 201-264. 2 vols. Jerusalem: American Academy for Jewish Research, 1980.

Gordon, Cyrus H. "Azitawadd's Phoenician Inscription." *Journal of Near Eastern Studies* 8 (1949), pp. 108-115.

————. *Ugaritic Textbook*. Analecta Orientalia, vol. 38. revised reprint. Rome: Biblical Institute Press, 1996.

Gray, George Buchanan. *A Critical and Exegetical Commentary on the Book of Job*. International Critical Commentary. Edinburgh: T. & T. Clark, 1921.

Green, Arthur. "The Zaddik as *Axis Mundi* in Later Judaism." *Journal of the American Academy of Religion* 45 (1977), pp. 327-347.

Greenberg, Joseph. *Foreign Words in the Bible Commentary of Rashi*. Jerusalem: By the author's widow, 1980.

Greenberg, Moshe. "Some Postulates of Biblical Criminal Law." In *Yehezkel Kaufmann Jubilee Volume*, pp. 5-28. Edited by M. Haran. Jerusalem: Magnes, 1960.

————. *Ezekiel 1-20*. Anchor Bible, vol. 22. Garden City, N.Y.: Doubleday & Co., 1981.

————. "Tanakh—Commentary: French Commentators." *Encyclopedia Miqra'it* 9:689-695 (in Hebrew).

Greenfield, Jonas C. "Cherethites and Pelethites." *Interpreter's Dictionary of the Bible* 1:557.

Greenspahn, Frederick E. "The Meaning of *'Ein Lo Domeh* and Similar Phrases in Medieval Biblical Exegesis." *AJS Review* 4 (1979), pp. 59-70.

Greenstein, Edward L. "Two Variations of Grammatical Parallelism in Canaanite Poetry and their Psycholinguistic Background." *Journal of the Ancient Near Eastern Society* 6 (1974), pp. 87-105.

————. "One More Step on the Staircase." *Ugarit Forschungen* 9 (1977), pp. 77-86.

————. "Theories of Modern Bible Translation." *Prooftexts* 3 (1983), pp. 9-39.

————. "Medieval Bible Commentaries." In *Back to the Sources*, pp. 213-259. Edited by Barry W. Holtz. New York: Summit Books, 1984.

Gross, Abraham. "Spanish Jewry and Rashi's Commentary on the Pentateuch." In *Rashi Studies*, pp. 27-55. Edited by Zvi Arie Steinfeld. Ramat-Gan: Bar-Ilan University Press, 1993 (in Hebrew).

Grossberg, Daniel. "Noun/Verb Parallelism: Syntactic or Asyntactic." *Journal of Biblical Literature* 99 (1980), pp. 481-488.

Grossman, Avraham. "Rashi—Biblical Exegesis." *Encyclopaedia Judaica* 13:1559-1562.

————. *The Early Sages of Ashkenaz*. 2^d ed. Jerusalem: Magnes, 1988 (in Hebrew).

————. "Marginal Notes and Addenda of R. Shemaiah and the Text of Rashi's Bible Commentary." *Tarbiz* 60 (1991), pp. 67-98 (in Hebrew).

————. "MS Leipzig 1 and Rashi's Commentary on the Bible." *Tarbiz* 61 (1992), pp. 205-315 (in Hebrew).

————. *The Early Sages of France*. 2^d ed. Jerusalem: Magnes, 1996 (in Hebrew).

————. "Exegesis of the Piyyut in Eleventh Century France." In *Rashi et la culture juive en France du Nord au moyen âge*, pp. 261-277. Edited by Gilbert Dahan, Gérard Nahon, Elic Nicolas. Paris & Louvain: Peeters, 1997.

————. "Rashi's Commentary on Psalms and Jewish-Christian Polemics." In *Studies in the Bible and Education Presented to Professor Moshe Ahrend*, pp. 59-74. Edited by Dov Rappel. Jerusalem: Touro College Press, 1996.

————. "The School of Literal Exegesis in Northern France." In *Hebrew Bible/ Old Testament: The History of Its Interpretation, Volume I: From the Beginnings to the Middle Ages (Until 1300)*, pp. 321-371. Edited by Magne Saebø. Göttingen: Vandenhoeck & Ruprecht, 2000.

Gruber, Mayer I. "Akkadian Inluences in the Book of Ezekiel." M.A. Essay, Columbia University, 1970.

————. "Havilah." *Encyclopaedia Judaica* 7:1493-1494.

————. "Scepter." *Encyclopaedia Judaica* 14:935.

————. "The Midrash in Biblical Research." In *The Solomon Goldman Lectures: Perspectives in Jewish Learning*, vol. 2, pp. 69-80. Edited by Nathaniel Stampfer. Chicago: Spertus College of Judaica Press, 1979.

————. *Aspects of Nonverbal Communication in the Ancient Near East*. Studia Pohl, no. 12. 2 vols. Rome: Biblical Institute Press, 1980.

————. "The Meaning of *'ōrāyĕtā'* in the Babylonian Talmud." *Hebrew Studies* 22 (1981), pp. 25-33.

————. "Ten Dance-Derived Expressions in the Hebrew Bible." *Biblica* 62 (1981), pp. 328-346.

————. "The Change in the Name of the Decalogue." *Beit Mikra* 26 (1981-82), pp. 16-21 (in Hebrew).

————. "The Many Faces of Hebrew *nāśā' pānîm* 'lift up the face'." *Zeitschrift für die alttestamentliche Wissenschaft* 95 (1983), pp. 252-260.

————. "The Motherhood of God in Second Isaiah." *Revue Biblique* 90 (1983), pp. 351-359.

————. "The Mishnah as Oral Torah: A Reconsideration." *Journal for the Study of Judaism* 15 (1984), pp. 112-122.

————. "Hebrew *qĕdēšāh* and her Canaanite and Akkadian Cognates." *Ugarit Forschungen* 18 (1986), 133-148.

————. "Hebrew *da'ăbôn nepeš* 'dryness of throat': From Symptom to Literary Convention." *Vetus Testamentum* 37 (1987), pp. 365-369.

————. "What Happened to Rashi's Pictures?" *Bodleian Library Record* 14, no. 2 (1992), pp. 111-124.

————. *Rashi's Commentary on Psalms 1-89 (Books I-III)*. University of South Florida Studies in the History of Judaism, no. 161. Atlanta: Scholars Press, 1998.

————. "Azabbim 'idols'." In *Dictionary of Deities and Demons in the Bible*, pp.127-128. Edited by Karel van der Toorn, Bob Becking, and Pieter W. van der Horst. 2ᵈ ed. Leiden: E. J. Brill, 1999.

————. "A Reexamination of the Charges Against Shechem son of Hamor." *Beit Mikra* 44 (1999), pp. 119-127 (in Hebrew).

————. Review of *Away from the Father's House: The Social Location of the na'ar and na'arah in Ancient Israel* by Carolyn S. Leeb. In *Jewish Quarterly Review*, new series, 93 (2003), pp. 20-23.

————. "Nuances of the Hebrew Root *'ny*." In *Menachem Cohen Festschrift*. Edited by Shmuel Vargon. Ramat-Gan: Bar-Ilan University Press, 2004.

Gruenwald, Ithamar. *From Apocalypticism to Gnosticism*. Beiträge zur Erforschung des Alten Testaments und des antiken Judentums, vol. 14. Frankfurt am Main: Peter Lang, 1988.

Gunkel, Hermann. *The Psalms: A Form-Critical Introduction*. Translated by M. Horner with introduction by James Muilenberg. Facet Books Biblical Series no. 19. Philadelphia: Fortress, 1967.

———. *Die Psalmen*. 5th ed. Göttingen: Vandenhoeck & Ruprecht, 1968.

Gutmann, Joshua. "Achish." *Encyclopaedia Judaica* 2:210-211.

Guttel, J. P. "Remarques sur le 'Pseudo-Raši' de Ta'anit." *Revue des Etudes Juives* 125 (1966), pp. 93-100.

Haberman, Abraham Meir. *Piyyute Rashi*. Jerusalem: Schocken, 1941.

———. "Piyyute Rashi." In *Sefer Rashi*, pp. 592-610. Edited by Yehudah Leib Ha-Kohen Fishman Maimon. 2d ed. Jerusalem: Mossad Harav Kook, 1956.

———. "Azharot, Azharah." *Encyclopaedia Judaica* 3:1007-1008.

Hailperin, Herman. *Rashi and the Christian Scholars*. Pittsburgh: University of Pittsburgh Press, 1963.

Hakam, Noah. "'nh." *Tarbiz* 69 (2000), pp. 441-444.

Halivni, David. "The First Three Pages of the Commentary on Ta'anit Attributed to Rashi." *Sinai* 43 (1958), pp. 211-222 (in Hebrew).

———. Concerning the Identity of the Commentary on Ta'anit Assigned to Rashi." *Sinai* 44 (1959), pp. 23-25 (in Hebrew).

———. *Peshat and Derash*. New York & Oxford: Oxford University Press, 1991.

Halperin, David Joel. *The Merkabah in Rabbinic Literature*. American Oriental Series, no. 62. New Haven: American Oriental Society, 1980.

———. *The Faces of the Chariot*. Tübingen: J.C.B. Mohr, 1988.

Haran, Menahem. "Biblical Studies." *Tarbiz* 39 (1969), pp. 109-136 (in Hebrew).

Hareuveni, Noga. *Nature in our Biblical Heritage*. Translated by Helen Frenkley. Kiryat Ono: Neot Kedumim, 1980.

Harris, Robert A. Review of *Rashi's Commentary on Psalms 1-89 (Books 1-III)* by Mayer I. Gruber. In *Hebrew Studies* 40 (1999), pp. 331-334.

Harrison, Roland Kenneth "Disease." In *International Standard Bible Encyclopedia*, vol. 1, p. 956. Edited by Geoffrey William Bromiley. 4 vols. Grand Rapids: Eerdmans,1979.

Hartman, Louis F., and Alexander Di Lella. *The Book of Daniel*. Anchor Bible, vol. 23. Garden City, N.Y.: Doubleday & Co., 1978.

Havlin, Shlomoh Zalman. "Haggahot Maimuniyyot." *Encyclopaedia Judaica* 7: 1110-1112.

———. "Isaac Ben Meir." *Encyclopaedia Judaica* 9:23-24.

Havlin, Shlomoh Zalman, ed. *Scha'arei Ziyyon of Rabbi Isaac Lattes Edited from Oxford MS Mich. 602 and Russian State Library MS Guenzburg 1336*, with introductions, indexes, explanations, notes and comments. This work is published as an addendum to Menahem ha-Meiri, *History of the Oral Law*, q.v.

Heilperin, Jehiel b. Solomon. *Seder ha-Dorot*. Karlsruhe: Loter, 1769.

———. *Seder ha-Dorot*. Warsaw: Lewin-Epstein, 1878.

Held, Moshe. "Additional Pairs of Words in Synonymous Parallelism in Biblical Hebrew and in Ugaritic." *Lešonénu* 18 (1953), pp. 144-160 (in Hebrew).

———. The YQTL-QTL (QTL-YQTL) Sequence of Identical Verbs in Biblical Hebrew and Ugaritic." In *Studies and Essays in Honor of Abraham A. Neuman*, pp. 281-290. Edited by Meir Ben-Horin, Bernard D. Weinryb, and Solomon Zeitlin. Leiden: E. J. Brill for Dropsie College, 1962.

———. "The Action-Result (Factitive-Passive) Sequence of Identical Verbs in Biblical Hebrew and Ugaritic." *Journal of Biblical Literature* 84 (1965), pp. 272-82.

———. "Studies in Comparative Semitic Lexicography." In *Studies in Honor of*

Benno Landsberger on his Seventy-Fifth Birthday April 21, 1965, pp. 395-406. Edited by Hans G. Güterbock and Thorkild Jacobsen. Assyriological Studies, no. 16. Chicago: University of Chicago Press, 1965.

―――. "The Root *zbl/sbl* in Akkadian, Ugaritic, and Biblical Hebrew." *Journal of the American Oriental Society* 88 (1968), pp. 90-96.

―――. "Rhetorical Questions in Ugaritic and Biblical Hebrew." *Eretz-Israel* 9 (1969), pp. 71-79.

―――. "Studies in Biblical Homonyms in the Light of Akkadian." *Journal of the Ancient Near Eastern Society* 3 (1970-71), pp. 46-55.

―――. "Pits and Pitfalls in Akkadian and Biblical Hebrew." *Journal of the Ancient Near Eastern Society* 5 (1973), pp. 173-190.

―――. Studies in Biblical Lexicography in the Light of Akkadian." *Eretz-Israel* 16 (1982), pp. 76-77 (in Hebrew).

―――. "Studies in Biblical Lexicography in the Light of Akkadian." *Studies in the Bible Dedicated to the Memory of U. Cassuto on the 100th Anniversary of His Birth*, pp. 104-126. Jerusalem: Magnes, 1987 (in Hebrew).

Herdner, Andrée. *Corpus des tablettes en cunéiformes alphabétiques découvertes à Ras Shamra-Ugarit de 1929 à 1939*. 2 vols. Paris: Geuthner, 1963.

Herr, Moshe David. "Midrash." *Encyclopaedia Judaica* 11:1507-1514.

Herzog, Eliezra. "The Triple Rhetorical Argument in the Latter Prophets." Ph.D. diss., New York: Jewish Theological Seminary of America, 1991.

Hildesheimer, Esriel. *Sefer Halakhot Gedolot, edited from mss. and with introduction and notes*. 3 vols. Jerusalem: Mekize Nirdamim, 1971-1988.

Hoffman, Yair. *Jeremiah*. Mikra LeYisrael. 2 vols. Tel Aviv: Am Oved/Jerusalem: Magnes, 2001 (in Hebrew).

Holladay, William L. *The Root šûbh in the Old Testament*. Leiden: E. J. Brill, 1958.

Holmgren, Virginia C. *Birdwalk Through the Bible*. New York: Seabury, 1972.

Hoyt, Robert. *Europe in the Middle Ages*. New York: Harcourt Brace, 1957.

Humbert, Paul. "Etendre la main." *Vetus Testamentum* 12 (1962), pp. 383-395.

Hurowitz, Victor (Avigdor). *I Have Built You an Exalted House*. Journal for the Study of the Old Testament Supplement Series, no. 115. Sheffield: JSOT Press, 1992.

―――. "Nursling, Advisor Architect? *'āmôn* and the Role of Wisdom in Proverbs 8, 22-31." *Biblica* 80 (1999), pp. 391-400.

Hurvitz, Avi. *The Transition Period in Biblical Hebrew*. Jerusalem: Bialik, 1972 (in Hebrew).

―――. "The Biblical Roots of a Talmudic Term: The Early History of the Concept *sedaqah* (=charity, alms)." In *Studies in Language*, nos. 2-3, pp. 155-160. Jerusalem: Institute of Jewish Studies, 1987 (in Hebrew).

―――. "Wisdom Vocabulary in the Hebrew Psalter: A Contribution to the Study of 'Wisdom Psalms'." *Vetus Testamentum* 38 (1988), pp. 41-51.

Hurwitz, Simeon, ed. *Machsor Vitry*. 2^d ed. Nürnberg: J. Bulka, 1923.

Hyman, Aaron. *Torah Hakketubah Wehammesurah*. 3 vols. Tel Aviv: Dvir, 1965 (in Hebrew).

Ibn Ezra, Abraham. Biblical Commentaries found in the Rabbinic Bible.

―――. *Sefer Sahot*. See Valle Rodriguez, Carlos.

Idelsohn, Abraham Z. *Jewish Liturgy and Its Development*. New York: Henry Holt & Co., 1932.

Ilan, Tal. *Integrating Women into the Second Temple History*. Tübingen: J.C.B. Mohr, 1999.

Jacob b. Zvi Hirsch of Mir. *'Ateret Zvi*. Vilna & Grodno: Jewish Community of Vilna Press, 1834.

Jaffee, Martin S. "The Taqqanah in Tannaitic Literature: Jurisprudence and the Construction of Rabbinic Memory." *Journal of Jewish Studies* 41 (1990), pp. 204-25.

Japhet, Sara. *The Ideology of the Book of Chronicles and Its Place in Biblical Thought*. Jerusalem: Bialik, 1977 (in Hebrew).

———. *The Commentary of Rabbi Samuel Ben Meir (Rashbam) On the Book of Job*. Jersualem: Magnes, 2000 (in Hebrew).

Japhet, Sara, and Robert B. Salters. *The Commentary of R. Samuel b. Meir* Rashbam on *Qoheleth*. Jerusalem: Magnes, 1985.

Jerome. *The Homilies of St. Jerome*, vol. 1. Translated by Marie Liguori Ewald. Washington: Catholic University of America, 1964.

Joseph b. Eliezer Bonfils. *Sophnath Paneah*. Edited by David Herzog. 2 vols. Heidelberg: Carl Winters, 1911-1930.

Joseph Ben Lev. *Responsa of Joseph Ben Lev*. 4 vols. Amsterdam: Moses Frankfurt, 1626.

———. *Responsa of Joseph Ben Lev*. 4 vols. Bene Berak, S.L.A., 1988.

Josephus. *Antiquities*.

Kadushin, Max. *Organic Thinking*. New York: Bloch, 1938.

———. *Worship and Ethics*. Evanston: Northwestern University Press, 1966.

———. *A Conceptual Approach to the Mekilta*. New York: Jonathan David Publishers for the Jewish Theological Seminary of America, 1969.

———. *The Rabbinic Mind*. 3^d ed. New York: Bloch, 1972.

Kalimi, Isaac. "History of Inerpretaton: The Book of Chronicles in Jewish Interpretation." *Revue Biblique* 105 (1998), pp. 5-41.

———. *The Book of Chronicles: Historical Writing and Literary Devices*. Biblical Encyclopaedia Library, vol. 18. Jerusalem: Mossad Bialik, 2000 (in Hebrew).

Kalmin, Richard. *Sages, Stories, Authors, and Editors in Rabbinic Babylonia*. Brown Judaic Studies, no. 300. Atlanta: Scholars Press, 1994.

Kamin, Sarah. "*Dúgmah* in Rashi's Commentary on Song of Songs." *Tarbiz* 52 (1983), pp. 41-58 (in Hebrew).

———. "Rashi's Commentary on the Song of Songs and the Jewish-Christian Polemic." *SHNATON* 7-8 (1984), pp. 218-248 (in Hebrew).

———. "A Latin Version of Rashi's Commentary on the *Song of Songs* (13th Century?)." *Tarbiz* 54 (1986), pp. 381-411 (in Hebrew).

———. *Rashi's Exegetical Categorization in Respect to the Distinction Between Peshat and Derash*. Jerusalem: Magnes, 1986 (in Hebrew).

Kamin, Sarah, and Avrom Saltman. *Secundum Salomonem*. Ramat-Gan: Bar-Ilan University Press, 1989.

Kapelrud, Arvid S. "Zarephath." *Interpreter's Dictionary of the Bible* 4: 935.

Kasher, Menahem. M. *Torah Shelemah: Genesis*, vol. 4. New York: American Biblical Encyclopedia Society, 1951 (in Hebrew).

Katzenelenbogen, Mordechai Leib. *Joshua and Judges with the Commentary of Rashi*. Jerusalem: Mossad Harav Kook, 1987 (in Hebrew).

Kaufmann, Yehezkel. *History of the Israelite Religion*. 4 vols. Jerusalem: Bialik, 1963 (in Hebrew).

———. *The Religion of Israel*. Translated and abridged by Moshe Greenberg. Chicago & London: University of Chicago Press, 1960.

Kirchheim, Raphael. *Ein Commentar zur Chronik aus dem 10ten Jahrhundert Zum Erstenmal Herausgegeben*. Frankfurt am Main: H. L. Brünner, 1874.

Kirkpatrick, Alexander Francis. *The Book of Psalms*. Cambridge Bible for Schools and Colleges. Cambridge: Cambridge University Press, 1902.
Kraemer, David. *The Mind of the Talmud*. New York: Oxford University Press, 1990.
Krauss, Samuel. *Greichische und Lateinische Lehnwörter im Talmud, Midrasch und Targum*. 2 vols. Berlin: Calvary, 1898-1899.
Krecher, Joachim. "Kommentare." *Reallexikon der Assyriologie* 6:188-191.
Kronberg, Nehemia. *Raschi als Exeget*. Breslau: Schatzky, 1882.
Kugel, James. L. *The Idea of Biblical Poetry*. New Haven & London: Yale University Press, 1981.
Kupfer, Efraim F. R. *Salomon Izḥaqi (Raši) Commentarius in Tractatum Moʿed Katan ad Fidem Codicus Hispansiensis*. Jerusalem: Mekize Nirdamim 1961 (in Hebrew).
Kutscher, Eduard Yechezkel. *A History of the Hebrew Language*. Edited by Raphael Kutscher. Leiden: E. J. Brill/ Jerusalem: Magnes, 1982.
Ladermann, Shulamith. "Parallel Texts in a Byzantine Christian Treatise and Sections of Midrash Attributed to Rabbi Moshe Hadarshan." *Tarbiz* 70 (2001), pp. 213-226 (in Hebrew).
Laing, Gordon Jennings. *Survivals of Roman Religion*. New York: Cooper Square Publishers, 1931.
Landa, Luis. "Rashi's Stories in the Rashi Commentary Printed in the Babylonian Talmud." *Eshel Beer Sheva* 3 (1986), pp. 101-17 (in Hebrew).
Landes, George M. "Linguistic Criteria and the Date of the Book of Jonah." *Eretz-Israel* 16 (1982), pp. 147-170.
Landsberg, Max. "Night." *Jewish Encyclopedia* 9:303-304.
Lange, Isaac S., ed. *The Torah Commentaries of R. Judah the Pious*. Jerusalem: By the editor, 1975 (in Hebrew).
Lasker, Daniel J. *Jewish Philosophical Polemics Against Christianity in the Middle Ages*. New York: Ktav, 1977.
Lattes, Isaac de. *Schaare Ẓion*. Edited by Solomon Buber. Jaroslau: Eisig Gräber, 1885.
Lehman, Manfred R. "Studies in the Exegetical *waw*." *Sinai* 85 (1979), pp. 200-210 (in Hebrew).
Lemke, Werner E. "Gehenna." In *Harper's Bible Dictionary*, p. 335. Edited by Paul J. Achtemeier. San Francisco: Harper & Row, 1985.
Leslie, Elmer A. *The Psalms*. New York: Abingdon, 1949.
Levenson, Jon D. *Sinai and Ẓion*. San Francisco: Harper & Row, 1986.
————. "The Sources of Torah: Psalm 119 and the Modes of Revelation in Second Temple Judaism." In *Ancient Israelite Religion*, pp. 574-559. Edited by Patrick D. Miller, et al. Philadelphia: Fortress, 1987.
————. *Creation and the Persistence of Evil*. San Francisco: Harper & Row, 1988.
Levias, Caspar. "Meturgeman." *Jewish Encyclopedia* 8:521.
Levin, Benjamin Menashe. "Rashi's *Responsum* Concerning 'kí is employed in four meanings'." In *Sefer Rashi*, pp. 489-495. Edited by Yehudah Leib Ha-Kohen Fishman Maimon. Jerusalem: Mossad Harav Kook, 1941 (in Hebrew).
Levine, Baruch. A. "Kippurim." *Eretz-Israel* 9 (1969), pp. 88-95 (in Hebrew).
Levinson, Bernard M., and Molly H. Zahn, "Revelation Regained: The Hermeneutics of kî and ʾim in the Temple Scroll." *Dead Sea Discoveries* 9 (2002), pp. 295-346.
Levita, Elias. *Massoreth Ha-Massoreth*. Edited with an English translation and Critical and Explanatory Notes by Christian David Ginsburg. London: Longmans, Green, Reader & Dyer, 1867; reprint, New York: Ktav, 1968.

Levy, Raphael. *Contribution à la lexicographie française selon d'anciens textes d'origine juive.* Syracuse, N.Y.: Syracuse University Press, 1960.

————. *Trésor de la langue des juifs français au moyen âge.* Austin: University of Texas Press, 1964.

Liber, Maurice. "Rashi." *Jewish Encyclopedia* 10:324-328.

————. *Rashi.* Translated by Adele Szold. Philadelphia: Jewish Publication Society, 1906.

Liberles, Robert. *Salo Wittmayer Baron: Architect of Jewish History.* Modern Jewish History Series, vol. 6. New York & London: New York University Press, 1995.

Lieberman, Saul. *Hayerushalmi Kiphshuto.* Jerusalem: Darom, 1934.

————. *Tosepheth Rishonim.* Jerusalem: Bamberger & Wahrmann, 1938.

————. *Hellenism in Jewish Palestine.* New York.: Jewish Theological Seminary of America, 1950.

————. *Tosefta Ki Fshutah.* Order Zeraim, pt. 2. New York: Jewish Theological Seminary of America, 1955.

Linville, James. "Rethinking the 'Exilic' Book of Kings." *Journal for the Study of the Old Testament* 75 (1997), pp. 21-42.

Lipschuetz, Eliezer Meir. *Rashi.* Warsaw: Tushiya, 1914 (in Hebrew).

Lockshin, Martin. *Rabbi Samuel ben Meir's Commentary on Genesis: An Annotated Translation.* Lewiston: Edwin Mellen Press, 1989.

————. *Rashbam's Commentary on Exodus: An Annotated Translation.* Brown Judaic Studies, no. 310. Atlanta: Scholars Press, 1997.

————. "'Rashbam' on Job: A Reconsideration." *Jewish Studies Quarterly* 8 (2001), pp. 80-104.

————. *Rashbam's Commentary on Leviticus and Numbers: An Annotated Translation.* Brown Judaic Studies, no. 330. Providence: Brown University, 2001.

Löw, Immanuel. *Die Flora der Jüden.* 4 vols. Vienna: R. Loewit, 1924-1934.

Loewenstamm, Samuel E. "The Expanded Colon in Ugaritic and Biblical Verse." *Journal of Semitic Studies* 14 (1969), pp. 176-196.

————. "Resheph." *Encyclopedia Miqra'it* 7: 437-441 (in Hebrew).

————. "zebul." *Encyclopedia Miqra'it* 2:907-908 (in Hebrew).

Loewinger, David Samuel, and Bernard Dov Weinryb. *Catalogue of the Hebrew Manuscripts in the Library of the Juedische-Theologisches Seminar im Breslau.* Publications of the Leo Baeck Institute, New York. Wiesbaden: Harrassowitz, 1965.

Lohfink, Norbert. "Enthielten die im Alten Testament bezeugten Klageriten eine Phase des Schweigens." *Vetus Testamentum* 12 (1962), pp. 260-277.

Lowe, James. H. *"Rashi" on the Pentateuch, Genesis.* 2 vols. London: Hebrew Compendium Publishing Co., 1928-1929.

Luria, Avraham. *Nisyonot Avraham.* Vilna: Mann, 1821.

Luria, Solomon. *Responsa.* Jerusalem: Yahdayw, 1983 (in Hebrew).

Luther, Martin. "Preface to the Psalter." In *Works of Martin Luther,* vol. 6, pp. 384-388. 6 vols. Philadelphia: Muhlenberg, 1932.

Luzatto, Samuel David. *Erläuterungen über einen Theil der Prophet und Hagiographen.* Lemberg; A. Isaak Menkes, 1876.

Maarsen, Isaac. *Parschandatha. The Commentary of Rashi on the Prophets and Hagiographa edited on the basis of several mansucrits and editions.* 3 vols. vol. 1. Amsterdam: M. Hertzberger, 1930; vol. 2. Jerusalem: Central Press, 1933. vol. 3. Jerusalem: Central Press, 1936.

————. "Raschi's Kommentar zu Sprüche und Job." *Monatsschrift für Geschichte und Wissenschaft des Judentums* 83 (1939), pp. 442-444.

Malter, Henry. *Saadiah Gaon: His Life and Works.* Philadelphia: Jewish Publication Society, 1921.

Malul, Meir. "Also I shook out my sleeve." *Beit Mikra* 31 (1986), pp. 17-22 (in Hebrew).

Mann, Jacob. *The Bible as Read and Preached in the Old Synagogue,* vol. 1. Cincinnati: By the author, 1940.

Margalioth, Ephraim Zalman. *Shem Ephraim.* Munkascz: Kahn, 1913.

Margalit, Baruch. *The Ugaritic Poem of Aqhat.* Berlin & New York: Walter de Gruyter, 1989.

Margalith, Othniel. "Dor and En-dor." *Zeitschrift für die alttestamentliche Wissenschaft* 97 (1985), pp. 109-111.

Marcus, David. "Some Antiphrastic Euphemisms for a Blind Person in Akkadian and Other Semitic Languages." *Journal of the American Oriental Society* 100 (1986), pp. 307-310.

Margolis, Reuven. *Nizozey Or.* Jerusalem: Mossad Harav Kook, 1065.

Marmura, Michael E. "Avicenna." In *Encyclopedia of Philosophy* 1:226- 229.

Mastin, B. A. "*waw explicativum* in 2 Kings viii 9." *Vetus Testamentum* 34 (1984), pp. 353-355.

May, R. A., ed. *Catalogue of the Hebrew Mansucripts in the Bodleian Library, Supplement of Addenda and Corrigenda to Vol. I A. of A. Neubauer's Catalogue Compiled Under the Direction of Malachi Beit-Arié.* Oxford: Clarendon Press, 1994.

McCarter, P. Kyle, Jr. *I Samuel.* Anchor Bible, vol. 8. Garden City, N.Y.: Doubleday & Co., 1980.

McCullough, W. Stewart. "Exegesis of Psalms 72-92, 94, 97-99, 101-119, 139." In *Interpreter's Bible,* vol. 4. Edited by George Arthur Buttrick. New York and Nashville: Abingdon, 1955.

———. "Wild Ox." *Interpreter's Dictionary of the Bible* 4: 843-844.

McFall, Leslie. *The Enigma of the Hebrew Verbal System: Solutions from Ewald to the Present Day.* Sheffield: Almond Press, 1982.

McKane, William. *Jeremiah.* vol. 2. International Critical Commentary. Edinburgh: T & T Clarke, 1996.

Meir b. Baruch of Rothenburg. *Sefer She'elot uTeshuvot Maharam.* Cremona: Vinceno Conti, 1557.

Meir ha-Kohen of Rothenburg. *Haggahot Maimuniyyot.* Found in the standard editions of Moses Maimonides, Mishneh Torah.

———. *Teshuvot Maimuniyyot.* Appendices to Meir ha-Kohen of Rothenburg, *Haggahot Maimuniyyot.*

Melamed, Ezra Zion. *Bible Commentaries.* 2 vols. Jerusalem: Magnes, 1975 (in Hebrew).

Menahem Azariah of Pano. *Responsa of Rabbenu Menahem Azariah of Pano.* Jerusalem: Salomon, 1963.

Menahem b. Aaron b. Zerah (1312-1385). *Zedah la-Derek.* Warsaw: Joshua Gershon Munk, 1879.

Menahem ha-Meiri. *History of the Oral Law.* Edited by Shlomo Zalman Havlin. 2^d ed. Jerusalem & Cleveland: Ofek Instiute, 1995 (in Hebrew).

Michel, Walter L. "SLMWT: Deep Darkness or Shadow of Death." *Biblical Research* 29 (1984), pp. 5-20.

Miesen, M. "Zür Geographie Palästinas." *Monatsschrift für Geschichte und Wissenschaft des Judentums* 74 (1930), pp. 135-136.

Mihelic, Joseph. "Sin, Wilderness of." *Interpreter's Dictionary of the Bible* 4:376.

———. "Zin, Wilderness of." *Interpreter's Dictionary of the Bible* 4:958-59

Milgrom, Jacob. *Cult and Conscience: The Asham and the Priestly Doctrine of Repentance.* Studies in Judaism in Late Antiquity, vol. 18. Leiden: E. J. Brill, 1976.

———. *Numbers.* The JPS Torah Commentary. Philadelphia: Jewish Publication Society, 1990.

———. *Leviticus 23-27*, Anchor Bible, vol. 3B. New York: Doubleday, 2000.

Milikowsky, Chaim. "'Seder Olam' and Jewish Chronography in the Hellenistic and Roman periods." *Proceedings of the American Academy for Jewish Research* 52 (1985), pp. 115-139.

Miqra'ot Gedolot. 4 vols. Venice: Daniel Bomberg, 1524-1526; reprint, Jerusalem: Makor, 1972.

Miqra'ot Gedolot on the Pentateuch and the Five Scrolls. 5 vols. Vilna: Romm, 1927.

Miqra'ot Gedolot on the Prophets and the Hagiographa. 3 vols. Jerusalem & Tel Aviv: Schocken, 1959.

Moldenke, Harold Norman, and Almah Moldenke. *Plants of the Bible.* Waltham, Mass.: Chronica Botanica, 1952.

Moran, William. L. "The Scandal of the Great Sin at Ugarit." *Journal of Near Eastern Studies* 18 (1959), pp. 280-281.

Moscati, Sabatino. *An Introduction to the Comparative Grammar of the Semitic Languages.* Wiesbaden: Harrassowitz, 1969.

Moses Ibn Danon. *Kelalim.*

Moses Maimonides (1135-1204). The Book of the Commandments.

Moses Nahmanides. "The Gate of Retribution." In *Collected Writings of Nahmanides*, pp. 264-320. Edited by Chaim Chavel. Jerusalem Mossad Harav Kook, 1963 (in Hebrew).

Mueller, Joël, ed. *Réponses faites par de célèbres rabins français et lorrains du XI et XII siècle.* Vienna: Loevy & Alkalay, 1881.

Muffs, Yochanan. *Love & Joy.* New York & Jerusalem: Jewish Theological Seminary of America, 1992.

Muilenberg, James. "The Linguistic and Rhetorical Usages of the Particle *kî* in the Old Testament." *Hebrew Union College Annual* 32 (1961), pp. 135-160.

Murphy, Roland E. "A Contribution to the Classification of Wisdom Psalms." In *Congress Volume: Bonn 1962*, pp. 156-177. Supplements to Vetus Testamentum, vol. 9. Leiden: E. J. Brill, 1963.

Myers, Jacob M. *II Chronicles.* Anchor Bible, vol. 13. Garden City, N.Y.: Doubleday & Co., 1965.

Mutius, Hans Georg von. *Rechtsentscheide Rachis aus Troyes (1040-1105).* Judentum und Umwelt, vols. 15/I-15/II. 2 vols. Frankfurt am Main: Peter Lang, 1986-87.

Neale, John Mason, and Richard Frederick Littledale. *A Commentary on the Psalms from Primitive and Medieval Writers.* 4 vols. London: Joseph Masters, 1869-1883.

Netzer, Nissan. "The Term 'Leshon X' for the Purpose of Providing Semantic Differentiation in Rashi's Commentary on the Bible." In *Proceedings of the Tenth World Congress of Jewish Studies (Jerusalem, August 16-24, 1989)*, Division D, Volume 1, pp. 93-100. Jerusalem: World Union of Jewish Studies, 1990 (in Hebrew).

Neubauer, Adolf. *La Géographie du Talmud.* Paris: M. Levy, 1868; reprint, Hildesheim: Georg Olms, 1967.

———. *Catalogue of the Hebrew Manuscripts in the Bodleian Library and in the College Libraries of Oxford.* Oxford: Clarendon Press, 1886.

Neubauer, Adolf, ed. *Medieval Jewish Chronicles and Chronological Notes.* 2 vols. Oxford: Clarendon Press, 1887-1895.

Neusner, Jacob. *A Life of Yohanan ben Zakkai ca. 1-80 C.E.* 2ᵈ ed. Studia Post Biblica, vol. 6. Leiden: E. J. Brill, 1970.

———. *Between Time and Eternity: The Essentials of Judaism.* Encino & Belmont, Calif.: Dickenson Publishing, 1975.

———. *Midrash as Literature: The Primacy of Documentary Discourse.* Lanham, Md.: University Press of America, 1987.

———. *Where the Talmud Comes from: A Talmudic Phenomenology.* University of South Florida Studies in the History of Judaism, no. 120. Atlanta: Scholars Press, 1995.

———. Review of *Salo Wittmayer Baron: Architect of Jewish History,* by Robert Liberles. In *Religion* 26 (1996), pp. 286-290.

———. *How Adin Steinsaltz Misrepresents the Talmud: Four False Propositions from his "Reference Guide."* University of South Florida Studies in the History of Judaism, no. 190. Atlanta: Scholars Press, 1998.

———. *How the Rabbis Liberated Women.* University of South Florida Studies in the History of Judaism, no. 191. Atlanta: Scholars Press, 1998.

———. *Rabbinic Narrative: A Documentary Perspective.* Brill Reference Library of Judaism. 4 vols. Leiden: Brill, 2003.

Newman, Louis Israel. *Jewish Influence on Christian Reform Movements.* Columbia University Oriental Studies, vol. 23. New York: Columbia University Press, 1925.

Norzi, Jedidiah Solomon Raphael b. Abraham. *Minhat Shai.* Found in *Miqra'ot Gedolot.*

Nutt, John W., ed. *Two Treatises on Verbs Containing Feeble or Double Letters by R. Jehudah Hayug of Fez.* London & Berlin: Asher & Co., 1870.

Obadiah of Bertinora (d. 1510). Commentary on Mishnah. Found in Mishnah. 7 vols. Vilna: Romm: 1887-1909.

O'Connell, Kevin J. "Exodus." In *Harper's Bible Dictionary,* pp. 288-291. Edited by Paul J. Achtemeier. San Francisco: Harper & Row, 1986.

Ogden, Graham S. "The 'Better'-Proverb (Tôb-Spruche), Rhetorical Criticism, and Qoheleth." *Journal of Biblical Literature* 96 (1977), pp. 489-505.

Oppenheim, A. Leo. *Letters from Mesopotamia.* Chicago & London: University of Chicago Press, 1967.

———. *Ancient Mesopotamia.* rev. ed. completed by Erica Reiner. Chicago & London: University of Chicago Press, 1977.

Oppenheim, Chaim, ed. "The Commentary by Joseph Hammeqanne with Annotations." *Beth Talmud* 3 (1883), pp. 10-15; 42-49 (in Hebrew).

Orlinsky, Harry M. *Notes to the New Translation of the Torah.* Philadelphia: Jewish Publication Society, 1969.

Palmoni, Jacob. *"'arbeh." Encyclopedia Miqra'it* 1:525.

Pardee, Dennis. *"yph* 'witness' in Hebrew and Ugaritic." *Vetus Testamentum* 28 (1970), pp. 204-213.

———. *Handbook of Ancient Hebrew Letters.* Society of Biblical Literature: Sources for Biblical Study. Chico: Scholars Press, 1982.

Pardo, David. *Hasde David: Tosefet Qedushah.* Jerusalem: Frumkin, 1890.

Parker, Simon B. "Rephaim." *Interpreter's Dictionary of the Bible Supplementary Volume,* p. 739.

Patrick, Dale. Review of *Aspects of Nonverbal Communication in the Ancient Near East,* by Mayer I. Gruber. In *Journal of Biblical Literature* 102 (1983), p. 289.

Paul, Shalom M. *Studies in the Book of the Covenant in the Light of Cuneiform and Biblical Law*. Vetus Testamentum Supplements, vol. 18. Leiden: E. J. Brill, 1970.

———. *Amos*. Hermeneia—A Critical and Historical Commentary on the Bible. Minneapolis: Fortress, 1991.

Penkower, Jordan S. "The End of Rashi's Commentary on Job: The Manuscripts and the Printed Versions" (forthcoming).

Perdue, Leo G. "Names of God in the Old Testament." In *Harper's Bible Dictionary*, pp. 685-687. Edited by Paul J. Achtemeier. San Francisco: Harper & Row, 1985.

Pines, A. L. "Concerning the Identity of the Author of the Commentary on Chronicles Attributed to Rashi." *Beit Mikra* 23 (1978), p. 122; p. 244 (in Hebrew).

Pines, Shlomo. "Avicenna." *Encyclopaedia Judaica* 3:955-959.

Plaut, W. Gunther. *The Torah: A Modern Commentary*, vol. 1: Genesis. Translated into Hebrew by Aviv Meltzer. Jerusalem: Hebrew Union College, 1988.

Pope, Marvin. *Job*. Anchor Bible, vol. 15. 3^d ed. Garden City, N.Y.: Doubleday & Co., 1973.

———. *The Song of Songs*. Anchor Bible, vol. 7C. Garden City, N.Y.: Doubleday & Co., 1977.

Porges, Nathan. "Censorship of Hebrew Books." *Jewish Encyclopedia* 3: 642-650.

Porton, Gary G. "Defining Midrash." In *The Study of Ancient Judaism*, vol. 1, pp. 55-92. Edited by Jacob Neusner. 2 vols. New York: Ktav, 1981.

Poznański, Samuel N. "Fragments from the Biblical Exegesis of Menachem bar Helbo. In *Nahum Sokolow Jubilee Volume*, pp. 389-439. Warsaw: Shuldberg, 1904.

———. *Kommentar zu Ezechiel und den XII kleinen Propheten von Eliezer aus Beaugency*. Warsaw: Mekize Nirdamim, 1913.

———. *Babylonische Geonim im nachgaonäischen Zeitalter nach handschriftlichen und gedruckten Quellen*. Schriften der Lehranstalt für die Wissenschaft des Judentums, Band IV, Heft 1.1. Berlin: Mayer & Müller, 1914.

———. "Who is the Rav Saadiah Mentioned by the French Bible Commentators?" *Ha-Goren* 9 (1923), pp. 69-89 (in Hebrew).

Press, Jesaias. "Beiträge zur historischen Geographie Palästinas." *Monatsschrift für Geschichte und Wissenschaft des Judentums* 73 (1929), pp. 52-57.

———. "Erwiderung." *Monatsschrift für Geschichte und Wissenschaft des Judentums* 74 (1930), pp. 136-137.

Price, Ira Maurice. *The Ancestry of Our English Bible*. 3^d rev. ed. by William A. Irwin and Allen P. Wikgren. New York: Harper & Brothers, 1956.

Pritchard, James. B. *The Ancient Near East in Pictures Relating to the Old Testament*. 2^d ed. with Supplement. Princeton: Princeton University Press, 1969.

———. *Ancient Near Eastern Texts Relating to the Old Testament*. 3^d ed. with Supplement. Princeton: Princeton University Press, 1969.

Rabbinovicz, Raphael. *Variae Lectiones in Mischnam et in Talmud Baylonicum (Diqduqe Soferim)*. 10 vols. Munich: E. Huber, 1867-1897.

Rabin, Chaim. "Massorah and 'Ad Litteras'." *Hebrew Studies* 26 (1985), pp. 81-91.

Rabinowitz, Louis Isaac. *The Social Life of the Jews in Northern France in the XII-XIV Centuries*. 2^d ed. New York: Hermon, 1972.

———. "Tefillin." *Encyclopaedia Judaica* 15:898-904.

Rad, Gerhard von. *Deuteronomy: A Commentary*. Old Testament Library. Philadelphia: Westminster, 1966.

Rainey, Anson F. "The Ancient Hebrew Prefix Conjugation in the Light of Amarna Canaanite." *Hebrew Studies* 27 (1986), pp. 4-19.

Reifmann, Jacob. "Various Studies on the Psalms Targum." *Beth Talmud* 2 (1882), pp. 151-157; 223-219 (in Hebrew).

————. "Notes on Rashi's Commentary." *Beth Talmud* 5 (1886), pp. 55-59 (in Hebrew).

Riché, Pierre. "Courants de Pensé dans la France du XIe Siècle." in *Rashi Studies*, pp. xxxi-xxxvi. Edited by Zvi Arie Steinfeld. Ramat-Gan: Bar-Ilan University Press, 1993.

Robinson, Alan. "Three Suggested Interpretations in Ps. LXXXIV." *Vetus Testamentum* 24 (1974), pp. 378-381.

Rogerson, John William, and John William McKay. *Psalms 51-100*. Cambridge Bible Commentary on the New English Bible. Cambridge: Cambridge University Press, 1977.

Rosen, Gilla. "Rashi's Commentary on Qoheleth: A Critical Edition According to Ms. J.T.S. L 778/1 With Textual Emendations from Other Manuscripts and First Editions, Including Citation of Sources." M.A. Thesis. Ramat-Gan: Bar-Ilan University, 1995.

Rosen, Michael S. "The Hebrew Commentary on Job in Ms. Jewish Theological Seminary, New York L 778 Attributed by Some to R. Samuel ben Meir: An Analysis of Its Sources and Consideration of Its Authorship" Ph.D. diss., University of London, 1994.

Rosenbaum, Morris Abraham, and Maurice Silbermann in collaboration with A. Blashki and L. Joseph. *Pentateuch with Targum Onkelos, Haphtaroth and Rashi's Commentary Translated into English and Annotated*. 5 vols. London: Shapiro, Vallentine & Co., 1929-1934.

Rosenthal, Erwin Isaak Jacob. "Anti-Christian Polemic in Medieval Bible Commentaries." *Journal of Jewish Studies* 11 (1960), pp. 115- 135.

Rosenthal, Judah M. "Anti-Christian Polemics in the Biblical Commentaries of Rashi." In Judah M. Rosenthal, *Studies in Texts in Jewish History, Literature and Religion*, pp. 101-116. 2 vols. Jerusalem: Rubin Mass, 1967.

————. "Seder Olam." *Encyclopaedia Judaica* 14:1091-1093.

————. "The Slavery Controversy and Judaism." *Conservative Judaism* 31, no. 3 (1977), pp. 69-79.

Rosin, David. *R. Samuel b. Mëir (Rashbam) als Schrifterkläre = Jahresbericht des Jüdisch-Theologischen Seminars Fraenkel'scher Stifftung*. Breslau: F. W. Jungfer, 1880.

————. *Reime und Gedichte des Abraham Ibn Esra: Aussergottesdienstliche Poesie, Heft IV = Jahresbericht des Jüdisch-Theologischen Seminars Fraenkel'scher Stifftung* 7. Breslau: Schottlaender, 1891.

Rosin, David, ed. *The Torah Commentary of R. Samuel b. Meir*. Breslau: Schottlaender, 1882 (in Hebrew).

Roth, Wolfgang M. W. "The Numerical Sequence x/x+1 in the Old Testament." *Vetus Testamentum* 12 (1962), pp. 300-311.

Sarna, Nahum M. "The Interchange of the Prepositions *bēt* and *min* in Biblical Hebrew." *Journal of Biblical Literature* 78 (1959), pp. 310-316.

————. "Psalms, Book of." *Encyclopaedia Judaica* 13: 1303-1322.

————. "Rahab." *Encyclopedia Miqra'it* 7:328-329 (in Hebrew).

Sassoon, David Solomon. *A History of the Jews in Baghdad*. Letchworth: Solomon David Sassoon, 1949.

————. *Ohel David*. 2 vols.: Oxford: Oxford University Press, 1932.

Schaeffer, Claude F.-A., ed. *Ugaritica V*. Paris: Imprimerie Nationale, 1968.

Schirmann, Jefim Hayyim. *Hebrew Poetry in Spain and Provence, vol. 2*. 2^d ed. Jerusalem: Mossad Bialik/Tel Aviv: Dvir, 1971 (in Hebrew).

————. "Joseph ben Solomon of Carcassone." *Encyclopaedia Judaica* 10:237.

Schochet, Elijah. *Animal Life in Jewish Tradition*. New York: Ktav, 1984.

Scholem, Gershom. *Jewish Gnosticism, Merkabah Mysticism and Talmudic Tradition*. 2^d ed. New York: Schocken, 1965.

Schoors, Antoon. "The Particle *kî*." *Old Testament Studies* 21 (1981), pp. 240-276.

Schremer, Adiel. "Concerning the Commentaries on Mo'ed Qaṭan Attributed to Rashi." In *Atara L' Haim: Studies in the Talmud and Medieval Rabbinic Literature in Honor of Professor Haim Zalman Dimitrovsky*, pp. 534-554. Edited by Daniel Boyarin, Shamma Friedman, Marc Hirshman, Menahem Schmelzer, Israel M. Ta-Shma. Jerusalem: Magnes, 2000 (in Hebrew).

Schwartz, Avrohom, and Yisroel Schwartz. *The Megilloth and Rashi's Commentary*. Hebrew Linear Classics. New York: Feldheim, 1983.

Schwarz, Arthur Zacharias. *Die Hebräische Handschriften der Nationalbibliothek in Wien*. Vienna: Ed. Strache, 1925.

Schwarz, Joseph. *A Descriptive Geography and Brief Historical Sketch of Palestine*. Translated by Isaac Leeser. Philadelphia: A. Hart, 1850.

Schwarzbaum, Haim. *The Mishle Shu'alim (Fox Fables) of Rabbi Berechiah Ha-Nakdan: A Study in Comparative Folklore and Fable Lore*. Kiron: Institute for Jewish and Arab Folklore Research, 1979.

Schwarzfuchs, Simon. "Reshit darko shel rashi." In *Rashi Studies*, pp. 177-183. Edited by Zvi Arie Steinfeld. Ramat-Gan: Bar-Ilan University Press, 1993.

Seligsohn, Max. "Isaac ben Samuel of Narbonne." *Jewish Encyclopedia* 6:630.

———. "Edom, Idumea." *Jewish Encyclopedia* 5:41.

———. "Elijah ben Menahem Ha-Zaken." *Jewish Encyclopedia* 5:131-132.

———. "Meshullam b. Nathan of Melun," *Jewish Encyclopedia* 8:503-504.

———. "Saadia ben Nahmani." *Jewish Encyclopedia* 10:586

———. "Shem in Rabbinical Literature." *Jewish Encyclopedia* 11: 1261-1262.

———. "Solomon ben Judah ha-Babli." *Jewish Encyclopedia* 11:453.

Sforno, Obadiah (1475-1550). *Commentary on the Book of Psalms*. Venice: Z. D. Gara, 1586 (in Hebrew).

Shapiro, Israel. "Commentaries on Rashi on the Torah." *Bitzaron* 2 (1940), pp. 426-436 (in Hebrew).

Shereshevsky, Esra. "Rashi and Christian Interpretations." *Jewish Quarterly Review*, new series, 61 (1970), pp. 76-86.

———. "Inversion in Rashi's Commentary." In *Gratz College Anniversary Volume*, pp. 263-268. Edited by I. David Passow and S. T. Lachs. Philadelphia: Gratz College, 1971.

———. *Rashi: The Man and His World*. New York: Sepher-Hermon, 1982.

Shoshana, Avraham. *The Book of Job with the Commentaries of Rashi, Rabbenu Jacob b. Meir Tam, and a disciple of Rashi*. Jerusalem: Ofeq Institute, 5760 [=1999] (in Hebrew).

Shukry, Zipporah. "The Wolf and the Fox in the Well." *Laographia* 22 (1963), pp. 491-97.

Signer, Michael A. "King/Messiah in Rashi's Exegesis of Psalm 2." *Prooftexts* 3 (1983), pp. 273-278.

Simon, Uriel. *Four Approaches to the Book of Psalms: From Saadya Gaon to Abraham Ibn Ezra*. Ramat-Gan: Bar-Ilan University Press, 1982 (in Hebrew).

Skinner, John. *A Critical and Exegetical Commentary on Genesis*. International Critical Commentary. 2^d ed. Edinburgh: T. & T. Clark, 1930.

Smalley, Beryl. *The Study of the Bible in the Middle Ages*. 3^d ed. Oxford: Clarendon Press, 1984.

Smith, John Thomas, Patrick Arthur Faulkner, and Anthony Emery. *Studies in*

Medieval Domestic Architecture. Edited by M. J. Swanton. London: Royal Archaeological Institute, 1975.

Soggin, J. Alberto. *Judges.* Old Testament Library. Philadelphia: Westminster, 1981.

Sokolow, Moshe. "Establishing the Text of Rashi's Commentary on the Book of Job." *Proceedings of the American Academy of Jewish Research* 48 (1981), pp. 19-35.

————. "The Commentary of Rashi on the Book of Job." In *Proceedings of the Eighth World Congress of Jewish Studies, Jerusalem August 16-21, 1981, Division A: The Period of the Bible,* pp. 139-144. Jerusalem: World Union of Jewish Studies, 1982.

————. Review of *Rashi's Commentary on Psalms 1-89 (Bookx I-III),* by Mayer I. Gruber. In *Jewish Book World* 16, no. 3 (1998), p. 57.

Soloveitchik, Haym. "Can Halakhic Texts Talk History?" *AJS Review* 3 (1978), pp. 153-196.

————. "Rashi." *Dictionary of the Middle Ages* 10:259-260. Edited by Joseph R. Strayer. 13 vols. New York: Scribner's, 1988.

Spanier, Arthur. "Zur Formengeschichte des altjüdischen Gebetes." *Monatsschrift für Geschichte und Wissenschaft des Judentums* 78 (1934), pp. 438-447.

Speiser, Ephraim Avigdor. *Genesis.* Anchor Bible, vol. 1. Garden City, N.Y.: Doubleday & Co., 1964.

————. "Census and Ritual Expiation in Mari and Israel." In *Oriental and Biblical Studies: Collected Writings of E. A. Speiser,* pp. 171-186. Edited by J. J. Finkelstein and M. Greenberg. Philadelphia: University of Pennsylvania Press, 1967.

————. "The Durative Hithpaʻel: A *tan* Form." In *Oriental and Biblical Studies: Collected Writings of E. A. Speiser,* pp. 506-514. Edited by J. J. Finkelstein and M. Greenberg. Philadelphia: University of Pennsylvania Press, 1967.

Sperber, Alexander. "Problems of the Masora." *Hebrew Union College Annual* 17 (1942-43), pp. 293-394.

Sperber, Daniel. "Weights and Measures in the Talmud." *Encyclopaedia Judaica* 16:388-390.

Sperling, S. David. "Rephaim." *Encyclopaedia Judaica* 14:79-80.

————. "Late Hebrew *ḥazāru* and Akkadian *saḫāru.*" *Journal of the Ancient Near Eastern Society* 5 (1973), pp. 397-404.

————. "Gen. 41:40: A New Interpretation." *Journal of the Ancient Near Eastern Society* 10 (1978), pp. 113-119.

Spinoza, Benedict. *Tractatus Theologico-Politicus.* Translated by Samuel Shirley. Leiden: E. J. Brill, 1989.

Stanton, Elizabeth Cady, ed. *The Woman's Bible.* 2 vols. New York: European Publishing Co., 1895-1898.

Steiner, Richard. "Saadia vs. Rashi: On the Shift from Meaning-Maximalism to Meaning-Minimalism in Medieval Biblical Lexicology." *Jewish Quarterly Review,* new series, 88 (1998), pp. 213-258.

Steinschneider, Moritz. *Jewish Literature from the Eighth to the Eighteenth Century.* London: Longman, Brown, Green, Longmans, & Roberts, 1857.

Steinsaltz, Adin. *Talmud: The Steinsaltz Edition: A Reference Guide.* New York: Random House, 1989.

Stemberger, Günter. *Introduction to the Talmud and the Midrash.* Translated and edited by Markus Bockmuehl. 2^d ed. Edinburgh: T. & T. Clark, 1996.

Strack, Hermann L. *Introduction to the Talmud and Midrash.* Philadelphia: Jewish Publication Society, 1931.

"Symposium: The *yiqtol* in Biblical Hebrew." *Hebrew Studies* 29 (1988), pp. 7-42.

Ta-Shma, Israel. "Isaac Ben Eliezer." *Encyclopaedia Judaica* 9:18-19.
———. "Jacob Ben Yakar." *Encyclopaedia Judaica* 9:1224
———. "Meshullam b. Nathan of Melun." *Encyclopaedia Judaica* 11:1403-1404.
———. "Solomon Ben Meir." *Encyclopaedia Judaica* 15:125.
———. "Tam, Jacob b. Meir." *Encyclopaedia Judaica* 15:779-781.
———. "Concerning Some Matters Pertaining to Mahzor Vitry." *Alei Sefer* 11 (1984), pp. 81-89 (in Hebrew).
———. "Bible Criticism in Early Medieval Franco-Germany." In *The Bible in Light of Its Interpreters: Studies in Memory of Sarah Kamin*, pp. 453-459. Edited by Sara Japhet. Jerusalem: Magnes, 1994 (in Hebrew).
———. "The Commentary on Chronicles in Ms. Munich 5." In *From the Collections of the Institute for Microfilmed Hebrew Manuscripts*, pp. 135-141. Edited by Avraham David. Jerusalem: Jewish National & University Library, 1996.
———. *Rabbi Moshe ha-Darshan and the Apocryphal Literature*. Studies in Jewish History and Literature. Jerusalem: Touro College, 2001.
Taitz, Emily. *The Jews of Medieval France*. Contributions to the Study of World History, no. 45. Westport, Ct.: Greenwood Press, 1994.
Talshir, Zipora. "From the Desk of the Author of Chronicles." *Cathedra* 102 (December 2001), pp. 188-190 (in Hebrew).
Taylor, William R. "Exegesis of Psalms 1-71, 93, 95-96, 100, 120-138, 140-150." In *Interpreter's Bible*, vol. 4. Edited by George Arthur Buttrick. New York and Nashville: Abingdon, 1955.
Tcherikover, Victor. *Hellenistic Civilization and the Jews*. Phildelphia: Jewish Publication Society, 1959.
Thomas, D. Winton. "ṣalmāwet in the Old Testament." *Journal of Semitic Studies* 7 (1962), pp. 191-200.
Thompson, John Arthur. *The Book of Jeremiah*. New International Commentary. Grand Rapids: Eerdmans, 1980.
Thucydides. *History of the Peloponnesian War Books I and II* with an English Translation by Charles Foster Smith. Loeb Classical Library. rev. ed. Cambridge, Mass.: Harvard University Press/ London: William Heinemann Ltd., 1928.
Touito, Elazar. "Concerning Rashbam's Method in his Commentary on the Pentateuch." *Tarbiz* 48 (1979), pp. 248-273 (in Hebrew).
———. "The Exegetical Method of Rashbam Against the Background of the Historical Reality of His Time." In *Studies in Rabbinic Literature, Bible, and Jewish History*, pp. 48-74. Edited by Y. Gilat, Ch. Levine, and Z. Rabinowitz. Ramat-Gan: Bar-Ilan University Press, 1982 (in Hebrew).
———. "Rashbam's Method in His Commentary on the Legal Portions of the Pentateuch." *Mile't* 2 (1984), pp. 275-288 (in Hebrew).
———. "Concerning the Meaning of the Term *teŝubat hamminim* in the Writings of our French Rabbis." *Sinai* 63 (1986), pp. 144- 148 (in Hebrew).
———. "Rashi's Commentary on Genesis 1-6 in the Context of Judeo-Christian Controversy." *Hebrew Union College Annual* 61 (1990), pp. 159-183.
———. "Does MS Leipzig 1 Really Reflect the Authentic Version of Rashi's Commentary on the Pentateuch?" *Tarbiz* 61 (1992), pp. 85-115 (in Hebrew).
Trible, Phyllis. *God and the Rhetoric of Sexuality*. Philadelphia: Fortress, 1978.
Tur-Sinai, Naftali H. *The Book of Job: A New Commentary*. Jerusalem: Kiryath Sepher, 1967.
Twersky, Isadore. *Introduction to the Code of Maimonides*. Yale Judaica Series, vol. 22. New Haven & London: Yale University Press, 1980.

Urbach, Ephraim Elimelech. *The Tosaphists.* 4th ed. 2 vols. Jerusalem: Mossad Bialik, 1980 (in Hebrew).

————. "How Did Rashi Merit the Title *Parshandata?*" In *Rashi 1040-1990: Homage à Ephraim E. Urbach,* pp.387-398. Edited by Gabrielle Sed-Rajna. Paris: Editions du Cerf, 1993 (in Hebrew).

Urbach, Ephraim Elimelech, ed. *Sefer Arugat Habosem, auctore R. Abraham b. R. Azriel (saec XIII) Tomus IV: Prolegomena et Indices.* Jerusalem: Mekize Nirdamim, 1963.

Valle Rodriguez, Carlos de, ed. and trans. *Sefer Sahot de Abraham ibn 'Ezra.* Bibliotheca Salamanticensis Dissertationes, 1. Salamanca: Universidad Pontifical, 1977

Veltheim-Lottum, Ludolf. *Kleine Weltgeschichte des städtischen Wohnhauses.* Heidelberg: L. Schneider, 1952.

Vogüé, Charles Jean, marquis de Melchior. *Corpus Inscriptionum Semiticarum, Pars Secunda: Inscriptiones Aramaicas Continens, Tomus I: Tabulae, Fasciculus Primums.* Paris: E. Reipublicae Typographeo, 1889.

Wagner, Max. *Die lexikalischen und grammatikalischen Aramaismen im alttestamentlichen Hebräischen.* Beiheft zur Zeitschrift für die alttestamentliche Wissenschaft, no. 96. Berlin: Toppelmann, 1966.

Watson, Wilfred G. E. *Classical Hebrew Poetry: A Guide to Its Techniques.* Journal of the Society of Old Testament Study Supplement Series, no. 26. Sheffield: JSOT Press, 1984.

————. "Reflexes of Akkadian Incantations in Hosea." *Vetus Testamentum* 34 (1984), 242-247.

Weinberg, M. "Die Partikel *ki* nach der Auslegung dest Talmuds." *Jahrbuch der Jüdisch-Literarischen Gesellschaft (Sitz: Frankfurt am Main)* 14 (1921), pp. 191-207.

Weinberger, Leon J. *Twilight of a Golden Age: Selected Poems of Abraham Ibn Ezra.* Tuscaloosa & London: University of Alabama Press, 1997.

Weinfeld, Moshe. *Deuteronomy 1-11.* Anchor Bible, vol. 5. New York: Doubleday, 1991.

Weinryb, Bernard D. "Rashi Against the Background of His Epoch." In *Rashi Anniversary Volume,* pp. 39-46. Edited by H. L. Ginsberg. New York: American Academy for Jewish Research, 1941.

Weiser, Artur. *The Psalms: A Commentary.* Translated by Herbert Hartwell. Old Testament Library. London: SCM Press, 1962.

Weiser, Asher. "The Commentary on Chronicles Attributed to Rashi." *Beit Mikra* 22 (1977), pp. 362-364 (in Hebrew).

Weiss, Benjamin. "Mishnat Ha-Middot." *Encyclopaedia Judaica* 12:109.

Weiss, Isaac Hirsch. "The Life of R. Salomon b. Isaac." *Beth Talmud* 2 (1882), pp. 33-44; 73-65; 97-101; 129-138; 161-166; 193-206; 231- 235; 264-257; 297-289 (in Hebrew).

————. *Dor Dor Wedorshayw.* 5 vols. New York & Berlin: Platt & Munkus, 1924.

Weiss, Raphael. *Mishshut baMiqra.* Jerusalem: Rubenstein, 1976 (in Hebrew).

Weisse, Joseph. "Concerning the Commentary of Rashi to Chronicles: Its Author, Date and Content." *Kerem Chemed* 5 (1841), pp. 232-244 (in Hebrew).

Wellhausen, Julius. *Prolegomena to the History of Ancient Israel.* Translated by J. Sutherland Black and Allan Menzies with reprint of the article "Israel" from the *Encyclopaedia Britannica.* Edinburgh: Adam & Charles Black, 1883.

Widmer, Gottfried. *Die Kommentare von Raschi, Ibn Esra, Radaq zu Joel.* Basel: Volksdruckerei, 1945.

Wiesenberg, Ephraim J. "A Note on *mizzeh* in Psalm lxxv 9." *Vetus Testamentum* 4 (1954), p. 434.

Wigoder, Geoffrey, ed. *The Illustrated Dictionary and Concordance of the Bible.* New York: Macmillan, 1986.

Wilmore, Sylvia Bruce. *Crows, Jays, Ravens, and their Relatives.* Middlebury, Vt.: Paul S. Eriksson, 1977.

Wilson, J. Robert, Clayton T. Beecham, and Elsie Reid Carrington. *Obstetrics and Gynaecology.* 4ᵗʰ ed. St. Louis, Mo.: C. V. Moshy, 1971.

Wolf, C. Umhau. "Yoke." *Interpreter's Dictionary of the Bible* 4:924-925.

Wright, George Ernest. "Sinai, Mount." *Interpreter's Dictionary of the Bible* 4:376-78.

Wright, J. S. "Divination." In *The Illustrated Bible Dictionary* 1:391. Edited by James Dixon Douglas. 3 vols. Leicester: Inter-Varsity, 1980.

Yadin, Yigal. "New Gleanings on Resheph from Ugarit." In *Biblical and Related Studies Presented to Samuel Iwry,* pp. 259-274. Edited by Ann Kort and Scot Morschauer. Winona Lake, Indiana: Eisenbrauns, 1985.

Yassif, Eli. "Sefer ha-Ma'asim." *Tarbiz* 53 (1984), pp. 427-428 (in Hebrew).

———. *The Hebrew Folktale: History, Genre, Meaning* (Jerusalem: Mossad Bialik/Ben-Gurion University of the Negev Press, 1994 (in Hebrew).

Yeivin, Israel. *Introduction to the Tiberian Masorah.* Translated by E. J. Revell. Society of Biblical Literature Masoretic Studies, no. 5. Chico: Scholars Press, 1980.

Zacuto, Abraham b. Samuel. *Sefer ha-Yuhasin.* Edited by A. H. Freimann 2ᵈ ed. Frankfurt am Main: Wahrman, 1924.

Zadok, Ran. "Notes on Esther." *Zeitschrift für die alttestamenliche Wissenschaft* 98 (1986), pp. 105-110.

Zeitlin, Solomon. "Rashi." *American Jewish Yearbook* 41 (1939-1940), pp. 111-140.

———. "Rashi and the Rabbinate." *Jewish Quarterly Review,* new series, 31 (1940-41), pp. 1-58.

Zevit, Ziony. "The So-called Interchangeability of the prepositions *b, l,* and *m(n)* in Northwest Semitic." *Journal of the Ancient Near Eastern Society* 7 (1975), pp. 103-112.

Zinberg, Israel. *A History of Jewish Literature.* Translated and edited by Bernard Martin. 12 vols. Cleveland: Case Western Reserve University Press, 1972.

Zobel, Moshe Nahum. "Conforte, David." *Encyclopaedia Judaica* 5:891-893.

Zohory, Menahem. *The Sources of Rashi's Halakic and Aggadic Midrashim in His Commentaries: Psalms.* Jerusalem: Cane, 1987 (in Hebrew).

———. *Rashi's Sources: Midrash Halakah and Midrash Aggadah in his Commentaries: Addenda and Corrigenda.* Jerusalem: Carmel, 1994 (in Hebrew).

———. *Grammarians and Their Writings in Rashi's Commentaries.* Jerusalem: Carmel, 1995 (in Hebrew).

———. *Quotations from Moshe ha-Darshan and the Liturgical Poems of Elazar ha-Qaliri in Rashi's Commentaries.* Jerusalem: Carmel, 1995 (in Hebrew).

Zunz, Leopold. "Salomon ben Isaac genannt Raschi." *Zeitschrift für die Wissenschaft des Judenthums,* 1822, pp. 277-333.

———. "Heisst Raschi Jarchi?" *Israelitische Annalen,* 1839, pp. 328-315; reprinted in Zunz, L. *Gesammelte Schriften,* vol. 3, pp. 100-105. Berlin: Louis Gerschel Verlag, 1875.

———. *Zur Geschichte und Literatur.* Berlin: Veit und Comp., 1845.

———. *Die Ritus des synagogalen Gottesdienstes.* 2ᵈ ed. Berlin: L. Lamm, 1919.

פירוש רש"י לספר תהילים

י"ל ע"פ כ"י וינה 220 עם מבוא, תרגום אנגלי,
הערות, מפתחות וביבליוגרפיה

ע"י

מאיר גרובר

In loving memory

of

ORI YESHAYAH AVIHAI
(16 Av 5758-29 Nisan 5759)

The LORD is my light and my salvation
(Ps. 27:1)

FOREWORD TO HEBREW SECTION

A critical edition of an ancient or medieval Hebrew text attempts to reproduce the text of the best surviving manuscript together with a critical apparatus. Such an edition supplies important variant readings from other old witnesses to the particular ancient or medieval composition.[1] Abraham Berliner twice attempted to produce such an edition of Rashi's Commentary on the Pentateuch. However, the number of old manuscripts extant was too great for Berliner to control them.[2] Isaac Maarsen attempted to produce a critical edition of Rashi's Commentary on Psalms. However, his edition[3] suffers from the fact that Maarsen did not accurately copy out either the manuscript he chose as the basis for his edition or the variants cited in his critical apparatus.[4] Typical is Maarsen's substitution of the abbreviation *wĕkû* for the manuscripts' *wĕgô*. Both abbreviations, many readers will recall, are the functional equivalent of our ellipsis dots at the end of an abbreviated quotation. Many readers will also recall that ancient and medieval Rabbinic texts employ the former abbreviation when the quotation is from a Rabbinic text and the latter abbreviation only when the citation is from a biblical text. This distinction, found in the sixty odd medieval mss. of Rashi's Commentary on Psalms, which I was priveleged to examine either in the original or in the microfilm copies in the Institute for Microfilms of Hebrew Manuscripts at the Jewish National and University Library at the Givat Ram Campus of the Hebrew University of Jerusalem, is not reflected in Maarsen's edition.

Another classical example of Maarsen's unfaithfulness to the task of correctly copying out Oxford Bodleian, Ms. Opp. 34, which was

---

[1] Classical examples include Saul Lieberman, *The Tosefta* (5 vols.; New York: Jewish Theological Seminary of America, 1955-1988); Bernard Mandelbaum, *Pesikta deRav Kahana* (2ᵈ ed.; 2 vols.; New York: Jewish Theological Seminary of America, 1987); Louis Finkelstein, *Sifra on Leviticus* (4 vols.; New York: Jewish Theological Seminary of America, 1983-1991).

[2] Abraham Berliner, *Raschi: Der Kommentar des Salomo b. Isak über den Pentateuch* (2ᵈ ed.; Frankfurt am Main: J. Kaufmann, 1905), pp. xv, 454.

[3] Isaac Maarsen, *Parshandatha, Part III: Psalms* (Jerusalem: Central Press, 1936)

[4] Jehudah Fries-Horeb, Review of *Parshandatha*, by Isaac Maarsen, in *Kirjath Sepher* 14 (1937-38), pp. 444-447.

his base ms., is his substitution of the letter *he*, an abbreviation for *haššēm* "the [divine] name" where Opp. 34 consistently abbreviates the divine name *YHWH* by means of *yy* as in modern Jewish prayer-books except that in Ms. Opp. 34 the *yy* is consistently underlined. In Ms. Leiden Scal. 1, as in the ms. we used, Vienna Heb. ms. 220, and in many other medieval mss., the standard abbreviation for the tetragrammaton is y*ʸ*y, usually but not always underlined.

Strange to relate, with respect to my earlier publication of an edition and translation of Rashi on Psalms 1-89,[5] Moshe Sokolow remarked:

> I am not comfortable with Gruber's decision to 'pietize' his text by changing all the "YAH" theophoric substantives into "KAH." I have never seen this in a medieval manuscript and am surprised that no apologia for it is provided in the foreward.[6]

In fact, no apology was in order on my part because, in fact, I simply adhere to the convention of Ms. Vienna 220, which, incidentally, is shared by Heb. Ms. Vatican Ebr. 94. These two important mss. do, in fact, avoid writing out the divine names *'elohim, 'elohenu, yah*, and they substitute for them *'eloqim, 'eloqenu* and *yaq*, respectively. Alternative strategies adopted by other medieval mss. of Rashi's commentary include omitting the *lamedh* from the word *'elohim* and calling attention to its absence by means of a circle over the initial aleph of the word *'elohim*. Among the mss. that employ the latter strategy are Oxford Bodleian Ms. Opp. 34 [the basis for Maarsen's edition] and Leipzig Stadtbibliothek, Ms. Wagenseil, B.H. 4.

Interestingly enough, Ms. Berlin Staatsbibliothek, Or. Fol. 1221 substitutes *'qym* with dot over the initial *'aleph* for *'elohim* at Ps. 138:1, indicating that out of respect for the divine name the *lamedh* has been omitted from *'elohim* at Ps. 138:1. Likewise, this ms. substitutes *'qy* with dot over the *q* for *'lhy* at Ps. 109: 1. This ms. combines the distinct strategies of Opp. 34, on the one hand (dotted *'aleph* instead of *'l*), and Vienna 220 and Vatican Ebr. 94 (*q* instead of *h*) on the other hand.[6] No less interesting is the strategy employed by Vienna Heb. Ms. 3. Here we have in all forms of the divine names *'l* and

[5] Mayer I. Gruber, *Rashi's Commentary on Psalms 1-89*, University of South Florida Studies in the History of Judaism, no. 161 (Atlanta: Scholars Press, 1998).

[6] Moshe Sokolow, Review of *Rashi's Commentary on Psalms 1-89 (Books I-III)*, by Mayer I. Gruber, in *Jewish Book World* 16, no. 3 (1998), p. 57.

'elohim the two letters *'l* combined while *h* is replaced by *q*. Alternative strategies are attested in Parma Ms. De Rossi 181/1 where, for example, at Ps. 90:1 *ha'elohim* becomes *hy*|*hym*. In the latter form the *yod* followed by a vertical stroke beginnng at the level of the preceding *yod* and extending above the line is a "pietization" (Sokolow's term) of the Scriptural text's *'l*, which the scribe construes as a divine name; similarly that same ms. pietizes *'l* to *y*| in Ps. 149:6. Madrid National Library Ms. 5470 exemplifies a similar strategy for avoding writing out the divine names, lest sacrilege be performed upon them in the course of an anti-Semitic book burning. The latter ms. substitutes for *'lhy* at Ps. 109:1 *'qy* with a vertical stroke over the *'aleph*; here again the *'aleph* with diacritic represents original *'l ; similarly* the Madrid ms. substitutes *'hynw* for *'elohenu*, and here again the initial *'aleph* with supralinear dot is a substitute for the divine name *'l*.

Were I not to correct the false impression that Prof. Soklow's review creates, my silence, possibly construed as acquiescence (so BT Bava Meṣi'a 37b), would lend credence to two falsehoods: 1) that I falsified the text; 2) that with respect to theophoric names and epithets my edition here presented, is a less than reliable transcription of the ms. I claim to have copied out accurately. With Job I insist, "My consolation is ... I have not withheld the words of the sacred [text of the ms.]" (Job. 6:10).

While I was able to examine some sixty mss., Maarsen utilized only six mss. and three printed editions. More recent, so-called "scientific editions" of Rashi's commentaries do not even pretend to copy out a particular medieval ms. Instead, relying upon several of the mss. and early printed editions regarded by scholars as most reliable, they create an eclectic text.[7] Louis Finkelstein, in the introduction to the second edition of his *Sifre on Deuteronomy*, goes so far as to use the term "puerility" to describe creating a new text and passing it off as a scientific edition.[8]

Relying upon both the criteria generally accepted among experts[9] and in consultation with experts, I chose Austrian National Library

----

[7] See Menahem Cohen, ed., *Mikra'ot Gedolot 'Haketer': Joshua-Judges and General Introduction* (Ramat-Gan: Bar-Ilan University Press, 1992), p. 84* (in Hebrew); Chaim Dov Chavel *The Commentaries of Rashi on the Torah* (Jerusalem: Mossad Harav Kook, 1983), pp. 14-15; Mordechai Leib Katzenelenbogen, *Joshua and Judges with the Commentary of Rashi* (Jerusalem: Mossad Harav Kook, 1987), pp. 7-8.

[8] Louis Finkelstein, *Sifre on Deuteronomy* (2ᵈ ed.; New York: Jewish Theological Seminary of America, 1969), p. ii.

Cod. Hebr. 220 as the basis for this edition. This beautiful ms. is written on vellum in three parallel columns of Ashkenazi cursive script. This ms. comes from *Ashkenaz,* i.e., the cultural and geographical sphere of Franco-Germany. Dated to the 13th or 14th century, this 276 page manuscript[10] consists of the text of the biblical commentaries written by or attributed to Rashi on all books of the Hebrew Bible with the exception of Chronicles. Apparently, the scribes responsible for our ms. anticipated the conclusion of many modern that Rashi did not write a commentary on the Book of Chronicles. Our ms. is typical of many medieval mss., which produce only the biblical commentaries of Rashi without the biblical text. The pages are 32.4 cm. × 42.3 cm. Each of the three columns of text is 31.5 cm from top to bottom while the width of the left, middle and right columns of text is 66 mm., 68 mm., and 67 mm., respectively. The manuscript is the work of two scribes, whose names are Menahem and Abraham. Menahem wrote out pp. 1v-22v; 95r-108v; 149r-152v; 182-276r while the remaining pages were penned by Abraham. The Commentary on Psalms begins in the center of the middle column on p. 208r and concludes two thirds of the way down in the middle column on p. 224r.

Dr. Michael Carasik, now associated with the University of Pennsylvania, copied out the Hebrew text of Rashi's Commentary on Psalms from a copy produced from a microfilm of the ms. at the Institute for Microfilms of Medieval Hebrew Manuscripts in Jerusalem. I accept full responsibility for any errors arising from my editing of Dr. Carasik's transcription. Significant variants or additions found in other medieval mss. are discussed in the notes to the translation. In some instances a variant reading is adopted in the translation, and this is indicated in the notes to the translation. Only in two places—Ps. 30:8 and Ps. 50:11—do I incorporate a correction in the transcription of the Hebrew text. In both instances the corrections, i.e., missing letters, are placed within square brackets.

In the transcription, abbreviations are indicated in the modern style with either a final apostrophe or double quotation marks between the last two letters of the abbreviation rather than in the style

---

[9] Abraham J. Levy, *Rashi's Commentary on Ezekiel 40-48* (Philadelphia: Dropsie College, 1931), pp. 1-64; Cohen, *Mikra'ot Gedolot 'Haketer: Joshua-Judges and General Introduction,* p. 84.

[10] Since in modern books the obverse (*recto*) and reverse (*verso*) are numbered separately, moderns would count 552 pages.

of the manuscript, which uses superscript dots. Hence for שׁנ with a dot over the נ we use שׁנ׳ and for כדא with a dot over each letter we use כד״א. The manuscript sometimes omits the dots from various abbreviations, especially with forms of the root אמר. Many of the abbreviations are not standard, but they simply reflect lack of space at the end of a line. Abbreviations common to our manuscript, which are not necessarily familiar even to experienced Hebraists, are listed in the table on p. 807. Characteristic of medieval Hebrew mss. is the practice of writing out the first few letters of a word to fill out a line. The complete word is written at the beginning of the next line. In the transcription this scribal practice is indicated by transcribing the word only once but underlining the repeated "fill" letters: e.g., מעשׂיכם. It is not possible to be perfectly accurate in this regard since sometimes partial letters are written to fill out the line. Chapter and verse numbers of the standard Hebrew text of the Bible have been added. The marginal chapter numbers and divisions in the manuscript do not always correspond to these. For example, Ps. 90 is designated Ps. 88 in the manuscript. The notes to the translation discuss the causes for these discrepancies (see, e.g., the discussion at Ps. 43 and at Ps. 118).

In some instances, Menahem the Scribe writes two words in reverse order and then indicates the correct order by adding above each of the words the Hebrew numerals ב (=2) and א (= 1). In accord with my desire to reproduce Menahem's version of the text, this practice appears also in the transcription.

The standard printed editions of medieval Hebrew commentaries generally employ a single dot (.) between the lemma and the comment and two dots (:) at the end of a comment or to mark a major division within the comment on a particular lemma. Menahem, on the other hand, is inconsistent. If a comment concludes at the end of a line, considerations of space may preclude punctuation. I attempt to reproduce Menahem's text exactly with all its inconsistencies in punctuation. However, for Menahem's single dot (·) and double dots (··) at the end of a comment I employ period (.) and colon (:) respectively as in the standard printed editions.

In the manuscript, the first word or phrase of each psalm is written in large letters. The transcription reflects this feature of the ms. On the other hand, Menahem uses no special script to set off the lemmas from the comments. However, in order to make the present edition more user-friendly, the lemmas are set in bold type.

An appendix at the end of the Hebrew section of this volume contains my transcription of the text of Rashi's commentary on Psalm 121 from the Second Rabbinic Bible (Venice: Bomberg, 1525), which is translated and discussed in the note to Ps. 121 on pp. 701–702. of the English section of this volume.

I dedicate this publication of the Hebrew text of Rashi's Commentary on Psalms to my late and beloved grandson Ori—may his soul be bound up in the bond of eternal life. I fervently pray that this edition of Rashi's Commentary on the fourth and fifth of the five books of the psalter will find favor in both the celestial and terrestrial academies as well as in the hearts and homes of curious souls throughout God's universe. It is my further prayer that this volume may indeed serve to perpetuate the memory of Ori son of Liat and David.

Mayer I. Gruber

ABBREVIATIONS EMPLOYED IN THE MANUSCRIPT

אמר	אמ'
בלעז = בצרפתית עתיקה	בל'
בלעז = בצרפתית עתיקה	בלע'
דבר אחר = פירוש אחר	ד"א
היום	היו'
הקדוש ברוך הוא	הק'
וגו = 'וגומר = ...	וגומ'
וכולה = ...	וכו'
ותירגם יונתן [בן עוזיאל]	ותי 'יו'
יהוה (tetragrammaton)	י'י
כמן דאת אמר = כפי שאתה אומר	כד"א
כולה = ...	כו'
כמו	כמ'
לומר	לומ'
לשון	לשו'
עניין אחר	ע"א
עבודה זרה; על זה	ע"ז
שנאמר	שנ'
תוספות = additions (not Rashi)	תו'
תירגם	תי'
תירגם יונתן [בן עוזיאל]	תי' יו'
תירגם יונתן [בן עוזיאל]	תי' יונ'

HEBREW TEXT OF RASHI'S COMMENTARY
ON PSALMS

א 1 אשרי האיש. בעשרת לשוני זמר נאמ' ספר זה. בניצוח. בניגון. במזמור. בשיר. בהלל. בתפילה. בברכה. בהודאה. **באשרי.** בהללויק'. כנגד עשרה בני אדם שאמרוהו. אדם. מלכי צדק. אברהם. משה. שלמה. אסף. ושלשה בני קרח. חלוקין על ידותון. יש אומרי' אדם היה היה כמה שכתוב בדברי הימים ויש אומ' אין ידותון שבספר הזה אלא על שם הדת והדינין של גזירות שעברו עליו ועל ישר': **אשרי האיש** אישריו ותהילותיו של אדם אלו הן אשר לא הלך בעצת רשעים. כי מתוך שלא הלך לא עמד ומתוך שלא עמד לא ישב : 2 **כי אם בתורת י"י חפצו.** הא למדת שמושב הלצים מביאו לידי ביטול תורה : **ובתורתו יהגה.** מתחילי' היא נקראת תורת י"י ומי שעמל בה תורתו נקראת : **יהגה.** כל לשון הגה בלב הוא. כד"א והגיון לבי לפניך. לבך יהגה אימה. כי סוד יהגה לבם : 3 **ועלהו לא יבול.** אפי' הפסולות שבו לצורך הוא. שיחתן של חכמים צריכה תלמוד. **לא יבול.** לשון כמש. לעז פלשטריר בלעז : 5 **על כן** וגו'. דבוק למקרא של אחריו. 6 **כי יודע י"י** וגו'. לפי שהוא יודע דרך הצדיקים ולפניו הוא להכירה תמיד **דרך רשעים** שנואה בעיניו ומעביר' מלפניו על כן תהא הקמת רגל **לרשעים** ליום הדין ולחטאים בעדת צדיקים :

ב 1 למה רגשו גוים. רבותינו דרשו את העניין על מלך המשיח. ולפי משמעו ולתשובת **המינין** נכון לפותרו על עצמו לעניין שני וישמעו פלשתים כי משחו ישר' את דוד עליהם למלך. ויקבצו **פלשתים** את מחניהם ונפלו בידו. ועליהם אמר למה רגשו גוים **ונתקבצו. ולאמים יהגו** בלבם **ריק** : 2 אשר **נתייצבו מלכי ארץ ורוזנים נוסדו יחד** וגו'. ומה היא העצה 3 **ננתקה את מוסרותימו.** אילו רצועות שקושרין העול בהם : 4 **ישחק. ילעג.** דבר לשון הווה הם משמשים : 5 **אז ידבר אלימו.** ומהו הדיבור. 6 **ואני נסכתי מלכי.** למה רגשתם. ואני **מיניתי** את זה לנסוך ולמלוך על הר ציון קדשי. 7 **אספרה אל חוק.** אמי' דוד לחק קצוב הוא מקובל עלי **לספר** זאת ולהודיע. **י"י אמר אלי.** על ידי נתן וגד ושמואל **בני אתה** ראש לישר' הקרויים בנים בני בכורי והם יתקיימו שכולם תלויין בך : **אני היום** שהמלכתיך עליהם. **ילדתיך** להיות קרוי בני וחביב עלי בכך בשבילים שני וידע דוד כי הכינו י"י. למלך על ישר' וכי נשאת מלכותו **בעבור** עמו ישר' מצינו במלכים החביבים לפניו שקראם בנים כמה שני בשלמה הוא יהיה לי לבן ואני **אהיה** לו לאב : 8 **שאל ממני.** התפלל אלי בכל עת שאתה בא להלחם באויביך. 9 **תרועם.** תרוצצם. **בשבט ברזל.** היא החרב. **תנפצם.** תשברם. וזה הוא לשון בכל המקרא. חרם המשובר בשברים דקים : 10 **ועתה מלכים השכילו.** נביאי ישר' אנשי רחמים ומוכחים אומ' העולם לסור מרעתם שהק' פושט יד לרעים ולטובים : 11 **ברעדה.** כשתבא אותה רעדה שבתוב בה אחזה רעדה חניפים תגילו ותשמחו אם עבדתם את י"י : 12 **נשקו בר.** זרזו עצמיכם בבור לבב. **פן יאנף.** יקצף. **ותאבדו דרך** כעניין שני ודרך רשעים תאבד : **כי יבער כמעט אפו.** כי ברגע מועט יבער אפו עליכם פתאום. ואותה שעה **אשרי כל חוסי בו.** יהיו נכרים אישורי החוסים בו :

ג 1 מזמור לדוד בברחו הרבה דרשות דרשו בני אגדה בדבר. רבותינו אמרו בתלמוד משאמר לו הנביא הנני מקים עליך רעה מתוך ביתך היה לו לבו סוער עבד או ממזר יקום עלי שאינו מרחם עלי. כיון שידע שבנו הוא **שמח.** ומדרש אגדה על שראה טכסיסו קיימת שהיו עבדיו **והכרייתי** והפלייתי שהם סנהדרין מחזיקין עליהם. כשאמ' להם קומו ונברחה מפני אבשלום. מה כתי' שם כל אשר יבחר אדוני המלך הנה עבדיך וכשבאו מחנים שובי בן נחש ומכיר בן עמיאל וברזילי יצאו לקראתו וכלכלוהו : 2 **רבים קמים עלי.** בני אדם גדולים בתורה גדולים בעושר גדולים בקומה. כגון שאול וילידי הרפה

דואג ואחיתופל: 3 **אין ישועתה לו באלקים.** לפי שבא על אשת איש: **אומרים לנפשי.** על
נפש. 6 **אני שכבתי ואישנה.** לבי אטום בדאגי ופחד **הקיצותי.** מדאגתי. כי בטחתי **בי״י**
שיסמכני: 8 **שני רשעים** גבורתם. **כי הכית את כל אויבי לחי.** מכת בזיון כד״א יתן למכהו
לחי. בשבט יכה על הלחי. ומדרש אגדה מכת הפה: כד״א ויצו אל ביתו ויחנק: 9 **לי״י**
הישועה. עליו להושיע את עבדיו ואת עמו. ועל עמו מוטל לברך ולהודו לו סלה:

ד 1 **למנצח בנגינות מזמור** מזמור זה יסד דוד שיאמרוהו בני לוי המנצח
בנגינות בשיר על הדוכן לשון ניצוח נופל למתחזקים בעבודה כעניין שני ויעמדו הלוים מבן
עשרים שנה ומעלה לנצח על מלאכת בית י״י: 2 **בצר הרחבת לי.** בימים שעברו עלי. ומעתה
חנני ושמע תפילתי: 3 **בני איש.** בני אברהם יצחק ויעקב **הק**רוּיים איש. באברהם נאמר
השב אשת האיש. ביצחק נאמ׳ מי האיש הלזה. ביעקב איש תם: **עד מה כבודי לכלימה.** עד
מתי אתם מבזים אותי ראיתי את בן ישי. בכרות עם בן ישי כי בוחר אתה לבן ישי. אין לי
שם. **תבקשו כזב.** תרדפו למצוא כזבים כגון זיפים שמלשינים עלי ולי הם מראים שלום.
וכיוצא בהם דיליטורין שהיו בימי שאול הלא דוד מסתתר בגבעת החכילה. וכן הרבה: 4
הפלה. הבדיל. 5 **רגזו.** חרדו מלפני הק׳ **ואל תחטאו. אמרו בלבבכם על משכבכם.** השיבו אל
לבבכם שהזהיר הק׳ על כך: 6 **זבחו זבחי צדק.** הצדיקו מעשיכם. והרי אתם כמקריבים
זבחים **ובטחו אל י״י** שישפיע לכם טובה. ואל תחטאו לו בשביל ממון שאתם מצפים לקבל
שכר מאת שאוּל: 7 **רבים אומרי׳ מי יראנו טוב.** להיות עשירים ומשיגי תאוה כאילו. **נסה**
עלינו. הרם עלינו לנס את אור פניך. לשון הרימו נס. אריס נסי. לשון נסי. אבל אני **אי**ני מקנא בהם 8
כי שמחה נתונה בלבי **מעת דגנם ותי**רושם של אומות **רבו.** בטחתי. אם למכעיסיו כך לעושי
רצונו על אחת כמה וכמה לעתיד שהו׳ יום קיבול שכרם: 9 **בשלום יחדיו.** אם היו ישר׳
בשלום יחדיו **אשכבה ואישן** הייתי שוכב וישן בטוח ולא הייתי ירא מכל צר ואויב: **לבדד.**
לשו׳ מבטח ושקט הוא שאינו צריך להושיב גייסות עמו:

ה 1 **אל הנחילות** מנחם פתר בכולן נחילות ועלמות גיתית ידותון כולן
לשון כלי זמר ונעימת המזמור היה לפי שיר הראוי לאותו הכלי **ו**מדרש אגדת הספר פירש
נחילות לשון נחלה. ואין זה משמעות התיבה וגם עניין המזמור אינו מדבר בנחלה ויתכן
לפתור נחילות לשון גייסות כמו נחיל של דבורים. תפלה בלשון גייסות אויבים הבאים על
ישר׳ ואמר המשורר את המזמור בשביל כל ישר׳: 2 **אמרי האזינה.** כשיש בי כח לומר צרכיי
לפניך. וכשאין בי כח להתפלל והדאגה עצורה בלבי: **בינה הגיגי. הבן** הגיון לבי. כן מפורש
במדרש. כל בינה שבמקרא הטעם תחת הבי״ת: 4 **בקר תשמע קולי.** בבקר אני קורא לך
עליהם שהוא עת משפט הרשעים כמה שני לבקרים אצמית כל רשעי ארץ. היה זרועם
לבקרים. כי בבקר בבקר יעבר. ונאה לך לאבד רשע מן העולם: **ולא יגורך** ולא יגור אצלך: 6
כי לא חפץ רשע אתה. ונאה לך לאבד רשע מן העולם: **ואצפה** שתעשה בהם משפט:
הוללים. משתטים 7 **איש דמים ומרמה.** זה עשו וזרעו. משתטים **ואני ברוב חסדך אבוא ביתך.**
להשתחוי להודות לך **ברוב חסדך** שהפלאת לי להראותינו נקמה מהם. 9 **שוררי.** **עיני**ני.
המצפים שנגבגוד בך **ותעזבנו.** **שוררי.** כמ׳ אשורנו ולא קרוב: 10 **כי אין בפיהו נכונה.**
נראים כאוהבים והם אויבים: **קרבם הות.** מחשבותם מרמה: **קבר פתוח גרונם** לבלוע יגיע
אחרים. כקבר הבולע ולבולע את הגוף: 11 **ממו**עצותיהם שהם יועצים על
ישר׳ ואז 12 **ישמחו** כל **חוסי בך** ואתה **תסך עלימו.** תגונן ותסוכך עלימו. **ויעלצו** בך. כשיראו 13
אשר **אתה תברך צדיק** יעקב וזרעו. **כצנה** המקפת שלש רוחות של אדם: **רצון.** נחת רוח.
תעטרנו. תסובבנו. כמו ושאול ואנשיו עוטרים אל דוד ואל אנשיו:

ו 1 **על השמינית** כינור של שמונה נימין ושמינית שמו וכן מצינו
בדברי הימים פלוני ובניו על השמינית לנצח: 3 **אומלל.** **נ**שחת ודל כח קוֹנפוֹנדוּס בלעז כמו
היהודים האומללים דעזרא: 4 **ואתה י״י עד מתי** תביט ואינך רופא: 5 **שובה** מחרונך. **חלצה**
נפשי. מחוליי: 7 **אסחה בכל לילה מטתי.** לשון סחי ומאוס. והיתה נבלתם כסוחה **ממ**איס
את מטתי בדמעות. **ערשי אמסה.** אלחלח וארטיב כמו מים. 8 **עששה.** לשון עששית.
לנטירנא. עין שמאורה כהה. ודומה לו כאילו רואה דרך זכוכית שכנגד עיניו: **עתקה.**

נתיישנה ונזדקנה עיני בַכֲהיית אור : **בכל צוררי.** בשביל צרות המצירין לי: 11 **יבשו ויבהלו**
וגו'. מהו **ישובו יבשו** פעם שנייה וגומ' א"ר יוחנן לעתיד לבא הק' דן את הרשעים של
אומות ומתחייבין לגיהנם והן מתרעמין עליו והק' מַחֲזירן וחוזר ומראה גליונים שלהם ודן
אותן ומתחייבים והוא מחזירן לגיהנם הרי בושה כפולה. ר' שמואל בר נחמני אמ' לעתיד
לבא כל אומה קוראה לאלקיה ואין עונה וקוראין להק' אומ' להם אילו הייתם
קוראים אלי תחילה הייתי עונה אבל עכשיו עשיתם ע"ז עיקר ואותי טפל איני עונה שני
ישועו ואין מוֹשיע. זו ע"ז. ואחר כך אל י"י ולא ענם. לכך נאמ' ישובו יבושו:

ז 1 **שגיון לדוד** מנחם אמר שגם זה אחת משמות הזמר על שם הכלי. וכן

פירש על שגיונות ורבותי' פירשו לשון משגה שהתודה והתפלל על השגיון. שאמ' שירה על
מפלתו של שאול כמה שני וידבר דוד לי'. וגו'. אבל לענין המזמור אינו מוכיח על כך. לפי
שהוא מדבר על עסקי האומות 9 **י'י ידין עמים** ואומ' אני שאמרו על עסקי ישוב בני שַבא
עליו על עונשו של שאול כמו שפירשו רבותי' שאמ' לו הק' על נטרד דואג האדומי על ידך
נהרג שָאול ובניו כולה כדאית' בחלק והפך דוד את תפילתו והתפלל שלא יפול ביד אויב. וכן
פתרונו משגה שר דוד לי'י על ששגג לומ' להק' למוסרו ביד אויב על דברי שאול שנהרג על ידו
ד"א על שגיון כנף המעיל אשר כרת לשאול. **כוש.** מה כושי משונה בעורו אף שאול משונה
במעשיו: 3 **פורק** לשון פרקן נזמי הזהב: 4 **אם עשיתי זאת** מה שמפרש אחריו. 5 **אם גמלתי**
שולמי רע. אם גמלתי כגמולו. **ואחלצה צוררי.** שיחתי את חליצתו בכרתי את כנף מעילו אם
השחית ולחלצו והעמידהו ריקם ובשנאה עשיתי אֶלָא להודיעו שהיה מסור בידי לַהֲרגו ולא
הרגתיו. **ואחלצה.** לשון הֲפשטת בגדים : 7 **קומה באפך** על שונאי. כגון ישבי ואחיו ופלשתים
ולא אמסר בידם. **והנשא** והתפאר להראות נקמת עברה בהתעברך עליהם **ועורה אלי.**
שאוכל לעשות בהם מִשפ' נקמה אשר צוית. **והכן צוית.** תָרועם בשבט ברזל. ואיבתי את
איביך. זה מצאתי במדרש : 8 **ועדת לאמים תסובבך.** אם יחזרו אחריך גייסות של אומות
להושיען. אל תשמע לקולם. התרחק מעליהם ושוב ושב במקומך במרום. **למרום שובה.**
להראות להם שידך על העליונה : 9 **י'י ידין עמים.** הפוך הדין מעליונו ותנהו על האומות. **ידין.**
לשון ייסורין. **שָפטני י'י כצדקי** ואת ישר' שפוט לפי מעשים טובים שבידם ולא לפי
העבירות. 10 **ותכונן צדיק. ובוחן לבות** אתה מי הוא הצדיק שתכוננהו. **אלקים צדיק.** כן
שמך. 12 **שופט צדיק.** שופט שהוא צדיק. 13 **ילטוש** הק' עליו וידרך קשתו. 14 **ולו.** לרשע
הכין הק' **כלי מות**: 15 **יחבל און.** לשון הריון. ולידה כמ' שמה חבלתך אמך : **הרה עמל וילד**
שקר. כל מה שהוא מולידו יגע הכל משקר בו שאינו מתקיים בידו מתלא אמ' כל מה
דמשקר מוליד פֶחתא נסבא : 18 **אודה י'י כצדקו.** כֲשיצדק הדין הגמור לשפוט הרשעי'
ברשעם:

ח 1 **על הגיתית** כלי זמר שבא מגת. שם מצוין לעשותו. ורבותי' אמרו

על אדום שעתידה לידרך כגת. כמה שני' פורה דרכתי לבדי. אך ענין המזמור אינו מוכיח 2
מה אדיר שמך. יותר מכדי מדת תחתונים. ואתה בעניינתך הגדולה. כו'. לא היו התחתונים
כדי שתשרה שכינתך ביניהם. **אשר הוד**ך ראוי שתתנהו **על השמים.** 3 ואתה בעניינתך לך **עוז**
מפי עוללים והכהנים שהם בני אדם גדילים בלכלוך ויונקי שדים. **עוללים.** לשון ועוללתי
בעפר קרני. ועל שם הלכלוך נקראו תינוקות עוללים. **למען צורריך.** להודיעם כי עמך אנחנו
להשבית חרפת **אויב ומתנקם.** האומרים לא טובים אתם משאר אומות : 4 **ואני כשאני**
רואה **שמיך** וגו'. אני תמיה בלבי 5 **מה אנוש כי תזכרנו.** 6 **ותחסרנהו מעט** וגו' שַנתַ כח
ביהושע להדמים החמה לייבש את הירדן. במשה לקרוע את הים ולעלות למרום. באליהו
להחיות את המת : 8 **צאנה ואלפים.** צאן ובקר כמו שגר אלפיך. יש מדרשי אגדו' ואינם
מתיישבין לפי סדר המֲקראות :

ט 1 **עלמות לבן** ראיתי במסורת שהוא תיבה אחת שהרי חיבר לה הוא

ינהגנו עלמות. פתרו פותרים וגם דונש מה שפתרו ואינם נראים בעיני. וראיתי בפסיקתא
שהענייני' מדבר בעמלק ועשו : גערת גוים אבדת רשע שמם מחית. ואומ' אני **למנצח עלמות**
לבן שיר זה לעתיד לבא לכשיתלבן ילדותן ושחרותן של ישר' ותגלה צדקתם ותקרב יֲשועתם

שימחה עשו וזרעו : **עלמות.** ילדות. **לבן.** כמו ללבן. ומנחם פתר עלמות לבן. נגינות ללמד.
עלמות. על שם כלי שיר ששמו עלמות. כמ' שאמור בספר זה על עֲלָמוֹת שיר : 2 **כל נפלאותיך.**
גאולה אחרונה החשובה כנגד כל הניסי' כמה שני לא יאמר עד אשר העלה וגו' : 5 **משפטי
ודיני.** יש תיבות כפולות במקרא ואין חילוק בינהם. משפטי ודיני בשמים עדי וסהדי
במרומים עצמי אפיקי גרמי נחשה כמטיל ברזל : **ישבת לכסא.** כסא המשפט. 6 **גערת
גוים.** עמלק. ראשית גוים. **אבדת רשע.** עשו. **שמם מחית.** כי מחה אמחה. 7 **האויב תמו כי
חרבות לנצח.** כי חרבות השנאה לנצח קם עליו בחרב חדה : ד"א **האויב תמו חרבי' לנצח.**
אותו אויב שחרבות שנאתו שנאתו עלינו לנצח היתה וזהו שני בו ועברתו שמרה נצח : זה עשו **עָרִים
נְתַשְׁתָּ.** כי תאמר אדום רוששנו וגו' : **אבד זכרם** אותה שעה 8 **וַי'י לעולם ישב** וגו'. שם שלם
וכסא שלם כמה כמה שני כסאו אבל קודם שיימחה יה' כי על יד כס יה' כס חסר ושם חסר. 6
והוא ישפוט תבל בצדק ומישרים. עד בא הקץ .היה רגיל לשפטם ברחמים לפי מישרים
המצויין בהן דן אותם בלילה כשהן ישינים מן העבירות : 10 **ויהי י'י משגב לדך.** לעתיד
כשיתכוין למשפט כסאו יהי משגב לישרי' שהן דכים. **לעתות בצרה.** עתים של צרה : 12 **זמרו
לי'י יושב ציון.** כשיחזיר ישיבתו לציון יזמרו לו כן : 13 **אותם זכר.** את הדמים אשר נשפכו
בישרי' : 14 **חנני י'י.** עכשיו בגולה. **מרוממי** בגאולתך : 16 **טבעו גוים.** זו הי התהילה אשר
אסַפֵּר : 17 **נודע י'י.** כל זה התהילה נודע י'י לבריות כי שליט הוא ומושל ונוקם לאויביו.
שהרי **משפט עשה** בהם **נוקש רשע.** **נכשל** רשע. **הגיון** זה נהגב זאת **סלה** 18 **לשאולה.** א"ר
נחמיה כל תיבה הצריכה למ"ד בתחילתה הטל לה ה"י בסופה כגון מצרימה. מדברה.
התיבון ליה והכתי' ישובו רשעים לשאולה. א"ר אבא בר זבדי למדרגה התחתונה של שאול.
ומהו ישובו לאחר שיצאו מגיהנם ויעמדו בדין ויתחייבו ישׁוּבו למדרגה תחתית של גיהנם.
19 **כי לא לנצח ישכח** ישר' **האביון** מַלְפָּנוּד עליהם מה שעיבדו בו. **ותקות עניים** לא **תאבד
לעד :** 20 **קומה י'י.** דוד מתפלל לפני המקום שיקום וימהר לעשות זאת : **אל יעז** עזו לאורך
ימים בגדולתו : 21 **מורה.** מרות ועול. ד"א
מורה השלכה. לשון ירה בים **ידעו גוים** שהם **אנוש** ולא אלקים לחיי' גבורתם שולטת : **י** 1
תעלים לעתות בצרה. תעלים עיניך לעיתי הצרה. 2 **ידלק.** ירדוף. כמו כי דלקת אחרי. **יתפשו
במזימות** שהרשעים חושבים עליהם : 3 **כי הלל רשע.** מוסב על למה תעמוד ברחוק. כי עתה
עשו הרשע מתהלל שמשיג כל תאות נפשו. **ובצע ברך נאץ י'י.** והגוזל שיבח את עצמו לאמר
נאץ את י'י ושלום יהיה לו. **ברך** כמו בֵּירֵך. לשון פעל. ותדע שאילו הָיָה שם דבר היה הטעם
למעלה באות הראשונה והיה נקוד פתח וזה נקוד קמץ וטעמו למטה ברי"ש. **ואל** תתמה על
ברך שלא אמ' אמ' ברך שהרבה תיבות יש משמשות כך כגון אויב חֵרֵף י'י. ולא נאמ' חירף : **רשע
כגובה אפו** כל מזמותיו. : 4 **בל ידרוש** הק'. כל מה שאעשה כי אין משפט : **אין
אלקים.** לית דין ולית דיין. 5 **יחילו.** יצליחו. ודומה לו על כן לא יחיל טובו : **מרום משפטיך
מנגדו.** מסולקי' ומרוחקים משפטי ייסורין ופורענות שלך מנגדו. שאינן באים עליו : **כל
צורריו** הוא יפיח בהם. בהפחת רוח הוא מפיח בהם והם נופלים מפניו : 6 **לדור ודור אשר לא
בְרַע.** לא תבא עלי רעה לדורותיי. 7 **וָתֹךְ.** לשון מחשבה רעה הלויה בתוכו תמיד : 8 **עיניו
לחילכה יצפונו.** עיניו של עשו עשו לישרי' שהם חיל יְאָרֹבוּ. **לחלכה.** עליך יעזוב חליכה. שניהם
במסורת כַה מלין המשמש במקום ד"י כגון ובכה ובעמך. תבונה תנצרכה. ככל אשר צויתי
אותכה. הנצבת עמכה. למדנו המסורת שְׁחֵילֶכָה כמ' חילך. חיל שלך. 10 **ידכה ישוח** כך דרך
האויב שמדכא ומשפיל עצמו וּמַקְטִין עצמו כדי שלא יהא ניכר. **ונפל בעצומיו חלכאים.** ראיתי
במסו' הגדולה חלכאים אחת מחמש עשרה תיבות שהם תיבה אחת ונקראת שתי תיבות
כמו בָּגַד. ותאמר לאה בגד אשדת למו. מלכם תדכאו. אף זה חלכאים. **חיל** של נשברים.
כאים. לשון נכאה לבב למותת. לשון נכאה כמ' נו"ן נראה וני"ך נקלה. למדנו נו"ן נכאה כמ' נו"ך
צדיק. ואם תאמר הנון מן השורש יוכיח עליו למען הכאות לב
ברמיזותיו וקריצותיו. לשון הגישו עצמויכם. **ד"א בעצומי.** עוצם עיניו חיל של עניים : על
ידי גבורי. .א"ר סימון אין הרשע מטיל בקילורום שלו אלא גיבורים כמותו שני ולגוברין
גברי חילא דבחילתיה אמר לכפתא משך מישך וגו' : 13 **על מה ניאץ רשע** להק' לפי שאומ'
בלבו לא תדרש : 14 **ראיתה** כמו שהוא עושה ואתה מחריש. **כי אתה** כן דרך שֶׁתַּבִּיט עמל
וכעס **לתת בידך.** בכחך אתה נותן יד לרשעים להצליח ברשעם : **עליך יעזב חילכה.** ישר'

עמך שהם חילך 15 **ורע תדרוש רשעו בל תמצא.** פֹּשעי ישר' כשרואים את הרשעים הם
עוזבים עליך המשא שתעשה דין ברשעים. 14 **יתום אתה היית עוזר.** בימים הראשונים. 15
שבור זרועו של עשו היה **הרשע.** פושעי ישר' כשרואים את הרשעים
מצליחים לבם נושאם לַהֲרשיע. אבל משתתבור את זרועם הַרשעים אם באת לדרוש רשעם
של רעי ישר' לא תמצאנו: 16 **יי' מלך לעולם ועד.** מאחר שאבדו גוים מארצו: 18 **לשפוט
יתום.** לעשות משפטם של ישר' היתומים והרכים: **בל יוסיף עוֹד לערוץ אנוש.** לכתת
ולשביר את האנשים וחולים:

יא 1 אֵיךְ תאמרו לנפשי **נודי** וגו'. זהו דוגמת כי גרשוני היום מהסתפח בנחלת
יי' שגרשוני מארץ לחוצה לארץ. וכאן הוא אומ' ב'י' חסיתי שַׁיחזירני להסתפח בנחלתו. איך
תאמרו אתם טורדין לנפשי: **נודי הַרְכֶם.** עברי הר שלכם את צפור הנודדת שטירדונך מכל
ההר כצפור הנודדת. נודו כת' שהוא נדרש נדרש אף בישר' שהאומות אומרים להם כן: 2 **כי הנה
הרשעים ידרכון קשת.** דואג ודיולטורי הדור המטילין איבה ביני ובין שאול. ידרכון לשונם
קשתם שקר. **כוננו חצם על יתר** הקשת. במסתר **לישרי לב.** דוד וכהני נוב: 3 **כי
השתות יהרסון** על ידיכם כהני יי' צדיקים שהם שתות של עולי. **צדיק מה פעל.** דוד שלא
חטא מה פעל בכל זאת. אתם תשאו עון ולא אֲנִי : 4 **יי' בהיכל קדשו** הרואה וובחן מַעשיכם
ואעפ"י **שבשמים כסאו** גבוה עינים **יחזה** אתכם בארץ: 5 **יי' צדיק יבחן.** ואם מפני שאני
לוקה ונרדף על ידיכם אתם מתהללים לאמר אלקים עזבן. לא כן הוא. אך כך מדתו של הקי'
לייסר ולנסות הצדיקים ולא את הרשעים. הפשתני הזה כל זמן שֶׁהוא יודע שפשתנו יפה
מקיש עליה. וכשאינה יפה ממעט בכתישתה לפי שמתנתקת. **שנאה נפשו פחים.** לשון פחמים: 6 **ימטר** עליהם בגיהנם **פחים.** לשון פחמים: **זלעפות.** לשון שגעון.
7 **כי צדיק** יי' **צדקות אהב.** וְאותם אשר **ישר יחזו פנימו.** וְרבותי' פתרו הרשעים ידרכון קשת
על שבנא וסיעתו. ופתרו לישרי לב חזקיה וסיעתו: **כי השתות יהרסון.** אם השתות יהרסון
על ידם צדיקים שַׁל עולם מה פעל. ואין סדר המקרא' נופל על מהדרש:

יב 1 עַל הַשְּׁמִינִית. כינור של שמונה נימין. 2 **כי פסו אמוני'.** הכל
משקרים בי. מרגלים את המקומו' אשר אנכי מתחבא שם ומגידים לשאול הלא דוד מסתתר
עמנו : 3 **בלב ולב.** בשני לבבות לי מראים שלום ויש שנאה טמונה בלבם: 5 **ללשוננו נגביר.**
לשוננו נתגבר 6 **משד עניים.** מחמת שוד עניים הנשדדים על ידיכם כגון אני ואנשיי וכהני
נוב. ומחמת **אנקת אביונים יאמר** יי' **עתה אקום** לעזרתכם **אשית בישע יפיח לו.** אשיתם
בישע. ידבר עליהם. **יפיח.** לשון דבור. הרבה יש בספר משלי ובחבקוק ויפח לקץ ולא יכזב: 7
אמרות יי' **אמרות טהורות** הן שיש בידו יכולת לקיימם. אבל אמרות בני אדם אינן אמרות
שהם מתים ואין בידם לקיים. **טהורות.** ברורות ומתקיימות. כל מה שמבטיח עושה והרי
הבטיחני ישועה ומלכות. **כסף צרוף.** הרי תם ככסף צרוף הגלוי לכל הארץ. **בעליל.** לשון גלוי
הוא בלשון משנה בין שֶׁנראה בעליל בין שלא נראה בעליל כו'. **שבעתים.** בלבם. 8 **אתה יי'
תשמרם.** שמור אותה בלבם. **תצרנו מן הדור** הזה שלא ילמדו דרכיהם להיות דֵּילטורין :
ד"א **תשמרם.** לאותם עניים ואביונים הנרדפים **מן הדור זו** שהם דילטורין: 9 **סביב רשעים
יתהלכון.** לטמון מוקשים להכשילני. מקנאתם שעינם רעה בגדולתי
שנלקחתי מאחרי הצאן לַמֶלֶךְ. **שבעתים.** מדרש אגדה יש ומיושב על הסדר. ר' יהושע דסכנין
בשם ר' לוי תינוקות שהיו בימי דוד טעמו טעם חטא היו יודעים אֶת התורה בארבעים
ותשע פנים לכל צד. וזהו שבעתים. והיה דוד מִתְפלל עליהם. רבונו של כל העולמים ראה
כמה תורתך ואמרתך ברורה ומזוקקת וזהו פתרון **כרום זלות לבני אדם.** כשמתרומם איש
הזולל בעיני אדם וזהו דוגמת האמור במקום אחר. אבן מאסו הבונים. ומדר' אגדה פתרו
בישר' לעתיד לבא כשיתרוממו. **יג** 2 **עד אנה.** ארבעה פעמים כנגד ארבע מלכיות. ובשביל כל
ישר' נאמ': 4 **פן אישן המות.** שהמיתה נקראת שינה וישנו שנת עולם:

יד 1 אמר נבל בלבו וגו'. דוד נתנבא על נבוכד נצר שעתיד ליכנס להיכל
ולהחריבו ואין אחד מכל חיילותיו מוחה בידו : **אין אלקים.** **השחיתו
והתעיבו עלילה.** מעללים. **נאלחו.** נהפכו: 3 כולו **סר** וגו'. אין איש בחיילותיו מוחה בידו :

לקילקול. 4 **הלא ידעו אוכלי עמי.** אשר נדמה להם כאוכלי לחם שטעמו טעם מאכל ערב.
שָׁסוּפם 5 **שם פחדו פחד.** שישתלם גמולו לבלשצר בנו לפחוד פחד כמו שני באדין מלכא
זיווהי שנוהי וַקטריה חרציה משתריין וַאַרְכֻבָתֵיה דא לדא נקשן. **כי אלקים בדור צדיק.**
בדורו של יכניה שהיו צדיקים: 6 **עצת עני תבישו.** אתם אומ' שעצעתם של ישר' בושה. על
שהם בוטחים בי'י. **כי י'י מחסהו** 7 אך יקרב היום שיתן מציון תשועת ישר' לעתיד ואז **יגל
יעקב** וגו':

טו 3 לא רגל כמו וירגל בעבדך: **וחרפה לא נשא על קרובו.** אם עבר קרובו
עבירה שיש בה עונש עונשו במשפט ולא נשא עליו חרפתו. שיהא פה למחרף לומ' כך עבר
פלוני קרובך וחפיתה עליו. 4 **נבזה בעיניו נמאס.** מי שהוא נבזה ברשעו נמאס בעיניו של
צדיק. כגון חזקיה שגירר עצמו אבי בבזיון **נשבע להרע** לעצמו **ולא ימיר** שבועתו קל
וחומר שאינו ממירה בדבר שֶׁאינו לרעתו: 5 **ושוחד לא לקח על נקי** להרשיע בדין להטות
משפט. ועוד פירשוהו רבותי' לא לקח שוחד על נקי. לנקותו בדינו קל וחומר שאינו לוקח
להטות המשפט. **לא ימוט לַעולם.** אם ימוט אין מטנו מיטת עולם אלא מתמוטט ועולה:

טז 1 מכתם לדוד רבותינו אמרו לדוד שהיה מך ותם. שהיה מכתו תמה
שנולד מהול. ואין שיטת המקרא נופל על המכתום כאן. יש מְזַמור שני בו לדוד מכתם. שם יש
לְפרש שיר זה לדוד שהיה מך ותם. אבל כאן נאמ' מכתם לדוד אין לפרש כן. ואומ' אני אחד
מן שמות הנעימה הזמר הוא וחלוק בנעימות השיר. 2 **אמרת לאדני אדני אתה** וגו'. לכנסת
ישר' אמ' דוד יש עליך לומ' אדני את' וידד על העליונה לכל הבא עלי: **טובתי בל עליך.**
טובות שאתה עושה לי לא עליך הם לגומלני כי לא בצדקתי אתה מטיב לי 3 **לקדושים אשר
בארץ המה** בשביל הקדושים אשר המה קבורים בארץ אשר התהלכו לפניך באמת. **אדירי כל
חפצי בם.** הם האדירים אשר כל חפצי וכל צרכיי נעשים בשבילם: 4 **ירבו עצבותם** וגו'. כל
זה אמרי לי'י ירבו עצבותם של המהירים בך המהירים וחרידים לעבודת אל אחר: **בל אסיך
נסכים מדם.** אני לא אהיה כמותם לזרוק דם לעֻ'יז שם עֻ'יז הוא 5 **י'י הוא
מנת חלקי וכוסי.** כל טובתי הימנו. אתה הוא אשר הניחותה ידי יד החלק
הטוב שני החיים והמות נתתי לפניך ובחרת בחיים. כאדם האוהב אחד מבניו ומניח ידו על
חלק הטוב. את זה בחר לך. **תומיך.** השפלת ידי על הגורל. לשון ימך המקרא ישפל כן הוא
נדרש בספרי'. וגם יש לפותרנו לשון תמיכה למדרש אגדה כמ' ויתמך יד אבין : 6 **חבלים נפלו
לי בנעימים.** כשנפל לי גורל ליפול בחלקך. חבל נעים הוא זה **אף עלי שפרה** נחלה כז': 7
אברך את י'י. עד כאן ניבא דוד על כנסת ישר' שתאמר כן. ועכשיו אומ' גם אני אברך את י'י
אשר יעצני לבחור בחיים וללכת בדרכיו. **אף לילות ייסרוני כליותי.** לַאהבה אותו. ורבותינו
פירשוהו על אברהם אבינו שלמד תורה מאליו עד שלא ניתנה. אך אנו צריכין ליישב
המקראות על סדרן: 8 **שויתי י'י לנגדי תמיד.** בכל מעשיי שמתי מוראו לנגד עיני.
כי מימיני הוא תמיד לעזרתי לבל אמוט. 9 **לכן שמח לבי** וגומ' לפי שאני בטוח 10 **כי לא
תעזוב נפשי לַשאול** שהרי בעון עבירה גדולה שהיתי בידי בשרתני גם י'י העביר חטאתך קל
וחומר שמעתה לא תעזבני בעון ממך : 11 **תודיעני ארח חיים.** לש' עתיד הוא ואינו לשון
תפלה. **את פניך.** שְמַחות אשר לפניך בכת הקרובה לך :

יז 2 מלפניך משפטי יצא. עבירות שביד' שאני ראוי להשפט עליהם
בייסורין יצאו מלפניך ולא יהיון לפניך בדין: **עיניך תחזינה מישרים.** אם יש בידי זכיות בהם
תחזינה עיניך: 3 **בחנת לבי. ופקדתו בלילה.** לעת הערב בעון בת שבע שני ויהי לעת הערב
ויקם דוד וגו'. **צרפתני.** נסיתני. **בל תמצא.** לא מצאת בי חפצך. **זמתי בל יעבור פי.** אם
תעלה עוד במחשבתי לבחון לפניך בל יעבור פי לומר עוד בחנני ונסני. כמ' שאמרתי כבר כמה
שני בחנני י'י ונסני. שאמ' דוד לפני הק' מפני מה אומ' אלקי אברהם ואין אומ' אלקי דוד.
אמ' לו אברהם בחנתיו בעשר נסיונות ונמצא שלם אמ' לפני בחנני ונסני כו' כדאיתי' במס'
שבת: 4 **לפעולות אדם בדבר שפתיך** וגו' 5 **תמוך אשורי** וגו'. מאז והלאה לכל פעולת אדם
שבאתי לפעול אני שמרתי בשביל דבר שפתיך ארחותיך פרץ לנטות מהם שלא אלך בהם. אך
לתמוך אשורי תמיד במעגלותיך ולא נמוטו מהם פעמי. את המישרים תחזינה עיניך

והמשפט מלפניך יצא : 6 **כי תעניני אל.** כי בטוח אני אשר תעניני : 7 **הפלא חסדיך מושיע**
בימינך את החוסים בך ממתקוממים עליהם : 8 **כאישון.** הוא השחור שבעין שהמאור תלוי
בו. ועל שם שחרוריתו הוא קרוי אישון. לשון חושך. והק' הכין לו שומר את ריסי העין
המכסין אותו תמיד : 9 **זו שדוני.** בשביל זאת שעשודדים אותי **אויבי** אשר **בנפש יקיפו עלי**
ליטול את נפשי. בחלבמו **ובשמנם** סגרו לבם ועיניהם טחו מהביט אל פעלך
ליראה מפניך : 10 **חלבמו סגרו.** בחלבמו ובשמנם סגרו לבם ועיניהם טחו מהביט אל פעלך
לפשוט **בארץ.** ונראה לי **שהתפלל** דוד תפילה זו לאחר מעשה שבא לידו של אוריה ויואב
וישר' היו בארץ בני עמון צרים על רבה ויירא דוד שלא יכשלו שם בשביל עבירה שבידו.
וישמעו פלשתים ומואב ואדום וכל שכני ארץ ישר' הרעים המצפים ליום אידם ויבאו
עליהם. 12 **יכסוף.** יחמוד. כמו כי נכסף נכספת : 13 **קדמה פניו** של אויב. **הכריעהו.** קפח את
רגליו ויכרע ויפול. **פלטה נפשי.** מכל רשע. שהוא **חרבך.** שאתה **משליטו** ליפרע מן
המחוייבים לך. 14 **ממתים ידך.** מן המתים בידיך על מטמך אני בוחר להיות **ממתים מחלד :**
אותם שמתים בזקנה משהעלו חלודה רדוללייאה בלי. ומן הצדיקים אשר **חלקם בחיים :**
וצפונך תמלא בטנם. ומאותם אשר תמלא מעיהם מטובך אשר צפנת ליראיך. **יתרם**
נכסיהם אשר ישאירו במותם : 15 **ואני בצדקתך אחזה פניך** לעתיד. אז בצדק אחזה פניך
משפטי הוצא מלפניך והצדקות שבידי אחוז ובהם **אחזה פניך. אשבעה בהקיץ תמונת'.**
אשבעה מראות תמונתך בהקיץ המתים משנתם :

יח 1 **ביום הציל** י' **אותו** וגו'. כשהזקין וכבר עברו עליו כל צרותיו ונצול
מהם. **ומכף שאול.** והלא שאול בכלל היה אלא לפי שהיה קשה עליו **ורדפו** יותר מכולם : 2
ארחמך. אהבך כדתרגומ' ואהבת ותרחם. 3 **סלעי.** שעזרתני בסלע המחלוקת כשהייתי
מצומצם בין שאול ואנשיו ליתפש כמ' שני' שאול ואנשיו עוטרים אל דוד וגו'. **ומצודתי** לשון
מבצר. **צורי.** לשון סלע. **אחסה בו.** אבריאייר אתכסה בצלו. כעניין שני מבלי מחסה חבקו
צור. שהסלעים כסוי ומגן להולכי **דרכים** מן הרוחות ומזרם גשמים : 4 **מהלל אקרא י'.**
בהילולים אתפלל לפניו תמיד לפי שבטוח אני שאיושע מאויבי : 5 **אפפוני חבלי מות.** מחנות
אויבים. כמו חבלי נביאים. אף הוא לשון גייסות שוטפים כנחל : 6 **חבלי שאול.**
כמו חבלי מות. **משרין** רשיעי. ואני מה הייתי **עושה** 7 **בצר לי.** אני קורא אל י' תמיד : 8
ותגעש ותרעש הארץ. כי משמש **בלשון** כאשר. כשחרה לו ובא לנקום נקמת עמו ועבדיו
מפרעה ועמו געשה ורעשה הארץ : 9 **עלה עשן באפו.** כן דרך כל חרון אף להעלות עשן
מנחיריו : 10 **ויט שמים וירד.** לעבור בארץ מצרים : 11 **וידא.** כמו כאשר ידאה הנשר :
12 **חשכת מים שבעבי שחקים.** הם **חשך** אשר **סביבותיו.** ושמא תאמר לפנים מן החשך אין
אור ת"ל 13 **מנוגה נגדו.** אשר נגדו ותוך מחיצתו. את **עביו** אשר סביבותיו בוקעים ועוברים
ברד וגחלי אש : 16 **ויראו**
אפיקי ים. כשנבקעו כל **מוסדות תבל.** טרעיפשיינ"ט. הברד בוקע **ועובר** על המצריים על ים סוף : 17
ישלח ממרום מלאכיו להציל את ישר' מן הים וממצרים : **ימשני.** לשון הוצאה כמ'
משיתיהו : 19 **יקדמוני.** אויבי היו מקדמין וממהרים לבא **על ביום אידי** : 21 **כצדקי.** לכתי
אחריך במדבר : **כבורי.** לשון נקי ובר לבב. ד"א **ישלח ממרום יקחני.** כנגד המחלוקת שבא אל אל שאול. וגו' : **כצדקי.**
שלא הרגתיו בכרתי את כנף מעילו : 23 **כי כל משפטיו לנגדי.** תמיד שמתי אותם על לבי ולנגד
עיניני. 26 **עם חסיד תתחסד.** כלומ' לפי שכן דרכיו לגמול מדה כנגד מדה : **חסיד.** תמים **נבר**
כנגד שלשה אבות תמים נאמן **עם עקש.** כנגד פרעה : 29 **כי אתה תאיר נרי.** כשנלחם בלילה בגדוד
עמלק הבא אל צקלג שני ויכם דוד מהנשף עד הערב למחרתם : 30 **כי בך.** במבטחך : 31
צרופה. ברורה מבטיח ועושה. 30 **ובאלקי אדלג שור** כשבא להלחם על יבוס ואמ' כל מכה
יבוסי והיה לראש לראש הבא יואב ברוש ורענן ועלה על החומה ונתלה בו. אמ' דוד הלמני
צדיק וגו'. קיצר לו הקי את החומה ודילג : 33 **ויתן תמים דרכי.** במדרש **תילים** : 34 **משוה רגלי כאילות.**
כל תקלה ומכשול עד שנעשה שלם וכבוש : 34 **משוה רגלי כאילות.** רגלי הנקבות עומדות יותר
משל זכרים : 35 **ונחתה קשת נחושה זרועתי.** כמו כי חצץ נחתו. והנו"ן אינה יסוד בתיבה
אלא כמ' נחלו נתלו. ונדרכה קשת נחושה על ידי זרעותיי. **ק**שתות של נחשת היו תלויות

לדוד בביתו ורואים אותם מלכי האומות ואומריי זה לזה וכי אתם סבורים שיש בו כח
לדורכן אין זה אלא **לַיַּיראנו.** והוא היה שומע ודורכן בפניהם: 36 **וַעֲנוַתֲךָ תַרבֵנֵי.** הרבית
מדת ענותך להתנהג בה עמי: 37 **תַרחִיב צַעֲדִי תַחתֵי.** המרחיב צעדיו אינו נוח ליפול. וכן
הוא אומ׳ בלכתך לא יצר צעדיך: **קַרסוּלי.** הם הרגלים מן האיסתוירין שקורין קביל״א
בלמטה: 41 **תִּתָּה לִי עֹרֶף.** פונים לי ערפה. ובורחים: 42 **יְשוּוֵעוּ** לעי״ז שלהם **וְאֵין מוֹשִיעַ.**
שאין בו יכולת חוזרים וקוראים אל י״י **וְלֹא עָנָם:** 43 **אֲרִיקָם.** כטיט הנרוק שאינו עב.
הם מריקים. לא הורק מכלי אל כלי: 44 **תְּפַלטֵנִי מֵרִיבֵי עָם.** שלא איענש בְדִינֵי ישר׳ להטות
משפט. ולא **לֵשֲעַבֵד** בישר׳ יותר מן הרשות: **תְּשִימֵנִי לרֹאש גוֹיִם** שאין עונש עליהם בהם. 45 **לֵשֵמַע**
אֹזֶן. אפיי שלא בפניי אלא **שֵיִשְמעוּ** שליחות **יִשָמעוּ אֵלִי.** יסורו אל משמעתי. והן נשמעים
לדברי. **יַכַחֲשוּ לִי.** מחמת יראה: 46 **יבוֹלוּ.** ילאו כמ׳ נבל תבל. מלאה תלאה. **וְיַחרגוּ.** לשו׳
אימה. כדמתרגמי ומחדרים אימה חרגת מותא: **מִמֵמגרוֹתֵיהֵם:** מחמת ייסורי מסגרת וכלא
שאני מייסרו בהם: 47 **חַי י״י** העושה לי זאת. 48 **הַנוֹתֵן נקָמוֹת לִי.** נותן בי כח להנקם מאויביי.
וַיַדבֵר. ויהרוג לשון דָבָר. **תַחתֵי.** במקומי. וחילופי. כעניין שני ואתן אדם תחתיך. נתתי כפרך
מצרים:

יט 2 **הַשָמַים** מספרים כבוד אל. המשורר עצמו פירש את הדבר 4 **אֵין**
אֹמֵר וְאֵין דְבָרִי׳. אין מדברים עם הבריות אלא מתון 5 **שֵבֵכֵל הָאָרֵץ יָצָא קָוָם** ומאירים
לבריות מתון כך מספרים הבריות כבוד אל ומודים ומברכים על **הַמֵאוֹרוֹת:** 3 **יוֹם לְיוֹם יַבִיעַ**
אֹמֵר. מעשה בראשית מתחדש מיום אל יום. לערב חמה שוקעת וזורחת לבקר. ומתון כך
יביעו הבריות אמרי שבח על ידי הימים והלילות שמורים את הבריות לשבח ולהודות: 5 **בֵכֵל**
הָאָרֵץ יָצָא קָוָם. השמים. שהם נמתחיי על פני כל הארץ. ומחמת כן **בֵקֵצֵה תֵבֵל מִילֵם.**
שהכל מדברים בנפלאות שהם רואים: **לַשֵמֵש שָם** הקי **אֹהֵל בָהֵם.** בשמים: 6 **וְהוּא כֵחָתָן**
יוֹצֵא מֵחוּפָתוֹ בכל בקר. וזהו שאמ׳ השמים מספרים כבוד אל: 7 **וּתקוּפָתוֹ.** הקפת סיבובו
מקצה אל קצה. **וְאֵין נֵסתָר מֵחַמָתוֹ.** אילמלא ניתן ברקיע התחתון לא היה אדם נסתר מפניו
מרוב **חַמִימוּתוֹ.** כמו שני בסוף העניין מאירת
עינים. ואומ׳ כי נר מצוה ותורה אור: **תוֹרַת י״י תמִימָה.** גם היא מאירה כשמש. כמו שני הַדִין וליהט אותם היום
הבא. אבל **תוֹרַת י״י** תמִימָה היא **מֵשִיבַת נֵפֵש.** ד״א **וְאֵין נֵסתָר מֵחַמָתוֹ.** ליום הַדִין וליהט אותם היום
וזורחת לכם יראי שמי וגו׳ **עֵדוּת י״י נֵאֱמָנָה.** נאמנה היא להעיד בלומדיה: **מֵשִיבַת נֵפֵש.**
משיבתו מדרכי מיתי׳ לדרכי חיים: 9 **בָרֵה.** מצהרת. תורת. עדות. פיקודי. מצות. משפטי.
ששה כנגד ששה סדרי משנה: 8 **מַחכִימַת פֵתִי.** נותנת חכמה לפתאים: 11 **וְנוֹפֵת צוּפִים** ומתק
צופים. 12 **בֵשָמרָם עֵקֵב רָב.** נַזהֵרתי בשמירתם בשביל רב טובך אשר צפנת: 13 **שְגִיאוֹת מִי**
יָבִין. אני נזהרתי בהם אבל אי איפשר להזהר שלא אשגה בהם: ואתה נקֵיני **מִנֵסתָרוֹת**
שנסתרו ממני ולא ידעתי בחטאי בשגגה: 14 **גַם מֵזֵדִים.** מן **הַזֵדוֹנוֹת:** **אָז אֵיתָם.** אהיה
תמים. מ״ן אמרו חכמים למה דוד דומה לכותי הַמֵחזֵר על הפתחים והם מערימים בדבר
מכל אדם. תנו לי מים לשתות דבר שאין בו חסרון כים. משיתנה אומ׳ יש כאן בצל קטן.
משיתנו לו אומ׳ יש בצל בלא מלח. משנתנו לו אומ׳ תנו לי מעט לחם שלא יזיק לי הבצל. כך
דוד בתחילה על השגגות ואחרכך על הזדונות ואחרכך על המרדים. פשעיי אילו המרדים
שמתכוין להכעיס. וכן הוא אומ׳ מלך מואב פשע בי: 15 **יַהיו לְרָצוֹן.** לפיוס. לרצותך

כ 2 **יַעַנך י״י:** **בֵיוֹם צָרָה** המזמור הזה על שם שהיה שולח את יואב ואת
ישר׳ למלחמה והיה עומד בירושלם ומתפלל עליהם כעניין שני טוב כי תהיה מעיר לעי׳ לעזור
ואמרו רבותי׳ אילמלא דוד לא עשה יואב מַלחמה: **שֵם אֱלֹקי יַעֲקֹב.** שהבטיחו בלכתו לחרן
ושמר הבטחתו. לכך נאמ׳ אלקי יעקב: 3 **מִקָדֵש.** מהיכל קדשו: **שֶהוּא שוכן שם:** 4 **יִדשֵנָה.**
לשון שומן. כמו ואכל ושבע ודשן. כלומ׳ יקבלם ברצון כעולות מחים: **מִנחוֹתֵיך וְעוֹלָתֵך.** הם
התפילות שאתם מתפללין במלחמה: 6 **נֵרַננָה בִישוּעָתֵך.** כשיושיע אותך הקי נרננה כולנו
להקי ובשם אלקינו **נֵדגֹל.** נתאסף ונעשה חיל: 7 **עַתָה יָדַעתִי.** זו היא הרננה שארנן עתה בתשועה זו
שבאה ליואב ולישראל ידעתי שחפץ המקום בי ויעננו **מֵשמֵי קָדשוֹ.** כי תשועתם היא
תשועתי: 8 **אֵלֵה בָרֵכֵב.** יש מן האומות בוטחים ברכב שלהם. ויש בוטחים בסוסיהם. אבל

אנחנו בשם י' נזכיר כי לו הישועה. נזכיר לשון הקטרה ותפילה. כמו מזכיר לבונה. את
אזכרתה. ולפיכך 9 המה כרעו ויפולו ואנחנו נקום ונתעורר:

כא 2 בעזך ישמח מלך. רבותי' פתרוהו על מלך המשיח. ונכון הדבר לפותרו
עוד על דוד עצמו. לתשובת המינין שפקרו בו: וארשת. לשון דיבור. ואין לו דמיון 4 כי
תקדמנו ברכות טובות. קודם ששאלתי ממך הקדמת לי ברכתך על ידי נתן הנביא והקימותי
את זרעך וגו'. והכינותי את כסא ממלכתו עד עולם: תשית לראשו עטרת פז. ויקח את
עטרת מלכם ותהי על ראש: 5 חיים שאל ממך. כשהייתי בורח לחוצה לארץ מפני שאול
הייתי מתפלל אתהלך לפני י' בארצות החיים: נתתה לו. שהשיבותני לארץ ישר': אורך
ימים. למלכותי. שאמרת והכינותי ממלכתו עד עולם: 7 תחדהו. לשון חדוה. את פניך. בגן
עדן. ורבותי' שדרשוהו במלך המשיח הביאו ראיה לדבר ועד עתיק יומין יתיב מטא
ולקדמוהי הקרבוהי. ואומ' והקרבתיו ונגש אליו: 8 בל ימוט. ובחסד עולם עליון הוא בוטח
שלא ימוט. לעת זעמך. 9 תמצא ידך לכל איביך. כל מכת ידך שיש לך להביא הבא על אויביך: 10 לעת
פניך. לעת זעמך. כאש יבלעם. תפילה היא זו: 11 פרימו מארץ תאבד. להק' הוא אומ'
ומתפלל. שיאבד פריו של עשו הרשע. שיחלקו ישר' את
עצמו. בל יוכלו לעשותה: 13 כי תשיתמו שכם. אשר תשית אותם לחלק. שיחלקו ישר' את
ממונם. כמה שני והיה אתננה וגו': במיתריך תכונן על פניהם. במיתרי קשתותיך תכונן
חיצך ותזמין לירות על פניהם:

כב 1 על אילת השחר. שם כלי שיר: ד"א על כנסת ישר' שהיא אילת
אהבים הנשקפה כמו שחר. ורבותינו דרשוהו באסתר: 2 למה עזבתני. עתיד' ללכת בגולה
ואמר דוד תפילה זו על העתיד: רחוק מישועתי ומדברי שאגותיי: 3 אקרא יומם. אני
קוראה לך מיום אל יום ואינך עונה: 4 ואתה קדוש ויושב לשמוע תהילות ישר'. מימים
קדמונים: 7 ואנכי תולעת ולא איש. כל ישר' מכנה כאיש אחד: 8 יפטירו. יפתחו. כמו פטר
רחם: 9 גל אל י'. כמו לגול. יש לאדם הגולל יהבו ומשאו אל יוצרו למען יפלטהו: 10 גוחי.
מוציאי ומושכי כמו כי יגיח ירדן וגו' מבטיחי על שדי אמי. זימנת לאדם שדים לישען
עליהם למחיה: 11 עליך השלכתי. נשלכתי מרחם. מאז הוצאתני מרחם. כד"א העמוסים
מני בטן. מאז נולדו השבטים. נשאם ונהלם: 13 פרים רבים. מלכיות חזקים. אבירי בשן. גם
הם לשון פרים בבשן. שהיו שמינים: כתרוני. סבבוני. 14 אריה
טורף. נובד נצר. 15 כדונג שעה הנמוחה מחום האש. 16 מלקוחי הם החיכים שקורין
פלייש. כשאדם מצר אין רוק מצוי בפיו: ולעפר מות. לדכאות מיתה. תשפתני. אתה
מושכני. לשון שפיתת קדירה. שפות הסיר: 17 כארי ידי ורגלי. כאילו הם מדוכאים בפי ארי.
וכן אמ' חזקיה כארי כן ישבר כל עצמותי: 18 אספר כל עצמותיי. כאב עצמי. המה יביטו
שמחים לאידי. 19 ועל לבושי ידון גורל. בוזזים את נכסינו: 20 איילותי. כחי. כמ' הייתי כגבר
אין אייל. וכמ' יש לאל ידי. 22 הושיעני מפי אריה. כאשר מקרני ראמים עניתני. זה האמרי
אשר כגובה ארזים גובהו. בהתאסף כל
כנסיותי וכן אומר להם 24 יראו י' הללוהו אילו הגרים. וכל זרע יעקב: 25 ענות עני צעקת
דל. כל ענייה שבמקרא לשון צעקה. ועוד יש לפותרו ענות לשון הכנעה. כמו לענות מפני
שהוא נכנע ומתפלל לפניך. 27 יאכלו ענוים. לעת הגאולה לימות המשיח: יחי לבבכם לעד.
כל זה אומר לפניהם: 28 יזכרו האומ' הרעה שמצאתנו כשיראו הטובה וישובו אל י': 29 כי
לי' המלוכה. כי יראו שהחזרת לך המלוכה והממשלה: 30 אכלו והשתחוו כל דשני ארץ.
הרי זה מקרא מסורס. אכלו ענוים כל משמני ארץ והשתחוו לי' בהלל והודייה על הטובה:
דשני ארץ. טוב חלב הארץ. כל זה יראו אפסי ארץ וישובו אל י': לפניו יכרעו כל מיתי
האומות מתוך גיהנם ולא ירחם עליהם לחיות את נפשם מגיהנם: ונפשו של כל אחד ואחד
לא חיה. לא יחיה ורבותינו דרשו המקרא הזה שהמתים לפני מיתתם בשעת נטילת נפש
רואים פני שכינה: 31 זרע יעבדנו וגו' זרע ישר' אשר תמיד עובדים אותו יסופר לי' לדור.
סרס המקרא ודרשהו. יסופר לדור אחרון לשם ולשבח את אשר עשה לאותו זרע 32 יבאו
הראשונים ויגידו צדקתו לעם הנולד כי עשה להם צדקה:

כג 1 **מזמור** אמרו רבותינו כל מקום שני מזמור לדוד מנגן <u>ואחרכך</u> שורה
עליו שכינה מזמור להביא רוח הקודש לדוד. וכל שנאמ' בו לדוד מזמור שרתה עליו שכינה
ואחרכך אמ' שירה : **ל"י רעי.** בטוח אני שלא אחסר כלום. 2 **בנאות דשא** בנאוה דשאים. לפי
שהתחיל <u>לדמות</u> מזונותיו למרעה בהמה שאמ' ל"י רועי. נופל על הלשון נאות דשא. ומזמור
זה אמ' דוד ביער חרת למה נקרא שמו יער חרת. שהיה מנוגב כחרש. והרטיבו הק' מטוב
<u>העולם</u> הבא : מדרש תילים. 3 **נפשי ישובב.** רוחי שהופך בצרות ובמנוסה ישובב לקדמותו :
במעגלי צדק. בדרכי מישור. שלא אפול ביד אויבי. 4 **בגיא צלמות.** בגיא חושך. ועל מדבר
ציף אמ' כל צלמות לשון חושך : פיר' דונש בן לברט. **שבטך ומשענתך.** ייסורין שבאו עלי
ומשען שאני בטוח על חסדך. שניהם **ינחמוני** שיהו לי לסלוח עון ובטוח אני 5 **תערוך לפני**
שולחן היא המלכות. **דשנת בשמן ראשי.** <u>כבר</u> נמשחתי על פיך למלך : **כוסי רוייה.** לשון
שובע :

כד 1 **ל"י הארץ** ארץ ישר' **תבל.** שאר ארצות. 2 **על ימים יסדה** שבעת
ימים מקיפין ארץ ישראל וארבע נהרות ירדן וירמוך קרמיון ופוגה : 3 **מי יעלה בהר ל"י.**
אעפ"יי שכל יושבי תבל שלו אין הכל כדאי לקרב אליו אלא 4 **נקי כפים** וגו'. **לא נשא לשוא**
נפשו. לא נשבע בשמו ובנפשו לשוא. מצינו לשון שבועה נופל על נפש שני נשבע ל"י צבאות
בנפשו. 6 **זה** שכך מעשיו הוא **דור דורשיו.** בימי שלמ' בני כשיבא
להכניס לבית קדשי <u>הקד</u>שים ודבקו השערים זה בזה אמ' עשרים וארבעה רננות ולא נענה
עד שאמ' אל תשב פני משיחך זכרה חסדי דוד עבדך : **פתחי עולם.** <u>פתח</u>ים שקדושתן
עולמית :

כה 1 **נפשי** אשא אכוין לבי : 3 **ריקם.** הגזלנים והחמסנים <u>המושיבים</u> את
העניים ריקם <u>מנכסיה</u>ם. כמ' ואחלצה צוררי ריקם. 7 **כחסדך זכור לי אתה.** הראוי לחסדך
תזכור לי. אילו מעשים טובים שבידי : 8 **טוב וישר ל"י** וחפץ להשדיר ברייותי : **על כן יורה**
חטאים בדרך תשובה. ד"א יורה חטאים. לרוצחים שני תכין לך וגו'. מקלט כתי' על פרשת
דרכים כו' : 11 **למען שמך** הרב סלח לעוני **כי רב הוא.** נאה לרב לסלוח עון רב. 12 **מי הוא**
הירא ל"י יורנו בדרך שהוא בחר. הוא דרך הטוב. 13 **נפשו בטוב תלין.** כשילין בקבר תלין
בטובה נפשו : 16 **כי יחיד אני** ועון רבים תלויה בי ולנגדן אני יחיד. לפיכך **פנה אלי וחנני.** כי
תפילתי צריכה לתשועת כל ישר'. 18 **ראה עניי ועמלי.** ועל ידיהם **שא לכל חטאותיי :** 19
שנאת חמס שלא כדין : 5 **קויתי כל היום** הוא העולם הזה שהוא יום לאומות ולילה לישר'.
6 **כי מעולם המה.** מימות אדם הראשון שאמרתי לו ביום אכלך ממנו מות תמות. ונתת לו
יום משלך שהוא אלף שנים :

כו 1 **שפטני** י'י. ובמקום אחר הוא אומ' אל תבא במשפט. אמ' דוד <u>כשאתה</u>
דן את הרשעים שפטני כי לפי הרשעים אני צדיק. וכשאתה דן את הצדיקים אל תביאני
במשפט. 4 **ועם נעלמים.** המכסים בסתר לעשות מעשיהם **לא אבוא.** איני רגיל לבא <u>להכנס</u>
עמם : 6 **בנקיון.** שאין גזל במצות שאני מקיים. לולב הגזול פסול. 7 **לשמיע.** כמו להשמיע.
כל נפלאותיך זה הלל שיש בו לשעבר ולהבא. ויש בו לגוג <u>ויש</u> בו לימות המשיח ויש בו לעתיד
לבא. 12 **רגלי עמדה במישור.** בדרך ישר :

כז 3 **בזאת** אני בוטח. במה שאמור למעלה ל"י מעוז חיי : 4 **ולבקר בהיכלו.**
ליראת שם כל בקר ובקר. כן פי' דונש. 5 **כי יצפני בסוכה** בטוח אני שיצפנני בבית מקדשו
ושנינו בסדר עולם שהמקרא הזה נאמ' על יואש בן אחזיה שהסתירתו יהושבעת אחותו
בעליית בית קדשי הקדשים כעניין שני ויהי אתה בבית ל"י מתחבא שש שנים : **בצור ירוממני**
העמיד על סלע רגליי : 6 **זבחי תרועה** זבחים שאומרים עליהם שיר : 8 **לך אמר לבי בקשו פני**
בשבילך בשליחותך אומר לבי בקשו כולכם ישר' את פני. ואני שומע לו. **את פניך ל"י אבקש :**
לך כמו הן אני כפיר לך אם לא לאל תריבון <u>במקומו.</u> אף כאן לך אמר לבי. במקומך בא אלי
לבי לומר כן : 9 **אל תט.** אל תכריע כמי ויט שמים : 10 **כי אבי ואמי עזבוני.** בשעת תשמיש
להנאתם נתכוונו כיון שגמרו הנאתם זה הופך פניו אילך וזו הופכת פניה אילך. **ול"י יאספני.**

קמו בי אותם עידי שקר וכילוני : לולא נקוד עליו. למדרש שדרשו רבותינו יודע אני שאתה
נותן שכר טוב לצדיקים לעולי הבא. אבל איני יודע אם יש לי חלק עמהם אם לאו. 14 ואם
לא תתקבל **תפילתי** חזור וקוה : **כח** 3 **אל תמשכני** עם אל תרגילני עם רשעים : 7 **ומשירי**
אהדינו. וזו היא ההודייה. 8 **יי' עוז לעמו** לאותם התלוים בי. והם כל בית ישר' בעת **שמעוז**
ישועות משיחו הוא :

כט 1 **הבו** **ליי'**. הכונו ליי' והכינו לו. אתם בני אילי הארץ. מכאן שאומרי'
אבות. **הבו ליי' כבוד ועז**. מכאן **שאומרים** גבורות. 2 **כבוד שמו**. זו **קדושת** השם. ויש
במזמור זה שמונה עשרה הזכרות. וכנגדן **תקנו** חכמים שמונה עשרה ברכות. 3 **קול יי' על**
המים. על ים סוף. ירעם משמים י' וגו'. בשעת מתן תורה צימצם את קולו
לפי כחן של ישר' שני והאלקים יעננו בקול. **בקולו** של משה : 5 **קול יי' שובר ארזים**. מלכי
האומות כענניין שני וירעם יי' **בקול** גדול על פלשתים וגו'. מי מקול יי' יחת אשור. בשעת מתן
תורה. כי מי כל בשר וגו'. ויחי. אתה שמעת וחיית. ואומות העולם שומעים ומתי' : 6
וירקידם כמו עגל. את הארזים ואת ההרים שבאו לשמוע מתן תורה ואומות העולם שומעים
ומתים. **לבנון ושריון**. שמות הרים : 7 **חוצב להבות אש**. רבותי' פירשו שהיה הדיבור של
עשרת הדברות יוצא בלהבות אש מפיו ונחקק על הלוחות כתבניתם : 8 **יחיל מדבר**. לשון חיל
כיולדה. **יחיל יי' מדבר קדש**. הוא מדבר סיני. כמו שאמרו רבותינו במס' שבת חמשה שמות
נקראו לו מדבר סיני מדבר צין. מדבר קדש. מדבר קדמות מדבר פארן. מדבר קדש
שנתקדשו ישר' עליו : 9 **קול יי' יחולל איילות**. יפחיד ויחיל לעתיד את האומות שהם עכשיו
עומדות בחוזק כאיילות כענניין שני משנה רגלי כאיילות. א"ר פנחס כאילים אין כתי' כאן
אלא **כאיילות** שרגלי הנקבות עומדות יותר משל זכרים. **ויחשוף יערות** כמו **מחשוף** הלבן.
קלף עצי היער. כלומר יפשיטם מכבודם משולי' כעצי יער שני אשר כגובה ארזים
גובהו. **ובהיכלו** שיבנה **כולו אומר כבוד**. הכל יקלסו שם ויאמרו 10 **יי' ישב** בגדולתו יחידי.
וגם עתה **וישב** יי' לבדו **מלך לעולם**. והאלילים כליל יחלף. אבל 11 **לעמו יתן עוז** וברכת
שלום. ורבותי' דרשוהו במתן תורה שנתפחדו ונתבהלו האומות ובאו להם אצל בלעם ואמר'
לו מה קול ההמון אשר שמענו שמא מבול הוא בא להביא לעולם. אמ' להם כבר נשבע שלא
יביא אלא קול ההמון אשר שמעתם הק' נותן תורה לעמו :

ל 1 **שיר חנכת** הבית. שיאמרוהו הלוים בחנוכת הבית בימי שלמה. 2
ארוממך יי' כי **דליתני**. הגבהתני. **ולא שמחת אויבי לי**. שהיו אומרי' אין לדוד חלק לעולם
הבא. וכשראו שבשבילו נפתחו **הדלתות** לארון שמחל הק' על אותו עון וגהפכו פני
שונאי דוד כשולי קדירה. שלא ארד לבור : 4 **מירדי בור**.
מרדתי לגיהנם. כמו ושב ורפא לו : 5 **זמרו ליי' חסידיו**. על מה שעשה לי. כי יכולים אתם
לחסות בו שייטיב לכם. ואפי' אתם שרוים בצרה אל תיראו. 6 **כי רגע** קטן **באפו**. וחיים
ארוכים יש בהרצותו ובהפייסו : 7 **ואני אמרתי בשלוי**. בשלוותי הייתי חושב לא **אמוט**
לעולם. אבל אין הדבר ברשותי כי אם ברשותו של הק'. 8 **ברצוני** העמיד את **הררי**. את
גדולתי ע[ל] להיות **עוז**. וכיון שהסתיר פניו ממני מיד **הייתי נבהל** 9 **ואקרא אליך ואתחנן**
תמיד לאמר לפניך. 10 **מה בצע בדמי** וגו'. ואתה שמעת קולי. 12 **והפכת מספדי למחול לי**.
ורבותי' דרשו כל המזמור הזה על מרדכי והמן בפסיקתא זוטא. **ואסתר** והמן 7 **ואני אמרתי**
בשלוי יאמר המן 9 **אליך אקרא** אמרה אסתר. כו' עד ש 11 **היה עוזר לי**. 12 **הפכת מספדי**
למחול לי אמר מרדכי וכל ישר' :

לא 6 **בידך** אפקיד רוחי. תמיד לפי שאתה פדית אותי מצרה. 7 **השומרים**
הבלי שוא. המצפים לתשועת ע"ז : 10 **עשׁה**. כהתה. לשון עששית שאדם נותן זכוכית לנגד
עיניו לראות לעבר הזכוכית דבר אין אותה מראה ברורה : 11 **ועצמי עששו** לשון רקב כאילו
אכלם עש. 12 **מכל צוררי**. מאת כל צוררי. **הייתי חרפה** לגידוף. **ולשכיני אני חרפה מאד**.
ופחד למיודעי. מתפחדים על קורותיי. 13 **ככלי אובד**. ההולך לאיבוד. כל לשני אבידה אין
הלשון נופל על לשון אבידה ועל בעל אבידה לומ' הוא אבד אותה אלא האבידה אובדת ממנו
כד"א אשר תאבד והאובדות לא בקשתם : 14 **דבת רבים**. עצת רבים. דבת פרלדי"ץ. לשני

דובב שפתי ישינים. וכן כל דבה שבמקרא. **מגור מסביב.** שמייראים ומפחדים אותי. **בהוסדם.** בהתייעצ׳: 16 **בידך עתותי.** עתים העוברות עלי על פיך הם ובגזירותיך. 18 **אל אבושה כי קראתיך.** אחרי אשר קראתיך אין נאה: **ידמו לשאול.** ישתתקו ויאלמו לשאול. 19 **הדוברות על צדיק עתק.** שאומרים עלי לשאול דוד מבקש רעתך. 20 **מה רב טובך.** ידעתי כי לעולם הבא יש שכר טוב ליריאיך. ומכל מקום בעולם הזה שהרשעים מקיפים אותם אני מתפלל 21 **שמסתירם בסתר פניך מרוכסי איש.** מחיבורי רעים המתקשרים יחד להרע להם: 22 **בעיר מצור.** בקעילה שאמר שאול עלי נסגר לבא בעיר דלתים ובריח. 23 **ואני אמרתי בחפזי.** כשיצאתי מקעילה ובאתי אל מדבר מעון והייתי נחפז ללכת מפני שאול כי הגישני ושאול ואנשיו עוטרים אלי ואל אנשיי לתפשם: אמרתי בלבי **נגרזתי.** נכרתי. לשון גרזן הכורת את העץ. על שם גזירתו נקרא גרזן כך פירש דונש: 24 **אמונים נוצר י׳׳י.** המאמינים בישועתו וסומכים עליו: **על יתר.** מדה במדה מכוונת כחץ על יתר הקשת. או יש לפתור **על יתר.** חבל כנגד חבל. קו כנגד קו:

לב 1 **משכיל** לדוד. אמרו חכמים כל מזמר שנאמ׳ בו משכיל על ידי תורגמן אמרו. **אשרי נשוי פשע.** שהק׳ נושא פשעו ומכסה חטאיו 2 **ולא יחשב לו עון.** ובלבד שלא תהא **ברוחו רמיה** להיות בדעתו לשוב אל קיאו: 3 **כי החרשתי.** מלהתודות על פשעי לפניך. **בלו עצמי** מרוב שיגגות אנחתי כל היו׳ שהייתי דואג מפני הפורענעת: 4 **כי יומם ולילה** היה כבד עלי למורא ידך וגזרותיך: **נהפך לשדי.** ליחלוחי שלי. וכן לשד השמן. לחלוח שמן כך פירשו דונש: **בחרבוני קיץ.** עד שיבש בחרוני הקיץ. מפני דאגת כובד ידך שהייתי דואג על חטאי. ולפיכך 5 **חטאתי אודיעך** תמיד. ולשונו הווה הוא. כי **אמרתי** טוב **אודה על פשעי** לי׳׳י. ועתה כשהודיתי ואמרתי לנתן הנביא חטאתי. **נשאת עון חטאתי** כענייין שני גם ל׳׳י העביר חטאתך וגו׳. 6 **לעת מצוא.** בהמצאך לקבל תפילתו. ומה היא זאת. **רק לשטף מים רבים** אשר **לא יגיעו אליו.** שלא יפול ביד האומות שהם כמים שוטפים: וכן מצינו שהתפלל דוד על זאת ואמי אפלה נא ביד י׳׳י כי רבים רחמיו. וביד אדם אל אפלה. 7 **אתה סתר לי.** להסתר בצלך מחמת פחד אויב. **רני פלט.** רנה של הצלה. **תסובבני.** לשון הווה הוא. סבבתני תמיד **רני פלט.** וכך אמרתי לי: 8 **אשכילך ואורך.** **איעצה.** ארמוז לך בעיניי מה תעשה. **איעצה.** לשון קיצות עין. כמו עוצם עיניו לחשוב תהפוכות בספר משלי: 9 **אל תהיו כסוס כפרד** שאינו מבין בין העושה לו טובה לעושה לו רעה. **כשאתה** ממתגו במתג הוא בולם את פיו ומכסכס את רסנו. וכשאתה מקרדו ומקרצפו ומעידו עדי ומייפהו הוא בולם. ואתה צריך לבלום ולסגור את פיו ולייסרו בייסורי׳ במתג: ורסן **בל קרוב אליך** שלא יקרב אליך להזיקך כשאתה מייפהו. **במתג ורסן עדיו לבלום.** בשעת עדיו שאתה מקרבו ומקרצפו אתה צריך לסגור במתג ורסן שלא יקרב אליך: **בלימה.** בלשון משנה לשון מסגר. רגליו מבולמות במסכת בכורות:

לג 2 **בנבל** עשור. של עשר מיני נעימה: 7 **כנד.** לשון גובה. וכן תי׳ אונקלוס נצבו כמ׳ נד. קמו כשור. וכן פירשו מנחם. ואין נד ונאד שוין: **נתן באוצרות תהומות.** תהומות באוצרות תחת הארץ: 14 **השגיח הביט** 15 **היוצר יחד לבם.** לב כולם יחד. ורבותי׳ הסיבוהו אל ממכון שבתו השגיח יחד לבם היוצרו. ודרשו שכולם נסקרין בסקירה אחת:

לד 1 **בשנותו** את טעמו כעניין שני ויתיו על דלתות השער וגו׳. וישנה את טעמו בעיניהם. **לפני אבימלך.** כן כל מלכי פלשתים נקראי׳ וכל מלכי מצרים פרעה. ואעפ״יי שמו אכיש קורין לו אבימלך: ומדרש אגדה שהיה צדיק כאבימלך שלא רצה להרג. ואנשיו אמרו לו הלא זה דוד מלך הארץ. כדאיתא במדרש תילים: 3 **בי׳׳י תתהלל נפשי.** מתפאר ומתהלל אני שיש שיש לי מתון כך יבינו אותם וישמעו: 5 **מגורותי.** לשו׳ פחד ויגר מואב: 6 **הביטו אליו ונהרו.** כל אותם שהביטו אליו מתוך צרתם נהרו והאירו פניהם: 9 **טעמו** דברו. 10 **יראו.** הוו יראים לשון ציוי: 11 **רשו.** לשון דלות. לשון דלות: 15 **בקש** במקומך **ורדפהו** במקום אחר. 18 **צעקו** הצדיקים וי׳׳י **שמע:** 20 **רבות רעות צדיק.** הרבה רעות ופחדים באים עליו. ומכולם

ניצל. 21 **שומר** הק' **כל עצמותיו**: 22 **תמותת** את הרשע הרעה שהוא עושה. **תמותת**. תמית:
23 **לא יאשמו**. לא יתחרטו לאמר אשמנו שחטינו בו:

לה 3 **והרק** הזדיין. **וסגור לקראת רודפיי**. הגן ביני וביניהם כמחיצה. 6 **חשך**
וחלקלקות. שניהם יחד כדי שיחליקו רגליהם בחלקלקו' והחושך אינו מניחם להשמר מן
ה**חלקלקות**. כד"א לכן יהי דרכם ב**חלקלקות** באפילה ידחו ונפלו בה: 7 **חפרו לנפשי** שוחה
ליפול בה: 8 **שואה** חשך. **ורשתו אשר טמן** כן דרך לטמון הרשת ולכסותו בקש או ב**עפר** כדי
שלא ירגיש בה העובר עליה. עד שנלכד בה: 9 **ונפשי תגיל**. כשאראם במפלתם: 10 **כל**
עצמותי יקלסוך על כן. כי עתה 11 **יקומון** עלי ת**מיד עד חמס** וגו': 13 **ותפילתי אל חיקי**
תשוב: 14 **כרע כאח לי התהלכתי** כאילו הן אחי ורעיי התהלכתי מיצר על צרתם **כאבל אם**
כבן המתאבל על אמו. או כאם המתאבלת על בנה. 15 **ובצלעי שמחו ונאספו**. אנשים פסחים.
נאספו עלי נכים. כמו שמתרגמי' נכה
חגירא. **קרעו ולא דמו**. אילו היו קורעין את בשרי לא היה דמי שותת לארץ. כשמלביניני פני:
16 **בחנפי לעגי מעוג**. בשביל חנופת של ליצנות. אכילה ושתייה: **כשמחניפים** לשאול בשביל
שיאכילם וישקם חורקים עלי שיניהם. **מעוג**. לשון אכילה. כמו אם יש לי מעוג **דאליהו**: 17
כמה תראה. כמה ארך אפים יש לפניך לראות כל אלה: **משואיהם** מחשך שלהם: 19 **יקרצו**
עין. הקורצים עין: 20 **על רגעי ארץ**. על דכאי ארץ. וכן רוגע הים. וכן עורי רגע. וכן פי' דונש.
האח האח. לשון מתהלל בתאות לבו. 23 **העירה והקיצה**. פמליא של מעלה לשפוט משפטי
מאוייביי:

לו 2 **נאם** פשע לרשע בקרב לבי וגו'. הרי זה מקרא מסורס יש בקרב לבי
שהפשעו הוא יצר הרע אומ' לרשע שלא יהא פחד אלקים לנגד עיניו: **בקרב לבי**. כאדם שאומ'
כמדומה אני. 3 **כי החליק** הפשע אל הרשע **חלקלקות בעיניו**. כדי שימצא הק' את עונו
לשנוא אותו. 4 **חדל ולהשכיל להטיב**. מנע עצמו מלהשכיל להטיב כי מעשיו: 5 **יתיצב על דרך**
לא טוב הק' נתן לפניו דרך הטוב ודרך הרע. והוא בוחר לו דרך לא טוב: 6 **י"י בהשמים**
חסדך. בשביל הרשעים הללו אתה מסלק חסד מן התחתונים. ומגביה **אמונתך עד שחקים**
לסלקה מבני אדם. 7 **וצדקתך** יקרה מן הבריות **כהררי אל**. בשביל מעשה הרשעים.
ומשפטיך באים לעולם עד **תהום רבה. אדם ובהמה תושיע י"י**. בני **אדם** שהם ערומים בדעת
כאדם הראשון ומשימים עצמם כבהמה בענוה אתה מושיע: 8 **מה יקר חסדך**. אינו כדיי
להימשיך על הרשעים הללו אבל **בני אדם** אשר **בצל כנפיך יחסיון** הם 9 **ירויון מדשן** וגו'. 12
אל תבואני רגל גאוה. אל תבא עמי רגל הרשעים הללו בעת קיבול השכר להיות חלקם עם
צדיקים. **ויד רשעים אל תנידני** ממקומי בבואי לירש משנה את חלקי ואת חלקו בטובה
כעניין שנאמ' לכן בארצם משנה יירשו. ואז 13 **שם נפלו פועלי און**. שם יבינו במפלתם ושם
דוחו ולא יוכלו קום:

לז 1 **אל תתחר** במרעים מוכיח את ישר' הוא שלא יתחרו בהצלחת
המרעים לעשות כמעשיהם. כמו **נאז** תתחרה את הסוסים לרוץ ב**מרוצתם**. אטיר בלעז.
ואל תקנא בעושי עולה. לעשות עולה כמותם. 3 **בטח בי"י**. ואל תאמר אם לא אגזול ו**אגנוב**
ואתן עיני בממון אחרים במה אתפרנס: **ועשה טוב**. ואז תשכון **ארץ** לאורך ימים **ותרעה**
אמונה. תאכל ותתפרנס שכר האמונה ש**האמנת** בהק' לסמוך עליו ולעשות טוב: 4 **והתענג**
אל י"י. התעדן בתפנוקי' על משענתו של הק': 5 **גל על י"י דרכך**. גלגל עליו כל צרכיך: 7 **דום**
לי"י. המתן לתשועתו. כמו אם כה יאמרו אלינו **דומו** דיהונתן: **והתחולל**. לשון תוחלת: **אל**
תתחר לומ' ארשיע כמותו ואצליח כמותו: 8 **הרף מאף ועזוב חימה**. הרף מהרשיע שלא יבא
עליך אף. **ועזוב** דבר המביא עליך חמתו של הק'. 9 **כי המרעים** שאתה רואה מצליחים עתה.
הם **יכרתון** 10 **ועוד מעט**. **כשתמתין** עוד מעט תראה כי אין הרשע. **והתבוננת על מקומו**.
ותסתכל על מקום שהיה שם **ואיננו** כי מת ואבד: 14 **חרב פתחו רשעים** תגר וחירום
מתחילין ה**רשעים** מאיליהן: 16 **טוב מעט לצדיק** טובים מעט אנשים שהולכים **מהמון**
רשעים. אמרפל וחביריו שהצליחו והרגו כל אותן האוכלוסים. 18 **יודע ימי תמימים**. מכיר
את מעשה ידיהם **ונחלתם** וקיבול שכרם מאתו **לעולם תהיה**: 20 **כיקר כרים**. כאור ענן בקר

הנראה שחרית מלבין על מרחבי בקעה. **כרים.** מישור. כמו כר נרחב. **אדם כיקר.** יקרות. ויש
פותרים **כיקר כרים.** כבכוד כבשים שמפטמים אותם לטבח: 21 **וצדיק חונן ונותן.** הק' שהוא
צדיק **וחונן** משלו **ונותן** לזה שהלוה לזה מה שהוא גוזל ממנו: 22 **כי מבורכיו** של צדיקו של
עולם **ירשו ארץ.** 23 **מצעדי גבר.** מי שהוא גבור ביראת הק'. לא יושלך. להיות
נעזב: 25 **נער הייתי.** שר העולם אמרו. דאילו דוד לא קש כולי האי. 26 **כל היום** הצדיק **חונן**
עניים **ומלוה** להם **וזרעו** זה שהיה זורע לצדקה סופו לברכה: 30 **פי צדיק יהגה** תחילה בלבו
חכמה לראות דין שפסוקה תורה לכל דבר ואחרכך **לשונו תדבר משפט:** 31 **לא תמעד**
אשוריו. לא יחליקו צעדיו: 35 **ומתערה** משריש. כמו ערות על יאור. ובלשון משנה יש הרבה.
אילן שנשפשח ומעורה בקליפה. **כאזרח רענן.** 37 **שמרתם.** הסתכלו בדרכי התמימים ללמד מעשיהם: **כי אחרית לאיש שלום.**
אם ראשית אין לו אחרית יש לו. אבל 38 **פושעים ורשעים נכרתו** ונשמדו הם **יחדיו:**

לח 1 **מזמור** **לדוד להזכיר.** לומרו בעת צרה להזכיר צרתם של ישר' לפני הק'
וכנגד כל ישר' אמרו: 3 **נחתו.** נזרקו. לשון ירקון. וכן נחתה קשת נחושה.
ואין הנו"ן שורש בתיבה. שאם כן היה לו לומ' ננחתו בי. **ותנחת.** לשון ותרד. ובזה הנו"ן
שורש בתיבה. 4 **מתום.** תמימות. כבדים: 5 **יכבדו.** אנטרין: 7 **נעויתי.** לשון אחותו עוית.
אקרופישון בל' : 8 **כסליי מלאו נקלה.** במחשבתי אני קל בעיני עצמי: 9 **נפוגותי.** נחלפתי
לשוני ויפג לבו : מאין הפוגות : 10 **כל תאותי** אתה יודע כל צרכיי: 11 **סחרחר:** מוקף יגון. וזה
מתיבות הכפולות. כמ' ירקרק אדמדם: סגלגל: חמרמרו: 12 **מנגד נגעי יעמרו.** אותם
שנראים לי כאוהבים בשעת הנאתם כשראים שהנגע בא עלי אין עומדי' לי בשעת דוחקי
אלא מנגד יעמדו ואינם עוזרים לי: **וקרוביי.** שמראים עצמם קרובים. 13 **ויבקשו.** מבקשים
מוקשים לי: **יהגו.** יחשובו: 14 **ואני כחרש.** ישר' שומעים חרפתם מן האומות ואינם
משיבים. ולמה 16 **כי לך הוחלתי.** שתגאלני ותושיעני מהם. 17 **כי אמרתי פן ישמחו לי.** לכן
אנו שותקים כי אנו אומרים בלבנו אם נשיב עזות שמא יראו במפלתנו וישמחו לנו במוט
רגלינו ויגדילו עלינו לומר הלא אתם מתפארים לתשועתכם: 18 **כי אני לצלע נכון.** לכך אנו
דואגים פן ישמחו לנו לפי שמלמדים אנו במכות ומוכנים ומזומנים לשבר תמיד. **ומכאובי**
לנגדי. מזומן הוא לבא אלי **תמיד.** 19 **כי עוני אגיד.** לבי מגיד לי עוני ולפיכך אני דואג וירא
מחטאתי שלא יגרום לי צלע ומכאוב: 20 **חיים עצמו.** מעצימים חיים בשלום ובטובה 21
תחת רדפי טוב. תחת שאנחנו דביקים בהק' ובמצותיו:

לט 1 **לידותון** שם אדם אחד מן המשוררים. וגם כלי שיר היה ששמו ידותון.
ומדרש אגדה על הדתות ועל הגזירות של צרה הנגזרות לישר': 2 **אמרתי אשמרה דרכי** וג'.
אנחנו היה בלבנו לשמור את עצמינו על כל הצרות הבאות עלינו. שלא נהרהר ונדבר קשה
אחר מדת הדין אעפ"י שהרשעים לנגדנו המצורים עלינו. 3 **ונאלמנו דומיה** ימים רבים וגם
החשינו **מטוב.** אפי' מדברי תורה מפני יראתם. ומתוך כך כאבינו **נעכר.** נבהל. ובשתיקתינו
4 קם **לבנו בקרבנו** ובהגיון לבנו בוער בנו כמו **אש** והי' גורם לנו שאנו מדברים בלשונינו לפניך
וזו היא שאנו מדברים 5 **הודיעני** י'י **קיצנו** עד מתי נהיה בצר' ונדע מתי אנחנו **חדילים**
ממנה: 6 **הנה טפחות.** מדודים המה ימי האדם כדבר הנמדד בטפחים כך ימי האדם
קצובים. וחלדנו וזקננתנו **כאין נגדך. חלד.** לשון חלודה. רזוליי"א בל'. **כל אדם** כל אדם **הבל**
ימיו ומצבו: 7 **אך בצלם** בחשך פירשו דונש לשון צלמות. **אך הבל** היא. אך הבל כל המייה
וגאוה שלהם: **צבר** תבואה בשדה כל ימות הקציר ואינו יודע מי אוספה לבית האסיף
האסיף ימות: 8 **ועתה מה קויתי.** מה היא השאילה אשר שאול ומייחל ממך אינה אלא 9
שממפשעי תצילני **וחרפת עשו הנבל אל תשימני.** הבא עלי נגעים ומכאובות שלא יוכל לומ'
לי אתם לוקים ואנו אין אנו לוקים. והתפילה הזאת גרמה להביא יישורי חלאים על
האומות: 10 **כי אתה עשית** שהבאת עלינו צרה יותר מכל האומות: 11 **מתגרת ידך.** ממורא
מכותיך. **תגרת** לשון ויגר מואב. והתי"ו יסוד נופל בתיבה כמ' תלונה תקומה תחינה. 12
בתוכחות הכתובות בתורה על עונינו שהעוינו לפניך ייסרתנו בהם: **ותמם כעש חמודנו.**

הרקבתנו בשריגו כבגד שאכלו **חמודו.** בשרו שהיא חמדתו : 14 **השע ממני.** הרף ידך מלהלקות. **ואבליגה. ואתחזקה** :

מ 2 **קוה קויתי** י' במצרים. ומזמור זה כנגד כל ישר' **ויט אלי** אזן. 3 **מבור שאון** מאסירים של מצרים ושאון המיתם : **מטיט היון.** מן הים. 5 **ושט כזב.** השטים מדרך היון. **כון.** הכין אשורי. צעדי : 4 **שיר חדש.** שירת הים. 5 **ושט כזב.** השטים מדרך הישר אחרי הכזב של ע"ז : 6 **נפלאתיך ומחשבותיך אלינו.** בשבילינו בראת עולמך. לנו קרעת הים. וחשבת מרחוק להטיב לנו : **אחרתנו** במדבר ארבעים שנה. **ומפני האמוריים** שגידעו את האילנות והחריבו ארצם כשנשמע שישראל יוצאים לרשת ארצם : **אין ערוך אליך** אין לדמות לו וכל מלך ומושיע : **אגידה ואדברה.** אם באתי להגיד ולדבר **עצמו מספר.** 7 **זבח ומנחה לא** שאלת : ביום מתן תורה כעניין שני ועתה אם שמוע תשמעו בקולי. **כרית.** עשיתם חלולו לשמוע 8 **אז** בשעת מתן תורה **אמרתי** לפניך **הנה באתי** במסורת בריתך נעשה ונשמע. ודבר זה **כתוב עלי** עדות **במגילת ספר.** בתורת משה : 9 **ותורתך בתוך מעי.** אף על הבאר. שירת דבורה. **לא אכלא.** לא אמנע. לשו' ויכלא הגשם. **לא תכלא רחמיך.** לא תמנע : 12 **יצרוני.** ישמרוני : 13 **אפפו.** סבבו : 15 **לספותה** לכלותה : כדמתרגמי' עד תם כל הדור. עד דסף. 16 **ישומו.** יתמהו. **על עקב בשתם.** כשיקבלו בושתם על עקב. **הכל** במדה שמדדו ובדרך שהלכו **למולי.** **על עקב.** אינְצֵישְׁטְרָאצְשׁ בלעז. **האמרים לי האח.** האומרים בשבילי האח. כשהצרה באה מתהללים באידינו : 18 כל **עני ואביון** שבתילים אינו אלא כנגד ישר' : **יחשב לי.** יתן לי לחשוב ענייתי ואביונותי להושיענו :

מא 2 **אל דל** חולה לבקרו לבקרו לקנויין שני מדוע אתה דל ככה דאמנן **ביום רעה.** זה גיהנם. ובעולם הזה מה שכרו. 3 **י'י ישמרהו.** למי שמבקרין ומטיב לו : 4 **על ערש דוי.** כשיחלה גם הוא יסעדנו. מהו **על ערש דוי.** זה יום שביעי של חולה שהוא דוה מאד כך נדרש באגדת תילים : **כל משכבו הפכת בחליו.** אף בשעה שחליו כבד עליו שנהפך כל מרגועו ומנוחתו 5 **אני אמרתי י'י חנני.** אני אין לי מבקרים לטובה. וכשאני צועק מתוך חוליי ואומר י'י חנני וגו' : 6 שמחים **אויביי** עלי ואומרים דבר **הרע לי. מתי ימו'** וגו' : 7 **שוא ידבר.** מראה עצמו כאילו הוא מיצר וכשהוא יושב לפניו **יקבוץ לבו** מחשבות **און** לעצמו מה רעה ידבר בצאתו. וכשיוצא לחוץ מדבר אותה 8 **עלי יחשבו** דבר הוא **רעה לי.** ומה היא המחשבה 9 **דבר בליעל יצוק בו.** כל רשעיות שעשה ישתפכו והואיל **אשר שכב לא יוסיף לקום.** כך מתקללים אותי : 10 **הגדיל עלי עקב.** מארב. כמו ואת עקבו מים לעים וגו' : 12 כשתחנני **ותקימני** אדע **כי חפצת** בי כאשר **לא יריע אויבי** עלי תרועה שמחה **עלי.** 13 ואראה **כי בתמי תמכת בי.** 14 **ברוך י'י.** כשאקום מחוליי אברכך כך :

מב 1 **לבני קרח** אסיר ואלקנה ואביאסף. הם היו תחילה בעצת אביהם. ובשעת המחלוקת פרשו. וכשנבלעו כל סביבותם ופתחה הארץ פיה נשאר מקומם בתוך פי הארץ כעניין שני ובני קרח לא מתו. ושם אמרו שירה ועלו ושם יסדו המזמורים הללו ושרת עליהם רוח הקודש ונתנבאו על הגליות ועל חורבן הבית ועל מלכות בית דוד : 2 **כאיל תערוג על אפיקי מים.** לשון ערג נופל על לשון קול כאשר יפול לשון נהם לארי ושקק לדוב וגעה לשוורים וצפצוף לעופות. אמרו רבותי' האילה הזאת חסידה שבחיות. שכשהחיות צמאות למים הם מתכנסות אצלה שתתלה עיניה למרום. מה היא עושה חופרת גומא ומכנסת קרניה לתוכה וגועה והק' מרחם עליה והתהום מעלה לה מים : **כאיל תערוג.** כאיילות תערוג לא נאמר אלא כאיל דבר הכת' בזכר ערוג על עסק המים כמו שפירשנו. והנקיבה כשהיא כורע' לילד רחמה צר והיא צועקת והק' **מרחם** עליה ומזמן לה נחש ומכישה בבית הרחם שלה ורחמה נפתח : 3 **מתי אבא ואראה פני אלקים** לעלות לרגל ונתנבא כאן על חורבן הבית ונאמר שלשה פעמים **מה תשתוחחי** כנגד שלש מלכיות שהן עתידות לבטל לעבודת המקדש וישר' צועקים **ונגאלים.** מלכות בבל ויון ואדום : **צמאה נפשי.** כנסת ישר' אומרת כן בגלות בבל : 4 **היתה דמעתי לחם.** מכאן שהצלת משביע את האדם ואינו מבקש לאכול. וכן הוא אומ' בחנה ותבכה ולא תאכל : 5 **אלה אזכרה.** **וכי אעבר בסך.** את זאת אני זוכרת **ונפשי** משתפכת בזוכרי עליית רגלים שהייתי עוברת בגדוד בני אדם

ו<u>מדדה</u> עמהם עד בית אלקים. סך. לשו' חשבון. סך לשון מחיצת בני אדם. סך לשון צבים
ועגלים. כמו מדדין עגלים וסייחים והאשה מדדה את בנה. ותיבה זו משמשת שתי תיבות
אדדה עמהם. כמו' ולא יכלו דברו לשלו' דבר עמו לשלום: המון חוגג. שהיו הולכים לחוג.
ומדרש אגדה לשי' יווני הוא שקורין לבריכת מים חוגגין. ועל ככה יסד הפייט עוצם המון
חוגג ו<u>שוטף</u> כנהר: 6 תשתוחחי. לשון כי <u>שחה</u> לעפר נפשינו. נשח כשהוא <u>מדבר</u> בלשון מתפעל
התיו חולקת את אותיות שרשי התיבה כדרך כל תיבה שיסודה שי"ן בתחילתה. הוחילי.
המתיני וצפי לגאולתך: 7 אזכרך מארץ ירדן. ממה שעשית לנו בירדן. והרי חרמון אחרי כל
הכעס <u>שהכעסנוך</u> בשטים הובשת לנו את הירדן. מהר מצער. מהר סיני שהוא צעיר לשאר
ההרים. אחר שהכעסנוך בו במעשה העגל סלחת לעווניני <u>והלכת</u> עמנו כל אלה אני זוכרת
ב<u>גלותי</u> שמענת מלהטיב לי. ו<u>גזרות</u>יך מתחדשות עלי זו אחר זו: 8 תהום אל תהום. צרה
קוראה לחברתה לקול צינוריך המקלחים עלי פורענות כמים שוטפים עד כי כל משבריך
וגליך עלי עברו: משבריך. לשון הים גלוי עולים למעלה ומשתברים ונופלים: 9 יומם יצוה
י'י: חסדו. יבא האור של גאולה ויצוה חסדו י'י לנו. ובלילה בחשך. הגלות והצרה יהי שירה
עמי תהי חניגתו בתוכנו. שירה לשון חנייה דמתרגמי' ויחן ושרא. וזו למדתי מתוך מסור'
הגדולה שחיבר את זה ויהי שירה חמשה ואלף באלפ"א בית"א של שתי תיבות החלוקים
בפתרונן לימדונו שאין זה לשון שיר ומדרש אגדה פותרו לשון שיר. וכך הוא פותרו שכך ישר'
אומרי' להקי' זכרנו מה שעשית לנו במצרים מצה אחת צויתנו ביום בערב הפסח ושמרנוה
ובלילה גאלתנו ושרנו לפניך שירה את ההלל. ועכשיו הרבה מצות אני שומרת ואין אתה
גואלני. ועל זאת 10 אמרה לאל סלעי למה שכחתני וגו': 11 ברצח בעצמותי חרפוני צוררי.
נדמה לי כאילו הורגים אותי כך עצור בעצמותי מה שאויבי מחרפים אותי: מג 1 מגוי לא
חסיד הוא אדם. שגר עשו בין שני צדיקים ולא למד ממעשיהם: שפטני. נקמני. 3 שלח
אורך ואמתך מלך המשיח שנדמה לאור שני ערכתי נר למשיחי ואליהו הנביא שהוא אמיתי.
נביא נאמן 4 אל אל. אל הקי' שהוא שמחת גילי:

מד 2 באזנינו שמענו כאן אתה למד שהיו מדברים בני קרח בשביל דורות
הללו הבאים אחריהם שאילו הם עצמם. שלא היה להם לומי' אבותינו סיפרו לנו שהרי הם
עצמם ראו ניסי המדבר והים והירדן ומלחמות <u>יהושע.</u> כך מפורש באגדת תילים. 3 תרע
לאומים. הרעותה לשבעה אומו' גדולות ושילחתם מפנינו. ואתה בידך וכאך הורשתם מתוך
ארצם ונטעת לאבותינו בתוכה: 5 צוה ישועות יעקב. עתה 6 נבוס קמינו. נרמוס אויבינו
לשון מתבוססת בדמיך והיו כגיבורים בוסים בטיט חוצות. 10 אף זנחת ותכלימנו. אף עתה
אשר זנחתנו ותכלימנו אנו בשמך נודה לעולם: 11 תשיבנו אחור וגו'. לשון הווה הוא. שסו
למו. בזזו נכסינו איש לו: 20 כי דכיתנו במקום תנין. כי זה משמש בלשון כאשר. ואף כאשר
השפלתנו בארץ ערבה ושוחה מדבר מקום תנין וכסית בצלמות. אם בכל זאת 21 שכחנו שם
אלקינו 22 הוא יחקור זאת כי הוא יודע תעלומות וגו'. 23 כצאן לטבחה. כצאן אל טבח:

מה 1 על שושנים לכבוד תלמידי חכמים ייסדו השיר שהם רכים
כשושנים ונאים כשושני ומרטיבים מעשים טובים כשושנים. משכיל על ידי תורגמן. שיר
ידידות שיר אהובים. שיר שבח להם להאהיבם על הבריות ולהאהיב תורתם עליהם: 2 רחש
לבי כך התחיל המשורר בשירו. הרחיץ בקרבי דבר טוב בשבחיך את התלמידי חכמים: רחש
לשי' נענוע וכן כל לשון שירוץ וריחוש: אומר אני מעשי למלך. השיר הזה שייסדתי ועשיתי
אני אומרו למי שהוא הגון למלך שני בי מלכים ימלוכו: לשוני צח בשירי. כעט סופר מהיר:
ראיתי ביסודו של ר' משה הדרשן מהיר לשון ערבי בקי: 3 יפיפית מבני אדם. העוסקי'
במלאכת חיי שעה. למה לפי שהוצק חן בשפתותיך להורות הוראות בהלכה: על כן ברכך. כמה שני לי'
עז לעמו יתן. ומה שכרו י'י יברך את עמו: 4 חגור חרבך על ירך להלחם מלחמתה של תורה. התורה
והיא הוד והיא הדרך: 5 על דבר אמת להורות כדת ולהתנהג בענות צדק ותורך. התורה.
ודבר אמת שתתעסוק בו היא תורה אותך טכסיס המלחמה לעשות ימינך נוראות. לפי שהזכיר
בלשון מלחמה נופל בו לשון הימין <u>המיומנת</u> להלחם: 6 חציך שנונים. בלב אויביך המלך.
הרי זה מקרא מסורס. מצינו שהתלמדים נקראים חצים. שני כחצים ביד גבור כן בני

הנעורים. ותלמידי חכמים המודיעים בהלכה קרויים אויבים זה לזה לפי שעה שנ' יבושו כי
ידברו את אויבים בשער. **עמים תחתיך יפולו.** ובשכר התורה יפלו האומות תחתיהם של
ישר': 7 **כסאך אלקים.** כסאך שר ושופט לעולם ועד. כעניין שנ' נתתיך אלקים לפרעה. ולמה
בשביל ששבט מישור מישור שבט מלכותך: שמשפטיך אמת וראוי אתה למלוך 8 **משחך שמן
ששון.** כל לשון גדולה נופל עליה לשון מרקחים קציעות: 9 **מר ואהלות קציעות.**
קדה מתרגמינן קציעתא. **כל בגדיך.** כל בגדותיך מרקיחים כריח בשמים. ומדרשו כל
בגידותיך וסירחוניך מ<u>ת</u>כפרים ומריחים ריח ערב: **מן היכלי שן.** מני שמחוך. היכלות אשר
מהיכלי שן משובחים ההיכלות המ<u>ת</u>וקנים לך בגן עדן לשמחך בהם: **מני שמחוך.** אשר
ממניהם שמחוני. הנותני שכרך. 10 **בנות מלכים** יהו מבקרות אותך כעניין שני ושרותיהם
מיניקותיך. **ביקרותיך.** ק"וף דגישה לפי שהוא לשון בקור. ואעפ"יי שכתוב יו"וד לפניה ראיתי
בניקוד רב סעדיה תיבה זו סדורה עם מי נתן למשיסה יעקב. שכת' יו"וד והס"מך מדגשת.
שגל. מלכה. אשתך תתיצב לימינך **בכתם אופיר.** שמעי כנסת ישר' וראי
דרך הטוב **והטי אזנך** לתורה **ושכחי עמך.** האומות שאת גדילה ביניהם. **ובית אביך.** ע"יז
שעבדו אבותיך מעבר הנהר: 12 **ויתאו המלך יפיך.** ואם תעשי כן י<u>ת</u>אוה הק' לנוי מעשיך: 13
ובת צור במנחה פניך יחלו. ובשכר זה תזכי שיביא ליך עשו הרשע אשכרים ודורון אותם
שהם עכשיו **עשירי עם:** 14 **כל כבודה בת מלך** וגו' זהו שנאמ' והביאו את כל אחיכם וגו'.
אותם שכל כבוד תלוי בהם והם כנסייה של מלך אשר נהגו עצמם בצניעיות עתה בגדיהם
חשובים ממשבצות זהב של כהנים גדולים: 15 **לרקמות תובל למלך** בבגדי רקמה יביאום
מנחה למלך על כל הארץ: **בתולות אחריה ריעותיה.** מן האומות ילכו אחריהם כעניין שני
והחזיקו בכנף איש יהודי. וגו'. לאמר נלכה עמכם כי שמענו אלקים עמכם **מובאות לך.** כלפי
הק' שאמ' המשורר 17 **תחת אבותיך** וגו'. לכל אחד מישראל אמ' 18 **אזכירך שמך** כלפי הק'
אמרו המשורר

מו   1 **על עלמות** שם כלי שיר בדברי הימים: 3 **במהיר ארץ** לעתיד לבא
ביום שני הארץ כבגד תבלה ראו בני קרח שנעשה להם שנבלעו כל סביבותם והם עמדו
באויר. ואמרו לישר' ברוח הקודש שדוגמת הנס הזה יהא עשוי להם לעתיד. ואמרו 4 **מימיו**
יגרשו רפש וחומר וטיט כמשפט: של הק' הנזכר בראש המזמור: 5
נהר פלגיו נהר גן עדן: 6 **לפנות בקר.** לעת הגאולה. רכבי המלחמה של
אומות **מז** 2 **תקעו כף.** התערבו יחד זה עם זה להריע להם **בקול רינה:** 4 **ידבר עמים
תחתינו.** יתן דבר באומות תחת נפשינו להיות חמתו מתגררת בהם ואנו ניצולים כעניין שני
נתתי כפרך מצרים וגו'. 5 **יבחר לנו** וגו' וי<u>ח</u>זירנו לתוכה ואז 6 **יתעלה בתרועה וקול שופר**
שנתקע לפניו בשיר על עולות וזבחי שלמים ונאמ' 7 **זמרו לאלקים** וגו': 9 **מלך אלקים על
הגוים.** כך יאמרו הכל **ישב על כסא קדשו.** עכשיו הכסא שלם והגדולה נצחת ויגידו כי 10
נאספו לעירו **נדיבי עמים.** שהתנדבו עצמם לטבח ולהרג על קדושת שמו : **עם אלהי אברהם.**
ש<u>ה</u>יה נדיב לב הראשון תחילה לגרים עתה נודע **כי לאלקים מגיני ארץ.** היכולת בידו להגן
על החוסים בו : **מח** 2 **בעיר אלקינו.** לעתיד לבא כשיבנה את עירו יהי בשבילם **גדול ומהולל:**
3 **יפה נוף.** עיר שהיא נוף יפה לשון נוף של אילן : ד"א כלילת יופי. שכן ב<u>ב</u>רכי הים קורין
לכלה נינפי. **משוש כל הארץ.** ומה היא משושה. **ירכתי צפון.** ירך המזבח צפונה ששם
שוחטין חטאות ואשמות. ומי ש<u>ה</u>וא עצב על עבירה שבידו מ<u>ב</u>יא חטאתו ואשמו ומתכפר לו :
והוא יוצא משם שמח ועל ידי הקרבנות טובה באה לעולם. **נודע למשגב.** כישישכון בה
לעתיד יאמרו כן. 5 **המלכים נועדו** להלחם עליה במלחמת גוג ומגוג **עברו יחדו.** 6 <u>למ</u>לחמה:
המה ראו את הק' יוצא ונ<u>ל</u>חם בגוים להם : 8 **ברוח קדים.** הוא לשון פורענות שהק' נפרע בו
מן הרשעים כמה שני יוצא ויולך י"י את הים ברוח קדים וגו'. וכן בצור רוח הקדים שברך בלב
ימים. ברוח קדים אפיצם לפני אויב: **אניות תרשיש.** הם שכיני צור היא אפריקיא ומאדום
היא. 9 **כאשר שמענו** הנחמות מפי הנביאים **כן ראינו:** 10 **דמינו חסדך** הנביא חוזר ומתפלל
להק' ואומר דמינו וקוינו אל חסדך לראות תשועתך זו **בקרב היכלך:** 11 **וכשמך כן תהילתך.**
כאשר שמך גדול כן תהילתך בפי כל. 12 **למען משפטיך.** שתעשה דין באומו' 13 **בני ציון.**
אתם הבונים אותה. **ספרו מגדליה.** לשון מניין. דעו כמה מגדלים ראוים לה. 14 **לחילה.**

לחומתה כמ' חיל וחומה. **פסגו ארמנותיה** הגביהו בירניותיה. כמו אשדות הפסגה. רמתא.
למען תספרו את גובהה ואת יופיה לדור שאחריכם 15 כאדם המנהיג את בנו קטן :

מט 2 **חלד** היא הארץ על שם שהיא נושנת. וחלודה רדולייא בלע' ורבותי'
פירשו על שם החולדה שהי' ביבשה ואינה בים. דתנו רבנן כל שיש ביבשה יש בים חוץ מן
החולדה : 3 **גם בני אדם. גם בני איש.** בני אברהם שנקרא האדם הגדול בענקים. בני ישמעאל ובני
קטורה. **גם בני איש.** בני נח שנקרא איש צדיק. **והגות לבי.** מחשבות לבי **תבונות** הם : 5
אטה למשל אזני. לדברי שנקראו משל הקדמוני. **אפתח** לכם **בכנור** את החידות. וזו היא
החידה. 6 **למה** אני צריך לירא **בימי רע.** ביום פקודת דיני' לפי שעון **עקביי יסובני** עוונות
שאני דש בעקביי. שאני מזלזל בהם שהם בעיני עבירו' קלות הן מרשיעות אותי בדין. וכל
שכן העמים 7 **הבוטחים** באמונה ומה בצע בממונם הלא 8 **אח** לא יוכל לפדות את אחיו
בממונו. לפי שאם באים איש לפדות אחיו 9 ויתייקר פדיון מכל הון. לפיכך על כרחך **חדל**
הוא **לעולם** מלפדותו 10 שיחיה לנצח **ולא יראה השחת. כי יראה חכמים ימותו** ואין
ניצולין מן המות לפיכך על כרחינו הוא חדל ליגע ולטרוח על פדיון אחיו. **חילם.** ממונם.
בחכמים נאמרה מיתה. ובכסיל ובער נאמרה אבידה שהגוף והנשמה אובדים 12 **קרבם
בתימו לעולם.** מחשבותם לבנות להם בתים שיתקיימו לעולם. **קראו בשמותם** את בתיהם.
שהם בונין למען יהיו להם לזיכרון כגון ניבראם שם העיר כשם בנו חנוך. אנטיוכס בנה
אנטוכיא. סליקוס בנה סליקיא. 14 לי שטות. **ואחריהם בפיהם ירצו סלה.** והבאים
אחריהם ידברו בהם ויספרו בפיהם מה אירע לראשונים. **ירצו** לשון הרצאת דברים.
ורבותינו פירשו **זה דרכם** של רשעים סופו לאיבוד אבל **כסל למו.** חלב יש למו על כסליהם
ומכסה את כליותם ואין יועצות אותו לשוב מרעתן. ושמא תאמר שכחה היא להם ששכחו
סופן למות ת"ל ואחריהם בפיהם ירצו. כלומ' יום אחריתם תמיד בפיהם ואין חרידים
ממנו : 15 **כצאן לשאול שתו.** כצאן המתאסף לדיר. גם הם **לשאול שתו** דגשות התי"יו במקום
תי"יו שניה לשאול שתתו. לשון שתותיה של שאול. למדריגה התחתונת. וכן שתו בשמים
פיהם. ולשונם הרע. **מות ירעם.** מלאך המות יאכלם. ואל תתמה על לשון אכילה שמצינו
במקום אחר יאכל בדי אכל בכור מות. **וירדו** בם **ישרים לבקר.** ליום הגאולה כשיזרח בוקרן של
ישרים והיו בודים בהם כמה שני ועשיתם רשעים וגו'. **וצורם לבלות שאול** צורתם של רשעים
תבלה את השאול גיהנם בלה והם אינם בלין : **מזבול לו.** מהיות להם מדור. והק' מוציא חמה
מנרתיקה ומלהטת אותם שני ולהט אותם היום הבא : 16 **אך אלקים יפדה נפשי.** אבל אני
שהטיתי אזן למשל אלקים יפדה את נפשי שלא אלך אל שאול. **כי יקחני** בחיי ללכת בדרכיו.
19 **כי נפשו בחייו יברך.** הרשע מברך נפשו בחיי ואומ' שלום עלי נפשי לא יאונך שום רע.
אבל אחרים אין אומרים עליו כן. **ויודוך כי תטיב לך.** ואתה אם תשמע לדברי הכל יודון כי
תיטיב לנפשך. ליי שר את דרכיך 20 **תבא עד דור אבותיו.** כשתשלים ימיך ותמות תבא
ותראה את דור הרשעים נידונין בגיהנם אשר **נצח לא יראו אור :** 21 **אדם ביקר לא יבין.** דרך
חיים נתונה לפניו שאם ילך בה הרי הוא נכבד ואינו מבין את הטוב :

נ 1 **אל אלקים** יי. ל'י האלקים ל'י שמו. **דבר ויקרא ארץ.** ול'י 2 **הופיע**
מציון שהוא **מכלל יופי. מכלל** שם דבר. פרמינט. ועל גאולת העתיד נתנבא. **ואל יחרש** על
דם עבדיו השפוך : 4 **יקרא אל השמים** לפקוד על שרי האומות שבמרום **ואל הארץ** לפקוד על
מלכי האדמה **לדין עמו:** לנקום נקמת עמו כמו כי ידין ל'י את עמו ודם עבדיו יקום : 5 **אספו
לי חסידי.** ועוד יקרא לשמים ולארץ שיאספו לו הגליות כעניין שני עורי צפון ובאי תימן :
כרתי ברית עלי זבח. שיקבלו התורה בברית וזבח כעניין שנאמ' הנה דם הברית אשר כרת
וגו'. 8 **לא על זבחיך אוכיחך.** אם אינך מביא לי זבחים ולא נגדי עולותיך תמיד. אינני שם
עיניי ולבי על כך : 9 **לא אקח מביתך פר.** לא שלך הם אלא שלי. **ממכלאותיך** הוא דיר הצאן.
כמו גזר ממכלא צאן : 10 **בהמות בהררי אלף.** הוא המתוקן לסעודת העתיד שהוא רועה אלף
הרים ליום ובכל יום הם צומחים 11 **וזיז שדי.** רמש השדה. זיז על שם שהם זזים ממקום
למקום. אישמומבמינט בל' עמד[י]. אני יודע את כולם : 13 **האוכל בשר** ופרים. לא אמרתי
לך זבח שאיני צריך לאכילה אלא נחת רוח לפני שאמרתי ונעשה רצוני 14 זבח לאלקים

תודה. התוודה על מעשיך ושוב אלי זהו זבח שאני נרציתי ללכת עמו : 19 **תצמיד מרמה.**
תרגיל אצלה רמיה לדבר רעה כו'. 14 זהו זבח שאני חפץ בו. ואחרכך **שלם לעליון נדריך.** כי
אז יַתַּקבלו לרצון : 16 **ותשא בריתי.** תורתי וַתִירץ עמו. נתרצתי ללכת עמו. 20 **בבן אַמך**
שאין לך וריב עמו שאינו יורש עמך. **דופי.** דבר גנאי. לדחות. לשון יַהָדפנו : 21 **דמיתי.** סבור
אתה שאהיה כמוך. להתרצות במעשיך הרעים : 23 **זובח תודה.** המביא לי זבח של תשובה
והודאה על עוונותיו הוא **יכבדני : ושם דרך.** השב לי בכל לב ושם לחוטאים לשוב אני
אראנו בישע רב :

נא 1 **חנני** 5 **וחטאתי נגדי תמיד.** מַתוֹך שאני מתחרט ודואג עליו נדמה לי
כאילו הוא כל שעה לפניי. לפיכך בידך אף מה שהרעתי לאוריה
לא חטאתי אלא לך. שהזהרת על הדבר : **למען תצדק בדברך.** כח היה בידי להתגבר על יצרי
אלא שַלא יאמרו העבד נצח רבו. שאמרתי לפניך בחנני ונסני ובחנתני ולא נַמצאתי שלם כדי
שתצדק אתה ולא אני : ד"א **למען תצדק בדברך.** אם תמחל לי תצדק בדינך. לנוכח כל
הרשעי' שאינן שבים אלא למודיך לומר אילו עַשינו תשובה לא הועלנו : 7 **הן בעון חוללתי**
ואיך לא אחטא. ועיקר יצירתי על ידי תשמיש הוא. שכמה עוונות באים על ידו. ד"א עיקר
יצירתי מזכר ונקיבה שכולם מלאי עון : יש מדרשים למקרא זה ואינן מתייישבין לפי עניין
המדבר במזמור : 8 **הן אמת חפצת.** והריני מודה על האמת כי חטאתי. **בטוחות.** אילו
הכליות שהן חלקות ובסתום חכמה תודיעני. ובלב שהוא סתום הודעתני חכמה להתוודות :
9 **תחטאני באזוב.** כמי שמטהר מצורע וטמא מת : 14 **השיבה לי ששון ישעך.** רוח הקודש
שנסתלקה מעלי. **נדיבה** לשון קצינות. 15 **אלמדה פושעים דרכיך.** ממני ילמדו וישובו אם
יראו שתתלה לי. 16 **הצילני מדמים.** שלא אמות בחרב על עונשו של אוריה שהרגתי. 17 **אדני**
שפתי תפתח. מחול לי ויהא לי פתחון פה להגיד תהילתך. 18 **כי לא תחפוץ זבח.** שאם תחפץ
אתננו לך : 20 **הטיבה** לבנות בית מקדשך בתוכה בימי שַלמה בני :

נב 3 **מה תתהלל** ותתפאר ברעה שאתה עושה אתה הגבור בתורה. **חסד**
אל כל היום להציל את הנרדף על ידך : ד"א **חסד אל כל היום.** ואם לא נתן לי יתנני אחרים :
4 **מלוטש.** מחודד. **עושה רמיה.** חותך הבשר עם השער : 7 **ויסחך.** ויעקרך **ושרשך.** ישרש
אחריך לעקור כל הַשרשים. אשרצינייר בלעז : 8 **ועליו ישחקו.** וזהו השחוק שיאמרו עליו 9
הנה זה **הגבר** אשר **לא** שם מבטחו בהק'. ראו מה עלתה בו : **יעוז בהוותו.** מתגבר היה
ברשעו. 10 **ואני** הנרדף עתה בידך אהיה **כזית רענן** בבניי ובני בניי **בבית** הק' : 11 **כי עשית**
כשתעשה לי זאת. וכלפי הק' אמר מקרא זה :

נג 1 **על מחלת** שם כלי שיר : ד"א על מחלתן של ישר' כשחרב הבית. וכבר
אמר מזמור אחר דוגמ' זה. אמר נבל בלבו כו'. המזמור הזה על חורבן הראשון. וזה על טיטוס בבית
שיני : 2 **אמר נבל בלבו.** כשנגזר הפרכות וחרבו דם אמי הרג את עצמו : 4 **כלו**
סג. לשון סיגים. **אין גם אחד** מכל חילו שמחה בידו. 5 **הלא** יש לידע לאוכל עמי כמאכל
לחם. וי"ל **לא קראו.** שסוף 6 שיפחדו שם פחד באחרית הימים **לא היה** זה כפחד הראשון
שאירע לבלשצר כי בגאולה זו **פיזר** הק' **עצמות חונך** החונים עלייך ירושלם שני המק בשרו
וגו'. **הבישות** אתה לי את אויביי כי מאסתם :

נד 3 **ובגבורתך** תדיננו. תנקום. כמו כי ידין את עמו. 7 **לשוררי**
לעוייני. לשון אשורנו ולא קרוב : **באמתך.** מתוך שאתה אמיתי וַאמרת ליפרע מהולכי רכיל
ורודפי הרג. לכך **המציתם :**

נה 3 **אריד** בשיחי. אתאונן בַצערי. כמו עוני ומרודי. ירדתי על ההרים : 4 **כי**
ימוטו עלי און. דואג וַאחיתופל מכריעים עלי עונות להורות שאני בן מות ומתירים את דמי :
5 **יחיל.** ידאג : 8 **הנה ארחיק** וגומ' 9 **יחישה מפלט לי.** אם היו לי כנפים הייתי מרחיק לנוד
וממהר להציל את נפשי מידם שהם **כרוח סועה.** עוקרת אילנות. כמו ויסע כעך. 10 **פלג**
לשונם. הבדילהן שלא ישמע אדם לשונם. **כי ראיתי חמס וריב** על ידם. 11 **יסובבוה.** החמס

והאון. 12 **הוות.** שבר. **תוך ומרמה.** לשון אונאה : 13 **כי לא אויב חרפני** מימיי שאושא
חרפתי שאתה מחרפני. לפי שאתה אדם גדול בתורה : 14 **אנוש כערכי.** חשוב <u>כמותי. מיודעי.</u>
כמו אלופי. לשון <u>ואדעך</u> בשם. ורביתיך : 15 **אשר יחדיו** היינו רגילים להמתיק **סוד** בתורה
ובבית אלקים היינו מהלכים **ברגש.** ברוב עם. בבתי מדרשי. 16 **מות עלימו.**
ישיא הק׳ עליהם את מלאך המות : **ישי.** יסכסך. מסית לשון השיאני ואוכל. **במגורם.**
במלונם. 18 **ערב ובקר וצהרים.** שחרית וערבית ומנחה. שלש תפילות : 19 **מקרב לי.** מן
המלחמה הבאה עלי. **כי ברבים** וגומ׳ כי זאת עשה לי בשביל הרבים שהן בעזרתי להתפלל
עלי. שני וכל ישר׳ ויהודה אוהבים את דוד : 20 **ישמע אל** לתפילותם של אותם רבים **ויענם**
המלך שהוא **יושב קדם. אשר אין חליפות למו.** לאותם הרשעים <u>הרודפים</u> אותי. אין נותנין
להם אף יום חליפות : אין חרידים מיום המיתה. 21 **שלח ידיו** זה הרשע אחיתופל **בשלמיו**
במי שהיה שלם ושלום עמו : **חלקו.** לשון חלקלקות. **מחמאות פיו.** לשון חמאה. והמ״ם
ראשונה יסוד נופל הוא כמ״ם של מעשר ומ״ם של מראה ומאמר : **וקרב לבו.** ולבו למלחמה :
<u>ו</u>**המה פתיחות.** מנחם פתר לשון חרבות. ואני אומר לשון קללה הוא בלשון ארמי כדאמרינן
כתב אמימר פתיחא עילויה. והוא שטר שמתא : 23 **יהבך.** משאך : רוח הקודש משיבה לו כן.
יכלכלך. יסבול משאך. לשון כילכול מתורגם בתרגום יוני׳ בר עזיאל מסובר : **מוט.** מעידת
רגל :

נו 1 **יונת אלם** רחוקים. כל עצמו אמר שהיה רחוק מארץ ישר׳ אצל
אכיש והיו אחיו של גלית מבקשים רשות מאכיש זה הלא זה זה מלך הארץ. והוא
היה ביניהם כיונה כונה אילמת : 2 **שאפני אנוש.** מצפים לבלעני. בלעו גולושיר כמ׳ שאפה רוח :
מרום. הק׳ שהוא מרום : 5 **באלקים אהלל דברו.** אף בשעה שהוא בא במדת הדין אהלל
דברו ואבטח בו : 6 **כל היום דברי יעצבו.** מעציבים אותי רודפיי עד שכל דברי פי עצב
וצעקה : 7 **יגורו יצפנו** המה אורבים ולנים במקום שהם מקום שאני אלך שם .ושומרים את
עקביי. טראצא בל׳ לרגלני ולהוליך את רודפיי שם. כל זה היה קובל על רשעי ישר׳ האורבים
לו ומאימתם ברח אצל אכיש. כשיודעים ומקום
דרך זאת ילך : 8 **על און פלט למו.** למצוא הצלה ועושר על דבר און ופשע ורשע : **פלט.** כמ׳
לפלט. **מצפים** שאומרים להרגני : 9 **נדי ספרתה.** ידעת מניין המקומות <u>שנד</u>דתי לברוח : **שים**
דמעתי בנאד שלך. ותהא שמורה לפניך : **הלא בספרתך.** הלא במנייניך תתנגה למנותה עם
שאר צרותייי : 11 **באלקים אהלל. בי״י אהלל.** על מדת הדין ועל מדת רחמים אהלל. 14 **באור**
החיים לשון ארץ ישראל :

נז 1 **למנצח** אל תשחת. כך כינה דוד המזמור הזה בשביל שהיה דוד קרוב
למות ויסד מזמור זה לאמר אל תשחת אותי י״י : 2 **חנני חנני.** שלא אהרג ולא איהרג. **עד**
יעבר הוות. עד תעבר הרעה : 4 **חרף שאפי.** יושיעני <u>מחרפת</u> שואפי האומר לבלעני : 5 **נפשי**
בתוך לבאים. אבנר ועמשא שהיו לבאים בתורה ואינם מוחים בשאול : **אשכבה לוהטים.**
אשכבה כלוהטים. בין הזיפים שלוהטים אחר יצר הרע ולשון הרע : 6 **רומה על השמים.**
הסתלק מן התחתונים שאינם כדיי לשרות ביניהם. ועל כל הארץ תתכבד בזו. 7 **כפף נפשי**
האויב **נפלו בתוכה.** סופו ליפול בתוכה : 8 **נכון לבי.** נאמן עמד במדת הדין ונאמן עמד במדת
הרחמים : 9 **עורה כבודי.** לא אישן שלש שעות כככבוד שאר מלכים : **עורה הנבל וכנור.** העירה
אותי אתה הנבל והכנור התלוי על מטתי פתוח לצד צפון. וכיון שמגיע חצות לילה רוח
צפונית מנשבת בו ודוד <u>עומד</u> ועוסק בתורה : **אעירה <u>שחר</u>.** אני מעורר את השחר. ואין השחר
מעוררני :

נח 1 **מכתם** שם נעימת שיר. 2 **האמנם אלם צדק תדברון** וגו׳. מזמור זה
אמר על שם שבא אל המעגל אשר שאול שוכב שם ולקח את החנית ואת הצפחת והלך לו
וקרא הלא תענה אבנר כלומ׳ הלא יש לך עתה להוכיח לשאול ולהראותו שעל חנם רודפני
שאילו רציתי הרגתיו. וכך אמר בשירו האמנם נאלם מפיכם הצדק שהיי לכם לדבר
המישרים שיש לכם לשפוט הצדק אשר תדברון : 3 **אף בלב עולות תפעלון.** ולא עוד אלא
שבלבבכם אתם חורשים רעה לפעול און וחמס. **עולות.** כמו עולות. כאשר יאמר משור

שוורים ומעיר עיירים. ושלשה עיירים להם שהן לשון עיר וקריה: **בארץ חמס ידיכם**
תפלסון. בתוך הארץ אתם מכריעים חמס ידכם. שהוא שוקל משקל רב: 4 **זרו רשעים**
מרחם. ממעי אמן הם נעשים זרים להק' כדרך שעשה עשו ויתרוצצו הבנים בקרבה. **זרו.**
נזרו כמו שמו שמם וימררוהו ורבו: רומו מעט. כולם לשון נפעלו: 5 **חמת למו.** ארס. יש
להם להרוג את הבריות כדמות ארס נחש. **כמו פתן חרש אשר יאטם אזנו:** הנחש כשהוא
מזקין נעשה חרש ואוטם את השנית בעפר שלא ישמע את הלחש שהחבר
משביעו שלא יזיק 6 **אשר לא ישמע** וגו'. מחובר במקרא שלפניו אוטם אזנו בשביל שלא
ישמע לקול מלחשיו: **חובר חברים** שיודע ללחש את הנחשים: 7 **מלתעות.** שינים הפנימיות
שקורין מישלרי"ש. הק' לנגדם כדי **שיתמוללו:** 9 **שבלול.** יש פותרין לימאצ"א ויש
פותרים מיישלי"ש. ויש פותרים כמ' שבולת מים: **תמס.** נמס והולך. תמ"ס. שם דבר הוא
והתי"ו בו יסוד נופל כמו ת"יו של תבל עשו: **נפל אשת.** טלפא בלע' שאין לה עינים. והיא
תנשמת דמתרגמין אשותא. כך פירשו רבותי'. ויש פותרים נפל של אשה: 10 **בטרם יבינו**
סירותיכם אטד בטרם ידעו קוצים רכים להיות אטדים קשים. עד שלא יגדלו בני הרשעים.
כמו חי כמו חרון. כלומר בגבורה ובחזק ובחרון יסערם הק' חי לשון גבור: 12 **ויאמר אדם**
אך פרי לצדיק. ואז תאמרו הבריות ודאי יש פירות ותשלום שכר במעשי הצדיקים. שנקם
האל נקמות. **יש אלקים.** דיין שופט ושעים **בארץ:**

נט 1 **אל תשחת** כך קרא שם המזמור על שם שהיה קרוב למות ולהיות
נשחת ומבקש רחמים על הדבר **וישמרו הבית.** כשאמרה להם מיכל חולה הוא והבריחתו
בלילה. 4 **יגורו עלי.** לנים בביתי לשמרני. 5 **בלי עון** לא חטאתי להם. **ויכוננו.** מזומנים
להרוג: 6 **הקיצה לפקוד כל הגוים.** את אלה הרשעים שפוט במשפט הגוים ועליהם **אל תחון:**
7 **ישובו לערב.** לא דיים מה שעשו ביום אלא אף לערב ישובו על רעתם לשמור שלא אברח
ואצא מן העיר. ומה עשו ביום הנה הם כל היום יביעו בפיהם לרגל עלי אל שאול. 8 **חרבות**
בשפתותיהם ואומרים בלבם מי ישמ' וגו' 9 **ואתה** יי' אשר **תלעג לכל גוים תשחק** גם לרשעים
הללו:

עוז 10 **אליך אשמרה.** עוזו ותוקפו של אויבי החזק עלי. אליך אשמורה
ואצפה לעזרני הימנו: 11 **יקדמני.** יקדים לי עזרתו קודם שתשלט בי יד שנאי: **יראני**
בשוררי מה שאני תאב לראות: 12 **אל תהרגם** שאין זו נקמה הנזכרת. **פן ישכחוה עמי.** כי
כל המתים משתכחים. אלא **הניעמו** מנכסיהם שיהו עניים והיא נקמה שתיזכר לאורך ימים.
13 **חטאת** של פיהם הוא **דבר שפתימו** ונלכדים בגאונם העניים הנרדפים על ידיהם מפני
האלה והכחש שהם מספרים. 14 **כלה** אותם בחמתך מלך השופט **וידעו כי** אתה **מושל**
ביעקב. 15 **וישובו לערב.** מחובר על מקרא העליון חטאת פימו הם מדברים ביום ולערב
שבים לארוב אותם שהלשינו עליהם. 16 **המה יניעון לאכול.** כאשר יעשון הכלבים כל הלילה
אם אינם שביעים שילינו מתוך שבעם וישנו 17 **ואני** כשאמלט מהם לבקר **אשיר עזך:**

ס 1 **על שושן** עדות מכתם לדוד ללמד. **מכתם לדוד** על עדותנו של סנהדרין
שנמשלו בשושנה שני שררך אגן וגו'. סוגה בשושנים. שנצרך שילמדוהו מה יעשה כשנלחם
עם ארם ושלח את יואב עליהם אמרו לו לא מבניו של יעקב אתם היכן הוא השבועה שנשבע
ללבן על הגל הזה. ולא ידע יואב מה להשיב בא לו אצל דוד אמ' לו כך אמרו לי בני ארם. באו
ושאלו את סנהדרין אמרו להם ולא הם עברו את השבועה שנ' מן ארם ינחני בלק מלך מואב
מהררי וגו'. ועוד כושן רשעתי' ארמי היה. **ויך יואב וישב את אדום** וגו'. שמונה עשר אלף
הכתובים במלכים. ובדברי הימים הרג אבישי פעם ראשונה ויואב שנים עשר אלף כשישב
מהכות את אדום: 2 **בהצותו.** כמ' בהצותם על יי': 3 **זנחתנו פרצתנו** הרבה צרות סבלנו בימי
השופטים מאויבינו סביב: **אנפת** קצפת עלינו. מעתה **תשוב** ברצונך לנו 4 **הרעשת** לנו ארצינו
בכמה גייסות פצמתה. שברתה אותה. ראיתי בדברי דונש שהוא לשון ערבי. אבל לא פירש
אותו. וביסודו של ר' משה הדרשן פירשו לשון קריעה וראיה הביא וקרא לו חלוני מתורגם
ופצים אך אני אומר ופצים שתירגם יונתן לשון יחלון "תיקון הוא ככל פתחים שיש לו
פצימין: **רפה שבריה.** לשון רפואה. ואף על פי שכתוב בה"י הרבה תיבות משמשות כן: **כי**

מטה. לשון שפלות: 5 **יין תרעלה** האוטם את הלב ועוטפו. רעל לשון עטיפה הוא כמ' והברושים הרעלו. ובלשון' משנה מדיות רעולות: 6 **נתת ליראיך נס.** נסיונות של צרות הרבה **להתנוסס** להיות מנוסים בהם אם יעמדו ביראתך: **מפני קושט.** לקשט מדותיך בעולם. כשנשתתן להם הטובה לא ידונו האומות אחריך אלא יקשטו ריביך ויאמרו יפה הטיב להם. כי הם עמדו לו בכמה נסיונות: 7 **יחלצון.** ינצלו מרעה. **הושיעה ימינך** אשר השיבותה אחור בהתחזק אויביהם עליהם: **וענני.** אם תענני יחלצו הם אני נלחם בשבילם. 8 **דבר בקדשו.** אשר אהיה מלך עליהם: **אעלוזה** בישועתו. **אחלקה שכם.** אחלק להם נכסי חלק בנכסי אויביהם. **ועמק סכות אמדד.** סוכות זה איני יודע מאיזו אומה היא. לא ידעתי שבאו לו ישר' כשנשסעו מרעמסס היכן הוא: 9 **לי גלעד.** למלוך עליהם. **מחוקקי.** שרים שלי: 10 **מואב סיר רחצי.** אשר ארחץ בהם כסיר של נחושת. המוכן לרחוץ בו. **עלי פלשת התרועעי.** התחברי על ממשלתי כי גת מארץ פלשתים וכן עזה. וכבשם דוד: 11 **מי יובילני** עתי **לעיר מצור** אם לא אתה תנצור ותעזור אותי. על מבצרי אדום. **מי יובילני** ומי ינחני עליהם. 12 **ולא תצא.** ואינך יוצא: 14 **יבוס.** ירמוס:

סא 3 **מקצה הארץ** אעפ"י שאני רחוק מאנשיי שאני משלח על אויביי למלחמה **אליך אקרא בעטוף לבי** עליהם. ועל מה אני קורא לך. **שתנחני בצור** שהוא רם וחזק ממני: 5 **אגורה באהלך עולמים.** זכני בעולם הזה ולעולם הבא 6 **נתת ירושת יראי שמך.** החזרת ערי ירושתם על ידי: 7 **ימים על ימי מלך תוסיף.** אם נגזר עלי למות בחור הוסף ימים על ימי עד ששנותיי יהיו שבעים שנה כמ' שנות דור ודור. 8 **ישב** המלך **לעולם לפני אלקים.** **חסד ואמת** שהוא עוסק בהם יהו **מזמנים** לנצרו: **מן.** בהזמנה כמו וימן ל"י קיקיון: 9 **כן אזמרה.** כמו **שתטיב** לי כך אזמרה שמך. להיותי משלם נדריי יום יום:

סב 1 **על ידותון** שם כלי **שיר.** ומדרש אגדה על הדתות ועל הדינין הנגזרים על ישר' מאויביהם. 2 **דומיה נפשי.** כמו דום ל"י והתחולל לו: 3 **ולא אמוט רבה.** מטות גדולה. ומדרש אגד' רבה גיהנם: 4 **תהותתו.** מנחם פירשו מגזירת התיו לאכלה ויתא ראשי עם. **עד אנה תהותתו על איש** ולי נראה שיש שלש לפותרני לשני הוות הוות ה"י ת"יו יסוד כאשר יאמר מן מת מות ומן התהוונת ולשו' רבים הוות ולשון מחשבת שבר ותרמית. **כקיר נטוי.** המוכן ליטול על בני אדם. 5 **משאתו.** לפי שאתם יגורים מן ה**א**דם שמא ימלוך וישלם לכם גמולכם: יעצתם להדיח עליו הרעה הזאת שהק' **בפיו** של כל אחד ואחד מהם **יברכו ובקרבם יקללו סלה:** 10 **אך הבל בני אדם** ואל תיראו מהם מאחר שהק' **מחסה לנו: במאזנים לעלות.** אם באו לעלות במאזנים הם והבל שוים. כן **פשוטו.** ומדרשו לענין הזוגות. 11 **חיל כי ינוב.** אם תראו רשעים **שממונם** מצליח וגדל אל תשיתו לב. **חיל.** ממון. **ינוב.** יצמח. לשון **תנובה:** 12 **אחת דבר אלקים** ששמעתי מתוכה **שתים.** ומה הן השתים. 13 **לשלם לאיש כמעשהו.** והשני כי **לך ה' החסד.** ומאיזה דבור שמענום ממנו שהק' **פוקד** עוונות ונוצר חסד שני פוקד עון אבות וגו'. וכן בטוח אני שישלם שכר טוב לצדיקים ופורענות לרשעים זו **למדתי** מיסודו של ר' משה הדרשן. ורבותי' דרשוהו בזכור ושמור בדיבור אחד נאמרו: 13 **לך ל'י החסד.** ומהו החסד. **כי אתה תשלם לאיש כמעשהו.** ולא מעשהו ממש. אלא מקצתו כענין שני כי אתה חשכת למטה מעוונינו. כן נדרש בהגדת תילים. ויש לפותרו כי לך ל'י חסד כי יש בידך לשלם לשון לאיש כמעשהו:

סג 1 **במדבר** יהודה. בורח מפני שאול. 2 **כמה לך בשרי.** לשון תאוה. ואין לו דמיון **בארץ צייה.** במדבר: 3 **כן בקדש חזיתיך** וגו'. כמו כאשר צמאתי לראות עזך וכבודך כדרך **שחזיתיך** במקדש. משכל שילה תשבע נפשי במראית עוזך וכבודך: 9 **בי תמכה ימינך.** שלא אפול: 10 **והמה** אויבי. **לשואה יבקשו נפשי.** באים עליו במארב ביום אפילה שלא ארגיש: 11 **יגירוהו על ידי חרב.** לשון גרירה. כמו המוגרים במורד: פרץ נחל מעם גר. 12 **והמלך ישמח.** על עצמו היה אומר. שהרי כבר היה נמשח: **יתהלל כל הנשבע בו.** כשיראו שתושיעני **יתהללו** ויתפארו כל הנדבקים בך ונשבעים בשמך: **כי יסכר.** יסתם כמו ויסכרו מעינות תהום

סד 2 **שמע** אלקים קולי **בשיחי.** מזמור זה דרשוהו בעלי אגדת תילים על דניאל שהושלך לגוב אריות. ויפה נופל כל לשון הַמזמור על האגדה. צפה דוד ברוח הקודש כל המאורע והתפלל עליו שדניאל מזרעו היה שנאמ' לחזקיה ומבניך אשר תוליד והיו סריסים בהיכל מלך בבל. אילו **חנניה** מישאל ועזריה : אילו האחשדרפנים שנתייעצו עליו שני אדיין סרכיא ואחשדרפניא הוו בען עילוי לאשכחא לדניאל וגו' . 3 **מרגשת פועלי און.** שהם מתרגשים לבקש לו עלילות מות. דכת' ארגישו על מלכי. 4 **דרכו חיצם.** הוא לשונם הרע : 5 **לירות במסתרים** הם יורו בחציהם 6 **יספרו לטמון מוקשים.** ידברו אל המלך בערמה דברים טמונים שאפי' המלך לא יבין למה היו עושי' כן. והם היו מתכוונים לטמון מוקשים לדניאל להלוך בהם. שאמרו לדריוש אתייעטו כל סרכי מלכותא לקיימא קיים מלכותא שלא יתפלל אדם תפילה לפני שום אלוק' חוץ ממך ל' יום. 7 **יחפשו עולות.** מבקשים עלילות כעניין שני הוו בעו עילוי להשכחא לדניאל. **טמנו** בלבם ולא גילו את **חופש** העלילות **המחופש** על ידם **וקרב** מחשבותם ועומק לבם. **וקרב איש** איש מהם. כל אחד טמן מחשבת : 8 **ויורם אלקים.** יורה אותם לגוב אריות. כדכת' ואמר מלכא גוברייא אילך די אכלו קורצוהי די דניאל ולגוב אריאותה רמוהי . 9 **ויכשילוהו עלימו לשונם.** הכשלון שדמו להכשיל עלימו נַהפך לשונם : **יתנודדו** בראשם. להניע בראשם ולשחק עליהם **כל ראה בם** : 11 **ישמח צדיק.** דניאל. **ויתהללו כל ישרי לב.** יתהללו על יושר לבם וישתבחו בעצמם כי בטוחים הם שהק' בעזרתם

סה 2 **לך דומיה** תהלה. השתיקה תהלה לך. לפי שאין קץ לשבחך. וַהמרבה בשבחך אינו אלא כגורע : **אלקים בציון.** אלקים השוכן בתוכם. ד"א **לך דומיה תהילה אלקים בציון** אַת אשר דוממת והחרשת על מַה שעשו אויביך בציון. תהילה היא שהיכולת בידו להנקם ואתה מאריך אף : 5 **אשרי מי אשר תבחר ותקרב.** אשר **ישכון בחצריך** : 6 **נוראות תעננו.** בצדק תעננו לעשות נוראות בגוים. 8 **משביח.** משפיל. וכן וחכם באחור ישבחנה : 9 **מוצאי בקר וערב תרנין** לך את הבריות יושבי הקצוות : בבקר יוצר המאורות. ובערב מעריב ערבי' : 10 **פקדת הארץ.** כשאתה חפץ להטיב אתה פוקד הארץ ומשקה אותה : **רבת תעשרנה.** הרבה אתה מעשרה מפלג שלך שהוא מלא מים. ותכין בו דגנם של יושבי הקצוות. כי בכן אַתה מכין אותה : 11 **ותלמיה** הם שורות המחרישה. **רווה.** כמו לרווה : **נחת גדודיה.** להניח גדודיה לעשות נחת לבריות אתה **ממוגגה** ברביבים של מטר. **תמוגגנה.** לשון המסה : 12 **עטרת שנת טובתך.** ועל ידי הגשמים אתה מעטר בכל טוב אמנה שנה שאתה חפץ להטיב : **ומעגליך.** הם השמים שהן אבק רגליך : **ירעפון.** ייטיפון. דָשֵן. שומן : 13 **ירעפו** השמים **בנאות המדבר** : 14 **לבשו כרים הצאן.** יתלבשו השרון ממערבה מן הצאן הבאים לרעות את הדשא אשר הצמיח המטר : **ועמקים יעטפו בר.** על ידי המטר. ואז **יתרועעו** הבריות וישירו :

סו 1 **הריעו** לאלקים כל הארץ. 5 **נורא עלילה.** יראוי על בני אדם פן ימצא להם פשע. כי כל מעשיהם גלויים לו : 6 **הפך ים ליבשה.** ים סוף. 7 **אל ירומו** אל תהי ידם רמה : 8 **ברכו עמים** אלקים על נפלאותיו 9 **שהוא שם בחיים נפשנו** ואינכם יכולים להשמיד אותנו : 10 **כי בחנתנו** בצרה גדולה. 11 **מועקה** לשון מסגר. וכבל הַמעיק והמצקיף : 12 **הרכבת אנוש לראשינו.** מלכי כל אומה ואומה : 13 **אבא ביתך.** בבנותינו בית המקדש נשלם נדרנו בגולה : 15 **מחים.** שמינים. לשון מוח : 16 **כל יראי אלקים** הם הגרים שיתגיירו : 17 **אליו פי קראתי.** כשהייני בגולה קראנוהו וסיפרנו רוממותו בלשוננו : **ורומם.** כמו ונתרומם : 18 **און אם ראיתי בלבי** וגו' . לא פעל עמנו כחטאותינו עשה עמנו כלא רואה וכלא שומע און שבלבנו : 19 **אכן** באמת יש לדעת 20 **אשר לא הסיר תפילתי** מלפניו **וחסדו** לא הסיר **מאתי** :

סז 2 **אלקים** יחננו ויברכנו. יאר פניו להראות פנים שוחקות לתת טל ומטר : 3 **לדעת בארץ דרכך** ידעו שמדתך להיטיב. ועל זה 4 **יודך** 5 **וישמחו וירננו. כי תשפוט** העולם במישור לזכות :

סח 2 **יקום** אלקים ויפוצו אויביך. עשו וכיוצא בו : 3 **כהנדוף** כהתנדף : כאשר
יתנדף העשן כן **תדפם** : 4 **וישישו בשמחה.** וזו היא המשוש והשמחה. וכן יאמרו 5 **שירו**
לאלקים: סלו. לשון שבח. וכן לא תסולה בכתם אופיר. וכן המסולאים בפז. **ביה שמו.** בשמו
שהוא יק׳. לשון **יראה** כדמתרגמי׳ דחילא׳ במימר דחילא דתקיף עלמא. וכן ביה צור עולמי׳
ארי בכן תתקפון במימר דחילא דתקיף עלמא. ואומ׳ המשורר **שבח** מלפניו וגורו מפניו
ועלזו. נחזו דוגמת האמור במקום אחר וגילו ברעדה : 6 **אבי יתומים** שנעשה אב לישרי שהם יתומים שני יתומים
היינו אב ואין אב : **ודין אלמנות.** שעושה משפטה של ירושלי׳ שני בה היתה כאלמנה : 7 **מושיב**
יחידי׳ ביתה. ישר׳ שהיו מפוזרים כינסם יחד איש איש מנדחו והושיבם בית שלום וכניסיא
שלימה : **מוציא אסירים בכושרות.** הוציא את ישר׳ ממצרים בחדש שהוא כשר להולכי
דרכים לא חמה ולא צנה : **אך סוררים.** מצרים. **שכנו צחיחה.** נשארה ארצם ציה וצמא : 9
זה סיני. גם הוא רעש : **מפני יי׳ אלקי ישראל :** 10 **גשם נדבות תניף** עוד זאת עשית אם
נצרכו לגשמים הניפות והטלת לנו גשמי נדבה תמיד : **נחלתך ונלאה אתה כוננת.** כשהייתה
נחלתך ארצך נלאה וצמאה למטר אתה כוננת בה : 11 **חיתך ישבו בה.** כמי׳ ואספו פלשתים
לחיה : ד״א כנסת ישר׳ קרויה בהמתו וחיתו של הקי׳ היא : **תכין בטובתך.** כשיצאו ישר׳
ממצרים הסיבותם ארבעים שנה במדבר. לפי שעמדו כנענים וגידעו את האילנות. ובתוך כך
שהלכו ישר׳ במדבר עמדו ותקנו הכל : 12 **יי׳ יתן אומר המבשרות הצבא רב.** עוד הוא ישמע
בקול **להשמיע** צבאות הגוים הרבים ומהו האומר 13 **מלכי צבאות ידדון ידדון.** כענינו שני
יתנדדו ויושלכו מתוך ארץ ישר׳ וכנסת ישר׳ שהיא **נות בית תחלק** את **שללכם.** כענינו שני
והיא סחרה ואתגננה : 14 **אם תשכבון בין שפתים** וגו׳. כל זה יאמר להם אם אתם שכבתם
בין התחומים והתעגנתם בתענוגים. זאת יונתני. כנסיתי. **כנפיה נחפה בכסף.** וגו׳. ומהו
הכסף והחרוץ. 15 **בפרש שדי** וגו׳. כשפירש הקי׳ תורתו לפניהם אשר המלכים נשלגים
ומתלבנים בה בארץ חשך וצלמות אז נחפה כנפיה בכסף. בכספה וחמדתה של תורה ומצות :
14 **כנפי יונה.** פלומש בלי׳. **ואברותיה.** כנפיה שמעופפות בהן : **בירקרק חרוץ.** פי׳ דונש בן
לברט החרוץ הוא הזהב אשר יובא מארץ החוילה ומארץ כוש. זהב טוב מאד מאד לא הוא
ירוק ולא הוא אדום. ולכך קוראו ירקרק כמו לבן באדמדם לא אדום ולא לבן לכך נכפל
ירקרק אדמדם : 15 **מלכים.** אילו תלמידי חכמים שני בתורה בי מלכים ימלוכו. **בפרש** לשוי
ופרשו **השמלה.** בוררין את הדבר כשמלה חדשה : 16 **הר אלקים. הר בשן.** והיכן פירשנו בהר
סיני שהוא הר אלקים. וסמוך לבשן בעבר הירדן : **הר גבנונים.** הר המיוחד בהרים : **גבנוני׳.**
לשון כל דבר גבוה קרוי גב הרים על שם גובהו כמי׳ ותבני לך גב. 17 **למה תרצדון.** כל זה
מוסב על יי׳ יתן אומ׳ אומ׳ עוד יאמר להם למה תרצדון הרים גבנונים למה תארובו הרים גבוהים
להשחית את ההר אשר **חמד האלקים לשבתו** הוא הר הבית. **אף** הוא **לנצח ישכון** שם.
קדושתו **קדושת** עולם משנבחר לשבתו לא שרת שכינתו במקום אחר : **תרצדון.** ראיתי
ביסודו של ר׳ משה הדרשן רצד הוא מארב בלשון ערבי אבל מנחם פתר **תרצדון** כמ׳ תרקדון.
אף אותו לשון נופל על השיטה הזאת : 18 **רכב אלקים רבותים** וגו׳. עוד זאת מוסב על יי׳
יתן אומר המבשרו וגו׳. להזכיר חיבת עצמו אף כשנגלה רכב אלקים רבותים של אלפים
שאנני. שננים מלכים חדים. וי׳י׳ היה ביניהם **בסיני בקודש:** אף שם 19 **עלית** אתה נגיד
עמי משה בן עמרם. **ושבית** את התורה. **ולקחת מתנות** מן **העליונים** לתתם לבני אדם. **אף**
סוררים לשכון יק׳. אף עוד גרמת ששכן הקי׳ במשכן בתוך עם שהיו סוררים וממרים
ומקציפין אותו : 20 **ברוך י׳י.** זה מן השיר האמור למעל׳. שירו לאלקים. **יעמוס לנו.** יתן לנו
ישועות רבות. מלוא עומס כאשר נוכל שאת : 21 **האל לנו למושעות.** אלקים הוא מושיע לנו.
ולפנינו יש הרבה תוצאות מיני מות. תוצאות ורכבי מות : 22 **אך** לא עלינו נותנם. אבל **ימחץ**
בהם **ראש אויביו קדקד שיער.** קדקד של עשו איש איש שעיר. **המתהלך** תמיד **באשמיו** ואינו
חוזר מרעתו. 23 **אמר י׳י מבשן אשיב** כי כן הבטיח להשיב אותנו מתוך אבירי בשן ומאי׳
הים : 24 **למען תמחץ רגליך.** כשישמחו את ראש האויב. תהא רגלינו בוקעות בדמים. **תמחץ**
לשוי בוקע בתוך הים. כמו מחצה וחלפה רקתו. כמו ודגרה ובקעה. ולשון משנה הוא. והיו
עולי רגלים בוקעין עד ארכובותיהם בדם. ד״א **תמחץ** כלי ששואבין בו יין הבור מחץ שמו.
במסי׳ ע״ז. ולשון **כלבך מדם האויבים. מנהו** תהא פרנסתו כדאמ׳ מאי׳ משמע דהאי מן

לַישְׁנָא דמזוני הוא כדכתי' אשר מנה את מאכלכם וגו'. 25 **רָאוּ הֲלִיכוֹתֶיךָ אֱלֹקִים.** לאילו נאה
לך להושיע. שֶׁרָאוּ הליכותיך בקדושתך בים. 26 **קִדְּמוּ שָׁרִים** לשורר לפניך שירת הים
וְאחריהם שבחו הנּוֹגְנִים אילו המלכים. **בְּתוֹךְ עֲלָמוֹת תּוֹפֵפוֹת.** עם מרים ונערותיה שלקחה
את התוף בידה ואמרו בשבחו 27 **בְּמַקְהֵלוֹת בָּרְכוּ אֱלֹקִים. מְקוֹר יִשְׂרָ'** אף עוברים ממעי
אמן : 28 **שָׁם בִּנְיָמִן צָעִיר. רֹדֵם.** נעשה רודה עליהן : רוֹדֵם. כמו רודֶם. ומשם זכה להיות להן
מלך לפי שירד תחילה בים וכן אמ' לו שמואל לשאול הלא אם קטן בעיניך ראש שבטי ישר'
אתה. ותיי' יו' שיבטא דבנימין עבר בימא בריש כל שבטיא : **שָׂרֵי יְהוּדָה רִגְמָתָם.** מתקנאים
בהם וזורקין אבנים. וכן **שָׂרֵי זְבֻלוּן** וְנַפְתָּלִי : רִגְמָתָם רקמתם. לשון ארגמן. כך חבר מנחם : 29 **צַוֵּה אֱלֹקִים עֻזֶּ** : ד"א רִגְמָתָם
לשו' רקמתם. לשון ארגמן. כך חבר מנחם : **עֻזָּה אֱלֹקִים.** עכשיו חוזר המשורר לִתְפִלָּתוֹ
שהתפלל יקום אלקים ויפוצו אויביו. **עֻזָּה אֱלֹקִים** והתגבר אשר כל אלה פעלת לנו. 30
וּמֵהֵיכָלְךָ עַל יְרוּשָׁלַ וגו'. וממה שיראו הַמְּלָכִים כבוד היכלך אשר על יְרוּשָׁלַ לך
דורון ושיי' : 31 **גְּעַר חַיַּת קָנֶה.** הוא עשו הנמשל כחזיר היער הדר בין הקנים : **עֲדַת אַבִּירִים**
בְּעֶגְלֵי עַמִּים. עד ששמנו ועשתו כפירים אבירים בתוך שאר אומות שאינם אלא כעגלים
לנגדם : **מִתְרַפֵּס בְּרַצֵּי כָסֶף.** אינם מתרצים לכל אדם אלא אם כן מרצה להם מעות : פִּזַּר
עַמִּים. פיזרון השבטים : כד"א אף חֹבֵב עמים. ותמיד **קְרָבוֹת יֶחְפָּצוּ.** חפצים להלחם בנו : 32
יֶאֱתָיוּ חַשְׁמַנִּים ואז כשתחריב עשו ויקום מלך המשיח יביאו לך דורונות ממצרים ומכוש :
מנחם פי' חשמנים שם מדינה. יושבי חשמונה. שם מדינה והפותרים פותרי' אותו לשון
דורון. 33 **שִׁירוּ לֵאלֹקִים.** שהראה את גודלו וגאל את עמו : 34 **הֵן יִתֵּן.** הן נותן. ורבותינו
דָּרְשׁוּ כל המזמור עד ברוך יי' יום יום על מתן תורה : וחיתך ישבו בה. ואני אין לבי מתיישב
לומ' ישבו בה בלשון נתיישבו בתורה : והֵהר חֶמֶד אלקים לשבתו. אין לבי מתיישב לדורשו
על הר סיני. שהרי לא לשבתו חמדו. ולא לשכון בו לנצח. וכאן כתוב ישכון לנצח. וכן מלכי
צבאות פי' כל מלאכי צבאות. ואין זה לשון המקרא. 36 **נוֹרָא אֱלֹקִים מִמִּקְדָּשֶׁיךָ.** ממה
שהחריבתו אתה יראוי שאומ' אם למקדשו לא נשא פנים קל וחומר לרשעי האומות :

סט 1 **עַל שׁוֹשַׁנִּים** על ישר' שהם שושנים בין החוחים שהחוחים מנקבין
אותם והתפלל עֲלֵיהֶם. 2 **כִּי בָאוּ מַיִם.** האומות. 3 **בִּיוֵן מְצוּלָה.** בבוץ ובטיט של מצולה :
שִׁבֹּלֶת מים. הוא שטף חוזק הנהר פיל בלעז : 4 **נָחַר** יבש. כמו ועצמי חרה מני חורב : **כָּלוּ**
עֵינַי. כל תוחלת ממושכה קרוייה כליון עינים. כמ' עינינו מצפות וכלות אליהם כל היום.
מכלות עינים. ועיני רשעים תכלינה. 5 **אֹיְבַי שֶׁקֶר** שנאים אותי על שאין אני רודף אחר שקר
שלהם לתפוש טעותם. **אָז יָשִׁיב** כשהן נאספים עלי אני מחשד אותם בממון שלא גזלתי
מהם : 7 **אַל יֵבֹשׁוּ בִּי קֹוֶיךָ.** אל תניחני בידם פן יבושו קוֹיך במה שמאורע בי. ויאמרו הלא
כה אירע למי שהיה תוחה קוה בהקי' : 9 **לְאֶחָי.** לעשו : 10 **קִנְאַת בֵּיתְךָ.** ראו החיבה שהנהגת בו בעוד
ביתך קיים ונתקנאו בי : 11 **וַתְּהִי לַחֲרָפוֹת לִי.** מה שאני בוכה ומתפלל ומתענה לפניך הם
מתלוצצים עלי : 14 **וַאֲנִי תְפִלָּתִי לְךָ.** יהי תפילתי עת רצון : 16 **וְאַל תֶּאְטַר עָלַי.** אל תסגור
עלי. **בְּאֵר פִּיהָ** של צרה נכרייה זו שפותחת את פיה לבלעני : תֶּאְטַר. כמ' אטר יד ימינו סגור יד
ימינו שאינו מִשְׁתַּמֵּשׁ בה. 19 **קָרְבָה אֶל נַפְשִׁי** קרב אל נפשי : **גְּאָלָה.** גאל אותה : 21 **וָאֲנוּשָׁה.**
ואאנש. ואחלה. כמ' כי אנושה מכותיה. וכמו ויאנש הילד דבר שבע. ואם תאמר היאך אי"לף
זו מְשַׁמֶּשֶׁת שורש ומשמשת שימוש המיסב הדבור אל המדבר. כך דרך תיבה שתחילתה
אי"לף כגון ואהב את יעקב. הרי היא כמ' אאהב. וכמ' אסף כל. כמ' אאסף :
לָנוֹד שיבאו לי אוהבים לנוד לי ולנחמני : 22 **בְּבָרוּתִי.** בסעודתי. כמו תבֵיי נא תָמָר אחותי
ואברה מידה : 25 **וְלִשְׁלוֹמִי'** כשיִּקָּווּ לשלומים הנה שלומם למוקש. 27 **כִּי אֵת הַעֲם אֲשֶׁר**
הִכִּיתָ אתה רוֹדָפוּ. אתה קצפת מעט. והם עזרו לרעה : **וְאֶל מַכְאוֹב חֲלָלֶיךָ יְסַפֵּרוּ** דבריהם
לבא בעצה נשחיתי בהיותם כואבים. 32 **וְתִיטַב** הילולי **מִשּׁוֹר פָּר.** הוא שור שהקריב אדם
הראשון שנברא בקומתו ובצביונו ובו ביום שנברא הביאו. שהשור בן יומו קרוי שור שנ'
שור או כשב או עז כי יולד. בו ביום נדמה לפר שהוא בן שלש שנים : **מַקְרִן מַפְרִיס.** קרנותיו
קדמו לפרסותיו שהרי בקומתו ובקרנותיו נברא. וראשו יצא מן הארץ תחילה כדרך כל
הנולדים הוצאיָתו הָאָרֶץ. נמצאו קרניו קֻדְמוֹת לרגליים :

ע 1 **למנצח** לדוד **להזכיר.** לשון תפילה כמו ואנחנו בשם י"י אֱלֹקינו נזכיר.
וכן בדברי הימים להזכיר ולהודות לַי"י. ובמדרש תילים משל למלך שכעס על צאנו
וסתר את הדיר והוציא את הצאן ואת הרועה. אחר זמן החזיר את הצאן ואת הרועה לא
הזכיר ובנה את הדיר. אמ' הרועה הרי הצאן מֻחֲזָר והדיר בנוי. ואני איני נזכר כך למעלה
מן העניין נאמ' כי אלקים יושיע ציון ואוהבי שמו ישכנו בה הרי הדיר הצאן בנוי והצאן כנוס
והרועה לא נזכר. לכך נאמ' לדוד להזכיר אלקים להצילני : 4 **ישובו על עקב בושתם.** מַדָה
במדה כמו שעשו לי **על עקב** באותו מעגל עצמו אינשיש טראצש : **האמרים** לי. עלי. **האח**
האח. לשון חדוה בראותו באויבנו כרצונו : 6 **חושה לי** לעזור :

עא 3 **בך י"י חסיתי** לבא תמיד באותו מעון. להנצל בתוכו מן הרודף.
צוית להושיעני. פעמים רבות הושעתני על ידי שלוחיך : 4 **וחומץ.** כמו חומס וכן אשרו
חמוץ. נגזל 6 **אתה גוזי.** גוחי. אתה מוציאי ומעבירי כמ' ויגז שלום. וכמ' כי גז חיש
ונעופה. 7 **כמופת הייתי לרבים** רבים ראו צָרוֹתי ודאגו פן תקראם דוגמתם צרתי. פן אהיה
להם לאות כאשר הוקרה לזה כן יקרה לנו כעניין שנא' והיה יחזקאל לכם לאות ולמופת 9
לעת זקנה. אם זקנתי בחטאים כלומ' שחטאתי הרבה : 10 **כי אמרו אויבי לי ונועצו יחדו**
11 **לאמר אלקים** עזבו ואין אנו נענשים עליו שכבר נכשל בעבירו. 14 **ואני תמיד איחל**
לתשועתך. **וכשתושיעיני** אוסיף על כל תהילותיך. 15 **לא ידעתי ספרות** של צדקות
ותשועות שעשית עמדי. 16 **אבוא בגבורות.** להודות ולהלל. 18 **לכל יבוא גבורתך.** לכל אשר
יבא אצלי אגיד גבורתך. 19 **וצדקתך אלקים** אשר היא עד **עד מרום.** שני מקראות הללו
מחוברים על 18 **אגיד זרועך לדור** : 23 **תרננה שפתי.** עם זמר קול הכנור כשאזמרה לך
בכנור :

עב 1 **לשלמה** על שלמה בנו התפלל תפילה זו שצפה ברוח הקודש שהוא
עתיד לשאול מאת הק' לב להבין לשמוע משפט : **משפטיך.** חכמת דיניך שצוית בתור'
וצדקתך לצדק את הדין : **מלך ובן מלך** שניהם בשלמה אמורים : ד"א **משפטיך למלך.**
הייסורין יהו כלים בי. **ובן מלך** עשה צדקה לבני שיהא שלום בימיו : 3 **ישאו הרים** בימיו **שלום**
לעם. ומהו שלום שההרים נושאים כשהן עושין פירות אין עין הבריות צרה וקורא אִיש
לרעהו אל תחת גפן ואל תחת תאינה : **וגבעות בצדקה.** וגבעות ישאו להם שלום בשביל
הצדקה שיעשה : ד"א **ישאו הרים.** שרים. וכן גבעות. אז ייראוך עם שמש. כמו שני אשא עיני אל ההרים 5
ייראוך עם שמש. כשיהיה לו שלום והשרים מביאין לו דורון ונותנין לו מַס. אז **ייראוך**
עם שמש. אז ישכימו את תפילתם עם הנץ החמה : 5 **לפני ירח.** לפני הלילה יקדימו תפילת
ערבית ואין ביטול מנחה : ד"א **ייראוך עם שמש.** ממנו ילמדו ישר' ליראה אותך כל ימי
השמש והירח לדור דורים. בעוד שהירח קיים והם לפניו. והרבה יש בלשון
משנה לפני הבית ושלא בפני הבית : **דור דורים** לעולם : 6 **ירד כמטר על גז.** ירד דברו על
עמד ובתוך לבם כמטר היורד על ירק הגזוז שהוא צריך למטר שגזזוהו כעניין שני דורים והנה
דורים. **ולפני ירח.** בעוד שהירח קיים והם לפניו. והרבה יש בלשון משנה לפני הבית ושלא
בפני הבית : **דור דורים** לעולם : 6 **ירד כמטר על גז.** ירד דברו על עמד ובתוך לבם כמטר
היורד על ירק הגזוז שהוא צריך למטר שגזזוהו כעניין שני לקש אחר גזי המלך :
זרזיף ארץ. לשון טיפים הוא בלשון ארמי. במס' יומא הוו מטו זרזיפי דַמַיא : 7 **יפרח**
בימיו צדיק. ישר'. **ורוב שלום** יפרח בימיו. ויהא שלום זה ארוך עד לא עולם. וכל תפילה זו
נתקיימה חוץ מדבר זה. לפי ששלמה חטא לא נמשכה מלכותו נמסרה לדוד על
תנאי אם ישמרו בניך בריתי. ישר' פרחו בימיו שנאמ' ישר' ויהוד' רבים כחול הים. ורוב
שלום היה בימיו שני וישב יהודה וישראל לבטח איש תחת גפנו וגו'. כל ימי שְׁלֹמֹה 8 **וירד מים**
ועד ים. כל ארץ יִשׂר' מים סוף ועד ים פלשתים **ומנהר עד אפסי ארץ.** כי הוא רודה בכל
עבר הנהר וגו' : 9 **ציים.** כתות של שרים כדמתרגמי' וצים מיד כתים. וסיע' יסתרון : 10
מלכי תרשיש ואיים מנחה ישיבו. כי אני תרשיש למלך בים אחת לשלש שנים תבוא אני
תרשיש. **מלכי שבא.** מלכת שבא. דורון. **אשכר.** 11 **כל גוים יעבדוהו.** וכל הארץ מביאים
מנחה לשלמה והמה מביאים איש מנחתו : 14 **מתוך ומחמס** ממכות ומגזל. **יגאל נפשם.**

על ידי משפט וצדקה אשר יעשה בהם. 15 ויחי שלמה ויתן לו הק' מזהב שבא. וכן היתה
לו. גם עושר גם כבוד אשר לא היה כמוך וגו' : ויתפלל בעדו תמיד וגו'. היא התפילה היא
הברכה. כשהק' אומ' לו לאדם ברוך תהיה בלשון תפילה הוא. 16 פיסת בר. לשון פסיון.
תוספת ורבוי ורבותי' פירשו בלשון גלוסקאות לימות המשיח. ד"א פיסת בר. לשון רצון כמ'
פיוס שהבריות מתפייסים ומתרצי' מאת הק' כשנותן שלום ושובע בעולם : ירעש כלבנון
פריו. חטני גסין כפריות האילן וככליות של שור שהיו בימי שמעון בן שטח : ויציצו
ישר' מעיר : מתוך ירושלם כעשב הארץ 17 יהי שמו של שלמה נזכר לעולם בעושרו
ובחכמתו. לפני שמש ינון שמו. כל ימי השמש יגדל שמו : ינון. לשון מלכות ושררה. כמ'
ואחריתו יהי מנון : ולניני. השליט על נכסיי אחרי : אמרו בלבם נינים יחד. מלכיהם יחד :
ויתברכו בו. אדם אומר לבנו תהא חכם ועשיר כשלמה : 18 ברוך י'י העושה נפלאות
גדולות ברדת האש מן השמים על ידי שלמה בני :

20 כלו תפילות דוד בן ישי : רבותי' דרשו כלו כל אילו
תפילות בן דוד. לכלול כל הספר על שם דוד. ואף מה שאמרו בני קרח ועשרה זקנים על
שם שהוא נקרא נעים זמירות ישר'. ויש לפתור כלו נסתיימו. כמו רומו מעט. שומו שמים.
ואם כן הוא למה לא נכתב המזמור במקומו ואין מוקדם ומאוחר בספר. ונראין הדברים
שלעת זקנותו כשהמליך את שלמה בנו אמרו :

עג 1 מזמור לאסף אך טוב לישר' אלקים. לפי שעניין המזמור מדבר בצרות
הבאות על ישר' לכך פתח בו כך. וזהו פי' שאעפ"י שאני זועק ומתמיה על צרותיהן של
ישר' ידעתי כי הק' טוב להם ולטובתו' הוא מביא להם את הרעה כדי לזכותם לחיי העולם
הבא. 2 ואני בטרם שומי זאת על לבי כמעט נטיו רגלי ושופכו אשורי לנטות מאחרי
המקום 3 כי הייתי מקנא בהוללים במערבבי דרכיהם אשר הייתי רואה את שלומם : 4 כי
אין חרצובות למותם. לשון אמירה. כמו פתח חרצובות רשע. מסגרי כבלי רשע. שאוסרין
בהם העניים אף כאן אין ייסורין למיתתן. המתים בהם מתים בריאים כאולם בלא
ייסורין. ורבותי' פי' בו נוטריקון שאין חרדים ועצבים מיום המיתה : ד"א שאין הק'
מאחר צביונם : בהוללים במערבבים. כמו סבאך מהיל במים : 6 לכן ענקתמו גאוה. בעבור
זה שאין ייסורין באין עליהם העינקתם גאוה לעלות על צוארם גסות הרוח. יעטף שית
חמס למו. החמס. שהן עושין עושה אותם שמינים ועוטף שתתיהם ועגבותיהם בעובי
שומן ובשר. 7 יצא מחלב עינימו. יותר ממה שלבם שוכח ומיחל ומצפה באה להם תאוות
עברו בהשגת ידם את תאות לבם : 8 ימיקו את רעיהם וידברו ברע עושק לעשוק אביונים
מרום ידברו. כמו פרעה וסנחריב ונבוכד נצר. פרעה אמ' מי י'י. סנחריב מי בכל אלקי
הארצות. נבוכד נצר אעלה על במותי עב. וזהו 9 שתו בשמים פיהם. 10 לכן ישוב עמו
הלום. לפי שעמו רואים דרך רשעים צלחה. ישובו. אל דרך הרשעים לאחוז בדרכיהם.
הלום. כמו מי הביאך הלום. פה : ומי מלא ימצו למו. ומים של פלג המלא הם דברי התורה
נחשבים למו תמצית ומזלזלין בהן. 11 הנה רשעים הם ועוברים על תורתו. ד"א איכה ידע אל
בהק' ותורתו אמת : 12 הנה רשעים הם ועוברים על תורתו. והרי הם שלוי עולם.
ומגדילים כח ועושר. ושלוי עולם לשון שלוה : השגו הגדילו. ומנחם פתר ישוב עמו הלום
ישוב הרשע להלום את עמו של הק' והראשון למדתי מדבריו של ר' מאיר בר' יצחק שליח
צבור זצ"ל. 13 אך ריק זכיתי לבי. כל זה מוסב על אמרם אויכה ידע אל. וגם אומ' אך
לריק ועל חנם אנו שומרים מצותיו 14 והרי אנו נגועים כל היום : ותוכחתי נראית תמיד
מבקר לבקר צרות מתחדשות 15 אם אמרתי אספרה כמו. אמ' אסף אם אמרתי בלבי
לספר הכל כמ' שהוי כל שעמו אומרים על זאת. הנה דור בניך בגדתי. כולם אנשים בוגדים
ורשעים. 16 ואחשבה בלבי לדעת זאת מה היא מדתו של הק' כן. עמל היא בעיני. נראית
היתה מדתו זאת עלי עמל ולא משפט. 17 עד אשר באתי אל מקדשי ואז הבנתי אחרית הרשעים שהוא לאבדון. ואמרתי מה
שאירע בסנחריב ואז הבנתי אחרית הרשעים שהוא לאבדון. ואמרתי 18 כל הטובה הבאה
להם חלקות הם. שהק' מחליק להם את הדרך שלהם שתהא נוחה וחלוקה למען לא יתנו

לב להשיב אליו ויאבדו : **אַךְ בַּחֲלָקוֹת תָּשִׁית לָמוֹ** כל הטובה הבאה להם שהרי סופם
הַפַּלְתָּם לְמַשּׁוּאוֹת : 19 **מִן בַּלָּהוֹת.** שדים : 20 **כְּחֲלוֹם מֵהָקִיץ.** כשינה שאין לה קץ שהיא
שנת עולם כך היתה להם : ויבא המלאך ויך במחנה אשור : **יְיָ בָּעִיר צַלְמָם תִּבְזֶה.** בירושלם
שהרעו שם נתבזה צלם שמם ונשרפו כולם : 21 **כִּי יִתְחַמֵּץ לְבָבִי.** בטרם ראיתי מפלה זו
ברוח הקודש היה לבי מתחמץ על דרך רשעים אשר צלחה : **וְכִלְיוֹתַי** הייתי משתונן. לשון
חרב שנון וכשהוא מתפעל התי"ו נתונה באמצע שרשי התיבה כדרך כל תיבה שתחילת
יסודה שי"ן : 22 **וַאֲנִי** הייתי **בַעַר** ולא הייתי יודע מה היא המדה. וכבהמה **הָיִיתִי עִמָּךְ.** 23
ואף **אֲנִי** אעפ"י שהייתי רואה כל זה **תָּמִיד** הייתי **עִמָּךְ** ולא זזתי מיראתך : **אָחַזְתָּ בְּיַד יְמִינִי.**
להחזיקני ביראתך כשקרבו רגלי לנטות מדרכיך. כמו שאמי למעלה כמעט נטיו רגלי : 24
תַּנְחֵנִי. נחיתני. לאחר שהשלמתו לסנחריב כל הכבוד שפסקת לו **תִּקָּחֵנִי** אֵלֶיךָ. טעם הרביע מבדיל ואחר לפרשו לשלמעלה הימנו. הפלאת נסים לישר' והחרבת את
סנחריב : 25 **מִי לִי בַשָּׁמָיִם.** שום מלאך שבחרת לאלוקי אלא אותך לבדי : 26 **כָּלָה שְׁאֵרִי.**
נתאוה בשרי **וּלְבָבִי** לך. **כָּלָה.** לשון תאוה. כמו כלתה נפשי לתשועתך : 27 **זוֹנֶה מִמֶּךָּ.** נפרד
ממך : 28 **מַלְאֲכוֹתֶיךָ.** שליחותיך. רוח הקודש הבא בקרבי לאומרו :

עד 1 **לָמָה** אֱלֹקִים זָנַחְתָּ לָנֶצַח. יֶעְשַׁן אַפְּךָ. כל הכועס עשן יוצא מנחיריו : 2 **קָנִיתָ קֶדֶם.** לפני בריית עולם. שני מעון היית לנו בדור ודור. בטרם הרים יולדו : **שָׁכַנְתָּ בּוֹ.**
תיקון הלשון הוא כמו זו חטאנו לו. והרי **הוּא** כמו אשר **שָׁכַנְתָּ בּוֹ** : 3 **הָרִימָה פְעָמֶיךָ**
לְמַשּׁוּאוֹת. לשון חורבן כמו שאייה. וכמו תשאה שממה : **נֵצַח** הגבה פעמיים ובהלות שלך
שיהו לאויביך למשואות נצח על כל אשר **הֵרַע** הָאוֹיֵב בבית המקדש. כך חברו מנחם עם
ותפעם רוחו : 4 **מוֹעֲדֶיךָ.** אילו בית המקדש שני בו ונועדתי עליך שם : **שָׂמוּ אוֹתֹתָם אֹתוֹת.**
כְּשֶׁגָּבְרָה ידי להחריבו אז שמו להם אותות קסמיהם שהם אותות אמת ומה הן הקסמים
קלקל בחצים שאל בתרפים : 5 **יִוָּדַע כְּמֵבִיא לְמַעְלָה בִּסֲבָךְ עֵץ קַרְדֻּמּוֹת.** יודע האויב
כשנמסכה בפתחי שער בית המקדש שהוא כמביא למעלה מכותיו ברקיע **נִמְנוּ** היה יודע
שהיה רואה העיר שהעץ מסבך ואוחז את הקרדומות ובולע כמו שאמרו רבותי' כולהו בלעתנהו
חדא תרעא דירושלם : **בְּסֲבָךְ עֵץ בַּקַּרְדֻּמּוֹת.** לשון נאחז בסבך. העץ סובך אותם ונסבכין בו
6 **וְעַתָּה** אעפ"י שהיה רואה שלפני הק' קשה לא **נִמְנַע** מלהום כל פתחיה ושעריה : **בְּכַשִּׁיל**
וְכֵילַפֹּת. כלי משחית של נגרים הם. ובקרדומות באו לך. תי' יוי' בן עוזי' ובכשילין : **כֵּילַפּוֹת.**
לשון ערבי הוא כך פי' דונש שהוא מכלי הנגרים. **יַהֲלֹמוּן** הָאוֹיְבִים : 8 **אָמְרוּ בְלִבָּם נִינָם**
יַחַד. כל מושליהם מחשבה אחת להם : **נִינָם** מושליהם : וכן ינון שמו. ואחריתו **יְהִי** מנון.
כראשונים כאחרונים להזדווג לפטרונון של ישר' תחילה ואחר יזדווגו להם. ותדע שהרי
שָׂרְפוּ כָל מוֹעֲדֵי יְיָ שהיו **בָאָרֶץ.** כל בתי **וַעַד** שלו. פלשתים החריבו שילה. נבוכד נצר החריב
בית ראשון. רומים החריבו בית שיני. בימים רבים שאנו בגולה נתנבא **אָסָף** על ימי הגלות : **עַד מָה.** עד מתי
נהיה בצרה זו : 11 **מִקֶּרֶב חֵיקְךָ כַלֵּה.** גרש לשון כלה גרש יגרש : 12 **וֵאלֹקִים מַלְכִּי מִקֶּדֶם.**
הלא אתה תשועתינו מאז : 13 **רָאשֵׁי תַנִּינִים.** הם מצרים שנקראו תנינים שני התנין הגדול
הרובץ בתוך יאוריו : 14 **רָאשֵׁי לִוְיָתָן.** פרעה נקרא כן שני יפקוד **יְיָ** בחרבו הקשה על לויתן
נחש בריח וגו'. **תִּתְּנֶנּוּ מַאֲכָל לְעַם לְצִיִּים.** נתת ממונן לעם לישר' לאוכלן. **לְצִיִּים.** לכתות.
וצבאות שהוצאת **צִיִּים.** סיעות. כמו שתירגם אונקלוס וצים מיד כתים. וסיעי : 15 **אַתָּה**
בקעת מעיינות מן הצור. **אַתָּה הוֹבַשְׁתָּ** את הירדן שהוא **נְהַר אֵיתָן** : 16 **לְךָ יוֹם אַף גָאַלְתָּ**
של ישר'. **וְאַף לְךָ לָיְלָה.** ועמך היה בצרות הלילה : 17 **אַתָּה הֲכִינוֹתָ מָאוֹר** וָאוֹרָה : **אַתָּה**
הִצַּבְתָּ גְּבוּלוֹת אָרֶץ בכל כך טוב. **קַיִץ וָחֹרֶף אַתָּה יְצַרְתָּם** הרי זה דוגמת שבועות קציר ישמר
לנו. לא שינית עליהם סוד השנים. 18 **זְכוֹר זֹאת.** ואחרי שכל תשועתינו בך זכור זאת
האויב אשר חירף בהשמידו אותנו : 19 **אַל תִּתֵּן לְחַיַּת.** לגדודי האומות. וכן ויאספו
פלשתי' לחיה : **נֶפֶשׁ תּוֹרֶךָ.** תור שלך. לשון תורי' ובני יונה. התור הזו משמת בן זוגה אינה
מזדוגה לאחר. כך ישר' לא החליפוך באל אחר אעפ"י שרחקת מהם. והיו כאלמנה. **חַיַּת**
עֲנִיֶּיךָ. נפש עניך : 20 **הַבֵּט לַבְּרִית** אשר כרתה לאבותינו : **נְאוֹת חָמָס.** נוה חמס לשו' מדור :
21 **אַל יָשֹׁב** מלפניך **דַּךְ נִכְלָם** בתפילתו. 22 **חֶרְפָּתְךָ.** גידופך :

עה 1 **למנצח אל תשחת** את ישר׳. 2 **הודינו לך אלקים** על הטובה **הודינו** אף על
הרעה **וקרוב** בפינו **שמך** תמיד. **ספרו** דורותינו **נפלאותיך** תמיד : 3 **כי אקח מועד** כשיש לנו
יום טוב. אין עסוקין בניבול הפה ובקלות ראש ככל הגוים. **אני מישרים אשפוט.** אנו
נותנין אל לבנו להלל ולשבח מעין המאורע ביום : 4 **נמוגים ארץ וכל יושביה.** ביום מתן
תורה כשהיו נמוגים ארץ וכל יושביה מתנאי שהתנית׳ עליהם במעשה בראשית שאם לא
יקבלו את התורה יחזרו לתוהו ובוהו. **אנכי** עמד ישר׳. **תכנתי עמודיה.** כשאמרתי נעשה
ונשמע : 5 **להוללים.** לרשעים המעורבבים : 7 **כי לא ממוצא** השמש **וממערבו ולא מן
המדברות** שאתם מפרשים בשיירות להרבות ממון. לא בכל אלה להרים קרן : 8 **כי אלקים
שופט** צדק על כל הרעה אשר עשיתם. **זה ישפיל וזה ירים.** הגבוהים ישפיל והנמוכים
ירים : 9 **כי כוס** <u>התרע</u>לה בידו **יין חמר.** חזק ויינש בלעז : **מלא מסך** הכוס מלא מזג.
מזוג. ולהשקות את כל הגוים : **ויגר מזה.** מזה הכוס יפיך ויקלח את משתיהם. לשון
המוגרים במורד 10 **ואני אגיד לעולם.** מאז והלאה את נקמתו ואת גבורתו. 11 **וכל קרני
רשעי׳** של עשו הרשע **אגדעם.** כעניין שני ונתתי נקמתי באדום ביד עמי ישר׳ יגדעו
קרן עשו. ואז **תרוממנה קרנות צדיק.** צדיקו של עולם ישראל שהם שבחו של הק׳ :

עו 1 **למנצח** בנגינות. 2 נודע ביהודה אלקים. 4 **שמה שבר רשפי קשת** של
סנחריב ואוכלוסיו : **רשפי קשת.** אין רשפי קשת לשון רשפי אש. שאין לשון רשפי אש נופל
בקשת. וזה רפי. ורשפי אש של דגש. ורשפי קשת לשון לשו׳ לחומי רשף <u>דמתרג</u>מינן עוף. וכן ובני
רשף יגביהו עוף. אף זה לשון חצים <u>המעופ</u>פים כעניין שנאמר ומחץ יעוף <u>ימס</u>. **שמה שבר
רשפי קשת.** חצים שהקשת מעופף : 5 **נאור אתה אדיר.** לשון נאר מקדשו. נארת ברית
עבדך. מנאר את אויביך וקמיך ומטאטאן מן העולם : **נאור** על שם מעשיו נקרא כמי׳ רחום
וחנון קנוא ונוקם על שם שהוא חונן <u>ושהוא</u> מרחם מקנא ושהו׳ נוקם : **אדיר
מהררי טרף.** חזק מעונקים. טורפים הגבוהים כהרים ולנגדך אין גבורתם נודעת : 6
אשתוללו כמי׳ השתוללו. כמו ואחריכן אתבדר אחיזיהו עם יהושפט כמי׳ התחבר ונגזר
אשתוללו מגזרת מוליך יועצי׳ שולל. והוא לשון משגה ושל. **כשוטים** שוגים. והיתי נופל
בלשו׳ מתפעל באמצע התיבה ככל התיבה שתחילת יסודה שיי׳׳: **נמ׳ שנתם** נרדמו בשינה.
לשון תנומה. **ולא מצאו** ידיהם נכוחה כשבאת ליפרע מהם : 7 **נרדם ורכב וסוס.** ויי׳ של
ורכב טפילה. כמו ואלה בני <u>צבען.</u> ואיה וענה ויי׳ של ואיה טפילה : 8 **מאז אפך.** משעה
שאתה כועס : 9 **משמים השמעת דין.** <u>כ</u>שנתנבא ישעיה על פורענותו של סנחריב ונתקיים
בו **ארץ** ישר׳ **שיראה** ממנו ואוכלוסיו. אז **שקט׳** 10 **בקום למשפט אלקים** לעשות <u>מ</u>שפט
באויביו. **להושיע** חזקיה וסיעתו : 11 **כי חמת אדם תודך.** <u>כ</u>עסם של רשעים גורם שהבריות
מודים להק׳ כשהן מראים כעסם והק׳ נפרע מהם שהכל מקלסין לפניו ואף הם עצמם
מקלסין כשהן רואי׳ שאין כעסן כלום. כמו שמצינו <u>בנ</u>בוכד נצר שהשליך חנניה מישאל
ועזריה לכבשן האש. מה נאמ׳ שם יהא שמיה דאלקא רבא מברך וגו׳. ועל ידי כן **שארית
החימות תחגור.** לשו׳ עכבה בלשון משנה. פגימת הסכין כדי שתחגור **תחגור.** ושמעתי
משמו של ר׳ אליעזר הגאון ב׳׳ר יצחק שהיה מביא <u>מ</u>קרא ׳׳ראיה זה לאותה משנה ויש
עוד לפתור חגירה כמשמעה לשון אזורה. ופי׳ לך נאה לחגור חימה ולעטות קנאה כי הכח
והיכולת שלך. ולשון שארית זהו מאחר שחמת אדם אינה כלום נשארו מל חגרות חימה
לך : 12 **נדרו ושלמו** נדריכם **כל סביביו.** השומעים תשועה זו. וכך עשו כמה שכת׳ תהיינה
חמש ערים בארץ מצרים מדברות שפת כנען ונשבעות לי׳׳י צבאות : **יובלו שי למור׳** למה
13 לפי שבעת חפצו **יבצור רוח נגידים.** רוח גסה של נדיבים וממעט גאונם : **יבצור.** ימעט.
כמו לא יבצר מהם. כל המזמור הזה מדבר על מפלת סנחריב. שלא מצינו אויב נופל
בירושלם אלא הוא :

עז 1 **למנצח** על ידותון. על הדתות ועל הדינין העוברים על ישר׳ : 3 **ידי**
מכתי. **לילה נגרה.** בגלות זה שהוא כלילה. היא נגרה לחה וטרי. **ולא תפוג** ולא תמיד
נגרתה : 4 **אזכרה אלקים** החסד שהיה רגיל לעשות לי בימי <u>חיבתי.</u> **אשיחה** באותן חסדים

וטובות. **ותתעטף רוחי.** פשמיר בלע'י : 5 **אחזת שמורות עיני.** שמורות. לשון <u>אשמורות</u>
הלילה. שאדם נעור <u>משנתו</u> ודעתו מיושבת עליו ולבו <u>חוזר</u> עליו. ואני איני כן בלילה זה של
גלות תמיד עיני נדבקות כאדם נרדם. האוטם לבי בצרות שאני רואה נפעמה רוחנו ואין
הדיבור בנו : 6 **חשבתי ימים מקדם** לזכור החסדי'ם אשר עשית את אבותינו : 7 **אזכרה**
נגינתי בלילה. כל הלילה. בימי הגלות הזה שהוא דומה ללילה אני זוכר את נגינותיי
שהייתי מנגן בבית המקדש : **ועם לבבי אשיחה.** שמא כלה חסדו. **9 האפס.** שמא כלה חסדו. **גמר אומר.** גזירת עולם
שלא ישוב <u>מחרונו</u> עוד. **10 השכח** להיות חונן : **חנות** לשון עשות ראות : ל"א **חנות.** חנינה :
אם קפץ באף רחמיו סלה : 11 **ואמר חלותי היא.** מחשבותי אומרות לי אין זאת אלא
להחלותי ולייראני לשוב אליו : **חלותי.** כמו לחלותי. **שנות ימין עליון.**
אשר נשתנית ימין עליון. לשון חולי וחיל : ועכשיו השיב אחור ימינו : 13 **והגית בכל**
פעלך. שעשית לנו כבר. 14 **בקודש דרכך** דרך מדתך לקדש את שמך בעולם לעשות דין
ברשעים : 17 **ראוך מים יחילו.** כשנגלית על הים : 18 **זורמו מים עבות** שחקים נטפו זרם
מים עבים : **חצציך.** לשון חצץ. כמ' מחצצים בין משאבים : חצציך. כמ' חציך : 19 **בגלגל.**
כמו בגלגל : **קול רעמיך** כגלגל על הים להום את מחנה מצרים : 20 **ועקבותיך לא נודעו.**
אין הפסיעות ניכרות על המים. **עקבותיך.** טראצש :

עח 1 **משכיל** לאסף האזינה עמי תורתי. 2 **במשל פי.** הם דברי תורה. 4 **לא**
נכחד מבניהם. וגם אנו לא נכחד מבניהם. של אבותינו מלהודיעם מה שסיפרו לנו : 7
כסלם. תוחלתם. וכן אם שמתי זהב כסלי. 8 **כאבותם** שהיו <u>במצרים</u> ובמדבר. 9 **בני**
אפרים שיצאו ממצרים בזרוע לפני הקץ ובטחו בגבורתם ובחיציהם. וסופן הפכו לנוס
ביום קרב כמפורש בדברי הימים ויהרגום אנשי גת הנולדים בארץ. **רומי.** משליכין
וזורקין. כמו רמה בים : 12 **נגד אבותם עשה פלא.** אחריכן כשהגיע הקץ אף הם ויוסיפו
לחטא. כמו <u>שמסיים</u> והולך : **נגד אבותם.** אברהם ויצחק ויעקב באו על הים והראה להם
הק'י היאך גואל את בניהם. 13 **כמו נד.** תל גבוה. כדמתרגמין נצבו כמו נד. כשור : 15 **יבקע**
צור. והכית בצור. וגו' : **וישק בתהומות רבה.** אף כשהיו בתוך הים שמימיו מלוחים
המתיק להם מעיינות בתוך התהום : 16 **ויורד כנהרות מים** שהיו נוזלים מן הבאר.
והנשיאים עושים שירטוט <u>במשענתם</u> והמים נמשכים אחריהם לכל <u>חניית</u> שבט ושבט
כעניין שנאמ' במחוקק במשענותם כמי שמפורש בארבעים ותשע מדות : 17 **למרות.** להק'י
להקניט. כמו ממרים הייתם. 20 **שאר.** בשר. 21 **ואש נשקה ביעקב.** כמו וברעו באפם :
לשון היסק והבערה כדכת'י ותבער בם אש י'י : 25 **לחם אבירים אכל איש.** <u>לחמכם</u> של
מלאכים : ד"א **אבירים איברים** איברים. שהיה נבלע באיברים ולא הוצרכו לנקבים : 26
יסע קדים. ורוח נסע ויגז שלום : 30 **לא זרו.** לא נעשו זרי' מתאוותם. כי כל תאוותם השיגו
עוד אוכלם בפיהם ועודנו הבשר בין שיניה'י טרם יכרת 31 ואף י'י חרה בעם : ד"א **לא זרו.**
לא נתרחקו מתאוותם עד שבאה <u>אליהם</u> הרעה והפורענות. 34 **ובחורי ישר'.** נבחרים
שבהם : והאספסוף שבהם הם הזקנים שנ'י אספה לי שבעים איש. **אם הרגם ודרשוהו** וגו'.
אף היא לא באמת אלא פיתוי הפה : ויכזבו בלשונם. 37 **ולבם לא נכון עמו.**
כן 38 **והוא רחום** להם וגם מכפר להם את עונם תמיד ולא <u>השחית</u> : **והרבה** פעמים רבות
להשיב אפו מהם. ואף אם הוא נפרע מהם לא העיר עליהם כל חמתו כי אם מעט מעט 39
לפי שזכור כי בשר המה ויצר הרע טמון בלבם. והוא **רוח הולך** כשימותו **ולא ישוב** אותו
רוח בהם לעולם הבא כשיחיו אין יצר הרע <u>שולט</u>. ולא יתכן לפרש **רוח הולך ולא ישוב.**
רוחם של חיים בהם. שאם אמרת כן כפרתה בתחיית המתים. וכן מפור' באגדת תילים. 40
כמה פעמים ימרוהו במדבר תמיד. 41 **התוו.** לשון סימן. כמו והתוית תיו וסימן הוא לשון
מופת ונסיון. בקשו ממנו אות וסימן. היש י'י בקרבנו אם אין : 45 **ותשחיתם** <u>שומטין</u> את
ביצתם. 47 **חנמל.** שם <u>הארבה.</u> ומדרשו בא חן ומל. היה מולל את ירק השדה והעשב
ואוכלן. 48 **ויסגר לברד בעירם.** כשהתחיל הברד לירד הבר'י המצרי מבריח את צאנו לבית
והברד נעשה למולו כמין כותל <u>והמצרי</u> שוחטו ונותנו על כתיפו <u>להוליכו</u> לבית ולאוכלו
והעוף בא ונוטלו ממנו. וזהו **ומקניהם לרשפים.** לעופות. כמו ובני רשף יגביהו עוף. וזהו

מדרשו ולפי פשוטו **לרשפים.** כמ' רשפי אש. כדכת' ואש מתלקחת בתוך הברד. 50 **יפלס**
נתיב לאפו. אעפ"י שבאף נשתלחו המכות לא שימשו אלא שליחותם מה שנצטוו להמית
המיתו. ולא הכל: בנתיבותם הלכו. **וחיתם** גופם. 55 **ויגרש מפניהם** שבעת אומות
באהליהם של גוים: 56 **וינסו. וימרו.** בימי השפטים: 57 **כקשת רמיה.** שאינו מורה חץ
למקו' שהמורה הפך: 61 **ויתן לשבי עוזו.** מסר הארון והלוחות ביד פלשתים: 63 **בחוריו**
אכלה אש. אש עברתו: **לא הוללו.** לא נֻכללו לאפריון וחופה שהבחורים מתו במלחמה.
הוללו. לשון הלולא בלשון ארמית. ורבותי' דרשוהו על נדב ואביהו' ואין לבי מתיישב
לפרשו כן שהרי כבר התחיל במשכן שילה: 64 **כהניו בחרב נפלו.** חפני ופנחס. **ואלמנותיו**
לא תבכינה. אף לאלמנות לא ניתן לבכותן שהרי אף היא מתה ביום השמועה שנאמ'
ותכרע ותלד כי נהפכו עליה צירה: 65 **מתרונן.** מתעורר ומתגבר כגיבור להקיץ מיינו:
מתרונן. לשון רינה הוא. 66 **ויך צריו אחור.** מכת אחוריים. בַטחורים ובעפלים והיא חרפת
גידוף להם לעולמים: 67 **וימאס באהל יוסף.** היא שילה שהיא בחלקו של יוסף: 69 **ויבן**
כמו רמים מקדשו כמו שמים וארץ שני בהן שתי ידים כמו מקדש יְיָ כוננו ידיך: ד"א כמו
שמים וארץ יסדו מה הם אין להם חליפין אף מקדש אין לו חליפים להשרות שם שכינה:
70 מִמֵכלאות צאן. דירי צאן. כמ' גזר ממכלא צאן. 71 **מאחר עולות הביאו** שהיה רועה
לאביו הצאן המניקות שהיה רחמני ומוציא הגדים תחילה ומאכיל ראשית העשבים
העליונים שהן רכים ומוציא התיישים אחריהם ואוכלין באמצע העשבים ואחרכך מוציא
הזקינות ואוכלות את שרשי העשבים. אמ' הקי' ראוי זה לרעות את עמי:

עט 1 **אָסָף** אלקים באו גוים בנחלתך. לעיים. ומהו מזמור קינה הוא. אלא
לפי שני' כלה י'י את חמתו. ובמה כלה. **ויצת אש בציון** וגי'. מזמור ושיר הוא ששפך את
חמתו על העצים ועל האבנים. ולא עשה כלייה בבניו: 2 **בשר חסידיך.** והלא רשעים היו
אלא משקיבלו פורענותם הרי הם חסידי' וכן הוא אומ' ונקלה אחיך לעיניך כיון שלקה
הרי הוא אחיך כך מפור' באגד'. **וקלס.** לשון דבה לדבר. כמו לַמשל: 5 **עד מה.** עד מתי.
תאנף. תקצף. **קנאתך.** חמתך שאתה מתקנא להנקם לשון אל קנא. אנפרנמנט בל': 11
הותר פתח אסורים: שלח מלאך ויתירהו: **בני תמותה.** בני הנהרגת עליך. **תמותה.**
אנמירינאיא בל'. ויש דוגמא בלשון חכמים מוטב שיאכלו ישר' בשר תמותות שחוטות ואל
יאכלו בשר תמותות נבילות. ופירשו רבותי' בשר מסוכנת שנשחטה במסי' קידושין:

פ 1 **עַל שׁוֹשַׁנִּים** על ישר' **עדות לאסף מזמור.** מזמור של עדות שרמז
להם בו שלש גליות והתפלל עליהם. שהרי נאמר במזמור זה שלש רגלים פעמים השיבנו
האר פניך ונושעה. ורמז לו בו שלש צרות העתידות לבא עליהם ממלכי ארם שני בימי יהוא
כי איבדם מלך ארם וישימם כעפר לדוש: 2 **רועה ישר'** מנהיג ופרנסם. **יוסף.** כל ישר'
נקראי' על שם יוסף לפי שהוא כילכלם בימי הרעב: **יושב הכרובים.** כמה שני' ונועדתי לך
שם: **הופיעה.** הראה את גבורתך. 3 **לפני אפרים ובנימן ומנשה.** כשהיו ישר' צריכין
לתשועתך אעפ"י שהן רשעים ואינן כדיי **עוררה את גבורתך. ולכה לישועתה לנו.** לך
ועליך להושיענו בין זכים ובין חבים. כמה שני' למשה ראה ראיתי וגו'. שתי ראיות הללו
למה. רואה אני שהן עתידים להכעיסני ואעפ"י ראיתי את **עוניים** מפני השבועה שנשבעתי
לאברהם ליצחק וליעקב. **אפרים.** במלחמת ארם כשצר על שומרון. ושלח מלאכים
לאחאב נשיך ובניך לי הם. כספך וזהבך לי הוא. **מנשה** בימי יהואש בן יהואחז שני כי ראה
י'י את עוני ישר'. וְהשיב את ערי ישר'. **בנימין** בימי אחשורוש שהיו מרדכי ואסתר בסכנה וכל הדור
תלוי בהן: **ולכה לישועתה לנו.** אין זה לשון הליכה אלא כמו ולך. וכן הוא במסורת ולכה
איפוא דיעקב. ולכה אין בשורה מוצאת. 4 **השיבנו** מגלות בבל
שהיה שם מרדכי 5 **עד מתי עשנת** בצרות מלכי יוון שַהצרו מאד לישר': 6 **האכלתם לחם**
דמעה. במצרים: **ותשקמו בדמעות שליש** בבבל. שהיו שם שבעים שנה שהן שליש של
רד"ו של מצרים זו לַמדתי מיסודו של ר' משה הדרשן. ועוד יש לפתור על שם שמלכות יוון
היתה הצרה השלישית. ואם תאמר רביעית היא שהרי קדמו מדי ופרס כל ע' שנה של בבל

אינן אלא גלות אחת. ומנחם פי' שליש שם כלי אחד <u>ששותין</u> בו. וכן פי' וכל בשליש עפר
הארץ : ורבותי פי' על שלש דמעות שהורידו עשו שני ויצעק צעקה הרי אחת. גדולה הרי
שתים. ומרה הרי שלש. ועליהם זכה לחיות על חרבו. שני והיה כאשר תריד : 7 תשימנו
מדון אתה שמת אותנו מדון לשכינינו <u>שהתגרו</u> בנו. ואויבנו בני יון. 8 השיבנו ונוושעה.
מבני יון : 9 גפן ממצרים תסיע. חזר ורמז על גלות רומיים. גפן ישר' אשר הסעת ממצרים
<u>עקרת</u> משם. כמו' ויסע כעץ כעץ תקוה. ואחרכך גרשתה שבעה גוים <u>ונטעתה</u> ישר' בארצם : 10
פנית לפניה את היושבים שם. ותשרש שרשיה השרישה שרשיה : 11 ועופיה כסו ארזי אל.
ארזים חזקים. כמו' מלכים אדירים : 12 תשלח קצירה: שלחה פאורותיה. כמו' ועשה
קציר : עד הים הגדול היה גבולה : ואל נהר יונקותיה. רחבה של ארץ ישראל ממדבר עד
הנהר נהר פרת : 13 למה פרצת גדירה של אותה הכרם. <u>וארוה כל עוברי דרך.</u> ליקטוה כל
הבא. כמו ארותי מורי. ובלשו' משנה כמלוא אורה וסלו : 14 יכרסמנה חזיר מיער. כמו
שדה שכירסמוה נמלים בלשון משנה והוא לשון נתיקה. מיער. העיי"ן תלויה בו זכו ישר'
הרי נעשו אויביהם כחית היאר שאין לה כח ביבשה. ובזמן שהפורענות נגזר עליהם מתגבר
עליהם כחית היער שהיא משחתת והורגת : חזיר מיער זה עשו. דכתי' בה אכלה ומדקה
ושארא ברגלה רפסה ויש לו קצת סימני טהרה. אף עשו יש לו זכות אבות : וזיז שדי כל
רמש האדמה. ולמה נקרא שמו זיז על שם שהוא זז ואוכלן והולך. ירענה רועה עליה ענפיה
ואוכלן : 16 וכנה אשר נטעה ימינך. המבוססת והמיושבת אשר נטעה ימינך. לשו' והשיבך
על כנך ועל בן אימצתה לך. ועל בן עשו שהיה חביב לאביו שהיה קורא אותו בני <u>אימצת</u>
גפן יעקב לך שני ואת אחיך תעבוד. עכשיו 17 היא שרופה באש וכסוחה. לשו' לא תזמור.
לא תכסא. תמיד הם אבודין והולכין מגערת פניך וזעפך : 18 תהי ידך על איש
ימינך. על עשו שהוא איש העומד לפרע <u>ממנו. ועל בן אדם</u> אשר אימצת להיות מושבו
משמני הארץ : 19 לא נסוג ממך לא תגרום לנו להיות נסוגים ממך : תחיינו. מן הגלות
ונכיר בטובתך ובגבורתך ואז נקרא בשמך 20 <u>יי' אלקים צבאות.</u> ג' אזכרות נאמר כאן
ובאמצעי ב' אזכרות ובראשון אזכרה אחת. הכל לפי חוזק החוזק הגליות והצרה והגאולה :

פא 1 למנצח על הגיתית כלי שיר הבא מגת. 3 כנור נעים עם נבל. ר' חייא
בר' חייא בר אבא אמ' נבל לזה הוא כנור. ור' שמעון אמ' נימין יתירות בין זה לזה. ולמה נקרא
שמו נבל שמנבל כל מיני זמר : 2 ת' הריעו בראש השנה 4 בחדש. בכסה.
יום מועד מוכן וקבוע לכך. וכן ליום הכסא יבוא לביתו. למועד הקבוע : 5 כי חוק לישר'
הוא מאת הק' לתקוע בראש השנה. והוא יום משפט להק': 6 עדות ביהוסף שמו. בראש
השנה יצא יוסף מבית האסורים. שפת לא ידעתי אשמע. מפורש במס' סוטה שלמדו
גבריאל שבעים לשון : 7 מדוד. מעבודת עבדו' בישול קדירות כדרך עבדים. מדוד קדירה
כמו והכה בכיור או בדוד : 8 בצרה קראת ואחלצך. כולם קראתם מצרת עבדות סבלות
מצרים ואחלץ אתכם : אענך בסתר רעם. אתה קראת בסתר ביני וביני ואני עניתיך בקול
רם. הודעתיך גבורותיי ונפלאותי בפרהסיא : אבחנך על מי מריבה. ואעפי"י שגלוי לפני
זכרון שאתם <u>עתידין</u> להמרות אותי במי מריבה : אך לפי פשוטו <u>נראה</u>
אענך כסתר רעם. דוגמת והיה והיה אשר יענה באש. אענך כמו שהיית להסתירך
ברעם <u>שהסתתרתיך</u> ביום רעם וצרה : 9 שמעה עמי. אחרי שכל זאת עשיתי לך כדי אתה
לשמוע לי : 11 הרחב פיך לשאול ממני כל תאות לבך. ואמלאהו. ככל אשר תשאל אמלא :
13 בשרירות לבם. במראית עיניהם. כמו' למען שוררי : 14 לו עמי שומע לי. עדיין אם הוא
רוצה לשוב ולשמוע אלי : 15 כמעט אויביהם אכניע. בשעת מועטת הייתי מכניע אויביי.
אשיב ידי. אשיב מכתי מעליכ' לתת אותה עליהם. ואז 16 משנאי יי יכחשו לי. ויהי עת
פורענותם לעולם. 17 ויאכילהו לישר'. ומצור השביעם דבש כשהלכו בדרכי כענין שני
וינקהו דבש מסלע :

פב 1 אלקים נצב בעדת אל. לראות אם אמת ישפוטו. ואתם הדיינין 2 עד
מתי תשפטו עול. 3 הצדיקו אם זכאי הוא בדין אל תהפכו דינו לחובה בשביל לשאת פני
הרשעים. 5 לא ידעו הדיינין המעוותים את הדין ולא יבינו אם בשביל העון הזה <u>יתהלכו</u>

בחשיכה וימוטו על כך **מוסדי ארץ** : 6 **אלקים אתם** מלאכים. כשנתתי תורה לישר' נתתיה
על מנת שאין שום מלאך שולט בכם : 7 **אכן כ**ָ**אדם ׳תמותון** "הראשון. אחרי אשר חיבלתם
מעשיכם כמוהו. **וכאחד** הראשונים אשר מתו כן **תפלו** מדרש אגד' **כאחד השרים** של מעלה
שני ׳פקד יַ׳׳י על צבא המרום במרום : 8 **קומה אלקים** שפטה בידך למשפט :

פג 2 אלקים אל דמי לך. אל תתן שתיקה לעוותתינו שאויבינו מריעים
לנו : 6 **עליך ברית יכרותו.** עיצה אינה עליך להשכיח את שמך שאין אתה קרוי אלקים
להם כי אם לנו. אלקי ישראל ומאחר 5 **שלא יזכר שם ישר' עוד** אף שַמך הגדול לא יזכר :
9 **גם אשור.** אף אשר שהיה משאר אומות שני מן הארץ ההיא יצא אשר שיצא מעצת דור
הפלגה כאן נלוה עמם לרעה. ד׳׳א **גם אשור** גם זה שהיה מסגל מתחילתו מעשרים טובים
שפירשו מעצת נמרוד. אף הוא חוזר להיות רשע. לכך נשתתף עמהם להחריב ביתך בר׳
רב׳: **היו זרוע** וגו'. כל אלה נתנו עזר' למואב ועמון ועמלק שכיניינו לבוא עלינו : 10 **עשה**
להם כמדין על ידי גדעון. **כסיסרא.** על ידי ברק. 11 **נשמדו בעין דאר:** איני יודע איזו מן
המלחמות היתה שם של גדעון או של ברק. **היו דומן לאדמה.** זבל מפוזר תי' יוני : 13 **אשר**
אמרו הגוים האלה האמורים למעלה אדום וישמעאלים וכל חבריריה'. **נרשה לנו את** נוה
בית **אלקים.** ומהו הגלגל הוא ראשי קוצים השדה
שקורי' קרדונ׳׳ש בל'. וכשמגיעין ימי החרף נתקים ונשחתים מאיליהם ופורחי' מעט מעט
ודומה לו הניתק כמו גלגלי אופן עגלה והרוח. **ובסופתך.** אישטורבלון בל' :

פד 2 מה ידידות משכנותיך כמה אהובות וחביבות משכנותיך 3
נכספה. נחמדה: **כלתה.** נתאוותה כמ׳ ותכל נפש דוד לצאת על אבשלום. **לחצרות** אלקי׳ כי
חרבו ועל הגלות אמרה : **לבי ובשרי ירננו.** יתפללו על זאת : 4 **גם צפור מצאה בית.**
בַחורבנו קננו בו הצפורים. ומדרש אגדה בבניינו מדבר. והצפור היא כנסת ישר'. **אשר**
שתה. שמה אפרוחיה'. : 5 **אשרי** מי שיגיע **בביתך** לישב. **ועוד יהללוך** בתוכו : 6 **עוז לו בך.**
אשר שם אותך עוז מבטחו : **מסילות בלבבם.** החושב בלבו מסילות דרכיו לייישר דרכו : 7
עוברי בעמק הבכא. אותם העוברים על דתך והנם **בעומקה** של גיהנם בבכי ויללה : **מעיין**
ישיתוהו בדמעות עיניהם. ואף **ברכות יעטה מורה.** מברכים ומודים לשמו. ואומ׳ יפה דן
אותנו ואמת דינו וברכות יעטה מורה יעטה אותנו **בדרך** הטוב ולא שמענו אליו : 8 **ילכו מחיל אל**
חיל. אותם הנזכרים למעלה יושבי ביתך אשר מסילות בלבבם. **ילכו מחיל אל חיל.** מבית
המדרש לבי הכנסת. **ויראה** אל צבאם וחילם **אל הק׳ בציון** : 9 **שמעה תפילתי** לבנות ביתך :
10 **מגיננו.** הוא בית המקדש **המ**גין עלינו : **והבט פני** דוד **משיחך.** והסתכל בחסדיו וטרחו
אשר טרח ויגע בבניינו : 11 **כי טוב יום בחצריך** ולמחר ימות מלחיות במקום אחר **אלף** :
בחרתי אלף ל**הסתופף** על הסף ועל המזוזה לשקוד. **מדור באהלי רשע.** מהיות דר באהלי
עשו הרשע להדבק בהם : 12 **כי שמש ומגן.** יש לפתור שמש כמשמעו. ומדרש תילים פותרו
לשון חומה :

פה 2 רצית ׳׳י ארצך אם שבת שבות יעקב 3 ונשאת עוונם וכסית חטאתם 4
ואספת עברתך מהם **והשבת מחרון אפך** אז רצית את ארצך. וכל זמן שלא תעשה
זאת אין ׳׳י ארצך ועולמך מתרצה : 5 **שובינו.** שוב אתה והשיבנו. 7 **הלא אתה** סוף סוף **תשוב**
ותחיינו. שהרי הבטחתנו כן על ידי נביאיך. 9 **אשמעה מה ידבר** אזכה לשמוע מה ידבר הק׳
כשידבר שלום אל עמו. **לשט**ות לחטוא לפניו : 11 **חסד ואמת נפגשו.**
כשיהיו ישר' דוברי' אמת ומן השמים יפגוש בהם החסד. **צדק ושלום נשקו.** הצדקה שהיו
ישר' עושין והשלום מאת הק׳ יהו נושקין זה לזה כלומ' והיה מעשה הצדקה שלום : 12
אמת מארץ תצמח. כשהיו ישראל נוהגין באמת וישקיפו משמים צדק שהם עושין בארץ :
13 **וגם** זה **יתן יתן הטוב** יפתח אוצרו הטוב ואת השמים לתת מטר כדי לעשות **ארצנו** את
יבולה : 14 **וישם לדרך** פעמיו. וישם הק׳ את הצדיק בדרכי פעמיו. שיתנהג בהם עם בניו :

פו 1 תפילה לדוד הטה ׳׳י אזנך : 2 **כי חסיד אני.** שאני שומע חרפתי
וגידופי ויש בידי יכולת להנקם ואני שותק. כך היא באגדת תילים : ד׳׳א פי' רבותינו

בברכות לא חֲסִיד אני שכל מלכי מזרח יושבין בכבודן לפני ואני ידי מלוכלכות בדם בשפיר
ובשליא וכו'. 3 **כל היום.** כל הגלות שהוא יום לאומות ולילה לישר' כך מפורש באגד'
תילים: 4 **נפשי אשא.** לבי אכוין. 8 **ואין כמעשיך.** המקדים עליונים לתחתונים: 10 **ועושה**
נפלאות אתה לבדך. עד שלא נבראו המלאכים נבראו שמים וארץ. לפיכך 9 **כל גוים אשר**
עשית יכבדו את שמך: 13 **מַשְׁאוֹל תחתיה.** דרך המנאפים לינתן בעומקה של שאול ומשם
הצלתני שאמ' לי נתן הנביא גם י"י הֶעֱבִיר חטאתך ולא תמות: 14 **זידים קמו עלי** דואג
ואחיתופל. **ולא שמוך לנגדם.** לא זכרו את אשר ראו שמשחני שמואל על פיך: 16 **לבן**
אמתך. בן האמה משפיל עצמו לפני אדוניו יותר **ממקנת הכסף.** שבן האמה יליד בית הוא
וגדל בחיק אדוניו: 17 **עשה עמי אות לטובה.** שיהא ניכר לאחרים שמחלת לי. **ויראו**
שונאי האות **ויבושו** ולא שמע לו הק' ליתן האות בימיו אלא בימי שלמה בנו שדבקו
שערים זה בזה ולא נפתחו עד שאמ' אל תשב פני משיחך. זכרה לחסדי דוד עבדך :

פז 1 לבני קרח **מזמור שיר יסודתו בהררי קדש.** יסודת מזמור זה על
הררי ציון וירושלם יסדו המשורר : 3 **נכבדות מדובר בך** את ירושלם. דברי כבוד נדברו בך
מפי הק'. ומה הן הנכבדות שאת **עיר האלקים סלה:** 4 **אזכיר רהב ובבל לידעי.** עוד זאת
דבר עליך. אזכיר את מצרים ואת בבל על יודעי **להביאם** מנחה כעניין שני והביאו את כל
אחיכם מכל הגוים מנחה לי"י וגו'. **הנה פלשת וצור עם כוש** גם הם מצרים ובבל יתנו לב
לבקש ולזכור על כל אחד ואחד **זה יולד שם.** זה היה ממשפחת הנולדים בציון כעניין שני
ואתם תלוקטו לאחד לאחד. 5 **ולציון יאמר איש איש יולד בה.** ולכשיביאום מנחה לציון
יאמר לה על כל אחד ואחד זה מאותם שגלו ממך **והוא יכוננה עליון.** והק'
יכוננה על כל העיירות למעלה. 6 **י"י יספור בכתב עמים.** מקרא מסורס הוא. גם לה האמור
בסופו מוסב כלפי ראשו י"י יספור **בכתב עמים סלה.** כלומר לעתיד. כשיכתוב הק' את
האומות לדראון ימנה את ישר' שבר הנבלעים בתוכן ואף הנאנסין ביניהם. ויוצאין מתוכן
ויאמר זה יולד מאותן שגלו ממן **מציון** ויברור אף אותם לו. וזהו שאמ' ישעיה וגם מהם אקח
לכהנים וללוי' אמר י"י. מן הגוים המביאים אותם מנחה אקח הנבלעים ביניהם ויהיו
כהנים ולוים שאינן ניכרין ולפני גלוים הם **אמר י"י.** והיכן אמר הנסתרות לי"י אלקינו : 7
ושרים כחוללים על זאת. **כל מעייני.** קריבי. **בך.** בישועתך : **כחוללים** לשון מחולות :

פח 1 למנצח **על מחלת לענות.** על חולת אהבה ועניין שהיא מעונה בייסורי
הגלות : **להימן האזרחי.** יהודה היה כמ' שהיה מיוחס בדברי הימים ובני זרח זמרי ואיתן
והימן ודרדע וכלכל חמשה. והן היו חכמים גדולים. כמ' שני בשלמה ויחכם מכל בני מחול
ויסדו מזמורים ונקבעו בספר תילים. לכן נקראו בני מחול : **משכיל.** כל מקום שני משכיל
על ידי תורגמן נאמ' שהיה הנביא מעמיד תורגמן לפניו. וכשהרוח באה בו אומ' את
הנבואה לתורגמן והוא משמיעה : 2 **יום צעקתי** וגם **בלילה** אני נכון עמך : 4 **כי שבעה**
ברעות נפשי. כל כנסת ישר' הוא אומ' : 5 **אין אייל.** אין כח. אין כח. כמו אייליותי לעזרתי חושה : 6
במתים חפשי. הנני בין המתים חפשי מן העולם וכלה שהן חפשים מן העולי : **מידך נגזרו.**
ממכותך נגזרו מן העולם : 7 **בבור תחתיות.** היא הגלות : 8 **סמכה.** נשענה עלי. **כל משבריך**
ענית סלה. משברים לשון גלי הים הם. כל סערות אפך בכולם ענית אותם תמיד : 9 **שתני**
תועבות למו. האומות שהייתי חשובה בעיניהם עכשיו אני נמאסת להם : **כלוא.** נחבש
בכלא ואיני יכול לצאת : 11 **הלמתים תעשה פלא.** לרשעים. שאף בחייהם קרויין מתים.
להם אתה עושה נסים : **אם רפאים יקומו יודוך.** בתמיה : 12 **היסופר בקבר חסדך.** אם
לספר שבחך בקבר : 16 **וגוע מנוער.** מתוך תשנוק. כמו וינער י"י את מצרים : **אימיך אפונה.**
מיושבת ומבוססת אימתך בלבי : **אפונה** לשון דבר דבור על אופניו. על מכונו : 19 **מיודעי**
מחשך. נחשכתי ונחדלתי מהם :

פט 1 משכיל **לאיתן האזרחי.** גם הוא אחד מחמשת אחים המשוררי'
ורבותי' פי' באברהם אבינו על שם מי הַעִיר ממזרח : 2 **אודיע אמונתך בפי** אַת שידעתיך
שאתה שומר אבטחתך ומאמן את דבריך : 3 **כי אמרתי עולם חסד יבנה.** סבור הייתי

שיהא עולם בנוי בחסדך. **ותכין אמונתך** בשמים שתהא נכונה ומקויימת. ומה היא
האמונה אותי הבטחת שהבטחת את דוד על ידי נתן הנביא לאמר 4 **כרתי ברית לבחירי** 5
להכין עד עולם זרעו: 6 **ויודו שמים פלאך י'י.** אם היית שומר אבטחתך **אף אמונתך.**
אמונת דבריך יורו **בקהל קדושים.** 8 בסוד רב של מלאכים. בהנשא גליו 10 **בשוא גליו**
תשבחם. תשפילם. וכן וחכם באחר ישבחנה. וכן משביח שאון ימים: 11 **רהב.** מצרים:
16 **יודעי תרועה** שמסדרין עליה מלכיות וזכרונות **ושופרות**: 18 **וברצונך** שאתה מתרצה
להם. אפיימנטר בלעז: 20 **לחסידיך.** נתן הנביא וגד החוזה: **שויתי עזרי** על דוד לעזור לו
תמיד: 23 **לא ישיא אויב.** לא יגבר עליו להיות לו כנושה: 28 **בכור אתנהו.** גדול אתנהו: 33
ופקדתי בשבט פשעם. כך אמ' לו נתן הנביא על שלמה אשר בהעוותו והוכחתיו בשבט
אנשים זה רזון בן **אלידע.** שעמד לשטן לו. ובנגעי בני אדם זה אשמדאי: שהשדים היו בני
אדם הראשון: 36 **אם לדוד אכזב.** לשוי לא יכזבו מימיו. פיילנצא: 38 **ועד בשחק נאמן.**
השמש והירח עדים לו שכל זמן שהם קיימים מלכותו קיימת: כמו ירמיה שאמ' אם תפרו
את בריתי היום ואת בריתי הלילה גם בריתי תופר את דוד עבדי: 39 **ואתה זנחת.** דקדקת
אחר בניו לחשוב עוונם את אשר זנחתם בימי 'ח'זקיהו: 40 **נארת.** בטלת 41 **כל**
גדירותיו שבנה בירושלם: **מבצריו.** הר הבית ומצודת ציון: 44 **אף תשיב צור חרבו.**
השיבות והפכת את חידוד **חרבו.** כמו חרבות צורים. וכן כל כלי יוצר עלייך לא יצלח: **לא**
הקמותו. לא העמדתו מליפול: 45 **השבת מטהרו.** וריח **זריחתו.** כמו צהרים דמתרגמין
טיהרא. וכמי וכעצם השמים לטוהר **לארץ מיגרת.** השפלתה והישחתה. כל לשון שחייה
בתרגו' יונתן מגר: 48 **זכור אני מה חלד.** מה זקנה יש לי. הלא מעט ימי. דיי לך שאתה
נפרע ממני במותי קצר ימים: **על מה שוא.** לחנם ולהבל **בראת כל בני אדם:** 51 **שאתי**
בחיקי כל עמים רבים בגולה אני נושא סבלם ומשאם: 52 **עקבות.** סופי מלך המשיח ולשון
משנה הוא. בעקבות חוצפא יסגא: 53 **ברוך י'י לעולם אמן ואמן.** על כל תשועה שעשה לנו:

צ 1 **תפילה** למשה איש **האלקים.** י"א מזמורים מכאן עד לדוד מזמור
כולם משה אמרן. וכנגדן בירך י"א ברכות בזאת הברכה: **מעון אתה היית**
לנו. מדור ומנוס לבוא שם **אתה היית לנו** מעולי כי אתה הייתה מקדם הכל: 2 **בטרם**
הרים יולדו. נבראו: ובטרם חוללת **ארץ ותבל. ומעולם** ראשון **עד עולם** אחרון **אתה אל.** 3
תשב אנוש עד דכא. מביא יסורין על האדם עד שאתה מחזירן להיות תשוש כח וקרוב
למות. **ותאמר** לו בייסורין **שובו בני אדם** מדרכיכם הרעים: 4 **כי אלף שנים בעיניך** וגו'.
וכשעלת תשובה בדעתך מתחילה יפה דנתה ובראתה אתה והשנים לכך לפי
שהיו בני האדם רבים שלא היו אלף שנים בעיניך אלא כיום עובר וחלוף **ומעט** מן הלילה
עמו. שהרי אמרת לאדם ליום הראשון כי ביום אכלך ממנו **מות** תמות וחיה תתק"ל שנים.
נמצא אלף שנים עולים ליום אחד שלם ומעט מן הלילה עמו: **כיום אתמול** שכבר עבר: 5
זרמתם שינה יהיו. חטפתם עכשיו לאותן השנים **והבאתם** לימים מועטים שאינן אלא
כשינת תנומה ששני הדורות שבעים שנה כמו שמפרש בסוף העניין ימי שנותינו בהם
שבעים שנה. והם חשובי' שינה אחת כעניין שני בשוב י'י את שיבת ציון היינו כחולמים
ועל שבעים של גלות נאמר **זרמתם.** לשון **שטיפה.** כמו זורם מים: **בבקר כחציר**
יחלוף. הנולד בלילה מת בבקר לסוף ימות השינה. ואם 6 **בבקר יציץ** חלף. ועד בוא השמש
ימולל ויבש. למה 7 **כי כלינו באפך** וגו'. ועל כל זאת 8 **שתה עוונתינו לנגדך:** ואת
עלומינו. חטאינו נעורינו שמתה **למאור פניך** למולך להביט בהם. **עלומינו.** נעורינו. כמו בן
מי זה העלם: 9 **פנו בעברתך** נפנו ועברו והלכו להם בעברתך. **כמו הגא.** כדיבור הממהר
לכלות: 10 **ימי שנותינו בהם שבעים שנה.** ימי שנותינו בעוונינו אלה ובעלומינו אלה ע'
שנה: **ואם בגבורות.** ואם הרבה גרמו ימיו שמונים שנה: **ורהבם עמל ואון.** וכל הגדולה
והשררה שיש לו לאדם בתוך הימים האלה אינן אלא עמל ואון. ולמה. **כי גז.** שהרי גז חיש
ונעופה. בתוך **עברת** אנו עפים ומתים: **גז.** לשון עברה. כמו נגוזו ועבר. וכן ויגז
שלוים: 11 **מי יודע עוז אפך.** בימים מועטים כאלה מי יקנה לו לב לדעת את עוז אפך
וליראה אותך. ואתה **כיראתך עברתך כאשר** אתה יראוי כן עברתך קשה ונפרע מן
החוטאים: 12 **למנות ימינו כן הודע.** כאשר בתחילה הודע בעולם את מניין ימינו ארוכים:

וכיון שנארי' ימים נוכל לקנות לב **ונביא** בתוכם **לבב חכמה. ונביא.** לשון הבאה : ד"א
למנות ימינו כן הודע ע' שנה עולה בגימטרי' ע' : 13 **שובה י"י** מחרון אפך **והנחם.** חשוב
מחשבה טובה **על עבדיך** : 14 **שבעינו בבקר חסדך.** ביום הגאולה והתשועה שהוא בקר
ואור לליל הצרה והאנחה : **ורננה ונשמחה בכל ימינו.** כלומר בכל הצרות שעברו עלינו
בימים אלה : 15 **שמחינו** לימות המשיח כמנין ימות שעיניתנו **בגלות** וכמנין **שנות אשר
ראינו רעה** : 17 **נעם י"י** אלקינו שכינתו **ותנ**נחומיו. **ומעשה ידינו כונן עלינו.** לשון תחנה
הוא. **כוננה.** כמו שאומ' שָׁפַטָה שֶׁמָרָה. **כוננהו.** כונן אותו. **ושני** פעמים כונן אותו ומעשה
ידינו כונן. על מלאכת המשכן שברכו לישר' והתפלל. שתשרה שכינה במעשה ידיהם
במשכן. ואחד שתהא ברכה במעשה ידיהם :

צא 1 יושב בסתר **עליון** הק' היושב בסתר השמים : ד"א מי שהוא חוסה
בסתר כנפי השכינה הוא יתלונן בצלו. שהקי' מגין עליו : הרי משה רבינו במזמור זה משיא
את בני אדם לחסות תחת כנפי השכינה : **שדי.** לשון חוזק. **בצל שדי.** כמו בצלו חמדתי
וישבתי : 2 **אומר לי"י** שהוא **מחסי.** ולמה אני אומר כן 3 **כי הוא יצילך** כל אדם **מפח יקוש** :
4 **באברתו.** כנף : **יסך** יסוכך : **תחסה.** תתכסה. **וסוחרה** היא צנה המקפת את האדם קרוב
לארבע רוחותיו. **סוחרה.** לשון סחור סחור : 6 **לא תירא** אם תבטח בו : **מחץ יעוף.** שד
המעופף כאן : 6 **מדבר. מקטב** שמות שדים הם זה מזיק בלילה וזה מזיק ביום בצהרים :
ישוד. ישדד. 7 **יפול מצדך.** לשון חנייה. כמו על פני כל אחיו נפל : **מצדך.** משמאלך יחנו
אלף שדים. **ואליך לא יגש.** אחד מהם להזיק : 8 **ושילומת.** כיליון. ולמה 9 **כי אתה** אמרת
י"י **מחסי.** והרי זה מקרא קצר : **עליון שמת מעוניך.** את הק' שמת מעוז מבטחך. 10 **לא
תאונה.** לא תקרא. וכן אנה לידו : 12 **פן תגוף.** פן תַכשל. וכן כל לשון נגיפה. אצופיר בל.

צב 1 מזמור שיר ליום השבת. שיר של לויס. **ליום השבת** שאומרים
אותו בשבתות והוא **מ**דבר בעניין העולם הבא שכולו שבת : 3 **להגיד בבקר חסדך.** בעת
הגאולה. **ואמונתך בלילות.** ובעוד צרת הגלות להאמין בך שתשמור אבטחתך כל זה נאה
וטוב : 4 **עלי עשור** כנור של עשרה נימין : 7 **איש בער ולא ידע** את האמור למטה : 8 **בפרוח
רשעים כמו עשב.** אינו יודע שפריחתם אינה אלא להשמידם עדי עד שמשלם לשנאיו על
פניהם להאבידם : 9 **ואתה מרום.** בכל משפטיך ידך על העליונה שהכל מצדיקים עליהם
דינך : 11 **בלותי בשמן רענן.** לבלותי בשמן של שררה. **בלותי.** לשון בלול בשמן : 12 **בשורי.**
בעויניי. כמ' שורריי. **בקמים עלי מריעים.** על הרשעים הקמים עלי : שמעו אזניי מאחורי
הפרגוד שלא יועילו לכלות אותנו שנתנו שכך שמעתי : 13 **צדיק כתמר יפרח** כתמר לעשות פירות
וכארז להחליף גזע. **שתולים בבית י"י.** 14 **שתולים בבית י"י.** 15 **ינובון.** יהיו הצדיקים : **דשנים**
שמנים ורעננים יהיו. ואז 16 **יגיד כי ישר י"י צורי** :

צג 1 י"י מלך גאות לבש. יאמרו לעתיד **אף תכון תבל** במולכו תשמח
הארץ : 3 **נשאו נהרות י"י.** לשון צעקה וקובלנות הוא : אהה **י"י.** הנה האומות השטופים
כנהרות נשאו קולם ויהמיון. ואת דור עמקי נבכיהם ישאו ויגברו תמיד להתנאות כנגדך :
4 **מקולות מים רבים** וגו'. כל לשון תומיד דכא. לשון עומק ושפלות. ידעתי אני כי יותר
מקולות מים רבים אשר יהמיי' עלינו ומאדירות משברי הים הזה **אדיר במרום** י"י וידך
תקיפה עליהם. 5 **עדותיך** שהעידו והבטיחו נביאיך **לביתך** שהוא **נוה קודש. נאמנו מאד
לביתך ולאורך ימים** היא מצפה להם. ואפיי' שארכו הימים נאמנים הם מאד. **נאוה.** כמו
נאות אלקים. נֵנָה ותדע שכל נאוה שבמקרא אינו מפיק א"לף לפי שהן לשון נוי. וזה מפיק
א"לף :

צד 1 אל נקמות י"י הראה וגלה לנו נקמתך : 4 **יתאמרו.** ישתבחו. כמו
האמרת היום : 8 **בינו בערים. האומ**ות שוטים שבעולם. 9 **הנוטע אֹזן.** שמא הק' שנטע אזן
לא ישמע צעקת עמו ועניין : 10 **הלא יוכיח.** ייסר אתכם על כך : 11 **י"י יודע** מחשבותיכם
שאתם סבורים להתגאות בנזר המלוכה. כי הבל הם : 12 **אשרי הגבר.** אשריהם הצדיקים
המעונין על ידיכם ובלבד שיהיו עסוקים בתורה ובמצוות : 13 **להשקיט לו מימי רע.** מימי

דין של גיהנם. עד שיראו שיכרה **שיכרה לרשע שחת**: 15 **כי עד צדק ישוב משפט** הייסורין שלהן
עד **שיצדיקו** בשבילם. ואחר המשפט **כל ישרי לב** יתקבצו כי נטלו שכרם: 17 **דומה.**
דומיה: 16 **מי יקום לי.** זכות מי תעורר לנו בין האומות המריעים הללו: 20 **היחברך כסא
הוות.** היוכל להדמות לך מלכות האומות היוצרי צלמים ומסכות של עמל: **עלי חק** בשביל
חק. להיות חוק להם עבודתם. 21 **יגדו.** יאספו גדודים עד נפש ישר' להרוג: **ירשיעו.** יחייבו
בדין להורגו. 23 **אונם.** אונס. כמו יצפון לבניו אונו:

צה 1 **לכו נרננה** לַיְיָ: 4 **ותועפות.** לשון גובה המעופף. 6 **ונברכה.** לשון
ויברך את הגמלים 7 **היום אם בקולו תשמעו**: 9 **בחנוני גם ראו פעלי.** בחנני חנם שכבר
ראו פעלי במצרים: 10 **ארבעים שנה אקוט בדור** קטתי עמהם. רבתי עמהן. לשון נקטה
נפשי ארבעים שנה להמיתי כי אמרתי **תועי לבב הם**: 11 **אל מנוחתי** לארץ ישר' ולירושלם
אשר קראתיה מנוחה שני' זאת מנוחתי עדי עד:

צו 1 **שירו** לַיְיָ **שיר חדש.** 7 **הבו לַיְיָ משפחות עמים.** ומה תתנו לו. **הבו לו
כבוד ועוז** 10 **יְיָ מלך** ירגזון עַמים. לעתיד לבא יהיה זה שיר **ידין עמים במישרים.** אותם
שיהפוך להם שפה ברורה: **במישרי'.** בזכיות: 11 **ירעם הים.** להרים קול בתהלי' 12 **כל
עצי היער.** כל שולטני האומות:

צז 1 **יְיָ מלך** **תגל הארץ** בנטלו המלכות מעשו ומזרעו. **תגל הארץ.** זהו
שאמ' יחזקאל כשתוב כל הארץ שממה אעשה לך. על עשו נתנבא כן: 4 **ברקיו.** זהרורין.
כמו למען יהיה לה ברק מרוטה. **ותחל.** לשון חיל כיולדה: 5 **כדונג.** המתלהלים
והמתפארי' בע"ז: 8 **משפטיך** בעי': 11 **אור זרוע לצדיק.** נקמתך. זריעה ממש מוכנת לצמוח
להם:

צח 1 **מזמור** שירו לַיְיָ. כל אלה לעתיד 8 **נהרות ימחאו כף.** הנביאים דברו
בלשון שהאזן שומעת. לא שיהא לַנהרות כף אלא לשון חדוה ושמחה:

צט 1 **יְיָ מלך** ירגזון עמים מדבר במלחמת גוג ומגוג. ואז ירגזון עמים
כענין שני וזאת תהיה המגפ'. **תנוט.** לשון נטוי רגלי: 4 **ועוז מלך.** מוסב על מקרא עליון: 3
יודו שמך. ויודו אַת עוז מלך האוהב משפט: 4 **אתה כוננת מישרים** פשרה ושימת אנשי'
בין אנשים כוננת: באומרך כי תראה חמור שונאך וגו'. כי תפגע שור אויבך וגו'. ומי הוא
הרואה את שונאו גומל לו חסד ולא יודבן לבו לחבקו ולַנשקו: תנחומא: 7 **בעמוד ענן ידבר
אליהם.** אף עם שמואל. וזהו שאמ' הרואה ותעניינה אותם ותאמרנה יש. ונראה הענן
קשור על פתחו. כד"א ויש אשר יהיה הענן. כדי"א ויש אשר יהיה הענן: 8 **אל נושא
היית** ישר' **היתה להם** בשבילם **ונקם** היית' **על עלילותם**: 6 **משה ואהרן** בשמעו נא המורים.
שמואל על שלא הדריך בניו בדרך הטובה מת בחור: 9 **כי קדוש יְיָ אלקינו.** על שהוא
מדקדק עם הצדיקים הוא מקודש בעולם. וכן הוא אומ' ונקדש בכבודי:

ק 1 **לתודה.** להודייה לאומרו על זבחי התודה. 2 **עבדו את יְיָ בשמחה** וכל
כך למה. 3 **דעו כי יְיָ הוא אלקים** שישלם לכם שכר פעולתכם. אבל עובדי ע"ז אין להם
לעבוד בשמחה שאין משתלמין שכר: **הוא עשנו ולא אנחנו.** כשלא היינו בעולם: 4 **בתודה**
בהודייה. 5 **ועד דור ודור** קיימת **אמונתו.** הבטחה שמבטיח ומאמין הבטחה:

קא 1 **לדוד** **מזמור חסד ומשפט אשירה.** כשאתה עושה עמי חסד אקלסך
ברוך הטוב והמטיב וכשאתי עושה עמי משפט אני אשיר ברוך דיין האמת. בין כך ובין כך
לך יְיָ אזמרה. 2 **אשכילה** אתן לב על דרך התמים **מתי תבא** אלי הדרך הישרה להתהלך
בה. **ואתהלך בתום לבבי** אף **בקרב ביתי** בהצנע כמי' בפרהסיא. **שטים.** לשון כי תשטה
אשתו. לסור מן הדרך. דישטולייטיש בלע' 4 **רע לא אדע.** לא אאהב ולא אכיר בדבר רע: 5
אותו לא אוכל שיהא חבירי שלא אלמד ממעשיו: 8 **לבקרים אצמית.** מדי יום יום אכרית
מעט מעט המחוייבים מיתה:

קב 1 **תפילה** לעני כי יעטוף בהתעטף נפשו בצרה: 4 **נחרו.** הנו"ן מְשמשת
כמו נו"ן נעשו נקבו. והוא לשון יובש. כמו ועצמי חרה מני חורב. נחר מפוח: 7 **לקאת.** שם
עוף. **ככוס חֲרבות.** שם עוף. את הכוס ואת השלך חרבות. מדברות. מדברות: דמיתי **לקאת מדבר.**
כך אנו נדודים ממקומינו ללכת בגולה. התבוננתי בעצמי: הנני **כצפור הבודד על**
גג. יושב באין בן זוג לבדו. **בודד.** יושב בדד: 9 **מהוללי** המתלוצצים בי לשון הוללות: **בי**
נשבעו. ראו ברעתי ונשבעים בי ואומרים אם לא כן יארע לי כמו שאירע לישרי. כה יעשה
לי כמו שעשה לישרי: 10 **בבכי מסכתי.** בדמעות מזגתי: 11 **כי נשאתני** תחילה והגבהתני.
ועתה השלכתני משמים ארץ. ואם לא נשאתני תחילה לא היתה חרפתי גדולה כל כך: 12
כצל נטוי לעת ערב. כשהצללים נוטים ונחשכה אין הצללים ניכרים אלא כלים והולכים.
13 **ואתה** אשר **לעולם תשב** ונשבעת לנו בך. כשם שאתה קיים כך יש עליך לקיימנו. 14
לפיכך **אתה תקום תרחם** את **ציון כי עת לחננה.** שכך הבטחת כי יראה כי אזלת יד והרי
אזלת יד: 15 **כי רצו עבדיך.** אהבו. **את אבניה ואת עפרה.** ומדר' אגדה כשיצא יכניה וגלותו
נשאו עמם מאבני ירושלם ועפרה לבנות שם בית הכנסת בבבל: 16 **ויראו גוים** את שמך
כשתושיע את עמך: 18 **הערער.** הצועק כמו צרי צעקת שבר יעוערו: ד"א **ערער.** הרוס
ונשחת. כמו ערו ערו: 19 **תכתב זאת.** כך יאמרו רואי התשועה תכתב התשועה הזאת לספר
אותה **לדור אחרון. ועם נברא.** ועם שנעשה בריא חדשה לצאת מעבדות לחירות ומאופל
לאור: 20 **אל ארץ הביט.** לראות בעוני עמו: 21 **תמותה.** חולה. אנמוריניאה בל': 24 **ענה**
בדרך חוזר לקובלנותו הראשון כי נשאתני ותשליכני: ימי כצל נטוי אויב **כחי בדרך.**
25 **אמר ליַיְ** אלי אתה. **אל תעלני בחצי ימי.** אל תסלק אותן להשמידנו מן האדמה ביד
אויבינו בחצי ימינו. ומה הן שנים כל ימות **דור דורים שנותיך** הבטחת לקיימנו לפניך כמ'
שכתוב בסוף הַמזמור ושנותיך לא יתמו. וזרע עֲבדיך לפניך יכון 26 **לפניהם.** מתחילה. 27
כלבוש תחליפם. כאדם ההופך את לבושו לפושטו: 28 **ואתה הוא.** אתה הוא העומד
וקיים:

קג 1 **ברכי** נפשי את יַיְ. הי ברכי יש כאן כנגד ה' עולמות שאדם דר בהן כמו
שאמרו רבותי' במסכת ברכות. גר במעי אמו אמ' שירה על הים. ינק משדי אמו אמ' שירה
על הים וכו': 5 **תתחדש כנשר נעורייכי.** כנשר הזה שמתחדש משנה לשנה כנפים ונוצה.
ויש מדרש אגדה על מין נשר שמשמזקין חוזר: [צט:7: **בעמוד ענן ידבר אליהם** אף עם
שמואל וזהו שני שני בזה הרואה ותעניניה אותם ותאמרנא יש. ונראה הענן קשור על
פתחו. כד"וא ויש אשר יהיה הענן. **שמרו עדותיו וחוק** אשר **נתן למו:** 8 **אל נושא** עון. ישר'
היתה להם ונוקם נקמות על עלילותם משה ואהרן נענשו בשמעו נא המורי.
שמואל על שלא הדריך בני בדרך ישר' הטובה מת בחור. 9 **קדוש יַיְ אלקינו.** על שהוא
מדקדק על הצדיקים הוא מקודש בעולם וכן הוא אומ' ונקדש בכבודי. בכבודיי.] **קג:7:**
יודיע דרכיו למשה. 14 **זכר כי עפר אנחנו.** זכור הוא ולא שכח שאנחנו עפר: ויודע 15
שאנוש כחציר ימיו וגו': 16 **רוח עברה.** חולי של מיתה. 19 **משלה.** מושלת 22 **כל מעשיו**
אשר הוא בכל המְקמות שממשלתו שם:

קד 1 **ברכי** נפשי 2 **עוטה אור כשלמה.** עוטה אור ברקיע שלמה: 4 **עושה**
מלאכיו רוחות. עושה את הרוחו' שלוחיו: 6 **תהום כלבוש כסיתו.** זהו דוגמת האמור
במקום אחר. בשומי ענן לבושו וגו'. **תהום.** היא ים. **על ההרים יעמדו מים.** אוקיינוס גבוה
מכל העולם עומד על הרים. וכן הוא אומ' הקורא למי הים וישפכם על פני הארץ. אין
שפיכה אלא מלמעלה למטה: 7 **מן גערתך ינוסון.** כשאמרת יקוו המים. ומאותו **קל יחפזון**
ונקוו 8 למקום אשר **יסדת להם:** 9 **גבול שמת** להם. החול אשר סביב שפתו: 12 **עליהם**
עוף השמים ישכון. על המעיינות מבין עפאים ענפי האילנות וכן עפיה נופל על פני
חציר וגו': 15 **ויין** אשר **ישמח לבב אנוש** גם אותו יוציא מן הארץ. ושמן **להצהיל פנים** בו.
ולחם אשר לבב אנוש יסעד: 16 **עצי יַיְ** בגן עדן: 17 **צפרים יקננו שם.** ישר' שנקראו
צפרים: **יקננו.** לשון קן צפור: 18 **הרים הגבוהים** ברא **ליעלים. מחסה.** כל לשון מחסה
לשון צל ומחבוא. שאדם מתכסה שם מן המטר ומן החמים אבריאמנט בל': 19 **למועדים.**

למנות בו זמנים ורגלים : **שמש ידע מבואו.** אבל ירח לא ידע מבואו. פעמים בא בארוכ'
פעמים בא בקצרה : 20 **תשת חשך ויהי לילה.** בכל יום אתה מעריב השמש <u>והיה</u> לילה.
ובו רומשת **כל חיתו יער.** 22 **תזריח השמש יאספון** במסתריהם ונחבאים מבני אדם. ואז
23 כל **אדם יצא לפעלו.** 24 **קנינך.** מקנה וקניין שלך. כמו קונה שמים וארץ : הכל קנוי
לך. 25 **רחב ידים.** רחב מקום לרגש בל' : 26 **לשחק בו.** שלש שעות ביום. כך אמרו רבותינו
במס' ע"ז : וכן מפורש בספר איוב. <u>התשחק</u> בו כצפור : 29 **תוסף רוחם.** לשון כליון כמו ספו
תמו : 30 **תשלח רוחך** בהחיות המתים. 32 **יגע בהרים ויעשנו** כמו שמפורש בסיני. והר
סיני עשן כולו : 33 **בעודי.** בעודני חי : 35 **יתמו חטאים. חוטאים :**

קה 1 הודו ליי' **קראו בשמו : עלילותיו.** מעלליו. 3 **התהללו בשם קדשו**
התפארו במעון שם קדשו שיש להם פטרון כמוהו. **התהללו.** פורווונטיץ בלעז : 8 **דבר צוה**
לאלף דור. התורה אשר צוה להודיעה בעולם לאחר אלף דור וראה שאין העולם מתקיים
בלא <u>תורה</u> והעביר מהם תתקע"ד דורות ויש לפותרו כפשוטו. **זכר** לישר' את **בריתו** אשר
צוה לשמור והבטיח לשמור להם **לאלף דור** כעניין שנאמ' שומר הברית והחסד לאהביו
<u>ולשומ</u>רי מצותיו לאלף דור : 11 **לאמר לך אתן** וגו'. הוא הברית אשר כרת להם : 13
ויתהלכו מגוי אל גוי. אברהם גר בארץ פלשתים ובמצרים ובאר' כנען. וכן יצחק וכן יעקב
כולם גרו מגרות לגרות : 14 **ויוכח עליהם מלכים.** וינגע יי' את פרעה. כי עצר עצר
לאבימלך : 15 **במשיחי.** בגדוליי. כל משיחי לשון גדולה ושררה : 16 **ויקרא רעב** כדי
להגלותם במצרים : **מטה לחם.** משען לחם : 17 **שלח לפניו איש.** יוסף הנמכר שם לעבד :
18 **ברזל באה נפשו.** אמ' רב הונא בר אידי שירתוע עשתה לו תחת זקנו שאם ירכין פניו
יהא ה<u>ש</u>ירתוע מכהו : 19 **עד עת בא דברו** של הק' לקיים גזירתו שיתגלגל הדבר וירדו ישר'
למצרים : **אמרת יי' צרפתהו.** בחנתהו ליוסף שנתנסה וכבש את יצרו באשת אדוניו. ועליה
נתייסר ונצרף בייסורין לתתו אל בית הסהר : 20 **שלח מלך** מצרים שלוחיו <u>ויתירוהו.</u> שלח
מושל עמים הוא פרעי **ויפתחהו :** 22 **בנפשו.** לשון חיבה הוא זה כמ' כמ' ונפש יהונתן נקשרה
בנפש דוד כשפתר החלום חיבבוהו כולם : 24 **ויפר** הק' **את עמו.** הפרה והרבה אותם. 28
לא מרו את דברו. המכות שצוה לבא עליהם. באו במצותו ולא שינו את דברם. 40 **שאל**
ויבא שלו. שאל ישר' בשר ויבא לו הק' שלוים : 41 **הלכו בציות נהר.** הלכו נהרות מן הבאר
בארץ ציה וצלמות. 42 **כי זכר** הק' **את דבר קדשו** אשר עם **אברהם עבדו** שהבטיחו
ואחריכן יצאו ברכוש גדול ודור רביעי ישובו הנה :

קו 1 הללו יק' 2 **מי ימלל גבורות יי'.** 4 **ברצון עמך.** בהרצותך לעמך : 7
<u>וימרו</u> **על ים.** הם היו מקטני אמנה. אמרו כשם שאנו עולין מצד זה כך מצרים עולין לצד
אחר ויבאו אחרינו עד שרמז הק' לים לים והקיאם ליבשה. אז <u>נירא</u> ישר' את מצרים מת על
שפת הים. לפיכך ויאמינו ב<u>יי</u>' אבל מתחילה לא האמינו : 13 **לא חכו לעצתו.** לא קוו לו. 14
ויתאוו תאוה מי שאכילנו בשר. 15 **וישלח רזון בנפשם.** ואף י"י חרה בעם : 16 **ויקנאו**
למשה. הכעיסוהו. כמ' הם קנאוני בלא אל. 18 **ותבער** בם **אש** ותאכל את מקריבי
הקטרת : 20 **אוכל עשב.** אין לך משוקץ ומתועב מן השור בשעה שהוא אוכל עשב שהוא
מוציא פרש רבה והוא מלוכלך בה : 24 **וימאסו בארץ חמדה.** בשילוח מרגלים והוציאו
דבה על הארץ : 26 **וישא ידו.** שבועה. 27 **להפיל זרעם בגוים.** מאותה שעה נגזר עליהם
חורבן הבית. שהרי ליל ט' באב בכו. ואמ' הק' הם בכו בכייה של חנם ואני אקבע ל<u>ה</u>ם
בכייה לדורות : 33 **כי המרו** משה ואהרן **את רוח** בשמעו נא המורים. **ויבטא בשפתיו.**
שבועה לכן לא ת<u>בי</u>או את הקהל הזה וגו'. 34 **לא השמידו** בימי יהושע **את העמים אשר**
אמר יי' להם לא תחיה כל נשמה : 38 **ויתנם ביד גוים.** בימי השופטי' בין שופט לשופט.
ויתנם ביד גוים. בימי השופטי' בין שופט לשופט. כגון עגלון וכושן רשעתים וסיסרא
ופלשתים ומדין : 43 **וימכו בעוונם.** נעשו שפלים בעוונם. 47 **הושיעם** גם עתה יי' **אלקינו :**

קז 1 הודו ליי' **כי טוב.** 2 **יאמרו גאולי יי'.** כשיפדם מיני **צר.** 4 **תעו במדבר.**
הולכי מדברות אף הם צריכין להודות. שהרי פעמים שהם תועים 5 **ורעבים וצמאים : 7**
וינחם. וינהגם. ל<u>פיכ</u>ך 8 **יודו ליי' חסדו :** 10 **יושבי חשך וצלמות.** אף האסורים בבית

הסוהר צריכין להודות כשיוצאין מבית אסיריהם : 11 **כי המרו אמרי אל.** אין פורענו' באה
על האדם אלא בעוונו. 16 **כי שבר דלתות נחשת** שהיו נעולים בפניהם. 17 **אוילים מדרך**
פשעם. מעוונותיהם יתענו בתחלואי ייסורין. אף הם מן הצריכין להודות. יש סימניות
בפרשה זו ובאים לידרוש במקום אכין ורקין למעט לומ' צעקו קודם גזר דין נענין. אחר גזר
דין אין נענין : 27 **יחוגו.** לשון **שבר** הוא. וכן בחגוי הסלע. וכן אדמת יהודה למצרים
לחגא : 30 וישכחו **כי ישתוקו** הגלים. **מחוז.** לשון גבול. ומנחי' חיברו עם מחזותנו את
שאול. גבולינו שלא יכנס בתחומינו. וכן מחזה מול מחזה. 33 **ישם נהרות למדבר.** נותן
יישובי האומות לחורבן : 34 **למלחה.** להיות בארץ מליחה מעשות פרי : 35 **ישם מדבר**
לאגם. נותן יישוב חרב לבניין ומחזירו לקדמתו : 39 **וימעטו וישוחו.** והם מתחילה היו
מועטים ושחים **מעוצר רעה ויגון** : 41 **וישם כצאן משפחות.** וישם האביון משפחות זרעו
רבים כצאן : 42 **קפצה.** סתמה. כמי לא תקפוץ את ידך :

קח 2 **נכון לבי** אלקים נאמן לבי נאמן עמך. **אף כבודי.** אף כבודי הוא שאני
משורר לך : ד"א **אף כבודי** אף לפי **כבודי** לא אמנע לשורר לך ולא אחלוק לעצמי כבוד : 3
עירה שחר. דרך שאר מלכים השחר מעורר ואני מעורר השחר שאני קם בחצות לילה
שהנבל ו"כנור מעוררני כמו שאמרו רבותינו כנור היה תלוי למעלה ממטתו של דוד. וכיון
שהגיע חצות לילה רוח צפונית מנשבת בו. והוא מנגן מאליו. 5 **מעל שמים.** וכתוב אחר
אומר עד שמים. פירשו רבותי' כאן בעושין לשמה כאן בעושין שלא לשמה : 7 **וענני.** שכל
עמך וידידיך תלויין בי : 8 **אלקים דבר בקדשו** שאמלוך. יבא **העת** ואעלוז בדברו : **אחלקה**
ארץ אויבי שכם. חלק לישר'. כמו שכם אחד על אחיך : **ועמק סוכות.** 10 **מואב סיר רחצי.**
כלומ' עבדיי ושמשיי בכל תשמיש שמשתמשין בי : **על אדום אשליך נעלי.** עבודתי שיהו
מלכיהם נועלין מנעליי ברגלי : **אתרועע.** ארים קול ליראם מפני : 11 **מי יובילני** לימות
המשיח לפשוט יד בעשו ובעריו מבצריו. **מי שנחני** כבר על אדום שהכיתי בהם בגיא מלח
י"ח אלף :

קט 1 **אלקי** על כל ישר' נאמ'. 2 **כי פי רשע.** עשו : 4 **תחת אהבתי** אותך
ישטנוני. **ואני תפילה.** ואני מתפלל אליך תמיד. 7 **בהשפטו** לפניך **יצא** מ**ד**יינך **רשע**
ומחוייב : 8 **פקדתו.** גדולתו פרוטטישא"ה : 10 **ושאלו ודרשו מחרבותיהם.** הכל ישאלו
עליהם מה זה נהייתה בפלוני ופלוני מתוך קול חורבה שיצא עליהם. **ודרשו** משמע אחרים
שהרי נקוד חטף קמ׳. וכן **ושאלו** מפי אחרים. משמע שישאלו עליהם אחרים : ויש עוד
לפתור **ושאלו** ממשקל חזק יהו משאלים על הפתחים : 11 **ינקש.** נוקש **לכל אשר לו.** ינקש
הנושה בכל אשר לו : אדם הטורח ומחזר ולהוט לעשות דבר נופל בו לשון מתנקש כלומ'
מטרף ומתלבט : כמו וארכובותיה דא לדא נקשן. וכן פן תנקש אחריהם. אף כאן יהיה
הנוקש מתנקש ומתלהט ומתחפש אחר ממון של זה : **נושה לכל אשר לו.** יהא נושה ונוגע
ונקרב כל אשר לו. שייט אצופיר בל'. יהי משפט הנושה נוקש ונשען על כל ממונו וזהו יעקב
הנושה בעשו את עבודתו שני ורב יעבד צעיר : 14 **עון. אבותיו.** עון שהעוה על אבותיו.
לאברהם גרע חמש שנים מחייו. לאביו גרם כהיון העינים : **וחטאת אמו אל תמח.** שהשחית
את רחמה. ושגרם להעלים יום קבורתה מן **הבריות** שלא יקללוה שיצא עשו ממנה. ומ**כ**ריסה כמה
שני׳ ותמת דבורה מינקת רבקה וגו'. ויקרא שמו אלון ב**כ**ות. בלשון יווני קורין לאחר אלון.
שאבל אחר היה ליעקב עם של דבורה שמתה אמו והעלימו מיתה'. 15 **יהיו העוונות האלה**
נגד י"י **תמיד. ויכרת מארץ זכרם** של עשו ואלופיו. 16 **אשר לא זכר עשות חסד.** לעשות
באבל אביו כמ' שעשה יעקב נזיד עדשים לנחם את יצחק שבאותו יום מת אברהם : **איש**
עני. ישראל 17 **ויאהב קללה.** קללתו של הקי' שכפר בו : 19 **תהי לו.** הקללה מעטה **כבגד.**
ולמזח. חגורה. וכן ומזיח אפיקים רפה. אזור החזקים פתח. 23 **כצל כנטותו** פתח. ונע ו**מטורף**.
ננערתי. לשון תשנוק וטירוף ואוטם כארבה שהוא נודד נודד ונע ו**מטורף**.

קי 1 **נאם יי לאדני** רבותינו דרשוהו באברהם אבינו ו**א**ני אפרשנו
כדבריהם שקראוהו הכל אדון. אדוני שמענו. אדוני שבזכרנו : **שב לימיני.** התעכב לישועתי.
והתחולל לה. אין ישיבה אלא עכבה. וכן הוא אומ' ותשבו בקדש ימים רבים : **לימיני**.

לתשועת ימיני: **עד אשית אויביך** אמרפל וחביריו: 2 **מטה עזך ישלח י"י**. מטה לשון משען.
כמו כל מטה לחם שבר. כשתשוב מן <u>המלחמה</u> אתה ואנשיך עייפים ורודפים שלח הקי את
מלכי צדק מלך שלם להוציא לחם ויין: **רדה** <u>ב</u>מלחמה **בקרב אויביך** לבטח: 3 **עמך נדבות**
ביום חילך. כשתאסוף חיל לרדוף אחריהם יתנדבו עמך ואוהבי לצאת עמך כמו שמצינו
וירק את חניכיו ולא יותר וענר ואשכול וממר' התנדבו מאליהם ללכת אחריו <u>בעזרתו</u>:
בהדרי קדש מרחם משחר זאת תהיה לך בזכות הדרות קדש שהיו בך מבטן אמך שהזכיר
בוראו בן שלש שנים: **מרחם משחר**. <u>מ</u>שפלת מן הרחם. כמו משילין פירו' דרך ארובה.
ואיכא דתני משחירין: **לך טל ילדותך**. לך יחשב ילדותך. דרכי יושר שהתנהגת בהם
בילדותך יהיו לך לנועם כטל זה שהוא נעים ונוח: 4 **נשבע י"י ולא ינחם**. לפי שהיה מתיירא
על האוכלוסין שהרג נאמ' לו אל תירא אברהם. לא ינחם על הטובה אשר דבר עליך: **אתה**
כהן לעולם על דברתי מלכי צדק. ממך תהיה המלכות <u>וה</u>כהונה להיות בניך יורשים את
שם אביהם בכהונה ומלכות שניתנה לו: **דברתי מלכי צדק**. יי"וד יתר. כמ' רבתי עם. **על**
דברתי מלכי צדק. על פקודת מלכי צדק: **אתה כהן**. יש במשמע כהן כהונה ושררה. כמו
ובני דוד כהנים היו: 5 **י"י** אשר היה **על יד ימינך** המלחמה **ומחץ ביום אפו** את הארבעה
מלכים הוא 6 **ידין בגוים מלא גויות** זו היא בשורת ברית בין הבתרים שנאמ' לו במצרים
וגם את הגוי אשר יעבודו דן אנכי. **מלא גויות**. מלא עצמות: **מלא גויות**. אסיפת פגרים מלא לשון
אסיפה. כמו קראו אחריך מלא. אשר יקרא עליו מלא רועים יחד עלי יתמלאון. והיכן דן
מלא גויות את מצרים מת על שפת הים: **מחץ ראש על ארץ רבה**. זו היא דוגמת חבקוק
מחצת ראש מבית רשע. ראש פרעה שהוא ראש ושר על ארץ גדולה ו<u>נחש</u>ובה על כל הארצות
כמה שנאמ' מושל מושל בכל הארץ הליכתו היתה שותה ולא היתה צריכה למי גשמים: 7 **מנחל בדרך**
ישתה. מינילוס ההר <u>ב</u>דרך הליכתו היתה שותה ולא היתה צריכה למי גשמים: **על כן**
ירים ראש. על כך היה מרים ראש ומתפאר יאור לי ואני עשיתיני: ע"א יש לפרש המזמור
בדוד. 1 **נאם י"י** על עסקי שאול אדוני כשהייתי נרדף. **שב לימיני** התעכב והמתן <u>לתש</u>ועתי.
לאדני. על אדוני. כמי ואמר פרעה לבני ישר'. וכמו וישאלו אנשי המקום לאשתו. אמלוך לי
אחי הוא: 2 **מטה עזך ישלח י"י מציון**. מעשים טובים המצויונין בידך: ד"א עוד תמלוך
בציון ושם ישוח לך מטה עוז. ואז תרדה בקרב אויביך: 3 **עמך נדבות ביום חילך**. עם
ישר' יתנדבו לעזרתך ביום שתעשה חיל כמו <u>ש</u>מפורש בדברי הימים שהיו <u>נק</u>בצים אליו
מכל שבט ושבט ובלכתו בלכתו אל צקלג נפלו עליו ממנשה וגומ' ומן הגדי אל דויד וגו': **בהדרי**
קדש. בשביל הדרות קדשה שהיו בך מנעוריך **לך טל ילדותך**. ילדות טובה שהיה בך ופרק
נאה תהיה לך כטל שהוא נעים וערב ותעשה לך פירות להצליחך. 4 <u>נשבע</u> **י"י** וגו'.
שהמלכותת תהא שלך עולמית. **אתה כהן לעולם**. ואיזו מן <u>ה</u>כהונות כהונה שהיא למעלה
<u>מ</u>כהונת מלכי צדק וזו היא כהונת מלכות שהיא למעלה מכהונה גדולה שהיא בשלשים
מעלות: **על דברתי מלכי צדק** כלומ' למעלה מפקודת <u>מ</u>לכי צדק שהיה כהן לאל עליון. ואם
תאמר אף הוא היה מלך מלכות על הגוים אינה חשובה מלוכה כנגד ישר'. 5 **י"י** יהיה תמיד
על יד ימינך להושיעך אשר **מחץ ביום אפו מלכים** שנלחמו עם אברהם ועם יהושע ועם
ברק. 6 **ידין בגוים מלא גויות**. ועוד בימי <u>צד</u>קיהו בנך ידין באוכלוסי סנחריב קיבוץ פגרים
מתים. וימחץ סנחריב שהיא ראשה של נינוה. ואשור שהיא **ארץ רבה** 7 אשר **מנחל בדרך**
הרי שותה שנתפאר שברתי אוכלוסיו מימי <u>היר</u>דן שני אני קריתי ושתיתי מים ואחריב בכף
פעמי. **על כן ירים ראש** היה משתבח ומתפאר בגודלו: לי"א **מנחל בדרך ישתה**. הוא סם
המות שהוא משקה משקה של דרך כל הארץ נתנב' דוד עליו שימות ברשעו. **על כן ירים ראש**.
כלומ' על אשר ירים. על אשר היה מרים ראש:

קי"א 1 **הללו יק'** אודה **י"י** <u>ב</u>כל לבב: 4 **זכר עשה לנפלאותיו**. קבע לישר'
שבתות וימים טובים ומצות וכתב בהן וזכרת כי עבד היית ב<u>מ</u>צרים לפי שהוא **חנון ורחום**
על בניו וחפץ להצדיקם: 5 **טרף**. מזון. 6 **כח מעשיו הגיד לעמו** כשנתן **להם נחלת גוים** אז
הודיעם כחו וגבורתו. ומדר' תנחומא כתב לישר' מעשה בראשית להודיעם שהארץ שלו
ובידו להושיב בה כל מי שירצה ולעקור אילו ולהושיב אחרים שלא יוכלו האומות לומ'
לישר' גזלנים אתם שכיבשתם את ארץ שבעת גוים: 8 **סמוכים** הם פיקודיו על סמך ע"ז

מחזקין הם בעונשין ואזהרות והפרשיות קבועות זו על זו כסדר ולדרוש. וזהו שאמ׳
שלמה שוקיו עמודי שש :

קיב 1 **הללויק׳** אשרי איש. 2 **דור ישרים** אשר יבורך. יהי זרעו. 4 **זרח**
בחשך אור. כמו הזריח. ומדרשו הוא עצמו כביכול נעשה להם אור כמה שני׳ **יְיָ אורי**
וישעי׳ 5 **טוב איש חונן ומלוה** וגו׳. שחונן דלים ומלוה להם. ואינו **מדקדק** לומ׳ אין יכולת
בידי׳ **ואת דבריו** הצריכין לו במאכל ומשתה וכסות. מכלכל במשפט ומידה וחס על נכסיו :
יכלכל דבריו. מנהיג חפציו. 7 **נכון לבו.** נאמן לבו ליוצרו. 8 **סמוך לבו.** נשען ובטוח על
הקי׳ : 10 **רשע יראה וכעס.** לשון פעל. כמו ויכעס. לפיכך נקוד חצי קמץ וחצי פתח וטעמו
למטה :

קיג 1 **הללו יק׳** הללו עבדי יְיָ. 5 **מי כַיְיָ אלקינו.** בשמים ובארץ שהיא
מגביה לשבת ומשפיל לראות: **מגביהי משפילי.** מקימי. **להושיבי. מושיבי.** כלם יְ״וד
יתירה בהם. 9 **עקרת הבית** ציון שהיא כעקרה יושיבנה **אם הבנים שמחה.** כי חלה גם
ילדה ציון את בניה :

קיד 1 **בצאת** ישראל ממצרים מעם לועז. עם שפת אחר שאינו לשני הקודש.
וחבירו את עם נועז לא תראה עם עמקי שפה וגו׳. וני׳ון ולמ׳׳ד **מתחלפות** זו בזו. כמו נשכה
שהיא לשכה בספר עזרא : 2 **היתה יהודה לקדשו.** לקח את יהודה לגורלו וחבלו וקדושתו.
ואף הם קדשו את שמו בירידת הים. כמו שלמדנו באגדה פסוק זה שקפץ נחשון לתוך
הים. ואמ׳ אני ארד תחילה כעניין שנאמר שרי יהודה רגמתם. וזהו שני היתה יהודה
לקדשו : 3 **הירדן יסוב לאחור** שכל מימי מראשית נבקעו : 7 **חולי הָאָרֶץ.** המחולל את
הארץ וי׳׳וד יתירי׳ בו כי׳׳וד המגביהי לשבת והוהפכי 8 **למעיְינו מים.** וי׳׳יו יתירה כמו
חיתו יער : למעין :

קטו 1 **לא לנו** יְיָ לא בשבילנו. ובכושר מעשינו תעשה עמנו. **כי לַשמך תן**
כבוד כדי 2 שלא יאמרו איה אלקיהם : 7 **ולא ימישון.** לשון ימושני אבי׳. 11 **יראי יְיָ.** אילו
הגרים :

קטז 1 **אהבתי** כי ישמע יְיָ. תאבתי שישמע יְיָ בקולי: 2 **ובימי אקרא** בימי
צרתי אקראנו ובימי גאולתי אשבחנו : 3 **חבלי מות** חבורות אויבים המבקשים להמיתנו :
חבלי מות חבלי שאול. גבולי שאול. 9 **בארצות החיים.** ארץ ישר׳ שגרשוני רודפי ממנה
בימי שאול ועל כרחם חזרתי : 10 **האמנתי כי אדבר.** האמנתי את דברי ציבא שאמ׳ על
מפיבשת ואז **אני עניתי מאד.** דברתי קשה ונעננתי לך : 11 **אני אמרתי בחפזי** לנוס מפני
אבשלום : כל האדם כוזב ובוגד באוהבו. כי ראיתי בני מבקש נפשי וכל ישר׳ גומלים לי
רעה תחת טובה ולפיכך האמנתי לציבא ואמרתי אף מפיבושת כוזב ובוגד בי. כל לשי כזב
אינו אלא חסרון מבטח שבטחו עליו. פיילנצא׳. ויש פותרי׳
אותו **אני אמרתי בחפזי** בסלע המחלוקות שהיה שאול ואנשיו עוטרים אלי ואל אנשי
לתופשני. ושם נאמ׳ ויהי דוד נחפז ללכת. שמואל הנביא שהוא נאמן
ונביא אף הוא כוזב **שמשחני** למלך : 14 **נגדה נא לכל עמו.** נגד כל עמו. 15 **יקר בעיני יְיָ.**
הראני הקי׳ שדבר קשה הוא וכבד בעיניו להמית את חסידיו : **המותה.** המות. כמו הביתה
החוצה : 16 **עבדך בן אמתך.** אינו דומה עבד תרבות לעבד הלקוח מן השוק : **פתחת**
למוסרי. התרת מעל צוארי מוסרות ומוטות : 17 **זבח תודה.** זבחי הודייה על הניסים
שעשית לי. 18 **נדריי.** קורבנותיי שנדרתי. 19 **בתוככי.** כמו בתוך :

קיז 1 **הללו** את יְיָ כל גוים. 2 **כי גבר עלינו חסדו.** כלומ׳ כי אנחנו אשר
גבר עלינו חסדו. **ואמת יְיָ לעולם.** ששמר אבטחתו שהבטיחו את האבות : **קיח** 1 **הודו ליְיָ.**
2 **יאמר נא ישר׳.** לפי שלעולם חסדו :

קיח 5 **מן המצר** קראתי יק' **ענני במרחב.** ענני במה שהייתי צדיק
שהוציאני ממיצר למרחב. וכמוהו אשר באש. שיורד אש מן השמים. וכן אענך בסתר רעם.
אסתירך מן הרעם: 8 **טוב לחסות ביי.** חסיון אינו **אלא** לשון אש אשר צל ודבר מועט הוא
ומבטח דבר בריא וסמך חזק. ואע"פ כן לחסות ביי טוב מהבטחת בני אדם. 10 **כל גוים**
סבבוני. אמילם. אכריתם. לשון ימולל ויבש: 12 **דעכו כאש קוצים.** כל לשון דעיכה לשון
קפיצה וניתור. ממהר להיות ניתר וניתק ממקומו על כן הוא נופל על לשון אש ועל לשון
מים כגון נדעכו ממקומם. וכן ימי נדעכו. וכן ונרו עלי ידעד. כדרך שלהבת הניתק' מן
הפתילה. ועולה למעלה כשהיא כבה: 13 **דחה דחיתני** אתה אויבי עשו: 14 **עזי וזמרת יק'**
ויהי לי לישועה. עזי י"וד יתירה כי לא מצינו במקרא עוזי חטף קמץ אלא שורק חוץ מג'
מקומות שהוא יסוד סמוך אצל וזמרת. ועל כרחיך וזמרת דבוק הוא לתיבת השם ואינך
יכול לפרשו כמו וזמרתי. ואל תתמה על ויהי לי לישועה שלא אמר היה לי לישועה שהרבה
כאלה במקרא. ואשר לא שם לבו ויעזוב את עבדיו היה לו לכתוב עזב: 15 **קול רינה וישועה**
תהיה לעתיד **באהלי צדיקי.** ומהו קול הרנה וישועה **ימין יי' עושה חיל.** ירננו יי': 16 **ימין יי'**
רוממה: 17 **לא אמות** אני כנסת ישר' כשאר האומות מיתת עולם: 18 **יסר**
יסרני בגלות. ושם נתכפרו עוונותי. **ולמות לא נתנני:** 19 **פתחו לי שערי צדק.** ואילו הן
שערי צדק. **השער** של בית המקדש שהוא ליי' **והצדיקים יבאו בו.** 21 ושם **אודך כי**
עניתני. מן הגליות: 22 **אבן מאסו הבונים.** עם שהיה שפל בין האומות: 23 **מאת יי' היתה**
זאת: כן יאמרו הכל:

26 **ברוך** הבא בשם **יי'.** יאמרו למביאי הבכורים ולעולי הרגלים:
ברכנוכם. ברכנו אתכם: 27 **אסרו חג בעבותים.** הזבחים והחגיגות שהיו קונין ובודקין
ממום וקושרין בכרעי מיטותיהן עד שיביאום בעזרה **לקרנות המזבח.** ויש לפתור כל
המזמו' **מלא אמות כי אחיה** בדוד עצמו: 18 **יסור יסרני יה'** על מעשה בת שבע. בייסורין
כגון ואת הכבשה ישלם ארבעתים. וששה חדשים נצטרע דוד: **ולמות לא נתנני.** שני גם יי'
העבי' חטאתך ולא תמות: 19 **פתחו לי שערי צדק.** ואילו הן שערי צדק אותן **השע**רים של
בתי כנסיות ובתי מדרשו' אשר הם ליי' והצדיקים באים בם. 21 **אודך כי עניתני.** מכאן
ואילך אמרו דוד ושמואל וישי ואחי דוד כמו שמפור' בערבי פסחים. מי שאמ' זה לא אמ'
זה:

קיט 1 **אשרי תמימי** דרך. 3 **אף לא פעלו עולה.** אשריהם הצדיקים
אם כל זה בהם: **בדרכיו הלכו.** אעפ"י שלא פעלו עוולה אין שבחם שלם אלא אם כן
בדרכיו הלכו. וכן הוא אומ' סור מרע ועשה טוב. אעפ"י שאתה סר מרע אין הכל שלם אלא
אם כן תעשה טוב. מדרש אגדה: 5 **אחלי יכונו דרכי.** א"ילף יסוד בתיבה הנופל ממנו
לפרקי' כגון א"ילף שבאחוותי באזניכם. וא"ילף שבאסוך שמן: **אחלי.** תפילותי. ואילו הן
שיכונו דרכי. וכן אחלי אדוני לפני הנביא. צורכי אדוני להתפלל שיהא לפני הנביא הלואי
בשומרון. ולשון אחליות בלעז שוהיט. כאדם האומר לחבירו הלואי והייתי עשיר. הלואי
והייתי חכם: 11 **בלבי צפנתי.** לא נתתיו לעזוב ולהשתכח ממני: 16 **אשתעשע** אתעסק.
כמו ישעה האדם אל עושהו. ואל ישעו בדברי שקר: 17 **גמול על עבדך.** דבר **שאחיה** בו.
גמול חסד: 18 **נפלאות מתורתך.** דברים מכוסין שאינן מפורשין בה: 19 **גר אנכי בארץ.**
ימי מועטין. **אל תסתר ממני** ממצוותיך הנעלמות שלא אוכל לקיימם: 18
מתורתך. נפלאי. מפירושי תורתך שאינן מפורשים בה: 20 **גרסה נפשי.** משתברת נפשי
מחמת תאוה. לשון גרש גרש כרמל. ומנחם חיבר **לתאבה** עם מתאב אנכי את
גאון יעקב. ושניהם לשון שבר: 22 **גול מעלי** לשון גילגול כמו ויגל את האבן. 23 **בי נדברו.**
אעפ"י שמלכי אומות העולם מתלוצצים עלי שאני עוסק בתורה. 24 **שעשועי.** עסקי: 25
כדברך. כמו שהבטחתני על ידי נתן הנביא טובה: 26 **דרכי ספרתי** לך את צרכיי ואת
חטאתי ואשר עניתני: 28 **דלפה נפשי** נטפה. כלומי נחסרת והולכת: 33 **ואצרנה עקב.**
אשמרנה בכל מעגלותיה ועקבי נתיבותיה. לשון עקיבים טראשש בל': 38 **הקם לעבדך**

אמרתך שהבטחתני : אשר ליראתך שאהיה אני וזרעי יראי שמך. שעל מנת כן הבטחתני.
אם ישמרו בניך וגו'. 39 העבר חרפתי. מחול לי על אותו עון ושוב לא יוכלו אויבי לחרפני
בו. כי משפטיך טובים. וכבר אני מקבל עלי לשלם את הכבשה ארבעתים : 41 תשועתך
תבוא לי כאמרתך שהבטחתני : 43 ואל תצל מפי דבר אמת. ואל תבדל מי פי דבר אמת כמו
ויצל אלקים את מקנה אביכם. יחלתי. קויתי : 45 ואתהלכה ברחבה בהלכה רווחת
ופשוטה בישר'. דרשתי. בקשתי : 49 זכור דבר אשר ייחלתי על ידי נתן הנביא לעבדך : 52
משפטיך לעולם. שאתה מביא ייסורין וחוזר מחמתן וסולם. ועל כן אתנחם : 54 בבית
מגורי. בבית דאגתי מגור מסביב ויגר מואב. 55 זכרתי בלילה. בעת צרה ואפילה. 56 זאת
היתה לי. עטרה ההולמת אותי ולעדות לי ולזרעי הראויים למלוך בשכר שפיקודיך
נצרתי. כך דרשוהו חכמי ישר'. 59 חשבתי דרכי. הפסד מצוה כנגד שכרה ושכר עבירה
כנגד הפסדה לפיכך ואשיבה רגלי אל עדותיך. כי ראיתי שהיא הטובה שבכולן : 61 חבלי
רשעים עיוְדוני. סיעות של רשעים שללוני. כמו יאכל עד. כך חברו מנחם. ויש לפותרו לשון
עוד. כמו עוד זה מדבר. כלומ' עוד נוספו ורבו עלי : 67 טרם אענה במצוותיך טרם הגיתי
בהם בבתי מדרשות. ועתה משעניתי הגיתי בהם תורתך שמרתי.
שהמדרש מלמדני לסור מן העבירה לכך אני מבקש ממך 66 טוב טעם ודעת למדני : טרם
אענה לשון שונה והוגה בבית המדרש הוא. כגון תעז לשוני אמרתך. וכן יכרת י"י לאיש
אשר יעשנה ער וענה מאהלי יעקב. ער בחכמים וענה בתלמידים : 69 טפלו עלי שקר
חברו עלי שקר. וכמו ותטפל על עווני : 71 טוב לי כי עניתי וגומ' טוב היה היה בעיניי
שנתייסרתי וענויתי למען אשוב מדרך רעה ואשמור חקיך : 74 יריאיך יראוני בטובה
וישמחו כי כגמולי גמולם שהרי מריראיך אני ולדברך יחלתי : 75 ואמונתך עניתני. בדין
עניתני : 78 כי שקר עותוני. כי על חנם הרשיעוני : 81 כלתה נפשי. איותה נפשי. 82 כלו
עיני. צופים תמיד עד תמו וכל'. 83 כנאד בקיטור. כנאד של עור המתייבש בעשן. 86 שקר
רדפוני. לשוא רדפוני אויביי : 96 לכל תכלה. לכל סיום דבר יש קץ וגבול. אבל מצוותך אין
קץ לתכליתה : 99 מכל מלמדי השכלתי. מזה למדתי קצת ומזה קצת. שיחה לי. כל
שיחתי היתה בהם : 103 נמלצו. נמתקו : 105 נר לרגלי דברך. כשאני בא להורותני אני רואה בתורה והיא
מפרשת אותי מן האיסור כנר הדלק ומציל את האדם מן הפחתים : 107 נעניתי. נעשיתי
שפל ועני. וכן וענה גאון ישר' בפניו. ותרגום וימאיך וכן לענות מפני. והעני חשוב כמת.
לפיכך חייני כדברך : 108 נדבות פי דברי ריצוי שפי מתנדב לך. כל לשון נדבה רצון הוא :
109 נפשי בכפי תמיד הרבה נסתכנתי בסכנות קרובי' למיתה. ואעפ"יכן תורתך
לא שכחתי : 112 לעולם עקב. על מעליהם ועל נתיבותיהם : 113 סעפים שנאתי. חושבי
מחשבות און. כמו לכן סעיפי ישיבוני. על שתי הסעיפים כשאתה קורא סעיפים הוא שם
המחשבה. וכשאתה קורא סעפים נופל הלשון על החושבים אותה : 117 ואשעה בחקיך
כמו ואל ישעו בדברי שקר : ד"א ואשעה לשון סיפור ושינון. כדמתרגמי' למשל ולשנינה
ולשועין. 118 סלית. רמסת. נתת למרמס כמו סלה כל אביריי : 120 סמר. לשו' תסמר
שערת בשרי. כאדם שעמדו שערותיו הריצייר בלע'. ממשפטיך יראתי. מפורענות
גזירותיך : 122 ערוב עבדך לשון הצלה גרנטיזא בל'. היה ערב בשבילי לנגד הרעה : 123
ולאמרת צדקתך שהבטחתני : 126 עת לעשות לי"י וגו'. מוסב על מקרא שלפניו. הבינני
ואדעה עדותיך. להבין עת לעשות לשמך איך יעשו שהפרו תורתך למצוא רצון וסליחה
תמצא להם ואעשה כן על עבירה שבידי. ורבותי' דרשו ממנו שעוברין על דברי תורה כדי
לעשות סייג וגדר לישר' כגון גדעון ואליהו בהר הכרמל שהקריבו בבמה : עוד ראיתיו נדרש
באגדה העושה תורתו עתים מיפר ברית שאדם צריך להיות יגע בתורה כל יהיום 2שעות'
127 על כן אהבתי וגו'. על אשר אהבתיך מצוותיך ראוי לך ללמדני עת רצון מה לעשות לך
ותרצני : יש על כן הרבה שפתרונם על אשר. כגון כי על כן ראיתי פניך כי על כן ידעת
חנותינו במדבר. על כן יתרה עשה וכו'. על כל זה אני כדיי שתרצה
תמחול לי : 129 פלאות עדותיך. מכוסים הם ונפלאים עדותיך מבני אדם. על כן נצרתם נפשי
שהרביתה מתן שכרן כגון שילוח הקן : כולם כי לא נודע איזה יכשר

130 **פתח דבריך יאיר.** תחילת דבריך האירו את לב ישר' שאתה **המבין פתאים** באומרך
אנכי יְיָ אלקיך אשר הוצאתיך הֻוֹדַעתם הטובה שעשית להם שְׁקֻנּיתם מבית עבדים לדעת
כי אַתה אדון להם ויקבלו אדנותך וַאֱלֹקוּתך. ואחריכן יחדתה אלקותך עליהם: לא יהיה
לך וגו'. ואחריכן גְזַרֻתָ את גזירותיך: ד"א **פתח דבריך יאיר.** תחילת דיבורך במעשה
בראשית יהי אור: **מבין פתאים.** מֶשֶׁם יבינו הכל ויפתחו בדברי תורה. תנחומא. 131
ואשאפה. לשון בליעה כמו שאפה רוח. 134 **פדיני מעושק אדם.** פדיני מעושקו של אדם
מיֵיצֶר הרע העושק את הבריות מדרך הטוב: 139 **צמתתני קנאתי.** הקנאה שאני מקנא
לשמך על השוכחים דבריך היא צומתת אותי ומקנטת אותי בהם: 148 **אשמורות.** חצי
הלילה שתי אשמורות. ולדברי האומ' שלש משמרות הוי הלילה היה דוד עומד ממטתו
בשליש הלילה ועוסק בתורה עד חצות כמו שני **לשיח באמרתך.** ומחצות ולהלן עוסק
בשירות ובתושבחות כמו שני חצות לילה אקום. להודות לך: 149 **כמשפטיך חייני.**
כתורתך וכמצוותיך הנהנאת ימי חיי: 150 **קרבו רודפי זימה.** עצת חטאיו הלכו בעצת
חטאיהם ומתרחקים מתורתך לקרב אל עצת חטאיהם: 151 **קרוב אתה.** רחוקים הללו
המתרחקים מתורתך אם ישובו מדרכם: 152 **קדם ידעתי מעדותיך.** קודם היות הדבר
יֵדַעתָי מתוך עדותיך. קדם ירשו את הארץ **צוית** על הבכורים וַתרֻומות ומעשרות. וקדם
הניחות להם מאויביהם **צוית** והיה בהניח יְיָ אלקיך לך להעמיד מלך ולהכרית עמלק
ולבנות בית הבחירה: **כי לעולם יסדתם.** כי על דברים העתידים להיות לסוף העולם
יסדתה עדותיך: 160 **ראש דברך אמת.** שכששמעו אומ' העולם אנכי ולא יהיה לך ולא
תשא אמרו הכל להנאתו ולכבודו. כיון שׁשׁמעוּ את אביך לא תרצח לא תנאף הודו על
ראש דברך שהוא אֱמֶת: 162 **שש אנכי על אמרתך** על הַבטָחתך שהבטחתני: ד"א **על
אמרתך** על אחת מאמרותיך הסתומות כַשֶׁאני מבין בה: ורבותינו דרשוהו על המילה
שהיה דוד בבית המרחץ. וראה עצמו בלא ציצית ובלא תפילין ובלא תורה. אמ' אוי לי
שאני ערום מכל מצוה. כיון שנסתכל במילה שמח ואמ' בצאתו שש אנכי על המילה
שתחילתה ניתנה באמירה ולא בדיבור שני ויאמר אלקים אל אברהם ואתה את בריתי
תשמר 164 **שבע ביום היללתיך.** שחרית שתים לפני קרית שמע ואחת לאחריה ובערב
שתים לפניה ושתים לאחריה: **על משפטי צדקך.** על קרית שמע שהיא דברי תורה. 166
שברתי. הוחלתי. 168 **כל דרכי נגדך.** אתה יודע כל דרכיי: 169 **כדברך הבינני:** דברי
תורתך הבינני כהילכתן וכהוויתן: 171 **תבענה.** תדברנה: 172 **תען לשוני** כל עניניה. לשון
קול רם הוא:

קכ 1 שיר המעלות שיאמרו הלוים אותו על חמש עשרה מעלות
היורדות מעזרת ישר' לעזרת נשים. ויש כאן ט"ו מזמורים של שיר המעלות. ורבותי' אמרו
שיסדן דוד להעלות את התהום כמ' שמפורש במס' סוכה: 2 **משפת שקר.** זרעו של עשו
הרשע שצדיין את הבריות בפֵיהם בעלילות רשע. 3 **מה יתן לך** הק' **ומה יוסיף לך** שמירות
ומחצות. והרי את נתונה לפנים משתי מחיצות. 4 **חצי גבור שנונים.** והרי את הורגת
במקום רחוק כחץ: **עם גחלי רתמים.** כל הגחלים כבים מבחוץ וכבים מבְפנים ואילו כבו
מבחוץ ולא כבו מבְפנים: ד"א **מה יתן לך.** מה סופו של הק' לגזור עליך חצי גבור עם גחלי
רתמים. חציו מלמעלה וגיהנם מלמטה. 5 **אויה לי.** אמרה כנסת ישר' כי כבר לקיתי
בגליות רבים. הרי **גרתי משך** עם בני יפת במלכות פרס ויון ומשך: 7 **אני שלום** עמהם **וכי
אדבר** עליהם שלום **המה** באים להלחם בי:

קכא 1 שיר למעלות אשא עיני אל ההרים:

קכב 1 שיר המעלות שמחתי באומרים לי. שמעתי בני אדם אומרים
מתי ימות זה וימלוך שלמה ויבנה בית המקדש ואני שמח: 2 **עומדות היו רגלינו**
במלחמה. בכל מקום בשביל **שעריך ירושלם** שעוסקין בהן בתורה: 3 **ירושלם הבנוי'**
כשיבנה שלמה בני בית המקדש לַתוכה תהא בנויה בשכינה ומקדש וארון ומקד' ומזבח:
כעיר שחוברה לה כשילה קשילה שדמה הכתוב זו לזו שנא' אל המנוחה ואל הנחלה. מנוחה זו
שֵׁילה. נחלה זו ירושלם. ורבותי' אמרו זו ירושלם בנויה בשמים ועתידה ירושלם שלמטה

להיות כמותה : 4 **ששם עלו שבטים.** אשר שם בשילה עלו שבטים. כשעלו ממצרים
והוקבע המשכן בתוכה : **שבטי יה׳** שהוא **עדות לישר׳** לפי שהיו האומות מליזין עליהם
כשיצאו ממצרים ואומ׳ עליהן שהן ממזרים. ואומ׳ אם בגופן שלטו המצרים בנשותיהן לא
כל שכן. אמ׳ הק׳ אני מעיד עליהן שהם בני אבותיה׳ הטיל שמו עליהם : לראובני. לשמעוני
תוסיף עליהם אותיות השם אחת מכאן ואחת מכאן נמצא השם הזה יק׳ עדות לישר׳ : 5
כי שמה ישבו כסאות למשפט וגו׳ כי גם בירושלם תשרה השכינה **וישבו** שם לשפוט בהם
את האומות : **כסאות לבית דוד.** כסאות מלוכה לבית דוד 6 **שאלו את שלום ירושלם.**
ואמרו לה **ישליו אהבך.** 7 **ויהי שלום בחילך.** 8 **למען אחי ישר׳ ורעי : אדברה נא גם אני**
דוד המלך **שלום בך** :

קכג 1 **שיר המעלות אליך** נשאתי היושבי בשמים. י״וד יתירה. 4
הלעג השאננים. לעג הגוים. השאננים : 3 **שבענו בוז.** שביזו את 4 **גיא היונים.** היא
ירושלם. **לגאיונים.** כת׳ חד. וקרינן תרי :

קכד 1 **שיר המעלות** לולי **י״י** שהיה לנו. 3 **בחרות אפם** בנו בחרות
כמו בעשות : 4 **נחלה.** לשון חולי. 7 **נפשינו נמלטה** מהם **כצפור** אשר נמלטה **מפח**
יוקשים :

קכה 1 **שיר המעלות** הבוטחים **בי״י** כהר ציון. הבוטחים **בי״י** לא ימוטו
כהר ציון אשר לא **ימוט.** כי 2 כאשר ירושלם הרים **סביב לה.** כן הק׳ **סביב לעמו** : 3 **כי לא**
ינוח שבט הרשע. כי לא יתן הק׳ ממשלי הרשעים לנוח על הצדיקים. למען כי הצדיקים
נזהרין לשלוח ידיהם בעולה. 5 **והמטים עקלקלותם** על החבריות למצוא עלילות רשע.
יוליכם י״י את פועלי האון :

קכו 1 **שיר המעלות** בשוב **י״י** את **שיבת ציון** מגלות בבל. נהיה
כחולמים. 4 **כאפיקים בנגב** כאפיקי מים בארץ יבישה : **שמלחלחין** אותה כן נהיה
מרטיבין בשובך את שבותינו. אשר 5 **הזורעים** בה בארץ ציה. **בדמעה** שדואגים וסבורים
שמא לא תצמח **ברינה** קוצרים על ידי אפיקי המים כשהם משולחין בה : 6 **והלוך ילך**
ובכה. כך ישר׳ זורעים לפניך צדקה בדמעה בגלות ויקצרוה ברנה כשתשלם שכרם לעתיד :

קכז 1 **שיר המעלות** לשלמה. שאמ׳ דוד על שלמה שצפה ברוח
הקודש שעתיד לבנות בית המקדש ובו ביום ישא את בת פרעה. ועל זה נאמ׳ על אפי ועל
חמתי היתה לי העיר הזאת למן היום אשר בנו אותי לכך אמ׳ המזמור הזה למה לך בני
לבנות בית ולסבור מאחרי המקום מאחר שאינו חפץ בה **לשוא עמלו בוניו בו. שוא שקד**
שומר על חנם צופה בה השומר : 2 **שוא לכם** בעלי אומניות המשכימים ומאחרים
למלאכתן ומתפרנסין בעצבון **ובגיעה בלחם העצבים.** של טורח. **כן יתן** הק׳ פרנסה למי
שמנדד שנתו בשבילו לעסוק בתורה : 3 **הנה נחלת י״י**
לו. לאותו האיש **בנים.** שיש לו תלמידים שהוא מעמיד שהם לו כבנים : **שכר פרי הבטן.**
שכר פרי התורה שבלבו שני כי נעים כי **תשמרם** בבטנך : 4 **כחצים ביד גבור** להלחם בם את
אויביו. **כן בני הנעורים.** התלמידים שאדם מעמיד בנעוריו. 5 **אשרי הגבר אשר מלא**
אשפתו מהם. מאותם חצים : **אשפה.** תיק החצים שקורי׳ קוייבר׳ : **לא יבושו כי ידברו**
אויבים בשער. תלמידי חכמים המנצחין זה עם זה בהלכה נראין כאויבים זה לזה :

קכח 1 **שיר המעלות** אשרי כל ירא **י״י** :

קכט 1 **שיר המעלות** רבת צררוני מנעורי. 3 **האריכו למ**ענ**יתם.** הוא
תלם המחרישה כמו כבחצי מענה צמד שדה. דשמואל. 6 **שקדמת שלף יבש.** שקודם
שישלפוה ויתלשוהו ממקומו הוא יבש : 7 **וחצנו מעמר.** כמו והביאו בניך בחוצן. **אי**שילא
בלעז. כמי גם חצני ניערתי :

קל 1 שיר המעלות ממעמקי׳ 4 כי **עמך הסליחה** לא נתת רשות לשליח
לסלוח כמו שני כי לא ישא לפשעכם: **למען תורא** על זאת שלא יהא אדם בטוח על סליחת
אחר: 6 **נפשי לי״י מ**שומרים **לבקר. שומרים לבקר.** מצפים
ונחוזרין ומצפים קץ אחר קץ:

קלא 1 שיר המעלות י״י לא גבה לבי. 2 שויתי ורוממתי עליך נפשי
כגמול שהוא נתון **עלי אמו: גמול.** יונק שדים. נפשי בקרבי עלי לנגדך
כ**יונק** שדי אמו:

קלב 1 שיר המעלות עינותו. עינוי נפשו. אשר טרח ועמל למצוא לך
מקום. 5 **עד אמצא מקום.** עד אדע היכן יהי מקום מקדשו: 6 **באפרתה** במקום החשוב
והמעולה. כמו תחו בן צוף **אפרתי.** חשוב אבגינוס: ד״א **שמעמנוה כאפרתה.** בספר
יהושע שבא **מאפרים**: בכל התחומים הוא אומר ותאר הגבול. וכאן הוא אומ׳ ועלה הגבול
ומחה אל כתף היבוסי **ירושלם**: נמצא ירושלים גבוה מכל ארץ ישר׳ והיא ראויה לבית
המקד׳ שני׳ וקמת ועלית אל המקום וגו׳: **מלמד** שבית המקדש גבוה מכל ארץ ישר׳. כך
נדרש בשחיטת קדשי: **מצאנוה בשדי יער.** בגבול בנימן **שנמשל** לחית היער שני בנימן זאב
יטרף: 7 **נבואה למשכנותיו.** שמה 10 **אל תשב פני משיחך.** שלמה בבאו להכניס שם
הארון: 12 **ועדותי זו אל**מדם. זו אשר אלמדם: 15 **צידה.** מזונה 18 **יציץ.** יאיר. כמו
ונוצצים כעין נחשת קלל:

קלג 1 שיר המעלות הנה מה טוב ומה נעים שבת אחי׳ **גם יחד.** שישב
הק׳ בבית הבחירה. עם ישר׳ הקרוויין אחים ורעים 2 **כשמן הטוב** שנמשח בני אהרן הכהן:
היורד מראשו וזקנו. אל פי ראש כתונתו שלו שהזקן שוכב על פי הכתונת 3 כן נעים **טל
חרמון** שגבוה על **הררי ציון.** והטל מחרמון יורד 3 **על הררי ציון** כ**שם** ששמן המשחה
לגדולה כן טל ציון ותפארת ולכבוד לישר׳. 2 **כשמן הטוב** 3 **כטל חרמון** כן זה כן זה. כמ׳
והיה כאם כהנה. ורבותי׳ דרשו שבת אחים במשה ואהרן לעניין בשמן המשחה
במס׳ הוריות כל המזמור. אבל יש בדברי תורה וקבלת משל **ומליצה** דברי חכמים
וחידותם. ועיקר שיר המעלות על בית המקדש נאמ׳:

קלד 1 שיר המעלות הנה ברכו את י״י:

קלה 1 הללויק׳ הללו את שם י״י. 7 **ברקים למטר עשה** הם זהרורי רקיע
המבריקים ומאירים לפני המטר שקורי׳ אלויידש׳ לשון מצאי׳ כלומ׳ אוצרות תיקן
לרוח. ושם הם מצויין לו במשלחתן לשלחם: 9 **בתוככי.** כמ׳ בתוכך: 13 **י״י שמך לעולם.**
בגדולתך ובממשלתך. אז כן היה עתה והיכולת בידך לדין ולנקום נקמתינו: 14 **כי ידין י״י
עמו.** ישפוט משפטיכם מאויביה: **יתנחם.** יתעשת: 20 **יראי י״י.** אילו הגרים:

קלו 1 הודו לי״י **כי טוב כל״ח.** עשרים וששה כי לעולם חסדו נאמרו במזמור
זה כנגד כ״ו דורות שהיה העולם בלא תורה. ונתקיים בחסדו של הק׳:

קלז 1 על נהרות בבל. שם **ישבנו.** כשירדנו בגולה ושאלם נבוכד נצר
שישירו לו כמ׳ שהיו משונרים על הדוכן 2 **על ערבים בתוכה** ערבי נחל: **ותוללינו.** מיני
כלי זמר. על שם שתולים אותם. כך פירש מנחם **ותוללינו שמחה.** ותוללינו של שמחה ויש
לפתור ותוללינו אויבנו. שהם **מהו**ללים אותנו ומתעתעים ומשטים בנו: לשון מהוללי בי
נשבעו 4 **איך נשיר** לא נשיר לא נאמר אלא איך נשיר. מלמד שעמדו לוים וקצצו בשיניהם
בהונות ידיהם לכך נאמ׳ איך נוכל עוד לשורר בתופים ובנבלים ובכנורות ובהונותינו
מקוטעים: יצחק: 5 **איך אשכחך.** כנסת ישר׳ אומרת כן. 6 **אם לא אעלה את ירושלם** אל
זכרון. אבל חורבנה אעלה להזכירו בראש כל שמחותי 7 **ערו ערו.** לשון חורבן. וכן חומות
בכל הרחבה ערער תתערער. וכן ערות יסוד. ואינו נופל אלא על דבר שעוקרין שרשיו מן
הארץ:

קלח 1 **לדוד** אודך בכל לבי. **נגד אלקים.** לעיני שרים : 2 **כי הגדלת על כל שמך
אמרתך.** שמך בעל גבורות קנוא ונוקם. ואתה אמרת הבטחת טובך וחסדך **הגדלת על כל
שמך** שאתי מעביר לנו על מדותיך וסולח לנו : 3 **תרהיבני.** הגדלתני : 4 **כי שמעו אמרי פיך.**
כששמעו אמרי פיך לא תרצח לא תנאף הודו על אנכי ולא יהיה לך ואמרו כדיי הוא
להקבילם עול מלכותו עליהם תחילה ואחרכך יגזור כל גזירותי : 6 **ידע.** ייסר. כמו ויודע
בהם אנשי <u>סוכות</u> : 8 **יגמור בעדי.** יסכים על ידי בקשותי : **מעשי ידיך.** בית הבחירה שני בו
כוננו ידיך :

קלט 1 **לדוד** מזמור י**'**י חקרתני ותדע. 2 **בנתה לרעי מרחוק.** בנתה <u>מרחוק</u>
למושכני אל ריעותך וחיבתך. **לרעי.** לחברני אליך : 3 **ארחי ורבעי זרית.** דרכי ושכני ורבצי
סיבבתה שאין לי לעשות דבר בלא ידיעתך : **זרית** לשון זר זהב סביב. כך חיברו מנחם
ורבותיי פירשו על טיפת תשמיש ש<u>הוולד</u> נוצר מן הברור שבה. ופירורי זרית לשון יזורה על
נוחו גפרית. ולשון זורה תבואה לברורה מן הפסולת שבה **הסכנת.** למדת : 5 **אחור וקדם.**
פנים ואחור. **כפכה.** אפך ורידוייך ד**ישט**ריי**ט** בלעז : 6 **פליאה דעת ממני** וגו'. מכוסה ונעלם
ממני 7 מקום לברוח מפניך : 9 **אשא כנפי שחר.** אם אשא לי כנפים כשחר הזה המבהיק
לפי שעה מסוף העולם ועד סופו כן <u>אמרה</u> לעוף עד כי אשכון **באחרית ים.** 11 **ואומר אך
חשך. ישופני.** אם אמרתי אהיה נסתר במחשך והחשך יחשיך עלי ולא תראני : **ישופני.**
לשון נשף. **ולילה אור בעדני.** והלילה יהא מאפל לנגדי. **אור** זה. לשון אופל הוא. כמו יפיץ
ענן אורו. וכן וכל כך ככבי אור וכן ויאר את הלילה 12 **גם** שם אין לי מנוס כי כל **חשך לא
יחשיך ממך כחשיכה כאורה** שניהם שוים לך : 13 **כליותי החושבים** כל מחשבותיי.
תסוככני. תסוככני : 15 **עושיתי בסתר.** בתשמיש. **בתחתיות ארץ.** במדור התחתון ש**במעי**
אמי : 16 **גולמי** ורקמתי ותבנית צורתי בטרם הולדי ובטרם בואי לעולם **ראו עיניך ועל
ספרך כולם יכתבו** וכל יצורי עפר כמוני כמוהם. גם כולם טרם יבראון יחדיו גלוים לפניך
ימים יוצרו ולא אחד. כל מעשה האדם ותכלית ימיו גלוים לפניו כאילו יוצרו כבר. ואעפ**"**י
שלא היה היה כאחד מכולם ולא היה עדיין כי אחד מהם בעולם ואילו הן פלאי מפעלי
אלקינו ומשפט גבורות שהעתידות גלויות לפניו טרם תצמחנה והבאות טרם תבואנה. וכן
הוא אומ' בטרם אצרך בבטן ידעתיך וגו' : תו' : **גלמי ראו עיניך** מאז בראת את העולם ראו
עיניך את גולמי הדורות הבאים : **ועל ספרך** ספר תולדות אדם שהראית לאדם הראשון
כולם יכתבו. נכתבו : **ימים יוצרו לא אחד בהם.** לסוף ימים רבים היו עתידין להיבראות
ולא היה בעדן אחד אחד נברא בהם. וזהו פי' לפי המסורת שכתוב **ולא** לפי המקרא שהוא נקרא
ולו. כך פי' **ימים יוצרו** הראהו ימים העתידים להיבראות בירר **אחד מהם** את יום השבת :
ד**"**א זה יום הכפורים לסליחה : 17 **ולי מה יקרו ריעך.** כנסת ישר' אומרת כן מה נכבדו
בעיני הק' הצדיקי' שבכל דור ודור. **ומה עצמו ראשיהם** חשבון ספרותיהם. לשון כי תשא
את ראש. 18 **אספרם מחול.** אם באתי <u>לספור</u> את טיב מעשיהם הטובים. **מחול ירביון.**
הקיצותי ועודי עמך. הנני באתני עתה לקץ הדורות אשר קצבת מאז עד היום. ועד דור זה
עמך וביראתך : לא נטיתי <u>מאחריך</u> וגו' : 19 **אם תקטול.** הלואי <u>תקטול</u> עשו הרשע : 20 **אשר
יאמרוך למזימה.** מזכירים שמך על כל <u>מחשבות</u> רעתם ומכניסן אלקונתך לעי**"**ז : **נש'ו.** כמו
נשאו. **לשוא.** נשאו <u>לשוא</u> אויבים את שמך : **עריך.** אויביך. 24 **אם דרך עוצב בי** אם דרך
מעצבה וקילקולם בי :

קמ 1 **למנצח** 2 חלצני מאדם רע. 3 יגורו מלחמות. יהיו מלחמות במגוריהם
ובמושבותם. 4 **עכשוב.** <u>עכביש.</u> איריינא בלעז : 6 **וחבלים פרשו רשת.** דרך הרשת לקשור
חבל ארוך בראשה. והצייד כשרואה העופות שוכנים תחת הרשת מושך חבל <u>והרשת</u> נופל
על העופות : **ליד מעגל** אצל נתיבותי ופעמיי. **ליד.** אצל. כמו ראו חלקת יואב אל ידי :
מאויי רשע. עשו הרשע : **זממו אל תפק.** מחשבתו לא יצליח. **ירומו סלה.** כי יתגאו סלה :
ורבותינו פי' זממו לשון רסן : כזה הזוממים את פי הגמל ולשון משנה הוא : **אל תפק.** אל
תוצא מלחיו : 10 **ראש מסבי עמל.** חבורות חשבון גדודי עשו <u>האומרים</u> עשו להסב אותי
מעליך. **עמל שפתימו** יכסם. 11 **גחלים.** של גיהנם. **במהמורות** <u>יפילם לבל יקומון</u> עוד.

במהמורות. במלחמות ותגר. לשון מַמרים הייתם. 12 **איש לשון.** עשו כי ציד בפיו. צד את
אביו בפיו. **יצודנו.** הרע אשר הוא עושה הוא יצודנו : 13 **ידעתי כי** סוף הדברים **יעשה י"י**
דין עם עני. ינקום נקמת עבדיו : 14 **אך** ימהר ויעשה כדי **שיודו צדיקים** לשמו :

קמא 1 **י"י קראתיך** חושה. 2 **משאת כפי.** מה שאני נשא כפי אליו : 3 **שיתה**
שמרה לפי. בהתפללי לפניך בהיותי מדבר צחות שיהיו לרצון : **דל שפתי** היא שפה
העליונה : 4 **את אישים.** עם אנשים. **ובל אלחם במנעמיהם.** ולא אהיה מסב בסעודתם : 5
יהלמוני צדיק חסד ויוכיחני טוב לי שיוכיחני וייסרני נביא אמת וצדיק שכל מהלומותיו
וְתוֹכחותיו חסד : **שמן ראש אל יניא ראשי.** שמן מלכות שהוצק על ראשי כמו שני דשנת
בשמן ראשי. אל יסיר את ראשי את מתוכחות הצדיק ללכת וללחום את פועלי האון : **כי עוד**
ותפילתי כי כל עוד ותפילתי בפי הרי היא בשביל רעותיהם של פועלי און שלא אכשל
בהם : 6 **נשמטו בידי סלע שופטיהם.** דייניהם ומנהיגיהם של אילו נשמטו מדרך הטוב.
בידי יצר הרע ולב האבן וקשה כסלע. **ושמעו** דברי הנעימים שאני מדבר במִצְוֹתיו שלהם'
ואינם שבים מדרכ' ורבותינו בברייתא דסיפרי דרשוהו במשה ואהרן שמתו על ידי הסלע.
אבל איני יכול ליישב המקרא ראשו לַסופו. וכמעט יש ליישבו ולומר אילו דומים לעקשו
אותן שמתו על ידי הסלע ועל ידיהם כי אילו שמעו אמרי נעמים ואינן שבים : 7 **כמ' פולח**
עצים **ובוקע בארץ.** כן **נפזרו עצמינו** להגיע לפתח המות בשביל רעותיהם של עוברי עבירה.
פולח. לשון בוקע. כמו יפלח כליותי : 8 **כי אליך עיני.** מוסב למקראות העליונים. שיתה
שמרה לפי ואל תט לבי וגו' כי אליך עיני. **אל תער נפשי** מלפניך. כמ' ותער כדה : 10 **יפלו**
במכמוריו רשעים. יפול הרשע עצמו במכמוריו שהוא פורש לרגלי :

קמב 1 **משכיל** לדוד **בהיותו במערה.** שכרת כנף המעיל לשאול. 4 **ואתה**
ידעת נתיבתי כמה מוקשים יש בה : 5 **אין לי מכיר.** אין בכל משרתי שאול שימחה בידו : 8
בי יכתירו צדיקים. בשבילי יכתירוך צדיקים ויודו לשמך. שאתה סומך יריאיך :

קמג 1 **מזמור** לדוד **י"י שמע תפילתי. באמונתך** להאמין הבטחה שהבטחתני :
3 **כי רדף אויב נפשי** כלומר אם חטאתי לך הרי לקיתי כל ישר' וכנגד כל ישר' נאמר מזמור זה : 5
זכרתי ימים מקדם. שהפלאת לנו ניסים רבים : 4 **ישתומם.** לשון אוטם ותמהון כמו ואשב
שם שבעת ימים משמים בתוכם : ותשב תמר שֹמֵמָה. 6 **בארץ עייפה.** גולה : 7 **כלתה**
רוחי המתאוה ואינו משיג קרוי כַליון עינים. וכליון רוח : 8 **בבקר.** בצמח הגאולה. 9 **אליך**
כסיתי. תלאותי אני מכסה מכל אדם להגיד אליך.

קמד 1 **לדוד ברוך** י"י **המלמד** : 2 **הרודד עמים תחתי.** הרוקע ושוטח את
עמי לרבוץ במקומו כמו שוטח לאומי. מגדיל אותם. **רודד** תרגו' של רוקע. כדמתרגמי'
וירקעו ורדידו. **ויש פותרי' הרודד עמים תחתי.** המחליש עמים תחתי עמי. אך בספר מדוייק
מוגה עמי. ומסורת עליו ג' סברין עמים וקריין עמי. ועל תחתי יש מסורת תחתי קרי : 3
מה אדם. מה עשו וישמעאל לפניך כי ידעתם כי הרבות להם גדולה : 7 **פצני.** הוציאני. ולשון
הצלה הוא. וכן הפוצה את דוד עבדו 10 **הנותן תשועה למלכי.** מדבר על סלע המחלוקת
שהיה דוד קרוב ליתפש ביד שאול. ובא מלאך אל שאול לאמר מהרה ולכה. הציל את
שאול מהיות שופך דם נקי ואת דוד מהיות נהרג. 11 **פצני והצילני** כאשר פציתה אז כן
פצֵנ עתה : 12 **אשר בנינו** עתה וגומ' כלומ' כי עתה דור זה כשר הוא : **בנינו כנטיעים.**
שאין בהם מום. כך הם מנוקים מעבירה. **בנותינו** גבוהות קומה נאה **כזויות** שלבית
אבנים. שזויות האבן מכוונות כנגד חבירתה ועולה למעלה עד שהזויות מיושרות
מחוטבות תבנית היכל. מהוללות בפי רואיהן ומדמין אותן לתבנית קומת ההיכל.
ורבותינו פירשו בנותינו זָויות. מתמלאות תאוה כזוית מזבח המליאות דם ואינן נבעלות
אלא לבעליהן 13 **מזוינו מלאים** זויות אוצרות מליאים כל טוב. **מפיקים מזן אל זן.** מזון
משנה לשנה : **מזן אל זן.** משעת אסיף מזון לשנה עד זמן אסיף מזון לשנה אחרת. **זן.**
גובירנ"א : **מאליפות מרובבות.** לאלפים ולרבבות עושות פרי : 14 **אלופינו מסובלי'.** גדולים
שבהם נסבלים על קטניהם שהקטנים נשמעים לאלופיהם ומתוך כך **אין פרץ** בנו. **ואין**

יוצאת אין שמוע' רעה יוצאת למרחוק. **ואין צווחה.** אין קול מהומת חרב ומלחמה. 15. **אשרי העם שככה לו.** שכל הטובה הזאת לו:

קמה 1 **תהלה לדוד** 4 דור לדור. ישבח מעשיך: 5 וגם אני הדר כבוד **הודך** אשיחה. 6 **ועזוז נוראותיך** יאמרו. דור לדור ואני גם אני **גדולתך אספרנה.** 7 **זכר רב טובך** יביעו דור לדור. 11 **וגבורתך ידברו** זה לזה לאמר טוב לנו. 12 **להודיע לבני האדם** גבורותיו והדר מלכותו של הק': 16 **ומשביע לכל חי רצון** כדי <u>פרנסתו</u> הוא משביעו את טובו ואת רצונו ואת ברכתו. **רצון.** אפיימנט: 21 **תהילת י'י** ידבר פי. וגם **כל בשר יברך** את שם קדשו:

קמו 1 **הללו יק'** הללי נפשי את י'י. 2 **בעודי.** בעוד אני חי. 4 **עשתונותיו** מחשבותיו. 5 **אשרי** מי **שאל יעקב** <u>בעזרו.</u> שהבטיחו הק' הנה אנכי עמך ושמרתיך והשיבותיך. ולמה אשריו 6 לפי שהוא **עושה שמים וארץ את הים.** וכיון שהכל שלו יש בידו לשומרו בים ובישבה. אבל מלך בשר ודם אם שומרו בישבה אינו יכול לשומרו בים: **השומר אמת לעולם.** לסוף דורות רבים הוא שומר ומקיים אמיתת הבטחתו: 9 **יעודד.** לשון כח: 10 **ימלוך לעולם י'י.** יקיים מלכותו בגאולת בניו:

קמז 1 **הללו יק'** **כי טוב זמרה אלקינו.** כי טוב לזמר לו: 9 **לבהמה לחמה.** מאכלה **לבני עורב.** פירשו רבותינו שהוא <u>אכזרי</u> על בניו והק' מזמן להם יתושין מתוך ציאתם ונכנסין לתוך פיהם. 10 **לא בגבורת יחפוץ** הק'. **לא בקלות מרוצה שוקי האדם ירצה.** 16 **כפור.** גלידא. 14 **חלב חטים.** טוב חטים שמינים: 17 **משליך קרחו כפתים.** המים מגלידין ונעשין פתיתין. ומדרש אגדה כפיתים הכל לפי משא הבריות העני לפי חוסר מלבושיו מיקל עליו: **מי יעמוד** שלא יהא צונן בקרח 18 **ישלח דברו וימסם.** לאותן פיתים: **ישב רוחו** מערבית להשבית הקרח **ויזלו מים:**

קמח 1 **הללו יק'** 3 **כוכבי אור.** כוכבי לילה. 6 **חוק נתן** בהם זה ישמש ביום וזה ישמש בלילה. **ולא יעבור** אותו חק. 7 **תנינים.** דגים גדולים. 8 **אש וברד.** גלאצא בל'. **וקיטור.** ענן. **שנאה** שקורי' ברואינא: **ורוח סערה העושה** את **דברו** ואת שליחותו. <u>ונאמרו</u> רבותי' שהדברים הללו היו תחילתן גנוזים בשמים ובא דוד והורידן לארץ לפי שהן מיני פורעניות ואין נאה להיות במגוריו של הק':

קמט 1 **הללו יק'** שירו לי'י שיר חדש: 6 **רוממות אל בגרונם** והם לחרב פיפיות בידם: 8 **בזיקין.** <u>שרשרות.</u> 9 **משפט כתוב.** ונתתי את נקמתי באדום וגו'. ואם תאמר עדיין לא נולד יחזקאל כשאמר דוד זאת נתנבא דוד על קץ הגאולה. וכשיבא הקץ כבר כתוב הוא המשפט זה ימים רבים:

קן 1 **הללו יק'** הללו אל בקדשו 4 **במנים ועוגב.** כלי שיר הם. 5 **צלצלי שמע** מצלתים המשמיעים קול. **שמע.** שם דבר הוא כמו שמע. ומפני האתנחתא הוא נקוד קמץ גדול. ולכך טעמו למעלה תחת הש"ין:

נשלם תהילים שבח לאל אלים

נספח

מזמור קכ״א מתוך מקראות גדולות הוצאת בומברג שנת 1525

מצאתי שיר למעלות רמז במזמור שני למעלות העולות לצדיקים לעתיד לבא מתחת עץ
החיים לכסא הכבוד דתניא בסיפרי שיר המעלות אין כתוב כאן אלא שיר למעלות שיר למי
שעתיד לעשות מעלות לצדיקים לעתיד לבא וזהו שיסד הקלירי ומתחתיהם שלשים מעלות
זו למעלה מזו עד כסא הכבוד טסות ועולות בשיח נעימות שיר המעלות :

INDICES

INDEX OF BIBLICAL SOURCES

INDEX OF ANCIENT BIBLICAL
MANUSCRIPTS & VERSIONS

INDEX OF RABBINIC SOURCES

INDEX OF OTHER ANCIENT & MEDIEVAL AUTHORITIES

INDEX OF MEDIEVAL MANUSCRIPTS

INDEX OF MODERN AUTHORITIES

906   INDEX OF MODERN AUTHORITIES

INDEX OF SUBJECTS AND TERMS

Lightning Source UK Ltd.
Milton Keynes UK
UKOW01f0650210917
309601UK00020B/534/P